Lecture Notes in Artificial Intelligence 5027

Edited by R. Goebel, J. Siekmann, and W. Wahlster

Subseries of Lecture Notes in Computer Science

Ngoc Thanh Nguyen   Leszek Borzemski
Adam Grzech   Moonis Ali (Eds.)

New Frontiers in Applied Artificial Intelligence

21st International Conference on
Industrial, Engineering and Other Applications of
Applied Intelligent Systems, IEA/AIE 2008
Wrocław, Poland, June 18-20, 2008
Proceedings

Springer

Series Editors

Randy Goebel, University of Alberta, Edmonton, Canada
Jörg Siekmann, University of Saarland, Saarbrücken, Germany
Wolfgang Wahlster, DFKI and University of Saarland, Saarbrücken, Germany

Volume Editors

Ngoc Thanh Nguyen
Leszek Borzemski
Adam Grzech
Wrocław University of Technology
Institute of Information Science and Engineering
Janiszewskiego 11/17, 50-370 Wrocław, Poland
E-mail: {Ngoc-Thanh.Nguyen, Leszek.Borzemski, Adam.Grzech}@pwr.wroc.pl

Moonis Ali
Texas State University–San Marcos
Department of Computer Science
Nueces 247, 601 University Drive, San Marcos, TX 78666-4616, USA
E-mail: ma04@txstate.edu

Library of Congress Control Number: 2008927855

CR Subject Classification (1998): I.2, F.1, F.2, I.5, F.4.1, D.2, H.4, H.2.8, H.5.2

LNCS Sublibrary: SL 7 – Artificial Intelligence

ISSN   0302-9743
ISBN-10   3-540-69045-X Springer Berlin Heidelberg New York
ISBN-13   978-3-540-69045-0 Springer Berlin Heidelberg New York

Springer is a part of Springer Science+Business Media

springer.com

© Springer-Verlag Berlin Heidelberg 2008
Printed in Germany

Typesetting: Camera-ready by author, data conversion by Scientific Publishing Services, Chennai, India
Printed on acid-free paper   SPIN: 12281435   06/3180   5 4 3 2 1 0

Preface

The 21st International Conference on Industrial, Engineering and Other Applications of Applied Intelligent Systems (IEA-AIE 2008) held in Wroclaw, Poland was an international scientific forum for researchers in the field of applied artificial intelligence. The presentations of the invited speakers and the authors focused on developing and employing methods and systems to solve real-life problems in all applied intelligence areas. The IEA-AIE conference series, chaired by Moonis Ali, has a very long tradition, and it is the first time it was hosted in Poland.

We received 302 papers from 52 countries. Each paper was sent to at least three Program Committee members for review. Although the general quality of the submissions was very high, only 90 best papers were selected for oral presentation and publication in the LNAI proceedings. The papers in the proceedings cover the following topics: computer vision, fuzzy system applications, robot, manufacturing, data mining and knowledge discovery, neural network, machine learning, natural language processing, Internet application, e-learning, heuristic search, application systems, agent-based system, evolutionary and genetic algorithms, knowledge management, and other applications.

These papers highlight new trends and frontiers of applied artificial intelligence and show how new research could lead to new and innovative applications. We hope you will find these works useful and inspiring for your own research.

We would like to express our sincere thanks to the Program Committee members and all the reviewers for their hard work, which helped us to select the highest quality papers for the conference.

The conference was organized by the Institute of Information Science and Engineering, Wroclaw University of Technology, in cooperation with the International Society of Applied Intelligence (ISAI). We would like to thank our main sponsors, ISAI and Wroclaw University of Technology. Our special thanks are due also to the other sponsors: American Association for Artificial Intelligence (AAAI); Association for Computing Machinery (ACM/SIGART); Canadian Society for the Computational Studies of Intelligence (CSCSI/SCEIO); European Neural Network Society (ENNS); International Neural Network Society (INNS); Japanese Society for Artificial Intelligence (JSAI); Taiwanese Association for Artificial Intelligence (TAAI); and Texas State University-San Marcos.

We wish to thank the members of the Program and Organizing Committees for their very substantial work, especially those who played essential roles: Radosław Katarzyniak (Organizing Chair), Ryszard Kowalczyk (Special Session Chair) and the organizers of the special sessions: Zbigniew Banaszak, Oleg Zaikin, Gordan Jezic, Dan Popescu, Costin Badica, Adrian Giurca, Heloisa de Arruda Camargo, Maria do Carmo Nicoletti, Estevam Rafael Hruschka Jr. and Abdelhamid Bouchachia.

Our special thanks go to the Foundation for Development of Wroclaw University of Technology for the efficient dealing with the registration and management issues.

We would like to thank the invited speakers for their interesting and informative talks of world-class standard. We cordially thank the authors for their valuable contributions as well as the other participants of this conference. The conference would not have been possible without their support.

Thanks are also due to the many experts who contributed to making the event a success.

March 2008   Ngoc Thanh Nguyen
Leszek Borzemski
Adam Grzech
Moonis Ali

Conference Organization

General Chair

Moonis Ali
Texas State University, San Marcos, USA

Program Chairs

Leszek Borzemski
Wroclaw University of Technology, Poland

Adam Grzech
Wroclaw University of Technology, Poland

Ngoc Thanh Nguyen
Wroclaw University of Technology, Poland

Local Organizing Chair

Radoslaw Katarzyniak
Wroclaw University of Technology, Poland

Special Session Chair

Ryszard Kowalczyk
Swinburne University of Technology, Australia

Local Organizing Committee

Gomes Eduardo	Adrianna Kozierkiewicz
Mariusz Fraś	Wojciech Lorkiewicz
Krzysztof Juszczyszyn	Grzegorz Popek
Anna Kozłowska	

Special Sessions

1 Knowledge-Driven Manufacturing Systems
   Zbigniew A. Banaszak and Oleg Zaikin

2 Joint Session on Adaptive Networked Systems and Fuzzy Knowledge Bases
   Costin Badica, Heloisa de Arruda Camargo et al.

3 Software Agents and Multi-agent Systems
   Gordan Jezic

Invited Speakers

Shyi-Ming Chen
National Taiwan University of Science and Technology, Taiwan

Lakhmi C. Jain,
University of South Australia, Australia

Janusz Kacprzyk
Polish Academy of Science, Poland

Ryszard Kowalczyk
Swinburne University of Technology, Australia

Edward Szczerbicki
Gdańsk University of Technology, Poland

Ning Zhong
Maebashi Institute of Technology, Japan

Krzysztof Zieliński
AGH-University of Science and Technology, Poland

International Program Committee

Araz, Ceyhun, Turkey
Arredondo, Tomas, Chile
Banaszak, Zbigniew, Poland
Bannister, Peter R., UK
Belli, Fevzi, Germany
Brezillon, Patrick, France
Burke, Edmund, UK
Chan, C.W., Hong Kong - China
Chang, Chir-Ho, Taiwan
Chang, Chuan-Yu, Taiwan
Chau, Kwokwing, Hong Kong - China
Chen, Shyi-Ming, Taiwan

Lee, Chang-Shing, Taiwan
Lee, Huey-Ming, Taiwan
Lee, Tsang-Yean, Taiwan
Li, Yanzhi, China
Liu, Fuyan, China
Loganantharaj, Raja, USA
Madani, Kurosh, France
Mejia-Lavalle, Manuel, Mexico
Mitra, Debasis, USA
Monostori, Laszlo, Hungary
Murphey, Yi Lu, USA
Neumann, Bernd, Germany

Cheng, Ching-Hsue, Taiwan
Chiang, Yu-min, Taiwan
Chien, Been-Chian, Taiwan
Chung, Paul W.H., UK
Clifton, David A., UK
Desimone, Roberto V., UK
Dreyfus, Gerard, France
Esposito, Floriana, Italy
Garrido, Antonio, Spain
Guesgen, Hans Werner, New Zealand
Hendtlass, Tim, Australia
Hesuan, Hu, China
Hong, Tzung-Pei, Taiwan
Honghai, Feng, Taiwan
Huang, Yi-Sheng, Taiwan
Huget, Phillipe M., France
Ito, Takayuki, Japan
Iwata, Shuichi, Japan
Jacquenet, Francois, France
Jiang, Dongxiang, China
Jo, Kang-Hyun, Korea
Jo, Guen Sik, Korea
Jozefczyk, Jerzy, Poland
Kaikhah, Khosrow, USA
Kinoshita, Tetsuo, Japan
Korbicz, Jozef, Poland
Kumar, Amruth N., USA
Kwasnicka, Halina, Poland

Nishida, Toyoaki, Japan
Nocera, Pascal, France
Okuno, Hiroshi G., Japan
Potter, Don, USA
Ramaswamy, Srini, USA
Randall, Marcus, Australia
Rau, Hsin, Taiwan
Rayward-Smith, Victor J., UK
Sanchez-Marra, Miquel, Spain
Sakurai, Shigeaki, Japan
Selim, Hasan, Turkey
Soares Correa da Silva, Flavio, Brazil
Sun, Jun, China
Suzuki, Kazuhiko, Japan
Swiatek, Jerzy, Poland
Tang, Ke, China
Treur, Jan, Netherlands
Vadera, Sunil, UK
Valtorta, Marco, USA
Vancza, Jozsef, Hungary
Viharos, Zsolt Janos, Hungary
Wang, Leuo-Hong, Taiwan
Williams, Graham J., Australia
Xu, Wenbo, China
Yang, Chunsheng, Canada
Yang, Don-Lin, Taiwan
Yubin, Yang, China

Program Committees of Special Sessions

Akerkar, Rajendra, India
Badic, Costin, Romania
Balic, Joze, Slovenia
Burdescu, Dumitru, Romania
Cojocaru, Dorian, Romania
Corchado, Juan, Spain
Dolgui, Alexandre, France
Dostal, Petr, Czech Republic
Ebecken, Nelson, Brazil
Ganzha, Maria, Poland
Gasevic, Dragan, Canada
Giurca, Adrian, Germany
Gomide, Fernando, Brazil
Hruschka, Eduardo, Brazil
Huljenic, Darko, Croatia
Kapus, Tatjana, Slovenia

Nawarecki, Edward, Poland
Nemeth, Gabor, Hungary
Paprzycki, Marcin, Poland
Popescu, Dan, Romania
Ramer, Arthur, Australia
Rasvan, Vladimir, Romania
Simoff, Simeon J, Australia
Sobecki, Janusz, Poland
Souza, Joao, Portugal
Stranjak, Armin, UK
Trigano, Philippe, France
Trzec, Krunoslav, Croatia
Vasilakos, Athanasios, Macedonia
Vellasco, Marley, Brazil
Virginias, Botond, UK
Vlaovic, Bostjan, Slovenia

Koppen, Mario, Japan
Krol, Dariusz, Poland
Kusek, Mario, Croatia
Menezes, Ronaldo, USA
Mohammadian, Masoud, Australia
Nalepa, Grzegorz J., Poland

Wagner, Ambrus, Hungary
Wagner, Gerd, Germany
Weber, Richard, Chile
Zagar, Mario, Croatia
Zaikin, Oleg, Poland
Zaremba, Marek, Canada

Additional Reviewers

Bocewicz, Grzegorz
Borzemski, Leszek
Fras, Dr. Mariusz
Jung, J. Jason
Juszczyszyn, Krzysztof
Kaplon, Tomasz
Katarzyniak, Radoslaw
Kiewra, Maciej
Kolaczek, Grzegorz
Makowska-Kaczmar, Urszula
Myszkowski, Pawel
Nowak, Ziemowit
Orłowski, Cezary
Prusiewicz, Agnieszka
Tabakow, Iwan
Zgrzywa, Aleksander

Table of Contents

Computer Vision

Fuzzy System Applications

Robot and Manufacturing

Data Mining and KDS

Neural Networks

Machine Learning

Natural Language Processing

Internet Application and Education

Heuristic Search

Application Systems

Agent-Based System

Other Applications

Special Session: Knowledge Driven Manufacturing Systems

Special Session: Joint Session on Adaptive Networked Systems and Fuzzy Knowledge Bases

Special Session: Software Agents and Multi-Agent Systems

Driver Assistance System Based on Monocular Vision

Yu-Min Chiang[1], No-Zen Hsu[2], and Kuan-Liang Lin[3]

[1,2,3] Department of Industrial Engineering and Management,
I-Shou University
No. 1, Sec. 1, Syuecheng Rd., Dashu Township,
Kaohsiung County, 840, Taiwan, R.O.C.
[1] ymchiang@isu.edu.tw, [2] m9420001@stmail.isu.edu.tw,
[3] m9620006@stmail.isu.edu.tw

Abstract. The rapid growing volume of traffic has a critical affect on economic development but causes large amount of traffic accidents. The paper attempts to develop a driver assistance system based on monocular vision. Main function of the system is to find a collision-free path by lane tracking and obstacle detection. The paper proposes a lane markings detection method which is applicable to variant illumination and complex outdoor environment. The built system will issue a warning signal when it detects a lane departure of the vehicle. For obstacle detection, we use gradient information to find the feature points of the object first and estimate the distance of the object by means of triangulation. Experimental results demonstrate the effectiveness of the proposed approach.

Keywords: driver assistance system, lane detection, lane tracking, obstacle detection, monocular vision.

1 Introduction

Automobiles became the basic transportation tools and brought lives of individuals and nations transforming during the 20th century. The rapid growing transportation has a critical affect on economic development. However, along with the growth of the automobile usage, the number of traffic accidents leading to fatalities and serious injures has been remarkable increases. Nowadays, traffic safety becomes an important social and economic problem. Sun, et al. mentioned at least one person dies in a vehicle crash every minute on average [1]. The hospital bill, damaged property, and other costs increase along with traffic accidents. The fatalities and injuries not only generate enormous cost for individual and household economy, but also cause huge loss of medical resources. Consequently, safer automobile travel and smoother traffic conditions are universally sought. In the past few years, considerable research has been carried out in the field of driver assistance systems (DAS) in order to reduce accident severity and injury as well as increase road safety and comfort. A complete DAS should be aware of all of the surroundings of the vehicle. These driver assistance systems use a sensor suite mounted in various positions of the vehicle. The most

N.T. Nguyen et al. (Eds.): IEA/AIE 2008, LNAI 5027, pp. 1–10, 2008.

common sensors are active sensors such as lasers, lidar, or radars [1]. The main advantage is that certain quantities (e.g. distance) can be measured directly requiring limited computing resources. However, active sensors have several drawbacks such as low spatial resolution, slow scanning speed, and high cost. On the other hand, optical sensors, such as CCD cameras, are usually referred to passive sensors. With the introduction of inexpensive cameras, we can have a wide field of view. Such visual information is very important in a number of related applications, such as traffic sign recognition [2, 3], lane detection [4-6], or obstacles detection [7-9].

Optical sensors have been widely applied to vehicle systems to increase driver's safety. Nevertheless, developing vision-based vehicle support systems is quite challenging due to variant illumination, complex outdoor environments, and unpredictable interactions between traffic participants, and messy background. The research presented in this paper is about a driver assistance system for vehicles on an on-board monocular camera. First concern of the research is about building a robust lane detection and tracking system, since lane detection and tracking is primary and essential for lane departure warning, driver-attention monitoring, lateral control, and autonomous driving.

The lane detection and tracking methods can be classified into region-based methods [10] and edge-based methods [11, 12]. Region-based methods often use color and texture as features for segmenting the road region. However, due to the uncontrolled illumination condition, the color of a road varies with time. It makes lane boundaries difficult to be precisely located. Meanwhile, the region-based lane detection methods are time-consuming. Hence, the research adopted an edge-based method and developed a novel and robust method for lane detection and tracking. In addition to detecting and tracking road lanes, this paper also addressed a distance measure method based on a monocular camera to detect obstacle in front of the vehicle to avoid collisions.

The rest of this paper is organized as follows. Section 2 describes the proposed lane detection and tracking approach. Section 3 presents the obstacle detection approach including a novel features detection method and a distance measure method based on a monocular camera. Experimental results are provided in Section 4, and Section 5 gives conclusions.

2   Lane Detection and Tracking Method

The purpose of the research is to find a collision-free vehicle guiding path to assist drivers keeping safety based on a computer vision system. For the vision system design, one colored camera is mounted in front of a vehicle for periodically acquiring images as the vehicle moves, as shown in Fig. 1. The height of the camera above the ground is h, and the tilt of the camera is the angle θ between the optical axis and the horizontal line. This research utilized a colored camera to grab images for the purpose of future extension. However, to decrease the image processing time for lane detection and tracking, the grabbed color images are transferred into gray images.

The paper addresses a lane markings detection method which is applicable to the situations involving varying illumination conditions and bad conditions of road paintings. Besides, it is suitable for identifying solid- and segmented- line lane markings. As the lane markings generally are slighter in intensity than the road surface, we can separate lane markings from road surface by means of a proper grey-level threshold. This threshold must be dynamically adjusted according to the changes in lighting.

Let I_L means the average grey level of the lane marking, I_R means the average grey level of the road, and T means the threshold used to separate land markings from the road surface. In the research, I_L was initially set to 255, which means the lane markings is pure white. Suppose the vehicle is initially located in a straight portion of the road and is approximately aligned with the road. The value of I_R was first defined by a window containing road surface (Fig. 2). The value of the threshold T was then obtained by the following equation:

$$T = (I_L + I_R)/2 \tag{1}$$

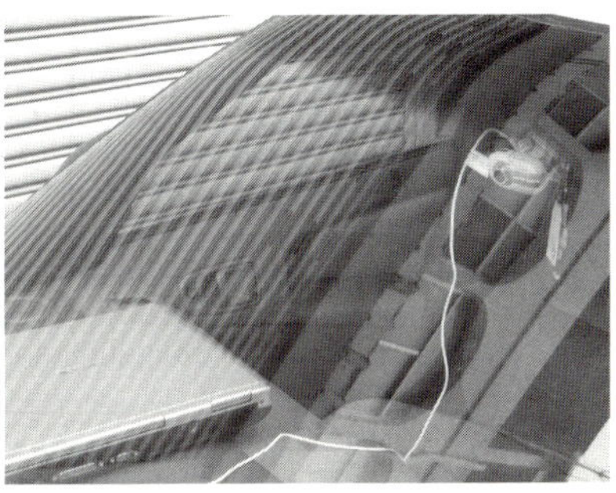

Fig. 1. Configuration of the vision system

Fig. 2. Window for defining the grey level of road

The scan direction for searching lane markings is shown in Fig. 3, which is from left to right and from bottom to top. If the grey level of a point P with coordinates (x, y) satisfies the following conditions, we consider P as a part of lane markings.

$$(I(x-1, y) < T) \& (I(x, y) > T) \& (I(x+1, y) > T) \& (I(x+2, y) > T) \tag{2}$$

where $I(x, y)$ means the grey level of pixel $P(x, y)$.

Once we detect the lane markings, we can further replace the value of I_L according to the grey level of the detected lane markings. Therefore, the value of I_L will be dynamically adjusted according to the illumination conditions of real environment.

If $P(x, y)$ lies on lane markings, we further scan the image along two lines, y-a and y+a, from left to right to find another point on the lane marking. In practical implementation, the value of a is set to 3. The orientation of the lane marking can be localized by these two points on the lane marking. Based on the fact that the curvatures of high speed roads are small [13], the lane boundaries can be approximated by a straight line within a short distance in a flat ground plane. Therefore, we track the extended lane along the found direction of the lane marking by a window with size 20x20 by a distance of 10 pixels. The lane tracking process is illustrated in Fig. 4. The windows with red borders indicate the end of the lane markings, and the window with green borders is the tracking window given above.

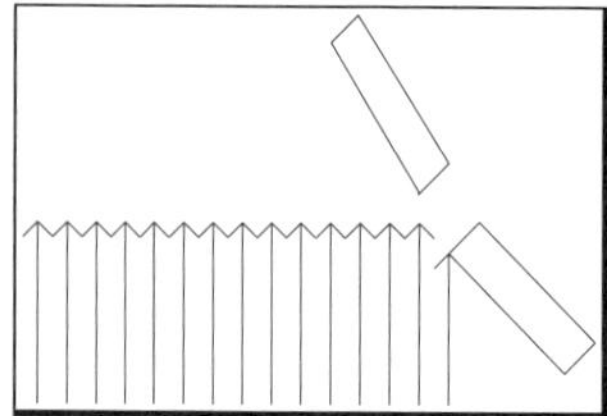

Fig. 3. Lane markings searching direction

Fig. 4. Lane tracking process

One safety driving behavior is to keep the vehicle at the center of the lane to avoid lateral collisions. If the vehicle stays at the center of the lane in a straight portion of the road, the orientations of left and right lane boundaries are expected symmetry ($\theta_l = \theta_r$), as depicted in Fig. 5. If the vehicle shifts to its right or left, the value of $|\theta_l - \theta_r|$ will get away from zero. As $|\theta_l - \theta_r|$ gets larger than a predefined threshold T_θ, we issue a lane departure warning signal to avoid an accident.

Fig. 5. Orientation of lane boundaries

3 Obstacle Detection Method

The research addressed an obstacle detection method based on a monocular camera. The objects of interest in front of the vehicle include other vehicles and stationary obstacles. Edge points appearing in the images are candidates for obstacles because they have large local variations in the grey level function, so we view them as feature points and propose an edge detection method called local k-means algorithm. Once the feature points of an object are found, we estimate the distance of the object by means of triangulation.

3.1 Feature Points Detection

This paper utilizes the gradient information to detect edge points. Pixels with steep gradient will be viewed as edge points. To avoid the influence caused by illumination altering, a local k-means algorithm is proposed to determine the value of the gradient threshold that is used for edge detection. In this research, we first found the edge points in vertical direction and then detected the horizontal edge points. For a vertical scan line, the pixels are divided into two clusters: one with steep gradient and the other with smooth gradient. Here the gradient in vertical direction is considered for image separation. Let $C1$ and $C2$ represent the mean value of the gradient in the two clusters, and GT represent the value of the gradient threshold. Assume the maximum gradient in vertical direction is $Gmax$. The steps of the local k-means algorithm for GT determination are illustrated as follows:

(1) Initialize the value of $C1$ to be $Gmax$, and the value of $C2$ to be 0.
(2) Repeat.
(3) Assign each pixel to the cluster to which the gradient is the most similar, based on the mean value of the gradients in the cluster.
(4) Update the cluster means, i.e., calculate the mean value of the gradients for each cluster.
(5) Until no change.

Once we obtain the mean value of the gradient in the two clusters by the above algorithm, the value of GT is calculated by the following Equation:

$$GT = (C1+C2)/2 \tag{3}$$

The pixels in the cluster with steep gradient are viewed as the vertical edge points. For a vertical edge point, we further detect the feature points along the horizontal direction by using the local k-means method. All the edge points in vertical direction and the horizontal direction are viewed as the feature points.

3.2 Camera Geometry

To obtain the depth information, the focal length of the camera must be known. The paper presents a simple way to acquire the focal length of the camera, as shown in Fig. 6. The parameters shown on Fig. 6 are:

f = the focal length of the camera
h = the height of the camera above the ground
O = the center of the camera
Q = the nearest point that can be seen by the camera in Z-axes
Z_Q = the z-coordinate of the point Q
Z_{max} = the distance in z-axis between the camera and the intersection of the optical axes and the ground
$IYmax$ = the y-coordinate of the projection of point Q on the image
θ = the angle between the optical axis of the camera and the horizontal
α = the angle between line OQ and the vertical
β = the angle between the optical axis and line OQ

Using the triangulation, the focal length of the lens can be found through Eq. (4) to Eq. (7).

$$\alpha = \tan^{-1}(Z_Q / h) \tag{4}$$

$$\theta = \tan^{-1}(h / Z_{max}) \tag{5}$$

$$\beta = \pi/2 - \alpha - \theta \tag{6}$$

$$f = IY_{max} / \tan(\beta) \tag{7}$$

Finally we can calculate the distance between the point P and the cameras in Z-axes. Figure 7 shows the triangulation for depth calculation.

$$\gamma = \tan^{-1}(IY / f) \tag{8}$$

$$\omega = \alpha + \beta - \lambda \tag{9}$$

$$z_P = h \cdot \tan(\omega) \tag{10}$$

The height of the feature point P also can be computed by means of triangulation similar to the above method. If the height is larger than the pre-determined threshold, we identify the object as an obstacle; otherwise, it belongs to the road surface.

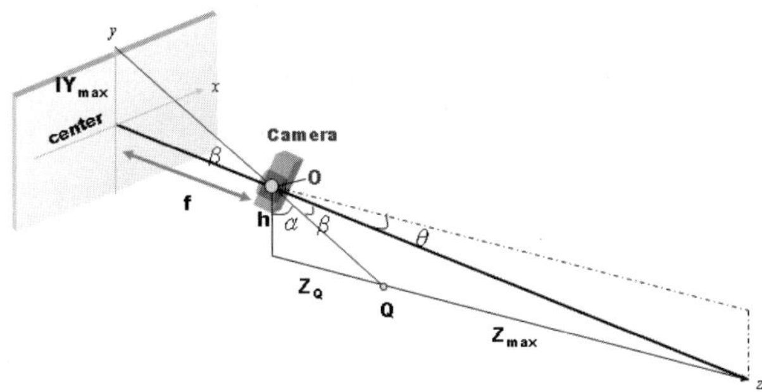

Fig. 6. Triangulation for focal length calculation

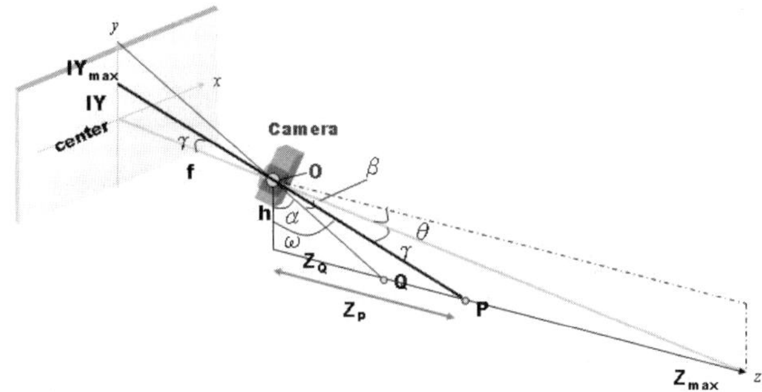

Fig. 7. Triangulation for depth calculation

4   Experimental Results

The sensing device described in Section 2 has been built with a 320x240 CMOS camera delivering 256 values in each of the red, green, and blue channel. We implemented the proposed algorithms using Borland C++ language and a personal computer with an Intel Pentium 4 CPU and 512 MB RAM. This vision set-up has been first tested in a laboratory environment for quantitative performance evaluation, and then it has been mounted near the front window of a vehicle for field test in real traffic conditions.

Fig. 8 shows the result of edge detection. For image size 320x240, the average time for feature points detection is 0.0156 sec based on 5 trials. The true positions of the target with respect to the cameras has been measured by a measuring tape, and compared with the positions computed by the proposed procedure in an indoor environment. We have totally taken 30 trials with a target on different distance in front of the set-up vision system. The range of distance is from 140 cm to 310 cm. The results are shown in Fig. 9, from which it indicates the proposed distance measure method performs well. The average error of depth is about 4.87 cm and the corresponding standard deviation is 1.59 cm.

Fig. 8. The result of edge detection

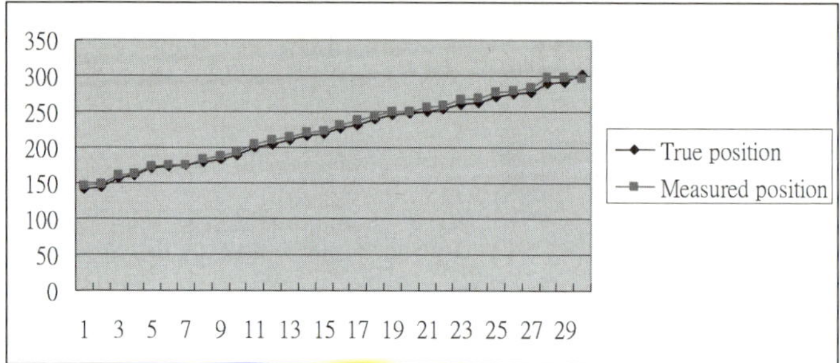

Fig. 9. Comparison of the true and the measured distance of a target

The performance of the lane detection and tracking method was thoroughly evaluated using a number of test drives on high ways in southern Taiwan. We took 31 images as the test samples. All the land markings can be exactly detected. Fig. 10 shows some of the lane markings searching results. Each end of the lane marking is bounded by a red window. The experimental results showed that the proposed method is robust against curved lanes and broken lanes in the captured road images. The average processing time for lane tracking is 0.0154 sec, which is quite matching the demand.

However, when calculating the orientation of the land marking, there are 4 images that couldn't be accurately tracked among the 31 images. One of the four samples is shown in Fig. 11. In the field, the solid- and segmented- line lane markings appear concurrently in front of the vehicle. It causes confusion in angle calculation.

Fig. 10. Lane markings searching results

Fig. 11. Lane tracking result with wrong orientation

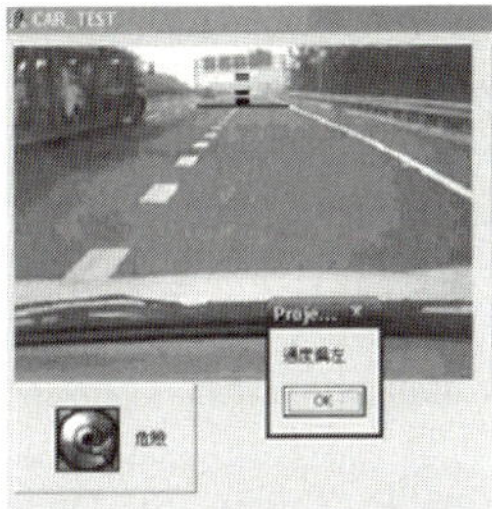

Fig. 12. Lane departure warning

An example of lane departure situation is depicted in Fig. 12. It can be observed that a lane departure warning signal is issued as the vehicle moves toward left.

5 Conclusions

The paper presents an active safety system for vehicles. We developed an automatic guided system of road vehicles based on monocular vision in order to enhance the driver's safety. In this research, we proposed a robust lane detection and tracking method which can quickly track the lane under varying illumination conditions. A warning signal is issued when the system detects the vehicle departing from the lane. The gradient information is utilized to detect the edge points. Followed by a k-means-like method, the feature points can be extracted. The 3-D position of an obstacle in front of the vehicle is computed by means of triangulation. Experimental results verify the effectiveness of the proposed approach. Currently, we are developing an automatic guidance system based on the proposed lane tracking and obstacle detection method. Future work will concentrate on building a complete driver assistance system that can be aware of all of the surroundings of the vehicle. Besides, the implemented system will be compared with the well-known DAS introduced in previous researches.

Acknowledgments

This research was supported by National Science Council of Taiwan, Republic of China, under the contract number NSC 95-2221-E-214-057-MY2.

References

1. Sun, Z., Bebis, G., Miller, R.: On-road vehicle detection using optical sensors: a review. In: The 7th International IEEE Conference on Intelligent Transportation Systems, pp. 585–590 (2004)
2. Zhou, Y., Xu, R., Hu, X., Ye, Q.: A robust lane detection and tracking method based on computer vision. Measurement Science and Technology 17(4), 736–745 (2006)
3. Piccioli, G., Michel, E.D., Parodi, P., Campani, M.: Robust method for road sign detection and recognition. Image and Vision Computing 14(3), 119–129 (1996)
4. Escalera, A.D.L., Armingol, J.M., Mata, M.: Traffic sign recognition and analysis for intelligent vehicles. Image and Vision Computing 21(3), 247–258 (2002)
5. Kluge, K., Thorpe, C.: The YARF System for Vision-Based Road Following. Journal of Mathematical and Computer Modelling 22, 213–233 (1995)
6. Broggi, A., Bertozzi, M., Fascioli, A.: Architectural Issues on Vision-Based Automatic Vehicle Guidance: The Experience of the ARGO Project. Real-Time Imaging 6(4), 313–324 (2000)
7. McCall, J.C., Trivedi, M.M.: Video-based lane estimation and tracking for driver assistance: survey, system, and evaluation. IEEE Transactions on Intelligent Transportation Systems 7(1), 20–37 (2006)
8. Gandhi, T., Devadiga, S., Kasturi, R., Camps, O.: Detection of obstacle on runways using ego-motion compensation and tracking of significant features. Image and Vision Computing 18(10), 805–815 (2000)
9. Stiller, C., Hipp, J., Rossig, C., Ewald, A.: Multisensor obstacle detection and tracking. Image and Vision Computing 18(5), 389–396 (2000)
10. Labayrade, R., Royere, C., Gruyer, D., Aubert, D.: Cooperative fusion for multi-obstacles detection with use of stereovision and laser scanner. Autonomous Robots 19(2), 117–140 (2005)
11. Paragios, N., Deriche, R.: Geodesic active contours and level sets for the detection and tracking of moving objects. IEEE Transactions on Pattern Analysis and Machine Intelligence 22(3), 266–280 (2000)
12. Bertozzi, M., Broggi, A.: GOLD: a parallel real-time stereo vision system for generic obstacle and lane detection. IEEE Trans. Image Process. 7, 62–81 (1998)
13. Beauvais, M., Lakshmanan, S.: CLARK: a heterogeneous sensor fusion method for finding lanes and obstacles. Image and Vision Computing 18, 397–413 (2000)
14. Jung, C.R., Kelber, C.R.: Lane following and lane departure using a linear-parabolic model. Image and Vision Computing 23(13), 1192–1202 (2005)

Particle Swarm Optimization for Object Recognition in Computer Vision[*]

Hugo A. Perlin, Heitor S. Lopes, and Tânia Mezzadri Centeno

Bioinformatics Laboratory, Federal University of Technology Paraná (UTFPR),
Av. 7 de setembro, 3165 80230-901, Curitiba (PR), Brazil
haperlin@gmail.com, hslopes@pesquisador.cnpq.br, mezzadri@utfpr.edu.br

Abstract. Particle Swarm Optimization (PSO) is an evolutionary computation technique frequently used for optimization tasks. This work aims at applying PSO for recognizing specific patterns in complex images. Experiments were done with gray level and color images, with and without noise. PSO was able to find predefined reference images, submitted to translation, rotation, scaling, occlusion, noise and change in the viewpoint in the landscape image. Several experiments were done to evaluate the performance of PSO. Results show that the proposed method is robust and very promising for real-world applications.

1   Introduction

Automatic pattern recognition in images is an important problem of computer vision, frequently found in industry, security, engineering and other areas. The main objective is to find specific objects (patterns or reference images) in a complex scene subject to degradation of quality. Many image processing methods have been used for this problem, mainly based on mathematical morphology or template matching [1]. Most image processing techniques are computationally expensive and too specific for certain types of images. Also, the lack of robustness limits their application to noisy images and when the object to be searched is occluded or randomly displaced/rotated in the scene. Overall, to achieve satisfactory performance for real-world applications, exhaustive search methods are inadequate and, then, heuristic methods can play an important role [2,3,4].

Particle Swarm Optimization (PSO) [5] is an evolutionary computation method, and has been successfully used for hard numerical and combinatorial optimization problems [6,7]. When compared with other heuristic optimization methods, PSO is easier to implement and tune parameters. PSO has been used very sparsely for image processing problems, mainly for image registration. This problem consists in aligning geometrically two images in such a way to optimize

---

[*] This work was partially supported by the Brazilian National Research Council – CNPq, under research grants nos. 309262/2007-0 to H.S. Lopes, and 477922/06-6 to T.M. Centeno. Authors also acknowledge the financial aid from CAPES as a scholarship to H.A. Perlin.

N.T. Nguyen et al. (Eds.): IEA/AIE 2008, LNAI 5027, pp. 11–21, 2008.
© Springer-Verlag Berlin Heidelberg 2008

(maximizing) a similarity measure. PSO was shown to be robust and efficient for this kind of optimization [8,9].

This work presents the implementation of PSO method for detecting objects in images in the context of computer vision. Given a pattern or reference image of an object, it is to be found anywhere in a target image (complex scene). Once found the object, its location is precisely determined in the target image, including planar coordinates, scale and rotation angle.

2   The Object Recognition Problem

Given two images, the first one containing a reference object (pattern), and the another as a target landscape where the object is supposed to be found, finding the pattern in the target is defined as finding the planar coordinates, rotation angle and scale factor. A possible solution is represented as 4-tuple: (x, y, s, θ), where x and y represent the planar coordinates of the center of the reference image relative to the landscape image, s is the scale factor, and θ is the rotation angle, relative to the coordinates system. Since the object can appear anywhere in the landscape, the set of all possible combinations is very large. Therefore, the problem can be stated as an optimization problem, so as to find appropriate values for (x, y, s, θ) that maximizes the similarity between the object and landscape images (see below).

In this work, the search space is limited by constraining the range of possible values for the variables of the problem, as follows: column $(0 \leq x < n)$, row $(0 \leq y < m)$, scale $(0.5 \leq s \leq 2.0)$, and rotation $(-\pi \leq \theta \leq \pi)$.

To evaluate possible solutions for the problem, it is necessary to define a measure of similarity between the reference and the landscape images. Some measures of similarity between images were proposed in the literature, such as mutual information and sum of the square of differences between pixels [8,9]. Since mutual information is computationally expensive and the other measure may give high values for similarity even when images are not correlated, we used in this work the absolute sum of differences between pixels.

A function that computes the difference between pixels of the reference image (RI) and the landscape image (LI) is called here "*Error*". Using such function a given solution can be evaluated by using the following equations:

$$Eval_{Sol} = \frac{(Error_{Max} - Error_{Sol})}{Error_{Max}} \tag{1}$$

$$Error_{Max} = 2^{nbits} * ((m * n) - Pinv) \tag{2}$$

$$Error_{Sol} = \sum_{i=0}^{n-1} \sum_{j=0}^{m-1} |RI(i, j) - LI(I, J)| \tag{3}$$

where: n and m are the dimensions (width and height) of the reference image; *nbits* is the number of bits used to represent gray levels; *Pinv* are pixels that belongs to the reference image, but doesn't belongs to the landscape image (they appear when the position of the reference image is near to the borders of landscape image); $Error_{Sol}$ is the sum of the difference of intensity between pixels of reference and landscape images, for the given solution.

The indices (I, J) of the pixels of the landscape image are obtained by the equations 4 and 5, where $ddX = j - \frac{Width_{RI}}{2}$ and $ddX = i - \frac{Heigth_{RI}}{2}$, and the values of x, y, s, θ belong to the candidate solution under evaluation.

$$I = y + s * (ddX * sin(-\theta) + ddY * cos(\theta)); \tag{4}$$

$$J = x + s * (ddX * cos(-\theta) + ddY * sin(\theta)); \tag{5}$$

The evaluation function (Equation 1) tends to 1, its maximum value, when the value of Equation 3 tends to 0. Therefore, an optimization method (in this case, PSO) can be used to maximize the value of the evaluation function, consequently minimizing the error between both reference and landscape images(Equation 3).

The previous definitions is for gray level images, although a similar principle can be used for color images. In this case, it is necessary to compute the matching error for each independent channel of the triplet RGB, as shown in the following equations:

$$Eval_{Sol} = \frac{(3 * Error_{Max} - (ErrorChannel_{Sol}))}{Error_{Max}} \tag{6}$$

$$ErrorChannel_{Sol} = \sum_{ch=1}^{3} \sum_{i=0}^{n-1} \sum_{j=0}^{m-1} |RI(i, j, ch) - LI(I, J)| \tag{7}$$

An important difference for the evaluation of color images is the range of values of Equation 6, from 0 to 3. However, this feature does not lead to significant differences in the recognition of objects in images. Considering that color images have three independent color channels, represented by the variable ch in the equation 7, the search for objects can be simplified if the landscape image is previously searched for large color discrepancies. This procedure can decrease the searchable size of the landscape image, thus significantly decreasing the computational effort.

3   Particle Swarm Optimization (PSO)

Particle Swarm Optimization (PSO) belongs to the group of heuristic methods known as swarm intelligence. PSO is an evolutionary computation method, like genetic algorithms, genetic programming, evolution strategies and ant colony optimization. PSO is inspired in the behavior of social agents, and was invented by Eberhart and Kennedy in 1995 [5]. The basic idea behind PSO is the simulation of a simplified social system, based on the collective behavior observed in bird flocking, bee swarming, and fish schooling, for instance. The individuals in these groups continuously adjust their position in the space while moving, so as to keep an average distance between neighbors. The behavior of a given individual affects the group and vice-versa. From the computational point of view, the swarm is composed by particles, which represent possible solutions for the problem. Particles "fly" over the hypersurface of the solution space, searching for the optimal solution.

At the beginning, the population of particles is randomly initialized. That is, their position in the search space, as well as their velocity (in all dimensions) are set randomly. Using a random number generator with uniform distribution, such initialization assures that any point in the search space can be reached. Each particle has a limited memory, and it is able to store the coordinates of its current position in the search space, as well as the position where it found the best solution to date (*pbest*), and the position of the best solution found by its neighbors (*lbest*) or by the whole swarm (*gbest*), depending on the implementation. *pbest* represents the knowledge acquired by the own particle during its navigation in the search space, also known as cognitive component. *gbest* or *lbest* represents the knowledge acquired by the group, also known as social component.

At each time step, the movement of particles is influenced by both its cognitive as well as its social components, as follows. Each particle has a velocity, which is modified according by the weighted influence of *pbest* and *gbest*. The larger is the difference between the current position of the particle to *pbest*, the more it is influenced to go towards it. The same occours for *gbest*. Equation (8) shows how the velocity of the i-th particle is updated in the next time step $(t + 1)$, according to its current position x_i^t at time t.

$$Vel_i^{t+1} = w * Vel_i^t + c_1 * r_1 * (pbest_i^t - x_i^t) + c_2 * r_2 * (gbest_i^t - x_i^t) \qquad (8)$$

where: w is the inertia moment, c_1 and c_2 are user-defined acceleration constants, r_1 and r_2 are uniformly distributed random numbers, and x_i represents the current solution.

Knowing the velocity of a given particle, it is possible to update its position in the search space at the next time step. This is done by Equation (9).

$$x_i^{t+1} = x_i^t + Vel_i^{t+1} \qquad (9)$$

The acceleration constants, c_1 and c_2, have a direct influence on the size of the step in the search space. Therefore, it is important to set such constants to appropriate values, aiming at an efficient exploration of the search space. A high value for c_1, local search is encouraged and the swarm tends to be clustered into small isolated groups, frequently with only one particle. On the other hand, with a high value for c_2, the swarm tends to be clustered in a local maximum, thus stagnating the search. As any other evolutionary computation method, the choice of optimal values for the control parameters is a difficult task and, usually, is problem-dependent.

The following steps summarize the standard PSO algorithm:

a) Initialize the swarm of particles with random values for each component of the solution vector (valid solution);
b) Evaluate the quality of the solution represented by each particle;

c) If the fitness of the current solution is better than *pbest* then update it with the current solution. If the current solution if better than *gbest* then update it with the current solution;

d) Compute the new velocity of particles according to Equation (8);

e) Compute the new position of particles (new solution) in the search space according to Equation (9);

f) If a stopping criterion is met, then stop. Otherwise, go to step (b). The stopping criterion can be a maximum number of iterations or a solution of satisfactory quality.

An additional step that can be used to improve performance of PSO is the use of some diversification method within the search process. When the swarm converges to a given region of the search space, very few improvement can be achieved. This is due to the lack of diversity of solutions in the swarm and can be observed when *gbest* stagnates for a number of iterations. In such situation, the easiest way to give chance of a further improvement of the PSO is to extinguish the swarm and restart PSO, but keeping the former *gbest*. This procedure is known as explosion, and was demonstrated to be of great utility for complex problems [6], allowing PSO to achieve better solutions, when compared with a PSO without explosions.

In fact, the PSO heuristics is easy to implement and does not require many computational resources for running. The most expensive part is always the evaluation of a candidate solution (particle).

4 Computational Experiments and Results

The standard PSO was implemented following the steps summarized in the section 3. A population of 40 particles, with random initialization, was used. Running parameters were set as the default values suggested in the literature: $c_1 = c_2 = 2$ and $w = 0.5$ The stopping criterion was set as reaching 800 iterations. Additionally, during the search, if premature convergence is detected, an explosion is performed [6]. In this work, premature convergence was defined as 20 iterations without improvement in *gbest*.

4.1 Experiment #1

The objective of this experiment is to investigate the sensitivity of the fitness function to changes in translation (x, y), scale (s) and rotation (θ). Translation for both x and y were changed, independently, in the range of $[-5.0..5.0]$, in steps of 0.1 pixel. Scale was changed in the range $[0.5..1.5]$, in steps of 0.001. Rotation was changed in the range of $[-0.0872..0.0871]$ in steps of 0.00001 radian. This is equivalent to -5 to $+5$ degrees. Several landscapes and reference images (grayscale and color) were used in this experiment. Results, in general, were equivalent. A representative result of this experiments is shown in Fig. 1, using Fig. 4(a) as landscape and 4(c) as reference.

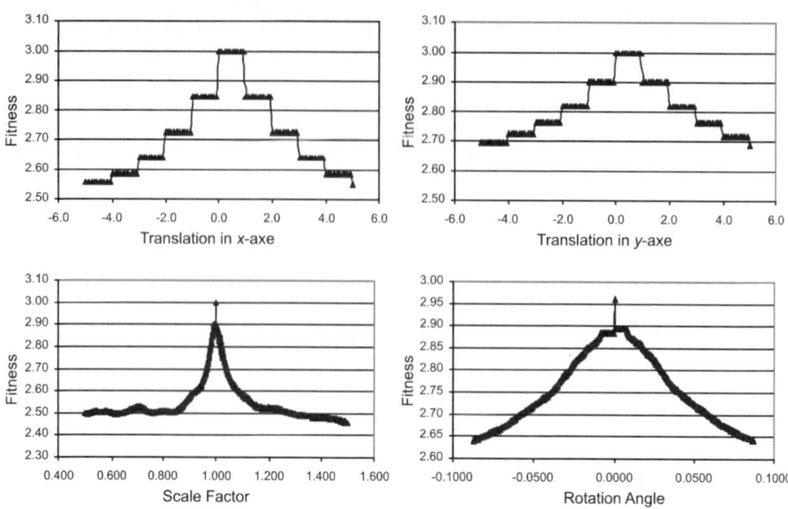

Fig. 1. Sensitivity analysis of the fitness function. Top: translation in axes x and y. Botton: scale and rotation.

4.2   Experiment #2

In this experiment the PSO was tested using a black-and-white reference image, shown in Fig. 2(a), having 69 x 148 pixels (from the work of [2]). Fig. 2(b) and Fig. 2(c) show the landscape images used, with the reference object translated and rotated, but with no change in scale.

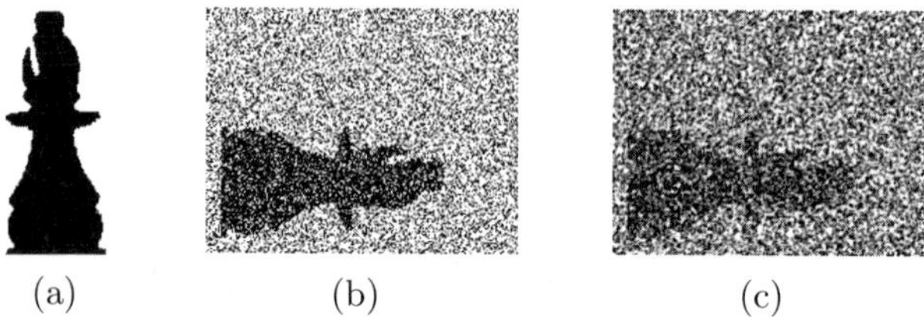

(a)   (b)   (c)

Fig. 2. (a) Reference image. (b) Landscape image with the pattern translated, rotated and degraded with noise. (c) Same landscape image of Fig. 2(b), but with more noise.

Gaussian noise was also added to the analysis image, but with a larger standard deviation (2.0). This experiment enabled to evaluate how PSO degrades its performance as noise increases.

To evaluate in what extent the proposed method is able to find the reference object, we added Gaussian noise to the landscape image. The Gaussian noise added had zero mean and standard deviation 0.5 and 2.0, for the landscape images of Fig. 2(b) and Fig. 2(c), respectively. The size of both landscape images was 208 x 150 pixels. In both cases, PSO found a good solution, shown in Tables 1 and 2. PSO easily found those solutions, converging with only 86 and 94

Table 1. Solution found by PSO for reference image of Fig. 2(a) and landscape image of Fig. 2(b)

Par.	Ref.	PSO	Error
y	84	84	0 %
x	106	107	0.94 %
s	1	1.006251	0.63 %
θ	-1.57	-1.565450	-0.29 %

Table 2. Solution found by PSO for reference image of Fig. 2(a) and landscape image of Fig. 2(c)

Par.	Ref.	PSO	Error
y	84	84	0 %
x	106	107	0.94 %
s	1	0.986482	-1.35 %
θ	-1.57	-1.571803	0.11 %

iterations, respectively, achieving a fitness of 0.735727 and 0.612881. In these tables, and in the following, "Par" refers to the elements of the 4-tuple of the image; "Ref" are the reference values; "PSO" refers to the values found by PSO; and "Error" is the percent of deviation of the solution found by PSO, regarding the reference values.

4.3   Experiment #3

To test the robustness of PSO in a more realistic situation, we used a gray level figure with several objects. The reference object, shown in Fig. 3(a) (238 x 269 pixels) is supposed to be found in the scene of Fig. 3(b) (496 x 347 pixels). It should be noted that the object is now translated, rotated, reduced and with a different viewpoint (in perspective). Besides, the reference object is partially occluded by another object (scissor) in the landscape. All these elements configures a hard task for an automatic object recognition system, since it is close to a real-world situation. PSO was able to find a satisfactory solution, shown in Fig. 3(c) (238 x 269 pixels), clipped from the original landscape image. The result parameters found by PSO was 133 and 209, to the x and y coordinates respectively, 0.533792153 for the scale factor and 0.69526328 to the rotation angle.

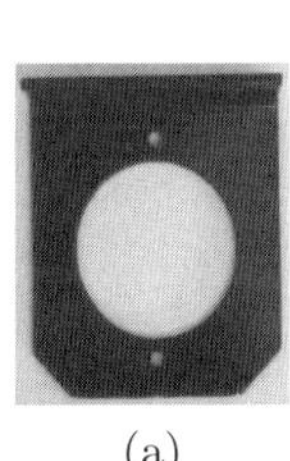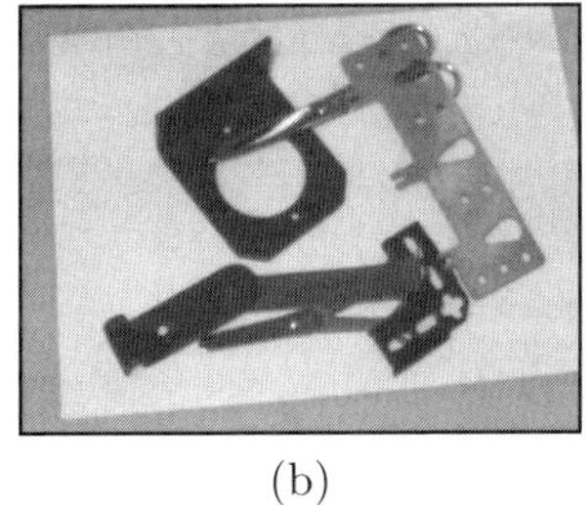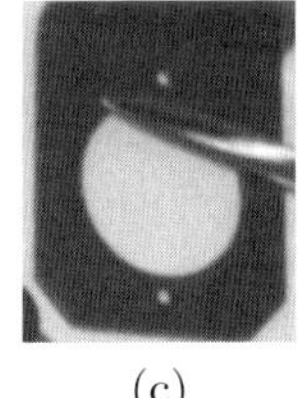

(a)   (b)   (c)

Fig. 3. (a) Reference image. (b) Landscape image. (c) Clip of the solution found by PSO.

4.4   Experiment #4

Besides gray scale images, we tested the proposed method with color images quantized with 24 bits. First, the reference image of Fig. 4(b) (76 x 83 pixels)

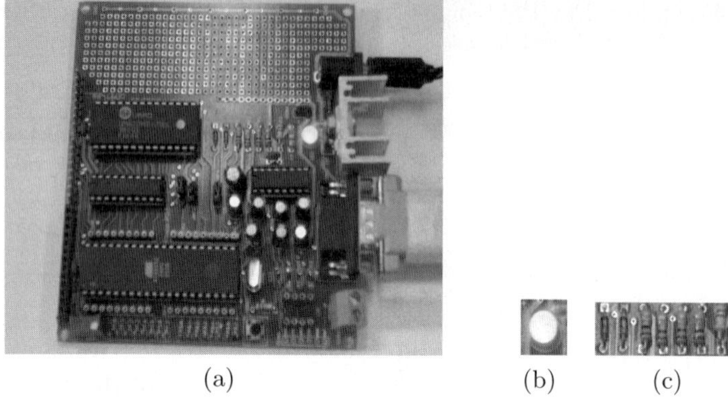

(a)   (b)   (c)

Fig. 4. (a) Color landscape image of a printed circuit board. (b) Reference image (bright led). (c) Reference image for experiment #1 (resistors).

Table 3. Comparison of the performance of PSO for gray scale and color versions of images of Fig. 4(a) and Fig. 4(b)

Type of Image	Avg. Fitness	Avg. Iter.	Avg. Expl.
Gray level	2.659252754	225.6	3.6
Color	2.911080048	191.5	3.4

and landscape image of Fig. 4(a) (800 x 600 pixels) were transformed to gray scale (using 8 bits) and submitted to PSO. Next, both color images were submitted to PSO in order to compare the effect of the decrement of the quantization level in the efficacy of PSO. Results are shown in Table 3 represent the average of 10 independent runs. The average fitness found for color images was larger than the corresponding for gray scale images. This suggests that, for this set of images, it is easier to find the object in a color image. In fact, it was intentionally selected the object with most discrepancy in the landscape (round, red and bright). However, when the image is converted to gray scale, there is no such discrepancy. Even so, PSO succeed to find the object, but with a larger effort, demonstrated by the average number of iterations necessary. The average number of explosions of the swarm was also larger for the gray scale image than for the color one. This is compatible with the larger difficulty imposed by the first case.

4.5   Experiment #5

In this experiment we used a large color image (1024 x 768 pixels) as landscape – see Fig. 5(a), and a small reference image (118 x 138 pixels) – see Fig. 5(b). The face of the reference figure has many details similar to other faces in the figure. Therefore, this experiment evaluated the ability of the proposed method to find an object in a complex scene with rich color details.

In this experiment, color Gaussian noise was added to the landscape image, in a percentage ranging from 5% to 75%. The objective of this test is to discover

(a)   (b)

Fig. 5. (a) Landscape figure of a complex scene. (b) Reference figure.

the limit of efficiency of the PSO. Table 4 shows the average results for 10 independent runs. As expected, the efficiency of PSO decreases as noise increases. A statistical analysis of data shows that this decrement is polynomial. In the same way, as a consequence of the increasing difficulty imposed by noise in the image, the average number of iterations increases also polynomially. The average number of explosions (restarts) is directly correlated to the number of iterations.

5   Discussion and Conclusions

In the experiment #1 it can be observed a difference in sensitivity for axes x and y. The larger sensitivity to translations in axis x is due to the specific features of the reference image 4(c), where elements are vertically positioned. The changes in the fitness function due to translation is in steps because pixels are discrete, although the PSO uses a resolution of tenths of a pixel. In this experiment it was also observed that changes in scale is much more critical than in translation or rotation. This fact suggests the possibility of using some kind of local search just to fine-tune the scale of a solution found by PSO.

Table 4. Results for different levels of color Gaussian noise in the landscape Fig. 5(a)

Noise	Avg. Fitness	Max. Fitness	Avg. Iter.	Avg. Expl.
5 %	2.70863165	2.85806349	208.6	3.6
10 %	2.59230251	2.74718357	267.4	6.1
20 %	2.53714739	2.55977623	198.0	4.6
30 %	2.23639087	2.32247749	248.3	5.1
50 %	2.09965423	2,15037207	229.6	5.4
75 %	1.93363241	1,97322669	418.2	15.2

Experiment #2 showed that PSO is robust, even in the presence of strong noise, when the reference image has a well-defined threshold with the background, typical of black-and-white images. Similarly, for color images, experiment #5 also showed the robustness of PSO, even for a complex scene with many details. The difficulty of the task is directly proportional to the amount of noise.

In the experiment #3 PSO showed its usefulness in a situation very close to real-world applications, specially in the industrial environment. PSO succeeded well in the experiment with a highly unfavorable conjunction of factors: displacement, rotation, reduction, occlusion and different viewpoint of the reference image.

Experiment #4 showed that the proposed method has more difficulty with images with less quantization levels. This suggests that it is easier to find patterns in color images because there is more information in the three channels than in a single gray level channel.

Overall, the problem of automatic object recognition in images is constantly found in industry, robotics, medicine, engineering, computer science and other areas. Therefore, efficient methods for dealing with this problem are always welcome. The proposed method, based on PSO, was shown to be a good alternative for the problem, and we believe it is specially suited for industrial applications, even in adverse situations.

To avoid parameter adjustments without prior knowledge of the behavior of the algorithm for each specific problem, future work will focus on a self-adaptive version of the PSO, inspired in a previous work with genetic algorithms [10]. Also, another evaluation functions will be tested so as to decrease computational effort and improve robustness.

Finally, we believe that the proposed method is promising, specially concerning the robustness and simplicity. Results suggest that this method can be used in a computer vision system for real-world object detection in images.

References

1. Jain, R., Kasturi, R., Schunck, B.G.: Machine Vision. McGraw-Hill, New York (1995)
2. Felizberto, M.K., Centeno, T.M., Lopes, H.S.: Object detection for computer vision using a robust genetic algorithm. In: Rothlauf, F., Branke, J., Cagnoni, S., Corne, D.W., Drechsler, R., Jin, Y., Machado, P., Marchiori, E., Romero, J., Smith, G.D., Squillero, G. (eds.) EvoWorkshops 2005. LNCS, vol. 3449, pp. 284–293. Springer, Heidelberg (2005)
3. Felizberto, M.K., Lopes, H.S., Centeno, T.M., Arruda, L.V.R.: An object detection and recognition system for weld bead extraction from digital radiographs. Comput. Vis. Image Unders. 102, 238–249 (2006)
4. Guerra, C., Pascucci, V.: Find line segments with tabu search. IEICE Trans. Inf. Syst. E84-D(12), 1739–1744 (2001)
5. Eberhart, R.C., Kennedy, J.: Swarm Intelligence. Morgan Kaufmann, San Francisco (2001)

6. Hembecker, F., Lopes, H.S., Godoy Jr., W.: Particle swarm optimization for the multidimensional knapsack problem. In: Min, G., Di Martino, B., Yang, L.T., Guo, M., Rünger, G. (eds.) ISPA Workshops 2006. LNCS, vol. 4331, pp. 358–365. Springer, Heidelberg (2006)
7. Lopes, H.S., Coelho, L.S.: Particle swarm optimization with fast local search for the blind traveling salesman problem. In: Proc. 5th Int. Conf. on Hybrid Intelligent Systems, pp. 245–250 (2005)
8. Talbi, H., Batouche, M.: Hybrid particle swam with differential evolution for multimodal image registration. In: Proc. IEEE Int. Conf. on Industrial Technology (ICIT), pp. 1568–1572 (2004)
9. Wachowiak, M.P., Smolíková, R., Zurada, J.M., Elmaghraby, E.: An approach to multimodal biomedical image registration utilizing particle swarm optimization. IEEE Trans. Evolut. Comput. 8(3), 289–301 (2004)
10. Maruo, M.H., Lopes, H.S., Delgado, M.R.B.S.: Self-Adapting Evolutionary Parameters: Encoding Aspects for Combinatorial Optimization Problems. In: Raidl, G.R., Gottlieb, J. (eds.) EvoCOP 2005. LNCS, vol. 3448, pp. 154–165. Springer, Heidelberg (2005)

Building Surface Refinement Using Cluster of Repeated Local Features by Cross Ratio

Hoang-Hon Trinh, Dae-Nyeon Kim, and Kang-Hyun Jo

Graduate School of Electrical Engineering, University of Ulsan, Korea
San 29, Mugeo-Dong, Nam-Ku, Ulsan 680 - 749, Korea
{hhtrinh,dnkim2005,jkh2008}@islab.ulsan.ac.kr

Abstract. This paper describes an approach to recognize building surfaces. A building image is analyzed to extract the natural characters such as the surfaces and their areas, vanishing points, wall region and a list of SIFT feature vectors. These characters are organized as a hierarchical system of features to describe a model of building and then stored in a database. Given a new image, the characters are computed in the same form with in database. Then the new image is compared against the database to choose the best candidate. A cross ratio based algorithm, a novel approach, is used to verify the correct match. Finally, the correct match is used to update the model of building. The experiments show that the approach method clearly decreases the size of database, obtains high recognition rate. Furthermore, the problem of multiple buildings can be solved by separately analyzing each surface of building.

Keywords: Repeated local feature recognition, building surface, cross ratio, vanishing point.

1   Introduction

The object recognition is performed by matching the features of a new image and the known images. The problems of object recognition as the size of database, object extraction, constructed features, method and constraint of match are challenging task because they directly effect to the robustness and the rate of recognition.

The role of above problems depends on the methods and the characters of objects. For example, in the appearance-based method [1,9,15], the object extraction and environment in the images are important. They strongly effect to the results. To improve the recognition rate, the method is performing with assumption that the object is handling [1] or appears in the black background. The number of models is usually so large because the object appeared many times with different rotated and scale poses [1] in the databse. The local feature-based method [3,4,6,7,15] is rapidly improved and widely used to recognize the object with the generality, robustness and easy learning. A major limitation of local feature-based method is that there are many stored descriptors in the database. One object is appeared several times. For each pose, hundreds of vector features

N.T. Nguyen et al. (Eds.): IEA/AIE 2008, LNAI 5027, pp. 22–31, 2008.

are stored. The method and constraint of match play an important role to reduce the mismatches. For searching the database, Euclidean or Mahalanobis distance is typically evaluated between the test feature and the stored ones. There are three constrained conditions for selecting the best match. The first one is a threshold-based constraint, two feature is matched together when their distance is below a certain threshold. So one test feature can get several matches. The second is nearest neighbor-based constraint, two features are matched if their distance is not only smallest but also below a certain threshold. With this constraint, a test feature can have only one match. The third constraint is similar to the second one, but the match will be rejected if the ratio between distances of the second nearest neighbor and the nearest neighbor is larger than a threshold [3]. This constraint selects a feature which strongly characterizes the object. Note that the third constraint is useful for searching the object in the general environment. It means that only one pose for each object is appeared in the database. But the robustness of recognition will be decreased when multiple appeared poses of each object are stored in the database like in [15,8]. Because the appeared poses will compete together, and many correct matches are ruled out. The multiple appeared poses in the database are also not suitable for applying the nearest neighbor-based constraint; because they will share the correct matches. Finally, the close pose of test image is selected by maximum number of local matches. The number of local matches sometimes includes the mismatches [15] or sometimes is counted after refining the correct matches [3]. The refinement as the last step of the recognition process is performed by the global transformation with epipolar geometry constraint for general 3D objects, or with homography for planar objects [2]. When the recognition process is performed with large size of database, it can be separated into two stages. In the first stage, the color histogram with slightly constraint is used to choose a small set of candidates (sub-candidate) from the database. The second stage is for refining the closest pose by local feature-based method [15]. In this paper, we concern about some problems of object recognition such as the size of database, object extraction, method and constraint of matching. Fig. 1 shows an overview of our method. We first obtain the building characters such as the surfaces and their areas, vertical and horizontal vanishing points, wall color histogram from the building image using our previous method [11,12]. The surface of building is represented by an area, wall color histogram with 32 bin-vector and a list of local feature vectors. The local feature is constructed by SIFT (Scale Invariant feature transformation, [3]) descriptors. After that a small number of candidates are chosen from database by matching the area and wall color histogram. Then the closest pose is refined by comparing the local feature vectors. Here, the threshold-based constraint is used to collect as much as possible the repeated features [15] which come from the similar principal components (PCs) such as the windows, doors or the wall region. The closest pose is defined as a stored surface with obtaining maximum number of matched features; of course there are many false correspondences. To refine the correspondences in the case

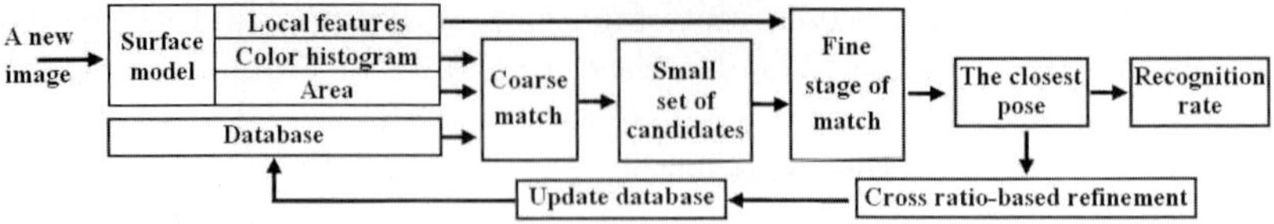

Fig. 1. An overview of proposed method

of small number of inliers, a novel method which based on the cross ratio is proposed. With high accuracy of positions of the correspondences, the features model is updated by an approximate vector. The frequently appeared features which are repeated in the different poses are kept and implemented after several times of updated performances. In this case, the recognition rate is increasing even that only one pose is stored in the database. The experiments show that the approach method clearly decreases the size of database, obtains high recognition rate. Furthermore, the problem of multiple buildings can be solved by separatively analyzing the surface of building.

2   Building Property Analysis

The building is extracted by the detected surfaces. each surface is described as an independent object. The method of surface detection was explained in detail in our previous works [11,12]; it contains 5 major steps as follows,

- Line segments were detected from the results of Canny edge detector.
- The segments of non-building pattern are roughly rejected by the contrast of two neighbor regions of that segment.
- MSAC (m-estimator sample consensus) algorithm is used for clustering segments into a common dominant vanishing point (DVP).
- The natural properties such as the density and co-existing appearances are used to refine the PC segments. And then the vertical segments are extended to across the image.
- The number of intersections between the vertical line and horizontal segments is counted to separate the building pattern into the independent surface. Finally, the boundaries of surface are fixed by the empirical conditions.

In the Fig. 2, the first row are the results of multiple buildings. The different colors represent the faces with different directions. The second row are the multiple face buildings. The last row shows that the proposed method is robust to the complex environment and general conditions.

Wall region detection was suggested by our previous works [10]. From the mesh of skewed parallelograms, the wall is grouped by the similar color skewed parallelogram. The color information of pixels of wall region is used to compute a hue histogram and quantize into 32 bins. Figs. 3(a,b,c) show an example of the wall detection and the hue color histogram.

Fig. 2. The results of surface detection

The keypoints and their SIFT [3] features are calculated as showing in Fig. 3(e). The keypoint which has the larger scale strongly characterizes rather than which has the smaller scale [10]. The difference of density of keypoints on the surfaces affect the recognition rate [15]. So the number of keypoints is proportional to its area. With the size 640x480 pixels of image and 700 keypoints for the maximum size of surface, the number of keypoints in each surface is calculated by $N = 700 \times \frac{S}{640 \times 480}$, where S is surface area. If the surface has more than N keypoints then just N keypoints which have largest scale are selected as shown in Fig. 3(f).

3   Cross Ratio-Based RANSAC for Refinement of Local Features

The RANSAC algorithm and general 2D projective matrix (general homography) are widely used to refine the correspondences [2] of planar objects. In practice, when a new image matches to the large database, some local features instead of being the correspondences they will be shared with the other models or the scene by randomly repeated local appearances. Therefore the number of correspondences (inliers) is markable decrease while the RANSAC algorithm and general 2D projective matrix (here, called general homography-based RANSAC) just bring into play the accurate result with larger than 50% inliers [2]. For the case of small number of inliers, Lowe [3] proposed the method using combination of affine transformation and Hough transform to refine the correct matches and obtained the high accurate result even there is 1% inliers. The method is

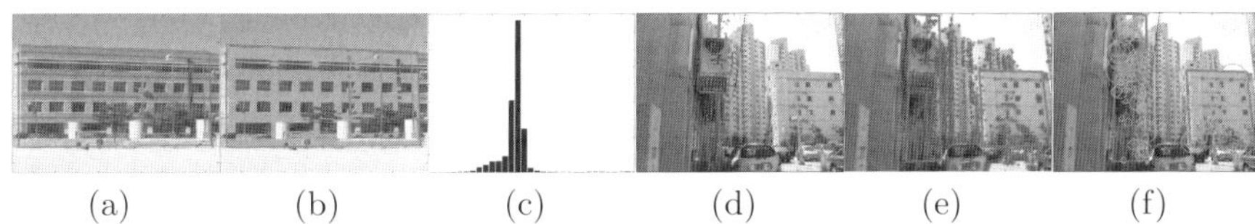

(a)   (b)   (c)   (d)   (e)   (f)

Fig. 3. (a) detected surface; (b) wall region; (c) hue color histogram; (d) original image; (e) detected surface and keypoints; (f) local region and keypoints

high accuracy when the object appearance is small or the object is so far from camera; because, in that case, the difference of geometry of affine transformation and general homography is not so far. In the case of building surface, the building is a large object with repeated structures so both of above methods are not suitable for refinement. To avoid that problem, Zhang et al. [15] lets slip the refinement step. The closest pose is selected by maximum number of matches including correspondences and false correspondences.

In this paper, a novel method is proposed by using cross ratio. Our method can refine the correspondences of large planar objects in the case of small percentages of inliers. The cross-ratio $\rho_{(ABCD)}$ of four collinear points A, B, C, D is defined as the "double ratio",

$$\rho_{(ABCD)} = \frac{CA}{CB} : \frac{DA}{DB} \tag{1}$$

If two segments intersect four concurrent lines at A, B, C, D and A', B', C', D' as in Fig. 4(a), then their cross ratios equal together,

$$\rho_{(ABCD)} = \rho_{(A'B'C'D')} \tag{2}$$

Now, we consider an artificial planar object as shown in Fig. 4(b) with four interest points $\{X_1, X_2, X_3, X_4\}$ and rectangular boundary. Let $\{P_i\}$ points be the projections of $\{X_i\}, (i = 1, ..., 4)$ on the bottom boundary. Therefore, four lines $P_i X_i$ parallel together. Assume that Figs. 4(c,d) are two poses of the above object which are built by general 2D projection. $\{x_i\}$ and $\{x_i'\}$ are the images of $\{X_i\}$ in the left and right poses. Similarly, $\{p_i\}$ and $\{p_i'\}$ are the images of $\{P_i\}$. In the left pose (Fig. 4(c)), Four lines $\{p_i x_i\}$ are concurrent at a vertical vanishing point. Let A, B, C, D be the intersections of $\{p_i x_i\}$, $i = 1, 2, 3, 4$, and the x-axis of the image, respectively. Now, two set of collinear points $\{A, B, C, D\}$ and $\{p_i\}$ are satisfied Eq. 2. So

$$\rho_{(ABCD)} = \rho_{(p_1, p_2, p_3, p_4)} \tag{3}$$

Similarly, for the right image (Fig. 4(d)),

$$\rho_{(A'B'C'D')} = \rho_{(p_1', p_2', p_3', p_4')} \tag{4}$$

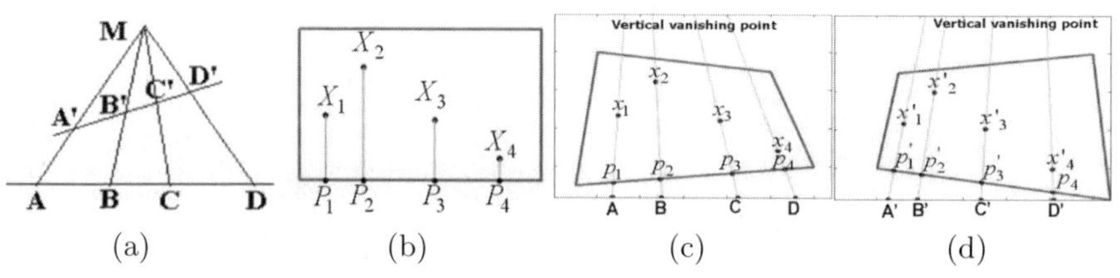

Fig. 4. The illustration of cross ratio-based method: (a) concurrent lines; (b) artificial object; (c, d) left and right poses

On the other hand, the sets of $\{p_i\}$ and $\{p_i'\}$ are projections of four collinear points $\{P_i\}$. So their cross ratio are invariant [2]; combining with Eqs. (3,4), we have

$$\frac{(x_C - x_A)(x_D - x_B)}{(x_D - x_A)(x_C - x_B)} = \frac{(x_{C'} - x_{A'})(x_{D'} - x_{B'})}{(x_{D'} - x_{A'})(x_{C'} - x_{B'})} \tag{5}$$

Note that, if $x_A > x_B > x_C > x_D$ then $x_{A'} > x_{B'} > x_{C'} > x_{D'}$. This order is considered as a constraint in our method.

Given two planar images with available vanishing points and N correspondences $\{X_i \longleftrightarrow X_i'\}$, $i = 1, 2, ..., N$; Let $\{x_i\}$ and $\{x_{i'}\}$ be projections of the correspondences on the x-axis of each image through the corresponding vanishing points, respectively. Randomly choosing a subset of three correspondences $\{A, B, C\}$ and $\{A', B', C'\}$, an error of cross ratio of the ith correspondence following x-axis is defined

$$e_i^x = \frac{(x_i - x_A)(x_C - x_B)}{(x_C - x_A)(x_i - x_B)} - \frac{(x_{i'} - x_{A'})(x_{C'} - x_{B'})}{(x_{C'} - x_{A'})(x_{i'} - x_{B'})} \tag{6}$$

Similar x-axis, on the y-axis, we get the error e_i^y.

Finally, the correspondences are refined by solving Eq. 7 with RANSAC method.

$$minimize \sum ((e_i^x)^2 + (e_i^y)^2); \quad i = 1, 2, ..., N \tag{7}$$

Here, the 2D problem is transformed into 1D problem. The number of loops of RANSAC in our case is smaller than homography method so the computational time is faster. The inliers then are refined by iterative weighted least mean squares method to get the 2D projective matrix. In Fig. 5(a), two poses with so far different direction of views from ZuBud data [8] directly matched together. 451 matches are obtained by threshold-based constraint. Fig. 5(b) shows that 21 inliers are obtained by affine transform method [3]. But many false correspondences are remained. Fig. 5(c) shows a false result with general homography-based RANSAC. Fig. 5(d) is an illustration of our method. Here, the false correspondences are strongly rejected so we got the good result even in the case of less than 6% inliers.

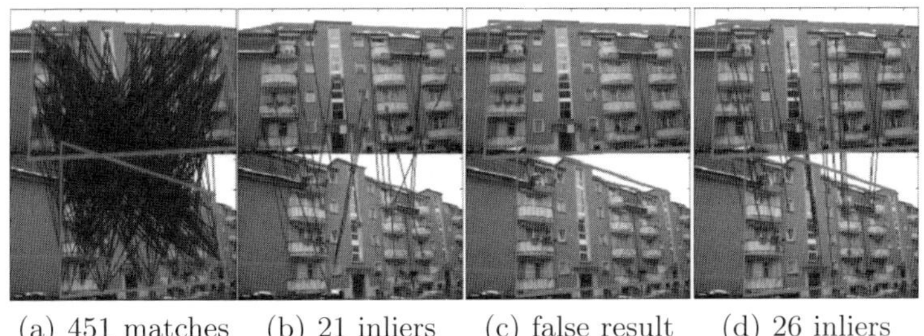

(a) 451 matches   (b) 21 inliers   (c) false result   (d) 26 inliers

Fig. 5. An example of result of proposed method and previous methods

4   Singular Value Decomposition (SVD)-Based Update of the Surface Model

Given $n \times 2$ matrix A, we use the singular value decomposition algorithm to decompose the matrix A. $A = U \sum V^T$, where $\sum = diag(\lambda_1, \lambda_2)$. Let a_1, a_2 be the columns of A, if distance from a_1 and a_2 is too small then $\lambda_1 \gg \lambda_2$ and $\lambda_2 \simeq 0$. In that case, matrix A is replaced by matrix $A' = U \sum' V^T$ where $\sum' = diag(\lambda_1, 0)$. Two columns a_1', a_2' equal together. Let $a = a_1' = a_2'$, a is called approximate vector of column a_1 and a_2 because distances from them are very small.

When the robot is working, the database is updated step-by-step as follows,

1. *Initial model*: The initial model is taken from a position of work space where the robot easily looks the building. If the building has more than one surface then all of them are stored in the database.
2. *The first update*: Just only the biggest area surface is chosen for matching to the database.
    - If the refinement is successful then the correspondences in the model is replaced by the approximate vectors. And assume that the ith building in the database is matched to the new image.
        - The remained surfaces of the new image are only matched to the remained ones of ith building. If the matching is successful then the matched surface is updated, otherwise that surface is added into the model of the ith building as a new surface.
        - The new image is stored at another place as an auxiliary model with indexing to the ith building.
    - If the refinement is not successful then the new image is added into the database.
3. *The next update*:
    - The correspondences are updated.
    - The new image is directly matched to the auxiliary model, and the new correspondences are also updated to the ith building by the obtained 2D transformative matrix.
    - The auxiliary model is replaced by the new image.
    - If the number of keypoints in the surface is larger N then some keypoints whose the updated times are smallest (not often appearance in the different poses) are ruled out.

The updating method can be used for both of supervised and unsupervised training the database. For the case of supervised training, if a new image of building which was not appeared in the database is analyzed then it will be ruled out. Or when the recognition or refinement process is false, the user decides to reject the new image. The updating process is prevented. In the unsupervised training, if a new image of building which was not appeared in the database is taken, then the recognition or refinement is be false. The new image is automatically added in database as a new building. And the database is automatically expanded and completed itself. Similarly, the color histogram is updated by the approximate vector.

5   Experiments

The proposed method has been experimented by supervised training for the urban image database contained 50 interest buildings and their neighborhoods. For each building, 22 poses are taken under general condition. The first pose is chosen as the initial database. 20 other images are used for training database. The remained one is used to test the algorithm. According to the scheme in Fig. 1, two criteria are issued to estimate the accuracy of system. the first one is the largest number of matches including correspondences and false correspondences. the second one is the correspondences after refinement.

Given a test surface, the recognition progress is divided into two stages. Firstly, using a ratio area and Euclidean distance of wall histogram, a small set of candidates is chosen from the database. In this paper, the thresholds of the ratio area and histogram distances are fixed by $[1/2, 2]$ and 1, respectively. Secondly, the recognition is refined by matching the SIFT features. We used threshold-base constraint to select the matches of a test feature. the test feature can have several matches which are satisfied,

$$d \leq 1.25 d_{smallest} \tag{8}$$

where d is Euclidean distance from the test to the features in database. For each of 50 test images, just only the biggest area surface is considered.

Here, 78 surfaces are detected for 50 initial poses in the database. The average area of detected surface is 52.73(%) the size of image. So each image contains about 369 keypoints and the database contains 18457 keypoints. That size is 6.775 times smaller than the database's size of the approach of W. Zhang [15]. In that approach, 5 poses for each building are stored in the database and each image contains around 500 keypoints. Table 1 shows the number of images of each building is stored in the database. The results show that the largest number of matching increases about 10(%) after each ten times of update. But the number of correspondences increases about 50(%) after ten times of update. Fig. 6 shows some examples of our results. For each sub-image, the above image is the test and the bottom building is the stored one. the first, second and third rows are the obtained correspondences of without update, after ten and twenty times update the database, respectively. The last one is the results matches including correspondences and false correspondences after twenty times update the database. We obtain 100(%) recognition rate for the observing test images with the updated database and the average number of sub-candidate database is 12.35. Furthermore, the problem of multiple buildings can be solved by separatively analyzing the surface of building.

Table 1. Number of images of each building in the database

Approach	# images for each building	Solved problem
Method of W. Zhang et al.[15]	5	Single building
Proposed method	1	Multiple buildings

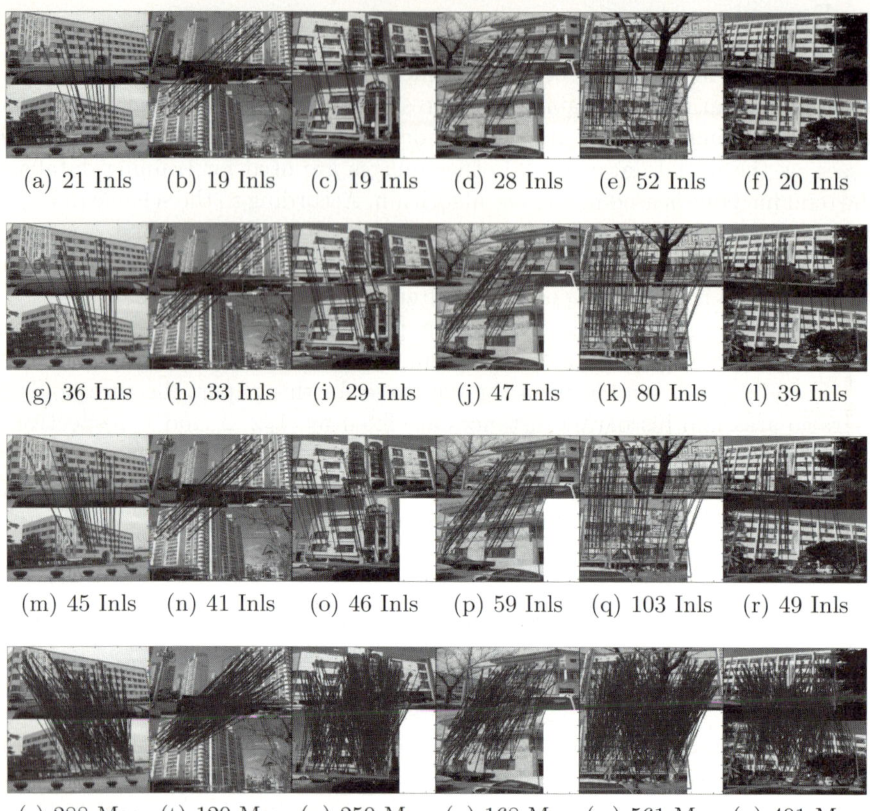

(a) 21 Inls   (b) 19 Inls   (c) 19 Inls   (d) 28 Inls   (e) 52 Inls   (f) 20 Inls

(g) 36 Inls   (h) 33 Inls   (i) 29 Inls   (j) 47 Inls   (k) 80 Inls   (l) 39 Inls

(m) 45 Inls   (n) 41 Inls   (o) 46 Inls   (p) 59 Inls   (q) 103 Inls   (r) 49 Inls

(s) 288 Mas   (t) 120 Mas   (u) 250 Mas   (v) 168 Mas   (w) 561 Mas   (x) 401 Mas

Fig. 6. Some examples of recognition results (inliers (Inls) and matches (Mas)); first row: without update; second and third rows: after 10 and 20 times of update; last row: number of matches after 20 time updating

6   Conclusions

A novel method is proposed for decreasing the size of database and increasing the recognition rate. Firstly, the geometrical and visual properties of building surface are extracted. each surface is represented by the vanishing points, area, wall color histogram and the list of local features. The multiple buildings in the image, a real case of urban environment, are segmented into the separate surfaces. Secondly, the invariant property of cross ratio of collinear points is used refine the correspondent points between a pair of images. It highly effect in the case of large planar objects with general homography and small number of inliers conditions. The transformation of 2D problem to 1D problem reduces the number of RANSAC loops. Finally, the SVD-based method is used for updating the database when the robot is working. The proposed method has performed the recognition the set of 50 buildings. All buildings are taken in Ulsan metropolitan city in South Korea under the general conditions. The results show that our method succeeds in the field of building recognition.

We are currently investing to apply the method for unsupervised training and robot's self-localization in urban environment.

Acknowledgements

The authors would like to thank to Ulsan Metropolitan City and MOCIE and MOE of Korean Government which partly supported this research through the NARC and post BK21 project at University of Ulsan.

References

1. Black, J., Jepsom, D.: Eigentracking: Robust Matching and Tracking of Articulated Objects Using a View-based Representation. IJCV 26(1), 63–84 (1998)
2. Hartley, R., Zisserman, A.: Multiple View Geometry in Computer Vision. Cambridge Uni. Press, Cambridge (2004)
3. Lowe, D.G.: Distinctive Image Features from Scale-invariant Keypoints. IJCV 60(2), 91–110 (2004)
4. Matas, J., Obdrzalek, S.: Object Recognition Methods based on Transformation Covariant Features. In: 12th European Signal Processing Conf. (2004)
5. Mikolajczyk, K., Schmid, C.: A Performance Evaluation of Local Descriptors. IEEE TPAMI 27(10) (October 2005)
6. Rothganger, F., Lazebnik, S., Schmid, C., Ponce, J.: 3D Object Modeling and Recognition Using Local Affine-Invariant Image Descriptors and Multi-View Spatial Constraints. IJCV 66(3), 231–259 (29) (2006)
7. Schaffalitzky, F., Zisserman, A.: Multi-view Matching for Unordered Image Sets, or 'How Do I Organize My Holiday Snaps?'. In: Heyden, A., Sparr, G., Nielsen, M., Johansen, P. (eds.) ECCV 2002. LNCS, vol. 2350, pp. 414–431. Springer, Heidelberg (2002)
8. Shao, H., Gool, L.V.: Zubud-zurich Buildings Database for Image Based Recognition, Swiss FI of Tech., Tech. report no.260 (2003)
9. Swets, D.L., Weng, J.J.: Using Discriminant Eigenfeatures for Image Ietrieval. IEEE Transactions on Pattern Analysis and Machine Intelligence 18(8), 831–836 (1996)
10. Trinh, H.H., Jo, K.H.: Image-based Structural Analysis of Building using Line Segments and their Geometrical Vanishing Points. In: SICE-ICASE, October 18-21 (2006)
11. Trinh, H.H., Kim, D.N., Jo, K.H.: Structure Analysis of Multiple Building for Mobile Robot Intelligence. In: SICE Proc., September 2007, Japan (2007)
12. Trinh, H.H., Kim, D.N., Jo, K.H.: Urban Building Detection and Analysis by Visual and Geometrical Features. In: ICCAS 2007, October 18-19, 2007, Seoul, Korea (2007)
13. Tuytelaars, T., Goedem, T., Van Gool, L.: Fast Wide Baseline Matching with Constrained Camera Position. In: CVPR, Washington, DC, pp. 24–29 (2004)
14. Zaboli, H., Rahmati, M.: An Improved Shock Graph Approach for Shape Recognition and Retrieval. In: Proceedings of the First Asia International Conference on Modelling & Simulation, pp. 438–443 (2007)
15. Zhang, W., Kosecka, J.: Hierarchical Building Recognition. In: IVC, May 2007, vol. 25, pp. 704–716. Daniel L. (2007)

Local Subspace-Based Denoising for Shot Boundary Detection

Xuefeng Pan[1,2,3], Yongdong Zhang[1,2], Jintao Li[1,2], Xiaoyuan Cao[1,2,3], and Sheng Tang[1,2]

[1] Virtual Reality Laboratory,
Institute of Computing Technology, Chinese Academy of Sciences,
Beijing, 100080, China
{xfpan, caoxiaoyuan, jtli, zhyd, ts}@ict.ac.cn
[2] The Key Laboratory of Intelligent Information Processing,
Institute of Computing Technology, Chinese Academy of Sciences,
Beijing 100080, China
[3] Graduate School of Chinese Academy of Sciences,
Beijing 100080, China

Abstract. Shot boundary detection (SBD) has long been an important problem in content based video analyzing. In existing works, researchers proposed kinds of methods to analyze the continuity of video sequence for SBD. However, the conventional methods focus on analyzing adjacent frame continuity information in some common feature space. The feature space for content representing and continuity computing is seldom specialized for different parts of video content. In this paper, we demonstrate the shortage of using common feature space, and propose a denoising method that can effectively restrain the in-shot change for SBD. A local subspace specialized for every period of video content is used to develop the denoising method. The experiment results show the proposed method can remove the noise effectively and promote the performance of SBD.

Keywords: subspace, denoising, shot boundary detection, SVD.

1 Introduction

As an important preprocessing step, video shot segmentation has attracted research ers' attention ever since the beginning of automatic video content analyzing [1]. A video shot consists of frame sequences captured by one camera in a single continuous action in time and space. It is the basic unit of video content. In order to segment the units from the video sequences, shot boundary detection (SBD) technique is introduced to find the boundaries of units automatically. Many SBD methods have been proposed and intensively reviewed in literatures [1]–[7].

Traditional SBD works are often rule based and only use the information of adjacent two frames. However, recent studies have shown the trends of introducing context information of more neighboring frames (e.g., [6], [7]) into SBD. Generally, the principle of SBD is to identify the discontinuities of visual content in a space of decision. In previous approaches, all frames in video are represented in one common

N.T. Nguyen et al. (Eds.): IEA/AIE 2008, LNAI 5027, pp. 32–41, 2008.

feature space (e.g., HSV color space). The mapping procedure to the final decision space is base on this kind of content representation. Sometimes, there are noises with a shot such as flash and motion. It is difficult to distinguish the discontinuities at the shot bound from the discontinuities brought by the noise in a common feature space. In such cases, it is necessary to find a way to remove the noise in the signal of video content. In this paper, a subspace-based method is proposed to remedy this problem. Each short period of video is represented using an individual subspace, named Local Subspace, generated from the contextual information. Then shot boundaries are detected in every specialized subspace. The experiment results show the Local Subspace based method can remove the noise effectively and promote the performance of SBD.

The rest of this paper is as follows: The shortage of representing all frames in one common space is analyzed in Section 2. Section 3 introduces the subspace-based method in detail. Experiments results and discussions are given in Section 4. In addition, Section 5 provides the major conclusions.

2   Shortage of Representing Visual Content in One Common Space

Various techniques such as intensity/color histograms [8]–[10], edge [11][12], motion [13]–[16] have been proposed to represent visual content in previous works. The experimental results in previous survey [3][4][17] show the complicated features usually cannot outperform simple histogram feature. So, only color histogram based visual content representation method is studied here.

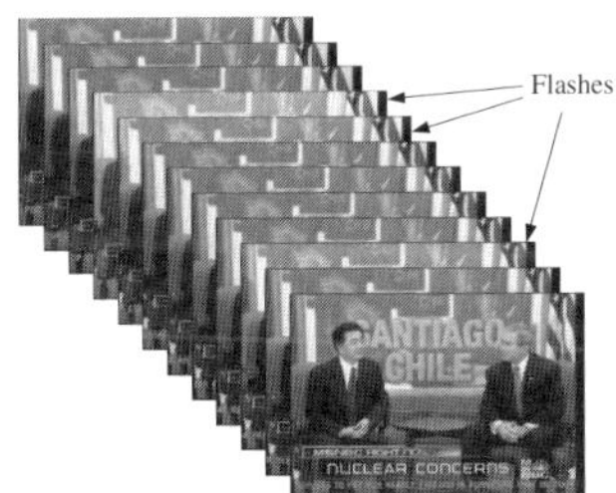

Fig. 1. Video sequence with three flashes. The sequence is taken from TRECVID2005 (20041120_ 110000_ MSNBC_MSNBCNEWS11_ENG.mpg, frame 6420-6450), only part of frames is shown here.

A classic problem in SBD is to distinguish the change within shots and at the shots boundaries. A familiar example is used to tell the flashes from abrupt shot boundaries. Flashes can remarkably influence the color or the intensity of pixels in video frames and bring discontinuity to video sequence. As a flash maintains a very short time, it influences just one or two frames in video sequence and often be mixed up with abrupt shot boundaries. Consider a video sequence with three flashlights as shown in Fig. 1. There are two flashes occur almost at the same time. They influence three adjacent frames in sequence. The other flash occurs alone and just influences one frame.

In Fig. 2, frames influenced by the three flashes are away from other frames in HSV space in the figure while other frames are well clustered. This figure demonstrates the significant influence of flashes on representing video content in HSV space. When there are no flashes, the same video contents are correctly represented in adjacent positions in HSV space. While flashes occurring, the contents are represented in positions away from usual one. This phenomena illustrates there may exit events (e.g., flash) which can change the feature representation in common feature spaces remarkably while leaving content untouched in video sequence. This means using the change in common space to detect the variation of video content may not be quite proper. Further discussion on distinguishing flashes from abrupt shot boundaries will show the shortage clearly.

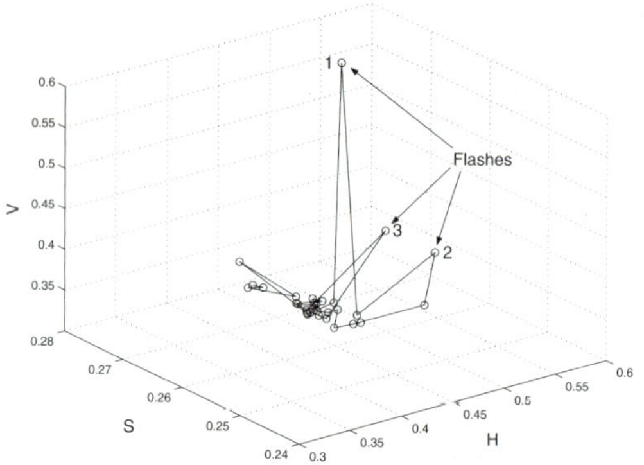

Fig. 2. Video sequence with three flashes represented in HSV color space (using the average HSV value of all pixels in every frame as coordinates). The frames influenced by three flashes are away from other frames in HSV space. Two flashes (1, 2) occurring almost at the same time influence three adjacent frames in sequence. The other flash (3) occurs alone just influences one frame.

A longer sequence that contains the sequence in Fig. 1 is used to analyze the issue of telling flashes from abrupt shot boundaries. The intersection of the Hue histogram is used as continuity value of two adjacent frames. The continuity of whole sequence is shown in Fig. 3. The continuity at shot boundary is often lower than that within a shot. So thresholds can be used to detect the boundaries. However, the influence brought by flashes makes the continuity value within a shot even lower than that at an abrupt boundary as shown in Fig. 3.

In order to surmount the obstacle, researchers improved the method in some way. In early years, the improvements were mainly centered on using adaptive thresholds [4]. At different parts of sequence, different thresholds are generated based on the continuity value of local frames. Recently, some contextual information based continuity computing methods are proposed [7]. The continuity of sequence is no longer based on the distance of only two adjacent frames in the feature space. The distances of all frame-pair in sequence context are used to detect shot boundary based on graph partition model in [7]. The graph partition models were also used in image segmentation [18] and video scenes detection [19][20].

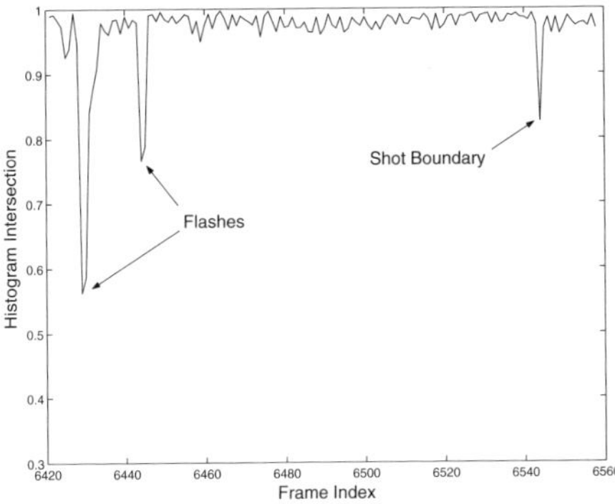

Fig. 3. The continuity of sequence (frame 6420-6560). The three flashes occur at frame 6428, 6430 and 6443. Because the first and second one occur almost at same time there are only two obvious undulations caused by flashes. Another undulation is caused by abrupt shot boundary occurring at frame 6553. There are three flashes and one abrupt shot boundary in the sequence.

Both kinds of methods only use contextual information after the visual content has been mapping to feature space. However, as shown in Fig. 2, the distance in feature space often cannot represent the actual similarity of visual content. That is because the common feature space is for the representation of all visual content we can see from the world but not for the specialized content. If there is some minor change in the frames of a sequence (e.g. flashes), even this kind of change is not in the main content of the sequence, the mapping of the frames to feature space will be remarkably changed. This kind of mapping is vulnerable to disturb in representing a specialized content. Therefore, we propose a subspace-based method to remedy this problem in this paper for SBD.

3 Local Subspace-Based Denoising

The subspace-based method proposed takes a step forward in using contextual information comparing with conventional methods. One individual frame subspace is created for every short period of visual content with the local information. The main visual content within a shot is stable and only changes dramatic at shot boundary. Therefore, the subspace for SBD should efficiently describe the main content of video sequence. In this paper, we use Singular Value Decomposition (SVD) to do this job.

3.1 Local Subspace Creating

Firstly, a frame in video sequence is taken as a vector, an array of all pixels' intense value in it. All frames in a sequence can form a nonnegative matrix with every column representing one frame. In another viewpoint, the images can also be regarded as signals in a high-dimensional pace. The main content of video sequence is represented by the main signal. In order to choose appropriate subspace for main content representation, the SVD is used to analyze the signal and noise in the sequence. According to the energy compaction property of the SVD, the large singular values represent the main signal in the sequence [21]. Therefore, the left singular vectors corresponding to large eigenvalue are used as basis of spaces, which represents the main content of video sequence.

Let S denotes a video sequence with m frames; the frame size is $h{\times}w$. The intense values of all $n{=}h{\times}w$ pixels in the ith frame are arrayed in row prior order to form a vector noted a_i. An $m{\times}n$ matrix $A = [a_1, a_2, a_3, \dots , a_m]$ is used to represent S. When we just consider the content of a short period video, there exists $m < n$. The SVD of A is as follows:

$$A = U \Sigma V^T = \sum_{k=1}^{l} u_k \sigma_k v_k^T \tag{1}$$

where $l = m = \min(m, n)$, $U = [u_1, u_2, u_3, \dots , u_m]$ is an $n \times m$ matrix having columns that are mutually orthonormal, $V = [v_1, v_2, v_3, \dots , v_m]$ is an $m \times m$ unitary matrix, and $\Sigma = \mathrm{diag}(\sigma_1, \sigma_2, \sigma_3, \dots , \sigma_m)$. The diagonal elements of Σ are called the singular values of A and are in decreasing order $\sigma_1 \geq \sigma_2 \geq \sigma_3 \dots \geq \sigma_m$. U is called the left singular matrix, and V is called the right singular matrix. The columns of U and V are called, respectively, the left and right singular vectors.

The sequence in Fig. 1 is used again here as example to illustrate how to create appropriate spaces for main content representing. The singular values and parts of visualized left singular vectors are shown in Fig. 4. From the figure, the energy of signal is obviously concentrated on the first singular value. So, the left singular vector v_1 according to the largest singular value is chosen as basis to create the eigenspace. The projection value pi of ith frame on v_1 is computed using

$$p_i = v_1 a_i \tag{2}$$

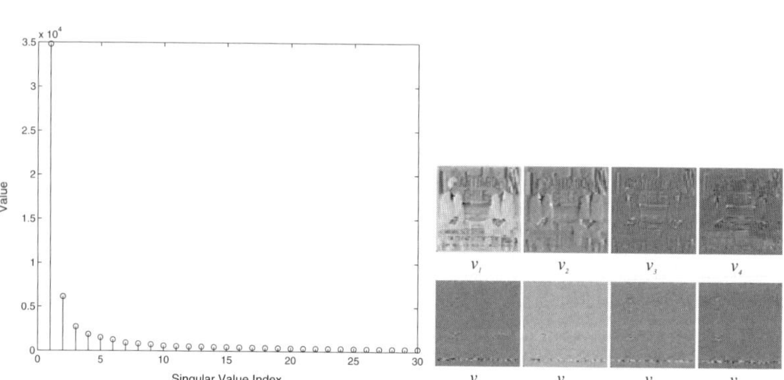

Fig. 4. The first 4 and last 4 visualized left singular vectors (frame 6420-6450). The frames are resized to 64×64. The singular vector according to singular value σ_i is labeled v_i.

The projection onto basis v_1 of frame 6420-6450 is given in Fig. 5. The noise brought by the two flashes is efficiently removed in the new subspace.

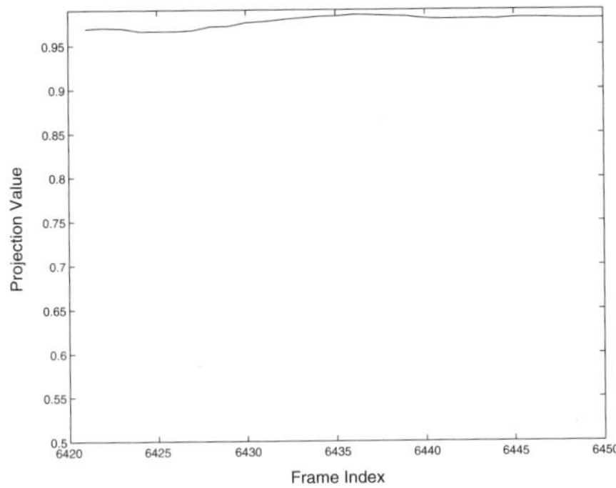

Fig. 5. The projection on basis v_1 (frame 6420-6450)

3.2 Local Subspace Refreshing

Usually, the video content is in continuously changing even with in one shot. Therefore, the subspace used for SBD should also keep changing with the content. If not doing so, one subspace generated from just period of video cannot describe the variation of whole content. In Fig. 6, the basis v_1 is generated from frame 6420-6450. When we project frame 6420-6560 on v_1, the projection value cannot reflect the changing in video content. For instants, at the shot boundary (frame 6543), the projection value does not fluctuate obviously. The projection value drops obviously from frame 6480 to 6490 according to a rapid camera zooming and tracking. This is to say when there is obvious change in video content, the subspace generated before the change is no longer useful in describing the content after the change.

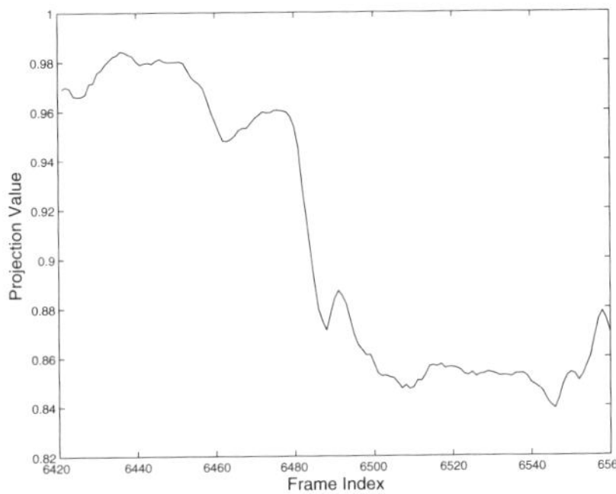

Fig. 6. The projection value generated using non-refreshed space. The basis v_1 is generated from frame 6420-6450. The frames 6420-6560 are projected on the non-refreshed basis.

Besides this, the difference of projection value is given in Fig. 7. The difference only fluctuates obviously from frame 6480 to 6490 according to the rapid camera zooming and tracking. After this camera action, the non-refreshed basis generated from 6420-6450 cannot describe the changing in content. The projection value fluctuates little despite of an abrupt shot boundary at frame 6543.

38   X. Pan et al.

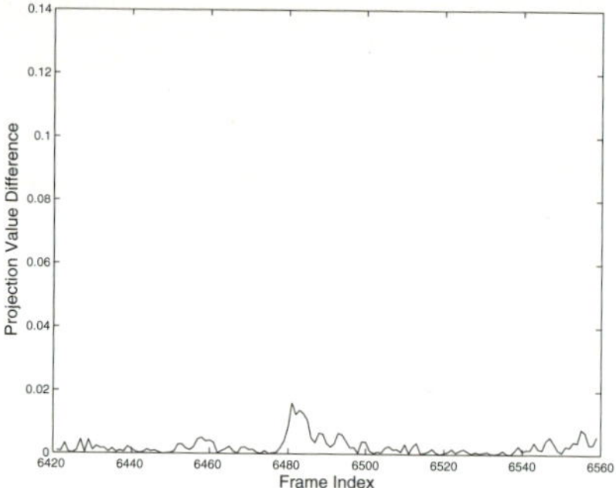

Fig. 7. The difference of projection value generated from frame 6420-6450 using non-refreshed spaces

Therefore, use one single subspace can not efficiently describe the changes of video content for SBD. It can not get better results than just use a common space. The key point is the subspace should be refreshed according to the changing local context. In practice, the local space is refreshed every k frame when there is no boundary detected in the duration. In case a boundary is detected, the local space is refreshed immediately. Then l adjacent frames are used to create the local space. The analyzing results of frame 6420-6560 in refreshed space are given in Fig. 8.

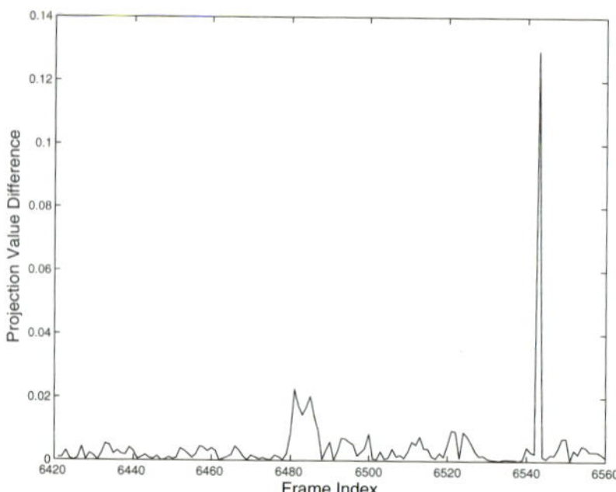

Fig. 8. The difference of projection value generated from frame 6420-6450 using refreshed spaces. When in refreshed space, $k=70$, $l=20$, the value also fluctuates from frame 6480 to 6490. Besides this, there is a much stronger pulse at frame 6543 representing the abrupt boundary.

In Fig. 8, when the subspace is refreshed every 70 frames, it can describe the change of video content within the frames effectively. In this way, the abrupt boundary at frame 6543 gives a remarkable pulse in Fig. 8. Besides this, the noise brought by the camera action makes much weaker fluctuates than the boundary. Therefore, we can tell the change at shot boundaries and the noises within shots apart with easy using refreshed subspace.

The results of using refreshed and not-refreshed methods on frame 6420-6450 are compared in Fig. 9.

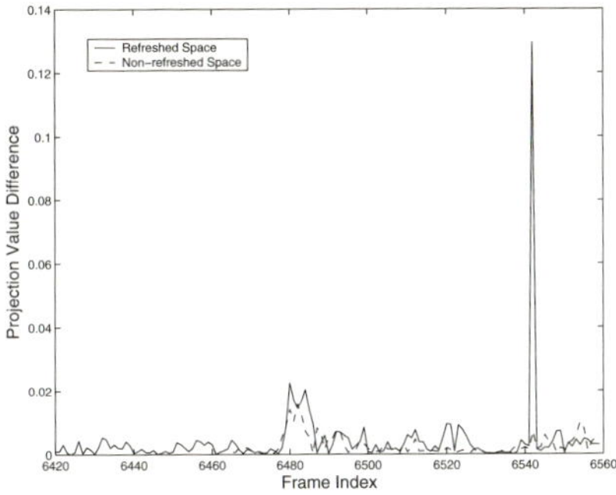

Fig. 9. The comparison of methods using refreshed (the solid line) and non-refreshed (the dashed line) spaces. In non-refreshed space, basis v_1 is generated from frame 6420-6450. The difference value only fluctuates obviously from frame 6480 to 6490 according to a rapid camera zooming and tracking. In refreshed spaces, the subspace keeps on refreshing from frame 6420-6450 every 70 frames.

In Fig. 9, the two curves represent the results of refreshing method and non-refreshing method individually. The curves are same until frame 6460. However, after that frame, the non-refreshed space cannot represent the change in video content. A strong pulse at frame 6543, which represents the abrupt boundary, only exists in refreshed space show the effectiveness of refreshing method in representing the changing contents for SBD. The noise can be efficiently distinguished from the signal brought by shot boundary.

A sequence from CNN (iraq.senate.vte.cnn) is used to compare the proposed method with the method in [22]. This video includes many scenes in war fields, so it is not easy to tell the shot bound from the noise caused by the camera action or objects moving. The result using both kinds of methods is given in Fig. 10.

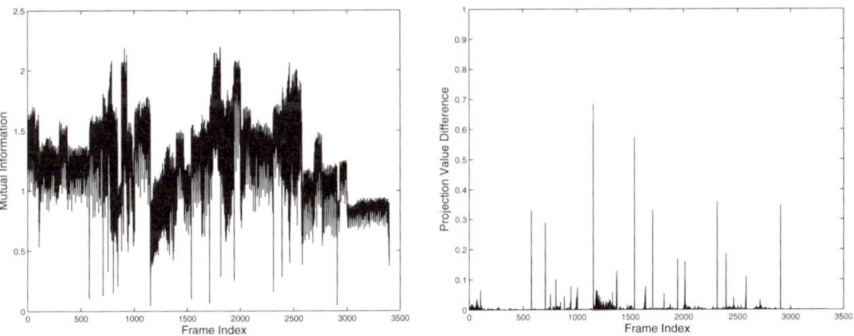

Fig. 10. The sequence is from CNN (bash.iraq.senate.vte.cnn). The left one is generated using MI. The Mutual Information (MI) is generated with method proposed in [22]. The right one is the difference of projection value generated using proposed method.

As there existing intense camera motion and object moving (war scenes), the gradual transitions are especially hard to tell from the noise. In MI based method, it is hard to find a proper threshold to tell shot boundary from the noise. In proposed method, to compute the difference of projection value, let $k=70$, $l=20$. The noise is effective removed. Only use a threshold (0.045), 12 abrupt boundaries and 7 gradual transitions are detected with 2 missed abrupt boundaries 3 false detected gradual transition.

4 Conclusion

In this paper, the shortage of using common feature space for SBD is demonstrated and analyzed. This may partly answer the question: why it is hard to choose appropriate thresholds for SBD in common feature space. Specialized subspace that keeps changing with the video content is used to detect the real shot boundary. Experiments show this kind of localized method can effectively restrain the noises with in the shots. As the local PCA can reveal the tangent space of perceptional manifold of video content [23], the projection to the subspace composed with eigenvectors of SVD can preserve the manifold structure of local content. We will analyze the video content according to the manifold structure of visual information in our future work.

Acknowledgements

This work is supported in part by the National High Technology and Research Development Program of China (863 Program, 2007AA01Z416), the National Key Basic Research Program of China (973 Program, 2007CB311100), Beijing New Star Project on Science and Technology (2007B071), and the National Natural Science Foundation of China (NSFC, 60773056).

The authors would like to thank the reviewers for their careful and constructive criticism of the original manuscript.

References

1. Smoliar, S.W., Zhang, H.-J.: Content-based video indexing and retrieval. IEEE Multimedia 1(2), 62–72 (1994)
2. Vasconcelos, A.L.: Statistical models of video structure for content analysis and characterization. IEEE Trans. Image Process. 9(1), 3–19 (2000)
3. Lienhart, R.: Reliable Dissolve Detection in videos: a survey and practitioner's guide. Int. J. Image Graph. 1(3), 469–486 (2001)
4. Hanjalic, A.: Shot-boundary detection: unraveled and resolved? IEEE Trans. Circuits Syst. Video Technol. 12(3), 90–105 (2002)
5. Albanese, A.C., Moscato, V., Sansone, L.: A formal model for video shot segmentation and its application via animate vision. Multimedia Tools Appl 24(3), 253–272 (2004)
6. Bescós, G.C., Martínez, J.M., Menendez, J.M., Cabrera, J.: A unified model for techniques on video shot transition detection. IEEE Trans. Multimedia 7(2), 293–307 (2005)
7. Yuan, J., Wang, H., Xiao, L., Zheng, W., Li, J., Lin, F., Zhang, B.: A Formal Study of Shot Boundary Detection. IEEE Trans. Circuits Syst. Video Technol. 17(2), 168–186 (2007)

8. Kikukawa, S.K.: Development of an automatic summary editing system for the audio visual resources. Trans. IEICE J75-A(2), 204–212 (1992)
9. Choubey, K., Raghavan, V.V.: Generic and fully automatic content-based image retrieval using color. Pattern Recog. Lett. 18(11–13), 1233–1240 (1997)
10. Zhang, J., Low, C.Y., Smoliar, S.W.: Video parsing and browsing using compressed data. Multimedia Tools Appl. 1(1), 89–111 (1995)
11. Zabih, J.M., Mai, K.: A Feature-Based Algorithm for Detecting and Classifying Scene Breaks. In: Proc. ACM Multimedia 1995, San Francisco, CA, pp. 189–200 (1995)
12. Zabih, J.M., Mai, K.: A Feature-based Algorithm for Detecting and Classification Production Effects. Multimedia Systems 7, 119–128 (1999)
13. Akutsu, Y.T., Hashimoto, H., Ohba, Y.: Video Indexing Using Motion Vectors. In: Proc. SPIE Visual Communications and Image Processing, vol. 1818, pp. 1522–1530 (1992)
14. Shahraray: Scene Change Detection and Content-Based Sampling of Video Sequences. In: Proc. SPIE Digital Video Compression, Algorithm and Technologies, vol. 2419, pp. 2–13 (1995)
15. Zhang, J., Kankanhalli, A., Smoliar, S.W.: Automatic Partitioning of Full-Motion Video. Multimedia Systems 1(1), 10–28 (1993)
16. Bouthemy, M.G., Ganansia, F.: A unified approach to shot change detection and camera motion characterization. IEEE Trans. Circuits Syst. Video Technol. 9(7), 1030–1044 (1999)
17. Gargi, R.K., Strayer, S.H.: Performance characterization of video-shot-change detection methods. IEEE Trans. Circuits Syst. Video Technol. 10(1), 1–13 (2000)
18. Shi, J.M.: Normalized cuts and image segmentation. IEEE Trans. Pattern Anal. Machine Intell. 22(8), 888–905 (2000)
19. Rasheed, M.S.: Detection and Representation of Scenes in Videos. IEEE Trans. Multimedia 7(6), 1097–1105 (2005)
20. Ngo, W., Ma, Y.F., Zhang, H.J.: Video summarization and Scene Detection by Graph Modeling. IEEE Trans. Circuits Syst. Video Technol. 15(2), 296–305 (2005)
21. Hu, S.: Digital Signal Processing, 2nd edn. Tsinghua University Press, Beijing (2003)
22. Černeková, I.P., Nikou, C.: Information theory-based shot cut/fade detection and video summarization. IEEE Trans. Circuits Syst. Video Technol. 16(1), 82–91 (2006)
23. Min, W., Lu, K., He, X.: Locality pursuit embedding. Pattern Recognition 37, 781–788 (2004)

Image Retrieval Using Modified Color Variation Co-occurrence Matrix

Yung-Fu Chen[1], Yung-Kuan Chan[2], Guo-Uei Chang[3], Meng-Chi Tsao[3],
Yu-Jhuang Syu[4], and Chuen-Horng Lin[3,4,*]

[1] Department of Health Services Administration, China Medical University, Taichung
404, Taiwan
yungfu@mail.cmu.edu.tw
[2] Department of Management of Information Systems, National Chung Hsing
University, Taichung 402, Taiwan
ykchan@nchu.edu.tw
[3] Department of Information Management and
[4] Institute of Computer Science and Information Technology, National Taichung
Institute of Technology, Taichung 404, Taiwan
{S1492B037,S1492B041,S18953108,linch}@ntit.edu.tw

Abstract. Texture is widely used as an important feature for content based image retrieval (CBIR). In this paper, color variation co-occurrence matrix (CVCM) modified from a previous investigation has been proposed for describing texture characteristics of an image. An image is processed and converted into four CVCMs based on overlapping 3 x 3 windows scanning from top to bottom and left to right. Each 3 x 3 window is divided into 4 grids with the central pixel located at four different corners. First, the original image with a size of N_x x N_y is converted into 4 motif matrices from individual scanning windows according to the traversal between the differences of four adjacent pixels. By contrasting to a previous method that 6 motif patterns were discriminated, an additional pattern was used to resolve ambiguity amounting to 7 motif patterns in total. By computing the probability of adjacent pattern pairs, an image retrieval system has been developed. The performance of the CVCM system was evaluated in the experiments using four different image sets. The experimental results reveal that the proposed CVCM-based image retrieval system outperforms the methods proposed by Huang and Dai and Jhanwar et al.

1 Introduction

Image retrieval plays an important role in several image database applications, such as office automation, medical image archiving, digital library, and geographic information systems [1]. Low-level features, such as spatial relations [2,9], colors [3-5,9], and textures [6-9], are extensively used to index image features of CBIR systems. Although color and texture attributes have been widely

---

* To whom correspondence should be addressed. No. 129, Sec. 3, Sanmin Rd.,
Taichung, Taiwan, R.O.C.; Tel.: 886-4-22195502; Fax: 886-4-22196311.

N.T. Nguyen et al. (Eds.): IEA/AIE 2008, LNAI 5027, pp. 42–51, 2008.

used in image retrieval, these attributes do not efficiently describe the spatial distribution of different texture patterns of an image resulting in unsatisfactory retrieval performance. In this study, we propose an attribute which describes the spatial relations among pixels and show that it is efficient for image retrieval.

Jhanwar et al. [7] proposed an image retrieval system using motif co-occurrence matrix (MCM) to describe texture patterns. However, it concerns only the adjacent pixels without overlapping. Four co-occurrence matrices used to achieve shift-invariance are constructed based on four $Nx/2$ x $Ny/2$ motif matrices by considering horizontal, vertical, and diagonal shifting of the original image having the size of Nx x Ny pixels. Besides, if two adjacent pixels having the same pixel value in a grid, the pattern is treated as ambiguous pattern and is simply discarded in the scheme proposed by Jhanwar et al. [7]. In order to better resolve the variation of adjacent pixel colors, this paper proposes an alternative scheme, namely color variation co-occurrence matrix (CVCM), for efficiently describing the texture attributes of an image. First, the scheme was modified to construct the co-occurrence matrices using overlapping scheme based on four Nx x Ny motif matrices that each of them has the size of 7 x 7 instead of 6 x 6 elements by treating ambiguous motifs as an alternative motif (motif 0). The results show that our proposed modified method significantly increases the retrieval performance tested using 4 image sets.

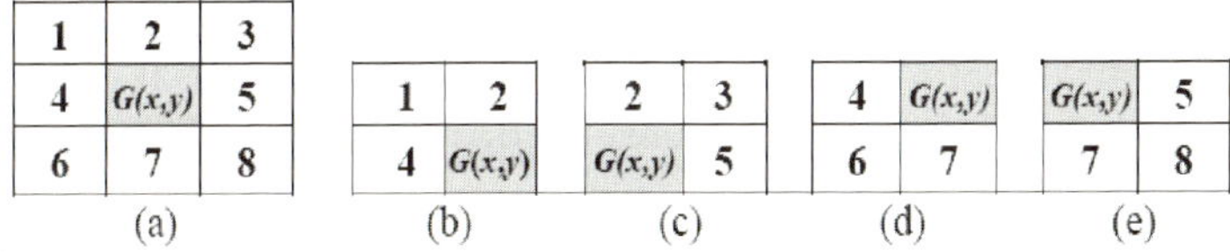

Fig. 1. (a) A 3 x 3 window can be divided into (b)-(e) four 2 x 2 grids with $G(x,y)$ located at four different corners

2   Motif Matrices of Scan Patterns

In this study, color variation co-occurrence matrix (CVCM) is proposed for representing the traversal of color difference for adjacent pixels in an image. Since each pixel has four neighboring pixels based on 4-neighborhood, four matrices that have the same size as the original image can be derived by using motifs of the scan patterns. Based on these four motif matrices, color variation co-occurrence matrix (CVCM) can be obtained with an element treated as a feature.

As shown in Fig. 1, a 3 x 3 window with the pixel $G(x,y)$ located at the center can be divided into four overlapped 2 x 2 grids with $G(x,y)$ located at 4 different corners, respectively. It contrasts to the previous investigation that non-overlapped grids were used to construct motif matrices [7]. These 2 x 2 grids are then replaced by motifs of scanning pattern traversing the grid in the optimal sense. The optimality of the scan is achieved by traversing the path with respect to the incremental difference in intensity along the scan path by minimizing the variation of the intensities at a local neighborhood. For example, by scanning the grid shown in Fig. 2(a) from the upper-left pixel $p1$, a U-shape motif is formed, Fig. 2(d). The distance from $p1$ to any pixel pi that has the shortest distance can be calculated from the following equation:

$$p(\Delta) = \min\left\{\|p_1 - p_i\|\right\}, \ i = 2, \ 3, \ 4. \tag{1}$$

The pixel p_i in turn will be used as the starting pixel for the next scan. For example, as shown in Fig. 2(b), p_3 is taken as the next starting point since its distance to p_1 is shortest. Its distances to other two pixels can be calculated in a similar way. The intermediate and final steps are shown in Figs. 2(c) and 2(d).

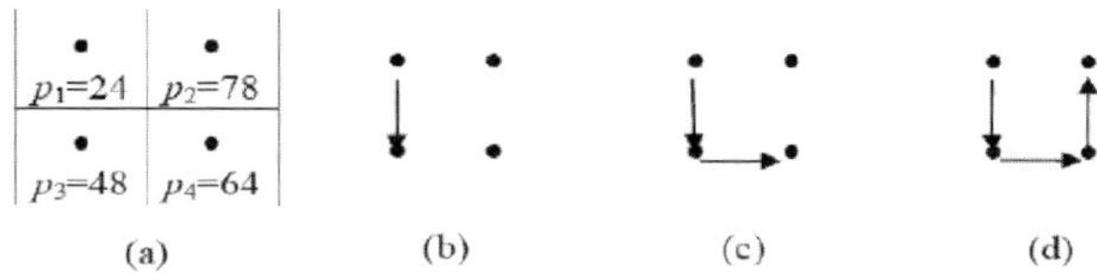

Fig. 2. Illustration of motif construction for a 2 x 2 grid

In general, there are 24 different scan patterns in total for a 2 x 2 grid if the traverse starts from four different corners along the paths. If only the scans starting from the top-left corner are considered, a complete family of space filling curve can be reduced to only 6 motif patterns, as shown in Fig. 3 (b)-(g) [7]. In order to resolve the ambiguous motif patterns mentioned in [7], motif 0 shown in Fig. 3(a) has been adopted to indicate special situations wherein a motif can not be formed due to the equivalence of two or more pixels. Hence, there are 7 motif patterns for constructing co-occurrence matrices with a size of 7 x 7 elements.

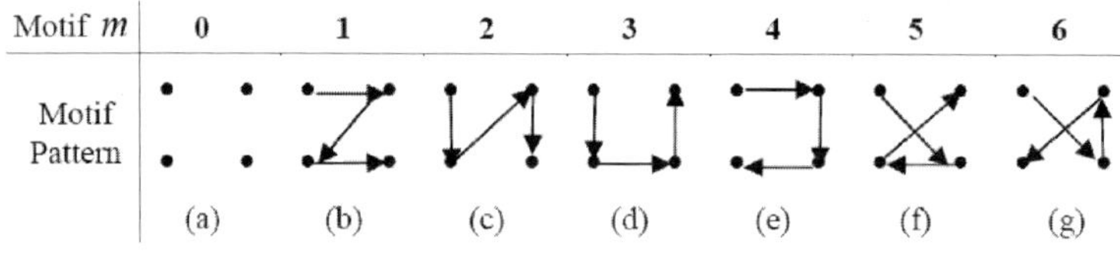

Fig. 3. Seven scanning patterns can be formed by scanning a 2 x 2 grid from its top-left corner

As shown in Fig. (4), the examples demonstrate various patterns of motif 0 in Fig. 3(a), in which all the four pixels or any two or three adjacent pixels have the same value in a grid. The patterns can be classified into ascending and descending patterns based on whether the values of scanning sequence are increased or decreased.

Motif 0	0-1	0-2	0-3	0-4	0-5
(a) Ascending Pattern	48 48 / 48 48	48 → 78 / 78 78	48 → 78 / 78 → 96	48 → 78 / 96 96	48 96 / 78 96
(b) Descending Pattern	96 96 / 96 96	78 → 48 / 48 48	96 → 78 / 78 → 48	96 → 78 / 48 48	96 48 / 78 → 48

Fig. 4. (a) Ascending and (b) descending scanning patterns for motif 0

3 Color Variation Co-occurrence Matrix (CVCM)

The conventional co-occurrence matrix calculates the probabilities of the occurrence of individual color patterns by considering a pixel and its adjacent ones with a certain distance. The probabilities are considered as the attributes of the image. In contrast, MCM and CVCM differ in that both schemes calculate the color distribution (scanning pattern) within two-dimensional motifs by representing it with a co-occurrence matrix $P_i[N_x,N_y]$. In another word, it considers the probability of the co-occurrence between the two adjacent motifs corresponding to a pixel (x, y) and its adjacent pixel $(x+\delta_x, y+\delta_y)$. The probability is then used as the attribute of image color variation. Given a spatial offset $(\delta_x;\delta_y)$, the co-occurrence probability between two motifs u and v can be computed for all possible co-occurring motif number pairs in a motif matrix.

After the image is processed and converted into motif patterns, four two-dimensional N_x x N_y matrix $P_i[N_x,N_y]$ for delineating motif scan patterns can be obtained. And then, if we consider the probability of the co-occurrence of the two motifs corresponding to a pixel (x, y) and its adjacent pixel $(x+\delta_x, y+\delta_y)$ with distances δ_x and δ_y on the x and y axes, respectively. The total number of co-occurring motifs of scan pattern pairs (u,v) with $u=0,1,\ldots 6$ and $v=0,1,\ldots 6$ is determined by:

$$M_i(u, v) = M_i(u, v\,|\delta_x, \delta_y) = M_i(P_i(x, y), P_i(x + \delta_x, y + \delta_y)) \qquad (2)$$

where $P_i(x,y) = u$ and $P_i(x+\delta_x, y+\delta_y) = v$ with $1\leq i \leq 4$, $1\leq x \leq N_x$, $1\leq y \leq N_y$, $1\leq x+\delta_x \leq N_x$, and $1\leq y+\delta_y \leq N_y$. The co-occurring probabilities of the ith motif matrix are determined by dividing $M_i(u,v)$ by the total number of counts across the co-occurrence matrix, as shown below:

$$m_i(u, v) = M_i(u, v)/N_i \qquad (3)$$

in which

$$N_i = \sum_{u=0}^{6}\sum_{v=0}^{6} M_i(u, v), \ 1 \leq i \leq 4 \qquad (4)$$

As a result, there will be four 7 x 7 two-dimensional CVCM matrices amounting to 4 x 7 x 7 = 196 elements used as attributes for image retrieval. For example, if we have an image with a size of 8 x 8 pixels shown in Fig. 5(a), four two-dimensional N_x x N_y motif matrices $P_i[N_x,N_y]$, Fig. 5(b), will be obtained for further calculation of 4 co-occurrence matrices, Fig. 5(c). In this example, by assuming δ_x and δ_y to be both 1, the total numbers of individual co-occurring motifs of the scan pattern $m_1[u,v]$ are shown in Fig. 5(b). A true-color image in which each pixel consists of three color components, i.e. R, G, and B, can be converted into three gray-level images. Hence, the CVCM of a color image is converted into three gray-level CVCM images.

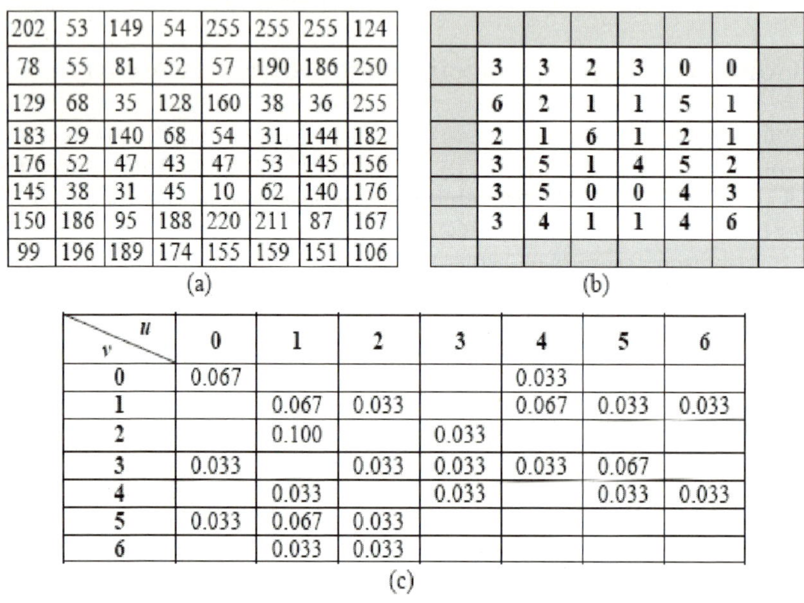

(a)

202	53	149	54	255	255	255	124
78	55	81	52	57	190	186	250
129	68	35	128	160	38	36	255
183	29	140	68	54	31	144	182
176	52	47	43	47	53	145	156
145	38	31	45	10	62	140	176
150	186	95	188	220	211	87	167
99	196	189	174	155	159	151	106

(b)

3	3	2	3	0	0
6	2	1	1	5	1
2	1	6	1	2	1
3	5	1	4	5	2
3	5	0	0	4	3
3	4	1	1	4	6

(c)

v \ u	0	1	2	3	4	5	6
0	0.067				0.033		
1		0.067	0.033		0.067	0.033	0.033
2		0.100		0.033			
3	0.033		0.033	0.033	0.033	0.067	
4		0.033		0.033		0.033	0.033
5	0.033	0.067	0.033				
6		0.033	0.033				

Fig. 5. (a) An 8 x 8 gray-scale image, (b) an example of motif matrix $P_1[6,6]$ and (c) its corresponding co-occurrence matrix $m_1[u,v]$

4   Image Retrieval System

Regardless the shift-variation influence of objects [9], CVCM is useful to describe the relationship between color and texture of an image. However, it is sensitive to the noise variation [9]. The similarity measure that we used for the purpose of retrieval was simply the summation of difference between the corresponding entries in the CVCM and an associated weight. When a query image Q is input to the retrieval system, the CVCM system compares the feature values of the query image with those of the images in database. The database images which have shortest distances to Q are delivered to the user. The similarity measure can be expressed as follow:

$$\Delta^{CVCM} = \Delta^R + \Delta^G + \Delta^B \tag{5}$$

where

$$\Delta^C = \sum_{i=1}^{4} \sum_{u=0}^{6} \sum_{v=0}^{6} \frac{\left| m_i^{Q_C}[u,v] - m_i^{D_C}[u,v] \right|}{m_i^{Q_C}[u,v] + m_i^{D_C}[u,v] + \nu} \tag{6}$$

in which C represents R, G, and B components, respectively, Q and D indicate the query and database images, and ν is a small number used to avoid possible numerical instabilities caused by zero denominator[7].

5 Experimental Results and Conclusions

The performance of the CVCM system is evaluated by experiments based on four image sets. In the first image set, an image pair is consisted of a query image and its corresponding database image. A query is deemed as successful if the corresponding image has been retrieved. Image Set 2 contains 112 gray-level texture images that each has a size of 512 x 512 pixels. Each image was partitioned into 16 non-overlapping images having the size of 128 x 128 pixels before experiments. For each query image, there are 15 corresponding images which are expected to be retrieved. The third image set was used by Jhanwar et al. [7] for testing the performance of their proposed method. It consists of 60 images that have been classified into 12 categories. Regarding the fourth image set, 1000 true-color natural images classified into 10 categories were used for the experiment to compare the performance of three methods.

In the first experiment, accuracy rate was used for evaluating retrieval performance, while in experiments 2, 3, and 4, precision and recall rates were applied. For each query in experiment 1, the system responds to the user L database images (I_i^d) that have the smallest distances to the query image I_i^q. If I_i^d is among the L responding database images, we say that the system correctly retrieves the desired image. Otherwise, it is considered as a failure. The accurate retrieval rate is used to evaluate the retrieval performance and is denoted as $ACC(\%)$. In contrast, the recall (R) and precision (P) rates are defined as follows [12]:

$$P(k) = n_k / L \tag{7}$$

$$R(k) = n_k / N \tag{8}$$

in which L indicates the number of retrieved images, n_k represents the number of relevant images which have been retrieved, and N is the number of all relevant images in the database.

Experiment 1. The first image set includes a database set, $SetD = \{I_1^d, I_2^d, I_3^d, ..., I_{1051}^d\}$, and a query set, $SetQ = \{I_1^q, I_2^q, I_3^q, ..., I_{1051}^q\}$ that each consists of 1051 true-color images. Some of the images were drawn out from videos and animations, in which each image pair (I_i^d, I_i^q) are randomly picked from the same video or animation. Most of these animations were downloaded from the websites (http://www.mcsh.kh.edu.tw and http://co25.mi.com.tw). Some other images were downloaded from http://wang.ist.su.du/IMAGE. The rest of the

(a)   (b)

Fig. 6. Examples of (a) query and (b) database images of Image Set 1

Table 1. Comparisons of accuracy rate $ACC(\%)$ among CVCM and the methods proposed by Huang and Dai and Jhanwar et al

$ACC(\%)$ L	1	2	3	4	5	10	20	30	50	100
Huang and Dai	65.3	72.2	74.7	77.0	78.1	83.5	86.2	88.4	92	94.7
Jhanwar et al.	62.4	70.7	74.8	76.6	79	84	87.7	90.2	92.3	94.6
CVCM	**66.4**	**74**	**76.7**	**78.4**	**80.2**	**85.5**	**89.8**	**91.6**	**93.6**	**96**

Table 2. A comparison of retrieval precision among three different methods

$P(\%)$ L	2	3	4	5	10	16
Huang and Dai [6]	84.7	80.3	77.0	74.6	66.2	57.0
Jhanwar et al. [7]	89.5	84.5	80.8	78.0	68.7	59.4
CVCM	**92.7**	**88.7**	**85.8**	**83.3**	**74.3**	**65.7**

images were scanned from natural images and trademark pictures. Fig. 6 shows some examples of the query and database images of this image set.

The retrieval accuracy for the proposed CVCM method was compared to the methods proposed by Huang and Dai [6] and Jhanwar et al. [7]. In this experiment, the spatial offset $(\delta_x, \delta_y)=(0,1)$. Table 1 compares the accuracy rates for CVCM and the other two approaches. As depicted in this table, CVCM outperforms the other two methods with respect to different number of responding images. As expected, since the CVCM concerns the adjacent pixel difference, better retrieval performance is achieved.

Experiment 2. Image Set 2 contains 112 gray-level texture images with the size of 512 x 512 pixels. The images are available on http://www.ux.his.no/~tranden /brodatz.html. Each image has been partitioned into 16 non-overlapping images with the size of 128 x 128 pixels before experiment. Fig. 7 (a) shows several examples of this image set. Table 2 compares the retrieval precision of three different approaches. The result demonstrates that CVCM system is capable of retrieving texture images with much better performance than the other two methods.

Table 3. Categories and number of images of individual categories for image set 3

Category	Buildings	Bark	Brick	Fabric	Flowers	Food	Leaves
Image No.	13	9	11	20	8	12	17
Category	Metal	Paintings	Sand	Stone	Terrain	Tile	Miscellaneous
Image No.	6	14	7	6	11	11	25

Fig. 7. Examples of images for (a) set 2, (b) set 3, and (c) set 4, respectively

Experiment 3. Table 3 shows the category and number of images of individual categories for image set 3. Examples of the image set are shown in Fig. 7(b).

Figs. 8(b) and 8(c) demonstrate the images retrieved by the method proposed by Jhanwar et al. [7] with color histogram [10] and MCM [7] used as two independent

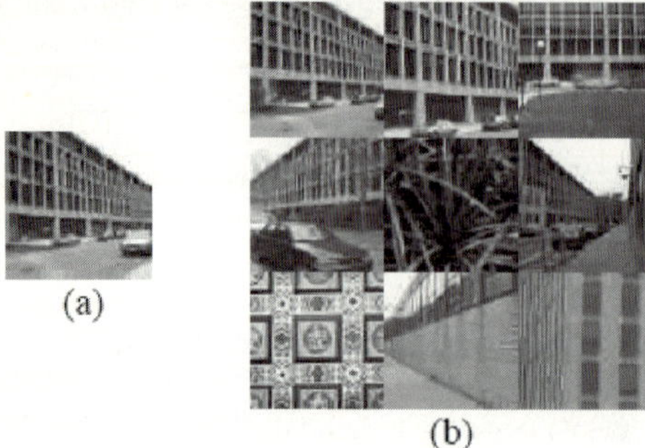

Fig. 8. (a) A query image and the retrieved images using the method proposed by (b) Jhanwar et al. and (c) the CVCM approach

Table 4. A comparison of retrieval precision among three methods for image set 4

Category	CVCM	Jhanwar et al.	Hung and Dai
African & Tribe	**0.5045**	0.4525	0.4240
Beach	0.4310	0.3975	**0.4455**
Building	**0.4500**	0.3735	0.4105
Bus	0.7900	0.7410	**0.8515**
Dinosaur	**0.9320**	0.9145	0.5865
Elephant	0.3185	0.3040	**0.4255**
Flower	0.8900	0.8515	**0.8975**
Horse	0.5495	0.5680	**0.5890**
Mountain & Glacier	**0.3050**	0.2925	0.2680
Food	**0.4340**	0.3695	0.4265
Average	**0.5605**	0.5264	0.5324

features and the proposed CVCM system, respectively. As shown in Fig. 8, both Jhanwar [7] and CVCM systems retrieved the same number of relevant images. Since the CVCM system is able to better recognize images with similar color distribution, the retrieved images are more similar and relevant to the query image and have lower ranks than the images retrieved by the approach proposed by Jhanwar et al. [7].

Experiment 4. The 4th image set contains 1000 true-color natural images classified into 10 categories that each contains 100 images. Fig. 7(c) demonstrates examples of individual categories. A comparison of three methods are presented in Table 4 with the number of returned images was set to $L=20$. As shown in this table, the proposed CVCM method achieves better precision rate than the other two methods.

In conclusion, color variation co-occurrence matrix (CVCM), a texture feature, has been proposed in this study for designing a system for image retrieval. CVCM is used to depict the variation relationship between the adjacent pixel colors. For experiments using 4 image sets, the results demonstrated that CVCM retrieval system achieves better retrieval performance based on accuracy, precision, and recall rates for different image sets.

References

1. Rui, Y., Huang, T.S.: Image Retrieval: Current Techniques, Promising Directions, and Open Issues. Journal of Visual Communication and Image Representation 10, 39–62 (1999)
2. Chun, Y.D., Seo, S.Y., Kim, N.C.: Image Retrieval Using BDIP and BVLC Moments. IEEE Transactions on Circuits and Systems for Video Technology 13, 951–957 (2003)
3. Chang, C.C., Chan, Y.K.: A Fast Filter for Image Retrieval Based on Color Features. In: Proc. SEMS, Baden-Baden, Germany, pp. 47–51 (2000)
4. Nezamabadi-Pour, H., Kabir, E.: Image Retrieval Using Histograms of Uni-color and Bi-color Blocks and Directional Changes in Intensity Gradient. Pattern Recognition Letters 25, 1547–1557 (2004)
5. Liapis, S., Tziritas, G.: Color and Texture Image Retrieval Using Chromaticity Histograms and Wavelet Frames. IEEE Transactions on Multimedia 6, 676–686 (2004)
6. Huang, P.W., Dai, S.K.: Image Retrieval by Texture Similarity. Pattern Recognition 36, 665–679 (2003)
7. Jhanwar, N., Chaudhurib, S., Seetharamanc, G., Zavidovique, B.: Content Based Image Retrieval Using Motif Co-occurrence Matrix. Image and Vision Computing 22, 1211–1220 (2004)
8. Liapis, S., Tziritas, G.: Color and Texture Image Retrieval Using Chromaticity Histograms and Wavelet Frames. IEEE Transactions on Multimedia 6, 676–686 (2004)
9. Lin, C.H., Chen, K.H., Chan, Y.K.: A Fast Image Retrieval System Based on Color-Space and Color-Texture Features. In: Gavrilova, M.L., Gervasi, O., Kumar, V., Tan, C.J.K., Taniar, D., Laganá, A., Mun, Y., Choo, H. (eds.) ICCSA 2006. LNCS, vol. 3984, pp. 384–393. Springer, Heidelberg (2006)
10. Pass, G., Zahib, R., Miller, J.: Comparing images Using Color Coherent Vector. In: The 4th ACM International Multimedia Conference, pp. 18–22 (1996)
11. Haralick, R.M., Shanmugam, K., Dinstein, I.: Texture Features for Image Classification. IEEE Transactions on Systems, Man and Cybernetics 3, 610–621 (1973)
12. Babu, G.P., Mehtre, B.M., Kankanhalli, M.S.: Color Indexing for Efficient Image Retrieval. Multimedia Tools and Applications 1, 327–348 (1995)

Tool Condition Monitoring Using the TSK Fuzzy Approach Based on Subtractive Clustering Method

Qun Ren[1], Marek Balazinski[1], Luc Baron[1], and Krzysztof Jemielniak[2]

[1] Mechanical Engineering Department, École Polytechnique de Montréal
C.P. 6079, succ. Centre-Ville, Montréal, Québec, Canada, H3C 3A7
{qun.ren, marek.balazinski, luc.baron}@polymtl.ca
[2] Faculty of Production Engineering, Warsaw University of Technology
Narbutta 86, 02-524 Warsaw, Poland
k.jemielniak@wip.pw.edu.pl

Abstract. This paper presents a tool condition monitoring approach using Takagi-Sugeno-Kang (TSK) fuzzy logic incorporating a subtractive clustering method. The experimental results show its effectiveness and satisfactory comparisons with several other artificial intelligence methods.

Keywords: tool condition monitoring, TSK fuzzy logic, subtractive clustering.

1 Introduction

Tool condition has a strong influence on the resulting surface finish and dimensional integrity of the workpiece, as well as vibration levels of the machine tool. The information obtained from tool wear monitoring can be used for several purposes that include: establishing tool change policy, economic optimization of machining operations, compensating for tool wear on-line and to some extent avoiding catastrophic tool failures [1]. Effective monitoring of a manufacturing process is essential for ensuring product quality and reducing production costs. Analysis, implementation and evaluation of machining processes present significant challenges to the manufacturing industry.

Cutting force measurement, currently the most reliable and accurate sensing method available in metal cutting, is one of the most commonly employed methods for on-line tool wear monitoring. It is frequently applied in turning processes because cutting force values are more sensitive to tool wear than other measurements such as vibration or acoustic emission [2].

In a tool condition monitoring system, real-time data are acquired from sensors located at different locations on the workpiece, tool and machine-tool, then a signal processing technique is used to extract valid data. A decision making system is then used to analyse the data and classify the results to make a reliable estimate of the state of the tool and consequently of the machined parts themselves [3].

Advanced signal processing techniques and artificial intelligence play a key role in the development of modern tool condition monitoring systems [4]. The most frequently chosen methods are neural network (NN) [5], Mamdani fuzzy logic (FL)

N.T. Nguyen et al. (Eds.): IEA/AIE 2008, LNAI 5027, pp. 52–61, 2008.

[6], [7], or a combination of NN with either Mamdani FL [8] or an automatic generating method, i.e., genetic algorithm (GA) [9]. All these methods have a similar objective – matching the estimate of average cutting tool wear with the directly measured wear value.

The aim of this paper is to present an effective tool wear monitoring method using the Takagi-Sugeno-Kang (TSK) fuzzy approach incorporating a subtractive clustering method [10] to accomplish the integration of multi-sensor information and tool wear information. It generates fuzzy rules directly from the input-output data acquired from sensors, and provides high accuracy and high reliability of the tool wear prediction over a range of cutting conditions.

This paper is divided into four sections. Section I contains tool wear monitoring development and some introductory remarks. Section II recalls the initial theoretical foundation: TSK fuzzy logic system (FLS), subtractive clustering method and least-square estimation. Section III is a specific turning case study. The experimental results show the effectiveness and advantages of the TSK fuzzy approach compared with other different artificial intelligence methods – NN, Mamdani FL and a neural network based fuzzy system (NF). Section IV contains concluding remarks and future research recommendations.

2   Theoretical Foundation

The proposed linguistic approach by Zadeh [11, 12], following the first "Fuzzy Sets" paper in 1965 [13], is effective and versatile in modeling ill-defined systems with fuzziness or fully-defined systems with realistic approximations. Later it is expanded into fuzzy systems modeling as a qualitative modeling approach. Qualitative modeling has the capability to model complex system behavior in such a qualitative way that the model is more effective and versatile in capturing the behavior of ill-defined systems with fuzziness or fully defined system with realistic approximation. In the literature, different modeling techniques can be found, and TSK FLS [14], [15] has attracted much attention.

2.1   TSK Fuzzy Logic System

TSK FLS was proposed in an effort to develop a systematic approach to generate fuzzy rules from a given input-output data set. This model consists of rules with fuzzy antecedents and a mathematical function in the consequent part. Usually the conclusion function is in the form of a dynamic linear equation [14], [15]. The antecedents divide the input space into a set of fuzzy regions, while consequents describe behaviours of the system in those regions. The main difference with more traditional [16] (Mamdani FL) fuzzy rules is that the consequents of the rules are a function of the values of the input variables. TSK FLSs are widely used for model-based control and model-based fault diagnosis. This is due to the model's properties; on one hand being a general non-linear approximator that can approximate every continuous mapping, and on the other hand being a piecewise linear model that is relatively easy to interpret [17] and whose linear sub-models can be exploited for control and fault detection [18].

A generalized type-1 TSK model can be described by fuzzy IF-THEN rules which represent input-output relations of a system. For an MISO first–order type-1 TSK model, its kth rule can be expressed as:

$$\textbf{IF } \; x_1 \; is \; Q_{1k} \; \textbf{ and } \; x_2 \; is \; Q_{2k} \; \textbf{ and } \; ... \; \textbf{ and } \; x_n \; is \; Q_{nk},$$

$$\textbf{THEN } \; Z \; is \; w^k = p_0^k + p_1^k x_1 + p_2^k x_2 + ... + p_n^k x_n \tag{1}$$

where x_1, x_2 ..., x_n and Z are linguistic variables; Q_1^k, Q_2^k, ..., and Q_n^k are the fuzzy sets on universe of discourses X_1, X_2 ..., and X_n, and $p_0^k, p_1^k, p_2^k, ..., p_n^k$ are regression parameters.

2.2 Subtractive Clustering Method

The structure of a fuzzy TSK model can be done manually based on knowledge about the target process or using data-driven techniques. Identification of the system using clustering involves formation of clusters in the data space and translation of these clusters into TSK rules such that the model obtained is close to the system to be identified.

The aim of Chiu's subtractive clustering identification algorithm [10] is to estimate both the number and initial location of cluster centers and extract the TSK fuzzy rules from input/output data. Subtractive clustering operates by finding the optimal data point to define a cluster centre based on the density of surrounding data points. This method is a fast clustering method designed for high dimension problems with a moderate number of data points. This is because its computation grows linearly with the data dimension and as the square of the number of data points. A brief description of Chiu's subtractive clustering method is as follows:

Consider a group of data points $\{x^1, x^2, ..., x^w\}$ for a specific class. The M dimensional feature space is normalized so that all data are bounded by a unit hypercube.

Then calculate potential P_i for each point as follows:

$$P_i = \sum_{j=1}^{w} e^{-\alpha \|x^i - x^j\|^2} \tag{2}$$

with $\alpha = 4 / r_a^2$ and r_a is the hypersphere cluster radius. Data points outside r_a have little influence on the potential. $\|\cdot\|$ denotes the Euclidean distance.

Thus, the measure of potential for a data point is a function of the distance to all other data points. A data point with many neighboring data points will have a high potential value. After the potential of every data point is computed, suppose $k = 1$ where k is a cluster counter. The data point with the maximum potential P_k^* with $P_k^* = P_1^*$ is selected as the first cluster center $x_k^* = x_1^*$. Then the potential of each data point x^i is revised using the formula

$$P_i = P_i - P_k^* e^{-\beta \|x^i - x_1^*\|^2} \tag{3}$$

with $\beta = 4/r_b^2$ and r_b is the hypersphere penalty radius. Thus, an amount representing the potential of each data point is subtracted as a function of its distance from x_1^* .

More generally, when the kth cluster center x_k^* has been identified, the potential of all data is revised using the formula:

$$P_i = P_i - P_k^* e^{-\beta \left\| x^i - x_k^* \right\|^2} \tag{4}$$

When the potential of all data points has been revised using (4), the data point x^t with the highest remaining potential is chosen as the next cluster center. The process of acquiring a new cluster center and revising potentials uses the following criteria:

if $\overline{P_t} > \varepsilon \overline{P_1^*}$ (ε is accept ratio)

    Accept x^t as the next cluster center, cluster counter $k = k + 1$, and continue.
else if $\overline{P_t} < \varepsilon \overline{P_1^*}$ (ε is reject ratio)

    Reject x^t and end the clustering process
else

    Let $d_{\min}$ = shortest of the distances between x^t and all previously found cluster

    centers.
    if $\dfrac{d_{\min}}{r_a} + \dfrac{P_t}{P_1^*} \geq 1$

        Accept x^t as the next cluster center. Cluster counter $k = k + 1$, and continue.
    else

        Reject x^t and set $P_t = 0$.

        Select x^t with the next highest potential as the new candidate cluster center
        and retest.
    end if
end if

The number of clusters obtained is the number of rules in the TSK FLS. Because Gaussian basis functions (GBFs) have the best approximation property [19], Gaussian functions are chosen as the MFs. A Gaussian MF can be expressed by the following formula for the vth variable:

$$Q_v^k = \exp\left[-\frac{1}{2} \left(\frac{x_v - x_v^{k*}}{\sigma} \right)^2 \right] \tag{5}$$

where x_v^{k*} is the mean of the vth input feature in the kth rule for $v \in [0, n]$. The standard deviation of Gaussian MF σ is given as

$$\sigma = \sqrt{1/2\alpha} \tag{6}$$

2.3 Least Square Estimation

For the first order model presented in this paper, the consequent functions are linear. In the method of Sugeno and Kang [15], least-square estimation is used to identify the consequent parameters of the TSK model, where the premise structure, premise parameters, consequent structure, and consequent parameters were identified and adjusted recursively. In a TSK FLS, rule premises are represented by an exponential membership function. The optimal consequent parameters $p_0^k, p_1^k, p_2^k, \ldots, p_n^k$ (coefficients of the polynomial function) in (1) for a given set of clusters are obtained using the least-square estimation method.

When certain input values x_1^0, x_2^0, ..., x_n^0 are given to the input variables x_1, x_2, ..., x_n, the conclusion from the kth rule (1) in a TSK model is a crisp value w^k:

$$w^k = p_0^k + p_1^k x_1^0 + p_2^k x_2^0 + \ldots + p_n^k x_n^0 \tag{7}$$

with a certain rule firing strength (weight) defined as

$$\alpha^k = \mu_1^k(x_1^0) \cap \mu_2^k(x_2^0) \cap \ldots \cap \mu_n^k(x_n^0) \tag{8}$$

where $\mu_1^k(x_1^0)$, $\mu_2^k(x_2^0)$, ..., $\mu_n^k(x_n^0)$ are membership grades for fuzzy sets Q_1^k, Q_2^k, ..., and Q_n^k in the kth rule. The symbol $\cap$ is a conjunction operator, which is a T-norm (the minimum operator $\wedge$ or the product operator $*$).

Moreover, the output of the model is computed (using *weighted average aggregation*) as

$$w = \frac{\sum_{k=1}^m \alpha^k w^k}{\sum_{k=1}^m \alpha^k} \tag{9}$$

Suppose

$$\beta^k = \frac{\alpha^k}{\sum_{k=1}^m \alpha^k} \tag{10}$$

Then, (9) can be converted into a linear least-square estimation problem, as

$$w = \sum_{k=1}^m \beta^k w^k \tag{11}$$

For a group of λ data vectors, the equations can be obtained as

$$\begin{aligned}
w^1 &= \beta_1^1(p_0^1 + p_1^1 x_1 + p_2^1 x_2 + \ldots + p_n^1 x_n) + \beta_1^2(p_0^2 + p_1^2 x_1 + p_2^2 x_2 + \ldots + p_n^2 x_n) + \cdots \\
&\quad + \beta_1^m(p_0^m + p_1^m x_1 + p_2^m x_2 + \ldots + p_n^m x_n)) \\
w^2 &= \beta_2^1(p_0^1 + p_1^1 x_1 + p_2^1 x_2 + \ldots + p_n^1 x_n) + \beta_2^2(p_0^2 + p_1^2 x_1 + p_2^2 x_2 + \ldots + p_n^2 x_n) + \cdots \\
&\quad + \beta_2^m(p_0^m + p_1^m x_1 + p_2^m x_2 + \ldots + p_n^m x_n)) \\
&\qquad\qquad\qquad\qquad \vdots \\
w^\lambda &= \beta_\lambda^1(p_0^1 + p_1^1 x_1 + p_2^1 x_2 + \ldots + p_n^1 x_n) + \beta_\lambda^2(p_0^2 + p_1^2 x_1 + p_2^2 x_2 + \ldots + p_n^2 x_n) + \cdots \\
&\quad + \beta_\lambda^m(p_0^m + p_1^m x_1 + p_2^m x_2 + \ldots + p_n^m x_n))
\end{aligned} \tag{12}$$

These equations can be represented as:

$$
\begin{bmatrix}
\beta_1^1 x_1 & \beta_1^1 x_2 \cdots \beta_1^1 x_n & \beta_1^1 & \cdots & \beta_1^m x_1 & \beta_1^m x_2 \cdots \beta_1^m x_n & \beta_1^m \\
\cdot & \cdot & \cdot & \cdots & \cdot & \cdot & \cdot \\
\cdot & \cdot & \cdot & \cdots & \cdot & \cdot & \cdot \\
\beta_\lambda^1 x_1 & \beta_\lambda^1 x_2 \cdots \beta_\lambda^1 \mu_{n1} & \beta_\lambda^1 & \cdots & \beta_\lambda^m x_1 & \beta_\lambda^m x_2 \cdots \beta_\lambda^m x_n & \beta_\lambda^m
\end{bmatrix}
\begin{bmatrix}
p_1^1 \\ p_2^1 \\ \vdots \\ p_n^1 \\ p_0^1 \\ \vdots \\ p_1^m \\ p_2^m \\ \vdots \\ p_n^m \\ p_0^m
\end{bmatrix}
=
\begin{bmatrix}
w^1 \\ w^2 \\ \cdot \\ \cdot \\ w^3
\end{bmatrix}
\tag{13}
$$

Using the standard notation $AP = W$, this becomes a least square estimation problem where A is a constant matrix (known), W is a matrix of output values (known) and P is a matrix of parameters to be estimated. The well-known pseudo-inverse solution that minimizes $\|AP - W\|^2$ is given by

$$
P = (A^T A)^{-1} A^T W
\tag{14}
$$

3   Case Study

The experiments described in this paper were conducted on a conventional lathe TUD-50. A CSRPR 2525 tool holder equipped with a TiN-Al$_2$O$_3$-TiCN coated sintered carbide insert SNUN 120408 was used in the test. To simulate factory floor conditions, six sets of cutting parameters were selected and applied in sequence as presented in Fig. 1. During machining, the feed force (F_f) and the cutting force (F_c) were recorded while the tool wear was manually measured after each test.

For our purposes tool wear (VB) was estimated from three input sources: f, F_f and F_c. The choice of input variables was based on the following two observations: F_f is independent of f, but rather depends on VB and the depth of cut, denoted a_p. Moreover, F_c depends on a_p and f, while being only weakly dependent on VB. So, in

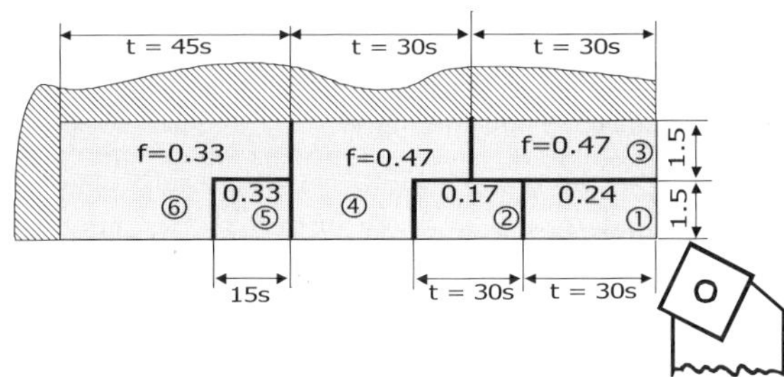

Fig. 1. Cutting parameters used in experiments, where f is feed rate and t is time

this paper f and the measurement F_c are used to determine a_p, and the measurement F_f is used to determine VB without requiring a_p as an input variable.

Cutting speed of each cut was selected to ensure approximately the same share in the tool wear. VB was measured after carrying out each sequence. The value for F_f and F_c were measured corresponding to a single cut using a Kistlter 9263 dynamometer during 5-s intervals while the cut was executed. Recent research has attempted to investigate the application of multiple sensors with complementing characteristics to provide a robust estimate of tool wear condition. Since the inserts used in the experiments had a soft, cobalt-enriched layer of substrate under the coating, the tool life had a tendency to end suddenly after this coating wore through.

The experiments were carried out until a tool failure occurred. Two experiments were carried out until a tool failure occurred. In the first tests (designated W5) 10 cycles were performed until a sudden rise of the flank wear VB occurred, reaching approximately 0.5 mm. In the second test (designated W7) failure of the coating resulted in chipping of the cutting edge at the end of 9th cycle. W5 was devised for TSK fuzzy rule identification, while W7 was used to verify the performance of the different monitoring system. Fig. 2 presents the cutting force components F_c and F_f versus VB obtained in the experiments.

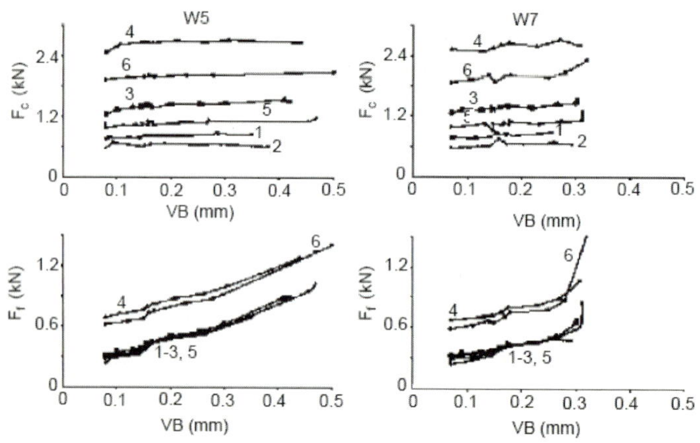

Fig. 2. Cutting force components F_c and F_f versus tool wear VB obtained in the experiments with six sets of cutting parameters shown in Fig.1

By using TSK fuzzy approach, a six rule TSK fuzzy model can be used to describe the tool wear condition with cutting feed, cutting force and feeding force as input variables. Table 1 lists the six cluster centers obtained by subtractive clustering method learning from the first experiment W5.

Table 1. Six cluster centers obtained by using subtractive clustering with the four parameters initialized as $r_a = 0.25$, $\varepsilon = 0.60$, $\overline{\varepsilon} = 1$, $\eta = 0.25$

Cluster	f (mm)	F_c (N)	F_f (N)	VB(mm)
1	0.47	1397	389	0.145
2	0.47	1392	442	0.165
3	0.33	1044	405	0.158
4	0.33	1051	349	0.135
5	0.47	1332	347	0.102
6	0.47	1455	508	0.2

Figure 3 summarizes results of tool wear conditioning from W5 (learning) and W7 (testing) and compares them with several different artificial intelligence methods described in [4], [9] applied to the same experimental arrangements.

For these four AI methods, the quality of the tool wear estimation was evaluated using root-mean-square-error (rmse):

$$rmse = \sqrt{\sum (VB_m - VB_e)^2 / N} \tag{15}$$

and maximum error (max):

$$\max = \max(VB_m - VB_e) \tag{16}$$

where VB_m, VB_e are measured and estimated flank wear respectively, and N is the number of patterns in the set (N = 71 for the experiment W5 and N = 66 for the experiment W7).

From Table 2, the TSK fuzzy approach has the lowest root-mean-square-error and the smallest maximum error.

Table 2. Summary of root-mean-square-error (rmse) and maximum error (max) form the experimental results with different AI methods

AI method	Learning (W5)		Testing (W7)	
	rmse (mm)	max (mm)	rmse (mm)	max (mm)
Neural Network	0.015	0.036	0.029	0.081
FDSS (Mamdani FL)	0.024	0.068	0.034	0.056
NF	0.014	0.030	0.030	0.081
TSK FL	0.011	0.023	0.015	0.037

The TSK fuzzy modeling program used for tool condition monitoring in this paper was developed by Geno-flou development group in Lab CAE at École Polytechnique de Montréal.

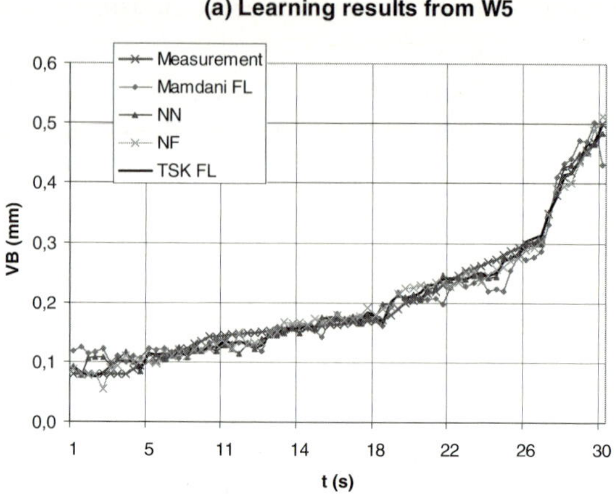

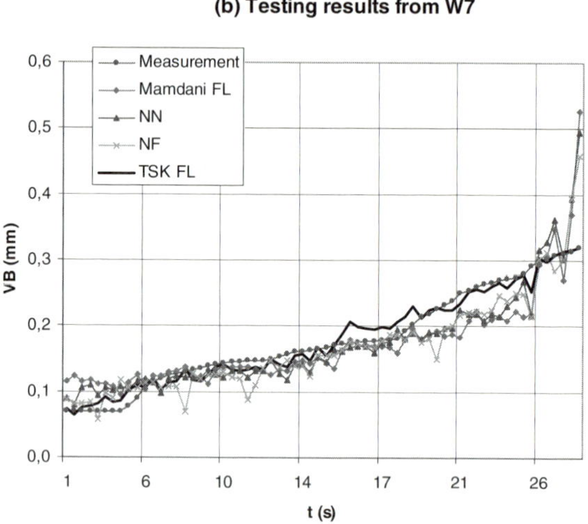

Fig. 3. Tool wear monitoring using different artificial intelligent methods: Mamdani FL, neural network (NN), neural network based fuzzy system (NF) and TSK fuzzy approach

4 Conclusion

A TSK fuzzy approach using subtractive clustering is described in detail in this article. It generates fuzzy rules directly from the input-output data acquired from sensors and provides high accuracy and high reliability of the tool wear prediction over a range of cutting conditions. The experimental results show its effectiveness and a satisfactory comparison with several other artificial intelligence methods.

References

1. El Gomayel, J.I., Bregger, K.D.: On-line Tool. Trans. of ASME. J. of Eng. in Industry 108(1), 44–47 (1988)
2. Du, R., Elbestawi, M.A., Wu, S.M.: Automated monitoring of manufacturing processes, Part 1 and Part 2. J. of Eng. In Industry 117, 121–141 (1995)
3. Balazinski, M., Bellerose, M., Czogala, E.: Application of fuzzy logic techniques to the selection of cutting parameters in machining processes. Fuzzy Sets and Systems 61, 301–317 (1994)
4. Balazinski, M., Czogala, E., Jemielniak, K., Leski, J.: Tool condition monitoring using artificial intelligence methods. Eng. App. of Art. Int. 15, 73–80 (2002)
5. Jemielniak, K., Kwiatkowski, L., Wrzosek, P.: Diagnosis of tool wear based on cutting forces and acoustic emission measures as inputs to neural network. J. of Int. Man. 9, 447–455 (1998)
6. Balazinski, M., Jcmielniak, K.: Tool conditions monitoring using fuzzy decision support system. In: VCIRP, AC 1998 Miedzeszyn, pp. 115–122 (1998)
7. Baron, L., Archiche, S., Balazinski, M.: Fuzzy decisions system knowledge base generation using a genetic algorithm. Int. J. of App. Reasoning 28(2-3), 125–148 (2001)
8. Li, X.L., Li, H.X., Guan, X.P., Du, R.: Fuzzy estimation of feed-cutting force from current measurement-a case study on intelligent tool wear condition monitoring. IEEE Trans. on Sys., Man and Cyb., Part C (Applications and Reviews) 34(4), 506–512 (2004)
9. Achiche, S., Balazinski, M., Baron, L., Jemielniak, K.: Tool wear monitoring using genetically-generated fuzzy knowledge bases. Eng. App. of Art. Int. 15(3-4), 303–314 (2002)
10. Chiu, S.L.: Fuzzy Model Identification Based on Cluster Estimation. J. on Int. Fuzzy Sys. 2, 267–278 (1994)
11. Zadeh, L.A.: Fuzzy Algorithm. Inf. and Contr. 12, 94–102 (1968)
12. Zadeh, L.A.: Outline of A New Approach to the Analysis of Complex Systems and Decision Processes. IEEE Trans. on Sys., Man, and Cyb. 3, 28–44 (1973)
13. Zadeh, L.A.: Fuzzy Sets. Inf. and Cont. 8, 338–353 (1965)
14. Takagi, T., Sugeno, M.: Fuzzy Identification of Systems and Its Applications to Modelling and Control. IEEE Trans. on Sys., Man, and Cyb. 15(1), 116–132 (1985)
15. Sugeno, M., Kang, G.: Structure Identification of Fuzzy Model. Fuzzy Sets and Systems 28(1), 15–33 (1988)
16. Mamdani, E.H., Assilian, S.: Applications of Fuzzy Algorithms for Control of Simple Dynamic Plant. Proc. Inst. Elec. Eng. 121, 1585–1588 (1974)
17. Johansen, T., Foss, B.: Identification of Non-Linear System Structure and Parameters Using Regime Decomposition. Automatic 31(2), 321–326 (1995)
18. Füssel, D., Ballé, P., Isermann, R.: Closed Loop Fault Diagnosis Based on A Nonlinear Process Model and Automatic Fuzzy Rule Generation. In: 4th IFAC Sym. on Fault Det., Sup. and Safety for Tech.1 Proc. (1997)
19. Wang, L.-X., Mendel, J.M.: Fuzzy basis functions, universal approximation, and orthogonal least-squares learning. IEEE Trans. on Neural Networks 3, 807–813 (1992)

Admissible Fuzzy Controller in L^2 Space[*]

Takashi Mitsuishi[1] and Yasunari Shidama[2]

[1] University of Marketing and Distribution Sciences, Kobe 651-2188, Japan
`takashi_mitsuishi@red.umds.ac.jp`
[2] Shinshu University, Nagano 380-8553, Japan

Abstract. This article presents a mathematical framework for studying the existence of optimal feedback control based on IF-THEN fuzzy
rules through approximate reasoning, and introduces the notion of an
admissible fuzzy controller. The framework consists of two propositions:
To guarantee the convergence of optimal solution, a set of fuzzy membership functions (admissible fuzzy controller) which are selected out of
L^2 space is convex and compact metrizable for the weak topology. And
assuming approximate reasoning to be a functional on the set of membership functions, its continuity is proved. Then, we show the existence of
a fuzzy controller which minimize (maximize) the integral performance
function of the nonlinear feedback system.

Keywords: Fuzzy control, Functional analysis, Feedback systems,
Optimization.

1   Introduction

The authors consider fuzzy optimal control problems as problems of finding the
minimum (maximum) value of the performance (cost) function with feedback law
constructed by some approximate reasoning, by treating control laws as problems
of function approximation. To compute an optimal solution by a successive function approximation, it is necessary to define the distance between fuzzy membership functions and to study its topological properties. For this end, the authors
defined some topologies in the set of fuzzy membership functions, and discussed
the compactness for the set that contains triangular, trapezoidal, and bell-shaped
fuzzy membership functions with gradients less than some positive value [1] [2].
This paper is continuation and extension of our research mentioned above. Instead of using function with strict conditions, such as those with gradients less
than some positive value, the membership functions are considered as elements of
L^2 space that is the Hilbert space of all square Lebesgue integrable functions.

The fuzzy feedback control discussed here is a nonlinear feedback control, in
which the feedback laws are determined by IF-THEN type fuzzy control rules
through modified product-sum-gravity method and Nakamori method. Since the
control given by Mamdani method might not change smoothly, it is pointed out

[*] The paper was supported in part by Grant-in-Aid for Young Scientists (B)
#19700225 from Japan Society for the Promotion of Science (JSPS).

N.T. Nguyen et al. (Eds.): IEA/AIE 2008, LNAI 5027, pp. 62–71, 2008.

that his method is not necessarily appropriate to express the human intuition. Then, Mizumoto recently proposed the product-sum-gravity method by replacing minimum with product and maximum with summation in Mamdani method [3]. And Nakamori proposed calculation of the aggregated fuzzy sets interpreted as possibility distribution of the output [4]. Nakamori method almost same as the Height defuzzification method that is both a very simple and very quick method.

Throughout this paper, $\mathbb{R}^n$ denotes the n-dimensional Euclidean space with the usual Euclidean norm $\|x\| = \left(\sum_{i=1}^n |x_i|^2\right)^{1/2}$, $x = (x_1, x_2, \ldots, x_n) \in \mathbb{R}^n$. For any $a, b \in \mathbb{R}$, we set lattice operations $a \vee b = \max(a, b)$ and $a \wedge b = \min(a, b)$.

2 Membership Function in L^2 Space

Let $L^2[a, b]$ be the real Hilbert space of all square Lebesgue integrable real functions on $[a, b]$. Consider the set $\mathcal{L}$ of membership functions defined by

$$\mathcal{L} = \{\mu \in L^2[a, b] : 0 \leq \mu(x) \leq 1 \text{ a.e. } x \in [a, b]\}.$$

Proposition 1. (a) $\mathcal{L}$ *is closed under the lattice operations* $\vee$ *and* $\wedge$. (b) *If* $0 \leq c \leq 1$ *and* $\mu \in \mathcal{L}$, *then* $c \wedge \mu, c \vee \mu, c\mu \in \mathcal{L}$. (c) $\mathcal{L}$ *is a convex subset of* $L^2[a, b]$. (d) $\mathcal{L}$ *is compact metrizable for the weak topology on* $L^2[a, b]$.

Proof. (a), (b) and (c) are obvious. (d) Since every convex, bounded, and norm closed subset of $L^2[a, b]$ is compact metrizable for the weak topology, it is sufficient to show that $\mathcal{L}$ is bounded and norm closed in $L^2[a, b]$. The boundedness of $\mathcal{L}$ can be easily proved. In order to prove that $\mathcal{L}$ is closed, assume that a sequence $\{\mu_n\} \subset \mathcal{L}$ converges to $\mu \in L^2[a, b]$ for the norm topology on $L^2[a, b]$. Then there exists a subsequence $\{\mu_{n_k}\}$ of $\{\mu_n\}$ which converges to μ almost everywhere on $[a, b]$. Hence it is easy to show that $0 \leq \mu(x) \leq 1$ a.e. $x \in [a, b]$, and this implies that $\mu \in \mathcal{L}$. Thus $\mathcal{L}$ is norm closed in $L^2[a, b]$. $\qquad\square$

In fuzzy control, the control variable is generated by a family of fuzzy membership functions through the gravity defuzzification. The gravity defuzzification M is defined by $M : \mu \mapsto M_\mu = \int_a^b x\mu(x)dx / \int_a^b \mu(x)dx$. To avoid making the denominator of the expression above equal to 0, we consider

$$\mathcal{L}_\delta = \left\{\mu \in \mathcal{L} : \int_a^b \mu(x)dx \geq \delta\right\} \quad (\delta > 0),$$

which is a slight modification of $\mathcal{L}$. If δ is taken small enough, it is possible to consider $\mathcal{L} = \mathcal{L}_\delta$ for practical applications. Then, the following corollary is obtained.

Corollary 1. (a) $\mathcal{L}_\delta$ *is closed under the lattice operation* $\vee$. (b) $\mathcal{L}_\delta$ *is a convex subset of* $L^2[a, b]$. (c) $\mathcal{L}_\delta$ *is compact metrizable for the weak topology.* (d) *The gravity defuzzification* M *is weakly continuous on* $\mathcal{L}_\delta$.

Proof. (a) is obvious. (b) Let $\mu, \mu' \in \mathcal{L}_\delta$ and $0 \leq \lambda \leq 1$. Then

$$\int_a^b (\lambda\mu(x) + (1 - \lambda)\mu'(x))dx \geq \lambda\delta + (1 - \lambda)\delta = \delta,$$

and hence $\lambda\mu + (1 - \lambda)\mu' \in \mathcal{L}_\delta$. Therefore $\mathcal{L}_\delta$ is convex.
(c) Let $\{\mu_n\}$ be a sequence in $\mathcal{L}_\delta$. Assume that $\mu_n \to \mu \in \mathcal{L}$ for the weak topology. Since $\mu_n \in \mathcal{L}_\delta$ for all $n \geq 1$,

$$\int_a^b \mu(x)dx = \lim_{n \to \infty} \int_a^b \mu_n(x)dx \geq \delta,$$

and this implies that $\mu \in \mathcal{L}_\delta$. Therefore, $\mathcal{L}_\delta$ is weakly closed in $\mathcal{L}$. Since $\mathcal{L}$ is compact metrizable for the weak topology by (d) of proposition 1, the same can be said of $\mathcal{L}_\delta$.
(d) Assume that a sequence $\{\mu_n\} \subset \mathcal{L}_\delta$ converges weakly to $\mu \in \mathcal{L}_\delta$, we have

$$\int_a^b x\mu_n(x)dx \to \int_a^b x\mu(x)dx \quad \text{and} \quad \int_a^b \mu_n(x)dx \to \int_a^b \mu(x)dx \quad (n \to \infty).$$

Put $M_{\mu_n} = \int_a^b x\mu_n(x)dx / \int_a^b \mu_n(x)dx$. Then, the weak continuity of M follows from the fact that a sequence $\{M_{\mu_n}\} \subset \mathbb{R}$ converges to $M_\mu \in \mathbb{R}$. $\qquad\square$

3　Fuzzy Controller

Assume the following m IF-THEN type fuzzy control rules are given.

Rule i:　*IF* x_1 *is* A_{i1} *and* ... x_n *is* A_{in}　*THEN* y *is* B_i $(i = 1, 2, \cdots, m)$　(1)

Here, m is the number of fuzzy production rules, and n is the number of premise variables $x_1, x_2, \ldots, x_n$. Let $\mu_{A_{ij}}$ $(i = 1, 2, \ldots, m; j = 1, 2, \ldots, n)$ be membership functions defined on a certain closed interval of the fuzzy set A_{ij}. Let μ_{B_i} $(i = 1, 2, \ldots, m)$ be membership functions defined on a certain closed interval of the fuzzy set B_i. For simplicity, we write "IF" and "THEN" parts in the rules by the following notation: $\mathcal{A}_i = (\mu_{A_{i1}}, \mu_{A_{i2}} \ldots, \mu_{A_{in}})$ $(i = 1, 2, \ldots, m)$, $\mathcal{A} = (\mathcal{A}_1, \mathcal{A}_2, \ldots, \mathcal{A}_m)$, $\mathcal{B} = (\mu_{B_1}, \mu_{B_2}, \ldots, \mu_{B_m})$.

Then, the IF-THEN type fuzzy control rules (1) is called a fuzzy controller, and is denoted by $(\mathcal{A}, \mathcal{B})$. In the rules, the pair of premise variable $x = (x_1, x_2, \ldots, x_n)$ is called an input information given to the fuzzy controller $(\mathcal{A}, \mathcal{B})$, and y is called a control variable.

Mamdani method (min-max-gravity method), product-sum-gravity method and Nakamori method are introduced in this section. Mamdani method is widely used in fuzzy controls because of its simplicity and comprehensibility. In the case that the membership functions are elements of L^2 space, Mamdani method is not necessarily continuous with respect to the weak topology on L^2. Since min-max gravity method uses minimun and maximum operations, because of their nonlinearity, the value of the agreement degree and the gravity might not change smoothly. In addition, it is pointed out that this method is not necessarily appropriate to express the human intuition. Then, Mizumoto proposed the product-sum-gravity method by replacing minimun with product and maximun with summation [3]. If given the input information $x = (x_1, x_2, \ldots, x_n)$ to the fuzzy controller $(\mathcal{A}, \mathcal{B})$, the procedure for inference is summarized as follows:

Procedure 1. The strength of each rule is calculated by

$$\alpha_{min\mathcal{A}_i}(x) = \bigwedge_{j=1}^{n} \mu_{A_{ij}}(x_j), \quad \alpha_{pro\mathcal{A}_i}(x) = \prod_{j=1}^{n} \mu_{A_{ij}}(x_j) \quad (i = 1, 2, \ldots, m).$$

Procedure 2. The control output of the each rule is calculated by

$$\beta_{min\mathcal{A}_i B_i}(x, y) = \alpha_{\mathcal{A}_i}(x) \wedge \mu_{B_i}(y) \quad (i = 1, 2, \ldots, m),$$

$$\beta_{pro\mathcal{A}_i B_i}(x, y) = \alpha_{\mathcal{A}_i}(x) \cdot \mu_{B_i}(y) \quad (i = 1, 2, \ldots, m)$$

where $\cdot$ indicates multiplication.

Procedure 3. The inference result of the entire rule, the aggregated control output for the input x is calculated by

$$\gamma_{max\mathcal{A}\mathcal{B}}(x, y) = \bigvee_{i=1}^{m} \beta_{\mathcal{A}_i B_i}(x, y), \quad \gamma_{sum\mathcal{A}\mathcal{B}}(x, y) = \sum_{i=1}^{m} \beta_{\mathcal{A}_i B_i}(x, y).$$

Nakamori fuzzy model [4] does not infer each rule, and defines the inference result of all rules as a weighted average of agreement degree as follows:

$$\gamma_{nak\mathcal{A}\mathcal{B}}(x, y) = \frac{\sum_{i=1}^{m} \beta_{pro\mathcal{A}_i B_i}(x, y)}{\sum_{i=1}^{m} \alpha_{\mathcal{A}_i}(x)}.$$

Procedure 4. Defuzzification stage. The center of gravity of the aggregated control output is calculated by

$$\rho_{\mathcal{A}\mathcal{B}}(x) = \frac{\int y \gamma_{\mathcal{A}\mathcal{B}}(x, y) dy}{\int \gamma_{\mathcal{A}\mathcal{B}}(x, y) dy}.$$

In the case that the membership functions are elements of L^2 space, the minimun clipping operator represented by β_{min} in the procedure 2 and the aggregation operator represented by γ_{max} in the procedure 3 are not necessarily continuous with respect to the weak topology on L^2 space. In this paper, we call the approximate reasoning without the minimun clipping operator β_{min} and the aggregation operator γ_{max}, *min-or-product-sum-gravity method*.

4   Application to Fuzzy Feedback Control

4.1   Nonlinear Feedback Control

$\mathbb{R}^n$ denotes the n-dimensional Euclidean space with the usual norm $\| \cdot \|$. Let $f(y, v) : \mathbb{R}^n \times \mathbb{R} \to \mathbb{R}^n$ be a (nonlinear) vector valued function which is Lipschitz continuous. In addition, assume that there exists a constant $M_f > 0$ such that $\|f(y,v)\| \le M_f (\|y\| + |v| + 1)$ for all $(y,v) \in \mathbb{R}^n \times \mathbb{R}$.

Consider a system given by the following state equation: $\dot{x}(t) = f(x(t), u(t))$, where $x(t)$ is the state and the control input $u(t)$ of the system is given by the state feedback $u(t) = \rho(x(t))$. For a sufficiently large $r > 0$, $B_r = \{x \in \mathbb{R}^n : \|x\| \le r\}$ denotes a bounded set containing all possible initial states x_0 of the system. Let T be a sufficiently large final time. Then, we have

Proposition 2. [6]. *Let $\rho : \mathbb{R}^n \to \mathbb{R}$ be a Lipschitz continuous function and $x_0 \in B_r$. Then, the state equation*

$$\dot{x}(t) = f(x(t), \rho(x(t))) \tag{2}$$

has a unique solution $x(t, x_0, \rho)$ on $[0, T]$ with the initial condition $x(0) = x_0$ such that the mapping $(t, x_0) \in [0, T] \times B_r \mapsto x(t, x_0, \rho)$ is continuous.

For any $r_2 > 0$, denote by Φ the set of Lipschitz continuous functions $\rho : \mathbb{R}^n \to \mathbb{R}$ satisfying $\sup_{u \in \mathbb{R}^n} |\rho(u)| \le r_2$. Then, the following (a) and (b) hold.
(a) For any $t \in [0, T], x_0 \in B_r$ and $\rho \in \Phi$, $\|x(t, x_0, \rho)\| \le r_1$, where

$$r_1 \equiv e^{M_f T} r + (e^{M_f T} - 1)(r_2 + 1). \tag{3}$$

(b) Let $\rho_1, \rho_2 \in \Phi$. Then, for any $t \in [0, T]$ and $x_0 \in B_r$,

$$\|x(t, x_0, \rho_1) - x(t, x_0, \rho_2)\| \le \frac{e^{L_f (1+L_{\rho_1})t} - 1}{1 + L_{\rho_1}} \sup_{u \in [-r_1, r_1]^n} |\rho_1(u) - \rho_2(u)|, \tag{4}$$

where L_f and L_{ρ_1} are the Lipschitz constants of f and ρ_1.

Let $(\mathcal{A}, \mathcal{B})$ be a fuzzy controller given by the IF-THEN type fuzzy control rules (1). We say that the system (2) is a *fuzzy feedback system* if the control function $u(t)$ is given by the state feedback $u(t) = \rho_{AB}(x(t))$, where $\rho_{AB}(x(t))$ is the amount of operation from the fuzzy controller $(\mathcal{A}, \mathcal{B})$ for the input information $x(t)$. In the following, fix $r_2 > 0$ and a final time T of the control. We also fix $\Delta_{ij} > 0$ $(1 \le i \le m; 1 \le j \le n)$ and $\delta > 0$. Put r_1 be the constant determined by (3). We define two sets of fuzzy membership functions:

$$F_{\Delta_{ij}} = \{\mu \in C[-r_1, r_1] : 0 \le \mu(x) \le 1 \text{ for } \forall x \in [-r_1, r_1],$$

$$|\mu(x) - \mu(x')| \le \Delta_{ij}|x - x'| \text{ for } \forall x, x' \in [-r_1, r_1]\}$$

$$G = \{\mu \in L^2[-r_2, r_2] : 0 \le \mu(x) \le 1 \text{ a.e. } x \in [-r_2, r_2]\}.$$

We assume that the fuzzy membership functions $\mu_{A_{ij}}$ in "IF" parts of the rules (1) belong to the set $F_{\Delta_{ij}}$. On the other hand, we also assume that the fuzzy membership functions μ_{B_i} in "THEN" parts of the rules (1) belong to the set G. Put

$$\mathcal{F} = \prod_{i=1}^{m} \left\{ \prod_{j=1}^{n} F_{\Delta_{ij}} \right\} \times G^m. \tag{5}$$

where G^m denotes the m times Cartesian product of G. Then, every element $(\mathcal{A}, \mathcal{B})$ of $\mathcal{F}$ is a fuzzy controller given by the IF-THEN type fuzzy control rules (1). By the Tychonoff theorem [5], $\mathcal{F}$ is compact and metrizable with respect to the product topology on $C[-r_1, r_1]^{mn} \times G^m$.

4.2   Application of Min-or-Product-Sum-Gravity Method

In the procedure 4 of the approximate reasoning, the amount of operation is obtained through the gravity defuzzification. To avoid making the denominator of the expression above equal to 0, for any $\delta > 0$, we consider the set:

$$\mathcal{F}_\delta = \left\{ (\mathcal{A}, \mathcal{B}) \in \mathcal{F} : \int_{-r_2}^{r_2} \gamma_{AB}(x, y)dy \geq \delta \text{ for } \forall x \in [-r_1, r_1]^n \right\}, \qquad (6)$$

which is a slight modification of $\mathcal{F}$. If δ is taken small enough, it is possible to consider $\mathcal{F} = \mathcal{F}_\delta$ for practical applications. We say that an element $(\mathcal{A}, \mathcal{B})$ of $\mathcal{F}_\delta$ is an *admissible fuzzy controller*. Then, we have the following

Proposition 3. *The set $\mathcal{F}_\delta$ of all admissible fuzzy controllers is compact and metrizable with respect to the product topology on $C[-r_1, r_1]^{mn} \times G^m$.*

Proof. We first note that a sequence $\{(\mathcal{A}^k, \mathcal{B}^k)\} \subset \mathcal{F}$ converges to $(\mathcal{A}, \mathcal{B})$ in $\mathcal{F}$ for the product topology if and only if, for each $i = 1, 2, \ldots, m$,

$$\|\alpha_{\mathcal{A}_i^k} - \alpha_{\mathcal{A}_i}\|_\infty \equiv \sup_{x \in [-r_1, r_1]^n} |\alpha_{\mathcal{A}_i^k}(x) - \alpha_{\mathcal{A}_i}(x)| \to 0$$

and $\mu_{B_i^k} \to \mu_{B_i}$ weakly on $L^2[-r_2, r_2]$ i.e. $\int_{-r_2}^{r_2} |\mu_{B_i^k}(y) - \mu_{B_i}(y)|^2 dy \to 0$.

Assume that a sequence $\{(\mathcal{A}^k, \mathcal{B}^k)\}$ in $\mathcal{F}_\delta$ converges to $(\mathcal{A}, \mathcal{B}) \in \mathcal{F}$. Fix $x \in [-r_1, r_1]^n$. Then, it is easy to show that

$$\int_{-r_2}^{r_2} \gamma_{AB}(x, y)dy = \lim_{k \to \infty} \int_{-r_2}^{r_2} \gamma_{A^k B^k}(x, y)dy \geq \delta,$$

and this implies $(\mathcal{A}, \mathcal{B}) \in \mathcal{F}_\delta$. Therefore, $\mathcal{F}_\delta$ is a closed subset of $\mathcal{F}$, and hence it is compact metrizable. $\qquad \Box$

In this case, for any admissible fuzzy controller $(\mathcal{A}, \mathcal{B}) \in \mathcal{F}_\delta$, the amount of operation $\rho_{mpsAB} : [-r_1, r_1]^n \to \mathbb{R}$ is constructed by min-or-product-sum-gravity method:

$$\rho_{mpsAB}(x) = \frac{\int_{-r_2}^{r_2} y\gamma_{AB}(x, y)dy}{\int_{-r_2}^{r_2} \gamma_{AB}(x, y)dy},$$

$$\alpha_{\mathcal{A}_i}(x) = \bigwedge_{j=1}^{n} \mu_{A_{ij}}(x_j) \text{ or } \prod_{j=1}^{n} \mu_{A_{ij}}(x_j) \quad (i = 1, 2, \ldots, m),$$

$$\beta_{A_i B_i}(x, y) = \alpha_{\mathcal{A}_i}(x) \cdot \mu_{B_i}(y) \ (i = 1, 2, \ldots, m) \text{ and } \gamma_{AB}(x, y) = \sum_{i=1}^{m} \beta_{A_i B_i}(x, y)$$

for each $x \in [-r_1, r_1]^n$ and $y \in [-r_2, r_2]$. Then, we have

Proposition 4. *Let $(\mathcal{A}, \mathcal{B}) \in \mathcal{F}_\delta$. Then, the following hold.* (a) *ρ_{mpsAB} is Lipschitz continuous on $[-r_1, r_1]^n$.* (b) *$|\rho_{mpsAB}(x)| \leq r_2$ for all $x \in [-r_1, r_1]^n$.*

Proof. (a) For any $x, x' \in [-r_1, r_1]^n$ and any $i = 1, 2, \ldots, m$, we have even if minimum operation or product operation is applied

$$|\alpha_{\mathcal{A}_i}(x) - \alpha_{\mathcal{A}_i}(x')| = n\Delta_i \|x - x'\|,$$

where Δ_i is the maximum of Lipschitz constants of the functions $\mu_{A_{ij}}$ ($j = 1, 2, \ldots, n$). Hence the mapping $\alpha_{\mathcal{A}_i}$ is Lipschitz continuous on $[-r_1, r_1]^n$. Noting that $|\mu_{B_i}(y)| \leq 1$, we have

$$|\beta_{\mathcal{A}_i \mathcal{B}_i}(x, y) - \beta_{\mathcal{A}_i \mathcal{B}_i}(x', y)| \leq n\Delta_i \|x - x'\|$$

and

$$|\gamma_{\mathcal{A}\mathcal{B}}(x, y) - \gamma_{\mathcal{A}\mathcal{B}}(x', y)| \leq m\Delta \|x - x'\|,$$

where $\Delta = \max\{n\Delta_1, n\Delta_2, \ldots, n\Delta_n\}$.

Noting that $\int_{-r_2}^{r_2} y\gamma_{\mathcal{A}\mathcal{B}}(x, y)dy \leq r_2^2$ and $\delta \leq \int_{-r_2}^{r_2} \gamma_{\mathcal{A}\mathcal{B}}(x, y)dy \leq 2r_2$ for all $x \in [-r_1, r_1]^n$ by (6), it follows that

$$|\rho_{mps\mathcal{A}\mathcal{B}}(x) - \rho_{mps\mathcal{A}\mathcal{B}}(x')| \leq \frac{2r_2^3 m\Delta}{\delta^2} \|x - x'\|,$$

and the Lipschitz continuity of $\rho_{\mathcal{A}\mathcal{B}}$ is proved.

(b) For any $y \in [-r_2, r_2]$, we have $y\gamma_{\mathcal{A}\mathcal{B}}(x, y) \leq r_2\gamma_{\mathcal{A}\mathcal{B}}(x, y)$. Noting that $\int_{-r_2}^{r_2} \gamma_{\mathcal{A}\mathcal{B}}(x, y)dy$ is non zero and

$$\int_{-r_2}^{r_2} y\gamma_{\mathcal{A}\mathcal{B}}(x, y)dy \leq r_2 \int_{-r_2}^{r_2} \gamma_{\mathcal{A}\mathcal{B}}(x, y)dy.$$

Then $|\rho_{mps\mathcal{A}\mathcal{B}}(x)| \leq r_2$ for all $x \in [-r_1, r_1]^n$. $\qquad\square$

4.3   Application of Nakamori Method

Similarly, in the case that Nakamori method is applied, to avoid making the denominators of the gravity defuzzification and the aggregation operator γ_{nak} equal to 0, for any $\varepsilon > 0$, $\sigma > 0$, we consider the set:

$$\mathcal{F}_{\varepsilon\sigma} = \left\{ (\mathcal{A}, \mathcal{B}) \in \mathcal{F} : \int_{-r_2}^{r_2} \gamma_{\mathcal{A}\mathcal{B}}(x, y)dy \geq \varepsilon, \sum_{i=1}^{m} \alpha_{\mathcal{A}_i}(x) \geq \sigma \text{ for } \forall x \in [-r_1, r_1]^n \right\}. \tag{7}$$

Then, we have following proposition

Proposition 5. *The set $\mathcal{F}_{\varepsilon\sigma}$ of all admissible fuzzy controllers is compact and metrizable with respect to the product topology on $C[-r_1, r_1]^{mn} \times G^m$.*

Proof. Omitted.

In this case, for any admissible fuzzy controller $(\mathcal{A}, \mathcal{B}) \in \mathcal{F}_{\varepsilon\sigma}$, the fuzzy output $\rho_{nm\mathcal{A}\mathcal{B}} : [-r_1, r_1]^n \to \mathbb{R}$ is constructed by Nakamori method:

$$\rho_{nm\mathcal{A}\mathcal{B}}(x) = \frac{\int_{-r_2}^{r_2} y\gamma_{\mathcal{A}\mathcal{B}}(x, y)dy}{\int_{-r_2}^{r_2} \gamma_{\mathcal{A}\mathcal{B}}(x, y)dy},$$

$$\alpha_{\mathcal{A}_i}(x) = \prod_{j=1}^{n} \mu_{A_{ij}}(x_j) \ (i = 1, 2, \ldots, m) \text{ and } \gamma_{AB}(x,y) = \frac{\sum_{i=1}^{m} \alpha_{\mathcal{A}_i}(x) \cdot \mu_{B_i}(y)}{\sum_{i=1}^{m} \alpha_{\mathcal{A}_i}(x)}$$

for each $x \in [-r_1, r_1]^n$ and $y \in [-r_2, r_2]$. Then, we have

Proposition 6. [7] *Let* $(\mathcal{A}, \mathcal{B}) \in \mathcal{F}_{\varepsilon\sigma}$. *Then,* $\rho_{nm\mathcal{A}\mathcal{B}}$ *is Lipschitz continuous on* $[-r_1, r_1]^n$, *and* $|\rho_{nm\mathcal{A}\mathcal{B}}(x)| \leq r_2$.

4.4 Existence of Unique Solution of State Equation

Let $(\mathcal{A}, \mathcal{B})$ be a fuzzy controller given by the IF-THEN type fuzzy control rules (1). We say that the system (2) is a fuzzy feedback system if the control function $u(t)$ is given by the state feedback $u(t) = \rho_{mps\mathcal{A}\mathcal{B}}(x(t))$ or $u(t) = \rho_{nm\mathcal{A}\mathcal{B}}(x(t))$, where $\rho_{mps\mathcal{A}\mathcal{B}}(x(t))$ and $\rho_{nm\mathcal{A}\mathcal{B}}(x(t))$ are the amount of operation from the fuzzy controller $(\mathcal{A}, \mathcal{B})$ for an input information $x(t)$.

Every bounded Lipschitz function can be extended to a bounded Lipschitz function without increasing its Lipschitz constant and bound. Let $(\mathcal{A}, \mathcal{B}) \in \mathcal{F}_\delta$. Then it follows from proposition 4 and the fact about bounded Lipschitz function that the extension $\tilde{\rho}_{mps\mathcal{A}\mathcal{B}}$ of $\rho_{mps\mathcal{A}\mathcal{B}}$ is Lipschitz continuous on $\mathbb{R}^n$ with the same Lipschitz constant of $\rho_{mps\mathcal{A}\mathcal{B}}$ and satisfies $\sup_{u \in \mathbb{R}^n} |\tilde{\rho}_{mps\mathcal{A}\mathcal{B}}(u)| \leq r_2$. Therefore, by proposition 2 the state equation (2) for the feedback law $\tilde{\rho}_{mps\mathcal{A}\mathcal{B}}$ has a unique solution $x(t, x_0, \tilde{\rho}_{mps\mathcal{A}\mathcal{B}})$ with the initial condition $x(0) = x_0$ [8]. Though the extension $\tilde{\rho}_{mps\mathcal{A}\mathcal{B}}$ of $\rho_{mps\mathcal{A}\mathcal{B}}$ is not unique in general, the solution $x(t, x_0, \tilde{\rho}_{mps\mathcal{A}\mathcal{B}})$ is uniquely determined by $\rho_{mps\mathcal{A}\mathcal{B}}$ using the inequality (4) of (b) of proposition 2. Consequently, in the following the extension $\tilde{\rho}_{mps\mathcal{A}\mathcal{B}}$ is written as $\rho_{mps\mathcal{A}\mathcal{B}}$ without confusion. The same fact about $\rho_{nm\mathcal{A}\mathcal{B}}$ is obtained in the same way as the case of $\rho_{mps\mathcal{A}\mathcal{B}}$.

5 Existence of Optimal Control

In this section, using an idea and framework mentioned in the previous section, the existence of optimal control based on fuzzy rules will be established.

The performance index of this control system for the feedback law ρ (ρ_{mps} or ρ_{nm}) in previous section is evaluated with the following integral performance function:

$$J = \int_{B_r} \int_0^T w(x(t, \zeta, \rho), \rho(x(t, \zeta, \rho)))dtd\zeta, \tag{8}$$

where $w : \mathbb{R}^n \times \mathbb{R} \to \mathbb{R}$ is a positive continuous function. The following theorems guarantee the existence of a rule set which minimizes the previous function (8).

Theorem 1 (Application of Min-or-product-sum-garavity method). *Put* $\rho = \rho_{mps}$. *The mapping*

$$(\mathcal{A}, \mathcal{B}) \in \mathcal{F}_\delta \mapsto \int_{B_r} \int_0^T w(x(t, \zeta, \rho_{AB}), \rho_{AB}(x(t, \zeta, \rho_{AB})))dtd\zeta \tag{9}$$

has a minimum value on the compact metric space $\mathcal{F}_\delta$ *defined by* (6).

Proof. Since compactness of $\mathcal{F}_\delta$ is already derived by proposition 3, it is sufficient to prove that the performance function is continuous on $\mathcal{F}_\delta$. Routine calculation gives the estimate

$$\sup_{x\in[-r_1,r_1]^n} |\rho_{\mathcal{A}^k\mathcal{B}^k}(x) - \rho_{\mathcal{AB}}(x)| \leq \frac{4mr_2^3}{\delta^2} \sum_{i=1}^m \|\alpha_{\mathcal{A}_i^k} - \alpha_{\mathcal{A}_i}\|_\infty$$

$$+ \frac{mr_2^2\sqrt{2r_2^2}}{\delta^2}\left(\frac{2}{\sqrt{3}}+1\right)\sum_{i=1}^m\left(\int_{-r_2}^{r_2} |\mu_{B_i^k}(y) - \mu_{B_i}(y)|^2 dy\right)^{\frac{1}{2}}.$$

Assume that $(\mathcal{A}^k,\mathcal{B}^k) \to (\mathcal{A},\mathcal{B})$ in $\mathcal{F}_\delta$ and fix $(t,\zeta) \in [0,T] \times B_r$. Then it follows from the estimate above that

$$\lim_{k\to\infty} \sup_{x\in[-r_1,r_1]^n} |\rho_{\mathcal{A}^k\mathcal{B}^k}(x) - \rho_{\mathcal{AB}}(x)| = 0. \tag{10}$$

Hence, by (b) of proposition 2,

$$\lim_{k\to\infty} \|x(t,\zeta,\rho_{\mathcal{A}^k\mathcal{B}^k}) - x(t,\zeta,\rho_{\mathcal{AB}})\| = 0. \tag{11}$$

Further, it follows from (10), (11) and (a) of proposition 2 that

$$\lim_{k\to\infty} \rho_{\mathcal{A}^k\mathcal{B}^k}(x(t,\zeta,\rho_{\mathcal{A}^k\mathcal{B}^k})) = \rho_{\mathcal{AB}}(x(t,\zeta,\rho_{\mathcal{AB}})). \tag{12}$$

Noting that $w : \mathbb{R}^n \times \mathbb{R} \to \mathbb{R}$ is positive and continuous, it follows from (11), (12) and the Lebesgue's dominated convergence theorem that the mapping (9) is continuous on the compact metric space $\mathcal{F}_\delta$. Thus it has a minimum (maximum) value on $\mathcal{F}_\delta$, and the proof is complete. $\qquad\square$

Theorem 2 (Application of Nakamori method). *Put* $\rho = \rho_{nm}$. *The mapping (9) has a minimum value on the compact metric space* $\mathcal{F}_{\varepsilon\sigma}$ *defined by (7).*

Proof. $\mathcal{F}_{\varepsilon\sigma}$ is compact by proposition 5. Only continuity of ρ_{nm} is proved. It is sufficient to prove that the performance function is continuous on $\mathcal{F}_{\varepsilon\sigma}$. Assume that $(\mathcal{A}^k,\mathcal{B}^k) \to (\mathcal{A},\mathcal{B})$ in $\mathcal{F}_{\varepsilon\sigma}$ and fix $(t,\zeta) \in [0,T] \times B_r$. Routine calculation gives the estimate

$$\sup_{x\in[-r_1,r_1]^n} |\rho_{\mathcal{A}^k\mathcal{B}^k}(x) - \rho_{\mathcal{AB}}(x)|$$

$$\leq \frac{\sqrt{2r_2}}{\varepsilon^2\sigma}\left(1+\frac{r_2}{\sqrt{3}}\right)\sum_{i=1}^m\left(\int_{-r_2}^{r_2} |\mu_{B_i^k}(y) - \mu_{B_i}(y)|^2 dy\right)^{\frac{1}{2}}$$

$$+ \frac{r_2(2+r_2)}{\varepsilon^2\sigma}\left(1+\frac{m}{\sigma}\right)\sum_{i=1}^m \|\alpha_{\mathcal{A}_i^k} - \alpha_{\mathcal{A}_i}\|_\infty \to 0 \qquad (k\to\infty)$$

Thus performance function has a minimum (maximum) value on $\mathcal{F}_{\varepsilon\sigma}$, and the proof is complete. $\qquad\square$

6   Conclusion

In this paper, we proved that there exists an optimal feedback control law in a nonlinear fuzzy feedback control system, in which the feedback laws are determined by IF-THEN type fuzzy rules through fuzzy approximate reasoning.

We proved that approximate reasoning is Lipschitz continuous composite function on the premise variables and continuous functional on the set of membership functions. Lipschitz continuity is one of the sufficient conditions for the existence of the unique solution of the state equation in the nonlinear feedback control. On the other, the continuity on the set of membership functions guarantees the existence of a rule set, in other words a pair of membership functions, which minimize the integral cost function with compactness of the set of membership functions. The compact admissible fuzzy controller $\mathcal{F}_\delta$ and $\mathcal{F}_{\varepsilon\sigma}$ in this paper includes the class of triangular, trapezoidal, and bell-shaped functions which are used in application generally.

It is recognized that in various applications it could be a useful tool in analyzing the convergence of fuzzy control rules modified recursively.

References

1. Shidama, Y., Yang, Y., Eguchi, M., Yamaura, H.: The compactness of a set of membership functions and its application to fuzzy optimal control. The Japan Society for Industrial and Applied Mathematics 1, 1–13 (1996)
2. Mitsuishi, T., Wasaki, K., Kawabe, J., Kawamoto, N.P., Shidama, Y.: Fuzzy optimal control in L^2 space. In: Proc. 7th IFAC Symposium Artificial Intelligence in Real-Time Control, pp. 173–177 (1998)
3. Mizumoto, M.M.: Improvement of fuzzy control (IV) - Case by product-sum-gravity method. In: Proc. 6th Fuzzy System Symposium, pp. 9–13 (1990)
4. Nakamori, Y., Ryoke, M.: Identification of fuzzy prediction models through hyper-ellipsoidal clustering. IEEE Transactions on Systems, Man and Cybernetics SMC-24(8), 1153–1173 (1994)
5. Dunford, N., Schwartz, J.T.: Linear Operators Part I: General Theory. John Wiley & Sons, New York (1988)
6. Mitsuishi, T., Kawabe, J., Wasaki, K., Shidama, Y.: Optimization of Fuzzy Feedback Control Determined by Product-Sum-Gravity Method. Journal of Nonlinear and Convex Analysis 1(2), 201–211 (2000)
7. Mitsuishi, T., Endou, N., Shidama, Y.: Continuity of Nakamori Fuzzy Model and Its Application to Optimal Feedback Control. In: Proc. IEEE International Conference on Systems, Man and Cybernetics, pp. 577–581 (2005)
8. Miller, R.K., Michel, A.N.: Ordinary Differential Equations. Academic Press, New York (1982)

Application of Fuzzy Cognitive Maps for Stock Market Modeling and Forecasting

Wojciech Froelich and Alicja Wakulicz-Deja

Institute of Computer Science, Silesian University
ul.Bedzinska 39, Sosnowiec, Poland

Abstract. In this paper, we investigated the possibility of discovering complex concepts for modeling and forecasting the stock market. We started from a short overview of existing domain knowledge and discussed the usefulness of well-known stock market indicators for predicting share prices. As opposed to other statistical or artificial intelligence approaches, we decided to concentrate on the modeling of cause and effect relationships among concepts within stock market behavior. After preliminary analysis, we made the case for the application of the resulting model for the forecasting stock market performance, using complex concepts that involve a mixture of diverse simple indicators and causal relationships. For the construction and evaluation of such complex concepts, we applied FCMs (fuzzy cognitive maps), a relatively easy approach that allows human interpretation of the results from the scheme. On the basis of the proposed formalism and the adapted evolutionary learning method, we have developed an FCM with the ability to support decisions relative to the stock exchange. We have verified the usefulness of the proposed approach using historical transactions of the Warsaw Stock Exchange.

1   Introduction

The problem of time series prediction has been a challenging task for researchers and practitioners for many years. The problem has been extensively investigated by applying domain knowledge[1], statistical theories[2], artificial intelligence techniques[3], and other approaches. Perhaps the best-known approach applies expert knowledge in the form of so-called fundamental[4] and technical[5] analysis. Both of the analyses operate by the application of numerous dedicated indicators.

There is a set of fundamental indicators that considers the economic situation of a company, macro-economic conditions of country, or even global conditions (e.g., prices of minerals). A typical example is the price/earnings indicator P/E that is the ratio of share price to the company's earnings at the considered period of time. The lower the P/E, the cheaper are the shares and the stronger is the indication to buy these shares.

The technical analysis assumes mostly that the fundamental information is usually discounted by the market, i.e., already accounted for in the price of a share. The technical indicators evaluate the behavior of share prices without any

N.T. Nguyen et al. (Eds.): IEA/AIE 2008, LNAI 5027, pp. 72–81, 2008.

reference to the economic situation. A simple example is the relative strength index (RSI) based on the number of ups and downs over a period of time: $RSI = 1 - \frac{1}{1+RS}$, $RS = \frac{u/n}{d/n}$, where: u = number of days up (share price higher than that of the previous day); d = number of days down (share price lower than that of the previous day); and n = number of days under consideration. The reasoning behind the RSI is expressed by the rule that states: if the RSI gradient is large, then sell; if the change in the RSI gradient changes from negative to positive, then buy. The decision attribute can be also expressed in fuzzy form, i.e., weak sell or strong buy. In spite of the existence of many indicators constructed mostly on the basis of domain knowledge, there is still no agreement among professional investors concerning which of the indicators are appropriate and when to use them. It is expected that the effectiveness of technical indicators depends on many factors, e.g., the country's economy and the political situation. We started our investigations by asking experts from five important financial institutions in Poland to complete a questionnaire. The experts were asked to evaluate, according to their experience, the usefulness of technical indicators for predicting movement of share prices. The results showed that the most frequently-used indicators are MACD and RSI and that WILIAMS and OBV are rarely used. Which indicator to use and when to use it are topics of ongoing discussion. The domain experts usually take into account a set of their favorite factors, mainly fundamental and technical indicators. Therefore, we would like to consider the situation in which more than one factor could have a cumulative causal effect on the share price.

The indicators can be evaluated by statistical methods. We evaluated some of the technical indicators on the basis of historical data obtained from the Warsaw Stock Exchange (Poland). We decided to apply some simple criteria, namely the Pearson's correlation and the achieved investment return, while using the recommendations generated by an indicator. The results of the analysis for the period from June 11, 2006, to June 11, 2007, for 274 companies are presented in Table 1. We calculated the correlation between a given indicator (first column) and the share prices of a particular stock. Then, the averages for all companies were computed and are shown in the second column of the table. The average investment return for all transactions recommended by the indicator and the

Table 1. Evaluation of technical indicators

Indicator (1)	Average Correlation (2)	Average return (3)	Max. return (4)	Min. return (5)
ROC	0,29	3,94%	1690%	-90%
MSI	-0,44	0,00%	223%	-89%
MACD	0,19	6,50%	376%	-66%
STS	0,30	0,95%	374%	-95%
MDM	0,15	-4,91%	6%	-36%
WILIAMS	0,38	7,26%	1614%	-88%

maximum and minimum returns for a single transaction are shown in columns 3,4, and 5, respectively. It is apparent from the Table 1 that the interpretation of the results is not obvious. On one hand, the application of indicators seems to be helpful for achieving high return values in some cases; on the other hand, the average investment return is rather disappointing. This means that the problem remains, i.e., when to use an indicator to achieve better returns, perhaps another indicator would do a better job, or should a new indicator be formulated. It could be also doubtful if the linear correlation reflects the nature of cause and effect relationships among considered factors.

The mutual dependencies among factors cannot be excluded. The dependencies among indicators, share prices (and, without doubt, other factors) are not simple one-to-one associations, but rather they involve more complex, causal structures that lead to a particular behavior of the market. It is also important to note the possibility of occurrences of known, cyclic phenomena that can be observed in market behavior. Therefore, our objective was to identify and develop such a model of the stock market that would be able to take into account these cyclic phenomena.

We would like to investigate the possibility of developing and applying an appropriate causal model to evaluate the effectiveness of stock market indicators and their various combinations. The advantage of causal modeling is the ability of the models to take into account cause and effect relationships among concepts or events. Although these types of relationships are difficult to develop using only statistical modeling, one of the known examples of the problem is the Simpson paradox[10]. While applying a causal model, there is a possibility of modeling and analyzing complex, indirect, causal dependencies, especially in cases in which the direct associations between concepts are difficult to identify. An introduction to causal and evidential modeling techniques can be found in[7]. A generalized, functional causal model and the model's relationship to probability theory are presented in the book of J. Pearl[10]. Among the very few reasonable approaches to causal modeling, it's also necessary to mention the causal modal logic proposed by Y. Shoham[8] and fuzzy evidential logic of R. Sun[9]. For the purpose of the stock market prediction problem, we have decided to apply a model expressed by fuzzy cognitive maps (FCMs)[13].

The intuitive and easy-to-interpret representation of an FCM is a directed graph, consisting of concepts (nodes) and cause-and-effect relationships (arcs) among them. The concepts represent states that are observable within the domain. The directions of arcs indicate the casual dependency between source and target concepts. The main difference between the Bayesian networks and FCM is that an FCM does not need to be an acyclic graph, i.e., a DAG (directed acyclic graph). The application of DCNs (the extension of FCMs) for the approximation of financial time series has been investigated in[19]. The proposed approach concentrates on the approximation capabilities of FCM (similar to the approach used in neural networks) and thus differs from our approach, which deals rather with the problem of causal impact of known indicators on the recommendation to buy, hold, or sell shares. In our previous research[20], we developed a system that is able to develop large number of concepts on the basis of information available from the web and tune their parameters appropriately with the expectation of being useful in the construction of FCMs. The proposed hybrid learning algorithm has led to promising results, but the necessity of dealing with many small similar FCMs makes the appropriate choice (which FCM to apply) to leave the decision to an expert.

2 Fuzzy Cognitive Maps

The idea of cognitive maps (CMs) has been introduced in psychology[11] and used primarily as a modeling tool in social sciences[12]. Fuzzy cognitive maps, introduced by Kosko[13], combine some of the features from fuzzy logic and neural networks in their representation schemes. There are many variations of the generic FCM model. The problem of modeling time delays between cause and effect concepts has been addressed in [14]. The limitation imposed by the linear cumulative nature of causal links has been significantly extended by the rule based fuzzy cognitive maps RBFCM[15]. The proposal of HO-FCMs[18] overcomes the problem of modeling high-order dynamics by adding memory to the concepts nodes. A review of the variations of FCMs and their operational methods can be found in [16]. There are also varying formal approaches to the description of FCMs.

For the targeted application, we propose the following model with the main intention to capture the observation - decision capabilities of FCM, so that every FCM can play the role of an agent situated in a dynamically changing environment. The FCM observes the market indicators and undertakes decisions that can affect market behavior. For the targeted application, we assume the following notation. Primarily, we present definitions of objects involved in every FCM, then we define its structure and present two basic modes of activity: exploitation and learning. Assume, the symbol U denotes the finite set of observations (objects or events) $u \in U$. The term concept will be understood, as a subset of observations $c \subset U$ described in any crisp or approximate way (for instance, intuitively, it can be defined beforehand by the center of a cluster in U and its neighborhood within a certain radius). The set of concepts is denoted by C. Now, we define a parameterized observation function:

$$\psi_{\bar{p}} : U \times C \to\, < -1, 1 > \tag{1}$$

where $\bar{p}$ is a vector of parameters. This way, it is possible to scale the observation values u to the $< -1, 1 >$ interval that reflects the so-called activation level of concept c. As assumed mostly in the literature, the activation value can be negative, and thus it is different from the value of the traditional fuzzy membership measure. For every concept c_i, we define its actual activation value (its state) denoted as $a_i \in\, < -1, 1 >$. Considering all concepts of FCM, a vector A is constructed (state vector). Every $a_i \in A$ in the state vector can be computed in two ways, i.e., applying the observation function (1) or on the basis of activation values of other concepts a_j, where $j \neq i$ (3). If time is considered, the respective objects will be complemented by the letter t. We define for every two concepts $c_i, c_j \in C$ a causal relation $r : c_i(t) \to c_j(t + \Delta t)$, that is described by the characteristic function $\mu(c_i, c_j)$. If $0 < \mu(c_i, c_j) \leq 1$, the causality is positive (the change of corresponding a_i causes the change of a_j in the same direction); if $-1 \leq \mu(c_i, c_j) < 0$, the causality is negative (in opposite direction, i.e. indicates that increasing of c_i causes the decreasing of c_j). Otherwise, when $\mu(c_i, c_j) = 0$, the two concepts are not in a causal relationship. The actual value of $\mu(c_i, c_j)$ at time step t will be denoted as a weight w_{ij} and stored in the two-dimensional matrix W.

The state of a fuzzy, cognitive map at a discrete time step $t \in< t_0, \ldots, t+n >$ is defined as a triple:

$$FCM = \langle C, A, W \rangle, \tag{2}$$

where C is the finite set of concepts; A is the vector of actual activation values assigned to concepts; and W is the weight matrix expressing the casual relations among every two concepts in the map. Let us now take a closer look at the activity of the FCM. The FCM can operate in two modes, i.e., 1) exploitation mode or 2) learning mode.

While in the exploitation mode, at the initial time step t_0, the vector $A(t_0)$ is computed by applying (1); then, at the following time steps, the FCM predicts the consecutive values of its state vector A. The value of $A(t + 1)$ is computed on the basis of the previous activation values of concepts and the transformation function:

$$a_i(t + 1) = a_i(t) + f\left(\sum_{j=1, j \neq i}^{n} w_{ij} a_{ij} \right), \tag{3}$$

where f is the threshold function that serves to reduce unbounded values to a strict range. It can be defined for instance as a sigmoid function: $f = \frac{1}{1+e^{-\lambda x}}$, in which the parameter λ determines the shape of the function. A discrete time simulation is performed by iteratively applying (3). During the iterative process, the state vector A may converge to the: a) fixed-point attractor (remains unchanged), b) limit cycle (A repeats), or c) chaotic attractor (A changes and repeating states never occur). This way the forward reasoning process is performed $A(t + 1) = W \times A(t)$. The values of weights in matrix W do not change in the exploitation mode.

There is a possibility that an expert could construct the entire FCM (definition of concepts, observation functions and values of weights). In such a case, there is no need to apply any machine learning technique. As mentioned in the first section, such an approach seems to be doubtful for the application targeted in our research, because the domain knowledge is not sufficient. The opposite approach is to learn almost all objects of the FCM structure, extract concepts from data, learn observation functions and weight matrix using machine learning techniques that can lead unfortunately to a large number of similar FCMs, which in most cases are difficult to select. Taking into account the above factors, we have decided to assume the set of concepts C and observation functions beforehand and to apply the evolutionary learning method only for the weights matrix W.

Given a set of concepts, learning FCM's weights can be basically of two types, i.e., adaptive[17] or evolutionary[16]. While performing adaptive type of learning, activation values for all concepts are computed on the basis of observation function $a_i(t) = \mu_{\bar{p}}(t)$ as defined in (1), at two consecutive time steps. For the concept i, the difference: $\Delta a_i = a_i(t) - a_i(t-1)$ is computed. The modification of weights is based mostly on the Hebian rule: $w_{ij}(t+1) = w_{ij}(t) + \alpha(t)[\Delta a_i \Delta a_j - w_{ij}(t)]$, where $\alpha(t) = \frac{0.1}{1 - t/1.1q}$ and q is the parameter. While applying genetic learning, the weights are modified by the genetic operators during the evolutionary process. In this case, the computation of the fitness function involves the evaluation of the entire FCM by measuring the sum of differences between observed $\mu_{\bar{p}}(t)$ and actual activity values $a_i(t)$ for all concepts.

$$err(FCM) = \sum_{j-1}^{k-1}\sum_{t=1}^{n}(\mu_{\bar{p}} - a_i(t)) \tag{4}$$

$$fitness(FCM) = \frac{1}{1 + err(FCM)} \tag{5}$$

where $n = card(C)$ and k is the number of observations read during one learning cycle.

3   Modeling Stock Market

Considering the above proposed notation, we have made the following assumptions for modeling the stock market and for computational simulations. We have decided to use, as source data, the set of historical transactions from the Warsaw Stock Exchange over the last eight years. This approach involves data in standard meta-stock format including: maximum and minimum share price, opening and closing price, and turnover. The raw data from the stock exchange have been pre-processed to prepare the file, which could play the role of an appropriate set of observations U for the considered FCM. One day's trading on the stock exchange refers to one record in the data file and observation vector u for FCM. It is, of course, not possible to take into account in our experiments the effects of transactions initiated by our system. We decided to use a fixed set of concepts, which has been chosen on the basis of the opinions of domain experts (previously discussed questionnaire) and our own experiences [20] with the FCM model. The number of concepts has been set to eight $card(C) = 8$, thus achieving the length of genotype equal to $8 \times 8 = 64$ genes that reflect the weights in matrix W. The set of concepts is the following C = { c_1 - share price, c_2 - turnover of the company, c_3 - indicator A/D, c_4 - indicator WILLIAMS, c_5 - indicator ROC, c_6 - WIG main index of Warsaw Stock Exchange, c_7 - turnover of WIG, c_8 - indicator OBV }. The concept c_1 is the target concept that refers to the predicted decision, the rest of the concepts corresponds to the actual conditions on the stock market. According to the set of concepts, the appropriate observation functions had to be appropriately implemented. The details of the computation of the technical indicators can be found in [5]. The values of source data had to be normalized to the $< -1, 1 >$ interval. For the observation function $\mu_{\bar{p}}$ we used only one parameter p_t for each concept to settle the time period for its computation for $< t - p_t, t >$, where t denotes the actual step of time. The entire considered period of time (eight years) has been divided into intervals (learning-exploiting cycles) consisting of r days. In every such interval, the data of the first k (4) days have been used to learn the population of FCMs (learning mode), and the rest $r - k$ days of the period are assumed as a testing period (exploitation mode).

3.1   Evolutionary Learning of FCM

For the learning process of FCM's weights, we have applied the evolutionary method[16] with the parameters $p_t = 5, r = 140, k = 40$. If the FCM achieves cycle attractor, the learning process is terminated immediately and the assumed learnig period is finished (the 100 days testing periods follows immediately). For the results presented in this paper the cardinality of population has been set to the constant number of 200 FCMs. Other parameters were: probability of mutation - 0.5, probability of crossover - 0.9, number of generations - 1000. After the learning period, the best (with respect to fitness function) achieved FCMs have been additionally filtered according to the strength of the causal relationships (matrix W) among concepts. Low values of weights, reflecting noise in the data or relationships of lower importance, undoubtedly disturbed the prediction capability of the map. After learning period, the filtering threshold $|w_{ij}| > 0.3$ was applied. The topology of one of the most frequent (considering diffcrent learning periods) FCMs for the KGHM Company is shown on Fig. (1). The abbreviation WIG stands for Warsaw Stock Exchange Index, and KGHM is a Polish copper mining and metallurgy company. The particular values of weights have been

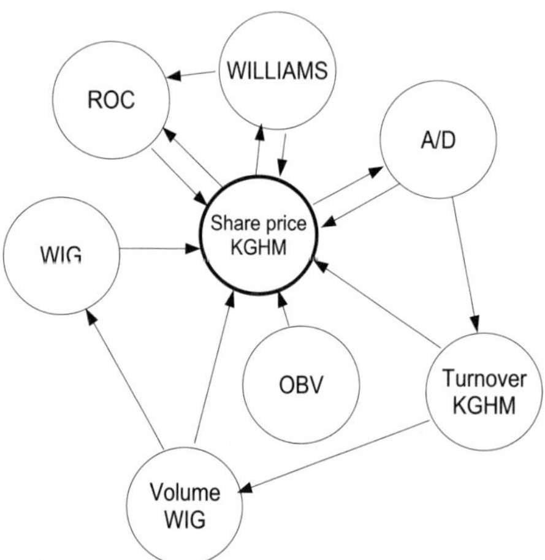

Fig. 1. Graphical interpretation of the achieved market model

intentionally omitted, due to their variance for different time periods. The FCMs have been also constructed for other companies. We have noticed surprisingly large differences among their topologies, and these differences suggest that more detailed studies of the dependency among companies' economic characteristics and the FCM causal models should be performed.

Notice that, while applying the FCM for one-step prediction, only direct relationships between concepts and KGHM share price can be considered. The length of time period Δt mapped to one simulation step can, of course, vary and is a parameter that must be set by an expert. However, in a generic model of FCM, this parameter should be the same for all relationships and cannot be modified after learning the FCM. In the discovered FCM, we achieved the model of weighted, shared, causal influences of technical indicators on the target c_1 concept.

3.2   Exploiting the FCM

The recommendation to buy, sell, or hold a share should be insensitive to noise, and the transactions should not be made immediately after detecting any change in target concept activation value. Therefore, the interval $< -1, 1 >$ of targeted c_1 concept (share price) activation value has been divided into 3 subintervals, namely $< -1, -0.3), < -0.3, 0.3), < 0.3, 1 >$ mapped to sell, hold, and buy, respectively. The achieved results for KGHM company (within a selected learning-exploiting period)have been presented in Fig. 2. The starting capital was 10000 zl(polish cuurency). The achieved investment return rate 12% at the end of the selected learning-exploitation period is quite interesting, especially taking into account the possible loss of 13% while following B&H (buy and hold) strategy. Notice, that the commissions have not been considered that in case of frequent transactions recommended by FCM can lead to significantly lower investment return. We consider to involve this criterion in future research while constructing the evaluation (fitness) function for FCMs.

After numerous experiments, we recognized two general types of periods of share price behavior in the stock market. The first type of period is characterized by stable market dynamics, whereas the dominant feature of the second type of period are sudden, relatively large price changes. Looking at the larger group of achieved prediction results, the first type situation (with lower price variations) seems to be more appropriate for the application of the FCM. In most cases, following the recommendations made by the FCM is better than the B&H strategy. The result for 3 selected companies (Debica, KGHM, Polimex) achieved within the other period of time (with stable and falling down WIG index) are shown in

Table 2. Comparison of investment strategies

Debica		KGHM		Polimex	
FCM	B&H	FCM	B&H	FCM	B&H
3.5%	-40%	64	-24	-0.6	-56

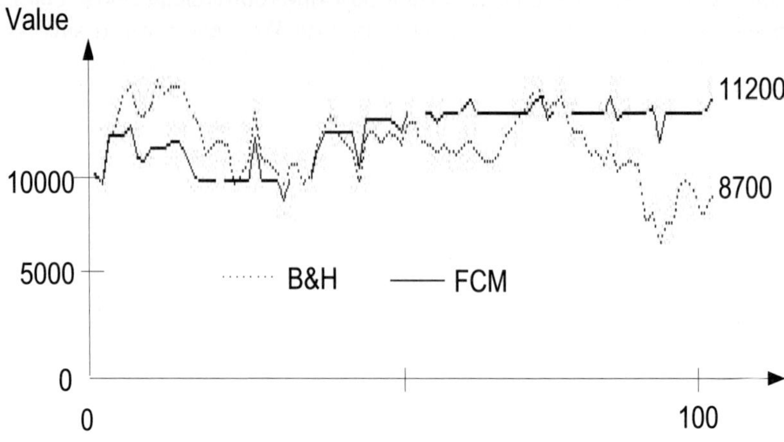

Fig. 2. Comparison of investment strategies for KGHM

Table 2. You can see that by following FCM recommandations it was possible to achieve benefit (KGHM) or avoid loss in case of other shares (Debica, Polimex).

4   Conclusion

In the presented research, we have designed a stock market decision support system based on the adapted model of fuzzy cognitive maps. We have combined the experts' domain knowledge and genetic learning method of the FCM for the construction of complex mixtures of simple indicators that can be useful in modeling and forecasting the stock market. On this basis, we have developed a practical system and achieved promising results that can be encouraging for the future research.

Acknowledgment. The research presented in this paper is planned to be supported by the European Union project: "Decision Support – New Generation Systems".

References

1. Elder, A.: Trading for a living: Psychology, Trading Tactics, Money Management. John Wiley & Sons, Chichester (1993)
2. Parikh, J.C.: Stochastic Processes and Financial Markets. Narosa Publishing House (2003)
3. Ehlers, J.: Cybernetic Analysis For Stock And Futures. John Willey & Sons, New York (2004)
4. Schwager, J.: Study Guide for Fundamental Analysis. John Wiley & Sons, Chichester (1995)

5. Pring, M.: Technical Analysis Explained. McGraw-Hill Company, New York (2004)
6. Vanstone, B., Tan, C.N.W.: A survey of the application of soft computing to investment and financial trading. In: Proceedings of the eighth Australian & New Zealand intelligent information systems conference (ANZIIS 2003), Sydney (2003)
7. Poole, D.: Learning, Bayesian Probability, Graphical Models, and Abduction. In: Flach, P., Kakas, A. (eds.) Abduction and Induction: essays on their relation and integration, Kluwer, Dordrecht (1998)
8. Shoham, Y.: Chronological Ignorance: Time, Nonmonotonicity, Necessity and Causal Theories, pp. 389–393. AAAI, Menlo Park (1986)
9. Sun, R.: Fuzzy Evidential Logic: a model of causality for commonsense reasoning. In: Proceedings of the Fourteenth Annual Conference of the Cognitive Scence Society (1992)
10. Pearl, J.: Causality, Models Reasoning and Inference. Cambridge University Press, Cambridge (2000)
11. Tollman, E.C.: Cognitive Maps in Rats and Men. The Psychological Review 55(3l), 189–208 (1948)
12. Axelrod, R.: Structure of Decision–The Cognitive Maps of Political Elites. Princeton University Press, Princeton (1976)
13. Kosko, B.: Fuzzy Cognitive Maps. International Journal of Man-Machine Studies 24(l), 65–75 (1986)
14. Park, K.S., Kim, S.H.: Fuzzy cognitive maps considering time relationships. International Journal Human-Computer Studies 42, 157–168 (1995)
15. Carvalho, J.P., Tome, J.A.B.: Rule Based Fuzzy Cognitive Maps - Fuzzy Causal Relations. In: Mohammadian, M. (ed.) Computational Intelligence for Modelling, Control and Automation: Evolutionary Computation & Fuzzy Logic for Intelligent Control, Knowledge Acquisition & Information Retrieval, IOS Press, Amsterdam (1999)
16. Stach, W., Kurgan, L.A., Pedrycz, W., Reformat, M.: Genetic learning of fuzzy cognitive maps. Fuzzy Sets and Systems 153(3), 371–401 (2005)
17. Huerga, A.V.: A balanced differential learning algorithm in fuzzy cognitive maps. In: Proceedings of the 16th International Workshop on Qualitative Reasoning (2002)
18. Stach, W., Kurgan, L.A., Pedrycz, W., Reformat, M.: Higher-order Fuzzy Cognitive Maps. In: Proceedings of NAFIPS 2006 (International Conference of the North American Fuzzy Information Processing Society (2006)
19. Koulouriotis, D.E., Diakoulakis, I.E., Emiris, D.M., Zopounidis, C.D.: Development of dynamic cognitive networks as complex systems approximators: validation in financial time series. Applied Soft Computing 5 (2005)
20. Froelich, W., Wakulicz-Deja, A.: Learning Fuzzy Cognitive Maps from the Web for the Stock Market Decision Support System. In: Proceedings of the 5th Atlantic Web Intelligence Conference - AWIC 2007, Fontainebleau, Advances In Soft Computing, vol. 43, pp. 106–111. Springer, Heidelberg (2007)

Fuzzy ARTMAP Neural Network for Classifying the Financial Health of a Firm

Anatoli Nachev

Information Systems, Dept. of Accountancy & Finance, National University of Ireland, Galway, Ireland
`anatoli.nachev@nuigalway.ie`

Abstract. In this paper, an application, based on data from a popular dataset, shows in an empirical form the strengths and weaknesses of fuzzy ARTMAP neural networks as predictor of corporate bankruptcy. This is an advantageous approach enabling fast learning, self-determination of the network structure and high prediction accuracy. Experiments showed that the fuzzy ARTMAP outperforms statistical techniques and the most popular backpropagation MLP neural networks, all applied to the same dataset. An exhaustive search procedure over the Altman's financial ratios leads to the conclusion that two of them are enough to obtain the highest prediction accuracy. The experiments also showed that the model is not sensitive to outliers of the dataset. Our research is the first to use fuzzy ARTMAP neural networks for bankruptcy prediction.

Keywords: data mining, neural networks, fuzzy ARTMAP.

1   Introduction

Financial analysis has developed a large number of techniques aimed at helping potential investors and decision makers. To estimate credit risk, investors usually apply scoring systems, which takes into account factors, such as leverage, earnings, reputation, etc. Due to lack of metrics and subjectiveness in estimates, sometimes decisions are unrealistic and not consistent.

Generally, a prediction of firm bankruptcy can be viewed as a pattern recognition problem, and as such, it could be solved by two approaches: structural, and empirical. The former derives the probability of a company for default, based on its characteristics and dynamics; the later approach relies on previous knowledge and relationships in that area, learns from existing data or experience, and deploys the statistical or other methods to predict corporate failure.

Empirical techniques used for bankruptcy prediction can be grouped into two broad categories [12]: (i) statistical and (ii) intelligent. Among statistical techniques, most popular are: linear discriminant analysis (LDA), multivariate discriminate analysis (MDA), quadratic discriminant analysis (QDA), logistic regression (logit) and factor analysis (FA). The most popular intelligent techniques are different neural network (NN) architectures, such as multi-layer perception (MLP), probabilistic neural networks (PNN), auto-associative neural network (AANN), self-organizing map

N.T. Nguyen et al. (Eds.): IEA/AIE 2008, LNAI 5027, pp. 82–91, 2008.

(SOM), learning vector quantization (LVQ) and cascade correlation neural network (Cascor). Other intelligent techniques include decision trees, case-based reasoning, evolutionary approaches, rough sets, soft computing (hybrid intelligent systems), operational research techniques including linear programming (LP), data envelopment analysis (DEA) and quadratic programming (QP), other intelligent techniques including support vector machine, fuzzy logic techniques.

LDA, MDA and logistic regression have been the most commonly used statistical models in this type of work. These techniques, however, have been sharply criticized because of assumptions about the linear separability, multivariate normality, and independence of the predictive variables, as these constraints are incompatible with the complex nature, boundaries, and interrelationships of majority of financial ratios [13]. To overcome these problems, the intelligent techniques have shown themselves to be more appropriate for that task.

The multilayer perceptron (MLP) is one of the most well known and widely used models of supervised NNs. MLP with one hidden layer can approximate any function but the size of this layer must be chosen only by an empirical method. The approach used in MLP implementations is totally empirical, and is not based on theoretical evidence as no complete theoretical explanation exists to obtain the optimal architecture of the MLP. Gallinari et al. [8] have demonstrated the relationship between LDA and MLP. Bell et al. [2], Hart [11], Yoon et al. [19], Curram and Mingers [7], and Wilson and Sharda [18] have compared the classifying power of different statistical tools and of MLP.

The aim of this paper is to show, in an empirical form, the strengths and weaknesses of the Fuzzy ARTMAP NN in the prediction of corporate failure. Our research is the first to use this type of neural networks for bankruptcy prediction.

2 Fuzzy ARTMAP Classifiers

A family of self-organizing neural networks for fast learning, pattern recognition, and prediction is based on the Adaptive Resonance Theory (ART) [10]. ART family includes both unsupervised: ART1, ART2, ART2-A, ART3, Fuzzy ART, Distributed ART; and supervised NNs: ARTMAP, ARTMAP-IC, Fuzzy ARTMAP, ART-EMAP, ARTMAP-FTR, distributed ARTMAP, and default ARTMAP systems.

By interconnecting two ART1 modules, ARTMAP was the first ART-based architecture suited for classification tasks [4]. ART2 was extended by Fuzzy-ART (FA), also capable of clustering real-valued patterns. ARTMAP was extended via Fuzzy-ARTMAP (FAM) to classify real-valued patterns [5]. FAM consists of two FA networks, ARTa and ARTb, bridged via an inter-ART module, as shown in Figure 1, and is capable of forming associative maps between clusters of its input and output domains in a supervised manner. The FA NN consists of two fully connected layers of nodes: an M-node input layer $F1$ and an N-node competitive layer $F2$. A set of real-valued weights $W=\{w_{ij}\in[0,1] : i=1, 2, ...,M; j=1, 2, ...,N\}$ is associated with the $F1$-to-$F2$ layer connections. Each $F2$ node j represents a recognition category that learns a prototype vector $w_j = (w_{1j}, w_{2j}, ...,w_{Mj})$. The $F2$ layer is connected, through learned associative links, to an L-node map field F^{ab}, where L is the number of classes in the output space. A set of binary weights W^{ab} is associated with the $F2$-to-F^{ab} connections.

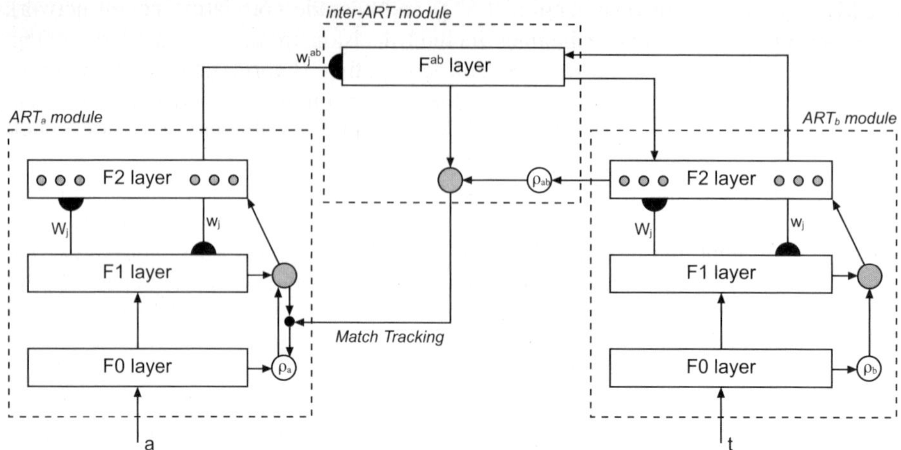

Fig. 1. Block diagram of Fuzzy ARTMAP, adapted from [5]

FAM classifiers perform supervised learning of the mapping between training set vectors *a* and output labels *t*, where $t_K = 1$ if *K* is the target class label for *a*, and zero elsewhere. The following algorithm describes FAM functioning [5, 9]:

1. *Initialization.* Initially, all the *F2* nodes are uncommitted, all weight values w_{ij} are initialized to 1. An *F2* node becomes committed when it is selected to code an input vector *a*, and is then linked to an F^{ab} node. Values of the learning rate $\beta \in [0,1]$, the choice $\alpha > 0$, and the baseline vigilance $\overline{\rho} \in [0,1]$ parameters are set.

2. *Input pattern coding.* When a training pair *(a,t)* is presented to the network, *a* undergoes a transformation called complement coding, which doubles its number of components. The complement-coded input pattern is defined by $A = (a, a^c) = (a_1, a_2, ...,a_m; a_1^c, a_2^c, ...,a_m^c)$, where $a_i^c = (1-a_i)$, and $a_i \in [0, 1]$. The vigilance parameter ρ is reset to its baseline value $\overline{\rho}$.

3. *Prototype selection.* Pattern *A* activates layer *F1* and is propagated through weighted connections *W* to layer *F2*. Activation of each node *j* in the *F2* layer is determined by the function:

$$T_j(A) = \frac{|A \wedge w_j|}{\alpha + |w_j|},$$ (1)

where $\wedge$ is the fuzzy AND operator, $(A \wedge w_j)_I \equiv min(A_i, w_{ij})$. The *F2* layer produces a binary, winner-take-all (WTA) pattern of activity $y=(y_1, y_2, ...,y_N)$ such that only the node *j=J* with the greatest activation value remains active. Node *J* propagates its top-down expectation, or prototype vector w_J, back onto *F1* and the vigilance test is performed. This test compares the degree of match between w_J and *A* against the dimensionless vigilance parameter ρ:

$$\frac{|A \wedge w_J|}{M} \geq \rho \tag{2}$$

If the test is passed, then node J remains active and resonance is said to occur. Otherwise, the network inhibits the active $F2$ node and searches for another node J that passes the vigilance test. If such a node does not exist, an uncommitted $F2$ node becomes active and undergoes learning.

4. *Class prediction.* Pattern t is fed to the map field F^{ab}, while the $F2$ category y learns to activate the map field via associative weights W^{ab}. The F^{ab} layer produces a binary pattern of activity $y^{ab} = (y_1^{ab}, y_2^{ab}, ...,y_L^{ab})$ in which the most active F^{ab} node K yields the class prediction. If node K constitutes an incorrect class prediction, then a match tracking signal raises the vigilance parameter ρ just enough to induce another search among $F2$ nodes in Step 3. This search continues until either an uncommitted $F2$ node becomes active, or a node J that has previously learned the correct class prediction K becomes active.

5. *Learning.* Learning input a involves updating prototype vector w_J, according to:

$$w_J' = \beta(A \wedge w_J) + (1 - \beta)w_J \tag{3}$$

where β is a fixed learning rate parameter. A new association between $F2$ node J and F^{ab} node K $(k(J) = K)$ is learned by setting $w_{Jk}^{ab} = 1$ for $k = K$, where K is the target class label for a, and 0 otherwise.

3 Research Design

Our objective was to investigate whether a trained FAM NN could find common characteristics of bankrupt firms, which distinguishes them from the viable firms and to be used to predict bankruptcy using financial data. Correctly categorizing a random sample of such firms as either currently healthy or currently bankrupt is taken as successful prediction. Secondly, we wanted to see how FAM NN parameters influence the predictive abilities of the model and to find their optimal values. Another objective was to investigate if usage of all Altman's ratios causes overtraining, that is to say, where the model learns all the samples but does not possess a generalizing capacity, a situation which is translated into a poor predictive capacity. Finally, we wanted to investigate if the FAM NN is sensitive to outliers. In statistics, an outlier is an observation that is numerically distant from the rest of the data. Outliers are considered as influential data as they can have a significant effect on a correct classification ability of the model.

In order to illustrate the use of the FAM NN as a predictor, we have made use of data that was published in previous studies, such as [15, 16, 17, 18]. Our research uses the results of those studies as a benchmark to compare those techniques with our approach. The dataset, based on the Moody's Industrial Manual, contains financial information for a total of 129 firms, of which 65 are bankrupt and the rest are solvent. The data entries have been randomly divided into two subsets: one for training, made up of 74 firms, of which 38 bankrupt and 36 non-bankrupt; another set for testing, made up of 55 firms, of which 27 bankrupt and 28 non-bankrupt. Our research uses the Altman's ratios [1] as they have been the most widely and consistently referenced and used to date by both researchers and practitioners: R1: Working Capital / Total Assets; R2: Retained Earnings / Total Assets; R3: Earnings Before Interest and Taxes ('EBIT) / Total Assets; R4: Market Value of Equity / Book Value of Total Debt; R5: Sales / Total Assets.

3.1 Preprocessing

One of the most common forms of preprocessing is linear rescaling of the input variables. Depending on the units in which each of these is expressed, they may have values which differ by several orders of magnitude. Such a disbalance can reduce the predictive abilities of the FAM model as some of the variables can dominate and suppress the others. By applying a linear transformation we arranged for all of the inputs to have similar values. Each of the input variables was treated independently, and for each variable x_i were calculated mean and variance using:

$$\overline{x}_i = \frac{1}{N}\sum_{n=1}^{N} x_i^n \; ; \quad \sigma_i^2 = \frac{1}{N-1}\sum_{n=1}^{N} (x_i^n - \overline{x}_i)^2 \tag{4}$$

where n labels the patterns. We then defined a set of rescaled variables by:

$$\tilde{x}_i^n = \frac{x_i^n - \overline{x}_i}{\sigma_i} \tag{5}$$

It is easy to see that the transformed variables have zero mean and unit standard deviation over the transformed set.

Another problem of the dataset is that it cannot be used directly as a FAM input as the NN requires M-dimensional vectors of floating point numbers in the interval *[0,1]*. The second preprocessing step, called normalization, maps the rescaled dataset into *[0,1]* using the transformation:

$$\hat{x}_i^n = \frac{(\tilde{x}_i^n - \tilde{x}_i^{min})}{(\tilde{x}_i^{max} - \tilde{x}_i^{min})} \tag{6}$$

where x_i^{max} and x_i^{min} are the max, and min values of the variable x_i, respectively. The normalization additionally reduces the disbalance between the variable values.

3.2 Reduction of Dimensionality

The principal motivation for that reduction of dimensionality is that a NN with fewer inputs has fewer adaptive parameters to be determined, and these are more likely to be properly constrained by a data set of limited size, leading to a network with better generalization properties. In addition, a NN with fewer weights may be faster to train. Clearly, in most situations such a reduction will result in loss of information. If too much information is lost, then the resulting reduction in performance cannot compensate any improvement arising from avoidance of overfitting.

One of the main goals in reduction of dimensionality is to ensure an optimal set of variables that avoids overfitting and maximize the FAM NN ability to discriminate between classes. There are various techniques to estimate discriminatory power of variables. Using univariate F-ratio analysis, Serrano [17] ranked the Altman's ratios and suggested that the second and third variables have a greater discriminatory power in contrast to the fifth one. The univariate analysis, however, helps a little to understand how combinations of variables would perform with a model. Another issue is that the optimal variable selection is different for different classification models, which means that there are no guarantees that an optimal set for a MLP NN would perform well with a FAM NN. Ideally, the optimal subset for a model can be selected by the exhaustive (brutal-force) search approach, which is a trivial general problem-solving technique that checks whether each subset-candidate satisfies the problem's statement. However, the cost of this technique is proportional to the number of candidates, which, in many practical problems, tends to grow very quickly as the size of the problem increases. If there are d possible variables, then since each can be present or absent, we have a total of 2^d possible subsets. The five Altman's variables yield 31 subsets, (all zeroes subset is ignored), which we find as an acceptable amount of candidates for experiments and the approach not very expensive computationally.

4 Empirical Results and Discussion

A series of tests was carried out in order to investigate how a trained FAM NN predicts bankruptcy using randomly ordered samples of the normalized training and testing datasets. In accordance with the exhaustive search strategy discussed above, 31 versions of the datasets were prepared for FAM simulations. They were indexed from 1 to 31 where 1 to 5 represented individual ratio subsets {R1} to {R5}; 6 to 15 – pairs of ratios {R1,R2}, {R1,R3} to {R4,R5}; 16 to 25 for triples - {R1,R2,R3}, {R1,R2,R4} to {R3,R4,R5}; 26 to 30 for quarters; and 31 for the full set {R1,R2,R3,R4,R5}. Each of those subsets was submitted to the FAM NN and iterated with 41 values of the vigilance parameter from 0 to 1 with increment 0.025 in order to investigated how level of focusing in details of the FAM search mechanism impacts the predictive ability of the model. Figure 2 shows a general picture of the obtained results. Circles of each steam represent different prediction accuracies obtained at different vigilance parameter values (note that there are many overlapping circles representing the same score).

The first conclusion from the experiments is that among the individual ratios (stems 1 to 5), R2 and R4 obtain highest scores: 80% and 76.4% respectively, which means that for the FAM model these two variables have highest discriminatory power. When FAM uses any of them, it outperforms the statistical LDA method [15] which scores 74.5%. Another interpretation of the results is that we can expect these two variables to be components of the subsets that provide highest scores. Indeed, the figure shows that the highest score is provided by {R2,R4} (stem 11) and the second highest is {R2,R4,R5} (stem 24), both contain R2 and R4. The optimal variable subset {R2,R4} provides score of 85.5% at some parameter values, which is the best obtained result published so far for that dataset. The second best {R2,R4,R5} equals the accuracy of the best MLP used by [17]. Table 1 shows the results obtained with

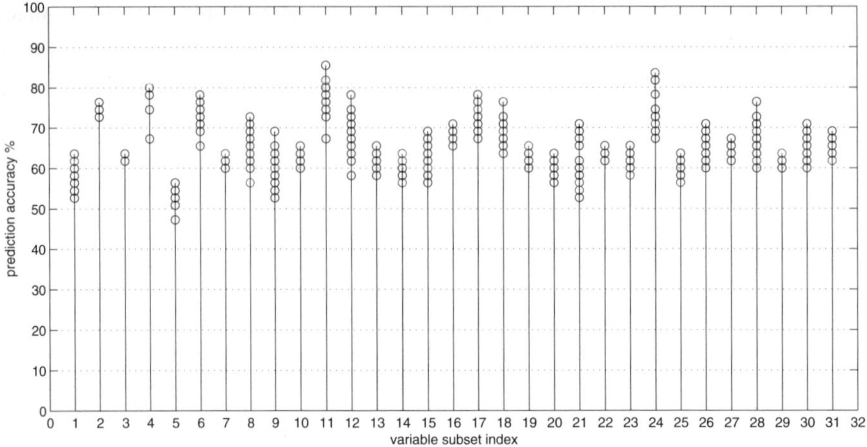

Fig. 2. This figure shows prediction accuracy obtained by submitting 31 subsets of the Altman's variables to the FAM NN with 41 different vigilance parameter values from 0 to 1 with increment of 0.025

the test by way of LDA, the single layer perceptron (SLP), the MLP used by [15], the MLP used by [17], and the MLP and the Athena neural model used by [16], as well as the score obtained by our FAM model. The table shows the misclassified firms by each of the models using the same dataset. Our FAM misclassifies 8, Serrano's MLP – 9, all other models – 10, except LDA that misclassifies 14.

Figure 3 provides more detailed view of scores obtained by the FAM NN using the subset-winner {R2,R4} with different values of ρ in the interval $[0,1]$. For majority of the values of the first half of the interval FAM steadily achieves 81.3% accuracy, whereas in the second half it has picks in 0.725 and 0.775 followed by declines at the end of the interval. The confusion matrix shows predicted vs. actual classifications with relevant percentage.

The next conclusion from the experiments is that the default values of the network parameters (except ρ) provide best NN performance and prediction accuracy. These values are as follows: baseline vigilance parameter $\rho_{test}=0$; signal rule parameter $\alpha=0.01$; and learning fraction parameter $\beta=1.0$. The vigilance parameter ρ determines the level of details in the prototype selection mechanism and therefore significantly affects the prediction accuracy of the model as discussed above.

Another series of experiments aimed to investigate if the FAM NN is sensitive to outliers. Outliers exist in almost all real data, such as the training dataset used in this study. We used the following criterion to mark outliers: If any value of a sample is more than 3 times by the standard deviation value away from the mean of the relevant variable, it is an outlier. All outliers were removed from the training dataset and a FAM NN was trained and tested again in the context of the experiments discussed above. Results showed no difference with those obtained so far, which leads to the conclusion that the FAM NN is not sensitive to the outliers of the dataset.

Table 1. This table shows the misclassified patterns obtained by the Fuzzy ARTMAP (FAM) and the results obtained with the test dataset by six different methods: Linear Discriminant Analysis (LDA) Single Layer Perceptron (SLP) and Multi Layer Perceptron (MPL[1]) by [15]; MLP[2] and Athena Neural Model (ANM) by [16]; and MLP[3] by [17]

pattern	1	2	3	4	5	6	7	8	9	10	11	12	13	14	15	16	17	18	19	20	21	22	23	24	25	26	27	28
FAM																	*	*		*	*				*			*
LDA																	*	*							*			
SLP																	*	*			*				*			
MLP[1]												*					*	*			*				*			
MLP[2]																	*	*			*				*			
ANM												*					*	*							*			
MLP[3]																	*	*			*				*			

pattern	29	30	31	32	33	34	35	36	37	38	39	40	41	42	43	44	45	46	47	48	49	50	51	52	53	54	55
FAM							*																			*	
LDA							*	*			*	*						*	*		*	*	*			*	*
SLD											*	*						*			*	*				*	
MLP[1]											*	*						*			*	*				*	
MLP[2]							*	*			*	*						*			*					*	
ANM											*	*						*			*	*				*	
MLP[3]											*										*	*				*	

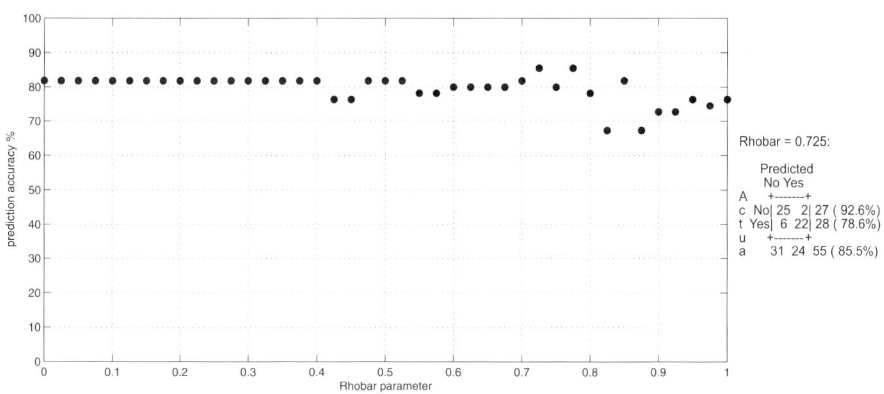

Fig. 3. Prediction accuracy obtained by FAM NN using variables {R2, R4} and 41 values of the Rhobar parameter from 0 to 1 with incremental step of 0.025. Highest score of 85.5% is obtained with parameter values 0.725 and 0.775. Confusion matrix is also provided.

Finally, the FAM NN was examined for efficiency in terms of training time, testing time and memory consumed for long-term memory (LTM) of the NN. Results show that the training and testing time for one session is less that 0.02 sec. and LTM less than 2.9 Kb regardless of variable subset or network parameter value. In fact the FAM model responds instantly, because of the one-pass learning as discussed above. In contrast, the most popular and widely used MLP NNs require multiple presentations (epochs) of the training set. For example, the Wilson & Sharda's study [18] covers a sample of 112 companies and the MLP achieves convergence after 100,000 training iterations; Coats and Fant's [6] MLP use a training set of 121 companies and achieve convergence after 1400 training cycles; Odom and Sharda [14] employed the Altman's ratios and used an MLP with training set of 74 companies, which achieves convergence after 191400 iterations that took 24 hours training. Those examples illustrate the efficiency of the FAM NN.

5   Conclusions

We present here a Fuzzy ARTMAP (FAM) neural network applied to a universal business problem: forecasting of failure of companies based on financial information. The commonly used statistical tool for such classification and prediction is the multiple discriminant analysis (MDA) of financial ratios, but this technique has limitations based on its assumptions of linear separability, multivariate normality, and independence of the predictive variables. A neural network, being free from such constraining assumptions, is able to achieve superior results. The most popular and widely used MLP neural networks outperform the MDA method, but their design is time–consuming because the user has to determine the network structure manually by tedious trails and errors. The MLP learning is also time-consuming, as it requires multiple presentations (epochs) of the training set. In contrast, the FAM neural network self-determines the appropriate layered structure, provides fast, one-pass online learning, and retains acquired knowledge while learning from novel patterns.

In order to illustrate the use of the FAM NN as a predictor, we have made use of data and financial ratios published in previous studies. The data preprocessing steps involved two transformations and reduction of dimensionality of the dataset. We applied the exhaustive search approach to find the optimal variable set for the FAM classifier. Our experiments showed that the financial ratios Retained Earnings / Total Assets and Market Value of Equity / Book Value of Total Debt provide highest discriminatory power. Using certain network parameter values, the FAM model scores 85.5% prediction accuracy, which outperforms MLPs applied to the same dataset. This is the highest score so far for that dataset. The experiments also showed that the FAM model is not sensitive to outliers of the dataset. The network efficiency was confirmed experimentally by training and testing times less that 0.02 sec. per session. Our research is the first to use Fuzzy ARTMAP neural networks for bankruptcy prediction.

References

1. Altman, E.: Financial Ratios, Discriminant Analysis, and the Prediction of Corporate Bankruptcy. Journal of Finance 23(4), 598–609 (1968)
2. Bell, T., Ribar, G., Verchio, J.R.: Neural Nets vs. Logistic Regression: a Comparison of each Model's Ability to Predict Commercial Bank Failures. In: Proc. of the 1990 Deloitte & Touche / University of Kansas Symposium on Auditing Problems, pp. 29–53 (1990)
3. Brigham, E.F., Gapenski, L.C.: Financial Management Theory and Practice. Dryden Press, New York (1991)

4. Carpenter, G., Grossberg, S., Reynolds, J.: ARTMAP: Supervised Real-Time Learning and Classification of Non-stationary Data by a Self-Organizing Neural Network. Neural Networks 6, 565–588 (1991)
5. Carpenter, G.A., Grossberg, S., Markuzon, N., Reynorlds, J.H., Rosen, D.B.: Fuzzy ARTMAP: A Neural Network Architecture for Incremental Supervised Learning of Analog Multidimensional Maps. IEEE Transaction on Neural Networks 3(5), 698–713 (1992)
6. Coats, P., Fant, L.: Recognizing Financial Distress Patterns Using Neural Network Tool. Financial Management, 142–155 (November 1993)
7. Curram, S., Mingers, J.: Neural Networks, Decision Tree Induction and Discriminant Analysis: an Empirical Comparison. Journal Operational Research 45(4), 440–450 (1994)
8. Gallinari, P., Thiria, S., Badran, F., Fogelman-Soulie, F.: On the Relations between Discriminant Analysis and Multilayer Perceptrons. Neural Networks 4, 349–360 (1991)
9. Granger, E., Rubin, A., Grossberg, S., Lavoie, P.: A What-and-Where Fusion Neural Network for Recognition and Tracking of Multiple Radar Emitters. Neural Networks 3, 325–344 (2001)
10. Grossberg, S.: Adaptive Pattern Recognition and Universal Encoding II: Feedback, expectation, olfaction, and illusions. Biological Cybernetics 23, 187–202 (1976)
11. Hart, A.: Using Neural Networks for Classification Task. Some Experiments on Datasets and Practical Advice. Journal Operational Research Society 43(3), 215–266 (1992)
12. Kumar, P., Ravi, V.: Bankruptcy Prediction in Banks and Firms via Statistical and Intelligent Techniques. European Journal of Operational Research 180(1), 1–28 (2007)
13. Lacher, R., Coats, P., Sharma, S., Fantc, L.L.F.: A Neural Network for Classifying the Financial Health of a Firm. European Journal of Operational Research 85, 53–65 (1995)
14. Odom, M., Sharda, R.L.: A Neural Network Model for Bankruptcy Prediction. In: Proceedings of the IEEE International Conference on Neural Networks, pp. 163–168 (1990)
15. Odom, M., Sharda, R.: A Neural Network Model for Bankruptcy Prediction. In: Trippi, R.R., Turban, E. (eds.) Neural Networks in Finance and Investing, Probus (1993)
16. Rahimian, E., Singh, S., Thammachacote, T., Virmani, R.: Bankruptcy prediction by neural networks. In: Trippi, R., Turban, E. (eds.) Neural Networks in Finance and Investing, Probus Publ., Chicago (1993)
17. Serrano-Cinca, C.: Self Organizing Neural Networks for Financial Diagnosis. Decision Support Systems 17, 227–238 (1996)
18. Wilson, R., Sharda, R.: Bankruptcy prediction using neural networks. Decision Support Systems 11, 431–447 (1994)
19. Yoon, Y., Swales, G., Margavio, T.: A Comparison of Discriminant Analysis versus Artificial Neural Networks. Journal Operational Research Society 44(1), 51–60 (1993)

Fuzzy Interpolative Reasoning Using Interval Type-2 Fuzzy Sets

Li-Wei Lee[1] and Shyi-Ming Chen[1,2]

[1] Department of Computer Science and Information Engineering,
National Taiwan University of Science and Technology, Taipei, Taiwan, R. O. C.
[2] Department of Computer Science and Information Engineering,
Jinwen University of Science and Technology, Taipei County, Taiwan, R. O. C.

Abstract. In this paper, we present a new fuzzy interpolative reasoning method using interval type-2 fuzzy sets. We calculate the ranking values through the reference points and the heights of the upper and the lower membership functions of interval type-2 fuzzy sets. By means of calculating the ranking values of the upper and the lower membership functions of interval type-2 fuzzy sets, we can use interval type-2 fuzzy sets to handle fuzzy interpolative reasoning in sparse fuzzy rule-based system in a more flexible manner.

Keywords: Fuzzy interpolative reasoning, interval type-2 fuzzy sets, ranking values.

1 Introduction

It is obvious that fuzzy rule interpolation is an important research topic of sparse fuzzy rule-based systems, where some fuzzy rules can be derived through their neighboring fuzzy rules to reduce the complexity of fuzzy rule bases. In recent years, some methods have been presented for dealing with fuzzy interpolative reasoning in sparse fuzzy rule-based systems [1]-[10], [12]-[18]. However, the existing fuzzy interpolative reasoning methods are based on type-1 fuzzy sets, which lack of flexibility. If we can handle fuzzy interpolative reasoning based on type-2 fuzzy sets in sparse fuzzy rule-based systems, then there is room for more flexibility, where the concept of type-2 fuzzy sets is originally introduced by Zadeh in 1975 [19].

In this paper, we present a new fuzzy interpolative reasoning method using interval type-2 fuzzy sets. We calculate the ranking values through the reference points and the heights of the upper and the lower membership functions of interval type-2 fuzzy sets. By means of calculating the ranking values of the upper and the lower membership functions of interval type-2 fuzzy sets, we can use interval type-2 fuzzy sets to handle fuzzy interpolative reasoning in sparse fuzzy rule-based systems in a more flexible manner.

The rest of this paper is organized as follows. In Section 2, we briefly review the basic concepts of interval type-2 fuzzy sets form [11]. In Section 3, we present the concept of ranking values of the upper and the lower membership functions of interval type-2 fuzzy sets. In Section 4, we present a new fuzzy interpolative reasoning method based on interval type-2 fuzz sets. In Section 5, we use an example

N.T. Nguyen et al. (Eds.): IEA/AIE 2008, LNAI 5027, pp. 92–101, 2008.

to illustrate the proposed fuzzy interpolative reasoning method. The conclusions are discussion in Section 6.

2 Basic Concepts of Interval Type-2 Fuzzy Sets

Type-2 fuzzy sets [11] can be regarded as an extension of type-1 fuzzy sets. In other words, type-1 fuzzy sets are special cases of type-2 fuzzy sets.

Definition 2.1 [11]: A type-2 fuzzy sets $\tilde{A}$ in the universe of discourse X can be described by a type-2 membership function $\mu_{\tilde{A}}$, shown as follows:

$$\tilde{A} = \{((x,u), \mu_{\tilde{A}}(x,u)) \mid x \in X, u \in J_X \subseteq [0,1], \text{and } 0 \leq \mu_{\tilde{A}}(x,u) \leq 1\}. \tag{1}$$

It should be noted that a type-2 fuzzy set $\tilde{A}$ also can be represented as follows:

$$\tilde{A} = \int_{x \in X} \int_{u \in J_X} \mu_{\tilde{A}}(x,u)/(x,u), \tag{2}$$

where $J_x \subseteq [0,1]$ and $\iint$ denotes the union over all admissible values of x and u.

In *Definition 2.1*, the first restriction that $\forall u \in J_x \subseteq [0,1]$ is consistent with the type-1 constraint that $0 \leq \mu_A(x) \leq 1$. The second restriction that $0 \leq \mu_{\tilde{A}}(x,u) \leq 1$ is consistent with the fact that the amplitudes of a membership functions should larger than or equal to zero and smaller than or equal to 1.

Definition 2.2 [11]: If all $\mu_{\tilde{A}}(x,u) = 1$, then $\tilde{A}$ is called an interval type-2 fuzzy set. An interval type-2 fuzzy set can be regarded as a special case of a type-2 fuzzy set shown in Eq. (2), as

$$\tilde{A} = \int_{x \in X} \int_{u \in J_X} 1/(x,u), \tag{3}$$

where $x \in X$, $u \in J_X$, $J_x \subseteq [0,1]$.

Definition 2.3 [11]: The upper membership function and the lower membership function of an interval type-2 fuzzy set are two type-1 membership functions, respectively.

3 Ranking Values of the Upper and the Lower Membership Functions of Interval Type-2 Fuzzy Sets

In this section, we present the concept of ranking values of the upper and the lower membership functions of interval type-2 fuzzy sets, respectively. For convenience, we only illustrate the concept of ranking values of the upper membership functions of interval type-2 fuzzy sets. The concept of ranking values of the lower membership functions of interval type-2 fuzzy sets also can be defined in the same way.

94   L.-W. Lee and S.-M. Chen

Let $\tilde{A}_1^U$, $\tilde{A}_2^U$, ..., and $\tilde{A}_n^U$ be the upper membership functions of the interval type-2 fuzzy sets $\tilde{A}_1$, $\tilde{A}_2$, ..., and $\tilde{A}_n$, respectively. An upper s-polygonal membership function $\tilde{A}_i^U$ can be represented as $\tilde{A}_i^U = (a_{i1}^U, a_{i2}^U, ..., a_{is}^U; H_1(\tilde{A}_i^U), ..., H_{s-2}(\tilde{A}_i^U))$, as shown in Fig. 1, where s denotes the number of edges in a polygon membership function, $H_r(\tilde{A}_i^U)$ denotes the rth height of the upper s-polygonal membership function $\tilde{A}_i^U$ (i.e., $1 \le r \le s\text{-}2$), $H_1(\tilde{A}_i^U) \in [0,1]$, ..., $H_{s-2}(\tilde{A}_i^U) \in [0,1]$, $s \ge 3$, and $1 \le i \le n$.

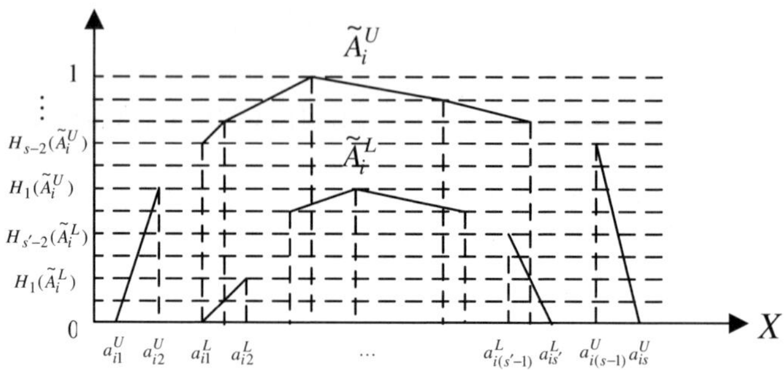

Fig. 1. The upper s-polygonal membership function $\tilde{A}_i^U$ and the lower s'-polygonal membership function $\tilde{A}_i^L$ of the interval type-2 fuzzy set $\tilde{A}_i$

It is obvious that the upper singleton membership function $\tilde{A}_i^U = (x; H(\tilde{A}_i^U))$ can be represented by a t-polygonal membership function $\tilde{A}_i^U = (x_1, x_2, ..., x_t; H_1(\tilde{A}_i^U), H_2(\tilde{A}_i^U), ..., H_{t-2}(\tilde{A}_i^U))$, where $H_r(\tilde{A}_i^U)$ denotes the rth height of the upper t-polygonal membership function $\tilde{A}_i^U$ (i.e., $1 \le r \le t\text{-}2$), $x_1 = x_2 = ... = x_t = x$, $H_1(\tilde{A}_i^U) = H_2(\tilde{A}_i^U) = ... = H_{t-2}(\tilde{A}_i^U)$, $H_1(\tilde{A}_i^U) \in [0,1]$, $H_2(\tilde{A}_i^U) \in [0,1]$, ..., $H_{t-2}(\tilde{A}_i^U) \in [0,1]$, t is even number and $t \ge 4$, and $1 \le i \le n$.

Definition 3.1: An upper s-polygonal membership function $\tilde{A}_i^U = (a_{i1}, a_{i2}, ..., a_{is}; H_1(\tilde{A}_i^U), ..., H_{s-2}(\tilde{A}_i^U))$ can be represented by an upper t-polygonal membership function $\tilde{A}_i^U = (a_{i1}', a_{i2}', ..., a_{it}'; H_1'(\tilde{A}_i^U), H_2'(\tilde{A}_i^U), ..., H_{t-2}'(\tilde{A}_i^U))$, where s is an odd number, $s \ge 3$, t is an even number, $t > s$, $a_{i1}' = a_{i1}$, $a_{i2}' = a_{i2}$, ..., $a_{i\lceil s/2 \rceil}' = a_{i(\lceil s/2 \rceil+1)}' = ... = a_{i(\lceil s/2 \rceil+t-s)}' = a_{i\lceil s/2 \rceil}$, $a_{i(\lceil s/2 \rceil+t-s+1)}' = a_{i(\lceil s/2 \rceil+1)}$, ..., $a_{it}' = a_{is}$, $H_1'(\tilde{A}_i^U) = H_1(\tilde{A}_i^U)$, ..., $H_{\lceil \frac{s-2}{2} \rceil}'(\tilde{A}_i^U) = H_{\lceil \frac{s-2}{2} \rceil+1}'(\tilde{A}_i^U) = ... = H_{\lceil \frac{s-2}{2} \rceil+t-s}'(\tilde{A}_i^U) = H_{\lceil \frac{s-2}{2} \rceil}(\tilde{A}_i^U)$, ..., $H_{t-2}'(\tilde{A}_i^U) = H_{s-2}(\tilde{A}_i^U)$, $H_r(\tilde{A}_i^U)$ denotes the rth height of the upper s-polygonal membership function $\tilde{A}_i^U$ (i.e., $1 \le r \le s\text{-}2$), and $H'_r(\tilde{A}_i^U)$ denotes the rth height of the upper t-polygonal membership function $\tilde{A}_i^U$ (i.e., $1 \le r \le t\text{-}2$).

Definition 3.2: An upper s-polygonal membership function $\tilde{A}_i^U = (a_{i1}, a_{i2}, ..., a_{is};$ $H_1(\tilde{A}_i^U), ..., H_{s\text{-}2}(\tilde{A}_i^U))$ can be represented by an upper t-polygonal membership function $\tilde{A}_i^U = (a'_{i1}, a'_{i2}, ..., a'_{it}; H'_1(\tilde{A}_i^U), H'_2(\tilde{A}_i^U), ..., H'_{t\text{-}2}(\tilde{A}_i^U))$, where s is an even number, $s \ge 4$, t is an even number, $t \ge s$, $a'_{i1} = a_{i1}$, $a'_{i2} = a_{i2}$, ..., $a'_{i\lceil s/2\rceil} = ... =$

$$a'_{i\lceil t/2\rceil} = a_{i\lceil s/2\rceil}, \quad a'_{i(\lceil t/2\rceil+1)} = ... = a'_{i(2\lceil t/2\rceil-\lceil s/2\rceil+1)} = a_{i(\lceil s/2\rceil+1)}, \quad ..., a'_{it} =$$

$$a_{is}, \quad H'_1(\tilde{A}_i^U) = H_1(\tilde{A}_i^U), \quad ..., \quad H'_{\left\lceil\frac{s-2}{2}\right\rceil}(\tilde{A}_i^U) = ... = H'_{\left\lceil\frac{t-2}{2}\right\rceil}(\tilde{A}_i^U)$$

$$= H'_{\left\lceil\frac{s-2}{2}\right\rceil}(\tilde{A}_i^U), H'_{\left\lceil\frac{t-2}{2}\right\rceil+1}(\tilde{A}_i^U) = ... = H'_{2\left\lceil\frac{t-2}{2}\right\rceil-\left\lceil\frac{s-2}{2}\right\rceil+1}(\tilde{A}_i^U) = H_{\left\lceil\frac{s-2}{2}\right\rceil+1}(\tilde{A}_i^U), ...,$$

$H'_{t\text{-}2}(\tilde{A}_i^U) = H_{s\text{-}2}(\tilde{A}_i^U)$, $H_r(\tilde{A}_i^U)$ denotes the rth height of the upper s-polygonal membership function $\tilde{A}_i^U$ (i.e., $1 \le r \le s\text{-}2$), and $H'_r(\tilde{A}_i^U)$ denotes the rth height of the upper t-polygonal membership function $\tilde{A}_i^U$ (i.e., $1 \le r \le t\text{-}2$).

Definition 3.3: An upper s-polygonal membership function $\tilde{A}_i^U$ can be represented by an upper t-polygonal membership function $\tilde{A}_i^U = (a_{i1}^U, a_{i2}^U, ..., a_{it}^U; H_1(\tilde{A}_i^U), H_2(\tilde{A}_i^U), ..., H_{t\text{-}2}(\tilde{A}_i^U))$, where t is an even number and $t \ge s$. The ranking value $Rank(\tilde{A}_i^U)$ of the upper t-polygonal membership function $\tilde{A}_i^U$ (i.e., t is an even number and $t \ge s$) is defined as follows:

$$Rank(\tilde{A}_i^U) = M_1(\tilde{A}_i^U) + M_2(\tilde{A}_i^U) + ... + M_{t\text{-}1}(\tilde{A}_i^U)$$

$$-\frac{1}{t}(S_1(\tilde{A}_i^U) + S_2(\tilde{A}_i^U) + ... + S_t(\tilde{A}_i^U)) \tag{4}$$

$$+ H_1(\tilde{A}_i^U) + H_2(\tilde{A}_i^U) + ... + H_{t\text{-}2}(\tilde{A}_i^U),$$

where $M_p(\tilde{A}_i^U)$ denotes the average of the set of the elements $\{a_{ip}^U, a_{i(p+1)}^U\}$ of the upper t-polygonal membership function $\tilde{A}_i^U$ (i.e., $M_p(\tilde{A}_i^U) = (a_{ip}^U + a_{i(p+1)}^U)/2$), $1 \le p \le t\text{-}1$, $S_q(\tilde{A}_i^U)$ denotes the standard deviation of the set of the elements $\{a_{iq}^U, a_{i(q+1)}^U\}$ of the upper t-polygonal membership function $\tilde{A}_i^U$ (i.e.,

$$S_q(\tilde{A}_i^U) = \sqrt{\frac{1}{2}\sum_{j=q}^{q+1}(a_{ij}^U - \frac{1}{2}\sum_{j=q}^{q+1} a_{ij}^U)^2}\ ), \quad 1 \le q \le t\text{-}1, \quad S_t(\tilde{A}_i^U)$$ denotes the standard deviation of the set of the elements $\{a_{i1}^U, a_{i2}^U, ..., a_{it}^U\}$ of the upper t-polygonal

membership function $\tilde{A}_i^U$ (i.e., $S_t(\tilde{A}_i^U) = \sqrt{\frac{1}{t}\sum_{j=1}^{t}(a_{ij}^U - \frac{1}{t}\sum_{j=1}^{t}a_{ij}^U)^2}$), $H_r(\tilde{A}_i^U)$ denotes

the rth height of the upper t-polygonal membership function $\tilde{A}_i^U$, $1 \leq r \leq t$-2, t is an even number and $t \geq s$. In general, we can use Eq. (4) as the general formula to calculate the ranking value of the upper t-polygonal membership function $\tilde{A}_i^U$, where $1 \leq i \leq n$.

For dealing with fuzzy interpolative reasoning in sparse fuzzy rule-based systems, we can calculate the ranking value of the interval type-2 fuzzy sets $\tilde{A}_i$ through the reference points and the heights of the upper membership function $\tilde{A}_i^U$ and the lower membership function $\tilde{A}_i^L$ of the interval type-2 fuzzy sets $\tilde{A}_i$. Then, the ranking value of the interval type-2 fuzzy sets $\tilde{A}_i$ can be calculated as follows:

$$Rank(\tilde{A}_i) = Rank(\tilde{A}_i^U) + Rank(\tilde{A}_i^L), \tag{5}$$

where $1 \leq i \leq n$.

In the next section, we will present a new fuzzy interpolative reasoning method in sparse rule-based systems based on interval type-2 fuzzy sets.

4 Fuzzy Interpolative Reasoning Method Based On Interval Type-2 Fuzzy Sets

A fuzzy interpolative reasoning scheme can be described by a modus ponens model, shown as follows:

$$\text{Observation} : X \text{ is } \tilde{A}$$
$$\text{Rules} : \text{if } X \text{ is } \tilde{A}_1, \text{ then } Y \text{ is } \tilde{B}_1$$
$$\text{if } X \text{ is } \tilde{A}_2, \text{ then } Y \text{ is } \tilde{B}_2$$
$$\overline{}$$
$$\text{Conclusion} : Y \text{ is } \tilde{B}$$

where X and Y are linguistic variables; $\tilde{A}_1$, $\tilde{A}$, $\tilde{A}_2$, $\tilde{B}_1$, $\tilde{B}_2$ and $\tilde{B}$ are interval type-2 fuzzy sets. The fuzzy interpolative reasoning scheme is shown in Fig. 2.

Based on Eq. (5), we can calculated the ranking values $Rank(\tilde{A}_1)$, $Rank(\tilde{A})$ and $Rank(\tilde{A}_2)$ of the interval type-2 fuzzy set $\tilde{A}_1$, $\tilde{A}$ and $\tilde{A}_2$, respectively. In order to perform fuzzy interpolative reasoning based on interval type-2 fuzzy sets, we define the "ranking proportional coefficient" λ_{Rank} among the fuzzy sets $\tilde{A}_1$, $\tilde{A}$ and $\tilde{A}_2$ as follows:

$$\lambda_{Rank} = \frac{Rank(\tilde{A}) - Rank(\tilde{A}_1)}{Rank(\tilde{A}_2) - Rank(\tilde{A}_1)}, \tag{6}$$

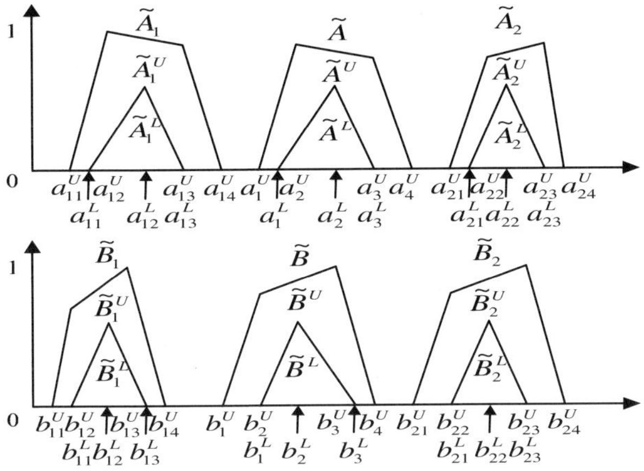

Fig. 2. Fuzzy interpolative reasoning scheme using interval type-2 fuzzy sets

where $Rank(\tilde{A}_2) - Rank(\tilde{A}_1) \neq 0$. Assume that $\tilde{A}_{11}, \tilde{A}_{21}, ..., \tilde{A}_{k1} \Rightarrow \tilde{B}_1$ and $\tilde{A}_{12}, \tilde{A}_{22}, ..., \tilde{A}_{k2} \Rightarrow \tilde{B}_2$ are two adjacent fuzzy rules with multiple antecedent fuzzy sets, $\tilde{A}_1$, $\tilde{A}_2$, ..., $\tilde{A}_k$ are the observations, $\tilde{B}$ is the fuzzy interpolative reasoning conclusion. Based on Eq. (5), we can calculate the ranking values $Rank(\tilde{A}_{i1})$, $Rank(\tilde{A}_i)$ and $Rank(\tilde{A}_{i2})$ of the interval type-2 fuzzy set $\tilde{A}_{i1}$, $\tilde{A}_i$ and $\tilde{A}_{i2}$, respectively, where $1 \leq i \leq k$. The ranking proportional coefficient $\lambda_{Rank(i)}$ among the interval type-2 fuzzy sets $\tilde{A}_{i1}$, $\tilde{A}_i$ and $\tilde{A}_{i2}$ is calculated as follows:

$$\lambda_{Rank(i)} = \frac{Rank(\tilde{A}_i) - Rank(\tilde{A}_{i1})}{Rank(\tilde{A}_{i2}) - Rank(\tilde{A}_{i1})}, \tag{7}$$

where $Rank(\tilde{A}_{i2}) - Rank(\tilde{A}_{i1}) \neq 0$ and $1 \leq i \leq k$. Then, the integral ranking proportional coefficient λ_{Rank} of the k-dimensional antecedents is calculated as follows:

$$\lambda_{Rank} = \frac{1}{k} \sum_{i}^{k} \lambda_{Rank(i)}, \tag{8}$$

where $k \geq 1$. In general, we use Eqs. (7) and (8) as general formulas for dealing with fuzzy interpolative reasoning based on interval type-2 fuzzy sets.

The proposed fuzzy interpolative reasoning method based on polygonal interval type-2 fuzzy sets is now presented as follows:

Step 1: If the upper membership functions $\tilde{A}_{i1}^U$, $\tilde{A}_i^U$, $\tilde{A}_{i2}^U$ and the lower membership functions $\tilde{A}_{i1}^L$, $\tilde{A}_i^L$, $\tilde{A}_{i2}^L$ of the k-dimensional antecedent interval type-2 fuzzy sets $\tilde{A}_{i1}$, $\tilde{A}_i$ and $\tilde{A}_{i2}$ of the fuzzy interpolative reasoning scheme are polygonal membership functions, where $1 \leq i \leq k$, then find the maximum number s of edges in the upper membership functions $\tilde{A}_{i1}^U$, $\tilde{A}_i^U$, $\tilde{A}_{i2}^U$ and the lower membership functions $\tilde{A}_{i1}^L$, $\tilde{A}_i^L$, $\tilde{A}_{i2}^L$ of the k-dimensional antecedent interval type-2 fuzzy sets $\tilde{A}_{i1}$, $\tilde{A}_i$ and $\tilde{A}_{i2}$ of the fuzzy interpolative reasoning scheme, where $1 \leq i \leq k$. Then, the upper membership functions $\tilde{A}_{i1}^U$, $\tilde{A}_i^U$, $\tilde{A}_{i2}^U$ and the lower membership functions $\tilde{A}_{i1}^L$, $\tilde{A}_i^L$, $\tilde{A}_{i2}^L$ of the k-dimensional antecedent interval type-2 fuzzy sets $\tilde{A}_{i1}$, $\tilde{A}_i$ and $\tilde{A}_{i2}$ of the fuzzy interpolative reasoning scheme are represented by t-polygonal membership functions, where $1 \leq i \leq k$, and if s is an odd number, $s \geq 3$, then $t = s + 1$; if s is an even number, $s \geq 4$, then $t = s$. Based on Eqs. (4) and (5), calculate the ranking values of the k-dimensional antecedent interval type-2 fuzzy sets $\tilde{A}_{i1}$, $\tilde{A}_i$ and $\tilde{A}_{i2}$ of the fuzzy interpolative reasoning scheme, respectively, where $1 \leq i \leq k$.

Step 2: Based on Eqs. (7) and (8), calculate the value of the integral ranking proportional coefficient λ_{Rank} among the k-dimensional antecedent interval type-2 fuzzy sets $\tilde{A}_{i1}$, $\tilde{A}_i$ and $\tilde{A}_{i2}$ of the fuzzy interpolative reasoning scheme, where $1 \leq i \leq k$.

Step 3: If the upper membership functions $\tilde{B}_1^U$, $\tilde{B}_2^U$ and the lower membership functions $\tilde{B}_1^L$, $\tilde{B}_2^L$ of the consequent interval type-2 fuzzy sets $\tilde{B}_1$, $\tilde{B}_2$ of the fuzzy interpolative reasoning scheme are polygonal membership functions, then find the maximum number s of edges in the upper membership functions $\tilde{B}_1^U$, $\tilde{B}_2^U$ and the lower membership functions $\tilde{B}_1^L$, $\tilde{B}_2^L$ of the consequent interval type-2 fuzzy sets $\tilde{B}_1$, $\tilde{B}_2$ of the fuzzy interpolative reasoning scheme. The upper membership functions $\tilde{B}_1^U$, $\tilde{B}_2^U$ and the lower membership functions $\tilde{B}_1^L$, $\tilde{B}_2^L$ of the consequent interval type-2 fuzzy sets $\tilde{B}_1$, $\tilde{B}_2$ of the fuzzy interpolative reasoning scheme are represented by t-polygonal membership functions, where if s is an odd number, $s \geq 3$, then $t = s + 1$; if s is an even number, $s \geq 4$, then $t = s$. Then, $\tilde{B}_1 = (\tilde{B}_1^U, \tilde{B}_1^L) = ((b_{11}^U, ..., b_{1t}^U; H_1(\tilde{B}_1^U), ..., H_{t-2}(\tilde{B}_1^U)), (b_{11}^L, ..., b_{1t}^L; H_1(\tilde{B}_1^L), ..., H_{t-2}(\tilde{B}_1^L)))$, $\tilde{B}_2 = (\tilde{B}_2^U, \tilde{B}_2^L) = ((b_{21}^U, ..., b_{2t}^U; H_1(\tilde{B}_2^U), ..., H_{t-2}(\tilde{B}_2^U)), (b_{21}^L, ..., b_{2t}^L; H_1(\tilde{B}_2^L), ..., H_{t-2}(\tilde{B}_2^L)))$, where $\tilde{B}_1$ and $\tilde{B}_2$ are the consequent interval type-2 fuzzy sets of the fuzzy interpolative reasoning scheme. Based on the value of the integral ranking proportional coefficient λ_{Rank} among the k-dimensional antecedent interval type-2 fuzzy sets $\tilde{A}_{i1}$, $\tilde{A}_i$ and $\tilde{A}_{i2}$, where $1 \leq i \leq k$, the fuzzy interpolative reasoning conclusion $\tilde{B}$ can be obtained, where $\tilde{B} = (\tilde{B}^U, \tilde{B}^L) = ((b_1^U, ..., b_t^U; H_1(\tilde{B}^U), ..., H_{t-2}(\tilde{B}^U)), (b_1^L, ..., b_t^L; H_1(\tilde{B}^L), ..., H_{t-2}(\tilde{B}^L)))$, shown as follows:

$$b_i^U = (1 - \lambda_{Rank}) \times b_{1i}^U + \lambda_{Rank} \times b_{2i}^U, \tag{9}$$

$$b_i^L = (1 - \lambda_{Rank}) \times b_{1i}^L + \lambda_{Rank} \times b_{2i}^L, \tag{10}$$

$$H_j(\tilde{B}^U) = (1 - \lambda_{Rank}) \times H_j(\tilde{B}_1^U) + \lambda_{Rank} \times H_j(\tilde{B}_2^U), \tag{11}$$

$$H_j(\tilde{B}^L) = (1 - \lambda_{Rank}) \times H_j(\tilde{B}_1^L) + \lambda_{Rank} \times H_j(\tilde{B}_2^L), \tag{12}$$

where $1 \leq i \leq t$, $1 \leq j \leq t\text{-}2$, and if s is an odd number, $s \geq 3$, then $t = s + 1$; if s is an even number, $s \geq 4$, then $t = s$.

5 Experimental Results

In this section, we use an example to illustrate the proposed fuzzy interpolative reasoning method.

Example 5.1: Let $\tilde{A}_1$, $\tilde{A}$, $\tilde{A}_2$, $\tilde{B}_1$ and $\tilde{B}_2$ be interval type-2 fuzzy sets of the fuzzy interpolative reasoning scheme, where

$\tilde{A}_1 = ((0, 5, 5, 6; 1, 1), (2, 4, 4, 5; 0.7, 0.7))$,

$\tilde{A} = ((7, 8, 8, 9; 1, 1), (7.5, 8, 8, 8.5; 0.7, 0.7))$,

$\tilde{A}_2 = ((11, 13, 13, 14; 1, 1), (11.5, 13, 13, 13.5; 0.7, 0.7))$,

$\tilde{B}_1 = ((0, 2, 2, 4; 1, 1), (1, 2, 2, 3; 0.8, 0.8))$,

$\tilde{B}_2 = ((10, 11, 11, 13; 1, 1), (10.5, 11, 11, 12; 0.7, 0.7))$.

We can see that the maximum number s of edges of the polygonal membership functions of the upper membership functions $\tilde{A}_1^U$, $\tilde{A}^U$, $\tilde{A}_2^U$ and the lower membership functions $\tilde{A}_1^L$, $\tilde{A}^L$, $\tilde{A}_2^L$ of the antecedent interval type-2 fuzzy sets $\tilde{A}_1$, $\tilde{A}$ and $\tilde{A}_2$ of the fuzzy interpolative reasoning scheme is 3 (i.e., $s = 3$). Then, the upper membership functions $\tilde{A}_1^U$, $\tilde{A}^U$, $\tilde{A}_2^U$ and the lower membership functions $\tilde{A}_1^L$, $\tilde{A}^L$, $\tilde{A}_2^L$ of the antecedent interval type-2 fuzzy sets $\tilde{A}_1$, $\tilde{A}$ and $\tilde{A}_2$ of the fuzzy interpolative reasoning scheme are represented by t-polygonal membership functions, where $t = s + 1 = 4$. Based on Eqs. (4) and (5), we can calculate the ranking values of the antecedent interval type-2 fuzzy sets $\tilde{A}_1$, $\tilde{A}$ and $\tilde{A}_2$ of the fuzzy interpolative reasoning scheme, respectively, where $Rank(\tilde{A}_1) = 25.92$, $Rank(\tilde{A}) = 50.76$ and $Rank(\tilde{A}_2) = 79.32$. Therefore, based on Eq. (6), we can calculate the ranking proportional coefficient λ_{Rank} among the antecedent interval type-2 fuzzy sets $\tilde{A}_1$, $\tilde{A}$ and $\tilde{A}_2$, where $\lambda_{Rank} = 0.47$. Based on Eqs. (9), (10), (11) and (12), we can get the fuzzy interpolative reasoning result $\tilde{B} = ((4.65, 6.19, 6.19, 8.19; 1, 1), (5.42, 6.19, 6.19, 7.19; 0.75, 0.75))$. The membership function curves of these interval type-2 fuzzy sets of the fuzzy interpolative reasoning scheme are shown in Fig. 3.

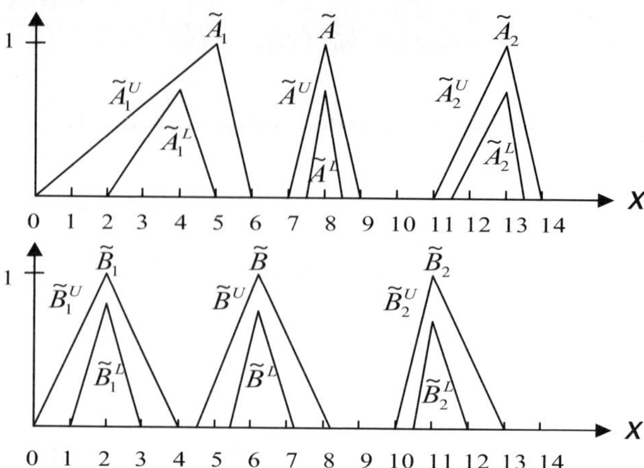

Fig. 3. Fuzzy interpolative reasoning scheme of Example 5.1

6 Conclusions

In this paper, we have presented a new fuzzy interpolative reasoning method based on interval type-2 fuzzy sets. We calculate the ranking values through the reference points and heights of the upper and the lower membership functions of interval type-2 fuzzy sets. By means of calculating the ranking values of the upper and the lower membership functions of interval type-2 fuzzy sets, the proposed fuzzy interpolative reasoning method can handle fuzzy interpolative reasoning in a more flexible and more intelligent manner.

Acknowledgements

This work was supported in part by the National Science Council, Republic of China, under Grant NSC 95-2221-E-011-116-MY2.

References

1. Baranyi, P., Gedeon, T.D., Koczy, L.T.: A General Interpolation Technique in Fuzzy Rule Bases with Arbitrary Membership Functions. In: Proceedings of the 1996 IEEE International Conference on Systems, Man, and Cybernetics, pp. 510–515 (1996)
2. Baranyi, P., Koczy, L.T., Gedeon, T.D.: A Generalized Concept for Fuzzy Rule Interpolative. IEEE Transactions on Fuzzy Systems 12(6), 820–837 (2004)
3. Baranyi, P., Tikk, D., Yam, Y., Koczy, L.T.: A New Method for Avoiding Abnormal Conclusion for α-cut Based Rule Interpolation. In: Proceedings of the 1999 IEEE International Conference on Fuzzy Systems, pp. 383–388 (1999)

4. Bouchon-Meunier, B., Marsala, C., Rifqi, M.: Interpolative Reasoning Based on Graduality. In: Proceedings of the 2000 IEEE International Conference on Fuzzy Systems, pp. 483–487 (2000)
5. Hsiao, W.H., Chen, S.M., Lee, C.H.: A New Interpolation Reasoning Method in Sparse Rule-Based Systems. Fuzzy Sets and Systems 93(1), 17–22 (1998)
6. Huang, Z.H., Shen, Q.: Fuzzy Interpolative Reasoning via Scale and Move Transformations. IEEE Transactions on Fuzzy Systems 14(2), 340–359 (2006)
7. Koczy, L.T., Hirota, K.: Interpolative Reasoning with Insufficient Evidence in Sparse Fuzzy Rule Bases. Information Sciences 71(1), 169–201 (1993)
8. Koczy, L.T., Hirota, K.: Approximate Reasoning by Linear Rule Interpolation and General Approximation. International Journal of Approximate Reasoning 9(3), 197–225 (1993)
9. Koczy, L.T., Hirota, K.: Size Reduction by Interpolation in Fuzzy Rule Bases. IEEE Transactions on Systems, Man, and Cybernetics 27(1), 14–25 (1997)
10. Li, Y.M., Huang, D.M., Tsang, E.C., Zhang, L.N.: Weighted Fuzzy Interpolative Reasoning Method. In: Proceedings of the Fourth International Conference on Machine Learning and Cybernetics, pp. 3104–3108 (2005)
11. Mendel, J.M., John, R.I., Liu, F.L.: Interval Type-2 Fuzzy Logical Systems Made Simple. IEEE Transactions on Fuzzy Systems 14(6), 808–821 (2006)
12. Qiao, W.Z., Mizumoto, M., Yan, S.Y.: An Improvement to Koczy and Hirota's Interpolative Reasoning in Sparse Fuzzy Rule Bases. International Journal of Approximate Reasoning 15(3), 185–201 (1996)
13. Shi, Y., Mizumoto, M.: Some Considerations on Koczy's Interpolative Reasoning Method. In: Proceedings of the 1995 IEEE International Conference on Fuzzy Systems, pp. 2117–2122 (1995)
14. Shi, Y., Mizumoto, M., Qiao, W.Z.: Reasoning Conditions on Koczy's Interpolative Reasoning Method in Sparse Fuzzy Rule Bases. Fuzzy Sets and Systems 75(1), 63–71 (1995)
15. Tikk, D., Baranyi, P.: Comprehensive Analysis of a New Fuzzy Rule Interpolation Method. IEEE Transactions on Fuzzy Systems 8(3), 281–296 (2000)
16. Vass, G., Kalmar, L., Koczy, L.T.: Extension of the Fuzzy Rule Interpolation Method. In: Proceedings of the International Conference on Fuzzy Sets Theory Applications, pp. 1–6 (1992)
17. Wong, K.W., Tikk, D., Gedeon, T.D.: Fuzzy Rule Interpolation for Multidimensional Input Spaces with Applications: A Case Study. IEEE Transactions on Fuzzy Systems 13(6), 809–819 (2005)
18. Yam, Y., Wong, M.L., Baranyi, P.: Interpolation with Function Space Representation of Membership Functions. IEEE Transactions on Fuzzy Systems 14(3), 398–411 (2006)
19. Zaheh, L.A.: The Concept of a Linguistic Variable and Its Application to Approximate Reasoning-1. Information Sciences 8(1), 199–249 (1975)

Fuzzy Measurement of the Number of Persons on the Basis of the Photographic Image

Dariusz Król[1] and Michał Lower[2]

[1] Institute of Applied Informatics, Wrocław University of Technology
Wyb. Wyspiańskiego 27, 50-370 Wrocław, Poland
`Dariusz.Krol@pwr.wroc.pl`
[2] Institute of Engineering Cybernetics, Wrocław University of Technology
Janiszewskiego 11/17, 50-370 Wrocław, Poland
`Michal.Lower@pwr.wroc.pl`

Abstract. The numbers of persons on the hall is often a base of the ventilation control system in big commercial buildings. The paper presents a method dedicated for the measurement of the number of persons on the basis of analysis the registered photographic images. A difference between consecutive frames is estimated in the presented method. Every 5 seconds a change in a frame is being evaluated towards previous one. Medium value of the changes for the period of a few minutes is proportional to the number of persons on the hall. For the implementation the algorithms based on fuzzy logic were used.

1   Introduction

The recognition of human interaction is a useful task in video processing, virtual reality, human-computer interaction, and robotics [10]. The idea of smart home, office and supermarket able to interpret the stream of activity has generated significant interest. Many vision systems suitable to analyse the activities are described [3]. From the other side these problems are complex and often fuzzy based solutions are proposed [2]. The automatic recognition of transport containers using image processing and fuzzy binarization is good example of new direction in modern applications [8].

The number of persons staying on the hall is often a base of the ventilation steering system in big commercial buildings. The minimum amount of air, which the system of the ventilation must replace, is described by norms. This amount is proportional to numbers of people in the room. Good ventilation to a considerable degree increases the comfort of staying in the building, however it is involving energy resources, which are directly translating into financial costs. We can expect the agreement from the system of steering that the amount of the swapping air will be reduced as much as is possible, when in the ventilated room not the thousand of persons but only several persons are located. Halls have their defined peculiarity. There are often rooms with big surface, foreseen for huge amounts of persons. However depending on a time of the day, the week or the year the number of persons staying on the hall can be different considerably.

N.T. Nguyen et al. (Eds.): IEA/AIE 2008, LNAI 5027, pp. 102–107, 2008.
© Springer-Verlag Berlin Heidelberg 2008

In order to fit the amount of traded air, fans are being a function of the steered productivity. The rotation speed of the fan is most often divided on e.g. three thresholds. Enclosing fans to individual thresholds is dependent on number of persons being on the hall. A method presented in the paper for measurement of number of persons on the hall is a result of experience and observation of the ventilation system led in one hypermarket in Poland. The control system developed by authors is expected to estimate the number of persons entering and leaving the hall of sale. In order to sum up persons sensors were installed in entrances and exits. In everyday observation of the system, up to the end of the day it was possible to notice the inaccuracy in calculations. At the moment of closing a shop when a hall of sale was empty, the system had noticed the plus or the minus several persons. These mistakes in the everyday exploitation were meaningless. Within the year, however, exceptional periods happened, e.g. during holidays of the Christmas. In this period in one moment a row of persons went the hall up. It turned out then that the system had summed a few hundred entering persons up as one and the mistake in summing persons increased. In the effect of such situations, in which on the hall of sale exceptionally large number of persons appeared, fans enclosed for minimum airing themselves. At present the price of digital photographic devices went considerably down and solutions based on these devices can become rival for others conceptions. Thus for the presented problem we decided to perform analysis of the photographic image from six model spaces of the building. On the basis of the photo registered every 5 seconds a change in every frame is being evaluated towards previous. We assumed that medium value of the changes from the period of one minute from six photo recorders was proportional to the amount of persons on the hall of sale. For the implementation the algorithms based on fuzzy logic were used.

2   The Concept of Measurement Method

At working on the measurement method reliable assumptions were adopted. Moving people in the shop have the same purpose and they are preserved in more or less similar way. People are moving with similar speed, they are stopping by bookshelves for few minutes. By bookshelves people are moving in the scope of minimum 10 cm. Sometimes they do uncharacteristic movements, generated by customers of the shop or the service events. In all day analysis of the image it is possible to observe occasional disruptions bound with the delivery of goods to bookshelves or with the maintenance work. We assumed that all the typical behaviour of customers connected with the shopping was a parameter pointing at the proper number of persons in the store. Atypical phenomena from a point of view of the measurement and the disruption bound with the delivery of goods to bookshelves or with the maintenance work should be filtered out. The observed speed of the changes of the number of people in the store during a few minutes does not influence measuring value in the significant way. However, such assumption will let minimize the influence by short uncharacteristic behaviours. In order to avoid the misconception connected with the influence of the delivery of goods on bookshelves or the maintenance work, we made up our mind for simultaneous measurements in a few places of the hall. A few measuring places e.g. six or more will let avoid the measurement from calculations from the place, in which the result in the significant scope is diverging. For the tested object six characteristic measuring places were chosen and it was assumed that measurements would be conducted the average in five minute time periods. On the basis of such a measurement person rate is being outlined for every photographic recorder. Every pointer is subjected to fuzzy analysis and on this base the number of person for every device is calculated. It is also assumed that distances between calculations are small that this value should be similar to previous one. In the consecutive stage two values are being rejected which are the most diverging from the last result. Remained results are the result of the measurement.

3   Person Rate Estimation

In the first stage of research, test photos were made in chosen characteristic points of the hall of sale. After analysis of photographs parameters of the required resolution, the scale of colours of the image and frequency of making photographs were determined. These parameters should guarantee to detect the movement of a person and at the same time should eliminate disruptions not resulting from this move. On the basis of observation we assumed that a movement in scope 10 cm was interesting. And so one pixel of the screen should match to the more or less 5 cm of the real image. In order to simplify fitting it is possible to assume that the head of a man in a photo should be located in a 5x5 square of pixels. We decided to limit the scope of used colours to 16 colours. Such a limitation will permit to eliminate the disruption from the little shifts connected with the illumination and at the same time to detect the majority of essential changes in the image.

The image is given in the form of the two-dimensional matrix, in which pixels of the image are individual elements. Value corresponding to the colour of the pixel is at the same time the value of the element of the matrix. In next steps photographs are being made and a difference is being enumerated between elements (1). The sum of the non-zero elements of the matrix is a value determining the number of persons in the shop. This value is an average from a period of fow minutes (e.g. 5 minutes). The following measure is used (2).

$$L^{nm} = \sum_{ij} x_{ij}, \; where \; x_{ij} = \begin{cases} 1 \Leftrightarrow a_{ij}^{nm} - a_{ij}^{n(m-1)} \neq 0 \\ 0 \Leftrightarrow a_{ij}^{nm} - a_{ij}^{n(m-1)} = 0 \end{cases} \tag{1}$$

$$L_k^n = \frac{\sum_m L^{nm}}{m} \tag{2}$$

In order to calculate the number of persons on the hall on the basis of mean value L_k^n, outlined from photographic images, we made up our mind for applying fuzzy algorithms. For every photographic recorder this value could be different. The value is depending on the specificity of the chosen place, the way of taking hold, sizes of photographed area. Therefore applying fuzzy reasoning oversimplified the pondered problem. For every photographic recorder membership functions were defined in relation to the number of persons in the shop where K^{nk} is the number of people on the hall on the n-th recorder. Experimentally, for every membership function three qualitative assessments determining the number of persons were defined: L - low number of persons, M - medium number of persons, H - high number of persons.

$$(L_k^n == H) \cap (K^{k-1} == H) \Rightarrow (K^{nk} = H)$$
$$(L_k^n == L) \cap (K^{k-1} == L) \Rightarrow (K^{nk} = L)$$
$$(L_k^n == M) \cap (K^{k-1} == M) \Rightarrow (K^{nk} = M)$$
$$(L_k^n == H) \cap (K^{k-1} == L) \Rightarrow (K^{nk} = M)$$
$$(L_k^n == H) \cap (K^{k-1} == M) \Rightarrow (K^{nk} = H) \qquad (3)$$
$$(L_k^n == M) \cap (K^{k-1} == L) \Rightarrow (K^{nk} = M)$$
$$(L_k^n == M) \cap (K^{k-1} == H) \Rightarrow (K^{nk} = M)$$
$$(L_k^n == L) \cap (K^{k-1} == H) \Rightarrow (K^{nk} = M)$$
$$(L_k^n == L) \cap (K^{k-1} == M) \Rightarrow (K^{nk} = L)$$

The rules (3) permit to convert the value L_k^n into the number of people. In order to eliminate disruptions, additional comparing of the value measured up with previous measuring value was introduced. We assumed that previous value of the measurement should not run away considerably from value measured later.

4   Results and Conclusions

The results of carried tests suggest that the fuzzy reasoning could be used successfully to measure the number of persons of big halls. In order to eliminate incorrect, accidental recommendations e.g. bound with the delivery of goods to bookshelves or with the maintenance work two measurements are being repelled. Formulating the rules we assumed that previous value of the measurement should not run away considerably from value measured up. And so two measurements most distant from the last result are eliminated. Remained value makes the base for enumerating the new result (4).

$$K^k = \frac{\sum_{n-2} K^{nk}}{n-2} \qquad (4)$$

The presented method of the measurement of the number of persons, was worked out to needs of the arrangement of the ventilation on the hall in the hypermarket. Laboratory tests demonstrated that the method of the measurement

Fig. 1. People flows at the front entrance

was enough accurate for the needs of the system of steering and the mistake resulting from estimating should not negatively influence the system.

For test purposes a number of persons moving in the entrance hall in one of buildings of the Wrocław University of Technology was being determined. In the absence of the other method of the measurement, the synonymous estimation of the measurement accuracy turned out difficult. It is possible, however, to state that general estimating was appropriate. The system pointed out the big number of people of the movement during recess. A tendency of the decreasing number of people was also observed on breaks and at evening hours. And so general recommendations of the system were in accordance with reality. However this experience showed that the presented method of the measurement could have wider applying, not only to commercial buildings. Some snapshots at the front entrance to the university building where the experiments were conducted are introduced in Fig. 1.

For the accuracy of the measurement a mechanical stiffness of fixing photographic recorders has a big meaning. If devices oscillate, even in the little step, it can change measuring signal for incorrect. In present study algorithms of disruptions eliminating the influence of this type were not developed.

The presented measurement system is easy to diagnostics. Introducing additional procedures controlling the technical efficiency of the system does not make the considerable problem. It is possible to equip the system of identifying the image with models of the background and it is possible to assess the technical efficiency of the recorder comparing the recorded image to the model. Such objects as halls of sale as a default are equipped with antitheft cameras, they more and more often use digital devices for monitoring. In such a situation the presented method can be an additional function and in the little step increases the cost of the entire installation. At the same time it should be noticed that the presented measurement method does not have excessive requirements of digital devices with respect to technical parameters taken. We expect that such measurement methods intended to counteract against analysis of the image will be becoming more and more rival with respect to traditional solutions.

References

1. Angelov, P., Xydeas, C.: Fuzzy systems design: Direct and indirect approaches. Soft Comput. 10, 836–849 (2006)
2. Borgi, A., Akdag, H.: Knowledge based supervised fuzzy classification: An application to image processing. Annals of Mathematics and Artificial Intelligence 32, 67–86 (2001)
3. Charif, H.N., McKenna, S.J.: Tracking the activity of participants in a meeting. Machine Vision and Applications 17(2), 83–93 (2006)
4. Ciliz, M.K.: Rule base reduction for knowledge-based fuzzy controllers with aplication to a vacuum cleaner. Expert Systems with Aplications 28, 175–184 (2005)
5. Cordon, O., Gomide, F., Herrera, F., Hoffmann, F., Magdalena, L.: Ten years of genetic fuzzy systems: Current framework and new trends. Fuzzy Sets and Systems 141, 5–31 (2004)
6. Du, T.C., Wolfe, P.M.: Implementation of fuzzy logic systems and neural networks in industry. Computers in Industry 32, 261–272 (1997)
7. Keller, J.M., Wand, X.: A Fuzzy Rule-Based Approach to Scene DDescription Involving Spatial Relationships. Computer Vision and Image Understanding 80, 21–41 (2000)
8. Kim, K.B., Cho, J.H.: Recognition of identifiers from shipping container images using fuzzy binarization and enhanced fuzzy RBF network. Soft Comput. 11, 213–220 (2007)
9. Li, W., Jiang, X., Wang, Y.: Road recognition for vision navigation of an autonomous vehicle by fuzzy reasoning. Fuzzy Sets and Systems 93, 275–280 (1998)
10. Park, S., Aggarwal, J.K.: A hierarchical Bayesian network for event recognition of human actions and interactions. Multimedia Systems 10, 164–179 (2004)
11. Pedrycz, W.: Special issue on fuzzy set technology in pattern recognition. Pattern Recognition Letters 17, 565–566 (1996)
12. Rezaee, M.R., Goedhart, B., Lelieveldt, B.P.F., Reiber, J.H.C.: Fuzzy feature selection. Pattern Recognition 32, 2011–2019 (1999)
13. Teodorovic, D.: Fuzzy logic systems for transportation engeneering: The state of the art. Transportation Research Part A 33, 337–364 (1999)
14. Tizhoosh, R.H.: Image thresholding using type II fuzzy sets. Pattern Recognition 38, 2363–2372 (2005)
15. Wu, J.K., Narasimhalu, D.: Fuzzy content-based retrieval in image databases. Information Processing & Management 34, 513–534 (1998)

A Cross-Platform Robotic Architecture for Autonomous Interactive Robots

Yasser F.O. Mohammad and Toyoaki Nishida

Nishida-Sumi Laboratory, Department of Intelligence Science and Technology,
Graduate School of Informatics, Kyoto University, Japan
`yasser@ii.ist.i.kyoto-u.ac.jp`, `nishida@i.kyoto-u.ac.jp`

Abstract. This paper reports the lowest level of specification of a new cross-platform robotic architecture for HRI applications called EICA. The main contribution of this paper is a thorough analysis of some of the challenges HRI applications impose on the underlying architecture, and the details of the reactive layer of the EICA architecture that was designed to meet those challenges emphasizing how low level attention focusing and action integration is implemented. The paper also describes the implementation of a listener robot that uses human-like nonverbal behavior during explanation scenarios using the proposed architecture and reports some encouraging results from experimenting with a simplified simulation of this robot.

1 Review and Motivation

Many researchers have studied robotic architectures for mobile autonomous robots. The proposed architectures can broadly be divided into reactive, deliberative, or hybrid architectures. One general problem with most hybrid architectures concerning real world interactions is the fixed pre-determined relation between deliberation and reaction [1], [2]. Interaction between humans in the real world utilizes many channels including verbal, and nonverbal channels. To manage those channels, the agent needs to have a variety of skills and abilities including dialog management, synchronization of verbal and nonverbal intended behavior, and efficient utilization of normal society-dependent unintended nonverbal behavior patterns. Those skills are managed in humans using both conscious and unconscious processes of a wide range of computational load. This suggests that implementing such behaviors in a robot will require integration of various technologies ranging from fast reactive processes to long term deliberative operations. The relation between the deliberative and reactive subsystems needed to implement natural interactivity is very difficult to be catched in well structured relations like deliberation as learning, deliberation as configuration, or reaction as advising usually found in hybrid architectures. On the other hand, most other autonomous applications used to measure the effectiveness of robotic architectures (like autonomous indoor and outdoor navigation, collecting empty cans, delivering Faxes, and underwater navigation) require a very well structured

N.T. Nguyen et al. (Eds.): IEA/AIE 2008, LNAI 5027, pp. 108–118, 2008.

relation between reaction and deliberation. To solve this problem the architecture should have a flexible relation between deliberation and reaction that is dictated by the task and the interaction context rather than the predetermined decision of the architecture designer.

Some researchers proposed architectures that are specially designed for interactive robots. Ishiguro et al. proposed a robotic architecture based on situated modules and reactive modules. While reactive modules represent the purely reactive part of the system, situated modules are higher levels modules programmed in a high-level language to provide specific behaviors to the robot. The situated modules are evaluated serially in an order controlled by the module controller. This module controller enables planning in the situated modules network rather than the internal representation which makes it easier to develop complex systems based on this architecture [3]. One problem of this approach is the serial nature of execution of situated modules which, while makes it easier to program the robot, limits its ability to perform multiple tasks at the same time which is necessary to achieve some tasks especially nonverbal interactive behaviors. Also there is no built-in support for attention focusing in this system.

Nicolescu and Mataric proposed a hierarchical architecture based on abstract virtual behaviors that tried to implement AI concepts like planning into behavior based systems. The basis for task representation is the behavior network construct which encodes complex, hierarchical plan-like strategies [4]. One problem of this work is the implicit inhibition links at the actuator level to prevent any two behaviors from being *active* at the same time even if the behavior network allows that, which decreases the benefits from the opportunistic execution option of the system when the active behavior commands can actually be combined to generate a final actuation command. Although this kind of limitation is typical to navigation and related problems in which the goal state is typically more important than the details of the behavior, it is not suitable for human-like natural interaction purposes in which the dynamics of the behavior are even more important than achieving a specific goal. For example, showing distraction by other activities in the peripheral visual field of the robot through partial eye movement can be an important signal in human robot interactions.

One general problem with most architectures that target interactive robots is the lack of proper intention modeling on the architectural level. In natural human-human communication intention communication is a crucial requirement for the success of the communication. Leaving such an important ingredient of the robot outside the architecture can lead to reinvention of intention management in different applications.

This analysis of existing HRI architectures revealed the following limitations:

- Lack of Intention Modeling in the architectural level.
- Fixed pre-specified relation between deliberation and reaction.
- Disallowing multiple behaviors from accessing the robot actuators at the same time.
- Lack of built-in attention focusing mechanisms in the architectural level.

To overcome the aforementioned problems, the authors designed and implemented a novel robotic architecture (EICA). In this paper the details of the lowest level of specification of this architecture is given with emphasize of presenting how the proposed architecture implements attention focusing and action integration in the lowest level of the system. A real world experiment with a humanoid robot developed using EICA is then presented.

2 L_0EICA

EICA is a behavioral hybrid architecture that specifies no predesigned relation between deliberation and reaction. The architecture has multiple levels of specification to make it possible to design the behaviors of the robot at any level of abstraction required for the task at hand while guaranteeing that all processes developed at whatever level of abstraction can be combined together in the final system using a fixed and simple action integration mechanism. A level of specification (LoS) is defined in EICA as a set of types and entities that can be used to build the computational processes of the robot at a specific level of abstraction. Levels of specification are arranged in a hierarchical structure where any process at a specific level of specification can use the types and entities of the lower levels of specification. In this paper only the lower level of specification L_0EICA is discussed.

Fig. 1 shows the lowest level of specification of the EICA architecture called L_0EICA. Every processing component in EICA must ultimately implement the *Active* interface. In that sense this type is equivalent to the *Behavior* abstraction

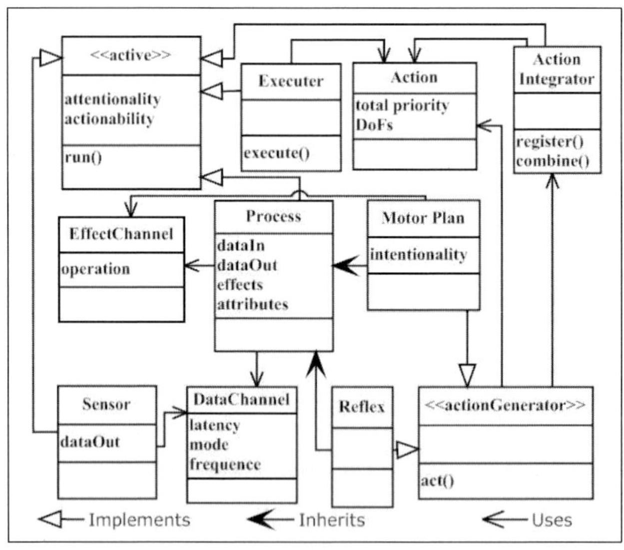

Fig. 1. L_0EICA

in BBS (behavior based systems) or the *Agent* abstraction in MAS (multi-agent systems). Every *Active* object has the following attributes:

Attentionality. A real number that specifies the relative attention that should be given to this process. This number is used to calculate the speed at which this process is allowed to run. As shown in Fig. 2, this attribute is connected to the output of the attention effect channel of the object.

Actionability. A real number specifying the activation level of the object. A zero or negative activation level prevents the object from execution. A positive actionability means that the process will be allowed to run but depending on the exact value of this attribute the effect of the object on other *active* objects is calculated. As shown in Fig. 2, this attribute is connected to the output of the action effect channel of the object.

Effects. A set of output ports that connect this object through effect channels to other active components of the system.

This specification for the *Active* type was inspired by the Abstract Behaviors of [4] although it was designed to be more general and to allow attention focusing at the lowest level of the architecture. By separating the actionability from the attentionality and allowing actionability to have a continuous range, EICA enables a form of attention focusing that is usually unavailable to behavioral systems. This separation allows the robot to select the active processes depending on the general context (by setting the actionability value) while still being able to assign the computation power according to the exact environmental and internal condition (by setting the attentionality value). The fact that the actionability is variable allows the system to use it to change the possible influence of various processes (through the operators of the effect channels) based on the current situation.

All *active* components are connected together through *effect channels*. Every *effect channel* has a set of n inputs that use continuous signaling and a single output that is continuously calculated from those inputs. This output is calculated according to the *operation* attribute of the *effect channel*. The currently implemented operations are:

- Max:$y = \max_{i=1:n} (x_i \,|\, a_i > \varepsilon)$
- Min:$y = \min_{i=1:n} (x_i \,|\, a_i > \varepsilon)$
- Avg: $y = \dfrac{\sum_{i=1}^{n} (a_i x_i)}{\sum_{i=1}^{n} (a_i)}$

Where x_i is an input port, a_i is the actionability of the object connected to port i and y is the output of the effect channel.

At this level of specification the types that can be used to directly implement the processing components of the robot are:

MotorPlan. Represents a simple reactive plan that generates a short path control mechanism from sensing to actuation. The action integration mechanism

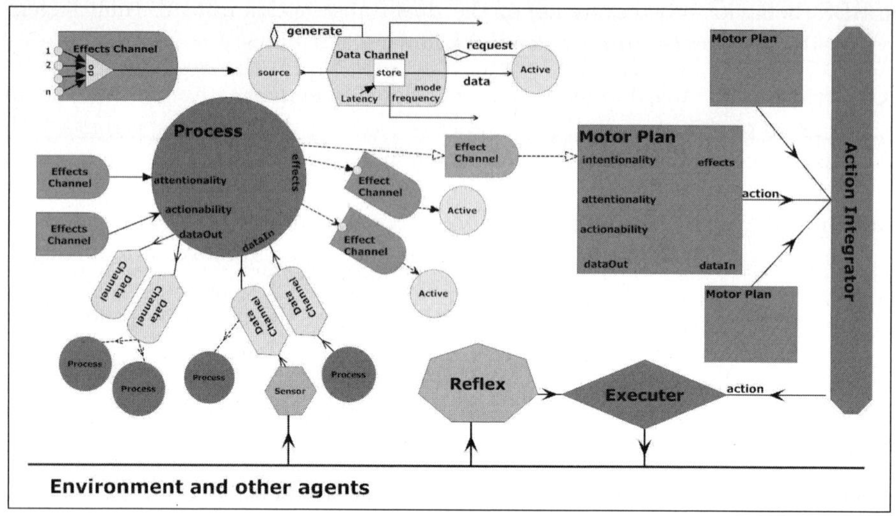

Fig. 2. Schematics of L_0EICA components

provides the means to integrate the actuation commands generated by all running *motor plans* into final commands sent to the executers to be applied to the robot actuators based on the *intentionality* assigned to every *motor plan*. This type of processes represents the reactive view of intention inspired by neuroscience and experimental psychology results regarding human intentional behavior [5]. The motor plans in EICA are more like reactive motor schema than traditional behaviors.

Process. Provides a higher level of control over the behavior of the robot by controlling the temporal evolution of the *intentionality* of various *motor plans*. As will be shown in the application presented in this paper, the interaction between multiple simple processes can generate arbitrary complex behavior. Processes in EICA are not allowed to generate action directly.

Reflex. A special type of processes that can bypass the action integrator and send direct commands to the executer(s). Reflexes provide safety services like collision avoidance during navigation, or safety measures to prevent any possible accidents to the interacting person due to any failures in other modules.

Sensor. An active entity intended to communicate with the hardware sensors of the robot directly. This kind of objects was introduced to provide a more efficient sensing capability to the robot by utilizing the latency property of the data channel component.

Various kinds of active components in the robot are connected together using *data channels* to exchange data. A *data channel* is a simple object that manages the generation and distribution of data from active objects in the system based on its mode of operation. In the *on demand* mode the *data channel* is usually passive until it receives a request from one of its output ports. The data item stored is sent to this port directly if the latency of this port is less than the time passed since the current data item was produced, otherwise the source process of the data channel is interrupted to generate a new data item to be stored and passed to the requester. This kind of *data on demand* is usually not available in behavioral systems, but it can improve the performance when sensing is an expensive operation as when using vision techniques. In the *continuous generation* mode the *data channel* interrupts the source process to generate data items every $1/frequency$ seconds. In the *interrupt* mode the data generated from the source are immediately sent to the output ports of which the *request* input is high with a frequency determined by the *latency* of this port. This mode of operation is useful in separating the preconditions of various processes from the execution core which enables more efficient implementation if the same preconditions are to be calculated by many processes.

Other than the aforementioned types of active entities, EICA has a central *Action Integrator* that receives actions from motor plans and uses the source's intentionality level as well as an assigned priority and mutuality for every DoF of the robot in the action to decide how to integrate it with actions from other motor plans using simple weighted averaging subject to mutuality constraints. This algorithm although very simple can generate a continuous range of integration possibilities ranging from pure action selection to potential field like action integration based on the parameters assigned by the various motor plans of the robot. The current implementation of EICA is done using standard C++, and is platform independent. The system is also suitable for implementation onboard and in a host server. It can be easily extended to support distributed implementation on multiple computers connected via a network. The EICA implementation is based on Object-Oriented design principles so every component in the system is implemented in a class. Implementing software EICA Applications is very simple: Inherit the appropriate classes from the EICA core system and override the abstract functions.

3   Example Implementations

Until now the EICA architecture was used to implement the TalkBack miniature robot reported in [6] and a humanoid listener robot reported here.

3.1   A Robot That Listens

The ability to use human-like nonverbal listening behavior is an advantage for humanoid robots that coexist with humans in the same social space. [7] implemented a robot that tries to use natural human like body language while listening to a human giving it road directions. In this work we try to build a general listener robot based on the EICA architecture. As a minimal design, only the head of the robot was controlled during this experiment. This decision was based on the hypothesis accepted by many researchers in the nonverbal human interaction community that gaze direction is one of the most important non-verbal behaviors involved in realizing natural listening in human-human close encounters [8].

The evaluation data was collected as follows:

1. Six different explanation scenarios were collected in which a person is explaining the procedure of operating a hypothetical machine that involves pressing three different buttons, rotating a knob, and noticing results in an LCD screen in front of a Robovie II robot while pretending that the robot is listening. The motion tracker's data was logged 460 times per second.
2. The log files were used as the input to the robot simulator and the behavior of the robot's head was analyzed.
3. For every scenario 20 new synthetic scenarios were generated by utilizing 20 different levels of noise. The behavior of the simulator was analyzed for every one of the resulting 120 scenarios and compared to the original performance.
4. The same system was used to drive the Robovie II robot and the final behavior was subjectively studied.

Four reactive motor plans were designed that encapsulate the possible interaction actions that the robot can generate, namely, looking around, following the human face, following the salient object in the environment, and looking at the same place the human is looking at. The sufficiency of those motor plans was based on the fact that in the current scenario the robot simply have no other place to look, and the necessity was confirmed empirically by the fact that the three behavioral processes needed to adjust the intentionality of all of these motor plans. Fig. 3 shows the complete design of the listener robot in this experiment.

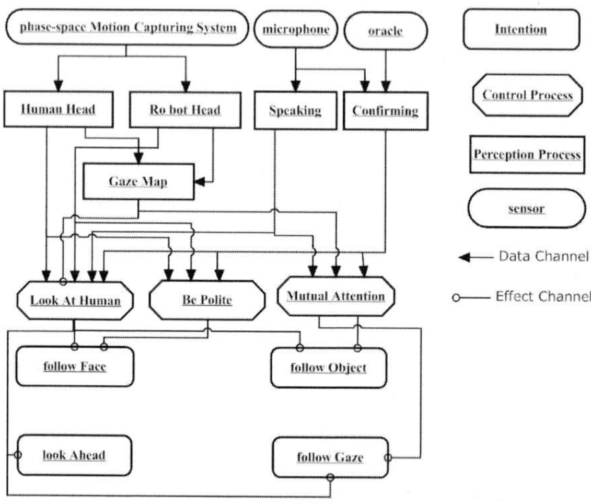

Fig. 3. The Design of the Listener Robot

The analysis of the mutual attention requirements showed the need of three behavioral processes. Two processes to generate an approach-escape mechanism controlling looking toward the human operator which is inspired by the *Approach-Avoidance* mechanism suggested in [8] in managing spacial distance in natural human-human situations. These processes were named Look-At-Human, and Be-Polite. A third process was needed to control the realization of the mutual attention behavior. This process was called Mutual-Intention. The details refer to [9]. A brief description of them is given here:

1. *Look-At-Human*: This process is responsible of generating an attractive virtual force that pulls the robot's head direction to the location of the human face. This process first checks the Gaze-Map's current modes and if their weights are less than a specific threshold for more than 10 seconds, while the human is speaking for more than 4 seconds , it increases the intentionality of the *followFace* motor plan and decreases the intentionality of the other three reactive motor plans based on the difference in angle between the line of sight of the human and the robot and the *Confirming* condition.
2. *Be-Polite*: This process works against the *Look-At-Human* process by decreasing the intentionality of the *followFace* motor plan in reverse proportion to the angle between the line of sight of the human and the robot depending on the period the human is speaking.
3. *Mutual-Attention*: This process increases the intentionality of the *followObject* or the intentionality of the *followGaze*. The rate of intentionality increase is determined based on the confirmation mode.

Five perception processes were needed to implement the aforementioned behavioral processes and motor plans:

1. *Human-Head*, which continuously updates a list containing the position and direction of the human head during the last 30 seconds sampled 50 times per second.
2. *Robot-Head*, which continuously updates a list containing the position and direction of the robot head during the last 30 seconds sampled 50 times per second.
3. *Gaze-Map*, which continuously updates a representation of the distribution of the human gaze both in the spacial and temporal dimensions. The spacial distribution is stored as a mixture-of-Gaussians like structure where the mean μ_i represents the location of an important object and the variance σ_i is a measure of the size of that object. The weight w_i represents the importance of the place according to the gaze of the human. The details of this process will not be given here due to lack of space, refer to [9] for details.
4. *Speaking*, which uses the power of the sound signal to detect the existence of human speech. The current implementation simply assumes there is a human speech whenever the sound signal is not zero. This was acceptable in the simulation but with real world data a more complex algorithm that utilizes fourier analysis will be used.
5. *Confirming*, which specifies whether or not the human is making a confirming action. Currently this value is manually added to the logged data.

Table 1. Comparison Between the Simulated and Natural Behavior

Item	Statistic	Simulation	H-H value
Mutual Gaze	Mean	31.5%	30%
	Std.Dev.	1.94%	–
Gaze Toward	Mean	77.87%	75%
Instructor	Std.Dev.	3.04%	–
Mutual	Mean	53.12%	–
Attention	Std.Dev.	4.66%	–

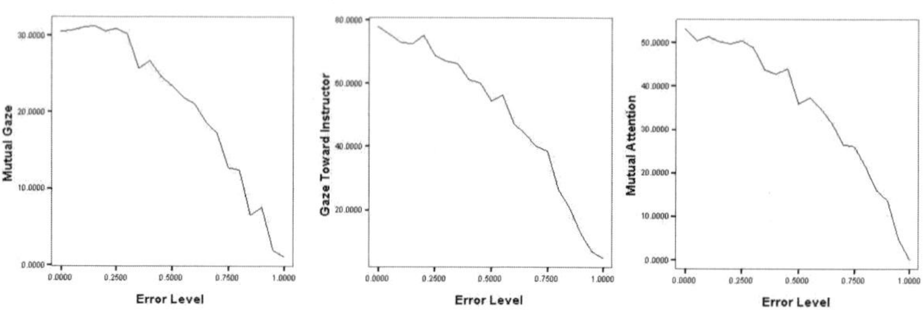

Fig. 4. Effect on the error level on the behavior of the robot

Some of the results of numerical simulations of the listening behavior of the robot are given in Table 1. The table shows the average time of performing four basic interactive behaviors obtained from the simulated robot in comparison to the known average values measured in human-human interaction situations. The source of the average time in the human-human case are reported from [8]. As the table shows the behavior of the robot is similar to the known average behavior in the human-human case for both mutual gaze and gaze toward instructor behaviors and the standard deviation in both cases is less than 7% of the mean value which predicts robust operation in real world situations. These results suggest that the proposed approach is at least applicable to implement natural listening behavior.

Fig. 4 shows the effect of increasing the error level on the percentage of time mutual gaze, gaze toward instructor, and mutual attention behaviors were recognized in the simulation. As expected the amount of time spent on these interactive behaviors decreases with increased error level although this decrease is not linear but can be well approximated with a quadratic function. Regression Analysis revealed that in the three cases the effect on the mean time spent doing the studied behavior grows with the quadrable of the inverse SNR (Signal to Noise ratio).

4   Limitations

Although L_0EICA provides a unified simple architecture for implementing behavioral control systems, and provides a consistent action integration mechanism, it has some limitations that will be targeted by higher levels of specifications. One such limitation is the lack of an explicit learning mechanism that enables the behavior of the robot to evolve over time. Although the architecture does allow the programmer to implement any learning algorithm as a set of processes that control the parameters of other running active components through effect channels, the architecture does not provide a specific learning framework to make this process easier. Another limitation is the lack of higher level planning-like structures that enable complex behaviors to be built easily from simpler ones. Again this higher level planning like structures can be implemented by the robot programmer in an ad-hoc fashion, but it would be better if the architecture itself can provide an easy way to implement such deliberative mechanisms. A third limitation of the current system that resulted from its generality is the lack of an explicit mechanism for reasoning about the believes and behaviors of interacting agents which is required to implement a theory of mind for the robot. Future work in EICA will target all of those limitations by providing higher levels of specifications compatible with L_0EICA.

5   Conclusion

This paper presented the design of the lowest level of specification of a new robotic architecture (EICA) that was designed to meet four basic limitations of available HRI architectures. Some of the novel features of the proposed architecture were shown and the implementation of a humanoid robot that uses nonverbal human like head movement during listening based on it is given. The experimentation with a simulated version of the robot revealed that EICA can indeed be used to develop interactive robots that achieve human-like nonverbal interaction capabilities and that the implemented system has a good noise rejection properties even though the underlying implementation is massively parallel. In the future the details of higher levels of specification of EICA that introduces planning-like capabilities to the system will be reported and tested in a complete version of the listener robot.

References

1. Arkin, R.C., Masahiro Fujita, T.T., Hasegawa, R.: An ethological and emotional basis for human-robot interaction, robotics and autonomous systems. Robotics and Autonomous Systems 42(3-4), 191–201 (2003)
2. Karim, S., Sonenberg, L., Tan, A.: A Hybrid Architecture Combining Reactive Plan Execution and Reactive Learning. In: Yang, Q., Webb, G. (eds.) PRICAI 2006. LNCS (LNAI), vol. 4099, pp. 200–211. Springer, Heidelberg (2006)
3. Ishiguro, H., Kanda, T., Kimoto, K., Ishida, T.: A robot architecture based on situated modules. In: IEEE/RSJ Conference on Intelligent Robots and Systems 1999 (IROS 1999), October 1999, vol. 3, pp. 1617–1624. IEEE, Los Alamitos (1999)
4. Nicolescu, M.N., Matarić, M.J.: A hierarchical architecture for behavior-based robots. In: AAMAS 2002: Proceedings of the first international joint conference on Autonomous agents and multiagent systems, pp. 227–233. ACM, New York (2002)

5. Mohammad, Y.F.O., Nishida, T.: A new, HRI inspired, view of intention. In: AAAI 2007 Workshop on Human Implications of Human-Robot Interactions, July 2007, pp. 21–27 (2007)
6. Mohammad, Y.F.O., Nishida, T.: Talkback: Feedback from a miniature robot. In: Twentieth Australian Joint Conference on Artificial Intelligence, December 2007, pp. 357–366 (2007)
7. Kanda, T., Kamasima, M., Imai, M., Ono, T., Sakamoto, D., Ishiguro, H., Anzai, Y.: A humanoid robot that pretends to listen to route guidance from a human. Autonomous Robots 22(1), 87–100 (2007)
8. Argyle, M.: Bodily Communication. New edn. Routledge (2001)
9. Mohammad, Y.F.O., Ohya, T., Hiramatsu, T., Sumi, Y., Nishida, T.: Embodiment of knowledge into the interaction and physical domains using robots. In: International Conference on Control, Automation and Systems, October 2007, pp. 737–744 (2007)

Match-Up Strategies for Job Shop Rescheduling

Patrick Moratori, Sanja Petrovic, and Antonio Vázquez

School of Computer Science, University of Nottingham, Nottingham, UK
{pbm, sxp, jav}@cs.nott.ac.uk

Abstract. We investigate the problem of integrating new rush orders into the current schedule of a real world job shop floor. Satisfactory rescheduling methods must keep stability of the shop, by introducing the fewest number of changes in the ordering of operations, while maintaining the same levels of the schedule performance criteria. This paper introduces a number of match-up strategies that modify only part of the schedule in order to accommodate new arriving jobs. These strategies are compared with the right-shift and the total-rescheduling methods, which are optimal regarding stability and performance, but ineffective for performance and stability, respectively. Statistical analysis indicates that the match-up strategies are comparable to right-shift for stability, and as good as total-rescheduling for performance.

1 Introduction

Job shop scheduling is defined as the problem of allocating a finite set of jobs on a finite set of machines subject to certain constraints. The traditional scheduling process considers static and deterministic future conditions. However, in the real world, disturbances often arise on the shop floor, such as the arrival of new jobs, rush orders, machine breakdowns, rework that has to be done, due dates changing etc. These require rescheduling of the initially allocated jobs [1]. The approaches to rescheduling can be classified into three groups [2]: (1) reactive approaches (also often named online scheduling) in which a job to be processed next is selected among the available jobs using only local information regarding the new job; (2) robust scheduling which creates a schedule in such a way that it absorbs the effect of disruptions on the shop floor; and (3) predictive-reactive scheduling in which a schedule which optimises shop floor performance is constructed first and then it is modified when a disruption occurs.

Match-up algorithms belong to the group of predictive-reactive approaches. They aim to change only a part of the initial schedule when a disturbance occurs, in such a way as to accommodate new disturbances and maintain both performance and stability of the shop floor. These algorithms have been mostly investigated in the context of single machine and flow shop problems. The studies presented in [3,4,5,6] describe a theoretical approach based on the economic's turnpike theory. The main idea consists in restoring the initial schedule as soon as possible, since it already has an optimal solution. However, these studies are restricted to single machine problems [3,5,6] and single stage with parallel

N.T. Nguyen et al. (Eds.): IEA/AIE 2008, LNAI 5027, pp. 119–128, 2008.

machines problems [4]. A branch and bound algorithm technique for match-up is presented in [7] to solve flow shop problems in which dispatching rules are selected for a match-up strategy.

Knowledge-based rescheduling systems have been investigated in the job shop context [8,9,10,11]. They resemble match-up approaches in that they also consider a part of the schedule for rescheduling. These methods consider, at every decision point, the most constrained part of the schedule. Then, they select, based on some stored knowledge, a rescheduling strategy. A drawback of these systems is that a single conflict (constraint violation) may be propagated in the remaining schedule, requiring several updates, which compromises the stability of the schedule. Another job shop scheduling problem with machine breakdown was investigated in [12]. In this study, the match-up approach is implicit because the developed heuristic collects affected jobs and right-shift them on the horizon. Another implicit match-up approach was presented in [13] in which a genetic algorithm considers both stability and performance measures to generate the optimal solution. However, the production environment is also restricted to single machine problems.

In this paper, we investigate rescheduling problems in the printing company Sherwood Press in Nottingham, UK. The scheduling of printing orders can be defined as a job shop problem with parallel machines. This scheduling problem is dynamic in the sense that new printing orders arrive every day and have to be integrated in the existing schedule.

Variants of a match-up algorithm, each in turn using a different strategy to define a rescheduling horizon, are proposed in this paper. The appropriate setting of the rescheduling horizon, which is the time window within which jobs are rescheduled to accommodate the new job, is essential for keeping the stability and performance of the schedule. The main contribution of this investigation is to propose and compare 8 strategies for the calculation of the rescheduling horizon. The proposed strategies are compared with the right-shift and the total-rescheduling methods, each in turn, by definition, is optimal regarding stability and performance, but ineffective for performance and stability, respectively. Statistical analysis indicates that the match-up strategies are comparable to right-shift for stability, and as good as total-rescheduling for performance.

A fuzzy multi-criteria genetic algorithm [14], previously developed for static problems, is used here for sequencing operations within the rescheduling horizon. The processing times are uncertain and represented by fuzzy numbers. Lot-sizing (splitting jobs into smaller lots), load balancing (a distribution of operations over parallel machines) and batching (grouping of similar operations to avoid setup) are also applied in order to improve the performance of the new generated schedule.

This paper is organized as follows. Section 2 introduces a real world job shop rescheduling problem present at Sherwood Press. Section 3 describes the main characteristics of the match-up algorithm for rescheduling. Section 4 discusses the experiments that were carried out to analyse the proposed algorithm. Section 5 describes the conclusions and future work.

2   Problem Statement

The job shop problem faced by Sherwood Press involves the allocation of a number of jobs on 18 machines, which are grouped into 7 work centres for printing, cutting, folding, card-inserting, embossing / debossing, gathering, and finishing. Some machines in the work centre are identical and are treated as parallel machines. Each job is subject to precedence constraints, i.e. it has a predefined sequence of machines on which it has to be processed. Each job is assigned a release and a due date which denote the time when the job has to start and finish its processing, respectively. The processing of a job on a machine is referred to as an operation. Each operation is assigned a processing time required on the machine. The following parameters are considered in the scheduling model: the release and due dates of jobs; the priority levels which define tolerance levels associated with the violation of the job due dates; and the setup times that are required on the printing machines when jobs of different colouring requirements are scheduled one after the other. In addition, the load balancing of parallel machines in the work centres was considered.

Five criteria are consider in the evaluation of performance of schedules: (1) the average weighted tardiness of jobs, (2) the number of tardy jobs, (3) the total setup time, (4) the total idle time of machines, and (5) the total flow time. The values of these metrics are mapped into satisfaction levels and aggregated into a final *Performance* measure (for more details see [14]). Since *Performance* is a measure of satisfaction, it has to be maximised.

Every day a new job (or jobs) arrives to be processed on the shop floor. The policy of the company is to keep the existing schedule unchanged for 2 days (48 hours). After that time the new job can start its processing. In this research, we consider new jobs that are rush orders. The task is to accommodate the new job in the existing schedule, as soon as possible, in such a way that the *Performance* of the new schedule is maintained together with the stability of the schedule. The stability measure introduced here, is based on the concept of sequence deviation presented in [12]. It is modified to consider parallel machines and to allow changing of the allocation of operations between the parallel machines.

Let M be the number of machines, O_i the number of operations that have to be processed on machine $i = 1, \ldots, M$. Let $Reward_{ij} = 1$ if the immediate successor of operation $j = 1, \ldots, O_i$ on machine i in the initial schedule remains a successor, although not necessarily an immediate one, in the new schedule, and 0 otherwise. To each machine i a measure of sequence stability, $Reward_i \in [0, 1]$ is assigned:

$$Reward_i = \sum_{j=1}^{O_i - 1} \frac{Reward_{ij}}{O_i - 1}. \tag{1}$$

In order to keep the sequence of operations on each machine as unchanged as possible, the sum of rewards of the machines has to be maximised. Since we are dealing with parallel machines, we consider the following special cases for the calculation of $Reward_i$:

1. If machine i is empty and stays empty after rescheduling then $Reward_i = 1$.

2. If machine i has originally just one operation and in the new schedule any number N, then $Reward_i = 1$.
3. If machine i is empty and any number N of operations are assigned to it in the new schedule, then $Reward_i = 0$.
4. If machine i has N operations and becomes empty in the new schedule, then $Reward_i = 0$.

The rationale of these rules is to penalise drastic changes in machine workload. In case 1, the rescheduling does not affect the workload of the machine which is highly rewarded. In case 2, the sequence of operations is not affected by adding any number of operations, since the original one is kept on the same machine. On the other hand, in case 3 and 4, the workload is completely changed resulting in $Reward_i = 0$.

The stability measure, used in this paper is defined as follows:

$$Stability = \frac{1}{M} \sum_{i=1}^{M} Reward_i. \tag{2}$$

3   Match-Up Strategies for Rescheduling

A match-up algorithm developed for the dynamic scheduling of rush orders will be presented in this section. The goal is to define a time horizon, within the initial schedule, that will be rescheduled in order to accommodate the new job. The already allocated operations, within the defined time horizon, and the new operations of the new job define the new scheduling problem. These operations are allocated new release and due dates in order to keep the schedule outside the defined time horizon unchanged. The pseudo-code of the developed algorithm is given in Fig. 1(a).

The match-up algorithm has three phases. In the first phase (step 1-2), the rescheduling horizon is defined. In the second phase (step 3-6), a new scheduling problem within the calculated horizon is defined. In the third phase (step 7), the feasibility of the solution is verified by checking possible overlaps between the unchanged part of the schedule (outside the rescheduling horizon) and the new generated solution (defined for the rescheduling horizon).

In the first phase, $initialStart$ is the time of the arrival of a new rush job increased by 48 hours required by the company. Fig. 1(b) shows using a Gantt chart an example of a new job arrival to the shop floor. The operations that have started before $initialStart$ must be completed before the rescheduling process begins. Therefore, in step 1, all the operations that are in processing at $initialStart$ are collected (in Fig. 1(b), jobs 5, 6 and 7 on machines M1, M3 and M4, respectively). The one with the highest completion time determines the $startPoint$ (job 7 on M4). All the operations that can be processed before the $startPoint$ will complete their processing (job 8 on M2 and job 6 on M5).

In order to calculate the $endPoint$ of the rescheduling horizon (step 2) the algorithm collects the idle times on the machines on which the new job requires processing. Four different strategies are introduced to collect the idle times:

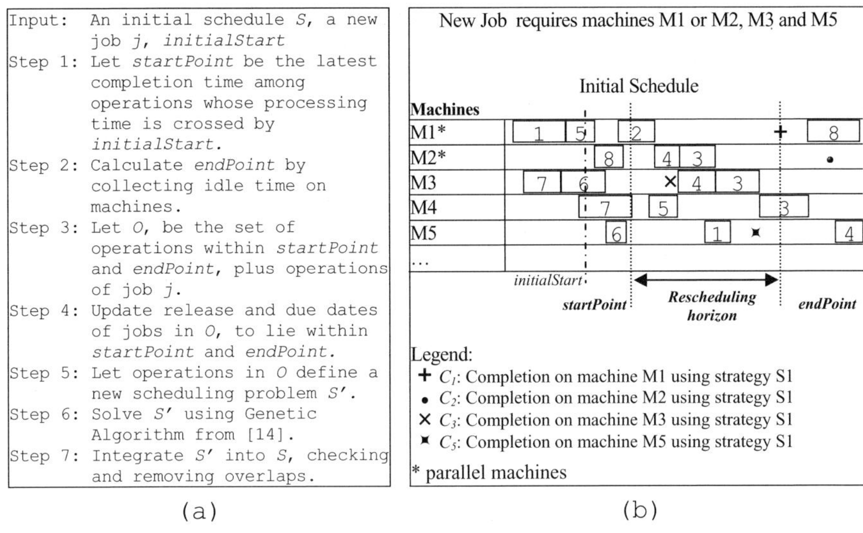

(a)

(b)

Fig. 1. Pseudocode (a), and example (b) of match-up approach

S1. Collect all available idle times on machines required by the new job (not necessarily as a single time period). The total idle time collected on each machine is equal to the required processing time of each new operation.

S2. Collect continuous idle times on each machine required for the new job.

S3. As S1, but considering the precedence constraints imposed by operations of the new job. The collection of the idle times for an operation j on a machine i starts after the completion time of the preceding operation $j - 1$.

S4. As S2, but considering the precedence constraints of the new job.

Let C_i be the completion time of a new job on machine i; then *endPoint* is defined as the maximum of C_i, $i = 1, \ldots, M$. In the case of parallel machines, there are several possible values of C_i. Just one of these is considered for the calculation of *endPoint*. In this way, we define 8 strategies: $S1 - S4$ that are as above and consider the earliest C_i among the parallel machines, and $S5 - S8$ are as $S1 - S4$, respectively, and consider the latest C_i among parallel machines. Fig. 3 demonstrates the idle time collection using the strategy S1 to set the rescheduling horizon. Since S1 is being used, the completion time of machine 1, that is earlier compared to the completion time on machine 2, denoted by C_1, is the one used to define *endPoint*. If the strategy S5 had been used instead of S1, then *endPoint* $= C_2$. Note that, in this example, machine 4 is not required by the new job.

All the operations between the *startPoint* and *endPoint* are collected together with the new job operations (step 3). Release and due dates of the jobs are set depending on the position of the jobs within the rescheduling horizon (step 4). This updating is necessary in order to keep the affected operations within the rescheduling horizon, and prevent their overlap with operations that are out of the rescheduling horizon. The collected operations define a new scheduling problem (step 5). This new problem is solved (step 6) using the same fuzzy multi-criteria genetic algorithm that was used to construct the initial schedule [14].

In the final phase (step 7) the partial schedule, contained within the rescheduling horizon of the initial schedule, is replaced by the schedule found in step 6. It may be the case that the latter extends out of the rescheduling horizon, and consequently, operations may overlap. Such cases are identified, and operations that are not within the rescheduling horizon are right-shifted to restore feasibility. Note that there is no need to consider overlaps with operations preceding the rescheduling horizon.

4   Experiments on Real World Data

Data sets obtained from Sherwood Press are used to test the *Performance* and *Stability* measures of the match-up algorithm. The scheduling planning horizon is 1 month. Saturation level (*sat*) is introduced as an indicator of idle time availability in the production shop, and is defined as the ratio between the sum of all required processing times and the makespan of the initial schedule. A small *sat* value indicates a highly saturated schedule, i.e. with a small amount of idle time.The saturation levels for each considered month are 3.67, 2.37 and 1.85. These values correspond to low, medium and high saturation levels respectively, i.e. $sat \in \{$low, medium, high$\}$. Different times of insertion of a new job, *insTime*, in the schedule were also investigated. In our experiments, $insTime \in \{$beginning, middle, end$\}$ where 'beginning", "middle" and "end" refer to a *startPoint* equal to 10%, 50% and 80%, respectively, of the makespan of the initial schedule. The size of a given job, *jobSize*, denotes the required number of operations. In our experiments $jobSize \in \{1, 2, 3, 4, 5\}$.

The initial schedule, for each month, was obtained using the Genetic Algorithm described in [14], with the objective of optimising the *Performance* measure. Each strategy S1-S8, as well as total-rescheduling and right-shift rescheduling are used for rescheduling. In total-rescheduling, all the remaining operations are rescheduled. In right-shift rescheduling, all operations after *startPoint* are right-shifted in the horizon to accommodate the new job. The *Performance* and *Stability* measures are recorded for each tested strategy on each problem.

The match-up algorithm and all rescheduling strategies were implemented in Visual C++. Testing was performed in a Windows XP environment on a PC Centrino Duo with 2.16 GHz and 1GB of RAM. Results are presented and analysed in the following section.

4.1   Analysis and Results

This section presents a statistical analysis of the effects of the problem parameters and the match-up strategies on *Performance* and *Stability*. In order to identify strengths and weaknesses of each rescheduling strategy, the overall results obtained by the match-up strategies, right-shift and total-rescheduling are presented. Interactions involving problem parameters will be also discussed.

Table 1. Results of the ANOVA test for *Performance* and *Stability*

		Performance		*Stability*	
		F value	P value	F value	P value
Main effects					
	Strategy	13.56	≤ 0.01	55.38	≤ 0.01
	sat	104.94	≤ 0.01	7.92	≤ 0.01
	jobSize	25.47	≤ 0.01	81.17	≤ 0.01
	insTime	18.24	≤ 0.01	108.40	≤ 0.01
Interactions					
	*Strategy*sat*	6.49	≤ 0.01	8.06	≤ 0.01
	*Strategy*jobSize*	0.66	0.94	2.15	≤ 0.01
	*Strategy*insTime*	5.86	≤ 0.01	14.83	≤ 0.01
	*sat*jobSize*	1.93	0.05	13.25	≤ 0.01
	*sat*insTime*	30.01	≤ 0.01	18.74	≤ 0.01
	*jobSize*insTime*	0.43	0.90	1.95	0.05
	R^2	0.71		0.83	

The statistical significance of the effects of problem parameters, match-up strategies, and the interactions among them on *Performance* and *Stability* was verified by means of the Analysis of Variance (ANOVA). ANOVA is a collection of models and procedures that allow for measurement of effects on a dependent variable (*Performance*, *Stability*) due to changes of one or more independent variables (Strategy, *sat, jobSize, insTime*) and their interactions. The summary of the ANOVA is given in Table 1, where the individual effects due to problem parameters and rescheduling strategy are labelled "main effects", whereas the combined effects of the possible pairs of variables are labelled "interactions". The $A * B$ notation refers to the interaction between parameters A and B. Values under the heading F value and P value are, the value of the Fisher statistic of the corresponding row effect, and the probability of this value being due to mere chance, respectively. Effects with a P value ≤ 0.05 are considered significant. The relatively large R^2 values for both metrics, *Performance* and *Stability*, is an indicator of the validity of the ANOVA test.

A pairwise comparison test (Bonferroni test, [15]) was carried out in order to identify those strategies that deliver higher *Performance* and *Stability* values. Results of the test are visually supported by the 95% confidence interval plots of Fig. 2(a), for *Performance*, and Fig. 2(b), for *Stability*. In each graph, the dot indicates the average value on the whole set of instances obtained by the corresponding strategy in the $x-$axis. The vertical lines denote the 95% confidence interval of the mean value. Statistical differences are immediately detected when there is no overlap between the confidence intervals of two or more strategies. Not surprisingly, the total rescheduling and right shift, deliver good values for *Performance* and *Stability*, respectively. This is achieved at the price of poor *Stability*, for the total-rescheduling strategy and poor *Performance* for right-shift. As the interval plots from Fig. 2 indicate, strategies S1-S4 are the most competent with respect to *Performance* and *Stability*, since they obtained the highest mean values. These results were confirmed by the adequate Bonferroni tests (details are not given here). The same figures and statistical tests also indicate that S1-S4 are statistically non distinguishable from the total-rescheduling

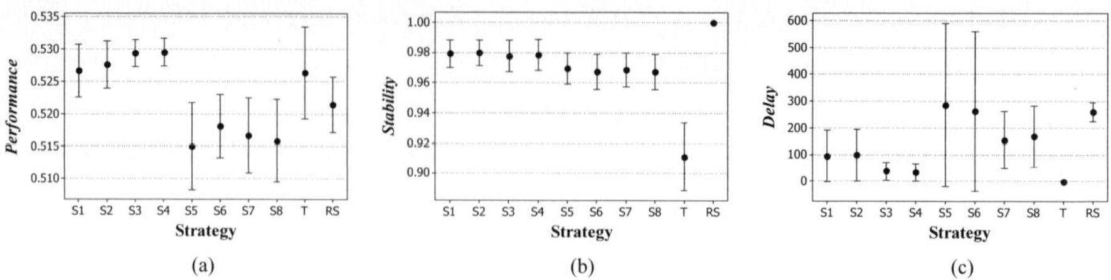

Fig. 2. Overall results obtained by each rescheduling strategy; in the x−axis, the strategy; in the y−axis the mean (dot) and 95% confidence interval (vertical bars) for *Performance* (a), *Stability* (b), and *Delay* (c)

strategy for *Performance* and from right-shift for *Stability*. Note that the latter always obtains, by definition a 100% stability. This result indicates that the newly introduced approaches, S1-S4, posses the best attributes of the two investigated extreme rescheduling approaches (total-rescheduling and right-shift), but do not exhibit their weaknesses.

Strategies S5-S8 obtain, overall, low *Performance* values. We have identified a significant correlation ($\rho = -0.42$) between *Performance* and the delay introduced after rescheduling. The *Delay* represents the time period of the overlap between the schedule within the identified time horizon for rescheduling and the initial schedule after it. This suggests that high delays caused by the rescheduling process are associated with low *Performance* values. This explains the low *Performance* values achieved by stratcgics S5-S8 which, as shown in Fig. 2(c), are the ones that lead to the largest *Delay* values. On the other hand, S3 and S4, which seem to be the best performers according to Fig. 2(a), cause the smallest delays.

Problem parameters *sat*, *jobSize* and *insTime*, have a significant influence on *Performance* and *Stability*. The nature of these effects can be observed in the 95% confidence interval plots in Fig. 3. The x−axis of each plot (a) and (d), (b) and (e), and (c) and (f), measures the level of *sat*, *jobSize* and *insTime*, respectively. The y−axis represent the average values of *Performance*, (a)-(c), and *Stability*, (d)-(f) over all rescheduling strategies (S1-S8, T and RS). The effect of these factors may be summarised as follows: in general, *Performance* and *Stability* values decrease when rescheduling is done on highly saturated schedules, rescheduling occurs at the beginning of the schedule, or when the inserted new job requires many operations.

The interactions between problem parameters and rescheduling strategies indicate what are the best approaches for a given problem type, i.e. for a certain combination of problem parameters. Given restrictions on paper length, we limit our discussion on this matter to mentioning that the relative ranks of the rescheduling strategies with respect to *Performance* and *Stability* values remain constant under different problem parameter combinations. Strategies S1-S4, for instance, do obtain the highest *Performance* and *Stability* values

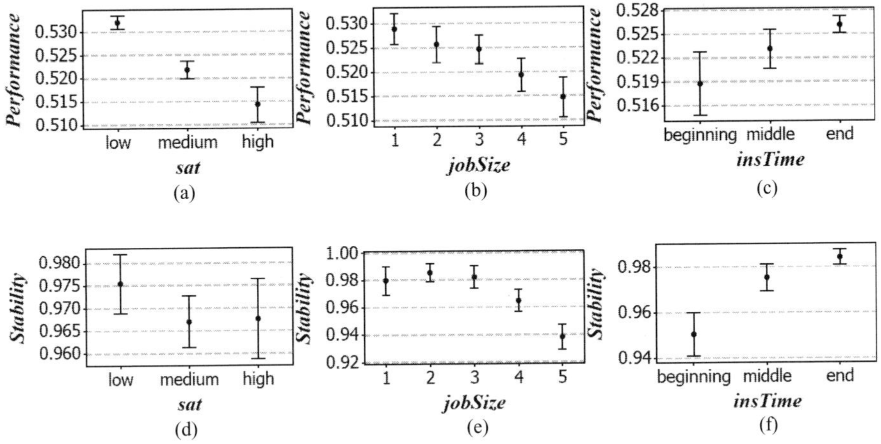

Fig. 3. Main average effects in *Performance* (a), (b), (c) and *Stability* (d), (e), (f) due to *sat*, *jobSize* and *insTime*, respectively

regardless of the problem parameters. Similarly, total-rescheduling and right-shift constantly obtain high *Performance* and low *Stability* values, and low *Performance* and high *Stability* values, respectively. Match-up strategies S1-S4 are, therefore, sensible approaches to the real world problems studied here.

5   Conclusion and Future Work

This paper investigates a real world job shop rescheduling problem from a printing company in Nottingham, UK. This problem is dynamic since new orders arrive every day and need to be integrated in the current schedule. A match-up algorithm, which accommodates new orders by using available idle times on machines, is proposed. The motivation of the match up algorithms is to modify only a part of the initial schedule in such a way that the stability and performance of the shop floor are kept. Several strategies to define rescheduling horizons were proposed and compared with basic strategies, including total rescheduling and the right-shift of operations. The obtained results were analysed and statistically validated. We conclude that the match-up approach provides a reasonable combination of stability and performance for the investigated real world job shop problem. It is as stable as the right shift method, and provides as good *Performance* values, as the total rescheduling approach.

Further work includes investigation of different additional types of disruptions on the shop floor such as order changes, new jobs arrivals that can be classified as non-rush orders, cancellation of jobs and rework required when the quality of a product is not satisfactory. In addition, the resources changes, such as machine breakdown and sickness of workers, will also be considered.

Acknowledgments. The authors acknowledge the support from the Engineering and Physics Science Research Council trough grant GR/R95319/01 and Sherwood Press Ltd, Nottingham, UK.

References

1. Vieira, G., Herrmann, J., Lin, E.: Rescheduling manufacturing systems: A framework of strategies, policies and methods. Journal of Scheduling 6(1), 39–62 (2003)
2. Aytug, H., Lawley, M., McKay, K., Mohan, S., Uzsoy, R.: Executing production schedules in the face of uncertainties: A review and some future directions. European Journal of Operational Research 161(1), 86–110 (2005)
3. Bean, J., Birge, J.: Match-up real-time scheduling. In: Proceedings of the Symposium on Real-Time Optimization in Automated Manufacturing Facilities, National Bureau of Standards, Special Publication 724, pp. 197–212 (1986)
4. Bean, J., Birge, J., Mittenthal, J., Noon, C.: Matchup scheduling with multiple resources, release dates and disruptions. Operations Research 39(3), 470–483 (1991)
5. Birge, J., Dempster, M.: Optimality conditions for match-up strategies in stochastic scheduling. Technical Report 92 - 58, Department of Industrial and Operations Engineering, The University of Michigan (1992)
6. Birge, J., Dempster, M.: Optimal match-up strategies in stochastic scheduling. Discrete Applied Mathematics 57(2-3), 105–120 (1995)
7. Akturk, M., Gorgulu, E.: Match-up scheduling under a machine breakdown. European Journal of Operational Research 112(1), 81–97 (1999)
8. Smith, S., Muscettola, N., Matthys, D., Ow, P., Potvin, J.: Opis: an opportunistic factory scheduling system. In: IEA/AIE 1990: Proceedings of the 3rd international conference on Industrial and engineering applications of artificial intelligence and expert systems, pp. 268–274. ACM Press, New York (1990)
9. Sadeh, N.: Micro-opportunistic scheduling: The micro-boss factory scheduler. In: Intelligent Scheduling, ch. 4, pp. 99–136. Morgan Kaufmann, San Francisco (1994)
10. Smith, S.: Reactive scheduling systems. In: Brown, D., Scherer, W. (eds.) Intelligent Scheduling Systems, Kluwer Academic Publishers, Dordrecht (1995)
11. Sun, J., Xue, D.: A dynamic reactive scheduling mechanism for responding to changes of production orders and manufacturing resources. Computers in Industry 46(2), 189–207 (2001)
12. Abumaizar, R., Svestka, J.: Rescheduling job shops under random disruptions. International Journal of Production Research 35(7), 2065–2082 (1997)
13. Wu, S., Storer, R., Chang, P.: One-machine rescheduling heuristics with efficiency and stability as criteria. Computers and Operations Research 20(1), 1–14 (1993)
14. Petrovic, S., Fayad, C., Petrovic, D., Burke, E., Kendall, G.: Fuzzy job shop scheduling with lot-sizing. Annals of Operations Research 159(1), 275–292 (2008)
15. Miller, R.: Simultaneous Statistical Inference. Springer, New York (1991)

Entropy Based Diversity Measures in Evolutionary Mobile Robot Navigation

Tomás Arredondo V., Wolfgang Freund, and César Muñoz

Universidad Técnica Federico Santa María, Valparaíso, Chile,
Departamento de Electrónica,
Casilla 110 V, Valparaíso, Chile
`tarredondo@elo.utfsm.cl`

Abstract. In this paper we analyze entropy based measures in various motivation and environmental configurations of mobile robot navigation in complex environments. These entropy based measures are used to probe and predict various environmental and robot configurations that can provide for the emergence of highly fit robotic behaviors. The robotic system uses a neural network to evaluate measurements from its sensors in order to establish its next behavior. Genetic algorithms, fuzzy based fitness and Action-based Environment Modeling (AEM) all take a part toward training the robot. The research performed shows the utility of using these entropy based measures toward providing the robot with good training conditions.

1 Introduction

A fundamental problem in robotics is navigation in unknown and unstructured environments. Extensive research has been made into this problem with the aid of various robotic architectures, sensors and processors. Behavior based robotics is an approach that in general does not consider the use of world models or complex symbolic knowledge. This design philosophy promotes the idea that robots should be low cost, built incrementally, capable of withstanding sensor and other noise, and without complex computers and communication systems. Behavior based learning systems typically include reinforcement learning, neural networks, genetic algorithms, fuzzy systems, case and memory based learning [1]. These biologically based mechanisms are capable novel complex behaviors which avoid local minima and have the ability to extrapolate from training information.

Recent research in behavior based robotics has focused on providing more natural and intuitive interfaces between robots and people [2,3]. One such interface decouples specific robot behavior using an intuitive interface based on biological motivations (e.g. curiosity, hunger, etc) [4,5].

It is well known that having diversity during training can provide for the emergence of more robust systems which are capable of coping with a variety of environmental challenges [6,7]. Early studies have shown that information theory can be used as an aid in analyzing robotic training performance [4]. Performing

N.T. Nguyen et al. (Eds.): IEA/AIE 2008, LNAI 5027, pp. 129–138, 2008.

a more extensive quantitative analysis of training diversity using such information theoretic based measures was something of interest to us. Toward this goal we investigate the capability of entropy based environmental and motivation diversity measures toward analyzing the outcome of several robotic navigation experiments.

In our work, robot navigation is performed in a simulator [8] by providing sensor values directly into a neural network that drives left and right motors. The robot uses infrared sensors which give limited information about the surroundings in which the robot is located. Action-based environmental modeling (AEM) is implemented with a small action set of four basic actions (e.g. go straight, turn left, turn right, turn around) in order to encode a sequence of actions based on sensor values. The search space of behaviors is huge and designing suitable behaviors by hand is very difficult [9] therefore we use a genetic algorithm (GA) within the simulator in order to find appropriate behaviors. The GA selects from a population of robots (neural networks) using a fuzzy fitness function that considers various robotic motivations such as: the need for exploration (curiosity), the need to conserve its battery (energy), the desire to determine its location (orientation), and the capacity to return to its initial position (homing).

This paper is organized as follows. Section 2 gives a description of the robotic system. Section 3 describes the entropy measures used for diversity evaluation. Section 4 introduces the experiments performed. In section 5 we describe and summarize our results. Finally, in section 6 some conclusions are drawn.

2 Robotics System Description

This section presents the robotic system used for these studies. The system has several different elements including: the robot simulator, action based environmental modeling, neural networks, GA, and fuzzy logic based fitness.

2.1 Robot Configuration

Our project uses a small simple robot which has two DC motors and eight (six front and two back) infrared proximity sensors used to detect nearby obstacles. These sensors provide 10 bit output values (with 6% random noise). These readings allow the robot to know in approximate form the distance to local obstacles. The simulator provides the readings for the robot sensors according to the robot position and the map (room) it is in. The simulator also has information for the different areas that the robot visits and the various obstacles detected in the room.

The robot internally generates a zone map in which the zones are marked with various values: obstacles are indicated with a value of -1, those not visited by the robot are marked with a 0 and the visited ones with a 1. During navigation, the robot executes 500 steps in each experiment, but not every step produces forward motion as some only rotate the robot. The robot is not constrained by its battery given that a 100% charge level allows more than 1000 steps.

2.2 Artificial Neural Network

The robot uses a neural network of the feed forward type with eight input neurons (one per sensor), five neurons in the hidden layer and two output neurons directly connected to the motors that produce the robot movement.

2.3 Action-Based Environmental Modeling

In order to reduce behavior search space, we use AEM based encoding to select the basic actions used by the robot to perform navigation:

- A1: Go 55 mm straight on.
- A2: Turn 30°left.
- A3: Turn 30°right.
- A4: Turn 180°right.

In AEM, a SOM [10] network is used by the robot to determine the room he is navigating in (localization). Robot navigation produces actions which are saved as action sequences. These action sequences are converted using chain coding into an environment vector. These vectors are fed into the SOM network for unsupervised learning. After training the SOM network associates a vector with one of its output nodes (r-nodes)[9]. We used inputs of 1000 steps for all rooms used in training, these were alternatingly presented to the SOM network for 10000 iterations, the network had a linear output layer of 128 r-nodes indicating the maximum possible number of rooms that could be identified.

2.4 Genetic Algorithm

A GA is used to find an optimal configuration of weights for the neural network. Each individual in the GA represents a neural network which is evolving with the passing of different generations. The GA uses the following parameters:

- Population size: 200.
- Crossover operator: Random crossover.
- Selection method: Elite strategy selection.
- Mutation rate P_{mut}: 1%.
- Generations: 90.

2.5 Fuzzy Fitness Calculation

Fuzzy logic (Fig.1) is used toward implementing a motivation based interface for determining robotic fitness. The motivation set (M) considered in this study includes: homing (m_1), curiosity (m_2), energy (m_3), and orientation (m_4). These motivations are used as input settings (between 0 and 1) prior to running each experiment [4].

The set of fitness criteria and the fuzzy variables that correspond to them are: proper action termination and escape from original neighborhood area (f_1), amount of area explored (f_2), percent of battery usage (f_3) and environment recognition (f_4). The values for these criteria are normalized (range from 0 to 1) and are calculated after the robot completes each run:

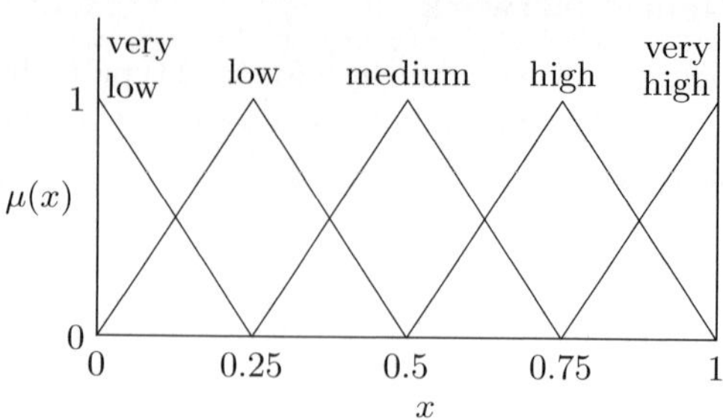

Fig. 1. Fuzzy membership functions

- f_1: a normalized final distance to home
- f_2: percentage area explored relative to the optimum
- f_3: estimated percent total energy consumption considering all steps taken
- f_4: determined by having the robot establish which room he is in (r-node versus the correct one), using the previously trained SOM network.

Four fuzzy variables with five triangular membership functions each are used ($4^5 = 1024$ different fuzzy rules) toward calculating robotic fitness. The membership functions used are given in Fig. 1. Sample fuzzy rules (numbers 9 and 10) are given as follows (here the K array is a simple increasing linear function):

if (f_1 == H) and (f_2 == L) and (f_3 == V.L.) and (f_4 == V.L.) then
$\quad$ f[9] = $m_1 f_1 K[4] + m_2 f_2 K[2] + m_3 f_3 K[1] + m_4 f_4 K[1]$
if (f_1 == V.H.) and (f_2 == L) and (f_3 == V.L.) and (f_4 == V.L.) then
$\quad$ f[10] = $m_1 f_1 K[5] + m_2 f_2 K[2] + m_3 f_3 K[1] + m_4 f_4 K[1]$

During training, a run environment (room) is selected and the *GA* initial robot population is randomly initialized. After this, each robot in the population performs its task (navigation and optionally environment recognition) and a set of fitness values corresponding to the performed task are obtained. Finally, robotic fitness is calculated using the fitness criteria information provided by the simulator and the different motivations at the time of exploration.

3   Entropy Measures

Entropy measures are used to measure environmental and motivation diversity [4]. These measures of diversity come from the well established definition of entropy as a measure of the uncertainty (which generates a diversity of outcomes) in a system [11,12].

3.1   Environmental Entropy

Environmental entropy is calculated using an extension of the local image entropy method [4]. In this method an estimation of the information content of

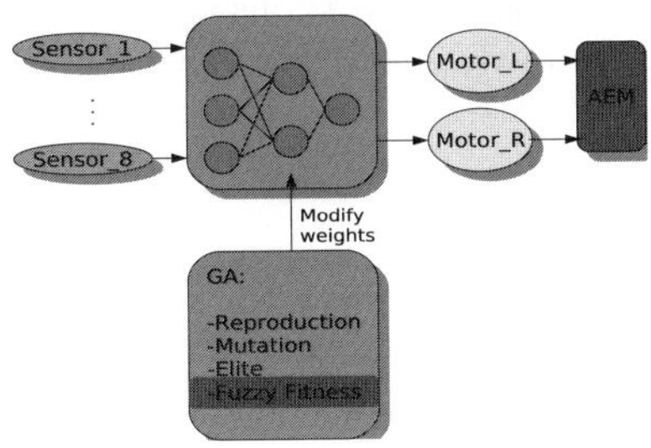

Fig. 2. System Overview

a pixel (x, y) based on a histogram of its neighborhood (w, h) pixel values is calculated as:

$$E_{w,h}(x, y) = -\sum_k p_{w,h}(k) \log p_{w,h}(k).$$

A region of an image (e.g. neighborhood) is interpreted as a signal of k different states with the local entropy $E_{w,h}(x, y)$ determining the observer's uncertainty about the signal [13].

To obtain a measure of an environments diversity (using a neighborhood window as given by w and h), we compute the average local image entropy for the room. Here the size of w and h are set using an uncertainty criteria of interest given the scale of the robot and obstacles in its path (e.g. a robots uncertainty of crossing a zone). In our current experiments we study this diversity measure to find neighborhood width and height settings which are successful in helping us predict better training environments.

Clearly if a neighborhood is empty or full the robot will have either no difficulty or no chance of traversing the terrain and hence the uncertainty for that neighborhood will be zero but if the neighborhood has some obstacles then its maximum uncertainty should be when $E_{w,h}(x, y) = 0.5$.

Obstacles were chosen at least as large as the robot size so as to preclude small checkered patterns which could also result in a local entropy value near 0.5 but would not make any sense in terms of our definition of traversing uncertainty (the robot clearly could not cross such a neighborhood).

3.2 Motivation Entropy

In order to calculate motivation entropy we first define a motivation set M as $\{m_1, m_2, \ldots, m_n\}$. Toward the calculation of motivation diversity $H(M)$, we consider the corresponding probabilities for $\{m_1, m_2, \ldots, m_n\}$ as $\{p_1, p_2, \ldots, p_n\}$. We compute the entropy of the random variable M using:

$$H(M) = -\sum_{i=1}^{n} p_i \log(p_i), \ where \ \sum_{i=1}^{n} p_i = 1.$$

Note that when $H(M) = 0$ the motivations are considered to have no diversity and for $n = 4$ the maximum diversity is when $M=\{0.25, 0.25, 0.25, 0.25\}$ and $H(M) = 2$.

4 Experimental Evaluation

Of interest to us was to study the impact of the entropy based diversity measures and their capability toward predicting a robot's ability to learn behaviors based on environmental and motivation diversity. Our results are verified based on an empirical model using multiple complete test runs given random motor and sensor noise.

All experiments had a training phase, in order to obtain the best weights for the NN, followed by a testing phase. The GA settings used in the training phase are given in section 2.4. The number of steps in each iteration was set to 1000 for the training phase, and 500 for the testing phase. The robot radius was 68.75 mm with a forward step size of 55 mm. The rooms are square (sides of 2750 mm) with various internal configurations of walls and obstacles. For mapping purposes rooms are divided into 2500 zones (each 55 mm by 55 mm).

Toward studying the diversity measures, we tested training in 15 different square rooms: r_1 - r_{15}. These rooms have an increasing number of obstacles in a fairly random distribution with the condition that any one obstacle should not preclude the robot from reaching any area of the room. Room r_1 has no obstacles, r_2 has only obstacle 1, r_3 has obstacle 1 (in the same place as in r_2) plus obstacle 2, and so on until r_{15} which contains obstacles 1 - 14. A room layout with the position of the obstacles (identified by its number) is shown in Fig. 3.

4.1 First Experiment: Environmental Diversity Measure

In order to analyze the sensitivity of the environmental diversity metric we first computed the average local image entropy of each room given different square window sizes (given as w or h). Fig.4 shows the average local entropy of each room given a range of window sizes from 10 to 250.

To evaluate the impact of environmental training diversity over the robots navigation behavior, we trained the robot in each room for 90 generations.

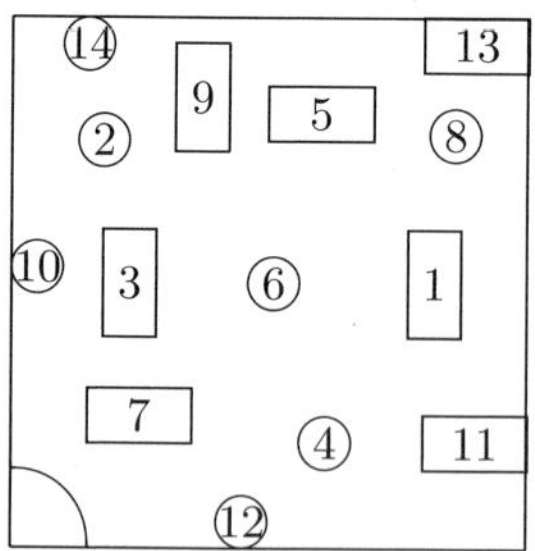

Fig. 3. Experiment 1 room layout (r_1-r_{15})

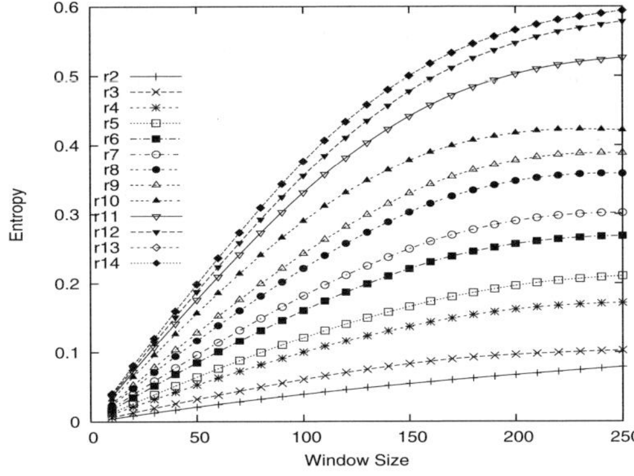

Fig. 4. Average local entropy for all rooms

We set the fuzzy motivations (m_1, m_2, m_3, m_4) as $(0, 1, 0, 0)$. After the training phase, the best individual from the GA population was selected to run its respective testing phase in rooms $r_1 - r_{10}$. During testing, rooms $r_{11} - r_{15}$ produced low fitness in all experiments, because of this small contribution we discarded these results from our analysis. A window size of 100 was used after analyzing window size results in Fig.4 and considering that the window size should correspond to the robot having close to a maximum traversal uncertainty when $E_{w,h}(x, y) = 0.5$.

4.2   Second Experiment: Motivation Diversity Measure

For this experiment, in order to see the effect of motivation diversity, we used 66 sets of fuzzy motivation criteria. Motivations (M) ranged from highly focused to more diverse. Average fitness values are given for motivations (m_1, m_2, m_3) ranging from $(0, 1, 0)$ to $(0.4, 0.3, 0.3)$ with values changing in increments of 0.1.

The population was trained for 90 generations in each of the rooms. During testing the best individual of the 90 generations was tested in all rooms and average fuzzy fitness values were calculated using the various fitness values $f_1 - f_3$.

5   Experimental Results

Ten complete runs were performed of each experiment (each run consisting of one training and 10 test executions) and only average values are reported in our results. Only ten runs are used given that obtained tests results were similar between runs.

5.1   First Experiment: Environmental Diversity

In Fig.5 we show the results of the testing phase after applying the respective training method specified for the environmental diversity experiment.

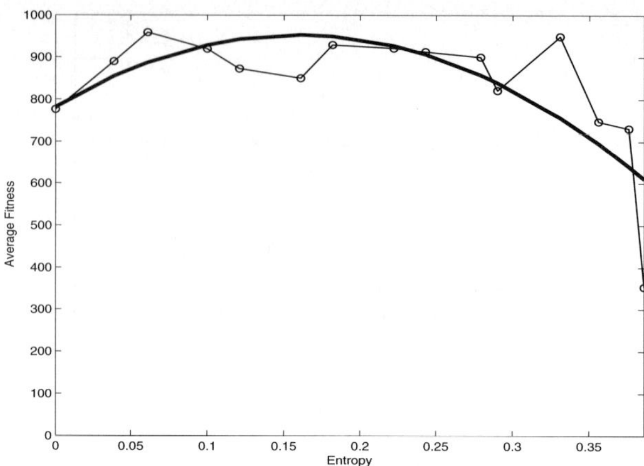

Fig. 5. Learning behavior given training rooms entropy

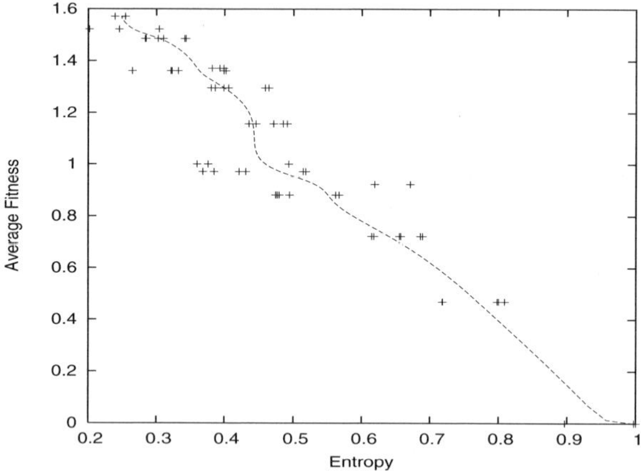

Fig. 6. Learning behavior given motivation diversity

5.2   Second Experiment: Motivation Diversity

In Fig.6 we show the results of the testing phase after applying the respective training method specified for the motivation diversity experiment.

6   Discussion

Average local image entropy can be seen as an effective measure of a training environments potential toward producing highly fit robots. As seen in Fig.4 the measure is sensitive to different window values but in our application a wide range of values could have been used. Our selection of neighborhood size was a reasonable as only very low values (around 10) show poor discriminancy.

Fig. 5 shows how the average fitness obtained during testing is clearly dependent on the diversity of the training room used. A training environment with too much environmental diversity is as unsuitable as one with not enough diversity.

Higher motivation diversity ($H(M)$) caused lower average score values. This is possibly due to the different and conflicting (e.g. orthogonal) requirements of the different motivations upon a small robotic *brain*. Even though obtained fitness was generally lower with more diverse motivations, the obtained behaviors (not shown due to space limitations) demonstrated very good capability (e.g. room exploration, battery usage, etc) and were in agreement with the specified motivations. Motivation diversity results are somewhat counter intuitive in that by diversifying motivation values one could naively expect higher overall fitness but this is clearly not the case due to system constraints.

7 Conclusions

Our entropy based measures are useful toward providing some understanding of complex systems such as robotic training environments. As seen by our test results, the average local image entropy measure is not very sensitive to differences in window size. The average local entropy measure also shows promise as an image diversity metric with potential usage in signal processing and pattern recognition. Fuzzy motivations are confirmed as an intuitive and user friendly mechanism for obtaining a wide range of different robotic behaviors. Using these entropy based measures it was possible to evaluate the effect of diversity on robotic fitness.

Future work includes hardware implementation and testing of these methods, utilizing fuzzy motivations within hybrid architectures, including environment recognition in motivation studies, parametric studies (e.g. linkages between motivations, testing different groups of GA parameters), add more actions to the robot and potential application in other areas of research.

Acknowledgements

This research was partially funded by the DGIP of UTFSM (230726).

References

1. Arkin, R.: Behavior-Based Robotics. MIT Press, Cambridge (1998)
2. Park, H., Kim, E., Kim, H.: Robot Competition Using Gesture Based Interface. In: Hromkovič, J., Nagl, M., Westfechtel, B. (eds.) WG 2004. LNCS, vol. 3353, pp. 131–133. Springer, Heidelberg (2004)
3. Jensen, B., Tomatis, N., Mayor, L., Drygajlo, A., Siegwart, R.: Robots Meet Humans - Interacion in Public Spaces. IEEE Transactions on Industrial Electronics 52(6), 1530–1546 (2006)

 4. Arredondo, T., Freund, W., Muñoz, C., Navarro, N., Quirós, F.: Learning Performance in Evolutionary Behavior Based Mobile Robot Navigation. In: Mery, D., Rueda, L. (eds.) PSIVT 2007. LNCS, vol. 4872, pp. 811–820. Springer, Heidelberg (2007)
 5. Huitt, W.: Motivation to learn: An overview. Educational Psychology Interactive (2001), http://chiron.valdosta.edu/whuitt/col/motivation/motivate.html
 6. Tan, K.C., Goh, C.K., Yang, Y.J., Lee, T.H.: Evolving better population distribution and exploration in evolutionary multi-objective optimization. European Journal of Operations Research 171, 463–495 (2006)
 7. Chalmers, D.J.: The evolution of learning: An experiment in genetic connectionism. In: Proceedings of the 1990 Connectionist Models Summer School, pp. 81–90. Morgan Kaufmann, San Mateo (1990)
 8. YAKS simulator website: http://www.his.se/iki/yaks
 9. Yamada, S.: Recognizing environments from action sequences using self-organizing maps. Applied Soft Computing 4, 35–47 (2004)
10. Teuvo, K.: The self-organizing map. Proceedings of the IEEE 79(9), 1464–1480 (1990)
11. Cover, T., Thomas, J.: Elements of Information Theory. Wiley, New York (1991)
12. Neelakanta, P.S.: Information-Theoretic Aspects of Neural Networks. CRC Press, Boca Raton (1999)
13. Handmann, U., Kalinke, T., Tzomakas, C., Werner, M., Weelen, W.v.: An image processing system for driver assistance. Image and Vision Computing 18, 367–376 (2000)

Intelligent System for Traffic Signs Recognition in Moving Vehicles

Bogusław Cyganek

AGH - University of Science and Technology
Al. Mickiewicza 30, 30-059 Kraków, Poland
`cyganek@uci.agh.edu.pl`

Abstract. Recognition of traffic signs by systems of the intelligent vehicles can increase safety and comfort of driving. It can be also used for highway inspection. In this paper we present architecture of such a system, with special focus on fast sign tracking method. In each frame an adaptive window is built around each area with high probability of existence of an object to be tracked. However, contrary to the mean-shift algorithm, it is not necessary to compute a centroid for each such object. Thus the method allows faster execution which is a key parameter for the real-time scene analysis.

1 Introduction

Automatic recognition of the traffic signs (TS) by systems of intelligent vehicles can help increase safety and comfort of driving. Such systems can be also used for highway maintenance activities. Known examples are systems developed by Daimler-Chrysler [9] or Siemens [16], for instance.

However, automatic recognition of TS is not a trivial task. There are many problems to be solved, such as operational conditions affecting the acquisition system (vibrations, dirt, harsh weather conditions, etc.), as well as insufficient computational resources at high demands on performance (response time, recognition quality).

In this paper we present the basic architecture and functionality of an intelligent system for TSs recognition in real-time. Details of its building modules can be found in publications [3-8]. We focus mainly on the cooperation of the different modules of the system, as well as on a tracking method, which is simple in implementation and fast in execution.

The works [3-14] and cited there references report many TS detection and/or classification systems. However, to the best of our knowledge publications on real-time tracking of TS are very scarce. A single TS detection and tracking system was reported by Fang et al. [11]. They propose a neural network system for detection of places with colour and shape characteristic to the TSs. Then, a fuzzy method is used for feature integration snd detection. Detected objects are tracked in the incoming frames with help on the Kalman filter. However, the system is tuned to detect only shapes of a certain size. Also the applied neural networks are tuned to detect only non distorted shapes. The system presented in this paper overcomes these difficulties.

N.T. Nguyen et al. (Eds.): IEA/AIE 2008, LNAI 5027, pp. 139–148, 2008.
© Springer-Verlag Berlin Heidelberg 2008

2 Architecture of the Road-Sign Recognition System

Fig. 1 presents architecture of the system for recognition of TSs. It consists of the four modules: the image acquisition, detection-tracking, registration and recognition. The acquisition module provides input images and (optionally) depth information.

Recognition usually consists of two separate steps: sign detection and then pictogram classification. The tracking module determines the main group to which a test object can belongs to. The second classifies a sign within its group. Two different methods has been devised for detection of the oval shape TSs ("B" - prohibition,

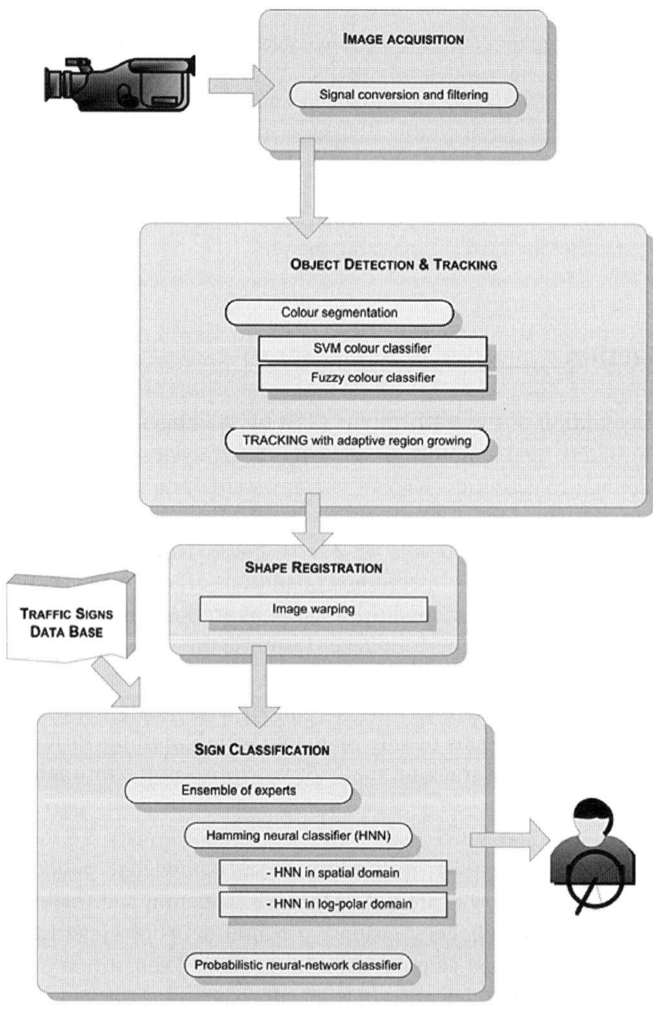

Fig. 1. Architecture of the traffic sign recognition system. There are four modules: image acquisition, object detection & tracking, shape registration, and classification.

Fig. 2. Timings analysis of the TS recognition process in intelligent Driving Assisting Systems

"C" - obligation), and all others [3-5]. However, a further improvement was attained after employment of the TSs tracking module, which is described in the next section.

A timing analysis allows assessment of the run-time system requirements (Fig. 2):

$$t_3 = \frac{s_1 - s_2}{v}, \text{ and } s_2 = t_{2_{min}} v,$$

(1)

where s_1 is a distance from which a sign is spotted by an image acquisition module, s_2 is a distance which will be passed by a vehicle during computation of the TSs recognition system, finally v is an average vehicle speed. The latter is assumed not to change very rapidly during the computation time. However, the most important factor is denoted by t_{2min}. This is a minimal allowable period of time from the moment of the system response to the moment of reaching a sign. Thus, it is a time left to a driver for reaction. For instance, if there is a STOP sign ahead, then a driver is assumed to bring his/her car into a stop position no further than a line of that sign. From the above we obtain that the computation time has to fulfil the following condition:

$$t_3 = \frac{s_1}{v} - t_{2_{min}}.$$

(2)

Table 1 contains some values for t_3 for two values of t_{2min}: 2s and 4s, respectively.

Table 1. Assessment of the max. computation time in respect to the sign acquisition distance s_1 and time left for reaction of a driver which is min. 2s or comfortable 4s (in parenthesis).

s_1 \ v	60 km/h	100 km/h	120 km/h
60 m	1.6 (-)	0.2 (-)	(-)
80 m	2.8 (0.8)	0.9 (-)	0.4 (-)
100 m	4 (2)	**1.6** (-)	1 (-)
120 m	5.2 (3.2)	**2.3** (0.3)	**1.6** (-)

It is evident that even with a very precise acquisition system which would be able to detect signs from a distance of 120 m or further, time left for reaction of the system is about 1.6s, which leaves only 2s for a driver for reaction. Thus, the run-time requirements on the system are very tight.

3 Traffic Signs Tracking

Traffic signs are characteristic of specific and well visible colours and shapes. These supply sufficient cues for detection and tracking. However, in real situations both colours and shape undergo great variations due to different factors such as projective distortions, occlusions, as well as colour variations due to aging, weather, camera characteristics, noise, etc. (see Fig. 7, for instance). There is also a trade off between accuracy and speed. Thus, high demands on the detection module.

Our observations and experiments led us to the conclusion that properly acquired colour information alone is sufficient for fast and acceptably accurate sign detection. Therefore colour segmentation constitutes a first stage of our detection module. In this respect three methods has been tested: The simple thresholding in the HSI space [5], the fuzzy segmentation [7], and the SVM classifiers in the one-class mode operating in the RGB space [3]. The former can be characterized by fastest execution and the simplest implementation. The latter shows more precise segmentation due to well known generalization abilities of the SVM. However, this is achieved at a cost of about 20% longer execution time and higher implementation complexity.

The commonly known mean shift tracking procedure climbs the estimated density gradient by recursive computation of the mean shift vector and translation of the centre of a mean shift kernel G. Thus, the locations of the kernel G are changed at each iteration step by a mean shift vector $\mathbf{m}$, forming a sequence $\{y_t\}$, as follows [0]:

$$\mathbf{m}_{(\delta,G)}\left(\mathbf{y}_t\right) = \mathbf{y}_{t+1} - \mathbf{y}_t = \sum_{j=1}^{M} \mathbf{x}_j g\left(\left\|\tfrac{\mathbf{y}_t - \mathbf{x}_j}{\delta}\right\|^2\right)\left[\sum_{j=1}^{M} g\left(\left\|\tfrac{\mathbf{y}_t - \mathbf{x}_j}{\delta}\right\|^2\right)\right]^{-1} - \mathbf{y}_t, \text{ for } t=1,2,\ldots, \tag{3}$$

where $\mathbf{m}_{(\delta,G)}(\mathbf{y}_t)$ denotes the mean shift vector for the kernel G, which is related to the profile g. Thus, the basic operation of the mean shift method is as follows:

1. Computation of the mean shift vector $\mathbf{m}$.
2. Shift of the kernel G by the mean shift vector $\mathbf{m}$.

It was proved by the mean shift procedure is convergent iff the kernel K has a convex and monotonically decreasing profile [2].

A modification to the above was proposed by Bradski in his CamShift method [0]. At each iteration and in a region R of an image the method assumes computation the statistical moments of the probability density. These are then used to position the region around a new centroid C of a "mass", which in effect moves that region toward the mode of the probability distribution p. Thus, in each iteration we have to compute

$$C = \left(\bar{x}, \bar{y}\right) = \left(\tfrac{m_{10}}{m_{00}}, \tfrac{m_{01}}{m_{00}}\right), \text{ where } m_{ab}\left(R\right) = \sum_{(x,y)\in R} x^a y^b p\left(x, y\right) \tag{4}$$

However, both formulations suffer from computational burden when considering a real-time implementation of the system. Therefore we propose a similar method which avoids iterative computation of the density kernel (3), as well as computation of the statistical moments (4). The main idea is to expand a rectangular window W in all eight direction around a place with high probability of existence of an object (see Fig. 3). Moreover, we do not assume that the tracked signal follows assumptions of the probability field. The only one requirement is that the tracked region is described by a nonnegative "mass" function μ for which we assume that the higher its value, the strongest belief that a pixel belongs to an object. Thus, μ follows rather rules of a fuzzy membership function, although it can be a probability field as well. Hence, the versatility of the method.

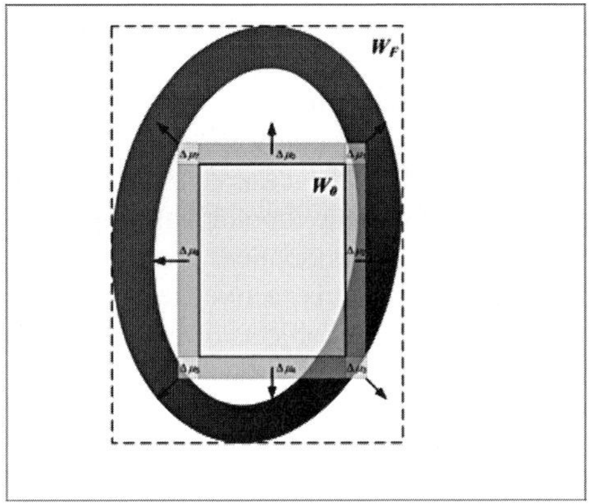

Fig. 3. Region growing technique for fast tracking – an initial window grows in all eight directions until a stopping criteria are reached (a)

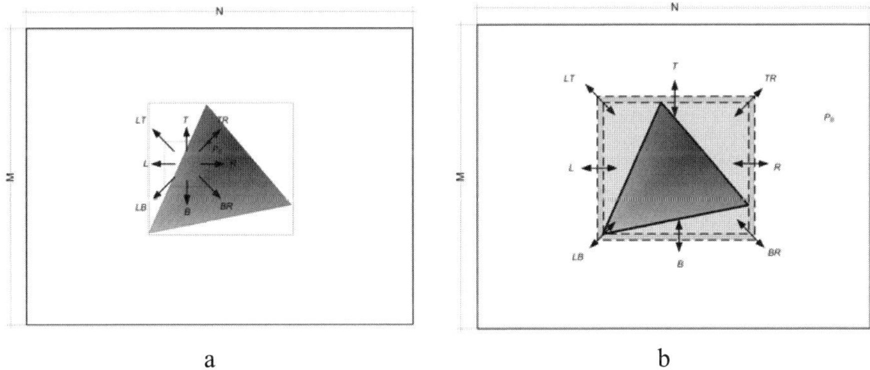

a   b

Fig. 4. Initial detection follows adaptive window growing (a). During tracking window can be inflated or deflated to follow actual position of the tracked object (b). If deflated below a minimal size then object is assumed to be lost.

Expansion in a given direction is possible iff there is a nonnegative increase in density of a new region. This is computed as a ratio of an object "mass" function divided by a number of pixels in a growing pane. In effect, starting from an initial size W_0 a final W_F is reached which encompasses tightly an object. In practice it is sufficient to set a minimal thresholds on a "mass" update in all direction of expansion to avoid division. That is a stop criteria in a direction k is expressed as follows:

$$\Delta\mu_k < \tau_k \, . \tag{5}$$

where denotes a threshold value τ_k. In our experiments in which μ was a fuzzy membership function conveying degree of a match of colour τ_k was in order of *0.1-10*.

The algorithm is guaranteed to stop either when condition (5) are reached in all directions or when borders of an image are touched. The last aspect concerns a chosen expansion step. Usually the expansion in each direction is done by one pixel at a time. This guarantees detection of compact objects. During tracking window can be inflated or deflated to follow actual position of the tracked object (Fig. 4). If deflated below a minimal size then object is assumed to be lost.

The problem gets complicated in the case of multi object tracking. In such an instance we need to take into account the topological properties of the tracked objects and their positions (Fig. 5). An image is divided into a number of tiles. With each tile a bit is associated. If it is set then a tile is 'active' for subsequent tracking procedure. Otherwise it is either not containing any objects or is already occupied.

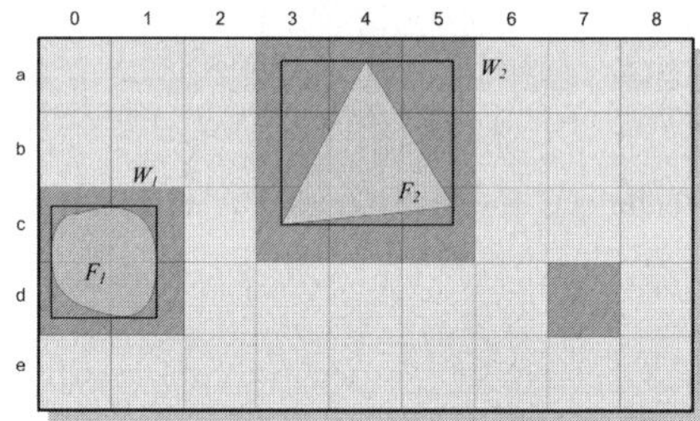

Fig. 5. Data structure for detection of multiple objects in a frame

Initially the bits for tiles are set in accordance with the membership functions μ computed for the whole image: If in a tile there is one or more pixels for which $\mu>0$, then such a tile is set as 'active'. For instance, objects F_1 and F_2 in Fig. 5, make the underlying tiles to be set as 'inactive', so the next run can find only new object in all tiles but those occupied for F_1 and F_2, respectively.

4   Experimental Results

The experimental system was installed in the Chrysler Voyager car. It is depicted in Fig. 6. It contains two Marlin C33 cameras on an adjustable tripod connected by the two IEEE 1394 links to the computer. Software was written in C++.

Fig. 7 presents tracking results obtained by our system. Depicted are three frames (Fig. 7a-c) from a video of a real traffic scene with tracking results (outlined) of a single sign B-36). Fig. 7d-f depict 2D fields of the membership functions μ denoting a degree of membership to a set of sign colours statistically gathered from real examples.

The system is able to process 640×480 colour frames in real time, i.e. at least 30 f/s. It is also resistant to noise and lighting variations due to noise suppression strategy in the construction of the membership functions.

Fig. 6. The experimental road signs recognition system installed in the car

Fig. 7. Results of a prohibitive sign traffic at rainy conditions. Original frames from the input 320x240 video (abc). Maps of fuzzy membership functions which are tracked (def). Detected and tracked signs (ghi).

Tracking of the warning sign A-17 is presented in Fig. 8. The colour images were acquired in rainy conditions. Maps of the fuzzy membership functions are visualized in Fig. 8def. Finally, detected and tracked sign by the adaptive window technique is depicted in Fig. 8ghi. However, some misalignments are visible which are due to non perfect segmentation of the input images. To cope with this phenomenon the classification module was designed to tolerate small deformations [3][8].

In the same way the system recognizes other groups of signs [8]. An average execution time of the pure software implementation of the system, and for 320×240 colour images, is ~0.2s per sign.

Fig. 8. Tracking of the warning sign A-17, school area, rainy conditions. Consecutive frames of a video frame (abc). Maps of the fuzzy membership functions (def). Detected and tracked sign with the adaptive window technique (ghi).

Fig. 9 presents recognition process of the B-2 traffic sign. The fuzzy membership map denoting colour distribution is visible in Fig. 9b, detected shapes in Fig. 9c. The data base of the most important prohibition signs used in this experiment is presented in Fig. 9d. Cropped object is visible in Fig. 9e, whereas the classified object from the data base is depicted in Fig. 9f.

System qualitative parameters were measured in terms of Precision (P) vs. Recall (R) factors. Results of these measurements are presented in Table 2 for compound system of neural classifiers [8].

The values of the recall parameter are affected mostly by performance of the detectors and in the lower degree by the classifiers. However, the parameters depend on specific settings as well as type and quality of the input images. Only results for

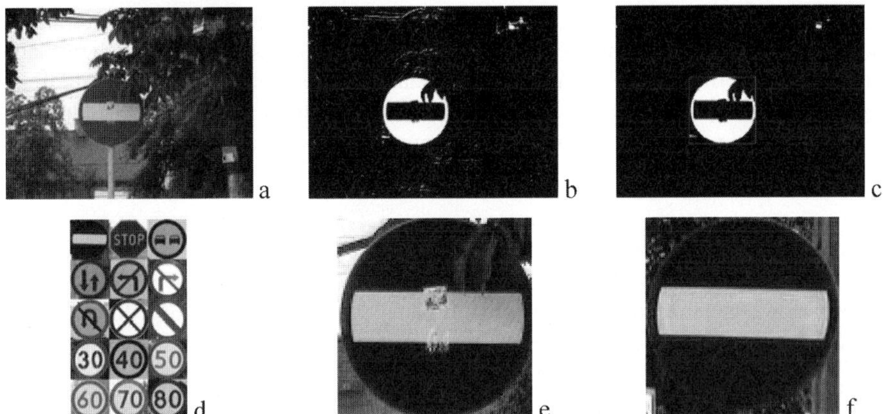

Fig. 9. Recognition of the B-2 traffic sign. Original image (a), the fuzzy membership map denoting colour distribution (b), detected object (c), data base of the most important prohibition signs used in this experiment. Detected object (e), classified object from the data base (f).

Table 2. Accuracy of recognition for different groups of signs: warning "A", prohibition "B", obligation "C", and information "D", daily conditions. Precision (P) versus recall (R). Used configuration of soft committee classifiers described in [8].

Group	Warning		Prohibition		Obligation		Information	
	P	R	P	R	P	R	P	R
	0.89	0.90	0.96	0.90	0.97	0.94	0.92	0.88

daily conditions are provided. Under night or worse weather conditions the recall parameter falls down due to segmentation method which relies on samples acquired in day light conditions. This is a subject of our further research.

5   Conclusions

The paper presents an intelligent system applied to the task of traffic signs recognition. Although designed for Polish conditions, it can be easily used in other conditions. The main assumptions are accuracy, fast execution, and easy maintenance. Therefore the system was designed to recognize signs based on prototypes provided from a formal specification or a limited number of real examples. Detection is based on colour information obtained from statistically significant amount of colour samples from real traffic objects. Nevertheless, further extensions of the method assume employment of the shape detection to facilitate detection.

Significant improvement to the detection was achieved with the novel tracking method which is based on the adaptive window growing technique. Its advantage is operation with any nonnegative map defining objects. For this purpose the probability fields or fuzzy measures can be used. The tracking module supplies enough information for a reliable detection of successive objects in the input video stream.

Sign classification is based on their pictograms. For this purpose a committee machine was designed with two groups of soft classifiers operating on deformable models of the prototypes [8]. Additionally, classification can done in the spatial and log-polar domains to cope with rotations [3]. The system shows high accuracy of recognition and real-time tracking with recognition speed of about up to five 320×240 colour frames per second in software implementation.

Acknowledgements

This work was supported from the Polish funds for scientific research in 2008.

References

1. Bradski, G.: Computer Vision Face Tracking For Use in a Perceptual User Interface. Intel Technical Report (1998)
2. Comaniciu, D., Meer, P.: Mean Shift: A Robust Approach Toward Feature Space Analysis. IEEE PAMI 24(5), 603–619 (2002)
3. Cyganek, B.: Circular Road Signs Recognition with Soft Classifiers. Integrated Computer-Aided Engineering 14(4), 323–343 (2007)
4. Cyganek, B.: Circular Road Signs Recognition with Affine Moment Invariants and the Probabilistic Neural Classifier. In: Beliczynski, B., Dzielinski, A., Iwanowski, M., Ribeiro, B. (eds.) ICANNGA 2007. LNCS, vol. 4432, pp. 508–516. Springer, Heidelberg (2007)
5. Cyganek, B.: Road Signs Recognition by the Scale-Space Template Matching in the Log-Polar Domain. In: Martí, J., Benedí, J.M., Mendonça, A.M., Serrat, J. (eds.) IbPRIA 2007. LNCS, vol. 4477, pp. 330–337. Springer, Heidelberg (2007)
6. Cyganek, B.: Real-Time Detection of the Triangular and Rectangular Shape Road Signs. In: Blanc-Talon, J., Philips, W., Popescu, D., Scheunders, P. (eds.) ACIVS 2007. LNCS, vol. 4678, pp. 744–755. Springer, Heidelberg (2007)
7. Cyganek, B.: Soft System for Road Sign Detection. Advances in Soft Computing 41, 316–326 (2007)
8. Cyganek, B.: Committee Machine for Road-Signs Classification. In: Rutkowski, L., Tadeusiewicz, R., Zadeh, L.A., Żurada, J.M. (eds.) ICAISC 2006. LNCS (LNAI), vol. 4029, pp. 583–592. Springer, Heidelberg (2006)
9. DaimlerChrysler, The Thinking Vehicle (2002), http://www.daimlerchrysler.com
10. Escalera de, A., Armingol, J.A.: Visual Sign Information Extraction and Identification by Deformable Models. IEEE Tr. On Int. Transportation Systems 5(2), 57–68 (2004)
11. Fang, C.-Y., Chen, S.-W., Fuh, C.-S.: Road-Sign Detection and Tracking. IEEE Transactions on Vehicular Technology 52(5), 1329–1341 (2003)
12. Gao, X.W., Podladchikova, L., Shaposhnikov, D., Hong, K., Shevtsova, N.: Recognition of traffic signs based on their colour and shape. J. Vis.Comm. & Image Repr. (2005)
13. Maldonado-Bascón, S., Lafuente-Arroyo, S., Gil-Jiménez, P., Gómez-Moreno, H., López-Ferreras, F.: Road-Sign Detection and Recognition Based on Support Vector Machines. IEEE Tr. on Intelligent Transportation Systems 8(2), 264–278 (2007)
14. Paclík, P., Novovičová, J., Duin, R.P.W.: Building road sign classifiers using a trainable similarity measure. IEEE Trans. on Int. Transportation Systems 7(3), 309–321 (2006)
15. Road Signs and Signalization. Directive of the Polish Ministry of Infrastructure, Internal Affairs and Administration (Dz. U. Nr 170, poz. 1393) (2002)
16. Siemens VDO (2007), http://usa.siemensvdo.com/topics/adas/traffic-sign-recognition/

Document Clustering Based on Spectral Clustering and Non-negative Matrix Factorization*

Lei Bao[1,2], Sheng Tang[2], Jintao Li[2], Yongdong Zhang[2], and Wei-ping Ye[1]

[1] Beijing Normal University, Beijing 100875, China
[2] Key Laboratory of Intelligent Information Processing, Institute of Computing Technology, Chinese Academy of Sciences, Beijing 100080, China
{baolei, ts, jtli, zhyd}@ict.ac.cn, bnuywp@yahoo.com

Abstract. In this paper, we propose a novel non-negative matrix factorization (NMF) to the affinity matrix for document clustering, which enforces non-negativity and orthogonality constraints simultaneously. With the help of orthogonality constraints, this NMF provides a solution to spectral clustering, which inherits the advantages of spectral clustering and presents a much more reasonable clustering interpretation than the previous NMF-based clustering methods. Furthermore, with the help of non-negativity constraints, the proposed method is also superior to traditional eigenvector-based spectral clustering, as it can inherit the benefits of NMF-based methods that the non-negative solution is institutive, from which the final clusters could be directly derived. As a result, the proposed method combines the advantages of spectral clustering and the NMF-based methods together, and hence outperforms both of them, which is demonstrated by experimental results on TDT2 and Reuters-21578 corpus.

Keywords: Document Clustering, Spectral Clustering, Non-negative Matrix Factorization.

1 Introduction

Document clustering is to divide a collection of documents into different clusters based on similarities of content. It has been widely used as a fundamental and effective tool for efficient organization, summarization, navigation and retrieval of large amount of documents, and attracted a lot of attention in recent years [1,2,3].

Spectral clustering, which doesn't make assumption on data distributions, is one of the most popular modern clustering algorithms. It represents document corpus as an undirected graph, and the task of clustering is transformed to find the best cuts of graph optimizing certain criterion functions, such as the ratio cut [4], average association [5], normalized cut [5] and min-max cut [6]. It can be proved that the top eigenvectors matrix of the graph affinity matrix, or a matrix derived from it, is the

* This research was supported by National Basic Research Program of China (973 Program, 2007CB311100), National High Technology and Research Development Program of China (863 Program, 2007AA01Z416), Beijing New Star Project on Science & Technology (2007B071).

N.T. Nguyen et al. (Eds.): IEA/AIE 2008, LNAI 5027, pp. 149–158, 2008.

solution to these optimization problems under relaxed conditions [7]. The rigorous mathematical derivation ensures that the eigenvectors matrix encodes the cluster information, which provides a reasonable clustering interpretation for the eigenvectors matrix. However, the real-valued eigenvectors matrix is not intuitive and doesn't directly correspond to individual clusters [2]. Consequently, traditional clustering methods in the real-valued matrix are necessary to get the final clusters.

Recently, document clustering based on non-negative matrix factorization (NMF) [8,9] has become popular for the intuitiveness of its non-negative solution. Xu et al. [2] proposed to represent each document as an additive combination of base topics, which are learned by NMF. Ding et al. [11] proposed an extension of NMF to the affinity matrix for clustering. The non-negative solutions provided by these NMF-based methods are much more intuitive than the real-valued ones, as the final clusters can be directly derived from these solutions. However, these methods lack a rigorous theoretical derivation to provide a reasonable clustering interpretation for their solutions and sometimes lead to unsatisfactory performances.

Based on the previous works, we propose a novel NMF to the affinity matrix for document clustering with non-negativity and orthogonality constraints simultaneously. With the help of additional orthogonality constraints, this NMF provides a non-negative solution to spectral clustering, which not only inherits the intuitiveness of the NMF-based methods, but also inherits the reasonable clustering interpretation of spectral clustering. Consequently, our method could combine the advantages of spectral clustering and NMF-based methods together, and outperform both of them.

2   A Brief Review

This section reviews spectral clustering and the previous NMF-based methods.

2.1   Spectral Clustering

Spectral clustering represents a document corpus $D = \{doc_1, doc_2, \cdots, doc_N\}$ as an undirected graph $G(V, E, W)$, where V, E, W denote the vertex set, the edge set, and the graph affinity matrix, respectively. Each vertex $v_i \in V$ represents a document doc_i, and each $edge(i, j) \in E$ is assigned an affinity score w_{ij} forming matrix W which reflects the similarity between doc_i and doc_j. The clustering task is consequently transformed to find the best cuts of the graph that optimize certain criterion functions. Here, we discuss two representative criterion functions: Average Association (AA) [5] and Normalized Cut (NC) [5]. The two criterion functions and their corresponding relaxed eigen-problems are summarized in Table 1, where $A_1, \cdots, A_K$ are the K disjoint sets (clusters) of V. $\overline{A}$ denotes the complement of $A \subset V$ and $|A|$ denotes the number of vertices in A. $cut(A, B)$ is the similarity between A and B calculated by $cut(A, B) = \sum_{i \in A, j \in B} w_{ij}$. $vol(A)$ is the weight of A calculated by $vol(A) = \sum_{i \in A} d_i$ where $d_i = \sum_{j=1}^{N} w_{ij}$. D is a diagonal matrix with $d_1, \cdots, d_N$ on the diagonal.

Table 1. Corresponding eigen-problems of AA and NC

Method	Average Association	Normalized Cut
Criterion Function	$\max\limits_{A_1,\cdots,A_K} \sum\limits_{i=1}^{K} \dfrac{cut(A_i,A_i)}{\lvert A_i\rvert}$	$\min\limits_{A_1,\cdots,A_K} \sum\limits_{i=1}^{K} \dfrac{cut(A_i,\overline{A_i})}{cut(A_i,V)}$
Indicator Matrix	$H \in \mathbb{R}^{N\times K}$ $h_{i,j} = \begin{cases} 1/\sqrt{\lvert A_j\rvert} & \text{if}\ \ i\in A_j \\ 0 & \text{otherwise} \end{cases}$	$H \in \mathbb{R}^{N\times K}$ $h_{i,j} = \begin{cases} 1/\sqrt{vol(A_j)} & \text{if}\ \ i\in A_j \\ 0 & \text{otherwise} \end{cases}$
Rewritten Problem	$\max\limits_{A_1,\cdots,A_K} Tr(H^TWH)$, s.t. $H^TH = I$ H defined as Indicator Matrix	$\max\limits_{A_1,\cdots,A_K} Tr(H^TWH)$, s.t. $H^TDH = I$ H defined as Indicator Matrix
Relaxed Problem	$\max\limits_{H\in\mathbb{R}^{N\times K}} Tr(H^TWH)$ s.t. $H^TH = I$	$\max\limits_{\widetilde{H}\in\mathbb{R}^{N\times K}} Tr(\widetilde{H}^T\widetilde{W}\widetilde{H})$ s.t. $\widetilde{H}^T\widetilde{H} = I$, where $\widetilde{H} = D^{1/2}H$, $\widetilde{W} = D^{-1/2}WD^{-1/2}$
Real-valued Solution	H : the eigenvectors of the K largest eigenvalues of W as columns	$\widetilde{H}$: the eigenvectors of the K largest eigenvalues of $\widetilde{W}$ as columns

From Table 1, we find that the relaxed problems for AA and NC are similar, and the only difference is that AA deals with W, while NC deals with $\widetilde{W}$. Here, we briefly explain some details of AA. The rewritten problem for AA is an NP-hard problem. However, when we relax it by allowing the elements of H to take arbitrary real values, the relaxed problem can be easily solved by applying Rayleigh Quotient Theorem [12]. The rigorous mathematical derivation ensure that as an approximation to indicator matrix, matrix H obtained by eigen-decomposition is interpretable and encodes the cluster information for the given document corpus. However, the solution H is not intuitive and doesn't directly indicate the cluster membership because of its real values. We have to use k-means on the rows of H to get the final cluster set.

2.2 Document Clustering by Non-negative Matrix Factorization

Given a document corpus with N documents and K clusters, [2] represents each document as a non-negative linear combination of K clusters centers which are also constrained to be non-negative. Translating this statement into mathematics, we have:

$$X \approx UV^T, \ \ s.t.\ U \geq 0, V \geq 0 \tag{1}$$

where $X = [\mathbf{x}_1,\mathbf{x}_2,\cdots,\mathbf{x}_N]$ is the term-document matrix and $\mathbf{x}_i$ represents the term-frequency vector of doc_i, $U = [\mathbf{u}_1,\mathbf{u}_2,\cdots,\mathbf{u}_K]$ and $\mathbf{u}_k$ represents the k'th cluster center, and $V^T = [\mathbf{v}_1,\mathbf{v}_2,\cdots,\mathbf{v}_N]$ and $\mathbf{v}_i$ is the linear coefficients of doc_i. Intuitively, by the NMF to X, we can assume the coefficient matrix V encodes some cluster information. Based on the assumption, we can assign doc_i to cluster k when $k = \arg\max\limits_{j} v_{ij}$.

In [11], Chris Ding proposed an extension of NMF to the graph affinity matrix:

$$W \approx HH^T, \ \ s.t.\ H \geq 0 \tag{2}$$

Where $W \in \mathbb{R}_+^{N \times N}$, $H \in \mathbb{R}_+^{N \times K}$ and we denote this NMF as NMF-HHt. The matrix H could be considered as an approximate solution to spectral clustering. Hence the final clusters are obtained by assigning doc_i to cluster k when $k = \arg\max_j h_{ij}$. However, from the derivation process in [11], we notice that the equivalence between NMF-HHt and spectral clustering is based on strict orthogonality constraints $H^T H = I$, and the constraints are hard to retain by NMF-HHt. As a result, the equivalence is hardly convincing and the clustering interpretation for H is unreasonable.

The NMF-based methods mentioned above benefit a lot from the intuitiveness of the non-negative solution. However, these methods lack a rigorous theoretical derivation to provide a reasonable clustering interpretation for their solutions, and sometimes lead to unsatisfactory performances.

3   The Proposed Method

The previous work motivates us to find a new NMF with a reasonable clustering interpretation, which is not only intuitive but also interpretable. Here, we propose a novel NMF to the affinity matrix with non-negativity and orthogonality constraints simultaneously. With the additional orthogonality constraints, this NMF is similar to eigen-decomposition but adds non-negativity constraints. Intuitively, the new NMF can provide a non-negative solution to spectral clustering. Given a corpus with N documents and K clusters ($K < N$), the factorization is expressed as follows:

$$W \approx PSP^T, \quad s.t.\ P \geq 0, S \geq 0, P^T P = I_K \tag{3}$$

where $W \in \mathbb{R}_+^{N \times N}$, $P \in \mathbb{R}_+^{N \times K}$, $S \in \mathbb{R}_+^{K \times K}$ is a diagonal matrix, and this NMF is denoted as NMF-PSPt in short. NMF-PSPt is transformed to the following optimization problem:

$$\min_{P \geq 0, S \geq 0} J_{NMF} = \min_{P \geq 0, S \geq 0} \left(\alpha \left\| W - PSP^T \right\|^2 + \beta \left\| P^T P - I_K \right\|^2 \right) \tag{4}$$

where α and β are positive constants. Since $\left\| W - PSP^T \right\|^2$ is the squared sum of $N \times N$ elements and $\left\| P^T P - I_K \right\|^2$ is the squared sum of $K \times K$ elements, we set $\alpha = \eta / (N \times N)$ and $\beta = (1 - \eta)/(K \times K)$ to keep evenness, where η ($0 < \eta \leq 1$) is a parameter to control the weight of constraint $P^T P = I_K$. The relationship between NMF-PSPt and spectral clustering is shown in the following theorem.

Theorem 1. The matrix P obtained by NMF-PSPt is an approximate solution to the relaxed optimizing problems for spectral clustering $\max_{H \in \mathbb{R}^{N \times K}} Tr(H^T W H)\ s.t.\ H^T H = I$.

Proof. Firstly, according to Eq.(3), W can be written as: $W = PSP^T + \theta$, where θ is a N-by-N matrix and its elements are negligible compared with PSP^T, which is ensured by the objective function J_{NMF} in Eq.(4). Since $Tr(H^T W H) = Tr(H^T(PSP^T)H) + Tr(H^T \theta H)$, we can relax the optimizing problems for spectral clustering as follows:

$$\max_{H \in \mathbb{R}^{N \times K}} Tr(H^T (PSP^T)H) \ s.t. \ H^T H = I \tag{5}$$

Then, since $P^T P = I_K$, PSP^T can be written as: $PSP^T = \sum_{i=1}^K s_i p_i p_i^T$, where $s_1, \cdots, s_K$ are diagonal elements of S, $p_1, \cdots, p_K$ are columns of P and satisfy: $p_i^T \cdot p_i = 1$, $p_i^T \cdot p_j = 1$. This means $p_1, \cdots, p_K$ are the K eigenvectors corresponding to the K largest eigenvalues $s_1, \cdots, s_K$ of PSP^T. Finally, based on Rayleigh Quotient Theorem, we can prove that P is a solution to Eq.(5) and an approximate solution to spectral clustering .   □

With Theorem 1, the solutions to spectral clustering can be equivalently carried out by NMF-PSPt, which ensures that the proposed method inherits the reasonable clustering interpretation of spectral clustering and is more interpretable and reliable than previous NMF-based methods. Furthermore, as the intuitiveness of non-negative solution, we can directly deduce the final clusters from P without an additional clustering operation, which is necessary for eigenvector-based spectral clustering. These mean NMF-PSPt combines the interpretation of spectral clustering and the intuitiveness of NMF-based methods together, overcomes the disadvantages of them.

3.1 Algorithm for Computing NMF-PSPt

The optimization for J_{NMF} can be completed by alternatively updating P and S until convergence. With fixed value of S, J_{NMF} becomes a quadratic form of $P : J_{NMF}(P)$. With fixed value of P, we get the quadratic form of $S : J_{NMF}(S)$. By referring to the algorithm derivation for symmetric convex coding [13], we deduced the following updating rules for P and S.

Theorem 2. The objective function $J_{NMF}(P)$ is decreasing under the updating rule,

$$P_{ik} = \tilde{P}_{ik} \left(\frac{\alpha \left[W \tilde{P} S \right]_{ik} + \beta \tilde{P}_{ik}}{\alpha \left[\tilde{P} S \tilde{P}^T \tilde{P} S \right]_{ik} + \beta \left[\tilde{P}^T \tilde{P} \right]_{ik}} \right)^{\frac{1}{4}} \tag{6}$$

Proof. Firstly, with the help of Jensen's inequality, convexity of the quadratic function and inequalities: $x^2 + y^2 \geq 2xy$, $x \geq 1 + \log x$, we can prove that the following equation is the auxiliary function (defined in [9]) for $J_{NMF}(P)$.

$$G(P, \tilde{P}) = \alpha \left(\sum_{ij} \left(W_{ij}^2 - 2W_{ij} \left[\tilde{P} S \tilde{P}^T \right]_{ij} \right) + 4 \sum_{ip} \tilde{P}_{ip} \log \frac{P_{ip}}{\tilde{P}_{ip}} \left[W \tilde{P} S \right]_{ip} + \sum_{ip} \frac{P_{ip}^4}{\tilde{P}_{ip}^3} \left[\tilde{P} S \tilde{P}^T \tilde{P} S \right]_{ip} \right)$$
$$+ \beta \left(\sum_{pq} \left(I_{pq}^2 - 2I_{pq} \left[\tilde{P}^T \tilde{P} \right]_{pq} \right) - 4 \sum_{ip} \tilde{P}_{ip} \log \frac{P_{ip}}{\tilde{P}_{ip}} \left[\tilde{P} I_K \right]_{ip} + \sum_{ip} \frac{P_{ip}^4}{\tilde{P}_{ip}^3} \left[\tilde{P} \tilde{P}^T \tilde{P} \right]_{ip} \right) \tag{7}$$

Then, taking the derivative of $G(P, P')$ w.r.t P_{ip}, and solving $\partial G(P, \tilde{P}) / \partial P_{ip} = 0$, we get that Eq.(6). Based on the Lemma of auxiliary function in [9], we can prove $J_{NMF}(P)$ is decreasing under the updating rule in Eq.(6).   □

Theorem 3. The objective function $J_{NMF}(S)$ is decreasing under the updating rule,

$$S_{kk} = \tilde{S}_{kk} \frac{\left[P^T W P \right]_{kk}}{\left[P^T P \tilde{S} P^T P \right]_{kk}} \tag{8}$$

Due to the space limit, we omit the proof of Theorem 3, which also can be analogously completed by introducing auxiliary function of $J_{NMF}(S)$.

Finally, we summarize the algorithm for computing NMF-PSPt as follows:

Step 1. Given an N-by-N graph affinity matrix W and a positive integer K, initialize N-by-K non-negative matrix P and K-by-K non-negative diagonal matrix.
Step 2. Update P and S by Eq.(6) and Eq.(8).
Step 3. Repeat Step 2 until convergence.

3.2 NMF-PSPt vs. Spectral Clustering and NMF-HHt

In this subsection, we use a simple and small document corpus to illustrate the document distributions derived by three different methods: the eigenvector-based AA method and two NMF-based methods based on NMF-HHt and NMF-PSPt. All the methods are focused on original affinity matrix W, and provide approximate solution to Average Association function. The small corpus is constructed by three topics from TDT2 corpus, which consist of 26, 15, and 43 documents respectively. Fig.1(a) shows matrix W, where each element is the cosine similarity between documents, and (b), (c) and (d) illustrate the data distributions derived by the three methods, where data points belonging to the same cluster are depicted by the same symbol. E_1, E_2, E_3 are the top three eigenvectors of W, H_1, H_2, H_3 are the column vectors of H obtained by NMF-HHt, and P_1, P_2, P_3 are the column vectors of P obtained by NMF-PSPt.

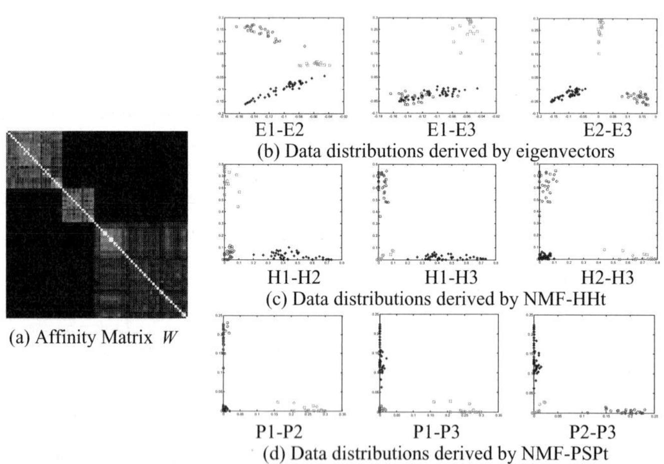

Fig. 1. Data distributions derived by eigenvectors, NMF-HHt and NMF-PSPt

From Fig. 1 we can observe that:

1. The small corpus can be easily separated as shown in Fig. 1(a). The within-cluster similarity is large and the between-cluster similarity is small. In fact, the three clusters are well separated by all the three methods as shown in Fig. 1(b), (c) and (d).
2. In Fig. 1(c) and (d), each data point is non-negative in all three directions, and the data points belonging to the same cluster spread along the same axis. However, in Fig. 1(b), each data point may take negative values in some directions, and the axes don't directly correspond to the clusters. As also discussed in [2], it shows the intuitiveness of non-negative solution.
3. Comparing Fig. 1(c) and (d), we find that the data points in Fig. 1(d) are much easier to be separated, as the data points of same cluster in Fig. 1(d) are more compact in same axis than those in Fig. 1(c). This fact verifies that, with the help of orthogonality constraints, the solution derived by NMF-PSPt is indeed more reliable and interpretable than that derived by NMF-HHt as mentioned in previous analysis.

4   Experimental Results

This section provides experimental evidences to show the effectiveness of our proposed algorithm in comparison with eigenvector-based spectral clustering algorithms [5] and previous NMF-based methods [2, 11].

4.1   Data Corpora

The standard corpora used in our experiments are TDT2[1] and Reuter-21578[2], which are benchmarks for document clustering. The TDT2 consists of English and Chinese documents from 9 news sources during the first half year of 1998 in 96 categories. The Reuters has 21,578 English documents in 135 categories. In our experiments, we used the English documents with unique category label, and excluded categories with less than 10 and more than 1,000 documents, leaving 5,333 documents in 52 categories for TDT2 and 2,710 documents in 40 categories for Reuters.

4.2   Performances Evaluations and Comparisons

As shown in Table 1, the essential difference between AA and NC is that NC applies the weights to W while AA does not. Therefore, we separate the two eigenvector-based methods, previous NMF-based methods and our proposed methods into two groups: one is non-normalized; the other is normalized, as showed in Table 2 and 3.

Non-normalized methods contain AA, NMF, AA-HHt and AA-PSPt. AA is eigenvector-based methods for Average Association function. NMF is the method proposed by [2] based on $X \approx UV^T$. AA-HHt and AA-PSPt are based on $W \approx HH^T$ and $W \approx PSP^T$, where w_{ij} is the cosine similarity between doc_i and doc_j.

Normalized methods contain NC, NMF-NCW, NC-HHt and NC-PSPt. NC is eigenvector-based methods for Normalized Cut function. NMF-NCW is the

---

156   L. Bao et al.

normalized NMF based on $XD^{-1/2} \approx UV^T$ [2]. NC-HHt and NC-PSPt are respectively based on $\widetilde{W} \approx HH^T$ and $\widetilde{W} \approx PSP^T$, where $\widetilde{W} = D^{-1/2}WD^{-1/2}$.

For performance measures, we selected the two metrics used in [2]: the accuracy (AC) and the normalized mutual information (MI) between the resulting clusters set and the ground truth set. The values of AC and MI are both within the range [0, 1], and the larger value represents the better performance.

As the evaluations in [2], we conducted our experiments for the cluster numbers ranging from 2 to 10. For each cluster number k, 20 tests were conducted on different randomly chosen clusters, and the final performance scores were the average of the 20 tests. For AA and NC, we applied k-means 10 times with different initial points and recorded the best result in terms of the objective function of k-means. Since NMF-based algorithms are affected by initialization, 10 trials were performed with different initial values and the trial with minimal criterion function value was chosen. In addition, the parameter η for AA-PSPt and NC-PSPt was set to 0.8. Table 2 and 3 respectively show the evaluation results of eight methods in two groups on TDT2 and Reuters. For each k, the best score in each group is shown in bold font.

Table 2. Performance comparisons on TDT2 corpus

K	Accuracy							
	Non-normalized algorithms				Normalized algorithms			
	AA	NMF	AA-HHt	AA-PSPt	NC	NMF-NCW	NC-HHt	NC-PSPt
2	0.8595	0.8465	0.8429	**0.9996**	**0.9987**	**0.9987**	**0.9987**	**0.9987**
3	0.8597	0.8404	0.8515	**0.9951**	0.9687	0.9413	0.9710	**0.9997**
4	0.7141	0.6884	0.6972	**0.9778**	0.9761	0.9532	0.9514	**0.9955**
5	0.7483	0.7280	0.7665	**0.9666**	0.9367	0.9503	0.9535	**0.9908**
6	0.7327	0.7279	0.7175	**0.9510**	0.8671	0.8958	0.8985	**0.9892**
7	0.7797	0.7588	0.7700	**0.9372**	0.9037	0.9280	0.9338	**0.9611**
8	0.7573	0.7413	0.7753	**0.9401**	0.8819	0.9253	0.9192	**0.9882**
9	0.7535	0.7546	0.7690	**0.9237**	0.8344	0.8696	0.8728	**0.9624**
10	0.7228	0.7426	0.7793	**0.9004**	0.9011	0.9310	0.9321	**0.9585**
avg.	0.7697	0.7587	0.7744	**0.9546**	0.9187	0.9326	0.9368	**0.9827**
K	Mutual Information							
	Non-normalized algorithms				Normalized algorithms			
	AA	NMF	AA-HHt	AA-PSPt	NC	NMF-NCW	NC-HHt	NC-PSPt
2	0.6953	0.6643	0.6640	**0.9961**	**0.9891**	0.9882	**0.9882**	0.9882
3	0.7598	0.7314	0.7545	**0.9497**	0.9426	0.9076	0.9430	**0.9968**
4	0.6377	0.6119	0.6171	**0.8790**	0.9486	0.9056	0.9035	**0.9676**
5	0.7163	0.6982	0.7179	**0.8986**	0.9240	0.9373	0.9352	**0.9776**
6	0.7254	0.7132	0.7084	**0.8871**	0.8598	0.8852	0.8840	**0.9749**
7	0.7952	0.7796	0.7758	**0.8906**	0.8959	0.9281	0.9272	**0.9473**
8	0.7973	0.7831	0.8003	**0.8970**	0.8911	0.9253	0.9168	**0.9756**
9	0.7954	0.8070	0.8114	**0.8842**	0.8538	0.8808	0.8859	**0.9473**
10	0.7876	0.7955	0.8083	**0.8689**	0.8834	0.9327	0.9308	**0.9699**
avg.	0.7456	0.7316	0.7397	**0.9057**	0.9098	0.9212	0.9238	**0.9717**

Table 3. Performance comparisons on Reuters corpus

K	Accuracy							
	Non-normalized algorithms				Normalized algorithms			
	AA	NMF	AA-HHt	AA-PSPt	NC	NMF-NCW	NC-HHt	NC-PSPt
2	0.7976	0.8400	0.8242	**0.9071**	0.8998	**0.9069**	0.8881	**0.9041**
3	0.7110	0.7335	0.7333	**0.8752**	**0.8714**	**0.8748**	0.8686	**0.8745**
4	0.7147	0.7091	0.7124	**0.7846**	0.7757	0.7824	0.7775	**0.8019**
5	0.6424	0.6608	0.6652	**0.7719**	0.7805	0.7723	0.7728	**0.8000**
6	0.5875	0.6113	0.6041	**0.7604**	0.6713	0.6866	0.6906	**0.7424**
7	0.5688	0.5982	0.6006	**0.7225**	0.7181	0.7339	0.7257	**0.8031**
8	0.5400	0.5635	0.5528	**0.6639**	0.6431	0.6637	0.6631	**0.7275**
9	0.5272	0.5444	0.5444	**0.6716**	0.6048	0.6137	0.6170	**0.7023**
10	0.4984	0.5476	0.5302	**0.6627**	0.6026	0.6380	0.6257	**0.6975**
avg.	0.6208	0.6454	0.6408	**0.7578**	0.7297	0.7414	0.7366	**0.7837**
K	Mutual Information							
	Non-normalized algorithms				Normalized algorithms			
	AA	NMF	AA-HHt	AA-PSPt	NC	NMF-NCW	NC-HHt	NC-PSPt
2	0.4564	0.5017	0.4716	**0.5736**	0.6183	**0.6380**	0.6085	0.6173
3	0.4419	0.4587	0.4504	**0.6163**	0.6847	**0.7069**	**0.7015**	0.7027
4	0.5771	0.5402	0.5395	**0.6015**	0.5761	0.5887	0.5841	**0.5989**
5	0.5471	0.5420	0.5397	**0.5829**	**0.6492**	0.6365	0.6389	**0.6484**
6	0.5281	0.5137	0.5120	**0.5802**	0.5941	0.6032	0.6011	**0.6287**
7	0.5066	0.4853	0.4856	**0.5249**	0.6324	0.6354	0.6277	**0.7032**
8	**0.5077**	0.4970	0.4848	0.4921	0.5883	0.5952	0.6000	**0.6291**
9	0.5104	0.4944	0.4950	**0.5347**	0.5588	0.5564	0.5595	**0.6079**
10	**0.4971**	0.4890	**0.4901**	0.4925	0.5718	0.5840	0.5768	**0.6234**
avg.	0.5080	0.5024	0.4965	**0.5554**	0.6082	0.6160	0.6108	**0.6400**

From Table 2 and 3, we observed that:

1. Most of normalized methods performed better than their corresponding non-normalized methods. This means that the normalization brings positive effects for spectral clustering (NC vs. AA) and the NMF-based methods (NMF-NCW vs. NMF, NC-HHt vs. AA-HHt, and NC-PSPt vs. AA-PSPt).

2. Comparing eigenvector-based spectral clustering with previous NMF-based methods in the same group (AA vs. NMF and AA-HHt, NC vs. NMF and NC-HHt), we notice that: 1) the intuitiveness of solution is important: although the eigenvector-based methods is more interpretable than the previous NMF-based methods, however the latter perform slightly better than the former on the whole because the real-valued solution of the former is not intuitive and leads to unsatisfactory performances; 2) a reasonable clustering interpretation is necessary: although the previous NMF-based methods are more intuitive than the eigenvector-based methods, they aren't obviously superior to the eigenvector-based methods and sometimes are inferior; the possible reason is that they lack a reasonable clustering interpretation. The above two facts motivate us to find a NMF with a reasonable clustering interpretation, which can combine both intuitiveness and interpretation together.

3. Obviously, our proposed methods (AA-PSPt and NC-PSPt) perform much better than other methods in the same group on most data sets. The results indicate that our method indeed combines the interpretation of spectral clustering and the intuitiveness

of NMF-based methods together, and brings outstanding improvements to the performances. Actually, the methods AA, AA-HHt and AA-PSPt (or NC, NC-HHt and NC-PSPt) all provide a solution to AA (or NC) criterion function under relaxed conditions; however, the non-negative and orthogonal solution provided by AA-PSPt (or NC-PSPt) may be much closer to the indicator matrix for spectral clustering, which is also non-negative and orthogonal simultaneously. That also explains the outstanding performances of our proposed methods.

5   Conclusions

In this paper, we have proposed a novel NMF to the affinity matrix with non-negativity and orthogonality constraints simultaneously, and also have presented the iterative algorithm for computing the new factorization. With the help of additional orthogonality constraints, the novel NMF provides a non-negative solution to spectral clustering, which combines the interpretation of spectral clustering and the intuitiveness of NMF-based methods together. The experimental evaluations demonstrate that the proposed method is much more efficient and effective than the eigenvector-based spectral clustering and the previous NMF-based methods.

References

1. Li, T., Ma, S., Ogihara, M.: Document Clustering via Adaptive Subspace Iteration. In: Proceedings of the 27th ACM SIGIR Conference, pp. 218–225 (2004)
2. Xu, W., Liu, X., Gong, Y.: Document Clustering Based on Non-Negative Matrix Factorization. In: Proceedings of the 26th ACM SIGIR Conference, pp. 267–273 (2003)
3. Xu, W., Liu, X., Gong, Y.: Document Clustering by Concept Factorization. In: Proceedings of the 27th ACM SIGIR Conference, pp. 202–209 (2004)
4. Chan, P.K., Schlag, D.F., Zien, J.Y.: Spectral K-way Ratio-cut Partitioning and Clustering. IEEE Trans. on CAD 13, 1088–1096 (1994)
5. Shi, J., Malik, J.: Normalized Cuts and Image Segmentation. IEEE Trans. on Pattern Analysis and Machine Intelligence 22, 888–905 (2000)
6. Ding, C., He, X., Zha, H., et al.: A Min-max Cut Algorithm for Graph Partitioning and Data Clustering. In: Proceedings of the 2001 IEEE ICDM Conference, pp. 107–114 (2001)
7. von Luxburg, U.: A Tutorial on Spectral Clustering. Technical Report No. TR-149, Max Planck Institute for Biological Cybernetics (2006)
8. Lee, D.D., Seung, H.S.: Learning the Parts of Objects by Non-negative Matrix Factorization. Nature 401, 788–791 (1999)
9. Lee, D.D., Seung, H.S.: Algorithms for Non-negative Matrix Factorization. Advances in Neural Information Processing Systems 13, 556–562 (2001)
10. Deerwester, S.C., Dumais, S.T., Landauer, T.K., et al.: Indexing by Latent Semantic Analysis. Journal of the American Society of Information Science 41, 391–407 (1990)
11. Ding, C., He, X., Simon, H.D.: On the Equivalence of Nonnegative Matrix Factorization and Spectral Clustering. In: Proceedings of the 2005 SIAM Data Mining Conference, pp. 606–610 (2005)
12. Lütkepohl, H.: Handbook of Matrices. Wiley, Chichester (1997)
13. Long, B., Zhang, A., Wu, X., et al.: Relational Clustering by Symmetric Convex Coding. In: Proceeding of the 24th International Conference on Machine Learning, pp. 680–687 (2007)

Application of Data Mining Algorithms to TCP throughput Prediction in HTTP Transactions

Leszek Borzemski, Marta Kliber, and Ziemowit Nowak

Institute of Information Science and Engineering, Wroclaw University of Technology,
Wybrzeze Wyspianskiego 27, 50-370 Wroclaw, Poland
{leszek.borzemski, ziemowit.nowak}@pwr.wroc.pl

Abstract. This paper presents a study of the application of data mining algorithms to the prediction of TCP throughput in HTTP transactions. We are using data mining models built on the basis of historic measurements of network performance gathered using WING system. These measurements reflect Web performance as experienced by the end-users located in Wroclaw, Poland. Data mining models are created using the algorithms available in *Microsoft SQL Server 2005* and *IBM Intelligent Miner* tools. Our results show that our data mining based TCP throughput prediction returns accurate results. The application of our method in building of so-called "best performance hit" operation mode of the search engines is proposed.

Keywords: data mining, TCP throughput prediction.

1 Introduction

The throughput prediction is important for efficiency of a wide range of tasks that includes: replica selection in a grid environment, selection of caches in Web content delivery services, mirror site selection for file downloading and selection for an overlay and multihomed networks as well as to provide peer-to-peer parallel downloads. The need of efficient work of these tasks requires answering the question: which transfer could be the fastest. In this work we are focused on the TCP throughput prediction in HTTP transaction. There exist two possible solutions to our question. The first one is a trial and error method. This one is very time consuming when TCP protocol is used, it is because the rerouting of an established TCP connection to a different network path or server can results in problems such as migration delays, packet reordering, and re-initialization of the congestion window. The bigger used infrastructure the longer it takes to find the best source or route. The second method is to know *apriori* which server or route connection should be established before actually starting the transfer and this is the place for the TCP throughput prediction.

We focus on predicting the throughput of a TCP transfer of middle large resources retrieved by a Web user. The reason is that the biggest data transfer in Web is done with the use of the TCP protocol and much of it is generated with Web browsers. For short TCP flows which are often limited by slow-start, the performance is determined by the Round-Trip Time and the presence of random losses, which can be based on direct and low-overhead measurements. The TCP throughput prediction for larger

N.T. Nguyen et al. (Eds.): IEA/AIE 2008, LNAI 5027, pp. 159–168, 2008.

data files is more complex because it depends on a large number of factors, including the transfer size, maximum sender and receiver windows, various path characteristics and the implementation of TCP at the end points.

We have designed and implemented a system that takes historic network measurements and applies to them the data mining algorithms. In this way the TCP throughput prediction models are created and forecasts can be generated for single input measurement. Prediction models change in time as a window of historic data, they are based on, slides. This way the models are updating window-by-window and always produce the most accurate outputs. The system offers four different models created with four different data mining algorithms: neural networks, decision trees, time series and regression.

The paper is structured as follows: Section 2 describes related works, Section 3 describes used measurements, Section 4 describes explored data mining algorithms and results achieved with each of algorithm, Section 5 presents the architecture of the throughput prediction system and Section 6 concludes our study and future works.

2   Related Works

The prediction of network performance has been always a challenging and topical problem [8, 9, 10, 13, 14]. The users need either a short-term or long-term forecasts. Short-term forecasting requires instantaneous measuring of network performance. In long-term forecasting we can apply less resource exhaustive monitoring and use historical information more extensively. There are many tools that focus on available bandwidth measurement of a network path. There are applications of statistical models like the auto-regressive moving average and the Markov-modulated Poisson process to predict future bandwidth [14]. Huang and Subhlok have developed the framework for an intelligent real-time throughput predictor based on knowledge of TCP patterns combined with heuristics [8]. DualPats system [9] makes throughput estimates based on an exponentially weighted moving average. Mirza et al. utilize machine learning approach [10]. This solution is based on SVR method and makes use of information from prior transfers for training and for forecasts requires measurements from lightweight probes.

Our focus is also to combine knowledge retrieved from historic measurements with current information about link state to accurately and efficiently predict TCP throughput with the use of APIs of professional data mining tools: *Microsoft SQL Server 2005* and *IBM Intelligent Miner*. These tools are used in our research and teaching. In our early work we proposed to employ some data mining algorithms to evaluate Internet and Web performance and reliability characteristics [4]. Extensive research in Internet paths performance was done by means of statistical data analysis [5, 6]. In [1] we introduced a new *Web performance mining* approach build around the clustering and decision trees algorithms to predict network weather. Generally, data mining based analysis of Internet and Web performance data seems to be very natural in searching of complex correlations in huge set of historic measurements data. For the needs of these research projects we have developed two measurement platforms WING [3] and MWING [2] for performing active measurements in Internet and Web.

3 Measurements

In our research we focus on Web performance from the end users perspective. End users explore Internet with browsers hence measurements that we use to the throughput prediction should take this facet into account. WING system [3, 5, 6] implemented for the needs of end-users located at Wroclaw University of Technology is a tool for conducting such measurements. WING is a network measurement system that measures end-to end Web performance path between the Web site and the end-user. It can trace all phases performed by the Web browser during the navigation procedure in the way which is shown in Figure 1. Tracing is done on the raw IP packages level and the entire communication between Web client and servers is reconstructed.

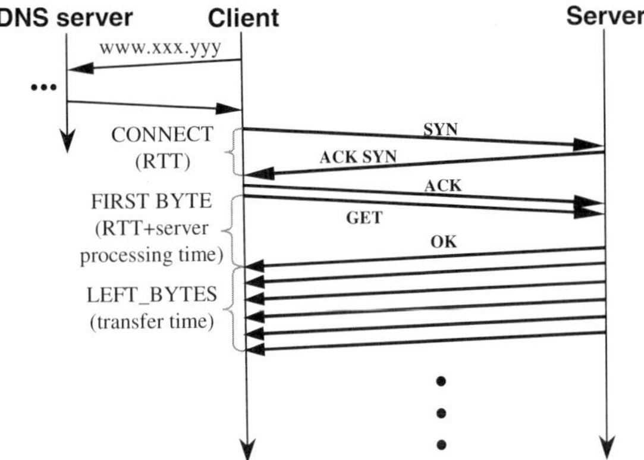

Fig. 1. The diagram of a Web transaction

Probing was performed from our university campus network by downloading the rfc1945.txt file from 50 Web servers ten times a day at regular intervals. Active measurements often use a special probing packet but we wanted to observe how the real browser (MS IE) manages the downloading, therefore we use the specific file as the probe. This file is not too small to measure the network throughput and at the same time not too big to overwhelm network paths. The data used in development of the throughput prediction system comes from time between 09/2002 and 07/2003 and was collected from servers distributed around the globe. For each of these servers about 1500 active measurements were performed.

Based on the gathered data, time intervals and transaction summary information of Web transaction were collected and include:

- ID – unique identifier,
- DATETIME - date and time of probing,
- CONNECT – time interval for setting the TCP connection with Web server,
- DNS – time interval for IP address resolving,
- FRSTBYTE – time between the end of issuing HTTP request to Web server and the beginning of obtaining of the first data packet,
- REDIRECTS – time between start of measurement and automatic redirection,

- INDEXFILE – time interval needed for HTML skeleton downloading,
- START_MS – time interval between the start of probing and sending a packet,
- IP_ADDRESS - IP address of Web server which was probed,
- PACKET_OK – number of received correct packets,
- PACKET_NOK - number of received incorrect packets,
- DNS2SYN – time between the end of DNS communication and start of the TCP connection to the Web server,
- ACK2GET – time between receiving the acknowledgement of the connection establishment and issuing a HTTP request,
- THROUGHPUT – throughput in kilobits per second,
- AVG_PING –average RTT based on three probes,
- WEEKDAY – day of the week when probing is taken,
- HOUR – hour when probing was taken,
- ERROR – bit flag for indicating probing error.

4 Data Mining Algorithms

At first we must formulate the throughput prediction problem. The situation is that there are lots of measurement data and complex throughput dependency to find. The proposed solution is to use data mining algorithms. This approach is very natural, since this technique is useful whenever correlations are searched in mass of data.

In our research we have used two data mining tools: *Microsoft SQL Server 2005* [16] and *IBM Intelligent Miner* [15]. These two systems provide four forecasting algorithms:

- Microsoft's Neural Networks,
- Microsoft's Decision Trees,
- Microsoft's Time Series,
- IBM's Transform Regression.

Examining each of these algorithms consisted of two steps performed for each algorithm variants where such exist. The first step was to determine the input data set. It is because, even though all data describe Web transaction, not all are as strongly correlated with the throughput as the others. Some of them even duplicate information carried by the others. The goal was to extract only these inputs that carry information which significantly affect prediction results. It results from the fact that inputs on which mining models will be based on are these which values are to be measured directly before prediction. The less we have to know to get the answer the faster we get it. The second step was to determine the values of algorithm parameters that give minimal prediction error.

Before models could be built some preparation was performed. Measurement data were cleaned and split into training and testing sets. Furthermore, the training set cardinality was established as the compromise between the accuracy and relevance. The bigger this set is the more cases are known, but the slower it takes to adapt to network changes. Hence finding the balance point was desired to be established.

The comparison of algorithms was prepared based on the mean square error (MSE) of gained predictions.

We present models, for each of these four algorithms, which achieved the best results in the meaning of the smallest MSE value.

4.1 Microsoft's Neural Networks

Neural networks algorithms give highly parameterized statistical models. They model non-linear and rather smooth correlations between input and output data [11]. Microsoft's Neural Networks algorithm works only with the discrete values. Since most of our data takes continuous values, it has been discretized. Microsoft offers automatic discretization with cluster or equal areas method. For each number of clusters for discretized attribute can be defined [16]. Researches showed that for our task discretization had minimal influence on achieved results. The best chosen input set for this algorithm is: CONNECT, FRSTBYTE, INDEXFILE, AVG_PING, DNS. A model built with this input set is called: model1. Additionally, model2 which is based on the set combined from only three from previous inputs, that is: CONNECT, FRSTBYTE, INDEXFILE gets MSE on a similar level. The training results for these two models are presented in Figure 2. The MSE achieved by both these models is equal to 0.17.

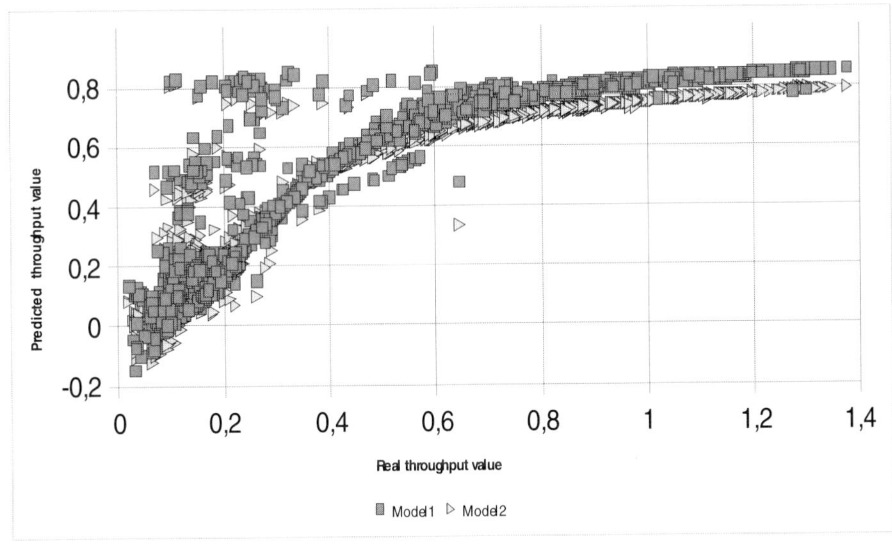

Fig. 2. The throughput prediction for two models of Microsoft's Neural Networks

Since Microsoft's Neural Networks allow only one hidden layer in the network, the only parameter of neural network structure was to determine: the number of neurons in hidden layer. Microsoft assumed that number of neurons in hidden layer should be determined using the following expression: hidden_node_ratio*sqrt(number of inputs * number of outputs). Our study of different hidden_node_ratio values has proven that for our aims the best value for number of neurons in hidden layer is when this parameter is set to value 2. The best Microsoft's Neural Network model with the best parameters values has MSE equal to 0.13.

4.2 Microsoft's Decision Trees

Decision tree is a widely used data mining algorithm. Its popularity is due to the easiness of result interpretation, possibility to represent arbitrarily compound correlations and a short time of decision making. This algorithm is used mostly in classification tasks, but also in regression and association problems as in SQL Server 2005 [16].

For the regression variant of Microsoft's Decision Trees, which works on both continuous and discrete values of data, the best set of input data consists of either three inputs: CONNECT, AVG_PING and DNS (model 1) or six inputs: INDEX-FILE, CONNECT, FIRESTBYTE, IP_ADDRESS, DNS and AVG_PING (model 2).

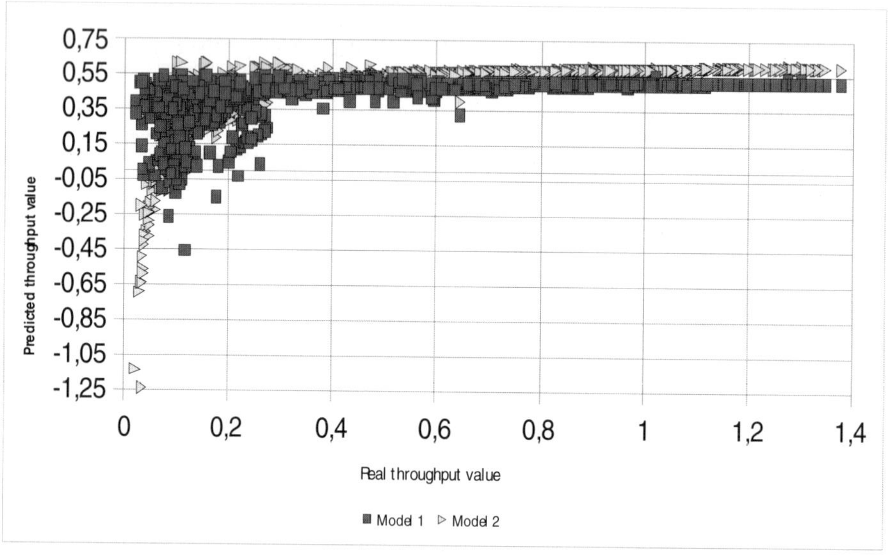

Fig. 3. The throughput prediction for two models of Microsoft's Decision Trees

The forecasts achieved for both model 1 and model 2 are presented in Figure 3. The results from both models form logarithmic plots. MSE for these two models is: 0.32 i 0.28, respectively.

Microsoft's solution allows to trace the strength of the relationships between input and output data. For the first model it was determined as AVG_PING, DNS and CONNECT; for the second model as IP_ADDRESS, INDEXFILE, DNS, AVG_PING, FRSTBYTE and CONNECT.

While preparing the forecasts the following information about the Web server was also analyzed:

  – address of Web server from which resource was downloaded,
  – two last parts of domain name included in URL,
  –IP address of the Web server,
  – autonomous system to which Web server belongs,
  – country and city where server is localized,
  – geographical longitude and latitude of server localization,
  – network name achieved from WHOIS databases.

However none of models employed this information. It is because the algorithms have not found strong enough correlation between this data and forecasted throughput to include it in the models.

The parameters of DT algorithm basically control of the growth of constructed decision tree. These parameters include complexity penalty which controls the number of splits, minimal support i.e. specify the minimal number of leaf cases that is required to generate a split, score method used to calculate split score and split method that is used to split a node.

Minimal support has very strong influence on the developed tree and even little decrease or increase of it can cause a change in the result tree. The best value of this parameter with minimum MSE achieved was 80 MSE. The worse results were achieved using the binary split method. The best solution would be to combine both methods.

4.3 Microsoft's Time Series

The time series analysis deals with the sequences of measurements. This algorithm works only on the continuous data so all discrete data had to be discarded [16]. To forecast not only the next and following outputs but also to identify the server for which the forecast is prepared, the time series must be built against the server for which the measurements were taken. Without such filtration the time series analysis for each server we could not be able to determine the server and therefore we could not be able to compare the throughput forecasts for the server for which the measurements were taken. Unfortunately, the computations were too complex and could not be efficiently performed on the computer used in our calculations. Moreover, analyzed series were too short to find patterns and accurately predict the output. Therefore further research for this algorithm is needed.

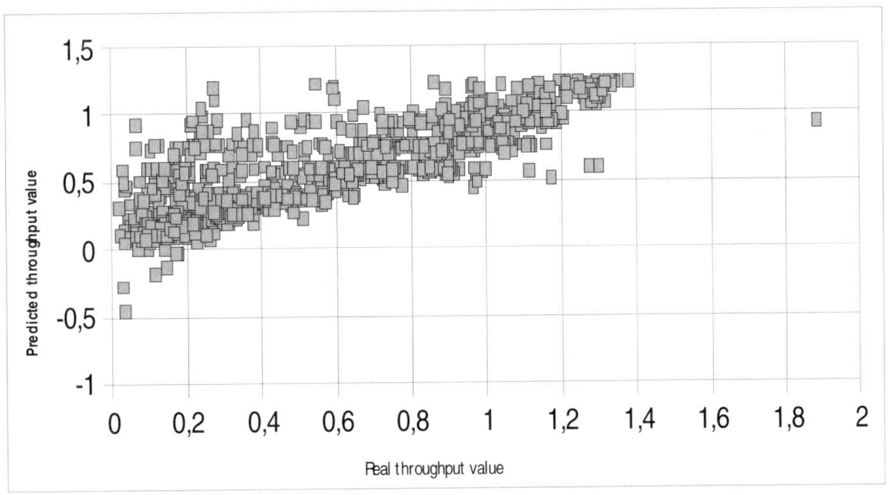

Fig. 4. The throughput prediction for Intelligent Miner Transform Regression

4.4 IBM's Transform Regression

Intelligent Miner modeling offers three variants of regression algorithms: linear, polynomial and transformed [12, 15]. Input set for which model returned minimal MSE was: CONNECT, DNS2SYN, DATETIME, PACKET_OK i START_MS. Nevertheless other input data combinations also returned very low MSE values. Figure 4 presents results for the following input set: CONNECT, DNS2SYN, HOUR, PACKET_OK and REDIRECTS.

The best results were achieved for the transform regression algorithm where the MSE was equal to 0. This algorithm is an IBM patented algorithm. It joins efficiency, nonparametrization and automatization of decision trees with the flexibility of neural networks. Polynomial regression that assumes polynomial and in particular linear relationship between inputs and output returned little higher MSE equal to 0.126.

5 Architecture of the throughput Prediction System

We are developing a service called Network Monitoring Broker (NMB) which can measure network performance, describe network characteristic and publish the forecasts of network behavior, especially for automatic network resource selection. We focus on end-to-end performance seen by end users of some virtual organization (like Grids or overlay networks) deployed over the set of network nodes linked by a mesh of Internet communication paths. One of the goals is to integrate NMB with the MWING measurement platform [2]. The reason was to have the direct connectivity to its database to use current measurements to update data mining models. It is because the prediction based on the best but outdated models is inaccurate or even erroneous.

The system is being implemented using the Microsoft's .NET platform. It makes connections with Microsoft's models by means of the ActiveX Data Objects Multidimensional for .NET and with IBM's model using a Visual Studio .NET plug-in to Intelligent Miner models. The system consists of three main components:

1. *User Interface* which is responsible for the communication to the user
2. *Processing Unit* formulating queries to appropriate data mining system based on user requests and delivers the output in a user-friendly messages
3. *Database* representing Microsoft and IBM data mining systems and their databases which store created mining models.

The system allows performing the throughput prediction with one of existing models and a training model with arbitrarily chosen data. Additionally, model can be exported to the PMML (Predictive Model Markup Language) script. PMML is XML-based language that enables the definition and sharing of data mining models between applications.

The system starts working when a user sends a request which contains the parameters that defines database, data mining model and data on which the prediction or training is performed. Data for the prediction task comes from the most recent measurement and for the training it is a set of measurements gathered for some period of time. When the Processing Unit receives request it sends a query for appropriate server for which request was retrieved. When a response comes it is formatted and returned to user.

Our early inspiration to the system development came from the need for supporting a Web user. The users commonly gain the Web resources (e.g. of files, sets of data, documents) with the usage of the search engines. Typically, the user is acting in the following three phases: the search made the search engine, the URL decision making made personally by the user, and the resource downloading from the target server. The user is receiving from the search engine the list of URLs pointing to the relevant resources that match the user query. The user try to evaluate the quality of found resources during the decision phase and by clicking on the suitable position on result list, selects the resource, which is likely right for him/her. Then the resource downloading starts and the resource gaining process ends.

However many times the page ranks are the same or similar, so we can target any page from the result list. Such situation may exits when we search resources in a duplicated content environment such as file mirroring system or content distribution network. Then we are mostly interested in determining the specific address to download the duplicated content from one of the listed servers in the least downloading time. Generally, the user has no chance to determine a priori which link has the best performance without the measurements of the server-to-client throughput at the moment of the decision making. In our approach we propose an automated so-called *"best performance hit"* link selection performed by the intermediary network prediction service based on its network performance knowledge collected through active measurements [7]. Then the result list is not returned to the user but analyzed by the intermediary service to determine the link with the best expected downloading performance and immediately reroute the user request directly to that link.

6 Conclusions

We have presented an empirical study how data mining can address the TCP throughput prediction issue in contemporary Web. We have used chosen data mining algorithms from two generic data mining tools, namely Microsoft SQL Server 2005 and IBM Intelligent Miner, to build the predictive performance models. Our study showed that the application of Microsoft's Time Series algorithm to our data requires further studies and as for now, the best results are achieved using the IBM's Transform Regression algorithm. We need to conclude that while simple prediction models work well, the system must be adaptive in their construction as the network behavior is changing. Such approach is assumed in our perspective throughput prediction system.

Acknowledgements

This work was supported by the Polish Ministry of Science and Higher Education under Grant No. N516 032 31/3359 (2006-2009).

References

1. Borzemski, L.: The Use of Data Mining to Predict Web performance. Cybernetics and Systems 37(6), 587–608 (2006)
2. Borzemski, L., Cichocki, Ł., Fraś, M., Kliber, M., Nowak, Z.: MWING: A Multiagent System for Web Site Measurements. In: Nguyen, N.T., Grzech, A., Howlett, R.J., Jain, L.C. (eds.) KES-AMSTA 2007. LNCS (LNAI), vol. 4496, pp. 278–287. Springer, Heidelberg (2007)
3. Borzemski, L., Cichocki, Ł., Nowak, Z.: WING: A System for Performance Measurement of WWW Service from the User's Point of View (in Polish). Studia Informatica 24(2A), 139–150 (2003)
4. Borzemski, L., Lubczyński, Ł., Nowak, Z.: Application of Data Mining for the Analysis of Internet Path Performance. In: Proc. of 12th Euromicro Conference on Parallel, Distributed and Network-Based Processing, pp. 54–59. IEEE Comp. Soc. Press, Los Alamitos (2004)
5. Borzemski, L., Nowak, Z.: Estimation of Throughput and TCP Round-Trip Times. In: 10th Polish Teletraffic Symposium PSRT 2003 (2003)
6. Borzemski, L., Nowak, Z.: An Empirical Study of Web Quality: Measuring the Web from Wrocław University of Technology Campus. In: Matera, M., Comai, S. (eds.) Engineering Advances of Web Applications, pp. 307–320. Rinton Press, Princeton, NJ (2004)
7. Borzemski, L., Nowak, Z.: Best performance hit: A Novel Method for Web Resource Gaining (in Polish). In: Kwiecień, A., Grzywak, A. (eds.) High Performance Computer Networks. Applications and Security, pp. 23–33. WKŁ, Warszawa (2005)
8. Huang, T., Subhlok, J.: Fast Pattern-Based Throughput Prediction for TCP Bulk Transfers. In: Proceedings of the Fifth IEEE International Symposium on Cluster Computing and the Grid, Washington, DC, USA, vol. 1, pp. 410–417 (2005)
9. Lu, D., Qiao, Z., Dinda, P.A., Bustamante, F.E.: Characterizing and Predicting TCP Throughput on the Wide Area Network Distributed Computing Systems. In: Proceedings 25th IEEE International Conference, pp. 414–424 (2005)
10. Mirza, M., Sommers, J., Barford, P., Zhu, X.: A Machine Learning Approach to TCP Throughput Prediction. In: ACM SIGMETRICS 2007 Proc., vol. 35, pp. 97–108 (2007)
11. Osowski, S.: Neural Networks (in Polish), Warsaw (1994)
12. Pednault, E.: Transform Regression and the Kolmogorov Superposition Theorem. In: Proc. of the Sixth SIAM International Conference on Data Mining, Bethesda, Maryland, April 20-22 (2006)
13. Qiao, Y., Skicewich, J., Dinda, P.: An Empirical Study of the Multiscale Predictability of Network Traffic. In: Proc. IEEE HPDC (2003)
14. Sang, A., Li, S.: A Predictability Analysis of Network Traffic. In: Proc. of the 2000 IEEE Computer and Comm Societies, Conf. on Computer Communications, pp. 342–351 (2000)
15. IBM DB2 Business Intelligence, http://publib.boulder.ibm.com infoceter/db2luw/v8/index.jsp
16. Microsoft SQL 2005 Data Mining Algorithms, http://msdn2.microsoft.com/en-us/library/ms175595.aspx

Incremental Mining with Prelarge Trees

Chun-Wei Lin[1], Tzung-Pei Hong[2,3], Wen-Hsiang Lu[1], and Been-Chian Chien[4]

[1] Department of Computer Science and Information Engineering
National Cheng Kung University
Tainan, 701, Taiwan, R.O.C.
{p7895122, whlu}@mail.ncku.edu.tw
[2] Department of Computer Science and Information Engineering
National University of Kaohsiung
Kaohsiung, 811, Taiwan, R.O.C.
tphong@nuk.edu.tw
[3] Department of Computer Science and Engineering
National Sun Yat-sen University
Kaohsiung, 804, Taiwan, R.O.C.
[4] Department of Computer Science and Information Engineering
National University of Tainan
Tainan, 700, Taiwan, R.O.C.
bcchien@mail.nutn.edu.tw

Abstract. In the past, we proposed a Fast Updated FP-tree (FUFP-tree) structure to efficiently handle new transactions and to make the tree-update process become easy. In this paper, we propose the structure of prelarge trees to incrementally mine association rules based on the concept of pre-large itemsets. Due to the properties of pre-large concepts, the proposed approach does not need to rescan the original database until a number of new transactions have been inserted. Experimental results also show that the proposed approach has a good performance for incrementally handling new transactions.

Keywords: data mining, association rule, FP-tree, pre-large tree, incremental mining.

1 Introduction

Finding association rules in transaction databases is most commonly seen in data mining. In the past, many algorithms for mining association rules from transactions were proposed [1][2][3][4][5][6][7][11][12], most of which were based on the Apriori algorithm [1]. They thus generated and tested candidate itemsets level-by-level. This may cause iterative database scans and high computational costs. Han *et al.* proposed the Frequent-Pattern-tree (FP-tree) structure for efficiently mining association rules without generation of candidate itemsets [8]. It compressed a database into a tree structure which stored only large items. The construction process was executed tuple by tuple, from the first transaction to the last one. After that, a recursive mining procedure called FP-Growth was executed to derive frequent patterns from the FP-tree. They showed the approach could have a better performance than the Apriori

N.T. Nguyen et al. (Eds.): IEA/AIE 2008, LNAI 5027, pp. 169–178, 2008.

approach. Hong *et al.* then modified the FP-tree structure and designed the fast updated frequent pattern trees (FUFP-trees) to efficiently handle newly inserted transactions based on the FUP concept [10]. The FUFP-tree structure was similar to the FP-tree structure except that the links between parent nodes and their child nodes were bi-directional. Besides, the counts of the sorted frequent items were also kept in the Header_Table of the FP-tree algorithm.

In this paper, we attempt to further modify the FUFP-tree algorithm for incremental mining based on the concept of pre-large itemsets [9]. A structure of prelarge tree is proposed and a mining algorithm based on the tree is provided to get the association rules. The structure keeps not only frequent items but also pre-large items. The proposed algorithm does not require rescanning the original databases to construct the prelarge tree until a number of new transactions have been processed. Experimental results also show that the proposed algorithm has a good performance for incrementally handling new transactions.

The remainder of this paper is organized as follows. Related works are reviewed in Section 2. The proposed Prelarge-tree mining algorithm is described in Section 3. An example to illustrate the proposed algorithm is given in Section 4. Experimental results for showing the performance of the proposed algorithm are provided in Section 5. Conclusions are finally given in Section 6.

2 Review of Related Works

2.1 The FUFP-Tree Algorithm

The FUFP-tree construction algorithm is based on the FP-tree algorithm [8]. The links between parent nodes and their child nodes are, however, bi-directional. Bi-directional linking will help fasten the process of item deletion in the maintenance process. Besides, the counts of the sorted frequent items are also kept in the Header_Table.

An FUFP tree must be built in advance from the original database before new transactions come. When new transactions are added, the FUFP-tree maintenance algorithm will process them to maintain the FUFP tree. It first partitions items into four parts according to whether they are large or small in the original database and in the new transactions. Each part is then processed in its own way. The Header_Table and the FUFP-tree are correspondingly updated whenever necessary.

In the process for updating the FUFP tree, item deletion is done before item insertion. When an originally large item becomes small, it is directly removed from the FUFP tree and its parent and child nodes are then linked together. On the contrary, when an originally small item becomes large, it is added to the end of the Header_Table and then inserted into the leaf nodes of the FUFP tree. It is reasonable to insert the item at the end of the Header_Table since when an originally small item becomes large due to the new transactions, its updated support is usually only a little larger than the minimum support. The FUFP tree can thus be least updated in this way, and the performance of the FUFP-tree maintenance algorithm can be greatly improved. The entire FUFP tree can then be re-constructed in a batch way when a sufficiently large number of transactions have been inserted.

2.2 The Pre-Large-Itemset Algorithm

Hong et *al.* proposed the pre-large concept to reduce the need of rescanning original database [9] for maintaining association rules. A pre-large itemset is not truly large, but may be large with a high probability in the future. A pre-large itemset was defined based on two support thresholds, a lower support threshold and an upper support threshold. The support ratio of an itemset must be larger than the upper support threshold in order to be considered large. On the other hand, the lower support threshold defines the lowest support ratio for an itemset to be treated as pre-large. An itemset with its support ratio below the lower threshold is thought of as a small itemset. Pre-large itemsets act like buffers in the incremental mining process and are used to reduce the movements of itemsets directly from large to small and vice-versa.

Considering an original database and transactions which are newly inserted by the two support thresholds, itemsets may fall into one of the following nine cases illustrated in Figure 1.

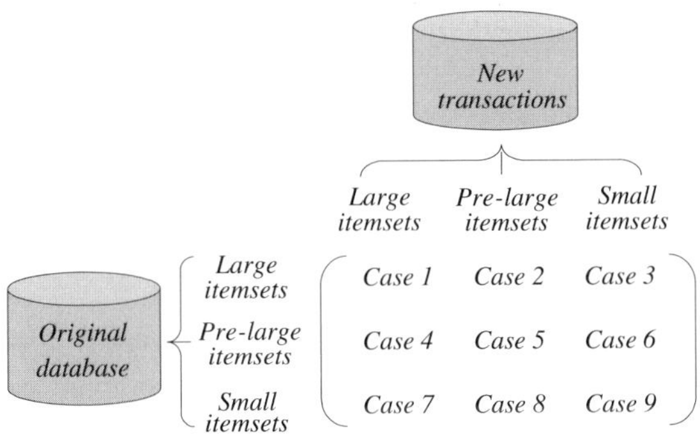

Fig. 1. Nine cases arising from adding new transactions to existing databases

Cases 1, 5, 6, 8 and 9 will not affect the final association rules according to the weighted average of the counts. Cases 2 and 3 may remove existing association rules, and cases 4 and 7 may add new association rules. If we retain all large and pre-large itemsets with their counts after each pass, then cases 2, 3 and case 4 can be handled easily. It has been formally shown that an itemset in Case 7 cannot possibly be large for the entire updated database as long as the number of transactions is smaller than the number f shown below [9]:

$$f = \left\lfloor \frac{(S_u - S_l)d}{1 - S_u} \right\rfloor,$$

where f is the safety number of the new transactions, S_u is the upper threshold, S_l is the lower threshold, and d is the number of original transactions.

3 The Proposed Incremental Mining Approach

A prelarge tree must be built in advance from the initially original database before new transactions come. Its initial construction is stated as follows. The database is first scanned to find the large items which have their supports larger than the upper support threshold and the pre-large items which have their minimum supports lie between the upper and lower support thresholds. Next, the large and the pre-large items are sorted in descending frequencies. The database is then scanned again to construct the prelarge tree according to the sorted order of large and pre-large items. The construction process is executed tuple by tuple, from the first transaction to the last one. After all transactions are processed, the prelarge tree is completely constructed. The frequency values of large items and pre-large items are kept in the Header_Table and Pre_Header_Table, respectively. Besides, a variable c is used to record the number of new transactions since the last re-scan of the original database with d transactions. Based on the proposed structure of prelarge trees, the details of the corresponding algorithm to maintain the structure for incremental mining is described below.

The prelarge-tree mining algorithm:

Input: An old database consisting of $(d+c)$ transactions, its corresponding Header_Table and Pre_Header_Table, its corresponding prelarge tree, a lower support threshold S_l, an upper support threshold S_u, and a set of t new transactions.

Output: A new prelarge tree for the updated database.

Step 1:   Calculate the safety number f of new transactions according to the following formula [9].

Step 2:   Scan the new transactions to get all the items and their counts.

Step 3:   Divide the items in the new transactions into three parts according to whether they are large (appearing in the Header_Table), pre-large (appearing in the Pre_Header_Table) or small (not in the Header_Table or in the Pre_Header_Table) in the original database.

Step 4:   For each item I which is large in the original database, do the following substeps (**Cases 1, 2** and **3**):

Substep 4-1: Set the new count $S^U(I)$ of I in the entire updated database as:
$$S^U(I) = S^D(I) + S^T(I),$$
where $S^D(I)$ is the count of I in the Header_Table (original database) and $S^T(I)$ is the count of I in the new transactions.

Substep 4-2: If $S^U(I)/(d+c+t) \geq S_u$, update the count of I in the Header_Table as $S^U(I)$, and put I in the set of *Insert_Items*, which will be further processed in STEP 8;

Otherwise, if $S_u > S^U(I)/(d+c+t) \geq S_l$, remove I from the Header_Table, put I in the head of Pre_Header_Table with its updated frequency $S^D(I)$, and keep I in the set of *Insert_Items*;

Otherwise, item I is still small after the database is updated; remove I from the Header_Table and connect each parent node of I directly to its child node in the prelarge tree.

Step 5: For each item I which is pre-large in the original database, do the following substeps (**Cases 4, 5** and **6**):

Substep 5-1: Set the new count $S^U(I)$ of I in the entire updated database as:
$$S^U(I) = S^D(I) + S^T(I),$$

Substep 5-2: If $S^U(I)/(d+c+t) \geq S_u$, item I will be large after the database is updated; remove I from the Pre_Hedaer_Table, put I with its new frequency $S^D(I)$ in the end of Header_Table, and put I in the set of *Insert_Items*;

Otherwise, if $S_u > S^U(I)/(d+c+t) \geq S_l$, item I is still pre-large after the database is updated; update I with its new frequency $S^D(I)$ in the Pre_Header_Table and put I in the set of *Insert_Items*;

Otherwise, remove item I from the Pre_Header_Table.

Step 6: For each item I which is neither large nor pre-large in the original database but large or pre-large in the new transactions (**Cases 7** and **8**), put I in the set of *Rescan_Items*, which is used when rescanning the database in STEP 7 is necessary.

Step 7: If $t + c \leq f$ or the set of *Rescan_Items* is *null*, then do nothing; Otherwise, do the following substeps for each item I in the set of *Rescan_Items*:

Substep 7-1: Rescan the original database to decide the original count $S^D(I)$ of I.

Substep 7-2: Set the new count $S^U(I)$ of I in the entire updated database as:
$$S^U(I) = S^D(I) + S^T(I),$$

Substep 7-3: If $S^U(I)/(d+c+t) \geq S_u$, item I will become large after the database is updated; put I in both the sets of *Insert_Items* and *Branch_Items* and insert the items in the *Branch_Items* to the end of the Header_Table according to the descending order of their updated counts;

Otherwise, if $S_u > S^U(I)/(d+c+t) \geq S_l$, item I will become pre-large after the database is update; put I in both the sets of *Insert_Items* and *Branch_Items*, and insert the items in the *Branch_Items* to the end of the Pre_Header_Table according to the descending order of their updated counts. Otherwise, do nothing.

Substep 7-4: For each original transaction with an item I existing in the *Branch_Items*, if I has not been at the corresponding branch of the prelarge tree for the transaction, insert I at the end of the branch and set its count as 1; Otherwise, add 1 to the count of the node I.

Substep 7-5: Otherwise, neglect I.

Step 8: For each new transaction with an item I existing in the *Insert_Items*, if I has not been at the corresponding branch of the prelarge tree for the new transaction, insert I at the end of the branch and set its count as 1; otherwise, add 1 to the count of the node I.

Step 9: If $t + c > f$, then set $d = d + t + c$ and set $c = 0$; otherwise, set $c = t + c$.

In the above algorithm, a corresponding branch is the branch generated from the large and pre-large items in a transaction and corresponding to the order of items appearing in the Header_Table and the Pre_Header_Table. Based on the prelarge tree, the desired association rules can then be found by the FP-Growth mining approach as proposed in [8] on only the large items.

4 An Example

In this session, an example is given to illustrate the proposed algorithm for maintaining a prelarge tree when new transactions are inserted. Table 1 shows a database to be used in the example. It contains 10 transactions and 9 items, denoted a to i.

Table 1. The original database in the example

Old database	
TID	Items
1	a, b, c, f, g
2	a, b, c, f, g
3	a, d, e, f, h
4	e, h, i
5	e, d, h, f
6	b, c, d
7	b, d, i
8	b, c, d
9	b, c, e, f, h
10	a, b, c, f, g

Assume the lower support threshold S_l is set at 30% and the upper one S_u at 50%. Here, not only the frequent items are kept in the prelarge tree but also the pre-large items. For the given database, the large items are b, c, f and d, and the pre-large items are a, e, h and g, from which the Header_Table and the Pre_Header_Table can be constructed. The prelarge tree is then formed from the database, the Header_Table and the Pre_Header_Table. The results are shown in Figure 2.

Here, we assume the three new transactions shown in Table 2 appear. The proposed prelarge-tree mining algorithm proceeds as follows. The variable c is initially set at 0.

Table 2. The three new transactions

Transaction No.	Items
1	a, b, c, e, f
2	e, h, i
3	d, e, f, h

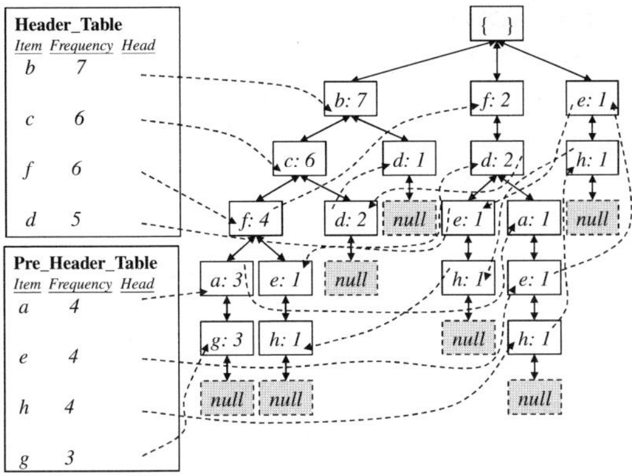

Fig. 2. The Header_Table, Pre_Header_Table and the prelarge tree constructed

The safety number f is first calculated as follows:

$$f = \left\lfloor \frac{(S_u - S_l)d}{1 - S_u} \right\rfloor = \left\lfloor \frac{(0.5 - 0.3)10}{1 - 0.5} \right\rfloor = 4.$$

The three new transactions are first scanned to get the items and their counts. All the items a to i are divided into three parts, $\{b\}\{c\}\{f\}\{d\}$, $\{a\}\{e\}\{h\}\{g\}$, and $\{i\}$ according to whether they are large (appearing in the Header_Table), pre-large (appearing in the Pre_Header_Table) or small in the original database. Each part is processed according the proposed prelarge-tree mining algorithm. The final results after STEP 9 are shown in Figure 3. Since $t (= 3) + c (= 0) < f (= 4)$, set $c = t + c = 3 + 0 = 3$. Note that the final value of c is 3 in this example and $f - c = 1$. This means that one more new transaction can be added without rescanning the original database for Case 7. Based on the prelarge tree shown in Figure 3, the desired large itemsets can then be found by the FP-Growth mining approach as proposed in [8] on only the large items.

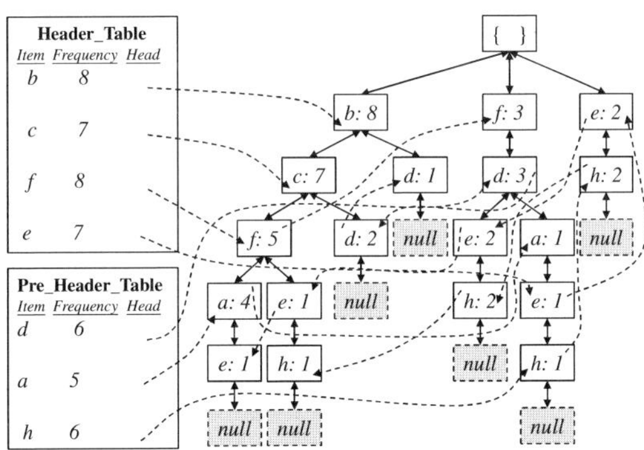

Fig. 3. The Header_Table, Pre_Header_Table and the prelarge tree after STEP 9

5   Experimental Results

Experiments were made to compare the performance of the batch FP-tree construction algorithm, the FUFP-tree mining algorithm and the prelarge-tree mining algorithm. A real dataset called BMS-POS [13] were used in the experiments. Each transaction in this dataset consisted of all the product categories purchased by a customer at one time. The first 500,000 transactions were extracted from the BMS-POS database to construct an initial tree structure. The value of the minimum support thresholds were set at 7% to 15% for the three mining algorithms, with 2% increment each time. The next 3,000 transactions were then used in incremental mining. For the prelarge-tree mining algorithm, the lower minimum support thresholds were set as the values of the minimum support threshold minus 0.8%, which are 6.2%, 8.2%, 10.2%. 12.2% and 14.2%, respectively. Figure 4 shows the execution times of the three algorithms for different threshold values.

It can be observed from Figure 4 that the proposed prelarge-tree mining algorithm ran faster than the other two. When the minimum support threshold was larger, the effects became more obvious. Note that the FUFP-tree mining algorithm and the prelarge-tree mining algorithm may generate a less concise tree than the FP-tree construction algorithm since the latter completely follows the sorted frequent items to build the tree. As mentioned above, when an originally small item becomes large due to new transactions, its updated support is usually only a little larger than the minimum support. The difference between the FP-tree, the FUFP-tree and the prelarge-tree structures (considering large items) will thus not be significant. For showing this effect, the comparison of the numbers of nodes for the three algorithms is given in Figure 5. It can be seen that the three algorithms generated nearly the same sizes of trees. The effectiveness of the prelarge-tree mining algorithm is thus acceptable.

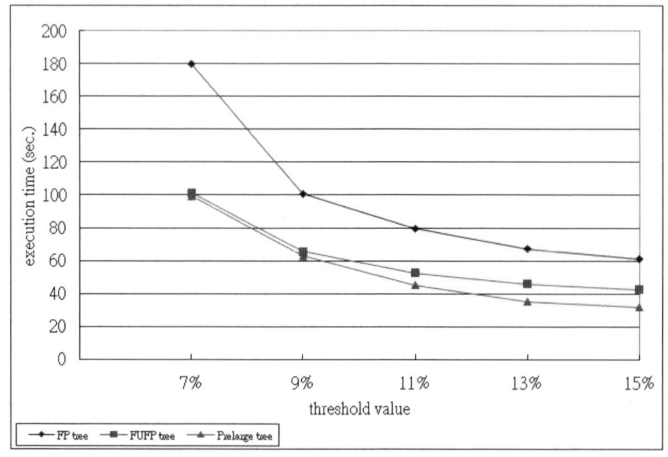

Fig. 4. The comparison of the execution times for different threshold values

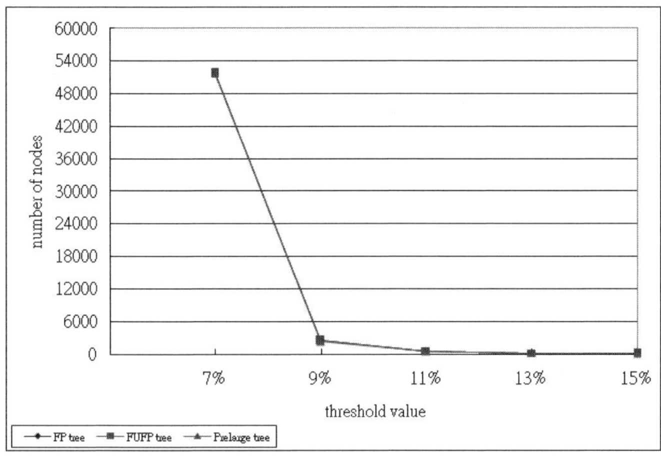

Fig. 5. The comparison of the numbers of nodes for different threshold values

6 Conclusion

In this paper, we have proposed a new incremental mining algorithm based on the concept of pre-large itemsets. The prelarge-tree structure is used to efficiently and effectively handle new transactions. Using two user-specified upper and lower support thresholds, the pre-large items act as a gap to avoid small items becoming large in the updated database when transactions are inserted. When new transactions are added, the proposed prelarge-tree mining algorithm processes them to maintain the prelarge tree. It first partitions items of new transactions into three parts according to whether they are large, pre-large or small in the original database. Each part is then processed in its own way. The Header_Table, the Pre_Header_Table, and the pre-large-tree are correspondingly updated whenever necessary.

Experimental results also show that the proposed prelarge-tree mining algorithm runs faster than the batch FP-tree and the FUFP-tree algorithm for handling new transactions and generates nearly the same number of frequent nodes as them. The proposed approach can thus achieve a good trade-off between execution time and tree complexity.

Acknowledgments. This research was supported by the National Science Council of the Republic of China under contract NSC 96-2221-E-390-003.

References

1. Agrawal, R., Imielinksi, T., Swami, A.: Mining association rules between sets of items in large database. In: The ACM SIGMOD Conference, pp. 207–216 (1993)
2. Agrawal, R., Srikant, R.: Fast algorithm for mining association rules. In: The International Conference on Very Large Data Bases, pp. 487–499 (1994)

3. Agrawal, R., Srikant, R.: Fast algorithm for mining association rules. In: The International Conference on Very Large Data Bases, pp. 487–499 (1994)
4. Agrawal, R., Srikant, R.: Mining sequential patterns. In: The Eleventh IEEE International Conference on Data Engineering, pp. 3–14 (1995)
5. Agrawal, R., Srikant, R., Vu, Q.: Mining association rules with item constraints. In: The Third International Conference on Knowledge Discovery in Databases and Data Mining, pp. 67–73 (1997)
6. Fukuda, T., Morimoto, Y., Morishita, S., Tokuyama, T.: Mining optimized association rules for numeric attributes. In: The ACM SIGACT-SIGMOD-SIGART Symposium on Principles of Database Systems, pp. 182–191 (1996)
7. Han, J., Fu, Y.: Discovery of multiple-level association rules from large database. In: The Twenty-first International Conference on Very Large Data Bases, pp. 420–431 (1995)
8. Han, J., Pei, J., Yin, Y.: Mining frequent patterns without candidate generation. In: The 2000 ACM SIGMOD International Conference on Management of Data, pp. 1–12 (2000)
9. Hong, T.P., Wang, C.Y., Tao, Y.H.: A new incremental data mining algorithm using pre-large itemsets. In: Intelligent Data Analysis, pp. 111–129 (2001)
10. Hong, T.P., Lin, C.W., Wu, Y.L.: Incrementally fast updated frequent pattern trees. Expert Systems with Applications (to appear)
11. Mannila, H.T., Verkamo, A.I.: Efficient algorithm for discovering association rules. In: The AAAI Workshop on Knowledge Discovery in Databases, pp. 181–192 (1994)
12. Park, J.S., Chen, M.S., Yu, P.S.: Using a hash-based method with transaction trimming for mining association rules. IEEE Transactions on Knowledge and Data Engineering, 812–825 (1997)
13. Zheng, Z., Kohavi, R., Mason, L.: Real world performance of association rule algorithms. In: The International Conference on Knowledge Discovery and Data Mining, pp. 401–406 (2001)

Learning Higher Accuracy Decision Trees from Concept Drifting Data Streams

Satoru Nishimura, Masahiro Terabe,
Kazuo Hashimoto, and Koichiro Mihara

Graduate School of Information Science, Tohoku University,
6-6-11-304 Aramaki-Aza-Aoba, Aoba-Ku, Sendai, Miyagi, 980-8579, Japan
{nishimura, terabe, kh, mihara}@aiet.ecei.tohoku.ac.jp

Abstract. In this paper, we propose to combine the naive-Bayes approach with CVFDT, which is known as one of the major algorithms to induce a high-accuracy decision tree from time-changing data streams. The proposed improvement, called $CVFDT_{NBC}$, induces a decision tree as CVFDT does, but contains naive-Bayes classifiers in the leaf nodes of the induced decision tree. The experiment using the artificially generated time-changing data streams shows that $CVFDT_{NBC}$ can induce a decision tree with more accuracy than CVFDT does.

Keywords: data stream, concept drift, decision tree, naive-Bayes classifiers, CVFDT.

1 Introduction

The recent development of sensor technologies and the rapid spread of the internet enable to obtain a huge amount of electronic data from the internet. Such data, as they arrive continuously but in various time intervals, are called a data stream[6]. Data stream can be viewed as stationary or non-stationary random process, whose total size of data is infinite in nature. To cope with such characteristics of data stream, a number of learning algorithms have been proposed so far.

Especially when a data stream is non-stationary, the model to be constructed changes over time. This time-variance is referred to as a concept drift. Learning algorithms should adapt the concept drift of the data stream under consideration.

Among methods to induce a classifier, a decision tree is one of the most widely accepted methods in the field of data mining for its fastness of learning and easiness of intuitive understanding.

Several algorithms have been proposed to induce a classifier from a data stream with concept drift as in [4,5,7,9,10,16]. Hulten et al. have proposed CVFDT (Concept-adapting Very Fast Decision Tree)[7] as the method to induce a decision tree. CVFDT is an incremental algorithm, and can induce a high-accuracy decision tree efficiently from a data stream with concept drift.

Kohavi et al. have proposed NBTree[11], which combines naive-Bayes approach[13] with C4.5[14], which is the major batch algorithm to induce a decision tree. NBTree induces a hybrid of decision tree classifiers and naive-Bayes

N.T. Nguyen et al. (Eds.): IEA/AIE 2008, LNAI 5027, pp. 179–188, 2008.
© Springer-Verlag Berlin Heidelberg 2008

classifiers (abbreviated as NBC in this paper), that is more compact and more accurate decision tree than the original C4.5 to predict the class of test example.

We propose an improvement to CVFDT, $CVFDT_{NBC}$ (CVFDT with naive-Bayes classifiers), for learning a high-accuracy decision tree from data streams with concept drift. $CVFDT_{NBC}$ applies NBCs in the leaf nodes of a decision tree induced by CVFDT. The resultant classifiers show more accurate performances than those by CVFDT with almost same training time, while preserving all the desirable properties of a decision tree.

2   Related Works

There are two ways to induce classifiers from data streams with concept drift. One is to induce a new decision tree periodically based on data stored at certain intervals by a batch algorithm, the other is to update an old decision tree based on the latest data by an incremental algorithm.

C4.5[14] is a batch algorithm that can induces a decision tree from massive data. Kohavi et al. have proposed NBTree[11] which applies NBCs to C4.5. NBTree can induce a more compact and more accurate decision tree than C4.5 does by applying NBCs to predict the class of example in the leaf nodes. To induce a decision tree from data streams with concept drift by a batch algorithm, we have to reconstruct a new decision tree in periodical time interval. It takes a certain amount of time to rebuild a new decision tree. Until a new decision tree is obtained, the data stream has to be processed with the old decision tree, which may have not reflected the most recent concept drift. This time lag causes a degradation in classification accuracy. Furthermore, the reconstruction of decision tree would be recommended whenever concept drift happens in data stream, however, it is difficult to predict an occurrence of concept drift. Unless reconstruction of decision tree is done in an appropriate interval, it will become another cause of degradation in classification accuracy.

CVFDT[7] is proposed as an incremental algorithm to induce a decision tree from a data stream with concept drift. Storing training examples in decision tree causes memory consumption and increase of process time, CVFDT only maintains frequencies of each combination on classes and attribute values at each node. CVFDT calculate information gain using frequencies. And, CVFDT uses the Hoeffding Bound to evaluate the validity of a splitting attribute estimated from the examples which reach the decision node. By the Hoeffding Bound, CVFDT can choose a precise and dependable splitting attribute. As a result, CVFDT can induce an accurate decision tree.

If concept drift happens, we have to make decision tree up to date to keep classification accuracy high. CVFDT reevaluate the validities of splitting attributes at each node periodically using the Hoeffding Bound. Once the splitting attribute of a node is considered as inappropriate, under the node CVFDT starts to generate an alternative subtree for the old subtree. When the alternative subtree becomes more accurate than the old subtree, CVFDT replace the old subtree with the alternative subtree.

3 CVFDT$_{\mathrm{NBC}}$ – CVFDT with Naive-Bayes Classifiers

Like C4.5[14], CVFDT[7] predicts the classes of test examples as the majority class of the leaf nodes that test examples reach. The utilized information to predict class is only the frequencies of each class, although frequencies of each combination of class and attribute value are stored under each leaf node of the decision tree. NBTree[11], however, shows that the accuracy of classifiers can be improved by constructing a hybrid of decision tree classifiers and NBCs.

Therefore, we propose CVFDT$_{\mathrm{NBC}}$ (CVFDT with naive-Bayes classifiers), which applies NBCs to the leaf nodes of a decision tree induced by CVFDT. To improve the accuracy of classifiers, CVFDT$_{\mathrm{NBC}}$ utilizes frequencies of each combination of class and attribute value of training examples assigned to each leaf node to classify test examples, which is the unused information in CVFDT.

Applying NBCs to the leaf nodes of a decision tree, we can divide an example space more finely. As a result of fine division of an example space, classifier shows high classification accuracy. Figure 1 shows an example that NBCs divide example space more finely.

For the sake of ease, we assume that the number of attributes is 2, and a decision tree of Fig.1(b) was learned after learning training examples shown in Fig.1(a). We assume that a decision tree shown in Fig.1(b) can't split any more because of the Hoeffding Bound.

Because decision trees classify test examples based on only class frequencies of training examples at leaf nodes, the decision tree couldn't learn training examples correctly shown in Fig.1(b). On the other hand, applying NBCs to the leaf nodes of a decision tree make it possible to divide an example space more finely using not only class frequencies of training examples but also information about attribute values at leaf nodes. As a result of fine division of an example space, we can learn training examples correctly shown in Fig.1(c)

When classifying a test example by a decision tree, CVFDT tests the example repeatedly based on a splitting attribute at each node from a root node to a leaf node, and finally predicts the class of a test example as the majority class of

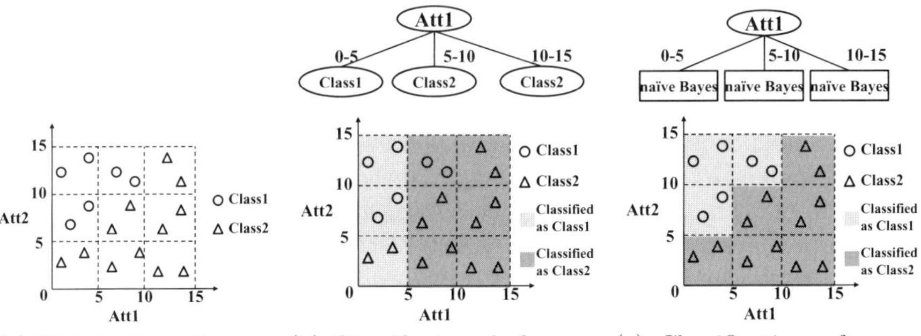

(a) Distribution of exam- (b) Classification before ap- (c) Classification after ap-
ple. plying NBCs. plying NBCs.

Fig. 1. The effect of applying NBCs

Table 1. The classification algorithm of CVFDT/CVFDT$_{\mathrm{NBC}}$

Input:	HT : HT is a decision tree induced by CVFDT/CVFDT$_{\mathrm{NBC}}$.
	e : e is a test example.
Output:	class : The class CVFDT/CVFDT$_{\mathrm{NBC}}$ predicts.

CVFDTClassify(HT,e)	**CVFDT$_{\mathrm{NBC}}$Classify(HT,e)**
l=DecisionTreeTraverse(HT, e)	l=DecisionTreeTraverse(HT,e)
Return Majority class of l.	class=NaiveBayesClassify(l,e)
	Return class.

the leaf node where the test example reaches. On the other hand, classification by CVFDT$_{\mathrm{NBC}}$ is different from CVFDT in that the class of a test example is predicted by one of the NBCs based on training examples' class frequencies and attributes' information assigned to a leaf node. NBC classifies a test example e as the class C that maximizes the probability $P(C|e)$ of (1).

$$P(C|e) \propto P(C) \prod_{i=1}^{d} P(e_i|C). \tag{1}$$

Here, e is an example, and e_i is the ith attribute value of the example e, d is the number of attributes. To classify test examples by NBCs, CVFDT$_{\mathrm{NBC}}$ uses both $P(C)$ and $P(e_i|C)$. Note that CVFDT holds this information. The amount of information maintained by CVFDT$_{\mathrm{NBC}}$ is the same as that of CVFDT. CVFDT$_{\mathrm{NBC}}$ does not request any bigger memory capacity than CVFDT.

Table 1 shows the classification algorithm of CVFDT and that of CVFDT$_{\mathrm{NBC}}$. DecisionTreeTraverse(HT, e) in Table 1 is the function that applies a decision tree HT to a test example e, and returns the leaf node l which the test example reaches. Meanwhile, NaiveBayesClassify(l, e) in Table 1 is the function, which applies NBC at the leaf node l which the test example e reaches, and returns the class that maximizes the probability estimated by the NBC.

NBCs are known as robust to irrelevant attributes, outliers and noise. Because NBC takes into account evidences from many attributes to predict the class of example, it works effectively even if dominant attributes for classification are not given. Although NBC assumes each attribute is independent, Domingos et al. proved that a NBC could achieve high accuracy, even if the assumption of attributes' independence doesn't hold, and shows sufficient accuracy from a few training examples[1]. Therefore, it is expected that CVFDT$_{\mathrm{NBC}}$ would show high accuracy from a few examples assigned to leaf nodes.

During the induction of a decision tree, CVFDT$_{\mathrm{NBC}}$ maintains essential information to introduce NBCs. Both the prior probability $P(C)$ and the posterior probability $P(e_i|C)$ are accumulated on each node naturally. The application of NBCs doesn't cause any overhead for training.

On the other hand, it is supposed that CVFDT$_{\mathrm{NBC}}$ takes more time to classify test examples than CVFDT. CVFDT just applies a decision tree to test examples in classification. However, CVFDT$_{\mathrm{NBC}}$ takes extra time to apply NBCs at the leaf node a test example reaches, in addition to the classification time of CVFDT. Thus, the time for classification by $\text{CVFDT}_{\text{NBC}}$ is longer than by CVFDT.

Like CVFDT, $\text{CVFDT}_{\text{NBC}}$ can deal with only nominal attributes.

4 Experiments

4.1 Experiment Settings

We conducted experiments to compare the performance of $\text{CVFDT}_{\text{NBC}}$ with CVFDT using artificially generated data streams whose characteristics could be adjusted by parameters. We chose two decision tree algorithms, a batch algorithm of C4.5 and an incremental algorithm of CVFDT, to compare with $\text{CVFDT}_{\text{NBC}}$. In our experiments, we used C4.5 Release 8[14], and CVFDT which is released in VFML[8]. The computer environment of the experiments is a 3.06GHz Pentium(R)4 machine with 2GB of RAM, running Fedora Core 6.

4.2 Data for Experiments

Following suggestions shown in Hulten et al.[7], we generate artificial data streams with concept drift to carry out performance tests. Every example e consists of d attributes and a class. Each attribute value e_i takes one of five values $\{0.1, 0.3, 0.5, 0.7, 0.9\}$. And the classes are binary, namely each class value is positive or negative.

Generation of Examples. First, examples are generated uniformly in a d-dimensional hypercube, where each attribute value is ranging from [0,1]. And we divide the example space into subspaces by the hyper plane (2).

$$\sum_{i=1}^{d} w_i e_i = w_0. \tag{2}$$

Let e_i as the ith attribute value of an example e and w_i as the weight given to the ith attribute. If an example e satisfies $\sum_{i=1}^{d} w_i e_i \geq w_0$, the example is labeled positive. And if an example satisfies $\sum_{i=1}^{d} w_i e_i < w_0$, the example is labeled negative. We can slide the hyper plane slightly and smoothly by changing the weight vector w. As a result of changing the weight vector, the class of some examples could change. That is how concept drifts are generated.

A weight w_i given to each attribute means the importance of the ith attribute for determining the class of example. For example, if all but one of the weights is zero, it means that the attribute with non-zero weight is the only one that contains information to decide the class of example. Namely, by changing the weight vector w, we can adjust the importance of each attribute to decide the class of example.

In our experiments, according to the left hand side of (2), we change the class of examples every $0.2w_0$. That is to say, depending on the left hand side of (2) which is determined by each attribute value e_i and each weight w_i, we label examples as positive if they satisfy $0 \leq \sum_{i=1}^{d} w_i e_i < 0.2w_0$, and as negative if they satisfy $0.2w_0 \leq \sum_{i=1}^{d} w_i e_i < 0.4w_0$, and as positive if they satisfy $0.4w_0 \leq \sum_{i=1}^{d} w_i e_i < 0.6w_0$ and so on.

After determining the class of example, every attribute value e_i is discretized into the midpoints of equally divided 5 intervals. And as a noise, we reversed 5% of examples' class.

Concept Drift. We initialize every weight w_i as 0.2, except for w_0 that was $w_0 = 0.25d$. Every 50,000 examples, we change the weights of the attributes which we want to drift by adding $0.007d\sigma_i$ to w_i, where σ_i is a direction of the change of the ith weight w_i. σ_i is initialized as 1, and is multiplied by -1 at 5% every 50,000 training examples. The domain of a weight is $0 \leq w_i \leq 0.2d$, and σ_i is multiplied by -1 before the weight goes out of the domain so that it always stays in $0 \leq w_i \leq 0.2d$.

Figure 2(a) shows the relation between the number of attributes and the degree of concept drift (drift level) where one attribute is drifted. Figure 3 shows the relation between the number of drifting attributes and the drift level where the number of attributes is 10. Here, the drifting attribute is the attribute whose weight changes after concept drift, and the drift level is a percentage of the test examples whose classes changed after concept drift. Figure 2(a) shows that the drift level is almost the same when the number of drifting attributes is same, and Fig.3 shows that the drift level rises as the number of drifting attributes increases.

4.3   Experimental Results

We prepared data streams which consist of 3,000,000 of training examples generated as mentioned above. Whenever every 10,000 examples are streamed in, we evaluated the classification accuracy, training time, and classification time of the induced classifier, by giving 100 test examples that represent the latest concept. Therefore, we will conduct 300 tests, and the classification accuracy, the training time for learning 10,000 training examples and the classification time for 100 test examples and the size of induced trees are given by the average of 300 tests. Concept drift is generated by changing the weight vector for every 50,000 training examples.

The parameters of CVFDT were the same as in Hulten et al.[7] and the parameters of C4.5 were default settings.

The Number of Attributes and Performance. Figure 2(a) shows the changes of classification errors when one attribute was drifted by changing the number of attributes d. CVFDT$_{\mathrm{NBC}}$ always achieved the lowest classification error. The classification error of CVFDT and C4.5 became lower as the number of attributes increased, but CVFDT$_{\mathrm{NBC}}$ didn't.

Because the problem becomes easier as the number of attributes increases, the classification error of CVFDT and C4.5 became lower. But CVFDT$_{\mathrm{NBC}}$ applies NBCs which uses all the attribute. Because of discretization of attribute value,

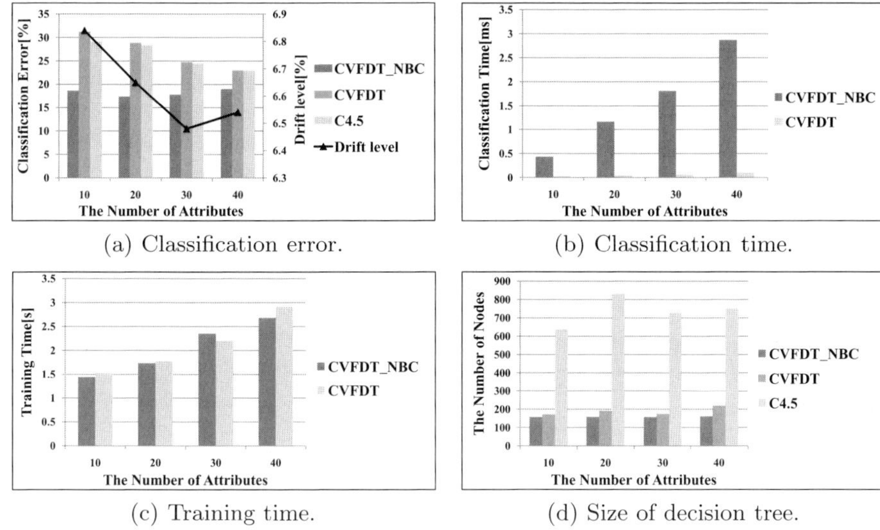

(a) Classification error.

(b) Classification time.

(c) Training time.

(d) Size of decision tree.

Fig. 2. Relation between the number of attributes and performance of classifiers

NBCs' performance degrade as the number of attributes increases. This is why $CVFDT_{NBC}$'s classification error didn't change.

Figure 2(b) shows the time taken to classify 100 test examples. $CVFDT_{NBC}$ took longer period of time to classify test examples than CVFDT did. $CVFDT_{NBC}$ needed longer time to classify test examples as the number of attributes d increased. Because of application of NBCs to the leaf nodes of a decision tree, $CVFDT_{NBC}$ takes extra time to apply NBCs to classify test examples.

NBCs, however, run fast in classification, the increase of processing time stayed very small. So the increase of classification time in $CVFDT_{NBC}$ should not be a big problem to cope with data stream, unless hundreds of test examples are made in a short time.

Figure 2(c) shows the time to learn 10,000 training examples. Using the information maintained at each node, $CVFDT_{NBC}$ can apply NBCs to the leaf nodes of a decision tree induced by CVFDT with no extra time. Therefore, training time of CVFDT and $CVFDT_{NBC}$ were almost same.

Figure 2(d) shows that decision trees induced by $CVFDT_{NBC}$ are almost same in size as CVFDT, and less than half of C4.5. $CVFDT_{NBC}$ induces single decision tree, and the size is smaller than that of C4.5, decision trees induced by $CVFDT_{NBC}$ are easy for human analysts to understand.

Drift Level and Performance. Next, we investigated classification error when the number of drifting attributes changes with the number of attributes set to 10. The result is shown in Fig.3. Figure 3 shows that $CVFDT_{NBC}$ achieved lower classification error than CVFDT at every drift level. It is observed that the improvement in classification accuracy of $CVFDT_{NBC}$ against CVFDT becomes smaller, as the number of drifting attributes increases. CVFDT classifies test

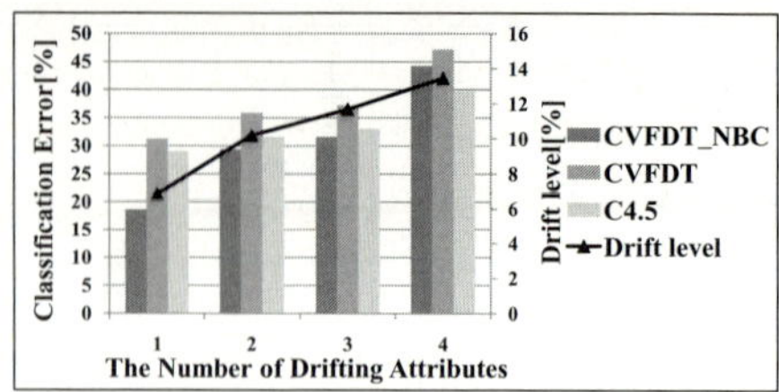

Fig. 3. The number of drifting attributes and classification error

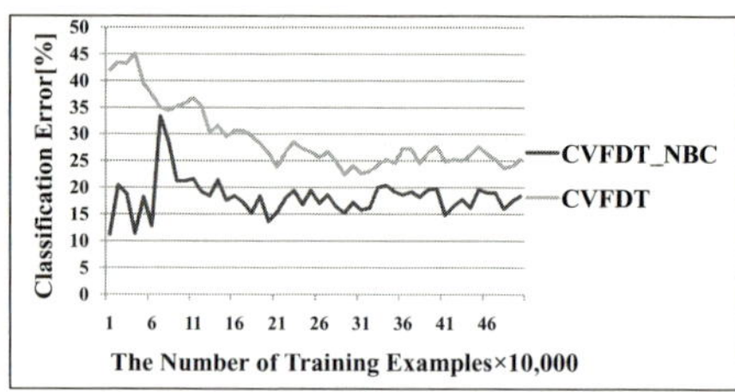

Fig. 4. Classification accuracy in early phase of data streams

examples as the class C which maximize the prior probability $P(C)$ in leaf nodes. On the other hand, because of NBCs applied to the leaf nodes, CVFDT$_{NBC}$ predicts the class of example based on not only the prior probability $P(C)$ but also the posterior probability $P(e_i|C)$, shown in (1). In such a case where the drift level is not high, CVFDT$_{NBC}$ could estimate classes correctly restraining the influences of concept drift by utilizing the posterior probability $P(e_i|C)$. But the effect of NBCs decreases as the drift level increases. This is why the advantage of CVFDT$_{NBC}$ over CVFDT shrinks.

Training Speed. We conducted the experiment to compare the classification accuracy of CVFDT$_{NBC}$ with CVFDT at early phase of learning. We generated artificial data streams consist of 500,000 training examples, and every time 10,000 training examples are learned, we gave 100 test examples to the induced classifiers. We repeated this procedure five times. In this experiment, the number of attributes was set to 20 with one attribute drifting. The result shown below is given by the average of five procedures. Figure 4 shows classification error of CVFDT and CVFDT$_{NBC}$ for every 10,000 examples were learned. CVFDT$_{NBC}$ has the advantage over CVFDT that it achieves high accuracy than CVFDT from the beginning of data stream, even in the region lower than 50,000 accumulated examples.

5   Conclusion and Future Work

NBTree improved the accuracy of classifiers by constructing a hybrid of decision tree classifiers and NBCs. Inspired by NBTree, we proposed the novel algorithm to induce a high-accuracy decision tree from a data stream with concept drift, called $CVFDT_{NBC}$, which applies NBCs to leaf nodes of a decision tree induced by CVFDT. With artificially generated data streams, we evaluated the performance of $CVFDT_{NBC}$.

The advantage of $CVFDT_{NBC}$ over CVFDT is that it achieves high accuracy in classification with almost the same training time and with the same amount of memory. Although the classification time increases to apply NBCs, the increase will stay within the allowable range for practical use. Through our experiments, we confirmed that $CVFDT_{NBC}$ could induce a higher-accuracy decision tree than CVFDT.

Different from other major methods such as Support Vector Machine[10] and an ensemble of decision trees[5], it is $CVFDT_{NBC}$'s strength that it could induce a single classifier which is easy for human analysts to understand. Furthermore, $CVFDT_{NBC}$ could obtain high-accuracy classifier, and it could achieve higher accuracy than CVFDT from early phase of data stream.

We conclude this paper by listing the future work as follows:

- **Application to the Real dataF.** We are studying on the identification of health conditions of the aged by monitoring their vital data using a variety of sensors. These data streams naturally contain concept drift as the observed health conditions change. We are planning to evaluate the performance of $CVFDT_{NBC}$ by applying to the above mentioned real data streams.
- **Handling Numeric AttributesF.** Like CVFDT, $CVFDT_{NBC}$ can't handle numeric attribute. There are two methods to handle numeric attributes. The first is assuming the normal distributions of numeric attributes[5], and the other is discretizing numeric attributes[4,14,15]. Among these methods, discretization of numeric attributes is the most suitable from both an accuracy and an efficiency standpoint. It is reported that entropy based discretization is the best method in [3,12]. As concept drift triggers the recalculation of the discretized intervals, it is necessary to develop an adaptive method to maintain the discretization the most appropriate. A dynamical modification of discretized intervals requires to store each examples' attribute value. How to save unnecessary memory capacity is another issue that needs to be addressed to obtain an discretization method from data stream with concept drift.

References

1. Domingos, P., Pazzani, M.: On the Optimality of the Simple Bayesian Classifiers under Zero-One Loss. Machine Learning 29, 103–130 (1997)
2. Domingos, P., Hulten, G.: Mining High-Speed Data Streams. In: Proceeding of the Sixth ACM SIGKDD International Conference on Knowledge Discovery and Data Mining, pp. 71–80 (2000)
3. Dougherty, J., Kohavi, R., Sahami, M.: Supervised and Unsupervised Discretization of Continuous Features. In: Proceedings of the Twelfth International Conference on Machine Learning, pp. 194–202 (1995)

4. Gama, J., Rocha, R., Medas, P.: Accurate Decision Trees for Mining High-speed Data Streams. In: Proceedings of the Nineth ACM SIGKDD International Conference on Knowledge Discovery and Data Mining, pp. 523–528 (2003)
5. Gama, J., Medas, P., Rodrigues, P.: Learning Decision Trees from Dynamic Data Streams. In: Proceedings of the 2005 ACM Symposium on Applied computing, pp. 573–577 (2005)
6. Han, J., Kamber, M.: Data Mining: Concepts and Techiniques, 2nd edn. Morgan Kaufmann, San Francisco (2006)
7. Hulten, G., Spencer, L., Domingos, P.: Mining Time-changing Data Stream. In: Proceedings of the Seventh ACM SIGKDD International Conference on Knowledge Discovery and Data mining, pp. 97–106 (2001)
8. Hulten, G., Domingos, P.: VFML – A Toolkit for Mining High-speed Time-changing Data Streams (2003), http://www.cs.washington.edu/dm/vfml/
9. Kubat, M., Widmer, G.: Adapting to Drift in Continuous Domains. In: Proceedings of the Eighth European Conference on Machine Learning, pp. 307–310 (1995)
10. Klinkenberg, R., Joachims, T.: Detecting Concept Drift with Support Vector Machines. In: Proceedings of the Seventeenth International Conference on Machine Learning, pp. 487–494 (2000)
11. Kohavi, R.: Scaling Up the Accuracy of Naive- Bayes Classifiers: a Decision-Tree Hybrid. In: Proceedings of the Second International Conference on Knowledge Discovery and Data Mining, pp. 202–207 (1996)
12. Kohavi, R., Sahami, M.: Error-Based and Entropy-Based Discretization of Continuous Features. In: Proceedings of the Second International Conference on Knowledge Discovery and Data Mining, pp. 114–119 (1996)
13. Langley, P., Iba, W., Thompson, K.: An Analysis of Bayesian Classifiers. In: Proceedings of the Tenth National Conference on Artificial Intelligence, pp. 223–228 (1992)
14. Quinlan, J.R.: C4.5: Programs for Machine Learning. Morgan Kaufmann, San Francisco (1993)
15. Quinlan, J.R.: Improved Use of Continuous Attributes in C4.5. Journal of Artificial Intelligence Research 4, 77–90 (1996)
16. Widmer, G., Kubat, M.: Learning in the Presence of Concept Drift and Hidden Contexts. Machine Learning 23, 69–101 (1996)

Recommending Software Artifacts from Repository Transactions

Joern David

Technical University Munich, Institute of Computer Science I1
Boltzmannstrasse 3, 85748 Garching, Germany
david@in.tum.de

Abstract. The central problem addressed by this interdisciplinary paper is to predict related software artifacts that are usually changed together by a developer. The working focus of programmers is revealed by means of their interactions with a software repository that receives a set of cohesive artifact changes within one commit transaction. This implicit knowledge of interdependent changes can be exploited in order to recommend likely further changes, given a set of already changed artifacts. We suggest a hybrid approach based on *Latent Semantic Indexing* (LSI) and machine learning methods to recommend software development artifacts, that is predicting a sequence of configuration items that were committed together. As opposed to related approaches to repository mining that are mostly based on symbolic methods like *Association Rule Mining* (ARM), our connectionist method is able to generalize onto unseen artifacts. Text analysis methods are employed to consider their textual attributes. We applied our technique to three publicly available datasets from the *PROMISE Repository of Software Engineering Databases*. The evaluation showed that the connectionist LSI-approach achieves a significantly higher recommendation accuracy than existing methods based on ARM. Even when generalizing onto unseen artifacts, our approach still provides an accuracy of up to 72.7% on the given datasets.

Keywords: Change impact analysis, recurrent neural networks, latent semantic indexing, repository mining, artifact recommendation.

1   Introduction

Change impact analysis is an activity within the field of change management that is meant for planning changes to be made to a system [3]. The predominant goal of the work at hand is to predict related software artifacts that are usually changed together due to their explicit or latent interdependencies. Typically software artifacts like requirement documents, use case diagrams or source code are managed as *configuration items* and are kept under version control. A *Configuration Management (CM) aggregate* [4], or shortly *commit set*, is a composite of configuration items that are committed within the same repository transaction. The software developers' working focuses should be learned

N.T. Nguyen et al. (Eds.): IEA/AIE 2008, LNAI 5027, pp. 189–198, 2008.

from their interaction with the artifact repository by means of *learning by example*. Developers deal with a work package of a software project and complete each of their working steps with a commit operation on the artifact repository. Especially two distinct tasks are to be solved by learning from the repository transaction data.

1. **Suggesting further changes:** Guiding a beginner or an experienced programmer who is unfamiliar with a certain subsystem and its configuration items. When a developer is working on a programming task, *relevant software artifacts* such as documentation, UML diagrams, code, multimedia files, etc. that might require corresponding changes should be *proactively* recommended: *"Programmers who changed these artifacts also changed.."* [18].
2. **Generalization:** The connectionist system should go beyond the state-of-art in guiding programmers, which is mostly based on symbolic association rules. The recommendation of related artifacts should even work for completely unlearned configuration items, which have not been under version control at the time of training. Based on their textual and conceptual similarity, the neural network provides a *content-based* assessment of unseen artifacts.

The combination of neural networks with *Latent Semantic Indexing* (LSI) is a novel and promising approach to change impact analysis, which is hardly investigated so far [17,8].

2   Related Work

Navigation and artifact recommendation as well as change impact analysis are highly relevant research areas [9,7,18]. In *"Mining Version Histories to Guide Software Changes"* Zimmermann et al. [18] applied association rule mining to analyze artifact changes that frequently occur together and thus are empirically related to each other. The current *situation* of a software developer is considered as a set of file changes that is used for mining association rules with a corresponding antecedent part *on the fly* (only on demand). The consequent parts of length one of all matching rules are ranked by confidence and are presented to the user. The implementation was done as an *Eclipse* plugin, such that the recommendations appear as a list in an integrated window of the development environment.

The main task of all recommendation systems is to discover the underlying functional interests that lead to common navigational activity among several users. Fu et al. already tried to exploit the tacit knowledge incorporated in the navigation history [5]. They propose an information recommendation system called *SurfLen*, which suggests interesting web pages to users. The underlying data mining technique is again association rule mining [2], which is used to discover *frequent 2-itemsets* containing web page URLs like $\{\{p, p_1\}, \{p, p_2\}, \ldots, \{p, p_n\}\}$. When the user is reading page p, then the associated pages $\{p_1, \ldots, p_n\}$ are recommended. So the items are URLs here and itemsets are ranked by an intersection measure $rank(U_i, S_j) = |U_i \cap S_j|$ between users' browsing histories $U_i = \{p_1, \ldots, p_m\}$ and mined frequent itemsets $S_j = \{p'_1, \ldots, p'_m\}$. The best k itemsets according to the $rank$-measure are recommended, when the current browsing history matches one of the stored ones.

The software *NavTracks* keeps track of the navigation history of software developers by forming associations between related files, as described in *Nav-Tracks: Supporting navigation in software maintenance* [16]. Its *symbolic algorithm* is based on navigation events and constructs associations between visited nodes. In the conducted case study, the navigation patterns of three users doing their everyday software maintenance tasks were captured. The *NavTracks* algorithm achieved an average accuracy of 29%, that is the next file was correctly recommended in 29% of the presented event streams respectively. Finally the industrial paper *"Empirical Software Change Impact Analysis using Singular Value Decomposition (SVD)"* [15] shows the use of SVD to analyze the changes in software project files that occur together. These are counted in a quadratic frequency matrix which is then decomposed by SVD in order to obtain the significances of the *association clusters*. These clusters indicate the strength of the associations between files. Likewise in the work at hand, a frequency matrix of keyterms and text units is computed and analyzed by SVD in a preprocessing step. This is a powerful method for removing redundancy and for eliciting the correlated latent concepts from an empirical dataset.

In both first named papers [18] and [5] the recommendation of software artifacts or web pages respectively is based on association rule mining. Thus useful *predictive information* in form of the artifact content is given away, if solely relying on symbolic items without consulting the similarity between artifacts. This drawback can be avoided by considering a rich representation of the visited entities instead of reducing them to meaningless unique identifiers.

3   The Recommendation Engine

The *Recurrent Neural Network* (RNN) is employed as enabling technology in this paper. The main purpose of the developed neural network model is to learn pairs of input and target sequences of coherent artifacts and to predict the most likely *target sequence* of related artifacts. Sequences of cohesive commit transactions upon a versioning repository are learned by the RNN in a supervised training process. Such a sequence is an ordered series of *multi-represented objects* $v_i \in V$ that consists of an input and target part $v_1, v_2, \ldots, v_k \mapsto v_{k+1}, v_{k+2}, \ldots, v_{k+m}$. Multi-represented objects [1] capture several attributes (aspects) of the same object like *Name*, *Identifier* and domain-specific attributes that store domain information: *FileType*, *FilePath*, *AuthorID*, etc. The values of these repository transaction descriptors are technically incorporated into a *Vector Space Model* (VSM) ([12], cp. section 4), which is an algebraic model equipped with a similarity measure where each dimension corresponds to a domain attribute. So configuration items are realized as multi-represented objects with a variable number of domain-specific attributes.

Sets A of committed software artifacts, the *Configuration Management aggregates*, are split into input and target part X and Y, where X runs through all subsets of A. This can be done in $n := \sum_{k=1}^{N-1} \binom{N}{k} = 2^N\text{-}2$ many ways, where $N := |A|$ is the cardinality of the commit set A. Apparently the training patterns P are obtained as mapping onto the complementary set of the generated CM-subsets: $P \equiv X \mapsto (A \setminus X)$. Since the RNN is a sequence processor, these sets are transformed into *sequences* by imposing an arbitrary but fixed lexicographical order onto the configuration items within each of the two parts X and Y. To be comparable with the ARM-based related work [18] and to reduce complexity, the target part of a sequence was also restricted to length one, which constrains the obtainable recall.

The neural prediction is computed on the basis of the recent *transaction history* $\boldsymbol{x}_{t-k}, \ldots, \boldsymbol{x}_t$ that reflects the user behavior. Figure 1 illustrates the topology and the information flow of the proposed recurrent neural network. $\boldsymbol{y}_{t+1}, \ldots, \boldsymbol{y}_{t+m}$ represents the associated sequence of target artifacts, which are predicted to correlate strongest with the observed user behavior. An important characteristics of the recurrent network design is its inherent temporal memory. Due to the *temporally unfolded network topology*, the RNN can learn the *sequential structure* of a set of node sequences. Thus the navigation behavior of the user is explicitly modeled in the *hidden state layer* $\boldsymbol{s}_{t-k}, \ldots, \boldsymbol{s}_{t+m-1}$. Its neuron records (the block arrows depicted in figure 1) serve as *hidden* and as *context units*, because $\boldsymbol{s}_{t-1}$ provides the context for the recursive computation of the subsequent hidden state $\boldsymbol{s}_t$. Thereby one input vector $\boldsymbol{x}_t$ or output vector $\boldsymbol{y}_{t+1}$ corresponds to one configuration item.

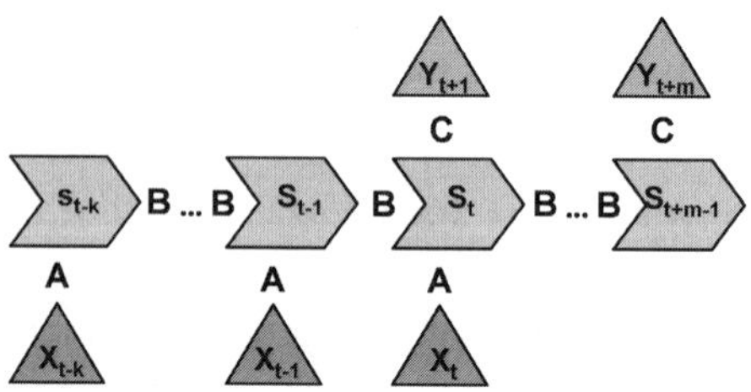

Fig. 1. Schematic topology of the proposed modular recurrent network RNN. The block arrows indicate the internal state transition $\boldsymbol{s}_t \to \boldsymbol{s}_{t+1}$. A, B and C are weight matrices. $\boldsymbol{x}_t$ is the external input vector at time t, $\boldsymbol{y}_{t+1}$ is the correspondingly predicted output vector. The depicted block arrow direction shows the forward propagation phase.

In order to process variably long node sequences $\boldsymbol{x}_{t-k}, \ldots, \boldsymbol{x}_t, \boldsymbol{y}_{t+1}, \ldots, \boldsymbol{y}_{t+m}$ as part of the same training set, we developed a modular recurrent neural network. The technical design of the RNN is defined by the following recurrent model of forward propagation.

- A is a $^h\mathbb{R}^{d_1}$, B is a $^h\mathbb{R}^h$ and C is a $^{d_2}\mathbb{R}^h$ matrix.
- d_1 is the dimensionality of the input- and d_2 is the dimensionality of the output feature space. f is a sigmoid activation function (logistic function).

- $h = dim(s_i)$ is the dimensionality of the state layer ($i = t\text{-}k,\dots,t\text{+}m$). h is independent from d_1 and d_2 and was set to $h = 20$ (experimentally determined) to provide sufficient network resources.

$$s_t \quad = \quad f(Bs_{t-1} + Ax_t) \tag{1}$$

$$o_{t+1} \quad = \quad f(Cs_t), \qquad f(x) = \frac{1}{1 + \exp(-x)} \tag{2}$$

$$o_{t+i} \xrightarrow{training} y_{t+i}, \ i = 1,\dots,m \tag{3}$$

As introduced above, $s_t \in S$ stands for the internal state at the discrete time step t. The crucial recurrent equation 1 combines an external input x_t with the previous state s_{t-1} to the subsequent state s_t, which indirectly depends on all foregoing external inputs $x_{t-k},\dots,x_{t-1}$ *and* internal states $s_{t-k},\dots,s_{t-1}$. In case of supervised network training, the target entities $y_{t+1},\dots,y_{t+m}$ are known, while during network application the *output sequence* $o_{t+1},\dots,o_{t+m}$ is computed solely based on the respective inputs. The RNN is trained with a modified *Backpropagation Through Time* (BPTT) algorithm [6] and is able to process variably dimensional vectors x_i and y_j. There are no further external inputs after t, since the observed input sequence is exhausted. For $t\text{+}1, t\text{+}2, \dots$ the network propagates activations $(s_t)_{t\in\mathbb{N}}$ only through the *state transition matrix* B of the *continuous internal state layer*, which enables infinitely long prediction sequences in theory. Independent of the length k of the input sequence or the length m of the target sequence, the weight matrices A, B and C are continuously adjusted in the training process (*online training*), because they are reused in every time step t. This implies that there are exactly three matrix instances for the training of all variably long sequences. During one training epoch, the network adapts at runtime to the individual structure of the respective node sequence with its input and target part. The advantage of the flexible network topology is that a prediction can still be computed when only a subsequence $(v_i, v_{i+1},\dots,v_k) \subset (v_1, v_2,\dots,v_k)$, $i > 1$, of the input part is available. This property is very useful for guiding programmers that start to explore a new working space, since the recommendation can be done incrementally. When observing an input (v_1, v_2) for example, v_3 is predicted and added to the current input sequence in turn. This extended input (v_1, v_2, v_3) is subsequently used as basis for the next recommendation and so on. In the operational application of the trained network, two functions are provided:

1. *Recognition and Recovery:* When presenting an input sequence of artifacts to the RNN that equals a set of trained configuration items, the remaining items of that CM aggregate are *recovered* and *recommended*.
2. *Generalization:* A virtually unknown sequence of software artifacts is fed into the RNN, which is then able to predict related artifacts that are most likely changed together.

4   Application to Textual Artifact Descriptors

Each artifact that contains unstructured text has to be transformed into a numerically processable representation. The content is considered by a text mining approach that provides a rich artifact representation with the semantics of the textual attributes of the repository transaction data, since conceptual similarity between artifacts is imposed thereby.

Rich Representation Based on Text Mining. In case of textual content, we apply well-known text mining methodologies for computing a numerical document representation. According to the vector space model [12], a feature vector $x \in \mathbb{R}^d$, $d := d_1$, (cp. section 3) is computed for each multi-represented object $v \in V$ of the knowledge base V (*bag-of-words* approach). The well-known preprocessing steps *stemming* [11] and *stop-word removal* were realized by the *Apache Lucene* indexing and search framework[1]. The vector space model can be refined by applying *Latent Semantic Indexing* [8] to the set of obtained feature vectors. Thereby a matrix $M_{i,j}$ of keyword frequencies per text unit (e.g. file paths, sentences, paragraphs, sections, documents) is spanned. The rows denote the frequency of occurrence for term i in text unit j, which is the textual content of an artifact in the knowledge base. In this case study, the text units are the file paths of the software artifacts and the terms are the single path components like the artifact name. The matrix is decomposed by *Singular Value Decomposition*, which is a generalization of the *Principal Component Analysis* (PCA) that determines the inherent key concepts that characterize all d-dimensional feature vectors. SVD is able to analyze the correlations among terms as well as the correlations between text units and comprised terms, which are described by a non-quadratic matrix. Thereby the term-frequency matrix $M = UDW^T$ is decomposed into two orthonormal matrices U and W and one diagonal matrix D. After *diagonalizing* that matrix M, the singular values $\sigma_j = D_{j,j}$ in the diagonal of the matrix D reveal the insignificant dimensions, which can be discarded. These k least informative dimensions with singular values $\sigma_{d-k}, \sigma_{d-k+1}, \ldots, \sigma_n$ are ignored by the transformation to a $(d\text{-}k)$-dimensional subspace. The resulting feature vectors $x_j \in \mathbb{R}^{d-k}$ represent the content of an artifact $v_j \in V$: $x_j^T := (W_{1,j}^T, W_{2,j}^T, \ldots, W_{d-k,j}^T)$, where $W_{i,j}^T$, $i = 1, \ldots, d\text{-}k$, $j = 1, \ldots, |V|$ are the entries of the transposed right-singular matrix. This global vector space model enables the RNN to learn the latent semantics of the domain knowledge.

Software Repository Transaction Data. We applied our recommendation technique to repositories of versioning data from three independent projects, namely *Nickle*, *XFree86* and *X.org* (http://{nickle.org, xfree86, x}.org). The used datasets stem from the *PROMISE Repository of Software Engineering Databases* [13], which is a collection of publicly available datasets and tools to serve researchers in building predictive software models (PSMs). Massey [10] has logged and analyzed the publicly available CVS archives of these projects

---

[1] http://lucene.apache.org

resulting in datasets with the same structure, such that we could conduct a uniform and comparable evaluation. The file names like *"INSTALL-X.org"* or *"Makefile"* (attribute *FilePath* in table 1) are the only content-based attributes of the CVS transaction data and are considered as text units in terms of section 4 for constructing the vector space model. The remainder of the attributes like *external* (boolean, author is different from submitting person) are mostly nominal and thus do not provide the possibility to compute similarity among their discrete values. On the other hand, the metric attributes *lines_added* and *lines_removed* revealed to be hardly significant and thus were excluded. Table 1 shows the schema of the logged repository transactions. Now the commit records

Table 1. Data schema of the repository transactions from the *XFree86 Project* concerning the configuration items with an excerpt of their attributes

FileType	FilePath	AuthorID	Revision	Commit Date
"code"	"config/imake/imake.c"	1	2.0	"2004-04-03 22:26:20"
"devel-doc"	"INSTALL-X.org"	1	1.6	"2005-02-11 03:02:53"
"doc"	"config/cf/Fresco.tmpl"	1	1.2	"2005-02-11 03:02:53"
"unknown"	"LABEL"	2	1.2	"2003-07-09 15:27:23"

were grouped according to their discrete commit dates, obtaining sets of artifacts that were committed by a specific author at the respective point of time (atomic). The contents of each *CM aggregate* were split into input and target sequences and one pair made up a single training pattern for the neural network.

5   Evaluation

Compared to association rule mining, which is a purely symbolic approach operating on atomic artifact identifiers, our connectionist technique paired with text mining methods is able to incorporate actual content into the learning and recommendation process. The association rule mining approach that is often used in related work [18] is not able to assess changes or visits of *new* artifacts in principle, since their (latent) semantics are ignored by the symbolic representation. On the other hand, we did not address source code fragments like done by Zimmermann et al. [18] but focused on versioned files in general, which are distinguished by type as listed in table 1.

For our case study we chose arbitrary subsets of 2,970 till 5,350 commit actions by 6 till 39 anonymous developers, depending on the respective project. The *generalization* accuracy for the target attribute *FilePath* was evaluated by arbitrary test sets with different numbers of configuration items from the three projects. The repository transaction data was arbitrarily split up into a training set of $\frac{7}{8}$ and a test set of $\frac{1}{8}$ of the relevant commit actions by interleaving (taking each 8th pattern). Since no internal order is specified on the *CM aggregates*, the artifacts of one commit set C are represented by the possible combinations of ordered input and target sequences making up one training pattern (*input* $\mapsto$ *target*). Thus the RNN learns the committed items as subsequences of the form $(C \supset (item^C_{i_1}, item^C_{i_2}, \ldots, item^C_{i_n}) \mapsto item^C_{j_1})$, where the target sequence only consists of one item. Despite the relatively short sequences of 3.3 configuration items per *CM aggregate* on average (*min* 1, *max* 34), we use a neural network for predicting related software artifacts because of its *generalization capability* [14]XX, which reveals its effect when visiting *unseen* artifacts that were not part of the training sequences. A successful recommendation is given, if a set of items $H := \{item_{i_1}, item_{i_2}, \ldots, item_{i_m}\} \subset C$ that was not trained before is presented and the network predicts one or several items of the complementary set $T := C \setminus \{item_{i_1}, item_{i_2}, \ldots, item_{i_m}\}$. In general, all items $u \in H$ of the input set are presented and one or several items $v \in T$ of the target subset are expected as correct recommendation, which counts as hit and is summed over all test cases.

The singular value decomposition of the term-document matrix as integral step of LSI succeeded to discover the latent semantic concepts of the textual attribute *FilePath* and optimized the term-frequency based *bag-of-words* approach. We were able to reduce the vector space dimensionality to $d'_1 = d_1 - k = 159$ by $k = 7$ while loosing only 1.06% of the variance in the training set (nearly lossless transform, *XFree* dataset). This was possible because high-dimensional bag-of-words vectors are usually *sparse*, that is to say those contain many 0-entries. More formally spoken, the term-document matrix $M \in \mathbb{R}^{d_1 \times |V|}$ (d_1 is the number of keyterms in the knowledge base) does not have full rank, but only $rank(M) = d_1 - k$. We did not conduct an actual dimension reduction with information loss by $k > 7$, because any removal of further dimensions led to a significant downgrade of the prediction accuracy[2].

Before presenting the quantitative results of our recommendation technique, we show two exemplary item recommendations generated from partially *unseen* commit histories of the *XFree* project. Both results were validated by hand using appropriate queries on the transaction database.

- *1 input, 1 target item:* **config/cf/xfree86.cf** $\mapsto$ **config/cf/xf86site.def**
  It stands to reason that *config/cf/xf86site.def* was predicted due to its conceptual similarity to the input item *config/cf/xfree86.cf* that resides in the same subdirectory *config/cf*, which is detected by LSI-based text mining.
- *2 input, 1 target item:* **Makefile.std, registry** $\mapsto$ **Imakefile**
  In this case the item *Imakefile* of type *build* was recommended, since the neural network had learned that committing the items *Makefile.std* and *registry* mostly implies committing the *Imakefile*, too.

We trained the network on up to 455 training patterns resulting from a basic set of 3,000 commits, whereupon the target items in all test sets could be inferred with a maximal accuracy of 72.72% in case of the *X.org* project. For the *Nickle* dataset we achieved an accuracy of 61.29% compared to 69.23% for the *XFree* dataset. Note that the residual training error could not be minimized completely (relative training error $0.25\% \leq \delta \leq 0.75\%$) and still might leave

---

[2] The smallest kept singular value $\sigma_{159} = 0.999 \approx \frac{6}{100}\sigma_1$ was still significant (X.org).

room for improvements. We did not strive for a perfect mapping of all training sequences in order to avoid overfitting. The significance of all results is quite high, since the dependent variable *FilePath* (attribute to be predicted) can take 167 (XFree) till 1047 (X.org) different values, depending on the project. Assuming an equal distribution of these values, guessing a single target item based on a given set of committed X.org project items would result in a hit probability of $1/1047 = 0.096\%$ on average. We suppose that even better results would be achievable in the presence of more meaningful and more predictive attributes than the path of a software artifact, which does not offer a variety of meaningful keyterms that would form a broad basis for textual similarity. The lack of rich content in the *FilePath* attribute, whose values mostly consist of only one till three terms, represents a deficiency compared to richer multi-represented domain objects.

6 Conclusion

We have introduced semantic learning and prediction of related artifact changes based on our *Recurrent Neural Network* (RNN). The RNN enables learning of variably long node sequences on graph-based and domain-specific knowledge bases such as transaction repositories. We trained the network on the cohesive configuration items of each commit set in a supervised manner leading to a recommender system that fulfills two main tasks:

1. ***Preventing Incomplete Change.*** Guidance of programmers by observing their working set and recommending related artifacts to prevent errors resulting from incomplete changes.
2. ***Inference of Related Artifacts.*** The learned dependencies among the items of each commit set are exploited by the RNN, which *generalizes* onto *unseen* software artifacts and thus even provides advice for new configuration items.

For both functionalities a knowledge representation based on *Latent Semantic Indexing* of text attributes builds the foundation for semantic recommendation. The evaluation was conducted by three independent datasets from the *PROMISE Repository of Software Engineering Databases* and revealed a prediction accuracy for partially unseen artifact sets of 67.75% altogether (maximum of 72.72% for the XFree project), based on a result space of 167 till 1047 different artifacts. Compared to existing methods based on association rule mining whose authors report accuracy values of about 26% till 50% [18], our approach even achieves a higher performance when applied to untrained item sets, which is not possible with symbolic techniques at all. For example, the evaluation of the *NavTracks* algorithm (cp. section 2) conducted by Singer, Robert and Storey [16] led to an accuracy of about 29%, based on the logged navigation pathways of three developers.

References

1. Achtert, E., Kriegel, H.-P., Pryakhin, A., Schubert, M.: Hierarchical density-based clustering for multi-represented objects. In: Workshop on Mining Complex Data (MCD 2005), ICDM, Houston, TX, Institute for Computer Science, University of Munich (2005)
2. Agrawal, R., Srikant, R.: Fast algorithms for mining association rules. In: Proc. of the 20th Int. Conf. on Very Large Data Bases, VLDB, Santiago, Chile (1994)
3. Bohner, S., Arnold, R.: Software change impact analysis, pp. 1–28. IEEE Computer Society Press, Los Alamitos (1996)
4. Bruegge, B., Dutoit, A.H.: Object-Oriented Software Engineering Using UML, Patterns, and Java. Prentice-Hall, Englewood Cliffs (2004)
5. Budzik, J., Fu, X., Hammond, K.J.: Mining navigation history for recommendation. In: Proceedings of the 5th international conference on Intelligent user interfaces, New Orleans, Louisiana, United States, pp. 106–112. ACM Press, New York (2000)
6. Callan, R.: Neuronale Netze im Klartext. Pearson Studium, London (2003)
7. Cubranic, D., Murphy, G.C.: Hipikat: Recommending pertinent software development artifacts. In: 25th International Conference on Software Engineering (ICSE 2003), pp. 408–418 (2003)
8. Deerwester, S., Dumais, S.T., Furnas, G.W., Harshman, R., Landauer, T.K.: Indexing by latent semantic analysis. Technical Report 6 (1990)
9. Gall, H., Hajek, K., Jazayeri, M.: Detection of logical coupling based on product release history. In: International Conference on Software Maintenance (ICSM 1998) (1998)
10. Massey, B.: Nickle repository transaction data, Computer Science Dept., Portland State University, Portland, OR, USA (2005)
11. Porter, M.: An algorithm for suffix stripping. Technical Report 3 (1980)
12. Salton, G., Wong, A., Yang, C.S.: A vector space model for automatic indexing. Communications of the ACM 18, 613–620 (1975)
13. Sayyad Shirabad, J., Menzies, T.: The PROMISE repository of software engineering databases. School of Information Technology and Engineering, University of Ottawa, Canada (2005)
14. Schmidhuber, J.: Discovering neural nets with low kolmogorov complexity and high generalization capability. Neural Networks 10, 857–873 (1997)
15. Sherriff, M., Lake, M., Williams, L.: Empirical software change impact analysis using singular value decomposition. IBM, North Carolina State University (2007), ftp://ftp.ncsu.edu/pub/unity/lockers/ftp/csc_anon/tech/2007/TR-2007-13.pdf
16. Singer, J., Elves, R., Storey, M.-A.: Navtracks: Supporting navigation in software maintenance. In: Proceedings of the International Conference on Software Maintenance (2005)
17. Syu, I., Lang, S.D., Deo, N.: Incorporating latent semantic indexing into a neural network model for information retrieval. In: Proceedings of the fifth international conference on Information and knowledge management, pp. 145–153 (1996)
18. Zimmermann, T., Weißgerber, P., Diehl, S., Zeller, A.: Mining version histories to guide software changes. In: International Conference on Software Engineering (ICSE 2004) (2004)

Ranking Links on the Web: Search and Surf Engines

Jean-Louis Lassez[1], Ryan Rossi[1], and Kumar Jeev[2]

[1] Coastal Carolina University, USA
{jlassez, raross}@coastal.edu
[2] Johns Hopkins University, USA
kjeev@cs.jhu.edu

Abstract. The main algorithms at the heart of search engines have focused on ranking and classifying sites. This is appropriate when we know what we are looking for and want it directly. Alternatively, we surf, in which case ranking and classifying links becomes the focus. We address this problem using a latent semantic analysis of the web. This technique allows us to rate, suppress or create links giving us a version of the web suitable for surfing. Furthermore, we show on benchmark examples that the performance of search algorithms such as PageRank is substantially improved as they work on an appropriately weighted graph.

Keywords: Search Engines, Surf Engines, Singular Value Decomposition, Heuristic Search, Intelligent Systems.

1 Introduction

The ergodic theorem and/or its associated iterative construction of principal eigenvectors forms the backbone of the main search algorithms on the web. (PageRank [1], HITS [2], SALSA [3]). The standard proofs of the ergodic theorem rely on the Perron Frobenius theorem, which implies the use of a certain amount of mathematical machinery and restrictive hypotheses. A new fundamentally simpler proof of the ergodic theorem was derived in [4]. In a second section we will show how this proof can be used to clarify the role played by Markov models, the Perron Frobenius theorem and Kirchhoff's Matrix Tree theorem in the design of search engines. In a short third section we make a case that the ranking of links should play a major role in the design of surf engines. In the fourth section we first recall how singular value decomposition is used to extract latent semantic features [5, 6]. In the next three subsections we apply this technique to automatically rate and update links, leading to improved efficiency for search algorithms, we then generate surf sessions and extract meta sites and target sites. This construction of meta sites and targets can be used to generate hubs and authorities [2] and the bipartite graphs defined in SALSA [3] and Trawling [7].

2 A Symbolic View: From Kirchhoff to Google

In this section we review the results from [4] and see how they relate to PageRank, SALSA, HITS and other algorithms that form the core of search engines.

N.T. Nguyen et al. (Eds.): IEA/AIE 2008, LNAI 5027, pp. 199–208, 2008.

In the patent application for PageRank we find the statements: "the rank of a page can be interpreted as the probability that a surfer will be at a particular page after following a large number of forward links. The iteration circulates the probability through the linked nodes like energy flows through a circuit and accumulates in important places." The first sentence shows that the web is considered as a Markov chain and that the ranking of sites is given as an application of the ergodic theorem [8], which indeed computes how frequently each site is visited by a surfer. The second sentence is related to Kirchhoff's [9] current law.

The proof of the ergodic theorem is most frequently given as an application of the Perron Frobenius theorem, which essentially states that the probabilities of being at a particular site are given as the coefficients of the principal eigenvector of the stochastic matrix associated to the Markov chain, which is computed as

$$\lim_{n \to \infty} M^n e, \quad \text{where } e \text{ is the unit vector}$$

The implementation of the PageRank algorithm uses this construction (as a foundation, there is more to the PageRank algorithm and to the Google search engine), as well as SALSA. So we have two separate problems to consider. One is the use of the Markov Chain model for the web, and the other is the use of the Perron Frobenius theorem as a basis for an implementation. Indeed alternative constructions for computing the most frequently visited sites have been proposed for instance based on Gauss Seidel [10]. And if Kleinberg's HITS algorithm is not based on the Markov Chain model or the ergodic theorem, it nevertheless makes systematic use of the Perron Frobenius theorem.

The ergodic theorem now plays a major role in computer science, but its complete proof is a challenge at least for undergraduate computer scientists. Indeed we have issues of convergence involving further theorems from analysis, computing eigenvalues which involves considerations of complex numbers, issues of uniqueness of solution which creates serious problems leading to restrictive hypotheses and further mathematical machinery [10].

In [11,12] it was shown that elimination theory, based on Tarski's meta theorem could be used to derive strikingly simple proofs of important theorems whose known proofs were very involved. This technique was applied in [4] to the ergodic theorem. We informally present here the essential result that allows us to present the ergodic theorem with minimal mathematical machinery and no overly restrictive hypotheses.

Let G be a graph representing a Markov chain where the nodes s_i are called states (or sites in our application) and the edges represent links between states.

Consider the system of equations below. The x_i are the probabilities of being in state i, while $p_{i,j}$ is the probability of moving from state i to state j. So if we are in state 2 with probability x_2, it is because we were previously in state 1 with probability x_1 and we transitioned with probability p_{12}, or we were in state 4 with probability x_4 and we transitioned to state 2 with probability p_{42}.

$$p_{21}x_2 + p_{31}x_3 + p_{41}x_4 = x_1$$

$$p_{12}x_1 + p_{42}x_4 = x_2$$

$$p_{13}x_1 = x_3$$

$$p_{34}x_3 = x_4$$

$$\sum x_i = 1$$

We solve this system by symbolic Gaussian elimination, using maple we find:

$$x_1 = p_{21}p_{34}p_{41} + p_{34}p_{42}p_{21} + p_{21}p_{31}p_{41} + p_{31}p_{42}p_{21}/\Sigma$$

$$x_2 = p_{31}p_{41}p_{12} + p_{31}p_{42}p_{12} + p_{34}p_{41}p_{12} + p_{34}p_{42}p_{12} + p_{13}p_{34}p_{42}/\Sigma$$

$$x_3 = p_{41}p_{21}p_{13} + p_{42}p_{21}p_{13}/\Sigma$$

$$x_4 = p_{21}p_{13}p_{34}/\Sigma$$

$$\Sigma = p_{21}p_{34}p_{41} + p_{34}p_{42}p_{21} + p_{21}p_{31}p_{41} + p_{31}p_{42}p_{21} + p_{31}p_{41}p_{12} + p_{31}p_{42}p_{12} +$$

$$p_{34}p_{41}p_{12} + p_{34}p_{42}p_{12} + p_{13}p_{34}p_{42} + p_{41}p_{21}p_{13} + p_{42}p_{21}p_{13} + p_{21}p_{13}p_{34}$$

A careful examination shows us that a monomial such as $p_{42}p_{21}p_{13}$ represents a reverse weighted spanning tree with root at s_3. So we see clearly how to compute a general solution: x_i will be equal to the quotient of the sums of the monomials corresponding to the reverse weighted spanning trees rooted at s_i by the sum of the monomials corresponding to all reverse weighted spanning trees.

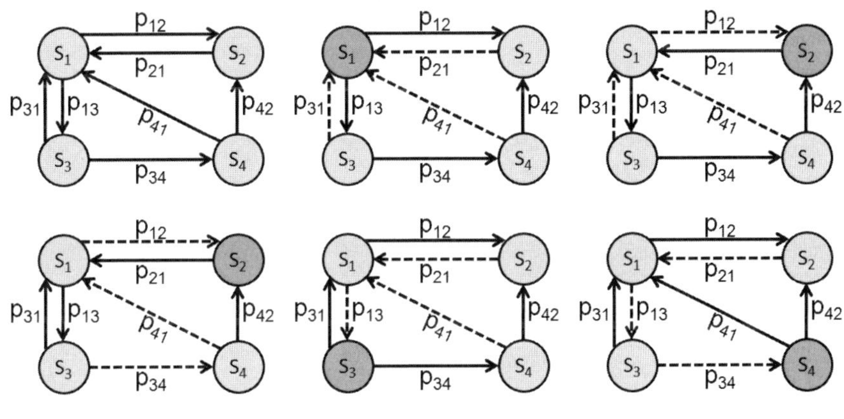

Fig. 1.

A simple induction will complete the proof whose details can be found in [4]. So we can present the ergodic theorem without any of the usual more complex machinery. We have the exact solution in a finite number of steps.

Also importantly we see that the only restrictive condition is that the denominator Σ is non null, that is we require that the graph admits at least one reverse spanning tree. That is an improvement on the use of Perron Frobenius which does not converge on a cycle as its largest eigenvalue has degree two. This causes restrictive conditions and makes the proof more complex, even though intuitively it is obvious that the solution is a uniform value for all sites. While with our proof we see that obviously all spanning trees are isomorphic and therefore all probabilities are equal.

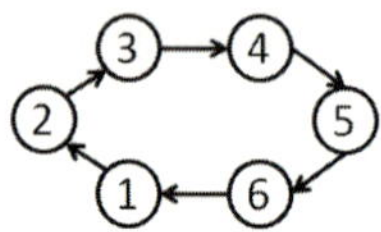

Fig. 2.

Furthermore, we see that if a graph has several "sinks" as described in the Google patent, then it cannot have a reverse spanning tree and the ergodic theorem will not apply. That is why in PageRank new links are added to get out of sinks, making the graph strongly connected.

3   From Search Engines to Surf Engines

If at the theoretical level some algorithms assume that links are given some weights or probabilities, in practice they are given a uniform probability distribution. It is however clear that all links are not "equal" and that a weighting of these links should improve the performance of search engines. This is a local ranking as shown in figure 3, where the question is "where can I go from here?"

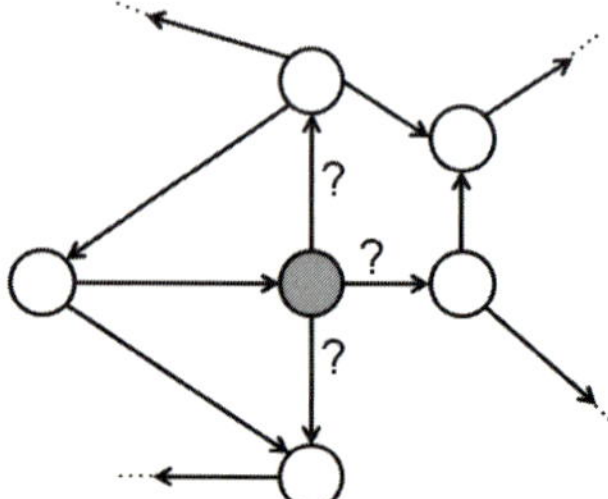

Fig. 3.

However if we consider the surfing aspect of search where we start a bit randomly and go window shopping on the sites, a ranking or rating of links should be of fundamental importance. This time the question is not "where can I go from here?" but rather "where *should* I go from here?" even if there is no link. This is particularly important for updating the graph, as illustrated in figure 4. The graph on the top-left represents the web at some point in time. Later new sites I,J,K,L are added with links to H and the sites C and G have updated their links adding one to H, as seen on the top-right graph. Now that H is clearly an important site, we would like to automatically update the graph, for instance by adding a link from A to H as shown in the graph at the bottom.

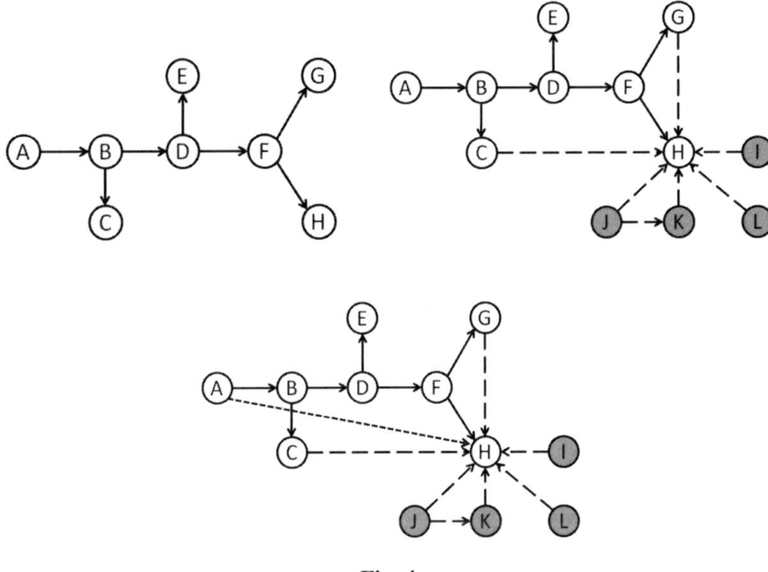

Fig. 4.

Finally an important question is raised when we rank the links globally, as opposed to locally. In figure 5 the importance of links is marked by the thickness of the arrow.

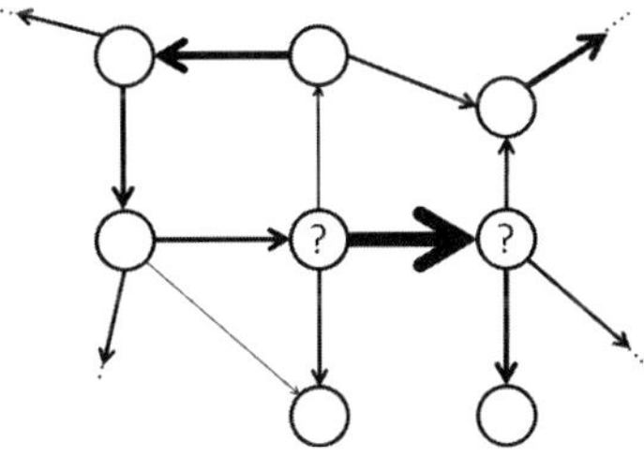

Fig. 5.

The question is: what is the nature of the sites which correspond to the most highly ranked links? We can expect them to be of some significance, and we will verify this at the end of the next section.

4 Latent Semantic Analysis of the Web

The seminal paper by Kleinberg [2] introduced the notion of Hubs and Authorities for sites on the web, and if it does not rely on the Markov Chain model, it is a remarkable application of the Perron Frobenius theorem, as it makes a double usage of its construction of principal eigenvectors.

We go one step further by considering the singular value decomposition which systematically computes all eigenvectors of MM^T and M^TM. Instead of using the eigenvectors to classify sites as in [2], we use them to rank the links by computing a new graph representation of the web.

4.1 Singular Value Decomposition

Let $M \in \Re^{nxm}$, we decompose M into three matrices using Singular Value Decomposition:

$$M = U\,S\,V^T$$

where $U \in \Re^{nxm}$, $S \in \Re^{mxm}$ and $V^T \in \Re^{mxm}$. The matrix S contains the singular values located in the $[i, i]_{1,..,n}$ cells in decreasing order of magnitude and all other cells contain zero. The eigenvectors of MM^T make up the columns of U and the eigenvectors of M^TM make up the columns of V. The matrices U and V are orthogonal, unitary and span vector spaces of dimension n and m, respectively. The inverses of U and V are their transposes.

$$\begin{bmatrix} | & | & & | \\ d_1^f & d_2^f & \cdots & d_k^f \\ | & | & & | \end{bmatrix} \begin{bmatrix} s_1 & 0 & 0 & 0 \\ 0 & s_2 & 0 & 0 \\ 0 & 0 & \ddots & 0 \\ 0 & 0 & 0 & s_k \end{bmatrix} \begin{bmatrix} — & d_1^c & — \\ — & d_2^c & — \\ & \vdots & \\ — & d_k^c & — \end{bmatrix}$$
$$\qquad\quad U \qquad\qquad\qquad S \qquad\qquad\qquad V^T$$

The columns of U are the *principal directions of the hubs* and the rows of V^T are the *principal directions of the authorities*. The principal directions are ordered according to the singular values and therefore according to the importance of their contribution to M.

The singular value decomposition is used by setting some singular values to zero, which implies that we approximate the matrix M by a matrix:

$$M_k = U_k\,S_k\,V_k^T$$

A fundamental theorem by Eckart and Young states that M_k is the closest rank-k least squares approximation of M [13]. This theorem can be used in two ways. To reduce noise by setting insignificant singular values to zero or by setting the majority of the singular values to zero and keeping only the few influential singular values in a manner similar to principal component analysis.

In latent semantic analysis we extract information about the relationships between sites as they change when we set all, but the most significant, singular values to zero.

The singular values in S provide contribution scores for the principal directions in U and V^T.

We use the terminology "principal direction" for the following reason. In zoomed clusters [14] it was shown that (assuming unit vectors) the principal eigenvector is an "iterated centroid" that is a version of the notion of centroid, where outliers are given a decreasing weight. The iterative centroid is the reason Kleinberg's HITS algorithm favors the most tightly knit communities.

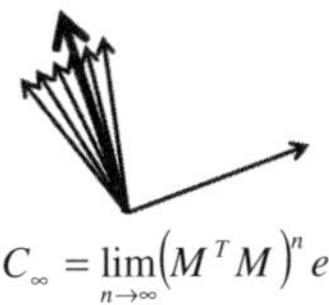

$$C_\infty = \lim_{n\to\infty}\left(M^T M\right)^n e$$

The iterative centroid penalizes outliers and gives more weight or influence to the tightly knit community.

4.2 Automatic Rating and Updating of Links

The datasets we used in these experiments came from Panayiotis Tsaparas at the University of Toronto [15]. The queries we selected were: "Movies", "Computational Geometry", "Death Penalty", "Abortion", "Gun Control" and "Genetic." We start with a set of web pages interconnected by links. The set of web pages can be represented as an adjacency matrix M of the hyperlink graph G, where $M_{i,j} = 1$ if there is a link from site i to site j, and $M_{i,j} = 0$ if there is no link between site i and j.

In these experiments we first compute the SVD of the adjacency matrix M from a given query and set all but five singular values to zero. We then compute M_5 a low rank approximation of M, to which corresponds a new graph G_5. To this new graph, we apply the inDegree and PageRank algorithms. We count the number of relevant sites among the first ten given by the algorithms. We then compare these results with the results on the original graph G, see table 1. There is clearly a significant improvement for both algorithms. This improvement is further illustrated in tables 2 and 3, where we show the top ten results for the "Movies" query in each situation. Similar results have been obtained with the other queries.

It is important to notice that we are not following a Markov model now because the matrix M_5 is not a stochastic matrix, it even can have negative numbers. It does not

Table 1. Quantitative relevance results before and after LSA on inDegree and PageRank

Queries	inDegree	LSA inDegree	PageRank	LSA PageRank
Movies	6	**10**	4	**10**
Computational Geometry	8	**10**	5	**10**
Death Penalty	9	**9**	6	**9**
Abortion	10	**10**	3	**10**
Gun Control	9	**10**	7	**10**
Genetic	9	**9**	6	**9**

correspond either to a Kirchhoff model as it does not fit a conservation system. However the values in M_5 represent the larger coordinates of the eigenvectors with the larger eigenvalues, and as such representative of the main directions of the graph.

Table 2. Ranking of sites from the "Movies" query using inDegree on the original graph compared with inDegree on the appropriately weighted graph in which LSA has been applied

Rank	inDegree	LSA inDegree
1	**Hollywood.com - Your entertainment**	**Hollywood.com - Your entertainment**
2	**Paramount Pictures**	**Film.com & Movie Reviews,**
3	**Film.com & Movie Reviews,**	**Paramount Pictures**
4	Welcome to mylifesaver.com	**Universal Studios**
5	**Disney.com -- Where the Magic**	**Disney.com -- Where the Magic**
6	**Universal Studios**	**Movies.com**
7	My Excite Start Page	**MGM - Home Page**
8	**Movies.com**	**All Movie Guide**
9	Lycos	**Boxoffice Magazine**
10	Google	**Batman Forever Movie**

Table 3. Ranking of sites from the "Movies" query using PageRank on the original graph compared with PageRank on the appropriately weighted graph in which LSA has been applied

Rank	PageRank	LSA PageRank
1	**GuideLive: Movies in Dallas**	**Hollywood.com - Your entertainment**
2	CitySearch.com	**Film.com & Movie Reviews,**
3	On Wisconsin	**Paramount Pictures**
4	CDOutpost.com	**Universal Studios**
5	**Ebert & Roeper and the Movies**	**Disney.com -- Where the Magic**
6	**Roger Ebert**	**Movies.com**
7	Sofcom Motoring	**MGM - Home Page**
8	**Hollywood.com - Your entertainment**	**All Movie Guide**
9	The Knoxville News	**Boxoffice Magazine**
10	Excite@Home: Career Opp.	**Gannett home page**

4.3 Surf Sessions

In a surf session we chose a starting site at random and follow the links with the highest weight. To generate the weights we first compute the SVD of the adjacency matrix from the movies query and set all but two hundred singular values to zero. We then compute M_{200}. We selected the site "Math in the Movies" at random and followed the link with the highest value. In this example we can check that all visited sites are relevant, we had similar cases with other random start sites, where even if a visited site did not appear to be relevant the following ones were. Such surf sessions help us validate the SVD technique that we proposed, as well as being a starting point for the design of surf engines.

Table 4. Surf session starting with the site "Math in the Movies" from the query "Movies"

Links	Surf Session
Start	http://world.std.com/~reinhold/mathmovies.html Math in the Movies
2	http://www.pithemovie.com Pi The Movie: Enter
3	http://www.mrcranky.com Movies and more movies!
4	http://ign.com IGN
5	http://www.allmovie.com All Movie Guide
6	http://www.chireader.com/movies Reader Guide: Movies
End	http://www.amctv.com American Movie Classics

4.4 Meta Sites and Targets

Assuming that a hub and a corresponding authority are of excellent quality, we could expect that they are directly linked. This is why in SALSA, Trawling and others, the relationship between hubs and authorities is given as a bipartite graph. In our setting we can expect that the links with the highest value connect sites of particular interest. Indeed we see from the tables that the sites from which the links originate are sites about sites, or meta sites, while those pointed to by the links are targets. Such sites are related to Kleinberg's Hubs and authorities, but they might be more specific and are computed differently, so we gave them different names to avoid confusion.

Table 5. Meta sites and Targets for the query "Computational Geometry"

Link Weight	Meta sites	Targets
1.92	"All" Engineering Resources on the Internet	Geometry in Action
1.85	Computational Geometry Pages: What's ancient?	Geometry in Action
1.60	Computational Geometry on the WWW	Geometry in Action
1.53	"All" Engineering Resources on the Internet	Directory of Computational Geometry Software
1.47	Computational Geometry Links	Geometry in Action
1.46	Computational Geometry Pages: What's ancient?	Directory of Computational Geometry Software
1.36	Computational Geometry Web Directories	Geometry in Action
1.35	"All" Engineering Resources on the Internet	The former CGAL home page
1.30	Computational Geometry Pages: What's ancient?	The former CGAL home page

5 Conclusion

We have shown that the ranking of links, using singular value decomposition, can have a beneficial effect on the ranking of sites, the discovery of meta sites, and can serve as a basis for the design of surf engines.

Acknowledgments. Parts of this paper were presented in Sapporo, Marseille and Paris, we thank Nicholas Spryratos, Yusuru Tanaka, Mohand Said Hacid, Michele Sebag for their comments and interest. Work supported by NSF Grant ATM-0521002.

References

1. Page, L., Brin, S., Motwani, R., Winograd, T.: The PageRank citation ranking: Bringing order to the web. Technical report, Stanford Digital Library Technologies Project, (1998)
2. Kleinberg, J.: Authoritative sources in a hyperlinked environment. In Proceedings of the 9th ACM-SIAM, SODA, (1998)
3. Lempel, R., Moran, S.: The stochastic approach for link-structure analysis (SALSA) and the TKC effect. In 9th International WWW Conference, (2000)
4. Jeev, K., Lassez, J-L.: Symbolic Stochastic Systems. AMCS, 321-328 (2004)
5. Berry, M.W., Browne, M.: Understanding Search Engines: Mathematical Modeling and Text Retrieval. SIAM, Philadelphia (2005)
6. Deerwester, S., Dumais, S., Landauer, T.K., Furnas, G., Harshman, R.: Indexing by latent semantic analysis. J. Amer. Soc. Info. Sci. 41, 391-407 (1990)
7. Kumar, S.R., Raghavan, P., Rajagopalan, S., Tomkins, A.: Trawling emerging cybercommunities automatically. In 8th International WWW Conference, (1999)
8. Markov, A. A., Rasprostranenie zakona bol'shih chisel na velichiny, zavisyaschie drug ot druga, Izvestiya Fiziko-matematicheskogo obschestva pri Kazanskom universitete, 2-ya seriya, tom 15, 9 4, 135-156 (1906).
9. Kirchhoff, G.: Über die Auflösung der Gleichungen, auf welche man bei der untersuchung der linearen verteilung galvanischer Ströme geführt wird. Ann. Phys. Chem. 72, 497-508 (1847)
10. Langville, A., Meyer, C.: Google's PageRank and Beyond: The science of search engine rankings. Princeton University Press, Princeton, New Jersey (2006)
11. Chandru, V., Lassez, J-L.: Qualitative Theorem Proving in Linear Constraints. Verification: Theory and Practice. 395-406 (2003)
12. Lassez, J-L.: From LP to LP: Programming with Constraints. In: Theoretical Aspects of Computer Software. LNCS, vol. 526, pp. 420-446. Springer, Heidelberg (1991)
13. Eckart, C., Young, G.: The approximation of one matrix by another of lower rank. Psychometrika. 1, 211-218 (1936)
14. Lassez, J-L., Karadeniz, T., Mukkamala, S.: Zoomed Clusters. ICONIP, 824-830 (2006)
15. Tsaparas, P.: Using non-linear dynamical systems for web searching and ranking. Principles of Database Systems, 59-69 (2004)

Cluster Analysis for Users' Modeling in Intelligent E-Learning Systems

Danuta Zakrzewska

Institute of Computer Science Technical University of Lodz, Wolczanska 215, 93-005
Lodz, Poland
dzakrz@ics.p.lodz.pl

Abstract. In the paper, the data driven approach for users' modeling in intelligent e-learning system is considered. Individual models are based on preferred learning styles dimensions, according to which students focus on different types of information and show different performances in educational process. Building individual models of learners allows for adjusting teaching paths and materials into their needs. In the presented approach, students are divided into groups by unsupervised classification. Application of two-phase hierarchical clustering algorithm which enables tutors to determine such parameters as maximal number of groups, clustering threshold and weights for different learning style dimensions is described. Experimental results connected with modeling real groups of students are discussed.

Keywords: Intelligent Systems in Education, Student Modeling, Data Mining.

1   Introduction

To obtain the assumed learning outcomes, educational software should not only fulfil pedagogical requirements, but should also be customized according to individual learners' preferences. The contents of courses, the way the information is presented as well as the order in which contents are organized and introduced, may play crucial role in users attitudes towards using educational software and taking active part in the learning process. Students are characterized by their own personal learning styles [1] and the performance of the distance education system depends on its adaptivity and personalization abilities.

In the paper, it is considered application of cluster analysis for students' modeling on the basis of their individual learning styles dimensions. In spite of approach consisting of assigning students into predefined groups without the possibility of updating (see [2,3]), unsupervised classification enables creating groups with similar preferences and tailoring the teaching contents into their requirements. It is proposed, the two-phase hierarchical algorithm, which allows tutors for choosing parameters corresponding to the courses' characteristic features. The paper is organised as follows. The relevant research is described in

N.T. Nguyen et al. (Eds.): IEA/AIE 2008, LNAI 5027, pp. 209–214, 2008.

the next section. Then, learners' modeling by learning styles dimensions is presented and the two-phase hierarchical clustering algorithm for users' grouping is described. In the following section, some experimental results on the real group of students as well as choice of clustering parameters are discussed. Finally, concluding remarks concerning evaluation of the applied algorithm as well as future research are presented.

2   Related Work

There exist several papers concerning students' modeling for the purpose of adaptive intelligent educational systems (see for example [4,5]). In the present work, it is considered using individual preferred learning styles as the basis for building learner models. The relationship of individual styles and distance education was examined by different researchers, who indicated learning styles as valuable features of users' models in a teaching process (see for example [6]). Graf & Kinshuk [7] showed that students with different learning styles have different needs and preferences. Rovai [8] stated that teaching methods should vary according to learning styles of learners, the significant impact of which, on Web based courses performances, was identified by Lu et al. [9] and Lee [10].

Authors examined different techniques for students' learning styles investigations. Alfonseca et al. [11] used descriptive statistics for student grouping in collaborative learning. García et al. [12] applied Bayesian networks for detecting students' learning styles on the basis of their behaviors. Xu et al. [13] built fuzzy models on the basis of learning activities and interaction history. Viola et al. [14] showed the effectiveness of data-driven methods for pattern extractions. In the current approach, data-driven models are built by cluster analysis. In [15], it was considered using Farthest First Traversal Algorithm, for data previously cleaned out from outliers by COF technique, to find out groups of students with similar learning styles dimensions. In that approach tutors had to determine the required number of learners' groups in advance. In the present paper, it is proposed to apply two-phase hierarchical algorithm, which deals with outliers and allows for determining weights for different learning styles dimensions, with number of clusters depending on a required threshold.

3   Students' Modeling

3.1   Learning Styles

There exist different models of learning styles such as Felder & Silverman [1], Kolb [16], and Honey & Mumford [17], to mention the most frequently used. In the present study, Felder and Silverman model, which is often used for providing adaptivity regarding learning styles in e-learning environments [14], has been chosen. It is based on *Index of Learning Style* (ILS) questionnaire, developed by Felder & Soloman [18].

The results of ILS questionnaire indicate preferences for four dimensions of the Felder & Silverman model: *active* vs *reflective*, *sensing* vs *intuitive*, *visual* vs *verbal*, *sequential* vs *global*. The index obtained by each student has the form of the odd integer from the interval [-11,11], assigned for all of the four dimensions. Each student, who filled ILS questionnaire, can be modeled by a vector SL of 4 integer attributes:

$$SL = (sl_1, sl_2, sl_3, sl_4) = (l_{ar}, l_{si}, l_{vv}, l_{sg}) \ , \tag{1}$$

where l_{ar} means scoring for *active* (if it has negative value) or *reflective* (if it is positive) learning style, and respectively l_{si}, l_{vv}, l_{sg} are points for all the other dimensions, with negative values in cases of *sensing, visual* or *sequential* learning styles, and positive values in cases of *intuitive, verbal* or *global* learning styles.

3.2 Two-Phase Hierarchical Algorithm

The problem statement, which consists of finding groups of students with similar learning styles preferences by unsupervised classification, imposes requirements for characteristic features of a clustering algorithm. The applied grouping technique should be fully self-generating and order independent with possibilities of changing threshold value as well as determining the significance of each attribute value (each learning style dimension may be of different importance for disparate courses). There should be no requirements for determining, in advance, the final number of clusters (the amount of learners' groups may change for different data), however it cannot exceed the maximal value, determined by a tutor. What is more, there should be included the possibility of developing students' models by adding other attributes (like color preferences for example), represented by variables of different types. The last feature may be fulfiled by using similarity measures for mixed type data. Finally, dealing with outliers, which usually signify outstanding students, will be an advantage of applied method.

To fulfil all of the requirements, two-phase hierarchical algorithm is proposed. The first stage consists of a single layer clustering, during the second phase clusters are formed into hierarchical structure. The steps of the algorithm may be described as follows:

Phase I: Single Layer Clustering
[Input]: A set of N students' *SL* data, clustering threshold T, maximal number of clusters $KMAX$, minimal clustering threshold $MINT$.
Step 1: Assign the first student SL_1 as the first cluster and its centroid, Repeat Step 2 and Step 3 for each student $SL_i, i = 2, ...N$:
Step 2: Calculate the similarity between student's *SL* and the centroid of each existing cluster,
Step 3: Assign the student into the closest cluster, for which the similarity is greater than T, otherwise SL_i initiates a new cluster
Step 4: If there exist clusters containing one element, repeat Step 2 and Step 3 until all cluster centroids stabilize,

[Output]: Set of clusters SCL
Phase II: Hierarchical Agglomerative Clustering
Step 1: Choose all the clusters containing one element and remove them from SCL, let they consist the set $SCL1$
Step 2: If number of clusters in SCL is less or equal to $KMAX$ then go to Step 4,
Step 3: Repeat: Merge the closest clusters according to centroids similarity, until number of clusters $KMAX$ is achieved
Step 4: For each cluster from $SCL1$, find the closest cluster from SCL, if similarity of their centroids is greater than $MINT$ then merge both clusters otherwise indicate clusters containing one element as an outlier.
[Output]: The set of clusters SCL and the set of outliers.

The clustering threshold T as well as minimal clustering threshold $MINT$ should be determined by requirements connected with the considered courses and should guarantee that students grouped into the same clusters are of sufficiently similar learning styles preferences. Maximal number of clusters $KMAX$ is connected with number of teaching paths that a tutor is able to prepare for the educational process. All the outliers require individual paths as it always happens with outstanding students.

The hierarchical clustering algorithm of this kind was presented in [19] for web page clustering, with divisive hierarchical approach in the second phase. Wang proved [20] that this kind of hierarchical clustering algorithm is independent of the order of the input data, if they are well normalized. Normalization of data is guaranteed by the properly defined similarity measure, which should also allow for using weights and for application into mixed types of data as it was stated at the beginning of this section. In the presented approach, it is proposed to use general similarity coefficient, introduced by Gower [21], that fulfils all the requirements formulated above and may be also applied to data points with missing values. Let SL_i, SL_j denote two d-dimensional objects. Then the general similarity coefficient sim_g is defined as:

$$sim_\mathrm{g}(SL_i, SL_j) = \frac{1}{\sum_{k=1}^{d} w_k} \sum_{k=1}^{d} w_k s_k \ , \tag{2}$$

where $d = 4$ in the considered case, s_k is the similarity of the k-th attribute of SL_i, SL_j and w_k is either one or zero depending on wether or not a comparison is valid for the k-th attribute of the two objects. For numerical attributes s_k is defined as

$$s_k = 1 - \frac{\mid sl_{i_k} - sl_{j_k} \mid}{R_k} \ , \tag{3}$$

where R_k is the range of k-th attribute. Similarity function defined by (2) may be also used for binary, nominal and categorical attributes, then s_k is determined in a different way. Using w_k enables assigning weights for different attributes, the ones not valid in the classification process should be equal to 0.

4   Experiments

Experiments were done on the real data sets of Computer Science students' learning styles. There were considered two data sets of 125 and 71 instances. The performance of the algorithm was checked, for different parameters. The results were compared with the ones obtained by using well known k-means and hierarchical Farthest First Traversal algorithm.

The investigations showed that the threshold value has the great influence on the quality of results and the number of clusters obtained; for $T = 0.9$, the algorithm assigned all the students, except outliers, into one cluster after the first phase; if $T = 0.92$ the number of clusters created was equal to two, and all the assignements were also done during the first phase. In the case of the high value of T, parameter $KMAX$ decides of the final number of clusters, for example if $T = 0.96$ number of groups obtained was equal to $KMAX$ value.

Examination of the technique, by using different values of weights, showed the big influence of each dimension on the final effects. Putting any of weights equal to zero, completely changed the structure of obtained groups. It means that in the e-learning system, there should be taken into account only these dimensions that are expected to have an influence on students' perception and activity during the course. The algorithm expressed also the big ability for finding outliers, comparing with the performance of Conectivity Outlier Factor algorithm considered in [15]. The structure of the groups received (clusters of different sizes), was similar to the ones obtained by hierarchical Farthest First Traversal, while k-means divided students into almost equal clusters. The presented approach, showed many advantages like dealing with outliers, possibility of using different parameters and flexible cluster structure, but evaluation of the obtained effects still needs investigations.

5   Conclusions

In the paper, it was considered application of the two-phase hierarchical algorithm for students' grouping according to their individual learning styles preferences. In the presented approach, clustering threshold and maximal number of required clusters decide of the obtained results. Tutors do not need to determine the exact number of students' groups and teaching paths that will be created. The proposed method allows for differentiating of the similarity function, by using weights or even not taking into account certain dimensions, that may not be important from the point of view of different courses. Experiments conducted so far, showed the good performance of the algorithm, also on the data sets containing outliers.

The future research will consist of further investigations of the algorithm, with the emphasis on the choice of parameters, usage of weights and application of different similarity functions, for different data sets, as well as of comparing its effectiveness with other algorithms.

References

1. Felder, R.M., Silverman, L.K.: Learning and teaching styles in engineering education. Eng. Educ. 78, 674–681 (1988)
2. Saarikoski, L., Salojärvi, S., Del Corso, D., Ovein, E.: The 3DE: an environment for the development of learner-oriented customized educational packages. In: Proc. of ITHET 2001, Kumamoto (2001)
3. Triantafillou, E., Pomportsis, A., Georgiadou, E.: AES-CS: Adaptive educational system base on cognitive styles. AH Workshop, Malaga, pp. 10–20 (2002)
4. Stash, N., Cristea, A., De Bra, P.: Authoring of learning styles in adaptive hypermedia: Problems and solutions. In: Proc. WWW Conf., pp. 114–123 (2004)
5. Brusilovsky, P., Peylo, C.: Adaptive and intelligent web-based educational systems. International Journal of Artificial Intelligence in Education 13, 156–169 (2003)
6. Felder, R., Brent, R.: Understanding student differences. J. Eng. Educ. 94, 57–72 (2005)
7. Graf, S., Kinshuk: Considering learning styles in learning managements systems: investigating the behavior of students in an online course. In: Proc. of the 1st IEEE Int. Workshop on Semantic Media Adaptation and Personalization, Athens (2006)
8. Rovai, A.P.: The relationships of communicator style, personality-based learning style and classroom community among online graduate students. Internet & Higher Education 6, 347–363 (2003)
9. Lu, J., Yu, C.S., Liu, C.: Learning style, learning patterns and learning performance in a WebCT-based MIS course. Inform. Manage. 40, 497–507 (2003)
10. Lee, M.: Profiling students adaptation styles in Web-based learning. Comput. Educ. 36, 121–132 (2001)
11. Alfonseca, E., Carro, R.M., Martin, E., Ortigosa, A., Paredes, P.: The impact of learning styles on student grouping for collaborative learning: a case study. User Model. User-Adap 16, 377–401 (2006)
12. García, P., Amandi, A., Schiaffino, S., Campo, M.: Evaluating Bayesian networks' precision for detecting students' learning styles. Comput. Educ. 49, 794–808 (2007)
13. Xu, D., Wang, H., Su, K.: Intelligent student profiling with fuzzy models. In: Proc. of HICSS 2002, Hawaii (2002)
14. Viola, S.R., Graf, S., Kinshuk, Leo, T.: Investigating relationships within the Index of Learning Styles: a data driven approach. Interactive Technology & Smart Education 4, 7–18 (2007)
15. Zakrzewska, D.: Cluster analysis for building personalized e-learning system. Pol. J. Environ. Stud. 16, 330–334 (2007)
16. Kolb, D.A.: Experiental Learning: Experience as a Source of Learning and Development. Prentice-Hall, Englewood Cliffs (1984)
17. Honey, P., Mumford, A.: The Manual of Learning Styles. Peter Honey, Maidenhead (1986)
18. Index of Learning Style Questionnaire, http://www.engr.ncsu.edu/learningstyles/ilsweb.html
19. Zha, Y., Yu, J.X., Hou, J.: Web Communities. Analysis and Construction. Springer, Berlin Heidelberg (2006)
20. Wang, L.: On competitive learning. IEEE T. Neural Networ. 8, 1214–1217 (1997)
21. Gower, J.: A general coefficient of similarity and some of its properties. Biometrics 27, 857–874 (1971)

An Empirical Investigation of the Use of a Neural Network Committee for Identifying the *Streptococcus Pneumoniae* Growth Phases in Batch Cultivations

Antonio C.L. Horta[1,*], Teresa C. Zangirolami[2], Maria do Carmo Nicoletti[3], Luciana Montera[1], Talita S. Carmo[4], and Viviane M. Gonçalves[4]

[1] PPG-Biotechnology - UFSCar, SP - Brazil
horta@iris.ufscar.br
[2] Dept. of Chemical Engineering - UFSCar, SP - Brazil
[3] Dept. of Computer Science - UFSCar, SP - Brazil
[4] Butantan Institute, SP - Brazil

Abstract. *Streptococcus pneumoniae* is a bacterial pathogen that causes many life-threatening diseases and an effective vaccine against this pathogen is still subject of research. These bacteria grow with low carbon dioxide production, which hinders the application of exhaust gas composition for on-line process monitoring. This work investigates the proposal of a committee of neural networks for identifying *Streptococcus pneumoniae* growth phases, to be used for on-line state inference. The committee results as well as the accuracy for predicting the culture phases are compared to the results of a unique neural network, for different input variables. The best configuration for the software was: a committee of three NN trained with two input attributes (optical density and mass of alkali solution), 200 epochs of training and log sigmoid as the activation function in the hidden layer as well as in the output layer.

Keywords: growth phase identification, neural network committee, batch cultivations, *Streptococcus pneumoniae*.

1 Introduction

The *Streptococcus pneumoniae* bacterium is one of the leading biological agents responsible for many human infections. According to [1], over one million children younger than 5 years die each year from pneumonia, with the *S. pneumoniae* being the main responsible for this infection. In Brazil the bacterium was the cause of 29,600 meningitis cases, causing 8,554 deaths between the years of 1983 and 2003. It is worth mentioning that the use of antibiotics for treating milder infections, such otitis and sinusitis, has contributed for the development of *S. pneumoniae* strains with multidrug resistance.

---

[*] Corresponding author.

N.T. Nguyen et al. (Eds.): IEA/AIE 2008, LNAI 5027, pp. 215–224, 2008.
© Springer-Verlag Berlin Heidelberg 2008

The numbers confirm the importance of seeking for a more effective large-scale treatment/vaccine against *S. pneumoniae*. The volume of production and the quality of vaccines directly influence the cost of treating the infections. There is an urgent need to low the production costs and, at the same time, increase the amount as well as the quality of vaccine production processes.

One way to improve the production processes is by means of establishing control strategies that maximize growth or product formation. Therefore, a deep understanding of how cells grow and synthesize products is required. According to [2], when a cultivation medium is inoculated with a bacterial strain, the microorganisms selectively absorb the nutrients, converting them into biomass and metabolites, such as carbon dioxide, ethanol, organic acids and others. A typical curve representing a microorganism growing during a batch process is showed in Figure 1, where the following phases can be identified: (1) lag, (2) exponential growth, (3) deceleration, (4) stationary and finally (5) death. The lag phase occurs immediately after the inoculation and it is a period related to the adaptation of the microorganism to the new environment. In the exponential growth phase, the microorganism is already adapted to the medium. They then grow exponentially in both mass and number of cells. In the deceleration phase, the microorganism growth rate diminishes as a consequence of two conditions: depletion of essential nutrients and accumulation of metabolites, which can inhibit growth. The stationary phase starts at the end of the deceleration phase, when the growth rate is zero (there is no cellular division) or when the death rate is equal to the growth rate. Even during this phase the cells are still active and can produce non-growth associated metabolites as antibiotics. The last phase in Figure 1 is the death phase in which the death rate surpasses the growth rate and the cell concentration decreases.

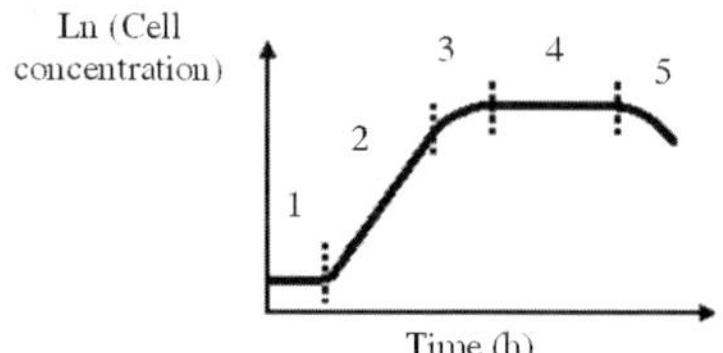

Fig. 1. Typical growth pattern of a bacterium population in a batch cultivation ([2])

The previous description of growth phases indicates how growth phase identification is crucial for process optimization. If the synthesis of the desired product is associated to a known phase of the growth curve, the cultivation conditions can be manipulated so that the period of time of this specific phase can be extended. On the other hand, anticipating the end of the process, when the microorganisms enter the stationary or death phases, is also important to minimize idle time in bioreactors operation. However, growth phase identification is not trivial even for an experienced observer. First of all, a clear definition of when one phase ends and the following starts is difficult to be established. Secondly, the choice of the dataset to be used for the identification of the growth phases must be carefully considered. Most relevant information is present in the variables directly related to cell growth, such as dry cell weight concentration and glucose consumption. However, these states can not be measured on-line during cultivations and thereby, they are not suitable for automatic phase identification. On the other hand, the mass of alkali solution added to control pH can be easily followed on-line, but it depends upon organic acids production which can be (or not) directly related to growth.

This paper describes the proposal of a neural network based software tool for the on-line detection of the cellular growth phase, based on on-line measures of a few process variables, in a batch bioreactor. Aiming at obtaining the most favorable operational conditions, the on-line identification of the growth phase will contribute by giving the necessary information for controlling the feed rate of the bioreactor. The proposed scheme can be further used for control and optimization of industrial processes, as part of a control system that dynamically changes the model that supervises the production of capsular polysaccharide in a bioreactor, based on the growth phase of the cultivation.

2   Experiments and Results

This section describes (a) how the laboratorial cultivation of *Streptococcus pneumoniae* were conducted; (b) how the data collected from the cultivations were prepared to be used by a backpropagation learning procedure and (c) how the neural networks were trained and evaluated as well as how the committee of NNs was defined and how it operates for the on-line identification of the growth phase in a *Streptococcus pneumoniae* batch cultivation.

(a) Bench Scale Cultivation of *Streptococcus Pneumoniae*

Microorganism: For the experiments described in this work, *Streptococcus pneumoniae* serotype 6B strain ST 433/03 was used, which was obtained from the Instituto Adolfo Lutz, Bacteriology Section, São Paulo, Brazil.

Cultivation Medium Composition and Preparation: Bench scale experiments were carried out using a variant of the Hoeprich medium, containing glucose as the main carbon and energy source; acid-hydrolyzed casein, dialyzed yeast extract, L-glutamine and asparagine as nitrogen sources, as well as several salts ([3], [4]).

Cultivation Conditions: The experiments were conducted in 5L-bioreactors BioFlo 2000 (New Brunswick Scientific Inc.), monitored by the LabView 7.1 program (National Instruments). The following cultivation conditions were employed: N_2 flow rate of 0.25 VVM, agitation speed of 100 rpm and temperature of 37°C. Frozen stock culture (-70°C) was used to inoculate 500 mL of the same medium. The culture was incubated for 13h at 37°C in atmosphere containing 5-10% of CO_2. The inoculum volume transferred into the bioreactor was enough to obtain an initial optical density (OD) of 0.2 at 600 nm. Polypropyleneglycol was used as antifoam agent when necessary (feed-on-demand). In order to maintain the broth at the desired pH (in the range of 7.4 to 7.6) and compensate the decrease in pH due to lactic acid formation, the addition of a sodium hydroxide solution (5 M) was automatically controlled. The acquisition of NaOH solution consumption data was performed by an electronic balance (APX-6001, Denver Instruments Company) connected to the acquisition system through a serial port (module Breakout Box RS 232). Data storage and monitoring interface were implemented in LabView 7.1 program, as well.

Analytical Methods: A culture sample was collected at each hour. An aliquote of 1 mL was immediately diluted after sample withdrawal and used for determination of the optical density (OD), measured as absorbance at 600 nm (Hitachi U-1800 Spectrophotometer). The remaining of the sample was centrifuged at 3.220 g, 4°C for 30 minutes and the supernatant was used for chemical analysis of glucose, lactic acid and PS concentrations. Biomass concentration was determined using the cell sediment, which was re-suspended in a 0.9% salt solution, centrifuged again and dried at 60°C until constant weight. The residual glucose and the lactic acid concentrations were measured directly from the supernatant, using the colorimeter method of glucose oxidase (Enz-Color Biodiagnstica, Brazil) and the HPLC, respectively. PS was determined by the quantification of rhamnose ([5]) after the dialysis against distilled water.

Description of the Experimental Data: Three *Streptococcus pneumoniae* cultures aiming at the production of capsular polysaccharide were conducted in bioreactors at the Fermentation Laboratory, Butantan Institute (São Paulo - Brazil). The data collected from the three bench scale experiments are referred in this paper as dataset $Ferm_2$, dataset $Ferm_5$ and dataset $Ferm_{11}$, respectively. The cultivation medium composition as well as the experimental procedure and preparation of each culture were very similar and for each cultivation process, the data was collected at one hour interval. Each of the three datasets contains 12 data instances; each data instance is described by the value of six variables, namely: Cell concentration (C_X) - it gives the dry cell mass concentration (not on-line); Glucose concentration (C_S) (not on-line); PS concentration (C_{PS}) - refers to the amount of the product of interest i.e., of capsular polysaccharide (not on-line); Lactic acid concentration (C_L) (not on-line); mass of sodium hydroxide solution consumed (NaOH) (on-line) and optical density (OD) - related to the cell concentration. The last variable, OD, can be taken as an on-line measurement since its value was obtained in less than 3 minutes after sample withdrawal.

(b) Preparing the Data for the Automatic Learning of the *Streptococcus Pneumoniae* Growth Phase

Data in each of the original dataset, i.e., $Ferm_2$, $Ferm_5$ and $Ferm_{11}$ went through a few modifications, as showed in Figure 2, aiming at its use by a neural network training algorithm. Due to the relatively low number of collected data instances (12 per experiment) as well as to the possibility of noise in the collected data, each dataset was input to a smoother/interpolator process (implemented as the perfect smoother described in [6]) that produced, for each input dataset, its extended smoothed version containing 55 instances. This process is represented on the left of Figure 2, where SM refers to the smoother procedure. The interpolating function used by the smoother was adjusted for interpolating a new data instance between two experimental instances, at the frequency of 12 minutes along the time axis. As the perfect smoother process requires a user-defined value for the parameter λ (the smoothing parameter), a few different values were tried and the one, which suited the best, was chosen.

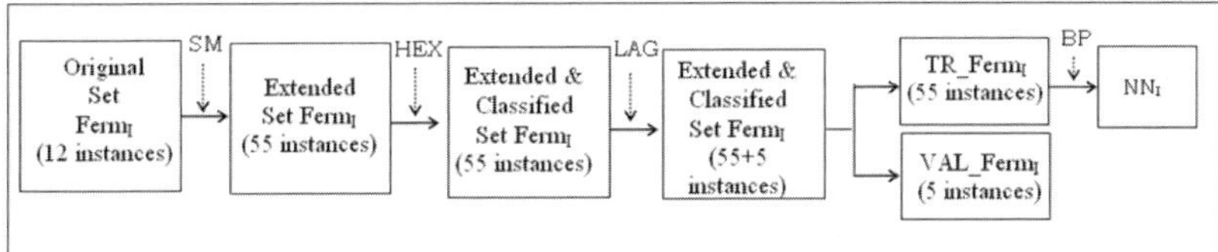

Fig. 2. The adopted scheme for preparing the data collected in each laboratorial experiment to be used for learning each individual network, NN_I (I = 2, 5, 11) where SM: smoother, HEX: human expert, LAG: introduction of artificially generated lag data and BP: backpropagation training, resulting in the neural network NN_I, further used as part of a committee. Data in VAL_Ferm_I (I = 2, 5, 11) are used for validation purposes, while in TR_Ferm_I for training of the NN's.

Typical results of the smoothing/interpolation process are represented in Figure 3, for the experimental dataset $Ferm_5$. The figure shows the 12 original data instances and the interpolated data as a curve based on the 55 values, for each of the six variables that describe each data instance.

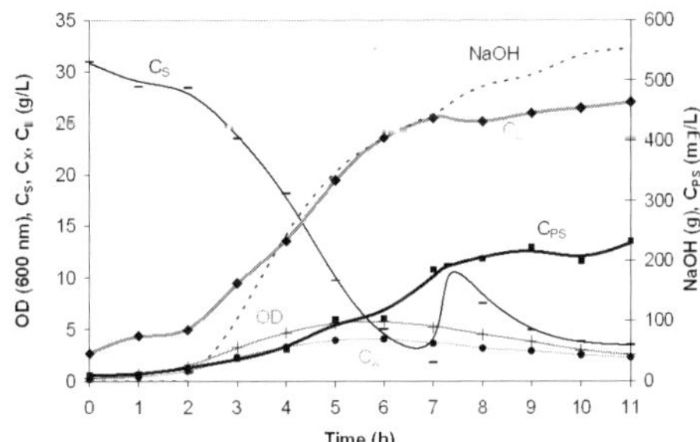

Fig. 3. Interpolation and smoothing of the experimental data from $Ferm_5$, with $\lambda = 8$ and INT = 12 (INT: time interval for interpolating a new instance). The symbols represent experimental data. The continuous lines represent the extended data. The dashed line refers to on-line measurements of NaOH solution consumed.

Since the bench scale experiments were started using well activated inoculum, the three *Streptococcus pneumoniae* cultivations did not have the lag phase. In order to have data representing the 5 phases of the canonical growth curve, data referring to a lag phase were artificially produced, as can be visualized in Figure 2. The optical density in the lag phase (OD_{lag}) was calculated for each time interval using eq.(1), where OD is the initial absorbance of the exponential phase, t_f is the total time of the lag phase and t_{lag} is the time interval.

The value of max was determined using data from the exponential growth phase for each experiment as the slope of the function Ln(OD) plotted against time. The value of μ_{maxlag} is the μ_{max} of the lag phase, determined for each time interval. The time length of the lag phase of each experiment was chosen between half hour and two hours; the choice was based on the information gathered from previous cultivations of the same microorganism and aiming at a more general setting, we decided to establish three different lag phase length: $t_{lag}^{Ferm_2} = 0.6$ h, $t_{lag}^{Ferm_5} = 0.8$ h and $t_{lag}^{Ferm_{11}} = 1$ h, $\mu_{MAX}^{Ferm_2} = 0.8$, $\mu_{MAX}^{Ferm_5} = 0.75$, $\mu_{MAX}^{Ferm_{11}} = 0.71$.

$$\frac{OD}{OD_{lag}} = e^{\left[\left(0.9 \cdot \mu_{MAX} \cdot \frac{t_{lag}}{t_f} + 0.1 \cdot \mu_{MAX}\right) \cdot (t_f - t_{lag})\right]} \tag{1}$$

The neural network algorithm chosen for learning to identify the growth process phase was the backpropagation, main due to its popularity and relative success in many different domains. The backpropagation is typically a supervised learning technique i.e., when used for classification tasks (as is the case in this work), requires that each data instance used in the training procedure has an associated class assigned to it. All the data instances underwent a manual class assignment process. A human expert, identified as HEX in Figure 2, classified each data instance of the extended datasets $Ferm_2$, $Ferm_5$ and $Ferm_{11}$ into one of the five possible phases. Each dataset was then modified, in order to include the phase associated to each instance, given by the expert.

The five phases were encoded using 1-of-5 coding, meaning that 5 binary (0/1) target variables corresponding to the 5 phases were coded at the end of each instance, in a process known as introduction of dummy variables. Each dummy variable was then given the value zero except for the one corresponding to the correct phase, which was given the value 1, as shows the examples in Table 1.

Table 1. The 1-of-5 coding used for codifying the five growth phases, when a data instance is described by two variables namely OD (optical density) and mass of NaOH solution

Time(h)	OD(600nm)	NaOH(g)	Phase	Time	OD	NaOH	Phase Representation
0.2	0.16	0	Lag	Lag	0.16	0	1 0 0 0 0
1.8	0.66	10.57	Exponential	1.8	0.66	10.57	0 1 0 0 0
3.8	3.61	133.76	Deceleration →	3.8	3.61	133.76	0 0 1 0 0
6.0	5.46	261.18	Stationary	6.0	5.46	261.18	0 0 0 1 0
10.40	3.93	396.95	Death	10.40	3.93	396.95	0 0 0 0 1

(c) The Training of Neural Networks the Committee *Versus* a Single NN

Traditional neural network algorithms such as backpropagation require the definition of the network architecture, prior to training. Generally speaking, these methods work well only when the network architecture is appropriately chosen. However, it is well known that there is no general answer to the problem of defining a neural network architecture for a given application. A common practice for defining a neural network architecture that suits a problem consists of defining several different architectures, training and evaluating each of them and then, choosing the one most appropriate for the problem ([7]).

The conducted experiments in learning how to identify the growth phase using neural networks were based on the common practice of trying different network architectures. A previous few experiments involving architectures with 2 and 3 hidden layers and a set of different number of hidden neurons per layer were tried. The initial experiments also tried different combinations of activation functions for hidden and output neurons. The combinations of activation functions tried for hidden and output neurons respectively were: (a) tangent-sigmoid and linear (b) log-sigmoid and linear (c) log-sigmoid and log-sigmoid. A few experiments that tried to identify the set of the most relevant variables for characterizing the growth phase were also conducted and among all the variable sets tried, particularly two have shown to be more relevant: OD, C_X, C_S, C_L, C_{PS}, NaOH, referred to as All and the subset OD, NaOH.

Two different approaches for using NNs were employed in the experiments: one referred to as a committee of NNs, which consisted in training a set of three neural networks (each NN was trained using only one of the three previously mentioned datasets) and composing them into a classification committee. The other was the traditional approach, in which a single NN was trained using the available training data. For the experiments of training the single network, a dataset contained all the data instances from TR_Ferm_2, TR_Ferm_5 and TR_Ferm_{11} was used (each TR_Ferm_I ($I = 2, 5, 11$) was obtained as described in Figure 2).

Figure 4 shows a detailed diagram of the procedure adopted for learning the NNs which compose the committee (i.e., NN_2, NN_5 and NN_{11}), and the single neural network (NN). The procedure adopted for using the committee of the three NNs for inferring the growth phase is: each of the three neural networks delivers an output data point and a counter module uses the frequency for calculating the system final output.

Due to the volume of data obtained, we decided to present the best results only i.e., the results obtained with (a) one hidden layer (b) the log-sigmoid as activation functions of both, hidden neurons and output neurons and (c) two sets of input variables: OD, NaOH and All. The effects of the number of hidden neurons on the results can also be seen in Figure 6. The results presented in Figure 6 are for the two architectures showed in Figure 5 i.e., one for two input variables, OD and NaOH, and the other the six input variables, OD, C_X, C_S, C_L, C_{PS} and NaOH (All). Both have five output neurons. In both architectures, all input nodes are connected to all hidden nodes and all hidden nodes are connected to all output nodes.

The programs that implement all the procedures described in this paper were written and run under a MatLab 6.5 (Mathworks) platform. The backpropagation was implemented using the Levenberg-Marquardt algorithm, with 200 epochs.

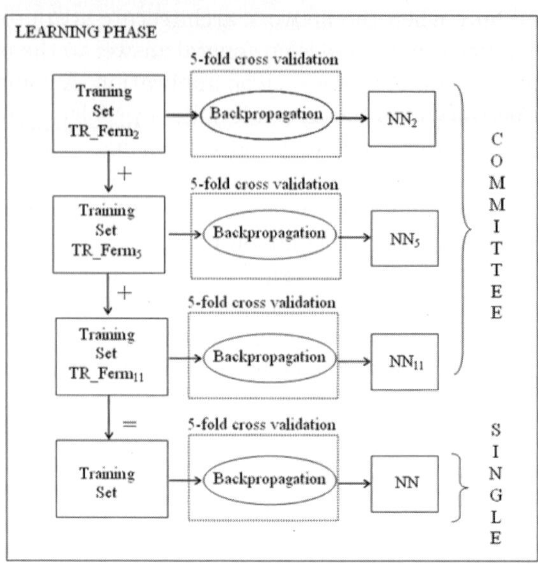

Fig. 4. The learning phase of the neural networks based on the extended classified training data

As depicted in Figure 4, for training each of the NNs used in the experiments, a 5-cross validation process was carried out. For each training dataset, among the five NNs constructed, the one with the best performance in the corresponding test set was chosen to be part of the committee. For validating both, the committee and the single NN accuracy, the dataset containing the data instances from the datasets VAL_Ferm_I (I = 2, 5, 11) (see Figure 2) was used and the results are showed in Figure 6. As can be seen in Figure 6, the performance of the committee was not as good as the single network, although the differences between both are not statistically significant. These results should be analyzed taking into consideration, on one hand, the fact the single NN was induced using the total amount of available data (i.e., data instances from the three datasets) and, as such, it generalizes over the three bench scale experiments. On the other hand, each neural network that is part of the committee represents a generalization of one single experiment.

A very interesting aspect of the committee, however, is a direct consequence of its inherent incremental nature, i.e., new NNs can be introduced into the committee, as experimental data becomes available, without any additional effort other than training the new network, using the new available data. Furthermore, this approach enables the committee to handle usual variations of the growth patterns from different cultivations that will become more relevant as the number of experimental datasets increases. When using a single network, however, the training process needs to be restarted again, from scratch, taking into consideration the previous as well as new experimental data.

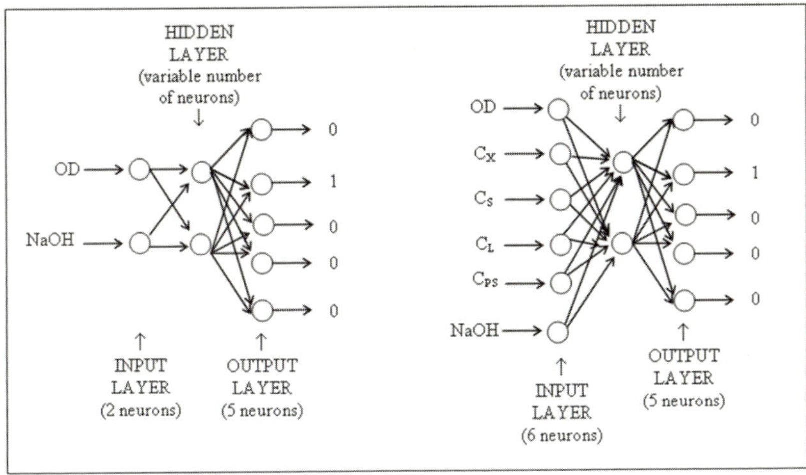

Fig. 5. The two NN architectures with the best results. The numbers of hidden nodes tried were: 2, 3, 4, 5, 6, 7, 10 and 15.

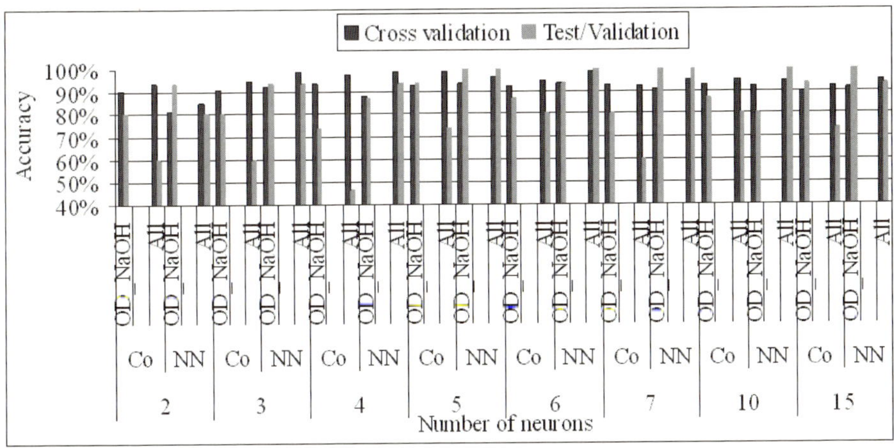

Fig. 6. Accuracy results from both: the committee (Co) and the single NN, for networks with two (OD and NaOH) and with six input (All) variables. Results from architectures using different number of hidden neurons are showed. All the networks have five output neurons.

Although the NNs trained with all attributes have a smaller cross validation error, one can see from the results shown at Figure 6 that the performance of their classification committee is very close to that observed for the committee of NNs trained only with the attributes OD and mass of NaOH solution, which are available on-line. This result is extremely important, since it indicates that the NNs committee generated with on-line inputs can be used as an on-line control tool.

3   Conclusions

This paper describes a non-conventional use of neural networks for identifying the growth phase of *Streptococcus pneumoniac*, in a bioreactor, aiming at the production of capsular polysaccharide. A committee of three neural networks has been proposed for the identification task and the results of both approaches, the committee and a single neural network, using empirical data, are compared. We believe that instead of using a single network to solve the identification problem, there are advantages in using a committee of such networks, each of them trained using data collected from a particular laboratorial experiments. Instead of having all the available data generalized into a unique network, the committee allows the generalization of each laboratorial experiment in a NN and a voting scheme based on frequency, for identification, which gives the identification process more flexibility. Also, the incremental aspect of the committee allows for new similar laboratorial experiments to be generalized as neural networks and included as part of the committee, without interference with the current committee. The experiments discussed in this paper will be further investigated, by repeating them using other NN training algorithms (such as constructive algorithms).

References

1. Bricks, L.F., Berezin, E.: Impact of pneumococcal conjugate vaccine on the prevention of invasive pneumococcal diseases. J. Pediatr (R. J.) 82(3 Suppl), S67–74 (2006)
2. Shuler, M.L., Kargi, F.: Bioprocess Engineering: Basic Concepts, 2nd edn. Prentice-Hall, Englewood Cliffs (2001)
3. Hoeprich, P.D.: Carbon-14 labeling of Diplococcus pncumoniae. J. Bacteriol. 69, 682–688 (1955)
4. Gonçalves, V.M., Zangirolami, T.C., Giordano, R.L.C., Raw, I., Tanizaki, M.M., Giordano, R.C.: Optimization of medium and culture conditions for capsular polysaccharide production by *Streptococcus pneumoniae* serotype 23F. Applied Microbiology and Biotechnology, Germany 59, 713–717 (2002)
5. Dische, Z., Shettles, B.: A specific color reaction of methylpentoses and a spectrophotometric micromethod for their determination. J. Biol. Chem. 175, 595–603 (1948)
6. Eilers, P.H.C.: A Perfect Smoother. Analytical Chemistry 75(14), 3631–3636 (2003)
7. Giordano, R.C., Bertini, J.R., Nicoletti, M.C., Giordano, R.L.C.: On-line filtering of CO_2 signals from a bioreactor gas outflow using a committee of constructive neural networks. Bioprocess and Biosystems Engineering (2007) (accepted for publication)

Suboptimal Nonlinear Predictive Control with MIMO Neural Hammerstein Models

Maciej Ławryńczuk

Institute of Control and Computation Engineering, Warsaw University of Technology
ul. Nowowiejska 15/19, 00-665 Warsaw, Poland
Tel.: +48 22 234-76-73
M.Lawrynczuk@ia.pw.edu.pl

Abstract. This paper describes a computationally efficient (suboptimal) nonlinear Model Predictive Control (MPC) algorithm with neural Hammerstein models. The Multi-Input Multi-Output (MIMO) dynamic model contains a steady-state nonlinear part realised by a set of neural networks in series with a linear dynamic part. The model is linearised on-line, as a result the MPC algorithm solves a quadratic programming problem. The algorithm gives control performance similar to that obtained in nonlinear MPC, which hinges on non-convex optimisation.

1 Introduction

Model Predictive Control (MPC) algorithms based on linear models have been successfully used for years in advanced industrial applications [11,15,16]. It is mainly because they can take into account constraints imposed on both process inputs (manipulated variables) and outputs (controlled variables), which usually decide on quality, economic efficiency and safety. Moreover, MPC techniques are very efficient in multivariable process control. Because properties of many processes are nonlinear, different nonlinear MPC approaches have been developed [7,12,16], for example MPC algorithms based on neural models [10,16,17].

This paper details a computationally efficient nonlinear MPC algorithm with neural Hammerstein models. The Multi-Input Multi-Output (MIMO) dynamic model contains a steady-state nonlinear part realised by a set of neural networks followed by a linear dynamic part. Hammerstein models can be used for control [9,13,14], although an inverse model is usually necessary. In the algorithm described in this paper the model is used on-line to find a local linearisation and a nonlinear free trajectory. Future control policy is calculated on-line from an easy to solve quadratic programming problem. In practice, the algorithm gives closed-loop performance comparable to that obtained in fully-fledged nonlinear MPC, in which nonlinear optimisation is repeated at each sampling instant.

Hammerstein structures can be efficiently used for modelling of various technological processes [1,4,9]. Different identification methods have been proposed: correlation methods [3], parametric methods [4] and non-parametric regression methods [5]. In the simplest case polynomials are used in the steady-state nonlinear part of the model. Unfortunately, such an approach has some disadvantages.

N.T. Nguyen et al. (Eds.): IEA/AIE 2008, LNAI 5027, pp. 225–234, 2008.

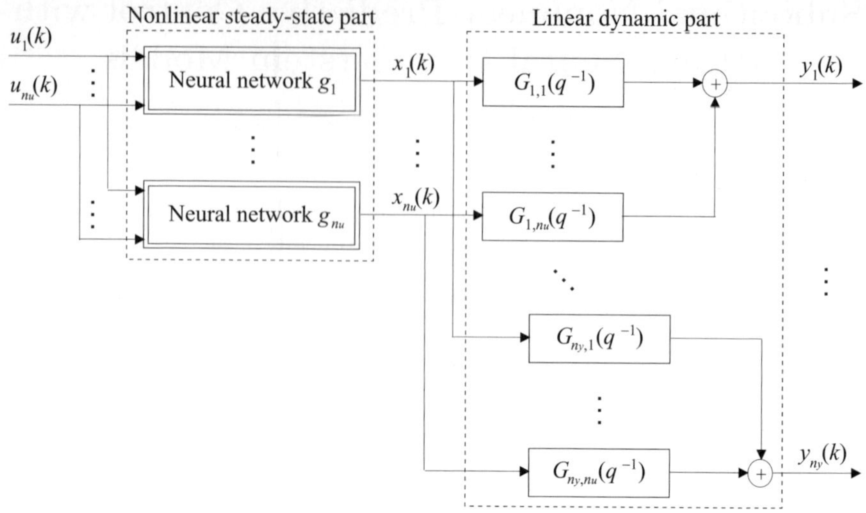

Fig. 1. Structure of the MIMO neural Hammerstein model

First of all, the accuracy of polynomial approximation is limited. Secondly, for MIMO processes polynomials have many parameters, the model is very complex.

In this paper neural networks are used in the steady-state nonlinear part of the Hammerstein model as an efficient alternative to the traditional polynomial approach, especially for MIMO processes. Such a model has a few advantages. Neural networks [6] are universal approximators, which means that a multilayer perceptron with at least one hidden layer can approximate any smooth function to an arbitrary degree of accuracy. Unlike polynomial approximations, neural approximations are very smooth. Moreover, neural networks have relatively small numbers of parameters and simple structures. Finally, computational complexity of identification algorithms for neural Hammerstein models is low [2,8].

2   MIMO Neural Hammerstein Models

Structure of the considered Multi-Input Multi-Output (MIMO) neural Hammerstein model is depicted in Fig. 1. The model has n_u inputs and n_y outputs, i.e. $u(t) \in \Re^{n_u}$, $y(t) \in \Re^{n_y}$. It consists of a nonlinear steady-state part

$$x(k) = g(u(k)) \tag{1}$$

where $g : \Re^{n_u} \longrightarrow \Re^{n_u}$, in series with a linear dynamic part

$$\boldsymbol{A}(q^{-1})y(k) = \boldsymbol{B}(q^{-1})x(k) \tag{2}$$

Auxiliary signals are denoted by $x(t) \in \Re^{n_u}$.

The steady-state nonlinear part of the model is comprised of n_u MultiLayer Perceptron (MLP) feedforward neural networks with one hidden layer and a linear output [6]. Outputs of neural networks are

$$x_n(k) = w_0^{2,n} + \sum_{i=1}^{K^n} w_i^{2,n} \varphi(z_i^n(k))$$ (3)

where

$$z_i^n(k) = w_{i,0}^{1,n} + \sum_{j=1}^{n_u} w_{i,j}^{1,n} u_n(k)$$ (4)

are sums of inputs of the ith hidden node, $\varphi : \Re \longrightarrow \Re$ is the nonlinear transfer function (e.g. hyperbolic tangent), K^n is the number of hidden nodes. Weights of the nth network $(n = 1, \ldots, n_u)$ are denoted by $w_{i,j}^{1,n}$, $i = 1, \ldots, K^n$, $j = 0, \ldots, n_u$, and $w_i^{2,n}$, $i = 0, \ldots, K^n$, for the first and the second layer, respectively.

The dynamic linear part (2) of the model is defined by polynomial matrices

$$\boldsymbol{A}(q^{-1}) = \begin{bmatrix} 1 + a_1^1 q^{-1} + \ldots + a_{n_A}^1 q^{-n_A} \ldots & & 0 \\ & \vdots & \ddots & \vdots \\ 0 & & \ldots 1 + a_1^{n_y} q^{-1} + \ldots + a_{n_A}^{n_y} q^{-n_A} \end{bmatrix}$$ (5)

and

$$\boldsymbol{B}(q^{-1}) = \begin{bmatrix} b_1^{1,1} q^{-1} + \ldots + b_{n_B}^{1,1} q^{-n_B} & \ldots & b_1^{1,n_u} q^{-1} + \ldots + b_{n_B}^{1,n_u} q^{-n_B} \\ \vdots & \ddots & \vdots \\ b_1^{n_y,1} q^{-1} + \ldots + b_{n_B}^{n_y,1} q^{-n_B} & \ldots & b_1^{n_y,n_u} q^{-1} + \ldots + b_{n_B}^{n_y,n_u} q^{-n_B} \end{bmatrix}$$ (6)

where q^{-1} is the backward shift operator. From (2), (5) and (6), the transfer function connecting the nth input of the dynamic part with the mth output $(n = 1, \ldots, n_u, m = 1, \ldots, n_y)$ is

$$G_{m,n}(q^{-1}) = \frac{b_1^{m,n} q^{-1} + \ldots + b_{n_B}^{m,n} q^{-n_B}}{1 + a_1^m q^{-1} + \ldots + a_{n_A}^m q^{-n_A}}$$ (7)

Outputs of the model can be described by the following equations

$$y_m(k) = \sum_{n=1}^{n_u} \sum_{l=1}^{n_B} b_l^{m,n} x_n(k-l) - \sum_{l=1}^{n_A} a_l^m y_m(k-l)$$ (8)

All things considered, outputs of the model can be expressed as

$$y_m(k) = f_m(u_1(k-1), \ldots, u_1(k-n_B), \ldots, u_{n_u}(k-1), \ldots, u_{n_u}(k-n_B),$$ (9)
$$y_m(k-1), \ldots, y_m(k-n_A)$$

where $f_m : \Re^{n_u n_B + n_A} \longrightarrow \Re$, $m = 1, \ldots, n_y$. From (3), (4) and (8) one has

$$y_m(k) = \sum_{n=1}^{n_u} \sum_{l=1}^{n_B} b_l^{m,n} \left[w_0^{2,n} + \sum_{i=1}^{K^n} w_i^{2,n} \varphi \left(w_{i,0}^{1,n} + \sum_{j=1}^{n_u} w_{i,j}^{1,n} u_n(k-l) \right) \right]$$ (10)
$$- \sum_{l=1}^{n_A} a_l^m y_m(k-l).$$

3   Model Predictive Control Algorithms

In MPC algorithms [11,16] at each consecutive sampling instant k a set of future control increments is calculated

$$\Delta \boldsymbol{u}(k) = \left[\Delta u^T(k|k)\ \Delta u^T(k+1|k)\ldots\Delta u^T(k+N_u-1|k)\right]^T \tag{11}$$

It is assumed that $\Delta u(k+p|k) = 0$ for $p \geq N_u$, where N_u is the control horizon. The objective is to minimise the differences between the reference trajectory $y^{ref}(k+p|k)$ and the predicted outputs values $\hat{y}(k+p|k)$ over the prediction horizon $N \geq N_u$. The following quadratic cost function is usually used

$$J(k) = \sum_{p=1}^{N} \left\|y^{ref}(k+p|k) - \hat{y}(k+p|k)\right\|_{\boldsymbol{M}_p}^2 + \sum_{p=0}^{N_u-1} \left\|\Delta u(k+p|k)\right\|_{\boldsymbol{\Lambda}_p}^2 \tag{12}$$

where $\boldsymbol{M}_p \geq 0$, $\boldsymbol{\Lambda}_p > 0$ are weighting matrices of dimensionality $n_y \times n_y$ and $n_u \times n_u$, respectively. Only the first n_u elements of the determined sequence (11) are applied to the process (i.e. the control moves for the current sampling instant k), the control law is then $u(k) = \Delta u(k|k) + u(k-1)$. At the next sampling instant, $k+1$, the output measurements are updated, the prediction is shifted one step forward and the whole procedure is repeated.

Future control increments are found on-line from the following optimisation problem (for simplicity of presentation hard output constraints [11,16] are used)

$$\min_{\Delta u(k|k)\ldots\Delta u(k+N_u-1|k)} \{J(k)\}$$

subject to

$$u^{\min} \leq u(k+p|k) \leq u^{\max}, \quad p = 0,\ldots,N_u-1 \tag{13}$$

$$-\Delta u^{\max} \leq \Delta u(k+p|k) \leq \Delta u^{\max}, \quad p = 0,\ldots,N_u-1$$

$$y^{\min} \leq \hat{y}(k+p|k) \leq y^{\max}, \quad p = 1,\ldots,N$$

where $u^{\min}$, $u^{\max}$, $\Delta u^{\max} \in \Re^{n_u}$, $y^{\min}$, $y^{\max} \in \Re^{n_y}$ define constraints.

4   Suboptimal MPC with Neural Hammerstein Models

4.1   Suboptimal MPC Quadratic Programming Problem

The prediction equation for $p = 1,\ldots,N$ is

$$\hat{y}(k+p|k) = y(k+p|k) + d(k) \tag{14}$$

where quantities $y(k+p|k)$ are calculated from a nonlinear model. Unmeasured disturbances $d(k)$ are assumed to be constant over the prediction horizon. They are estimated from

$$d(k) = y(k) - y(k|k-1) \tag{15}$$

where $y(k)$ are measured while $y(k|k-1)$ are calculated from the model.

If for prediction a nonlinear neural Hammerstein model is used without any simplifications, the nonlinear MPC optimisation problem (13) has to be solved on-line at each sampling instant. Although in theory such an approach seems to be potentially very precise, it has limited applicability because computational burden of nonlinear MPC is enormous and it may terminate in local minima. That is why the MPC scheme with Nonlinear Prediction and Linearisation (MPC-NPL) [10,16,17] is adopted here. At each sampling instant k the neural Hammerstein model is used on-line twice: to find a local linearisation and a nonlinear free trajectory. The output prediction is expressed as the sum of a forced trajectory, which depends only on the future (on future control moves) and a free trajectory $\boldsymbol{y}^0(k)$, which depends only on the past

$$\hat{\boldsymbol{y}}(k) = \boldsymbol{G}(k)\Delta\boldsymbol{u}(k) + \boldsymbol{y}^0(k) \tag{16}$$

where

$$\hat{\boldsymbol{y}}(k) = \begin{bmatrix} \hat{y}(k+1|k) \\ \vdots \\ \hat{y}(k+N|k) \end{bmatrix}, \quad \boldsymbol{y}^0(k) = \begin{bmatrix} y^0(k+1|k) \\ \vdots \\ y^0(k+N|k) \end{bmatrix} \tag{17}$$

are vectors of length $n_y N$. The dynamic matrix $\boldsymbol{G}(k)$ of dimensionality $n_y N \times n_u N_u$ is calculated on-line taking into account the current state of the plant

$$\boldsymbol{G}(k) = \begin{bmatrix} \boldsymbol{S}_1(k) & 0 & \cdots & 0 \\ \boldsymbol{S}_2(k) & \boldsymbol{S}_1(k) & \cdots & 0 \\ \vdots & \vdots & \ddots & \vdots \\ \boldsymbol{S}_N(k) & \boldsymbol{S}_{N-1}(k) & \cdots & \boldsymbol{S}_{N-N_u+1}(k) \end{bmatrix} \tag{18}$$

It contains step-response coefficients of the local linear approximation of the nonlinear Hammerstein model. Step-response submatrices are

$$\boldsymbol{S}_j(k) = \begin{bmatrix} s_j^{1,1}(k) & \cdots & s_j^{1,n_u}(k) \\ \vdots & \ddots & \vdots \\ s_j^{n_y,1}(k) & \cdots & s_j^{n_y,n_u}(k) \end{bmatrix} \tag{19}$$

Thanks to using the suboptimal prediction (16), the optimisation problem (13) becomes the following quadratic programming task

$$\min_{\Delta\boldsymbol{u}(k)} \left\{ \left\| \boldsymbol{y}^{ref}(k) - \boldsymbol{G}(k)\Delta\boldsymbol{u}(k) - \boldsymbol{y}^0(k) \right\|_{\boldsymbol{M}}^2 + \left\| \Delta\boldsymbol{u}(k) \right\|_{\boldsymbol{\Lambda}}^2 \right\}$$

subject to

$$\boldsymbol{u}^{\min} \le \boldsymbol{J}\Delta\boldsymbol{u}(k) + \boldsymbol{u}^{k-1}(k) \le \boldsymbol{u}^{\max} \tag{20}$$

$$-\Delta\boldsymbol{u}^{\max} \le \Delta\boldsymbol{u}(k) \le \Delta\boldsymbol{u}^{\max}$$

$$\boldsymbol{y}^{\min} \le \boldsymbol{G}(k)\Delta\boldsymbol{u}(k) + \boldsymbol{y}^0(k) \le \boldsymbol{y}^{\max}$$

where

$$\boldsymbol{y}^{ref}(k) = \begin{bmatrix} y^{ref}(k+1|k) \\ \vdots \\ y^{ref}(k+N|k) \end{bmatrix}, \quad \boldsymbol{y}^{\min} = \begin{bmatrix} y^{\min} \\ \vdots \\ y^{\min} \end{bmatrix}, \quad \boldsymbol{y}^{\max} = \begin{bmatrix} y^{\max} \\ \vdots \\ y^{\max} \end{bmatrix} \tag{21}$$

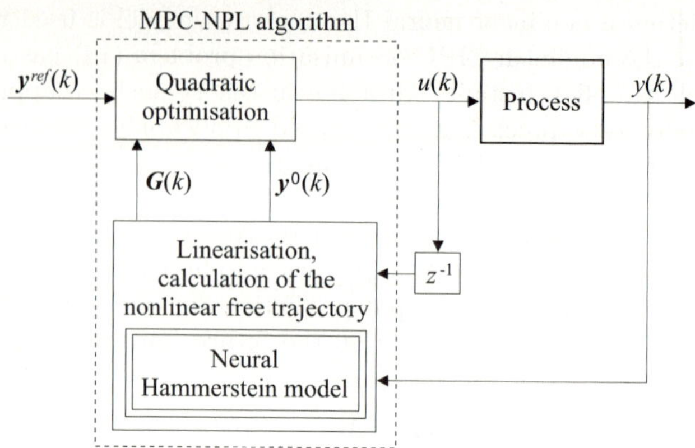

Fig. 2. Structure of the MPC algorithm with Nonlinear Prediction and Linearisation

are vectors of length $n_y N$,

$$
\boldsymbol{u}^{\min} = \begin{bmatrix} u^{\min} \\ \vdots \\ u^{\min} \end{bmatrix}, \qquad \boldsymbol{u}^{\max} = \begin{bmatrix} u^{\max} \\ \vdots \\ u^{\max} \end{bmatrix}
$$

$$
\Delta\boldsymbol{u}^{\max} = \begin{bmatrix} \Delta u^{\max} \\ \vdots \\ \Delta u^{\max} \end{bmatrix}, \quad \boldsymbol{u}^{k-1}(k) = \begin{bmatrix} u(k-1) \\ \vdots \\ u(k-1) \end{bmatrix}
\tag{22}
$$

are vectors of length $n_u N_u$, $\boldsymbol{M} = diag(\boldsymbol{M}_1, \dots, \boldsymbol{M}_N)$, $\boldsymbol{\Lambda} = diag(\boldsymbol{\Lambda}_0, \dots, \boldsymbol{\Lambda}_{N_u-1})$ are weighting matrices of dimensionality $n_y N \times n_y N$ and $n_u N_u \times n_u N_u$, respectively, and

$$
\boldsymbol{J} = \begin{bmatrix}
\boldsymbol{I}_{n_u \times n_u} & \boldsymbol{0}_{n_u \times n_u} & \boldsymbol{0}_{n_u \times n_u} & \cdots & \boldsymbol{0}_{n_u \times n_u} \\
\boldsymbol{I}_{n_u \times n_u} & \boldsymbol{I}_{n_u \times n_u} & \boldsymbol{0}_{n_u \times n_u} & \cdots & \boldsymbol{0}_{n_u \times n_u} \\
\vdots & \vdots & \vdots & \ddots & \vdots \\
\boldsymbol{I}_{n_u \times n_u} & \boldsymbol{I}_{n_u \times n_u} & \boldsymbol{I}_{n_u \times n_u} & \cdots & \boldsymbol{I}_{n_u \times n_u}
\end{bmatrix}
\tag{23}
$$

is the matrix of dimensionality $n_u N_u \times n_u N_u$ comprised of identity and zeros submatrices of dimensionality $n_u \times n_u$. In order to cope with infeasibility problems, output constraints can be softened by means of slack variables [11,16].

Structure of the MPC-NPL algorithm is depicted in Fig. 2. At each sampling instant k the following steps are repeated:

1. Linearisation of the neural Hammerstein models: obtain the matrix $\boldsymbol{G}(k)$.
2. Find the nonlinear free trajectory $\boldsymbol{y}^0(k)$ using the neural Hammerstein model.
3. Solve the quadratic programming problem (20) to determine $\Delta\boldsymbol{u}(k)$.
4. Apply $u(k) = \Delta u(k|k) + u(k-1)$.
5. Set $k := k + 1$, go to step 1.

4.2 On-Line Linearisation and the Free Trajectory Calculation

Defining n_y linearisation points as vectors comprised of past input and output signal values corresponding to the arguments of the Hammerstein model (9)

$$\bar{\boldsymbol{x}}_m(k) = [\bar{u}_1^T(k-1)\ldots\bar{u}_1^T(k-n_B)\ldots\bar{u}_{n_u}^T(k-1)\ldots\bar{u}_{n_u}^T(k-n_B), \tag{24}$$

$$\bar{y}_m(k-1)\ldots\bar{y}_m(k-n_A)]^T$$

where $m = 1,\ldots,n_y$ and using Taylor series expansion at these points, the linear approximation of the model, obtained at a sampling instant k, is expressed as

$$\boldsymbol{A}(q^{-1})y(k) = \widetilde{\boldsymbol{B}}(k,q^{-1})u(k) \tag{25}$$

where

$$\widetilde{\boldsymbol{B}}(k,q^{-1}) = \tag{26}$$

$$\begin{bmatrix} \tilde{b}_1^{1,1}(k)q^{-1} + \ldots + \tilde{b}_{n_B}^{1,1}(k)q^{-n_B} & \cdots & \tilde{b}_1^{1,n_u}(k)q^{-1} + \ldots + \tilde{b}_{n_B}^{1,n_u}(k)q^{-n_B} \\ \vdots & \ddots & \vdots \\ \tilde{b}_1^{n_y,1}(k)q^{-1} + \ldots + \tilde{b}_{n_B}^{n_y,1}(k)q^{-n_B} & \cdots & \tilde{b}_1^{n_y,n_u}(k)q^{-1} + \ldots + \tilde{b}_{n_B}^{n_y,n_u}(k)q^{-n_B} \end{bmatrix}$$

Taking into account the structure of the neural Hammerstein model given by (10), coefficients of the linearised model are

$$\tilde{b}_l^{m,n}(k) = b_l^{m,n} \sum_{i=1}^{K^n} w_i^{2,n} \frac{\mathrm{d}\varphi(z_i^n(\bar{\boldsymbol{x}}_m(k)))}{\mathrm{d}z_i^n(\bar{\boldsymbol{x}}_m(k))} w_{i,n}^{1,n} \tag{27}$$

If hyperbolic tangent is used as the nonlinear transfer function φ in the hidden layer of steady-state part of the model, $\frac{\mathrm{d}\varphi(z_i^n(\bar{\boldsymbol{x}}_m(k)))}{\mathrm{d}z_i^n(\bar{\boldsymbol{x}}_m(k))} = 1 - \tanh^2(z_i^n(\bar{\boldsymbol{x}}_m(k)))$.

Step-response coefficients of the linearised model comprising the dynamic matrix $\boldsymbol{G}(k)$ given by (18) are determined from

$$s_j^{m,n}(k) = \sum_{i=1}^{\min(j,n_B)} \tilde{b}_i^{m,n}(k) - \sum_{i=1}^{\min(j-1,n_A)} a_i^m s_{j-i}^{m,n}(k) \tag{28}$$

The nonlinear free trajectory $y_m^0(k+p|k)$, $p = 1,\ldots,N$, $m = 1,\ldots,n_y$ is calculated on-line recursively from the prediction equation (14) using the neural Hammerstein model (10). Because the free trajectory depends only on the past, no changes in the control signal from a sampling instant k onwards are assumed

$$y_m^0(k+p|k) = \sum_{n=1}^{n_u} \left[\sum_{l=1}^{I_{uf}(p)} b_l^{m,n} w_0^{2,n} + \sum_{i=1}^{K^n} w_i^{2,n}\varphi\left(w_{i,0}^{1,n} + \sum_{j=1}^{n_u} w_{i,j}^{1,n} u_n(k-1)\right) \right. \tag{29}$$

$$+ \sum_{l=I_{uf}(p)+1}^{n_B} b_l^{m,n} w_0^{2,n} + \sum_{i=1}^{K^n} w_i^{2,n}\varphi\left(w_{i,0}^{1,n} + \sum_{j=1}^{n_u} w_{i,j}^{1,n} u_n(k-l+p)\right) \Bigg]$$

$$- \sum_{l=1}^{I_{yp}(p)} a_l^m y_m^0(k-l+p|h) - \sum_{l=I_{yp}(p)+1}^{n_A} a_l^m y_m(k-l+p) + d_m(k)$$

where $I_{uf}(p) = \max(\min(p,n_B),0)$, $I_{yp}(p) = \min(p-1,n_A)$.

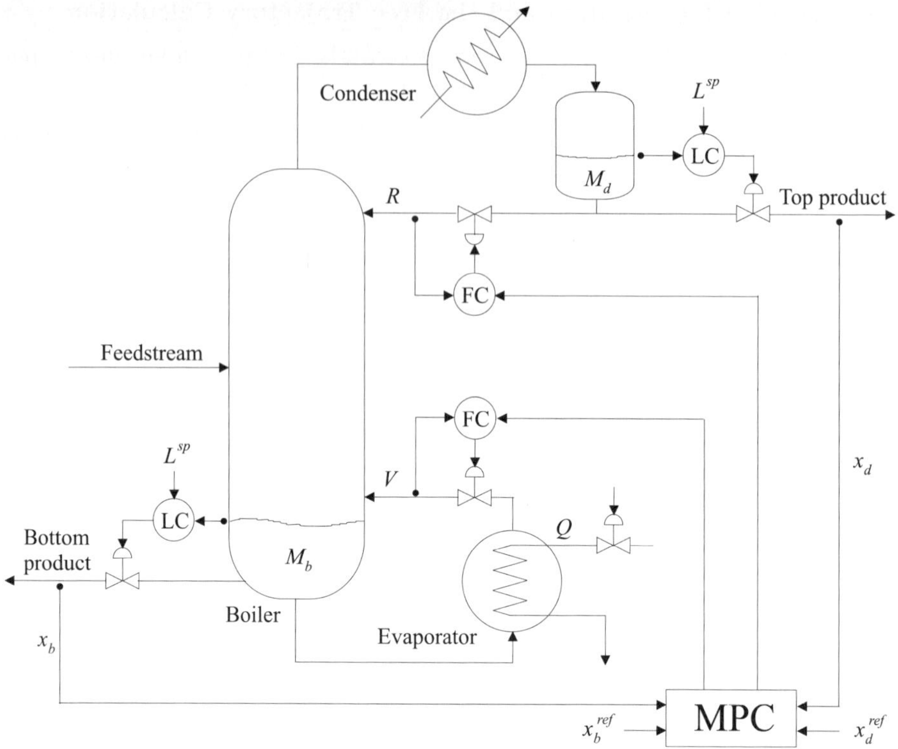

Fig. 3. Distillation column control system structure

5 Simulation Results

The process under consideration is a methanol-water distillation column shown
in Fig. 3. From the perspective of supervisory MPC algorithms, the plant has two
manipulated variables: R – the reflux stream flow rate, V – the vapour stream
flow rate and two controlled variables: x_d – the composition of the top product,
x_b – the composition of the bottom product.

The considered distillation column exhibits significantly nonlinear behaviour,
both steady-state and dynamic properties are nonlinear. The process has very
strong cross-couplings. Time-constants of top and bottom parts of the process are
different. Because of significantly nonlinear nature of the process, it is natural
to use nonlinear MPC. Simulation results of MPC algorithms with black-box
neural models applied to the distillation column are presented in [10].

Three models of the process are used. The fundamental model is used as
the real process during simulations. An identification procedure is carried out,
a linear model and a neural Hammerstein model are obtained. Both empirical
models have input arguments determined by $n_A^m = n_B^{m,n} = 2$, $m = 1, 2$, $n = 1, 2$,
in the Hammerstein model steady-state neural parts contain $K^n = 4$ hidden
nodes. Sampling time of MPC is 1 min. Parameters of MPC are $N = 10$, $N_u = 3$,

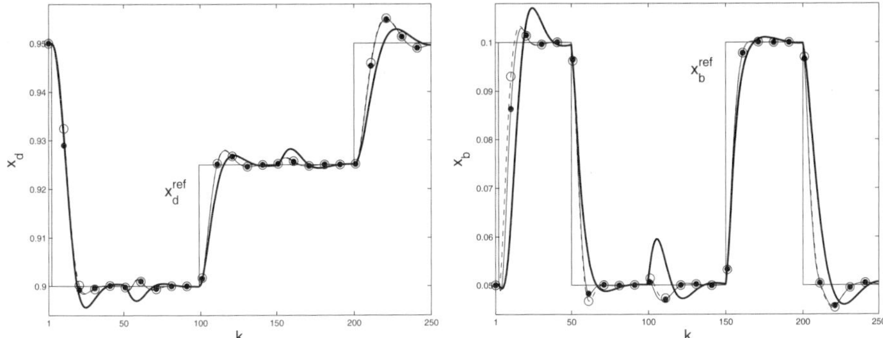

Fig. 4. Simulation results: the MPC algorithm with the linear model (*thick solid line*), the MPC-NO algorithm (*solid-pointed line*) and the MPC-NPL algorithm (*dashed-circled line*) with the same neural Hammerstein model

$M_p = diag(5, 0.5)$, $\Lambda_p = diag(1.5, 1.5)$. Manipulated variables are constrained: $R^{\min} = R_0 - 20 \ kmol/h$, $R^{\max} = R_0 + 20 \ kmol/h$, $V^{\min} = V_0 - 20 \ kmol/h$, $V^{\max} = V_0 + 20 \ kmol/h$ where $R_0 = 33.3634 \ kmol/h$, $V_0 = 83.3636 \ kmol/h$.

Three MPC schemes are compared: the MPC algorithm with a linear model and two MPC algorithms with the same neural Hammerstein model: the MPC algorithm with Nonlinear Optimisation (MPC-NO) and the discussed MPC-NPL algorithm. Simulation results are depicted in Fig. 4 for given reference trajectories (x_d^{ref}, x_b^{ref}). The linear algorithm is slower than nonlinear ones, it gives bigger overshoot. On the other hand, closed-loop performance obtained in the suboptimal MPC-NPL algorithm with quadratic programming is practically the same as in the computationally prohibitive MPC-NO approach in which at each sampling instant a nonlinear optimisation problem has to be solved on-line.

6   Conclusions

Accuracy, computational burden and reliability of nonlinear MPC are determined by the structure of the model and the way it is used on-line. Fundamental models, although potentially very precise, are usually not suitable for on-line control because they are very complicated and may lead to numerical problems resulting, for example, from ill-conditioning or stiffness. Among numerous types of models, Hammerstein structures can be efficiently used for modelling of various technological processes. Typically, polynomial steady-state approximation is used, which has limited accuracy. Moreover, for MIMO processes the number of coefficients is usually big. A neural Hammerstein model is a sound alternative to the classical polynomial-based Hammerstein structure. Neural networks can precisely approximate steady-state properties of the process, they have relatively small numbers of parameters and simple structures. Moreover, a neural Hammerstein model is also a reasonable alternative to a neural black-box model.

Neural Hammerstein models can be efficiently used in the suboptimal MPC-NPL algorithm. It has many advantages: reliability, computational efficiency and closed-loop accuracy. A numerically reliable quadratic programming procedure is used on-line, the necessity of repeating nonlinear optimisation at each sampling instant is avoided. Although suboptimal, in practice the algorithm gives performance comparable to that obtained in MPC with nonlinear optimisation.

Acknowledgement. This work was supported by Polish national budget funds 2007-2009 for science as a research project.

References

1. Aoubi, M.: Comparison between the dynamic multi-layered perceptron and generalised Hammerstein model for experimental identification of the loading process in diesel engines. Control Engineering Practice 6, 271–279 (1998)
2. Al-Duwaish, H., Karim, M.N., Chandrasekar, V.: Hammerstein model identification by multilayer feedforward neural networks. International Journal of Systems Science 28, 49–54 (1997)
3. Billings, S.A., Fakhouri, S.Y.: Identification of systems containing linear dynamic and static nonlinear elements. Automatica 18, 15–26 (1982)
4. Eskinat, E., Johnson, S., Luyben, W.L.: Use of Hammerstein models in identification of nonlinear systems. AIChE Journal 37, 255–268 (1991)
5. Greblicki, W.: Non-parametric orthogonal series identification Hammerstein systems. International Journal of Systems Science 20, 2355–2367 (1989)
6. Haykin, S.: Neural networks – a comprehensive foundation. Prentice-Hall, Englewood Cliffs (1999)
7. Henson, M.A.: Nonlinear model predictive control. current status and future directions. Computers and Chemical Engineering 23, 187–202 (1998)
8. Janczak, A.: Neural network approach for identification of Hammerstein systems. International Journal of Control 76, 1749–1766 (2003)
9. Ling, W.M., Rivera, D.: Nonlinear black-box identification of distillation column models – design variable selection for model performance enhancement. International Journal of Applied Mathematics and Computer Science 8, 793–813 (1998)
10. Ławryńczuk, M.: A family of model predictive control algorithms with artificial neural networks. International Journal of Applied Mathematics and Computer Science 17, 217–232 (2007)
11. Maciejowski, J.M.: Predictive control with constraints. Prentice-Hall, Englewood Cliffs (2002)
12. Morari, M., Lee, J.H.: Model predictive control: past, present and future. Computers and Chemical Engineering 23, 667–682 (1999)
13. Nešić, D., Mareels, I.M.Y.: Dead-beat control of a simple Hammerstein models. IEEE Transactions on Automatic Control 43, 1184–1188 (1998)
14. Patwardhan, R.S., Lakshminarayanan, S., Shah, S.L.: Constrained nonlinear MPC usnig Hammerstein and Wiener models. AIChE Journal 44, 1611–1622 (1998)
15. Qin, S.J., Badgwell, T.A.: A survey of industrial model predictive control technology. Control Engineering Practice 11, 733–764 (2003)
16. Tatjewski, P.: Advanced control of industrial processes, Structures and algorithms. Springer, London (2007)
17. Tatjewski, P., Ławryńczuk, M.: Soft computing in model-based predictive control. Int. Journal of Applied Mathematics and Computer Science. 16, 101–120 (2006)

Test Case Generation from QR Models*

Harald Brandl and Franz Wotawa**

Institut für Softwaretechnologie
Technische Universität Graz
Inffeldgasse 16b/2
A-8010 Graz, Austria

Abstract. In this paper we present the application of AI to automated test case generation. In particular we introduce a technique for deriving abstract test cases from qualitative models. In the case of reactive systems, the behavior of the device depends on its internal state and the perception of the environment via its sensors. Such systems are well suited for modeling with using Qualitative Reasoning methods. Qualitative Reasoning enables one to specify system behavior that also acquires changing environmental conditions and hence provides a good foundation to derive more realistic test cases. In the first part of this paper we give a short introduction to Qualitative Reasoning and Garp3, the tool we use for model creation and simulation. We also present a method for modeling differential equations within Garp3. In the second part we deal with abstract test case generation from QR models and present first results obtained.

Keywords: Model-based Reasoning - Qualitative Reasoning - Model-based Testing - Embedded Systems.

1   Introduction

Autonomous systems have to operate in their environment for a possibly long time and they are not as easy accessible as a PC connected to the internet. Therefore, it is very important to test such systems thoroughly so that a high degree of availability and correctness can be assured. This kind of systems heavily depend on their environment and hence testing them has to consider environmental interactions.

Since the effort of testing increases with system complexity an automation of the process is desirable. In a traditional approach a test engineer tries to think of all possible use cases and exceptional behaviors and creates a set of test cases. A more beneficial way provides automated test case generation from formal specifications. Here the specification can be checked against certain requirements and in many cases can be executed using simulation tools. This supports the validation process and may discover design errors at an early stage of the engineering

---

* This work has been supported by the FIT-IT research project *Self Properties in Autonomous Systems(SEPIAS)* which is funded by BMVIT and the FFG.
** Authors are listed in alphabetical order.

N.T. Nguyen et al. (Eds.): IEA/AIE 2008, LNAI 5027, pp. 235–244, 2008.

process. After the specification has been approved automated test generation techniques produce test cases that obey certain coverage criteria. Test coverage may also be tailored due to a distinct test purpose. Such tools generate abstract test cases that have to be refined subsequently in order to be executable on the implementation under test. In order to determine if an implementation conforms to a specification, model based testing theory requires the definition of a conformance relation. There are well known ones, like conformance relations for Labelled Transition Systems by Jan Tretmans [10].

This paper deals with Qualitative Reasoning (QR) and its use for QR model creation and test case generation. Systems comprising components that interact with each other via continuous quantities can be well described with QR models. For instance this is the case for reactive systems that act upon their internal state and the state of the environment. Our test case generation algorithm uses the simulation result and a test purpose as input and generates a set of abstract test cases as output.

QR models express continuous behavior of quantities as claimed by the continuity law [4]. Thus values change as a function of time and have to be steady and differentiable. Software systems are not constraint to this demand because variables can take any value in its range. In embedded system domains software could be specified in some formal language whereas the physical components of the device and its environment are modeled with Garp3. The QR model delivers sensor inputs and in collaboration with the formal system model gives verdicts upon the behavior of the device.

Within our real-world application we are using for providing a case-study of our test case generation approach the following scenario is of importance. Suppose the QR model simulates night conditions and a low battery. Then the activation of a system component drawing a high current could be an undesired behavior leading to a fail verdict. As example we consider an autonomous system for tracking container units. The task of the system is to collect GPS data on demand or at intervals and transmit them to a server under consideration of system constraints. For example if the charge level in the battery is low and there is a second device in near field range, the system may send information via a wireless network to the adjacent device which in turn sends it to the server. This alternative consumed less energy and is a better solution than sending data directly via GSM at the risk of falling below the limit voltage of the CPU causing a reset. Figure 1 shows a block diagram of the system. We consider the energy supply of the system as small example. The model captures the battery and an external supply source and is presented in Section 6. The next section gives a short introduction to QR and Garp3, the tool used for model creation and simulation.

2   Qualitative Reasoning

QR is an AI Technique with the purpose to reason about systems with incomplete knowledge. In knowledge based systems which comprise a set of facts and

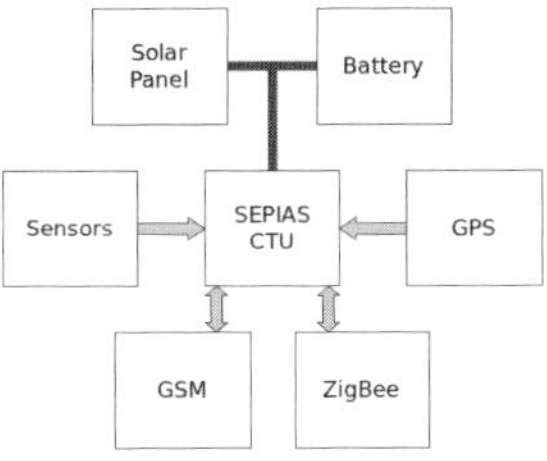

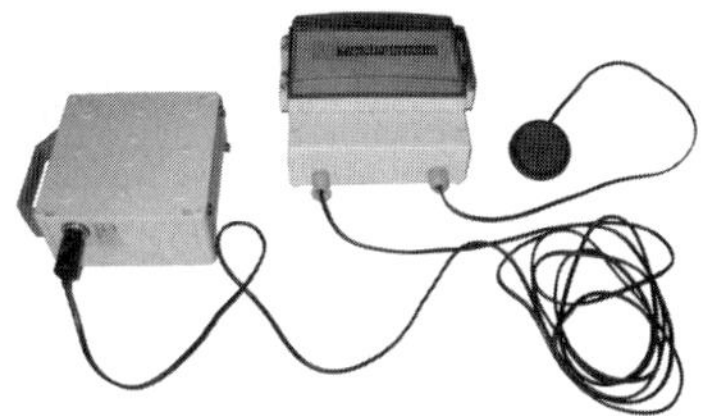

Fig. 1. Block Diagram of a container tracking unit

Fig. 2. The implemented prototype of the container tracking unit

rules in some kind of logical notation the system's behavior is constrained by what is deduceable from inference rules. If the designer of the knowledge base does not consider a specific detail of the system, many desired system behaviors won't be inferable because of the closed world assumption (what is not known is considered to be false).

The behavior of a QR system is generated through simulation. The simulation engine takes the system description as input and derives everything possible regarding the system's boundary conditions. In QR, systems are described in a qualitative manner. Numerical values of system quantities are mapped to points and intervals as proposed by Forbus [4]. For instance we consider the qualitative behavior of water in terms of temperature. The physical quantity temperature is continuous on the real numbers. Of course the possible values are bounded due to physical constraints. Within this boundaries that are marked by limit values water shows different behavior with changing temperatures. Below zero degree Celsius it is frozen, at zero degree it is melting, above zero degree it is liquid and at around 100 degree, depending on the pressure, it starts boiling. Above 100 degree Celsius water changes to steam. This example illustrates how quantities are subdivided into points and intervals. Two adjacent intervals are separated by a point, called landmark. In QR the property of a quantity within an interval is considered to be the same. Only when an interval is left across one of its landmarks, the quantity's property changes. For example water has the property to be liquid between the landmarks melting and boiling.

Time is represented as a sequence of temporally ordered states of behavior. States are left if a quantity changes its value. Within a state nothing can be said about time. Hence QR methods provide a coarse representation of time but accurate enough to describe the causal relations.

In addition to capture the important quantities the relations between them have to be investigated for building proper models. In mathematics systems can be described with differential equations. Ben Kuipers introduced a qualitative representation of ordinary differential equations (ODE), called qualitative differential equations (QDE) [8]. This notation describes how quantities evolve over time from a qualitative point of view. Simulation tools like QSIM [7] process such equations as input and produce a state space representation of the solution as output.

Another approach is followed by the tool GARP3 developed by Bert Bredeweg et al. [3]. This tool is based on the Qualitative Process Theory by Forbus [4] which enables one to build QR models with graphical elements that are connected via certain kinds of relations. There is no need to acquire the system's behavior with differential equations. The system is rather modeled in an more intuitive way like humans are used to think about a system's behavior. Humans look at systems and learn about their functioning by comprehending the causal dependencies between the system parts. This relational knowledge about system parts can be modeled with Garp3 and subsequent simulation exhibits the system's behavior.

Sometimes we already know the behavior of a system part and we are interested in the compound behavior with the remaining system. So we have to go the opposite direction and find a Garp3 model for a known behavior. Then this model can be integrated in an existing model and simulation will reveal further insights to the compound system's behavior. Section 3.1 presents as example the modeling of a sine oscillation.

3   Garp3

Garp3 is implemented in SWI Prolog and provides every means to build and inspect QR models. An elaborate description of the functions can be found in the user manual [1], and [2] provides a user guide for building proper models.

The main issues will be shortly mentioned. In Garp3 a model is comprised of a set of model fragments which are the basic units that describe behavior where two types can be distinguished: static and process model fragments. A third one called *agent* enables one to model exogenous influences on the system. Static fragments represent behavior that is time invariant e.g. proportional relations between quantities like that the amount of water in a vessel is proportional to the water level. A dynamic fragment introduces changes via influences between quantities, for example a positive flow rate into a vessel will increase the amount of liquid and hence the liquid level over time.

Usually systems except simple ones are comprised of several model fragments that become active when certain boundary conditions are met. In Garp3 such conditions are represented with red modeling primitives e.g. a red arrow on a quantity's value. This has the effect that the fragment only gets active if the marked value is reached. Everything red in a model fragment depicts a set of conditions that all have to be met. Blue symbols stand for consequences that become new facts in the knowledge base if they don't contradict existing facts and the fragment gets active. This enables the designer to partition the system domain into qualitative equivalence classes that can be captured within model fragments. During simulation the set of fragments collected in a library get active and inactive as the system evolves over time.

Within a model fragment the main modeling primitives are entities, quantities, proportionalities, a set of ordinal relations, and in dynamic model fragments additional influences. Entities are the components of the system that have certain properties expressed through associated quantities. For example the entity

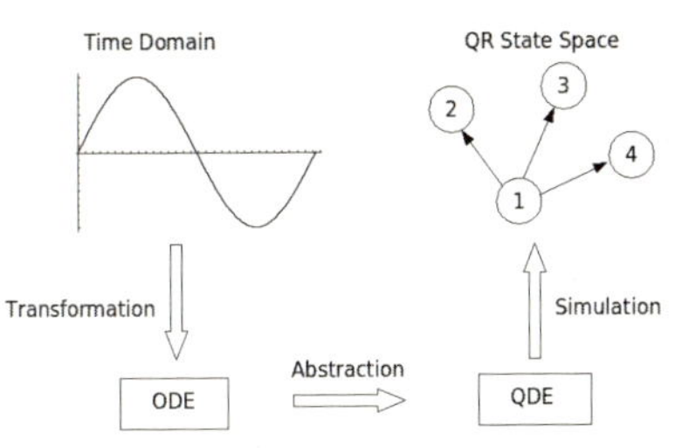

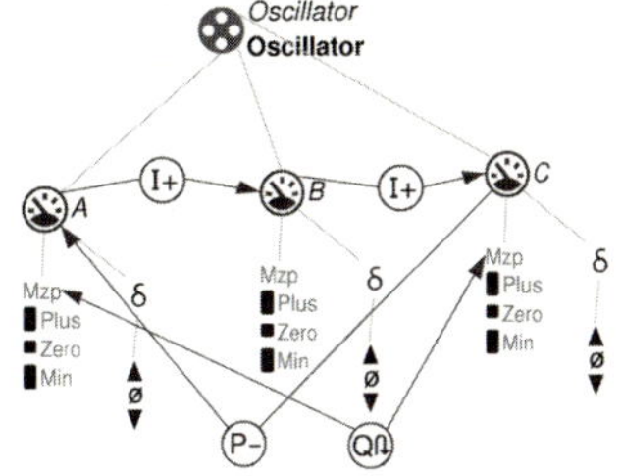

Fig. 3. Getting QR Models from Mathematical Behavior Descriptions

Fig. 4. Model Fragment for an Oscillator

battery has the quantities voltage, current, and charge. Proportionalities establish a mathematical relation between two quantities in the form of monotonic increasing or decreasing functions. The graphical syntax Garp3 uses relies on notations of Qualitative Process Theory. For example $P+(Q1; Q2)$ expresses that a change of $Q2$ causes a change of $Q1$ in the same direction. A proportionality with a minus sign states that a change of the cause quantity induces a change in the opposite direction of the effected quantity. Ordinal relations called *inequalities* provide means to constrain possible behavior. Influences cause dynamic changes of the system and provide means for integration. With scenarios the initial state of the system is captured and is along with a library of model fragments describing the system the input to the simulation engine.

3.1   Modelling Cyclic Behavior from Differential Equations

The motivation for modeling cycles with Garp3 comes from the need to represent repetitive behavior like day/night cycles. Garp3 is intended for building component based models for systems where the interactions between system parts can be investigated. In the case of black box systems where only the external properties are observable it is often very difficult to find a component model for it. One has to "invent" quantities with appropriate relations that express the system accurately. This applies for instance for a simple sine oscillation. In the following a method for modeling such cases with Garp3 is presented. Figure 3 depicts the process.

Either the modeler starts from the behavior in time domain or already has a set of differential equations for it. We assume the first case for a sine oscillation. At first we have to find a differential equation that describes the oscillation. Therefor we transform the sine function into Laplace domain, see equation 1.

$$y(t) = cos(a \cdot t) \circ\!\!\!-\!\!\!\bullet \ \frac{a}{s^2 + a^2} = Y(s) \implies s^2 \cdot Y(s) + a^2 \cdot Y(s) - a = 0 \quad (1)$$

By using the linearity of the Laplace transformation $\mathcal{L}$, and Equation 1 we obtain the differential equation:

$$y''(t) + y(t) = 0 \quad with \quad y(0) = 0, \ y'(0) = a \quad where$$

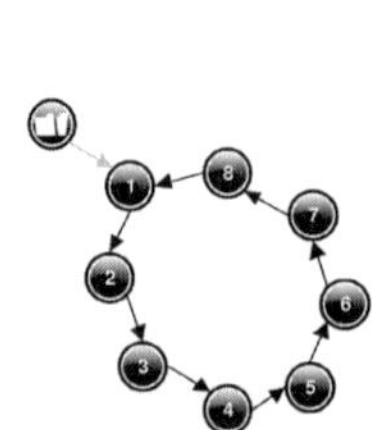

Fig. 5. Cycle in the state chart of the oscillator

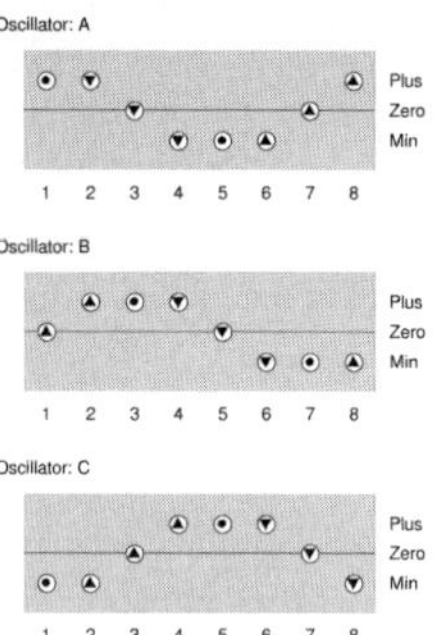

Fig. 6. Value history of the oscillator simulation

$$\mathcal{L}^{-1}\{s^2 \cdot Y(s) - s \cdot y(0) - y'(0)\} = y''(t) \;\; and \;\; \mathcal{L}^{-1}\{s \cdot Y(s) - y(0)\} = y'(t)$$

In order to build a Garp3 model out of a set of differential equations they have to be rewritten in their integral form. That is achieved by applying the integration operator $\int$ as often until the highest order derivation of all terms is zero. Applied to our example we get the following equation: $y(t) + \iint y(t) \cdot dt = 0$. This property is required because Garp3 only offers an operator to represent integration by influences. An influence from quantity A to B states that $B = \int A \cdot dt$. Now we can turn to Garp3 and create a model fragment from the following equations: $I+(B,A)$; $I+(C,B)$; $P-(A,C)$ with the correspondences: $A \Leftrightarrow y(t)$; $B \Leftrightarrow \int y(t) \cdot dt$; $C \Leftrightarrow \iint y(t) \cdot dt$. Figure 4 shows the model fragment for the integral equation. The method of building *integration chains* with auxiliary quantities is a means for representing any order of integration and hence for representing ordinary differential equations of any order. The QDE's state that there is a negative proportionality from C to A. It is observable that the relations between the quantities form a loop. In terms of control theory each integration step causes a phase shift of -90°. After twofold integration the phase shift at quantity C is -180°. Through the negative proportionality back to A this is turned into a positive feedback with 0° phase shift causing the undamped oscillation. Figure 5 depicts the cycle in the state graph and Figure 6 the corresponding value history. The presented method enables one to model any ordinary differential equation in Garp3 which to our best knowledge has not been published before.

4   Test Case Generation from Garp3 Models

In order to test reactive systems it is necessary to model the system environment. Hence the specification consists of a formal system model and a model reflecting the environment. These two models are executed in parallel while influencing each other. Therefore, we define interaction points that are a subset of the quantities in the Garp3 model. The quantities are partitioned into three sets, whereas the view is from the system side: input, output, and hidden. Input quantities are refined to concrete sensor inputs for the system and system outputs are abstracted to output quantities influencing the environment. So the set of interaction points is the set of all quantities but the hidden quantities. A test case consists of a system and an environment part. If both of them reach a pass state the test case gives a pass verdict, otherwise it has failed. In this work we introduce a method for specifying test cases for the environment.

The simulation output of a QR model is a state space representation of all possible behaviors that may evolve over time starting from an initial scenario. This generated state space can get quite big and so a designer has virtually no chance to find a certain path that leads to a distinct state or a set of paths that lead to a set of states. We apply model checking techniques to find state sequences that satisfy certain requirements.

The simulation output is an unlabeled transition system as all information is stored in the states. We denote the set of states by S. Every quantity in the set of quantities Q of the simulation output has an associated quantity space. QS denotes the set of quantity spaces, where qs maps each quantity to its according quantity space: $qs : Q \rightarrow QS$. Each state in the state space binds all quantities to a distinct value and delta: $v : S \times Q \rightarrow qs(Q)$ and $\delta : S \times Q \rightarrow \{min, zero, plus\}$. The *delta* of a value stands for its direction of change over time, $\delta \sim \frac{\partial value}{\partial t}$. If there is a transition between two states, then either a value or a delta for some quantity changes. This is expressed with the predicate $Transition(s_1, s_2)$:

$$\forall s_1, s_2 \in S : \; Transition(s_1, s_2) \rightarrow$$
$$\exists q : (v(s_1, q) \neq v(s_2, q) \vee \delta(s_1, q) \neq \delta(s_2, q)) \wedge CR(s_1, s_2)$$

where the predicate CR denotes the continuity rule proposed by Johan De Kleer and John Seely Brown [6]. The rule states that a qualitative value as a function of time cannot jump over values in its domain. It has to change continuously. As all state transitions computed by the QR engine follow the continuity rule we get that on every transition from a state to a successor state at least one quantity changes its value or direction. Otherwise the two states would be qualitatively equivalent. The unlabeled transition system can be converted to a labeled one by writing on each outgoing state transition the values and deltas of the successor state. As we will see this complete labeling is not necessary since only certain labels are of interest. These labels occur in the specification of the test purpose and represent defined properties. The aim is to transform the unlabeled graph of the specification into a labeled one with the symbols of the test purpose as labels. This allows to compute the synchronous product of the test purpose with the specification to generate the complete test graph.

4.1   Test Purpose

A test purpose is described in a XML file containing property definitions and a regular expression. The alphabet of the regular expression describing the test purpose corresponds to a set of properties of model quantities. For example a property of a battery could be that its charge is greater than zero (*battery : charge gt zero*). This property denotes a value relation where *Battery* is the entity name, *charge* is the name of the quantity, *gt* is the relation operator, and *zero* is a value in the quantity's domain.

The second relation type like (*battery : charge dx eq min*) determined by the *dx* keyword considers the δ of quantities. The relation operator is defined for *lt, le, eq, gt*, and *ge* relations.

A symbol identifies a property set comprising the conjunction of several properties. In addition the XML file provides a section for defining global properties. They are added to the input properties when enabled by setting a *global* attribute to true. The regular expression that completely specifies the test purpose consists of the defined symbols and operators allowed in regular expressions. The equivalent deterministic automaton accepts all symbol sequences that lead to an accept state.

Suppose we are interested in the the cyclic occurrence of a property *a*, e.g., for three times and thereafter a path leading to property *b*. The regular expression $([\hat{}a] * a)\{3\}[\hat{}b] * b$ describes such a test purpose.

4.2 Construction of the Complete Test Graph and Extraction of Test Cases

The computed LTS is not stored in a new graph data structure but is rather an extension of the existing unlabeled state graph. So we have two LTS with the same alphabet and hence the product of them can be computed. The synchronous product of the test purpose and the specification is computed with a depth first search algorithm. On this new LTS an algorithm for determining the set of states that lead to an accept state is applied. The method employs Tarjan's algorithm for computing the set of strongly connected components as a framework [9].

A strongly connected component is defined as a subset of graph states, inside which every pair of states can reach each other via transitions to states inside the set. A directed graph with possible cycles partitioned in its SCCs is a directed acyclic graph (DAG) with the set of SCCs as nodes.

Finally a depth first search applied to the complete test graph yields a set of state sequences that lead to an accepting state. This search starts from the set of accepting states, traverses the graph in reverse direction and stops if the initial state is reached. Branches with cycles are cut off because otherwise the search would not terminate. This is no restriction because if it is desired to test cyclic behavior one can write a test purpose that specifies the number of times the cycle is run through.

5 Discussion and Related Research

Tretmans [10] described test case generation for Labeled Transition Systems (LTS). The paper focused on Input-Output-LTS (IOLTS) and introduced conformance relations for them. Jard and Jeron [5] presented a tool for automatic conformance test generation from formal specifications. They used IOLTS as

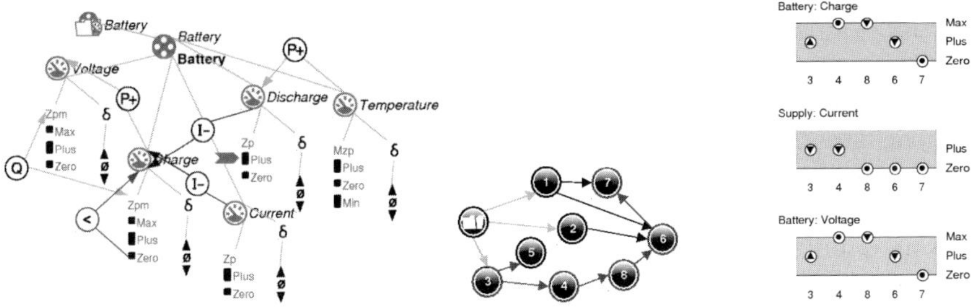

Fig. 7. Battery Model Fragment   **Fig. 8.** Battery State Chart   **Fig. 9.** Battery Value History

formal models and defined the *ioco* conformance relation for weak input enabled systems. In contrast to this approaches we use symbolic labels on state transitions which makes it comparable to Symbolic Transition Systems (STS).

This work presents a method for building Garp3 models from given ordinary differential equations (ODEs). Furthermore we propose to use qualitative models for test case generation. Generated test suites cover many environmental interactions that increase the probability of detecting errors. The advantage of using QR techniques is that behavior is generated by simulation of a system model. This enables one to specify systems on a high abstraction level in a compact form.

6   Results

The model fragment in Figure 7 describes the discharge behavior of a battery. The battery is continuously discharged by a current drawn by an external load or due to a certain discharge rate which depends on the temperature. Another model fragment introduces an external charge current. We consider a simple scenario where the temperature and the load current are constant, and the charge current decreases. Suppose we are interested in all paths leading to states where the battery gets empty. Of course the condition to meet this test purpose is satisfied. The following listing depicts the output of our tool when applied to our running example: $\{\{0, 3, 4, 8, 6, 7\}, \{0, 2, 6, 7\}, \{0, 1, 6, 7\}, \{0, 1, 7\}\}$. Figure 9 shows the value history for the first path.

We modeled the whole system comprising a solar panel, a battery, and the environment with day/night cycles and changing temperatures with Garp3. We derived relevant test cases from this model and showed that our technique works for any Garp3 specification.

7   Summary

For testing reactive systems which heavily interact with their environments it is not only necessary to have a specification and a model of their behavior but also to have an accurate model of the environments. These models are often available as set of differential equations which represent the relevant aspects of the physical world. Hence, an approach which allows us for generating test cases using environmental knowledge together with system knowledge will improve the quality of test cases because otherwise it is very likely to oversee possible interactions. In this paper we presented a technique which allows for generating test cases from qualitative models. We further showed how quantitative models can be represented in Garp3. For the purpose of test case generation we introduced the concept of test purposes which allows for focusing the test case generation process. Moreover, we give first results of our approach. Further research include the evaluation of the obtained results using our example application.

References

1. Bouwer, A., Liem, J., Bredeweg, B.: User Manual for Single-User Version of QR Workbench. Naturnet-Redime, STREP project co-funded by the European Commission within the Sixth Framework Programme (2002-2006), p. 1 (2005) (Project no. 004074. Project deliverable D4.2.1)
2. Bredeweg, B., Liem, J., Bouwer, A., Salles, P.: Curriculum for learning about QR modelling. Naturnet-Redime, STREP project co-funded by the European Commission within the Sixth Framework Programme (2002-2006) (2005) (Project no. 004074. Project deliverable D6.9.1)
3. Bredeweg, B., Bouwer, A., Jellema, J., Bertels, D., Linnebank, F.F., Liem, J.: Garp3 - a new workbench for qualitative reasoning and modelling. In: Proceedings of 20th International Workshop on Qualitative Reasoning (QR-2006), Hannover, New Hampshire, USA, pp. 21–28 (2006)
4. Forbus, K.D.: Qualitative process theory. Artif. Intell. 24(1-3), 85–168 (1984)
5. Jard, C., Jeron, T.: TGV: theory, principles and algorithms. International Journal on Software Tools for Technology Transfer (STTT) 7(4), 297–315 (2004)
6. De Kleer, J., Brown, J.S.: A qualitative physics based on confluences. Artif. Intell. 24(1-3), 7–83 (1984)
7. Kuipers, B.: Qualitative simulation. Artificial Intelligence 26, 289–338 (1986), Reprinted In: Weld, D., De Kleer, J. (eds.): Qualitative Reasoning about Physical Systems, pp. 236–260. Morgan Kaufmann, San Francisco (1990)
8. Kuipers, B.: Qualitative simulation: Then and now. Artificial Intelligence 59(1-2), 133–140 (1993)
9. Morel, P., Jeron, T.: Test Generation Derived from Model-Checking. In: Halbwachs, N., Peled, D.A. (eds.) CAV 1999. LNCS, vol. 1633, pp. 108–121. Springer, Heidelberg (1999)
10. Tretmans, J.: Test generation with inputs, outputs, and quiescence. In: Margaria, T., Steffen, B. (eds.) TACAS 1996. LNCS, vol. 1055, pp. 127–146. Springer, Heidelberg (1996)

Shape-Based Human Activity Recognition Using Independent Component Analysis and Hidden Markov Model

Md. Zia Uddin, J.J. Lee, and T.-S. Kim

Department of Biomedical Engineering, Kyung Hee University,
1 Seochun-ri, Kiheung-eup, Yongin-si, Kyunggi-do, Republic of South Korea, 446-701
`ziauddin@khu.ac.kr, ljj@khu.ac.kr, tskim@khu.ac.kr`

Abstract. In this paper, a novel human activity recognition method is proposed which utilizes independent components of activity shape information from image sequences and Hidden Markov Model (HMM) for recognition. Activities are represented by feature vectors from Independent Component Analysis (ICA) on video images and based on these features, recognition is achieved by trained HMMs of activities. Our recognition performance has been compared to the conventional method where Principle Component Analysis (PCA) is typically used to derive activity shape features. Our results show that superior recognition is achieved with our proposed method especially for activities (e.g., skipping) that cannot be easily recognized by the conventional method.

Keywords: PCA, ICA, K-means, LBG, HMM.

1 Introduction

Recently human activity recognition is becoming an intensive field to study and research due to an interest in proactive computing. A system that can recognize various human activities has many important applications such as automated surveillance systems and smart home healthcare applications [1, 2]. In general, human activities in images can be represented in two categories based on their features: one includes shape features and another motion features such as optical flow. In this paper, we focus on shape features and their improved representation via ICA. Conventionally, most previous recognition works have used PCA to extract shape features of activities [1, 2]. Basically, PCA focuses on global representation of the shape features based on the second-order statistics. Recently another statistical approach called ICA exploiting higher order statistics for face recognition [3, 4]. It is proved that ICA features are very effective to describe local features. Thus our proposed approach is to use ICA to describe local information of activity shapes more effectively than PCA.

As for recognition, due to successful applications of HMM in speech recognition [5, 6], recently HMM has been adopted in the human activity research field as well [1, 2, 7]. Once human activities are represented in features via PCA or ICA, HMM can be effectively used for human activity recognition, since it is a most suitable technique for recognizing time sequential feature information. Our results show that superior recognition is achieved with our proposed method, in which IC features are

N.T. Nguyen et al. (Eds.): IEA/AIE 2008, LNAI 5027, pp. 245–254, 2008.

combined with HMM, especially for activities (e.g., skipping) that cannot be easily recognized by the conventional PC-based HMM method.

2 Related Works

In recent years, many recognition methods are proposed for human activity recognition. In [1] and [2], Niu and Abdel-Mottaleb used PC-based shape features to build HMM for recognition. They combined motion features with shape. In [7], Yamato et al. proposed 2D mesh features and a HMM based approach to recognize several tennis activities in time sequential images. In [8], Carlsson and Sullivan proposed another shape based approach to recognize forehand and backhand strokes from tennis video clips. For each person in each image sequence one key-frame per stroke was defined and using that one other frames in the sequence, depicting the same activity posture, were found. In [9], a view independent approach is proposed for classification and identification of human posture. The authors used 2D shapes captured by multiple cameras and shape description using a 3D shape descriptor. The descriptions were used for learning and recognition by SVM. In [10], Nakata proposed a multi-resolutional optical flow based method for recognition. He applied the Burt-Anderson pyramid approach to extract useful features consist of multi-resolutional optical flows. In [11], Sun et al. used affine motion parameters and optical flow features to build HMM for recognition. In our case, we propose a shape-based approach of using ICA in combination with HMM for the first time to recognize human activities.

3 Methods

We discuss video image preprocessing for shape feature extraction in Section 3.1. In sections 3.2 and 3.3, shape feature extraction methods via PCA and ICA are discussed respectively. PCA/ICA features extracted from sequential images are converted to a sequence of symbols, which correspond to the codewords of a code book. In Section 3.4, we present the codebook generation schemes using vector quantization where two methods are described. Two codebook structures are discussed and their performances are compared. Section 3.5 gives an overview of HMM models that are used for recognition using shape features. In learning HMM, the symbol sequences obtained from the training image sequences of each activity are used to optimize the corresponding HMM. In recognition, the symbol sequence is applied to all the HMMs and one is chosen that gives the maximum likelihood. Fig. 1 shows overall architecture of the proposed system where T represents the number of testing shape images, N number of trained HMMs, and L likelihoods.

3.1 Video Image Preprocessing

A simple Gaussian probability distribution function, i.e. (1), is used to subtract background from a recent frame to extract a Region of Interest (ROI).

$$P(R(x, y)) = \frac{1}{C} \sum_{i=1}^{C} \frac{1}{\sqrt{2\pi\sigma^2}} \exp(\frac{-(R(x, y) - B_i(x, y))^2}{2\sigma^2}) \qquad (1)$$

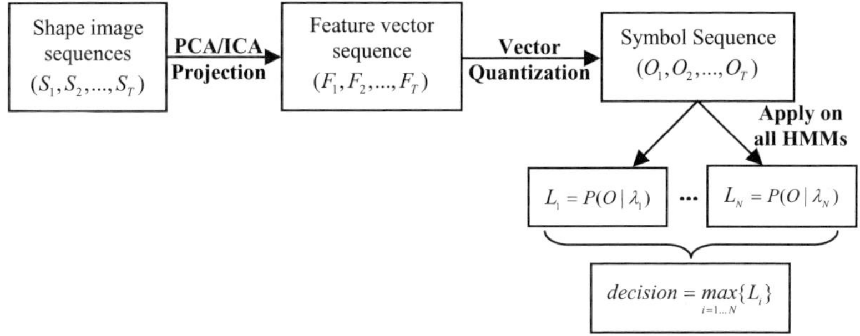

Fig. 1. Architecture of activity recognition using our proposed approach

where C is the number of background images. $P(R(x, y))$ is the probability of being background of a pixel in x and y position of the recent frame. $B_i(x, y)$ and $R(x, y)$ is the intensity value of pixel in x and y position of the ith background image and the recent frame respectively. To extract ROI, the recent frame is converted to binary according to (2) using a threshold Th. The value of Th is experimentally determined on the basis of the result from (1). To get better binary shapes, median filtering is applied to remove noise after adjusting Th. Fig. 2 (c) shows ROI of a sample frame and Fig. 3 a sequence of generalized ROIs from an image sequence of walking.

$$BI(x, y) = \begin{cases} 1 & P(R(x, y)) \leq Th \\ 0 & P(R(x, y)) > Th \end{cases} \tag{2}$$

where BI is the resultant binary image after applying a threshold Th.

To apply PCA or ICA to extract activity features from these ROIs, every normalized ROI is represented as a row vector where the dimension of the vector is equal to

(a)   (b)   (c)

Fig. 2. (a) Background image, (b) Frame from a walking sequence, and (c) ROI with rectangle

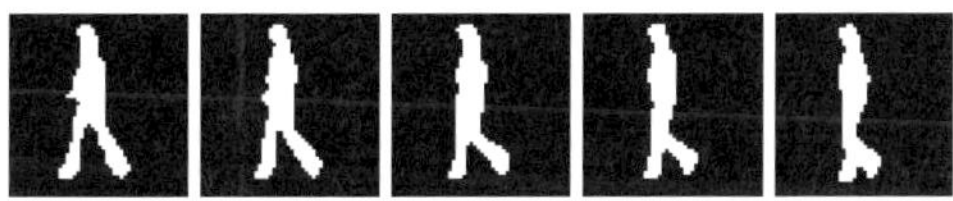

Fig. 3. Generalized ROIs from a walking sequence

the number of pixels in an entire image. Preprocessing steps are necessary before applying PCA or ICA algorithm on the images. The first step is to make all the training vectors to zero mean. Then PCA or ICA algorithm is applied on the zero mean input vectors. Defining T as a number of shape images and $X_1, X_2, ..., X_T$ the sequential shape images, the mean shape image vector $\bar{X}$ is subtracted from each shape vector to make it a zero mean vector $\tilde{X}_i$ according to (3) where $1 \le i \le T$.

$$\tilde{X}_i = (X_i - \bar{X}) \tag{3}$$

3.2 Shape Feature Extraction Using PCA

PCA basis images for human shape images represent global information of activities. Fig. 4 depicts 10 basis images after PCA is applied on 750 images of 5 activities: namely walking, running, skipping, right hand, and both hand waving. It shows some global features representing frequently moving parts of human body in all activities.

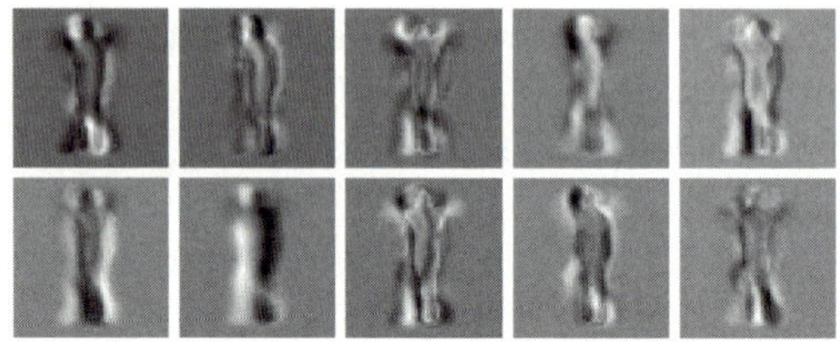

Fig. 4. Ten PCs from all activity shape images including walking, running, skipping, right hand, and both hand waving

The principle component representation of a shape image vector $\tilde{X}_i$ is as follows.

$$P_i = \tilde{X}_i E_m \tag{4}$$

where P_i is the PCA projection of ith image. E_m is the top m eigenvectors corresponding to the first top eigenvalues of descending order.

3.3 Shape Feature Extraction Using ICA

The ICA algorithm finds the statistically independent basis images. The basic idea of ICA is to represent a set of random observed variables using basis function where the components are statistically independent. If S is collection of basis images and X is collection of input images then the relation between X and S is modeled as (5).

$$X = MS \tag{5}$$

where M represents an unknown linear mixing matrix of full rank.

The ICA algorithm learns the weight matrix W, which is inverse of the mixing matrix M. W is used to recover a set of independent basis images S. ICA basis images focus on the local feature information rather than global information as in PCA. Fig. 5 shows 10 ICA basis images from the feature space of all activity shape images where high contrast parts represent local human body components such as legs and hands that are used frequently in all activities. Before applying ICA, PCA can be used to reduce dimension of total training image data. ICA algorithm is performed on E_m as follows.

$$S = W E_m^T \tag{6}$$

$$E_m^T = W^{-1} S \tag{7}$$

$$X_r = V W^{-1} S \tag{8}$$

where V is projection of images X on E_m and X_r the reconstructed original images.

The independent component representation I_i of ith shape vector $\tilde{X}_i$ from an activity image sequence can be expressed as

$$I_i = \tilde{X}_i E_m W^{-1}. \tag{9}$$

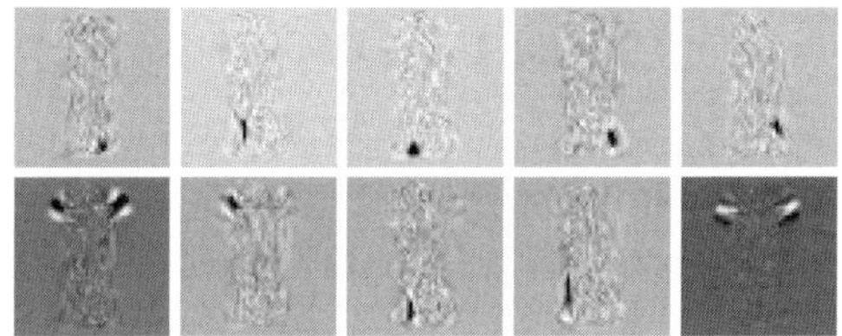

Fig. 5. Ten ICs from all activity shape images

3.4 Vector Quantization

We symbolize feature vectors obtained using ICA or PCA before applying to train or recognize by HMM. An efficient codebook of vectors can be generated using vector quantization from training vectors. In our experiment, we have used two vector quantization algorithms: namely ordinary K-means clustering and Linde, Buzo, and Gray (LBG)'s clustering algorithm [12]. In both of them, first initial selection of centroids is obtained. In case of the K-means clustering, until a convergence criterion is met, for every sample it seeks the nearest centroid, assign the sample to the cluster, and compute the center of that cluster again. However, in case of LBG, recomputation is done after assigning all samples to new clusters. In LBG, initialization is done by splitting the centroid of whole dataset. It starts with the codeword size of one and recursively splits into two codewords. After splitting, optimization of the centroids is done to reduce the distortion. Since it follows binary splitting methods, the size of the codebook must be power of two. In case of the K-means, the overall performance varies due to the selection of the initial random centroids. On the contrary, LBG starts from splitting the centroid of entire dataset, thus there is less variation in performance.

When a codebook is designed, the index numbers of the codewords are used as symbols to apply on HMM. As long as a feature vector is available then the index number of the closest codeword from the codebook is the symbol for that replace. Hence every shape image is going to be assigned a symbol. If there are K image sequences of T length then there will be K sequences of T length symbols. The symbols are the observations, O. Fig. 6 shows the codebook generation and symbol selection from codebook using IC features.

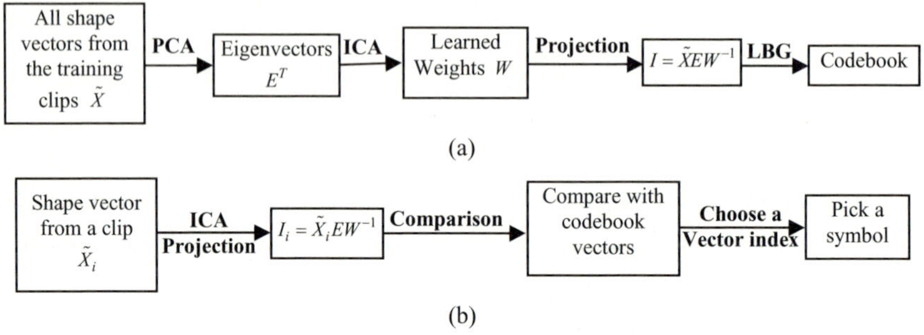

Fig. 6. (a) Codebook generation and (b) Symbol selection

3.5 Activity Modeling and Training Using HMM

A generic HMM can be expressed as $\lambda = \{\Xi, \pi, A, B\}$ where Ξ denotes possible states, π the initial probability of the states, A the transition probability matrix between hidden states where state transition probability a_{ij} represents the probability of changing state from i to j, and B observation symbols' probability from every state where the probability $b_j(O)$ indicates the probability of observing the symbols O from state j. Before recognition, a distinct HMM is trained for every activity. If the number of activities is N then there will be a dictionary $(\lambda_1, \lambda_2, ... \lambda_N)$ of N models. We used the Baum-Welch algorithm for HMM parameter estimation [13]. The parameter estimation of observation sequence O is shown from (10) to (13).

$$\xi_t(i, j) = \frac{\alpha_t(i) a_{ij} b_j(O_{t+1}) \beta_{t+1}(j)}{\sum_{i=1}^{q} \sum_{j=1}^{q} \alpha_t(i) a_{ij} b_j(O_{t+1}) \beta_{t+1}(j)} \tag{10}$$

$$\gamma_t(i) = \sum_{j=1}^{q} \xi_t(i, j) \tag{11}$$

$$\hat{a}_{ij} = \frac{\sum_{t=1}^{T-1} \xi_t(i, j)}{\sum_{t=1}^{T} \gamma_t(i)} \tag{12}$$

$$\hat{b}_j(d) = \frac{\sum_{\substack{t=1 \\ O_t = d}}^{T-1} \gamma_t(j)}{\sum_{t=1}^{T} \gamma_t(j)} \tag{13}$$

where $\xi_t(i,j)$ represents the probability of staying in a state i at time t and a state j at time $t+1$. $\gamma_t(i)$ is the probability of staying in the state i at time t. α and β are the forward and backward variables respectively that are calculated from transition and observation matrix. $\hat{a}_{ij}$ is the estimated transition probability from the state i to the state j and $\hat{b}_j(d)$ the estimated observation probability of symbol d from the state j. q is the number of states used in the models.

Four-state left to right model is used for each activity. Since we start training from the first state hence π is assigned as $\{1,0,0,0\}$. For B, the possible number of observations from every state is the number of vectors in the codebook. In each model, we applied uniform observation and transition probability from the states before training. The total transition and observation probability from any state is one. Fig. 7 shows the structure and transition probabilities of an ICA-based running HMM before and after training with the codebook size of 32.

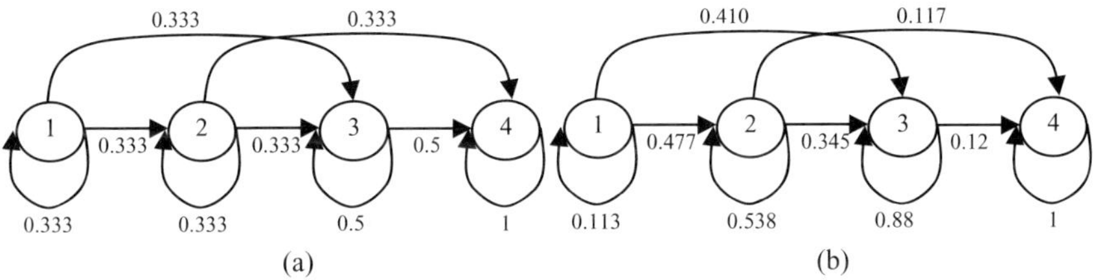

Fig. 7. Running HMM structure and transition probabilities (a) before and (b) after training

To test observation sequence O, we have to find the appropriate HMM with the highest likelihood. The following equation represents the likelihood of an observation sequence O at time t using a forward variable α where a model λ is given.

$$P(O \mid \lambda) = \sum_{i=1}^{q} \alpha_t(i) \tag{14}$$

4 Experimental Results

Five activities have been recognized using our proposed approach: namely walk, run, skip, right hand wave, and both hand wave. Every sequence consists of 10 images. A total of 15 sequences from every activity are used to build feature space and for training corresponding HMM. Hence, the whole database consists of total 750 images. After applying ICA on PCA, 150 features are taken in feature space as it is known that the more number of features results in the better performance. We have tested its performance using four different sizes of the codebook: namely 8, 16, 32 and 64. Two types of codebook generation schemes are used: K-means and LBG. A total 180 sequences are used for testing the models. Table 1 and Table 2 show the recognition results using ordinary K-means and LBG respectively. Graphical performance using only the LBG codebook is shown in Fig. 8.

Table 1. Recognition result using the K-means codebook

Codebook size	Activity	Recognition rate (PCA)	Mean	Standard deviation	Recognition rate (ICA)	Mean	Standard deviation
8	Walk	89.09 %			76.36 %		
	Run	62.5			65		
	Skip	38.09	72.60	22.63	47.61	73.70	18.35
	RHW	80			84		
	BHW	93.33			95.56		
16	Walk	96.36			96.36		
	Run	95			95		
	Skip	42.85	83.02	22.64	42.85	83.55	23
	RHW	92			88		
	BHW	88.89			95.56		
32	Walk	100			100		
	Run	100			100		
	Skip	66.67	90.40	13.77	66.67	92.09	14.31
	RHW	92			96		
	BHW	93.33			97.78		
64	Walk	94.54			98.18		
	Run	100			100		
	Skip	57.14	88.23	17.64	57.14	88.57	17.83
	RHW	92			92		
	BHW	97.48			95.56		

 * RHW=Right Hand Wave.
** BHW=Both Hand Wave.

Table 2. Recognition result using the LBG codebook

Codebook size	Activity	Recognition rate (PCA)	Mean	Standard deviation	Recognition rate (ICA)	Mean	Standard deviation
8	Walk	94.54%			94.54%		
	Run	67.5			87.5		
	Skip	57.14	77.52	14.96	66.67	83.43	10.28
	RHW	84			84		
	BHW	84.44			84.44		
16	Walk	96.36			96.36		
	Run	82.5			85		
	Skip	47.61	79.25	19.17	66.67	84.36	12.61
	RHW	92			96		
	BHW	77.78			77.78		
32	Walk	100			100		
	Run	100			100		
	Skip	66.67	90.40	13.77	85.71	95.89	5.93
	RHW	92			96		
	BHW	93.33			97.78		
64	Walk	98.18			100		
	Run	100			100		
	Skip	66.67	89.23	13.45	85.71	94.66	6.02
	RHW	88			92		
	BHW	93.33			95.56		

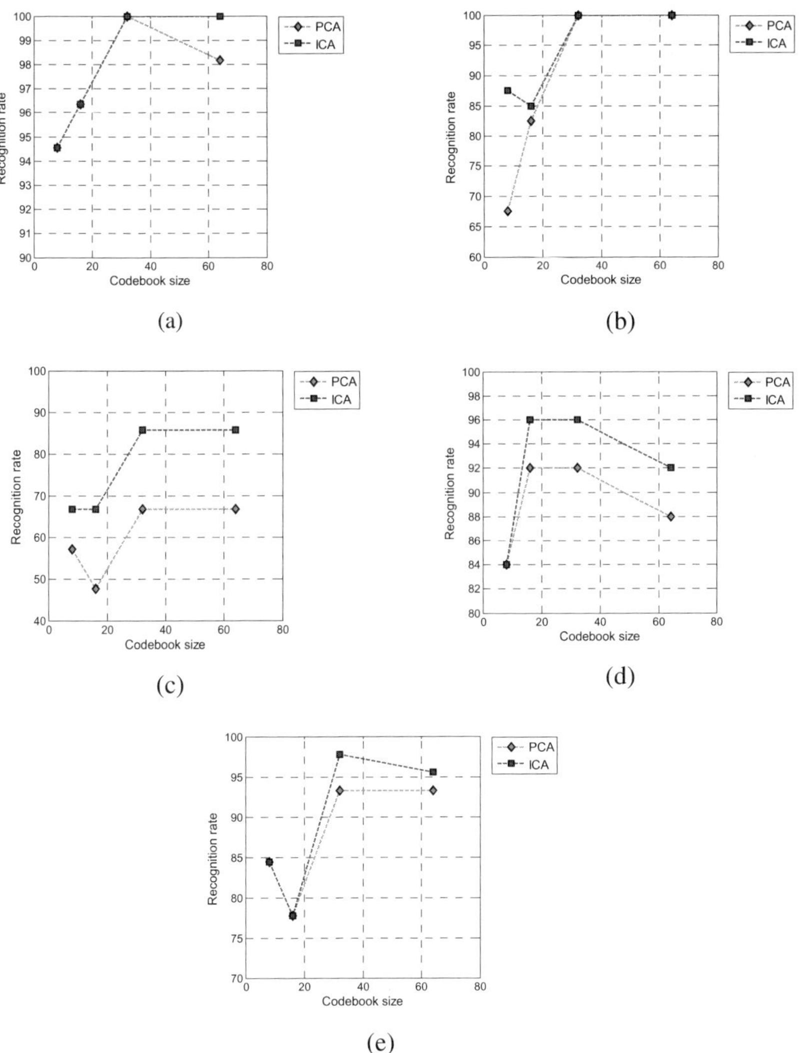

Fig. 8. Recognition performance of (a) walking, (b) running, (c) skipping, (d) right hand waving, and (e) both hand waving

5 Conclusions

We have presented a new IC-based HMM approach for human activity recognition. With local shape features from ICA, our results show much improved performance than other conventional shape based activity recognition approaches. Especially in case of skipping, we have obtained from 68% to 86% improvement in recognition rate. Experimental results show that the optimal codebook size for overall recognition of five activities is greater than 30. For more robust human activity recognition, we plan to include motion information with the proposed IC shape features.

Acknowledgement

This research was supported by the MKE (Ministry of Knowledge Economy), Korea, under the ITRC (Information Technology Research Center) support program supervised by the IITA (Institute of Information Technology Advancement) (IITA-2008-(C1090-0801-0002)).

References

1. Niu, F., Abdel-Mottaleb, M.: View-Invariant Human Activity Recognition Based on Shape and Motion Features. In: Proceedings of the IEEE Sixth International Symposium on Multimedia Software Engineering, pp. 546-556 (2004)
2. Niu, F., Abdel-Mottaleb, M.: HMM-Based Segmentation and Recognition of Human Activities from Video Sequences. In: Proceedings of IEEE International Conference on Multimedia and Expo, pp. 804-807 (2005)
3. Bartlett, M., Movellan, J., Sejnowski, T.: Face recognition by independent component analysis. In: IEEE Transactions on Neural Networks, vol. 13, pp. 1450-1464 (2002)
4. Yang, J., Zhang, D., Yang, J. Y.: Is ICA Significantly Better than PCA for Face Recognition?. In: Proceedings of IEEE International Conference on Computer Vision, pp. 198-203 (2005)
5. Lawrence, R., Rabiner, A.: Tutorial on Hidden Markov Models and Selected Applications in Speech Recognition. In: Proceedings of the IEEE, 77(2), pp. 257-286 (1989)
6. Bregler, C., König, Y.: Eigenlips for Robust Speech Recognition. In: Proceedings of the IEEE International Conference on Acoustics, Speech, and Signal, Processing, pp. 669-672 (1994)
7. Yamato, J., Ohya, J., Ishii, K.: Recognizing Human Action in Time-Sequential Images using Hidden Markov Model. In: Proceedings of IEEE International Conference on Computer Vision and Pattern Recognition, pp. 379-385 (1992)
8. Carlsson, S., Sullivan, J.: Action Recognition by Shape Matching to Key Frames. In: IEEE Computer Society Workshop on Models versus Exemplars in Computer Vision, pp. 263-270 (2002)
9. Cohen, I., Li, H.: Inference of Human Postures by Classification of 3D Human Body Shape. In: IEEE International Workshop on Analysis and Modeling of Faces and Gestures, pp. 74-81 (2003)
10. Nakata, T.: Recognizing Human Activities in Video by Multi-resolutional Optical Flow. In: International Conference on Intelligent Robots and Systems, pp. 1793-1798 (2006)
11. Sun, X., Chen, C., Manjunath, B. S.: Probabilistic Motion Parameter Models for Human Activity Recognition. In: 16th International Conference on Pattern recognition, pp. 443-450 (2002)
12. Linde, Y., Buzo, A., Gray, R.: An Algorithm for Vector Quantizer Design. In: IEEE Transaction on Communications, vol. 28(1), pp. 84–94 (1980)
13. Iwai, Y., Hata, T., Yachida, M.: Gesture Recognition based on Subspace Method and Hidden Markov Model. In: Proceedings of the IEEE/RSJ International Conference on Intelligent Robots and Systems, pp. 960-966 (1997)

Potential Distribution Modelling Using Machine Learning

Ana C. Lorena[1], Marinez F. de Siqueira[2], Renato De Giovanni[2],
André C.P.L.F. de Carvalho[3], and Ronaldo C. Prati[3]

[1] Centro de Matemática, Computação e Cognição,
Universidade Federal do ABC, Santo André - SP - Brazil
ana.lorena@ufabc.edu.br
[2] Centro de Referência em Informação Ambiental
Campinas - SP - Brazil
{marinez,renato}@cria.org.br
[3] Instituto de Ciências Matemáticas e de Computação,
Universidade de São Paulo, São Carlos - SP- Brazil
{andre,prati}@icmc.usp.br

Abstract. Potential distribution modelling has been widely used to predict and to understand the geographical distribution of species. These models are generally produced by retrieving the environmental conditions where the species is known to be present or absent and feeding this data into a modelling algorithm. This paper investigates the use of Machine Learning techniques in the potential distribution modelling of plant species *Stryphnodendron obovatum* Benth (MIMOSACEAE). Three techniques were used: Support Vector Machines, Genetic Algorithms and Decision Trees. Each technique was able to extract a different representation of the relations between the environmental conditions and the distribution profile of the species being considered.

Keywords: Ecological niche modelling, Potential distribution modelling, Machine Learning.

1 Introduction

Potential distribution models allow to better understand the influence and relationship of environmental conditions in the distribution of species. For this reason, distribution models have been used in different types of analysis, such as indicating areas for environmental conservation [1,2], evaluating the risk of harmful proliferation of invasive species [3,4], studying the impact of environmental changes in biodiversity [5,6,7,8], indicating the course of diseases spreading [9], among others.

Brazil has a vast biodiversity with large data gaps that can be explored by modelling techniques. These techniques can help monitoring, preserving and developing strategies for the sustainable use of natural resources.

One of the first initiatives to build a generic software framework for potential distribution modelling has been initially carried out by the Reference Center

N.T. Nguyen et al. (Eds.): IEA/AIE 2008, LNAI 5027, pp. 255–264, 2008.

on Environmental Information (CRIA). CRIA develops *openModeller*[1], an open source tool for static modelling of spatial distribution. *openModeller* receives as input a set of occurrence points and a set of environmental layers. Different algorithms within the same framework can be used to produce potential distribution models and also rasters with the potential distribution of species. Among the algorithms currently available in *openModeller* are GARP (Genetic Algorithm for Rule Set Production) [10] and, more recently, SVMs (Support Vector Machines) [11].

This paper compares three Machine Learning (ML) techniques in the modelling of *Stryphnodendron obovatum*. ML is a research field from Computational Intelligence concerned with the development of techniques that can extract knowledge from datasets [12]. This knowledge is represented in the form of a model, providing a compact description of the given data and allowing predictions for new data. ML algorithms are pointed as promising tools in modelling and prediction of species distribution [13]. GARP [10], which combines rules with the use of a Genetic Algorithm [14], is an example of successful use of ML in this area.

The techniques compared in this paper are: Decision Trees (DTs) [15], SVMs and GARP. Each of these techniques has advantages and disadvantages in the prediction of species distribution, which will be analyzed in this paper.

This paper is organized as follows: Section 2 presents some related studies in ecological niche modelling. Sections 3 and 4 presents the materials and methods used in the experimental study. Section 5 shows the experimental results obtained. Finally, Section 6 concludes this paper and presents some future research directions.

2   Related Bibliography

Numerous methods used to model the distribution of species are based in the concept of fundamental niche [16]. The fundamental niche of a species is a set of environmental conditions within which the species is able to survive, not taking into account other factors such as competition, predation and parasitism [17]. The objective is to use a correlative approach [18] to model the fundamental niche based on abiotic conditions provided as environmental data rasters. Among examples of environmental data, one can mention temperature, precipitation and topography. Generated models can then be used to predict regions where the species may potentially be able to survive [17].

The modeling process has several steps. First, it is necessary to find the corresponding environmental conditions associated with each species occurrence point. Occurrence points are usually provided as coordinates (pairs of longitude and latitude) in a certain reference system. Environmental data is provided as a set of georeferrenced rasters that are previously selected by a species expert or by generic pre-analysis tools.

In general, species occurrence data are significantly unbalanced in terms of the proportion of presence and absence data [13]. This happens because it is easier

---

[1] `http://openModeller.cria.org.br`

and more usual for specialists to record the presence of a species, resulting in few absence data. An alternative frequently used to overcome this limitation is to generate "pseudo-absence" data [10].

The ML field opens up several possibilities to achieve better results in species distribution modelling. Depending on the technique used, results can lead to greater accuracy, or models can be simpler to understand, and sometimes even if the accuracy is not the best one, it may still be competitive but achieved in a significantly shorter time. Among some studies from literature which successfully used ML techniques in the species distribution modelling problem one can mention [19,20,10,21,6,22,23,24].

This work presents the results of three different ML techniques to model the distribution of a Brazilian species using a large set of environmental rasters, presence points collected with Global Positioning System (GPS), and "pseudo-absence" points randomly generated in biomes where the species is unlikely to occur. In particular, the dataset generation process is new compared to previous work performed in potential distribution modelling.

3   Dataset Preparation

All presence points (50 records) for *Stryphnodendron obovatum* were collected using a rapid survey technique [25,26] inside São Paulo State, Brazil, during the period of 1999-2001 using GPS with a precision of approximately $100m^2$.

Stryphnodendron obovatum is a small tree typical of the Brazilian Savannah. Since the species is only known to occur in this biome, the same number of absence points (50 records) were randomly generated using an ArcView[2] extension (random point generation v.1.3) inside areas of Atlantic Rain Forest from the São Paulo State. The vegetation map used for this task came from the Biota[3] Database. This technique tried to minimize possible errors by discarding random points that were located within less than 1.5 Km from the border between the Atlantic Rain Forest and Savannah biomes.

A total number of 73 attributes were selected among climate, topographic and vegetation index layers. The climate data layers came from the Worldclim[4] [27] current conditions dataset (1950-2000) in 30 arc-second resolution grids. Climate variables included monthly total precipitation, monthly minimum and maximum temperature and Bioclimatics layers also available at Worldclim. Topographic layers included aspect, slope, elevation, flow water direction and accumulation, and a topographic index of land. All topographic layers are derived from a 30 arc-second digital elevation model of the world and they all came from the HYDRO1k project[5]. The vegetation index layers are a monthly mosaic of Normalized Difference Vegetation Index (NDVI) generated by Souza et al. [28] in 2005 (NASA[6]). NDVI index is used to estimate a large number of vegetation

---

[2] http://www.esri.com/software/arcview/
[3] http://www.biota.org.br/
[4] http://www.worldclim.org/
[5] http://www.usgs.gov/
[6] http://visibleearth.nasa.gov/

properties, typical examples include the Leaf Area Index, biomass, chlorophyll concentration in leaves, plant productivity, fractional vegetation cover, accumulated rainfall, etc. No pre-processing techniques were used to remove possibly redundant data.

A summary of the dataset used in the experiments can be found in Table 1. This table presents the number of examples in the dataset ($\sharp$Data), the number of attributes ($\sharp$Attrib. - all continuous valued), the distribution of examples per class (%ex./class) and the error rate of the majority class classifier (ME).

Table 1. Dataset main characteristics

$\sharp$**Data**	$\sharp$**Attrib.**	**% ex./class**	**ME**
100	73	50% presence	50%
		50% absence	

4   Machine Learning Techniques

This section presents the ML techniques used in this paper.

4.1   Decision Trees

Decision Trees (DTs) organize the knowledge extracted from data in a recursive hierarchical structure composed of nodes and branches [15]. Each internal node represents an attribute and is associated to a test relevant for data classification and the leaf nodes of the tree correspond to the classes. The branches represent each of the possible results of the applied tests. A new data point can be classified following the nodes and branches accordingly until a leaf node is reached.

The DT induction process aims to maximize the correct classification of all the training data provided. To avoid overfitting, a pruning phase is usually applied to the trained tree. It prunes ramifications which have low expressive power according to some criterion, like the expected error rate [29].

One advantage of DTs is the comprehensibility of the classification structures generated. For each new data, it is possible to verify which attributes determined the final classification. DTs may be, nevertheless, not robust to inputs with high dimensions (with a large number of attributes).

4.2   Support Vector Machines

Support Vector Machines are based on concepts from the Statistical Learning Theory [30]. Given a dataset T composed of n pairs $(\mathbf{x}_i, y_i)$, in which $\mathbf{x}_i \in \Re^m$ and $y_i \in \{-1, +1\}$, SVMs seek for a hyper plane $\mathbf{w} \cdot \mathbf{\Phi}(\mathbf{x}) + b = 0$ able to separate the data in T with minimum error and which also maximizes the margin of separation between the classes. $\mathbf{\Phi}$ represents a mapping function, which maps the data in T to a space of higher dimension, such that the classes become linearly separable. Maximizing the margin is equivalent to minimizing the norm $\|\mathbf{w}\|$ [11]. The following optimization problem is then solved:

$$\text{Minimize: } \|\mathbf{w}\|^2 + C \sum_{i=1}^{n} \xi_i$$

$$\text{With the restrictions: } \begin{cases} \xi_i \geq 0 \\ y_i \left(\mathbf{w} \cdot \Phi(\mathbf{x}_i) + b \right) \geq 1 - \xi_i \end{cases}$$

in which C is a regularization constant which imposes a different weight for training in relation to the model complexity and ξ_i are slack variables. The restrictions are imposed in order to ensure that no training data should be within the margins of separation. However, they are relaxed by the slack variables in order to avoid an overfitting to the training data and also to deal with noisy data. The number of training errors and data within the margins is controlled by the minimization of the term $\sum_{i=1}^{n} \xi_i$. The decision frontier generated is given by Equation 1.

$$f(\mathbf{x}) = \sum_{\mathbf{x_i} \in i=1:n} y_i \alpha_i \Phi(\mathbf{x_i}) \cdot \Phi(\mathbf{x}) + b \tag{1}$$

in which the constants α_i are named Lagrange variables and are determined in the optimization process. The dot product $\Phi(\mathbf{x}_i) \cdot \Phi(\mathbf{x})$ is performed by Kernel functions, which are usually simpler than the mapping function. Some of the most used Kernel functions are the Gaussian or RBF (Radial-Basis Function) functions.

SVMs have good generalization ability. Besides, SVMs also stand out for their robustness to high dimensional data. Their main deficiency concerns the difficulty of interpreting the generated model.

4.3   GARP

GARP is an algorithm that was specifically developed in the context of ecological niche modelling. A GARP model consists of a set of mathematical rules based on the environment conditions. Given a specific environment condition, if all rules are satisfied then the model predicts presence of the species. Four types of rules are possible: atomic, logistic regression, bioclimatic envelope, and negated bioclimatic envelope.

Each set of rules is an individual of a population in the typical context of a genetic algorithm. GARP generates an initial population which is evaluated in each iteration to check if the problem converged to a solution. Genetic operators (join, cross-over and mutation) are applied in the beginning of each new iteration based on the best individuals from previous steps to produce a new population.

GARP is therefore a non-deterministic algorithm that produces boolean responses (present/absent) for each different environment condition. This experiment used the GARP Best Subsets technique which selects the 10 best GARP models out of 100 models. By aggregating 10 GARP models, a GARP Best Subsets model produces more outputs than just a boolean response. The probability of presence in a specific condition is proportional to the number of GARP models that predicts presence for the species.

5 Experiments

In order to provide a better estimate of the performance of the algorithms used in this paper, the dataset described in Section 3 was divided with the 10-fold stratified cross-validation methodology.

Experiments with SVMs were performed with the LibSVM tool [31] currently available from *openModeller*. DTs were generated with the C4.5 algorithm [15]. They are currently being evaluated for future inclusion in *openModeller*. The GARP models were generated with the DesktopGARP Best Subsets implementation available in *openModeller*. For all techniques, default parameter values were used and a probabilistic output was obtained.

As the GAs results depend of the initial population, GARP was executed thirty times for each training/test dataset partition and the reported results correspond to the average error rates obtained in these runs.

The training datasets provided to SVM were normalized with zero mean and unit variance. GARP used its own scale normalization in the training datasets based on the minimum and maximum values of each environmental layer. In both cases, the test datasets were pre-processed according to the normalization factors extracted from their corresponding training data.

5.1 Results

The error rates and AUC (Area Under the ROC Curve) values for DTs, SVMs and GARP are presented in Table 2. The error rates and AUC values illustrated are the mean of the measures obtained in the 10-fold cross-validation process. Their standard-deviation rates are indicated in parenthesis. The best error rate and AUC obtained are highlighted in boldface and the worst in italics.

Table 2. Error and AUC rates

Technique	Error rate	AUC
DT	14.0 (9.7)	89.8 (9.3)
SVM	**9.0 (8.8)**	**95.2 (5.8)**
GARP	*14.6 (8.3)*	*88.6 (8.2)*

5.2 Discussion

Comparing the results presented in Table 2, SVMs performed better, showing a lower error rate and a higher AUC value. GARP, on the other hand, showed the worst performance, while DTs presented an average performance, although it can be considered closer to the GARP performance. Nevertheless, comparing the results statistically with the Friedman test for multiple comparisons [32], no statistical differences were found among the performance of the three techniques considered, at 95% of confidence level.

For SVMs and GARP, already implemented under the *openModeller* framework, it is possible to plot distribution maps based on the predictions of the generated models. As one of the objectives of this work is to verify the ability of the predictors, while the occurrence points from the São Paulo state were used in the induction of the models, the resulting predictions were projected in all of Brazil. Using all dataset to obtain the models, the obtained maps are presented in Figure 1. In both maps, light colors represents absence of the species and dark colors represents a high confidence in the presence of the species. Intermediate colors represent different degrees of confidence in the presence of the species in the given region.

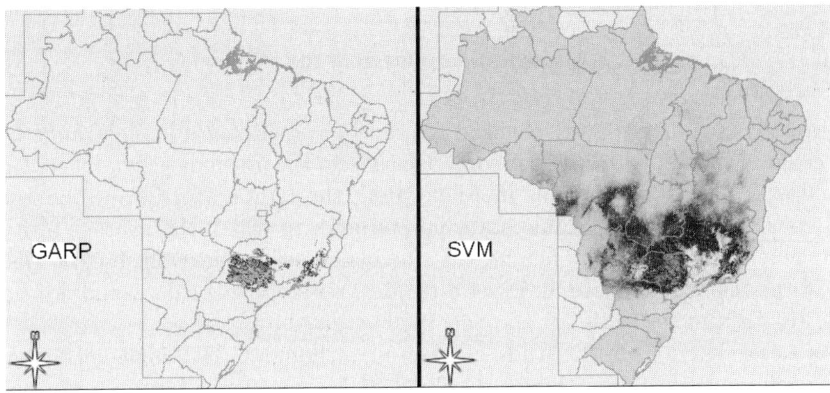

Fig. 1. Distribution maps generated by GARP and SVM

Stryphnodendron obovatum is typical of Brazilian Savanah and is present in almost all central Brazil and in the Southeast Savanah areas. Although the generated models do not reflect the total known distribution of the species, the SVM resulting map shows a potential distribution closer to the known distribution of the analyzed species. GARP showed more restricted predictions, practically restricted to the São Paulo state. GARP was then more sensitive to the information present in the training dataset, such that the generated rules were too specific for this particular region, both ambiently and geographically. These results indicate a higher generalization ability of SVMs concerning the known distribution of the species.

Although it is not currently possible to plot maps for DTs, one interesting feature of this technique is the comprehensibility of the generated model. For instance, using the whole dataset to generate a DT and translating the tree structure into rules, a set of eight rules was obtained. It is a compact set of rules, which is quite easy to interpret. Figure 2 presents three of the generated rules. Rules R1 and R2 cover almost 40% of the absence class, while rule R6 covers 36% of the presence class.

Analyzing the produced rules according to the data from the São Paulo state (which is the data contained in the used dataset), R1 can be considered plausible. Since the used points in São Paulo are more or less in the southern limits of the species known distribution, it would not be expected to find the species in

> **R1: if** (min temperature of August ≤ 10.8°C)
>   **then** the species is absent
> **R2: if** (min temperature of August > 10.8°C)
>   **and** (elevation ≤ 402m)
>   **then** the species is absent
> **R6: if** (min temperature of August > 10.8°C)
>   **and** (elevation > 402m)
>   **and** (NDVI September/2000 > 167)
>   **and** (min temperature of the coldest month > 9.5°C)
>   and (average max temperature of December ≤ 29.9°C)
>   **then** the species is present

Fig. 2. Classification rules from the DT model

environments colder than that. Rule R2 can be considered a little strange from the ecological perspective, but it correctly reflects the given dataset. An ecologist would expect that for terrains more elevated, the temperature would be lower. But considering the São Paulo state points used, in which the average altitude is, in general, around 400m height, the rule makes sense. Nevertheless, for points out of the São Paulo State, in lower altitudes, possibly this rule would not hold. Rule R6 also makes sense for the São Paulo state data.

As a conclusion from the study conducted, although GARP is one of the most employed modelling algorithms in Ecology, SVMs achieved a better performance considering unseen data. DTs, on the other hand, have the advantage of generating comprehensible classification rules, which is interesting for biologists in order to validate the generated model or to infer new knowledge from the generated rules.

6   Conclusion

This work presented a study comparing the use of three ML techniques to model the potential distribution of *Stryphnodendron obovatum*, a species from the Brazilian Savannah. The techniques used were GARP, SVMs and DTs.

Although GARP is the most used modelling technique in environmental studies, the results obtained indicate SVMs as a promising technique concerning the ability to generalize well to new data. Furthermore, DTs obtained classification rules in accordance to what was expected for the potential distribution of the considered species in the São Paulo state and will be considered for future inclusion in the *openModeller* modelling tool.

As future work, other techniques commonly used in potential distribution modelling, besides ML techniques, will also be included in a comparative study. Other comparison measures will also be included in this work, as the time spent in the models' generation and in the obtainment of predictions.

Acknowledgments

To the financial support of the Brazilian Research Agencies FAPESP and CNPq.

References

1. Egbert, S.L., Peterson, A.T., Sanchez-Cordero, C., Price, K.P.: Modeling conservation priorities in Veracruz, Mexico. In: GIS in natural resource management: Balancing the technical-political equation, pp. 141–150 (1998)
2. Ortega-Huerta, M.A., Peterson, A.T.: Modelling spatial patterns of biodiversity for conservation prioritization in north-eastern Mexico. Diversity and Distributions 10, 39–54 (2004)
3. Peterson, A.T., Vieglais, D.A.: Predicting species invasions using ecological niche modeling: New approaches from bioinformatics attack a pressing problem. BioScience 51(5), 363–371 (2001)
4. Peterson, A.T., Papes, M., Kluza, D.A.: Predicting the potential invasive distributions of four alien plant species in north America. Weed Science 51(6), 863–868 (2003)
5. Huntley, B., Berry, P.M., Cramer, W., McDonald, A.P.: Modelling present and potential future ranges of some european higher plants using climate response surfaces. J. Biogeography 22, 967–1001 (1995)
6. Pearson, R.G., Dawson, T.P., Berry, P.M., Harrison, P.A.: Species: A spatial evaluation of climate impact on the envelope of species. Ecological Modelling 154, 289–300 (2002)
7. Peterson, A.T., Ortega-Huerta, M.A., Bartley, J., Sanchez-Cordero, V., Buddemeier, R.H., Stockwell, D.R.B.: Future projections for mexican faunas under global climate change scenarios. Nature 416, 626–629 (2002)
8. Guisan, A., Thuiller, W.: Predicting species distribution: offering more than simple habitat models. Ecology Letters 8, 993–1009 (2005)
9. Peterson, A.T., Sanchez-Cordero, V., Beard, C.B., Ramsey, J.M.: Ecologic niche modeling and potential reservoirs for chagas disease, Mexico. Emerging Infectious Diseases 8, 662–667 (2002)
10. Stockwell, D.R.B., Peters, D.P.: The GARP modelling system: Problems and solutions to automated spatial prediction. International Journal of Geographic Information Systems 13, 143–158 (1999)
11. Cristianini, N., Shawe-Taylor, J.: An Introduction to Support Vector Machines and other kernel-based learning methods. Cambridge University Press, Cambridge (2000)
12. Mitchell, T.: Machine Learning. McGraw-Hill, New York (1997)
13. Elith, J., Graham, C.H., Anderson, R.P., Dudík, M., Ferrier, S., Guisan, A., Hijmans, R.J., Huettmann, F., Leathwick, J.R., Lehmann, A., Li, J., Lohmann, L.G., Loiselle, B.A., Manion, G., Moritz, C., Nakamura, M., Nakazawa, Y., Overton, J.McC., Peterson, A.T., Phillips, S.J., Richardson, K.S., Scachetti-Pereira, R., Schapire, R.E., Soberón, J., Williams, S., Wisz, M.S., Zimmermann, N.E.: Novel methods improve prediction of species' distributions from occurrence data. Ecography 29, 129–151 (2006)
14. Mitchell, M.: An introduction to Genetic Algorithms. MIT Press, Cambridge (1999)
15. Quinlan, J.R.: Induction of decision trees. Machine Learning 1(1), 81–106 (1986)
16. Peterson, A.T.: Predicting species' geographic distributions based on ecological niche modeling. Condor 103(3), 599–605 (2001)
17. Siqueira, M.F.: Uso de modelagem de nicho fundamental na avaliação do padrão de distribuição geográfica de espécies vegetais. PhD thesis, Escola de Engenharia de São Carlos, Universidade de São Paulo, São Carlos (2005) (in Portuguese)

18. Soberón, J., Peterson, A.T.: Interpretation of models of fundamental ecological niches and species distributional areas. In: Biodiversity Informatics (2005)
19. Fielding, A.H.: Machine learning methods for ecological applications. Kluwer Academic, Dordrecht (1999)
20. Lek, S., Guegan, J.F.: Artificial neural networks as a tool in ecological modelling: an introduction. Ecological Modelling 120, 65–73 (1999)
21. Ath, G.D., Fabricius, K.E.: Classification and regression trees: a powerful yet simple technique for ecological data analysis. Ecol. 81(11), 3178–3192 (2000)
22. Pearson, R.G., Dawson, T.P., Liu, C.: Modelling species distribution in britain: a hierarchical integration of climate and land-cover data. Ecography 27, 285–298 (2004)
23. Siqueira, M.F.D., Peterson, A.T.: Consequences of global climate change for geographic distributions of cerrado tree species. Biota Neotropica 3(2) (2003), http://www.biotaneotropica.org.br/v3n2/pt/ abstract?article+BN00803022003
24. Guo, Q., Kelly, M., Graham, C.H.: Support vector machines for predicting distribution of sudden oak death in California. Ecol. Modelling 182, 75–90 (2005)
25. Ratter, J.A., Bridgewater, S., Ribeiro, J.F., Dias, T.A.B., Silva, M.R.: Distribuição das espécies lenhosas da fitofisionomia cerrado sentido restrito nos estados compreendidos no bioma cerrado. Boletim do Herbário Ezechias Paulo Heringer 5, 5–43 (2000) (in portuguese)
26. Durigan, G., Siqueira, M.F., Franco, G.A.D.C., Bridgewater, S., Ratter, J.A.: The vegetation of priority areas for cerrado conservation in são paulo state, brazil. Edinburgh Journal of Botany 60, 217–241 (2003)
27. Hijmans, R.J., Cameron, S.E., Parra, J.L., Jones, P.G., Jarvis, A.: Very high resolution interpolated climate surfaces for global land areas. International Journal of Climatology 25, 1965–1978 (2005)
28. Souza, A.L.F., Giarola, A., Gondim, M.A.: Aplicao de mascaramento de nuvens e correção atmosférica na geração do índice de vegetação por diferença normalizada no cptec/inpe. In: XIV Cong. Brasileiro de Agrometeorologia (2005) (in portuguese)
29. Quilan, J.R.: C4.5 Programs for Machine Learning. Morgan Kaufmann, San Francisco (1988)
30. Vapnik, V.N.: The nature of Statistical learning theory. Springer, New York (1995)
31. Chang, C.C., Lin, C.J.: LIBSVM: a library for support vector machines (2004), http://www.csie.ntu.edu.tw/~cjlin/libsvm/
32. Demsar, J.: Statistical comparisons of classifiers over multiple datasets. Journal of Machine Learning Research 7, 1–30 (2006)

A Cluster-Based Classification Approach to Semantic Role Labeling

Necati E. Ozgencil, Nancy McCracken, and Kishan Mehrotra

Syracuse University
Syracuse, NY 13244-4100
{neozgenc,njm,kishan}@ecs.syr.edu

Abstract. In this paper, a new approach for multi-class classification problems is applied to the Semantic Role Labeling (SRL) problem, which is an important task for natural language processing systems to achieve better semantic understanding of text. The new approach applies to any classification problem with large feature sets. Data is partitioned using clusters on a subset of the features. A multi-label classifier is then trained individually on each cluster, using automatic feature selection to customize the larger feature set for the cluster. This algorithm is applied to the Semantic Role Labeling problem and achieves improvements in accuracy for both the argument identification classifier and the argument labeling classifier.

Keywords: Machine Learning, Natural Language Processing, Clustering, Classification.

1 Introduction

The focus of the research described in this paper is to develop a machine learning technique for classification tasks with large number of features. Throughout the paper, for classification, we use support vector machines (SVM). In particular, we use libSVM, an open source SVM package [1] that uses the *one versus one* classification approach for multi-label problems, selecting the radial basis functions kernel.

It has been observed that features suited for one group of data may not be suitable for the other set. This property is also known as cross-talk and in our approach we wish to minimize the cross-talk effect. For example, for the semantic role labeling problem, Pradhan et al. [2] state that:

> Error analysis showed that some features specifically suited for one argument class, for example, core arguments, tend to hurt performance on some adjunctive arguments.

Some researchers argue that SVM classification is robust and therefore it does not make any sense to select separate set of features for a classification problem (within the same system). We argue that, as observed by Pradhan et al., by selecting a difference set of features for each classification problem we help the

N.T. Nguyen et al. (Eds.): IEA/AIE 2008, LNAI 5027, pp. 265–275, 2008.
© Springer-Verlag Berlin Heidelberg 2008

system because some features may be of local importance only. This argument is very easy to justify when the measure of decision making is the *average distance*. That is, there are features that have a large impact (have a large distance measure) on a certain decision when used in a subset of the features, but the same average distance measure may look quite small in the overall feature space. Benefits of this approach are demonstrated for a much studied application area – the Semantic Role labeling (SRL) problem.

In section 2, we present our proposed method. In section 3, we provide a brief introduction to the SRL problem followed by our analysis. In section 4, we describe the overall results for the SRL problem including the constraint satisfaction module and compare these results with results obtained by other researchers.

2   Cluster-Based Classification

In this paper, we propose cluster-based classification, a new approach to solve a classification problem. To minimize the cross-talk effect clustering is a natural approach. As argued earlier some features may be of local importance only. Therefore, we select separate set of features for a classification problem even though it has been argued that SVM classification is robust.

Given a training set, our classification algorithm uses the following steps, each of which is briefly described below:

- use a clustering algorithm to divide the training set into "similar" clusters. Use an appropriate similarity measure involving *some* features of the overall problem; disregard the class labels themselves,
- to maximize the classification accuracy within each cluster, prune some outlying examples,
- use an automatic feature selection for individual clusters,
- produce separate classifiers for each cluster.

By breaking the task into clusters, we not only can improve the accuracy of classification, but also improve the time complexity of the automatic feature selection, making it more feasible to train on large data sets. Furthermore, the time of the testing function improves, resulting in a more practical classification technique.

2.1   Clustering

Clustering, an unsupervised learning procedure to find a *structure* in a collection of unlabeled data, is the first step in our proposed scheme. Self-organizing-maps and k-mean are two of the best known clustering algorithms [3]. In experiments with the SRL problem, we have found that $k-$mean clustering is fast and gives comparable results when compared with self-organizing-maps. Hence, throughout this paper we use $k-$mean clustering.

An important component of the clustering process is the choice and appropriateness of the distance measure. Feature values of the SRL problem are discrete and nominal, therefore, the traditional Euclidean distance measure for continuous features is not appropriate. We use instead a variation of the Hamming distance in which the similarity between two examples, represented as feature vectors, is the normalized value of number of features that have the same values. Similarity between two clusters is computed as the average of all pair-wise similarities between examples of two clusters.

To select a subset of features for clustering, we evaluate the performance of one feature at a time and select the best ℓ features out of the given set; where ℓ is a pre-specified integer.

Although we do not use class label information during clustering, we might expect that all instances belonging to a class also belong to only one cluster. In practice this does not happen.

This is generally the case for the SRL problem discussed in the following section.

2.2 Cluster Cleaning

Cluster cleaning is essentially removal of "outliers" for improved classification. In this paper it is guided by two principles: a cluster must not contain stray examples of a class and a cluster should be sufficiently large. These two rules are implemented as follows.

1. Number of examples in a cluster should be more than α, if not, the cluster is removed and its observations are put into other clusters based on the similarity metric, and
2. number of examples of a class in a cluster should be more than γ, if not, the examples of that class are removed from the cluster,

where α and γ are two positive integers. Appropriate values of α and γ are chosen based on performance on the validation set. The two steps improve the overall performance of the classification procedure and reduce the training time.

2.3 Feature Selection

For the classification task one feature set might give the best performance for one cluster while it might give poor performance for another cluster. To automatically select appropriate features for each cluster from the set of all features first we use a genetic algorithm [4,5] to find an initial subset and second, we apply a bi-directional local search to further improve the subset obtained in the first stage. We found this hybrid approach to be less time consuming than the genetic algorithm by itself as well as providing better results than a standard bi-directional search. Results used to evaluate feature selection were based on wrapper methods, for which we used the development set of the training data.

2.4 Testing Algorithm

In order to classify a (new) example the algorithm first finds its closest cluster (the example is said to "visit" the cluster that it is closest to). The classifier of that cluster is then used to decide the class label of the example.

3   Semantic Role Labeling System

SRL is the process of annotating the predicate-argument structure in text with semantic labels [6]. This task is important to the natural language processing community to understand the meaning of text by identifying the event structures of the sentence. These events come from the predicates of the text, usually verbs, and the process of identifying the semantic roles of the predicates will answer the Who, What, When, How and Why questions of events described in the text. In recent years, statistical approaches to the SRL task have been made possible by the annotation of large corpora with semantic role labels in both Propbank [7] and in FrameNet [8]. These resources have been used as the training data for the SRL problem and have been the subject of significant research over the last several years, including the shared task of CoNLL in 2004 and 2005 [9] and one of the tasks of Senseval in 2004 [10]. Throughout the paper, we use the training data and evaluation function from CoNLL 2005. For purposes of this investigation, we restrict the syntactic information to Charniak parse trees [11]and the features to fifteen primarily based on the works of [12,6].

3.1   Previous Work

The SRL problem has been described extensively in [7] for the Propbank corpus. In this corpus, the semantic role labels are annotated using core argument labels (Arg0 through Arg5), adjunctive argument labels (such as ArgM-TMP and ArgM-MNR), and some additional less frequent labels such as the reference and continuation labels.

A variety of machine learning methods have been used to train multi-label classifiers for the argument labeling part of the problem such as the linearly interpolated relative frequency models by Gildea and Jurafsky [12], support vector machines (SVM), decision trees, maximum entropy, and conditional random fields. A summary of the types of classifiers used in the CoNLL 2005 shared task is presented in [9].

In addition, there has been some variety in how the classifiers have been applied to the argument labeling problem. For example, in [13], the learning classifier is based on a Winnow update rule incorporated in SnoW [14] and the resulting scores are used for constraint optimization with an integer linear programming (ILP) approach. In [15], a log-linear model is used to find the probability of each label, and these probabilities are used in a joint re-ranking model to find the best overall labeling for each predicate. In these works, classifiers uses the same overall feature set.

There has also been work by several authors investigating the use of different feature sets, and many systems combine different syntactic views. For example, Pradhan et al.,[2], focus on features from a combinatory categorial grammar parser and on combining syntactic views from different parsers. An SVM classifier is trained for each role-label, and each one can have a different feature set.

Many researchers have used an architecture, as shown in Figure 1, that uses: (1) *candidate generator* – a process involving the preparation of candidate constituents to be given a semantic role label, (2) *the identification task* – a bi-label

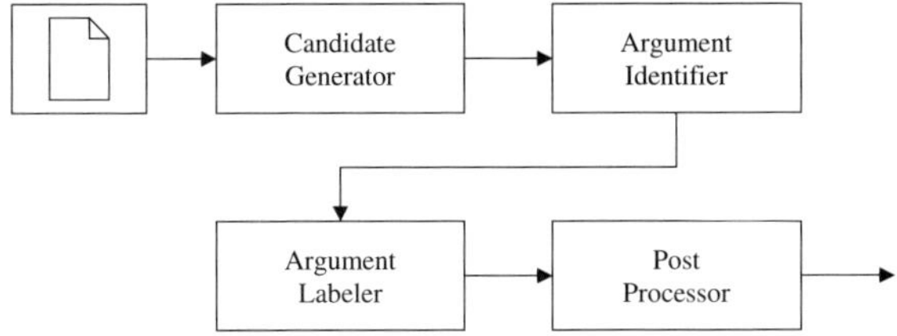

Fig. 1. Block Diagram of Semantic role labeling system

classification task whose goal is identification of syntactic constituents that are semantic roles for a given predicate, (3) *argument label classifier* – a multi-label classification task of giving the correct semantic role to arguments identified in the previous task, and (4) *post processing* – application of constraint resolution across the semantic role labels of a predicate.

The Propbank dataset as defined in the CoNLL 2005 shared task, has three parts; the training set, the validation (development) set and the test set, with 39,832 sentences, 1,346 sentences and 2,416 sentences, respectively. We use Charniak parser data, which has the highest alignment percentage among other parsers, to generate argument candidates.

3.2   Argument Identification Module

The candidate-generator module generates many more "negative" predicate-argument pairs than positive; our data set contains approximately 233 thousand positive and 3.8 million negative examples. The functionality of the argument-identification task is to label as "positive" only those candidates that are "true" arguments. As this imbalance is well-known to be a problem for training classifiers, we use a two-step argument identification procedure, as shown in Figure 2. The objective of the *pruner* is to eliminate most of the negative examples so that the classifier used in the second module, the *identifier*, has a balanced training data set. The pruner eliminates "easy-to-identify" negative examples and its output labeled "positive" becomes input to the identifier.

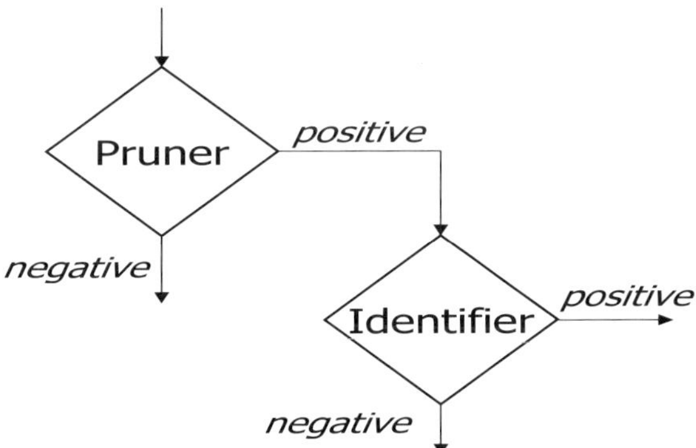

Fig. 2. Two-step diagram of argument label identifier

The pruner needs to have very high recall, reasonable precision and be fast; achieved by a simple classifier with only one feature – the Short-Path.

The pruner is trained using all positive examples and only 1% of the negative examples. The classifier, so obtained, correctly classifies positive examples as positive 99% and 97% of the times on the training and test sets and approximately 7% and of the negative examples are misclassified as positive (resulting in the $F_{\beta=1} = 66\%$ and 62% for the training and test sets respectively[1] and also meets the condition of being fast.

The Identifier – The pruner removes 'easy' negative examples and only the 'difficult' negative examples are used to train the identifier; i.e., we use fewer but *more important* negative examples to train the identifier.

The identifier is a cluster-based binary classifier and to train it 233,247 positive examples and 235,522 negative examples are used. For clustering we use the five best features, namely the Phrase Type, Short Path, Position, Voice and Subcategory. Accuracy on the validation set attains its maximum value when number of clusters is 9. For each cluster the feature selection process maximizes the $F_{\beta=1}$ measure of each classifier on the validation set; each cluster has its own SVM classifier. Table 2 summarizes the performance of the two-step approach on the label identification task on the test set and Table 1 summarizes performance of the identifier, cluster by cluster, on the test set.

Table 1. Indentifier's performance on the test set for each cluster

Cluster Number	Training Set Number of Examples	Test Set Number of Examples	$F_{\beta=1}$
1	23,928	1,422	0.932
2	7,785	440	0.872
3	140,503	8,065	0.860
4	13,066	786	0.822
5	125,358	7,308	0.904
6	7,814	392	0.812
7	17,450	1,048	0.918
8	48,116	2,937	0.928
9	84,749	4,752	0.826
Overall	**468,769**	**27,150**	**88.19%**

For comparison, we use a single SVM system and train the pruner by using all positive examples and randomly selected 20% ($\sim$ 700k) of the negative examples. By using the new pruning technique and the cluster based classification, we improved the testing performance from $F_{\beta=1} = 84.67\%$ to $F_{\beta=1} = 86.66\%$.

The pruner is very fast and the entire label identification task takes only 640 seconds for the test set, compared with 8,255 seconds in the single SVM system.

---

[1] When $\beta = 1$, the F measure is defined to be the harmonic mean of precision and recall.

Table 2. Performance of the two-step identification method on the test set by using cluster based classification

	Prediction		
Fact	Positive	Negative	
Positive	11,625	1,527	13,152
Negative	2,053	201,527	
	13,678		

Prec. = 84.99%, Recall = 88.39%, $F_{\beta=1}$ = 86.66%

Thus, the proposed scheme significantly reduces the test time and improves the performance.

3.3   Argument Labeling Task

The argument labeling task is to assign appropriate class labels to the arguments identified by identification module. It is not always the case that only true arguments come to the label classifier module. Some candidates are falsely identified as argument. For these cases, any decision to label them to one of the existing classes will be wrong. To overcome this problem the "NULL" class label is added to the current 52 existing classes.

In the dataset A0 and A1 are two dominant classes whereas some class labels, such as AA and AM, are rarely represented. We use k-mean clustering to partition the training set using eight features[2]. To select the appropriate number of clusters, we conducted a series of experiments with k value ranging from 6 to 13 and tested the performance on the validation set. Based on the experiment the best performance is obtained for $k = 9$.

The cluster refining constants α and γ were also obtained based on empirical results. Based on these results we chose $\gamma = 5$. As a consequence of cluster cleaning, 120 examples were removed from the training set (only 0.05% of the entire training data set). An informal examination of removed examples showed that about one fourth could be annotation errors (with the caveat that these were not judged by a trained annotator) and the remainder were divided between examples with incorrect parse trees and correct examples that were occurrences of rare syntactic structure.

The clustering process partitions the data set into 9 clusters, each contains a different number of examples and class labels. Table 3 describes two representative clusters and class memberships in each cluster.

Table 3 shows that 91% of the observations of class A0 belong to cluster 1. This cluster also contains all of the 13 observations of class AA and is also represented by observations of class A1 and C-A0. We infer that the observations belonging to these classes are close to each other (as measured in terms of five features used in clustering). Observations belonging to class A1 are mostly found in clusters

---

[2] Predicate, Phrase Type, Path, Position, Voice, Subcategory, Head Word, and Temporal Word.

Table 3. Contents of Clusters 1 and 6

Class Label	Count	Cluster %	Class %	Class Label	Count	Cluster %	Class%
NULL	2,091	2,50%	15,69%	NULL	3,007	8,27%	22,56%
A0	54,810	65,42%	90,85%	A0	2,319	6,38%	3,84%
A1	23,250	27,75%	29,30%	A1	3,464	9,53%	4,37%
A2	1,910	2,28%	10,06%	A2	8,821	24,27%	46,48%
A3	158	0,19%	4,98%	A3	2,232	6,14%	70,32%
AM-LOC	193	0,23%	3,39%	A4	2,394	6,59%	93,85%
AM-MNR	132	0,16%	2,12%	AM-LOC	3,691	10,15%	64,80%
AM-TMP	1,058	1,26%	6,59%	AM-TMP	4,445	12,23%	27,70%
Rest	178	0.21%		Rest	5,975	16,44%	
Total	83,780			Total	83,780		

5 and 1 (43% and 29.30%, respectively). Cluster 5 also contains all observations of class AM-REC and high proportion of observations of class A2; indicating that these classes are also close to each other. Cluster 6 (see Table 3) is very informative, as it contains classes A2, A3, and A4, and AM-EXT, AM-LOC, AM-MNR, AM-PRD, C-A2 and C-AM-MNR in high proportion and indicates that elements in this cluster are difficult to distinguish. This is further substantiated by percent of correct classification for this cluster which is lowest among all clusters at 79.4% as seen in Table 3. Only by selecting additional new features one is able to achieve good classification for this cluster.

After clustering, the feature selection algorithm chooses a set of features from the overall set for each cluster. The differences between the clusters can also be seen in these individual feature sets, although the results are not always intuitive. For example, Short Path is selected for cluster #2 and #7 only and Temporal Cue Words is used by all clusters.

Table 4 shows the final set of clusters with accuracies before and after feature selection. Again we compare the new cluster based classification approach with a single SVM system, which had an accuracy of 88.37% (see Table 6). It can be seen that we obtain 1.4% better accuracy by applying cluster based classification technique.

3.4   Post Processor (Constraint Satisfaction) Module

In a sentence, for a given predicate there could be more than one candidates, say ℓ. These candidates are required to satisfy the following constraints:

1. A constituent cannot have more than one argument label,
2. An argument label cannot be assigned to more than one constituents,
3. If two constituents have argument labels, they cannot have any overlap,
4. No argument can overlap the predicate.

Constraint 4 is guaranteed by the candidate generator module. To satisfy the remaining three constraints, we use a simple greedy approach (other optimization techniques have been used to satisfy the constraints, as indicated in the previous works section).

Table 4. Clustering Based Classification for Argument Labeling Task

Cluster Number	Number of Examples	Test Set Accuracy	
		Before Feature Selection	After Feature Selection
1	4,704	0.932	0.938
2	784	0.800	0.825
3	1,722	0.868	0.882
4	921	0.849	0.849
5	2,241	0.951	0.952
6	1,653	0.770	0.794
7	105	0.852	0.876
8	112	0.819	0.848
9	910	0.841	0.891
Overall	**13,152**	**88.46%**	**89.77%**
SVM			**88.37%**

To meet the constraints listed above desired input for the post processor module consists of probability estimates of an argument belonging to each class. In libSVM tool, these are calculated from probability estimates generated by $\frac{q \times (q-1)}{2}$ binary classifiers. We iteratively choose the largest probability value in the probability matrix so obtained. As long as the probability is above a predetermined threshold θ, we assign the associated class label to the constituent and remove column to satisfy the constraint #2. We also remove the corresponding row to satisfy the constraint #1. To satisfy the constraint #3, we remove all rows which overlap with the selected constituent.

If a high value of θ is chosen (say (0.8)), then precision is high but the recall value is low. And if θ is assigned a small value, then the precision is low while recall is high. Based on a set of experiments, we have found that $\theta = 0.45$ gives the highest $F_{\beta=1}$ value for the validation set.

4   Overall Results for the SRL Problem

In the CoNLL 2005 Shared task, to test the performance of the SRL system the WSJ test data was used. In addition, another test set, called the "Brown Test Set", was also used with intent to measure performance of the system in other unseen corpuses. We have tested our SRL system on the Brown Test set as well. The final results are summarized in Table 5.

Scores of the all participants of the CoNLL 2005 shared task are given in [16] in which the performance was measured as the weighted average of the WSJ and Brown test. Four systems perform as good or better than our current system. But, all of these four systems use *multiple* parsers such as Charniak with different parameters, Collins and UPC. By eliminating parsing errors they improve the overall score. We expect that our system will compete very favorably with these four systems with multiple parsers.

Table 5. Overall results of the CBC system on the development set and the test sets

	Precision	Recall	$F_{\beta=1}$
Development	80.63	71.23	75.64
WSJ	82.36	73.23	77.52
Brown	72.56	61.09	66.33
WSJ+Brown	81.16	71.60	**76.08**

Following table from Koomen et al. [17] reports single parser results on the validation set.

Table 6. Results reported by [17] on single parsers

	Precision	Recall	$F_{\beta=1}$
Charniak-1	75.40%	74.13%	74.76%
Charniak-2	74,21%	73.06%	73.63%
Charniak-3	73.52%	72.31%	72.91%
Charniak-4	74.29%	72.92%	73.60%
Charniak-5	72.57%	71.40%	71.98%
Collins	73.89%	70.11%	71.95%
Joint Inference	80.05%	74.83%	77.35%

We obtain approximately 2% better accuracy on the validation data and 1.5% better accuracy on test data than reported in this table for individual parsers.

5   Conclusion

The proposed cluster based classification method has several advantages. It improves the overall classification performance, the test time is significantly smaller. This is mostly due to the reason that in the usual SVM decision procedure for the SRL problem all one-to-one classification rules are evaluated for all 53 classes whereas in CBC each cluster has much smaller number of classes. An additional by-product of CBC is that it allows us to investigate the clusters. For example, we noted that cluster 6 in the labeling task has the poorest performance, and we also can find the reason and potential solutions. For example, SRL researchers can identify some new features that can be used to separate classes within cluster 6.

References

1. Chang, C.-C., Lin, C.-J.: LIBSVM: a library for support vector machines (2001), http://www.csie.ntu.edu.tw/libsvm
2. Pradhan, S., Ward, W., Hacioglu, K., Martin, J., Jurafsky, D.: Semantic role labeling using different syntactic views. In: ACL (2005)
3. Mehrotra, K., Mohan, C.K., Ranka, S.: Elements of Artificial Neural Networks. MIT Press, Cambridge (1996)

4. Vafaie, H., DeJong, K.: Robust feature selection algorithms. Proc. 5th Intl. Conf. on Tools with Artifical Intelligence, 356–363 (1993)
5. Ritthoff, O., Klinkenberg, R., Fischer, S., Mierswa, I.: A hybrid approach to feature selection and generation using an evolutionary algorithm. Technical Report CI-127/02, Collaborative Research Center 531, University of Dortmund, Dortmund, Germany (2002), ISSN (1433)-3325
6. Pradhan, S., Hacioglu, K., Krugler, V., Ward, W., Martin, J.H., Jurafsky, D.: Support vector learning for semantic argument classification. Machine Learning Journal, Special issue of Speech and Natural Language Processing 60(1-3), 11–39 (2005)
7. Palmer, M., Gildea, D., Kingsbury, P.: The proposition bank: A corpus annotated with semantic roles. Journal of Computational Linguistics 31(1), 71–106 (2005)
8. Baker, C.F., Fillmore, C.J., Lowe, J.B.: The Berkeley FrameNet project. In: Proceedings of the COLING-ACL, Montreal, Canada (1998)
9. Carreras, X., Màrquez, L.: Introduction to the conll-2005 shared task: Semantic role labeling. In: Proceedings of the COLING-ACL, Montreal, Canada (2005)
10. SENSEVAL-3: Third international workshop on the evaluation of systems for the semantic analysis of text. Association for Computational Linguistics, Barcelona, Spain (2004)
11. Charniak, E.: A maximum-entropy-inspired parser. In: Proceedings of the first conference on North American chapter of the Association for Computational Linguistics, pp. 132–139. Morgan Kaufmann Publishers Inc., San Francisco (2000)
12. Gildea, D., Jurafsky, D.: Automatic labeling of semantic roles. Computational Linguistics 28(3), 245–288 (2002)
13. Punyakanok, V., Roth, D., Yih, W., Zimak, D.: Semantic role labeling via integer linear programming inference. In: Proceedings of COLING-2004 (2004)
14. Roth, D.: Learning to resolve natural language ambiguities: A unified approach. In: Proceedings of AAAI, pp. 806–813 (2004)
15. Toutanova, K., Haghighi, A., Manning, C.D.: Joint learning improves semantic role labeling. In: Proceedings of the Association for Computational Linguistics 43rd annual meeting (ACL2005), Ann Arbor, MI (2005)
16. Carreras, X., Màrquez, L.: Introduction to the CoNLL-2005 shared task: Semantic role labeling. In: Proceedings of the Ninth Conference on Computational Natural Language Learning (CoNLL-2005), Ann Arbor, Michigan, June 2005, Association for Computational Linguistics (2005)
17. Koomen, P., Punyakanok, V., Roth, D., Yih, W.-t.: Generalized inference with multiple semantic role labeling systems. In: Proceedings of the Ninth Conference on Computational Natural Language Learning (CoNLL-2005), Ann Arbor, Michigan, June 2005, pp. 181–184. Association for Computational Linguistics (2005)

Data Reduction Algorithm for Machine Learning and Data Mining

Ireneusz Czarnowski and Piotr Jędrzejowicz

Department of Information Systems, Gdynia Maritime University
Morska 83, 81-225 Gdynia, Poland
{irek, pj}@am.gdynia.pl

Abstract. The paper proposes an approach to data reduction. The data reduction procedures are of vital importance to machine learning and data mining. To solve the data reduction problems the agent-based population learning algorithm was used. The proposed approach has been used to reduce the original dataset in two dimensions including selection of reference instances and removal of irrelevant attributes. To validate the approach the computational experiment has been carried out. Presentation and discussion of experiment results conclude the paper.

1   Introduction

In the supervised learning, a machine-learning algorithm is shown a training set, which is a collection of training examples called instances. After learning from the training set, the learning algorithm is presented with additional input vectors, and the algorithm should generalize, that is to decide what the output value should be.

It is well known that in order to avoid excessive storage and time complexity and to improve generalization accuracy by avoiding noise and overfitting, it is often advisable to reduce original training set by selecting the most representative information [18]. Reducing the size of the dataset can result in:

- increasing capabilities and generalization properties of the classification model,
- reducing space complexity of the classification problem,
- decreasing the required computational time,
- diminishing the size of formulas obtained by an induction algorithm on the reduced data sets [2].

Data reduction can be achieved by selecting instances and by selecting features. Instance reduction, often referred to as the selection of reference vectors, becomes especially important in case of large data sets, since overcoming storage and complexity constraints might become computationally very expensive. Although a variety of instance reduction methods has been so far proposed in the literature (see, for example the review [18], [19]), no single approach can be considered as superior nor guaranteeing satisfactory results in terms of the learning error reduction or increased efficiency of the supervised learning.

N.T. Nguyen et al. (Eds.): IEA/AIE 2008, LNAI 5027, pp. 276–285, 2008.

Equally important is the reduction of the number of features by removing features that are irrelevant for classification results. In the real-world situations, relevant features are often unknown a priori and, therefore, many features are introduced with a view to better represent the domain [4]. Many of these features are not only irrelevant from the point of view of classification results but also can have a negative influence on the accuracy and on the required learning time of the classifier. The presence of redundant features introduces unnecessary noise to the data mining analysis and results in the increased computational complexity of the learning process. As it has been observed in [14], the number of instances needed to assure the required classification accuracy grows exponentially with the number or irrelevant features present. The feature selection problem belongs to the group of NP-hard problem [10], [17].

The idea of simultaneously reducing both discussed dimensions of the training dataset has been recently investigated in [7], [14]. In both papers the suggested approach was based on using genetic algorithm to train the respective classifiers. In [17] the data reduction problem was combined with the belief revision in the adaptive classification systems. The belief revision is understood as modification and updating of the dataset in two dimensions. The modification and the updating of the dataset occur in the adaptive classification systems when the size of the dataset increases or when the dataset is huge and a decision system operates on subset of data.

In this paper we show that there is still a room for improving data reduction techniques. The proposed approach is an agent-based population learning algorithm for data reduction.

The paper is organized as follows. Section 2 reviews briefly the data reduction problem and data reduction algorithms. Section 3 provides details of the proposed approach. To validate it the computational experiment has been planned and carried out. Its results are presented and discussed in Section 4. Finally, in the last section some conclusions are drawn and direction for future research is suggested.

2   Data Reduction Algorithms

2.1   Selection of Reference Instances

Instance reduction problem concerns removing a number of instances from the original training set T and thus producing the reduced training set S. Let N denote the number of instances in T and n - the number of attributes. Total length of each instance (i.e. training example) is equal to $n + 1$, where element numbered $n + 1$ contains the output value. Let also $X = \{x_{ij}\}$ $(i = 1, \ldots, N, j = 1, \ldots, n + 1)$ denotes the matrix of $n + 1$ columns and N rows containing values of all instances from T.

Usually, instance reduction algorithms are based on a distance calculation between instances in the training set. In such case selected instances, which are situated close to the centre of clusters of similar instances, serve as the reference instances. The approach requires using some clustering algorithms. Other approaches, known as similarity-based methods, remove an instance if it has the same output class as its k nearest neighbors assuming that all neighbourhood instances will be, after all, correctly classified. The third group of methods tries to eliminate training examples basing on some removal criteria that need to be fulfilled [3], [18]. Instances reduction problem, often referred to as the prototype selection problem, can be also solved by heuristics or random search [1], [2], [15].

In [3] the instances reduction is achieved based on calculating, for each instance from the original set, the value of its similarity coefficient, and then grouping instances into clusters consisting of instances with identical values of this coefficient, selecting the representation of instances for each cluster and removing the remaining instances. Finally, the selected reference vectors produce the reduced training set. In [3] it was shown that such an approach can result in reducing the number of instances and still preserving a quality of the data mining results. It was also demonstrated that in some cases reducing the training set size can increase efficiency of the supervised learning.

The data reduction approach, proposed in this paper, uses the above technique to identify clusters instances, with identical values of similarity coefficient, from which the references vectors are next selected by the agent-based population learning algorithm. The grouping of instances is based on the following steps:

Step 1. Transform X normalizing value of each x_{ij} into interval $[0, 1]$ and then rounding it to the nearest integer, that is 0 or 1.

Step 2. Calculate for each instance from the original training set the value of its similarity coefficient I_i:

$$I_i = \sum_{j=1}^{n+1} x_{ij} s_j, i = 1, \ldots, N, \tag{1}$$

where:

$$s_j = \sum_{i=1}^{N} x_{ij}, j = 1, \ldots, n+1. \tag{2}$$

Step 3. Map input vectors (i.e. rows from X) into t clusters denoted as Y_v, $v = 1, \ldots, t$. Each cluster contains input vectors with identical value of the similarity coefficient I and t is a number of different values of I.

In next step the reference vectors are selected based on the following rules:

- If $|Y_v| = 1$ then $S = S \cup Y_v$.
- If $|Y_v| > 1$ then $S = S \cup \{x_j^v\}$, where x_j^v are reference instances from the cluster Y_v. In this paper these reference vectors are selected by the agent-based population learning algorithm.

2.2 Feature Selection

Equally important, as the selection of reference instances, is the reduction of the number of features and the identification of irrelevant or redundant features. The problem of finding optimal subset of features is NP-hard [17]. Feature selection method based on enumeration and review of all subset of features leads directly to finding the best one. However this procedure is very time consuming and in majority of cases not feasible. The statistical methods evaluate independently each attribute. Other approaches attempt to evaluate and rank some subsets of features that were generated by heuristics, random or genetic search procedures. All feature selection methods that have been so far proposed, try to find the best subset of features satisfying certain criterion. This can be the classifier error rate, information entropy, dependence measure, consistency measure or distance measure. The discussion of the feature selection approaches can be found in [4], [13], [19].

3   Agent-Based Data Reduction

To overcome some of the difficulties posed by computational complexity of the data reduction problem it is proposed to apply the population-based approach with optimizing procedures implemented as an asynchronous team of agents (A-Team), originally introduced by Talukdar [16].

An A-Team is a collection of software agents that cooperate to solve a problem by dynamically evolving a population of solutions also called individuals. Each agent contains some problems solving skills and is representing an optimizing procedure. All the agents can work asynchronously and in parallel. During their works agents cooperate to construct or find a solution by selecting and modifying solutions, which are drawn from the shared common memory and store them back after attempted improvement. Generally, A-Team is based on a common memory containing the population of temporary solutions to the problem to be solved. In our case the shared memory is used to store a population of solutions to the data reduction problem.

In this paper an approach to data reduction, based on a dedicated team of agents and denoted as *IFS* (*Instance and Feature Selection*), is proposed and validated. The *IFS* functionality is realized by two main types of agents. The first one - *optimizing agents*, are implementation of the improvement algorithms, which aim at improving the current solution. Each *optimizing agent* represents a single improvement algorithm. The second one, called as *solution manager*, is responsible for managing of the common memory and maintenance and updating of individuals in the common memory. The *optimizing agents* cooperate to find the better solution with the *solution manager* and work in parallel. Each *optimization agent* sends a request to the *solution manager* who replies by sending a single individual from the shared memory i.e. that in proposed approach each *optimizing agent* operates on a single individual (solution). The solutions forwarded to *optimizing agents* for improvement are randomly drowned by the *solution manager*.

Each *optimizing agent* tries to improve quality of the solution provided by the *solution manager*. After the stopping criterion has been met the resulting individual is sent back to *solution manager*, which, in turn, updates common memory by replacing the randomly selected worse individual with the improved one.

The *solution manager* role is to manage the population of solutions, which at the initial phase is generated randomly and stored in the shared memory. After the initial population of solutions has been generated the *solution manager* runs the procedure producing clusters of potential reference instances using the algorithm described in Section 2.1.

Also to assure the required diversity the initial population of solutions is drawn in such a way that random individuals represent different numbers of reference instances in each cluster and different numbers of features. Finally, the population contains individuals representing solutions of the data reduction problem. Each individual consists of:

- The list of numbers of selected reference instances. The list, on the first t positions, defines how many elements from Y_v are contained in the cluster v, the next positions represent input vector number from Y_v.
- The list of numbers of selected features.
- The values of the quality factors including: the classification accuracy of the solution, the percentage of compression of the training set and the number of rules. To obtain value of these parameters the C 4.5 [12] classification tool is used. For each decision tree produced by the C 4.5 the size of the respective tree is calculated and recorded.

To solve the data reduction problem four types of optimizing agents representing different improvement procedures have been implemented.

The first procedure - local search with tabu list modifies the current solution by removing the randomly selected reference vector from the randomly chosen cluster and replacing it with some other randomly chosen reference vector thus far not included within the improved solution. The modification takes place providing the vector to be replaced is not on the tabu list. After the modification the newly added reference vector is placed on the tabu list and remains there for a given number of iterations. This number depends on the cluster size and decreases for smaller clusters.

The second procedure - local search, modifies the current solution either by removing the randomly selected reference vector from the randomly chosen cluster and by adding some other randomly chosen reference vector thus far not included within the improved solution.

The third procedure improves a solution by changing, randomly, numbers on the feature list. The algorithm runs similarity the first procedure except that the procedure modifies the current solution by removing the random selected feature number and replacing it with some other randomly chosen feature number thus for not included within the improved solution. The modification takes place providing the feature to be replaced is not on the tabu list and after the modification the newly added feature is placed on the tabu list.

The fourth procedure modifies a solution by changing values on both lists - of reference vectors and features. Direction of change is random and has identical probability. When the list of reference vector is modified, then the randomly selected reference vector from the randomly chosen cluster is removed and other randomly chosen reference vector thus far not included within the improved solution is added. In case of changing the feature lists the procedure modifies the current solution by removing the random selected feature number and replacing it with some other randomly chosen feature number thus for not included within the improved solution, or by adding to the current solution a new feature number which is not represented within the improved individual. Adding and removing a feature number is a random move executed with equal probabilities.

In each of the above cases the modified solution replaces the current one if it is evaluated as a better one using the classification accuracy. If, during the search, an agent successfully improves the received solution then it stops and the improved solution is sent back to the *solution manager*. Otherwise, agents stop searching for an improvement after having completed the prescribed number of iterations.

From technical point of view the *IFS* was implemented using JADE-Based A-Team (JABAT) environment. JABAT, based on JAVA code, is a middleware supporting the construction of the dedicated A-Team architecture than can be used for solving a variety of computationally hard optimization problems. More details concerning the JABAT is included in [8].

4   Computational Experiment Results

To validate the proposed approach several benchmark classification problems have been solved. Datasets for each problem have been obtained from [11]. They include: Cleveland heart disease (303 instances, 13 attributes, 2 classes), credit approval (690, 15, 2), Wisconsin breast cancer (699, 9, 2), sonar problem (208, 60, 2) and adult (30162, 14, 2).

Experiment plan has been based on the 10-cross-validation approach. For each run the respective training set T has been then reduced to a subset S containing reference vectors with relevant features only. Each reference vectors set has been, in turn, used to produce a decision tree. This has been evaluated from the point of view of the classification accuracy. Each decision tree has been created using only the instances in S and each C 4.5 classifier has been trained without pruned leaves and with pruned leaves. In case of the sonar problem the experiment has been carried out using the available training and test sets. Training set has been reduced as in all remaining cases.

For each benchmarking problem the experiment has been repeated 30 times and the reported values of the quality measures have been averaged over all runs. All optimization agents have been allowed to continue iterating until 100 iterations have been performed. The common memory size was set to 100 individuals. The number of iterations and the size of common memory have been set out experimentally at the fine-tuning phase.

Experiment results are shown in Table 1. The results have been averaged over all experiment runs carried. Table 1 show accuracy of classification performed on the test set by the trained C 4.5 classifier without pruned leaves and with pruned leaves. Additionally, Table 1 includes the average number of rules and the average size of the resulting tree. The results in Table 1 are presented for following cases:

A - Classification accuracy (percentage of rightly classified instances) - all instances from the original dataset with all features.
B - Classification accuracy - all instances from the original dataset with the reduced number of features produced by the *wrapper* technique [4], [9], where subsets of features are evaluated using the C 4.5 algorithm.
C - Classification accuracy - reference vectors with all features. Reference vectors have been selected using the approach described in Section 2.1
D - Classification accuracy - as in C with the *wrapper*-based selection of features.
E - Classification accuracy - reference vectors and feature selection as proposed in Section 3.

Table 1. Average classification accuracy (%), average number of rules and average size of the decision tree

	pruned leaves					unpruned leaves				
Problem	A	B	C	D	E	A	B	C	D	E
	Average accuracy (%)									
credit	84.9	77.2	90.7	81.3	92.6	83.2	74.8	90.4	76.7	90.9
cancer	94.6	94.4	97.4	95.0	98.1	95.0	94.4	98.4	86.5	97.9
heart	77.9	79.9	91.2	81.7	93.0	76.9	79.5	92.4	81.3	92.2
sonar	74.0	72.1	83.7	78.4	87.5	74.0	71.2	83.7	76.4	88.8
adult	83.2	80.1	83.9	83.3	86.1	81.4	82.4	83.5	82.4	85.3
average	82.43	80.74	89.05	83.94	91.46	82.1	81.70	89.50	81.40	91.05
	Average number of rules									
credit	12.0	36.0	16.4	15.5	10.5	54.0	75.0	24.5	15.4	13.9
cancer	15.0	8.0	8.2	2.3	6.5	20.0	19.0	12.8	2.7	7.7
heart	17.0	11.0	17.6	8.7	11.5	44.0	26.0	23.8	8.4	14.3
sonar	8.0	10.0	9.0	16.0	11.0	8.0	12.0	10.0	14.0	11.4
adult	215.3	225	37.2	45.5	23.4	274	197.2	34.6	52.4	27.4
	Average size of the tree									
credit	23.0	71.0	31.8	30.0	20.0	107.0	149.0	48.0	29.8	26.8
cancer	29.0	15.0	15.4	3.6	12.0	39.0	37.0	24.6	4.4	14.3
heart	33.0	21.0	34.3	16.4	22.0	87.0	35.0	46.6	15.8	27.6
sonar	15.0	20.0	17.0	19.0	21.0	15.0	25.0	19.0	17.0	21.8
adult	1432	654	87.6	40.5	28.4	1765	721	94.2	68.2	32.1

What is even more important the proposed agent-based data reduction technique is very competitive with respect to classification accuracy in comparison with other classifiers and other approaches to data reduction. This is shown in Table 2 where the results obtained in the described above computational experiment are compared with the classification and data reduction techniques reported in the literature. The column $|S|/|T|$ in Table 2 shows what percentage of the original training set has been retained by the respective reduction algorithm.

Table 2. Performance comparison of different classifiers and instance reduction algorithms

Approach	cancer		heart		credit		sonar	
	Accur.	$\|S\|/\|T\|$	Accur.	$\|S\|/\|T\|$	Accur.	$\|S\|/\|T\|$	Accur.	$\|S\|/\|T\|$
IFS	98.1%	20%	93.0%	60%	92.6%	30%	88.8%	90%
K-NN [18]	96.28%	100%	81.19%	100%	84.78%	100%	58.8% [14]	100%
CNN [18]	95.71%	7.09%	73.95%	30.84%	77.68%	24.22%	74.12%	32.85%
SNN [18]	93.85%	8.35%	76.25%	33.88%	81.31%	28.38%	79.81%	28.26%
IB2 [18]	95.71%	7.09%	73.96%	30.29%	78.26%	24.15%	80.88%	33.87%
IB3 [18]	96.57%	3.47%	81.16%	11.11%	85.22%	4.78%	69.38%	12.02%
DROP3 [18]	96.14%	3.58%	80.84%	12.76%	83.91%	5.96%	78%	26.87%
RMHC [15]	70.9%	7%	82.3%	3%	-	-	-	-
GA-KJ [14]	95.5%	33.4%	74.7%	33.1%	-	-	55.3%	52.6%
1NN+RELIEF [13]	72.12%	100%	77.85%	100%	79.57%	100%	-	-
IB3+RELIEF [13]	73.25%	100%	79.94%	100%	71.75%	100%	-	-
ID3+FSS [9]	94.53%	100%	-	-	-	-	-	-
ID3 [5]	94.3%	100%	-	-	-	-	-	-
C 4.5+BFS [5]	95.28%	100%	-	-	-	-	-	-
C 4.5 [7]	94,7%	100%	77.8%	100%	85.5%	100%	76.9%	100%

It can be observed that the proposed approach guarantees good classification results together with quite a satisfactory reduction of the original dataset. In case of all of the considered problems data reduction have increased the classification accuracy as compared with accuracy obtained by training the C 4.5 classifier using the original dataset. Gains in classification accuracy seem to be quite substantial. On average, classifiers based on original training sets produce average classification accuracy of 82.43% and 82.1%, for pruned and unpruned leaves, respectively, while the proposed approach to instance and feature reduction assures accuracy of 91.46% and 91.05%. In case of the *sonar* problem, considered to be a difficult one, the improvement is even more spectacular (from the average accuracy of 74% to the accuracy of 88.8%). The classification accuracy improvement can be also observed for *adult* problem (for which the reported accuracy on UCI is 84.25% [11]). In this case the C 4.5 classifier, based on the reduced training set, produces average classification accuracy 86.1% and 85.3%, for pruned and unpruned leaves, respectively. The experiment results show also that the proposed approach to feature reduction results in better classification accuracy as compared to accuracy obtained through applying the wrapper technique.

On the other hand, the experiment results show that the data reduction can result in a decreased complexity and size of the decision tree as compared with the decision tree created using the full dataset. It can be concluded that the proposed approach to data reduction results in a decreasing complexity of knowledge representation as well as in a reduction of computation time required. This remains true not only for decision trees but also for other machine learning techniques.

5   Conclusion

Main contribution of the paper is proposing and validating an agent-based approach for data reduction. Effective and dependable data reduction procedures are of vital importance to machine learning and data mining. Computational experiment results support authors' claim that reducing training set size still preserves basic features of the analyzed data. Agent-based approach to data reduction allows taking advantage of synergetic effect of cooperation between different agent types.

The proposed technique extends the range of available instance reduction algorithms. Moreover, it is shown that the proposed algorithm can be, for some problems, competitive in comparison with other existing techniques. Properties of the proposed algorithm should be further studied. The proposed approach should be further validated using different classifiers and, possibly, new improvement schemes.

References

1. Aarts, E.H.L., Korst, J.: Simulated Annealing and Boltzmann Machines. John Wiley, Chichester (1989)
2. Cano, J.R., Herrera, F., Lozano, M.: On the Combination of Evolutionary Algorithms and Stratified Strategies for Training Set Selection in Data Mining. Pattern Recognition Letters. Elsevier, Amsterdam (in press, 2004)
3. Czarnowski, I., Jędrzejowicz, P.: An Approach to Instance Reduction in Supervised Learning. In: Coenen, F., Preece, A., Macintosh, A. (eds.) Research and Development in Intelligent Systems, vol. XX, pp. 267–282. Springer, London (2004)
4. Dash, M., Liu, H.: Feature Selection for Classification. Intelligence Data Analysis 1(3), 131–156 (1997)
5. Duch, W.: Results - Comparison of Classification. Nicolaus Copernicus University (2002), http://www.is.umk.pl/projects/datasets.html
6. Glover, F.: Tabu search. Part I and II. ORSA Journal of Computing 1(3), Summer (1990) and 2(1) Winter (1990)
7. Ishibuchi, H., Nakashima, T., Nii, M.: Learning of Neural Networks with GA-based Instance Selection. In: IFSA World Congress and 20th NAFIPS International Conference, vol. 4, pp. 2102–2107 (2001)
8. Barbucha, D., Czarnowski, I., Jędrzejowicz, P., Ratajczak-Ropel, E., Wierzbowska, I.: JADE-Based A-Team as a Tool for Implementing Population-Based Algorithms. In: Chen, Y., Abraham, A. (eds.) Proceedings of the Sixth International Conference on Intelligent Systems Design and Applications (ISDA 2006), vol. 3, pp. 144–149. IEEE Computer Society, Los Alamitos (2006)
9. Kohavi, R., John, G.H.: Wrappers for Feature Subset Selection. Artificial Intelligence 97(1-2), 273–324 (1997)

10. Meiri, R., Zahavi, J.: Using Simulated Annealing to Optimize the Feature Selection Problem in Marketing Applications. European Journal of Operational Research 17(3), 842–858 (2006)
11. Merz, C.J., Murphy, M.: UCI Repository of Machine Learning Databases. University of California, Department of Information and Computer Science, Irvine, CA (1998), http://www.ics.uci.edu/mlearn/MLRepository.html
12. Quinlan, J.R.: C4.5: Programs for Machine Learning. Morgan Kaufmann, SanMateo
13. Raman, B., Ioerger, T.R.: Enhancing learning using feature and example selection. Journal of Machine Learning Research (in press, 2003)
14. Rozsypal, A., Kubat, M.: Selecting Representative Examples and Attributes by a Genetic Algorithm. Intelligent Data Analysis 7(4), 291–304 (2003)
15. Skalak, D.B.: Prototype and Feature Selection by Sampling and Random Mutation Hill Climbing Algorithm. In: International Conference on Machine Learning, pp. 293–301 (1994)
16. Talukdar, S., Baerentzen, L., Gove, A., de Souza, P.: Asynchronous Teams: Cooperation Schemes for Autonomous. Computer-Based Agents. Technical Report EDRC 18-59-96, Carnegie Mellon University, Pittsburgh (1996)
17. Wroblewski, J.: Adaptacyjne metody klasyfikacji obiektów. PhD thesis, University of Warsaw, Warsaw (in Polish, 2001)
18. Wilson, D.R., Martinez, T.R.: Reduction Techniques for Instance-based Learning Algorithm. Machine Learning 33-3, 257–286 (2000)
19. Zongker, D., Jain, A.: Algorithm for Feature Selection: An Evaluation. In: International Conference on Pattern Recognition, ICPR 1996, pp. 18–22 (1996)

A New Word Clustering Method for Building N-Gram Language Models in Continuous Speech Recognition Systems

Mohammad Bahrani, Hossein Sameti, Nazila Hafezi, and Saeedeh Momtazi

Speech Processing Lab, Computer Engineering Department,
Sharif University of Technology, Tehran, Iran
{bahrani, sameti, hafezi, momtazi}@ce.sharif.edu

Abstract. In this paper a new method for automatic word clustering is presented. We used this method for building n-gram language models for Persian continuous speech recognition (CSR) systems. In this method, each word is specified by a feature vector that represents the statistics of parts of speech (POS) of that word. The feature vectors are clustered by k-means algorithm. Using this method causes a reduction in time complexity which is a defect in other automatic clustering methods. Also, the problem of high perplexity in manual clustering methods is abated. The experimental results are based on "Persian Text Corpus" which contains about 9 million words. The extracted language models are evaluated by the perplexity criterion and the results show that a considerable reduction in perplexity has been achieved. Also reduction in word error rate of CSR system is about 16% compared with a manual clustering method.

Keywords: Class n-gram Models, Continuous Speech Recognition, Part Of Speech, Persian Text Corpus, Word Clustering.

1 Introduction

One of the most efficient methods for improving the accuracy of continuous speech recognition system is using language information (statistical, grammatical, etc). There are many methods for incorporating language models in speech recognition. The main method is incorporating statistical language models that appear as n-gram models [1], [2].

In n-gram language models we assume that the probability of occurrence of one word in a text depends on just n-1 previous words [3]. In every language, for extracting this kind of language models, a large amount of data is required. The more amounts of data, the more correct estimations of n-gram models.

Unfortunately, collecting data and providing a suitable text corpus for the Persian language is in its primary stages and the amount of data is not enough. Therefore extracted n-gram models will be too sparse.

One of the ways for solving this problem is using word clustering methods [2]. It means that we can use the statistics between clusters of words instead of the statistics

N.T. Nguyen et al. (Eds.): IEA/AIE 2008, LNAI 5027, pp. 286–293, 2008.

between words, when the word-based n-gram models are not accurate enough. The n-gram language models that are constructed with these methods are called "class-based n-gram models".

For example, consider this sentence: "He woke up Sunday morning at 7 a.m.". For computing the bigram statistics between the words of the sentence, we should use the statistics between "Sunday" and "morning" but you see that there is little difference between (Sunday, morning), (Monday, morning) or (Sunday, night), etc. because the functions of these words are similar in language.

The idea of word clustering comes from here. We can assign similar words in one unique class and use the statistics between classes instead of words. For achieving this goal and clustering words, the simplest method is clustering them according to their part of speech (POS) tags [4]. This means that the words with similar POS tags (nouns, adjectives, verbs, prepositions, etc) can be assigned in a particular class.

Beside this manual word clustering method, there are other methods which cluster the words automatically [5], [6]. In most of them, the clustering process is based on the perplexity criterion.

In this research, a new method has been used for automatic word clustering in order to build a suitable language model. This method is a concatenation of two different methods: the automatic word clustering and the manual (POS-based) word clustering.

The text corpus that we used for building the language models is "Persian Text Corpus" [13]. This corpus and its features are introduced in the next section. Section 3 deals with the different methods of word clustering. Our new method and its advantages are discussed in section 4. The experimental results go on in fifth section. Finally, in section 6, concluding remarks are made.

2   Persian Text Corpus

In this research, we have used the first edition of "Persian Text Corpus", the only available text corpus in Persian.

"Persian Text Corpus" contains of various types of Persian texts, including about 9 million words annotated with POS tags. The texts of this Corpus are gathered from various data sources (like newspapers, magazines, journals, books, letters, handwritten texts, scenarios, news and etc.). The whole set of this data is a complete set of Persian contemporary texts. The texts are about different subjects like politics, art, culture, economics, sport, stories and etc.

All files of "Persian Text Corpus" are in text (.txt) format. For every ".txt" file, there is a file in ".lbl" format which contains the words of ".txt" file plus a tag per word. These tags which include one or more characters, show the syntactic category (POS) and -if it is necessary- the syntactic or semantic subcategories of words.

Generally, 882 POS tags have been used in "Persian Text Corpus". Not only is this number of POS tags very large, but also some of them are so detailed and some of them are rarely used. Therefore after revising the POS tags and extracting the statistics of each tag, we have classified them into 164 classes -based on the syntactic similarity between them- and assigned a general tag for each new class. By this mean the number of POS tags is reduced and infrequent tags are assigned to more general classes.

For those tags which were infrequent and were not included in any defined class, we have assigned a new tag, named "IGNORE".

For the end of a sentence which is the start of the next sentence, another tag is assigned named "NULL". In processing the sentences of corpus, where there was one of the end of a sentence symbols ('.', '?', '!' and ':') we supposed that there is a NULL tag there. After considering all above conditions, the size of tag set was reduced to 166 POS tags and we have replaced the detailed POS tags with the new general ones.

3   Class-Based N-Gram Models

As we discussed in the introduction, because of the lack of data in text corpus, we have to use the "class-based n-gram models". In these models the n-gram probability of word w_n given word sequence $w_1w_2...w_{n-1}$ that are assigned to classes $c_1c_2...c_n$ is calculated as follows [2]:

$$P(w_n \mid w_1w_2 \cdots w_{n-1}) = P(c_n \mid c_1c_2 \cdots c_{n-1}).P(w_n \mid c_n) \tag{1}$$

For clustering words and determining the cluster of each word, there are two different forms. The first form is automatic clustering and the second one is manual clustering. In ordinary automatic word clustering, the goal is to optimize the perplexity or the average mutual information between classes. Brown's [5] and Martin's [6] algorithms are the most famous automatic word clustering algorithms. But the time complexity of them is very high and especially when the vocabulary size or the number of clusters is large, these types of word clustering algorithm are costly.

In other methods, each word is represented as a feature vector and the clustering procedure is accomplished based on the similarity between those vectors. Korkmaz algorithm [7] is the most prevalent algorithm that uses words feature vector. This algorithm uses the bigram probabilities of each word as its feature vector.

The manual word clustering methods are usually based on the POS or semantic categories of words. POS-based n-gram models can be extracted from text corpora which have POS tags for words [4], [12].

Because every word can have different POSs in different sentences, each word can be assigned to more than one class by this method. This defect leads to high perplexity of language in comparison with automatic methods. Table 1 shows a comparison between automatic and manual techniques:

Table 1. The comparison between automatic and manual clustering

	Automatic Clustering	Manual Clustering
Time Complexity	Very High	Very Low
Perplexity	Low	High
Number of Clusters for each Word	Only One Cluster	More than One Cluster

Considering the above table, you see that there are some problems in using each of these methods. In automatic word clustering algorithms that optimize the perplexity, the time complexity is very high. Also in the POS-based manual word clustering algorithm the perplexity of language is high and one word may be assigned to more than one class.

To tackle these problems successfully, according to this comparison, a new idea has been proposed. We decided to merge these two methods and reached a new method for word clustering which obeys the disciplines of automatic word clustering and has the concept of manual word clustering. According to the results, the new method leads to highlighting the advantages and abates the problems of both previous methods.

4 A New Word Clustering Method

As we discussed in previous sections, in Persian language, every single word can get different POS tags in different contexts based on its syntactic function and its meaning. The POS tags statistics for each word have been extracted from "Persian Text Corpus" through the following steps:

Step 1. The varieties of words and the frequency of occurrence of them in "Persian Text Corpus" were extracted.
Step 2. The 20000 most frequent words were defined as the "vocabulary" of system; the other words were considered as "out of vocabulary".
Step 3. The number of occurrence of each POS tag for each word of vocabulary was extracted. As we decreased the number of POS tags to 166, the result of this step is saved in a 20000*166 matrix which we called "POS Matrix".

For example, the word "zib/" (زیب) in "Persian Text Corpus" has three different POS tags according to the text which it has been used in. It appears as non-quantitative simple adverb (ADV_NQ_SIM) 9 times, singular private noun (N_SING_PR) 7 times and simple adjective (ADJ_SIM) 420 times. The statistics of other POS tags for this word are zero. Therefore the row of POS matrix for "zib/" has three non-zero elements (9, 7 and 420) and has zero values in all other elements.

As another example, we discuss about the word (مرد). As in Persian language we use Arabic script, short vowels are not written and capitalization is not used. So the word (مرد) has several POS tags, based on its pronunciation and meaning. In "Persian Text Corpus", it appears as common single noun (N_SING_COM) 1201 times and as simple adjective (ADJ_SIM) 32 times when it is pronounced as "mard" (man) and it appears as verb with simple past tense (V_PA_SIM) 47 times when it is pronounced as "mord" (died). It is necessary to mention that because separating the statistics of Persian homograph words is very difficult, it was not considered in this research.

We want to use the fact that every word can appear with different POS tags, for word classification. Let us suppose that each row of POS matrix is the feature vector of related word. These vectors are used for word clustering. The reason that we use these vectors for word clustering is obvious, based on the above examples. Clearly, two words that have the same POS tags distribution have similar feature vectors and both of them should be assigned to one class. For example, all verbs with simple past tense are classified in one class and all singular common nouns are assigned in another one.

In this research, we use k-means clustering algorithm for clustering the words. At the first step, primary clusters of words are made and the centroid of each cluster is computed. Then we continue the clustering process with k-means algorithm. It means that we compute the distances between each vector and the centriods of all clusters. Then the centroid that has minimum distance to the vector is updated according below [14]:

$$\mathbf{c}^{(t+1)} = \mathbf{c}^{(t)} + \varepsilon(t)(\mathbf{w} - \mathbf{c}^{(t)})$$

(2)

Where $\mathbf{c}^t$ is the nearest centroid with word vector $\mathbf{w}$ at iteration t and $\varepsilon(t)$ is a non-increasing function of t.

The process of computing the distances between each vector and the centroids and updating the centroids will be continued until no change appears in the results of two consequential iterations or until a given number of iterations is fulfilled.

The cosine distance (equation 3) is used for computing the distances between the word vectors $\mathbf{w}$ and $\mathbf{v}$:

$$d(\mathbf{w}, \mathbf{v}) = \cos^{-1} \frac{\mathbf{w} \cdot \mathbf{v}}{|\mathbf{w}||\mathbf{v}|}$$

(3)

In k-means algorithm the number of clusters should be predefined. We assumed different numbers of clusters for implementing our new clustering method.

The most important advantages of this algorithm in comparison with other automatic word clustering algorithms (like Martin's and Brown's algorithms) are its low time complexity and using POS tags for assigning each word to a cluster. Table 2 shows a comparison between time complexities of our clustering algorithm, the Brown's algorithm [5] and the Martin's algorithm [6]. In this table N, V, C and d represent corpus size, vocabulary size, number of classes, and dimension of feature vectors respectively.

Table 2. A comparison between time complexities of our clustering method, Brown's algorithm and Martin's

Our method	$O(VCd)$
Brown's algorithm	$O(V^3)$
Martin's algorithm	$O(N+VC^2)$

Also, with this method each word appears in just one cluster. In other techniques that use the feature vector for each word (like Korkmaz algorithm), the bigram statistics of each word are used as the feature vector. In these techniques if the size of vocabulary is large, the dimension of feature vectors become too large and it makes the clustering procedure very complicated, while in our word clustering method the dimension of feature vectors are small and independent of the size of vocabulary.

After the clustering process, we have built n-gram language models for word classes instead of words. The training set for clustering words is about 380000 sentences of "Persian Text Corpus" which is about 8 million words. We have built only the class bigram and class trigram language models in this research, because of the small size of our corpus.

Suppose that we partition a vocabulary of V words into C classes. Then the class bigram model has $C(C-1)$ independent parameters of the form $P(C_n|C_{n-1})$, $C-1$ parameters of the form $P(C_n)$, V parameters of the form $P(w_n)$, plus V parameters for determining the class of each word. Beside the class bigram model parameters, the class trigram model also has $C^2(C-1)$ independent parameters of the form $P(C_n|C_{n-1}C_{n-2})$.

5 Experimental Results

The class language models extracted from our word clustering method are tested for evaluating two different criteria: perplexity and word error rate of a CSR system. We computed the perplexity based on class bigram and class trigram models on a test set of the last 43800 sentences (about 1 million words) of "Persian Text Corpus" not included in training data. The perplexity can be computed by equation (4) as follows:

$$PP = \hat{P}(w_1 w_2 w_3 \cdots w_m)^{-1/m} \tag{4}$$

In this equation m is the number of words in test set and $w_1 w_2 w_3 \cdots w_m$ show the words sequence of test set. $\hat{P}(w_1 w_2 w_3 \cdots w_m)$ can be computed by equations (5) and (6) for the bigram and trigram models respectively.

$$PP_{bi} = \left(\prod_{i=1}^{m} \hat{P}(w_i \mid w_{i-1}) \right)^{-1/m} \tag{5}$$

$$PP_{tri} = \left(\prod_{i=1}^{m} \hat{P}(w_i \mid w_{i-1} w_{i-2}) \right)^{-1/m} \tag{6}$$

In these equations, $\hat{P}(w_i \mid w_{i-1})$ and $\hat{P}(w_i \mid w_{i-1} w_{i-2})$ are computed by equation (1).

Table 3 shows the perplexity of "Persian Text Corpus" based on class bigram and class trigram models with different number of classes.

Table 3. The perplexity of "Persian Text Corpus" based on class bigram and class trigram models with different number of classes

Language Model	Num. of Classes	Perplexity
Class Bigram	100	739
	200	699
	300	652
	500	683
Class Trigram	100	681
	200	644
	300	589
	500	651
POS-based Bigram	166	990
Martin's Algorithm (Bigram)	200	502

For comparing the new clustering method with manual POS-based one and Martin's algorithm, the last two rows of table 3 show the perplexity using manual method and Martin's algorithm. According to this table, there is an obvious reduction in perplexity using our suggested clustering method compared with manual method.

To evaluate our statistical language models in CSR system, we used SHARIF speech recognition system [9], which is a Persian speaker independent continuous speech recognition system. This system performs modeling of monophones using Hidden Markov Model (HMM) and utilizes the word search algorithm described in [10] for word recognition. In this algorithm, while recognizing the phonemes, the lexicon tree is also searched in order to find the best word sequence according to the phoneme sequence.

To run experiments, the HMMs were trained for each 30 phonemes of Persian language using 5940 sentences (about 5 hours of read speech) of FARSDAT speech database [11]. We performed the experiments on 140 sentences of FARSDAT database which don't overlap with the training data.

In general, in speech recognition systems, the language model score can be combined with acoustic model score through two methods: "during search" and "at the end of search" [8]. In this paper we have used "during search" method. In "during search" method when the search process recognizes a new word within expanding the different hypothesis, the new hypothesis score is computed via multiplication of following three terms: the n-gram score of new word, the acoustic model score of new word and current hypothesis score.

Table 4 presents the word error rates (WER) obtained when incorporating different class n-gram models in the CSR system. The last two rows show the results using POS-based method and Martin's algorithm. The results show that about 16% reduction in word error rates has been achieved compared with POS-based manual method.

Table 4. The word error rate obtained by incorporating different class n-gram models in CSR system

Language Model	Num. of Classes	WER [%]
Class Bigram	100	24.45
	200	24.33
	300	24.02
	500	24.35
Class Trigram	100	23.87
	200	23.40
	300	22.98
	500	23.32
POS-based Bigram	166	27.36
Martin's Algorithm (Bigram)	200	23.90

6   Concluding Remarks

In this paper we presented a new automatic word clustering technique based on POS tags. The class n-gram language models have been extracted from the clustering results and evaluated in our continuous speech recognition system. The time complexity of this method is lower than other automatic methods and it is easy to implement. The perplexity of language and word error rate of CSR system reduced considerably.

References

1. Huang, X., Alleva, F., Hon, H., Hwang, M., Lee, K., Rosenfield, R.: The SPHINX-II Speech Recognition System: An Overview. Computer Speech and Langauge 2, 137–148 (1993)
2. Young, S.J., Jansen, J., Odell, J.J., Ollason, D., Woodland, P.C.: The HTK Hidden Markov Model Toolkit Book (1995)
3. Rabiner, L., Juang, B.H.: Fundamentals of Speech Recognition. Prentice Hall, New Jersey (1993)
4. Heeman, P.A.: POS tagging versus Classes in Language Modeling, Proc. 6th Workshop on Very Large Corpora, August 1998, pp. 179–187 (1998)
5. Brown, P., Della Pietra, V., de Souza, P., Lai, J., Mercer, R.L.: Class-based n-gram models of natural language. Computational Linguistics 18(4), 467–479 (1992)
6. Martin, S., Liermann, J., Ney, H.: Algorithms for bigram and trigram word clustering. Speech Communication 24, 19–37 (1998)
7. Korkmaz, E.E., Ucoluk, G.: A Method for Improving Automatic Word Categorization, Workshop on Computational Natural Language Learning, Madrid, Spain, pp. 43–49 (1997)
8. Harper, M.P., Jamieson, L.H., Mitchell, C.D., Ying, G.: Integrating Language Models with Speech Recognition. In: AAAI-94 Workshop on the Integration of Natural Language and Speech Processing, August 1994, pp. 139–146 (1994)
9. Babaali, B., Sameti, H.: The Sharif Speaker-Independent Large Vocabulary Speech Recognition System. In: The 2nd Workshop on Information Technology & Its Disciplines, Kish Island, Iran, February 24-26 (2004)
10. Ney, H., Haeb-Umbach, R., Tran, B.H., Oerder, M.: Improvements in Beam Search for 10000-Word Continuous Speech Recognition, IEEE Int. In· Conf. on Acoustics, Speech and Signal Processing, pp. 13–16 (1992)
11. Bijankhan, M.: FARSDAT-The Speech Database of Farsi Spoken Language. In: Proc. The 5th Australian Int. Conf. on Speech Science and Tech., Perth, vol. 2 (1994)
12. Bahrani, M., Samet, H., Hafezi, N., Movasagh, H.: Building and Incorporating Language Models for Persian Continuous Speech Recognition Systems. In: Proc. 5th international conference on Language Resources and Evaluation, Genoa, Italy, pp. 101–104 (2006)
13. BijanKhan, M.: Persian Text Corpus, Technical report, Research Center of Intelligent Signal Processing (2004)
14. Fritzke, B.: Some competitive learning methods, System Biophysics Institute for Neural Computation Ruhr-Universität Bochum (1997),
`ftp://ftp.neuroinformatik.ruhr-unibochum.de/pub/software/NN/DemoGNG/sclm.ps.gz`

Integrating Topic Estimation and Dialogue History for Domain Selection in Multi-domain Spoken Dialogue Systems

Satoshi Ikeda, Kazunori Komatani, Tetsuya Ogata, and Hiroshi G. Okuno

Graduate School of Informatics, Kyoto University, Kyoto, Japan
{sikeda, komatani, ogata, okuno}@kuis.kyoto-u.ac.jp

Abstract. We present a method of robust domain selection against out-of-grammar (OOG) utterances in multi-domain spoken dialogue systems. These utterances cause language-understanding errors because of a limited set of grammar and vocabulary of the systems, and deteriorate the domain selection. This is critical for multi-domain spoken dialogue systems to determine a system's response. We first define a *topic* as a domain from which the user wants to retrieve information, and estimate it as the user's intention. This topic estimation is enabled by using a large amount of sentences collected from the Web and Latent Semantic Mapping (LSM). The results are reliable even for OOG utterances. We then integrated both the topic estimation results and the dialogue history to construct a robust domain classifier against OOG utterances. The idea of integration is based on the fact that the reliability of the dialogue history is often impeded by language-understanding errors caused by OOG utterances, from which using topic estimation obtains useful information. Experimental results using 2191 utterances showed that our integrated method reduced domain selection errors by 14.3%.

1 Introduction

More and more novices are using spoken dialogue systems through telephones. They often experience difficulties in using such systems because of automatic speech recognition (ASR) errors. These kinds of errors are often caused by *out-of-grammar utterances*, i.e., those containing expressions that systems cannot accept by their grammar and vocabulary for language-understanding.

This is an increasingly important issue for multi-domain spoken dialogue systems because they deal with various tasks. We define a *domain* as a sub-system in a multi-domain spoken dialogue system. **Domain selection**, i.e., determining which sub-system in the multi-domain systems should respond to a user's request, is essential for such systems. We previously presented a framework of the domain selection that uses dialogue history [1]. However, when the user's utterance is out-of-grammar, this method cannot be used to determine the unique domain that should respond to the utterance because it can obtain no useful information from such utterances.

N.T. Nguyen et al. (Eds.): IEA/AIE 2008, LNAI 5027, pp. 294–304, 2008.
© Springer-Verlag Berlin Heidelberg 2008

To solve this problem, we adopted the following two approaches:

1. Topic estimation using large amounts of texts collected from the Web and Latent Semantic Mapping (LSM) [2] (described in Section 3.1).
2. Integrating the topic estimation result and dialogue history (described in Section 3.2).

We defined a "topic" as a domain about which users want to find more information, and we estimated it as the user's intention. Using these results is a reliable way to select domains even for out-of-grammar utterances. The topic estimation and use of dialogue history have complementary information. The topic estimation uses only information obtained from a single utterance while dialogue history takes the context into consideration. On the other hand, dialogue history is often damaged by language-understanding errors caused by out-of-grammar utterances while topic estimation results are relatively reliable for such utterances. Therefore, integrating the topic estimation and the dialogue history should reduce the number of domain selection errors.

2 Managing Out-of-Grammar Utterances in Multi-domain Spoken Dialogue Systems

2.1 Architecture of Multi-domain Spoken Dialogue Systems

Multi-domain spoken dialogue systems deal with various tasks, such as searching for restaurants and retrieving bus information. They can deal with user's various requests by a single interface. A problem of this system was that a large amount of effort was required to develop it. To reduce the amount of effort needed, Lin *et al.* have proposed an architecture with domain extensibility [3], which enables system developers to design each domain independently. This architecture is composed of several domains and a central module that selects an appropriate domain (**domain selection**) to generate a response. Because a central module does not manage the dialogues and each domain does, domain selection is a process that is essential to keep the independence of each domain. Our multi-domain spoken dialogue system is based on this architecture, and, as shown in Figure 1, it has five domains.

2.2 Definition of Topics for Managing Out-of-Grammar Utterances

Out-of-grammar utterances cause language-understanding errors because of their limited set of grammar and vocabulary, and they also damage the domain selection. We define *in-domain utterances* as utterances that any of the domains in a multi-domain system accept, and *out-of-grammar utterances* as the utterances that none of the domains in the system do. Therefore, out-of-grammar utterances cannot be treated in either conventional frameworks [3,4] or our previous system [1].

To reduce the domain selection errors, we define the term *"topic"* for out-of-grammar utterances. A *topic* is defined as a domain from which users want

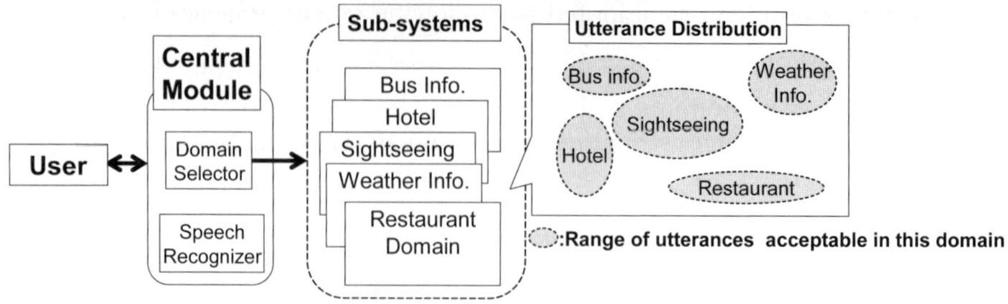

Fig. 1. Architecture for multi-domain spoken dialogue system

Fig. 2. Relation between domains and topics

to retrieve information, and we estimate it as the user's intention. The relation between domains and topics is shown in Figure 2.

Lane *et al.* developed a method for detecting utterances whose topics cannot be handled by the system [5]. They estimated topics and detected such utterances with Support Vector Machine or a linear discriminant analysis. However, their method lacks domain extensibility because they require dialogue corpora to be collected in advance, and this required a lot of effort. Our method does not disrupt domain extensibility because it automatically collects training data from the Web texts and does not need to collect dialogue corpora in advance.

2.3   Robust Domain Selection against Out-of-Grammar Utterances

We previously presented a domain classifier based on a 3-class categorization [1]: (i) the domain in which a previous response was made, (ii) the domain in which the ASR results with the highest score for language-understanding can be accepted, and (iii) other domains. Conventional methods [3,4] considered only the former two. However, when the user's utterance is out-of-grammar, the language-understanding errors mean that this method cannot determine the unique domain that should respond to the utterance. An example of such a situation is shown in Figure 3. Here, the utterance U2 relates to the restaurant domain, but ASR errors occurred because of the *out-of-vocabulary word*, which is not included in the vocabulary for language-understanding. As a result of the error, the domain with the highest score for language-understanding in U2 is the

U1: **Tell me the address of Holiday Inn.** (domain: hotel)
S1: The address of Holiday Inn is ...
U2: **I want Tamanohikari near there.** (domain: restaurant)
  *Tamanohikari (name of liquor) is an out-of-vocabulary word, and
  misrecognized as a spot of Tamba-bashi (name of place). (domain: sightseeing)*
S2 (by method [1]): I do not understand what you said. (domain: others)
S2 (by our method): I do not understand what you said. You can ask about
  several conditions such as location, price and food type about restaurants.
  For example, you can say "Tell me restaurants near the Gion area". (domain:
  restaurant)

Fig. 3. Example of dialogue including out-of-grammar utterances

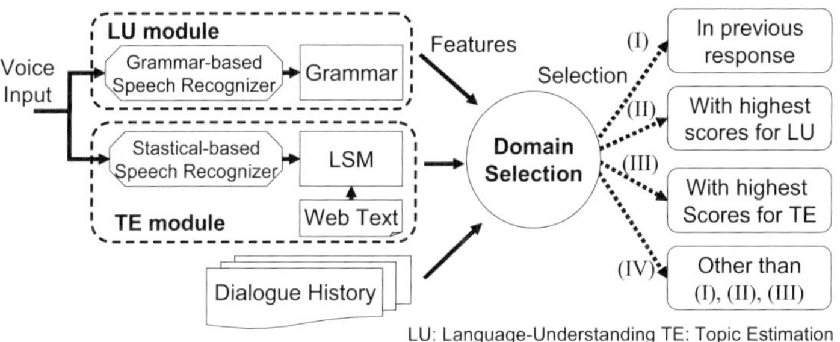

Fig. 4. Overview of domain selection

sightseeing domain. In this case, the domain that should ideally be selected is
neither the previous domain (hotel) nor the domain with the highest score for
language-understanding (sightseeing). The system can detect (iii) on the basis
of our previous method [1], but, as the concrete domain is not determined, it
cannot generate a concrete response, shown as S2 (by method [1]).

We integrated the topic estimation with the domain selection using the dialogue history presented in our previous paper [1]. The overview of our domain
selection is shown in Figure 4. In addition to our previous features about dialogue history and language-understanding results [1], we introduced features
obtained by topic estimation. These features improve the accuracy of the domain selection for out-of-grammar utterances. Then, we define domain selection
as the following 4-class categorization: the same (I) and (II) as (i) and (ii) of
the method [1], (III) the domain with the highest score for topic estimation, and
(IV) other domains. This 4-class categorization increases the number of utterances for which the system can select a uniquely correct domain, which enables
the system to generate a concrete response. This is shown as S2 (by our method)
in Figure 3: The system does not accept the language-understanding results for
U2 containing errors, and provides help messages based on the domain (in this
case, restaurant) derived from the topic estimation result.

3   Domain Selection Using Dialogue History and Topic Estimation

3.1   Topic Estimation with Domain Extensibility

We estimated topics by calculating the closeness between the user's utterance and the training data collected from the Web by using LSM [6]. The topic estimation module in Figure 4 shows a brief overview of the topic estimation process. Our system has five topics corresponding to each domain (restaurant, sightseeing, bus information, hotel, and weather information) and the command topic, which corresponds to the command utterances for the system such as "yes" and "undo". Estimating topic is a process that consists of the following two parts. More details were presented in our previous paper [6].

Collecting training data from the Web: We collected Web texts for each of the five topics except for the command topic by using a tool for developing language models [7]. First, we manually prepared about 10 keywords and several hundred sentences related to the topic. Then, the tool automatically retrieved 100,000 sentences related to the topic by using the keywords while filtering out irrelevant sentences based on the prepared sentences. We added 10,000 sentences, which were generated by each domain grammar, to this training data. For the command topic, we manually prepared 175 sentences as training data. We randomly divided the training data into d sets ($d = 20$) for each topic, and we made up the training documents.

Using LSM to remove the effect of noise from the training data: We used LSM [2] because the training data collected from the Web contain documents with other topics as noise. Latent Semantic Mapping is suitable for expressing the conceptual topic of a document. It removes the effect of noise from such data and allows for robust topic estimation. We first constructed the co-occurrence matrix, $M \times N$, between the words and the training documents, where M is the vocabulary size, and N is the total number of documents. We applied the singular value decomposition to the matrix and calculated the k-dimensional vectors of all the documents. The size of the co-occurrence matrix we constructed was $M = 67533$, $N = 120$, and $k = 50$.

The degree of closeness between a topic and a user's utterance is defined as the maximum cosine distance between the k-dimensional vector of an ASR result of a user's utterance and that of d training documents related to the topic. This ASR for topic estimation uses a statistical language model trained with the collected Web texts, unlike the grammar-based one used for the ASR for language-understanding. The resulting topic is the one with the highest score of closeness to a user's utterance.

3.2   Integrating Dialogue History and Topic Estimation

We define domain selection as the following 4-class categorization: (I) the previous domain, (II) the domain with highest score for language-understanding, (III)

Table 1. Features representing confidence in previous domain

P1: number of affirmatives after entering the domain
P2: number of negations after entering the domain
P3: whether tasks have been completed in the domain (whether to enter "requesting detailed information" in database search task)
P4: whether the domain appeared before
P5: number of changed slots after entering the domain
P6: number of turns after entering the domain
P7: ratio of changed slots ($= $ P5/P6)
P8: ratio of user's negative answers ($= $ P2/(P1 + P2))
P9: ratio of user's negative answers in the domain ($= $ P2/P6)
P10: states in tasks

Table 2. Features of ASR results

U1: acoustic score of the best candidate of ASR results for LU interpreted in (I)
U2: posteriori probability of N-best candidates of ASR results for LU interpreted in (I)
U3: average of words' confidence score for the best candidate in (I)
U4: acoustic score of the best candidate of ASR results for LU in (II)
U5: posteriori probability of N-best candidates of ASR results for LU interpreted in (II)
U6: average of words' confidence score for the best candidate of ASR results for LU in (II)
U7: difference of acoustic scores between candidates selected as (I) and (II) ($= $ U1-U4)
U8: ratio between posteriori probability of N-best candidates in (I) and that in (II) ($= $ U2/U5)
U9: ratio between averages of words' confidence scores for the best candidate in (I) and that in (II) ($= $ U3/U6)

LU: Language Understanding.

the domain with highest score for topic estimation, and (IV) other domains. We constructed a domain classifier using machine learning. Here, we describe the features used to construct it.

In addition to the information listed in Table 1, 2, and 3, which was used in our previous work [1], we adopted the features listed in Table 4. Using this information enables the system to select correct domains for out-of-grammar utterances. The features from T1 to T6 are defined so that they represent the confidence in the topic estimation result. We defined the confidence measure of topic T used in T2 and T4 as $CM_T = closeness_T / \sum_j closeness_{t_j}$, where T and t_j are topics handled by the system, and $closeness_t$ is the degree of closeness between topic t and the user's utterance. We also adopted the features from T7 to T9 to represent the relation between (I), (II) and (III). For example, if the topic estimation result is the same as (I), the system prefers (I). We defined feature T10 because an utterance whose duration is too short often causes errors in the estimation of the topic. The features from T11 to T13 represent whether

Table 3. Features representing situations after domain selection

C1: dialogue state after selecting (I)
C2: whether the language-understanding result is affirmative after selecting (I)
C3: whether the language-understanding result is negative after selecting (I)
C4: number of changed slots after selecting (I)
C5: number of common slots (name of place, here) changed after selecting (I)
C6: dialogue state after selecting (II)
C7: whether the language-understanding result is affirmative after selecting (II)
C8: whether the language-understanding result is negative after selecting (II)
C9: number of changed slots after selecting (II)
C10: number of common slots (name of place, here) changed after selecting (II)
C11: whether (II) has appeared before

Table 4. Features of topic estimation result

T1: closeness between (III) and ASR result for TE
T2: confidence measure of (III)
T3: closeness between (II) and ASR result for TE
T4: confidence measure of (II)
T5: difference of closeness to ASR result for TE between (II) and (III) (= T1 - T3)
T6: difference of confidence measures between (II) and (III) (= T2 - T4)
T7: whether (III) is the same as (II)
T8: whether (III) is the same as (I)
T9: whether (III) is the same as "command"
T10: duration of ASR result for TE (number of phoneme in recognition result)
T11: acoustic score of ASR result for TE
T12: difference of acoustic scores per phoneme between candidates selected as (III) and (I) (= (T11 - U1)/T10)
T13: difference of acoustic scores per phoneme between candidates selected as (III) and (II) (= (T11 - U4)/T10)

TE: Topic Estimation.

the user's utterance is out-of-grammar [8]. If the user's utterance seems so, the system does not prefer (II).

4   Experimental Evaluation

4.1   Dialogue Data for Evaluation

We evaluated our method by using the dialogue data that was collected from 10 subjects [1]. It contains 2191 utterances. This data was collected by using following procedure. First, to get accustomed to the timing to speak, the subjects used the system by following a sample scenario. They then used the system by following three scenarios, where at least three domains were mentioned.

We used Julian, a grammar-based speech recognizer [9], for the language understanding. Its grammar rules correspond to those used in the language-understanding modules in each domain. We also used Julius, a statistical-based

Table 5. Features survived after feature selection

Our method	P2, P3, P4, P5, P6, P7, P9, P10, U2, U3, U5, U6, C3, C6, C8, C10, C11, T2, T3, T4, T5, T7, T8, T9, T10, T11, T12
Baseline method	P1, P4, P5, P8, P9, P10, U1, U2, U3, U5, U6, U7, U9, C8, C9, C11

speech recognizer [9], for estimating the topic. Its language model was constructed from the training data collected for the topic estimation. A 3000-state Phonetic Tied-Mixture (PTM) model [9] was used as an acoustic model. The ASR accuracies were 63.3% and 69.6% for each.

We used C5.0 [10] as a classifier. To construct it, we used features selected by the backward stepwise selection, in which a feature survives if the performance in the domain classification is degraded when it is removed from a feature set one by one. In our method, we selected from the features listed in Table 1, 2, 3, and 4. Table 5 lists the selected features. The performance was calculated with a 10-fold cross validation. Accuracies for domain selection were calculated per utterance. When there were several domains that had the same score after domain selection, one domain was randomly selected from them.

Reference labels of the domain selection were given by hand for each utterance on the basis of domains the system had selected and transcriptions of the user's utterances:

Label (I): When the correct domain for a user's utterance is the same as the domain in which the previous system's response was made.

Label (II): Except for case (I), when the correct domain for a user's utterance is the domain in which an ASR result for language understanding in the N-best candidates with the highest score can be interpreted.

Label (III): Except for case (I) and (II), when the correct domain for a user's utterance is the domain that has the maximum closeness to an ASR result used for topic estimation.

Label (IV): Cases other than (I), (II), and (III).

4.2   Evaluation of Domain Selection

We first calculated the accuracy for domain selection in our method. Table 6 lists the classification results in our method as a confusion matrix. There were 464 domain selection errors in our method. Using our method enabled the system to successfully select correct domains for 37 of 131 utterances of (III). For these utterances, the conventional method cannot be used to select the correct domain. For example, we can select a domain correctly by using topic estimation results even for the utterance with Label (III) "Is any bus for *Kyoudaiseimonmae (a name of place)* in service?", which contains out-of-vocabulary words "in service". Nevertheless, the recall rate for (III) was not so high because the number of the utterances of (I) was much larger than that of (III) and the classifier was trained as most of utterances are classified as (I). Our method could also be used to select the correct domain for 84 of 238 utterances of (IV). These are the utterances

Table 6. Confusion matrix in our domain selection

Reference label \ Output	(I)	(II)	(III)	(IV)	Total (recall)
(I): in previous response	1348	34	23	37	1442 (93.5%)
(II): with highest score for LU	93	$258 + 10^{\dagger}$	14	5	380 (67.9%)
(III): with highest score for TE	81	7	37	6	131 (28.2%)
(IV): others	130	11	13	84	238 (35.5%)
Total	1652	320	87	132	2191
(precision)	(81.6%)	(80.6%)	(42.5%)	(63.6%)	(78.8%)

LU: Language Understanding TE: Topic Estimation.
†: These include 10 errors because of random selection when there were several domains having the same highest scores.

Table 7. Comparison between our method and baseline method (Output/Reference label)

Method\Output	(I): previous	(II): with highest score for LU	(IV): others	Total
Baseline	1303/1442	238/380	131/369	1672/2191
Our method	1348/1442	258/380	140/369	1746/2191

in which dialogue history is not reliable. In fact, the investigation for these 84 utterances correctly classified as (IV) revealed that 83 domain selection results of their previous utterances were incorrect. By detecting (IV), we can avoid successive domain selection errors.

We also compared the performance of our method with that of the baseline method described below:

Baseline method: A domain was selected on the basis of our previous method [1]. After we had merged utterances with Labels (III) and (IV), we constructed a 3-class domain classifier by using the dialogue data described in Section 4.1. We used features selected from the ones listed in Table 1, 2, and 3. These are listed in Table 5.

Table 7 lists the classification accuracy per their reference labels when it was calculated using the baseline conditions (3-class classification). The error rate of domain selection in the baseline method was 23.7% ($= 519/2191$), and that in our method was 20.3% ($= 445/2191$). The error reduction rate was 14.3% ($= 74/519$). Adopting the features obtained by the topic estimation results improved the accuracies for all labels from the baseline.

These results also showed that our method selects a uniquely correct domain for more utterances than a baseline method does. As listed in Table 7, the number of utterances for which the system selected uniquely correct domains in the baseline method was 1541 ($= 1303 + 238$). On the other hand, as listed in Table 6, that in our method was 1643 ($= 1348 + 258 + 37$). This represents an increase of 102 utterances from the baseline method.

We have discussed which features played an important role in the domain classifier and calculated how the number of errors increased when each feature was removed. Table 8 lists the top 10 features which increased the number of

Table 8. Increased number of errors when feature was removed

Removed feature	U8	P9	T7	U6	T2	C8	U3	P5	T10	T12
Increased number of errors	86	67	62	58	47	43	40	40	37	33

errors when it was removed. Four features related to topic estimation are listed here, and they show that features obtained from the topic estimation were useful for domain selection.

5   Conclusion

We developed a method of robust domain selection against out-of-grammar utterances in multi-domain spoken dialogue systems. By integrating the topic estimation results and dialogue history, using our method enables the system to generate correct responses for utterances that the system cannot accept. The experimental results using 2191 utterances showed that our method successfully reduced domain selection errors by 14.3% compared to a baseline method.

There are still some issues for developing the robust multi-domain system against out-of-grammar utterances. When the system selects either (III), the domain with the highest score for topic estimation, or (IV), other domains, it obtains no language-understanding result. Thus, we need to develop effective dialogue management, such as providing help messages, on the basis of the selected domain information.

Acknowledgements. We are grateful to Mr. Teruhisa Misu and Prof. Tatsuya Kawahara of Kyoto University for allowing us to use the document-collecting program they developed [7]. We are also grateful to Dr. Mikio Nakano of Honda Research Institute Japan and Mr. Naoyuki Kanda for their cooperation in developing the multi-domain system used to collect the evaluation data.

References

1. Komatani, K., Kanda, N., Nakano, M., Nakadai, K., Tsujino, H., Ogata, T., Okuno, H.G.: Multi-domain spoken dialogue system with extensibility and robustness against speech recognition errors. In: Proc. SIGDial, pp. 9–17 (2006)
2. Bellegarda, J.R.: Latent semantic mapping. IEEE Signal Processing Mag. 22(5), 70–80 (2005)
3. Lin, B., Wang, H., Lee, L.: A distributed agent architecture for intelligent multi-domain spoken dialogue systems. In: Proc. ASRU (1999)
4. O'Neill, I., Hanna, P., Liu, X., McTear, M.: Cross domain dialogue modelling: an object-based approach. In: Proc. ICSLP, pp. 205–208 (2004)
5. Lane, I.R., Kawahara, T., Matsui, T., Nakamura, S.: Topic classification and verification modeling for out-of-domain utterance detection. In: Proc. ICSLP, pp. 2197–2200 (2004)

6. Ikeda, S., Komatani, K., Ogata, T., Okuno, H.G.: Topic estimation with domain extensibility for guiding user's out-of-grammar utterance in multi-domain spoken dialogue systems. In: Proc. Interspeech, pp. 2561–2564 (2007)
7. Misu, T., Kawahara, T.: A bootstrapping approach for developing language model of new spoken dialogue systems by selecting Web texts. In: Proc. ICSLP, pp. 9–12 (2006)
8. Komatani, K., Fukubayashi, Y., Ogata, T., Okuno, H.G.: Introducing utterance verification in spoken dialogue system to improve dynamic help generation for novice users. In: Proc. SIGDial, pp. 202–205 (2007)
9. Kawahara, T., Lee, A., Takeda, K., Itou, K., Shikano, K.: Recent progress of open-source LVCSR engine Julius and Japanese model repository. In: Proc. ICSLP, pp. 3069–3072 (2004)
10. Quinlan, J.R.: C4.5: Programs for Machine Learning. Morgan Kaufmann, San Mateo (1993), http://www.rulequest.com/see5-info.html

The Effect of Emotional Speech on a Smart-Home Application

Theodoros Kostoulas, Iosif Mporas, Todor Ganchev, and Nikos Fakotakis

Artificial Intelligence Group, Wire Communications Laboratory,
Electrical and Computer Engineering Department,
University of Patras, 26500 Rion-Patras, Greece
{tkost, imporas, tganchev, fakotaki}@wcl.ee.upatras.gr

Abstract. The present work studies the effect of emotional speech on a smart-home application. Specifically, we evaluate the recognition performance of the automatic speech recognition component of a smart-home dialogue system for various categories of emotional speech. The experimental results reveal that word recognition rate for emotional speech varies significantly across different emotion categories.

Keywords: speech recognition, emotional speech, dialogue systems.

1 Introduction

The use of spoken dialogue applications has been increased over the last decade. It is common that services such as info-kiosks, telephone centers and smart-home applications are supported by multimodal dialogue systems. The challenge in technology is to provide user-friendly human-machine interaction, which guarantees robust performance in variety of environmental conditions or behavioral styles.

To this end, a number of spoken dialogue systems have been reported. Most of them focus on designing various techniques concerning the dialogue flow between the user and the system. In [1] an adaptive mixed initiative spoken dialogue system (MIMIC) that provides movie show-time information is described. MIMIC has been implemented as a general framework for information query systems, by decoupling its initiative module from the goal selection process, while allowing the outcome of both processes to jointly determine the response strategies employed. In [2] MiPad, a wireless personal digital assistant is presented. It fully integrates continuous speech recognition and spoken language understanding. In [3] a multimodal application's architecture is described. This architecture combines finite-state multimodal language processing, a speech-act based multimodal dialogue manager, dynamic multimodal output generation and user-tailored text planning, so as to enable rapid prototyping of multimodal interfaces with flexible input and adaptive output. The application provides a mobile multimodal speech-pen interface to restaurant and subway information. In [4] a multimodal dialogue system using reinforcement learning for in-car scenarios is demonstrated. The baseline system is built around the DIPPER dialogue manager [5]. The DIPPER dialogue manager is initially used to conduct

N.T. Nguyen et al. (Eds.): IEA/AIE 2008, LNAI 5027, pp. 305–310, 2008.

information-seeking dialogues with a user, such as finding a particular hotel and restaurant, using hand-coded dialogue strategies. The task and user interface modules of a multimodal dialogue system development platform are presented in [6]. The system is evaluated for a travel reservation task.

The aforementioned approaches try to meet the needs for successful interaction experiences through: *(a)* Keeping track of the overall interaction of the user with the dialogue system, with a view to ensuring steady process towards task completion, and *(b)* proper management of mixed initiative interaction. The basic component that determines the performance of a dialogue system is the automatic speech recognition (ASR) component. In [7] Rotaru et al. examined dependencies between speech recognition problems and users' emotions. Moreover, previous ASR experiments prove that the user's emotional state affects significantly the recognition performance. In [8] Steeneken and Hansen performed experiments on speech data characterized by different kind of difficulties. The results show the strong effect of emotions on the performance of the speech recognizer. In [9] Polzin and Waibel demonstrated that automatic speech recognition accuracy varies significantly depending on the emotional state of the speaker. Their research focused on performing experimentations on five major emotion categories {*neutral, happiness, sadness, fear, anger*}. Further experiments, realizing emotion-specific modeling, improved the word accuracy of the speech recognition system, when faced with emotional speech. Athanaselis et al. addressed the task of recognizing emotional speech by using a language model based on increased representation of emotional utterances [10].

In the present work, we study the effect of emotional speech recognition on smart-home application. Specifically, we examine the variation in the speech recognition performance for a variety of emotion categories. The present research is important for providing estimation about the potential gain of ASR performance that can be obtained, if an emotion recognition component is incorporated into our application.

2 The Spoken Dialogue System of the LOGOS Project

The scope of the LOGOS project is to research and develop a smart-home automation system that offers user-friendly access to information, entertainment devices and provides the means for controlling intelligent appliances installed in a smart-home environment. Fig. 1 illustrates the overall architecture of the LOGOS system, and the interface to various appliances, such as high definition television (HDTV), DVD player, mobile phone, etc. The multimodal user interface of that system allows the home devices and appliances to be controlled via the usual infrared remote control device, PC keyboard, or spoken language. In the present study, we focus on the speech interface and the spoken dialogue interaction.

Fig.1 presents in detail the architecture of the spoken dialogue interaction sub-system, which functions as follows: The speech is captured by a microphone array, which tracks the position of the user as s/he moves. Next, the preprocessed speech signal is fed to the speech and speaker recognition components that identify the command and the speaker, respectively. The dialogue manager generates feedback to the user, according to the interpretation of commands received from the speech understanding component, the device status and other information. This feedback is

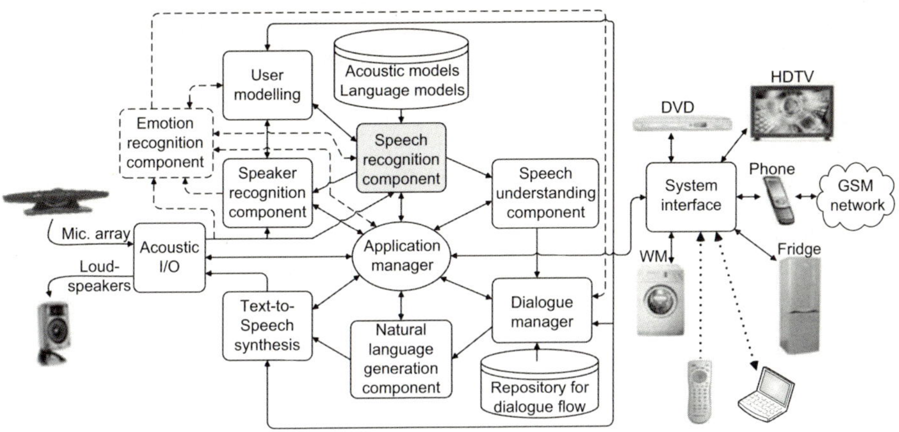

Fig. 1. The LOGOS system

delivered via the text-to-speech component, which is fed by the natural language generation component. All components of the spoken dialogue system are deployed on a personal computer, and the communication with the intelligent appliances is performed through a set-top box, which provides the interface to the intelligent appliances.

The smart-home system is designed with open architecture, which allows new components to be added for extending the system's functionality. One such addition could be an emotion recognition component (in Fig. 1 it is shown with dashed-line box), which could contribute to significant improvement of the user-friendliness of the system, as well as of its overall performance. By utilizing the feedback from this component, which ideally would capture the emotional state of the users, the system will be able to select an emotion-specific acoustic model, for improving the speech recognition performance, or to steer the dialogue flow accordingly.

3 Experiments and Results

For examining the operational performance of the smart-home dialogue system under the effect of the emotional state of the user the open source Sphinx III [11] speech recognition engine was employed. A general purpose acoustic model trained over the Wall Street Journal database [12] was utilized. Speech data, consisting of recordings of 16 kHz and resolution of 16-bit, were frame blocked from a sliding window of 512 samples and further parameterized. For the parameterization, the 13 first cepstral coefficients were computed from 40 Mel filters covering the frequency range [130, 6800] Hz, as well as their first and second derivative coefficients. The acoustic model consists of 3-state left-to-right HMM phone models, with each state modeled by a mixture of 8 continuous Gaussian distributions. The number of tied states was set to 4000. No automatic gain control or variance normalization was applied.

In order to capture the variation of the recognition performance across the numerous emotional speaking styles, we used, as test data, the Emotional Prosody Speech and Transcripts database [13]. It consists of recordings of professional actors reading series of semantically neutral utterances (dates and numbers) spanning fourteen distinct emotional categories. The full set of emotional categories are *anxiety, boredom, cold anger, contempt, despair, disgust, elation, happy, hot anger, interest, panic, pride, sadness, shame,* and *neutral.* The recordings were down-sampled to 16 kHz, 16-bit, single-channel format, following the specifications of the acoustic model. Finally, each speech file of the database was segmented to smaller ones, resulting one single emotional state per file. The segmentation was accomplished according to the annotation files provided with the database.

During recognition process a unigram language model, consisting of the list of words that appear in the Emotional Prosody Speech and Transcripts database, was constructed. Each single-emotion speech file was pre-processed and parameterized identically to the acoustic model training data. The decoder's language weight was set to 9.5. The rest of the decoder's parameters held their default values. We used uniform setup for all the emotional classes.

The speech recognition results for the fourteenth emotional classes as well as for neutral (conversational speaking style) are shown in Table 1. The first column provides the number of words that existed in the test set for each emotion. The second column shows the number of words that were not recognized, including word substitutions, insertions and deletions. The last column provides the speech recognition performance in terms of percentage of word error rate (WER).

Table 1. Speech recognition results for different emotional categories

Emotion	# Words	# Errors	WER (%)
Neutral	1787	111	6.21
Shame	736	69	9.38
Interest	818	86	10.51
Boredom	853	95	11.14
Pride	722	91	12.60
Sadness	766	102	13.32
Despair	875	136	15.54
Anxiety	884	141	15.95
Cold Anger	746	129	17.29
Happy	830	170	20.48
Disgust	850	176	20.71
Contempt	796	188	23.62
Panic	673	237	35.22
Elation	747	271	36.28
Hot Anger	347	153	44.09

As Table 1 presents, emotional speaking affects significantly the speech recognition performance. Neutral speaking style presents the highest performance, which was expected since the utilized acoustic model was trained purely with neutral speech. In fact, the ASR performance depends on a number of speech characteristics, such as: voice quality, speaking rate, manner of articulation, intensity, pitch range, and these differ among emotional and neutral speech. Emotional states, such as happiness, panic and hot anger, are characterized by: high speaking rate, breathy voice quality, tense articulation, high intensity and wide pitch range [14]. In addition,

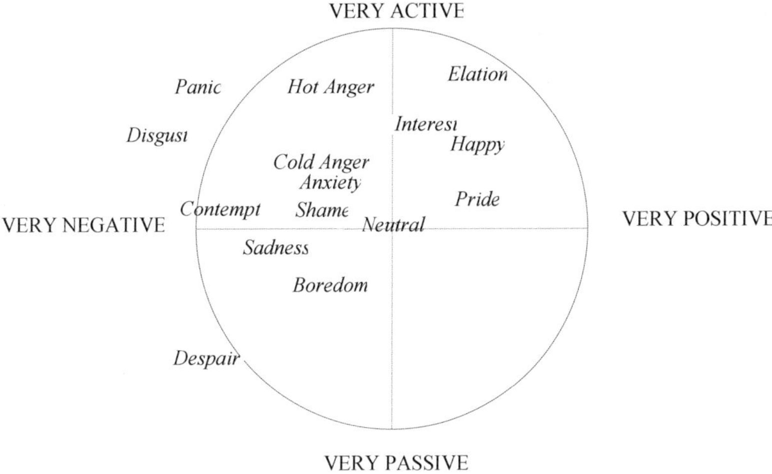

Fig. 2. Emotion categories used, mapped in the activation-evaluation space

physiological changes affect the air flow propagation and impose using non-linear speech features to model the corresponding emotional speech [15]. Thus, it is logical such emotion categories to present significantly higher WER than the one reported for the neutral utterances.

On the other hand, emotion categories, such as sadness and shame, present lower increase of the WER. Previous studies conducted on emotion recognition from speech had shown that these emotions differ less from neutral speech, since they present low speaking rate, regular voice quality and slurring articulation [14]. As observed in Fig. 2 the WER results conform to the position of the aforementioned emotion categories in the activation-evaluation space [16]. As more active the emotional speech is, either positive or negative, so the WER increases.

4   Conclusions

In this paper we studied the performance of a speech recognizer for emotional speech. The experimental results show significant variation in the WER reported across different emotion categories. The results suggest the potential gain of ASR performance which can be achieved when reliable emotion recognition component is incorporated into the dialogue system. We deem that emotion-specific or emotion-adapted acoustic models for the ASR would improve the recognition performance of the verbal content of emotional speech [9, 10], thus enhance human-computer interaction.

Acknowledgments. This work was partially supported by the LOGOS project (*A general architecture for speech recognition and user friendly dialogue interaction for advanced commercial applications*), which is funded by the General Secretariat for Research and Technology of the Greek Ministry of Development.

References

1. Chu-Carroll, J.: MIMIC: An adaptive mixed initiative spoken dialogue system for information queries. In: Proc. of the 6th ACL Conference on Applied Natural Language Processing, Seattle, WA, pp. 97–104 (2000)
2. Huang, X., Acero, A., Chelba, C., Deng, L., Duchene, D., Goodman, J., Hon, H.-W., Jacoby, D., Jiang, L., Loynd, R., Mahajan, M., Mau, P., Meredith, S., Mughal, S., Neto, S., Plumpe, M., Wand, K., Wang, Y.: MIPAD: A next generation PDA prototype. In: Proc. ICSLP, Beijing, China, pp. 33–36 (2000)
3. Johnston, M., Bangalore, S., Vasireddy, G., Stent, A., Ehlen, P., Walker, M., Whittaker, S., Maloor, P.: MATCH: An architecture for multimodal dialogue systems. In: Proc. of the 40th Annu. Meeting of the Association for Computational Linguistics, pp. 376–383 (2002)
4. Lemon, O., Georgila, K., Stuttle, M.: An ISU dialogue system exhibiting reinforcement learning of dialogue policies: generic slot-filling in the TALK in-car system. In: EACL (demo session) (2006)
5. Bos, J., Klein, E., Lemon, O., Oka, T.: DIPPER: Description and Formalisation of an Information-State Update Dialogue System Architecture. In: 4th SIGdial Workshop on Discourse and Dialogue, Sapporo, pp. 115–124 (2003)
6. Potamianos, A., Fosler-Lussier, E., Ammicht, E., Peraklakis, M.: Information seeking spoken dialogue systems Part II: Multimodal Dialogue. IEEE Transactions on Multimedia 9(3), 550–566 (2007)
7. Rotaru, M., Litman, D.J., Forbes-Riley, K.: Interactions between Speech Recognition Problems and User Emotions. In: Proc. Interspeech 2005, pp. 2481–2484 (2005)
8. Steeneken, H.J.M., Hansen, J.H.L.: Speech under stress conditions: Overview of the effect of speech production and on system performance. In: ICASSP 1999, vol. 4, pp. 2079–2082 (1999)
9. Polzin, S.T., Waibel, A.: Pronunciation variations in emotional speech. In: Strik, H., Kessens, J.M., Wester, M. (eds.) Modeling pronunciation variation for automatic speech recognition. Proceedings of the ESCA Workshop, pp. 103–108 (1998)
10. Athanaselis, T., Bakamidis, S., Dologlou, I., Cowie, R., Douglas-Cowie, E., Cox, C.: ASR for emotional speech: Clarifying the issues and enhancing performance. Neural Networks 18, 437–444 (2005)
11. Lee, K.-F., Hon, H.-W., Reddy, R.: An overview of the SPHINX speech recognition system. IEEE Transactions on Acoustics, Speech and Signal processing 38(1), 35–45 (1990)
12. Paul, D., Baker, J.: The design of the wall street journal-based CSR corpus. In: Proceedings of ARPA Speech and Natural Language Workshop, ARPA, pp. 357–362 (1992)
13. University of Pennsylvania, Linguistic Data Consortium, Emotional Prosody Speech, http://www.ldc.uppen.edu/Catalog/CatalogEntry.jsp?cataloId=LDC2002S28
14. Cowie, R., Douglas-Cowie, E., Tsapatsoulis, N., Votsis, G., Kollias, S., Fellenz, W., Taylor, J.G.: Emotion recognition in human-computer interaction. IEEE Signal Processing Magazine 18(1), 32–80 (2001)
15. Guojun, Z., Hansen, J.H.L., Kaiser, J.F.: Nonlinear feature based classification of speech under stress. IEEE Transactions on Speech and Audio Processing 9, 201–216 (2001)
16. Whissell, C.: The dictionary of Affect in Language. In: Plutchik, R., Kellerman, H. (eds.) Emotion: Theory, research and experience, vol. 4, Academic Press, New York (1989)

Another Face of Search Engine: Web Search API's[*]

Harshit Kumar[1] and Sanggil Kang[2]

[1] DERI, National University of Ireland, Galway
`harshitkumar@suwon.ac.kr`
[2] Computer Science and Information Engineering, Inha University, 253 Younhyun-dong,
Nam-gu, Incheon, South Korea
`sgkang@inha.ac.kr`

Abstract. Since search engine development requires building an index which is a tedious and space consuming process. Now-a-days all major search engines provide developers access to their resources through a set of APIs. In this paper we try to answer the following questions. What differences exist between search engines and their associated search APIs? Does search APIs really surrogate for the actual search engine within the research domain? If yes, then which APIs is more suitable? For our experiments, we have used the following search engines and their web search APIs: Yahoo, Google, MSN, and Naver. Our experimental results will help researchers to choose appropriate web search APIs that suit their requirements.

Keywords: Search Engine, Search API, Google, MSN, Naver, Yahoo.

1 Introduction

Lately researchers have been using web interface of search engine [11] or search engine query logs [3] for their research. The basic trouble with these two approaches is that they are manual and tedious. In the year 2002, Google introduced a free SOAP-based search API (Application Programming Interface) [1] that allows public to access their index and further augment it to suit their requirements. Later Yahoo, Naver, and MSN also allowed free access to their index through the public interface of APIs. Researchers now make use of the web search APIs for the collection of data for their experiments. Most of the research works have used Google search API [12, 13] and very few have used either Yahoo [8, 12] or MSN search API [9, 12]. In this paper, we have made an attempt to provide collectively the differences among search results from web interface of search engine and search APIs. We report the following differences: freshness, accuracy, ranking, and the number of results and difference of index.

We have used the search APIs of Google, Yahoo, MSN, and Naver. These APIs have their own limitations regarding the number of queries per day that can be issued,

[*] This research was partly supported by the Ministry of Information and Communication, Korea, under the College Information Technology Research Center Support Program, grant number IITA-2006-C1090-0603-0031 and by the K-net project under the EU Seventh Frame Programme, grant number FP7-215584.

N.T. Nguyen et al. (Eds.): IEA/AIE 2008, LNAI 5027, pp. 311–320, 2008.
© Springer-Verlag Berlin Heidelberg 2008

the number of results that they return, etc. Moreover, the search engine does not provide any support for these APIs and most of the information is covert, which leaves users of these APIs wondering about how the APIs interact with the server of search engine?, which index do they access? The results in this paper address the above questions. For evaluation, we have compared the results between two faces of search engine using Discounted Cumulative Gain [2] (DCG), Cumulative Gain [2] (CG), Average Rank [3] (AR), and Kendall-Tau distance [4].

The paper is organized as follows. Next, we discuss the related work which is followed by the evaluation metrics in Section 3. Section 4 has a discussion about experimental results along with analysis. We conclude in Section 5.

2 Related Work

A recent work [5] compares web search results from WUI (Web Search Interface) and web search APIs. It compares how consistent is the index for Google, Yahoo, and MSN APIs with the WUI. We, on the other hand, have a different goal; moreover our evaluation metrics are also different. They claim that their work is the first analysis of the results produced by the Google, MSN, and Yahoo API and WUI interfaces. We also vouch for their claim.

We have found many studies that have used Google API [8], Yahoo API [12] for their research work, and MSN API [9]. There exists one study [10] that compared Google API with Google Search engine. They have shown that the search results from two different Google interfaces: Google API and Google search engine vary in range, structure, and availability. They fail to provide any measurement for the above quantities. We have tried to express the above quantities in number and shown that how much they vary in range, structure, and availability? Most of the studies just compare the results of their proposed method to the search engine using the search engine API. This is the only domain in which search engine API has been exploited. In a recent work [12], the author has listed the issues to be considered while submitting a query to an API. He cautioned that API occasionally fails to return a valid result for a user query, special characters in user query are not supported by APIs. And the number of results beyond the maximum value (2147483647) fails to return a valid response.

Some of the studies [11] copy the results from search engine for the evaluation purpose which is a tedious job. Our work automatically observes user behavior for calculating evaluation metrics. i.e. we store the results returned by the API, user clicked URLs which is used for calculating the values of DCG, CG, AR, and Kendall-Tau distance.

3 Evaluation Metrics

The metric Average Rank (AR) is used for measuring the quality of personalized search. The AR of a query q is defined as shown in Eq. (1).

$$AR_q = 1/|V| \sum_{p \in V} R(p) \tag{1}$$

where $R(p)$ is the rank of URL p, and V is the set of URLs clicked by the user. Second metric that we used for measuring the quality of results is Cumulative Gain (CG). A higher value of Gain Vector symbolizes more relevant results and vice versa. For example, if the highest value of CG is 20 in scenario1 and 12 in scenario 2, that implies scenario1 has high relevant results compared to scenario 2. The CG Vector is calculated as shown in Eq. (3).

$$CG = \begin{cases} G(1) & \text{if } i = 1 \\ CG(i-1) + G(i) & \text{otherwise} \end{cases} \tag{3}$$

Third metric used for measuring the ranking quality is Discounted Cumulative Gain (DCG) as seen in Eq. (4). DCG is particularly useful when results are evaluated at different relevance levels (highly relevant, relevant, and not relevant) by assigning them different gain values. The idea behind DCG is, the greater the rank, the less accessible that URL is.

$$DCG = \begin{cases} G(1) & \text{if } i = 1 \\ DCG(i-1) + G(i)/\log_b(i) & \text{otherwise} \end{cases} \tag{4}$$

For the purpose of this experiment, we have used 3 different relevance levels; $G(i)=2$ for highly relevant result and $G(i)=1$ for relevant result and $G(i)=0$ for not relevant result. Also b is the parameter of penalization; we have taken value 2 for b. To measure the similarity between two lists, we have used a variant of Kendall-Tau distance. Kendall-Tau in its original form cannot be used to compare the results of two search engines because it compares two lists over the same elements. The modified Kendall-Tau that suits our requirements is presented below

$$K^{(p)}(\tau_1,\tau_2) = \sum_{\{i,j\} \in P(\tau_1,\tau_2)} \bar{K}_{i,j}^{(p)}(\tau_1,\tau_2) \tag{5}$$

where τ_1 and τ_2 are the top k lists, and P is the union of all unordered pairs of τ_1 and τ_2. The optimal approach chooses $p=0$. The value of $K_{(i,j)}(\tau_1, \tau_2)$ is calculated by formulating the following four cases:

Case I: i and j appear in both top k lists.
      (a) i being ahead of j, then the value $K_{(i,j)}(\tau_1, \tau_2)$is 0.
      (b) In one list, i is ahead of j and in another list j is ahead of i, the value of
        $K_{(i,j)}(\tau_1, \tau_2)$is 1.
Case II: i and j both appear in one list and either of them appears in other top k list.
      (a) if i is ahead of j in one top k list, then the value $K_{(i,j)}(\tau_1, \tau_2)$is 1 else 0.
Case III: i appear in one list and j appears in another list.
      (a) The value of $K_{(i,j)}(\tau_1, \tau_2)$is 1.
Case IV: i and j both appear in one list.
      (a) The value of $K_{(i,j)}(\tau_1, \tau_2)$ is 1.
So as to compare the results over a range, we normalized the value $K_{(i,j)}$ using Eq. (6).

$$K = 1 - (K^{(0)}(\tau_1,\tau_2)/k^2) \tag{6}$$

4 Experiment

Before explaining the experiments, it is important to explain the test collection that was used. An experiment evaluation was carried out using NPL [6] test collection which is available for free from Glasgow IR resources. The NPL test collection is a collection of 93 queries with their descriptions. Fifteen people from different labs at Inha University and Suwon University participated as relevance assessors. They were free to choose any of the 39 queries out of the available 93 queries. However, they have to construct the query term from the given query descriptions. The queries were issued to 8 search engines (4 web search engines and 4 search APIs based search engine). We observed different results for the same query. It is just because different users had different notions for a query description and they inputted different query terms. The experiments were carried out for a period of 3 months from Mid January 2007 to end of March 2007. The total number of queries issued was 450, out of which 80% had the same query description but different query terms were formulated by the user.

The section below gives an introduction to web search APIs and precisely define what we intend to present in this study which is followed by the experiment results.

4.1 Web Search API

In this section, we briefly explain about the search APIs that we used for our work. We developed an interface using Java technologies, HTML Tidy [7], DOM API, and Apache to carry out the experiment. The interface is named Exclusively Your's. It receives a query from the user, forwards the query to the search engine server, and then receives a result set. The result set comprises of URLs, snippets, and title. The result set is then rendered on the browser. Everywhere in the paper result set means a set of URLs. Note that the result set is different from that returned by the web interface of search engine. This can be due to several reasons which we wish to explore in this study. Individual user information such as query issued, results returned (snippets, title), total number of results, and web pages clicked by user were logged in the MS access database which were analyzed later for experiments.

Table 1 presents the list of top 10 titles returned for a query "web search API" requested to web search engine and exclusively yours. Note that both interfaces return the same set of URLs but their rankings are different. For instance, the title "Google Web API" (position 3) has higher ranking in the results from Google search engine whereas the title "Yahoo * Services[1]" has the same rank (position 1, 2) in both interfaces. And the title "MSN Live search API" (position 9) has higher ranking in Exclusively Your's. One thing is sure that the index used by Google search engine and search APIs is not same. Now the obvious question arises, which API is better among Yahoo, Google, MSN, and Naver and which search API results are close to its associated search engine results? We try to answer the questions in the following section.

---

[1] Yahoo * Services means the sequence of strings enclosed inside Yahoo and Service. In this case, it is Yahoo Search Documentation for Yahoo Web Services and Yahoo Search Web Services.

Table 1. Thr representation of URL titles returned by Google search engine and exclusively yours (Google) for query "web search API"

Position	Google search engine	Exclusively yours (Google)
1	Web Search Documentation for Yahoo! Search Web Services	**Web Search** Documentation for Yahoo! **Search Web** Services
2	Yahoo! Search Web Services	Yahoo! **Search Web** Services
3	Google Web APIs	Alexa **Web Search** Platform
4	Google AJAX Search API - Google Code	Build a Site **Search** with Yahoo! **Search Web** Services
5	Alexa Web Search Platform	Google AJAX **Search API** - Google Code
6	Build a Site Search with Yahoo! Search Web Services	Unofficial Guide to Ask's **Web Search API** - Antezeta
7	» Unofficial Guide to Ask's Web Search API - Antezeta	Decrypting Ask's **Web Search API** - Antezeta
8	» Decrypting Ask's Web Search API - Antezeta	Alexa **Web Search API** - Programmable-Web Profile
9	Alexa Web Search API - Programmable-Web Profile	Live **Search API**, Version 1.1
10	Live Search API, Version 1.1	Windows Live Dev

Table 2. Comparison of Google, Yahoo, Msn and ,Naver web search APIs. Here NL means no limit, NS means no similalrity (50% similar), MS means mostly similar (80% similar), MS* means mostly similar (>90%), and M means many language support.

Comparison Parameter	SE API (G)	SE API (Y)	SE API (MSN)	SE API(N)
No. of query term	NL	NL	NL	NL
No. of results	NL	NL	NL	100
Result Format	Set of URL	Set of URL	Set of URL	XML file
Link:URL	Fewer links	Lots of Links	Moderate Links	NA
No. of queries/day	1000	5000	10000	NL
Result Similarity	MS	MS*	NS	MS*
Development Language	M	M	Microsoft Technologies	M
Repetition of Results	Y	Y	Y	N

4.2 Results and Discussion

In the first set of results, we compare among the search APIs and try to answer the first question i.e. which search API is better and easier to use. In the second set, we compare search API with its associated search engine and report the freshness of results and quality of results using DCG, CG, Average Rank, and Kendall Tau evaluation metrics.

Table 2 lists the comparison of search APIs across various comparison parameters which are listed in the 1st column. The first row compares search engine (SE) APIs for the number of query terms that they can receive. For all the four SE APIs, there is no limit (NL) on the number of query terms i.e. user can enter as many terms as the user wants. The number of results returned by Naver SE API is restricted to 100 and all

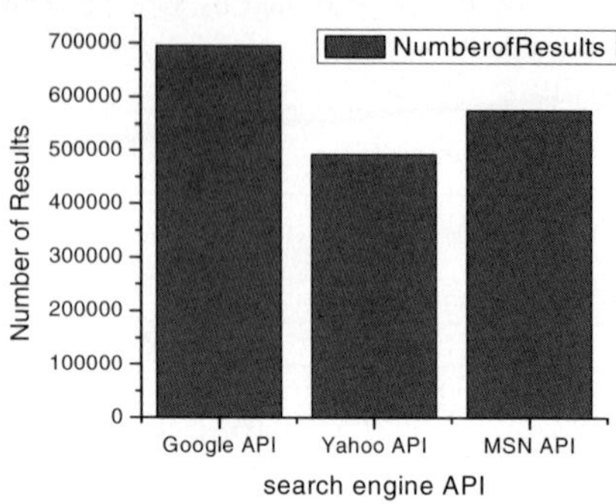

Fig. 1. Number of Results returned by search engine APIs

other SE APIs return infinite number of results. However, the number of results beyond the maximum value (2147483647) fails to return a valid response.

From the graph in Fig. 1, we can see that Google SE API returns on an average more number of results than any other API. This graph is an average of total number of results over all the queries issued by our assessors. This suggests that Google API uses a bigger index among all the APIs which is exactly not true. The explanation follows in the next paragraph.

We were interested to know the number of repetitions in the results from Google API. So, we observed that Google API returns a large number of results but this comes with a lot of repetitions. For instance, the query "AUSDM 2006" issued to Google search API which we issued in March 2007 returned 230 results. The first 100 results were unique with few repetitions. The results from 101 to 110 were exactly similar to results from 91 to 100. The same phenomenon carried on until 221 to 230. Now we wanted to know if Google also shows the same behavior. To verify our doubt, we requested the same query "AUSDM 2006" to Google search engine which returned 346 results out of which 123 were unique. This indicates that Google search engine returns large number of results on the face but actually it is not the real scenario. We also noticed one peculiar behavior: if we issue the same query again, then 20% and 13% of the queries receive different number of results for Google and Yahoo API, respectively. All the APIs return a set of URL, snippet, and title for a user requested query. Whereas, Naver API returns a XML file which imposes an extra burden on the developer to parse the file and extract title, URL, and snippet. There is of course the advantage that the programmer is free to choose any language for parsing XML file. Google and Yahoo search APIs can be used in almost all the languages, on the other hand MSN API only works with Microsoft technologies. The developers who are not comfortable with MSN API will prefer not to choose MSN API. Sometimes the XML file returned by Naver API is not properly formatted which causes many XML parsing APIs to reject the file as not a proper XML compatible version. This is a serious problem with Naver API. To workaround this problem, we avoided using XML parser API and opened XML file as a stream of bytes. We stored the stream of bytes in a string and then parsed the string using string related functions for extracting URL, snippets, title, etc.

The query link: URL returns the number of in-inks that point to a URL. For example, the query "link: www.inha.ac.kr" will return the list of URLs that has an outgoing link to www.inha.ac.kr or in other words it returns the number of in-links to www.inha.ac.kr. Naver API does not support this type of query and Yahoo API is the most supportive i.e. it returns the maximum number of in-links. MSN API and Google API provide a list of few incoming links. There is a limit on the number of the queries that can be requested in one day. Google, Yahoo and MSN API impose a limit of 1000, 5000 and 10000 respectively. Naver API does not impose any such limit.

4.3 Freshness of Results Comparison between API and Search Engine

This section evaluates the similarity between the results from the search API and search engine. Fig. 2 presents the Kendall-tau distance between the two lists: one list comprises top 20 URLs returned from the search API and the other list comprises top 20 URLs returned from the associated search engine. We can see that the Naver API results are almost similar to Naver search engine and that MSN API shows a lot of dissimilarity. The plots in Fig 5 (a), (b), (c), and (d) clearly ascertain the previous statement. If we rank the four web search APIs on the basis of similarity of result set, Naver will be a clear winner followed by Yahoo, Google, and MSN API at the last. The results in Table 2 also support the above statement. In other words, it shows that Naver API returns the freshest results almost same as returned by the search engine. However, there is a caveat here. If we issue the same query again, then 13% of the queries return different number of results for Yahoo API.

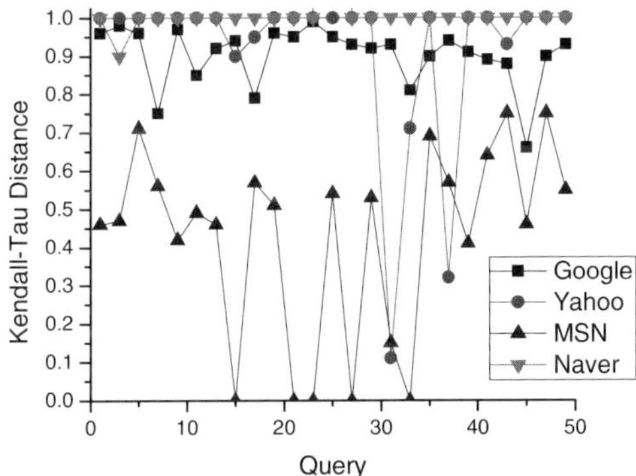

Fig. 2. Kendall-Tau Plot for 50 queries issued to search engine and their associated APIs

4.4 Quality of Results Comparison between APIs

Quality of Results measures how much relevant the returned URL is? To measure the quality, we have used evaluation measures CG, DCG, and AR. AR measures quality on a binary relevance whereas CG and DCG measure the relevance of returned result at more than two relevance levels. Moreover, AR can only be used to compare a search engine with its API but not with another API or with another search engine. Note that in this study we do not intend to compare search engines.

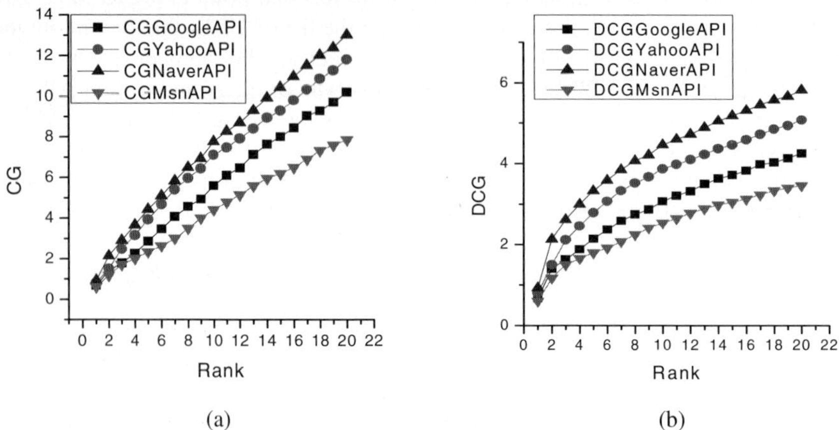

(a)   (b)

Fig. 3. (a) Rank vs. CG for search API, (b) Rank vs. DCG for search API

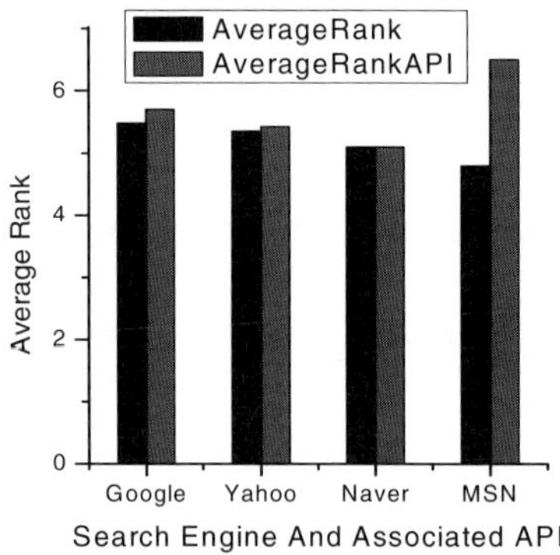

Fig. 4. AR plot for search engine and associated search API

The CG (DCG) plot in Fig, 3 (a) and (b) is plotted as an average CG (DCG) over all the queries. It appears that the Naver API returns high quality of results which is followed by Yahoo API. Note that there is not much difference in the first 10 results from Naver and Yahoo API. The difference increases as assessor evaluates the higher ranked results. The explanation is that the first 10 results might be same or different but assessors evaluated them at almost the same relevance level. However, Naver API returns better results in the 11-20 rank and hence it's CG or DCG value exceeds the Yahoo CG or DCG value. Also the MSN API returns better result in the beginning but later Google APIs takes over. In this case, it is only the first 2 or 3 results which were better but later results were not better than Google.

The comparison of AR between search engine and its API is plotted in Fig. 4. It shows that the Google and its API differ by an AR of 4%, Yahoo and its API differ by 1.3%, Naver and its API by 0% and MSN and its API by 35%. The AR values suggest that the Naver and its' API results are exactly same, which means the Naver search API uses the same index for searching as used by the Naver search engine. While, there is a huge difference in AR between search results from MSN and MSN API. This indicates that the MSN API is using an older index or a smaller index. The research work carried out by [5] has shown that the API indexes are not older, but they are probably smaller.

4.5 Quality of Results Comparison between Search Engines and Its APIs

Fig. 5(c) and (d) support Fig. 4(a) and (b) that Yahoo, Yahoo API and Naver, Naver API have the same search quality. However there is a small difference for yahoo API which is not visible because of averaging. Fig. 5(a) presents the plot of CG between Google and Google API. This plot in addition to the plot of Fig. 4(a) gives us a clear picture of differences between top 20 results. The similar plots for MSN, Naver, and Yahoo is shown in Fig. 5(b), 5 (c), and 5 (d), respectively. From Fig. 5(a) and 5(b), it is apparent that the Google and yahoo API use a different index which is not better than the index used by original search engine. As seen in Fig. 5(d), for Yahoo, the first 10 results have same CG value and the later 10 results have a small difference. The results from MSN show a very strange behavior. The MSM API returns more relevant top 10 results where MSM search engine returns highly relevant next 10 (i.e. from 11 to 20) results. The plot in Fig. 5(c) again ascertains that the Naver API and the Naver search engine use the same index.

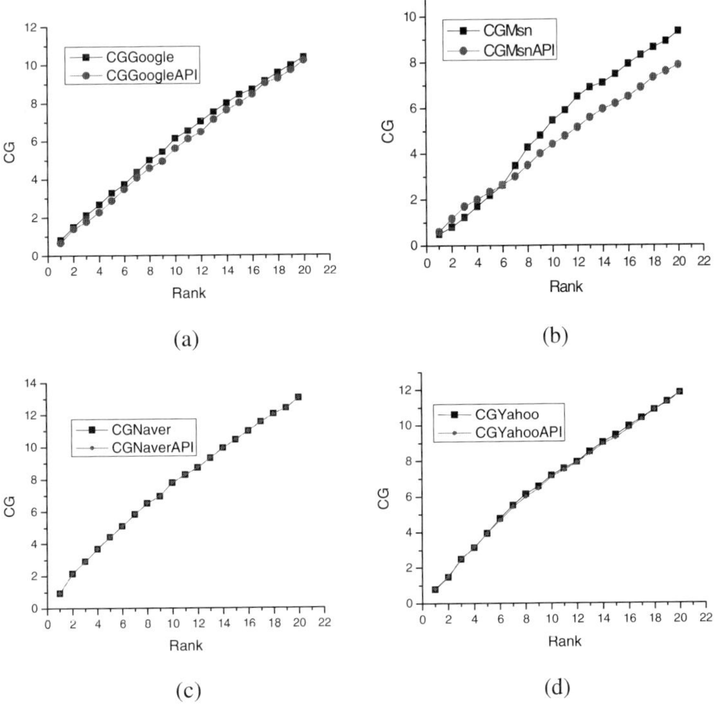

Fig. 5. (a), (b), (c), and (d) show CG-Rank plot between Google, MSN, Naver, and Yahoo

5   Conclusion

In this paper, we investigated how well an API surrogates for the original search engine. The results suggest that, Naver API very closely surrogates Naver search engine. However there are few drawbacks that the Naver API returns only 100 results and the result quality is lowest among all the APIs. This means, if a researcher is interested in more than 100 results or better search result quality, he should not go with Naver API. On the other hand, Yahoo API is very consistent and its results match closely to the Yahoo search engine but not an exact match. It has another advantage that the result quality is the 2nd best after Naver API. MSN API is very restrictive and works with Microsoft technologies only. Moreover there is a 34% difference in AR between the search results from MSN and MSN API.

References

1. http://code.google.com/apis/soapsearch/
2. Järvelin, K., Kekäläinen, J.: Cumulated gain-based evaluation of IR techniques. In: TOIS, pp. 422–446 (2002)
3. Dou, Z.: A Large-scale Evaluation and Analysis of Personalized Search Strategies. In: WWW 16, pp. 581–590 (2007)
4. Fagin, R., Kumar, R., Sivakumar, D.: Comparing top k lists. SIAM Journal on Discrete Mathematics, 134–160 (2003)
5. McCown, F., Nelson, M.: Agreeing to Disagree: Search Engines and Their Public Interfaces. In: JCDL 2007, pp. 309–318 (2007)
6. http://ir.dcs.gla.ac.uk/resources/test_collections/npl/
7. http://tidy.sourceforge.net/
8. Diaj, F., Metzler, D.: Improving the estimation of relevance models using large external corpora. In: SIGIR, pp. 154–161 (2006)
9. http://project.carrot2.org/publications/carrot2-dresden-2007.pdf
10. Mayr, P., Tosques, F.: Google Web APIs – An instrument for Webometric Analyses? In: ISSI 2005 (2005), retrieved from
    http://www.ib.hu-berlin.de/%7Emayr/arbeiten/ISSI2005_Mayr_Toques.pdf
11. Guha, R., McCool, R., Miller, E.: Semantic Search. In: WWW 2003, pp. 700–709 (2003)
12. Ong, J.: The Predictability Problem, PhD Thesis,
    http://tertius.net.au/~shade/math/doctoral_thesis.pdf
13. Kumar, H., Park, S., Kang, S.: A Personalized URL Re-ranking Methodology using User's Browsing Behavior. In: KES-AMSTA 2008, pp. 212–221 (2008)

The Consistency and Conformance of Web Document Collection Based on Heterogeneous DAC Graph

Marek Kopel and Aleksander Zgrzywa

Wrocław University of Technology, Poland
{kopel, zgrzywa}@pwr.wroc.pl

Abstract. The heterogeneous DAC graph is an extension to a traditional, homogeneous graph representing a Web document collection. In DAC graph, beside documents' relationships, the relationships between documents, authors and concepts can be modeled. The document-author-concept relationships' model is used to measure consistency and conformance of a Web document collection.

Keywords: Web document collection, consistency, conformance, heterogeneous graph, relationship.

1 Introduction (Relationships in WWW)

The most obvious and common model of a Web document collection is a directed graph as pointed out in [1]. The graph model idea was derived from the hyperlinked documents' environment so that nodes in the Web graph represent documents and the directed edges represent the hyperlinks anchored in one document and linking to another. The graph model for today Web is so self-evident, that Tim Berners-Lee mentioned recently in his blog ([2]), in reference to the present-day Web: "I called this graph the Semantic Web, but maybe it should have been Giant Global Graph!".

Since the Web was growing bigger and finding relevant documents in it was getting harder the graph model was used to improve the accuracy of Web search results. The most known information retrieval algorithms for searching the Web - HITS [3] and PageRank [4] - benefit from documents' hyperlinking relationship. Since 2001, when Tim Berners-Lee's vision of Semantic Web went worldwide by [5], WWW is on its way to become the machine-readable Web and serves more and more semantically enriched information. Today we can acquire from the Web much more information on two documents' relationship than just the fact that they are hyperlinked.

Using link's attributes *rel* and *rev* author of a Web document can define type of the relationship with the linked document. As recommended in [6] the relationship may concern navigation in a document collection (types: *start*, *prev*, *next*, **contents, index**), structure (types: *chapter*, *section*, *subsection*, *appendix*, **glossary**) or other meta information (types: **copyright, help**). According to [7] users may extend this collection of relationships if the extensions will be defined in their own namespace and their names will be qualified names. This means that using a proper ontology user can define the relationship in as many ways as it is needed.

N.T. Nguyen et al. (Eds.): IEA/AIE 2008, LNAI 5027, pp. 321–330, 2008.

In hypertext environment also the relationship between authors of Web documents can be defined. Using FOAF vocabulary ([8]) the relationships among people are defined by *<foaf:knows>* tag. If the fact of knowing people is not enough, a more detailed description of human relationships can be defined using XFN ([10]). With this microformat it is possible to provide specific information about type of document authors' relationship, such as: friendship (*contact, acquaintance, friend*), family (*child, parent, sibling, spouse, kin*), professional (*co-worker, colleague*), physical (*met*), geographical (*co-resident, neighbor*) and romantic (*muse, crush, date, sweetheart*).

Another interesting meta data that is being enclosed in vast amount of new Web documents are, so called, tags as described in [9]. Tags (or categories - in reference to blogs) are keywords considered relevant and assigned to a document by its author. Using e.g. *rel-tag* microformat ([10]) it is possible for author to create folksonomies - a step toward collaborative ontologies or replacement of traditional, hierarchical approach of top-down taxonomies.

2   Heterogeneous DAC Graph

The formats described above are used in the Internet quite broadly, especially in the services that follow the idea of Web 2.0. The term Web 2.0 ([11]) refers to web-based communities and services which aim to facilitate creativity, collaboration, and sharing among users. Provided that Web users are becoming as important as the documents they are publishing, the present-day Web, when modeled as graph, should consist of at least two types of nodes: documents and authors.

On the other hand, current trends in classification and information retrieval for multimedia Web documents concern using tags, i.e. the idea of keywords known from text documents. This in conjunction with projects like WordNet ([12]) or more semantic oriented like SIMILE ([13]), DBpedia ([14]) or most recent LinkingOpenData cannot be overrated and must be included in a modern Web model.

In this paper for modeling the Web a heterogeneous DAC graph is used (see fig. 1.A). The DAC graph consists of the nodes of three types: document, author and concept. The edges between nodes model the relationships among nodes of three types. Most of the relationships can be acquired directly from the Web data. The rest of the relationships can be derived from the acquired relationships.

3   Consistency and Conformance

In order to improve Web search results using DAC graph 2 measures for Web document collections are proposed. The measures are consistency and conformance. Consistency of a document collection refers to the collection's inner similarity of the documents concerning their subject. The subject of documents is similar if they are similarly tagged, i.e. their authors assigned to them the same tags or categories (in the context of Web 2.0) or documents have the same keywords in their corresponding metadata files (in the context of digital libraries).

Conformance of a Web document collection is a measure concerning document authors' relationship. The intuition here is that authors with strong relationship often are coauthors of a document and thus agree on some subjects. The relationship may also come out of authors citing and referencing of each other's documents. At some amount the conformance may also concern trust in Web document authors based on the idea of Web of Trust as proposed in [15].

Previous works in the author's Ph.D. thesis research showed that dealing with documents and authors ([15]) or documents and weighing terms ([16]) alone is not enough to obtain precise measures for improving searching, filtering or classification. In this paper the measures of consistency and conformance are proposed for document-author-concept environment modeled by a heterogeneous DAC graph.

4   Relationships in DAC Graph

Constructing a DAC graph is the main problem discussed in this paper. Identifying nodes in the graph is equivalent to identifying single documents, authors and concepts in the Web. Using the semantically enriched information this is a relatively easy task. However discovering relationships among the three types of nodes including all aspects of their connection is not so easy.

Since, in a specific case, the DAC graph may be a complete graph we should be able to establish at least 6 types of relationships (if symmetric) – each type of node with each other type and itself.

4.1   Document-Document Relationship

The relationship between documents is the same relationship that exists in a simple, homogeneous graph with only document as nodes. The relationship is influenced by the fact that one document links to another. The strength of the relationship is established on the number of links between two documents. It can be also distinguished whether one document is cited by the other or it is just "see also" or "next" type of link. In addition the impact on the strength of the relationship between two documents may have the *rel* and *rev* attributes of the link. It is intuitive that values of the attributes like *prev*, *next*, *section* and *subsection* should affect the relationship to be stronger than the values like *appendix*, **glossary**, **copyright** or *help*.

4.2   Author-Author Relationship

The relationship of traditional documents' authors can be established on the number of documents they were coauthors of. This will work for research papers published as PDF or documents from digital libraries. In Semantic Web authors' relationship is expressed more explicitly. We can use FOAF and XFN metadata to weight Web users relationships by assigning different impact factors to different combinations of relation types, e.g. relationship declared by XFN *rel="friend met co-worker"* should be stronger than *rel="acquaintance neighbor"*. The value of this relationship may also be influenced by measures like duration, frequency or intensity, used in social network analysis ([17]). Another approach is measuring the relationship strength as a user's Agent Trust in Personal Web of Trust ([15]).

4.3 Concept-Concept Relationship

The Semantic Web's promise was to give access to machine-readable data and ontologies to let machines inference. For most domains of knowledge ontologies are graphs of concepts. Provided with that structure, a distance between two concepts can be established. The strength of a relationship between two concepts is their similarity, which is the inverse of their distance. However in many cases Web data lack a proper ontology. This is where a folksonomy can be used. Though in folksonomies the distance between two concepts is not as easy to establish as it is in ontologies, the concepts relationship's strength can be evaluated on their co-occurring use for tagging a document. So the more documents are tagged with both of the tags (assigned both of the concepts), the stronger the concepts' relationship is.

4.4 Document-Author Relationship

The relationship between a document and its single author is self-evident. If there is more than one author of a single document then the relationship's strength is divided among those authors. However, since an author is also a user that uses a Web document, there can exist a relationship between the two even if the author (user) is not the creator of the document. The relationship may be a User Rank or an Agent Rank for the document estimated according to the trust in documents' authors derived from a Web of Trust as proposed in [15]. Another information that should impact the document-author(user) relationship is the user's ranks used in collaborative filtering systems or the user's comments on the document.

4.5 Document-Concept Relationship

Similarly to the above a relationship between a Web document and a tag (concept) assigned to it is obvious. The relationship's strength is distributed among all the concepts that tag the document. But again, there is more to it than the fact of assigning a tag to a document. To verify if a document was tagged properly a tag weighting may me carried out. The tags that are better weighting terms for the document (e.g. based on the *tf-idf* measure [18]) should have stronger relationship with it. On the other hand if a tag is commonly used to tag documents then it is not a good descriptor. So the rarely used tags should be related stronger to documents they are assigned to than the commonly used tags.

4.6 Author-Concept Relationship

This type of relationship can be established indirectly through documents that have a tag assigned by their author. This will be a redundant information in a DAC graph. However the presented algorithm will not use the original information and the derived one at the same time.

5   The Algorithm

In order to establish consistency and conformance of a document collection, an algorithm for establishing consistent and conformable subcollections is needed. And in order to find out what the subcollections are a method for dividing the collection into a consistency collection and a conformance collection must be presented. Eventually, the dividing algorithm needs the DAC relationships' values as input.

5.1   DAC Relationships' Values

Currently the algorithms is being implemented for experiments on the Wordpress blogging platform. For this implementation the formulas for estimating the relationships' values are defined as follows.

$$rel(d_i,d_j) = \frac{cite(d_i,d_j) + @ b\log(b_i,d_i) + @ b\log(b_i,d_j)}{cite(d_i,*) + cite(*,d_j) + @ b\log(b_i,*)} \; . \tag{1}$$

Value of the relationship between document d_i and d_j (1) depends on the number the documents cite each other (*cite*) in the relation to all the citations they include and the fact that the documents appear on the same blog b_i (*@blog*) in relation to the size of the blog.

$$rel(a_i,a_j) = \frac{2*coauthor(a_i,a_j)}{coauthor(a_i,*) + coauthor(*,a_j)} \; . \tag{2}$$

Value of the relationship between authors a_i and a_j (2) depends on the number the coauthored documents (*coauthor*) in relation to all the coauthored documents with anybody.

$$rel(c_i,c_j) = \frac{2*cooccur(c_i,c_j)}{cooccur(c_i,*) + cooccur(*,c_j)} \; . \tag{3}$$

Value of the relationship between concepts c_i and c_j (3) depends on the number of tagging a document with both c_i and c_j tags (*cooccur*) in relation to all the documents tagged with any tag co-occurring with c_i or c_j.

$$rel(a_i,d_i) = \frac{author(a_i,d_i)}{author(*,d_i)} \; . \tag{4}$$

Value of the relationship between author a_i and document d_i (4) depends on the fact of the author a_i being a coauthor of document d_i (*author*) in relation to all the coauthors of this document.

$$rel(d_i,c_i) = \frac{2*tagged(d_i,c_i)}{tagged(d_i,*) + tagged(*,c_i)} \; . \tag{5}$$

Value of the relationship between document d_i and concept c_i (5) is the combination of the inverse of the number of tags assigned to the document (*tagged*) and the inverse of the number of tags used in the system.

$$rel(a_i,c_i) = \frac{author(a_i,d_i)*tagged(d_i,c_i)}{author(a_i,*)+tagged(*,c_i)}. \tag{6}$$

Value of the relationship between author a_i and concept c_i (6) is the combination of the values from (4) and (5). Experiment results are expected to verify those formulas.

5.2 Consistency Collection and Conformance Collection

As stated earlier consistency of a document collection is established on the basis of relationships among documents and concepts, since there relationship reflect the subject similarity of the documents. On the other hand, the conformance of a document collection takes into the account only the relationships among documents and authors as the relationships indicate the agreement between authors on some subjects described in their documents. Therefore to measure the consistency and conformance the DAC graph (fig. 1.A) must be divided into two graphs: a document-concept graph (fig. 1.B) and the a document-author graph (fig. 1.C) that represent the consistency aspect and the conformance aspect of the collection respectively.

It may not be evident why use a DAC graph, when it is sufficient to use document-author graph and document-concept graph separately to evaluate the consistency and the conformance measures. The main reason and benefit of using the three type nodes graph is that when the division is made some of the relationships may have been left

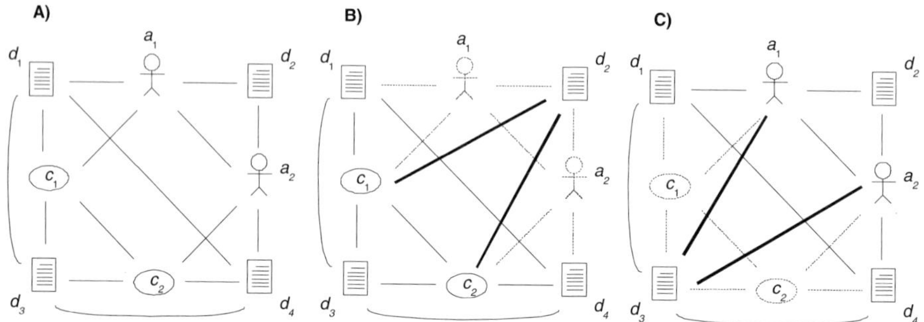

Fig. 1. A) is a fragment of a DAC graph of a Web document collection with 4 document nodes, 2 author nodes and 2 document nodes. The edges represent relationships of different type and different value. B) is a representation of the consistency collection for the collection from A). It is created by removing author nodes along with any edges they were connected to (shown by dotted lines). But before authors are removed, their relationship with documents and concepts are used to derive a direct relationship between documents and concepts if the relationship could not be established before (shown by thick lines). C) is a representation of the conformance collection which is analogical to B), but instead of the author nodes – the concept nodes are removed and new direct relationships between documents and authors are estimated.

out. For example let us take the case presented in fig. 1. If the consistency collection (fig. 1.B) is formed only by removing author nodes and their edges, the document d_2 would be separated from the rest of the collection by not having any direct relationships with any of the rest documents and concepts. But even though the direct relationship for this node were not found, they can be established using the indirect relationships in the DAC graph. The established relationship between document d_2 and concept c_1 was derived from the indirect relationship in which author a_1 was a proxy. The same way the relationship between document d_2 and concept c_2 was derived from the a_2 proxy relationships. This way the document d_2 stays in a relationships with the rest of the collection which would not be possible when using graph of two type nodes separately.

The intuition for establishing a derived document-concept relationship in the aspect of consistency is that the author of the document may have used the concept to tag the document. The relationship was not represented in the DAC graph because the author had not used a specific tag for this document. But the author may have used other tags that have very strong relationships with this specific tag. E.g. this may be the case when some authors use two different tags meant for the same subject, but luckily other authors use both of the tags for the subject (so the relationship between the two tags is strong). The calculated value of the derived relationship should only be influenced by the proxy authors who use the concept frequently for other documents and the concept is strongly related to the concepts used for tagging the document. This is what the derived relationship is intended to reflect.

The intuition and this part of algorithm work in the same way for the conformance aspect of the collection. This means that some document-author relationships may be derived from an indirect concept proxy relationships (thick lines in fig. 1.C). And the proxy concepts should impact the relationship only in the relation to authors that created the document and have a strong relationship with the author.

5.3 Derived Relationships' Values

To estimate the value of direct relationships, derived during the division a document collection into a consistency collection and a conformance collection, all the one node proxy, indirect relationships must be taken into the account.

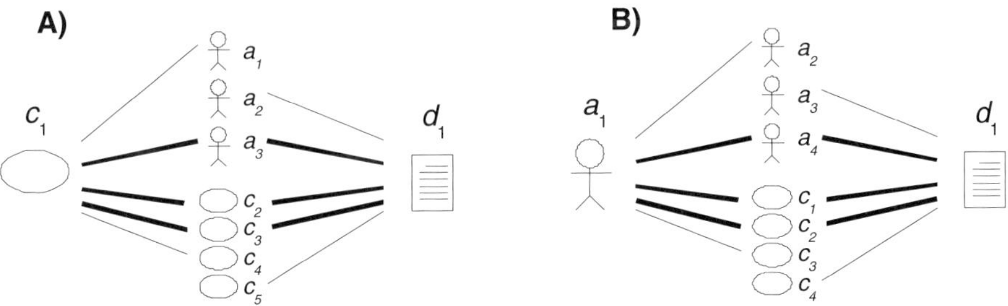

Fig. 2. A) is a fragment of a DAC graph representing some relationships of concept c_1 and document d_1. The relationships that can be used for establishing a direct relationship between concept c_1 and document d_1 are drawn with thick lines. B) is an analogical to A) fragment of a DAC graph but showing relationships that can be used for establishing a direct relationship between author a_1 and document d_1.

Calculation of the values of derived relationships in the context of consistency is presented below. The execution of the algorithm iterates all the author that are proxy nodes for the indirect relationship (a_3 from fig 2.A) and all proxy concept nodes (c_2, c_3 from fig 2.A).

Algorithm for calculating the value of a direct relationship between concept c_1 and document d_1 (see fig. 2.A). The value is a calculated using the values of authors' and concepts' relationships that form one node proxy paths linking the concept and the document (thick lines in fig. 2.A).

```
For all authors a_i that have relationships with both
concept c_1 and document d_1

    For all concepts c_i that have relationships with
    both concept c_1 and document d_1

        rel(c_1,d_1)      +=      rel(c_1,a_i)*rel(a_i,d_1)*

                                  rel(c_1,c_i)*rel(c_i,d_1)
```

The algorithm for calculating indirect relationships in the context of conformance is analogical to the above one and it operates on the relationships of the author-document indirect relationship's proxy nodes (drawn with thick lines on fig 2.B).

5.4 Consistent and Conformable Subcollections

Current approach considers using graph clustering algorithm for establishing consistent subcollection and conformable subcollection. The graph clustering is carried out for the consistency collection graph and the conformance collection graph.

In this case the heterogeneous nature of the graphs does not matter since the input for the algorithm are only the relationships' values. The output of the algorithm are clusters of the nodes. Only the biggest clusters are taken into account. The document nodes in the biggest cluster in the output, when the input was a consistency collection graph, is the consistent subcollection. Analogically, the output biggest cluster's document nodes are the conformable subcollection, if the conformance collection graph was given as an input for the clustering algorithm.

5.5 Consistency and Conformance Measures

Provided a method for establishing consistent and conformable subcollections the consistency and conformance measures for the collection can defined.

$$consistency = \frac{card(cons\_sub(C))}{card(C)}. \tag{7}$$

where: C – Web document collection, $cons\_subc(C)$ – consistent subcollection of C

It shows that consistency measure (7) is depending directly on the consistent subcollection establishing algorithm. It is equal to one if and only if the established consistent subcollection is the input collection itself. In analogical way we define conformance measure (8).

$$conformance = \frac{card(conf\_sub(C))}{card(C)}.\tag{8}$$

where: C – Web document collection, $conf\_subc(C)$ – conformable subcollection of C.

6 Conclusions and Future Work

So far the DAC graph is used as an undirected graph and thus the relationships are modeled to be symmetric. But a hyperlink or a citation is not a symmetric relationship. The same thing is with authors' and concepts' relationships. Future works shall focus on this issue.

When deriving a direct relationship from an indirect relationship only the paths with one proxy node are taken into account. It is planned to examine the behavior of the relationship values when n proxy nodes' relationships are used for deriving.

For current experiments the Markov Cluster Algorithm, presented in [19] and [20], is used as the graph clustering algorithm. Although other graph clustering algorithms' influence on the method is also planned to be examined, it is more likely that further research will consider another approach. The approach is using the maximum clique technique, known from graph theory, where the clique would be the output subcollection. Of course the main problem in using the technique directly to the consistency and conformance collections' graphs is that the graphs are almost always complete graphs, which is the requirement for the clustering algorithms. The maximum clique only uses the existence of an edge information and not it's value, so a threshold can be introduced. The edges with the value not exceeding the threshold will be removed from the graph and then the maximum clique technique can be used.

References

1. Brin, S., Page, L.: The anatomy of a large-scale hypertextual Web search engine. Computer Networks and ISDN Systems 30, 107–117 (1998)
2. Berners-Lee, T.: Timbl's blog | Decentralized Information Group (DIG) Breadcrumbs
3. Kleinberg, J.M.: Authoritative sources in a hyperlinked environment. Journal of the ACM 46, 604–632 (1999)
4. Page, L., et al.: The pagerank citation ranking: Bringing order to the web. Technical report, Stanford Digital Library Technologies Project, 1998 (1998)
5. Berners-Lee, T., Hendler, J., Lassila, O.: The semantic Web. Scientific American 284, 28–37 (2001)
6. Raggett, D., Le Hors, A., Jacobs, I.: HTML 4.01 Specification. W3C Recommendation REC-html401-19991224, World Wide Web Consortium (W3C) (December 1999)
7. Axelsson, J., et al.: XHTML 2.0. W3C Working Draft 26 July 2006, World-Wide Web Consortium (2006)
8. Ding, L., et al.: How the Semantic Web is Being Used: An Analysis of FOAF Documents. In: HICSS 2005. Proceedings of the 38th Annual Hawaii International Conference on System Sciences, p. 113 (2005)
9. Voß, J.: Tagging, Folksonomy & Co - Renaissance of Manual Indexing, cs/0701072v2 (2007)

10. Allsopp, J.: Microformats: Empowering Your Markup for Web 2.0. Friends of ED
11. O'Reilly, T.: What Is Web 2.0: Design Patterns and Business Models for the Next Generation of Software, Marzec (2007)
12. Fellbaum, C.: Wordnet: An Electronic Lexical Database. MIT Press, Cambridge (1998)
13. Mazzocchi, S., Garland, S.: Simile: Practical Metadata for the Semantic Web. XML. com (2005)
14. Auer, S., et al.: DBpedia: A Nucleus for a Web of Open Data. In: 6th International Semantic Web Conference, November 2007, Busan, Korea (2007)
15. Kopel, M., Kazienko, P.: Application of Agent-Based Personal Web of Trust to Local Document Ranking. In: Nguyen, N.T., Grzech, A., Howlett, R.J., Jain, L.C. (eds.) KES-AMSTA 2007. LNCS (LNAI), vol. 4496, p. 288. Springer, Heidelberg (2007)
16. Kopel, M., Danilowicz, C.: Method of completing the consistency graph of a hyperlinked document collection. In: Intelligent technologies for inconsistent knowledge processing, Magill: Advanced Knowledge International, pp. 145–161 (2004)
17. Wasserman, S., Faust, K.: Social Network Analysis: Methods and Applications. Cambridge University Press, Cambridge (1994)
18. Salton, G., McGill, M.J.: Introduction to Modern Information Retrieval. McGraw-Hill, New York (1986)
19. van Dongen, S.: Graph clustering by flow simulation (PhD dissertation), Utrecht, The Netherlands, University of Utrecht, p. 169 (2000)
20. Brandes, U., Gaertler, M., Wagner, D.: Experiments on graph clustering algorithms (2003)

Pedagogical Protocols Selection Automatic Assistance

Paola Britos, Zulma Cataldi, Enrique Sierra, and Ramón García-Martínez

Software & Knowledge Engineering Center. Buenos Aires Institute of Technology
PhD on Computer Science Program. School of Computer Science. University of La Plata
Intelligent Systems Laboratory. School of Engineering. University of Buenos Aires
Educational Informatics Laboratory. School of Engineering. University of Buenos Aires
Intelligent Systems in Engineering Group. School of Engineering. University of Comahue
`rgm@itba.edu.ar`

Abstract. The preliminary results presented in this paper corresponds to a research project oriented to the search of the relationship between the predilection of students concerning learning style and the pedagogical protocols used by the human tutors (professors during the first courses of the Computer Engineering undergraduate Program) by using intelligent systems tools.

1   Introduction

In the tutor module of an intelligent tutoring system, the main sub module contains the pedagogical protocols, which are made up of two basic components: the profile analyzer and the database of pedagogical protocols available in the system. The system has a database of pedagogical protocols [Salgueiro et al., 2005]. Its use will be subordinated to the availability of the contents in the knowledge module, although the lesson always can be generated for some of the available protocols. In order to collect data about the way in which each student learns lists of learning styles will be used as well as tools for data collection. Beginning with the provided information by each student [Felder, 1988; Figueroa, 2003], his or her learning style will be determined. Afterwards, in a second step, the learning style will be linked to the pedagogical protocol. The Felder [1988] list is a validated tool that allows obtaining solid data from students. After giving a questionnaire to the students, we will try to get data records on different sets by using the intelligent systems based tools (such as SOM and TDIDT) in order to obtain a relationship between the preferences of the students and pedagogical protocols. From a statistically significant sample of students for which the lists of complete learning styles had been taken, we will try to see if the learning styles can be grouped according to the education techniques or pedagogical protocols. This will allow correlating the preference of the student with the most suitable pedagogical protocol in the system. As the selection of the pedagogical protocol is one of the elements to determine, it is desired to group the students in families with common characteristics. Therefore the research presented is oriented towards the search of the relationship between the predilection of students concerning learning style and the pedagogical protocols used by the human tutors (professors).

N.T. Nguyen et al. (Eds.): IEA/AIE 2008, LNAI 5027, pp. 331–336, 2008.

2 The Problem

During the first courses of the computer engineering undergraduate program at the University of Buenos Aires, the number of human tutors in Programming Area is usually not enough: the students/tutors ratio is very high and there is a great heterogeneity in the acquired knowledge and background of students. The main idea behind this paper is to describe a system that could emulate a human tutor in the process of helping a student to select a course according to his learning preferences. Thus, the tutor will be able to provide student with a high level of flexibility for the selection of the most adequate tutorial type. This could be a feasible solution to the stated problem.

3 Proposed Solution

The proposed solution can be achieved using the Self Organizing Maps (SOM) neural networks (also known with the name Kohonen [2001] maps) that make a "determined clustering" or grouping action according to common characteristic of the original set of individuals. Once obtained the resulting groups of SOM network an induction algorithm will be used to find the rules that characterize each one of these groups. In this case the algorithms to be used will belong to the family of Top-Down Induction Trees (TDIT) algorithms. Although several algorithms exist that make these functions, a very complete one is Quinlan´s C4.5 [Quinlan, 1993], an extension of algorithm ID3 (Induction Decision Trees) also proposed by Quinlan [Quinlan, 1987]. Its objective is to generate a decision tree and the inference rules that characterize this tree. In this particular case, the C4.5 will take as input the data of the students already clustered by SOM and the output will be the rules describing each cluster.

Once obtaining the smallest amount of rules by pruning the tree to avoid over fitting, we move to another stage of the analysis in which, by means of an inference process, we found the relation between the SOM clusters and the pedagogical protocols available. In order to carry out the inference, additional data concerning to the performance of students with different protocols of education in the courses under study were used. The scheme of the solution can be seen as follows: we start from a student population for which we have their preferences concerning learning styles through the lists of Felder, we form groups of students by using SOM, a table is generated using the previously classified students, using all the attributes that describe them and the cluster predicted by SOM, then a TDIDT algorithm is used to generate the rules that best describe each cluster, relating a particular cluster not only with all its attributes, as in the table of classified students, but also with a set of rules.

In the inference of the pedagogic protocol stage we try to relate the groups generated by SOM to the pedagogical protocols by training a Back propagation type neural network. In order to find the relationship between the learning style and the pedagogical protocol that best fits each group, the basic protocols described by Perkins [Perkins, 1995] in Theory One were used: [a] The *didactic or skillful instruction*: It satisfies a need that arises within the framework of the instruction in order to expand the repertoire of student knowledge [b] *The training*: It satisfies the need to make sure the student will have an effective practice, [c] *Socratic education*: This type of instruction is applied to provide educational aid to the student to include/understand certain concepts by himself and to give him the opportunity to investigate and learn how to do it, all by himself.

4 The Experiments

Two courses (A and B) will be taken belonging to the area of Programming. The only fundamental difference between both of them was centered in the form of education, that is to say, in the pedagogical protocol used in the classes. From this frame of reference, two courses were evaluated according to the control variables raised by García [1995]. The variables raised for the reference courses are the following ones: [a] Similar contents of the courses, [b] Similar schedules, [c] Similar bibliography used for references, [c] Random entrance of the students, without preference defined to some course, [d] Similar previous formation of the assistants and instructors in charge of practical works, [e] Similar didactic tools and [f] Way in which the class is dictated, where each one of the tutors presents the classes based on the pedagogical protocol that turns out more natural to carry out to him.

The possible options are defined in Theory One and that are analyzed in this investigation, independently of the needs or preferences of individualized students. Two more particular hypotheses arise from this main one: (a) The composition of styles of learning (needs and preferences of students) of each student determine the style of education (or pedagogical protocol) (b) Those students for whom the education style does not agree with their preference, show difficulties in the approval of the taught subjects. From the second hypothesis it is given off that for the approved students, the protocol preferred by most of them will have to be the one that agrees with the one used in class by the tutor, whereas for the failed ones, the protocol must be inverted for most of them.

In order to validate this affirmation a network of Back propagation type was trained with the following characteristics: [1] the approved students of the course with professor who dictates in Socratic style and the most of the failed ones of the course with professor who dictates in skillful way and the network is trained considering as output the Socratic protocol, [2] the approved students of the course with professor who dictates in skillful style plus the failed ones of the course with professor who dictates in Socratic way and the network is trained considering the output exit as skillful protocol. In order to suppress the "data noise" the training is carried out in the previously indicated way due to the fact that the groups that are outside the analysis contribute to increase the data noise (those students that approved with any protocol which will be considered "indifferent" and those that failed by lack of study or other reasons) and hope that the error of the tool is minor than the percentage of elements that are outside the analysis.

Therefore, each generated cluster will be analyzed in the following way: [a] approved students: [a1] majority class is related the correct protocol selection, [a2] minority class is related to the indifferent selection; and [b] failed students: [b1] majority class is related to inverted protocol selection, [b2] minority class is related to lack of study. Now we look to relate the forms of education and the learning styles. Following the hypothesis: failed students who do not belong to the main cluster predicted by SOM must have a different preference concerning a pedagogical protocol (inverted in this case) from the one the professor used when they attended the classes. Obtained information may be used by a sub module gives a ranking of best suitable pedagogical protocol, in descendent order with respect to the preference for the selected student.

The fundamental steps for the experimental design are described in Table 1 where it starts with the data capture from the students (to lists of learning styles) and it is used them like entrance for the training of a neural network of SOM type to generate the different groups. Soon the rules identify what describes these groups by means of the TDIDT algorithms.

Table 1. Steps for the experimental design

Step	Input	Action	Output
1	Data recollection from students	Use Felder tool on students	Result of the Felder tool.
2	Felder tool result	SOM Training	Students Clusters
3	Cluster + Felder tool results.	Use C4.5 algorithm	Rules describing each generated cluster and the corresponding decision tree.
4	Academic perform-ance	Academic data grid	Academic grid
5	Result of the Felder tool + Academic grid + Clusters	Analysis of the cluster and determination of reprobated students.	Reprobated Student List for each cluster.
6	Result of the Felder tool.	Back propagation training	Determination of the training error and the data out of analysis. Find the relation between learning style and pedagogic protocol.

If the amount of clusters is very high, it may occur that it does not exists a correlation between so many pedagogical protocols and clusters, since it is started from the hypothesis that 3 pedagogical protocols exist (the proposed by Theory One). The number of clusters which is expected to get will be annotated between two and three. The results obtained from SOM were two clusters of data with all the attributes: Cluster 1 with 6 (5%) and Cluster 2 with 114 (95%). The result is within the awaited amount of clusters and therefore the experimental data, they agree in the amount of clusters generated. As all the data are categorical, the generated rules will not have any range for them (for example: the continuous data). In order to find the attributes with greater gain of information, it is required to use the first N passages of the TDIDT Algorithm. In this case, the first nine were taken and the rules appear in Table 2.

The Intelligent Tutorial System requires minor amount of information to select the pedagogical protocol of the student and with easier access information (it is simpler to know the answers of some key questions in the list that the answers to the entire questionnaire). Training this way it is managed to suppress the "noise" that contributes the

Table 2. Resulting rules to cross the tree generated by the C4.5 Algorithm

Rule	Antecedent	Consequent
Rule 1	**If** "Normally they consider me: Extrovert"	**Then** Cluster 2
Rule 2	**If** "Normally they don't consider me Reserved neither Extroverted"	**Then** Cluster 1
Rule 3	**If** "I Remember easily: Something that I have thought much"	**Then** Cluster 2
Rule 4	**If** "I don't remember easily something that I have thought much or something that I did"	**Then** Cluster 1
Rule 5	**If** "I learn: To a normal rate, methodically. If I make an effort , it profit".	**Then** Cluster 2
Rule 6	**If** "I do not learn to a normal rate, not methodically neither disordered"	**Then** Cluster 1
Rule 7	**If** "When I think about what I did yesterday, most of the times I think about: Images"	**Then** Cluster 2
Rule 8	**If** "When I think about what I did yesterday, most of the times I think about: Words"	**Then** Cluster 2
Rule 9	**If** "When I think about what I did yesterday, most of the times I don't think about words neither images"	**Then** Cluster 1

groups that are outside the analysis. In Table 3 the results of the students discriminated by courses can be seen, counting total students, students failed classified as belonging to the cluster in opposition to the one of the majority and the percentage that relates the failed and approved students that in addition are bad classified.

For this experience the network of the Backpropagation type trained and a ranking (scale) of pedagogical protocols most adapted for a particular situation was obtained, in order to give flexibility to the module that stores the contents.

Table 3. Summary of percentage obtained for the analysis of students, by courses

Observed Characteristic	Course A	Course B
Total of Students (For this study)	47	53
Students who reprobated the partial evaluation and were in a course with different pedagogical protocol	30	0
Students who approved the partial evaluation were in a course with different pedagogical protocol (inverted)	10	33
Approved students (no mattering about the protocol)	7	20
Reprobated students respect to the approved ones, within the subgroup badly classified	75%	0%

For the training of the Back propagation network 67% of the data (qualifications) were used randomly whereas 33% of the remaining data were used to validate the generated model. After more than 100 training of 1000 cycles each one, where it was carried out in order to diminish the error in the resulting network, it was reached the conclusion that the optimal values for the parameters of the network are those that are seen on Table 3.

Table 4. Neural Net Training Results

Characteristic	Value
% Error (Training group)	3.75%
% Error (Validation group)	2.00%
Network characteristics	
Input neuron	13
First hidden layer neurons	20
Second hidden layer neurons	20
Output neurons	2

This training is valid since the error of the tool (3,75% for the set of training and 2,00 % for the validation set) is minor than the error of the elements that were outside the analysis, which represents the students who did not approve because lack of study, although the pedagogical protocol agreed with the preference of the student (who is 25%). Therefore it is possible to conclude that: [a] course B is related to cluster 1: since the errors induced by elements of cluster 2 within the course are in a 75% or in other words, the network classifies to 75% of the students failed in the course and [b] course A is related to cluster 2: since another possible allocation in this case does not exist and in addition the percentage error of classification and reprobation is of 0%. The obtained results agree with the affirmations of Perkins, where the Back propagation network predicts that most of the failed students must have received classes using another pedagogical protocol. Socratic protocol is related with Cluster 2 and Magistral protocol is related with Cluster 1.

5 Preliminary Conclusions

The preliminary research described in this paper tend to provide to the field of the Intelligent Tutorial Systems a tool, to facilitate the automatic selection of the suitable pedagogical protocol, according to the student preferences.

When validating the model against the real data, as much for the data triangulation as the training of the neural networks that support the model, it was found that the data adapted very satisfactorily to the preliminary test conditions became not only a theoretical tool, but also a validated instrument to help the selection of the best course pedagogical protocol according to student strengths.

Next research step will focus on verifying experimentally the expectation that right selection of the pedagogical protocol will imply the improvement of the student population engineering undergraduate program course performance.

Acknowledgements

The authors would like to thank the National Agency for Science Research Promotion; Argentine, Grant ANPCyT, BID 1728/OC-AR PICT 02-13533 for supporting partially this research.

References

Felder, R., Silverman, L.: Learning Styles and Teaching Styles in Engineering Education. Engr. Education 78(7), 674–681 (1988)

Figueroa, N., Lage, F., Cataldi, Z., Denazis, J.: Evaluation of the experiences for improvement of the process of learning in initial subjet of the computer science careeer. In: Proc. Int. Conf. on Eng. and Computer Educ. ICECE 2003, March 16-19, 2003, San Paulo, Brazil (2003)

García, M.: El paradigma de Pensamiento del profesor. Editorial CEAC, Barcelona (1995)

Kohonen, T.: Self-Organizing Maps, 3rd edn. Springer, Heidelberg (2001)

Quinlan, J.: Simplifying Decision Trees. Simplifying Decision Trees. International Journal of Man-Machine Studies 27(3), 221–234 (1987)

Quinlan, J.: C4.5: Programs for Machine Learning. Morgan Kaufmann, San Francisco (1993)

Salgueiro, F., Costa, G., Cataldi, Z., García-Martinez, R., Lage, F.: Sistemas Inteligentes para el Modelado del Tutor. In: Salgueiro, F., Costa, G., Cataldi, Z., García-Martinez, R. (eds.) Proc. GCETE, Brazil, p. 63 (2005)

Oates, T.: The Effects of Training Set Size on Decision Tree Complexity. In: Proc. 14th International Conference on Machine Learning (1997)

Perkins, D.: Smart schools. A division of Simon & Schuster, Inc., The Free Press (1995)

Lagrangian-Based Solution Approaches for a Resource-Constrained Parallel Machine Scheduling Problem with Machine Eligibility Restrictions

Emrah B. Edis[1], Ceyhun Araz[1], and Irem Ozkarahan[2]

[1] Dokuz Eylul University, Department of Industrial Engineering, 35100, Izmir, Turkey
{emrah.edis, ceyhun.araz}@deu.edu.tr
[2] Troy University, Computer Science Department, Montgomery, AL 36103-4419, USA
iozkarahan@troy.edu

Abstract. This study is motivated by a real world scheduling problem in an injection molding department of an electrical appliance company. In this paper, a resource-constrained parallel machine scheduling problem with machine eligibility restrictions is investigated. For the problem, an integer linear program is developed with the objective of minimizing total flow time. Based on this model, a Lagrangian-based solution approach with a subgradient optimization procedure has been proposed. Additionally, a problem-specific heuristic algorithm is developed to obtain near-optimal solutions. Through randomly generated instances of the problem, it is demonstrated that the proposed algorithms generate not only very tight lower bounds but also efficient results with a small optimality gap.

Keywords: Parallel machine scheduling, Resource constraints, Machine eligibility, Lagrangian relaxation, Subgradient optimization.

1 Introduction

In most of parallel machine scheduling (PMS) studies, the only considered resources are machines [1,2]. However, in real-life manufacturing systems, jobs may also require *additional resources* such as machine operators, tools, pallets etc. [1]. A common example of additional resources is the cross-trained workers that perform different tasks associated with different machines [3]. In real-world PMS environments, jobs may often not be processed on any of the available machines but rather must be processed on a machine belonging to a specific subset of the machines [2]. This situation, called *machine eligibility restrictions*, is also widely encountered in real scheduling environments. This study deals with a resource constrained parallel machine scheduling problem (RCPMSP) including machine eligibility restrictions.

PMS problems have received a lot of attention in the literature. A limited number of these studies were devoted to RCPMSPs. In an earlier study, Blazewicz et al. [4] classified the resource constrained scheduling problems in terms of problem complexity and resource specifications. Edis and Ozkarahan [5] present a brief review on RCPMSPs. Daniels et al. [3] and Ruiz-Torres and Centeno [6] consider a fixed

N.T. Nguyen et al. (Eds.): IEA/AIE 2008, LNAI 5027, pp. 337–346, 2008.

amount of an additional resource is dedicated to every machine along the scheduling horizon. However, this static assignment reduces the flexibility of the additional resource. A number of papers [e.g.,7,8,9,10] studied parallel-dedicated machine environments, i.e., the set of jobs that will be processed on each machine is predetermined. This situation also reduces the flexibility of the system considering only allocation of additional resources to the machines. Some papers [e.g.,1,11] deal with identical machines. Finally, a few papers [12,13,14] including machine eligibility restrictions assume that only the number of auxiliary equipment (e.g., dies) is limited instead of considering a common shared resource (e.g., machine operators).

The machine scheduling problems are inherently difficult to solve via classical integer programming (IP) methods because of their combinatorial nature. When the additional resource constraints are the case, scheduling problems become more complex. Since the use of exact methods is impractical for most real-world applications, it may be preferable to obtain rapid, easily applicable and near-optimal solutions. Hence, it is important to develop effective heuristics for these problems.

Lagrangian relaxation is a mathematical programming technique used in constrained optimization. Since Lagrangian relaxation algorithms offer a lower bound (in minimization) to the original problem, it is often used as a measure of efficiency of the schedule obtained by a proposed heuristic. Lagrangian relaxation often generates infeasible solutions. However, one can easily adjust the infeasible solution to obtain a feasible schedule by using a Lagrangian heuristic [15]. Although many studies [e.g.,1,15,16] have used Lagrangian relaxation for PMS problems; to the best of our knowledge, only Ventura and Kim [1], which also motivates our study, use Lagrangian relaxation for a RCPMSP with identical machines. However, they do not consider machine eligibility restrictions.

Differently from previous studies, our paper considers machine eligibility restrictions and common shared resource cases together, and proposes two heuristics for the considered RCPMSP. The first one is a Lagrangian-based algorithm which adjusts infeasible solutions of Lagrangian Relaxation Problem (LRP) to obtain feasible schedules, while the second one is a problem-based heuristic. Lagrangian relaxation has also been used to obtain tight lower bounds. Through randomly generated test problems, it is demonstrated that the proposed algorithms produce not only very tight lower bounds but also efficient results with small optimality gap.

The rest of the paper is organized as follows. In Section 2, a 0-1 IP model with its LRP for the considered RCPMSP is presented. Section 3 is devoted to explain proposed algorithms, i.e., a Lagrangian-based solution approach (LSA) with the subgradient optimization procedure and a problem-specific heuristic (PSH). Computational results are given and discussed in Section 4. Finally, Section 5 summarizes the paper and outlines the directions for the future research.

2   Integer Programming Model of the Problem

This section presents an IP model for a RCPMSP with machine eligibility restrictions which is motivated by a real life scheduling problem of injection molding machines in an electrical appliance company.

In the molding shop, there are a series of injection-molding machines on which dies can be mounted according to their compatibilities. In the plant, only one unit is available from each type of die. Therefore, the parts that share the same die cannot be processed at the same time interval.

A fixed number of machine operators are responsible for unloading parts from the machines, inspecting them, trimming excess material, and putting the parts into containers. These tasks may not require an operator's full attention at one machine. Based on data collected on work content, there are three types of processes:

1. *manually operated processes* –requires exactly one operator along the processing.
2. *semi-automated processes* – one operator can deal with two machines.
3. *fully-automated processes* – no operator is required during the processing.

The basic assumption in this problem is the parts that share the same die constitute a *job string*. The IP model is also based on the following assumptions:
1. All jobs are available for processing at time zero.
2. A machine can process at most one job at a time.
3. All processing times of job strings are assumed to be equal.
4. Operator requirements are fixed; i.e., no operators, one-half, or exactly one.
5. Operators are continuously available for the specified scheduling horizon.
6. Operator transfer times between machines are negligible.
7. Time window for scheduling of jobs are fixed to unit periods.
8. All the operators are fully cross-trained workers.

The proposed IP model and its LRP are given in the following sections.

2.1 Integer Programming Model

The following notation is used within the formulation of IP model.

Indices and Parameters

i: index of job strings (or dies) to be scheduled. $i = 1, ..., n$
j: index of parallel machines. $j = 1, ..., m$
t: index of time periods in the scheduling horizon. $t = 1, ..., T$
res_i: the amount of operator required by job i.
b: available number of operators for the scheduling horizon.

$$M_{ij} = \begin{cases} 1, & \text{if machine } j \text{ is compatible with job } i \\ 0, & \text{otherwise.} \end{cases}$$

Decision Variables

$$x_{ijt} = \begin{cases} 1, & \text{if job } i \text{ is processed on machine } j \text{ at time interval } [t-1, t) \\ 0, & \text{otherwise.} \end{cases}$$

Using this notation, the following IP model is developed:

$$\text{minimize} \quad \sum_{i=1}^{n} \sum_{j=1}^{m} \sum_{t=1}^{T} t\, x_{ijt} \tag{1}$$

subject to:

$$\sum_{i=1}^{n} x_{ijt} \leq 1 \qquad j = 1, ..., m \; ; t = 1, ..., T \tag{2}$$

$$\sum_{j=1}^{m} x_{ijt} \leq 1 \qquad i = 1, ..., n \; ; t = 1, ..., T \tag{3}$$

$$\sum_{i=1}^{n} \sum_{j=1}^{m} res_i \, x_{ijt} \leq b \qquad t = 1, ..., T \tag{4}$$

$$\sum_{j=1}^{m} \sum_{t=1}^{T} x_{ijt} = 1 \qquad i = 1, ..., n \tag{5}$$

$$\sum_{t=1}^{T} x_{ijt} \leq M_{ij} \qquad i = 1, ..., n \; ; j = 1, ..., m \tag{6}$$

$$x_{ijt} \in \{0,1\} \qquad i = 1, ..., n \; ; j = 1, ..., m \; ; t = 1, ..., T \tag{7}$$

The objective function (1) minimizes total flow time. Constraints (2) ensure that no more than one job can be assigned to any machine at any time interval. Constraints (3) guarantee that each job can be processed on only one machine at any time interval. Constraints (4) ensure that total number of operators assigned to jobs at any time interval is less than or equal to the available number of operators, b. Constraints (5) guarantee that each job must be processed. Constraints (6) ensure that a job cannot be assigned to an incompatible machine. Finally (7) states that all x_{ijt} are 0-1 variables.

2.2 Lagrangian Relaxation of the Problem

Lagrangian relaxation is an approach to handle computationally hard IP problems. Specifically, some sets of difficult constraints are dualized to create a LRP which is easier to solve [1]. In our problem, constraint set (4) is dualized so that the associated LRP has a special structure and can be easily solved. By relaxing constraint set (4), the following problem is obtained:

$$(\text{LRP}) \; Z_D(\lambda) = \text{minimize} \sum_{i=1}^{n} \sum_{j=1}^{m} \sum_{t=1}^{T} t \, x_{ijt} + \sum_{t=1}^{T} \lambda_t \left[\sum_{i=1}^{n} \sum_{j=1}^{m} res_i x_{ijt} - b \right] \tag{8}$$

subject to (2), (3), (5), (6), and (7).

where $\lambda = [\lambda_t]$ is the set of nonnegative Lagrangian multipliers for constraint set (4).

The objective of the Lagrangian dual program (LDP) is then to find $\lambda = [\lambda_t]$ that makes the lower bound as large as possible, i.e.,

$$(\text{LDP}) \quad \text{maximize} \quad Z_D(\lambda)$$

$$\text{subject to} \quad \lambda \geq 0 \tag{9}$$

To determine the optimal values of $\lambda = [\lambda_t]$, a subgradient optimization procedure is applied. The following section gives the proposed heuristic algorithms and the details of the subgradient optimization procedure.

3   Heuristic Algorithms and Subgradient Optimization Procedure

In the remainder of the paper, the following additional notation is used:

J	set of jobs
NRJ	set of non-resource jobs
$NRSJ_t$	set of non-resource jobs processed at time t
RJ	set of resource-jobs
RSJ_t	set of resource jobs processed at time t
M	set of machines
ME_i	eligible machine set of job i
R_t	the current usage of operators at time t
NM_i	the total number of eligible machines that job i can be processed on
LFJ	least flexible job first
MFJ	most flexible job first
UB^r	updated upper bound at iteration r of subgradient optimization procedure
LB^r	updated lower bound at iteration r of subgradient optimization procedure

As stated above, the jobs are separated to two sub-sets: NRJ and RJ. A non-resource job requires no operator during its process, while a resource-job necessitates a pre-determined amount of operator during its operation. Note that, LFJ is a well-known dispatching rule for PMS problems with machine eligibility restrictions [2].

3.1   Lagrangian-Based Solution Approach (LSA)

The proposed LSA involves three basic components. The first one is the initial heuristic (IH) which constructs an initial feasible solution. The second one is the Lagrangian heuristic (LH) that transforms the infeasible schedule obtained from LRP to a feasible one. Finally, the last component, subgradient optimization procedure, is an iterative procedure with two main goals: to maximize the LB^r obtained from LRP and to update the UB^r by applying LH to LRP through the consecutive iterations.

Initial Heuristic (IH). The aim of IH is to provide an initial upper bound (i.e., UB^0) for the subgradient procedure. Feasible period length obtained by the solution of IH is employed to determine length of scheduling horizon, T, to be used in LRP and PSH.

- *Step* 1. Arrange the jobs in set J in decreasing order of res_i. If there are more than one job with same res_i, arrange them in non-decreasing order of NM_i, i.e., apply LFJ rule. It is assumed that, the jobs are indexed by their rank in the arranged list. Note that $[i]$ denotes the job with index i in the arranged list.
- *Step* 2. Set $R_t = 0$, for all t; $x_{ijt} = 0$, for all i, j, t; set $i{=}1, j{=}1, t{=}1$.
- *Step* 3. Assign job $[i]$ to machine j at time t if the following conditions are satisfied:
  (i) $R_t + res_{[i]} \leq b$ (ii) $j \in ME_{[i]}$ (iii) $\sum_{l=1}^{n} x_{ljt} = 0$. Update $x_{[i]jt} = 1$, $R_t = R_t + res_{[i]}$, $i{=}i{+}1$ and go to Step 5. Otherwise, go to next step.
- *Step* 4. If $j \geq m$, set $t{=}t{+}1, j{=}1$; otherwise, $j{=}j{+}1$. Go to Step 3.
- *Step* 5. If $i{>}n$, $z^0 = \sum_{i=1}^{n} \sum_{j=1}^{m} \sum_{t=1}^{T} t x_{ijt}$,STOP. Otherwise, set $j{=}1, t{=}1$.Go to Step 3.

Lagrangian Heuristic (LH). In LH, we take the solution to the current LRP and attempt to convert it into a feasible solution for the original problem by suitable adjustments. This feasible solution constitutes an upper bound on the optimal solution [17]. This upper bound is used to update UB^r through the iterations of subgradient procedure. The proposed LH takes R_t and x_{ijt} values from LRP at each step of the subgradient optimization procedure.

- *Step* 1. If $R_t \leq b$ for all t, go to Step 14. Otherwise, pick the period t with maximum R_t. If a tie occurs, assign the latest period among the alternatives as t.
- *Step* 2. Arrange the jobs in set RSJ_t in decreasing order of NM_i. (i.e., apply the MFJ rule. It chooses the job that can be processed on the largest number of machines.) Break ties arbitrarily. It is assumed that, jobs are indexed by their rank in the arranged list (Note that $[i]$ denotes the job with index i in the arranged list). Set $i=1$.
- *Step* 3. If $i \leq n(RSJ_t)$, where $n(RSJ_t)$ denotes the number of elements in set RSJ_t, set $t^*=1$, $j=1$; go to next step. Otherwise, determine the current feasible period length, say t^c, and pick current machine of job $[i]$, say $v \in M$. Set $i=1$, go to Step 7.
- *Step* 4. If $t^* < t$, go to next step. Otherwise, $i=i+1$, go to Step 3.
- *Step* 5. Assign job $[i]$ to machine j at time t^* if following conditions are satisfied:
  (i) $R_{t^*} + res_{[i]} \leq b$ (ii) $j \in ME_{[i]}$ (iii) $\sum_{l=1}^{n} x_{ljt^*} = 0$. Update $x_{[i]jt} = 0$, $x_{[i]jt^*} = 1$,
  $R_t = R_t - res_{[i]}$, $R_{t^*} = R_{t^*} + res_{[i]}$, and go to Step 1. Otherwise, go to next step.
- *Step* 6. If $j \geq m$, set $j=1$, $t^* = t^* + 1$, go to Step 4. Otherwise, $j = j+1$. Go to Step 5.
- *Step* 7. If $i \leq n(RSJ_t)$, set $t^{**}=1$, go to next step. Otherwise, set $i=1$, $j=1$, $t^{***}=t+1$, go to Step 12.
- *Step* 8. Arrange the jobs in $NRSJ_{t^{**}}$ by applying MFJ rule. Break ties arbitrarily. Again, assume that the jobs are indexed by their rank in the arranged list. Set $k = 1$.
- *Step* 9. If $t^{**} \leq t_c$, go to next step. Otherwise, $i = i + 1$, go to Step 7.
- *Step* 10. If $k \leq n(NRSJ_{t^{**}})$, go to next step. Otherwise, $t^{**} = t^{**} + 1$, go to Step 8.
- *Step* 11. Interchange job $[i]$ on machine v at time t with job $[k]$ on machine j at time t^{**} if following conditions are satisfied: (i) $j \in ME_{[i]}$, $v \in ME_{[k]}$ (ii) $R_{t^{**}} + res_{[i]} \leq b$.
  Update $x_{[i]vt} = 0$, $x_{[i]jt^{**}} = 1$, $x_{[k]jt^{**}} = 0$, $x_{[k]vt} = 1$ $R_t = R_t - res_{[i]}$, $R_{t^{**}} = R_{t^{**}} + res_{[i]}$
  go to Step 1. Otherwise, $k=k+1$, go to Step 10.
- *Step* 12. If $j > m$, set $j=1$, $t^{***} = t^{***} + 1$; go to next step. Otherwise, go to next step.
- *Step* 13. Assign job $[i]$ to machine j at time t^{***} if following conditions are satisfied:
  (i) $R_{t^{***}} + res_{[i]} \leq b$ (ii) $j \in ME_{[i]}$ (iii) $\sum_{l=1}^{n} x_{ljt^{***}} = 0$. Update $x_{[i]jt} = 0$, $x_{[i]jt^{***}} = 1$,
  $R_t = R_t - res_{[i]}$, $R_{t^{***}} = R_{t^{***}} + res_{[i]}$, go to Step 1. Otherwise, $j=j+1$, go to Step 12.
- *Step* 14. Arrange the jobs in NRJ by increasing order of their job number. It is again assumed that, the jobs are indexed by their rank in the arranged list. Set $g=1$.
- *Step* 15. If $g \leq n(NRJ)$, say the current period of job $[g]$ is t' and set $t''=1$, go to next step. Otherwise, $z = \sum_{i=1}^{n} \sum_{j=1}^{m} \sum_{t=1}^{t_c} t\, x_{ijt}$, STOP.
- *Step* 16. If $t'' < t'$, set $j=1$, go to next step. Otherwise, $g=g+1$, go to Step 15.

- *Step* 17. If $j > m$, set $t'' = t'' + 1$, go to Step 16. Otherwise, go to next step.
- *Step* 18. Assign job $[g]$ to machine j at time t'' if following conditions are satisfied:
  (i) $j \in ME_{[g]}$ (ii) $\sum_{l=1}^{n} x_{ljt''} = 0$. Update $x_{[g]jt''} = 1$, $x_{[g]jt'} = 0$; $g = g+1$, go to Step 15. Otherwise, $j = j+1$, go to Step 17.

Subgradient Optimization Procedure. Subgradient optimization is used to both maximize the lower bound obtained from LRP and update the upper bound by applying LH. The details of the subgradient optimization algorithm are provided below. A similar notation of [1] is used within this procedure.

1. Set initial values for Lagrangian multipliers, iteration counter and bounds: $\lambda_t = 0$ for all t, $r = 1$, $LB^0 = 0$, $UB^0 = z^0$; where z^0 is obtained from IH.

2. Solve LRP with the current set of multipliers (λ_t^r). Let x_{ijt}^r be the solution values and $Z_D(\lambda^r)$ the optimal objective function value of LRP.

3. Update the lower bound: $LB^r = \max\left\{LB^{r-1}, Z_D(\lambda^r)\right\}$.

4. If LRP generates a feasible solution, set $\bar{x}_{ijt}^r = x_{ijt}^r$. Otherwise, generate a feasible solution $\bar{x}_{ijt}^r$ with objective function value $z(\bar{x}_{ijt}^r)$ from LH.

5. Update the upper bound: $UB^r = \min\left\{UB^{r-1}, z(\bar{x}_{ijt}^r)\right\}$

6. If $(UB^r - LB^r) \le \varepsilon$, STOP. Otherwise, go to Step 7.

7. Calculate the subgradients evaluated at the current solution:
   $$G_t^r = \sum_{i=1}^{n} \sum_{j=1}^{m} (res_i \, x_{ijt}^r) - b \; ; \; t = 1, \dots, T$$

8. Determine the step size : $T^r = \pi^r (UB^r - LB^r)/\sum_{t=1}^{T} G_t^{r^2}$

9. Update the λ_t using: $\lambda_t^{r+1} = \max\left\{0, \lambda_t^r + T^r G_t^r\right\}$ $t = 1, \dots, T$

10. Set the iteration number ($r = r + 1$), and go to Step 2.

After a preliminary computational test, it was found that the best convergence criterion is to set $\pi^1 = 2$. If LB^r and UB^r do not improve during 10 consecutive subgradient iterations, the value of π^r is divided by two. In Step 6, if the error (i.e., $UB^r - LB^r$) becomes less than or equal to ε ($\varepsilon = 0.999$), the subgradient procedure is terminated. Since the value of objective function should be integer, $UB^r - LB^r < 1$ indicates that LSA converges to an optimal solution. If the procedure is not stopped with the error, we terminate it when π^r gets smaller than 0.0005.

3.2 Problem Specific Heuristic (PSH)

The aim of PSH is to find near-optimal solutions to the considered RCPMSP.

- *Step* 1. Set $x_{ijt} = 0$ for all i, j, t; $R_t = 0$, for all t. Arrange the jobs in set RJ in non-decreasing order of res_i. If there are more than one job with same res_i, arrange them with LFJ rule. It is again assumed that, the jobs are indexed by their rank in the arranged list. Remember that $[i]$ denotes the job with index i in the arranged list. Set $i=1, j=1, t=1$.

- *Step* 2. Assign job $[i]$ to machine j at time t if the following conditions are satisfied: (i) $R_t + res_{[i]} \le b$ (ii) $j \in ME_{[i]}$. (iii) $\sum_{l=1}^{n} x_{ljt} = 0$. Update $x_{[i]jt} = 1$, $R_t = R_t + res_{[i]}$, $i=i+1$ and go to Step 4. Otherwise, go to next step.
- *Step* 3. If $j \ge m$, $t = t + 1$, $j = 1$. Otherwise, $j=j+1$, go to Step 2.
- *Step* 4. If $i > n(RJ)$, go to Step 5. Otherwise, $j=1$, $t=1$, go to Step 2.
- *Step* 5. Arrange the jobs in *NRJ* with LFJ rule. It is again assumed that, the jobs are indexed by their rank in the arranged list. Set $i=1, j=1, t=1$.
- *Step* 6. Assign job $[i]$ to machine j at time t if the following conditions are satisfied: (i) $j \in ME_{[i]}$ (ii) $\sum_{l=1}^{n} x_{ljt} = 0$. Update $x_{[i]jt} = 1$, $i=i+1$, go to Step 8. Otherwise, go to next step.
- *Step* 7. If $j \ge m$, $t = t+1$, $j=1$. Otherwise, $j=j+1$. Go to Step 6.
- *Step* 8. If $i > n(NRJ)$, $z^{PSH} = \sum_{i=1}^{n} \sum_{j=1}^{m} \sum_{t=1}^{T} t\, x_{ijt}$, STOP. Otherwise, $j=1$, $t=1$, go to Step 6.

4   Computational Results

The LSA and PSH given in the previous section are coded in OPLScript [18]. OPLScript is a script language that composes and controls OPL models. OPL Studio 3.7 [18] is the development environment of OPLScript. All generated problems are implemented in OPL Studio 3.7 using a Pentium D 3.4 Ghz 4 GB RAM computer.

We considered two sets of instances: 50 and 100 jobs. Two levels of processing flexibility for the machines are determined using the process flexibility index (F_p) defined in [19]. For all test instances, the cases that have F_p higher than 0.65 are defined as high processing flexibility cases, whereas the others that have a F_p less than 0.35 are considered as low processing flexibility cases. The number of machines is selected as three, five and eight. The number of operators available is taken as one, two and three with respect to the number of machines. For each combination of parameters, 30 test problems were solved. For all problems, operator requirements of jobs are generated from a discrete uniform distribution for the values 0, 0.5 and 1.

Table 1 summarizes the computational results for LSA and PSH. To investigate the effectiveness of heuristics, we gathered average number of iterations, CPU time, maximum and average gap percent and number of optimal solutions.

The results show that LSA gives good results based on average percent deviation which represents the mean gap percent between the lower bound and upper bound obtained by subgradient optimization procedure. It should also be noted that subgradient optimization procedure produces very tight lower bounds for almost all cases. The LSA attained less than 1% deviation from the optimal solution in 169 problems out of 240 test problems. The average gap percent for all problems is 0.77. It should be also noted that LSA gives relatively better results in case of low processing flexibility environments. While LSA reaches less than 1% deviation from the optimal solution in 60.83% of test problems with high flexibility, it ensures less than %1 deviation in 80.00% of test problems with low flexibility.

Table 1. The Computational Results

n	m	# of Oper. (b)	Proc. Flex. (F_p)	Lagrangian-based Solution Approach (LSA)				Problem Specific Heuristic (PSH)	
				Avg. # of Iter.	Avg. Time(s)	Max.% (UB-LB)/LB	Avg.% (UB-LB)/LB	Max.% (UB-LB)/LB	Avg.% (UB-LB)/LB
50	3	1	Low	148.70	21.86	2.92	0.97 (9)	11.25	2.70 (4)
			High	167.87	33.77	4.61	1.91 (3)	4.57	1.00 (11)
	5	2	Low	88.40	9.33	1.00	0.26 (20)	11.11	2.12 (3)
			High	120.50	19.06	1.02	0.35 (16)	1.02	0.42 (13)
100	5	2	Low	167.93	95.97	1.09	0.63 (0)	3.69	1.03 (1)
			High	162.83	132.33	1.59	1.03 (1)	1.71	0.34 (6)
	8	3	Low	150.73	88.40	1.09	0.52 (4)	3.58	0.81 (1)
			High	144.00	121.68	1.00	0.47 (7)	1.10	0.27 (15)

PSH also gives good results. PSH attained less than 1% deviation from the optimal solution in 157 out of 240 test problems. The average percent deviation for all problems is 1.08 %. Different from LSA, PSH provides relatively better results in case of high processing flexibility. While the number of problems that PSH reached less than 1% deviation is 60 (50%) among 120 problems with low flexibility, it provides less than %1 deviation in 97 (80.33%) out of 120 problems with high process flexibility. These results show that LSA provides superior performance than PSH in low flexibility cases whereas PSH performs better when the process flexibility is high. The average gap measures given in Table 1 also confirm this outcome.

It should also be highlighted in Table 1 that the LSA gives the solutions within a timely fashion for all cases. Note that CPU time of PSH is negligible.

In Table 1, the numbers in parentheses represent the number of times that the algorithms achieved optimal solutions. Although the aim of the proposed heuristics is to reach near-optimal solutions, LSA and PSH attained optimal solutions in 60 and 54 test problems, respectively. When both heuristics are considered together, we reached the optimal solutions in 85 out of 240 test problems.

Clearly, the considered problem can also be tried to solve by using some optimization software. However one can easily observe that such tools may not handle large problem sizes (e.g., 100 or more jobs) and may fail to find a solution (even feasible) in a reasonable time. This is one of the reasons why we developed heuristic algorithms for this problem.

5   Conclusion and Future Research

This paper has addressed a RCPMSP with machine eligibility restrictions. We constructed a 0-1 IP model and proposed a Lagrangian-based solution approach (LSA) that involves an IH, a LH and a subgradient optimization procedure to obtain tight lower bounds and near optimal solutions. A problem specific heuristic (PSH) is also proposed. By means of randomly generated instances of the problem, it is showed that the proposed algorithms produce not only very tight lower bounds but also efficient results with a small optimality gap. LSA gives superior results in low flexible machine environments, while PSH is relatively better in high flexible ones.

This research can be extended to problems with more jobs, machines and resource types and to the cases with different objectives and non-equal processing times.

References

1. Ventura, J.A., Kim, D.: Parallel Machine Scheduling with Earliness-Tardiness Penalties and Additional Resource Constraints. Comput. Oper. Res. 30, 1945–1958 (2003)
2. Pinedo, M.: Scheduling Theory, Algorithms and Systems. Prentice-Hall, Englewood Cliffs (1995)
3. Daniels, R.L., Hua, S.Y., Webster, S.: Heuristics for Parallel-Machine Flexible-Resource Scheduling Problems with Unspecified Job Assignment. Comput. Oper. Res. 26, 143–155 (1999)
4. Blazewicz, J., Lenstra, J.K., Rinnooy Kan, A.H.G.: Scheduling subject to Resource Constraints: Classification and Complexity. Discrete Appl. Math. 5, 11–24 (1983)
5. Edis, E.B., Ozkarahan, I.: Parallel Machine Scheduling with Additional Resources: A Brief Review of the Literature. In: The 11th IFAC Intl. Symposium CEFIS 2007, Istanbul, Turkey, pp. 381–386 (2007)
6. Ruiz-Torres, A.J., Centeno, G.: Scheduling with Flexible Resources in Parallel Work centers to Minimize Maximum Completion Time. Comput. Oper. Res. 34, 48–69 (2007)
7. Daniels, R.L., Hoopes, B.J., Mazzola, J.B.: An Analysis of Heuristics for the Parallel-Machine Flexible-Resource Scheduling Problem. Ann. Oper. Res. 70, 439–472 (1997)
8. Daniels, R.L., Hoopes, B.J., Mazzola, J.B.: Scheduling Parallel Manufacturing Cells with Resource Flexibility. Manage. Sci. 42(9), 1260–1276 (1996)
9. Kellerer, H., Strusevisch, V.A.: Scheduling Problems for Parallel Dedicated Machines under Multiple Resource Constraints. Discrete Appl. Math. 133, 45–68 (2004)
10. Li, Y., Wang, F., Lim, A.: Resource Constraints Machine Scheduling: A Genetic Algorithm Approach. In: The 2003 Congress on Evolutionary Computation CEC 2003, vol. 2, pp. 1080–1085. IEEE Press, Los Alamitos (2003)
11. Ventura, J.A., Kim, D.: Parallel Machine Scheduling About an Unrestricted Due Date and Additional Resource Constraints. IIE Trans. 32, 147–153 (2000)
12. Tamaki, H., Hasegawa, Y., Kozasa, J., Araki, M.: Application of Search Methods to Scheduling Problem in Plastics Forming Plant: A Binary Representation Approach. In: Proceedings of 32nd Conference on Decision and Control, pp. 3845–3850. IEEE Press, Los Alamitos (1993)
13. Chen, J.-F.: Unrelated Parallel Machine Scheduling with Secondary Resource Constraints. Int J. Adv. Manuf. Tech. 26, 285–292 (2005)
14. Chen, J.-F., Wu, T.-H.: Total Tardiness Minimization on Unrelated Parallel Machine Scheduling with Auxiliary Equipment Constraints. Omega- Int. J. Manage. S. 34, 81–89 (2006)
15. Luh, P.B., Hoitomt, D.J.: Scheduling of Manufacturing Systems Using the Lagrangian Relaxation Technique. IEEE T. Automat. Contr. 38(7), 1066–1079 (1993)
16. Martello, S., Soumis, F., Toth, P.: Exact and Approximation Algorithms for Makespan Minimization on Unrelated Parallel Machines. Discrete Appl. Math. 75, 169–188 (1997)
17. Beasley, J.E.: Lagrangean Relaxation. In: Reeves, C.R. (ed.) Modern Heuristic Techniques for Combinatorial Problems, McGraw-Hill, UK (1995)
18. ILOG OPL Studio 3.7, Language Manual, ILOG S.A, France (2003)
19. Vairaktarakis, G.L., Cai, X.: The Value of Processing Flexibility in Multipurpose Machines. IIE Trans. 35, 763–774 (2003)

A Hierarchy of Twofold Resource Allocation Automata Supporting Optimal Web Polling

Ole-Christoffer Granmo[1] and B. John Oommen[2]

[1] Dept. of ICT, University of Agder, Grimstad, Norway
[2] School of Computer Science, Carleton University, Ottawa, Canada[*]

Abstract. We consider the problem of polling web pages as a strategy for monitoring the world wide web. The problem consists of repeatedly polling a selection of web pages so that changes that occur over time are detected. In particular, we consider the case where we are constrained to poll a *maximum* number of web pages per unit of time. Thus, the issue at stake is one of determining which web pages are to be polled, and we attempt to do it in a manner that maximizes the number of changes detected. We solve the problem by first modelling it as a *Stochastic Non-linear Fractional Knapsack Problem*. We then present a completely new on-line Learning Automata (LA) system, namely, the *Hierarchy of Twofold Resource Allocation Automata* (H-TRAA), whose primitive component is a *Twofold Resource Allocation Automaton* (TRAA). Both the TRAA and the H-TRAA have been proven to be asymptotically optimal. Finally, we demonstrate empirically that H-TRAA provides *orders of magnitude* faster convergence compared to the LAKG which represents the state-of-the-art. Further, in contrast to the LAKG, H-TRAA scales sub-linearly. Based on these results, we believe that the H-TRAA has a tremendous potential to handle demanding real-world applications, particularly those which deal with the world wide web.

Keywords: *Web Polling, Learning Automata, Stochastic Optimization.*

1 Introduction

The world wide web is an extremely vast resource-thirsty field, which probably consumes a major portion of the computing resources available today. Searching, updating and examining web-pages is, undoubtedly, one of the primary tasks done by both individuals and companies today. This, in turn, leads to numerous extremely interesting real-life resource allocation and scheduling problems, and in this paper, we study one such problem, the so-called "Web polling" problem.

Web page monitoring consists of repeatedly polling a selection of web pages so that the user can detect changes that occur over time. Clearly, as this task can be prohibitively expensive, in practical applications, the system imposes a constraint on the *maximum* number of web pages that can be polled per unit of

---

[*] *Chancellor's Professor*; *Fellow : IEEE* and *Fellow : IAPR*. The Author also holds an *Adjunct Professorship* with the Dept. of ICT, University of Agder, Norway.

N.T. Nguyen et al. (Eds.): IEA/AIE 2008, LNAI 5027, pp. 347–358, 2008.

time. This bound is dictated by the governing communication bandwidth, and by the speed limitations associated with the processing. Since only a fraction of the web pages can be polled within a given unit of time, the problem which the system's analyst encounters is one of determining which web pages are to be polled. In such cases, a reasonable choice of action is to choose web pages in a manner that maximizes the number of changes detected, and the optimal allocation of the resources involves trial-and-failure. Web pages may change with varying frequencies (that are unknown to the decision maker), and changes appear more or less randomly. Furthermore, as argued elsewhere, the probability that an individual web page poll uncovers a change on its own decreases monotonically with the polling frequency used for that web page [1].

We shall utilize the model of the Stochastic Non-linear Fractional Equality Knapsack (NEFK) problem to model the present problem, and once such a formalization has been established, we shall allude to the LA solution of the NEFK to solve web-polling problems.

In order to appreciate the qualities of the Stochastic NEFK Problem, it is beneficial to view the problem in light of the classical *linear* Fractional Knapsack (FK) Problem. Indeed, the Stochastic NEFK Problem generalizes the latter problem in two significant ways. Both of the problems are *briefly* defined below.

The Linear Fractional Knapsack (FK) Problem: The linear FK problem is a classical continuous optimization problem which also has applications within the field of resource allocation. The problem involves n materials of different value v_i per unit volume, $1 \leq i \leq n$, where each material is available in a certain amount $x_i \leq b_i$. Let $f_i(x_i)$ denote the value of the amount x_i of material i, i.e., $f_i(x_i) = v_i x_i$. The problem is to fill a knapsack of fixed volume c with the material mix $\boldsymbol{x} = [x_1, \ldots, x_n]$ of maximal value $\sum_1^n f_i(x_i)$ [2].

The Nonlinear Equality FK (NEFK) Problem: One important extension of the above classical problem is the *Nonlinear Equality* FK problem with a separable and concave objective function. The problem can be stated as follows [3]:

$$\text{maximize } f(\boldsymbol{x}) = \sum_1^n f_i(x_i)$$
$$\text{subject to } \sum_1^n x_i = c \text{ and } \forall i \in \{1, \ldots, n\}, x_i \geq 0.$$

Note that since the objective function is considered to be concave, the value function $f_i(x_i)$ of each material is also concave. This means that the derivatives of the material value functions $f_i(x_i)$ with respect to x_i, (hereafter denoted f_i'), are non-increasing.

The Stochastic NEFK Problem: In this paper we generalize the above NEFK problem. First of all, we let the material value per unit volume for any x_i be a *probability* function $p_i(x_i)$. Furthermore, we consider the distribution of $p_i(x_i)$ to be *unknown*. That is, each time an amount x_i of material i is placed in the knapsack, we are only allowed to observe an instantiation of $p_i(x_i)$ at x_i, and not $p_i(x_i)$ itself. As an additional complication, $p_i(x_i)$ is nonlinear in the sense that it decreases monotonically with x_i, i.e., $x_{i_1} \leq x_{i_2} \Leftrightarrow p_i(x_{i_1}) \geq p_i(x_{i_2})$. Given this stochastic environment, we intend to devise an on-line incremental scheme that learns the mix of materials of maximal *expected* value, through a series of informed guesses.

Stochastic Knapsack Problems — State-of-the-Art: The first reported generic treatment of the stochastic NEFK problem itself can be found in [1]. Various instantiations of the problem have, however, appeared sporadically, particularly within the web monitoring domain. In these latter instantiations, the unknown parameters are *estimated* by means of a tracking phase where web pages are polled mainly for estimation purposes [4]. One major disadvantage of such an approach is that the parameter estimation phase significantly delays the implementation of an optimal solution. This disadvantage is further aggravated in *dynamic* environments where the optimal solution changes over time, introducing the need for parameter re-estimation [1].

Learning Automata (LA): In contrast to the above approaches, we base our work on the principles of LA [5]. LA have been used to model biological systems [6], and have attracted considerable interest in the last decade because they can learn the optimal actions when operating in (or interacting with) unknown stochastic environments. Furthermore, they combine rapid and accurate convergence with low computational complexity.

The novel Learning Automata Knapsack Game (LAKG) scheme that we proposed in [1] does not rely on estimating parameters, and can be used to solve the stochastic NEFK problem in both static and dynamic settings. Indeed, empirical results verify that the LAKG finds the optimal solution with arbitrary accuracy, guided by the principle of Lagrange Multipliers. Furthermore, the empirical results show that the performance of the LAKG is superior to that of parameter-estimation-based schemes, both in static and dynamic environments. Accordingly, we believe that the LAKG can be considered to represent the state-of-the-art when it concerns the stochastic NEFK problem. This landmark is now extended to develop the TRAA, and its hierarchical version, the H-TRAA.

Contributions of This Paper: The contributions of this paper are the following: (1) We report the first *analytical* results for schemes that solve the optimal web-polling problem using a formal solution to the Stochastic NEFK Problem. (2) We propose a novel scheme for the *two-material* resource allocation, namely, the *Twofold Resource Allocation Automaton (TRAA)*. (3) We provide convergence results for the TRAA.(4) We report the first *hierarchical* solution to the Stochastic NEFK Problem, based on a hierarchy of TRAAs, namely, H-TRAA. (5) We verify empirically that H-TRAA provides orders of magnitude faster convergence compared to LAKG.

2   A Hierarchy of Twofold Resource Allocation Automata

In order to put our work in the right perspective, we start this section by providing a brief review of the concepts found in [1] - which are also relevant for more "primitive" variants of the knapsack problem.

As indicated in the introduction, solving the classical linear FK problem involves finding the most valuable mix $x^* = [x_1^*, \ldots, x_n^*]$ of n materials that fits within a knapsack of fixed capacity c. The material value per unit volume for each material i is given as a constant v_i, and each material is available in a certain amount $x_i \leq b_i$, $1 \leq i \leq n$. Accordingly, the value of the amount x_i of material i, $f_i(x_i) = v_i x_i$, is linear with respect to x_i. In other words, the derivative of $f_i(x_i)$ — i.e., the material value per unit volume — is fixed: $f_i'(x_i) = v_i$. Because *fractions* of materials can be placed in the knapsack, the following greedy algorithm from [2] finds the most valuable mix: *Take as much as possible of the material that is most valuable per unit volume. If there is still room, take as much as possible of the next most valuable material. Continue until the knapsack is full.*

Let us now generalize this and assume that the material unit volume values are *random* variables with *constant* and *known* distributions. Furthermore, for the sake of conceptual clarity, let us only consider binary variables that *either* instantiate to the values of 0 or 1. Since the unit volume values are random, let p_i denote the probability of the unit volume value $v_i = 1$ for material i, $1 \leq i \leq n$, which means that the probability of the unit volume value $v_i = 0$ becomes $1 - p_i$. With some insight, it becomes evident that under such conditions, the above greedy strategy can again be used to maximize the *expected* value of the knapsack, simply by selecting material based on the *expected* unit volume values, $E[v_i] = 0 \times (1 - p_i) + 1 \times p_i$, rather than actual unit volume values.

The above indicated solution is, of course, inadequate when the p_i's are unknown. Furthermore, the problem becomes even more challenging when the p_i's are no longer constant, but rather depend on their respective material amounts x_i, $1 \leq i \leq n$. Let $p_i(x_i)$ denote the probability that the current unit volume value of material i is $v_i = 1$, given that the amount x_i has already been placed in the knapsack. Then, the expected value per unit volume of material i, $1 \leq i \leq n$, becomes $E[v_i] = 0 \times [1 - p_i(x_i)] + 1 \times p_i(x_i) = p_i(x_i)$, and accordingly, the expected value of the amount x_i becomes $f_i(x_i) = \int_0^{x_i} p_i(u)du$.

Our aim, then, is to find a scheme that moves towards optimizing the following NEFK problem on-line:

$$\text{maximize } f(\boldsymbol{x}) = \sum_1^n f_i(x_i), \text{where} f_i(x_i) = \int_0^{x_i} p_i(u)du, \text{ and } p_i(x_i) = f_i'(x_i),$$
$$\text{subject to } \sum_1^n x_i = c \text{ and } \forall i \in \{1, \ldots, n\}, x_i \geq 0.$$

Note that we allow only instantiations of the material values per unit volume to be observed. That is, each time an amount x_i of material i is placed in the knapsack, an instantiation v_i at x_i is observed.

Because of the above intricacies, we approach the problem by relying on informed material mix *guesses*, i.e., by experimenting with different material mixes and learning from the resulting random unit volume value outcomes. We shall assume that x_i is any number in the interval $(0, 1)$. The question of generalizing this will be considered later. The crucial issue that we have to address, then, is that of determining how to change our current guesses on x_i, $1 \leq i \leq n$. We shall attempt to do this in a discretized manner by subdividing the unit interval into N points $\{\frac{1}{N+1}, \frac{2}{N+1}, \ldots, \frac{N}{N+1}\}$, where N is the resolution of the learning scheme. It turns out that a larger value of N ultimately implies a more accurate solution to the knapsack problem.

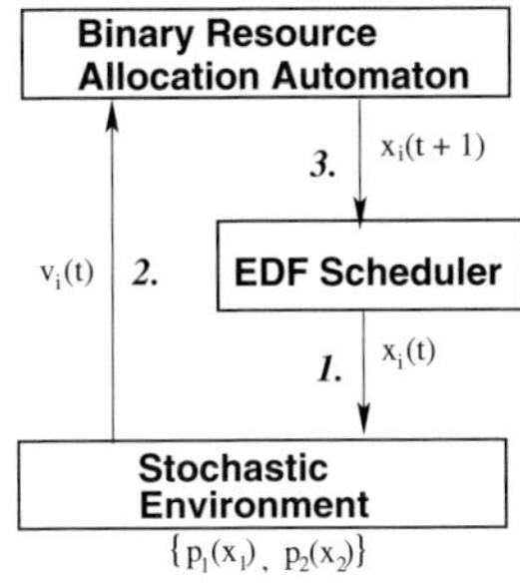

Fig. 1. The Twofold Resource Allocation Automaton (TRAA)

2.1   Details of the TRAA Solution

We first present our LA based solution to *two-material* Stochastic NEFK Problems. The two-material solution forms a critical part of the hierarchic scheme for multiple materials that is presented subsequently. As illustrated in Fig. 1, our solution to two-material problems constitutes of the following three modules.

Stochastic Environment: The *Stochastic Environment* for the two-material case can be characterized by: (1) The capacity c of the knapsack, and (2) two material unit volume value probability functions $p_1(x_1)$ and $p_2(x_2)$. In brief, if the amount x_i of material i is suggested to the Stochastic Environment, the Environment replies with a unit volume value $v_i = 1$ with probability $p_i(x_i)$ and a unit volume value $v_i = 0$ with probability $1 - p_i(x_i)$, $i \in \{1,2\}$. It should be emphasized that to render the problem both interesting and non-trivial, we assume that $p_i(x_i)$ is unknown to the TRAA.

Twofold Resource Allocation Automaton: The scheme which attempts to learn the optimal allocation $\boldsymbol{x}^* = [x_1^*, x_2^*]$ can be described as follows. A finite fixed structure automaton with the states $s(t) \in \{1, 2, \ldots, N\}$ is used to decide the allocation of resources among the two materials. Let the current state of the automaton be $s(t)$. Furthermore, let $q_{s(t)}$ refer to the fraction $\frac{s(t)}{N+1}$, and let $r_{s(t)}$ refer to the fraction: $1 - q_{s(t)}$. Then the automaton's current guess is $\boldsymbol{x} = [q_{s(t)}, r_{s(t)}]$. If the Stochastic Environment tells the automaton that the unit volume value of material i is $v_i(t)$ at time t, the automaton updates its state as follows:

$$s(t+1) := s(t) + 1 \ \textbf{If} \qquad \textbf{rand}() \leq r_{s(t)} \text{ and } v_i(t) = 1 \qquad (1)$$
$$\text{and } 1 \leq s_i(t) < N \text{ and } i = 1$$
$$s(t+1) := s(t) - 1 \ \textbf{If} \qquad \textbf{rand}() \leq q_{s(t)} \text{ and } v_i(t) = 1 \qquad (2)$$
$$\text{and } 1 < s_i(t) \leq N \text{ and } i = 2$$
$$s(t+1) := s(t) \qquad \textbf{Otherwise} \qquad (3).$$

Notice how the stochastic state transitions are designed to offset the learning bias introduced by accessing the materials with frequencies proportional to $\boldsymbol{x} = [q_{s(t)}, r_{s(t)}]$. Also observe that the overall learning scheme does not produce any absorbing states, and is, accordingly, ergodic supporting dynamic environments.

Finally, after the automaton has had the opportunity to change its state, it provides the output $\boldsymbol{x} = [q_{s(t+1)}, r_{s(t+1)}]$ to an EDF Scheduler. That is, it outputs the material amounts that have been changed.

Earliest Deadline First (EDF) Scheduler: The EDF Scheduler takes material amounts $\boldsymbol{x} = [x_1, \ldots, x_n]$ as its input (for the two-material case the input is $\boldsymbol{x} = [x_1, x_2]$). The purpose of the Scheduler is to: (1) provide accesses to the Stochastic Environment in a sequential manner, and (2) make sure that the unit volume value functions are accessed with frequencies proportional to $\boldsymbol{x}$.

The reader should note that our scheme does not rely on accessing the unit volume value functions sequentially with frequencies proportional to $\boldsymbol{x}$ for solving the knapsack problem. However, this restriction is obviously essential for solving the problem *incrementally* and *on-line* (or rather in a "real-time" manner).

Lemma 1. *The material mix $\boldsymbol{x} = [x_1, \ldots, x_n]$ is a solution to a given Stochastic NEFK Problem if (1) the derivatives of the expected material amount values are all equal at $\boldsymbol{x}$, (2) the mix fills the knapsack, and (3) every material amount is positive, i.e.:*

$$f_1'(x_1) = \cdots = f_n'(x_n)$$
$$\textstyle\sum_1^n x_i = c \text{ and } \forall i \in \{1, \ldots, n\}, x_i \geq 0.$$

The above lemma is based on the well-known principle of Lagrange Multipliers [7], and its proof is therefore omitted here for the sake of brevity. We will instead provide our main result for the *two-material* problem and the TRAA. For the two-material problem, let $\boldsymbol{x}^* = [x_1^*, x_2^*]$ denote a solution, as defined above. Note that since x_2^* can be obtained from x_1^*, we will concentrate on finding x_1^*.

Theorem 1. *The TRAA solution scheme specified by (1)–(3) is asymptotically optimal. I.e., as the resolution, N, is increased indefinitely, the expected value of the TRAA output, $x_1(t)$, converges towards the solution of the problem, x_1^*:*

$$\lim_{N \to \infty} \lim_{t \to \infty} E[x_1(t)] \to x_1^*.$$

Proof. The proof is quite involved and is found in [8]. It is omitted here in the interest of brevity. $\qquad\square$

2.2   Details of the H-TRAA Solution

In this section we propose a hierarchical scheme for solving n-material problems. The scheme takes advantage of the TRAA's ability to solve two-material problems asymptotically, by organizing them hierarchically.

2.2.1   H-TRAA Construction.

The hierarchy of TRAAs, which we hereafter will refer to as H-TRAA, is constructed as follows[1]. First of all, the hierarchy is organized as a balanced binary tree with depth $D = \log_2(n)$. Each node in the hierarchy can be related to three entities: (1) a set of materials, (2) a partitioning of the material set into two subsets of equal size, and (3) a dedicated TRAA that allocates a given amount of resources among the two subsets.

---

[1] We assume that $n = 2^\gamma, \gamma \in \mathbb{N}^+$, for the sake of clarity.

Root Node: The hierarchy root (at depth 1) is assigned the complete set of materials $S_{1,1} = \{1, \ldots, n\}$. These n materials are partitioned into two disjoint and exhaustive subsets of equal size: $S_{2,1}$ and $S_{2,2}$. An associated TRAA, $T_{1,1}$, decides how to divide the full knapsack capacity c (which, for the sake of notational correctness will be referred to as $c_{1,1}$) among the two subsets. That is, subset $S_{2,1}$ receives the capacity $c_{2,1}$ and subset $S_{2,2}$ receives the capacity $c_{2,2}$, with $c_{2,1} + c_{2,2} = c_{1,1}$. Accordingly, *this* TRAA is given the power to prioritize one subset of the materials at the expense of the other.

Nodes at Depth d: Node $j \in \{1, \ldots, 2^{d-1}\}$ at depth d (where $1 < d \leq D$) refers to: (1) the material subset $S_{d,j}$, (2) a partitioning of $S_{d,j}$ into the subsets $S_{d+1,2j-1}$ and $S_{d+1,2j}$, and (3) a dedicated TRAA, $T_{d,j}$. Observe that since level $D + 1$ of the H-TRAA is non-existent, we use the convention that $S_{D+1,2j-1}$ and $S_{D+1,2j}$ refer to the primitive materials being processed by the leaf TRAA, $T_{D,j}$. Assume that the materials in $S_{d,j}$ has, as a set, been assigned the capacity $c_{d,j}$. The dedicated TRAA, then, decides how to allocate the assigned capacity $c_{d,j}$ among the subsets $S_{d+1,2j-1}$ and $S_{d+1,2j}$. That is, subset $S_{d+1,2j-1}$ receives the capacity $c_{d+1,2j-1}$ and subset $S_{d+1,2j}$ receives the capacity $c_{d+1,2j}$, with $c_{d+,2j-1} + c_{d+1,2j} = c_{d,j}$.

At depth D, then, each individual material can be separately assigned a fraction of the overall capacity by way of recursion, using the above allocation scheme.

2.2.2 Interaction of H-TRAA with EDF Scheduler and Environment.

As in the single TRAA case, H-TRAA interacts with an EDF Scheduler, which suggests which unit volume value function $p_i(x_i)$ to access next. A response is then generated from the Stochastic Environment using $p_i(x_i)$. This response is given to all the TRAAs that were involved in determining the material amount x_i, that is, the TRAAs in the hierarchy that have allocated capacacity to a material subset that contains material i. Finally, a new candidate material mix $x = [x_1, \ldots, x_n]$ is suggested by the H-TRAA to the EDF Scheduler.

2.2.3 Analysis of the H-TRAA Solution.

In the previous section we stated the asymptotic optimality of the individual TRAA. We will now consider the H-TRAA and its optimality. In brief, it turns out that when each individual TRAA in the hierarchy has solved its own two-material problem, a solution to the complete n-material Knapsack Problem has also been produced.

Theorem 2. *Let $T_{d,j}$ be an arbitrary TRAA at level d of the H-TRAA associated with the node whose index is j. Then, if every single TRAA, $T_{d,j}$, in the H-TRAA has found a local solution with proportions $c_{d+1,2j-1}$ and $c_{d+1,2j}$ satisfying $f'_{d+1,2j-1}(c_{d+1,2j-1}) = f'_{d+1,2j}(c_{d+1,2j})$, the overall Knapsack Problem involving n materials that are hierarchically placed in $\log_2 n$ levels of TRAAs, also attains the global optimum solution.*

Proof. The proof of this theorem is also quite deep. It is included in [8], and omitted here due to space limitations. $\qquad\square$

3 Experimental Results: Optimal Web Polling

Having obtained a formal solution to the model in which we set the NEFK, we shall now demonstrate how we can utilize this solution for the current problem being studied, namely, the optimal web-polling problem.

Although several nonlinear criterion functions for measuring web monitoring performance have been proposed in the literature (e.g., see [4, 9]), from a broader viewpoint they are mainly built around the basic concept of *update detection probability*, i.e., the probability that polling a web page results in new information being discovered. Therefore, for the purpose of clarification and for the sake of conceptual clarity, we will use the update detection probability as the token of interest in this paper. To further define our notion of web monitoring performance, we consider that time is discrete, with the time interval length T to be the atomic unit of decision making. In each time interval every single web page i has a constant probability q_i of remaining *unchanged*[2]. Furthermore, when a web page is updated/changed, the update is available for detection only until the web page is updated again. After that, the original update is considered lost. For instance, each time a newspaper web page is updated, previous news items are replaced by the most recent ones.

In the following, we will denote the update detection probability of a web page i as d_i. Under the above conditions, d_i depends on the frequency, x_i, that the page is polled with, and is modeled using the following expression: $d_i(x_i) = 1 - q_i^{\frac{1}{x_i}}$. By way of example, consider the scenario that a web page remains unchanged in any single time step with probability 0.5. Then polling the web page uncovers new information with probability $1 - 0.5^3 = 0.875$ if the web page is polled every 3rd time step (i.e., with frequency $\frac{1}{3}$) and $1 - 0.5^2 = 0.75$ if the web page is polled every 2nd time step. As seen, increasing the polling frequency reduces the probability of discovering new information on each polling.

Given the above considerations, our aim is to find the page polling frequencies $\boldsymbol{x}$ that maximize the expected number of pollings uncovering new information:

$$\text{maximize } \sum_1^n x_i \times d_i(x_i)$$
$$\text{subject to } \sum_1^n x_i = c \text{ and } \forall i = 1, \ldots, n, x_i \geq 0$$

Note that in the general web monitoring case, we are not able to observe $d_i(x_i)$ or q_i directly — polling a web page only reveals whether the web page has been updated *at least once* since our last As such, web monitoring forms a proof-of-concept application for resource allocation in unknown stochastic environments.

3.1 H-TRAA Solution

In order to find a H-TRAA Solution to the above problem we must define the Stochastic Environment that the LA are to interact with. As seen in Sect. 2,

---

[2] Note that in our empirical results, we also report high monitoring performance even with changing q_i. The high performance can be explained by the adaptation ability of our scheme.

the Stochastic Environment consists of the unit volume value functions $\mathcal{F}' = \{f'_1(x_1), f'_2(x_2), \ldots, f'_n(x_n)\}$, which are unknown to H-TRAA. We identify the nature of these functions by applying the principle of Lagrange multipliers to the above maximization problem. In short, after some simplification, it can be seen that the following conditions characterize the optimal solution:

$$d_1(x_1) = d_2(x_2) = \cdots = d_n(x_n)$$
$$\sum_1^n x_i = c \text{ and } \forall i = 1, \ldots, n, x_i \geq 0$$

Since we are not able to observe $d_i(x_i)$ or q_i directly, we base our definition of $\mathcal{F}'$ on the result of polling web pages. Briefly stated, we want $f'_i(x_i)$ to instantiate to the value 0 with probability $1 - d_i(x_i)$ and to the value 1 with probability $d_i(x_i)$. Accordingly, if the web page i is polled and i has been updated since our last polling, then we consider $f'_i(x_i)$ to have been instantiated to 1. And, if the web page i is unchanged, we consider $f'_i(x_i)$ to have been instantiated to 0.

3.2 Empirical Results

We here evaluate our learning scheme by comparing it with four classical policies using synthetic data. We have implemented the following classical policies.

Uniform: The uniform policy allocates monitoring resources uniformly across all web pages. This is the only classical policy of the four that can be applied directly in an unknown environment.

Proportional: In the proportional policy, the allocation of monitoring resources to web pages is proportional to the update frequencies of the web pages. Accordingly, this policy requires that the web page update frequencies are known.

Estimator: The estimator policy handles unknown web update frequencies by polling web pages *uniformly* in a parameter estimation phase, with the purpose of estimating update frequencies. After the parameter estimation phase, the proportional policy is applied, however, based on the estimated frequencies.

Optimal: This policy requires that update frequencies are known, and finds the optimal solution based on the principle of Lagrange multipliers [4, 9].

To evaluate web resource allocation policies, recent research advocates Zipf-like distributions [10] to generate realistic web page update frequencies [4, 9]. Thus, for our experiments, web pages are considered ranked according to their update frequencies, and the update probability of a web page is calculated from its rank. We use the following function to determine the update probability of a web page: $q_k(\alpha, \beta) = \frac{\alpha}{k^\beta}$. In this case, k refers to the web page of rank k and the parameter β determines the skewed-ness of the distribution, while $\alpha \in [0.0, 1.0]$ represents the magnitude of the update probabilities.

As we will see in the following, it turns out that one of the strengths of the H-TRAA is its ability to take advantage of so-called spatial dependencies among materials. In the above experimental setup, materials are spatially related in the sense that the updating probabilities decreases with the rank-index k. In order to starve the H-TRAA from this information, we opted to perturb this spatial structure. Each perturbation swapped the updating probabilities of a randomly selected material and the material succeeding it in the ranking.

3.2.1 Configuring H-TRAA.

H-TRAA can be configured by various means. First of all, the material amount space $(0, 1)$ need not be discretized uniformly. Instead, a nonlinear material amount space can be formed, as done for LAKG in [1]. Furthermore, the discretization resolution N must also be set for each TRAA, possibly varying from TRAA to TRAA in the hierarchy. In short, the performance achieved for a particular problem can be optimized using these different means of configuring H-TRAA. In this section, however, our goal is to evaluate the overall performance of H-TRAA, without fine tuning. Therefore, we will only use a linear material amount space, as specified in Sect. 2. Furthermore, we will use the same resolution $N = 500$ for all the TRAAs in the hierarchy, independently of the specific knapsack problem at hand. Thus, our aim is to ensure a fair comparison with the present state of the art, namely, LAKG.[3]

3.2.2 Static Environments.

The most difficult class of static environments we simulate is an environment with a highly skewed web page update distribution ($\beta = 1.5$) combined with a high update probability ($\alpha = 0.9$). In such an environment, the optimal policy performs significantly better than the proportional policy, and so any scheme that converges towards a proportional policy solution will not reach optimal performance. In short, both LAKG and H-TRAA breach the performance boundary set by the proportional policy, and converges towards near optimal solutions. Also, for all the tested environments, H-TRAA converges slightly quicker than LAKG.

3.2.3 Dynamic Environments.

A dynamically changing environment is particularly challenging because the optimal solution is time dependent. In such cases, the current resource allocation solution should be modified according to the environmental changes. When, additionally, the environment and its characteristics are unknown, any changes must first be learned before any meaningful modification can take place.

In order to simulate a dynamic environment, we change the ranking of the web pages at every r^{th} web page poll — a single web page is selected by sampling from the current Zipf-distribution, and this web page switches rank with the succeeding web page in the ranking. As a result, the Zipf-distribution also changes. This means that the web monitor is allowed to conduct r web page polls before the environment changes. Fig. 2(a) demonstrates the ability of our scheme to re-learn in a switching environment for $r = 80,000$. As seen, the H-TRAA quickly recovers after the environment has changed, and then moves towards a new near optimal solution. Also, H-TRAA outperforms LAKG.

---

[3] Since we in this paper emphasize speed of learning, we will presently utilize material unit values of both 0 and 1 (the state transitions for unit value 0 is obtained by inverting the state transitions of the individual TRAAs from Sect. 2).

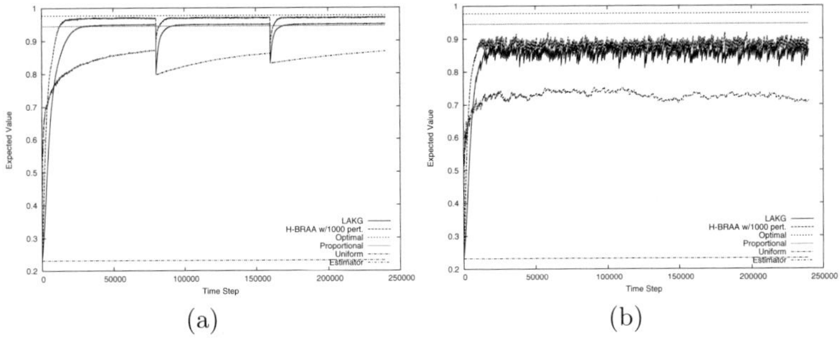

Fig. 2. The dynamic $(\alpha = 0.9, \beta = 1.5)$-environments

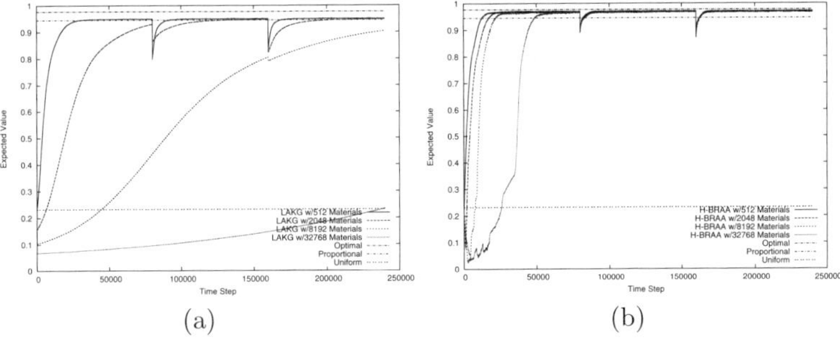

Fig. 3. Scalability of LAKG and H-TRAA

In the previous dynamic environment, the H-TRAA was able to fully recover to a near-optimal solution because of the low frequency of environmental changes. Fig. 2(b) demonstrates the behavior of the automata in a case when this frequency is increased to $r = 1,000$. As seen, the automata still quickly and steadily improve the initial solution, but are obviously never allowed to reach an optimal solution. However, note how the quickly changing environment is not able to hinder the automata stabilizing on a solution superior to the solutions found by the estimator scheme. Again, H-TRAA performs better than LAKG.

3.2.4 Scalability. One of the motivations for designing H-TRAA was improved scalability by means of hierarchical learning. As seen in Fig. 3(a), extending the number of materials significantly increases the convergence time of LAKG. An increased initial learning phase may be unproblematic in cases where the system will run correspondingly longer, adapting to less dramatic changes as they occur. However, as also seen from the figure, the adaptation speed increases with the number of materials too, when LAKG is used. H-TRAA, however, is far less affected by the number of materials. In Fig. 3(b) we observe that the initial learning phase is orders of magnitude faster than what can be achieved with LAKG. Furthermore, the impact on adaptation speed is negligible!

4 Conclusions and Further Work

In this paper, we have considered the optimal web polling problem. Our problem has been that of determining which web pages are to be polled, in a manner that maximizes the number of changes detected. To solve the problem, we first modelled it as a *Stochastic Non-linear Fractional Knapsack Problem*. We then presented a completely new on-line Learning Automata (LA) system, namely, the *Hierarchy of Twofold Resource Allocation Automata* (H-TRAA), whose primitive component is a *Twofold Resource Allocation Automaton* (TRAA). Comprehensive experimental results demonstrated that performance of H-TRAA is superior to the previous state-of-the-art scheme, LAKG. We have also demonstrated that the H-TRAA scheme adapts to switching web distribution functions, allowing us to operate in dynamic environments. Finally, we also provided empirical evidence to show that H-TRAAs possess a sub-linear scaling property. In our further work, we aim to develop alternate LA-based solutions for different classes of knapsack problems, including the NP-hard integer knapsack problem.

References

1. Granmo, O.C., Oommen, B.J., Myrer, S.A., Olsen, M.G.: Learning Automata-based Solutions to the Nonlinear Fractional Knapsack Problem with Applications to Optimal Resource Allocation. IEEE Transactions on Systems, Man, and Cybernetics, Part B (2006)
2. Black, P.E.: Fractional knapsack problem. Dictionary of Algorithms and Data Structures (2004)
3. Kellerer, H., Pferschy, U., Pisinger, D.: Knapsack Problems. Springer, Heidelberg (2004)
4. Pandey, S., Ramamritham, K., Chakrabarti, S.: Monitoring the Dynamic Web to Respond to Continuous Queries. In: 12th International World Wide Web Conference, pp. 659–668. ACM Press, New York (2003)
5. Narendra, K.S., Thathachar, M.A.L.: Learning Automata: An Introduction. Prentice-Hall, Englewood Cliffs (1989)
6. Tsetlin, M.L.: Automaton Theory and Modeling of Biological Systems. Academic Press, London (1973)
7. Bretthauer, K.M., Shetty, B.: The Nonlinear Knapsack Problem — Algorithms and Applications. European Journal of Operational Research 138, 459–472 (2002)
8. Granmo, O.C., Oommen, B.J.: Solving stochastic nonlinear resource allocation problem s using a hierarchy of twofold resource allocation automata (submitted for publication, 2007)
9. Wolf, J.L., Squillante, M.S., Sethuraman, J., Ozsen, K.: Optimal Crawling Strategies for Web Search Engines. In: 11th International World Wide Web Conference, pp. 136–147. ACM Press, New York (2002)
10. Zipf, G.: Human Behavior and the Principle of Least Effort. Addison-Wesley, Reading (1949)

A Heuristic Search for Optimal Parameter Values of Three Biokinetic Growth Models for Describing Batch Cultivations of *Streptococcus Pneumoniae* in Bioreactors

Luciana Montera[1,*], Antonio C.L. Horta[1], Teresa C. Zangirolami[2],
Maria do Carmo Nicoletti[3], Talita S. Carmo[4], and Viviane M. Gonçalves[4]

[1] PPG-Biotechnology - UFSCar, SP - Brazil
`montera@dc.ufscar.br`
[2] Dept. of Chemical Engineering - UFSCar, SP - Brazil
[3] Dept. of Computer Science - UFSCar, SP - Brazil
[4] Butantan Institute, SP - Brazil

Abstract. Simulated annealing (SA) is a stochastic search procedure which can lead to a reliable optimization method. This work describes a dynamic mathematical model for *Streptococcus pneumoniae* batch cultivations containing 8 unknown parameters, which were calibrated by a SA algorithm through the minimization of an evaluation function based on the performance of the model on real experimental data. Three kinetic expressions, the Monod, Moser and Tessier equations, commonly employed to describe microbial growth were tested in the model simulations. SA convergence was achieved after 13810 interactions (about 10 minutes of computing time) and the Tessier equation was identified as the kinetic expression which provided the best fit to the cultivation dataset used for parameter estimation. The model comprising the Tessier equation, estimated parameter values supplied by SA and mass balance equations was further validated by comparing the simulated results to 3 experimental datasets from new cultivations carried out in similar conditions.

Keywords: simulated annealing, microbial growth models, biokinetic parameters estimation.

1 Introduction

Estimation of model parameters is the most difficult task on the development of mathematical expressions capable of describing chemical and biochemical processes. Levenberg Marquardt is an example of a traditional deterministic global optimization method used for parameter estimation [1]. More recently, the usage of stochastic optimization methods such as genetic algorithm (GA) or simulated annealing (SA) to handle parameter estimation in large, non-linear models has increased [2]. Although some publications address the application of GA for

---

[*] Corresponding author.

N.T. Nguyen et al. (Eds.): IEA/AIE 2008, LNAI 5027, pp. 359–368, 2008.

coupling simulation and parameter calibration in dynamic, non-linear models, typical of biochemical processes ([1], [3]), studies about parameter estimation mediated by SA in dynamic, biological systems have not been reported yet. This paper describes the application of SA for parameter estimation of dynamic, non-structured models of *Streptococcus pneumoniae* batch cultivations for conjugated vaccine production. Capsular polysaccharide (PS) is a component of the bacterial cell wall and plays a key role on the protection provided by the vaccine. Large-scale PS production is carried out in submerged, anaerobic cultivations of *S. pneumoniae*. Although its growth requirements and metabolism have already been well characteryzed [4], it is still a challenge to maintain optimal cultivation conditions during *S. pneumoniae* growth, mainly due to the huge amount of lactic acid accumulated in the medium, which, in turn, affects cell growth and PS formation. Consequently, the production of low cost, high quality vaccines relies on the modeling, monitoring and control of PS production process. Besides the investigation of SA as a more effective way of determining biokinetic parameter values associated to microbial growth models, three different kinetic models which are particularly very popular for the description of microbial growth in suspension were considered: Monod, Tessier and Moser models [5]. For each model, the search for an optimal set of its parameter values was conducted by simulated annealing, directed by an evaluation function based on the performance of the model on empirical data. The three models, customized by their own optimal set of parameter values, were then used in a comparative analysis of their modeling capability.

2 Material and Methods

This section describes the procedures used in the laboratory cultivations as well as the strategy adopted to increase the amount of data, which provided the empirical data used in the experiments described in Section 4.

Experimental Data from Batch Cultivations of *Streptococcus pneumoniae* Microorganism, Cultivation Medium Composition and Analytical Methods: The four experiments were conducted at the Biotechnology Center of Butantan Institute (S. Paulo - Brazil), using *Streptococcus pneumoniae* serotype 6B strain ST 433/03, which was obtained from Adolfo Lutz Institute, Bacteriology Section, SP, Brazil. A variant of the Hoeprich medium, containing glucose as the main carbon source, dialyzed yeast extract and other aminoacids as nitrogen sources and salts was employed in all experiments. Detailed information about the medium composition analytical methods is given by [4].

Experimental Procedure: The experiments were conducted in 5L BioFlo 2000 bioreactors, monitored by the LabView 7.1 program. Table 1 summarizes the cultivation conditions employed at each experiment, which were very similar. In this paper, the experiments as well as the data collected in each of them are referred to as $Ferm_2$, $Ferm_5$, $Ferm_{10}$ and $Ferm_{11}$.

Table 1. Experimental conditions adopted in batch cultivations of *S. pneumoniae*. Overpressure of the cultivation vessel was kept at 0.1 bar for all experiments.

	$Ferm_2$	$Ferm_5$	$Ferm_{10}$	$Ferm_{11}$
Temperature (°C)	37	37	37	36
N_2 flow rate (L/min)	1.0	1.0	0.5	1.5
pH	7.2-7.0	7.3-7.0	7.6-7.1	7.4-7.2
Agitation speed (rpm)	200	200	100	250
Bioreactor volume (L)	5.0	8.8	2.0	8.8
Initial glucose concentration (g/L)	30	30	15	30

Handling Laboratory Experimental Data

The data was collected at one-hour interval yielding 6-8 data instances per batch, which were described by the values of four variables, namely: Cell concentration (C_X); Glucose concentration (C_S); PS concentration (C_{PS}) and Lactic acid concentration (C_L). The data in the original dataset $Ferm_5$, which was used for parameter calibration, went through a few modifications aiming at both, to increase of the number of data instances as well as to remove noisy data by means of interpolation and smoothing, respectively. The dataset $Ferm_5$ was input to a smoother/interpolator process (implemented as the perfect smoother, described in [6]) that produced an extended smoothed version of this dataset, also referred as $Ferm_5$. The interpolating function used by the smoother was adjusted for interpolating 29 new data instances between two experimental instances (INT = 2). The number of the original dataset instances, 8, was extended to 211. As the perfect smoother process requires a user-defined value for the parameter (the smoothing parameter), a few different values were tried and the one which suited the best ($\lambda = 8$) was chosen.

3 *S. pneumoniae* Growth Modeling

To achieve satisfactory results during a microbial cultivation, some strategies aiming at the process optimization should be considered. Most of the available optimization strategies are based on the appropriate use of mathematical models that describe a particular microbial growth. The models are based on kinetic expressions which relate the specific growth rate of the microorganisms to the limiting substrate concentration and on a set of differential equations describing the substrate consumption, biomass and product formation.

There are several simple empirical expressions that are currently used to describe the growth kinetics in bioprocesses [5]. As mentioned earlier in this paper, the search for the optimal kinetic growth parameter values was conducted in relation to three different empirical expressions, namely, Monod, Tessier and Moser models. This section describes the assumptions, the relevant parameters as well the main equations related to each model. Assuming that the cell growth is limited only by the substrate concentration (glucose, in the experiments), the cell growth rate (represented by μ) can be described by the Monod equation (1).

$$\mu = \frac{\mu_{MAX} \cdot C_S}{K_S + C_S} \tag{1}$$

The Monod equation (1) describes substrate-limited growth only when the growth and population density are low. Two other equations assume that the cell growth is limited only by the substrate concentration, and are known as Tessier and Moser, described by eq. (2) and eq. (3), respectively. The model proposed by Moser is an extension of the Monod equation and it is generally regarded as superior in fitting due to its extra parameter, the exponent n. On the other hand, while the Monod equation was inspired in the enzymatic kinectic rate expression deduced by Michaelis-Menten, the kinetic expression formulated by Tessier is purely empirical [5].

$$\mu = \mu_{MAX} \cdot \left(1 - e^{-KC_S}\right) \tag{2}$$

$$\mu = \frac{\mu_{MAX} \cdot C_S^n}{K_S + C_S^n} \tag{3}$$

In order to grow, microorganisms consume nutrients from the medium (substrate). Part of the substrate is used as energy and carbon source by the microorganisms for the building of new cells and the remaining is converted into other products. In a system, the concentrations of cells, substrate and products through time are described by the mass balance equations. Considering the *S. pneumoniae* cultivation where glucose is the limiting substrate and lactic acid and capsular polysaccharide are the main products, the equations (4) to (7) express the mass balances for the key variables as a set of ordinary differential equations (ODEs) dependent on the time t. Consider, for example, eq. (4). For specific values of μ, k_d and the initial condition $C_X = C_X(t_0)$ (at a time $t = t_0$), given a set of values t_k, $t_0 \le t_k \le t_{end}$, solving the equations means to integrate them at the interval of time defined by t_k, $t_0 \le t_k \le t_{end}$, in order to find the corresponding $C_{X(t)}$ value at each time t^1. Table 2 describes each variable and parameter involved in equations (1) to (7).

$$\frac{dC_X}{dt} = (\mu - k_d) \cdot C_X \tag{4}$$

$$\frac{dC_S}{dt} = \left(\frac{\mu}{Y_{XS}} + m\right) \cdot C_X \tag{5}$$

$$\frac{dC_S}{dt} = \left(\frac{\mu}{Y_{XL}}\right) \cdot C_X \tag{6}$$

$$\frac{dC_{PS}}{dt} = \left(\frac{\mu}{Y_{XP}} + \beta\right) \cdot C_X \tag{7}$$

---

[1] In the experiments described in Section 4, to solve the differential equations the ode45 MATLAB function was used, which implements the Runge-Kutta (4,5) method.

Table 2. Variables and parameter used in equations (1) to (7)

Variables			
C_X(g/L)	C_S(g/L)	C_L(g/L)	C_{PS}(mg/L)
Cell conc.	Glucose conc.	Lactic acid conc.	Polysaccharide conc.
Parameters			
Y_{XS} (g/g), Y_{XL} (g/g), Y_{XP} (g/mg)	Yield coefficients for cell formation on glucose consumed (Y_{XS}) or for polysaccharide (Y_{XP}) and lactic acid (Y_{XL}) production per mass of cells		
$M(h-1)$ (g/mg)	Maintenance coefficient		
$K_d(h-1)$	Death constant		
$\mu_{MAX}(h-1)$	Maximum specific growth rate		
$K_S(g/L)$	Saturation constant		
$\beta(mgPL \cdot gX - 1 \cdot h - 1)$	Non-growth-related product formation coefficient, Luedeking and Piret model [5]		
K	Exponential decay constant (Tessier model)		

In the specific case of the *S. pneumoniae* cultivation, its growth kinetics (μ) was assumed to be defined by one of the three cell growth rate equations (i.e., eqs. (1), (2) or (3)). For each growth rate expression tested together with the mass balances to fit experimental data, the main challenge was to establish an appropriate set of parameter values for the chosen model. In most cases the parameter values are not known; they must be determined by computational routines that, based on the comparison between experimental and estimated values, try to establish an optimum set of parameter values. In this context, "optimum set of parameter values" should be understood as the set of values that enables the best fit of the model to the experimental data.

4   The Use of Simulated Annealing for Determining Optimal Parameter Values of Three Microbial Growth Models

This section describes the procedures for parameter estimation and model validation. Initially the three selected growth models had their parameter values adjusted by a heuristic algorithm, using the experimental data described in $Ferm_5$. The best model, i.e., the one among the three that better represented the data, was then validated trying to identify its adequacy for modeling similar (but new) *S. pneumoniae* cultures represented by datasets $Ferm_2$, $Ferm_{10}$ and $Ferm_{11}$.

Simulated annealing (SA) is a stochastic search procedure suitable for finding global minimum (or maximum) of functions. It is mainly used for finding the best solution to a function in a large search space when deterministic methods are not suitable. The use of SA in the experiments described in this section aims at finding an optimal (or quasi-optimal) set of values for the main parameters used by the three non-structured growth models associated to the ODEs, so to adjust each model to the experimental data $Ferm_5$. For each time stamp, the objective function to be optimized by the SA represents the difference between the estimated and the experimental values for variables C_X, C_S, C_L and C_{PS}. As the aim is to adjust the model to best 'fit' the experimental data, the objective function chosen is the quadratic error sum of the variables, as described by following equation, where C_{model} and C_{exp} represent, respectively, the 4-uple of variable values predicted by the model and the 4-uple of variable values experimentally measured.

$$F(C_{model}, C_{exp}) = \sum_{t=initial}^{final} ((C_{X(t)}^{model} - C_{X(t)}^{exp})^2 + (C_{S(t)}^{model} - C_{S(t)}^{exp})^2 +$$

$$(C_{L(t)}^{model} - C_{L(t)}^{exp})^2 + (C_{PS(t)}^{model} - C_{PS(t)}^{exp})^2)$$

Where $C_{X(t)}^{model}$, $C_{S(t)}^{model}$, $C_{L(t)}^{model}$, $C_{PS(t)}^{model}$: model estimated values for biomass, glucose, lactic acid and capsular polysaccharide concentrations at a time t, respectively and $C_{X(t)}^{exp}$, $C_{S(t)}^{exp}$, $C_{L(t)}^{exp}$, $C_{PS(t)}^{exp}$: experimental values for biomass, glucose, lactic acid and capsular polysaccharide concentrations at the same time t, respectively.

To assess the adequacy of a model for describing the behavior of a system, it is necessary first to estimate a reasonably 'good' value for its parameters. The determination of optimized parameter values can be done by analytical methods such as the Simplex [7] or the Newton method. Although these methods can quickly find a minimum (or maximum) of a function, the value can be a local minimum (or maximum). Also, analytical methods can be quite complicated to be implemented and, in general, they are limited when dealing with variable restrictions. As an alternative to analytical methods there are the heuristic methods, which are based on search procedures throughout the space of all possible solutions, aiming at finding an optimal (or near optimal) solution. The SA is one of such heuristic methods and its canonical pseudocode is given in Figure 1. The algorithm resembles the hill climbing search; in its inner loop, however, instead of choosing the best move, it picks up a random move[2].

The algorithm starts by choosing a random candidate solution, i.e., a set of values for the model parameters (p_1, p_2, ..., p_n as shown Table 3). This solution is referred to as *cur_param*. Any random value is acceptable, provided it is within the restriction interval of the corresponding parameter (see Lower and Upper bounds in Table 3). Next, the cost associated with the *cur_param* solution is calculated. At each step of the algorithm, a new candidate solution, identified as *new_param* is randomly chosen in the neighborhood of the current solution, such that the restriction intervals are respected and, in addition, the following condition on the parameter values is satisfied, for all parameters: $cur\_param[p_i]*0 \leq new\_param[p_i] \leq cur\_param[p_i]*2$. The new solution cost is then calculated and both solutions have their cost compared; the one with the smaller cost becomes the current solution. However, there is a chance of the *new_param*, even with a higher cost, to become the current solution which is dependent on both,

---

[2] The function *random()* in the SA pseudocode, return a random integer value.

```
procedure SA
   begin
       cur_param = choose_param(param_restrictions)
       cur_param_cost = cost(cur_param)
       T = 10000
       decreasing_factor = 0.999
       while (T > 0.01) do
          new_param = choose_param_neighbor(cur_param,param_restrictions)
          param_new_cost = cost(param_new)
          if (new_param_cost < param_cur_cost) then
              cur_param = new_param   // change the current set of parameter values
              cur_param_cost = new_param_cost
          else
              num = randon (  )
              if (num < exp^(-ΔE/T)) then
                  cur_param = new_param
                  cur_param_cost = new_param_cost
          T = T × decreasing_factor // decreasing the temperature
   end
```

Fig. 1. The SA pseudocode

the temperature T and the difference in cost between the new and the current solution, represented by $\triangle$E.

The decision of accepting a solution with higher cost is an attempt to prevent the SA of finding a good solution that, in fact, is just local (a local maximum or a local minimum) by enlarging the search space covered during the algorithm search. As can be observed in the algorithm pseudocode, as the temperature T decreases, the probability P of accepting 'higher-cost' solutions also decreases, fact that guarantees the algorithm convergence. The initial values for variables T and *decreasing_factor* must be empirically determined since they control the number of interactions the algorithm performs and, consequently, play an important role in its convergence. The initial values of 10,000 and 0.999 for T and *decreasing_factor*, respectively, used in the implemented SA were established after a reasonable number of executions.

Table 3 presents the estimated values found for the parameters belonging to Monod, Tessier and Moser expressions as well as for the ones included in the mass balances. The table shows the lower and the upper bounds of each parameter (i.e., the parameter restrictions) as well.

Table 3. Parameter restrictions and parameter values of Monod, Tessier and Moser expressions and mass balance equations found by SA

	Parameters								
	p_1 K_s	p_2 m	p_3 K_d	p_4 Y_{XS}	p_5 Y_{XP}	p_6 μ_{MAX}	p_7 Y_{XL}	p_8 β	p_9 N
Lower Bound	0.01	0.0001	0.0001	0.1	0.1	0.45	0.0001	0.1	0.0001
Upper Bound	6	0.5	0.5	0.8	0.5	0.85	0.4	50	10
Monod	0.38	0.0004	0.0005	0.13	0.15	0.55	0.19	11	-
Tessier	0.14	0.001	0.01	0.14	0.13	0.6	0.18	8.6	-
Moser	0.01	0.0002	0.002	0.13	0.17	0.47	0.16	13	0.0014

Table 4. Values of the objective function for each kinetic model tested

	Monod	Tessier	Moser
$F(C_{model}, C_{exp})$	73.2	38.2	71.4

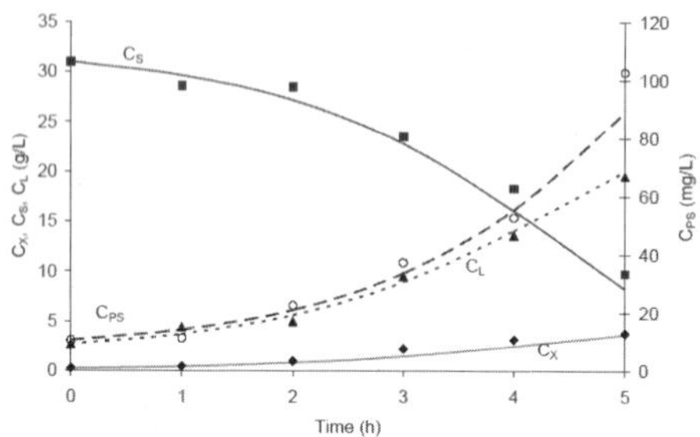

Fig. 2. Simulated (represented by lines) and experimental (represented by symbols) values of the *S. pneumoniae* cultivation main variables using the Tessier growth rate expression. Data from the cultivation $Ferm_5$ was used for parameter calibration.

Based on the value of the objective function ($F(C_{model}, C_{exp})$) associated to each model (Table 4), the Tessier model was identified as the one that best described biomass formation, glucose consumption, P_S and lactic acid production of the batch *S. pneumoniae* cultivation represented by $Ferm_5$. Figure 2 shows the predicted values, using the Tessier expression, for variables cell concentration (C_X), glucose concentration (C_S), lactic acid concentration (C_L) and capsular polysaccharide concentration (C_{PS}) together with the experimental data.

The implemented SA algorithm was very efficient, running 13810 iterations in approximately 10 minutes (in a machine with a Pentium 4 processor with 1GB of memory). The number of 13810 iterations was enough to guarantee the SA convergence, which is not dependent on the initial parameter values, as some estimation algorithms are [8].

Next, Tessier model was validated, by examining its adequacy in describing three other similar experiments (datasets $Ferm_2$, $Ferm_{10}$ and $Ferm_{11}$). As the experimental C_L values for cultivation $Ferm_2$ were not measured due to technical problems, this attribute was not included in the objective function when the adequacy of the Tessier model for describing the experiment $Ferm_2$ was examined.

Figure 3 (a), (b) and (c) compares experimental data and predicted values for the cultivations $Ferm_{11}$, $Ferm_{10}$ and $Ferm_2$, respectively. The model predicted values were estimated by solving the set of ODEs for the Tessier model as the kinetic expression, with the parameter values tuned by the SA using the data from $Ferm_5$. Only the values of initial conditions were changed to fit the model to the new data. In Table 5, the accuracy of the model on describing different datasets

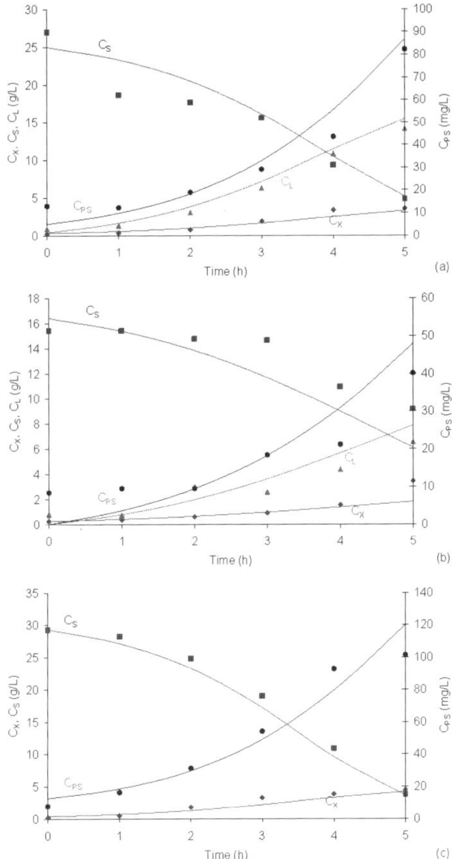

Fig. 3. Validation of the Tessier model using the parameter values estimated by SA for three cultivations of *S. pneumoniae* performed in similar conditions: (a) $Ferm_{11}$ (b) $Ferm_{10}$ (c) $Ferm_2$. Simulated values represented by lines; experimental values represented by symbols.

generated in similar cultivation conditions can be evaluated by analyzing the error between experimental and simulated data for the different validation tests performed. In Figure 3, it can be observed that the model, together with the estimated parameter values supplied by SA, provides a fairly good description of the time-profiles for all variables. It is also clear that the lack of accuracy of the experimental data, mainly at the beginning of the experiments, can affect the evaluation of the model performance. This difficulty in obtaining more accurate measurements of experimental data is generally attributed to the lack of sensitivity of some analytical procedures, mainly of those employed for determining cell and metabolite at low concentrations.

Table 5. Values of the objective function for each dataset

Cultivation dataset	$Ferm_2$	$Ferm_5$	$Ferm_{10}$	$Ferm_{11}$
Objective Function value (excluding lactic acid)	1.25	1.03	8.47	1.66

Comparing the objective function values obtained for $Ferm_2$ and $Ferm_{11}$ with the one calculated for $Ferm_5$, which was used for parameter calibration (Table 5), it is possible to state that the model validation was successful for datasets $Ferm_2$ and $Ferm_{11}$. However, the objective function value for $Ferm_{10}$ was significantly higher. In fact, Table 1 shows that $Ferm_{10}$ was carried out under fairly different conditions of bioreactor volume, agitation speed and initial glucose concentration, what could explain the poor description provided by the model.

5   Conclusion

Simulated annealing is a good choice for a robust optimization procedure. The proposed model (and its set of parameters) was successfully validated and its mass balance equations could be easily modified to simulated more promising bioreactor operation forms, such as fed-batch operation. The simulations could be extremely useful for identifying optima cultivation conditions for achieving higher PS concentration, lower acid lactic formation and, consequently, better process yield and productivity.

References

1. Moles, C.G., Mendes, P., Banga, J.R.: Parameter estimation in biochemical pathways: a comparison of global optimization methods. Genome Res. 13, 2467–2474 (2003)
2. Bonilla-Petriciolet, A., Bravo-Sánchez, U.I., Castillo-Borja, F., Zapiain-Salinas, J.G., Soto-Bernal, J.J.: The performance of simulated annealing parameter estimation for vapor-liquid equilibrium modeling. Br. J. of Chem. Eng. 24, 151–162 (2007)
3. Rodriguez-Fernandez, M., Mendes, P., Banga, J.R.: A hybrid approach for efficient and robust parameter estimation in biochemical pathways. BioSystems 83, 248–265 (2006)
4. Gonçalves, V.M., Zangirolami, T.C., Giordano, R.L.C., Raw, I., Tanizaki, M.M., Giordano, R.C.: Optimization of medium and cultivation conditions for capsular polysaccharide production by Streptococcus pneumoniae serotype 23F. Appl. Microbiol. Biotechnol. 59, 713–717 (2002)
5. Shuler, M.L., Kargi, F.: Bioprocess engineering: basic concepts. Prentice-Hall, Englewood Cliffs (2001)
6. Eilers, P.H.C.: A Perfect Smoother. Analytical Chemistry 75(14), 3631–3636 (2003)
7. Nelder, J.A., Mead, R.: A simplex method for function minimization. Comput. Journal 7, 308–313 (1965)
8. Nelles, O.: Nonlinear system identification: from classical approaches to neural networks and fuzzy models. Springer, Germany (2001)

Efficient Handling of Relational Database Combinatorial Queries Using CSPs

Malek Mouhoub and Chang Feng

University of Regina
Wascana Parkway, Regina, SK, Canada, S4S 0A2
{mouhoubm, feng202c}@cs.uregina.ca

Abstract. A combinatorial query is a request for tuples from multiple relations that satisfy a conjunction of constraints on tuple attribute values. Managing combinatorial queries using the traditional database systems is very challenging due to the combinatorial nature of the problem. Indeed, for queries involving a large number of constraints, relations and tuples, the response time to satisfy these queries becomes an issue. To overcome this difficulty in practice we propose a new model integrating the Constraint Satisfaction Problem (CSP) framework into the database systems. Indeed, CSPs are very popular for solving combinatorial problems and have demonstrated their ability to tackle, in an efficient manner, real life large scale applications under constraints. In order to compare the performance in response time of our CSP-based model with the traditional way for handling combinatorial queries and implemented by MS SQL Server, we have conducted several experiments on large size databases. The results are very promizing and show the superiority of our method comparing to the traditional one.

1 Introduction

It is generally acknowledged that relational databases have become the most significant and the main platform [1] to implement data management and query searching in practice. The efficiency and veracity for query solving is acquiring more concerns and has been improved among various database systems. However, along with the complex requirement for query from the customer, a problem is triggered: the conventional relational database system often fails to obtain answers to the combinatorial query efficiently. Indeed, current Relational Database Management Systems (RDBMS) require a lot of time effort in answering complex combinatorial queries. [2] has given an accurate definition of a combinatorial query: *a request for tuples from multiple relations that satisfy a conjunction of constraints on tuple attribute values.* The following example illustrates the above definition.

Example 1. Let us assume we have a relational database containing three tables describing computer equipments: CPU (*CPU_id*, Price, Frequency, Quality), Memory (*Memory_id*, Price, Frequency, Quality), and Motherboard (*Motherboard_id*, Price, Frequency, Quality).

N.T. Nguyen et al. (Eds.): IEA/AIE 2008, LNAI 5027, pp. 369–378, 2008.

CPU_id	Price	Freq	Quality
1	200	5	80
2	500	10	80
3	1100	8	90
4	2000	15	95

Mem_id	Price	Freq	Quality
1	1000	7	80
2	900	9	90
3	800	10	90
4	1000	15	100

Mboard_id	Price	Freq	Quality
1	100	6	50
2	200	6	50
3	300	11	80
4	400	15	70

```
Select CPU_id, Memory_id,Motherboard_id
From CPU, Memory, Motherboard  Where
 CPU.Price + Memory.Price + Motherboard.Price < 1500
 And CPU.Frequency + Memory.Frequency + Motherboard.Frequency < 30
 And CPU.Quality + Memory.Quality + Motherboard.Quality < 250
```

Fig. 1. An example of a combinatorial query

Figure 1 illustrates the three tables and an example of a related combinatorial query. Here the combinatorial query involves a conjunction of three arithmetic constraints on attributes of the three tables.

Although a variety of query evaluation technologies such as hash-join [3], sorted-join, pair-wise join [4,1] have been implemented into the relational model attempting to optimize searching process, the effect is extremely unsatisfactory since most of them concentrate on handling simple constraints, not the complex ones [2,3,5,6]. For instance, in example 1 the arithmetic query involves a conjunction of three constraints that should be satisfied together. This requires higher complexity and selectivity [6] since the traditional model has to perform further complex combinatorial computations after searching for each sub query (corresponding to each of these 3 constraints) which will cost more time effort. In order to overcome this difficulty in practice, we propose in this paper a model that integrates the Constraint Satisfaction Problem (CSP) framework in the relational database system. Indeed, CSPs are very powerful for representing and solving discrete combinatorial problems. In the past three decades, CSPs have demonstrated their ability to efficiently tackle large size real-life applications, such as scheduling and planning problems, natural language processing, business applications and scene analysis. More precisely, a CSP consists of a finite set of variables with finite domains, and a finite set of constraints restricting the possible combinations of variable values [7,8]. A solution tuple to a CSP is a set of assigned values to variables that satisfy all the constraints. Since a CSP is known to be an NP-hard problem in general[1], a backtrack search algorithm of exponential time cost is needed to find a complete solution. In order to overcome this difficulty in practice, constraint propagation techniques have been proposed [7,9,11,10]. The goal of theses techniques is to reduce the size of the search space before and during the backtrack search. Note that some work on CSPs and databases has already been proposed in the literature. For instance, in [12] an analysis of the similarities between database theories and CSPs has been conducted. Later, [2] has proposed a general framework for modeling the combinatorial aspect, when dealing with relational databases, into a CSP. Query searching has then been improved by CSP

---

[1] There are special cases where CSPs are solved in polynomial time, for instance, the case where a CSP network is a tree [9,10].

techniques. Other work on using CSP search techniques to improve query searching has been reported in [13,14,15].

In this paper, our aim is to improve combinatorial query searching using the CSP framework. Experimental tests comparing our model to the the MS SQL Sever demonstrate the superiority in time efficiency of our model when dealing with complex queries and large databases.

In the next section we will show how can the CSP framework be integrated within the RDBMS. Section 3 describes the details of our solving method. Section 4 provides the structure of the RDBMS with the CSP module. The experimental tests we conducted to evaluate the performance of our model are reported in section 5. We finally conclude in section 6 with some remarks and possible future work.

2   Mapping a Database with the Combinatorial Query into a CSP

There are many similarities between the structure of a database and the CSP model. Each table within the database can be considered as a relation (or a CSP constraint) where the table attributes correspond to the variables involved by the constraint. The domain of each variable corresponds to the range of values of the corresponding attribute. The combinatorial query is here an arithmetic constraint of the related CSP. For instance, the database of example 1 with the combinatorial query can be mapped into the CSP defined as follows.

- **Variables:** CPU.Price, CPU.Frequency, CPU.Quality, Memory_id.Price, Memory_id.Frequency, Memory_id.Quality, Motherboard_id.Price, Motherboard_id.Frequency and Motherboard_id.Price.
- **Domains:** Domains of the above variables. For instance the domain of the variable CPU.Price is equal to $\{200, 500, 1100, 2000\}$.
- **Constraints:**
  - **Semantic Constraints:**
    * CPU(*CPU_id*, Price, Frequency, Quality)
    * Memory(*Memory_id*, Price, Frequency, Quality)
    * Motherboard(*Motherboard_id*, Price, Quality)
  - **Arithmetic constraint:**
    ```
    CPU.Price + Memory.Price + Mother.Price < 1500
    And CPU.Frequency + Memory.Frequency + Motherboard.Frequency < 30
    And CPU.Quality + Memory.Quality + Motherboard.Quality < 250
    ```

After this conversion into a CSP, we can use CSP search techniques, that we will describe in the next section, in order to handle the combinatorial query in an efficient manner.

3   Solving Method

As we mentioned before in introduction, solving a CSP requires a backtrack search algorithm of exponential time cost. In order to overcome this difficulty in practice, local consistency techniques have been proposed [7,9,11,10]. The goal of theses techniques is to reduce the size of the search space before and during the backtrack search. More precisely, local consistency consists of checking to see if a consistency is satisfied on a subset of variables. If the local consistency is not successful then the entire CSP is not consistent. In the other case many values that are locally inconsistent will be removed which will reduce the size of the search space. Various local consistency techniques have been proposed [7]: node consistency which checks the consistency according to unary constraint of each variable, arc consistency which checks the consistency between any subset sharing one constraint, path consistency which checks the consistency between any subset sharing two constraints ..., etc. In this paper we use arc consistency in our solving method as follows.

1. First, arc consistency is applied on all the variables to reduce their domains. If a given variable domain is empty then the CSP is inconsistent (this will save us the next phase) which means that the query cannot be satisfied.
2. A backtrack search algorithm using arc consistency [7,9] is then performed as follows. We select at each time a variable and assign a value to it. Arc consistency is then performed on the domains of the non assigned variables in order to remove some inconsistent values and reduce the size of the search space. If one variable domain becomes empty then assign another value to the current variable or backtrack to the previously assigned variable in order to assign another value to this latter. This backtrack search process will continue until all the variables are assigned values in which case we obtain a solution (satisfaction of the combinatorial query) or the entire search space has been explored without success. Note that during the backtrack search variables are selected following the *most constrained first* policy. This rule consists of picking the variable that appears in the largest number of constraints.

In the general case, arc consistency [7] works as follows. Given a constraint $C(X_1, \ldots, X_p)$ then arc consistency is enforced through C on the set $X_1, \ldots, X_p$ as follows. Each value $v \in D(X_i)$ $(1 \leq i \leq n)$ is removed if it does not have a support (value such that C is satisfied) in at least one domain $D(X_j)$ $(1 \leq j \leq n$ and $j \neq i)$. $D(X_i)$ and $D(X_j)$ are the domains of X_i and X_j respectively.

Before we present the details of the arc consistency algorithm, let us see with the following examples how arc consistency, through arithmetic and semantic constraints, is used to reduce the domains of the different attributes in both phases of our solving method.

Example 2. Let us consider the database of example 1. The domain of the variable CPU.Price is equal to $\{200, 500, 1100, 2000\}$. Using arc consistency with the subquery `CPU.Price + Memory.Price + Mother.Price < 1500`, we can remove the values 1100 and 2000 from the domain of CPU.price. Indeed there are no values in the domains of Memory.Price and Mother.Price such that the above arithmetic constraint is satisfied for 1100 and 2000.

Example 3. Let us now take another example where each attribute has a large number of values within a given range. For example let us consider the following ranges for the attributes of the table CPU. `200 <= Price <= 2000.` `5 <= Frequency <= 15.` `80 <= Quality <=95`. Using the above range for Price and the subquery:

```
CPU.Price + Memory.Price + Mother.Price < 1500
```

we can first reduce, the range of the attribute CPU.Price as follows `200 <= CPU.Price < 1500`. When using the attributes Memory.Price and Motherboard.Price we reduce the upper bound of the above range as follows.

```
CPU.Price < 1500 - [Min(Memory.Price) + Min(Motherboard.Price)]
          < 1500 - [800 + 100]
          < 600
```

We will finally obtain the following range for CPU.Price: `200 <= CPU.Price < 600`.

During the second phase of our solving method arc consistency is used through arithmetic and semantic constraints. The following example shows how an assignment of a value to a variable, during backtrack search, is propagated using arc consistency through the arithmetic constraint to update the domains (ranges) of the non assigned variables which will reduce the size of the search space.

Example 4. Let us consider the arithmetic constraint $A + B + C < 100$, where the domains of A, B and C are respectively: $[10, 80]$, $[20, 90]$ and $[20, 70]$. Using arc consistency we will reduce the domains of A and B as follows. $10 < A < 100 - (20 + 20) = 60$. $20 < B < 100 - (10 + 20) = 70$. Suppose now that, during the search, we first assign the value 50 to A. Through arc consistency and the above arithmetic constraint, the domain of B will be updated as follows: $20 < B < 100 - (50 + 20) = 30$.

Example 5. Let us consider the previous example and assume that we have the following semantic constraints (corresponding to three tables): Table1$(A, D, \ldots)$, Table2$(B, E, \ldots)$ and Table3$(C, F, \ldots)$. After assigning the value 50 to A as shown above in example 4, the domain of B will be reduced to $[20,30]$. Now through the semantic constraint Table1 all the tuples where $A \neq 50$ should be removed from Table1. Also, through Table2 all tuples where $B \notin [20,30]$ will be removed from Table2. This will reduce the domains of D, E and F.

Arc consistency is enforced with an arc consistency algorithm. In the past three decades several arc consistency algorithms have been developed. However most of these algorithms deal with binary constraints [11,16,17,18,19,20]. In the case of n-ary constraints there are three types of algorithms [7].

- Generalized Arc Consistency: for general non binary constraints.
- Global constraints: for constraints involving all the variables of a given CSP (such as the constraint $allDifferent(X_1, \ldots, X_n)$ which means that the values assigned to each of the variables $X_1, \ldots, X_n$ should be mutually different).
- Bounds-Consistency: which is a weaker (but less expensive) form of arc consistency. It consists of applying arc consistency to the upper and lower bounds of the variable domains. Examples 3 and 4 above use a form of bounds-consistency which motivates our choice of this type of algorithm for arithmetic constraints as shown below.

Algorithm GAC

1. Given a constraint network $CN = (X, C)$
      (*X: set of variables, C: set of constraints between variables*)
2. $Q \leftarrow \{(i, j) \mid i \in C \wedge j \in vars(C)\}$
3.   (*vars(C)* is the list of variables involved by C)
4.   **While** $Q \neq Nil$ **Do**
5. $Q \leftarrow Q - \{(i, j)\}$
6.   **If** $REVISE(i, j)$ **Then**
7.   **If** $Domain(j) = Nil$ **Then** return false
8. $Q \leftarrow Q \sqcup \{(k, l) \mid k \in C \wedge j \in vars(k)$
9. $\wedge\, l \in vars(k) \wedge k \neq i \wedge j \neq l\}$
10.   **End-If**
11.   **End-While**
12. Return true

Function $REVISE(i, j)$
(REVISE for bound consistency)
  1$domainSize \leftarrow |Domain(j)|$
  2**While** $|Domain(j)| > 0$
     $\wedge \neg seekSupportArc(i, j, min(j))$ **Do**
  3. remove $min(j)$ from $Domain(j)$
  4**End-While**
  5**While** $|Domain(j)| > 1$
     $\wedge \neg seekSupportArc(i, j, max(j))$ **Do**
  6. remove $min(j)$ from $Domain(j)$
  7**End-While**
  8Return $domainSize \neq |Domain(j)|$

Function $REVISE(i, j)$
(REVISE for handling semantic constraints)
  1. $REVISE \leftarrow false$
  2. $nbElts \leftarrow |Domain(j)|$
  3. **For** each value $a \in Domain(j)$ **Do**
  4.   **If** $\neg seekSupport(i, j, a)$ **Then**
  5.   remove a from $Domain_j$
  6. $REVISE \leftarrow true$
  7.   **End-If**
  8. **End-For**

Fig. 2. GAC algorithm and Revise for bound consistency (bottom left) and for handling semantic constraints (bottom right)

In our work we use the improved generalized arc consistency (GAC) algorithm [21] for semantic constraints (since this algorithm is dedicated for positive table constraints) and the bound consistency algorithm for discrete CSPs [22] in the case of arithmetic constraints. More precisely, bounds consistency is first used through arithmetic constraints to reduce the bounds of the different domains of variables. The improved GAC [21] is then used through the semantic constraints to reduce more the domains of the attributes. Let us describe now the details of our method. The basic GAC algorithm [23,21] is described in figure 2. This algorithm enforces the arc consistency on all variables domains. GAC starts with all possible pairs (i, j) where j is a variable involved by the constraint i. Each pair is then processed, through the function $REVISE$ as follows. Each value v of the domain of j should have a value supporting it (such that the constraint j is satisfied) on the domain on every variable involved by i otherwise v will be removed. If there is a change in the domain of j (after removing values without support) after calling the function $REVISE$ then this change should be propagated to all the other variables sharing a constraint with j.

When used with arithmetic constraints (as a bound consistency algorithm) C constains the list of arithmetic constraints and the *REVISE* function (the function that does the actual revision of the domains) is defined as shown in figure 2 [22]. In the other case where GAC is used with semantic constraints C contains these arithmetic constraints and the *REVISE* function is defined as shown in the bottom right of figure 2 [21]. In the function *REVISE* (for bound consistency) of figure 2, the function *seekSupportArc* (respectively the function *seekSupport* of *REVISE* for semantic constraints in figure 2) is called to find a support for a given variable with a particular value.

4   Structure of the RDBMS with the CSP Module

Figure 3 presents the architecture of the module handling combinatorial queries. In the CSP module, the CSP converter translates the query and the other information obtained for the database such as the semantic constraints into a CSP. The solver contains the solving techniques we described in the previous section.

More precisely, in the traditional RDBMS model the query submitted by the user through the user interface is first received by the query parser which will transform the string form of the query into query objects that will be handled by the query processor. Regularly, the query optimizer will choose the appropriate query solving plan (query execution order with the least estimated cost) and send the execution request to the interpreter. The interpreter will then handle the request and implements the input/output operations by driving storage engine.

In the case of the RDBMS model integrating the CSP module, once the combinatorial query is parsed by the query parser, it is sent to the CSP module. The converter will convert the query (including the arithmetic constraints) and the semantic constraints obtained from the database into the CSP. The solver will then solve it and send the solution to the execution interpreter.

5   Experimentation

In order to compare the time performance of our query processor with one of the most advanced relational databases (MS SQL server 2005) we run several tests on randomly generated databases and take the running time in seconds needed (by our method and MS SQL) to satisfy the query. The tests are conducted on a IBM T42 with a P4 1.7 GHz processor and 512 MB RAM memory, running Windows XP. Each database and its corresponding combinatorial query are randomly generated according to the following parameters: T (the number of tables withing the database), R and C (respectively the number of rows and columns of each table within the database); and P the constraint tightness. This last parameter defines how easy|hard is the CSP corresponding to the generatcd database. More precisely, the constraint tightness P of a given constraint is defined as "*the fraction of all possible pairs of intervals from the domains of the variables (involved by the constraint) that are not allowed by the constraint [24].*" According to this definition, the value of P is between 0 and 1. Easy problems are those where the tightness is small and hard problems correspond to a high tightness value.

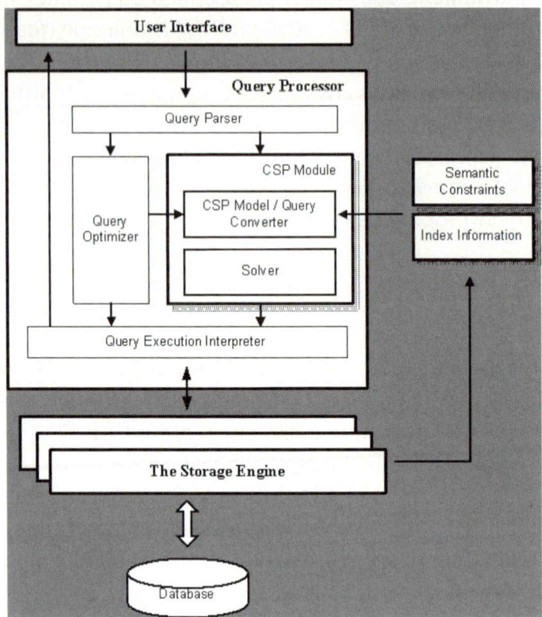

Fig. 3. Relational database model with the CSP module

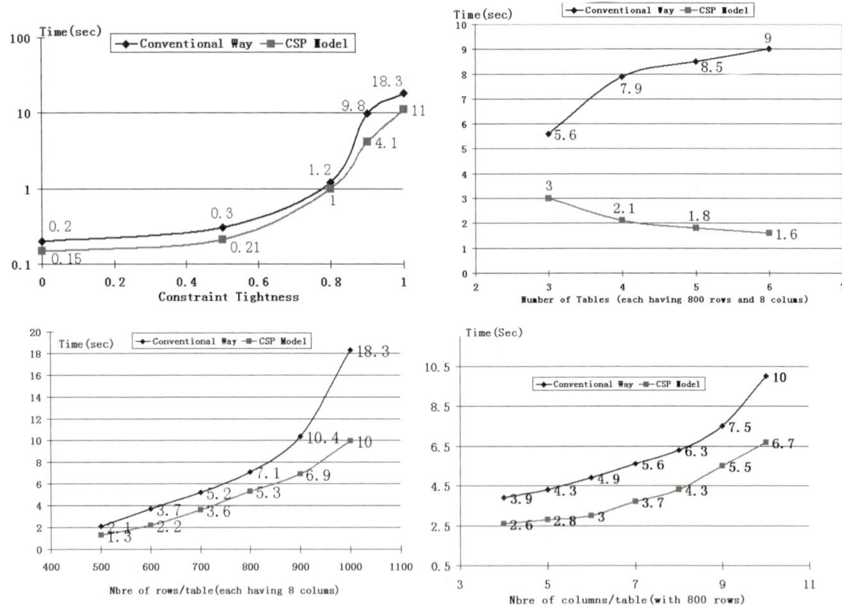

Fig. 4. Test results when varying the tightness (top left), the number of tables (top right), the number of rows (bottom left) and the number of columns (bottom right)

The top left chart of figure 4 presents tests performed when varying the tightness P. T, R and C are respectively equal to 3, 800 and 8. As we notice on the chart, when T is below 0.8 (the case where %80 of the possibilities are not solutions) the 2 methods have similar running time. However when T is more than 0.8 (which corresponds to hard problems where only few possibilitites are solutions) we can see the superiority of our method over the traditional model. The other three charts of figure 4 correspond to the situation where we vary T, R and C respectively. In all these 3 cases we can easily see that our method outperforms MS SQL (especially when R or T increases). Note that in the case where T is greater than 3 (in the top right chart of figure 4), the problem becomes inconsistent (the query cannot be satisfied). In this particular case, our method detects the inconsistency before the backtrack search (see step 1 of our solving method in Section 3). Since the backtrack search phase is saved in this case, the total running time is even better than the case where T is equal to 3.

6 Conclusion and Future Work

CSPs are a very powerful framework to deal with discrete combinatorial problems. In this paper we apply CSPs in order to solve a particular case of combinatorial applications consisting of satisfying a combinatorial query. More precisely our method translates the combinatorial query with the database information into a CSP. CSP techniques including constraint propagation and backtrack search are then used to satisfy the query by looking for a possible solution to the CSP. In order to demonstrate the efficiency in practice of our method, we conducted different tests on large databases and compared the running time needed by our method and the well known SQL server 2000 in order to satisfy combinatorial queries. The results of the tests demonstrate the superiority of our method for all the cases.

In the near future, we intend to integrate other search methods such local search techniques and genetic algorithms in order to speed up the query search process. Indeed, we believe that while these approximation algorithms do not guarantee a complete solution they can be very useful in case we want an answer within a short time.

References

1. Atzeni, P., Antonellis, V.D.: Relational database theory. Benjamin-Cummings Publishing Co (1993)
2. Liu, C., Foster, I.T.: A framework and algorithms for applying constraint solving within relational databases. In: W(C)LP 2005, pp. 147–158 (2005)
3. Revesz, P.: Introduction to Constraint Databases. Springer, New York (2002)
4. Chuang, L., Yang, L., Foster, I.T.: Efficient relational joins with arithmetic constraints on multiple attributes. In: IDEAS, pp. 210–220 (2005)
5. Vardi, M.Y.: The complexity of relational query languages. In: Annual ACM Symposium on Theory of Computing (1982)
6. Chandra, A.: Structure and complexity of relational queries. In: The 21st IEEE Symposium, pp. 333–347 (1980)
7. Dechter, R.: Constraint Processing. Morgan Kaufmann, San Francisco (2003)

8. Hentenryck, P.V.: Constraint Satisfaction in Logic Programming. MIT Press, Cambridge (1989)
9. Haralick, R., Elliott, G.: Increasing tree search efficiency for Constraint Satisfaction Problems. Artificial Intelligence 14, 263–313 (1980)
10. Mackworth, A.K., Freuder, E.: The complexity of some polynomial network-consistency algorithms for constraint satisfaction problems. Artificial Intelligence 25, 65–74 (1985)
11. Mackworth, A.K.: Consistency in networks of relations. Artificial Intelligence 8, 99–118 (1977)
12. Vardi, M.Y.: Constraint sastisfaction and database theory: A tutorial. In: PODS 2000 (2000)
13. Swami, A.: Optimization of large join queries: combining heuristics and combinatorial techniques. In: The 1989 ACM SIGMOD international conference on Management of data, pp. 367–376 (1989)
14. Jarke, M., Koch, J.: Query optimization in database systems. In: ACM Computing Surveys (CSUR), pp. 111–152 (1984)
15. Miguel, I., Shen, Q.: Solution techniques for constraint satisfaction problems: Foundations. Artificial Intelligence Review 15(4) (2001)
16. Mohr, R., Henderson, T.: Arc and path consistency revisited. Artificial Intelligence 28, 225–233 (1986)
17. Bessière, C.: Arc-consistency and arc-consistency again. Artificial Intelligence 65, 179–190 (1994)
18. Bessière, C., Freuder, E., Regin, J.: Using inference to reduce arc consistency computation. In: IJCAI 1995, Montréal, Canada, pp. 592–598 (1995)
19. Zhang, Y., Yap, R.H.C.: Making ac-3 an optimal algorithm. In: Seventeenth International Joint Conference on Artificial Intelligence (IJCAI 2001), Seattle, WA, pp. 316–321 (2001)
20. Bessière, C., Régin, J.C.: Refining the basic constraint propagation algorithm. In: Seventeenth International Joint Conference on Artificial Intelligence (IJCAI 2001), Seattle, WA, pp. 309–315 (2001)
21. Lecoutre, C., Radoslaw, S.: Generalized arc consistency for positive table constraints. In: Benhamou, F. (ed.) CP 2006. LNCS, vol. 4204, pp. 284–298. Springer, Heidelberg (2006)
22. Lecoutre, C., Vion, J.: Bound consistencies for the csp. In: Proceeding of the second international workshop Constraint Propagation And Implementation (CPAI 2005) held with the 10th International Conference on Principles and Practice of Constraint Programming (CP 2005), Sitges, Spain (September 2005)
23. Mackworth, A.K.: On reading sketch maps. In: IJCAI 1977, pp. 598–606 (1977)
24. Sabin, D., Freuder, E.C.: Contradicting conventional wisdom in constraint satisfaction. In: Proc. 11th ECAI, Amsterdam, Holland, pp. 125–129 (1994)

Maintaining Population Diversity in Evolution Strategy for Engineering Problems

Roman Dębski, Rafał Dreżewski, and Marek Kisiel-Dorohinicki

Department of Computer Science
AGH University of Science and Technology, Kraków, Poland
{drezew,doroh}@agh.edu.pl

Abstract. In the paper three new mechanisms for maintaining population diversity in (μ, λ)-evolution strategies are introduced: deterministic modification of standard deviations, crowding, and elitism. The proposed mechanisms are experimentally verified with the use of optimal shape designing of rotating variable-thickness annular elastic discs problem.

Keywords: evolution strategies, maintaining population diversity, optimal shape design.

1 Introduction

Many engineering tasks lead to the global optimization problems, which in most cases cannot be solved by traditional methods. In such a situation one can use (meta)heuristic computational techniques such as *evolutionary algorithms*. This term covers a wide range of search and optimization methods, based on analogies to Darwinian model of evolutionary processes. Particularly interesting from the engineering problems point of view are evolution strategies. They are most often used for solving continuous optimization problems and are distinguished by a real-valued representation, Gaussian mutation with auto-adaptation as the main variation operator, and deterministic selection scheme [2,8].

The paper discusses the application of evolution strategies to optimal shape designing of a rotating variable-thickness annular disc—the optimal shape means here the one corresponding to the maximal elastic carrying capacity of the disc [6]. The main goal of the paper is to present some modifications of "classical" evolution strategies mainly focused on maintaining population diversity and thus protecting the searching process from getting stuck in a local extrema. Maintaining population diversity seems to be the problem of vast importance in this case.

The paper is organized as follows. Classical evolution strategies and proposed mechanisms for maintaining population diversity (i.e. deterministic modification of standard deviations, crowding and elitism) are described in section 2. Section 3 presents the optimization problem: the design of rotating variable-thickness annular elastic disc, proposed representation of the solutions, and the model used to evaluate their quality (fitness). Selected experimental results with the proposed (μ, λ)-evolution strategy with additional mechanisms conclude the work.

N.T. Nguyen et al. (Eds.): IEA/AIE 2008, LNAI 5027, pp. 379–387, 2008.

2 Evolution Strategies

Evolution strategies (ES) were developed by Rechenberg and Schwefel in the 1960s at the Technical University of Berlin. The first applications were aimed at hydrodynamical problems like shape optimization of a bended pipe and drag minimization of a joint plate [3]. ES is a special instance of an evolutionary algorithm characterized by real-valued vector representation, Gaussian mutation as main variation operator, self-adaptation of mutation rate, and deterministic selection mechanisms.

2.1 Classical Approach

Algorithmic framework of contemporary evolution strategies may be described with the use of following notation [7]:

- $(\mu + \lambda)$-ES generates λ offspring from μ parents and selects the μ best individuals from $\mu + \lambda$ (parents and offspring) individuals $(1 \leq \mu \leq \lambda)$,
- (μ, λ)-ES denotes an ES that each time step generates λ offspring from μ parents and selects the μ best individuals only from λ (offspring) individuals $(1 \leq \mu \leq \lambda)$.

The individuals in a population consist of the objective variables vector $\boldsymbol{x}$ and a vector of *strategy parameters* $\boldsymbol{\sigma}$, where σ_i denotes the standard deviation used when applying a zero-mean Gaussian mutation to the i-th component in parent vector. These parameters are incorporated into the representation of individual in order to obtain evolutionary *self-adaptation* of an ES [8,1]. The mutation operator changes strategy parameters according to:

$$\sigma_i' = \sigma_i \exp(\tau_0 N(0,1) + \tau N_i(0,1)) \tag{1}$$

and the objective variables (a simplified case of uncorrelated mutations):

$$x_i' = x_i + N(0, \sigma_i') \tag{2}$$

where the constant $\tau \propto \dfrac{1}{\sqrt{2\sqrt{n}}}$, $\tau_0 \propto \dfrac{1}{\sqrt{2n}}$, $N(0,1)$ is a standard Gaussian random variable sampled once for all n dimensions and $N_i(0,1)$ is a standard Gaussian random variable sampled for each of the n dimensions.

If the number of parents $\mu > 1$, the objective variables and internal strategy parameters can be recombined with usual recombination operators, for example *intermediate recombination* [4], which acts on two parents $\boldsymbol{x_1}$ and $\boldsymbol{x_2}$ and creates an offspring $\boldsymbol{x'}$ as the weighted average:

$$x_i' = \alpha x_{1i} + (1 - \alpha)x_{2i} \tag{3}$$

where $\alpha \in [0,1]$ and $i = 1, \ldots, n$. The same may be applied to standard deviations:

$$\sigma_i' = \alpha \sigma_{1i} + (1 - \alpha)\sigma_{2i} \tag{4}$$

It is not necessary to apply the same recombination operator for objective variables and standard deviations. For example one can use *discrete recombination* for standard deviations and *intermediate recombination* for objective variables.

2.2 Maintaining Population Diversity Mechanisms

An evolutionary algorithm works properly (in terms of searching for a global solution) if the population consists of individuals different enough, i.e. the so-called diversity in the population is preserved. Yet many algorithms tend to prematurely loose this useful diversity and, as a result, there is possibility that population gets stuck in some local extrema instead of searching for a global one. To avoid this undesirable behavior in classical ES the mechanism of self-adaptation, as described above, was proposed. Yet this mechanism proves often not sufficient for very complex multi-modal problems.

In [5] the additional mutation operator was introduced. It improved obtained results, however it turned out that this additional mutation was still insufficient in the case of highly multi-modal problems of shape designing. The new mechanisms for maintaining population diversity in ES introduced in this paper include:

M1: the new mechanism of modifying standard deviation. Standard deviation is changed deterministically, in the following way:

$$\sigma'(\phi) = \sigma_{max} - (\sigma_{max} - \sigma_{min})\frac{(\phi - \phi_{min})^2}{(\phi_{max} - \phi_{min})^2} \tag{5}$$

where:

$\sigma_{max}, \sigma_{min}$ are predefined values of maximal and minimal mutation standard deviation;

ϕ_{max}, ϕ_{min} are maximal and minimal fitness found in all past generations.

The above function causes that the standard deviation of "poor" solutions is increased, so their children can "jump" in the solution space with greater probability. There are of course different function with the same characteristic and the one presented above was chosen arbitrary.

M2: the mechanism of crowding. The next generation population of μ individuals is generated from the population of λ individuals in the following way. The individuals in the offspring population are sorted on the basis of their fitness values. The best individual from the offspring population is added to the next generation population. Then the next individual is added to the population only if its Gaussian norm based distance from all k individuals already added to the population is greater than:

$$k \cdot d_{min} \cdot \left(1 - \left(\frac{t}{t_{max}}\right)^2\right), \quad \text{for } t = 1, 2, \ldots t_{max}. \tag{6}$$

where k is the number of individuals already present in the new generation population, d_{min} is the minimal distance between two individuals, t_{max} is the predefined maximal number of generations, and t is the actual number of generation. The third component of the above equation $\left(1 - \left(\frac{t}{t_{max}}\right)^2\right)$ is decreasing as the number of generation increases (the analogy to "temperature" in simulated annealing technique). This mechanism works in such a

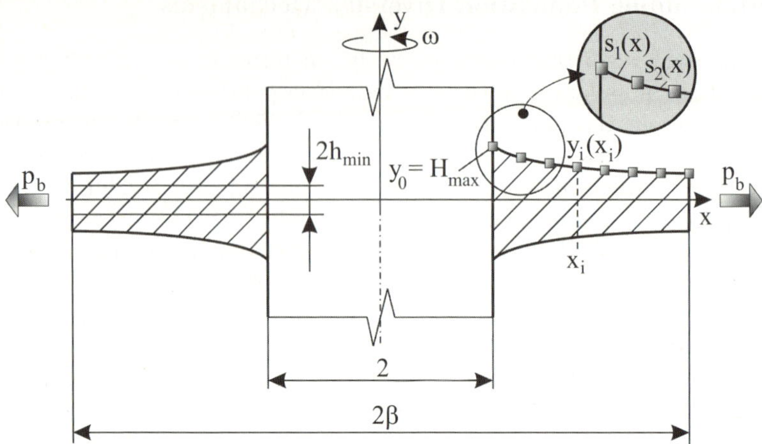

Fig. 1. Annular disc under consideration and its profile representation

way that "good" individuals can be more "crowded" than the "poor" ones but this restriction is loosen as the current number of generation increases. Thanks to this we can promote population diversity—individuals located in basins of attraction of "poor" local minima can not be crowded but they can be moved to the next generation population of μ individuals.

M3: elitism mechanism. The best individual from the population of μ parents is always moved to the population of λ offspring.

3   The Optimization Problem

The most important assumptions about the physical model of the discussed design problem are as follows [6]:

1. We consider an annular elastic disc of variable thickness $h = h(r)$ rotating with constant angular velocity ω and subject to uniform traction p_b at the outer radius b. The disc is clamped at the inner radius a.
2. The classical theory of thin discs with small gradient dh/dr is assumed and hence the stresses t_{ry} and s_y are neglected[1].
3. The material is linear-elastic with Young's modulus E, Poisson's ratio ν and subject to the Huber-Mises-Hencky (H-M-H) yield condition.
4. The small-strain theory is adopted.

The profile of the disc is represented by the 3rd order spline built on equidistant nodes (see fig. 1), where a dimensionless radius $x = r/a$ was introduced.

---

[1] In this paper we use t and r symbols to denote the stresses instead of τ and σ, which are usually used in the literature, because the latter ones are already used in the evolution strategies description.

After introducing basic equations one may formulate the optimization problem by defining a decision variables vector, a feasible region and an objective function. The decision variables vector:

$$\mathbf{Y} = (y_1, y_2, \ldots, y_n) \in M \subset \mathbf{R}^n \tag{7}$$

represents the shape of the disc in n equidistant points.

The feasible region:

$$M = \{\mathbf{Y} \in \mathbf{R}^n \mid k_d \cdot h_{min} \le y_j \le k_g \cdot H_{max} \quad \forall j = 1, \ldots, n\} \tag{8}$$

assumes that the disc is clamped at the inner radius having there fixed thickness ($y_0 = H_{max}$) and that the disc can be neither too thin (not thinner than $k_d \cdot h_{min}$) nor too thick (not thicker than $k_g \cdot H_{max}$). Objective function is described by the following formula:

$$\Phi = \left\{ c \left[\frac{1}{\beta - 1} \int_1^\beta s_i(x)\, dx \right] + (1 - c)\sqrt{p^2 + \Omega^2} \right\} \to max \tag{9}$$

where $0 \le c \le 1$ makes it possible to set the importance of each of the two criteria taken into account. The first of them (with the multiplier c) is connected with the equalization of the stress intensity and the second one with the external loadings (it is worth noting that if $c = 0$ this criterion becomes a simple maximization of elastic carrying capacity). Such a generalization is very helpful in estimating the limit carrying capacity or decohesive carrying capacity.

4   Experimental Results

Optimal shapes in the meaning of criterion (9) conected with different ratio Ω/p were presented in [6]. Below only the analysis of the proposed mechanisms is discussed.

All the results of experiments presented in this section were obtained for the following values of the systems' parameters (the definitions of these parameters can be found in [5]): $\beta = 2$, $H_{max}/h_{min} = 5$, $p/\Omega = 0$, $k_d = 0.9$, $k_g = 1.1$, $\nu = 0.3$, $s_0/E = 0.001$, $c = 1$, $\mu = 15$, $\lambda = 100$, $\sigma_{min} = 10^{-6}$, $\sigma_{max} = 1$, $d_{min} = 0.13$.

The results for the basic version of the algorithm are presented in the figure 2. It can be observed that the population diversity is not maintained very well in this case. Usually it is quite quickly reduced after 20–30 (sometimes after about 100–150) generations. In the first case there is usually an individual with high fitness value (as compared to other individuals within the population) within the population but with very low standard deviation values. In such a case the population is quite quickly composed of the clones of such individual, the algorithm loses the population diversity and the abilities to explore the search space—usually the results obtained in such a case are very poor.

In the second case (when the population diversity falls down after 100–150 time steps) the algorithm locates the basin of attraction of one of the local

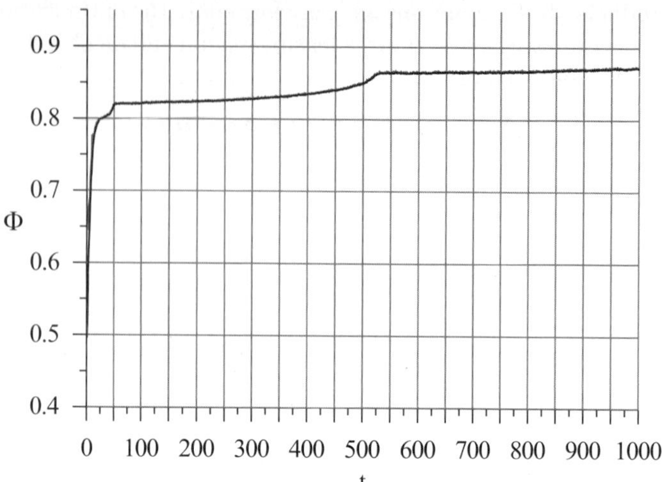

Fig. 2. Minimum, average and maximum value of the objective function for the base algorithm (with no additional mechanisms)

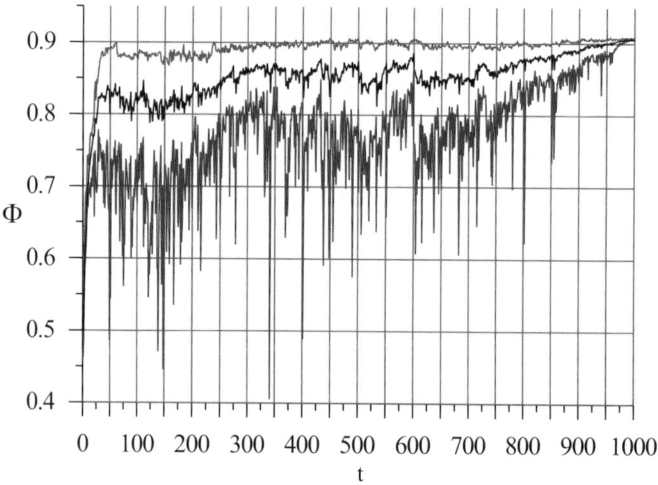

Fig. 3. Minimum (bottom line), average (middle line) and maximum (top line) value of the objective function for mechanism $M2$ (crowding)

maxima. The population diversity is very low but the standard deviations are such that there is still the possibility of locating basins of attraction of other maxima (the values of standard deviations are analyzed in [6,5]). Sometimes the algorithm locates the basin of attraction of quite "good" maxima but generally results obtained are not satisfying.

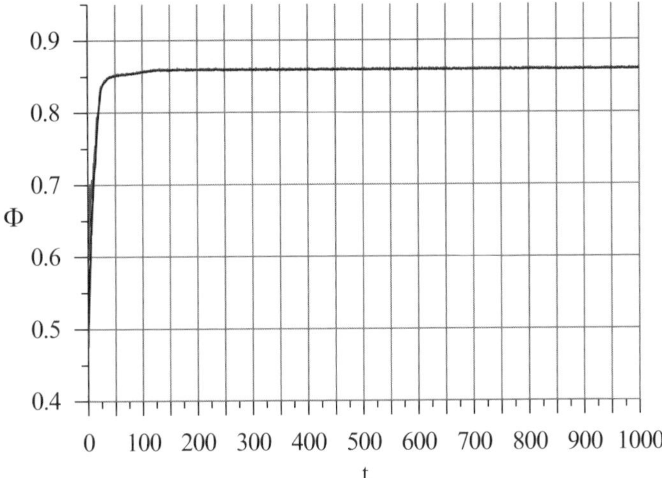

Fig. 4. Minimum, average and maximum value of the objective function for mechanism $M3$ (elitism)

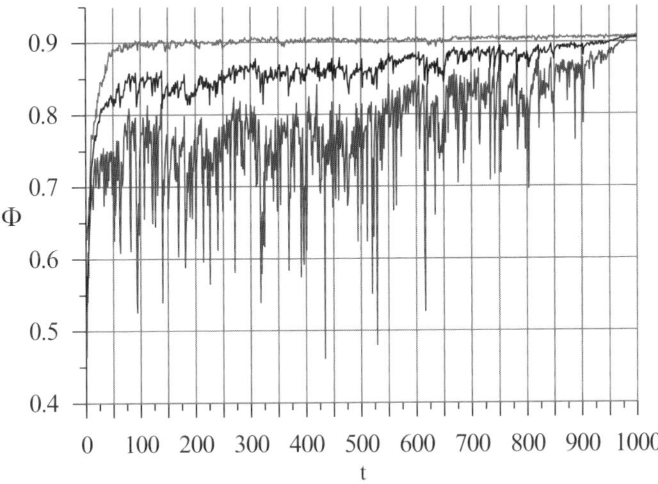

Fig. 5. Minimum (bottom line), average (middle line) and maximum (top line) value of the objective function for combined mechanisms $M2$ and $M3$ (crowding and elitism)

The additional operators presented in [5] had not greatly improved the results, and there still had been the tendency to lose the population diversity during optimization.

It was observed that the mechanism $M1$ (the deterministic standard deviation modification) applied separately led to worse final results as compared to the base algorithm. The main problem was related to the lack of convergence—the

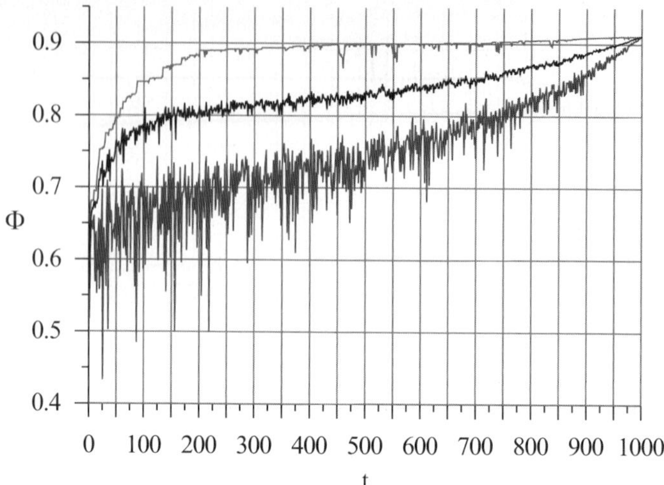

Fig. 6. Minimum (bottom line), average (middle line) and maximum (top line) value of the objective function for combined mechanisms $M1$, $M2$ and $M3$ (the deterministic standard deviation modification, crowding and elitism)

algorithm with the deterministic standard deviation modifications resembled random walk.

The use of the mechanism of crowding ($M2$) results in better results when the diversity of the population is considered but additionally causes that the algorithm is not "stable"—there are chaotic changes of the fitness values within the population (see fig. 3). When we additionally introduce the elitism mechanism ($M2$) the chaotic fluctuations of the fitness values disappear—the algorithm works "stable" (fig. 5). The application of all three mechanisms together (see fig. 5) results in maintaining population diversity, there are no chaotic changes in fitness values of the individuals, and additionally the possibility of dominating the whole population by the copies of the individual with small fitness value and small values of standard deviations is reduced. Also in this case the average results obtained are the best.

5   Concluding Remarks

Many tasks related to optimal designing cannot be solved by the use of classical methods (e.g. calculus of variations) because of various reasons. It is the case for example when there is no strict mathematical model of a problem (e.g. the mapping between the decisive variables and the objective function is unknown). In such a situation the optimization process is performed as a sequence of evaluations of possible solutions. When the domain space make the complete searching impossible one can use some heuristic methods to control the algorithm of candidate solutions selecting, like evolutionary algorithms or simulated annealing.

Both the techniques in their classic forms usually do not work correctly in problems with many local extrema. In case of evolutionary algorithms one of the key problems is related to maintaining population diversity.

In the paper the following three modifications to the classic (μ, λ)-ES were discussed: deterministic modification of standard deviations, crowding and elitism. The analysis was based on the results of the shape optimization of rotating variable-thickness annular elastic disc. The results clearly show that only the simultaneous use of all these three mechanisms help to maintain population diversity and, in consequence, lead to a more stable searching processes and finally—better solutions. Future research could concentrate on the further verification of the proposed mechanisms. Other engineering problems should be considered for this purpose.

References

1. Bäck, T., Fogel, D., Whitley, D., Angeline, P.: Mutation. In: Bäck, T., Fogel, D., Michalewicz, Z. (eds.) Handbook of Evolutionary Computation, IOP Publishing and Oxford University Press (1997)
2. Bäck, T., Schwefel, H.-P.: An overview of evolutionary algorithms for parameter optimisation. Evolutionary Computation 1(1) (1993)
3. Bäck, T., Schwefel, H.-P.: Evolutionary computation: An overview. In: Proceedings of the Third IEEE Conference on Evolutionary Computation, IEEE Press, Piscataway NJ (1996)
4. Booker, L., Fogel, D., Whitley, D., Angeline, P.: Recombination. In: Bäck, T., Fogel, D., Michalewicz, Z. (eds.) Handbook of Evolutionary Computation, IOP Publishing and Oxford University Press (1997)
5. Dębski, R., Dreżewski, R., Kisiel-Dorohinicki, M.: Preserving diversity in evolution strategy for shape design of rotating elastic disc. In: Proceedings of the 6th Conference on Evolutionary Algorithms and Global Optimization (KAEiOG 2003), University of Zielona Góra (2003)
6. Dębski, R., Woźniak, G., Dreżewski, R., Kisiel-Dorohinicki, M.: Evolutionary strategy for shape design of rotating variable-thickness annular elastic disc. In: Proceedings of the Symposium on Methods of Artificial Intelligence (AI-METH 2002), Gliwice, Silesian University of Technology (2002)
7. Rudolph, G.: Evolution strategies. In: Bäck, T., Fogel, D., Michalewicz, Z. (eds.) Handbook of Evolutionary Computation, IOP Publishing and Oxford University Press (1997)
8. Schwefel, H.-P.: Numerical Optimization of Computer Models. John Willey & Sons, Ltd., Chichester (1981)

Clustering of Gene Expression Data with
Quantum-Behaved Particle Swarm Optimization

Wei Chen, Jun Sun, Yanrui Ding, Wei Fang, and Wenbo Xu

School of Information Technology, Jiangnan University
No. 1800, Lihu Avenue, Wuxi, Jiangsu P.R. China
chenwei_0906@yahoo.com.cn, sunjun_wx@hotmail.com,
yr_ding@yahoo.com.cn

Abstract. Based on the previously proposed Quantum-behaved Particle Swarm Optimization (QPSO) algorithm, in this paper, we focus on the application of QPSO in gene expression data clustering which can be reduced to an optimization problem. The proposed clustering algorithm partitions the N patterns of the gene expression dataset into user-defined K categories to minimize the fitness function of Total Within-Cluster Variation. Thus a partition with high performance is obtained. The experiment results on four gene expression data sets show that our QPSO-based clustering algorithm will be an effective and promising tool for gene expression data analysis.

1 Introduction

In the past a few years, clustering algorithms have been effectively applied in molecular biology for gene expression data analysis [1]. With the development of DNA microarray technology, researchers can obtain thousands of gene expression data simultaneously under different specific conditions. In an attempt to analysis such massive biological data, clustering algorithms are used to partition genes into groups according to the similarity between their expression profiles. The goal of the clustering process is to identify the genes with the same functions or the same regulatory mechanisms.

Many clustering algorithms have been proposed for gene expression data analysis. The hierarchical clustering is one of the earlier methods to apply in clustering of gene expression data. Eisen et al. used a variant of the hierarchical average-link clustering algorithms to identify groups of co-regulated yeast genes [2]. However, the hierarchy of the algorithm is greatly affected by the minor change of the given data, which makes the clustering show the lack of robustness and nonuniqueness. K-means [3] is one of another popular methods used in gene expression data analysis due to its high computational performances. But it might converge to a local optimum, and its results is quite subject to the random initialization process, which means that different runs of K-means on the same data set might produce different clusters. As one kind of neural network, self-organizing map (SOM) which presents high-dimensional data by the low dimensional data has also been applied in gene expression data clustering [4]. However it always produce an unbalanced solution and it is difficult to find clear clustering boundaries from results of the SOM.

N.T. Nguyen et al. (Eds.): IEA/AIE 2008, LNAI 5027, pp. 388–396, 2008.

In recent years, many researchers have employed evolutionary algorithms for clustering. The fundamental strategy of such clustering approaches is to imitate the evolution process of nature and improve the solutions of clustering from one generation to the next. For an instance, Krishna and Murty proposed a new clustering method called Genetic K-means Algorithm (GKA) [5], which hybridizes a genetic algorithm with the K-means algorithm. Based on the GKA, Lu Y et al. proposed Fast Genetic K-means Algorithm (FGKA) and Incremental Genetic K-means Algorithm (IGKA) for analyzing gene expression data [6-8].

More recently, Particle Swarm Optimization (PSO)[9], a population-based random search technique motivated by the behavior of organisms such as fishing schooling and bird flock, has been applied to data clustering [10]. In this paper, we'll propose a novel clustering algorithm for gene expression data based on our previously proposed Quantum-Behaved Particle Swarm Optimization (QPSO) Algorithm inspired by quantum mechanics [11-13]. Our motivation is based on the fact that as a global convergent algorithm, due to its stronger search ability, QPSO may be a promising method in gene expression data clustering, which can be reduced to a multi-modal optimization problem. The QPSO-based clustering algorithm partition the N patterns of the gene expression dataset into user-defined K categories to minimize the fitness function of Total Within-Cluster Variation. Thus a partition with high performance is obtained.

The rest part of the paper is organized as follows. Section 2 gives a brief introduction to PSO and QPSO algorithms, followed by Section 3 presenting how to use QPSO as a clustering algorithm. In Section 4, we describe four gene expression data sets used in our experiments. Section 5 is the experiment results and the paper is concluded in Section 6.

2   QPSO Algorithm

Particle Swarm Optimization (PSO) was originally proposed by J. Kennedy and R. Eberhart [9]. The underlying motivation for the development of PSO algorithm was social behavior of animals such as bird flocking, fish schooling, and swarm theory. In the Standard PSO with S individuals, each individual is treated as a volume-less particle in the D-dimensional space, with the position and velocity of ith particle represented as $X_i = (X_{i1}, X_{i2}, \cdots, X_{iD})$ and $V_i = (V_{i1}, V_{i2}, \cdots, V_{iD})$. The particles move according to the following equation:

$$V_{id} = w \cdot V_{id} + c_1 \cdot rand(\cdot) \cdot (P_{id} - X_{id}) + c_2 \cdot Rand(\cdot) \cdot (P_g - X_{id}) \qquad (1)$$

$$X_{id} = X_{id} + V_{id} \qquad (2)$$

where c_1 and c_2 are positive constant and rand() and Rand() are two uniform random functions within [0,1]. Parameter w is the inertia weight introduced to accelerate the convergence speed of the PSO. Vector $P_i = (P_{i1}, P_{i2}, \cdots, P_{iD})$ is the best previous position (the position giving the best fitness value) of particle i called **personal best position**, and vector $P_g = (P_{g1}, P_{g2}, \cdots, P_{gD})$ is the position of the best particle among all the particles in the population and called **global best position**.

In the previous work presented in [11-13], we proposed a novel variant form of PSO, Quantum-behaved Particle Swarm Optimization algorithm (QPSO), which was inspired by Quantum Mechanics and seems to a promising optimization problem solver. In QPSO, the particle moves according to the following equation:

$$X_{id} = p_{id} \pm \alpha |mbest_d - X_{id}| \ln(1/u), \quad u = Rand() \tag{3}$$

where *mbest* is the mean of personal best positions among the particles, that is

$$mbest = \frac{1}{M}\sum_{i=1}^{M} P_i = \left(\frac{1}{M}\sum_{i=1}^{M} P_{i1}, \quad \frac{1}{M}\sum_{i=1}^{M} P_{i2}, \quad \cdots, \quad \frac{1}{M}\sum_{i=1}^{M} P_{id}\right) \tag{4}$$

and p_{id} is determined by $p_{id} = \varphi \cdot P_{id} + (1-\varphi) \cdot P_{gd}$, $\varphi = rand()$. φ is a random number distributed uniformly on $[0,1]$ and u is another uniformly-distributed random number within $[0,1]$ and α is a parameter of QPSO called Contraction-Expansion Coefficient. The stochastic evolution equation (3) comes from a quantum δ potential well model proposed in [11]. One may refer to references [11-13] for the origin and development of QSPO.

The procedure of Quantum-behaved Particle Swarm Optimization (QPSO) Algorithm in [13] is outlined as follows:

QPSO Algorithm
Initialize particles with random position X_i=X[i][:];
Let personal best position P_i=P[i][:]=X_i;
while termination criterion is not met **do**
    Compute the mean best position mbest[:] by equation (4);
    for i=1 to swarm size S

      if f(X_i)<f(P_i) **then** P_i=X_i; **endif**
      Find the P_g=P[g][:] across the swarm;
      for d=1 to D
        fi=rand(0,1); u=rand(0,1);
        p=fi*P[i][d]+(1-fi)*P_g[d];
        if (rand(0,1)>0.5
          X[i][d]=p+α*abs(mbest[d]-X[i][d])*ln(1/u);
        else
          X[i][d]=p-α*abs(mbest[d]-X[i][d])*ln(1/u);
            endif
      endfor
    endfor
endwhile

3   QPSO Clustering Algorithm

The problem of clustering gene expression data consists of N genes and their corresponding N patterns. Each pattern is a vector of D dimensions recording the expression levels of the genes under each of the D monitored conditions or at each of the D time points. The goal of using QPSO clustering algorithm is to partition the patterns into user-defined K categories, such that this partition minimizes the fitness function of the algorithm. One of the most important components of a clustering algorithm is the measure of similarity used to determine how close two patterns are to one another. In our QPSO clustering algorithm, we group gene patterns into their corresponding categories based on Euclidean distance as similarity measure. Data vectors within a cluster have small Euclidean distances from one another, and are associated with one centroid vector, which represents the "midpoint" of that cluster.

In the context of the clustering, a single particle of QPSO represents the K cluster centroid vectors. That is, each particle X_i is constructed as follows:

$$X_i = (M_{i1}, \cdots M_{ij}, \cdots M_{iK}) \tag{5}$$

where M_{ij} refers to the j-th cluster centroid vector of the i-th particle in cluster C_{ij}, which is the subset of data patterns in cluster j of particle i. Therefore, a swarm represents a number of candidate clusterings for the current gene expression data patterns.

It is vital to select an appropriate fitness function for the QPSO clustering algorithm. The fitness function is used to evaluate the quality of every particle to determine the best solution for the given optimization problem. For our clustering algorithm, it is used to evaluate the rationality and the correctness of the partition to the given gene expression dataset according to every particle. Originally we use the quantization error in [10]:

$$J_e = \frac{\sum_{j=1}^{K} [\sum_{\forall Z_p \in C_{ij}} d(Z_p, M_{ij}) / |C_{ij}|]}{K} \tag{6}$$

as the fitness function of the clustering algorithm, where d denotes the Euclidean distances, Z_p denotes the p-th data patterns, M_{ij} denotes the j-th cluster centroid vector of the i-th particle and $|C_{ij}|$ is the number of data vectors belonging to cluster C_{ij}. But we found that the QPSO clustering algorithm using J_e as its fitness function always produces an unbalanced partition of the dataset, i.e. most of the patterns are grouped into some categories and some categories are empty. For improving the result of the clustering, we select the Total Within-Cluster Variation (TWCV) proposed in [7] to substitute the quantization error as the new fitness function, which is defined as follows:

$$TWCV = \sum_{n=1}^{N} \sum_{d=1}^{D} z_{nd}^2 - \sum_{j=1}^{K} \frac{1}{|C_{ij}|} \sum_{d=1}^{D} SF_{jd}^2 \tag{7}$$

where SF_{jd} is the sum of the d-th features of all the patterns in cluster C_{ij}.

Based on above design of the algorithm, the QPSO clustering process can be concluded as follows:

1. Initialize each particle to contain K randomly selected cluster centroids.
2. For $t = 1$ to t_{max} do
    (1) For each particle i do
    (2) For each expression pattern Z_p
        a. Calculate the Euclidean distance $d(Z_p, M_{ij})$ to all cluster centroids C_{ij}
        b. Assign Z_p to cluster C_{ij} such that
        $$d(Z_p, M_{ij}) = \min_{\forall c=1,\cdots,K}\{d(Z_p, M_{ic})\}$$
        c. Calculate the fitness using equation (7)
    (3) Update the global best and local best positions
    (4) Update the cluster centroids using equations (3)

where t_{max} is the maximum number of iterations.

4 Gene Expression Data Sets

The four data sets used to conduct our experiments are the rat CNS data set, the galactose GAL data set and two yeast cell cycle data subsets with 384 and 237 genes respectively.

1. The rat CNS data set

The rat CNS data set was obtained by reverse transcription-coupled PCR to study the expression levels of 112 genes during rat central nervous system development over nine time points. These 112 genes were selected from four gene families according to prior knowledge of biology by Wen et al [14]. We use this 112×9 microarray as one of our experimental datasets and take these four functional categories as external standard categories.

2. The GAL data set

For exploring gene expression regulation information in the pathway of galactose utilization in the yeast saccharomyces cerevisiae and interaction between genes and proteins, four replicated hybridizations were performed for each cDNA array experiment to generate the GAL microarray by Ideker et al [15]. Yeung et al used a subset of 205 genes, whose expression patterns reflect four functional categories in the Gene Ontology (GO) listings in [16]. We use this 205×20 microarray as the second experimental data set, and the four categories are used as our external knowledge.

3. The yeast cell data set

The yeast cell data set shows the fluctuation of expression levels of approximately 6000 genes over approximately two cell cycles (17 time points). By visual inspection of the raw data, Cho et al identified 420 genes showing significant variation over the course of the cell cycle [17]. Yeung et al selected 384 genes achieving peak in only one phase from the subset of 420 genes, and obtained five standard categories by grouping the genes achieving peak at the same phase into one category [18]. On the other hand, Tavazioe et al found that 237 genes from the subset could be grouped into 4 functional categories through searching for the protein sequence database of MIPS [3]. We use these two 384×17 and 237×17 microarrays as the third and the fourth experimental data sets. The corresponding five and four functional categories are used as external standard categories.

5 Experiment Results

For validating the new method of clustering, this section compares the results of K-means, PSO and QPSO clustering algorithms on four gene expression data sets presented in Section 4. In our experiments, the population number of PSO and QPSO is set to 30 and the maximum number of iterations is 500. For PSO, $c_1 = c_2 = 2$, w is decreased linearly from 0.9 to 0.4 with the iterations. For QPSO, α is also decreased linearly from 1.0 to 0.5 with the iterations. For each experiment in this study, we record the results of each clustering algorithm by averaging 30 independent runs of the algorithm.

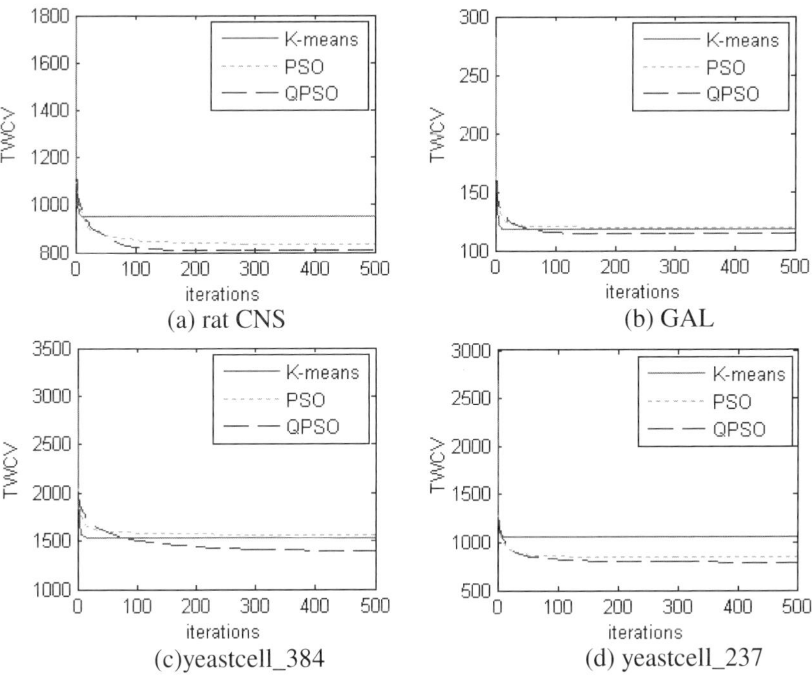

Fig. 1. Comparison of convergence process of the three competitor algorithm on four data sets

Fig 1 shows the convergence behavior of three clustering algorithms based on four gene expression data sets, respectively. Obviously, the K-means algorithm exhibits a faster, but premature convergence to a lager value of TWCV. While the QPSO algorithm had slower convergence, but to a better value of TWCV. To the comparison between PSO and QPSO, it can be seen that QPSO algorithm converges to better values of TWCV on all of the four experimental data sets, while PSO algorithm even has worse convergence performance than K-means algorithm on the second and the third data sets because of its premature problem. It illustrates that the QPSO clustering algorithm has the best global convergence. Table 1 shows the values of TWCV in our experiments and we can also see that the QPSO algorithm has the best convergence result.

Table 1. Comparison of TWCVs of the three competitor algorithm on four data sets

	K-means		PSO		QPSO	
	min	mean	min	mean	min	mean
rat CNS	807.24	950.18	807.24	835.53	807.24	808.07
GAL	113.96	117.88	114.12	119.39	114.11	114.16
yeastcell_384	1386.4	1531.6	1488.1	1562.2	1379.1	1395.8
yeastcell_237	789.46	1053.5	802.54	837.78	789.46	790.26

Table 2. Adjusted Rand indices and their standard deviations on four data sets

	K-means		PSO		QPSO	
	std	mean	std	mean	std	mean
rat CNS	0.0214	0.3563	0.0156	0.4232	0.0095	0.4651
GAL	0.0323	0.9023	0.0315	0.9132	0.0158	0.9557
yeastcell_384	0.0410	0.6384	0.0168	0.6827	0.0087	0.6834
yeastcell_237	0.0188	0.6899	0.0104	0.6881	0.0011	0.6903

The adjusted Rand index [19] is used in our experiments to assess the degree of agreement between the partition of the clustering algorithm and the partition based on the standard categories. The adjusted Rand index has the maximum value of 1, which means perfect agreement between the external criterion and the clustering result. A higher adjusted Rand index means a higher correspondence to the gold standard. Table 2 shows the adjusted Rand indices between the results of the three clustering algorithms and the external standard partitions corresponding to the four data sets. The mean Rand indices of the QPSO clustering algorithm are higher than those of the K-means algorithm and the PSO clustering algorithm. It illustrates that the clustering algorithm using QPSO can always obtain an excellent partition of the given gene expression data set with high correspondence to the partition based on the standard categories. The standard deviations of the adjusted Rand indices on the four data sets in our experiment are also given in Table 2.

6   Conclusions

In this paper, we propose a new clustering algorithm based on Quantum-Behaved particle swarm optimization and apply it in gene expression data analysis. Four gene expression data sets, including the rat CNS data set, the GAL data set and two yeast cell data sets are selected to validate the performance of the QPSO clustering algorithm. The experiments show that the new method always obtains partitions with outstanding effect and will be a promising tool for gene expression data clustering.

References

1. Shamir, R., Sharan, R.: Approaches to clustering gene expression data. In: Jiang, T., Smith, T., Xu, Y., Zhang, M.Q. (eds.) Current Topics in Computational Biology, MIT press, Cambridge (2001)
2. Eisen, M.B., Spellman, P.T., Brown, P.O., Botstein, D.: Cluster analysis and display of genome-wide expression patterns. Proc. Natl. Acad. Sci. USA 95, 14 863–14 868
3. Tavazoie, S., Hughes, J.D., Campbell, M.J., Cho, R.J., Church, G.M.: Systematic determination of genetic network architecture. Nat. Genet. 22, 281–285 (1999)
4. Tamayo, P., Slonim, D., Mesirov, J., Zhu, Q., Kitareewan, S., Dmitrovsky, E., Lander, E.S., Golub, T.R.: Interpreting patterns of gene expression with self-organizing maps: methods and application to hematopoietic differentiation. Proc. Natl Acad. Sci. USA 96, 2907–2912
5. Krishna, K., Murty, M.: Genetic K-means algorithm. IEEE Transactions on Systems, Man and Cybernetics-Part B: Cybernetics 29, 433–439 (1999)
6. Lu, Y., Lu, S., Fotouhi, F., Deng, Y., Brown, S.: FGKA: A Fast Genetic K-means Algorithm, March 2004 (2004)
7. Lu, Y., Lu, S., Fotouhi, F., Deng, Y., Brown, S.: Fast genetic K-means algorithm and its application in gene expression data analysis. Wayne State University, Detroit (2003)
8. Lu, Y., Lu, S., Fotouhi, F., Deng, Y., Brown, S.: Incremental genetic K-means algorithm and its application in gene expression data analysis. BMC Bioinformatics 5, 172 (2004)
9. Kennedy, J., Eberhart, R.: Particle Swarm Optimization. In: Proc. IEEE int. Conf. On Neural Network, pp. 1942–1948 (1995)
10. van der Merwe, D.W., Engelbrecht, A.P.: Data Clustering using Particle Swarm Optimization[J/OL]. In: Proc. 2003 Congress on Evolutionary Computation, Piscataway, NJ, pp. 215–220 (2003)
11. Sun, J., Feng, B., Xu, W.-B.: Particle Swarm Optimization with Particles Having Quantum Behavior. In: Proc. 2004 Congress on Evolutionary Computation, Piscataway, NJ, pp. 325–331 (2004)
12. Sun, J., Xu, W.-B., Feng, B.: A Global Search Strategy of Quantum-behaved Particle Swarm Optimization. In: Proc. 2004 IEEE Conference on Cybernetics and Intelligent Systems, Singapore, pp. 111–116 (2004)
13. Sun, J., Xu, W.-B., Feng, B.: Adaptive Parameter Control for Quantum-behaved Particle Swarm Optimization on Individual Level. In: Proc. 2005 IEEE International Conference on Systems, Man and Cybernetics, Piscataway, NJ, pp. 3049–3054 (2005)
14. Wen, X.L., Fuhrman, S., Michaels, G.S., et al.: Large-scale temporal gene expression mapping of central nervous system development. Proc Natl. Acad. Sci. USA 95(1), 334–339 (1998)

15. Ideker, T., Thorsson, V., Ranish, J.A., et al.: Integrated genomic and proteomic analyses of a systemically perturbed metabolic network. Science 292(5518), 929–943 (2001)
16. Yeung, K.Y., Medvedovic, M., Bumgarner, R.E.: Clustering gene expression data with repeated measurements. Genome Biology 4(5), R34 (2003)
17. Cho, R.J., Campbell, M.J., Winzeler, E.A., et al.: A genome-wide transcriptional analysis of the mitotic cell cycle. Molecular Cell 2(1), 65–73 (1998)
18. Yeung, K.Y., Haynor, D.R., Ruzzo, W.: Validating clustering for gene expression data. Bioinformatics 17(4), 309–318 (2001)
19. Hubert, L., Arabie, P.: Comparing partitions. J. Classification, 193–218 (1985)

Ant Colony Optimization for the Single Machine Total Earliness Tardiness Scheduling Problem

Rym M'Hallah[1] and Ali Alhajraf[2]

[1] Department of Statistics and Operations Research, Kuwait University, P.O. Box 5969, Safat 13060, Kuwait
mhallah@kuc01.kuniv.edu.kw
[2] af_alhajraf@kuc01.kuniv.edu.kw

Abstract. This paper proposes an ant colony optimization hybrid heuristic (ACH) for the total earliness tardiness single machine scheduling problem where jobs have different processing times and distinct due dates, and the machine can not be idle. ACH is an ant colony system with daemon actions that intensify the search around good quality solutions. The computational results show the effectiveness of ACH.

Keywords: *ant colonies, earliness, tardiness, scheduling, heuristics.*

1   Introduction

The globalization of the world's economy along with the internet's development have induced many changes in today's industries. These changes have shifted the industry from mass to just-in-time production. Subsequently, competitors are now forced to satisfy their customers' demands as close as possible to their due-dates. Missing a demand's due-date may result in the loss of the customer or in penalties whereas satisfying a client's demand earlier than its due-date may cause unwanted inventory or product deterioration. Thus, companies need to minimize the total earliness tardiness (TET) of scheduled jobs.

The NP hard single machine TET scheduling problem, $1|d_j| \sum E_j + T_j$, consists in searching for an optimal sequence of a set $N = \{1, \ldots, n\}$ of independent jobs to be scheduled on a single machine. Each job is characterized by its processing time p_j and due date d_j. All jobs are ready for processing at time zero and job preemption is not allowed. Furthermore, no idle time is allowed on the machine whose capacity is limited compared to demand. For a particular permutation of N, the completion time C_j of job $j, j \in N$, is the sum of the processing times of the subset of jobs that precede j including j. Job j is early if $C_j \leq d_j$ with earliness $E_j = max\{0, d_j - C_j\}$, but is tardy if $C_j > d_j$ with tardiness $T_j = max\{0, C_j - d_j\}$. To be on time, jobs with close due dates have to compete for the same time slot [3]. Thus, only small sized instances of the mixed integer linear model of the problem can be solved exactly [14].

The $1|d_j| \sum E_j + T_j$ problem has been tackled using exact and approximate algorithms. Exact methods are based on dynamic programming [1] and branch

N.T. Nguyen et al. (Eds.): IEA/AIE 2008, LNAI 5027, pp. 397–407, 2008.

and bound [12] whereas approximate ones are based on dispatching rules and metaheuristics. Ow and Morton [15] present a filtered beam search –with no backtracking– that uses a linear and an exponential priority rule to guide the search. Almeida and Centeno [3] combine tabu search, simulated annealing, and hill climbing to generate near optima. Ventura and Radhakrishnan [20] apply Lagrangean relaxation and subgradient optimization to their binary formulation. Valente and Alves [18] design a dispatching rule and a greedy algorithm based on a lookahead parameter. Valente and Alves [19] compare their filtered and recovering beam search to existing heuristics. Finally, M'Hallah [14] proposes a hybrid heuristic (HH) that combines local (dispatching rules, hill climbing and simulated annealing) and global (genetic algorithms) search.

This paper tackles the $1|d_j|\sum E_j + T_j$ using a heuristic inspired from ant colony optimization (ACO). ACO, which mimics the foraging behavior of real ants [2], converges to optimality under certain conditions [8]. It has been successfully applied to a large variety of combinatorial optimization problems [4] including single machine [6], flow shop [21], and job shop [10] scheduling. Its widespread application is due to its success in addressing the two competing goals of metaheuristics: exploration and exploitation. Exploration or evolution allows diversification of the solution space whereas exploitation or learning preserves the good parts of near optima and intensifies the search around them.

Section 2 explains the basic mechanisms of ant colony algorithms. Section 3 details the proposed heuristic. Section 4 tunes its parameters and evaluates its performance. Finally, section 5 is a summary.

2 Ant Colony Algorithms

ACO mimics the behavior of real ants, which are known for their complex social behavior and cooperative work despite their blindness [5]. Ants identify the shortest path between their nest and a food source without using any visual cue [7]. They exchange information regarding a food source by laying, on their path between their nest and a food source, an odorous chemical substance, pheromone. Different ants searching for food at a later time sense the pheromone left by earlier ants and tend to follow a trail with a strong pheromone concentration in hope that it leads them to a food source fast. They choose their path by a probabilistic decision biased by the amount of pheromone: the larger the amount of pheromone on the trail, the higher the probability that ants follow it. In the absence of a pheromone trail, ants move randomly. As time evolves, shorter paths between the nest and a food source have a high traffic density whereas pheromone evaporates along low-density paths. This behavior leads to a self-reinforcing process, which in turn leads to the identification of the shortest path between the nest and a food source [2].

The most frequently applied ACO algorithms are the ant system (AS) and the ant colony system (ACS). When applied to the traveling salesman problem [8], AS positions a set $\mathbf{A}$ of ants randomly on the network. An ant $h \in \mathbf{A}$ moves from a node i to a node j according to a probability p_{ij}^h, which depends on η_{ij}, the arc's attractiveness according to its contribution toward the objective function, and on π_{ij}, the learned desirability of moving from i to j :

$$p_{ij}^h = \begin{cases} \pi_{ij}^\alpha \eta_{ij}^\beta / (\sum_{j' \in N_i^h} \pi_{ij'}^\alpha \eta_{ij'}^\beta) & \text{if } j \in N_i^h \\ 0 & \text{otherwise,} \end{cases} \tag{1}$$

where N_i^h is the feasible set of destinations of h when located at node i, and α and β are two parameters that weigh the relative importance of π_{ij} and η_{ij}. Once all ants have completed their tours, the length of each tour is evaluated, and the pheromone amounts on the network are updated using evaporation and deposit. Evaporation reduces all pheromone amounts on the network by a constant evaporation rate $\varphi \in (0, 1]$:

$$\pi_{ij} = (1 - \varphi)\pi_{ij}. \tag{2}$$

Pheromone deposit increases the pheromone level of each traveled network arc (i, j) :

$$\pi_{ij} = \pi_{ij} + \sum_{h \in \mathbf{A}} \Delta\pi_{ij}^h. \tag{3}$$

That is, every time an ant $h \in \mathbf{A}$ travels (i, j), π_{ij} increases by $\Delta\pi_{ij}^h$, which is a function of z_h, the solution value of h. Subsequently, AS repositions the ants randomly in the system where ant $h \in \mathbf{A}$ moves from i to j according to the updated p_{ij}^h. The process is repeated until the stopping criterion is met.

AS does not use any centralized daemon actions; i.e., actions not performed by the ants but by an external agent [7]. For real ants, daemon actions can be the wind moving a food source closer or further, floods forbidding some paths, etc. [7]. In artificial systems, daemon actions can be simple such as depositing additional pheromone along the path followed by the incumbent, or more elaborate such as local search procedures to improve the population's fitness, to prohibit some paths, or to reinforce a set of complex constraints [6,7,17].

ACS is a more sophisticated version of AS combining exploration and exploitation [5,16] . Ant $h \in \mathbf{A}$ moves from i to j according to p_{ij}^h, which reflects a trade-off between the exploration of new connections and the exploitation of available information [7]. ACS generates a random number q and compares it to q_0, an ACS parameter. If $q \leq q_0$, then ACS chooses j such that

$$\pi_{ij}^\alpha \eta_{ij}^\beta = \max_{j' \in N_i^h} \{\pi_{ij'}^\alpha \eta_{ij'}^\beta\} \tag{4}$$

i.e., ACS exploits the available knowledge, choosing the best option with respect to the weighted heuristic and pheromone information. Otherwise, ACS applies a controlled exploration as in AS; i.e., it computes p_{ij}^h using (1). Once all ants have completed their tours, ACS updates the pheromone levels using (2) and (3). In addition, to diversify the solution space and avoid premature convergence, ACS applies an online step-by-step pheromone trail update (including both pheromone evaporation and deposit) [7]. Each time ant h moves from i to j, ACS decreases the pheromone amount on the arc (i, j) making it less attractive to the following ants:

$$\pi_{ij} = (1 - \varphi)\pi_{ij} + \varphi\pi_0,$$

where π_0 is a lower bound on the pheromone amount along (i, j). Finally, to exploit the available information, ACS applies a daemon action which updates the pheromone level along the path traveled by the ant corresponding to the current incumbent solution.

Different variations of AS and ACS have been applied to scheduling problems. Liao and Juan [11] introduce a new initial pheromone trail parameter to ACO and apply it to the single machine weighted tardiness scheduling problem with sequence-dependent setup times. Tasgetiren et al. [17] test a swarm optimization algorithm, that uses a smallest position value and variable neighborhood search (VNS) as daemon actions, on the permutation flow shop problem with the objective of minimizing both the makespan and the total flow time. Gutjahra and Rauner [9] apply ACO to a dynamic regional nurse scheduling problem where the daily assignment of pool nurses to public hospitals takes into account many soft and hard constraints (eg., shift dates and times, working patterns, nurses qualifications, nurses and hospitals preferences, and costs). Ross and Dini [16] propose an ACS for a flexible manufacturing system in a job-shop environment with routing flexibility, sequence-dependent setup and transportation time. Lo et al. [13] present a modified AS for the precedence and resource-constrained multiprocessor scheduling problems where AS solves the scheduling problems while a dynamic heuristic assigns jobs to processors, and satisfies the time-dependency structure. Herein, an ant colony heuristic (ACH) is proposed for the $1|d_j| \sum E_j + T_j$.

3   The Proposed Heuristic

ACH assimilates the move of an ant from i to j to assigning job j to position i. An ant stops when it schedules all n jobs. Initially, the system constructs $\mathbf{A}$ by choosing $m = |\mathbf{A}|$ random sequences of the n jobs, and assigning each of them to an ant. It evaluates z_h, the TET of ant h, $h \in \mathbf{A}$, and identifies the best current solution h^* whose value $\overline{z} = \min_{h=1,m} \{z_h\}$.

ACH quantifies its acquired knowledge about the problem by setting π_{ij} equal to the proportion of times job j appears in position i in the best $m/5$ ants of the current generation. It then builds m new artificial ants. It sets ant h, $h \in \mathbf{A}$, equal to the empty sequence, and $N_1^h = N$, where N_i^h is the set of candidate jobs for position i for ant h, which has the ordered set of jobs $\overline{N}_{i-1}^h$ assigned in positions $1, \ldots, i - 1$. That is, $N_i^h \bigcup \overline{N}_{i-1}^h = N$.

For ant h, the assignment of job j to position i depends on the acquired knowledge π_{ij} and the assignment's attractiveness

$$\eta_{ij} = 1 - (E_j + T_j)/ \max_{j' \in N_i^h} \{E_{j'} + T_{j'}\}. \tag{5}$$

ACH draws a random number q from the continuous Uniform$[0,1]$, and compares it to q_0, a threshold level for intensification. If $q \leq q_0$, ACH chooses j according to (4); otherwise, it opts for the best local option choosing the job j with the largest opportunity; that is, $\eta_{ij} = \max_{j' \in N_i^h} \{\eta_{ij'}\}$. It defines the set of jobs that remain to be positioned setting $\overline{N}_i^h = \overline{N}_{i-1}^h \setminus \{j\}$, and the set of positioned jobs as $N_{i+1}^h = N_i^h \bigcup\{j\}$. It continues this process till all jobs have been assigned.

Subsequently, ACH updates the learned desirability π_{ij} using pheromone evaporation and deposit. If job j is assigned to position i, then ACH sets

$$\pi_{ij} = (1 - \varphi)\pi_{ij} + \varphi(1 - (E_j + T_j)/z_h). \tag{6}$$

The amount of pheromone deposited is proportional to the impact of assigning j to i on z_h. The smaller $(E_j + T_j)$ relative to z_h, the higher is the amount of pheromone deposited.

Once the m ants are obtained, the populations of the current and the previous generations are merged, and the best m ants are retained for further investigation. Indeed, each of the best m ants is subject to an intensified search. Ant h, $h \in \mathbf{A}$, is subject to $(n - 1)$ two-opt swaps. If any of the $n - 1$ neighbors improves z_h, then it replaces h in the current generation. This intensification step, or daemon action, is needed to speed ACH's convergence.

Finally, ACH applies a global pheromone update. For every (i, j), it evaporates the pheromone using (2), and deposits Δ_{ij}, where Δ_{ij} is the proportion of times j has been assigned to i in the best $m/5$ ants of the current generation. Subsequently, ACH updates h^* and $\overline{z}$, and repeats these steps for a prefixed number of generations, n_g. A summary of ACH is given in Algorithm 1.

4   Computational Results

The objective of the computational experimentation is twofold: (i) to tune ACH's parameters and investigate their impact on ACH's performance, and (ii) to compare ACH's performance to a standard ACO algorithm (AS) and to the solutions obtained by Cplex. ACH and AS are coded using Fortran, under the Microsoft Developer Studio platform whereas Cplex is evoked from GAMS. All computation is undertaken on a Pentium IV 3.0 GHz and 512 MB of RAM.

To tune ACH's parameters, we set $n = 10, 20, 30$; $n_g = 10, 50, 100, 300$; $m = 100, 500, 1000, 2000, 5000, 10000$; $q_0 = .1, .3, .5, .7, .9$; $\rho = .1, .3, .5, .7, .9$; and $(\alpha, \beta) = (1, 1), (1, 2), (2, 1)$. For each possible combination of these parameters and level n, we generate ten instances as in [15]; that is, the processing times and due dates are random integers from the Uniform $[1, 12]$, and $[.65\overline{p}, 1.15\overline{p}]$, respectively, where $\overline{p} = \sum_{j \in N} p_j$. We run each instance ten times using ACH, and compute RT, the average run time (in seconds) over the ten replications, and the performance ratio $r = \overline{z}/z^*$, where $\overline{z}$ is ACH's average solution value over the ten replications, and z^* is the exact solution value obtained via Cplex.

Algorithm 1. Detailed algorithm of ACH

Initialization
1. For $h = 1, \ldots, m$
   (a) Set ant h to a random permutation of the n jobs.
   (b) Compute z_h, the total earliness tardiness of h.
2. Set $\overline{z} = \min_{h=1,m} \{z_h\}$, and h^* the ant whose $z_{h^*} = \overline{z}$.
3. Set $g = 1$.
4. Set π_{ij}, the learned desirability of assigning job j to position i, to the proportion of times job j appears in position i in the best $m/5$ ants of the current generation.

Iterative Step
1. For $h = 1, \ldots, m$
   (a) Set $N_1^h = N$, $\overline{N}_0^h = \emptyset$.
   (b) For $i = 1, \ldots, n$
       – Generate a random number q from the continuous Uniform[0,1].
       – If $q \leq q_0$, choose j according to (4); else, choose $j \ni \eta_{ij} = \max_{j' \in N_i^h} \{\eta_{ij'}\}$.

       – Set $\overline{N}_i^h = \overline{N}_{i-1}^h \setminus \{j\}$, and $N_{i+1}^h = N_i^h \bigcup \{j\}$.
   (c) Update π_{ij} using (6).
2. Choose the best m ants out of the m ants of the current generation and the m ants of the previous generation.
3. For $h = 1, \ldots, m$
   (a) Generate $(n-1)$ neighbors of ant h using two-opt swaps;
   (b) Choose the best out of the n solutions to replace h in the current generation.
4. Determine Δ_{ij}, the proportion of times j has been assigned to i in the best $m/5$ ants of the current generation.
5. Set $\pi_{ij} = (1 - \varphi)\pi_{ij} + \Delta_{ij}$.
6. Update h^* and $\overline{z}$.
7. Set $g = g + 1$.

Stopping condition
   If $g > n_g$, stop; otherwise, goto the **iterative step**.

Figures 1 and 2 show that increasing n_g and m improves r; thus improves ACH's opportunity to converge toward a global optimum; however, this occurs at the cost of a larger runtime. They further indicate that setting $n_g = 300$ and $m = 5000$ seems a reasonable tradeoff between solution quality and runtime. ACH is using a relatively large number of ants; however opting for $m = 10$ with $n_g = 300$ yields an average r equal to 1.065 versus 1.016 when $m = 5000$. This is most likely due to the competition of the jobs for the same time slots on the machine, and the resulting myopic decisions of the ants.

Figure 3 shows that there is no clear rule of thumb to privileging either the accumulated knowledge or the local heuristic information for different population sizes. For example, $\alpha = \beta = 1$ is a better alternative when $4000 \leq m \leq 6000$, but is not the best strategy for lower or higher values of m. It is therefore recommended that preliminary testing be undertaken prior to setting α and β.

Figure 4 displays the effect of q_0 and φ on ACH's performance. Even though no clear rule of thumb applies, some general guidelines can be established. A high φ may cause too much pheromone evaporation along good paths and too much pheromone deposit along undesirable ones; thus, good quality knowledge may be lost while myopic decisions are strengthened. Indeed, for TET, a "good" position for a job strongly depends on the jobs assigned to the preceding positions. On the

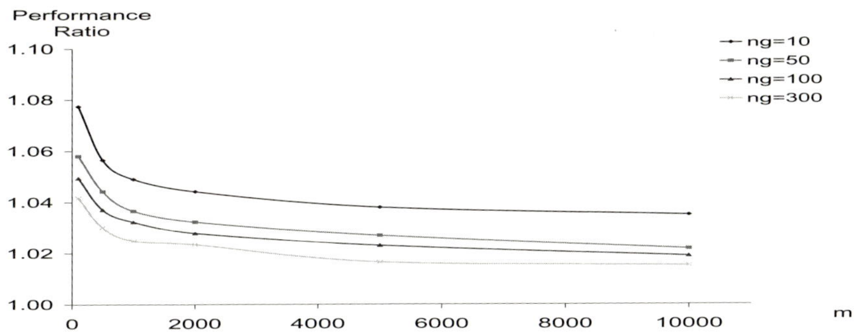

Fig. 1. ACH's solution quality as n_g and m vary $(n = 20, \alpha = \beta = 1, \varphi = 0.9, q_0 = .1)$

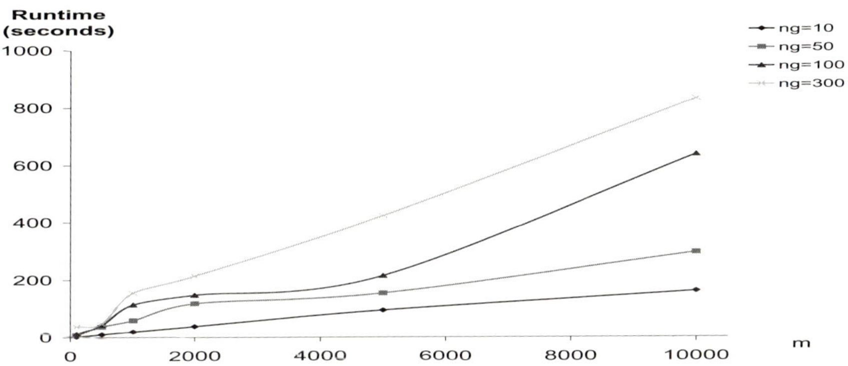

Fig. 2. ACH's Runtime as n_g and m vary $(n = 20, \alpha = \beta = 1, \phi = 0.9, q_0 = .1)$

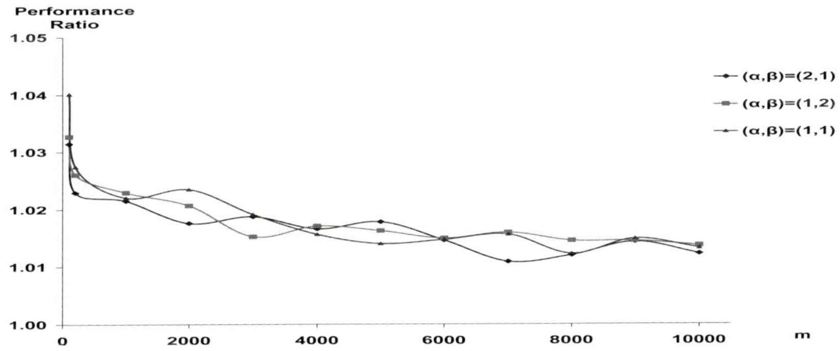

Fig. 3. ACH's Performance as (α, β) varies $(n = 20, n_g = 300, q_0 = 0.9, \varphi = 0.9)$

other hand, a low φ limits the acquisition of new knowledge and relies heavily on available information; thus, may cause premature convergence and stagnation

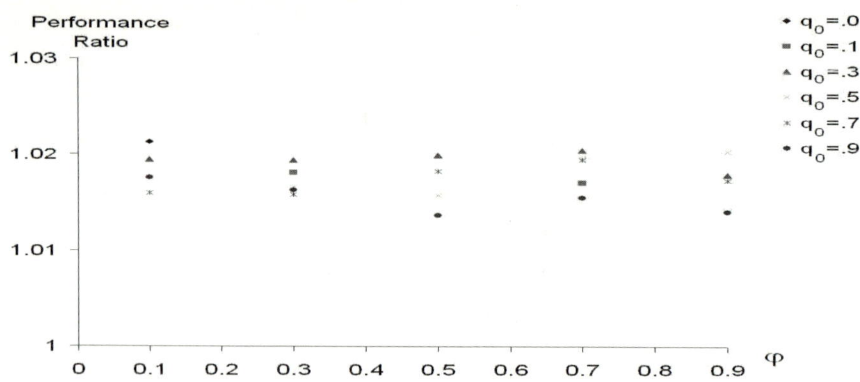

Fig. 4. ACH's Performance as q_0 and φ vary ($n = 20, \alpha = \beta = 1, n_g = 300, m = 5000$)

of the algorithm. $\varphi = 0.5$ seems to offer a good balance between pheromone evaporation and deposit; i.e., between maintaining prior knowledge and using newly acquired information (obtained via heuristic information).

A high q_0 enhances the use of available knowledge, and limits relying on local search. It guides ACH toward the best decision according to a weighted version of the accumulated (pheromone) and acquired (heuristic) knowledge. On the other hand, a very low q_0 encourages a guided exploration of the search space where the search is biased towards more promising areas (guided by prior knowledge). Despite few exceptions, setting $q_0 = 0.9$, and $\varphi = .5$ seems to yields good results.

ACH's runtime, whose evolution as a function of n is illustrated in Figure 5, can be approximated by $RT = .2127n^{2.2314}$ when $m = 5000$ and $n_g = 300$. Initially, ACH creates, evaluates, and sorts m ants. In addition, in each of the n_g generations, ACH undertakes the following steps. It creates another m ants, where each ant requires n comparisons. It then sorts $2m$ ants in $O(2mlog(2m))$. Finally, it applies a two-opt neighborhood search for each of the best m ants, where each search requires $(n - 1)nm$ operations. Subsequently, the number of operations undertaken by ACH is $O(2n_g(n^2 + m(n + log(2m))))$.

The performance ratios for $n = 10, 20$, and 30 are on average around 1.01 when $m = 5000, n_g = 300, \varphi = 0.5$, $q_0 = 0.9$, and $\alpha = \beta = 1$, with the average r equaling the median. The average r is 1.00 for $n = 10$, 1.01 for $n = 20$ and 1.02 for $n = 30$. This is expected since m and n_g are fixed; thus, the smaller the problem size, the higher the chances of ACH to find the global optimum.

ACH's convergence rate may be improved as follows. The initial sequences being randomly generated in Step 1(a) of the initialization step of ACH may be substituted by their best neighbors obtained via simulated annealing or tabu search. In addition, in Step 3(a) of the iterative step, the $n - 1$ neighbors can be obtained by applying a simulated annealing $n - 1$ times to the current ant h.

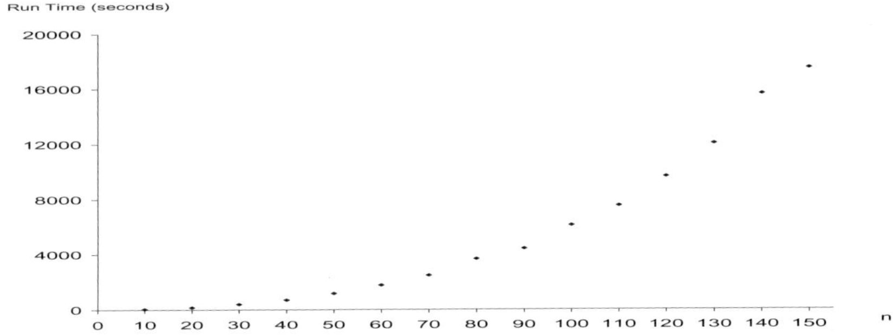

Fig. 5. ACH's Run Time as n increases ($\alpha = \beta = 1, n_g = 300, m = 5000, q_0 = .9, \varphi = .1$)

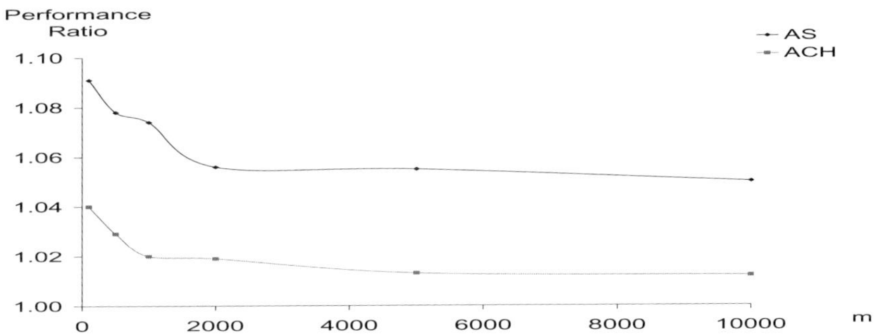

Fig. 6. Comparison of ACH and AS's performance as m increases ($\alpha = \beta = 1, n_g = 300, q_0 = .9, \varphi = .1, n = 20$)

These modifications will intensify the search around promising areas and improve the quality of the knowledge being propagated through ACH's generations.

The comparison of ACH to AS shows that hybridization improved ACH's performance. The average improvement is 4.5% and reaches 5.4% when $m = 1000$; yet, this improvement is independent of the problem size. Figure 6 further shows that ACH yields consistently better results than AS.

5   Conclusion

This paper proposes an ant colony optimization hybrid heuristic for the minimum total earliness tardiness single machine scheduling problem with distinct deterministic due dates. The heuristic is a modified ant colony system with daemon actions that intensify the search in promising areas. The computational results illustrate the heuristic's good performance. The heuristic can be further enhanced if implemented as a parallel algorithm.

References

1. Abdul-Razaq, T.S., Potts, C.N.: Dynamic programming state-space relaxation for single machine scheduling. Journal of the Operational Research Society 39, 141–152 (1988)
2. Albritton, M.D., McMullen, P.R.: Optimal product design using a colony of virtual ants. European Journal of Operational Research 176, 498–520 (2007)
3. Almeida, M.T., Centeno, M.: A composite heuristic for the single machine early tardy job scheduling problem. Computers & Operations Research 25, 535–625 (1998)
4. Bullnheimer, B., Hartl, R.F., Strauss, C.: An improved ant system algorithm for the vehicle routing problem. Annals of Operations Research 89, 319–328 (1999)
5. Dorigo, M., Stützle, T.: Ant Colony Optimization. MIT Press, Cambridge (2004)
6. Gagné, C., Price, W.L., Gravel, M.: Comparing an ACO algorithm with other heuristics for the single machine scheduling problem with sequence-dependent setup times. Journal of the Operational Research Society 53, 895–906 (2002)
7. García-Martínez, C., Cordón, O., Herrera, F.: A taxonomy and an empirical analysis of multiple objective ant colony optimization algorithms for the bi-criteria TSP. European Journal of Operational Research 180, 116–148 (2007)
8. Gutjahr, W.J.: A graph-based ant system and its convergence. Future Generation Computer Systems 16, 873–888 (2000)
9. Gutjahr, W.J., Rauner, M.S.: An ACO algorithm for a dynamic regional nurse-scheduling problem in Austria. Computers & Operations Research 34, 642–666 (2007)
10. Heinonen, J., Pettersson, F.: Hybrid ant colony optimization and visibility studies applied to a job-shop scheduling problem. Applied Mathematics and Computation 187(2), 989–998 (2007)
11. Liao, C.J., Juan, H.C.: An ant colony optimization for single-machine tardiness scheduling with sequence-dependent setups. Computers & Operations Research 34, 1899–1909 (2007)
12. Liaw, C.F.: A branch and bound algorithm for the single machine earliness and tardiness scheduling problem. Computers & Operations Research 26, 679–693 (1999)
13. Lo, S.T., Chen, R.M., Huang, Y.M., Wu, C.L.: Multiprocessor system scheduling with precedence and resource constraints using an enhanced ant colony system. Expert Systems with Applications 34(3), 2071–2081 (2008)
14. M'Hallah, R.: Minimizing Total Earliness and Tardiness on a Single Machine Using a Hybrid Heuristic. Computers & Operations Research 34(10), 3126–3142 (2007)
15. Ow, P.S., Morton, E.T.: The single machine early/tardy problem. Management Science 35, 177–191 (1989)
16. Rossi, A., Dini, G.: Flexible job-shop scheduling with routing flexibility and separable setup times using ant colony optimisation method. Robotics and Computer-Integrated Manufacturing 23, 503–516 (2007)
17. Tasgetiren, M.F., Liang, Y., Sevkli, M., Gencyilmaz, G.: A particle swarm optimization algorithm for makespan and total flowtime minimization in the permutation flowshop sequencing problem. European Journal of Operational Research 177, 1930–1947 (2007)
18. Valente, J.M.S., Alves, R.A.F.S.: Filtered and Recovering beam search algorithms for the early/tardy scheduling problem with no idle time. Computers & Industrial Engineering 48(2), 363–375 (2005)

19. Valente, J.M.S., Alves, R.A.F.S.: Improved heuristics for the early/tardy scheduling problem with no idle time. Computers & Operations Research 32(3), 557–569 (2005)
20. Ventura, J.A., Radhakrishnan, S.: Single machine scheduling with symetric earliness and tardiness penalties. European Journal of Operational Research 144, 598–612 (2003)
21. Ying, G.C., Liao, C.J.: Ant colony system for permutation flow-shop sequencing. Computers & Operations Research 31, 791–801 (2004)

Tuning Constrained Objects

Ricardo Soto[1,2] and Laurent Granvilliers[1]

[1] LINA, CNRS, Université de Nantes, France
[2] Escuela de Ingeniería Informática
Pontificia Universidad Católica de Valparaíso, Chile
{ricardo.soto,laurent.granvilliers}@univ-nantes.fr

Abstract. Constrained objects provide a suitable object-oriented style for modeling systems under constraints. A set of classes is defined to represent a problem, whose state is then controlled by a constraint satisfaction engine. This engine is commonly a black-box based on a predefined and non-customizable search strategy. This system rigidity, of course, does not allow users to tune models in order to improve the search process. In this paper we target this issue by presenting an extensible formalism to define a wide range of search options so as to customize, improve and/or analyze the search process of constrained object models.

Keywords: Constraint Programming, Heuristic Search.

1 Introduction

The constrained object modeling paradigm [12,3] offers a suitable way to describe CSPs (Constraint Satisfaction Problems) whose structure is inherently compositional. An object-oriented style is provided to capture the structure of the problem in a natural manner. A class represent an element of the composition and the whole set of classes represents the entire CSP (see Section 2).

Classes encapsulate the variables and constraints of the problem. Variables can include a range of possible values called domain; and constraints are posted to restrict the combination of values that variables can adopt. Usual data structures and control abstractions can also be included to enrich the model. Finally, the search process is performed by a black-box engine with embedded constraint satisfaction algorithms.

The searching phase as much as the modeling activities is an important part of the problem resolution. An appropriate selection of the value or variable ordering may be determinant to perform an efficient searching process. A correct consistency level used may impact too, the search space can be pruned in order to reduce the search time [13].

A formalism to define these search options has not been studied yet (for constrained objects). There is no mechanism for selecting the value or variable ordering; and no means exist for defining the consistency level used by constraints.

In this paper we present a simple formalism to define these search options. Value and variable ordering as well as consistency levels can be chosen by a

N.T. Nguyen et al. (Eds.): IEA/AIE 2008, LNAI 5027, pp. 408–414, 2008.

simple parameter. This capability will make users able to tune, customize and/or improve the resolution process of constrained object models.

This work has been designed as part of the s-COMMA [2] system, a solver-independent architecture for modeling CSP. Here, one s-COMMA model can be mapped to four different solvers: Gecode/J [1], ECLiPSe [7], RealPaver [6] and GNU Prolog [4]. Let us mention that an important capability of this architecture (also present in others state-of-the-art modeling languages [9,8,5]) is to allow users to test one model with different solvers, the aim is to know which solver is the best for the model. The addition of search functionalities clearly improve this capability. Many possibilities of experimentation arise, the user will be able to test different combinations of search options in different solvers. As a result, a wider vision of the solvers' behavior can be obtained.

This paper is organized as follows: Section 2 gives an overview of s-COMMA models. Section 3 shows how models can be tuned defining the value or variable ordering. Section 4 explains the means for selecting the different consistency levels. Extensibility mechanisms are introduced in Section 5, followed by conclusions and future work.

2   s-COMMA Overview

Let us give an overview of an s-COMMA model by means of a CSP from the engineering field. Consider the task of configuring an industrial mixer [11]. Figure 1 shows the composition of the system. The mixer is composed of a vessel and an agitator. A cooler and a condensor are the components of the vessel. At the end, the agitator includes an engine, an impeller and a shaft.

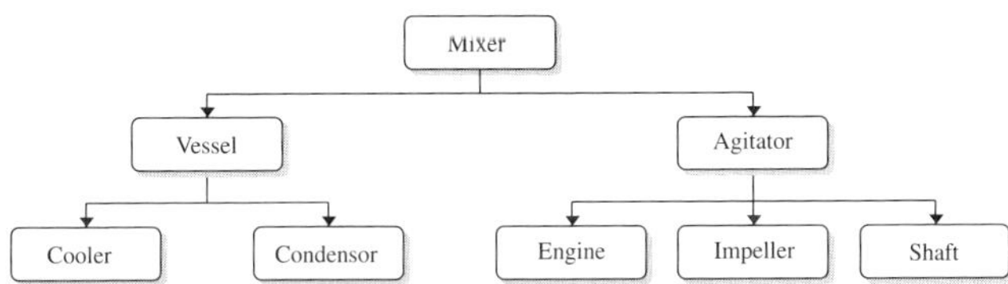

Fig. 1. The Mixer Problem

An s-COMMA model for the mixer problem is as follows. Each part of the composition is represented by a class. For instance, the class shown below at line 1 represents the Mixer.

```
1. class Mixer {
2.    Agitator  a;
3.    Vessel    v;
4.    constraint design {
5.       a.i.rps      <= v.diameter/a.i.diameter;
6.       a.i.diameter <= a.i.ratio*v.diameter;
7.    }
8. }
```

```
9.  class Agitator {
10.    Engine   e;
11.    Impeller i;
12.    Shaft    s;
13.    constraint power {
14.       e.power >= 2*i.power;
15.    }
16. }
```

The `Mixer` class is composed by two attributes, `a` is an instance of the class `Agitator` and `v` is an instance of the class `Vessel`. A constraint zone called `design` is defined to post two constraints. As in common object-oriented languages we use a dot notation to refer to attributes[1] of objects, e.g. `v.diameter` refer to the attribute `diameter` of the `Vessel` object called v; `a.i.rps` refer to the attribute `rps` of the `Impeller` object i which is an attribute of the `Agitator` object called a. The class `Agitator` has a similar definition, three objects are declared, the e object represents the engine of the system, i describes the impeller and s represents the shaft. Finally, a constraint zone called `power` is stated to post a constraint between the `power` attributes of the engine and the impeller.

Below, the class `Impeller` and the class `Engine` are described, both are simple classes without objects, just `real` decision variables are included. Remaining classes can be defined in the same way[2].

```
17. class Impeller {              23.   class Engine {
18.    real  power;               24.      real   power;
19.    real  diameter;            25.   }
20.    real  rps;
21.    real  ratio;
22. }
```

3   Value and Variable Ordering

The exploration of the space of values that variables can adopt is performed by backtracking procedures [13]. These algorithms try to assign values to the variables until the right value is found i.e., a value that satisfy the constraints. Several experiments [13,14] have demonstrated that the ordering in which variables are selected for this variable-value assignment can notably improve the performance of the search process. Many heuristic to define this ordering have been investigated, the most solver-supported of them are the following:

- min-dom-size: Selects the variable with the smallest domain size.
- max-dom-size: Selects the variable with the largest domain size.
- min-val: Selects the variable with the smallest value in its domain.
- max-val: Selects the variable with the greatest value in its domain.
- min-regret-min-dif: Selects the variable that has the smallest difference between the smallest value and the second-smallest value of its domain.
- min-regret-max-dif: Selects the variable that has the greatest difference between the smallest value and the second-smallest value of its domain.
- max-regret-min-dif: Selects the variable that has the smallest difference between the largest value and the second-largest value of its domain.
- max-regret-max-dif: Selects the variable that has the greatest difference between the largest value and the second-largest value of its domain.

---

[1] Attributes may be objects or decision variables.
[2] Let us notice that a detailed explanation of s-COMMA models can be found in the user's manual available at [2].

Once the variable ordering is selected, a variable may have many potential values for an assignment. The order in which these values are tried can have a considerable impact too. For example, if the right value is chosen on the first try for each variable, a solution can be found without performing backtracks [13]. The most solver-supported heuristic for this ordering are the following:

- min-val: Selects the smallest value.
- med-val: Selects the median value.
- max-val: Selects the maximal value.

Let us now come back to the Mixer problem. To define these search options we have four possibilities: (1) To select the variable ordering, (2) to select the value ordering, (3) to select both or (4) do not select any option, in this case the search will be performed using the default search provided by the solver. The four cases are shown below.

```
// variable ordering selected          // value ordering selected
class Mixer [min-dom-size] {           class Mixer [min-val] {
  ...                                    ...

// both selections                     // no selection
class Mixer [min-dom-size,min-val] {   class Mixer {
  ...                                    ...
```

Due to the searching process is performed for the entire problem, we cannot select different search options for each class. So, if more than one class includes a search option, just the option of the main class[3] will be taken.

4 Consistency Level

The use of an appropriate consistency technique can also improve the exploration process. Backtracking procedures can be complemented with consistency algorithms so as to detect failures earlier; and as consequence to avoid the inspection of useless spaces. This task is in general performed by variants of an arc-consistency algorithm [13,14] embedded in the search engine of the solver. We provide two consistency levels, the bound and the domain consistency:

- bound: An arc-consistency algorithm is used to reduce the domain of involved variables, but just the bounds of the variables' domain are updated.
- domain: An arc-consistency algorithm is used to reduce the domain of involved variables. The full domain of variables is updated.

These options can be defined using a simple parameter, we provide three cases: (1) To select the consistency level for a class, (2) to select the consistency level for an object; and (3) to select the consistency level for a constraint. Let us note that cases 1 and 2 lead to a "cascade effect" i.e., the selected option will be inherited by objects and constraints belonging to the composition. Only

---

[3] The main class is the first class defined in the model, this default option can be changed adding the reserved word **main** to the head of the class.

objects and constraints with their own option do not inherit, they keep their own selected option.

Let us look at the next example. The class `Mixer` has a `domain` consistency level. The "cascade effect" will set the objects and constraints of the mixer's composition (Vessel, Agitator, Cooler, Condenser, etc.) with the `domain` option, except for the `Engine` object `e` and the constraint `e.power >= 2*i.power` which keep their own option (`bound` consistency). Using this effect we profit of the object-oriented style to avoid defining the search option for constraints one by one.

```
// tuned class                          // tuned object & tuned constraint
class Mixer [domain] {                  class Agitator {
  Agitator  a;                            [bound] Engine e;
  Vessel    v;                            Impeller i;
  constraint design {                     Shaft    s;
    a.i.rps <= v.diameter/a.i.diameter;   constraint power {
    a.i.diameter <= a.i.ratio*v.diameter;   [bound] e.power >= 2*i.power;
    ...                                     ...
```

Let us note that the combination of consistency level with value and variable ordering is allowed.

```
class Mixer [min-dom-size,min-val,domain] {
  ...
```

5   Extensibility

Extensibility is an important requirement of solver-independent languages. The idea is to make the architecture adaptable to further up-grades of the solver. Let us consider that three new search options are introduced in the Gecode/J solver. A variable ordering called BVAR_NONE, which selects the leftmost variable (no heuristic). A value ordering called BVAL_SPLIT_MIN, which selects the first value of the lower half of the domain; and the ICL_VAL consistency level, which performs the Gecode value consistency (a naive consistency [1]).

One of the possible ways to use these new search options from s-COMMA is to update its grammar and to recompile it by hand. In addition we need to redefine the Gecode/J translator, the translation of the new options from the modeling language to the solver language must be included. In order to avoid this hard task we introduce an extension mechanism to add new search options. The list of search options initially provided by s-COMMA can be extended by defining an extension file.

An extension file is composed by one or more main blocks (see Figure 2). A main block defines the solver where the new functionalities will be defined (extensions for more than one solver can be defined in the same file). Inside a main block we define the blocks for the search options: a `Variable-Ordering` block, a `Value-Ordering` block, and a `Consistency-Level` block. In each block we define the rules of the translation. The grammar of the rule is as follows:
⟨s-COMMA-option⟩ -> ⟨solver-option⟩ ;.

```
// extension file                  // using the new options
GecodeJ {                          class Mixer [first,lower-half] {
  Variable-Ordering {                [value] Agitator  a;
    first -> BVAR_NONE;              Vessel    v;
  }                                  constraint design {
  Value-Ordering {                     [value] a.i.rps <= v.diameter/a.i.diameter;
    lower-half -> BVAL_SPLIT_MIN;       [value] a.i.diameter <= a.i.ratio*v.diameter;
  }                                  }
  Consistency-Level {              }
    value -> ICL_VAL;
  }
}
```

Fig. 2. Extension for Gecode/J and the class `Mixer` using the new options

On the translation process the $\langle s\text{-}COMMA\text{-}option\rangle$ will be translated to the $\langle solver\text{-}option\rangle$. Figure 2 shows the use of these new options. The variable ordering `BVAR_NONE` can be chosen using the parameter `first`. The value ordering `BVAL_SPLIT_MIN` can be selected using `lower-half`; and the `ICL_VAL` consistency level is used by means of `value`.

6   Conclusion and Future Work

A simple formalism to tune constrained object models has been presented. Different alternatives for improving the search process can be defined by a simple parameter. Many combinations of value and variable ordering with consistency levels can be chosen. The latter can be defined over different elements of the model: class consistency level, object consistency level and constraint consistency level. In this stage, a "cascade effect" is provided to avoid rework.

The extension mechanism introduced is an important feature of the system. New search options can be introduced by means of an extension file. This capability make the s-COMMA architecture adaptable to further up-grades of the solvers.

The formalism introduced here is ongoing work, and we believe there is a considerable scope for future work, such as the addition of search-tree exploration options (as in OPL [15]). The investigation of parameters to tune numeric CSPs such as the box and hull consistency [10] will be useful too.

References

1. Gecode System, http://www.gecode.org
2. s-COMMA System, http://www.inf.ucv.cl/~rsoto/s-comma
3. Borning, A.H.: The Programming Languages Aspects of ThingLab, a Constraint-Oriented Simulation Laboratory. ACM TOPLAS 3(4), 353–387 (1981)
4. Diaz, D., Codognet, P.: The gnu prolog system and its implementation. In: SAC (2), pp. 728–732 (2000)
5. Frisch, A.M., et al.: The design of essence: A constraint language for specifying combinatorial problems. In: IJCAI, pp. 80–87 (2007)

6. Granvilliers, L., et al.: Algorithm 852: Realpaver: an interval solver using constraint satisfaction techniques. ACM Trans. Math. Softw. 32(1), 138–156 (2006)
7. Wallace, M., et al.: Eclipse: A platform for constraint logic programming (1997)
8. Nethercote, N., et al.: Minizinc: Towards a standard cp modelling language. In: Bessière, C. (ed.) CP 2007. LNCS, vol. 4741, Springer, Heidelberg (2007)
9. Rafeh, R., et al.: From zinc to design model. In: PADL, pp. 215–229 (2007)
10. Rossi, F.: Handbook of Constraint Programming. Elsevier, Amsterdam (2006)
11. Gelle, E., Faltings, B.: Solving mixed and conditional constraint satisfaction problems. Constraints 8(2), 107–141 (2003)
12. Jayaraman, B., Tambay, P.Y.: Constrained Objects for Modeling Complex Structures. In: OOPSLA, Minneapolis, USA (2000)
13. Apt, K.R.: Principles of Constraint Programming. Cambridge Press (2003)
14. Dechter, R.: Constraint Processing. Elsevier, Amsterdam (2003)
15. Van Hentenryck, P.: The OPL Language. The MIT Press, Cambridge (1999)

Ontology-Driven Approximate Duplicate Elimination of Postal Addresses

Matteo Cristani and Alessio Gugole

University of Verona,
37134 Verona
`matteo.cristani@univr.it`

Abstract. In several common real-life cases of usage of postal address databases an important problem that is often necessary to solve is the one of duplicate elimination. This may occur because a database of addresses is merged to another one, for instance during a joint-venture or a fusion between two companies, so that two or more than two addresses are the same.

Though a trivial approach based upon identification can be used in principle, this attempt would indeed fail in any concrete case, in particular for postal addresses, because the same address can be written in several different ways so that an approximate approach can be adopted successfully, under the condition that the duplicate elimination is correctly performed. We identify an ontology-driven approach for postal addresses which solves the problem in an approximate fashion. The algorithm is based upon a modification of the Levenshtein distance, obtained by introducing the notion of admissible abbreviation, and has a threefold outcome: eliminate duplicates, do not eliminate duplicates, undecided.

1   Introduction

The string matching problem (SMP) is an important type of string problems which has historically been very relevant to the development of Computer Science investigations in the past thirty years. We define SMP as follows.

Consider an alphabet Σ, and two strings x and y on Σ, $x, y \in \Sigma^*$. We name *string matching* the problem of computing the first position of y where a substring x' of y occurs[1] such that $x = x'$.

A generalisation of SMP is the Approximate String Matching Problem (ASMP). To define this problem we need to introduce two specific notions, the notion of *error* and the notion of *measure of an error*. An error is a transformation τ of a string x into a string x'. The inverse transformation is the inverse error. A measure of errors is a function from errors to non negative numbers that satisfies the axioms of Euclidean distance, namely:

---

[1] A string x occurs at a position n within a string y when x is a substring of y starting at the n-th character of y.

N.T. Nguyen et al. (Eds.): IEA/AIE 2008, LNAI 5027, pp. 415–424, 2008.
© Springer-Verlag Berlin Heidelberg 2008

- The measure of an error (x, y) is zero *iff* $x = y$;
- The measure of an error (x, y) is identical to the measure of an error (y, x);
- If the measure of an error (x, y) is m_1 and the measure of an error (y, z) is m_2, then the measure of the error (x, z) is m, such that $m \leq m_1 + m_2$.

Formally, an *approximate string matching framework* (ASMF) is a triple $\langle \Sigma, \delta, t \rangle$, where Σ is an alphabet, δ is a measure of errors defined among strings in Σ^* and t is a positive integer called the error threshold. Given an ASMF $F = \langle \Sigma, \delta, t \rangle$, two strings x and y, we define Approximate String Matching Problem as the problem of finding the position of the first substring x' of y such that the measure of the error (x, x') is less than or equal to t.

Clearly, independently of the distance used to measure errors, if a framework has a threshold $t = 0$ (degenerated ASMF), only SMP without approximations can be defined. Moreover, once fixed a threshold t we can only reveal errors between strings of length greater than or equal to t.

In a not degenerated ASMF, the method used to measure errors, and the maximum value of the measure of errors (the threshold t) actually defines the framework itself. We can define the error measure in two parts: (a) the error typology and (b) the weights of the error types. In particular (a) is the classification of the types of errors that can be identified, and for each type, the method used to identify the error in a string pair, and (b) is a function that associates a non negative real number to each error type that is used to envelope the total measure of error in a string match. We usually assume that the interpretation of errors in a string match are governed by a *compositional semantics*, so that the total error is a linear combination of the number of errors and their weights. In this paper we only address problems in which the above assumption is true. Formally a typed ASMF is a 4-tuple $\langle \Sigma, \Delta, W, T \rangle$ where Σ is an alphabet, Δ is a (finite) set of n measures of errors, T is a set of cardinality $n + 1$ of thresholds, and W is a set of weights for the error measure. We name total error measure the weighted sum of the errors in a string match between x and y, and redefine the ASMP as the problem of finding the position of the first substring x' such that the error measures are all less than or equal of their corresponding threshold and so does the total error. We say that a semantics like the above defined one is purely compositional when the fact that all the local error thresholds are not overwhelmed implies that the total error threshold is not overwhelmed as well. In general non-purely compositional semantics are much more interesting than purely compositional ones.

The classical method to measure errors is the Hamming distance [5]. The Hamming distance is defined firstly between two strings of equal length as the number of positions for which the corresponding symbols are different. A simple extension to Hamming distance, that is applicable also to strings of different length is the Levenshtein distance [12] also known as the Edit Distance. This measure consists in counting (and possibly weighting) the events that bring from one string to the other one. The classical version of this measure employs four methods for editing: (a) insertion, (b) deletion, (c) substitution and (d) swap. A reduced version of Edit distance is the Longest Common Subsequence distance [3] defined as the number of insertions and deletions needed to transform one string into the other one. In particular, it can be proved that Levenshtein distance can be reduced to Longest Common Subsequence distance. This is simply obtained by transforming a substitution into a sequence of one insertion and one deletion or vice versa, and analogously for swap. Clearly, Longest Common Subsequence distance will be higher for those errors that include one substitution or one swap, but if we assign different weights to substitutions and swap operations in Edit Distance we can make the two distances equal.

Several extensions have been proposed in the current literature of Information Theory, like those used to analyse the case of trees [15] or the generalisation of the above technique to graphs [4].

Two major application areas have been considered in literature: molecular biology (see for instance, [6]) and OCR/OMR technologies [14].

In this paper we present an application of edit distance to a classical database problem: data duplicate elimination. The reason for which we need an error metric in this application is that we aim at deduplicating records that contain anagraphic data, and we shall perform an analysis in which the pivot of duplicate elimination (the field of the records that discriminates corresponding records) is a postal address.

Though weighted edit distance results interesting in general, in this specific case we can prove, by experimental evidence, that it does make any particular enhancement with respect to simple direct correspondence or Hamming distance. However, a modified version, that includes *admissible abbreviations*, based upon a taxonomy of terms that can be used for *types of places*[2], namely the names street, square, avenue, and so on that qualify a toponym. In this paper we shall refer to the class of admissible abbreviations for Italian Postal Addresses.

This in not a novel approach as based upon the employment of structured taxonomies, in particular terminological hierarchies. In data warehouse research a similar approach has been used for duplicate elimination [2]. Their results have been extended and specialised for the peculiar case of duplicate elimination in Postal Addresses, an application case that does not exist yet. The importance of this case lies on the fact that our method can be fruitfully applied also in the case in which the number of duplicates is quite low, due to the particular form of the problem. Moreover we enhanced the Ananthakrishna approach with preprocessing steps based on partial hierarchies. This novelty produces an important performance and accuracy enhancement which could not be forecasted a priori.

The rest of this paper is organised as follows. In Section 2 we introduce an extension to weighted Levenshtein distance to include reference of admissible abbreviations for Italian Postal Addresses, and focus upon the ways in which this approach can be generalised to addresses in other countries, and to other contexts than Postal Addresses. In particular, Section 2.1 introduces an error measure based upon admissible abbreviation that is called Ontology-driven Edit Distance, Section 2.2 describes the approach used for the specific case of postal

---

[2] The reference literature does not identify a specific commonly accepted name. We therefore prefer the generic name types of places, which is defined here explicitly.

addresses and describes the parameter fixing activities for that case. In Section 3 we present an experimental activity aimed at proving that the adopted strategy is fruitful. This activity consisted in employing a technology that *normalises* addresses, namely finds each address into a database of addresses written in a normal form, that is the one established as correct by Postal Authority, and comparing the results of this normalisation to the duplicate elimination based upon modified edit distance. The trial shows that in performance terms the normalisation-based approach is slower than our method, and very close in terms of accuracy, making our approach practically preferable to the normalisation-based one.

2   Extended Edit Distance: The Case of Postal Addresses

First of all, let us introduce the problem by making an example of what we mean with duplicate elimination in postal addresses, or to be precise, in anagraphic databases with postal address pivot.

In Table 1 we show one record that is not yet been normalised, i.e. reduced to a version corrected based upon an archive of correct pairs $\langle t, T \rangle$ with t type of place and T toponym and then its normalised version.

The duplicate elimination process requires that we are cleverly able to distinguish between a case like the one in Table 2 where the records are duplicate.

The case of Table 3 shows two records that are not duplicate.

The above examples show that we need to address two major issues:

- Admissible abbreviations, like A. which is admissible for Alessio in the example, and v. that is admissible for 'Via' (Street) as in example of Table 1.
- Different relevance of errors depending on the field in which they occur.

2.1   Admissible Abbreviations and Ontology-Driven Edit Distance

We have developed a specific terminology that is characteristic of the problem as posed (Italian Addresses) and partly officially released by National Postal

Table 1. The effects of normalisation. NF indicates that the address is in normal form.

Status	Name	Family name	Type of place	Toponym	Number	ZIP Code
	Alessio	Gugole	v.	G. Mazzini	81	37059
NF	Alessio	Gugole	via	Giuseppe Mazzini	81	37059

Table 2. Records that are duplicate

Name	Family name	Type of place	Toponym	Number	ZIP Code	City	County
Alessio	Gugole	via	Pio XII	81	37059	Zevio	VR
A.	Gugole	via	Pio XII	81	37059	null	VR

Table 3. Records that are not duplicate

Name	Family name	Type of place	Toponym	Number	ZIP Code	City	County
Alessio	Gugole	via	Pio XII	81	37059	Zevio	VR
A.	Gugole	via	Pio XII	null	37059	Zevio	VR

Service. This work is the result of a collaboration between the Department of Computer Science of the University of Verona and the Company Address s.r.l. that is part of the Italian National Postal Service, and the official list of admissible abbreviations is a product of National Postal Service itself. In Table 4 we report the first fragment of the table of admissible abbreviations for the Italian Addresses.

The names can be abbreviated as well, and the number (street number) and ZIP code can be omitted. Obviously, the Type of Place abbreviation has a different weight, depending on its ambiguity. In particular, the abbreviation 'v.' can be used for Via, Viale, Vicolo and so on. If we use the admissible abbreviations that are unambiguous, the weight of the error is 0, if we use inadmissible abbreviations the weights are higher. Conversely, the abbreviation of a single name has a low weight, as well as the omission of number but the simultaneous abbreviation of name and omission of number will produce a higher error measure. The same happens for ZIP code. In other terms, the semantics we look for is compositional but not purely compositional.

Admissible abbreviations are set up for Names by means of an archive of Italian names. In Italy, however, there are two established linguistic minorities (German and French) and a few increasing immigrant minorities, mainly speaking either English or Arabic. It is evident that a complete name abbreviation reference is not possible. However, we can employ hyphenation similarity traditional techniques based on N-grams (for a recent analysis of the current literature see [13], that is not a survey but contains a quite well organised section on open problems and typical techniques) to identify the language in which the name is indeed written. Clearly, since the length of such texts is very short, consisting in fact in a maximum of three words, we have an accuracy degree of 58%[3] that can be improved if we exclude (or associate to low probability) close Latin languages like Spanish and Portuguese, to 73%. The adopted method is, therefore, to use a list of Italian names only when an efficient N-gram (we used 4-grams) technique detects a likely Italian string; otherwise the scheme is to accept only abbreviations of length one.

For instance, Alessio can be abbreviated into A., but since this can happen for Alessandro as well, if we have two Alessio Gugole in the same address, we have a completely certain match; if we have two Alessio Gugole with the same address with omitted ZIP or number we have a very likely match, with both omitted in one address, rather likely match; if one address is associated to A. Gugole and

---

[3] This is the result of a preliminary experiment, but it is also coherent with the achievements of research investigations actually focussing on this specific theme.

the other one to Alessio Gugole with the same toponym and number then they match, with the same toponym and different number they do not match, with one with omitted match they rather likely match.

Family names cannot be abbreviated. Conversely we cannot use a list of admissible Italian family names, because the number is too high (more than 300.000) making it inconvenient to use such techniques. Therefore we use a detector based upon a short list formed by the first 3000 family names, a number that can be managed conveniently. The result is a partial test, based upon approximate string match with traditional Edit Distance. This part of the algorithm returns either a match or a mismatch. In case of mismatch we do not eliminate duplicates, in case of match we set up the correction, which can be for both terms.

Cristani and Gugole are too far away in Edit Distance to potentially match, but Cristani and Crestani (a typical misspelling) are very close. However, Cristani and Crestani are both family names in the group of 3000 most common Italian family names, so they may match, but also may not match. Cristani and Christani are close in edit distance, but Christani does not pass the test for being an Italian word. Therefore, we do not look for it in the dictionary, we find Cristani and match Christani with Cristani, identifying this as an error.

The difficult part is the analysis of toponyms. There are several different admissible ways of writing down toponyms, and it is impossible to provide a complete analysis. A first pruning can be performed by employing abbreviation method for names, since the most common toponyms in Italy are dedicated to famous individuals. However, at least 60% of the actual addresses do not match with the above definition. Therefore, the only possible approach is to measure their distance by means of a relevance pattern identification. The method consists in finding a pattern that results in the first and in the second of the potentially matching toponyms, until no more pattern is found. When the rest of the single toponyms match by abbreviation, we assume match, when they do not we compute a probability based upon the measure of the Edit Distance of the rest.

For instance, if Type of Place is "Strada" and Toponym is "Le Grazie" in an address, and in a potentially matching one we have "S." as Type of Place, and "L. Grazie" for Toponym, they match.

Analogously we have a list of Italian cities and Counties which are used as terminological bases for measuring extended Edit distance in those cases.

By the above reasoning, it is clear that no algorithm can perform effectively without a reference to a database of actual toponyms. In fact the method we propose here is used in real-world applications as a preprocessing step. We measured an improvement to the performances of 17.8% when using our method as a preprocessing step.

2.2 Fixing the Parameters of Postal Address Version of Ontology-Driven Edit Distance

The highest difficulty with our approach is in fixing the parameters of the algorithm. In particular, the weights of the measures. Clearly, the only possible method for parameter fixing is empirical. After a first battery of trials to fix

Table 4. Admissible abbreviation: first fragment

OFFICIAL	ABBREVIATED	OFFICIAL	ABBREVIATED
ACCESSO	ACC.	CONTRADA	C.DA
AEROPORTO	AEROP.	CORSETTO	C.TTO
ALINEA	ALIN.	CORSIA	CORS.
ALZAIA	ALZ.	CORSO	C.SO
ANDRONA	ANDR.	CORTICELLA	C.LLA
ANDRONE	ANDR.	CORTILE	CORT.
ANGIPORTO	ANGIP.	CUPA VICINALE	CUPA VIC.
ARCHIVOLTO	ARC.	DARSENA	DARS.
ARGINE	ARG.	DEPOSITO	DEP.
AUTOSTRADA	AUTOSTR.	DIRAMAZIONE	DIRAM.
AVENUE	AV.	DIRAMAZIONI	DIRAM.
BACINO	BAC.	DISCESA	DISC.
BAGLIO	BAGL.	DISTACCO	DIST.
BALCONATA	BALC.	EMICICLO	EMIC.
BALUARDO	BAL.	ESEDRA	ESED.
BANCHINA	BANC.	EXTRAURBANA	EXURB
BARBARIA	BARB.	FONDACO	FOND.
BASTIONE	BAST.	FONDAMENTA	FONDAM.
BASTIONI	BAST.	FORNICE	FORN.
BELVEDERE	BELV.	FOSSATO	FOSS.
BORGATA	BO.TA	FRAZIONE	FRAZ.
BORGHETTO	B.TO	GALLERIA	GALL.
BORGO	B.GO	GRADINATA	GRAD.
BORGOLOCO	BORG.	GRADINI	GRAD.
BOULEVARD	BLVD	INTERNO	INT.

Table 5. Table of weights for the fields

FIELD	WEIGHT
Name	0.1
Family name	0.4
Type of Place	0.3
Toponym	0.8
Number	0.9
ZIP Code	0.8
City	0.4
County	0.3

the parameters we found, in three independent trials, values with a standard deviation of 0.003 as in Table 5.

Our implementation, of which we omit here programming details for the sake of space, and for clarity of presentation, is based upon the identification of two different thresholds. One for the duplicate records, initially set up at the value 0.5, and a second threshold for not duplicate initially fixed at the value 0.8. The method classifies as duplicate those records that form an error whose measure is less than or equal to the low threshold, and as not duplicate those which are greater than the high threshold. After having used our approach as a preprocessing step, the application checks whether the algorithm made its own decision, and if any, assumes it. In the case in which the preprocessing step concludes with no answer, the application starts by normalising the two addresses and match the normalised versions.

After the tests, the above thresholds have been set up to more realistic values 0.15 and 0.21. On those values we obtained the above mentioned incremental performance.

Summarising, the method consists in computing an extended Edit distance for each field, where the measure of errors is based on the four cases of classical Edit distance, plus the abbreviations based on a set of admissible ones. We then compute the weighted sum of the measures, and compare the result to the thresholds above. We use therefore three types of Edit distance: classic (indicated by e_p for Type of Place and e_x for Number, e_z for ZIP Code), extended by an abbreviation system (indicated by E_n for Names and E_t for Toponyms, E_c for cities E_a for counties) and mixed (indicated by ϵ_f for family names).

$$U = 0.15 \leq 0.1 \cdot E_n + 0.4 \cdot \epsilon_f + 0.3 \cdot E_t + 0.8 \cdot e_p + 0.9 \cdot e_x + 0.8 \cdot e_z + 0.4 \cdot E_c + 0.3 \cdot E_a \leq 0.21$$

3   Experimental Results

We have set up an experimental trial based upon the method of extracting a certain number of addresses at random from white pages, and maliciously modifying a controlled percentage by hands, whilst a bigger group is modified automatically with an algorithm that reproduces the distance distribution of known real cases. In Table 6 we report a small fragment of the database used for the test[4].

The records in Table 6 are normalised, namely no errors and no abbreviations appear onto them. In Table 7 we report the same addresses maliciously modified for our tests. The test has been performed as follows:

1. We formed a corpus of records from white pages;
2. We maliciously modify the records by inserting abbreviations and errors;
3. We mark up those records that are duplicate within the second group with some of the first group;
4. We mix up the two sets and eliminate at random a subset of records;
5. We perform the algorithm by itself, and as a preprocessing step;
6. We perform an algorithm based upon pure normalisation;
7. We compare computational performances and accuracy.

Regarding accuracy, the algorithm based upon normalisation and the one which employs our approach as a preprocessing step show identical accuracy. Conversely, our algorithm is, by itself, very inaccurate, being able to classify a total of 37% of the cases.

For computational performances we observe that the behaviour need an analysis on more than one single test, and in fact this has been done upon seven different extraction. The performance figure for small sizes is rather similar, being close to a linear complexity with growth factor 1.4. Conversely, for larger sample set, the performance of the method based upon our approach as a preprocessing step performs much better, being close to a linear complexity with the above mentioned growth factor, whilst the normalisation algorithm tends to a quadratic curve with 2.1 as growth factor.

---

[4] Clearly, the names used here and the addresses are masked onto false ones for self-evident privacy reasons, but the tests have been performed with real data.

Table 6. A fragment of the test sample

	Name	Family name	Type of Place	Toponym	Number	ZIP Code	City	County
1	Alessio	Gugole	via	Pio XII	81	37059	Zevio	VR
2	Alessio	Gugole	via	Pio XII	81	37059	Zevio	VR
3	Alberto	Gugole	via	Pio XII	85	37059	Zevio	VR
4	Eugenio	Peretti	via	Croce	29	37050	Oppeano	VR
5	Andrea	Pasetto	via	Albero	6	37056	Salizzole	VR
6	Valerio	Pasetto	via	Albero	6	37056	Salizzole	VR
7	Maurizio	Pasetto	via	Albero	12	37056	Salizzole	VR

Table 7. A fragment of the test sample after abbreviation and error insertion

	Name	Family name	Type of Place	Toponym	Number	ZIP Code	City	County
1	Alessio	Gugole	v.	Pio XII	81	37059	Zevio	VR
2	A.	Gugole	v.	Pio XII	81	37059	Zevio	VR
3	A.	Gugole	v.	Pio XII	85	37059	Zevio	VR
4	Eugenio	Pereti	vai	Croce	29		Oppeano	VR
5	Anrea	Pasetto	via	Albero	6	37056	Salizzole	VR
6	Valerio	Paseto	va	Albero	6	37100	Saliziole	VR
7	Marco	Pasetto	via	Albe	12	37056	Salizole	VR
8	Francesco	Saggioro	via	I Magio	21	37050	Oppeano	VR
9	Federico	Saggioro	via	I Maggio	19	37050	Opeano	VR

The analysis did not exhibit false positive examples, but this possibly depends on the limited number of error types that the experimental trial could manage for practical reasons of experiment settings. A larger case set could exhibit also false positive cases, but addressing this needs a very complex framework that does not appear necessary, due to the very good performance and accuracy results obtained with this sample sets.

4   Conclusions and Further Work

We described a method for improving the performance of duplicate elimination algorithms for Italian Postal Addresses. The investigation has shown that the performance of accurate algorithms for duplicate elimination of Postal Addresses can be significantly improved (17.8%) by the usage of our Ontology-driven approach that considers various semantic aspects related to both language and domain of usage.

There are several ways in which this research can be taken further. First of all, we can apply the same approach to cases other than Postal Addresses, or Postal Addresses in other languages. In particular two experiments are taking place at the moment, one with Portuguese and the other one with Polish. One different case is the one in which the duplicate elimination is performed in a database where the document to be aligned are more complicated that Postal Addresses, like in Digital Libraries.

We are also applying similar techniques to medical archive duplicate elimination, which is particularly interesting in view of the diffcrence between diagnostic and post-diagnostic analyses.

Acknowledgements

We gratefully thank the Address s.r.l. company that financially supported this work.

References

1. VLDB 2002. In: Proceedings of 28th International Conference on Very Large Data Bases, Hong Kong, China, August 20-23, 2002, Morgan Kaufmann, San Francisco (2002)
2. Ananthakrishna, R., Chaudhuri, S., Ganti, V.: Eliminating fuzzy duplicates in data warehouses. In: VLDB [1], pp. 586–597 (2002)
3. Apostolico, A., Guerra, C.: The longest common subsequence problem revisited. Algorithmica 2, 316–336 (1987)
4. Bunke, H.: On a relation between graph edit distance and maximum common subgraph. Pattern Recognition Letters 18(8), 689–694 (1997)
5. Hamming, R.W.: Error detecting and error correcting codes. Bell System Technology Journal 29, 147–160 (1950)
6. Jiang, T., Lin, G., Ma, B., Zhang, K.: A general edit distance between rna structures. Journal of Computational Biology 9(2), 371–388 (2002)
7. Lee, C.-S., Jian, Z.-W., Huang, L.-K.: A fuzzy ontology and its application to news summarization. IEEE Transactions on Systems, Man and Cybernetics Part B 35(5), 859–880 (2005)
8. Lee, C.-S., Jiang, C.-C., Hsieh, T.-C.: A genetic fuzzy agent using ontology model for meeting scheduling system. Information Sciences 176(9), 1131–1155 (2006)
9. Lee, C.-S., Kao, Y.-F., Kuo, Y.-H., Wang, M.-H.: Automated ontology construction for unstructured text documents. Data and Knowledge Engineering 60(3), 547–566 (2007)
10. Lee, C.-S., Wang, M.-H., Chen, J.-J.: Ontology-based intelligent decision support agent for cmmi project monitoring and control. International Journal of Approximate Reasoning (2007)
11. Lee, C.-S., Wang, M.-H.: Ontology-based computational intelligent multi-agent and its application to cmmi assessment. Applied Intelligence (2007)
12. Levenshtein, V.I.: Binary codes capable of correcting deletions, insertions, and reversals. Soviet Physics Doklady 10(8), 707–710 (1966)
13. McNamee, P., Mayfield, J.: Character n-gram tokenization for european language text retrieval. Inf. Retr. 7(1-2), 73–97 (2004)
14. Oncina, J., Sebban, M.: Learning stochastic edit distance: Application in hand-written character recognition. Pattern Recognition 39(9), 1575–1587 (2006)
15. Zhang, K., Shasha, D.: Simple fast algorithms for the editing distance between trees and related problems. SIAM J. Comput. 18(6), 1245–1262 (1989)

A Knowledge-Based System for Fashion Trend Forecasting

Paola Mello[1], Sergio Storari[2], and Bernardo Valli[3]

[1] DEIS - University of Bologna
Viale Risorgimento, 2 – 40136 – Bologna, Italy
pmello@deis.unibo.it
[2] ENDIF - University of Ferrara
Via Saragat, 1 – 44100 – Ferrara, Italy
sergio.storari@unife.it
[3] Faculty of Sociology - University of Urbino "Carlo Bo"'
Via Saffi, 15 – 61029 – Urbino, Italy
image@imagelab.w3n.it

Abstract. In this paper, we show how artificial intelligence techniques can be applied for the forecasting of trends in the high creative domain of fashion.

We describe a knowledge-based system that, starting from a set of keywords and pictures representing the concepts on which a fashion stylist chooses to base a new collection, is able to automatically create a trend forecast composed by the set of colors that better express these target concepts.

In order to model the knowledge used by the system to forecast trends, we experimented Bayesian networks. This kind of model is learned from a dataset of past trends by using different algorithms. We show how Bayesian networks can be used to make the forecast and the experiments made in order to evaluate their performances.

1 Introduction

There are sectors where the use of models is very important; in fact they can help in the comprehension of the surroundings and in the discovery of the natural laws in different sciences: Biology, Genetics, Chemistry, Physics. Among sectors where this knowledge modeling can be very interesting, we find the field of fashion, in particular the sphere of trends' valuation. In this field, stylists and marketing experts study past trends and, according to their experience, formulate a forecasting on trends that will lead the next years' collection. This study could prove to be very difficult and complicated both for experienced stylists and for small and medium companies that can only count on limited resources and experiences.

In this paper, we describe our research activity aimed at investigating if artificial intelligence may be useful to support the stylist in the creative process which starts with the analysis of past fashion trends and ends with the forecasting of the new ones. In particular, we focused our attention on the creation of color proposals made by color stylists for the spun-yarn industries working in the fashion market. The creation of such proposals is highly influenced by the stylist creativity and experience and it is so

N.T. Nguyen et al. (Eds.): IEA/AIE 2008, LNAI 5027, pp. 425–434, 2008.

complex that only under widely simplifying hypothesis we could imagine to introduce partially creative elements combining Artificial Intelligence techniques as, for example, knowledge-based systems and data mining.

Knowledge-based systems are able to solve problems in a limited domain but with performances similar to the ones of a human expert of the same domain. For this reason, a knowledge-based system seems suitable to support stylists and industry users in the creation of color proposal based on the analysis of past trends. One problem of such systems is knowledge acquisition because very often it can not be made manually, e.g. by making questions and interviews to the domain experts, in a easy and clear way. This is the case of the fashion domain as reported by Aarold Cohen [3]: "I concluded that color is one of those things that we do not exactly "think" about; what I mean is that we have ways of manipulating it in the head, but the manipulation does not follow the more regular traffic of externalization into verbal constructs.....". In order to overcome this limitation, data mining proposes several techniques to learn the knowledge base in a symbolic or sub-symbolic format from examples. Nowadays data mining techniques are widely used from a practical point of view to take advantage of the knowledge contained in databases.

In the light of these considerations, in this article we propose an hybrid approach based on knowledge-based systems and data mining to support the creation of color proposal in fashion.

The paper is organized as follows. The analysis of the process followed by a stylist to create a color proposal and the identification of where a support system may be useful is described in Section 2. Section 3 presents the data mining techniques that we evaluated as suitable for learning a knowledge base to be used in the support system. Section 4 and Section 5 describe respectively the experiments made to test the performance of the learned knowledge and how we use such knowledge to build a first prototype of the color proposal knowledge-based system. Conclusions follow in Section 6.

2   Analysis of the Creative Process

Stylists use different creative processes to define a color/tissue proposal. Among them, in this paper we focus on the one used by an Italian stylist. This process, similar to the one used by other stylists worldwide, was analyzed in details by the ImageLab [6] staff, in order to better understand its phases and the more important information. From this analysis emerged that the process starts from the choice of some words and/or concepts taken by the stylist as the keywords of a new color proposal. As second step, the stylist associates to these words/concepts one or more pictures taken from various sources such as, for example, TV, journals, books and photos. In the third and last step, the stylist chooses more or less ten colors and some tissues that in his/her opinion better represent the words, concepts and pictures chosen in the previous steps.

In this paper we propose to use a knowledge-based system to support the stylist in this last step of the creative process. In more details, the system should have the knowledge necessary to choose, among all the colors, the ones that better express the words, concepts and pictures chosen by the stylist. In the project we decided to elicit such knowledge from a collection of color proposals used in the past (named Proposal

Dataset PD). Each proposal contains: a set of words and concepts, the picture that has been associated to such words and concepts, and the set of chosen colors.

Pictures have been digitalized in 16M colors. In order to decrease the complexity of the classification models, we decided to reduce the number of colors to 64, switching from 8bit to 2 bit for each RGB canal (the space has been subdivided in 64 cubes and all the colors belonging to a cube have been associated to the color in the cube center)[1].

Given a picture, the frequency of each of the 64 colors is represented by the number of points that have a color which belongs in its color cube. Color frequencies have been discretized subdividing it by the highest color frequency in the picture (obtaining a relative frequency FR between 0 and 1) and assigning to it class N (not present) if $FR = 0$, B (low frequency) if $0 < FR \leq 0.25$, M (medium frequency) if $0.25 < FR \leq 0.5$, MA (medium high frequency) if $0.5 < FR \leq 0.75$ and A (high frequency) if $FR > 0.75$.

In the first experiments, these information have been digitally represented as follows:

- Words and concepts are modeled by boolean variables: a variable is True(False) if the word or concept it represents has(has not) been chosen in a color proposal;
- The 64 discretized color frequencies of the picture represented by the variables $S6\_1 - S6\_64$ (N = not present, B = low , M = medium, MA = medium high, A = high);
- The chosen colors have been represented by 64 tonalities and considered as boolean variables $C6\_1 - C6\_64$: a variable is True if the one or more colors of such tonality have been chosen in the proposal, otherwise False.

PD contains 153 color proposals. Some of them are incomplete as they contain only words/concepts and chosen colors. In the experiments we used 29 words/concepts (Frivolousness, Sensuality, Nature, Metropolitan, Relax, etc.).

3 Data Mining Techniques for Supporting Color Proposals

Data mining concerns the automatic or semiautomatic exploration and analysis of data in order to discover meaningful, previously unknown, nontrivial and potentially useful knowledge. Data mining techniques can be subdivided in symbolic, if the extracted knowledge has a symbolic representation and can be easily understood by a human, and sub-simbolic, if the knowledge can only be understood by a computer.

In our experiments, described in Section 4, we decided to focus on symbolic techniques for learning classifiers. We focus on classification because we see the problem of proposing or not a color C given the words/concepts WC and the picture colors S, chosen by the stylist, as a binary classification of the variable C in *to propose* and *not to propose* based on the values of the variables in WC and S. Moreover, we chosen the symbolic approach because, since the extracted knowledge is explicit, it is possible to explain to the user how a color has been proposed or not. Sub-symbolic techniques does not offer such advantage but will be tested in future experiments to compare their performance w.r.t. the symbolic ones.

---

[1] The expert has considered this approximation acceptable because the suggestion of a particular limited range of colors is useful to guide him in the definition of the specific color to choose.

Among the symbolic learning techniques, we tested Bayesian Networks [12]. A Bayesian network [12] is an appropriate method for dealing with uncertainty and probability, that are typical of real-life applications. A Bayesian network is a directed, acyclic graph (DAG) whose nodes represent domain variables and arcs represent probabilistic relations among them. In a Bayesian network each node is conditionally independent from any subset of nodes that are not its descendants, given its parents.

By means of Bayesian networks, we can use information about the values of some variables to obtain probabilities for other variables. A probabilistic inference takes place once the probabilities functions of each node conditioned to just its parents are given. These are usually represented in a tabled form, named Conditional Probability Table (CPT). Given a training set of examples, learning a Bayesian network is the problem of finding the structure of the direct acyclic graph and the CPT associated with each node that best match (according to some scoring metric) the dataset. Optimality is evaluated with respect to a given scoring metric. A procedure for searching among possible structures is needed.

The K2 algorithm [4] is a typical search and score method. It starts by assuming that a node has no parents, after which, in every step it adds incrementally the parent whose addition mostly increases the probability of the resulting structure. K2 stops adding parents to the nodes when the addition of a single parent cannot increase the probability of the network given the data.

In the "Experiments" section, we will describe how we learned Bayesian networks from the available dataset by using the K2 algorithm and how we evaluated the classification performance of such networks.

4   Experiments

This section describes the preparation of the datasets (Section 4.2), how we evaluate the performance of a learned Bayesian network (Section 4.4) and the performance results achieved by using different datasets and learning algorithms (Section 4.5).

4.1   Data Mining and Bayesian Network Tools

The Weka suite [14] (Waikato Environment for Knowledge Analysis), developed by the Waikato University of New Zeland, is a collection of machine learning algorithms. The suite, developed in Java, proposes a graphical user interface for easily accessing a lot of different algorithms, several pre-processing and post-processing methods, and some results visualization tools.

In our research, we used the Weka Bayesian network learning algorithms, available in the $classifiers$ group, and, in particular, the K2 algorithm implementation of Weka to learn a network and to analyze its performance. Moreover we saved the Bayesian network model in a Weka format. This model is then used by the knowledge-based system prototype, described in Section 5, to analyze a new case and classify a specific color as *to propose* or *not to propose*.

For the graphical visualization of the Bayesian network we used an opensource software named Genie [5].

4.2   Dataset Preparation

In order to prepare the dataset for the data ming algorithms we followed several steps. In the first, we applied two filters: a filter to remove the variables which represent the colors in the picture $S6\_1 - S6\_64$, obtaining a dataset containing only words/concepts and the chosen colors $C6\_1 - C6\_64$ (the *nopicture* label is added to the dataset name if this filter is applied); a filter to remove the color proposals which contain missing values (the *nomiss* label is added to the dataset name if this filter is applied). Applying this filters we created two datasets: PD_nomiss, used to evaluate the contribute that all the available information can give to the color classification; $PD\_nopicture\_nomiss$, used to evaluate the contribute that only the words/concepts can give to the color classification after the removal of the picture related information.

As described in Section 3, the aim is to build a classifier for each color. Since we have 64 colors $C6\_1 - C6\_64$, we learned 64 classifiers for the PD_nomiss dataset and 64 for the $PD\_nopicture\_nomiss$ dataset (for each classifier we have a dataset in which the class attribute is $C6\_i$ and the information used to make the classification are in the words/concepts and (eventually) the picture colors attributes).

4.3   Using the Bayesian Network Knowledge

As previously described in Section 3, in order to use a Bayesian network for the classification of a target variable, it is necessary to assign a value to some or all the other domain variables. In our domain, the target variable is a color *to propose* or *not to propose*, while the other domain variables are the words/concepts (set as T if chosen, F otherwise) and the picture color frequencies. As an example, Figure 1 shows in Genie the network learned from the PD_nomiss dataset for the $C6\_20$ color.

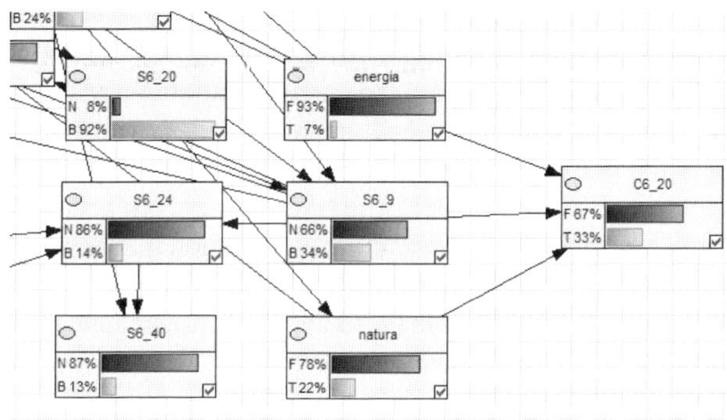

Fig. 1. Bayesian network model in Genie

Every node has associated an *a priori* probability for each admitted attribute value computed by mean of a statistical analysis of the dataset. As shown in Figure 1, the $C6\_20$ target node has two possible values: T that corresponds to the *to propose* output and F that corresponds to the *not to propose* output. Moreover, this node has three parent nodes: *natura*, associated to the nature concept; *energia*, associated to energy concept; $S6\_9$, associated to the frequency of the picture color number 9.

Given the choice of a set of words/concepts and of a picture, if we want to use the Bayesian network for classifying the target color as *to propose* or *not to propose* we assign a value to the word/concept and the picture color attributes according to the user choice. Given value assignments, Bayesian network inference algorithms are capable to propagate the probabilities on the network and change the probability of the allowable values of the target color (*to propose* or *not to propose*).

Figure 2 shows an example of this kind of probability propagation.

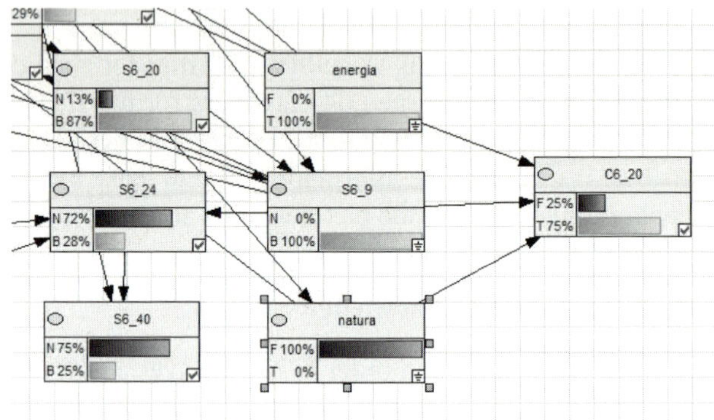

Fig. 2. Inference in the Bayesian network model

4.4   Performance Evaluation of a Learned Color Classifier

In order to evaluate the classification performance of a model, we created a confusion matrix and derived from it some performance indexes.

Given a dataset of classified examples and a classification model, the confusion matrix is used to compare the original classifications w.r.t. the ones proposed by the model. In our experiments the dataset of classified examples is represent by the set of past color proposals, the classification model is a Bayesian network used to classify a specific color as *to propose* or *not to propose* and the confusion matrix appear as shown in Table 1.

The cell names inside the confusion matrix have the following meaning: CNP = Correctly Not Proposed; ENP = Erroneously Not Proposed; EP = Erroneously Proposed; CP = Correctly Proposed.

The cell values are used to compute four performance indexes: $Accuracy = CP/(CP + EP)$ where this index expresses the percentage of times a color has been correctly proposed over the total times it has been proposed; $Sensitivity = CP/(CP + ENP)$ where this index expresses the percentage of times a color has been correctly proposed over the total times it had to be proposed; $Specificity = CNP/(CNP + EP)$ where this index expresses the percentage of times a color has been correctly not proposed over the time it had not to be proposed; $Falsealarmrate = 1 - Specificity$

Table 1. Confusion matrix

		Classification made by the Bayesian network	
		Not to propose	**To propose**
Real choice	**Not to propose**	CNP	EP
(made by the stylist)	**To propose**	ENP	CP

where this index expresses the percentage of times a color has been erroneously proposed over the time it had not to be proposed.

The accuracy has been also evaluated as the number of correct classifications over the total number of cases: $AccClass = (CNP + CP)/(CNP + CP + EP + ENP)$.

These indexes consider two different points of view: the first four are dedicated to stylists which prefer a model with high correctness of the *to propose* classification (an approach similar to the one proposed in [8]); The last index is dedicated to stylists which assign the same importance to the *to propose* and *not to propose* classifications, so they prefer a model with high performance for both of them.

4.5   Results

The results shown in this section have been achieved by the K2 Bayesian network learning algorithms and evaluated by using the 10-fold cross validation. The dataset used in the experiments were PD_nomiss (D1 for short) and $PD\_nopicture\_nomiss$ (D2 for short).

The K2 learning algorithm has been used with the option $initAsNaiveBayes$ set as $false$ (named $k2\_false$) and as $true$ (named $k2\_true$). When this option is set as $true$ (default), the initial network structure used in the learning is NaiveBayes like, with an arrow starting from the class attribute to each of the non-class attributes. When this option is set as $false$, the initial network has no arcs. The score function has been set as $BAYES$.

The results are shown in Table 2: since for each combination of dataset and algorithm we have learned 64 Bayesian networks (one for each color), in this table we show the average of the performance indexes achieved for all the colors (Accuracy (ACC), Sensitivity (SENS), Specificity (SPEC), False Alarm rate (FA) and AccClass (ACL)).

Table 2. Results of the K2_false and K2_true algorithms

	$K2\_false$ on D1	$K2\_false$ on D2	$K2\_true$ on D1	$K2\_true$ on D2
ACC	0.621	0.417	0.546	0.418
SENS	0.724	0.339	0.547	0.440
SPEC	0.632	0.749	0.691	0.720
FA	0.368	0.251	0.309	0.281
ACL	0.746	0.732	0.671	0.560

Analyzing these results, we observe that the Bayesian networks learned from the dataset which contains only the words/concepts chosen by the stylist (D2) achieve worst classification performances than the ones learned from the dataset which contains also the colors of the pictures (D1). Picture information are then effectively useful to perform good colors forecasting. Moreover we observe that the performance achieved by

$k2\_false$ are better than the $k2\_true$ one. Following these considerations the classification models used in the knowledge-based system, described in Section 5, are the ones learned by $k2\_false$ on D1.

Select the picture [　　　　　　　　　　　　　] Select

	Name	Color	Algorithm	Proposed
sensualita	Color 1		K2_false	
energia	Color 2		K2_false	
tradizione	Color 3		K2_false	
	Color 4		K2_false	
eleganza	Color 5		K2_false	
dolcezza	Color 6		K2_false	
	Color 7		K2_false	
glaciale	Color 8		K2_false	
frivolezza	Color 9		K2_false	
	Color 10		K2_false	
☑ relax	Color 11		K2_false	
sensibilita	Color 12		K2_false	
	Color 13		K2_false	
originalita	Color 14		K2_false	
	Color 15		K2_false	
☑ natura	Color 16		K2_false	
arte	Color 17		K2_false	
	Color 18		K2_false	
prezioso	Color 19		K2_false	
fluido	Color 20		K2_false	
	Color 21		K2_false	
molteplicita	Color 22		K2_false	
immensita	Color 23		K2_false	
	Color 24		K2_false	
intimita	Color 25		K2_false	
sportivo	Color 26		K2_false	
	Color 27		K2_false	
passione	Color 28		K2_false	
fragilita	Color 29		K2_false	
	Color 30		K2_false	
metropolitano	Color 31		K2_false	
magnetico	Color 32		K2_false	
emozione			Evaluate	

Fig. 3. Graphic user interface of the prototype

5   First Prototype

Following the experiment results, described in Section 4.5, we choose the 64 Byesian networks learned by $k2\_false$ on D1 as knowledge to use in the first prototype of the color proposal supporting system.

The interaction between the user and the knowledge base is managed by the graphic user interface (GUI) shown in Figure 3 that allows: the definition of a new color proposal creation request; the consultation of the knowledge base to create a color proposal; the visualization of the color proposal.

The definition of a new color proposal request is made by the user selecting: in the checkboxs on left side of the GUI the words/concepts on which the proposal should be focused; in the top of the GUI the file which specifies the frequencies of the color inside the picture that the user has associated to the words/concepts previously chosen. This choice is made by the user considering, for example, his/her experience, current trends and personal taste.

When the *Evaluate* button is pressed, the system creates the new color proposal following several steps. In the first, it creates the new color proposal request in the format described in Section 2 (extraction of other attributes from the pictures will be considered in future works).

This request is then sent to the 64 Bayesian networks that, following the inference methodology described in Section 4.3, classify each color as *to propose* and *not to propose*. The inference engine that interprets the Bayesian networks to make the classification is the one implemented in the $weka.classifiers.BayesNet$ class of Weka [14]. The set of colors proposed by the system is shown in the right side of the GUI.

6   Conclusions and Discussion

In this paper we presented a knowledge-based system that is able to create automatically the forecasting of trends in fashion represented by the colors to use in a new collection. In order to reach this goal, at first we have analyzed the creative process followed by a stylist, identifying a set of words/concepts and a picture as the most significant information used by him/her to make the forecast.

As second step we used data mining techniques for eliciting, from a dataset of past color proposals, the knowledge necessary to create a new proposal. Finally we developed a prototype of a knowledge-based system that effectively uses the elicited knowledge to support the color proposal creation.

The stylist that has supplied the starting dataset has found the elicited knowledge and the performance results very interesting. In particular in her opinion it is valuable the ability of the Bayesian network to make explicit the words/concepts and picture colors most influencing each color choice. Moreover, she confirmed that many of such probabilistic models are effectively consistent with her choices. She considered these models useful also for other reasons: they can be used by pret-a-porter stylists to analyze successful fashion collections in order to find the most appropriated color combinations; they can be used by high fashion stylists to differentiate their collection from the high distribution fashion collections proposing something "original".

Beside Bayesian networks, Decision tree [13] learning techniques have also been tested on the dataset of color proposals. In the experiments, described in [10], Bayesian networks have achieved the best predictive performances.

Among the necessary future steps we consider important to increment the number of color proposals in the dataset used to elicit the system knowledge base and to make a deep analysis of the informative value of pictures.

Despite the achieved results, we are aware that the application domain is very complex and that the combination of knowledge-based systems and data mining only under widely simplifying hypotheses could be considered a real creative process.

The aim of creating such creative systems is the goal of a research area of artificial intelligence named Computational Creativity [11][2]. This high interdisciplinary area (computer science, notional psychology, philosophy and art) does not fall within the areas that have the intention to suggest "problems' solution" but it is part of the areas that aim at the generation of "manufactures" of value: different artificial intelligence techniques are used to produce these manufactures, to value them through an "utility function" and to select some of them.

Systems based on creativity rules have been proposed in different application fields: in melodies, for the improvisation of jazz music ([7]Philip Johnson - Laird - University of Princeton); in art, for the creation of paintings (AARON [1] by Harold Cohen University of California); in theorems, for the discovery of mathematical rules (AM [9] Douglas Lenat Stanford University).

In spite of all these applications, as we know, computational creativity has never been applied to fashion and in particular to the forecasting of trends for color selection. For this reason we consider the work described in this paper as a first step on the development a real creative system for fashion.

Acknowledgments. This research activity has been partially funded by the Italian Cofin 2003 project (prot. 2003141985). We would like to thank Ornella Bignami (Elementi Moda s.r.l.), Alessandro Di Caro (ImageLab), Erika D'Amico (ImageLab), Emanuela Ciuffoli (ImageLab), Enrico Betti (ImageLab), Elena Giliberti (ImageLab), Beatrice Universo (ImageLab) and Enrico Munari (University of Ferrara) for their precious help in the research.

References

1. Aaron. Home Page:
   `http://www.kurzweilcyberart.com/aaron/history.html`
2. Boden, M.: Agents and Creativity. Communications of the ACM (1994)
3. Cohen, H.: The further exploits of aaron, painter. Stanford Humanities Review 4(2) (1994)
4. Cooper, G., Herskovits, E.: A bayesian method for the induction of probabilistic networks from data. Machine Learning 9, 309–347 (1992)
5. Genie. Home Page: `http://genie.sis.pitt.edu/`
6. Imagelab, universita' di urbino. Home Page: `http://imagelab.w3n.it/`
7. Johnson-Laird, P.: Jazz Improvisation: A theory at the computational level. Representing Musical Structure. Academic Press, London (1991)
8. Lavrac, N.: Machine learning for data mining in medicine. In: Horn, W., Shahar, Y., Lindberg, G., Andreassen, S., Wyatt, J.C. (eds.) AIMDM 1999. LNCS (LNAI), vol. 1620, pp. 47–64. Springer, Heidelberg (1999)
9. Lenat, D.B., Brown, J.S.: Why am and eurisko appear to work. Artif. Intell. 23(3), 269–294 (1984)
10. Mello, P., Storari, S., Valli, B.: Application of machine learning techniques for the forecasting of fashion trends. Intelligenza Artificiale (to appear, 2008)
11. Minsky, M.: The Society of Mind. Simon and Schster, New York (1986)
12. Pearl, J., Russell, S.: Bayesian networks. In: Arbib, M.A. (ed.) The Handbook of Brain Theory and Neural Networks, MIT Press, Cambridge (2003)
13. Quinlan, R.: Induction of decision trees. Machine Learning 1(1), 81–106 (1986)
14. Witten, I.H., Eibe, F.: Data Mining: Practical machine learning tools and techniques. Morgan Kaufmann, San Francisco (2005)

Planning with Multiple-Components in OMPS

Amedeo Cesta, Simone Fratini, and Federico Pecora

ISTC-CNR, National Research Council of Italy
Institute for Cognitive Science and Technology
Rome, Italy
{name.surname}@istc.cnr.it

Abstract. This paper presents OMPS, a new timeline-based software architecture for planning and scheduling whose features support software development for space mission planning applications. The architecture is based on the notions of domain components entities whose properties may vary in time and which model one or more physical subsystems which are relevant to a given planning context. Decisions can be taken on components, and constraints among decisions modify the components' behaviors in time. This paper presents the general features of OMPS and an example of how the architecture support development of complex applications.

1 Introduction

This paper describes OMPS, the "Open Multi-component Planning and Scheduling architecture". The general goal in OMPS is to provide a development environment for enabling the design and implementation of timeline-based planning and scheduling systems. This work is an evolution of previous work on a planner called OMP [1], which proposed a uniform view of state variable and resource timelines to integrate Planning & Scheduling (P&S). While the OMP experience lead to a proof of concept solver for small scale demonstration, the current development of OMPS is taking place within the Advanced Planning and Scheduling Initiative (APSI) of the European Space Agency (ESA). The aim of the APSI project is to generalize the approach to mission planning decision support by creating a software framework that facilitates product development. By inheriting our previous experience in developing planning and scheduling support tools for ESA (namely with the MEXAR, MEXAR2 and RAXEM systems [2], currently in active duty at ESA's control center) we lead to a substantial effort both in re-engineering and in extending our previous work.

The OMPS architecture is not only influenced by constraint-based reasoning work, but introduces also the notion of domain *components* as a primitive entity for knowledge modeling. Components are entities whose properties may vary in time and which model one or more physical subsystems which are relevant to a given planning context. Decisions can be taken on components, and constraints among decisions modify the components' behaviors in time. Components provide the means to achieve modular decision support tool development. A component can be designed to incorporate into a constraint-based reasoning framework entire decisional modules which have been developed independently.

N.T. Nguyen et al. (Eds.): IEA/AIE 2008, LNAI 5027, pp. 435–445, 2008.

Related Work. Most research in planning uses the representation formalism defined in the various evolutions of PDDL [3], where causal knowledge is expressed in the form of precondition-effect rules that represent actions performed by an executor (e.g., a robot). HSTS [4] departs from this approach, and is inspired by classical control theory: planning focuses on features of the world that vary over time. Specific constraints, called *compatibilities*, rule out undesired behaviors from the possible temporal evolution of the modeled features. HSTS has been the first architecture to propose a modeling language with explicit representation of timelines, using the concept of state variables.

2   Components and Behaviors

In OMPS, a *component* is an entity that has a set of possible temporal evolutions over an interval of time $\mathcal{H}$. The component's evolutions over time are named *behaviors*. Behaviors are modeled as temporal functions over $\mathcal{H}$, and can be defined over continuous time or as stepwise constant functions of time. It is in general possible to provide different representations for a component's behaviors, depending on (1) the chosen temporal model (continuous vs. discrete, or time point based vs. interval based), (2) the nature of the function's range $\mathcal{D}$ (finite vs. infinite, continuous vs. discrete, symbolic vs. numeric) and (3) the type of function which describes a behavior (general, piecewise linear, piecewise constant, impulsive and so on).

Not every function over a given temporal interval can be taken as a valid behavior for a component. The evolution of components in time is subject to "physical" constraints (or approximations thereof). We call *consistent* behaviors the ones that actually correspond to a possible evolution in time according to the real-world characteristics of the entity we are modeling. A component's consistent behaviors are defined by means of *consistency features*. In essence, a consistency feature is a function f^C which determines which behaviors adhere to physical attributes of the real-world entity modeled by the component.

It is in general possible to have many different representations of a component's consistency features: either explicit (e.g., tables or allowed bounds) or implicit (e.g., constraints, assertions, and so on). For instance, let us model a light bulb component. A light bulb's behaviors can take three values: "on", "off" and "burned". Supposing the light bulb cannot be fixed, a rule could state that any behavior that takes the value "burned" at a time t is consistent if and only if such a value is taken also for any time $t' > t$. This is a declarative approach to describing the consistency feature f^C. Different actual representations for this function can be used, depending also on the representation of the behavior.

A few more concrete examples of components and their associated consistency features are the following.

State variable. *Behaviors*: piecewise constant functions over a finite, discrete set of symbols which represent the *values* that can be taken by the state variable. Each behavior represents a different sequence of values taken by the component. *Consistency Features*: a set of sequence constraints, i.e., a set of rules that specify which transitions between allowed values are legal, and a set of lower and upper bounds on the duration of each allowed value. The model can be for instance represented as a timed automaton (e.g., the three state variables in Figure 1). Note that a distinguishing feature of a state variable is that not all the transitions between its values are allowed.

Resource (renewable). *Behaviors*: integer or real functions of time, piecewise, linear, exponential or even more complex, depending on the model you want to set up. Each behavior represents a different profile of resource consumption. *Consistency Feature*: minimum and maximum availability. Each behavior is consistent if it lies between the minimum and maximum availability during the entire planning interval. Note that a distinguishing feature of a resource is that there are bounds of availability.

The component-based nature of OMPS allows to accommodate pre-existing solving component into larger planning contexts. For instance, it is possible to incorporate the MEXAR2 application [2] as a component, the consistency property of which is not computed directly on the values taken by the behaviors, but as a function of those behaviors.[1]

3   Component Decisions

Now that we have defined the concept of component as the fundamental building block of the OMPS architecture, the next step is to define how component behaviors can be altered (within the physical constraints imposed by consistency features).

We define a *component decision* as a pair $\langle \tau, \nu \rangle$, where τ is a given *temporal element*, and ν is a *value*. Specifically, τ can be: (a) a time instant (TI) t representing a moment in time; (b) a time interval (TIN), a pair of TIs defining an interval $[t_s, t_e)$ such that $t_e > t_s$. The specific form of the value ν depends on the type of component on which the decision is defined. For instance, this can be an amount of resource usage for a resource component, or a disjunction of allowed values for a state variable.

Regardless of the type of component, the value of any component decision can contain *parameters*. In OMPS, parameters can be numeric or enumerations, and can be used to express complex values, such as "transmit(?bitrate)" for a state variable which models a communications system. Further details on value parameters will be given in the following section.

Overall, a component decision is something that happens somewhere in time and modifies a component's behaviors as described by the value ν. In OMPS, the consequences of these decisions are computed by the components by means an *update function* f^U. This is a function which determines how the component's behaviors change as a consequence of a given decision. In other words, a decision changes a component's set of behaviors, and f^U describes how. A decision could state for instance "keep all the behaviors that are equal to d' in t_1" and another decision could state "all the behaviors must be equal to d'' after t_2". Given a decision on a component with a given set of behaviors, the update function computes the resulting set.

Let us instantiate the concept of decision for the two types of components we have introduced so far.

---

[1] Basically, it is computed as the difference between external uploads and the downloaded amount stated by the values taken by the behaviors. See [2] for details on the MEXAR2 application.

State variable. *Temporal element*: a TIN. *Value*: a subset of values that can be taken by the state variable (the range of its behaviors) in the given time frame. *Update Function*: this kind of decision for a state variable implies the choice of values in a given time interval. In this case the subset of values are meant as a disjunction of allowed values in the given time interval. Applying a decision on a set of behaviors entails that all behaviors that do not take any of the chosen values in the given interval are excluded from the set.

Resource (renewable). *Temporal element*: a TIN. *Value*: quantity of resource allocated in the given interval — a decision is basically an *activity*, an amount of allocated resource in a time interval. *Update Function*: the resource profile is modified by taking into account this allocation. Outside the specified interval the profile is not affected.

4 Domain Theory

So far, we have defined components in isolation. When components are put together to model a real domain they cannot be considered as reciprocally decoupled, rather we need to take into account the fact that they influence each other's behavior.

In OMPS, it is possible to specify such inter-component relations in what we call a *domain theory*. Specifically, given a set of components, a domain theory is a function f^{DT} which defines how decisions taken on one component affect the behaviors of *other* components. Just as a consistency feature f^C describes which behaviors are allowed with respect to the features of a single component, the domain theory specifies which of the behaviors belonging to all modeled components are concurrently admissible.

In practice, a domain theory is a collection of *synchronizations*. A synchronization essentially represents a rule stating that a certain decision on a given component (called the *reference* component) can lead to the application of a new decision on another component (called *target* component). More specifically, a synchronization has the form $\langle C_i, V \rangle \longrightarrow \langle C_j, V', R \rangle$, where: C_i is the reference component; V is the value of a component decision on C_i which makes the synchronization applicable; C_j is the target component on which a new decision with value V' will be imposed; and R is a set of *relations* which bind the reference and target decisions.

Example. In order to clarify how inter-component relationships are modeled as a domain theory, we use a running example.

Problem definition. The planning problem consists in deciding data transmission commands from a satellite orbiting Mars to Earth within given ground station visibility windows. The spacecraft's orbits for the entire mission are given, and are not subject to planning. The fundamental elements which constitute the system are: the satellite's Transmission System (TS), which can be either in "transmit mode" on a given ground station or idle; the satellite's Pointing System (PS); and the satellite's battery (BAT). In addition, an external, uncontrollable set of properties is also given, namely Ground Station Visibility (GSV) and Solar Flux (SF). Station visibility windows are intervals of time in which given ground stations are available for transmission, while the solar flux represents the amount of power generated by the solar panels given the spacecraft's orbit. Since the orbits are given for the entire mission, the power provided by the solar flux is a given function of time $sf(t)$. The satellite's battery accumulates power through the solar flux and is discharged every time the satellite is slewing or transmitting data. Finally, it is required that the spacecraft's battery is never discharged beyond a given minimum power level (in order to always maintain a minimum level of charge in case an emergency manoeuvre needs to be performed).

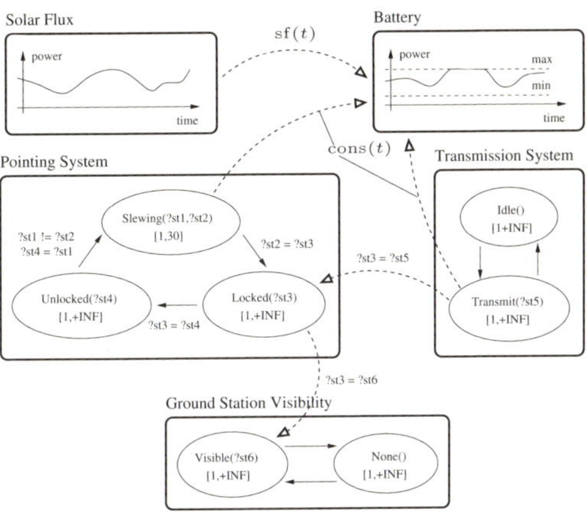

Fig. 1. Domain theory for the running example

Problem reduction. Instantiation this example into the OMPS framework thus equates to defining five components:

PS, TS and GSV. The spacecraft's pointing and transmission systems, as well as station visibility are modeled with three state variables. The consistency features of these state variables (possible states, bounds on their duration, and allowed transitions) are depicted in Figure 1. The figure also shows the synchronizations involving the three components: one states that the value "locked(?st3)" on component PS requires the value "visible(?st6)" on component GSV (where ?st3 = ?st6, i.e., the two values must refer to the same station); another synchronization asserts that transmitting on a certain station requires the PS component to be locked on that station; lastly, both slewing and transmission entail the use of a constant amount of power from the battery.

SF. The solar flux is modeled as a simple profile. Given that the flight dynamics of the spacecraft are given (i.e., the angle of incidence of the Sun's radiation with the solar panels is given), the profile of the solar flux resource is given function time $sf(t)$ which is not subject to changes. Thus, decisions are never imposed on this component (i.e., the SF component has only one behavior), rather its behavior is solely responsible for determining power production on the battery (through the synchronization between the SF and BAT components).

BAT. The spacecraft's battery component is modeled as follows. Its consistency features are a maximum and minimum power level (max, min), the former representing the battery's maximum capacity, the latter representing the battery's minimum depth of discharge. The BAT component's behavior is a temporal function $bat(t)$ representing the battery's level of charge. The consequences of power consumption $cons(t)$ (resulting from decisions on TS and PS components) and productions $sf(t)$ (from solar arrays), are calculated by the updating function as $bat(t) = L_0 + \alpha \int_0^t (sf(t) - cons(t))dt$ when $bat(t) \leq max$, and as $bat(t) = max$ otherwise (where L_0 is the initial charge of the battery at the beginning of the planning horizon and α is a constant parameter which approximates the charging profile).

In the example above, we have employed both state variables an ad-hoc component. Notice that this latter component is essentially an extension of a reusable resource: whereas a reusable resource's update function is trivially the sum operator, the BAT's update function calculates the consequences of activities as per the above integration over the planning horizon.

5   Decision Network

The fundamental tool for defining dependencies among component decisions are *relations*, of which OMPS provides three types; *temporal*, *value* and *parameter* relations.

Given two component decisions, a *temporal relation* is a constraint among the temporal elements of the two decisions. A temporal relation among two decisions A and B can prescribe temporal requirements such as those modeled by Allen's interval algebra [5], e.g., A EQUALS B, or A OVERLAPS [l,u] B.

A *value relation* between two component decisions is a constraint among the values of the two decisions. A value relation among two decisions A and B can prescribe requirements such as A EQUALS B, or A DIFFERENT B (meaning that the value of decision A must be equal to or different from the value of decision B).

Lastly, a *parameter relation* among component decisions is a constraint among the values of the parameters of the two decisions. Such relations can prescribe linear inequalities between parameter variables. For instance, a parameter constraint between two decisions with values "available(?antenna, ?bandwidth)" and "transmit(?bitrate)" can be used to express the requirement that transmission should not use more than half the available bandwidth, i.e., $?bitrate \leq 0.5 \cdot ?bandwidth$.

Component decisions and relations are maintained in a *decision network*: given a set of components $\mathcal{C}$, a decision network is a graph $\langle V, E \rangle$, where each vertex $\delta_C \in V$ is a component decisions defined on a component $C \in \mathcal{C}$, and each edge $(\delta_{C^i}^m, \delta_{C^j}^n)$ is a temporal, value or parameter relation among component decisions $\delta_{C^i}^m$ and $\delta_{C^j}^n$.

We now define the concepts of *initial condition* and *goal*. An initial condition for our problem consists in a set of value choices for the GSV state variable. These decisions reflect the visibility windows given by the Earth's position with respect to the (given) orbit of the satellite. Notice that the allowed values of the GSV component are not references for a synchronization, thus they cannot lead to the insertion in the plan of new component decisions.

Conversely, a goal consists in a set of component decisions which are intended to trigger the solving strategy to exploit the domain theory's synchronizations to synthesize decisions. In our example, this set consists in value choices on the TS component which assert a desired number of "transmit(?st5)" values. Notice that these value choices can be allocated flexibly on the timeline.

In general, the characterizing feature of decisions which define an initial condition is that these decisions do not lead to application of the domain theory. Conversely, goals directly or indirectly entail the need to apply synchronizations in order to reach domain theory compliance. This mechanism is the core of the solving process described in the following section.

6   Reasoning about Timelines in OMPS

OMPS implements a solving strategy which is based on the notion of *timeline*. A timeline is defined for a component as an ordered sequence of its values. A component's timeline is defined by the set of decisions imposed on that component. Timelines represent the *consequences* of the component decisions over the time axis, i.e., a timeline for a component is the collection of all its behaviors as obtained by applying the f^U function given the component decisions taken on it.

The overall solving process implemented in OMPS is composed of three main steps, namely *domain theory application*, *timeline management* and *solution extraction*. Indeed, a fundamental principle of the OMPS approach is its *timeline-driven* solving process.

Domain Theory Application. Component decisions possess an attribute which changes during the solving process, namely whether or not a decision is *justified*. OMPS's domain application step consists in iteratively tagging decisions as justified according to the following rules (iterated over all decisions δ in the decision network):

1. If δ *unifies with another decision in the network*, then mark δ as justified;
2. If δ's value *unifies with the reference value of a synchronization in the domain theory*, then mark δ as justified and add the target decision(s) and relations to the decision network;
3. If δ *does not unify with any reference value in the domain theory*, mark δ as justified.

Timeline Management. Timeline management is a collection of procedures which are necessary to go from a decision network to a completely instantiated set of behaviors. These behaviors ultimately represent a solution to the planning problem. Timeline management may introduce new component decisions as well as new relations to the decision network. For this reason, the OMPS solving process iterates domain theory application and timeline management steps until the decision network is fully justified and a consistent set of behaviors can be extracted from all component timelines. The specific procedures which compose timeline management are *timeline extraction, timeline scheduling* and *timeline completion*. Let us describe these three steps in detail.

The outcome of the domain theory application step is a decision network where all decisions are justified. Nevertheless, since every component decision's temporal element (which can be a TI or TIN) is maintained in an underlying flexible temporal network, these decisions are not fixed in time, rather they are free to move between the temporal bounds obtained as a consequence of the temporal relations imposed on the temporal elements. For this reason, a timeline must be *extracted* from the decision network, i.e., the flexible placement of temporal elements implies the need of synthesizing a total ordering among floating decisions. Specifically, this process depends on the component for which extraction is performed. For a resource, for instance, the timeline is computed by ordering the allocated activities and summing the requirements of those that overlap. For a state variable, the effects of temporally overlapping decision are computed by intersecting the required values, to obtain (if possible) in each time interval a value which complies with all the decisions that overlap during the time interval.

In the current implementation, we follow for every type of component an earliest start-time (EST) approach, i.e., we have a timeline where all component decisions are assumed to occur at their earliest start time and last the shortest time possible.

Once a timeline is extracted, it can present *flaws* and *inconsistencies*. The first of these features depends on the fact that decisions imposed on the state variable do not result in a complete coverage of the planning horizon with decisions. A flaw is a segment of time in which no decision has been taken, thus the state variable within this segment of time is not constrained to take on certain values, rather it can, in principle, assume any one of its allowed values. The process of deciding which value(s) are admissible with respect to the state variable's internal consistency features (i.e., the component's f^C function) is clearly a non-trivial process. Indeed, this is precisely the objective of *timeline completion*.

Notice that timeline completion is required for components such as state variables, where not all intervals of time are necessarily covered by a decision. Conversely, reusable resources as we have defined them in this paper cannot present flaws (an interval of time in which no decision is taken implies that the resource is simply unused).When invoked, timeline completion adds new decisions to the plan.

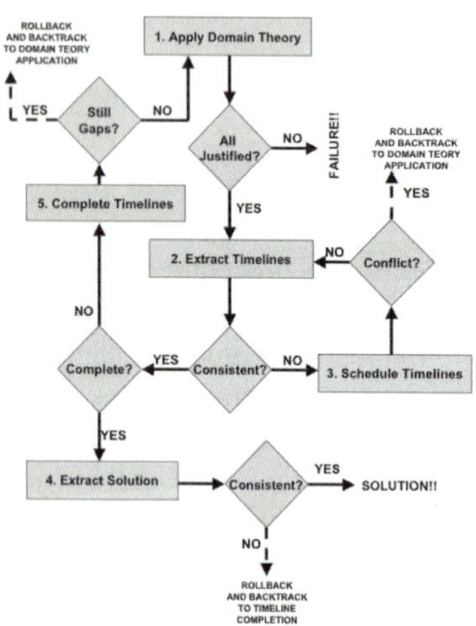

Fig. 2. The OMPS solving process

In addition to flaws, inconsistencies can arise in the timeline. The nature of inconsistencies depends on the specific component we are dealing with. In the case of state variables, an inconsistency occurs when two or more value choices whose intersection is empty overlap in time. As opposed to flaws, inconsistencies do not require the generation of additional component decisions, rather they can be resolved by posting further temporal constraints. For instance, two decisions $(A(x), B(y))$ and $(C(z))$ which overlap in time lead to an inconsistency which can be resolved by imposing a temporal relation which forces $(C(z))$ to occur either after or before $(A(x), B(y))$. In the case of the BAT component mentioned earlier, an inconsistency occurs when slewing and/or transmission decisions have lead to a situation in which $\text{bat}(t) \leq \min$ for some $t \in \mathcal{H}$. As in the previous example, BAT inconsistencies can be resolved by posting temporal constraints between the over-consuming activities. In general, we call the process of resolving inconsistencies *timeline scheduling*.

The scheduling process deals with the problem of resolving inconsistencies. Once again, the process depends on the component. For a resource, activity overlapping results in an inconsistency if the combined usage of the overlapping activities requires more than the resource's capacity. For a state variable, any overlapping of decision that requires a conflicting set of decisions must be avoided. The timeline scheduling process adds constraints to the decision network to avoid such inconsistencies through a constraint posting algorithm [6].

Solution Extraction. Once domain application and timeline management have successfully converged on a set of timelines with no inconsistencies or flaws, the next step is to extract from the timelines one or more consistent behaviors. Recall that a behavior is one particular choice of values for each temporal segment in a component's timeline. The previous domain theory application and timeline management steps have filtered out all behaviors that are not, respectively, consistent with respect to the domain theory and the components' consistency features. Solution extraction deals with the problem of determining a consistent set of fully instantiated behaviors for every component. Since every segment of a timeline potentially represents a disjunction of values, solution extraction must choose specific behaviors consistently. Furthermore, not all values in timeline segments are fully instantiated with respect to parameters, thus solution extraction must also take into account the consistent instantiation of values across all components.

Overall Solving Process. In the current OMPS solver the previously illustrated steps are interleaved as sketched in Figure 2. The first step in the planning process is domain theory application, whose aim is to support non-justified decisions. If there is no way to support all the decisions in the plan, the algorithm fails.

Once every decision has been supported, the solver tries to extract a timeline for each component. At this point, it can happen that some timelines are not consistent, meaning that there exists a time interval over which conflicting decisions overlap (an inconsistency). In such a situation, a scheduling step is triggered. If the scheduler cannot solve all conflicts, the solver backtracks directly to domain theory application, and searches for a different way of supporting goals.

If the solver manages to extract a conflict-free set of timelines, it then triggers a timeline-completion step on any timeline which is found to have flaws. It may happen that some timelines cannot be completed. In this case, the solver backtracks again to the previous domain theory application step, and again searches for a way of justifying all decisions. If the completion step succeeds for all timelines, the solver returns to domain theory application, as timeline completion has added decisions which are not justified.

Once all timelines are conflict-free and complete, the solver is ready to extract behaviors. If behavior extraction fails, the solver attempts to backtrack to timeline completion. Finally, the whole process ends when the solver succeeds in extracting at least one behavior for each timeline. This collection of mutually consistent behaviors represents a fully instantiated solution to the planning problem.

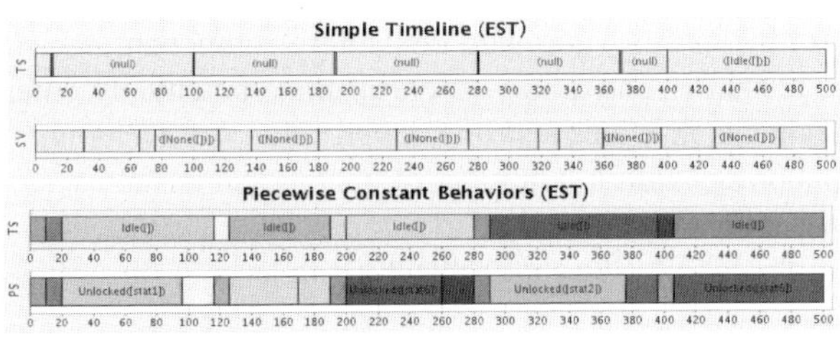

Fig. 3. Timelines and behaviors for the TS and GSV state variables

Example. Going back to our running example, the timelines of the GSV and TS components resulting from the application of a set of initial condition and goal decisions are shown in Figure 3 (top). Notice that the GSV timeline is fully defined, since it represents the evolution in time of station visibility given the fully defined flight dynamics of the satellite. The TS timeline contains five "transmit" value choices, through which we represent our goal. These value choices are allocated within flexible time bounds (the figure shows an EST timeline for the component, in which these decisions are anchored to their earliest start time and duration). As opposed to the GSV timeline, the TS timeline contains flaws, and it is precisely these flaws that will be "filled" by the solving algorithm. In addition, the application during the solving process of the synchronization between the GSV and PS components that will determine the construction of the PS's timeline (which is completely void of component decisions in the initial situation), reflecting the fact that it is necessary to point the satellite towards the visible target before initiating transmission. The behaviors extracted from the TS and PS components' timelines after applying this solving procedure on our example are shown in Figure 3 (bottom).

7   Conclusions

In this article we have given a preliminary overview of OMPS, an approach which draws from and attempts to generalize our previous experience in mission planning tool development for ESA [2] and to extend our previous work on the OMP planning system [1].

A distinctive feature of the OMPS architecture is that it provides a framework for reasoning about any entity which can be modeled as a component, i.e., as a set of properties that vary in time. This includes "classical" concepts such as state variables (as defined in HSTS [4] and studied also in subsequent work [7,8]), and renewable or consumable resources [6]. OMPS's component-oriented nature allows to modularize the reasoning algorithms that are specific to each type of component within the component itself, e.g., profile-based scheduling routines for resource inconsistency resolution are implemented within the resource component itself. This facilitates the process of including previously implemented/deployed ad-hoc components within the framework. We have given an example of this in this paper with the battery component, which essentially extends a reusable resource. The ability to encapsulate potentially complex modules within OMPS components provides a strong added value in developing real-world planning systems. This brings with it a number of operational advantages, such as fast-prototyping, prototype reliability (a particularly important feature in the space domain) and software scalability. Finally, the approach allows to leverage the efficiency of problem de-composition.

Acknowledgments. The authors are currently supported by European Space Agency (ESA) within the Advanced Planning and Scheduling Initiative (APSI). APSI partners are VEGA GmbH, ONERA, University of Milan and ISTC-CNR. Thanks to Angelo Oddi and Gabriella Cortellessa for their constant support, and to Carlo Matteo Scalzo for contributing an implementation of the battery component.

References

1. Cesta, A., Fratini, F.: Controlling Complex Physical Systems Through Planning and Scheduling Integration. In: Ali, M., Esposito, F. (eds.) IEA/AIE 2005. LNCS (LNAI), vol. 3533, pp. 197–207. Springer, Heidelberg (2005)
2. Cesta, A., Cortellessa, G., Fratini, S., Oddi, A., Policella, N.: An innovative product for space mission planning – an *a posteriori* evaluation. In: ICAPS-2007. Proceedings of the 17th International Conference on Automated Planning & Scheduling (2007)
3. Fox, M., Long, D.: PDDL2.1: An extension to PDDL for expressing temporal planning domains. J. Artif. Intell. Res (JAIR) 20, 61–124 (2003)
4. Muscettola, N., Smith, S., Cesta, A., D'Aloisi, D.: Coordinating Space Telescope Operations in an Integrated Planning and Scheduling Architecture. IEEE Control Systems 12(1), 28–37 (1992)
5. Allen, J.: Maintaining knowledge about temporal intervals. Communications of the ACM 26(11), 832–843 (1983)
6. Cesta, A., Oddi, A., Smith, S.F.: A Constraint-based method for Project Scheduling with Time Windows. Journal of Heuristics 8(1), 109–136 (2002)
7. Jonsson, A., Morris, P., Muscettola, N., Rajan, K., Smith, B.: Planning in Interplanetary Space: Theory and Practice. In: AIPS-2000. Proceedings of the Fifth Int. Conf. on Artificial Intelligence Planning and Scheduling (2000)
8. Frank, J., Jónsson, A.: Constraint-based attribute and interval planning. Constraints 8(4), 339–364 (2003)

The Contact Scheduling Process of the Galileo Navigation System

Tiago Franco[1], Flávio Moreira[1], Stewart Hall[2], and Henrique Oliveira[1]

[1] Critical Software S.A., [2] SciSys
tjpgfranco@criticalsoftware.com,
flavio.moreira@criticalsoftware.com,
stewart.hall@scisys.co.uk,
hja-oliveira@criticalsoftware.com

Abstract. Galileo [1] is a joint initiative of the European Commission and the European Space Agency (ESA) for the development of a Global Satellite Navigation System. This system will provide a highly accurate, guaranteed global positioning service under civilian control. The fully deployed Galileo system consists of 30 satellites (27 operational + 3 spares) and 5 globally distributed ground stations. The Spacecraft Constellation Planning Facility is the element responsible for generating the plans of contacts between satellites and ground stations for the entire constellation for the purpose of maintenance and corrective actions. This element includes the Contact Scheduler, the component with the scheduling functionalities of generating conflict free Contact Plans. This document describes the Galileo's contact scheduling problem, the design and implementation of the scheduler and the validation results.

Keywords: Planning and Scheduling, Heuristic Search.

1 Introduction

Due to the complex nature of the Galileo constellation operations, where one contact per orbit for each spacecraft must be achieved through 5 Telemetry, Tracking and Control (TT&C) stations (Fig. 1), the planning functions are an important component of the GCS (Galileo Ground Control Segment). The GCS architecture includes a Spacecraft Constellation Planning Facility (SCPF) to perform all satellite operations planning. This GCS specific short-term planning function is coordinated with, and is subordinated to, the overall mission planning function within the Ground Mission Segment (GMS). In addition to planning the timeline of operational activities for the entire constellation and for the GCS itself, the SCPF is also responsible for the scheduling of satellite-ground contacts.

This document presents the SCPF's Contact Scheduler's process, designed in [2].

N.T. Nguyen et al. (Eds.): IEA/AIE 2008, LNAI 5027, pp. 446–455, 2008.

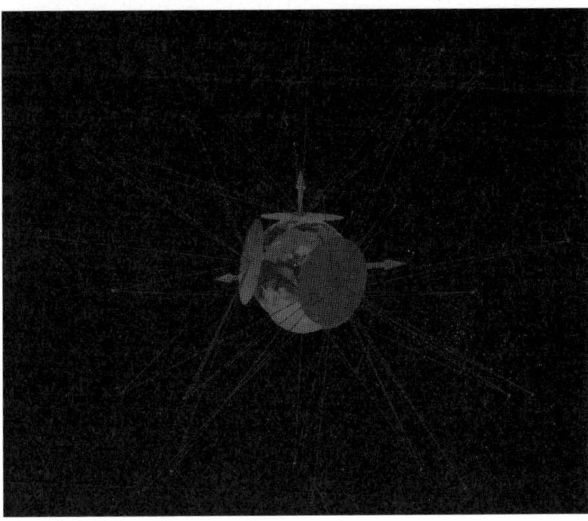

Fig. 1. Snapshot of the Galileo System's configuration. Each arrow represents the location of a ground station and the circles show its communication span. A line connects a spacecraft with a station if they are within radiometric range.

2   The Contact Scheduling Problem

The Galileo System will be implemented in two phases: In-orbit Validation (IOV) and Full Operational Contact (FOC). In IOV four spacecrafts will be distributed in two orbits and will be operated by two ground stations. The nominal Galileo Constellation in the FOC phase comprises 30 spacecraft in a Walker 27/3/1[1] configuration, plus 3 in-orbit spares. To operate the FOC constellation 5 Ground Stations were previously identified.

During the FOC phase, individual satellites will eventually fail and be replaced by the in-orbit spare. In order to re-instate in-orbit redundancy, this will be followed by launch of 2 additional satellites into the affected orbital plane. In addition the deployment of the FOC constellation will take place over a relatively short period of time and most satellites will reach end-of-life at the same time. In both situations the constellation may reach 40 spacecrafts.

The Contact Scheduling Process should therefore be configurable to support considerably more than the nominal 30 satellites, although performance requirements demanded validation of the CSH against the nominal 30 satellite scenario.

Spacecrafts are in circular orbits and a station can't always communicate with a particular spacecraft. The station needs to have radiometric *visibility* with a spacecraft in order to communicate. Additionally a ground-station can only contact one spacecraft at a time and vice-versa.

---

[1] Notation for labelling satellite orbits from J.G Walker. The pattern is fully specified by giving the inclination and the three parameters – t / p / f (where t = total number of satellites, p = no of planes, and f = relative spacing between satellites in adjacent planes). For the Galileo constellation there are 27 active satellites in 3 planes. Note that for Galileo the required inclination is 56 deg.

Under certain circumstances contacts may not occur because there is a spacecraft *event* that prevents contacts (eclipse, blinding, etc.). If a visibility intercepts an event between the same spacecraft and station it needs to be split/trimmed.

Spacecraft Operations may be classified as:

- Routine Operations
- Special Operations
- Contingency Operations

Routine operations will be performed either via the spacecraft's on-board command queue or during a *routine contact* of configurable duration (30 – 90 minutes) once per orbit period (14.5 hrs). Routine contacts are used to periodically download telemetry data and must be scheduled within a single visibility window: no hand-over between stations is permitted. For each routine contact a *backup contact* may be scheduled. This will increase the system's tolerance to failure and shall be a configurable behaviour. Usually backup contacts perform the exact tasks of the corresponding routine and are scheduled to occur within a different ground station.

Special operations include commissioning, planned anomaly investigation, manoeuvres and on-board software loads. In previous phases of Galileo definition, it has been assumed that a maximum of 4 spacecraft are expected to be in special operations simultaneously. Special operations must be performed under operator control and this may require the scheduling of a *special contact*. Special contacts may be exclusive or non-exclusive. To allow an optimized usage of resources the system supports the interception of two non-exclusive contacts between the same spacecraft and ground-station. This feature is called *aggregation* and may be enabled or disabled. Exclusive contacts can't aggregate with other contacts and routine contacts are always non-exclusive.

Backup contacts are triggered if a routine contact could not occur. This situation happens mainly when a ground station fails. It is highly improbable that two ground stations fail at the same time. For this reason it may be desirable to aggregate backup contacts of different spacecrafts if the corresponding routines are planned to occur in different stations. This feature is called *backup-backup aggregation* and this option can also enabled or disable.

Contingency operations are, by definition, un-planned. The intention is that there should be sufficient un-allocated visibility within the contact schedule to allow the operations team to activate an ad-hoc contact using this spare resource within the schedule to perform first line anomaly investigation. Any such ad-hoc contacts are not placed by the Contact Scheduler Process but handled entirely within the SCCF or by the SCPF operator by manually inserting contingency contacts where there is spare resource. Subsequent actions would then be incorporated as special contacts either at the next planning cycle or through emergency re-planning.

The essence of the Galileo's contact scheduling problem is to generate a contact schedule that accommodates all routine, backup and special contact requirements for 30+ satellites using 5 globally distributed ground stations, taking into account station availability, spacecraft visibilities and events.

For the nominal FOC constellation this approximates to 50 routine contacts per day. Up to 4 spacecraft may be in special operations at any one time, for which special contacts may also require scheduling.

It is noted that unlike low earth orbiting missions, for which "passes" are typically short (10 minutes), the visibility window of a Galileo satellite over a given ground station may be as long as 18 hours. Contacts will therefore only use part of a visibility – the problem is to ensure that all spacecraft are visited within a single 14.5 hr orbit period.

The Mission Management (MM) [3] Study was carried out by SciSys during 2001-2 under ESA's ARTES-IV programme [4]. Its objective was to develop an integrated suite of tools supporting off-line mission planning and automated ground-based schedule execution for the management of mission operations for spacecraft fleets and constellations. It was primarily concerned with operations that were relatively unconstrained (e.g. for communications or navigation missions). The Galileo constellation was used as a case study.

Of specific interest in the current context is that the Mission Management tool-set provides support for the generation of contact plans for constellations of Medium Earth Orbit (MEO^2) satellites, where there are multiple satellites and ground-stations. This includes both the generation of predicted visibilities from satellite orbit vectors, and the scheduling of available ground station resources to match contact requirements.

A prototype Contact Scheduler was developed during the MM study. This software was a constraint solver algorithm [5] based on the OPL Studio product from ILOG [0]. It demonstrated that as the number of spacecraft to be scheduled increases, there is a non-linear and significant increase in the time taken to reach a first solution. Hence, a solution can be produced for 3 or 4 spacecraft within a few seconds but 27 spacecraft can take up to 30 minutes.

The study showed that Galileo contact planning is not highly constrained, that a constraint-solver solution was unnecessarily complex and slow compared to the performance requirements for the SCPF contact scheduler. This led to the conclusion that, having characterized the scheduling problem, it would be possible to specify and build a specific solution to support the Contact Scheduler, rather than relying on generic constraint-based frameworks provided by third party commercial off-the-shelf (COTS) products. This engineered component for the Galileo ground-segment could use a simpler, deterministic^3 process to generate the contact plan. The planning constraints can then be used to validate the contact plan. This approach should be simpler to develop and offer much faster planning times than a constraint-solver solution.

3   The Galileo's Contact Scheduling Process

The Contact Scheduling Process' objective is the generation of a contact plan that satisfies all routine and special contact requirements for the next planning period.

---

^{2} Medium Earth Orbit (MEO), sometimes called Intermediate Circular Orbit (ICO), is the region of space around the Earth above low Earth orbit (2,000 kilometres (1,243 mi)) and below geostationary orbit (35,786 kilometres (22,236 mi)) – in Wikipedia.

^{3} Constraint-based algorithms are deterministic; however, because they are a class of AI sort-and-search algorithm, one cannot follow its processing path from run-to-run; they are, from a verification point-of-view, non-deterministic.

Typically the planning period will be configurable, but of the order of 7 days, and updated on a daily planning cycle.

From the results drawn from the MM Study it was concluded that the SCPF's Contact Scheduling Process should be under the AI classification of an informed, non-optimal and non-complete search algorithm. The process is informed because it uses several domain specific heuristics in the search of a solution and is non-optimal because it does not guarantee that a best solution is found. The process is also non-complete because it doesn't guarantee that a solution is provided, even if there is one. It is assumed that if the CSH can not find a solution then the problem is strongly constrained and something must be wrong with the provided inputs.

This approach was able to grant valid contact plans for a weak constrained problem and respect the demanding performance requirements of the Galileo's planning activities.

3.1 Process Inputs (Specification of the Search Problem)

The Contact Scheduling Process receives planning requirements and constraints from other elements of the Galileo's Ground Segment. These inputs are then processed and a valid contact plan is generated by the process. The inputs are as follows:

- Station Availability [or non-availability]. This is used to mark stations that are not available due to planned maintenance or other operational reasons. This means that during the non-available period a given station will not be able to communicate with any spacecraft.
- Satellite Visibilities. The radiometric visibilities between each spacecraft and ground-station.
- Spacecraft/Station Events data is provided as orbit events. This is used to inform that during a given time period the communication between a particular spacecraft and a specific station can not be established. Events summarize information about eclipses, blinding, etc.
- Special Contact Requirements. Provide planning requests for critical operations.
- The Previous Contact Plan is read to retrieve the last planned contact for each spacecraft at the start of the period to be scheduled.
- Time-window. The CSH provides a plan for the given Time-Window (first and last day of the contact plan).

3.2 Process Outline

The CSH is not an exhaustive search algorithm[4] - it performs a simple depth search without backtracking. It uses a set of heuristics to guide the process through the search space. The most relevant heuristic is the sequential execution of the process steps. The contact requirements are sequentially satisfied according to their contact type. This can be observed in the following picture:

---

[4] Exhaustive search algorithms guarantee that if there is a solution, it will be found (giving enough time).

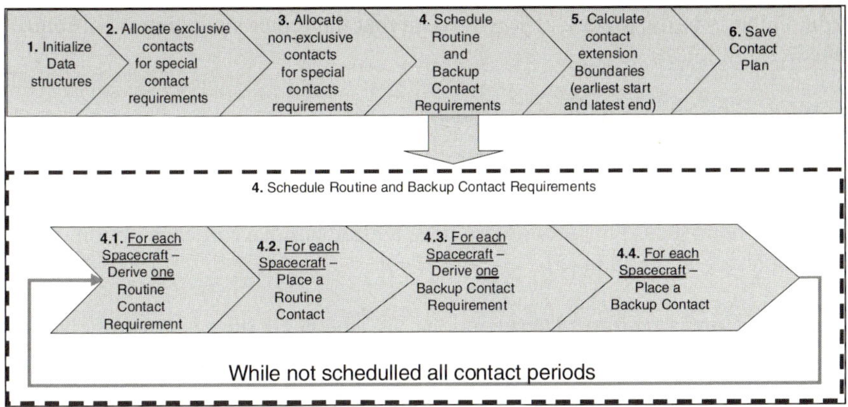

Fig. 2. Contact Scheduler Process outline

The process first loads the inputs and builds its internal data structures (1). It then satisfies the Exclusive Contact Requirements (2) because, from the operations perspective, these are the contacts with most impact. Hereafter non-exclusive Special Contacts are scheduled (3). Because these are non-exclusive aggregation of contacts for the same spacecraft occurs if allowed by the configuration options. After that the process interactively satisfies routine and backup contact requirements (4). In (4.2) and (4.4) the process sorts the requirements by the number of solutions (i.e. compatible spacecraft visibilities) that exist in the search space. This forces the most constrained requirements to be satisfied first. In step (5) the limit for the extension of the scheduled contact is calculated. This information is used by the operator to make adjustments in the final contact plan. Finally (6) the process saves the resulting contact plan in an XML format.

If a contact is impossible to schedule, mostly because the problem is too constrained, the CSH will report it. This will allow the operator to manually find a solution or lower the constraints on the contact requirements. Unscheduled Special or Backup Contact Requirements will not abort the CSH process, since these types of contacts do not have an impact on other Contact Requirements. However a Routine Contact Requirement for a given spacecraft is always dependent on the previous Routine Contact Requirement of the same spacecraft, in order to guarantee some periodicity among routine contacts for each spacecraft. For this reason if a Routine Contact Requirement can not be satisfied the CSH will stop the scheduling process and report the problem.

An unscheduled routine contact can abort the execution of the process without a valid solution. This is a critical issue because without backtracking the algorithm can abort in abnormally constrained scenarios. For this reason the scheduling heuristic was enhanced with *repair strategies*. The repair strategies are used to relax the constraints of a contact that would otherwise be impossible to schedule. Three repair strategies are supported for unscheduled routine contacts:

1 Schedule the contact in a wider time frame.
2 Move a conflicting contact.
3 Reduce the duration of the contact to the minimum allowed.

During the tests of the process it was verified that the repair strategies are infrequently applied.

3.3 Process Configuration

Additional configuration options were introduced into the Contact Scheduling Process. These options either impose new constraints or provide weights to the Contact Scheduler's heuristics. This section provides a brief summary of each option. Detailed information can be found in [2].

Spacecraft Configuration. These options are specified on a spacecraft basis and have impact only in the contacts scheduled for that spacecraft.

- Period. This option designates the frequency of routine and backup contacts.
- Routine Duration. The Routine Duration, like the term states, identifies the duration of the routine contact.
- Minimum Routine Duration. This option represents the shortest duration that a routine contact can have. This parameter is used only when all repair strategies to schedule a routine contact were applied to and didn't result in a solution.
- Backup Duration. The duration of the spacecrafts' backup contacts.
- Backup Offset. States the amount of time needed to detect that a routine contact has failed and perform the necessary operations to trigger the respective backup.
- Maximum Backup Offset. While the Backup Offset designates the lower bound limit for the start of a backup contact, this option represents how late a backup contact can start.
- Tolerance. Used to specify the amount of time that the routine contact may deviate from the preferred start time (as determined by the configured Period), but it is only used before routine repair techniques are applied.
- Max Interval. This is the maximum time interval allowed for the scheduling of a routine contact. It is only used when it is not possible to schedule a routine near the expected start time.

Station Configuration. Ground Stations have only one configuration property: station preference. This weighting is used to schedule more contacts in stations with better communication channels or lower operational costs.

Process Configuration. These configuration options have an impact in the overall CSH behaviour.

- Slot Size. The CSH internally divides time into slots. This configuration has impact in both the performance of the process and the quality of the contact plan.
- Station Setup Time. The time required by a station to internally setup for a contact.
- Special Contact Aggregation. This flag indicates if aggregation is to be performed and its priority.
- Backup Contact Aggregation. Same option but for backup contacts.
- Backup Contact Scheduling. Enable or disable the scheduling of backup contacts.

- Station Exclusion for Backup Contacts. It may be desirable to disallow the scheduling of a backup contact in the same station of the corresponding routine.
- Aggregation Coefficient. Weighting of the priority of contact aggregation.
- Elevation Coefficient. Weighting for the importance of elevation quality in the resulting contact plan.
- Periodicity Coefficient. Routine Contacts for period n+1 are expected to start near n+P, where P is the periodicity of each spacecraft. This coefficient specifies the impact that this property will have during the selection of a time frame for the scheduling of Routine Contacts.
- Size of Visibility Coefficient. It may be preferable to have most contacts within the same spacecraft visibility and leave other visibilities intact for large and rare contingency operations. Or it may be preferable to have small time gaps within the contact plan for small and regular contingency operations. This weighting refers to the relevance that the size of the visibility has for contact scheduling.
- Station Coefficient. Station preference is used to identify the preferred stations. This weighting refers to the importance that station preferences shall have when selecting a possible contact.

These configuration options are expected to affect both the performance and the ability of the CSH to generate a contact plan. Validation activities were conducted to identify the impact of each one. The following section describes how the CSH was implemented and validated and states the results of validation activities.

4 The Contact Scheduler's Performance

The Mission Management Study showed that a complete and optimal scheduling algorithm for the Galileo problem takes near 30 minutes to provide a solution. This performance is not acceptable because it is required [10] that the CSH must be able to produce a contact plan for a 7 days period in less than 7 minutes.

The alternative proposed consisted in a non-complete scheduling process and an early stage validation to assess the performance and ability of the CSH in the production of valid contact plans. Without this verification the risk of the software being unable to generate a useful contact plan in a responsive manner was high. For this reason, a prototype of the Contact Scheduler was implemented in two stages: the first to validate the performance and correctness of the process and the second to evaluate the impact of each configuration option. In each stage a Validation Report was produced to formally evaluate the conclusions of the corresponding validation phase.

The first development stage implemented only the features that strongly constrain the contact scheduling process. For example, aggregation and slot scoring were not implemented because they are mostly used to ease the contact scheduling process. Validation was performed against a pessimistic scenario, with a considerable number of spacecraft events and station unavailabilities. It was considered that if this configuration was able to produce a valid contact plan, then the Contact Scheduling Process is valid because the other possible configurations will be less constrained and more likely to succeed. The first version of the Validation Report [8] concluded that the CSH was able to successfully generate a Contact Plan, for 7 days, in a highly constrained scenario, in less than 5 seconds.

The second version of the CSH prototype implemented the full scheduling process and the corresponding Validation Report [9] provides detailed information about the impact that each configuration option has in the scheduling process. The report's conclusions and recommendations of the validation phase are separated in two topics: operational software and operational practice.

The operational software topic groups recommendations that should be considered for the development of the operational version of the CSH. For example, due to the excellent performance of the scheduling process, it is recommended that the slot size should have a fixed value of 1 minute, a value lower than the 5 minutes required.

The recommendations stated as operational practice focus on configuration values that shall be considered by the operator in the effective version of the Contact Scheduler. For example, to deal with situations where one station is preferred for planned contact scheduling, its preference shall be set to 1. But for a scenario where one station is preferred only for contingency operations, its preference shall be to 0 and the remaining stations to 1. For any of these two options the station preference weighting shall be 1.

It was also observed in the second validation phase that the configuration options have minimal impact on the performance of the CSH. The execution time of the process was never above 7 seconds.

5 Conclusions

The Galileo constellation will consist in 27 operational spacecrafts and 3 spares. The constellation will be managed by 5 ground stations in different geographic locations. Maintenance and corrective spacecraft contacts will be performed and need to be planned in advance.

The contact planning procedures include three activities: the processing of planning requests, the generation of a contact plan and the assignment of tasks to scheduled contact. Within the SCPF the Contact Scheduler (CSH) is the component responsible for the generation of a contact plan after the planning requests.

The CSH implements a contact scheduling process designed with the experience acquired from the Mission Management Study [3]. This study concluded that an optimal and complete scheduling process would not respect the performance requirements of the SCPF. In addition, the scheduling of contacts for the Galileo constellation system is not a strongly constrained problem.

With the interpretation of the SCPF requirements it was possible to identify a set of heuristics to design a non-optimal non-complete Contact Scheduling Process. The process exposes several configuration options to tweak its behaviour and produce a better contact plan.

The CSH was validated in two different stages. The first validation focused in the performance of the process and the ability to produce (or not) a valid contact plan for a strongly constrained scenario. The process was able to produce a contact plan in less than 5 seconds, while the SCPF's performance requirements imposed a limit of 7 minutes. The second validation phase was performed against 28 scenarios focused on the impact of each configuration option. Several operational software and practice recommendations were provided and the adoption of each one for the operational version of the CSH is currently under discussion.

This experience shows that the design of non-optimal non-complete depth-search algorithm for the Galileo scheduling problem was a success.

References

1. European Commission, European Space Agency: High Level Mission Definition, version 3.0 (2002)
   http://ec.europa.eu/dgs/energy_transport/galileo/doc/galileo_hld_v3_23_09_02.pdf
2. Moreira, F., Hall, S., Franco, T.: GAL-TN-SSL-SCPF-I-000001, Contact Scheduling Process Specification, Issue 1.1. Galileo Detail Design Document (2006)
3. SciSys: S7350/REP/001, Mission Management Team, ARTES IV: Mission Management Study Final Report (2003)
4. ESA ARTES IV Programme (2007),
   http://telecom.esa.int/telecom/www/object/index.cfm?fobjectid=5363
5. Russell, S., Norvig, P.: Artificial Intelligence: A Modern Approach, ch. 5, 2nd edn. Prentice Hall, Englewood Cliffs (2003)
6. ILOG OPL-CPLEX Development System, http://www.ilog.com/products/oplstudio/
7. Gurari, E.: Backtracking algorithms CIS 680: DATA STRUCTURES: ch. 19: Backtracking Algorithms (1999)
8. Franco, T.: GAL-RPT-CSW-SCPF-R/0002 Contact Scheduler Prototype Development Report – Issue 1.1, Galileo Validation Report, 04-04 (2007)
9. Franco, T.: GAL-RPT-CSW-SCPF-R/0002 Contact Scheduler Prototype Development Report – Issue 2.0, Galileo Validation Report, 04-10 (2007)
10. EADS Astrium. GAL-REQ-ASTU-SCPF-R/0121 GCS Element Requirements Document for the Spacecraft Constellation Facility – Issue 3.0, Galileo Requirements Document (2007)

Novel Extension of $k-TSP$ Algorithm for Microarray Classification

Marcin Czajkowski and Marek Kretowski

Faculty of Computer Science, Białystok Technical University
Wiejska 45a, 15-351 Białystok, Poland
{mczajk,mkret}@wi.pb.edu.pl

Abstract. This paper presents a new method, referred as $Weight\ k-TSP$, which generates simple and accurate decision rules that can be widely used for classifying gene expression data. The proposed method extends previous approaches: TSP and $k-TSP$ algorithms by considering weight pairwise mRNA comparisons and percentage changes of gene expressions in different classes. Both rankings have been modified as well as decision rules, however the concept of "relative expression reversals" is retained. New solutions to match analyzed datasets more accurately were also included. Experimental validation was performed on several human microarray datasets and obtained results are promising.

1 Introduction

DNA chips provide tens of thousands of genes expression levels in single experiment [6,11]. Recently, microarray technology have been widely used to assist diagnosis and to discriminate cancer samples from normal ones [1,2,4]. Through analysis of gene expressions, some marker genes are found which later on can be used to build medical decision-support systems. However, finding a meaningful and robust classification rule is a real challenge, since in different studies of the same cancer, diverse genes consider to be marked [14]. The analysis of DNA microarrays poses also a large number of statistical problems, in which we can specify two main issues - dimensionality and redundancy.

DNA microarrays produce massive quantities of information which is difficult for analysis and interpretation. Unfortunately, the number of samples (denoted by N) comparing to number of features (genes, P) remains quite small and usually not exceeded one or two hundreds - it is the well known *"small N, large P problem"* [15,16]. Considering some dimensionality reduction (i.e. feature selection) seems to be reasonable, especially when it influences the model complexity [9]. Among other solutions, increasing sample size and joining datasets could be mentioned, nevertheless there are some difficulties in consistency of resulting data [21].

Analyzing many attributes can easily cause a classifier to overfit training data [5]. Hopefully, most of genes are known to be irrelevant for an accurate classification. That is why the gene selection prior the classification not only simplifies

N.T. Nguyen et al. (Eds.): IEA/AIE 2008, LNAI 5027, pp. 456–465, 2008.

calculations and model complexity, but also removes noise and decreases the computation time which is also relevant. Furthermore, experiments have shown that in most of cases the gene selection improves accuracy of the following classification [12].

Many standard classification approaches including statistical learning and pattern recognition methods are applied to microarray data [17]. However, the specificity of gene expression data causes rising new algorithms or extensions of the existing methods. Recently, many methods based on Support Vector Machines (SVM) [19], have been proposed [13,22]. Neural networks [3] and decision trees [8] are also commonly applied in microarray classification. Unfortunately, most of these methods generate very complex diagnostic rules based on many expression values. From a medical point of view they are very difficult to understand and interpret.

In this paper, we propose an extension of $k - TSP$ [18] (k-Top Scoring Pairs), which originates from the TSP algorithm [7]. The presented solution (denoted as $Weight\ k - TSP$) is focused on relative gene expression values and pairwise comparisons between two genes expression levels. By involving only few genes and generating simple decision rules, classification results can be easily analyzed and interpreted. In general, TSP and $k - TSP$ accuracy is relatively high, although these original algorithms, in contrast to $Weight\ k - TSP$, can not be tuned to reflect the specificity of different cancer datasets. It can be expected that this way the classification precision can be improved. The proposed method extends original solutions by considering weight pairwise mRNA comparisons and percentage changes of gene expressions in different classes. Both ranking have been modified as well as decision rules, however the concept of "relative expression reversals" have still retained.

The rest of the paper is organized as follows. In the next section both TSP and $k - TSP$ algorithms are briefly recalled and the $Weight\ k - TSP$ method is presented. In section 3 the proposed approach is experimentally validated on real microarray datasets. The paper is concluded in the last section and possible future works are presented.

2   A Family of TSP Algorithms

All variants from the family of the TSP methods are applied according to the classical supervised learning framework. In the first step based on the training dataset created from the gene expression profiles with the verified diagnosis, the top scoring pairs are generated. This process is illustrated in Fig. 1. In the next step, the obtained classifier can be applied to a new microarray sample with unknown decision. Only selected genes are analyzed and TSP−based prediction is made (Fig. 2).

2.1   TSP

Top Scoring Pairs (TSP) method was presented by Donald Geman [7] and is based on pairwise comparisons of gene expression values. Despite its simplicity

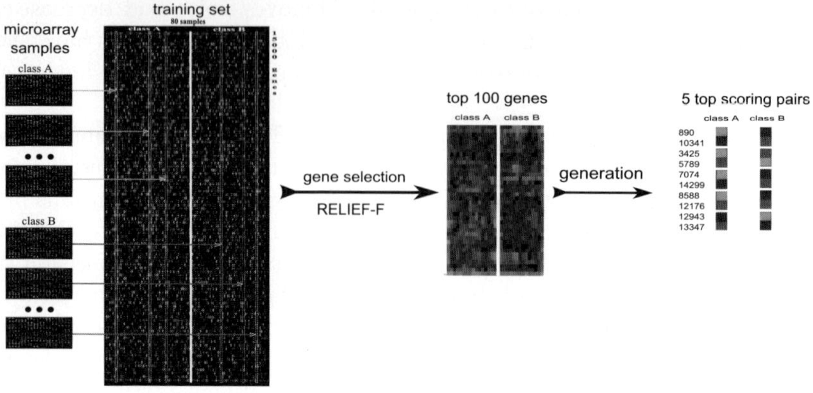

Fig. 1. Building TSP-based decision rules on the training dataset

comparing to other methods, classification rates for TSP are comparable or even exceed other classifiers [7]. Discrimination between two classes depends on finding matching pairs of genes that achieve the highest ranking value called "score".

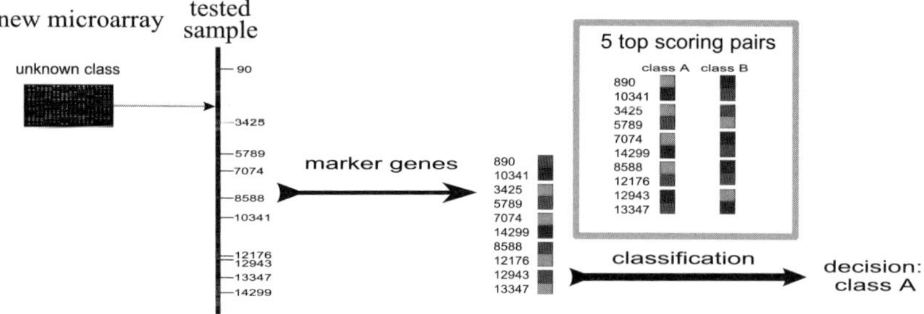

Fig. 2. Testing a new sample with the TSP classifier based on the selected genes

Considering the object containing P genes and N samples participating in the training microarray dataset, a $P \times N$ matrix X can be developed:

$$X = \begin{pmatrix} x_{11} & x_{12} & \dots & x_{1N} \\ x_{21} & x_{22} & \dots & x_{2N} \\ \vdots & \vdots & \ddots & \vdots \\ x_{P1} & x_{P2} & \dots & x_{PN} \end{pmatrix},$$

in which the expression value of i-th gene from the n-th sample is denoted by x_{ij}. Each row represents observations of a particular gene over N training samples, and each column represents a gene expression profile composed from P genes. Each profile has a true class label denoted $C_m \in C = \{C_1, \dots, C_M\}$. For the simplicity of calculations it is assumed that there are only two classes ($M = 2$) and profiles with indices from 1 to N_1 ($N_1 < N$) belong to the first class (C_1) and profiles from range $\langle N_1 + 1, N \rangle$ to the second class (C_2).

TSP method focuses on gene pair matching (i, j) ($i, j \in \{1, \ldots, P\}, i \neq j$) for which there is the highest difference in the probability of an event $x_{in} < x_{jn}$ ($n = 1, 2, \ldots, N$) between class C_1 and C_2. For each pair of genes (i, j) two probabilities are calculated $p_{ij}(C_1)$ and $p_{ij}(C_2)$:

$$p_{ij}(C_1) = \frac{1}{|C_1|} \sum_{n=1}^{N_1} I(x_{in} < x_{jn}) \,, \tag{1}$$

$$p_{ij}(C_2) = \frac{1}{|C_2|} \sum_{n=N_1+1}^{N} I(x_{in} < x_{jn}) \,, \tag{2}$$

where $|C_m|$ denotes a number of profiles from class C_m and $I(x_{in} < x_{jn})$ is the indicator function defined as:

$$I(x_{in} < x_{jn}) = \begin{cases} 1, & \text{if } x_{in} < x_{jn} \\ 0, & \text{if } x_{in} \geq x_{jn} \end{cases} . \tag{3}$$

TSP is a rank-based method, so for each pair of genes (i, j) the "score" denoted Δ_{ij} is calculated:

$$\Delta_{ij} = |p_{ij}(C_1) - p_{ij}(C_2)| . \tag{4}$$

In the next step of the algorithm pairs with the highest score are chosen. There should be only one top pair in the TSP method, however it is possible that multiple gene pairs achieve the same top score. A secondary ranking based on the rank differences in each class and sample is used to eliminate draws.

For each top-scoring gene pair (i, j) the "average rank difference" in both C_1 and C_2 are computed and defined as:

$$\gamma_{ij}(C_1) = \frac{\sum_{n=1}^{N_1}(x_{in} - x_{jn})}{|C_1|} \,, \tag{5}$$

$$\gamma_{ij}(C_2) = \frac{\sum_{n=N_1+1}^{N}(x_{in} - x_{jn})}{|C_2|} . \tag{6}$$

Value of this second rank for each pair of genes (i, j) is defined as:

$$\tau_{ij} = |\gamma_{ij}(C_1) - \gamma_{ij}(C_2)| \,, \tag{7}$$

and the algorithm chooses a pair with the highest score.

The TSP classifier prediction is made by comparing the expression values from two genes (i, j) marked as "top scoring pair" with a test sample (i_{new}, j_{new}). If we observe that $p_{ij}(C_1) \geq p_{ij}(C_2)$ and $x_{inew} < x_{jnew}$, then TSP votes for class C_1, however if $x_{inew} \geq x_{jnew}$ then TSP votes for class C_2. An opposite situation is when $p_{ij}(C_1) < p_{ij}(C_2)$, cause if $x_{inew} < x_{jnew}$ TSP votes for C_1 and if $x_{inew} \geq x_{jnew}$ TSP chooses C_2. In other words, if $p_{ij}(C_1) \geq p_{ij}(C_2)$ then:

$$y_{new} = h_{TSP}(new) = \begin{cases} C_1, & \text{if } x_{inew} < x_{jnew} \\ C_2, & \text{if } x_{inew} \geq x_{jnew} \end{cases}, \tag{8}$$

where h_{TSP} is a prediction result. Opposite situation is when $p_{ij}(C_1) < p_{ij}(C_2)$.

2.2 k-TSP

A $k-TSP$ classifier proposed by Aik Choon Tan [18] is a simple extension of the original TSP algorithm. The main feature that differ those two methods is the number of top scoring pairs included in final prediction. In the TSP method there can be only one pair of genes and in $k-TSP$ classifier the upper bound denoted as k can be set up before the classification. The parameter k is determined by a cross-validation and in any prediction the $k-TSP$ classifier uses no more than k top scoring disjoint gene pairs that have the highest score. Both primary and secondary rankings (equations (4) and (7)) remain unchanged.

The classification decision is made by comparing the expression values for each pair of genes (i_u, j_u) $(u = 1, \ldots, k)$ with a *new* test sample. The $k-TSP$ classifier denoted as h_{k-TSP} based on individual classifiers $h_u(new)$ employs a majority voting to obtain the final prediction of y_{new}, however each vote has the same wage:

$$y_{new} = h_{k-TSP}(new) = argmax \sum_{u=1}^{k} I(h_u(new) = C_i), \tag{9}$$

where $C_i \in C$, and

$$I(h_u(new) = C_i) = \begin{cases} 1, & \text{if } h_u(new) = C_i \\ 0, & \text{otherwise} \end{cases}. \tag{10}$$

Meaning of $h_u(new)$ is the same as in the equation (8).

2.3 Weight k-TSP

In classification $Weight\ k-TSP$ all rankings have been changed, comparing to TSP and $k-TSP$. Therefore, the selection of top scoring pairs, and the prediction is different than in TSP or $k-TSP$ classifier. The main reason that motivates research on extensions of the $k-TSP$ algorithm is its limitation in finding appropriate top scoring pairs. There are two factors that could cause it. First factor that hampers finding appropriate top scoring pairs is connected to the relatively high computational complexity, which for these methods is $\theta(N * P^2)$. Microarray datasets contain huge amounts of data and the feature selection is usually applied before the actual classification. However, $k-TSP$ sensitivity to the feature selection and small size of datasets may effect rank calculations and decrease accuracy. This is linked with the second factor which is a small number of features having similar expression values and being opposite to each other in different classes. Depending on data and preprocessing method, expression values can be very different and genes can have values for example from 0 to 10000.

Let us hypothetically assume that for some tested cancer samples two genes are responsible $G1$ and $G2$. Suppose that in healthy samples from training dataset genes the expression levels are in a range $G1 < 0, 50 >$, $G2 < 6000, 9000 >$ and in cancer sample: $G1 < 1000, 2000 >$, $G2 < 2500, 4000 >$. Method $k-TSP$ and TSP will never mark these genes as "top scoring pair" because among all classes $G1$ is smaller then $G2$. It might choose them with other genes, by making more top pairs, but it will not be so accurate and can cause problems in interpretability. A solution for this type of situations could be comparison of percentage changes of gene expression in pairs among different classes.

Considering that S represents average values quotient genes in each pair from K training samples (K determined by a cross-validation). For each pair of genes (i, j) $(i, j \in \{1, \ldots, P\}, i \neq j)$ single element from S can be described as:

$$S_{ij} = \frac{\sum_{m=1}^{K} x_{im}/x_{jm}}{K} . \tag{11}$$

$Weight\ k-TSP$ is focused on finding pairs of genes (i, j) that have the highest difference in probability of event $\{x_{in}/x_{jn} < S_{ij}\}$ $(n = 1, 2, \ldots, N)$ between class C_1 and C_2. For each pair of genes (i, j) two probabilities are calculated $p_{ij}(C_1)$ and $p_{ij}(C_2)$:

$$p_{ij}(C_1) = \frac{1}{|C_1|} \sum_{n=1}^{N_1} I(x_{in}/x_{jn} < S_{ij}) , \tag{12}$$

$$p_{ij}(C_2) = \frac{1}{|C_2|} \sum_{n=N_1+1}^{N} I(x_{in}/x_{jn} < S_{ij}) , \tag{13}$$

where $I(x_{in}/x_{jn} < S_{ij})$ is the indicator function defined as:

$$I(x_{in}/x_{jn} < S_{ij}) = \begin{cases} 1, & \text{if } x_{in}/x_{jn} < S_{ij} \\ 0, & \text{if } x_{in}/x_{jn} \geq S_{ij} \end{cases} . \tag{14}$$

Similarly to $k-TSP$, $Weigh\ k-TSP$ is a rank-based method, so for each pair of genes (i, j) the calculated score denoted Δ_{ij}, where:

$$\Delta_{i,j} = |p_{ij}(C_1) - p_{ij}(C_2)| . \tag{15}$$

Secondary ranking which used in TSP and $k-TSP$ in case of an equal score has also been modified, since there are exceptions that could discriminate genes with low values of expression. Again, considering the assumption that for some tested cancer two pairs of genes denoted $F1$ and $F2$, having the same primary ranking, are responsible. Suppose in all training dataset samples, genes expression values for these pairs are in range $F1 < 0, 1000 >$, $F2 < 3000, 9000 >$. Pair $F1$ may create more interesting decision rules and improve prediction than $F2$ because genes have changed their expression values from low level to high. In pair denoted $F2$, genes expression levels have stayed in high or very high range among all samples and should not be classified as a top scoring pair. However TSP and $k - TSP$ algorithm would choose $F2$ pair because of its rankings that compares only value differences. Proposed modifications do not discriminate genes with low values of expression and would mark $F1$ as a top scoring pair. To eliminate problem of very small values (near 0) to dividend divisor - average S was added, so all values belong to range $\langle 0, 1 \rangle$:

$$\gamma_{ij}(C_m) = \frac{\sum_{n \in C_m} \frac{x_{in}/x_{jn}}{S_{ij} + x_{in}/x_{jn}}}{|C_m|}, \tag{16}$$

where $|C_m|$ denote number of profiles in C_m. Value of this second rank for each par of genes (i, j) is defined as:

$$\tau_{ij} = |\gamma_{ij}(C_1) - \gamma_{ij}(C_2)|. \tag{17}$$

Similarly to previous solution the algorithm chooses pair with the largest score.

Final prediction is similar to presented earlier in TSP and $k - TSP$ algorithm and is based on voting. However unweighed majority voting was extended by adding weight and mixed decision rules, which for some datasets improved accuracy. The equations (9) and (10) for unweighed majority voting are still valid in $Weight\ k - TSP$, however there were changes in $h_u(new)$. If $p_{ij}(C_1) \geq p_{ij}(C_2)$ then:

$$h_u(new) = \begin{cases} C_1, & \text{if } x_{inew}/x_{jnew} < S_{ij} \\ C_2, & \text{if } x_{inew}/x_{jnew} \geq S_{ij} \end{cases}, \tag{18}$$

where x_{inew} denote an expression level of i-th gene from sample named new. Opposite situation is when $p_{ij}(C_1) < p_{ij}(C_2)$. In wage voting - equation (9) also has changed. If $p_{ij}(C_1) > p_{ij}(C_2)$ then:

$$I_{wg}(h_u(new) = C_i) = \begin{cases} \frac{S_{ij}}{S_{ij} + x_{inew}/x_{jnew}}, & \text{if } h_u(new) = C_i \\ 0, & \text{otherwise} \end{cases}. \tag{19}$$

If $p_{ij}(C_1) \leq p_{ij}(C_2)$, wage changes:

$$I_{wg}(h_u(new) = C_i) = \begin{cases} \frac{x_{inew}/x_{jnew}}{S_{ij} + x_{inew}/x_{jnew}}, & \text{if } h_u(new) = C_i \\ 0, & \text{otherwise} \end{cases}. \tag{20}$$

3   Experimental Results

3.1   Setup

Performance of $Weight\ k - TSP$ classifier was investigated on public available microarray datasets described in Table 1. All datasets come from Kent Ridge

Table 1. Binary class gene expression datasets

Datasets	Genes	Class 1	Class 2
Leukemia	7129	47(all)	25(aml)
Breast Cancer	24481	51(n)	46(r)
CNS	7129	39(f)	21(s)
Colon Tumor	2000	22(n)	40(t)
Prostate Cancer	12600	59(n)	77(t)
Lung Cancer	12533	31(mpm)	150(adca)
Lymphoma	4026	23(a)	24(g)

Table 2. Classifiers accuracy results tested with WEKA software

Classifiers	Datasets							Average
	ALL-AML	BC	CNS	CT	PC	LC	DLBCL	
Naive Bayes	97.05	78.94	76.66	74.19	23.52	99.32	97.87	78,22
RBF Network	97.05	78.94	75.00	85.48	79.41	98.65	95.74	**87,18**
SMO	94.11	68.42	81.66	88.70	26.47	99.32	97.87	79,5
AdaBoostMI	91.17	63.15	73.33	79.03	44.11	81.87	91.48	74,87
Bagging	94.11	63.15	76.66	82.25	41.17	95.97	85.10	76,91
J48	91.17	47.36	75.00	79.03	29.41	77.18	80.85	68,57
Random Forest	73.52	89.47	76.66	85.48	73.52	96.64	97.87	84,73
JRip	91.17	52.63	70.00	72.58	29.41	97.98	78.72	70,35

Bio-medical Dataset Repository and are related to studies of human cancer, including: leukemia, breast cancer, central nervous system, colon tumor, prostate cancer, lung cancer and lymphoma. Comparison $Weight\ k - TSP$ with several popular classifiers like: SMO, NB, RBF Network, ADA, Bagging, J48, Random Forest and JRip was performed on WEKA [20] - data mining software. $Weight$ $k - TSP$ and TSP-family classifiers were implemented and tested on the MLP software. Before classification, gene selection Relief-F [10] with neighbours k=10 and sample size 100 was applied.

Typical normalization was also performed: $a'_i = \frac{(a_i - a_{i_{min}})}{(a_{i_{max}} - a_{i_{min}})}$, where a_i is an expression level of i-th gene, $a_{i_{max}}$ is maximal and $a_{i_{min}}$ is a minimal value in dataset. For all classifiers default parameters, proposed in WEKA and recommend in [18]; typically 10 runs and 10 folds in crossvalidation were used.

3.2 Outcome

Results of experiments are shown in Table 1 and Table 2. Table 2 summarizes the results for 8 different classifiers on 7 binary classification problems, tested on WEKA software. Based on the results: the RBF Network (87,18) and Random Forest (84,73) yield the best accuracy averaged over the 7 problems and SVM (79,50) outperformed other methods in 4 of the 7 cases. However in terms of

Table 3. Classifiers accuracy results tested with MLP software

Classifiers	ALL-AML	BC	CNS	CT	PC	LC	DLBCL	Average
TSP	85,29	73,68	57,49	79,59	76,47	97,98	86,30	79,54
std. dev.	1,49	0,00	4,17	2,13	0,00	0,00	2,86	1,69
k-TSP	92,05	78,94	**59,33**	84,66	82,35	98,25	94,35	84,28
std. dev.	2,79	0,00	5,16	2,86	0,00	0,56	2,13	1,76
Weight TSP	91,17	73,68	58,33	84,73	82,35	84,63	86,40	81,68
std. dev.	0,00	0,00	5,77	2,54	0,00	1,49	2,78	1,64
Weight k-TSP	**93,52**	**84,21**	58,50	**87,61**	**89,11**	**98,38**	**97,95**	**87,04**
std. dev.	1,86	1,49	2,65	1,72	3,41	0,56	1,34	1,83

efficiency and simplicity $Weight\ k - TSP$ and TSP-family methods are superior. Table 3 summarizes the results for TSP-family classifiers on the 7 binary classification problems - implemented and tested on MLP software.

To appropriately compare $Weight\ k - TSP$ to TSP method, $Weight\ TSP$ was implemented. It can be observed that $Weight\ TSP$ and $Weight\ k - TSP$ accuracy is slightly increased in almost every tested database and in terms of efficiency and simplicity it is similar to TSP-family classifiers.

4   Conclusion and Future Works

This paper presents extension of TSP and $k - TSP$ classifier called $Weight\ k - TSP$. Main concept of this method is weight pairwise mRNA comparisons and percentage changes in gene expression in different classes. By concentrating in $Weight\ k - TSP$ on a relative gene expression changes between tested samples and by building novel prediction rules - the increase of the average classification accuracy was observed. In terms of efficiency and simplicity $Weight\ k - TSP$ is similar to TSP-family methods however it is superior to other classifiers like SVM and Naive Bayes.

TSP-family classifiers and several different machine learning methods was compared on 7 gene expression datasets involving human cancers. From results, $Weight\ k - TSP$ perform approximately the same as the RBF Network classifier and it was more accuracy then other methods on these data, however $Weight\ k - TSP$ provides simple decision rules usually involving few genes which have clear biological connections to adequate cancer types.

Furthermore, many possible improvement for $Weight\ k - TSP$ still exist. One direction of current research is to use discrete data of "present", "absent" or "marginal" gene expression values. Tests for finding marker genes that occurred most often in top pairs are also performed and superficial results are very promising.

Acknowledgments. This work was supported by the grant W/WI/5/05 from Białystok Technical University.

References

1. Alizadeh, A.A.: Distinct types of diffuse large B-cell lymphoma identified by gene expression profiling. Nature 403, 503–511 (2000)
2. Bittner, M., Meltzer, P., Chen, Y.: Molecular classification of cutaneous malignant melanoma by gene expression profiling. Nature 406, 536–540 (2000)
3. Cho, H.S., Kim, T.S., Wee, J.W.: cDNA Microarray Data Based Classification of Cancers Using Neural Networks and Genetic Algorithms. Nanotech 1 (2003)
4. Dhanasekaran, S.M.: Delineation of prognostic biomarkers in prostate cancer. Nature 412, 822–826 (2001)
5. Duda, R.O., Heart, P.E., Stork, D.G.: Pattern Classification, 2nd edn. J. Wiley, New York (2001)
6. Duggan, D.J., Bittner, M., Chen, Y., Meltzer, P., Trent, J.M.: Expression profiling using cDNA microarrays. Nature Genetics Supplement 21, 10–14 (1999)
7. Geman, D., d'Avignon, C., Naiman, D.Q., Winslow, R.L.: Classifying Gene Expression Profiles from Pairwise mRNA Comparisons. Statistical Applications in Genetics and Molecular Biology 3(1), 19 (2007)
8. Grześ, M., Krętowski, M.: Decision Tree Approach to Microarray Data Analysis. Biocybernetics and Biomedical Engineering 27(3), 29–42 (2007)
9. Hastie, T., Tibshirani, R., Friedman, J.H.: The Elements of Statistical Learning. Springer, Heidelberg (2001)
10. Kononenko, I.: Estimating Attributes: Analysis and Extensions of RELIEF. In: European Conference on Machine Learning, pp. 171–182 (1994)
11. Lipschutz, R.J., Fodor, S.P.A., Gingeras, T.R., Lockhart, D.J.: High density synthetic oligonucleotide arrays. Nature Genetics Supplement 21, 20–24 (1999)
12. Lu, Y., Han, J.: Cancer classification using gene expression data. Information Systems 28(4), 243–268 (2003)
13. Mao, Y., Zhou, X., Pi, D., Sun, Y., Wong, S.T.C.: Multiclass Cancer Classification by Using Fuzzy Support Vector Machine and Binary Decision Tree With Gene Selection. J. Biomed. Biotechnol., 160–171 (2005)
14. Nelson, P.S.: Predicting prostate cancer behavior using transcript profiles. Journal of Urology 172, S28–S32 (2004)
15. Sebastiani, P., Gussoni, E., Kohane, I.S., Ramoni, M.F : Statistical challenges in functional genomics. Statistical Science 18(1), 33–70 (2003)
16. Simon, R., Radmacher, M.D., Dobbin, K., McShane, L.M.: Pitfalls in the use of DNA microarray data for diagnostic and prognostic classification. Journal of the National Cancer Institute 95, 14–18 (2003)
17. Speed, T.: Statistical Analysis of Gene Expression Microarray Data. Chapman & Hall/CRC, New York (2003)
18. Tan, A.C., Naiman, D.Q., Xu, L., Winslow, R.L., Geman, D.: Simple decision rules for classifying human cancers from gene expression profiles. Bioinformatics 21, 3896–3904 (2005)
19. Vapnik, V.N.: Statistical Learning Theory. Wiley, New York (1998)
20. Witten, I.H., Frank, E.: Data Mining: Practical machine learning tools and techniques, 2nd edn. Morgan Kaufmann, San Francisco (2005)
21. Tan, X.L., Naiman, A.C., Geman, D.Q., Windslow, D., Robust, R.L.: Prostate cancer marker genes emerge from direct integration of inter-study microarray data. Bioinformatics 21(20), 3905–3911 (2005)
22. Zhang, C., Li, P., Rajendran, A., Deng, Y., Chen, D.: Parallelization of multicategory support vector machines (PMC-SVM) from classifying microarray data. BMC Bioinformatics (2006)

Simultaneous Vehicle and Crew Scheduling for Extra Urban Transports

Benoît Laurent[1,2] and Jin-Kao Hao[2]

[1] Perinfo SA, 41 avenue Jean Jaurès, 67000 Strasbourg, France
blaurent@perinfo.com
[2] LERIA, Université d'Angers, 2 boulevard Lavoisier, 49045 Angers Cedex 01, France
jin-kao.hao@univ-angers.fr

Abstract. We present a *simultaneous* approach to solve the integrated vehicle and crew scheduling problem in an extra urban context. We consider the single depot case with a *heterogeneous* fleet of vehicles. We propose a constraint based model which is subsequently solved by a Greedy Randomized Adaptive Search Procedure. The construction phase of each initial solution relies on constraint programming techniques, while the local search phase exploits a powerful neighborhood exploration mechanism. The computational experiments conducted on real-world instances show the effectiveness and the flexibility of the approach compared with the classical sequential vehicle and crew scheduling.

1 Introduction

Crews and vehicles are the main resources to provide services in transport systems. The way these resources are employed directly impacts the quality of service and the cost of the whole transport system. It is thus primordial to optimize the utilization of these resources in any transportation scheduling systems.

The conventional crew and vehicle scheduling process is the *sequential* approach which determines first the vehicles schedule and then the crews schedule. This separation is mainly due to the complexity of each sub-problem. Indeed, the Multi-Depot Vehicle Scheduling Problem (MDVSP) is known to be NP-hard. The Bus Driver Scheduling Problem (BDSP) is usually modeled as a Set Covering or Set Partitioning Problem, both being NP-hard.

In the early 1980s, Ball et al. criticized this sequential approach [1], but the first real *integrated* solutions, in which vehicles and crews are simultaneously scheduled, were only developed in 1995 [5]. This integrated management of both resources demonstrated its efficiency in [6] where relief locations, i.e. places where a driver can be relieved by a colleague, are spatially distant. Integration is also profitable when a driver is not allowed to change from one vehicle to another.

The most popular approach to tackle the integrated scheduling problem is undoubtedly integer linear programming (ILP). In [5], Freling *et al.* suggest, for the single depot case, an ILP formulation comprising a quasi-assignment structure for the vehicle scheduling, a set partitioning model for the crew scheduling, and a set of binding constraints. The solution approach is an approximated method

N.T. Nguyen et al. (Eds.): IEA/AIE 2008, LNAI 5027, pp. 466–475, 2008.

combining Lagrangian heuristics and column generation. The first exact algorithm is described in [9]. Both aspects, crew and vehicle, are modeled by a set partitioning formulation. However, the branch-and-cut-and-price algorithm proposed can only solve small instances up to 20 trips. Another interesting exact solution for the single depot case is presented by Haase *et al.* in [8] where scenarios up to 150 trips are solved. For larger problems, a heuristic is employed to solve scenarios of 350 trips within 3 hours of CPU time.

Gaffi and Nonato in [6] were the first to address the integrated VCSP in the multiple-depot case. Like Freling and coauthors, they make use of Lagrangian relaxation and column generation. Once again, they confirmed the dominance of the simultaneous scheduling of crews and vehicles over the sequential approach on scenarios of Italian public transit operators. However, they observed that computational time remained a critical issue: it takes more than 24 hours to solve an instance of 257 trips. Recently, in [11], the models and algorithms introduced in [4] were successfully extended to tackle the integrated vehicle and crew scheduling problem with multiple depots.

The simultaneous approach begins to cover the gap between the academic world and the business world. It is now included in commercial packages like Hastus' suite (see [3]) or Microbus 2 (see [2]).

Although efficient and flexible solutions based on metaheuristics were successfully developed to deal with vehicle or driver scheduling separately, to the best of our knowledge, no similar study is reported in the literature for the integrated driver and vehicle scheduling problem.

In this paper, we propose a new heuristic approach for the simultaneous vehicle and crew scheduling problem. In our situation, all vehicles are parked within the same depot. However, the problem is more general than the usual single depot case which imposes a homogeneous fleet of vehicles. Here, the vehicles may belong to different categories. The first contribution of this work is the introduction of a new model relying on the constraint satisfaction and optimization problem. This constraint based model has the main advantage of being intuitive and natural. It also offers much flexibility in terms of solution approaches since various metaheuristics can be developed. For the solution purpose, we implemented a Greedy Randomized Adaptive Search Procedure (GRASP) which constitutes, to our knowledge, the first application of metaheuristics to this problem. Within our GRASP algorithm, constraint programming techniques are used to build initial solutions. Improvements of these solutions are achieved with a local search algorithm which embeds a powerful "ejection chain" neighborhood exploration mechanism. The whole approach is assessed on a set of 7 real-world instances and compared with the conventional sequential methodology, clearly showing the superiority of the simultaneous scheduling approach.

2   Vehicle and Crew Scheduling: Problem Presentation

Given a set of trips within a one-day horizon, a set of drivers, a fleet of vehicles parked at a given depot, a set of workday types, the Vehicle and Crew Scheduling

Problem consists in determining a minimum cost schedule for crews and vehicles, such that generated duties are feasible and mutually compatible.

The trips are characterized by starting and ending locations with corresponding times. Each trip must be served by certain types (categories) of vehicles. Travel times between all pairs of locations are also known. The transfers without passengers between trips, or either coming from or returning to the depot are called deadheads. The other inputs concern the availability of vehicles in each category. Similar bounds exist for the crews. The workday types are defined by labor regulations. As mentioned in the introduction, crews and vehicles are supposed to share the same depot where all duties start and end.

The vehicle part of the problem consists in assigning a vehicle to each trip while satisfying the following constraints:

- **Category constraints.** The vehicle must belong to the required category (type). A hierarchy between types is defined so as to allow upgrades if no vehicle of the required type is available.
- **Feasible sequences constraints.** each vehicle must have enough time between consecutive trips to move from one to the other.

A sequence of compatible trips starting and ending at the depot, thus performed by the same vehicle, defines a vehicle block. Along these blocks, relief opportunities are time-place pairs defining when and where a driver can be relieved by a colleague. A portion of work between two relief points is thus necessarily accomplished by the same crew and defines a task, a piece of work being a sequence of tasks without interruption on a single vehicle. In our case, reliefs take place at the depot. In this context, pieces of work and vehicle blocks coincide.

The tasks from the vehicle scheduling phase are then assigned to crew members to compose crew duties. The following constraints must be satisfied (only a subset is presented here for the purpose of simplicity):

- **Maximum spread time.** For crew members, the duration between the pick-up time of the first trip and the drop-down time of the last one, must be less than or equal to the maximum spread time allowed.
- **Maximum working time.** For crew members, the total working time, corresponding to driving and possibly maintenance tasks, does not exceed the bound specified in each driver's contract.
- **Changeovers.** Depending on the companies, drivers are allowed or not to change from a vehicle to another during their duty.

Like many previously studied crew and vehicle scheduling problems, the cost structure for our problem is composed of fixed and operational costs. For evident economic reasons, the most important objective is to reduce the number of working drivers and running vehicles. In order to further reduce costs, it is also useful to minimize idle time and deadheads. For simplicity reasons, we do not mention these latter objectives in the rest of the paper.

3 Problem Formulation

In this part, we introduce an original formulation inspired by the study reported in [12] relying on a constraint satisfaction and optimization model. This constraint-based formulation offers a natural modeling of the initial problem and provides a flexible basis to implement various metaheuristics.

Notations. Let $\mathcal{T}$ be the set of trips, numbered according to increasing starting time. The bounds for the vehicles and for each workday types being provided, we can define $\mathcal{D}$ and $\mathcal{V}$ the sets of drivers and vehicles respectively. Let T, D and V be the associated cardinalities. Given $t \in \mathcal{T}$, $d \in \mathcal{D}$, $v \in \mathcal{V}$, we define the notations figuring in Table 1 to formalize the constraints and objectives.

Table 1. Notations

$Cat(t)$	set of categories (types) of vehicle that can serve trip t
$cat(v)$	category (type) of vehicle v
$st(t), et(t)$	respectively start and end time of trip t
$S_{\max}(d)$	maximum spread time allowed for driver d
$W_{\max}(d)$	maximum working time allowed for driver d
$VC_{\max}(d)$	maximum number of vehicle changes for driver d

We also use the following notations to handle "driver-vehicle to trip" assignments:

- $wd(d) = 1 \Leftrightarrow d$ is assigned to at least one trip,
- $vu(v) = 1 \Leftrightarrow v$ is assigned to at least one trip,
- $Seq(d)$ is the set of pairs (t_k, t_l) that $d \in \mathcal{D}$ handles consecutively.

Finally, $dh'(t_k, t_l), wt'(t_k, t_l)$ and $Seq'(d)$ are similar to $dh(t_k, t_l), wt(t_k, t_l)$ and $Seq(d)$ respectively, except that they take into account a stop at the depot between trips.

3.1 Decision Variables and Domains

In our problem, we aim to simultaneously assign a couple (driver and vehicle) to each trip. Therefore, we define the set of decision variables as the set of trips $\mathcal{T}$. Naturally, the associated value domain $\mathcal{I}_k$ for each variable corresponds to driver-vehicle pairs. Initially, all domains $\mathcal{I}_k$ are equal to $\mathcal{I} = \mathcal{D} \times \mathcal{V}$. The set of constraints is exposed in section 3.2, the pursued objectives in section 3.3.

3.2 Constraints

This section provides a mathematical definition of the types of constraints.

Category constraints

$$\forall t \in \mathcal{T}, \forall v \in \mathcal{V},\ t = (.,v), \quad CATEGORY(t,v) \Leftrightarrow cat(v) \in Cat(t)$$

Feasible sequences constraints

$$\forall\, d \in \mathcal{D}, \forall\, (t_k, t_l) \in \mathcal{T}^2,\ t_k = (d, .),\ t_l = (d, .),\ t_k \prec t_l,$$

$$FEASIBLE\_D(t_k, t_l, d) \Leftrightarrow \begin{cases} compat(t_k, t_l) \ \wedge\ (t_k, t_l) \in Seq(d) \\ \vee \\ compat'(t_k, t_l) \end{cases}$$

Similar constraints exist for the vehicles.

Maximum spread time constraints

$$\forall\, d \in \mathcal{D}, \forall\, (t_k, t_l) \in \mathcal{T}^2,\ t_k = (d, .),\ t_l = (d, .),\ t_k \prec t_l,$$

$$MAX\_SPREAD(t_k, t_l, d) \Leftrightarrow (et(t_l) - st(t_k)) \le S_{\max}(d)$$

Maximum working time constraints

$$\forall\, d \in \mathcal{D}, MAX\_WORK(t_k, t_l, d) \Leftrightarrow$$

$$\sum_{t_k \in \mathcal{T},\ t_k = (d, .)} (et(t_k) - st(t_k)) + \sum_{(t_k, t_l) \in Seq(d)} dh(t_k, t_l) + \sum_{(t_k, t_l) \in Seq'(d)} dh'(t_k, t_l) \le W_{\max}(d)$$

Changeovers constraints

$$\forall\, d \in \mathcal{D},\ CHANGEOVERS \Leftrightarrow |\{v\ \in \mathcal{V}\ |\ \exists t_k \in \mathcal{T}, t_k = (d, v)\}| \le VC_{\max}(d)$$

Constraints will be used to pre-process the value domains of the variables and to build the initial schedules.

3.3   Objectives

The following two objectives are considered: minimization of the number of working drivers and vehicles.

$$f_1 = Min \sum_{d \in \mathcal{D}} wd(d) \text{ and } f_2 = Min \sum_{v \in \mathcal{V}} vu(v)$$

These objectives will be combined into a weighted evaluation function which is used by the GRASP algorithm (see section 4.4).

4   Solution Approach

4.1   Constraint Based Pre-processing

The number of potential assignments is exponential subject to the cardinality of the set of decision variables and to the cardinality of the domains. To reduce this number, we borrow filtering techniques from constraint programming [14].

The node consistency property allows to remove from domains all values that are inconsistent with at least one constraint. Let us consider, for example, the CATEGORY constraints:

$$\forall\, t_k \in \mathcal{T}, \forall\, (d, v) \in \mathcal{I},\ cat(v)\ \notin Cat(t_k), \Rightarrow (d, v) \notin \mathcal{I}_k$$

For a given trip, all pairs including vehicles forbidden for category reasons are removed from the trip's domain.

4.2 General Algorithm

GRASP is a multi-start metaheuristic for combinatorial problems, in which each iteration consists basically of two phases: construction and local search. The skeleton of the procedure is described in Algorithm 1. Our construction phase, detailed in subsection 4.3, relies on constraint programming techniques. The resulting solution is then improved by a local search algorithm (see subsection 4.4) embedding a powerful neighborhood exploration mechanism.

Algorithm 1: Greedy randomized adaptive search procedure

Data   : f evaluation function, it_{max} maximum number of iterations, restricted candidate list
Result : Best solution found f^*
begin
    /* x^* is the best solution found so far and $f^* = f(x^*)$*/ ;
    $f^* \leftarrow \infty$;
    while $it \leq it_{max}$ **do**
        /* Generate a greedy randomized solution x */ ;
        $x \leftarrow$ greedy_rand() /* See Section 4.3 */;
        /* Apply a local search algorithm, x_l is a local minimum */ ;
        $x_l \leftarrow$ descent() /* See Section 4.4 */;
        /* Record best solution */ ;
        if $f(x_l) \leq f^*$ **then**
            $f^* \leftarrow f(x_l)$;
            $x^* \leftarrow x_l$;
        end
        /* Increment number of iterations */ ;
        $it \leftarrow it + 1$;
    end
end

4.3 Initial Schedule

The initial solution aims to find a feasible crew and vehicle schedule by assigning a driver-vehicle pair to each decision variable (trip) while satisfying all the constraints. For this purpose, we developed a constructive greedy heuristic sketched hereafter. The strategy employed here is similar to the Best Fit Decreasing Strategy developed for the Bin Packing Problem [13].

At each step of the greedy construction step, a trip is picked from a restricted candidate list of fixed size. This list contains the most-constrained trips. The selected trip is then assigned a value (a driver-vehicle pair) that can handle it.

After each assignment, a forward checking procedure is applied to prevent future conflicts. It performs arc consistency between the currently instantiated variable and the not-yet instantiated ones. Considering the MAX_SPREAD constraints for example, when a driver-vehicle pair (d_k, v_k) is assigned to a variable t_k, all pairs including d_k are removed from the domain of the variables bound to t_k within constraints of type MAX_SPREAD.

$$\forall\, t_j \in \mathcal{T},\ (et(t_k) - st(t_j) \geq S_{max}(d_k)) \ \Rightarrow\ \forall v \in \mathcal{V},\ (d_k, v) \notin \mathcal{I}_j$$

This forward-checking process is similarly applied to the other constraints.

4.4   Improvement by Local Search

Search Space. A configuration σ is a *consistent assignment* of "driver-vehicle" pairs in $\mathcal{I}$ to trips in $\mathcal{T}$. The search space Ω is then defined as the set of all such assignments. Notice that our representation remedies in essence, i.e. without any additional constraint, some drawbacks raised by sct partitioning or set covering models largely used for the Crew Scheduling Problem. The former is rather hard to solve and is often relaxed in the set covering formulation while the latter can lead to over-covered trips (see [10] for instance).

Evaluation Function. In order to guide the algorithm to visit the search space, one needs a function to evaluate the configurations. The quality of a configuration σ is estimated through a weighted aggregation of the different objectives.

$$\forall \sigma \in \Omega, \quad f(\sigma) = w_1 \times f_1(\sigma) + w_2 \times f_2(\sigma)$$

$w_i > 0\ (i{=}1,2)$ are the weights associated to the two vehicle and driver objectives.

Neighborhood Operator. The neighborhood is one of the most important component of any local search algorithm. In our case, we have experimented several neighborhoods using different principles such as one-change (changing the value of a variable), swap (exchanging the values of two variables), change-and-repair and ejection chain. Among these alternatives, the neighborhood based on ejection chain proves clearly to be the most powerful.

The principle of ejection chains was introduced in [7] and defined in a very general way. An ejection chain is initiated by selecting a set of elements to undergo a change of state. The result of this change leads to identifying a collection of other sets, with the property that the elements of at least one must be "ejected from" their current state. In our case, we devised an ejection chain as follows:

> 1. pick a trip (variable) at random,
> 2. pick a new driver-vehicle pair,
> 3. if assigning the pair to the trip does not create any conflict,
>   the assignment becomes effective, otherwise, a new driver-
>   vehicle pair is assigned to all the trips in conflict if a consis-
>   tent assignment is possible. As a last resort, these conflicting
>   variables are unassigned.

5 Computational Experiments

In this section, we assess the usefulness of our *integrated approach* and compare it with the *conventional sequential approach*. For this purpose, we carry
out a series of experimentations using a set of data instances coming from real
situations.

5.1 Data and Experimental Settings

Computational experiments were based on 7 real-world instances representing
different workloads. The main characteristics of these instances are shown in
Table 2 (Left Part), namely, the number of scheduled trips, available drivers
and vehicles. Notice that the size of these instances are comparable to those
mentioned in previous studies (see Section 1).

In our experimentations, all drivers are subjected to the same rules, namely a
maximum working time of 9:00 and a maximum spread time of 12:00.
Changeovers are not allowed. Two types of vehicles are considered with the
following hierarchy: vehicles of type 2 can handle trips of type 1 or 2, whereas
vehicles of type 1 are dedicated to type 1 only.

Our search procedures were coded in C++, compiled with VC++ 8.0 (flag
-O3), on a PC running Windows XP (1Go RAM, 2.8Ghz). For the sequential
approach, we developed a Branch & Bound algorithm on a multi-commodity
flow model for the vehicle part and on a set covering model for the crew part
(see [10]). For our GRASP procedure, 20 independent runs were carried out on
each instance with different random seeds, each run being limited to 10 minutes
of CPU time.

Concerning the tuning of GRASP, after some preliminary experimentations,
we obtained the best results with the following set of parameters: 10 iterations
($it_{max}=10$ in Algorithm 1), a size of 5 for the restricted candidate list, a stop
criterion for each local search set to $100 \times T$ iterations without improvement.

5.2 Comparison between Sequential and Integrated Scheduling

The right part of Table 2 displays the results of the sequential and the integrated
approach on the 7 data sets. For each instance, we report the number of required

drivers and vehicles[1]. Figures for the simultaneous approach correspond to the best solution over the 20 runs (mean and standard deviation between brackets).

From Table 2, we can make two main comments. First, one observes that the integrated approach always outperforms the sequential one except for 2 instances where both approaches furnish equivalent results. In particular, the savings in terms of number of drivers are significant with up to 5 in two cases (cor_67 and dij_159). The sequential approach provides a lower bound for the number of vehicles that is always reached in the integrated solutions. Across the 7 instances, the results are also quite stable with very small standard deviations.

Second, the integrated approach is more powerful than the sequential one in the sense that the sequential approach failed to solve the instance "opt_215" while solutions are possible when crews and vehicles are considered simultaneously. Indeed, when the sequential scheduling is applied to this instance, the vehicle phase results in a schedule with no relief opportunity along one bus duty and consequently leads to an insolvable problem for the driver scheduling part.

Table 2. Comparison between sequential and simultaneous scheduling

	Trips	Drivers	Vehicles		Sequential		Simultaneous	
			type 1	type 2	drivers	vehicles	drivers	vehicles
bea_59	59	20	11	5	18	16	**16** (16.0, 0.0)	16 (16.0, 0.0)
cor_67	67	20	18	0	20	15	**15** (15.8, 0.4)	15 (15.0, 0.0)
cha_105	105	25	14	10	22	22	22 (22.0, 0.0)	22 (22.0, 0.0)
sem_151	151	30	18	12	27	27	27 (27.0, 0.0)	27 (27.0, 0.0)
dij_159	159	36	20	20	34	29	**29** (29.0, 0.0)	29 (29.0, 0.0)
otp_215	215	50	50	0	-	48	**49** (49.0, 0.0)	49 (49.0, 0.0)
aux_249	249	50	35	12	48	44	**46** (46.8, 0.4)	44 (44.0, 0.0)

These results show the dominance of the integrated approach over the sequential one. A more complete assessment would compare the results with tight lower bounds, which are unfortunately unavailable yet.

6 Conclusion

In this paper, we proposed a new heuristic for a simultaneous drivers and vehicles scheduling problem in an extra-urban area. The assumptions retained are suitable to tackle practical problems in rural areas. The ability of managing a heterogeneous fleet for a given depot is thus especially relevant.

The problem formulation as a constraint satisfaction and optimization model proves to be a very flexible framework for designing heuristic algorithms. From this model, we developed a solution procedure relying on a Greedy Randomized Adaptive Search Procedure which integrates constraint programming techniques and a powerful neighborhood based local search. This proposed approach constitutes the first application of metaheuristics to this difficult application.

---

[1] Information related to the total duration of deadheads and idle periods is also available, but not reported here.

The computational study carried out on a set of real-world instances clearly shows the dominance of the integrated approach over the conventional sequential one. In particular, a simultaneous schedule of drivers and vehicles achieves better utilization of both resources. Moreover, in some cases, the integrated approach is indispensable, especially when relief opportunities are rare.

Finally, let us mention that the general solution approach shown in the paper is also suitable for dynamic adjustment of schedules by local re-optimization.

Acknowledgments. This work was partially supported by the French Ministry for Research and Education through a CIFRE contract (number 176/2004). The reviewers of the paper are greatly acknowledged for their helpful comments.

References

1. Ball, M., Bodin, L., Dial, R.: A matching based heuristic for scheduling mass transit crews and vehicles. Transportation Science 17, 4–31 (1983)
2. Borndoerfer, R., Loebel, A., Weider, S.: A bundle method for integrated multi-depot vehicle and duty scheduling in public transit. TR 04-14 (2004)
3. Dallaire, A., Fleurent, C., Rousseau, J.M.: Dynamic Constraint Generation in CrewOpt, a Column Generation Approach for Transit Crew Scheduling. In: Voß, S., Daduna, J.R. (eds.) Computer-Aided Scheduling of Public Transport (CASPT), pp. 73–90. Springer, Berlin (2004)
4. Freling, R.: Models and Techniques for Integrating Vehicle and Crew Scheduling. PhD thesis, Tinbergen Institute, Erasmus University Rotterdam (1997)
5. Freling, R., Boender, G., Paixão, J.M.P.: An integrated approach to vehicle and crew scheduling. Technical Report 9503/A, Economie Institute, Erasmus University Rotterdam, Rotterdam (1995)
6. Gaffi, A., Nonato, M.: An integrated approach to the extra-urban crew and vehicle scheduling problem. In: Wilson, N.H.M. (ed.) Computer-Aided Transit Scheduling, pp. 103–128. Springer, Berlin (1999)
7. Glover, F.: Ejection chains, reference structures and alternating path methods for traveling salesman problems. Discrete Applied Math. 65(1-3), 223–253 (1996)
8. Haase, K., Desaulniers, G., Desrosiers, J.: Simultaneous vehicle and crew scheduling in urban mass transit systems. Transportation Science 35(3), 286–303 (2001)
9. Haase, K., Friberg, C.: An exact branch and cut algorithm for the vehicle and crew scheduling problem. In: Wilson, N.H.M. (ed.) Computer-Aided Transit Scheduling, pp. 63–80. Springer, Berlin (1999)
10. Huisman, D.: Integrated and Dynamic Vehicle and Crew Scheduling. PhD thesis, Tinbergen Institute, Erasmus University Rotterdam (2004)
11. Huisman, D., Freling, R., Wagelmans, A.P.M.: Multiple-depot integrated vehicle and crew scheduling. Trans. Sci. 39, 491–502 (2005)
12. Laurent, B., Hao, J.K.: Simultaneous vehicle and driver scheduling: a case study in a limousine rental company. Computers & Industrial Engineering 53(3), 542–558 (2007)
13. Martello, S., Toth, P.: Knapsack Problems: Algorithms and Computer Implementations. Wiley, New York (1990)
14. Tsang, E.: Foundations of Constraint Satisfaction. Academic Press, London (1993)

SitCom: Virtual Smart-Room Environment for Multi-modal Perceptual Systems

Jan Cuřín and Jan Kleindienst

IBM Research, Voice Technologies and Systems,
V Parku 4/2294, Praha 4, Czech Republic
{jan_curin,jankle}@cz.ibm.com

Abstract. In this paper we present a novel approach for building intelligent services in smart rooms - i.e. spaces equipped with different sets of sensors, including audio and visual perception. Designing such multi-modal perceptual systems is a non-trivial task which involves interdisciplinary effort dealing with integration of voice and image recognition technologies, situation modeling middleware and context-aware multi-user interfaces into robust and self-manageable software framework.

The inherent complexity associated with building such systems aiming at perception and understanding of behavior of people in smart spaces makes it a very difficult undertaking. Hence this fresh research arena currently suffers with immature architectural models, weak system testability, and challenging component maintainability. In addition, traditional methodologies of design lifecycle such as "bottom-up" or "top-down" fall short because of the aspects mentioned.

Keywords: architecture, simulation, multi-modal fusion, perceptual systems, visualization, smart spaces, situation modeling.

1 Introduction

In this paper, we advocate for an approach we have used successfully in two large projects - one dealing with building intelligent meeting room services, the other with domotic perceptual services for elderly. The proposed approach is based on the recommendation to designers to concentrate first on the key part of the architecture, i.e. situation modeling. They do so by using a special tool we have developed and which we describe in this paper. It is because the situation modeling is at the heart of any multimodal perceptual system - it processes events from sensory/perceptual subsystems to acquire high-level knowledge, and serves such information to top-level services and agents, which in turn take advantage of understanding the situations, roles and relationships of people and objects in the environment. For example, if a meeting agent knows that Mr. X is in the conference room with ongoing meeting, it may choose to divert the calls for Mr. X and automatically provide performation about his further availability.

The paper is organized as follows: Section 2 introduces problems and tasks addressed by this paper, Section 3 shortly describes the reference architecture

N.T. Nguyen et al. (Eds.): IEA/AIE 2008, LNAI 5027, pp. 476–485, 2008.

for multimodal perceptual systems; Section 4 presents the SITCOM tool and its internal representation supporting development of applications within this architecture. Whereas Sections 5 and 6 illustrate two uses cases. Section 7 concludes the article by summarizing features of the proposed system.

2   Motivation and Related Work

The construction of contextual services demands an interdisciplinary effort because the situation modeling layer typically sits between two infrastructure parts: the environment sensing part and the application logic. Thus, even a simple service built for an intelligent room requires at least three different developer roles, each with a different set of skills:

- **Perceptual Technology Providers** supply sensing components such as person trackers, sound and speech recognizers, activity detectors, etc. to see, hear, and feel the environment. The skills needed here include signal processing, pattern recognition, statistical modeling, etc.
- **Context Model Builders** make models that synthesize the flood of information acquired by the sensing layer into semantically higher-level information suitable to user services. Here, the skills are skewed towards probabilistic modeling, inferencing, logic, etc.
- **Service Developers** construct the context-aware services by using the abstracted information from the context model (the situation modeling layer). Needed skills are application logic and user interface design; multi-modal user interfaces typically require yet an additional set of roles and skills.

upon starting, the service developer does not, typically, have access to a fully-equipped room with sensors, nor does she have the technology for detecting people and meetings. But for an initial prototype of such a service, pre-recorded input data may suffice.

A service developer then talks to context-model builder to define what new contextual abstractions will be needed, and which can be reused from an existing catalogue. The context-model builder in turn talks to technology providers to verify that capturing the requested environment state is within state-of-the art of the sensing technology. If not, there is still a possibility to synthesize the requested information from other sensors under a given quality of service; for example, the number of people in a room may be inferred through sound and speech analysis in case no video analysis technology is available.

We needed a development environment where all these roles meet and which would rationalize the above process and make the communication between those roles efficient and straightforward. It has also to facilitate the design of the entire system with partially complete and manually designed scenario data, helping with the boostrapping of the entire context-aware application.

During the initial expertise phase, we have identified three reliable pervasive computing systems satisfying a majority of our criteria: UbiREAL [1], Context

Toolkit [2], and Gaia [3]. But in contrast to these systems, which integrate contextual information directly from various sensors, we needed a system which relies on information provided by more complex perceptual components, i.e. more complex context-acquisition components such as person trackers and speech recognizers. A body tracker might be at once capable of detecting location, heading and posture of persons, identifying them, and tracking subjects of their interest. These circumstances lead us to idea of separating the concept of perceptual components and into another abstraction - the situation modeling. Defining and modeling situations based on a wide range of context-acquisition components was not supported by other environments such as UbiREAL and Context Toolkit, so we decided to implement a new framework, called SITCOM and described in Section 4. Our system is used as an integrator for the perceptual components providers and it is capable of dynamically exchanging perceptual components of the same kind, as well as enabling the seamless replacement of these components by simulators, a requirement from service developers.

3   Reference Architecture Model

As we already mentioned, one of the key feature of our approach was to effectively separate the effort of different development groups (in the one of the projects it was 15 partners) facilitating the possibility of easy integration. These requirements resulted in the layered architecture design—*Reference Architecture Model* [4,5]. The *Reference Architecture Model* provides a collection of structuring principles, specifications and *Application Programming Interfaces* (APIs) that govern the assemblage of components into highly distributed and heterogeneous interoperable systems. See schema in Figure 1(a).

Each level derives new information from the abstraction of the information processed and data flow characteristics such as latency and bandwidth, based on the functional requirements from the system design phase.

The components at the **Logical Sensors and Actuators** layer are either sensors feeding their data to the upper layers, or various actuators, such as output devices receiving data or steering mechanisms receiving control instructions. The aim of this layer is to organize the sensors and actuators into classes with well-defined and well-described functionality, to make them available remotely over a network and to standardize their data access.

The **Perceptual Component** layer [6] extracts meaningful events from continuous streams of video, audio and other sensor signals. Perceptual Components provide interpretation of data streams coming from various logical sensors and provides a collection of well-defined APIs that allow replacing one technology engine for another. These components still process information in a linear fashion, i.e. from sensors to higher level semantics.

The **Situation Modeling** layer is the place where the situation context received from audio and video sensors is processed and modeled. The context information acquired by the components at this layer helps services to respond better to varying user activities and environmental changes.

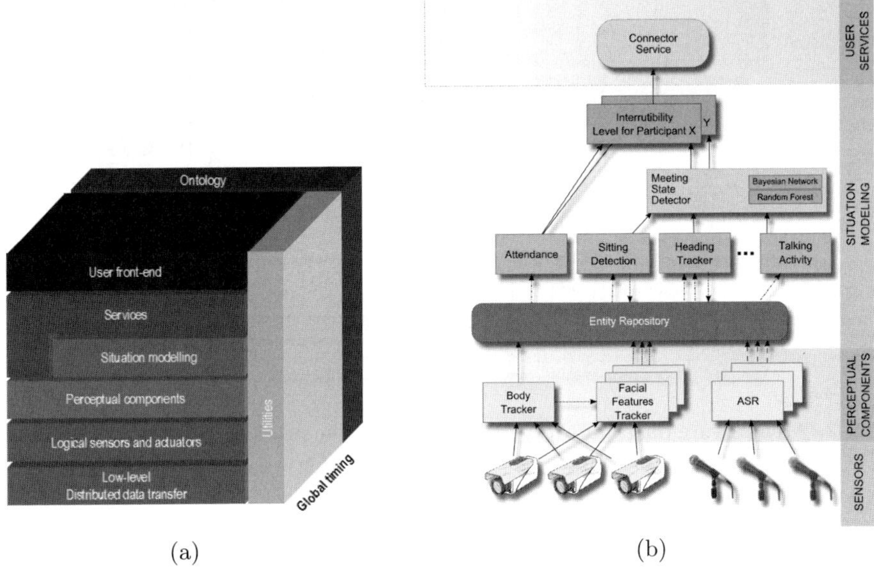

Fig. 1. Schemas of (a) the Reference architecture model and (b) the data flow in the CHIL meeting scenario

The **User Services** are implemented as software agents and manage interactions with humans by means of user services hosted on various interaction devices. The components at this level are responsible for communication with the user and presenting the appropriate information at appropriate time-spatial interaction spots. The *User Services* utilize the contextual information available from the situation modeling layer.

4   SitCom - Tool for Building Virtual Smart Rooms

This section introduces the core tool supporting the whole development cycle of multimodal perceptual systems – SITCOM. SITCOM (**Sit**uation **Com**poser for Smart Environments) is a 3D simulator tool and runtime for development of context-aware applications and services. Context-aware applications draw data from the surrounding environment (such as there is an ongoing meeting in the room, a person location, body posture, etc.) and their behavior depends on the respective situation (e.g. while in meeting silent the phone). In SITCOM, the environment characteristics are captured by Situations Models that receive input events from a) real sensor inputs (cameras, microphones, proximity sensors...), b) simulated data, c) combination of real and simulated input. SITCOM allows to combine the situation models into hierarchies to provide event filtering, aggregation, induction and thus construct higher-level meaning and reasoning functionality. Through the IDE controls, SITCOM facilitates the capture and/or creation of situations (e.g. 10 min sequence of several people meeting in a

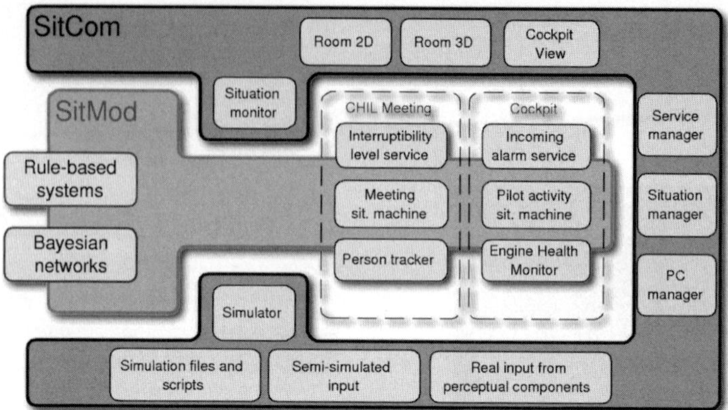

Fig. 2. Architecture diagram overview of SITCOM, the Situation Composer, and SIT-MOD, the Situation Model framework

conference room) and their subsequent realistic rendering as 3D scenarios. These scenarios can be re-played to invoke situations relevant for the application behavior, and thus provide mechanism for systematic testing of the context-aware application under different environmental conditions. The key feature is that we keep the portability between virtual and real devices.

4.1   SitCom Deployment Scenarios

In the reference architecture model, SITCOM itself plugs into the layer of situation modeling. So it sees the service layer as its upper layer, and the perceptual components as its lower layer. Also, as SITCOM itself is a framework for modeling systems enabling plugging diverse situation modeling technologies, it is split into two distinct parts: the simulation framework, named SITCOM, and the actual situation modeling being developed, named SITMOD (**Sit**uation **Mod**eling). In Figure 2, the two parts are clearly separated.

SITMOD (and modules plugged into it) is the portion of the system to be deployed into the field. During simulation, but also once deployed, the SITMOD run-time runs situation models for multiple and possibly unrelated scenarios. E.g. in Figure 2, a meeting and a cockpit scenario are running at the same time.

We found it very useful to be able to switch back and forth between simulated and recorded data, as for debugging some situations, we can run the experiment up to a point, and then we can interfere with the recorded data using synthetic data, so as to test the situation model and the service. This makes the test of *what if* scenarios very quick and simple.

4.2   Internal Representation Structures

SITCOM relies on data representation structures, which are specially designed to bridge context information and pervasive services in smart spaces. The basic unit visible at the context-acquisition level is an entity. An *entity* is characterized by a type (e.g., person, whiteboard, room) and its access to a set of property streams. A *property stream* represents a set of events for a particular aspect of the entity. As an example, properties for an entity of the type person are location (indicating the physical location of the person), heading (tracking direction the person is looking at), and identity (i.e. a stream sending events about the identification of the person). At the *Situation Modeling* layer, entities are stored in a container called entity repository. The *Entity repository* is capable of triggering events upon creation and registration of new entities. Accordingly, situation models and services can be notified about changes for a particular *entity* or its *property*, based on an appropriately designed subscription mechanisms.

For processing the contextual information, we introduce the abstraction of *situation machines*. *Situation machines* (SM) interpret information inferred from observing entities in the entity repository and current states of other situations. As SMs may use different techniques, such as rule-based or statistical approach, SITCOM can accommodate a mix of models at the same time. We give examples of situation machines and their hierarchies later in the text.

5   Use Case I: CHIL

In this section we demonstrate the use of SITCOM tool for the CHIL project. **CHIL** - *Computers in the Human Interaction Loop* - was an integrated project (IP 506909) under the European Commission's Sixth Framework Programme finished in October 2007. The aim of this project was to create environments in which computers serve humans in office or home environment providing non-obtrusive context-aware services.

Let us describe the SITCOM framework on a connector scenario proposed and exploited in [7]. The connector service is responsible for detecting acceptable interruptions (phone call, SMS, targeted audio, etc.) of a particular person in the "smart" office. During the meeting, for example, a member of the audience might be interrupted by a message during the presentation, whereas the service blocks any calls for the meeting presenter.

Our smart office is equipped with multiple cameras and microphones on the *sensor* level. The audio and video data are streamed into the following *perceptual components*, as depicted in Figure 1:

- **Body Tracker** is a video-based tracker providing 3D coordinates of the head centroid for each person in the room;
- **Facial Features Tracker** is a video-based face visibility detector, providing nose visibility for each participant from each camera;
- **Automatic Speech Recognition** is providing speech transcription for each participant in the room.

Figure 3 shows the rendering of the aggregated information in a $2D$ fashion for people locations, headings, their speech activity as well as if they are sitting or not. The $3D$ is useful when annotating information, as it's a more natural view to assess if the meeting is going on or not. Note also the view indicating the output of the sensors (in this case the cameras), which is useful for perceptual component developers to assess the quality of their output.

To plug into the architecture outlined in Section 3, we have designed a situation model to support needs of the connector service. The key task in this case is to detect if there is an ongoing meeting in the smart room.

We used the following set of situation machines:

- **Attendance** tracks the number of participants in the room;
- **Motion Detection** reports how many participants have moved over a certain distance threshold in a given time period;
- **Heading Tracker** infers the head orientation for each person from her position and face visibility for all cameras;
- **Attention Direction** tracks the number of participants looking towards the same spot, using their heading information;
- **Sitting Detection** infers whether a particular person is sitting or not from the Z (height) coordinate;
- **Talking Activity** tracks duration of speech activity and number of speaker changes in a given period;
- **Meeting State Detector** infers the current state of the meeting in the room;
- **Interruptibility Level** selects the level of *interruptibility* of a particular participant according to the current meeting state and the current speaker.

The actual implementation of particular situation machine can be part of the Java runtime or it can be a standalone module using a remote API. We had investigated the use of statistical classification module for meeting state recognition.

In particular, the actual detection of current state of the meeting is based on output labels produced by the perceptual components, which do further processing and combination of sensor outputs. We use the facts produced by perceptual components and other situation machines to determine the meeting states.

The results for distinguishing between two states (meeting / no meeting) reached reasonable accuracy of 95.9% [8]. This experiment started on simulated data (generated by SITCOM), later replaced by recording from smart rooms. Finaly, we were able to run the trained model in real-time environment with possibility to switch between three body tracking components provided by different partners.

6   Use Case II: NetCarity

Another more recent use case based on the approach advocated in this paper is NetCarity project. **NetCarity** is an ongoing integrated project supported by the European Community under the Sixth Framework Programme (IST-2006-045508). The aim of this project is investigating and testing technologies which

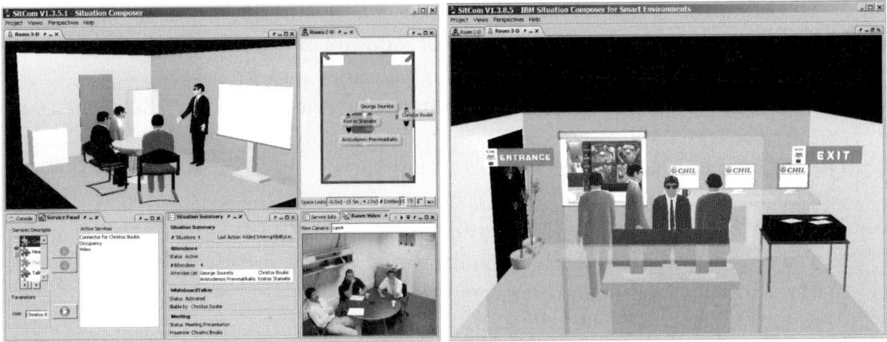

Fig. 3. GUI of SITCOM environment for smart office and demo booth

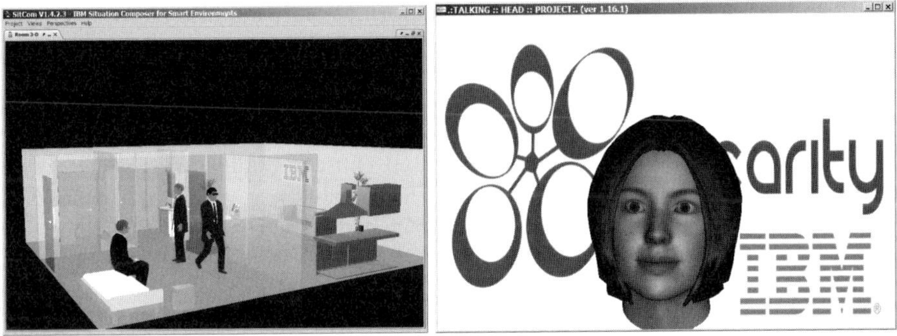

Fig. 4. SITCOM's 3D visualization of smart home and Talking Head interface

will help elderly people to improve their well being, independence, safety and health at home.

The idea of this project is to equip homes of NetCarity clients by a variable set of perceptual technologies and connect them to the central point providing various types of services. The most important activity of the central service point, called *NetCarity Server* (NCS), is to "keep an eye" on the client health and safety exploiting different perceptual technologies, i.e. acoustic event detector, body tracker.

This project is currently in its first stage when the technologies are still under development, but service provider are already eager to try prototypes and discuss deployment of feature functions with possible clients. We have created a SITCOM virtual smart home and several scenarios simulating essential situations in inhabitants' life.

The following sensors, actuators and perceptual components are being simulated in the virtual home environment:

- **Motion Detectors** are installed in each room, monitoring movement in the space.
- **Fire Detector** sensor detecting fire in the flat.

- **Gas Detector** sensor detecting leaking gas in the flat.
- **Remote Door Lock** sensor/actuator capable of reporting open/closed status of the door and locking/unlocking the door's lock.
- **Scene Acoustic Analyzer** analyzing noise and sounds in the scene, such as, someone is walking, speaking, laughing, door is opening/closing.
- **Body Tracker** is a video-based tracker providing 2D coordinates for each person in the room.
- **Talking Head** actuator giving audio/visual feedback to the inhabitant. It serves as a communication channel from the NetCarity server and as a humanoid interface to other services; see Figure 4.

The example of situation machine is:

- **Fall-down Detector** perceptual component detecting that the inhabitant may be in dangerous situation, for example (s)he felt down and is unable to call for help. It uses and combines information from different sensors and detectors.

In the actual implementation the sensors and actuator in client home are controlled by a *Residential Gateway* (RGW) which is connected to the Net-Carity Server by a secure and authenticated channel, called *NetCarity Secure Channel* (NCSC). In the simulated case, the residential gateway is replaced by the SITCOM run-time connected to NetCarity Server via the NCSC connection. There is no difference in behavior or data types between simulated and real-live smart home from the NetCarity Server side. Multiple instances of SITCOM run-times can simulate a whole network of smart homes and their residential gateways. This setup is currently used for tuning NetCarity Server's rule-based system, fall-detector and acoustic scene analysis modules, and for verification of proposed communication schemes. Beside the visual feedback during the development, the 3D visualization obviously serves also as a good demonstration platform.

7   Conclusion

This paper advocated for a novel approach in building multimodal perceptual systems. As a key tool, we have introduced SITCOM – an extensible Java toolkit to help in all phases of the development of non-trivial life-cycle of context-aware services. We equipped SITCOM with a set of functionalities that we found beneficial in development of perceptual applications:

- simulates the environment and the perceptual input (manually created or recorded scenarios)
- provides 2D and 3D visualization of the scenes, situations, and scenarios
- works as the middleware between user services and the layer of perception (situation modeling)
- serves as IDE for repetitive testing of context-aware services and applications by replaying recorded or simulated scenarios

– provides portability between virtual and real devices
– serves as a tool for annotation of recorded data

The SITCOM environment was successfully applied during the whole development cycle of the CHIL platform and it is now helping to bootstrap the NetCarity system. It has also been demonstrated in various venues; see screen-shots of SITCOM GUI in Figures 3 and 4.

In many ways, having an integrated tool specialized for context-aware applications has been helpful to identify necessary pieces for the application, like the needed room information, specific sensor information, or the definition of the participants roles. Our tool is in use on 10+ sites, and has seen plug-ins written by multiple developers, who have e.g. integrated a rule-based situation modeling, as well as multiple perceptual components.

References

1. Nishikawa, H., Yamamoto, S., Tamai, M., Nishigaki, K., Kitani, T., Shibata, N., Yasumoto, K., Ito, M.: UbiREAL: Realistic smartspace simulator for systematic testing. In: Dourish, P., Friday, A. (eds.) UbiComp 2006. LNCS, vol. 4206, pp. 459–476. Springer, Heidelberg (2006)
2. Dey, A., Salber, D., Abowd, G.: A conceptual framework and a toolkit for supporting the rapid prototyping of context-aware applications. Human-Computer Interaction (HCI) Journal 16, 97–166 (2001)
3. Roman, M., Hess, C.K., Cerqueira, R., Ranganathan, A., Campbell, R.H., Nahrstedt, K.: Gaia: A middleware infrastructure to enable active spaces. In: IEEE Pervasive Computing, October–December, pp. 74–83 (2002)
4. CHIL Consortium. The CHIL reference model architecture for multi-modal perceptual systems (2007), `http://chil.server.de/servlet/is/6503/`
5. Kleindienst, J., Curín, J., Fleury, P.: Reference architecture for multi-modal perceptual systems: Tooling for application development. In: Proceedings of 3rd IET International Conference on Intelligent Environments (IE 2007), Ulm, Germany (September 2007)
6. Crowley, J.L., Coutaz, J., Rey, G., Reignier, P.: Perceptual components for context aware computing. In: Borriello, G., Holmquist, L.E. (eds.) UbiComp 2002. LNCS, vol. 2498, Springer, Heidelberg (2002)
7. Danninger, M., Robles, E., Takayama, L., Wang, Q., Kluge, T., Nass, C., Stiefelhagen, R.: The connector service - predicting availability in mobile contexts. In: Proc. of the 3rd Joint Workshop on Multimodal Interaction and Related Machine Learning Algorithms (MLMI), Washington DC, US (2006)
8. Curín, J., Fleury, P., Kleindienst, J., Kessl, R.: Meeting state recognition from visual and aural labels. In: Popescu-Belis, A., Renals, S., Bourlard, H. (eds.) MLMI 2007, vol. 4892, pp. 24–35. Springer, Heidelberg (2008)

Optimizing Building's Environments Performance Using Intelligent Systems

E. Sierra, A. Hossian, D. Rodríguez, M. García-Martínez, P. Britos,
and R. García-Martínez

Software & Knowledge Engineering Center. Buenos Aires Institute of Technology
Confluencia Academic Unit, National University of Technology- University of Comahue
School of Architecture. University of Buenos Aires.
Intelligent Systems Laboratory. School of Engineering. University of Buenos Aires
rgm@itba.edu.ar

Abstract. This article describes an intelligent system architecture that based on neural networks, expert systems and negotiating agents technologies is designed to optimize intelligent building's performance. By understanding a building as a dynamic entity capable of adapting itself not only to changing environmental conditions but also to occupant's living habits, high standards of comfort and user satisfaction can be achieved. Results are promising and encourage further research in the field of artificial intelligence applications in building automation systems.

1 Introduction

According to the latest definitions internationally accepted for an "intelligent building", this is a building highly adaptable to the changing conditions of its environment [Krainier, 1996]. But, in an overall concept of comfort, the idea of adaptation to changing environmental conditions may be not enough. Building systems are constructed in order to provide comfortable living conditions for the persons who live in them. It is well known that people usually differ in their personal perceptions of comfort conditions. To some extent, the sensation of comfort is an individual one and it is normally affected by cultural issues. Thus, the idea behind this research is to find techniques based on artificial intelligence in order to provide design recommendations for comfort systems in buildings so that these buildings can also be highly adaptable in terms of the comfort conditions desired by their users. In a few words, a building must "learn" to change its performance not only as a function of environmental conditions, but also as a consequence of preferences set by the people who live in it. The majority of recent developments in building energy management systems (BEMS) followed the advances made in computer technology, such as genetic algorithms and neural networks. Other methods have also been proposed including empirical models [Yao, 2004], weighted linguistic fuzzy rules [Alcala, 2005; Sierra, 2007], simulation optimization [Fong, 2006] and online adaptive control [Wang, 2001].

N.T. Nguyen et al. (Eds.): IEA/AIE 2008, LNAI 5027, pp. 486–491, 2008.

2 The Proposed Intelligent System Architecture

According to the latest trends in the field, intelligence in building systems tends to be distributed [So, 1999]. The proposed intelligent system architecture is shown in Figure 1. There is a main computer where the functions of monitoring, visualizing and recording parameters is carried out while the regulation functions are left to the local controllers located throughout the building [Wong, 2001]. These controllers are responsible for taking over local control tasks in the zone they serve. To accomplish its function, the centralized computer contains a database that keeps track of relevant information concerning building user's preferences. For instance, this database keeps records of time, date, number of persons in a room, current temperature and humidity values, as well as temperature and humidity values desired by users. In order to do this, temperature and humidity input panels are located in the different rooms. Each user can eventually set them to what he or she thinks is an ideal comfort condition. As comfort perception is an individual sensation, the database in the main computer keeps track of every individual requirement.

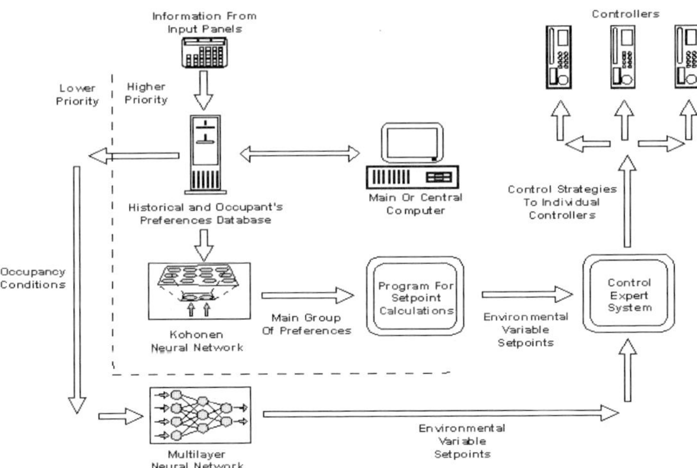

Fig. 1. Intelligent System Architecture, where the negotiating agent resides in main computer

The information contained in the user's requirements database for a given room is applied to a neural network of the self organizational maps of Kohonen (SOM) [Rich & Knight, 1991; Hilera & Martinez, 1995] type, which is used to cluster all the user's requirements and discard all those groups of requirements which are not relevant in terms of their approximation to the main cluster of preferences. Once a unique group of requirements is selected, their values are applied as input to a program which provides the limits as well as the average value for a particular environmental variable. This value is used as reference or set-point for the local control strategies set by an expert system which runs on the main computer. This expert system takes decisions concerning control strategies which are used to activate, deactivate or tune the individual controllers. The information about relevant occupancy and setting conditions, as well as the final values of environmental variables is used to train a multi-layer neural network which outcomes will provide ideal environmental values in case of absence of occupants or of preference information given by them. In any case, set-points assigned to comfort variables provided by the analysis of user's desired environmental conditions is given priority over any automatic calculation of these conditions.

3 Energy Saving Conditions

A very important issue in intelligent buildings technology is related to energy saving policies [Sierra *et al*, 2004]. Optimization procedures carried out to cut off energy consumption rates are not only justified in terms of operation costs reduction but also because of the environmental benefits implied in the adoption of energy saving strategies. In order to accomplish previously mentioned optimization procedures, an expert system [García-Martinez & Britos, 2004] containing rules that perform energy saving strategies is set up in the central computer. However, it is necessary to verify if the rules defined in the energy saving expert system may eventually alter the comfort conditions established by the control strategy expert system. As it is shown on Figure 2, there is an intelligent negotiation agent [Allen *et al.*, 1991; Conry *et al.*, 1988; Ferber & Drougol, 1992] which runs in the central computer created to determine whether the application of energy saving strategies will: a) not affect current comfort conditions in a given space (not affected) b) affect current comfort conditions but within the limits found by the SOM neural network based upon preference information provided by occupants (partially affected) c) affect current comfort conditions beyond the limits set by occupant's requirements (fully affected). The policy applied by the intelligent negotiation agent in the different situations mentioned earlier can be summarized as follows: [a] if comfort conditions are not affected, rules defining energy saving strategies are given the highest priority; [b] if comfort conditions are partially affected, rules defining energy saving strategies are given an intermediate priority, just lower than the priority given to the rules that regulate the operation of main control actuators and [c] if comfort conditions are fully affected, rules defining energy saving strategies are given the lowest priority.

In summary, the intelligent negotiation agent was given a number of rules which express the desired energy saving policy (constraints) based on the building conditions. The occurrence of certain events inside the building (e.g. a temperature raises above a permitted upper limit) will trigger the appropriate rule within the agent. The agent executes the rule(s), with the purpose of readjusting the environmental conditions to some preferred set of values. The triggered rule(s) will cause a set of actions to be immediately executed. After the previously described negotiation policy has been applied, the control expert system located in the main central computer has an updated rule base which can be used to set up the operation mode of local controllers (on, off, normal) and tune them accordingly, for example, by determining the appropriate set-point for the control variable.

4 An Example

With the purpose of providing an example that illustrates the functionality of the proposed intelligent system, the operation of the air – handling system will be described. It is assumed that the HVAC engineer has already designed the air handler in terms of laying out the ductwork, appropriately sizing the fan and heating and cooling coils, and selecting the proper dampers, damper actuators and motor contactor. From this design a system diagram has been constructed as shown in Figure 3.

The designations DA and VA stand for damper and valve actuators, respectively, C is for electrical contactor and H/C and C/C represent the heating and cooling coils. When building zone building served by the air –handler is "occupied", i.e., the current date and time fall within a certain schedule, the system is said to be in occupied mode. In this mode, the fan is started and the heating and cooling valves and dampers are modulated so as to maintain the set-point temperature in the zone. This is called the "normal" operating condition. Control strategies describe how specific subsystems are to be controlled.

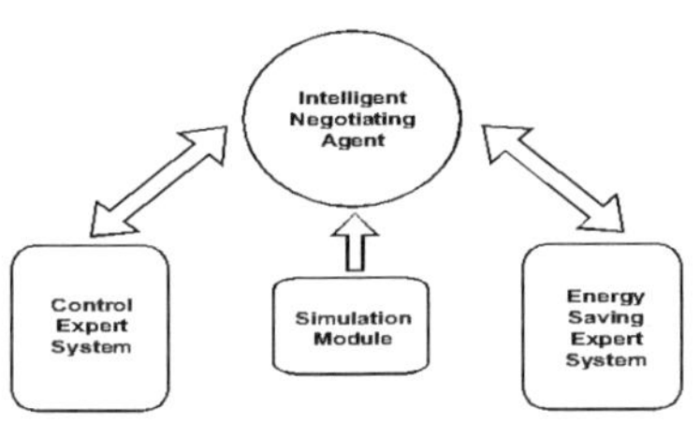

Fig. 2. Negotiation Control and Energy Saving Rules

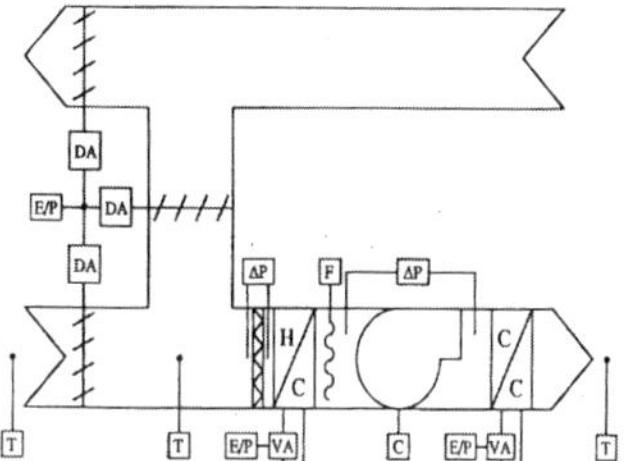

Fig. 3. System Diagram for the Air Handler

Thus, some of the rules contained in the rule base of the control expert system will be stated as follows:

```
IF       the date and time fall within the specified schedule
THEN     the system shall enter the occupied mode.

IF       the system is in the occupied mode,
THEN     the supply fan shall be turned on,
AND      the normally closed cooling valves and air dampers shall be controlled by a se-
         quenced PI (Proportional plus Integral) controller to maintain the room air tempera-
         ture set-point to 70 °F.

IF       the date and time fall outside of the specified schedule
AND      the room air temperature exceeds 55 ºF
THEN     the system shall enter the unoccupied mode.

IF       the system is in the unoccupied mode
THEN     the supply fan shall be turned off, the heating valve shall be set to fully open and
         the cooling valve and outside air dampers shall be set to fully closed.

IF       the date and time fall outside of the specified schedule
AND      the room air temperature is less than or equal to 55 ºF,
THEN     the system shall enter setback mode.

IF       the system is in the setback mode,
THEN     the system will remain in this mode until the room air temperature exceeds 60 ºF.
```

Energy saving strategies were designed in order to diminish energy consumption levels while keeping a satisfying response to the building energy demand profiles:

Dry Bulb Economizer Control:

```
IF        the system is in occupied mode
AND       the outside air temperature rises above 65 ºF, the dry bulb economizer set-point
THEN      the outside air damper will be set to a constant position of 20%.
```

Mixed Air Low Limit Control:

```
IF        the system is in occupied mode
AND       the mixed air temperature drops from 40 to 30 ºF,
THEN      a proportional (P) control algorithm shall modulate the outside air dampers from 100
          to 0%. Mixed air low limit control shall have priority over dry bulb economizer
          control.
```

Free cooling:

```
IF        the system is in unoccupied mode AND the room air temperature exceeds 65 ºF
AND       the outside air temperature equals to or is less than 55 ºF,
THEN      the supply fan shall be turned on the heating and cooling valves shall be set to
          fully closed and the outside air dampers shall be set to fully open.
```

As previously stated, the system tries to capture the occupants' preferences by modifying the set-points of control variables to users' demands.

5   Implementation and Results

A prototype of the proposed intelligent system has been implemented in CLIPS, a tool for developing expert systems. Neural network and negotiating agent algorithms have been programmed in C++. The system prototype has been tested in the building of the Ministry of Education, located in the city of Neuquén, Argentina. This building has been designed with a high degree of intelligence. After almost a year of continuous tuning and adjusting procedures, the most updated prototype of the system was put to work. The people who work in this public building was strongly encouraged to fill out surveys about the building's performance. The comments of users who admitted positive changes in comfort conditions were confirmed by a survey. The survey outcomes were: 75 % percent of users were very satisfied with the performance of the new system, 20 % were just satisfied and 5% not satisfied. Such results encourage advancing in this direction of optimizing the operative and control strategies carried out by the developed system.

6   Conclusions

Techniques of artificial intelligence have been used in many decision, control and automation systems in the last twenty years. Building systems have not been an exception. In this direction, the intelligent system that is proposed in this article tries to contribute in the field of intelligent buildings optimization, by transforming them in a dynamic space, with high standards of comfort and occupant's satisfaction. In this sense, the ability inherent to intelligent systems that are capable of learning from their own environment plays a very important role in the achievement of these building performance optimization goals. Furthermore, results obtained as a consequence of the proposed system implementation are very encouraging. Thus, further research and development work in the field deserves particular attention.

7 Implications

The open architecture of the system allows for easy and continuous updates and unlimited expandability. Therefore, the model's design allows for its application to a large number of building categories. Finally, it was clearly illustrated that an adequate combination of intelligent technologies and expert knowledge has significant potential for improving building energy management, since it has the capability of modulating, with the assistance of rules, intelligent interventions.

References

Alcala, R., Casillas, J., Cordon, O., Gonzalez, A., Herrera, F.: A genetic rule weighting and selection process for fuzzy control and heating, ventilating and air conditioning systems. Artificial intelligence 18, 279–296 (2005)

Allen, J.F., Kautz, H., Pelavin, R.N., Tenenberg, J.D.: Reasoning About Plans. Morgan Kaufmann Publishers, Inc., San Mateo, California (1991)

Conry, S.E., Meyer, R.A., Lesser, V.R.: Multistage negotiation in distributed planning. In: En Bond, A., Gasser, L. (eds.) Readings in Distributed Artificial Intelligence, Morgan Kaufmann Publishers, Inc., San Mateo, California (1988)

Ferber, J., Drougol, A.: Using reactive multiagent systems in simulation and problem solving. In: Avouris, N.M., Gasser, L. (eds.) Distributed Artificial Intelligence: Theroy and Praxis, Kluwer Academic Press, Dordrecht (1992)

Fong, K.F., Hanby, V.I., Chow, T.T.: HVAC system optimisation for energy management by evolutionary programming. Energy & Buildings 38, 220–231 (2006)

García Martínez, R., Britos, P.: Ingeniería de Sistemas Expertos. Editorial Nueva Librería. 649 páginas (2004), ISBN 987-1104-15-4

Hilera, J., Martínez, V.: Redes Neuronales Artificiales. Fundamentos, modelos y aplicaciones. RA-MA, Madrid (1995)

Krainier, A.: Toward smart buildings, Architectural Assn. Graduate School, Environment & Energy Studies Program (1996)

Rich, E., Knight, K.: Introduction to Artificial Networks. Mac Graw-Hill Publications, New York (1991)

Sierra, E., Hossian, A., Britos, P., Rodriguez, D., Garcia Martinez, R.: Fuzzy Control for improving energy management within indoor building environments. In: Proceedings CERMA 2007 Electronics, Robotics & Automative Mechanics Conference, pp. 412–416. IEEE Computer Society Press, Los Alamitos (2007)

Sierra, E., Hossian, A., Labriola, C., García Martínez, R.: Optimal Design of Constructions: A Preliminary Model. In: Proceedings of the World Renewable Energy Congress (WREC 2004), Denver, Colorado, Estados Unidos (2004)

So, A.: Intelligent building systems. Kluwer Academic Press, Dordrecht (1999)

Wang, S., Burnet, J.: Online adaptive control for optimizing variable speed pumps of indirect water-cooled systems. Applied Thermal energy 21, 1083–1103 (2001)

Wong, K.: The Intelligent Building Index: IBI manual: version 2. Asian Institute of Intelligent Buildings, Hong Kong (2001)

Yao, Y., Lian, Z., Hou, Z., Zhou, X.: Optimal operation of a large cooling system based on an empirical model. Applied Thermal Energy 24, 2303–2321 (2004)

Individualism and Collectivism in Trade Agents

Gert Jan Hofstede[1], Catholijn M. Jonker[2], and Tim Verwaart[3]

[1] Wageningen University, Postbus 9109, 6700 HB Wageningen
`gertjan.hofstede@wur.nl`
[2] Delft University of Technology, Mekelweg 4, 2628 CD Delft
`c.m.jonker@tudelft.nl`
[3] LEI Wageningen UR, Postbus 29703, 2502 LS den Haag
`tim.verwaart@wur.nl`

Abstract. Agent-Based Modeling can contribute to the understanding of international trade processes. Models for the effects of culture and cultural differences on agent behavior are required for realistic agent-based simulation of international trade. This paper makes a step toward modeling of culture in agents. The focus is one of the five dimensions of culture according to Hofstede: individualism versus collectivism. The paper presents an analysis based on social science literature about national cultures. For cultural differentiation of agent behavior, rules are formulated for individualist versus collectivist agent behavior with respect to negotiations, cooperation or defection in the delivery phase of transactions, trade partner selection, and trust. Example computations demonstrate the feasibility in multi-agent simulations.

Keywords: culture, negotiation, deceit, trust, simulation.

1 Introduction

Agent-Based Economics (ABE) studies economic processes as interactions of individual actors [1]. Cultural differences are known to have their effects on international business interactions and on trust between business partners [2]. Gorobets and Nooteboom [3] argue on the basis of a multi-agent simulation that different economic systems could be viable in societies with different levels of trust. Models of culture-bound agents will advance the understanding through ABE of intercultural trade processes as well as differences in trade processes across cultures.

Culture has different aspects or dimensions [4]. The current paper focuses on the widely recognized distinction between individualistic and collectivistic cultures. Section 2 presents this distinction as it is described in the social sciences. Section 3 analyzes its effect on trade processes as the basis for the formal modeling in section 4. Section 5 presents example computations. The results and future directions of this research are discussed in section 6.

2 The Cultural Dimension of Individualism and Collectivism

People are gregarious by nature. But the life conditions of societies vary, and they have adapted accordingly. Hunter-gatherers live in small bands, usually consisting of a few

N.T. Nguyen et al. (Eds.): IEA/AIE 2008, LNAI 5027, pp. 492–501, 2008.

nuclear families. In agricultural societies, larger units have developed, and the people may live in extended families or clans. This is still the default model of social organization in most of the world, although it is being put under strain by urbanization. In modern, affluent industrial societies people tend to revert to nuclear families. The variation in basic group size and cohesion between societies has been shown by sociologists, e.g., in the distinction between *Gemeinschaft* (community) and *Gesellschaft* (society) that Tönnies introduced as early as 1887 [5]. In a *Gemeinschaft*, people share everything, both material and immaterial, whereas in a *Gesellschaft,* private property and other individual-centered institutions are possible. This variation has been confirmed by social psychological cross-national studies of practices or values, for instance the work of Triandis [6] and Hofstede [4]. These authors speak of the distinction between *individualism* and *collectivism* that serves as this section's caption. Another independent confirmation comes from the World Values Survey by political scientist Inglehart and colleagues. Minkov [7] showed that the individualist – collectivist continuum is visible in Inglehart's survey data. He names it universalism versus exclusionism.

Recently the dimension has also become the main ingredient of theories about cross-cultural business, e.g., in the work of Trompenaars [8] who posits a number of dimensions of culture that were shown by Smith *et al.* [9] to be correlated with the dimension of individualism versus collectivism. Trompenaars' dimensions relate to individual versus community, universalist versus particularist reasoning, affective versus neutral emotional style, specific versus diffuse communication, performance versus ascription, sequential versus synchronous time use, and control versus acceptance of nature, each mentioned in the same direction of the individualism – collectivism continuum. The relevance of this particular dimension of culture to the management literature lies in the fact that Anglo countries are at the extreme individualist end of the scale, and so business partners from almost any country they try to do business with are bound to have more collectivist cultures.

Variation along the dimension of collectivism versus individualism also affects value systems and the functioning of institutions aside from the family, such as education, religion, politics and trade. Hofstede [4] incorporates a host of other studies that confirm the occurrence of the dimension and its relevance to many societal phenomena. These include the kind of processes that occur in trade relations: whether to show one's cards or not, whether to confront the other party or not, how to distribute favors, and the like. Table 1 shows typical distinctions, relevant for trade.

Table 1. Some distinctions between norms in collectivist and individualist societies

Collectivist	Individualist
Maintain harmony, avoid confrontation	Speak your mind
High-context, implicit communication	Low-context, explicit communication
Use the word "we"	Use the word "I"
Show favor to in-group customers	Treat all customers equally
No business without a personal relation	Task is more important than a good relation
A relation brings rights and obligations	Mutual advantage is the basis of relations
Relations are given	Build and maintain relations actively
Save face for in-group	Keep self-respect
Responsible for group interests	Responsible for personal interests

Source: Hofstede [4].

One typical distinction between individualist and collectivist practices is that to collectivist mindsets, relations are more important than business – and so, business tends to be done among friends and family, in contexts that to individualistic mindsets do not seem fit for business. In an individualistic society there tends to be a strict separation between various spheres of life, e.g., family, business, and leisure. In a collectivistic society, one tends to do all of these things with the same extended group of people. The term "in-group" is often used to denote this kind of self-evident unit of social life at large as it exists in collectivist societies. Finding new trading partners and establishing a working relationship with them, is not easy in these societies. The usual way is to use existing business relationships. In the very collectivist Chinese culture, the term *guanxi* denotes the social network that allows extending business contacts [10]. The term consists of two Chinese characters: *guan* (gate) and *xi* (connection). In individualistic societies a roughly equivalent notion is *social capital*.

Individualism is associated with direct, low-context communication while collectivism is associated with indirect, roundabout, high-context communication. In psychological terms, people from individualistic societies are on average more extraverted. This was indeed found by Hofstede and McCrae [11].

According to Hofstede and Hofstede [12] the world's countries have a wide continuum of scores on the dimension. The rough pattern, exceptions omitted, is as follows: at the collectivist end of the scale we find Central America, Pakistan, Indonesia, and the South East Asian tigers with China. Moderately collectivistic are Latin America, Africa, Latin and Balkan Europe. Moderately individualistic are India, Arab countries, and Central Europe. Individualistic are West- and North Europe. The most individualistic countries of all are those of the Anglo world. Importantly, Hofstede's own data as well as replications show that countries' orientation on this dimensions shift towards more extreme individualism with increases in wealth, and towards more collectivist values with increasing poverty. Individualism can thus be interpreted as an adaptation to wealth. Yet the dependency is not complete. There exist cultures that remain rather collectivist despite wealth, such as Japan, or rather individualist despite poverty, such as India.

3   Individualism and Collectivism in Trade Processes

Figure 1 presents a model of trade processes. This model is based on the Trust and Tracing game [13], a human gaming simulation of supply chain processes. The participants negotiate contracts about commodities with invisible quality attributes. Before entering negotiations, agents have to select each other as partners, based on their trade goals (sell or buy?; which commodity?; which quality?) and knowledge about potential partners. Once a contract has been agreed upon, traders can either cooperate (deliver truthfully) or try and use an opportunity to defect. Upon delivery the receiver can either trust or put the delivery to the test, the latter usually at some cost where trust is for free. The delivery and trust decisions are based on personal preferences and cultural background, as well as beliefs about the trade partner and the trade environment. In future research the Trust and Tracing game trading game can serve as an instrument to validate the models presented in this paper.

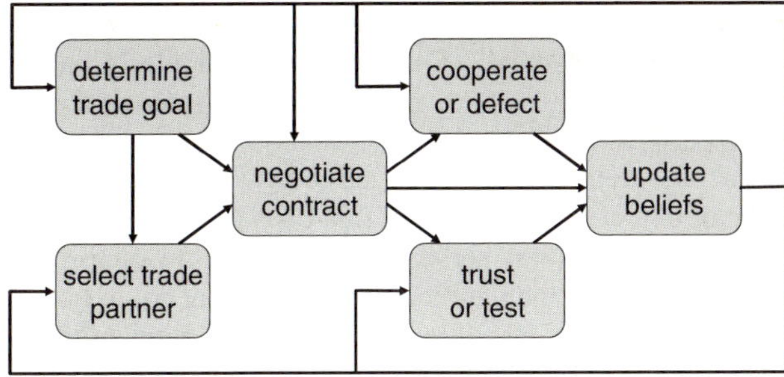

Fig. 1. Processes and internal information flows of trading agents

Experience from negotiation and delivery processes may change a trader's beliefs. In this paper we limit ourselves to beliefs about trade partners. We distinguish three beliefs. The belief about another agent's *fairness* represents an agent's expectation that a fair contract can be negotiated. The belief about another agent's *trustworthiness* represents an agent's expectation that the other will cooperate. The belief about *benevolence* represents an agent's expectation that the other will trust.

Table 1 in the previous section displays relevant distinctions for trade between individualistic and collectivistic societies. The remainder of this section analyses the effects of this dimension of culture on the trade processes depicted in Figure 1.

Negotiation behavior. To a collectivist mindset, negotiation has to be preceded by the formation of a relationship. If that goes wrong there will be no negotiation. During the negotiation, collectivist traders discriminate between in-group and out-group partners. They feel obliged to be more modest (or realistic, following their in-group's rules) in their first proposal to an in-group partner, are more hesitant to break off negotiations with in-group partners, and will try to maintain harmony as long as the opponent follows the in-group rules. When doing business with individualist traders the collectivists may be shocked by their opponent's explicit communication. Breaking the rules asks for a reaction. The style of that reaction may be furious, or they might never explicitly say anything, but just avoid the other from now on.

The first reply to a new proposal from an in-group partner will be modest, but there is no need to be modest to an out-group partner. If an out-group partner replies with no or small concession, negotiation is likely to be broken off, where an in-group partner or an acquainted relation would get a second chance.

In a collectivist mind the responsibility for in-group welfare and the compliance with in-group rules always play a prominent role. A collectivist will accept benefits for his in-group rather than his personal advantage as a convincing argument. Individualists have one thing in mind during negotiations: their own personal interest. This might be the material advantage of the deal in question, or the development of new trust relations with perspectives of future deals, or just the pleasant conversation during the negotiations, or the satisfaction of winning the game, but one thing stands for sure: individualists only pursue private interests. So individualist traders are not very modest in their negotiations, nor will they give in for the purpose of maintaining harmony. If they are not aware of the cultural differences when trading with collectivists, they may be upset by the lack of explicit communication, or they may upset their opponents by being too explicit, or by talking business before the relationship has been established and acknowledged. They are not particularly patient or impatient negotiators, but behave patiently as long as it serves their interest.

Truthful or untruthful delivery. After an agreement has been reached, it comes to delivery. Traders can defect or cooperate in this phase. For instance, if the quality of the commodity is invisible at first sight, a supplier can be opportunistic and try to deliver a lower quality product than agreed upon. By doing so, in both collectivist and individualist societies deceivers takes the risk of serious damage to the relation with their partner if the deceit be revealed. However, in collectivist societies there is the extra sanction of shame, so there is damage to the relations with other possible customers as well. Furthermore, the shame will not be restricted to the deceiver, but will hit his relatives, friends, and business associates too. Therefore, a collectivistic supplier takes extra care not to deceive in-group business partners.

In collectivist societies the thresholds for opportunistic behavior, trust and forgiveness are based on group memberships and norms. In individualist societies these properties are based on personal relations and the personal interests in these relations. Traders in individualist societies do not have to fear the social sanctioning system in case their opportunistic behavior is revealed. For individualist traders, decisions to deceive, to trust, and to forgive are motivated by personal interest in the relation, be it in the framework of the current transaction or in the long run. Their personal relations represent their social capital.

Trust or Distrust. Being aware of the sanctioning mechanisms in case of deceit, and for the sake of maintaining harmony, traders in collectivist societies show trust toward in-group suppliers. Following the rules of their societies, and trying to maintain harmony, they also tend to show trust toward out-group partners when they have had long lasting relations. Not being trusted by a business partner puts pressure on the perceived relation. Especially in collectivist societies, showing distrust does serious damage to relations.

Individual trust is more relevant in individualist societies than it is in collectivist societies. Group membership is the main item for collectivist traders, individual relations are the main item for individualist traders. In individualist societies, customers cannot rely on social sanctioning systems, so they depend on their personal judgment and will be more careful to trust. Although suppliers in individualist societies do not like to be distrusted, they will more easily accept a trade partner tracing their trustworthiness than collectivist suppliers.

Maintenance of Beliefs about Partners. The acceptability of trade partners and the estimate of their trustworthiness are primarily based on group membership in collectivist societies. In addition, and for individualist societies in particular, the experience of previous deals counts, be it personal experience or the experience of others (reputation). For both individualists and collectivists, negotiations resulting in an agreement increase the partner's acceptability, and failing negotiations decrease it. The weight of reputation compared to personal experience is stronger in collectivist societies than it is in individualist societies.

The individualism dimension of culture does not influence the extent to which negotiation success influences the belief about a partner's trustworthiness. However, the negative effect of revealed deceit is stronger in collectivist societies than it is individualist societies. Whenever deceit by out-group suppliers is revealed, collectivists will be unforgiving toward the deceivers and the groups they belong to. The deceived and their relations will exclude the deceivers and their relations from business for some time.

For an individualist trader, partner's acceptability after revealed deceit will be determined by future interests, but of course the estimate of partner's trustworthiness is decreased.

Partner selection. The question "whom do I deal with?" is important for collectivist traders. They prefer to do business with in-group members, or will have to familiarize with out-group trade partners before doing business. Business is only possible if some personal relation exists. With respect to out-group relations the traders benefit from information exchange in the in-group. On the other hand they are accountable to their in-group for their out-group relations. Questionable relations weaken their position. Collectivist traders do not take the initiative to propose to others than in-group members and existing business relations. Upon a proposal made by a previously unknown counterparty, a collectivist trader will only respond if the proposal is framed in a socially acceptable way, for instance introduced through a common relation.

Individualist traders feel free to enter into negotiations on the basis of new proposals and take the initiative to propose to new partners. Taking initiatives and starting new business in one's own interest is respected in individualist societies, but on the other hand individualists will value personal trust relations, as these relations represent the social capital that they acquired by investments, and that is not given to them like in collectivist societies. When entering into negotiations with new partners, individualists do not like proposals that appeal to common group membership. An individualist trader proposing business to a collectivist trader may be surprised by the refusal of the other, not realizing that business is only possible after an introduction by a common relation, or some other way to get familiarized before explicitly considering business proposals.

4   Representation in Agents

Building on the analysis in section 3, the present section formalizes rules for culture dependent agent behavior in trade, with respect to the individualism dimension.

Simulation of the negotiation process follows the negotiation architecture of Jonker and Treur [14]. The architecture defines negotiation processes in terms of utility functions, and parameters of the negotiation process: negotiation speed, impatience factor, allowable gap between own bid and partner's bid, concession factor, configuration tolerance, and some parameters for financial aspects.

Impatience is modeled as the likelihood that an agent will break off negotiations if the utility of a partner's bid is below the critical cut-off value or if the partner makes not enough progress. The first two rules express that impatience is moderated by common group membership and trust relations, relative to the extent that an agent is collectivist. All real valued parameters are normalized in the interval [0, 1]. Finally, the rules apply to sellers – for buyers replace benevolence with trustworthiness.

```
/* 1 have patience if in-group partners make unrealistic bids */
if cultural_script_contains(individualism_index(I: Real))
    and current_negotiation(C: Trader, X: Integer, L: Commodity_list)
    and current_round(X)
    and partner_model_contains_belief(C, group_distance, D: Real)
    and partner_model_contains_belief(C, benevolence, B: Real)
    and agent_trait_value(impatience, P: Real)
    and agent_trait_value(cut_off_value, M: Real)
    and others_bid_utility_in_round(U: Real, X)
    and U < M
    and random(0, 1, Z: Real)
    and P * (1 - (1-I)*max(1-D,B)) * 0.5 > Z
then stop_negotiation(C, X, L, gap);

/* 2 have patience if in-group partners make little concessions */
if cultural_script_contains(individualism_index(I: Real))
    and current_negotiation(C: Trader, X: Integer, L: Commodity_list)
    and current_round(X)
    and X > 3
    and partner_model_contains_belief(C: Trader, group_distance, D: Real)
    and partner_model_contains_belief(C: Trader, benevolence, B: Real)
    and agent_trait_value(impatience, P: Real)
    and agent_trait_value(minimal_progress, M: Real)
    and progress_in_bids(X-3, X, N: Real)
    and N < M
    and random(0, 1, Z: Real)
    and P * (1 - (1-I)*max(1-D,B)) * 0.5 > Z
then stop_negotiation(C, X, L, no_accommodation);
```

The minimum utility that an agent will accept depends on the concession factor. The following rule expresses that collectivists give less negotiation room to strangers.

```
/* 3 collectivist agents are indulgent only to in-group partners */
if cultural_script_contains(individualism_index(I: Real))
    and current_negotiation(C: Trader, X: Integer, L: Commodity_list)
    and partner_model_contains_belief(C, group_distance, D: Real)
    and partner_model_contains_belief(C, benevolence, B: Real)
    and agent_trait_value(concession_factor, F: Real)
then minimum_utility (1-F*(I + (1-I)*max(1-D,B)));
```

Deceit occurs in both collectivist and individualist societies, but for collectivistic agents, the threshold to deceive depends on group distance. The following rule only models the influence of group distance. In the eventual decision to deceive or not, other factors - such as personal relations - play a role as well, but we do not model these factors to depend on individualism versus collectivism.

```
/* 4 collectivist agents: opportunism increases with group distance */
if cultural_script_contains(individualism_index(I: Real))
    and current_negotiation(C: Trader, X: Integer, L: Commodity_list)
    and partner_model_contains_belief(C, group_distance, D: Real)
    and agent_trait_value(honesty, H: Real)
then deceit_treshold( H*(1-(1-I)*D) );
```

When a deal has been closed, the agents have to decide whether to trust the delivery or to put it to the test (*trace* it). In both types of societies, the decision is based on the personal trust relation between agents. Agents are less likely to trace as trust increases. However, in collectivist societies tracing in-group members is even less likely done. The decision is modeled as follows in the simulation agents.

```
/* 5 collectivist agents hesitate to trace in-group partners */
if deal_in_round(C: Trader, B: Bid, X: Integer)
    and current_round(X)
    and cultural_script_contains(individualism_index(I: Real))
    and partner_model_contains_belief(C, group_distance, D: Real)
    and partner_model_contains_belief(C: Trader, trustworthiness, T: Real)
    and random (0, 1, Z: Real)
    and (1-T)*(I+(1-I)*D) > Z
then to_be_traced(B: Bid);
```

The beliefs about partner's trustworthiness and benevolence are updated in the simulation, using the experience based trust update function

$$t_{C,x} = (1-\delta^+)t_{C,x-1} + \delta^+ e_{C,x}, \ \ if \ e_{C,x} > t_{C,x-1}\,,$$
$$t_{C,x} = (1-\delta^-)t_{C,x-1} + \delta^- e_{C,x}, \ \ if \ e_{C,x} \leq t_{C,x-1}\,.$$

(1)

$t_{C,x}$ represents the new value of an agent's trust in partner C, $t_{C,x-1}$ represents the value before the last experience, and $e_{C,x}$ represents the value of the last experience. δ^+ and δ^- are in the interval $(0,1)$, and $\delta^+ = \varepsilon\delta^-$, with $0 < \varepsilon < 1$: a negative experience has more impact than a positive one. The value of the endowment coefficient ε is a personal trait. It will usually be closer to 1 in individualist societies than in collectivist societies, as individualists expect more opportunism and distrust.

```
/* 6 the endowment effect is stronger in collectivist societies */
if cultural_script_contains (individualism_index(I: Real))
    and agent_trait_value(base_endowment_coefficient, E: Real)
    and agent_trait_value(collectivist_endowment_coefficient, F: Real)
then agent_trait_value (endowment_coefficient, E*I + F*(1-I) );
```

After a negotiation the fairness belief is updated in a similar way as trust is. In case of a successful negotiation, the utility of the deal is taken as experience value. If the negotiation is broken off without a deal, the experience value equals 0.

Update information originates from own experience or shared information (reputation). The experience value equals 0 in case of revealed deceit, 1 otherwise. For shared information, which is especially important for collectivist agents, δ^+ and δ^- are multiplied by the maximum of the information source's believed trustworthiness and (1-individualism_index)(1-group_distance) of the source.

The following is an example of an update rule for partner beliefs.

```
/* 7 process shared information for positive experience */
if info_from_about(S: Trader, C: trader, R: Trait, V: Real)
    and cultural_script_contains(individualism_index(I: Real))
    and partner_model_contains_belief(S, group_distance, D: Real)
    and partner_model_contains_belief(S, trustworthiness, T: Real)
    and partner_model_contains_belief(C, R, Z: Real)
    and agent_trait_value(base_negative_update_factor, U: Real)
    and agent_trait_value(endowment_coefficient, E: Real)
```

500   G.J. Hofstede, C.M. Jonker, and T. Verwaart

```
    and V > Z
    and P = E * U * max(T,(1-I)*(1-D))
then modify_partner_belief_in_round_source(C, R, (1-P)*Z + P*V , X, S);
```

The following rule expresses the acceptability of another agent as partner for future deals. An agent tries and selects the most acceptable partner that is available for the next negotiation, i.e., not currently negotiating with another agent.

```
/* 8 collectivists: relations are important for partner selection */
if cultural_script_contains(individualism_index(I: Real))
    and partner_model_contains_belief(C: Trader, group_distance, D: Real)
    and partner_model_contains_belief(C: Trader, benevolence, B: Real)
    and partner_model_contains_belief(C: Trader, fairness, F: Real)
then acceptability (C, I*F + (1-I)*max(1-D,B) );
```

5   Simulation Examples

Table 2 presents results of multi-agent simulations of trade in populations of 8 suppliers and 8 customers. The agents apply the rules presented in section 4.

Simulations in populations with collectivist agents belonging to different groups typically show the distribution of run **1** in Table 2: in-group trade. Individualist agents rapidly develop networks of preferred relations, on which they trade very efficiently. In mixed settings like run **2**, the individualists develop the same pattern, but collectivist agents stick to their in-group trade. However, in run **3** where no in-group partners are available, the collectivist agents develop the individual relations pattern. Group *C* agents can find in-group partners in run **4** and show the collectivist pattern, while the other collectivist agents develop the individual relations pattern.

Table 2. Number of successful transactions in simultations with 8 suppliers and 8 customers

1. Customers / Suppliers

		collectivist gr *A*				collectivist gr *B*			
		C1	C2	C3	C4	C5	C6	C7	C8
collectivist	S1	9	7	5	3	0	0	0	0
group *A*	S2	3	8	9	3	1	0	0	0
	S3	5	6	5	4	0	0	0	0
	S4	2	3	5	11	0	0	0	0
collectivist	S5	0	0	0	0	4	5	5	4
group *B*	S6	0	0	0	0	6	6	5	5
	S7	0	0	0	0	8	4	6	6
	S8	0	0	0	0	8	7	8	9

2. Customers / Suppliers

		individualist				collectivist gr *A*			
		C1	C2	C3	C4	C5	C6	C7	C8
individualist	S1	3	2	24	0	0	0	0	0
	S2	1	0	0	12	0	1	0	1
	S3	0	16	1	2	0	0	0	0
	S4	14	2	0	7	0	0	0	0
collectivist	S5	0	0	0	0	5	6	6	6
group *A*	S6	0	0	0	0	8	3	5	6
	S7	0	0	0	0	5	7	5	8
	S8	0	1	0	0	8	7	5	4

3. Customers / Suppliers

		individualist				collectivist gr *A*			
		C1	C2	C3	C4	C5	C6	C7	C8
individualist	S1	1	25	1	0	0	0	0	0
	S2	9	1	0	5	1	0	3	6
	S3	0	0	2	0	0	0	9	4
	S4	2	0	0	1	15	3	5	0
collectivist	S5	1	0	0	0	0	20	0	0
group *B*	S6	0	1	1	17	0	0	4	0
	S7	5	0	4	0	1	0	1	9
	S8	1	0	18	0	1	0	1	1

4. Customers / Suppliers

		collectivist gr *C*				collectivist gr *B*			
		C1	C2	C3	C4	C5	C6	C7	C8
collectivist	S1	6	7	7	5	0	0	0	0
group *C*	S2	9	3	4	8	0	0	0	0
	S3	4	7	6	6	0	0	1	0
	S4	4	5	5	6	0	0	0	0
collectivist	S5	0	0	0	0	17	0	1	1
group *A*	S6	0	0	0	0	1	0	1	16
	S7	0	0	0	0	0	23	1	1
	S8	0	0	1	2	1	15	1	2

6 Conclusion

The experiments correspond to the hypotheses in that trade goes smoothly when all traders are collectivistic, and have group relations, or when all agents are individualists. In mixed settings where buyers and sellers can be either collectivistic or individualistic, collectivist traders end up trading with in-group partners.

The work presented in this paper shows that the approach to vary cultural dependent behavior in trade processes in simulations, leads to behavior that corresponds to human behavior in trade simulation games [13]. Therefore, the paper shows that agent-based simulation contributes to the understanding of international trade processes.

Future work is (1) to develop models and study the effects of Hofstede's other dimensions of culture, using the same approach, (2) to integrate the models for the separate dimensions, and (3) to validate the models in human experiments.

Applications of this work are (1) as a tool for research in supply chains and institutional economics, (2) for education and training in business schools and multinational corporations, and (3) negotiation support systems.

Acknowledgement. The authors thank John Wolters for engineering the simulation.

References

1. Tesfatsion, L., Judd, K.L.: Handbook of Computational Economics, Agent-Based Economics, vol. 2. North-Holland, Amsterdam (2006)
2. Ghauri, P.N., Usunier, J.-C.: International Business Negotiations. Elsevier, Oxford (2003)
3. Gorobets, A., Nooteboom, B.: Agent Based Modeling of Trust Between Firms in Markets. In: Bruun, C. (ed.) AE 2006. LNEMS, vol. 584, pp. 121–132. Springer, Heidelberg (2006)
4. Hofstede, G.: Culture's Consequences, 2nd edn. Sage, Thousand Oaks (2001)
5. Tönnies, F.: Community and society. Harper & Row, New York. Original publ. 1887 (1963)
6. Triandis, H.C.: Individualism and collectivism. Westview, Boulder (1995)
7. Minkov, M.: What makes us different and similar: a new interpretation of the World Values Survey and other cross-cultural data. Klasika I stil, Sofia (2007)
8. Trompenaars, F.: Riding the waves of culture: understanding cultural diversity in business. Economist Books, London (1993)
9. Smith, P.B., Dugan, F., Trompenaars, F.: National culture and the values of organizational employees: A dimensional analysis across 43 nations. Journal of Cross-Cultural Psychology 27, 231–246 (1996)
10. Lu, H.: The role of guanxi in buyer-seller relationships in China. Wageningen Academic Publishers, Wageningen (2007)
11. Hofstede, G., McCrae, R.R.: Personality and culture revisited: linking traits and dimensions of culture. Cross-cultural research 38(1), 52–88 (2004)
12. Hofstede, G., Hofstede, G.J.: Cultures and Organizations. McGraw Hill, New York (2005)
13. Meijer, S., Hofstede, G.J., Beers, G., Omta, S.W.F.: Trust and Tracing game: learning about transactions and embeddedness in a trade network. Production Planning and Control 17, 569–583 (2006)
14. Jonker, C.M., Treur, J.: An Agent Architecture for Multi-Attribute Negotiation. In: Nebel, B. (ed.) Proceedings of the 17th International Joint Conference on AI, IJCAI 2001, pp. 1195–1201. Morgan Kaufman, San Francisco (2001)

Adding Attentional Capabilities Features to an Intelligent Virtual Agent

P. Brunny Troncoso[1,2], P. Ricardo Imbert[1], and Angélica de Antonio[1]

[1] Decoroso Crespo Laboratory, Computer Science School,
Universidad Politécnica de Madrid
28660 Boadilla del Monte (Madrid), Spain
[2] Information Systems Department, Universidad del Bío Bío,
Avda. Collao 1202, Concepción, Chile
btroncos@ubiobio.cl,{rimbert,angelica}@fi.upm.es

Abstract. Attention is defined as a mechanism that organizes and structures the operation of the person's basic cognitive processes; it has been studied from different paradigms; among them, attentional capability is related to: the quantity of stimulus a person can attend at the same time; the intensity (concentration) of his attention to them; and, the time period that this attention can be kept. We propose an attentional capability representation for Intelligent Virtual Agents (IVAs) designed with personality and emotional features through COGNITIVA. Our agent is embodied, has goals and plans to meet by performing specific actions. The proposal simulates concentration levels and intensity on performing an action, to modify agent's sensorial channels thresholds and to limit these activities according to the activation level of the organism. The aim is to provide our agent with both more believability and natural behavior, improving the user-IVA interaction and the user's presence on the system.

Keywords: Intelligent Virtual Agent, Intelligent Interfaces.

1 Attention and Intelligent Virtual Agent (IVA) Behavior

Human beings use the attention mechanism to articulate the different and possible mental processes, selecting the more interesting ones and checking its execution.

When a person's attentional processes are running, the current task is more efficiently executed and the person is more receptive to specific and appropriate stimulus. So, attention is viewed like the mechanism directly implicated in the activation and well working of processes and operations of selection, distribution and maintenance of psychological activities [1].

Cognitive psychologists and, lately, neurophysiologists have expansively studied human attention, coinciding on recognizing three aspects of attention as fundamental: selection, awareness, and control [2].

Attention is defined like a main mechanism –with limited capability– which inhibits or stimulates well defined stimulus according to specific needs of the individual (objectives), acting as a control mechanism in order to both orienting

N.T. Nguyen et al. (Eds.): IEA/AIE 2008, LNAI 5027, pp. 502–512, 2008.

conscious activity and taking control of the hierarchy organization of the information generation process [3, 4].

Attention has been studied from different paradigms, and, its taxonomy includes selective attention, attentional capability, divided attention and others. Attentional capability is related to: the quantity of stimulus a person can attend at the same time; the intensity (concentration) of his attention to them; and, the range of time that this attention can be kept without oscillation [2, 3, 4]. This capability is a personal attribute of an individual, specific for each one, but susceptible to be changed by training (increasing it) or disuse (decreasing it).

We have studied the psychologist of attention, trying to identify elements of theory, models and components useful to help us in the formulation of an attentional capability representation for an IVA.

Our focus is oriented to simulate one part of human attentional behavior on an embodied agent which habit a graphic virtual environment; the agent is designed through COGNITIVA [5], an agent architecture that allow us to provide it with personality features and emotions. The agent's perceptual machine works based on the Human-like Hearing Perception Model, presented by Herrero and de Antonio [6].

Our interest is focus on providing an IVA with a synthetic attentional capability mechanism; the agent needs this mechanism to interact with objects, avatars and other agents in its virtual word, performing its usual activities. The IVA do not have any kind of interaction with real word, there are no front-end devices capturing images or sounds from external environment; all interactions are inside its environment and users take avatars to introduce their self in the virtual word.

Human beings have a personal attentional capability which allows them to perform parallel activities, either conscious or automatic. An automatic action – a reflex– performed a response in presence of specific stimulus; a conscious action forces the individual to be in control of what are doing. We have considered both kinds of actions in our proposal, and a mechanism to transform in automatics some conscious actions previously marked by the designer.

Human attentional capability is related with both the concentration level that the individual can achieve performing an action and the time that can sustain this attention avoiding signifier fluctuations on it. We proposed mechanism and structures that allows us to simulate concentration for an IVA, considering it as a transitory state of his behavior.

We related concentration with the activation level of the IVA's body: activation level can limit the concentration level possible to achieve by the agent, and at the same time, each concentration level requires a specific organism's activation level.

On the other hand, the concentration achieved focuses the attention in some specific stimulus –needed for the current action– and changed the sensorial channels thresholds inhibiting the IVA's normal perception; when this happen the agent can only perceive stimulus that exceeded these new perceptual limits.

Our proposal tried to provide the agent both more credibility and natural behavior, improving the user-IVA interaction, motivating him to invest more time and effort using the system.

2   Related Work

The research range is broad, so we will present the three more usual ways to work with attention in computational fields:

2.1   Attentional Aware Systems (AAS) and Attentional User Interfaces (AUI)

Interaction with computer has changed in the last years since the initial paradigm of several users sharing a computer with a text interface coming to the more actual paradigm of an unique user working in a personal computer with a graphical user interface (GUI), to arrive at the paradigm presented in Vertegaal et al. [7] a multiparty relationship among user and the computational devices, because the existence of several communication channel between their.

Current systems have a number of actives computational devices surrounding the user, devices that are part of a computer network. On the other hand, users are part of a community that is trying to capture their attention by those devices [7]. This situation causes a bombardment of interruptions which necessitate speedy answers from the user, who is distracted from his current work. So, AAS emerging as systems capable to both recollect information about attentional user focus in a specific time and modify the information showed adjusting it to the previous information [8].

Research in AAS is mainly focus on establishing the correct moment to interrupt the user with new information; nevertheless, AAS can refresh the information dynamically in an attractive way for users, according to their interests [2].

Closely related to AAS, there is the Attentive User Interface (AUI) which "is a user interface that dynamically prioritizes the information it presents to its users, such that information processing resources of both user and system are optimally distributed across a set of tasks" [9]. AUIs use sensors to select the point where the users would focus their work, by extra input channels can check user presence, glace, orientation, oral activity, nearly, etc. [9, 10].

Toet [11] showed us that "attentive displays can be particularly useful in domains with tasks that require visual, spatial and causal reasoning". These domains share five features [12]: (1) objects are spatially distributed; (2) the domain is dynamic; (3) objects causally interact with each other; (4) such interactions can be traced along chains of cause; and (5) predicting the future evolution of a system in the domain.

Finally, an AUI research group at Microsoft has worked defining human attention as a central point for construct, organize and improve computational and communicational systems, trying to give it more intelligent interfaces [13].

2.2   Visual and Auditory Attention

Currently, visual and auditory attention research showed a deep work, integrated with neurophysiology and neurophysiology (among others), mainly studying how to reproduce –partially– visual selective attention mechanisms. The central point is oriented to visual reconnaissance of real objects or people in the scenes captured by front-end devices.

Some researchers have been studying biological systems and applying neuronal networks to formulate and implement computational model of visual attention [14, 15, 16, 17, 18, 19]. Some of them, imitating basics aspect of human vision, have proposed bottom-up computational models of visual attention and can formulate saliency map of the scene. Inside this paradigm, some ones have proposed models which include top-down processing, for example: Itti [16] presented his PhD thesis "Models of Bottom-up and Top-down Visual Attention"; Machnouh y Tarroux [20] proposed a visual architecture that include bottom-up and top-down visions to identity –according previously define goals– saliency regions of the scene; KanWoo Lee et al. [21], proposed a computational model for selective visual attention based on neurophysics evidence, which was implemented on the "Interactive Spiking Neural Network" and use bottom-up and top-down inputs.

On the other hand, Wrigley and Brown [22] have presented a computational model of auditory selective attention which try to reproduced –a small scale– the real auditory selective attention mechanisms, and is based on ASA (Auditory Scene Analysis), a model of auditory analysis previously proposed by Bregman in 1990.

2.3   Attention in Virtual Agents

Kim et al. [23] have proposed a visual and auditory perception-attention computational model which use bottom-up and top-down factors on selection; Hill [24, 25] presented an extension of it that has been implemented and tested for virtual humans as part of MRE project [26] of the Institute for Creative Technologies, USA. Kim et al. [23] have developed a complete work, integrating top-down and bottom-up features. Nevertheless, the virtual human have not personality or emotions and play the role of a pilot into a flight simulator, because that its interaction with the environment is limited.

Gu et al. [27] have showed a computational model that includes a blindness attentional feature; their model use attention as an input filter which allow the processing only for the selected subset. Their visual human attention model has both a bottom-up and a top-down filter building a saliency map of the real word scenes.

Peters et al. [28] presented a work oriented to embodied agents with synthetic vision, giving it the capability of perceive when another agent's attention is oriented to itself. Peter's agent can perceive both the gaze and body orientation of others agents in the environment and infer hypothesis about reasons, wish or intentions.

3   Simulating IVA Attentional Capability

3.1   The IVA's Actions

One agent's scheduler responsibility –defined by COGNITIVA– [5, 29] is scheduling the actions proposed as plans by the reactive processes, the deliberative and the social layers, in the IVA's Agenda. The Agenda is an action sequence sorted by their time of execution, order based on their priority. The scheduler selects in every cycle (considering an agent as a continuous *perception-cognition-action* cycle) the next action to be executed and sends it to the agent's effectors [5, 29].

Among all the actions received at a given moment, the scheduler selects the one to be sent to the effectors for its execution, keeping the rest ordered in the Agenda to be executed later. Then, the perception expectations related to that action are updated. If the expectations are fulfilled after the action execution, the execution of the rest of the actions of the Agenda will continue; otherwise, the execution of the scheduled actions will be questioned and the Agenda will be possibly restructured.

The virtual agent manages a finite set of actions to try to transform the conditions of its surrounded environment or its own state according to its interests or its goals; let us define this set as: $Ac = \{ac_0, ac_1, \dots\}$.

Any element of this set consists of (1) some *preconditions*, which must be verified in order to the action execution; they are of paramount importance for the scheduler to consider the parallelization of the execution of some actions; (2) an *operator*, which will be executed when it arrives to the effectors; (3) the *action consequences*, state –desirable or not– expected after the execution of the action; (4) the *expectations* about the action's execution; and (5) the *private attribute* set of the action.

The private attribute set contains: a *caducity date*, i.e. the time limit to execute the action once it has been proposed; the *automatic nature* of the action (could be true or false); action's *current condition* (automatic or conscious); the *successful action's executions quantification* (seq); the action's *performance difficulty degree*[1]; and, finally, the time stamp for the *last successful performance*.

3.2   Automatic and Conscious Actions for an IVA

Psychology has studied divided attention by the use of the *double work* paradigm; according to it, simultaneous execution of two different tasks is: easy, if they need little attention (both are automatic); more difficult if they need more attention (increasing mistakes); and almost impossible if both need attentional resources.

Therefore, we have divided the IVA's actions between: *automatic*, those ones that need minimal attentional resources because they have been well learned by the agent and they are executed in an unconscious way; and *conscious*, the ones that need attentional resources in each stage of the activity to be correctly performed.

The agent could perform successfully two or more actions (a limited number) at the same time if they are automatic, for example: walk, talk and watch around; however, conscious actions performance will be limited by the agent's capabilities and resource availability. While it is good practice to perform only one conscious action at the same time, the agent may try to play two if has sufficient resources available.

---

[1] For the performance difficulty degree we have arbitrarily defined three progressive levels: high, medium and low but, if necessary, these levels could be easily customized in design time.

Obviously, in real life a person performs partially-automatic actions. These actions are in progress to become automatic because of its repetitive execution, but need some attentional resources yet. To model this characteristic, some of the IVA's conscious actions –defined by the designer– *would become automatics by extensive performing*. Nevertheless, not every conscious action can be gradually transformed in an automatic one. It is a designer's duty to define correctly which ones will become automatic by practice, depending –mainly– on the environment's context.

To make a conscious action to acquire a new automatic condition, the action must have both automatic nature and a minimal –arbitrary– amount of successful executions (mseq). mseq, is defined by the system's designer and must be an integer greater than zero; the designer will define intermediate limits too, seq_{low} and seq_{med}, which allow the definition of certain learning levels:

Table 1. Definition of learning levels

Training level	Succesful execution quantification (seq)
Low	$0 < seq \leq seq_{low}$
Medium	$seq_{low} < seq \leq seq_{med}$
High	$seq_{med} < seq \leq mseq$

If $seq \geq mseq$, the action is defined like automatic.

On the other hand, to simulate the non-continuous practice effect in the IVA's practice level, a degradation function over the seq ($degraseq$) have been included, based on the timestamp of the last successful performance. If the time period since this timestamp overpasses a predefined $\Delta t'$ the value of seg will be decreased. So, $degraseq$ is defined as:

$$degraseq(seq) = \begin{cases} 0; & if\ seq = 0 \\ seq; & if\ \Delta t < \Delta t' \\ seq - 1; ioc. \end{cases} \quad (1)$$

In this case, while the seq value is increased by one every time a successful performance of the action takes place, the $degraseq$ function acts in the opposite way, decreasing the seq value by one after a certain non-practice period of time. The low limit will be obviously zero.

In order to define for the agent the required concentration levels to perform an action, we defined a classification table that relate the action perform difficult degree with the action training level in this action, showed in the next section.

3.3   Concentration an Attentional Capability of the IVA

The divided attention model, proposed by Kahneman [30], says there are tasks which need more mental effort than other. Effort is related to the person's mental work general capability, but there are different individual factors that can increase or decrease this capability; among others: concentration, arousal and experience.

Concentration is defined by psychologists as the attentional resources continuously applied during a time period to perform a task. Through concentration, attention highlights one specific situation in the personal consciousness, giving more energy and dedication to it. A human needs both attention and concentration to reach a good intellectual performance and, in this way, to facilitate the development of human mind processes.

We have modeled the agent's concentration as a transitory state of its personal model, and as such has been included in the extension that we propose for the agent's architecture, which means that it must include: a name, a quantitative and a qualitative domains, and a semantic model [5, 29].

On the one hand, the quantitative domain accepts values in the real numbers interval $[0, 1]$, with 0 related to the no-presence of the transitory state and 1 to its full presence. On the other hand, for the qualitative domain associated to this quantitative domain we have used the same set of fuzzy labels, defined and used in the functional specification of COGNITIVA described in [5, 29]; in this way, the qualitative domain used is both homogeneous and context free. The relationship between both domains has been defined univocally through the semantic model showed in figure 1.

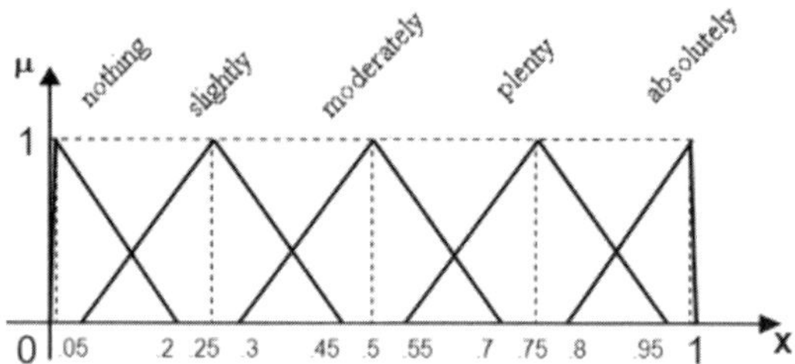

Fig. 1. Semantic Model for a transitive state

Is possible to assign the needed concentration level for the development of an action over two related values: Action Difficulty Degree and SEQ, and using the semantic model of transitory states to assign it, as is showed in table 2:

Table 2. Concentration required to performer an action

Action difficulty degree	SEQ	Concentration required
High	Low	Absolutely
High	Medium	Plenty
High	High	Moderately
Medium	Low	Absolutely
Medium	medium	Moderately
Medium	High	Moderately
Low	Low	Moderately
Low	Medium	Slightly
Low	High	Slightly

Those values would be useful to set up for the agent both: the activation level and the adjustment of the perceptive threshold of its sensorial channels; as we see later.

3.4   Activation Level, Concentration and Sensorial Thresholds

Arousal is the physiological and psychological state of being awake. From the biological point of view, the arousal of a person –sometimes called "activity level"– is the most important deciding factor for the individual attention; is related to the receptiveness and answerable that the nervous system has in a particular moment in time front the entire environment stimulus [2].

The activation level will have a notorious influence in the processing capability of an organism and, as a result in its attentional capability [25]. A person in activation can: has a higher attention level; give a better response to the environment stimulus; perform better complex tasks; and, concentrate attention for longer period of time [2].

Defining the activation level of the agent as a transitory state of its own personal model [9, 10] we can use the semantic model (see figure 1) for agent's belief.

Table 3. Activation Quantitative Measurement

Action Level Arousal	Arousal Qualitative Measurement	Activation Quantitative Measurement
Alert	Absolutely	1.0
Relax	Plenty	0.75
Sleepiness	Moderately	0.50
Asleep	Slightly	0.25

The higher concentration level, the higher required arousal level; this increases the sensorial channels thresholds too, as is showed later. Each level of concentration required –at least– a similar activation level; on the other hand, a specific activation level limits the concentration level to attain –at most– to the equivalent activation level. The table 4 show us the relationship among concentration and activation levels:

Table 4. Relationship among concentration and activation

Concentration Level	Activation Level (Arousal)
Absolutely	Alert
Plenty	Relax
Moderately	Sleepiness
Slightly	Asleep

A high concentration level on the current action modifies the sensorial channels thresholds; concentrated in the task the agent can perceive only closer visual stimulus, strident or aloud sounds and so on. Concentration avoid to distract the attention for everyone environment stimulus, just strong stimulus can overtake the –imposed by concentration– sensorial channels thresholds.

IVA's sensorial channels have associated a number of perceptive parameters used to describe the agent's perception and related with the synthetic perceptive model applied [4]. There is a thresholds range defined by two constant values to each channel: the upper limit and the lower limit. Nevertheless, when is necessary these can be temporally modified.

The finite set of thresholds is described by $U = \{u_0, u_1, \ldots\}$, where each element u_i represent a particular perceptive parameter for a well defined channel. Every element of the set is well defined by a data structure; and, although all parameters are numeric type, everyone has a singular interpretation that allows us to drive the agent's thresholds of each sensorial channel.

Of course, a reactive reaction can suddenly interrupt its current activity if the organizer demands it, forcing the reestablishment of standard values for concentration and sensorial channels, not to the arousal. Any strong emotion (i.e., panic) or an intense physical sensation (i.e., pain) can generate an attentional temporary blockade of senses; that is possible modifying the sense thresholds in a way to stop –almost by complete– the perception of any stimulus for a pre-establish and delimited time.

Finished the activity, attentional resources are free, the concentration level decrease and sensorial channels threshold return to their usual values.

4 Conclusions and Future Work

We have proposed a representation of Attentional Capability for an IVA which is based over on the Kahneman Attentional Capability Model, from the psychologist of attention. The idea of attentional resources and capability, concentration, activation levels and sensorial channels thresholds are inspired from it.

The proposal was applied to an agent modeled with personality and emotions through COGNITIVA; the mechanism that simulates different features related to the attentional capability of the embodied agent has clearly established the relationships among its different features.

The testing of our proposal for an IVA is currently in progress; for this purpose, the virtual environment and the experimental situations are well defined and in building and testing process.

References

[1] García Sevilla, J.: Psicología de la Atención. Ed: Síntesis (1997)
[2] Roda, C., Thomas, J.: Attention aware systems: Theories, applications and research agenda. Computers in Human Behaviour 22, 557–587 (2006)
[3] Rosselló i Mir, J.: Psicología de la Atención. Ed: Pirámide (1998)
[4] Styles, E.: The Psychology of Attention. Ed. Psychology Press (2006)

[5] Imbert, R., Antonio, A.D.: COGNITIVA: A Context Independent Cognitive Architecture for Agents Combining Rational and Emotional Behaviours. In: 5th. WSEAS Int. Conf. on Multimedia, Internet and Video Technologies. Corfu, Greece (2005)

[6] Herrero, P., Antonio, A.d.: Introducing Human-like Hearing Perception in Intelligent Virtual Agents. In: 2nd. International Joint Conference on Autonomous Agents and Multiagent Systems (2003)

[7] Vertegaal, R., Shell, J.S., Chen, D., Mamuji, A.: Designing for augmented attention: Towards a framework for attentive user interfaces. Computers in Human Behaviour 22, 771–789 (2006)

[8] Rapp, D.N.: The value of attention aware systems in educational settings. Computers in Human Behaviour 22, 603–614 (2006)

[9] Vertegaal, R.: Attentive User Interfaces. Communications of the ACM 46(3), 30–33 (2003)

[10] Vertegaal, R.: Designing Attentive Interfaces. In: Proceedings of the Eye Tracking Research & Application Symposium, ETRA 2002, USA (2002)

[11] Toet, A.: Gaze directed displays as an enabling technology for attention aware systems. special issue: Attention aware systems, Computers in Human Behavior 22, 615–647 (2006)

[12] Narayanan, N.H., Yoon, D.: Reactive information displays. In: Proceedings of INTERACT 2003: Ninth IFIP TC 13 international conference on human-computer interaction, pp. 244–251. IOS Press, Amsterdam, The Netherlands (2003)

[13] Horvitz, E., Kadie, C.M., Paek, T., Hovel, D.: Models of Attention in Computing and Communication: From Principles to Applications. Adaptative Systems and Interaction, Microsoft Research (2003) (accessed 10-27-2007), http://research.microsoft.com/~horvitz/cacm-attention.htm

[14] Chokshi, K., Panchev, C., Wermter, S., Taylor, J.G.: Knowing What and Where: A Computational Model for Visual Attention. In: Proceedings of the International Joint Conference on Neural Networks, Budapest, Hungary (2004)

[15] Indivari, G., Mrer, R., Kramer, J.: Active Vision Using an Analog VLSI Model of Selective Attention. IEEE Transactions on circuits and systems II: Analog and Digital Signal processing 48(5) (2001)

[16] Itti, L.: PhD. Dissertation: Models of Bottom-Up and Top-Down Visual Attention. California Institute of Technology, Pasadena, California (2000)

[17] Itti, L., Koch, C.: A saliency-based search mechanism for overt and covert shifts of visual attention. Vision Research 40(10), 1489–1506 (2000)

[18] Itti, L., Koch, C., Niebur, E.: A model of saliency-based visual attention for rapid scene analysis. IEEE Transactions on Pattern Analysis and Machine Intelligence 20(11), 1254–1259 (1998)

[19] Kohonen, T.: A Computational Model of Visual Attention. In: International Joint Conference on Neural Networks (2003)

[20] Machrouh, J., Tarraoux, P.: Attentional Mechanisms for Interactive Image Exploration. EURASIP Journal on Applied Signal Processing 14, 2391–2396 (2005)

[21] Lee, K., Buxton, H., Feng, J.: Cue-Guided Search: A Computational Model of Selective Attention (2005)

[22] Wrigley, S., Brown, G.: A Computational Model of Auditory Selective Attention. IEEE Transactions on Neural Netwoks 15(5), 1151–1163 (2004)

[23] Kim, Y., Van Velsen, M., Hill Jr., R.: Modeling Dynamic Perceptual Attention in Complex Virtual Environments. In: Conference on Intelligent Virtual Agent 2005, pp. 266–277 (2005)

[24] Hill, R.: Perceptual Attention in Virtual Humans: Towar Realistic and Believable Gaze Behaviours. In: Proceedings of the AAAI Fall Symposium on Simulating Human Agents, California, USA, pp. 46–52 (2000)
[25] Hill, R.: Modeling Perceptual Attention in Virtual Humans. In: Proceedings of the 8th Conference on Computer Generated Forces and Behavioral Representation, Florida, USA (1999)
[26] Hill, R., Gratch, J., Marsella, S., Rickel, J., Swartout, W., Traum, D.: Virtual Humans in the Mission Rehearsal Exercise System. Knstliche Intelligenz (KI Journal). Special issue on Embodied Conversational Agents (2003)
[27] Gu, E., Stocker, C., Badler, N.I.: Do You See What Eyes See? Implementing Inattentional blindess. In: The 5th. International Working Conference on Intelligent Virtual Agents, Greece (2005)
[28] Peters, C., Pelachaud, C., Bevacqua, E., Mancini, M., Poggi, I.: A Model of Attention and Interest Using Gaze Behaviour. In: The 5th. International Working Conference on Intelligent Virtual Agents (2005)
[29] Imbert, R., Antonio, A.D.: When Emotion Does Not Mean Loss of Control. In: Panayiotopoulos, T., Gratch, J., Aylett, R.S., Ballin, D., Olivier, P., Rist, T. (eds.) IVA 2005. LNCS (LNAI), vol. 3661, pp. 152–165. Springer, Heidelberg (2005)
[30] Kahneman, D.: Attention and Effort. Prentice-Hall, Englewood Cliffs (1973)

Adaptive Power Management Based on Reinforcement Learning for Embedded System

Cheng-ting Liu and Roy Chaoming Hsu

Department of Computer Science and Information Engineering
National Chiayi University, No.300, Syue-fu Road,
60004, Chiayi City, Taiwan, R.O.C.
rchsu@mail.ncyu.edu.tw

Abstract. In this study, an adaptive power management method based on reinforcement learning is proposed to improve the energy utilization and battery endurance for resource-limited embedded systems. A simulator which traces battery endurance and device operations is developed to examine the proposed method. Experimental results show that, in terms of battery efficiency and endurance, the performance of our proposed method is better than the traditional power management techniques, such as static power management method.

Keywords: adaptive power management, embedded system, reinforcement learning.

1 Introduction

In recent years, mobile communication devices and portable apparatus, powered by battery, has proliferated rapidly. With the limited energy resource provided by the battery, energy saving and efficiency is becoming an important issue in designing new embedded system products, such as PDA, cell phone, remote sensor devices and even satellite, etc. Even though some of the devices might be powered by renewable power sources, such as solar and wind energy, and the renewable energy can be stored in battery for later use, energy resources are still limited when they are carried by human being or are deployed to severe environment. The conditions of limited resource may be varied for different devices due to different design purpose for operating in different environment. For example, cell phone requires a battery to operate for several days before the battery energy is exhausted, while a sensor deployed in a remote area, might need renewable solar energy such that the sensor might be survived for several months by the battery charged using solar cell in sunny days. Hence, power management scheme in efficiently utilizing battery and in extending battery life for these embedded devices plays a crucial role in embedded system design.

For this reason, power management (PM) methods must be introduced and experimented in designing embedded system. Various PM platforms have been proposed by recent research [2-6]. Classification of PM method varies from component-level design to system-level framework [7, 8]. System-level PM approach usually relies on

N.T. Nguyen et al. (Eds.): IEA/AIE 2008, LNAI 5027, pp. 513–522, 2008.

software running on OS or goes along with some customized interface to implement PM on a given system. ACPI, a system-level framework PM interface protocol, is designed by Intel for commercial multi-purpose computer, such as desktop computer, and its peripherals. However, due to its inherent complexity, the protocol is not suitable for single-purpose resource-constrained embedded systems. IO-centric power management design by shutting down the devices after certain time instance can be considered as component-level platform, which is more suitable for low-end and resource-constrained embedded systems. The adaptive time-out policy [6] employs general shutdown strategy to flexibly determine the proper time instance to switch device's operation power from high to low until a request is received by the PM to switch back to high working power.

System-level PM approach is utilized in this proposed work. A battery simulator with accurate battery behavior model [11], is adopted as our battery model for experiment with our proposed power management scheme. The complete description of the reinforcement learning based PM method and the experimental results will be shown in the following sections.

2   Method Design

General speaking, an adaptive PM shall include an observer in monitoring the system and related resources, a management policy for deciding appropriate actions to the system according to different conditions, and a controller in exercising the decided actions to achieve operational state transition based the built-in policy [7, 8]. We assume major devices of an embedded system must be controlled by power manager in a PM method such that the power states of devices, built on resource-limited embed system, are managed by the power manager. Assuming there are two observable system states, service request rate from application and the percentage of energy remained in battery. The service request rate, denoted as ρ, is normalized and ranges from 0 to 100% with resolution of 1%, which stands for idle and full request capacity, respectively, for devices to be serviced. The percentage of energy remained in battery is represented by the notation δ, while the battery is modeled as an ideal rechargeable power source with a small internal resistance. The battery model is designed as a reservoir for energy, while the battery's discharge is considered as leakage with leakage rate following the Ohm's law and voltage distributed rule. The notations ρ and δ are the observable system states consisting of S, the system state vector. A round (or run), denoted as B, is considered to be ended once the battery is running out where the source voltage is lower than the device operational voltage and δ is equal to 0 in consequence. The action set A is defined as control signal of the device's power, which is consisted of a_{high} and a_{low}, i.e., $A=\{ a_{high} , a_{low} \}$, which represents high power and low power status, respectively, for each device. The power status of each device is regarded as an action from power manager's decision, which also indicates the assigned power consumption at given time instant for the battery discharge model. The time stamp is denoted as τ, with resolution of one minute for each stamp. Based on these observable states (ρ, δ), actions, and the defined parameters, a Q-learning algorithm is utilized for adaptive power management as shown in Fig. 1.

DPM-AGENT algorithm
1   initialize Q table entry for each (s, a) pair and reward, $B \leftarrow 1$
2   do
3       $\tau \leftarrow 1$
4   observe the current state (ρ, δ)
                (ρ: service request rate state, δ: battery remain power state)
5   while the end of run is false
6   adjust policy Π with given Q
                select action a with given Π
                execute **Battery.doDischarge**(a)
7   observe the new state (ρ', δ')
8   **Learner**[(ρ', δ'), a, R]
9   (ρ, δ) $\leftarrow$ (ρ', δ')
10              $\tau \leftarrow \tau + 1$
11   end while loop
12   get the reward R for the current run B
13      $B \leftarrow B + 1$
14   if the current run $\neq$ the assigned training number then go 2:
15 end do loop

Fig. 1. Power Management Agent Algorithm with Reinforcement Learning

In the beginning the first run ($B = 1$), the battery is full, power manager observes the initial state at the first time stamp (step $\tau = 1$, line 1), as line 4 in Fig. 1. Then, as in line 5, the PM method runs into the main loop for each run. In line 6, depending on the current Q, the policy, Π, is adjusted, and action a is selected with a given Π. Then, in line 8, Q-learning training rule (update rule, the *Learner* function) learns the information from observed states for building up Q table. The learning rule of the *Learner* function will be described in details later. The update rule of Q-learning is described in equation (1). State updates in line 9 and the step is increased by one in line 10. When δ is lower than 0, the current run is over and the learning reward will be calculated according to the service achievement rate of last run. The time step obtained at the end of each run represents the endurance time of the battery. Assuming that the battery can be charged immediately to the full scale for next run's operation and the PM algorithm then goes back with the new policy applied at the next run.

The learner's function, *Learner* ($\bullet$), in line 8, is composed of the following equations (1) to (5). According to the Q value of action from last run, denoted as Q_{B-1}, value of action of the current run, Q_B, is updated by (1)

$$Q_B (s, a) = (1 - \alpha) Q_{B-1}(s, a) + \alpha[R_B + \max_{a'} Q_{B-1}(s', a')] \qquad (1)$$

where α is learning rate in the interval (0,1). For series of run, the value of α is slightly decreased to achieve a proper value determined by the inverse of the number of (s,a) pair visited. Going through the learning phase in (1), the policy's decision is

$$\Pi_{B+1} = \begin{cases} \Pi_B + L; & Q_B > Q_{B-1}(1 + \varepsilon) \\ \Pi_B - L; & Q_B < Q_{B-1}(1 - \varepsilon) \\ \Pi_B; & \text{otherwise} \end{cases} \qquad (2)$$

where policy Π is a step-function as the threshold level corresponding to ρ for deciding which action to be taken, and L is step size of Π. Π_B is denoted as the current policy. Without loss of generality, L is assigned with value of $0.1\Pi_B$. At the end of each B, the next policy Π_{B+1} is determined by increasing or decreasing Π_B by L according to the comparison of value of action of the current and previous run, plus or minus by a small quantity, ε, which is a constant parameter with assigned value 0.5, herein. The next policy Π_{B+1} will be unchanged, otherwise. The equation of action selection is given by

$$a_\tau = \begin{cases} a_{High}; & \rho_\tau \geq \Pi_\tau \\ a_{Low}; & \text{otherwise} \end{cases} \qquad (3)$$

where the *High* power action will selected by turning device power state into high power (a_{high}) if current ρ larger than or equal to step level Π, while the *Low* power action will selected otherwise. The evaluation of service achievability, η, for a certain run is given by

$$\eta = \Sigma_{\tau \in B}[\rho_\tau a_\tau] / \eta_0 \qquad (4)$$

where η_0 is the sum of the total service request rate for the given run, i.e., $\eta_0 = \Sigma_{\tau \in B}[\rho_\tau]$. And the reward value for a certain round is obtained by

$$R_B = \eta \Delta_B - \varphi \qquad (5)$$

where Δ_B is the B_{th} battery's endurance time which is obtained by the time step τ at the end of the run. φ is assigned as the average value of Δ_B among all learning runs. If $\eta\Delta_B$ is higher than φ, the leaner will obtain a positive reward; on the other hand, if $\eta\Delta_B$ is smaller than φ, the leaner will obtain a punishment, i.e., negative reward. Hence, the appropriate action will be exercised and reward be given by going through learning phase from (1) through (5). In next section, the overall simulation environment will be described.

3   Simulation Configuration

To show how well the Q-learning algorithm's effectiveness in managing power adaptively, a simulation platform consists of the battery model (*BM*) as a battery behavior, service requester model (*SR*) as application software behavior, the service provider (*SP*) as servomechanisms behavior, the response monitor (*RM*) as the user interface, and the power manager (*PMR*) as an intelligent agent behavior are designed using the platform block diagram as in Fig. 2.

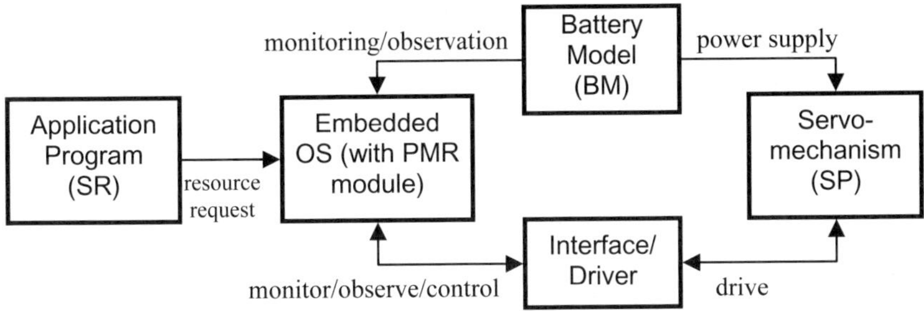

Fig. 2. The system block diagram of simulation model for the Q-learning based power management method

In Fig. 2, the *SR* generates a sequence of quantity of job for a segment of time interval in terms of service request rate, ρ, which is one of the environment state observed by the *PMR*. To know how well the proposed PM does, every job generated by the SR in the sequence is assumed independent and is dropped when it is done. The value of ρ, the service request rate as describes in section 2, is generated by applying sinusoid wave and by adding a white Gaussian noise as (6).

$$\rho(\tau) = A\,[1 + \sin(\,n_1\omega\tau\,)] + n_2 \tag{6}$$

where A and ω are controlling and normalizing parameters for the sinusoid wave, τ is time step, n_2 is a uniform random number which randomizes for every time step, and n_1 is random number which randomizes every 1000 time steps, such that ρ is a time-varying function with period follows ω. Fig. 3 shows portion of the service request profile, $\rho(\tau)$, as the dotted line. *SP* behaves like a controllable bi-power-state device, i.e., it can be switched to hi-power or low-power by the *PMR* by observing the ρ_τ as in. (3). When *SP* operates on hi-power (a_{High}), its service achievability is labeled

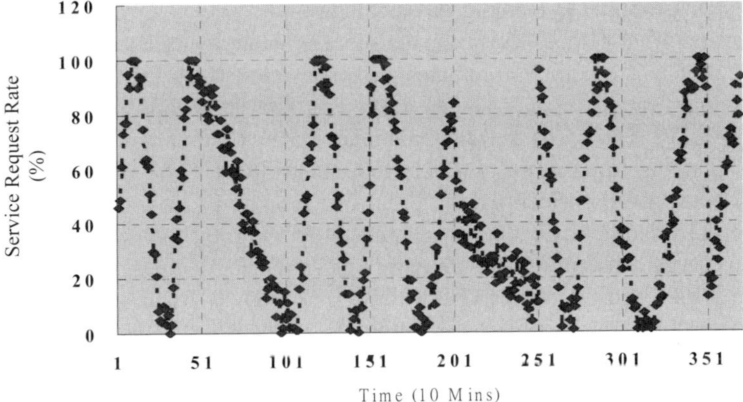

Fig. 3. The trace of service requested rate

100%, i.e., all of the jobs will be accepted and running. Similarly, if *SP* operates on low-power (a_{Low}), half of the jobs are serviced. Battery model of the simulator is defined as a rechargeable battery with maximum capacity of 2400 mAH and nominal operation voltage of 2.4V. In this simulation, it is assumed that the exhausted battery is to be charged to 2400 mAH immediately once the battery's capacity is exhausted. The endurance time, Δ, of battery is defined as the time interval from the time when the battery is fully charged to the time when the battery is exhausted. The Q-learning based PM method is designed in section 2 and the relationships of each block diagram of the simulation system are all well-defined now. The simulation and experimental results of the proposed method will be discussed in the following section.

4 Result and Discussion

To demonstrate the performance of energy saving and efficiency in extending battery life, the Q-Learning based PM method was applied to the simulation model defined above for embedded system. The experiment for measuring the endurance time of battery was conducted with the following scenarios:

1.   The system always operates on high power consumption (abbreviated as *always high* hereafter),
2.   The system operates with the proposed Q-Learning PM method.

The same service request profile as (6) is feed into the simulation system for both test scenarios. Experimental results of above scenarios are shown in Fig. 4-6. Fig. 4 shows the trace of the decided policy value for a period of time instants, where the action of high-power status is selected whenever service request value is higher than the profile and the job requested by *SR* is completed with high energy consumption. On the contrary, action of low-power consumption is selected once the service request value is lower than the profile. According to Fig. 5, the battery endurance time obtained by the proposed Q-learning PM method (bold black) is always about 1.5 times of the *always high* method. However, the shortest battery endurance time obtained by the *always high* is around 700 minutes (red thin line), which indicates that even the service request rate is light, as shown in the first bottom of Fig 3, the energy is consumed the most worst. The average endurance time of the *always high* and the proposed Q-learning PM method is calculated and is about 777.6 minutes and 1126.8 minutes, respectively, which exhibits that our proposed Q-learning PM method is effective in extending the battery's endurance time. Fig. 6 shows the results of accumulating energy consumption by summing up all the energy consumed in each run for the *always high* and the proposed Q-learning PM method. It can be seen from Fig 6 that the accumulating energy consumption of our proposed Q-learning PM method (bold blue line) consumes less than the *always high* method (thin red line), which indicates that our proposed Q-learning PM method performs better in energy consumption than that of the *always high* static method.

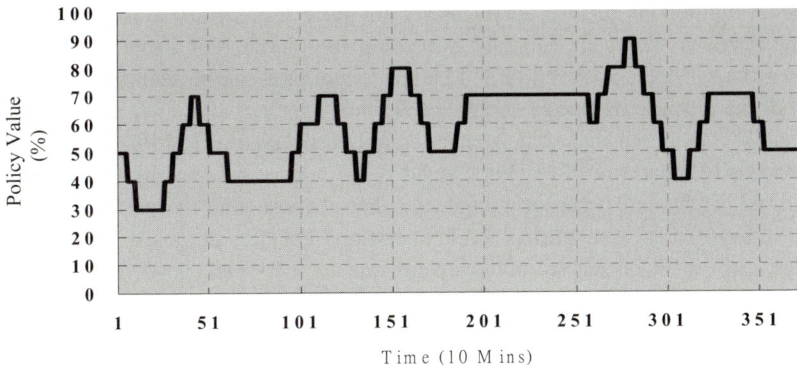

Fig. 4. The trace of the decided policy value

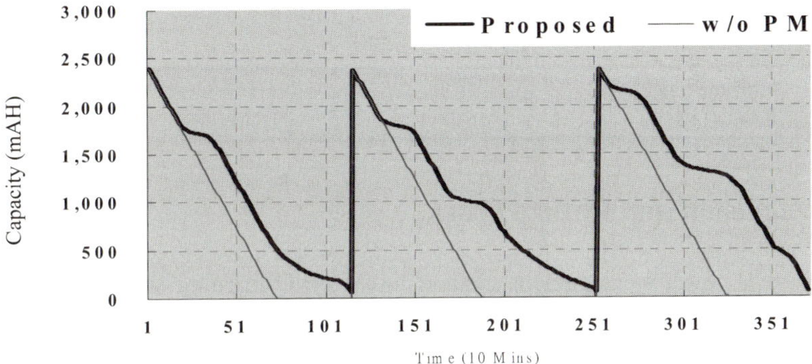

Fig. 5. Endurance trace of two different power management methods

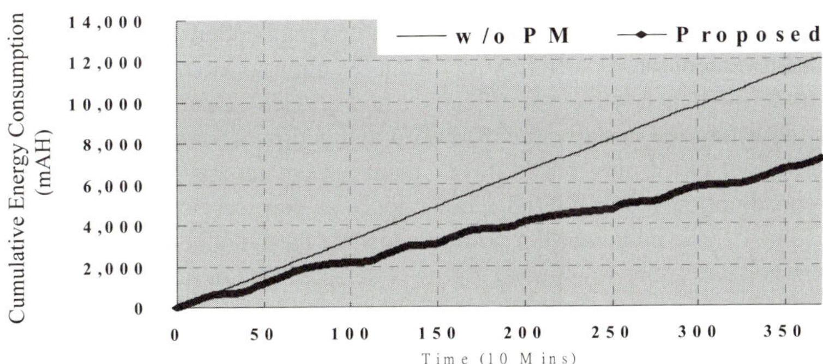

Fig. 6. The cumulative energy consumption trace of two different power management methods

The evaluation of service achievability for both test scenarios is also conducted and the result is shown in Table 1. According to column 4 of Table 1, the trade-off between the service achievability and battery endurance can be seen from the simulation. For the purpose of energy saving, power management will decrease some service achievability such that that some request might be delayed or lost. On the other hand, our proposed Q-learning PM method regards the service achievability as a portion of reward, as in (5), and it can be guaranteed that at most time the performance is still higher than 60% of the *always high* operation. For the proposed Q-learning PM method, only 30% of service achievement rate is sacrificed, however, the battery's endurance time is extended.

Table 1. Power Consumption and Service Achievement Rate of always high and the proposed Q-learning PM method

	Test 50 rounds		
	Total Endurance Time (10 min)	scaled with *always high* method	Average service achievability (%)
always high	38880	1	99
the proposed PM method	56300	1.40	73

5 Conclusion and Future Work

An adaptive power management method based on Q-learning suited for embedded system is proposed in this study. Experimental results show that through learning phases of the proposed Q-learning based PM method, the battery endurance time can be extended to more than 1.5 times of the *always high* method. The Q-learning based power management method can gradually approach the optimal conditions by learning step by step. Even the service achievement rate is decreasing, the embedded system also can maintain on the range from 58% to 85% operational during the 7_{th} to 50_{th} battery run. For applications on resource-limited embedded system, 70% average service achievement rate is sufficient to obtain the appropriate response.

The trade-off between energy efficiency and service achievability can be simply tuned by adjusting the initial value of reward and action according to the experiments of the proposed Q-learning based power management method. The reason is that if energy consumption is considered more important than service achievability, larger reward value of low-power-action will be added to the Q-value. The policy level will increase whenever more low-power status is selected and assigned such that the action of selecting hi-power-status is more difficult, and in consequence, the less energy will be consumed.

Furthermore, a solar panel model can be added to our proposed simulation platform such that a simulated embedded system with renewable power source, played as the exact battery charger, can be established. And the ideal charger assumption addressed by the above sections can be omitted. Then a better adaptive PM method can be designed utilizing the simulation model which is not only targeted for discharging phase, but also suited for charging period.

References

1. Benini, L., Bogliolo, A., Micheli, G.: A survey of Design Techniques for System-Level Dynamic Power Management. IEEE Transactions on Very Large Scale Integration Systems 8(3), 299–316 (2000)
2. Carreras, M., Yuh, J., Batlle, J., Ridao, P.: A Behavior-Based Scheme Using Reinforcement Learning for Autonomous Underwater Vehicles. IEEE Journal of Oceanic Engineering 30(2), 416–427 (2005)
3. Chen, W.-z., Zheng, H.: Analysis of Power Saving Effect for Dynamic Power Management. In: Proc. of the 2nd IEEE/ASME International Conference, pp. 1–4 (2006)
4. Cho, Y., Chang, N.: Energy-Aware Clock-Frequency Assignment in Microprocessors and Memory Devices for Dynamic Voltage Scaling. IEEE Transactions on Computer-Aided Design of Integrated Circuits and System 26(6), 1030–1040 (2002)
5. Chung, E.-Y., Benini, L., Bogliolo, A., Lu, Y.-H., Micheli, G.: Dynamic Power Management for Non-stationary Service Requests. IEEE Transactions on Computers 51(11), 1345–1361 (2002)
6. Dhiman, G., Rosing, T.S.: Dynamic Power Management Using Machine Learning. In: International Conference on Computer-Aided Design, San Jose, CA (2006)
7. Ernst, D., Glavic, M., Wehenkel, L.: Power Systems Stability Control: Reinforcement Learning Framework. IEEE Transactions on Power Systems 19(1), 427–435 (2004)
8. Irani, S., Shukla, S., Gupta, R.: Competitive Analysis of Dynamic Power Management Strategies for Systems with Multiple Power Saving States. In: Proc. of the Design, Automation and Test in Europe Conference and Exhibition (2002)
9. Li, M., Wu, X., Yao, R., Yan, X.: Q DPM: An Efficient Model-free Dynamic Power Management Technique. In: Proc. of the Design, Automation and Test in Europe Conference and Exhibition (2005)
10. Lu, Y.-H., Micheli, G.: Comparing System-Level Power Management Policies. IEEE Transactions Design and Test of Computers 18(2), 10–19 (2001)
11. Qiu, Q., Wu, Q., Pedram, M.: Stochastic Modeling of a Power-Managed System- Construction and Optimization. IEEE Transactions on Computer-Aided Design of Integrated Circuits and System 20(10), 1200–1217 (2001)
12. Rong, P., Pedram, M.: Battery-Aware Power Management Based on Markovian Decision Processes. IEEE Transactions on Computer-Aided Design of Integrated Circuits and System 25(7), 1337–1349 (2006)
13. Cheng, S.-H., Wang, K.: An Adaptive Hybrid Dynamic Power Management Method for Handheld Devices. In: Proc. of the IEEE International Conference on Sensor Networks, Ubiquitous and Trustworthy Computing (2006)
14. Simunic, T., Benini, L.: Event-Driven Power Management. IEEE Transactions on Computer-Aided Design of Integrated Circuits and System 20(7), 840–857 (2001)

15. Sutton, R.S., Barto, A.G.: Reinforcement Learning: An Introduction. MIT Press, Cambridge (1998)
16. Tynan, R., O'Kane, D.M.D., O'Hare, G.: Agents for Wireless Sensor Network Power Management. In: Proc. of International Conference on Parallel Processing Workshops (2006)
17. Viswanathan, L.P., Monie, E.C.: Reinforcement Temporal Difference Learning Scheme for Dynamic Energy Management in Embedded Systems. In: Proc. of the 19th International Conference on VLSI Design (2006)
18. Vlachogiannis, J.G., Hatziargyriou, N.D.: Reinforcement Learning for Reactive Power Control. IEEE Transactions on Power Systems 19(3), 1317–1325 (2004)

Hybrid MAS GIS Coastal Systems Modeling Methodology

Dominique Urbani and Marielle Delhom

SPE LAB - UMR CNRS 6134 - University of Corsica
Quartier Grossetti - 20250 Corté - France
durbani@laposte.net, delhom@univ-corse.fr

Abstract. Submitted to the combination of a growing anthropogenic pressure, pollution and the increase of health required standards, the costal and ponds' ecosystems are endangered involving the decline of traditional sea activities. In this paper we present a methodology to build a distributed artificial intelligent based model dedicated to interactions between watershed and activities in coastal areas. Organizing the coastal systems into a hierarchy, following a multi-agents approach, we build a generic model of each system's stakeholder. We focus on modeling the influences of the watershed activities on sea farming. Using a geographic information system, we explicit how to take advantages of the spatiotemporal ground data to fit the simulations to the specificities of each targeted site.

Keywords: multi-agent system, geographic information system, environmental science, coastal ecosystem, sea farm, decision support systems.

1 Introduction

From long range observations of interactions between men and their milieu we notice that unconsidered augmentation of nature exploitation affects ecosystems up to their death.

The whole Corsican context is a typical case of preserved areas that will be shortly living a large economical growth with a major impact on environment.

Among other factors, the openness of more territories to urbanization and the new exploitation of abandoned cultivated areas increase the anthropogenic pressure on the preserved ecosystems in the Corsican eastern coastal plain and menace thousand years old ponds' sea farms.

The consequences of a growth of the activities are an eutrophication of water, proliferations of toxic algae, an augmentation of the concentrations of heavy metals and other contaminants. The resulting water quality deterioration weaks the wild life and undermines the durability of traditional activities based on the exploitation of the natural resources.

Today, the impact of harder life conditions on the coastal ecosystems exploiters activities is still not well known. The economical actors concerned by these changes are in quest of tools to understand and to foresee the possible consequences on their

N.T. Nguyen et al. (Eds.): IEA/AIE 2008, LNAI 5027, pp. 523–530, 2008.

business [1]. These tools could be useful to find new ways to manage the growth and help decision makers to preserve strategic areas before the imminent economic boom, and limit the negative consequences on the coastal ecosystems and the traditional activities.

In this paper we propose a methodology based on a distributed artificial intelligence paradigm to model the interactions between human activities in the watershed and the coastal systems. This multi-agents system (MAS) model takes into account the increase of pollution due to the economical boom, the impact on the water quality and wild life, and finally the consequences on the traditional business of the milieu's exploiters: fisheries, aquaculture and seashell farming. We propose to use a geographic information system (GIS) to take into account the spatiotemporal data of the targeted sites.

The model will be used in future works to build a simulator and a decision support system to help the decision makers to find a way ensuring the continued existence of the traditional activities in coastal areas, guaranteeing the ecosystems' preservation, insuring a sustainable development of the territories.

2 Methodology

The modeling methodology exposed in this paper is a continuation of our works on the SMAG (Système Multi-Agents Géographique) platform architecture dedicated to the development of hybrid MAS-GIS decision support systems [2]. This architecture, based on a multi-agents approach, was specially fitted to model and to simulate heterogeneous systems with a strong spatial component and interactions between numerous stakeholders [2].

SMAG is a modular hybrid architecture based on 2 units:

- The first unit is dedicated to model the behaviors of the systems and the stakeholders according to a multi-agents system (MAS) approach.
- The second unit based on geographic information system (GIS) allows taking into account the spatiotemporal data of the targeted sites. It provides tools to define scenarios of simulations and plan the experimentations.

In this paper, we use CORMGIS (the first operational SMAG compliant platform [3]) to implement the agents of the coastal systems. CORMGIS multi-agent module is based on extensions of the Agricultural Research Centre for International Development (CIRAD) CORMAS (COmmon-pool Resources and Multi-Agent Systems) multi-agents platform [4], whereas its GIS module is implemented by ArcGIS, the ESRI company [5] GIS software. The CORMGIS extensions to CORMAS enable to plan experimentations, to connect to the geographic databases, and provide interfaces dedicated to the interactions with stakeholders, experts and decision makers. CORMAS is a MAS platform focused on models for natural renewable resource management, based on the VisualWorks programming environment which allows the development of applications in the object-oriented programming language SmallTalk. CORMAS pre-defined entities are SmallTalk generic classes from which, by specialization and refining, users can create specific entities for their own model. We used CORMGIS to build a decision support system dedicated to the fresh water problem and to highlight the influence of the social interactions during the water shortage in the north of Corsica [6] [7].

2.1 Sea Farm Modeling

We build our coastal multi-agents model taking into account the basic elements allowing simulating the sea farm activities at the lot scale (bag or rack of seashells, fishes or shrimps lot). This approach is based on both observations of the farmers' practices and the use of existing models about animals' growth and ecosystems. Our work consists in developing a library of models representing the different types of animals and species (ostrea edulis, crassostrea angulata, crassostrea gigas, mussels, european seabass, gilt-head bream), about the stockbreeding methods and about how the farmers use the marine space.

This modeling task follows a typological organization into a hierarchy of sea farming activities. Analyzing the system we pass from animals lots, to the farm, and then to a whole rearing area with several farms in a bottom up approach. We build a model with three levels of abstraction fitted to the available data and the territories' specificities. In the first level of abstraction, the agents are built reusing existing well-tried models. Restricting our works to the sea farming fundamental elements, we propose a generic framework usable to study most of aquaculture situations.

To build faithful and trustable models, we finely observe the animals' biological cycles, the breeding steps, the farmers' activities and the sanitary regulator's making decisions process. We first focus on modeling oysters farming. Oysters are filter-feeders (5l/h) shells inhabiting water depths of between 8 and 25 feet. They are pro-tandric, which means that during their first year they spawn as males (releasing sperm into the water). As they grow larger, they release eggs, as females, producing up to 100 million eggs annually. The larvae, which find suitable sites on which to settle, are called 'spat'. Oysters are fished from their beds, or cultivated by the sea farmers to the size of 'spat'. They may be allowed to mature further to form "seed" oysters. In sea farms they are put in racks or bags and held above the bottom. The oysters are harvested by lifting the bags or racks to the surface and removing mature oysters. Sea farmers move the oysters in their concession according to the water quality and the size of the shells.

2.2 Sea Farm Agents Identification

The CORMGIS based agents implementing the basic models of the sea farming activities can be classified in three categories:

- The Colony agents describe a set of same age animals reared together. These agents take into account the animals' biological cycles and growth models.
- The Farmer agents describe the sea farms; they manage the different animals' sets breeding, controlling the spatial uses of the marine concessions. All theirs actions are guided to reach their main goal witch is the economic viability of the exploitation.
- The MarineAdministor agents describe the actions of the regulators. These agents are useful to take into account the sanitary [8] and maritime space occupation rules. They can prohibit the commercialization of farm's production because of

pollutions and forbid some pools to preserve the environment. They have a major influence on the exploiters activities and their economics sustainability.

2.3 Watershed Activities Modeling

Considering the model finality, we must take into account the pollution emitted by the watershed occupants, the soils uses, and laws governing the area. We model the economic growth using a logic model linked to the area's population, economy and laws.

The rules [9] applied to the occupants of the watershed impact the system in many ways:

- The land uses are subject to administrative agreement and the agricultural rejections are limited. These constraints are determining factors of the agricultural growth.
- Administrative regulations frame the localization and the rejections of agro-industrial companies such as stockbreeding, food industries, manufactures.
- Regulators influence the system, protecting or opening new areas to tourism and residences building. Due to the real estate developers interest for the wild areas and coastal zones, these decisions have a major impact on the ecosystems preservation.

2.4 Watershed Activities Agents Identification

Based on the CORMGIS platform, the agents implementing the watershed activities, growth and regulation can be classified in four categories:

- The Cultivator agents use the soils to grow plants and extensive cattle breeding.
- The Industrial agents describe the agro industrial pollution emitters such as factories, intensive breeding and wastewater treatment plants.
- The Mansion agents represent the isolated inhabitants. They influence the system as small but numerous sources of pollution rejects and they exert an important pressure on wild and coastal areas.
- The Regulator agents limit the pollution rejections, open areas to building, allow agro-industrial settlement, and rule the agricultural activities.

2.5 Environment Modeling

The ground environmental model must take into account the water pollutions diffusion process; from the sources to the aquatic animals, through the soils, contaminating the hydrological system. Our model must be able to differentiate the nature of the contaminants: heavy metals, pesticides, domestic wastes.

The marine environmental model must take into account the contaminant concentrations and their consequences on the algae proliferation and the wild ecosystem.

The multi-agents formalization of the marine and ground environmental system is concretized by two agents' patterns. A GroundParcel agent represents a homogenous ground area taking into account the land cover and the contaminants loads and diffusion [7]. A MarineParcel agent represents a homogenous marine zone taking into account the contaminants loads and diffusion, the water eutrophication, and the algae proliferations.

The CORMGIS platform provides generic agent patterns to model the space. A spatial agent can either represent a grid parcel or an irregular area. In the aim of our works, modeling the pollution (emission & diffusion) and the proliferation of toxic algae are the most relevant things in this step.

2.6 Implementing Agents Using CORMGIS

At the beginning of the simulations, the agents are implemented creating one instance for each element constituting the coastal system. They are instances of the classes modeling each category of agent's patterns. The pattern classes (GroundParcel, Colony, etc) are derived from CORMGIS generic agents' classes that include all the attributes and methods essential to run and drive simulations [2]. 24 hours appears to be relevant step time as the least common factor of the agents' rhythms.

According to our organization into a hierarchy of the coastal system, our agent based model shown in Figure 1 is structured with three levels of abstraction:

1. Basic agents: Animals, ground and sea parcels, mansions, industries.
2. A Cultivator agent manages many ground parcels, while a SeaFarmer agent rears many Colony agent located in different sea parcels.
3. The Regulators agents control the Cultivators and SeaFarmers agents.

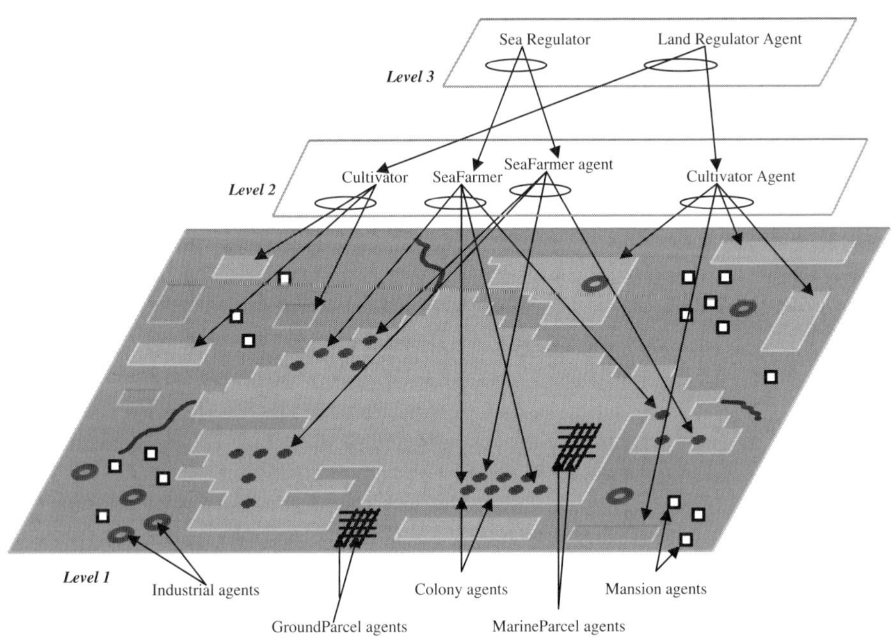

Fig. 1. Three layered agents based hierarchical model

CORMGIS is a native hybrid MAS GIS platform thought to use géodatabase and store the experimentations results. This platform provides a complete framework to model agents of environmental systems, and run simulations.

2.7 Sea Farms and Watershed Activities Interactions

The identification of the interactions' mechanism between the watershed and the costal ecosystems and sea farms is a key point of this work.

The pollutions resulting from the watershed activities modify the water quality in the coastal areas and obviously affect the sea farms. The models must take into account the concentrations of pathogen elements during the whole animals' growth. The animals' step of development is the main factor controlling their growth speeds, and the rates of morbidity [10]. The animals' loads of pollutants also depend of the different organs' growth speeds and ability to accumulate contaminants [11].

The activities in the watershed not only damage the live conditions in the breeding by their direct contaminants emissions, but also because their wastes induce an eutrophication of water and the proliferations of toxic algae.

Pollutions impose to farmers additional works and expenses: use of medicines, and more animals moving and handling. These new costs reduce the exploiter's benefits. Moreover an increasing animals' death rate, and a non commercialization of the production due to excessive water pollution, weigh down again the breeding profitability and endanger the future of sea farms.

3 Spatiotemporal Data Processing

Our model architecture and genericity imply an important work to prepare the spatiotemporal data required by the simulator to study the targeted sites. This importance is strengthened by the fact that the coastal systems and the sea farms are naturally highly dependant from two factors varying in space and time: weather and water quality.

Thus it's necessary to add to the system behavior agent based model, a complete toolbox dedicated to the definition and shaping of territory raw data [12]. The CORMGIS modular platform provide via its ArcGIS GIS based unit a complete suite to manage the spatiotemporal data.

Spatiotemporal data processing must occur before and after the simulation runs:

- The pre-experimentation spatiotemporal data processing works consists in collecting and getting into shape information about the territories. These geodata are first used at the beginning simulation to instance agents from the behavioral models as shown figure 2. The experimenters must also define collections of events (scenarios) supposed to occur during the simulations. The scenarios must take into account the systems' temporal and spatial modifications: weather, land covers, agro-industries, inhabitants, administrative and environmental rules, interactions between stakeholders. During simulations, the events are triggers to force instantiations of new agents and force the systems' inputs.
- The post-experimentation processing consists in analyzing the spatiotemporal data generated during the simulations. This work is necessary to highlight the key factors of the territories' dynamics, and to provide explicit documents about future to the systems' stakeholders and decision makers. Furthermore these results can be used to define scenarios for next simulations.

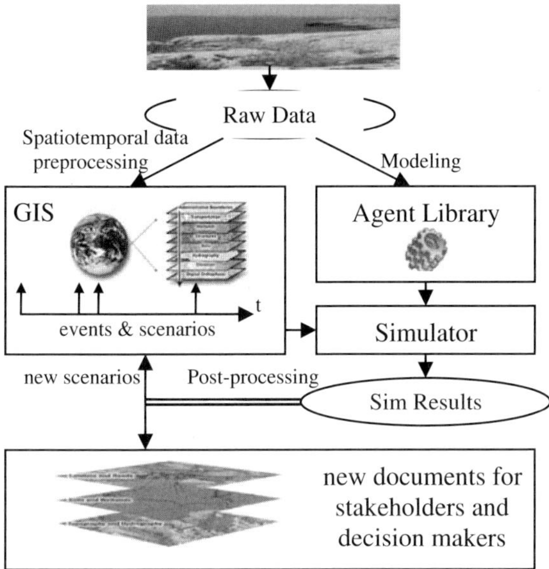

Fig. 2. Spatiotemporal data pre & post processing

Using a GIS permits to use sharply exact data to describe the target territories: stakeholders' localization and attributes, administrative and legal rules governing precisely each area, environmental conditions. The native layered data organization in GIS allows taking into account the different levels in the territories' management we identified during the models building step. Thus the systems can easily be considered at different levels of abstraction for both management and modeling.

4   Conclusion

The study and simulation of interactions in the coastal systems imply to take into account the spatiotemporal data and constraints. A generic multi-agent based behavioral modeling approach must be conduced jointly to spatiotemporal data processing works to fit to each territory. The use of the CORMGIS platform allows taking into account different levels of abstraction and to fit to data or systems' knowledge lacks.

The sea farm problematic is bordering the anthropogenic and wild ecosystems, at the confluence of the marine and land worlds, meeting point of the nature dependent and independent activities, is emblematic of both the complex interactions between watershed and coastal systems, and the tools' expectancies to find a way toward a sustainable development. Following our methodology we build a model fitted to answer to the sea farmers' and the managers expectancies. The first simulations dedicated to the study of the Corsican east plain confirm the relevance of our hybrid MAS GIS approach of the coastal systems.

Our future works will first focus on extending our library of agents to take into account more stakeholders, and then on studying new targeted sites.

References

[1] Copping, A., Khangaonkar, T.: Managing a Developing Estuary Integration of Hydrodynamic Models, Ecological Understanding, and Resource Management. In: Estuarine Research Federation's 19th Conf., Rhode Island (2007)

[2] Urbani, D.: Development of a new MAS GIS hybrid approach for Decision Support Systems; application to water management, Ph. D. these, University of Corsica (2006)

[3] Urbani, D., Delhom, M.: A Decision Support System for the Water Management in Mediterranean Islands based on a Multi-Agent System. In: Proceedings of IEEE - AISTA 2004 conference, Kirchberg - Luxembourg (November 2004)

[4] Bousquet, F., Bakam, I., Proton, H., Le Page, C.: Cormas: common-pool resources and multi-agent Systems. In: Mira, J., Moonis, A., de Pobil, A.P. (eds.) IEA/AIE 1998. LNCS, vol. 1416, pp. 826–838. Springer, Heidelberg (1998)

[5] ArcGIS description, http://www.esri.com/

[6] Urbani, D., Delhom, M.: Water Management Policy Selection Using a Decision Support System Based on a Multi-agent System. In: Proceedings 9th Congress of the Italian, Association for Artificial Intelligence, Milan, Italy, September 21-23 (2005)

[7] Urbani, D., Delhom, M.: Water Management Using a New Hybrid Multi-Agents System – Geographic Information System Decision Support System Framework. In: IEEE International Symposium on Environment Identities and Mediterranean area (July 2006)

[8] Directive 2006/88/EC of the European Parliament on animal health requirements for aquaculture animals and products

[9] Directive 2000/60/EC of the European Parliament establishing a framework for Community action in the field of water policy

[10] Deskshenieks, M., Hofmann, E., Klinck, J., Powell, E.: Quantifying the Effects of Environmental Change on an Oyster Population: A Modeling Study. Estuaries 23(5), 593–610 (2000)

[11] Apeti, D.A.: A Model for Bioaccumulation of Metals in Crassostrea virginica from Apalachicola Bay, Florida. American Journal of Environmental Sciences 1(3), 239–248 (2005)

[12] Urbani, D., Delhom, M.: Gestion intégrée de l'alimentation en eau à l'aide d'un système hybride SMA-SIG. In: Conférence SIG 2005 – ESRI France – Issy les Moulineaux, France (2005)

A Hybrid Multi-agent Model for Financial Markets

Stephen Chen[1], Jonathan Tien[2], and Brenda Spotton Visano[3]

[1] School of Information Technology, York University
4700 Keele Street, Toronto, Ontario M3J 1P3
`sychen@yorku.ca`
[2] Engineering Physics, McMaster University
1280 Main Street West, Hamilton, Ontario L8S 4L9
`tienj2@mcmaster.ca`
[3] School of Public Policy and Administration, Economics, Atkinson Faculty, York University
4700 Keele Street, Toronto, Ontario M3J 1P3
`spotton@yorku.ca`

Abstract. Economic models attempt to represent the aggregate behaviour of individual actors engaged in an economic activity. To ensure tractability in the subsequent mathematics, restrictive assumptions on the modelled phenomena are often required. Economic features that cannot be modelled mathematically can be difficult to verify experimentally. The hybrid multi-agent model developed here starts as an exact representation of a mathematics-based, multi-agent economics model, and then a more qualitative feature is added. Unlike purely qualitative studies, the effects of this additional feature can then be observed within an environment that has been experimentally demonstrated to be quantitatively accurate. The hybrid model is thus able to integrate both rigid mathematical assumptions and intuitive qualitative features, and the presented experimental data provides new insight into the potential role of social investors during market manias and bubbles.

Keywords: Multi-Agent Model, Financial Market Modelling, Social Investors.

1 Introduction

From an economic modelling perspective, our primary interest is to measure the effects of social investors on the time path of market prices. The actions of social investors are inherently based on qualitative features which are ill-suited to rigid mathematical models. However, it can be difficult to obtain experimental results for a qualitative investor model. Our initial work with multi-agent models showed the correct qualitative responses to the qualitative actions of the social investors [1], so we are presently motivated to embed the potential effects of social investors into a more quantitatively accurate financial model.

In real-world financial markets, trading dynamics produce a non-standard distribution of market returns – there is an excess kurtosis of outsized losses and gains. Recent multi-agent models [2,3,12-14] have been able to successfully replicate this quantitative feature of real-world markets. However, the extremes of market returns

N.T. Nguyen et al. (Eds.): IEA/AIE 2008, LNAI 5027, pp. 531–540, 2008.

that are observed during manias and bubbles have not been meaningfully replicated by multi-agent models that use investors who trade solely on economic information. By adding the unique and highly destabilizing influence of social investors to an existing multi-agent model, we hope to extend the range of the successfully modelled phenomena to include market manias and bubbles.

We start by developing a new computer simulation of the model presented by Lux and Marchesi [12-14]. This multi-agent model is simulated entirely by mathematical equations that describe the aggregate agent behaviour. To develop a market price, this model only needs to know *how many* agents are pursuing the various trading strategies, and not *which* actual agents are in the various states. Thus, the model requires no individual "agents" – it is not a true multi-agent model in the artificial intelligence sense.

A hybrid multi-agent model has been developed from the Lux and Marchesi model by creating agents and randomly assigning them the states that are represented in the mathematical model. After each time step of the original model, the required agent transitions are applied to randomly selected agents. At this point, the agents are "slaves" to the governing equations of the original model. However, once the agents exist, they can also be used as independent agents in a connected multi-agent model.

The "true" multi-agent model involves three classes of agents – fundamentalists, chartists, and social investors. Pursuing quantitatively-based trading strategies, the fundamentalists and chartists represent the two agent classes that are present in the original Lux and Marchesi model. These are not independent agents in the sense that their behaviour is controlled by the aggregating mathematical equations. The social investors however are independent agents that pursue qualitative trading strategies that are programmed at the individual agent level.

The resulting hybrid multi-agent model thus has two components. The first is a set of "simulated" agents that are controlled by aggregating mathematical equations. The second is a set of independent agents whose actions affect the state variables used in the previous mathematical equations. The overall system thus benefits from being able to model and measure the effects of both collective, quantitative behaviours and individual, qualitative behaviours.

By including both sets of behaviours in the hybrid multi-agent model, it is possible to obtain relevant, quantitative data that can realistically measure the effects of the highly qualitative decisions that are made by the social investors. In particular, the measured effects demonstrate that reasonably small increases in social investor participation can have thoroughly destabilizing effects on an otherwise stable and (mostly) efficient financial market. This initial result presents a highly promising direction for future economics research into modelling the nature and effects of increased market participation.

Before these future research directions are discussed in more detail, this paper starts with a brief review of multi-agent models for economic modelling in section 2. A description of the importance of our research from an economics perspective is presented in section 3. Highlights from our development of the Lux and Marchesi model are presented in section 4 and our analysis of this model is presented in section 5. Our hybrid multi-agent model is then developed in section 6, and the newly available quantitative analysis of social investors is presented in section 7. The discussion of the initial results and future research directions are then carried out in section 8 before we finish with a summary in section 9.

2 Background

Recent multi-agent models of financial markets tend to study the interaction of two classes of agents which represent fundamentalists and chartists only (e.g. [2,3,12-14]). In these models, both the fundamentalists and the chartists base their decisions to trade on economic information alone. The fundamentalist class estimates expected future profitability of the underlying firm and extracts capital gains by trading when current market prices deviate from the estimate. The chartist class will use the past history of prices to predict future movements (assuming repetitive time trends). These price charts allow noise traders to indirectly capture a "herding" market psychology that may move markets independently, if temporarily, away from fundamental values.

These two classes of "traditional" investors base their decisions on quantitative economic data such as the current market price of the stock, the expected future value of the stock, and the recent rate of change in the observed market price. To begin to capture some of the social aspects of investing, we introduce investors into the new model who base their trading decisions on the qualitative features such as the popularity of the investment activity alone. If a social investor sees a large number of other investors buying, then a social investor will buy as well. Conversely and symmetrically, a social investor seeing a large number of sellers will sell.

The expanding or shrinking participation that results from social investment activity differs importantly from the "herding" represented by the inclusion of a chartist class. Chartists are usually very sophisticated investors who may use charts and technical analysis to exploit (short-term) price changes. While these price changes motivate herding by chartists that then result in further price changes, such models can at best only indirectly capture the dynamics of social interaction. Our model of social investors is that they are economically uninformed investors – their investment decisions are not based on any financial information at all. The effects of social investors on a financial market are less predictable, and the model we build in this paper has the potential to capture the effects of social interactions more directly.

In particular, we hypothesize that increases in market participation are an important feature associated with market manias and bubbles. We further hypothesize that a significant portion of the new market participants will be less informed investors – investors who have little understanding of economic fundamentals and their relationship to stock prices. We have modelled these economically less informed investors as social investors. The effects of an influx of social investors has been discussed qualitatively with respect to the recent internet bubble (e.g. [15,16]), and the quantitative analysis conducted in this paper adds significantly to this previous work.

3 An Economic Perspective

In conventional models of prices in competitive financial markets, the price of equities reflects fully and accurately the existing information on the income earning potential of an asset. This "efficient market" outcome as explored by Fama [4-7] suggests that the present discounted value of the expected future income over the life of the asset—its "fundamental value"—will ultimately govern the asset's market price. Deviations from this so-called "fundamental value" will only be temporary – speculators capable of estimating the true fundamental value will quickly arbitrage away any implicit capital gains. Deviations may appear as the result of new information about future profitability and, as such, represent the disequilibrium adjustment to a new equilibrium with prices again equal to the now altered fundamental value.

Although intuitively appealing and consistent with a long-standing tradition in finance that acknowledges the importance of "value investing" [17], actual price movements and the resulting distribution of returns do not appear to adhere to the strict predictions of the efficient markets hypothesis. Explanations for persistent deviations from estimated fundamental values include various explanations for a "bubble" in stock prices. A "bubble" occurs when competitive bidding, motivated by repetitive and self-fulfilling expectations of capital gains, drives up a given asset's price in excess of what would otherwise be warranted by a fundamental value. The bubble may be driven by the presence of "noise" traders (i.e. "chartists"). Chartists attempt to exploit short-term momentum in the movement of stock prices, and their actions (e.g. buying when prices are rising, and selling when prices are falling) can exaggerate any movement in prices.

The presence of noise traders alters, however, neither the ultimate equilibrium market price for stocks (as fixed by the fundamental value of the underlying assets) nor the fact that the market will eventually reach it. In the extant literature, the formal introduction of "noise" traders creates a mean-reverting market dynamic to explain temporary deviations from fundamentals [10,11]. The presence of noise traders can confound market dynamics to such an extent that under some conditions or for some time, it is profitable for the more sophisticated traders to disregard the intrinsic value of the asset, follow the herd, and thus contribute to the asset bubble that results [8]. It has also been suggested that herding may explain the excess kurtosis observable in high-frequency market data [2].

Since these traders base their decisions solely on objective market information, the more traditional financial models exclude by assumption the possibility that the investment activity may also be a social activity. In situations where individuals are motivated to belong to a group, the possibility of fads, fashions, and other forms of collective behaviour can exist. Spotton Visano [16] suggests that investing in equity markets is not immune from social influences, especially when investors face true uncertainty. Consistent with the early views of financial markets as "voting machines" when the future is uncertain [9,16], Spotton Visano's result explains the fad and contagion dimensions of investing which relate to Lynch's [15] explanations of the recent internet "bubble".

When objective information is incomplete and individuals base investment decisions on social rather than economic information, outcomes become contingent on the collective assessment of the objective situation, and these outcomes are no longer uniquely identifiable independent of this collective opinion. Attempts to model this heterogeneity of investment behaviour and multiplicity of interdependent outcomes render the mathematics so complex as to threaten the tractability of the typical highly aggregated dynamic model. By presenting an opportunity to analyze the effects of different agent behaviours (and especially quantitative behaviours), there are significant potential benefits in using hybrid multi-agent models to simulate the actions of a financial market.

4 The Base Model

Lux and Marchesi [12-14] have developed a multi-agent model that can generate a time series of prices which accurately reflects the returns observed in actual stock markets. The key feature of real-world returns that had been difficult to model previously was the existence of excess kurtosis – compared to a normal distribution of returns, real-world returns are more likely to have unusually large gains and losses. By being able to quantitatively simulate the observed features of real-world returns, the multi-agent model is viewed as a viable explanation for the roles and interactions of multiple investment strategies.

The key features of the Lux and Marchesi model relate to the trading strategies and interactions of two classes of investors. These investor classes include the fundamentalists and the chartists, and the chartists are further divided into two subclasses which represent optimistic chartists and pessimistic chartists. The (aggregate) actions of each investor class lead to a price pressure component, and the subsequent changes in price affect the future actions of the investors. The two key features of the model which allow it to accurately produce simulated prices are the mechanisms which allow investors to switch trading strategies and the method used to specify price changes at any given time step.

$$\frac{dn_c^+}{dt} = \left(n_c^- * p_{-+} - n_c^+ * p_{+-}\right)\left(\frac{1-n_f}{N}\right) + n_f * (\frac{n_c^+}{N}) * p_{f+} - n_c^+ * (\frac{n_f}{N}) * p_{+f} - \left(p_{exit-}r_{newc}\right) * n_c^+ \qquad (1)$$

For example, equation (1) shows equation (1) from [12]. This aggregate equation governs the change in the number of optimistic chartists over time. It considers the number of optimistic chartists, pessimistic chartists, fundamentalists, and several global transition probabilities. However, these transition probabilities are not applied to individual, independent agents – the transitions occur at the aggregate level. The number of agents which undergo a transition is known, but the specific agents which have had a transition are not known. For this reason, we do not view the Lux and Marchesi model as a true multi-agent model in the artificial intelligence sense – it is primarily a mathematical model (that models the action of multiple agents).

$$\pi_{\uparrow p} = \max[0, \beta(ED + \mu)] \qquad (2)$$

Equation (2) above is part of equation (2.4) in [14]. This equation effects price changes as a function of excess demand (ED). The μ term is random noise, so this equation allows probabilistic behaviours to be modelled by the simulation. Arguably, this noise term is the only feature that distinguishes the Lux and Marchesi "multi-agent" model from a pure mathematical model.

With a few "tuning" parameters (e.g. β which affects the probability of price changes and p_{exit} which represents the probability that investors will exit the market), the Lux and Marchesi model is able to replicate several quantitative features that are observed in the returns of real-world markets. These features include the unit root property, the fat tail property, and volatility clustering [14]. Before adding the extremes observed during market manias and bubbles, it is important to ensure that our model can replicate these key features of real-world markets.

5 Model Implementation and Sensitivity Testing

The Lux and Marchesi model has been implemented using the equations from [12,14]. Table 1 presents the parameters we used – we attempted to use the same parameter values as Lux and Marchesi, but we needed some minor variations to achieve the desired price dynamics. In addition to market stability, the parameters were selected to allow/create meaningful price fluctuations (see Figure 1).

Table 1. Parameter and values used to implement the Lux and Marchesi model. Values for the number of chartists (optimistic and pessimistic) and fundamentalists are the initial values.

Parameter	Description	(Initial) Value
N	Number of total agents	500
n_c	Number of chartists	5
n_f	Number of fundamentalists	495
n^+_c	Number of optimistic chartists	3
n^-_c	Number of pessimistic chartists	2
t	Assets moved by chartists	0.02
a	Probability to exit market	0.15
γ	Fundamentalist reaction intensity	0.01
β	Price adjustment velocity	6
v_1	Infection velocity	3
v_2	Reaction velocity	2
a_1	Strength of opinion index	0.6
a_2	Strength of price movements	0.2
a_3	Reaction intensity	0.5
r	Nominal dividends	0.004
s	Discount factor	0.75

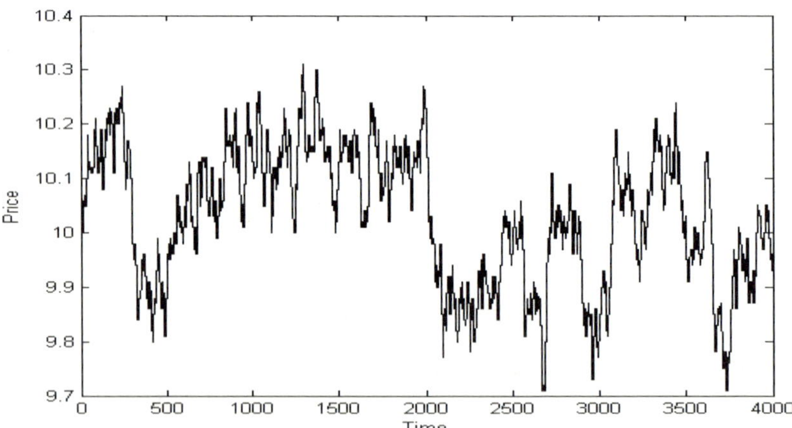

Fig. 1. Example of price dynamics in the Lux and Marchesi model. Although prices are stable overall (representing the unit root), large deviations can occur (representing the excess kurtosis and clustered volatility).

Lux and Marchesi present several possible parameter settings [12,14], so there is clearly some variation allowed. To test the model's sensitivity to each parameter, we ran simulations with the values given in Table 1 for every parameter except for one. We then recorded the range of values for this parameter which still led to a stable financial market (see Table 2). It should be noted that this sensitivity testing only considers market stability (e.g. the unit root property) and does not necessarily mean that other features of the market (e.g. excess kurtosis and clustered volatility) were produced for all values in the given parameter ranges.

Table 2. If all other parameters are those given in Table 1, the approximate parameter ranges given below will also lead to a stable model

Parameter	Stable Values
t	0.01-0.04
a	0.00-0.19
γ	0.0001-0.068
β	0.0001-12
v_1	0.0001-200
v_2	> 1.6
a_1	0-5.8
a_2	0-1.2
a_3	0-0.8
r	0-400
s	> 0

6   Adding Social Investors to Create the Hybrid Model

As has been discussed before, the Lux and Marchesi model [12-14] is not a true multi-agent model in the artificial intelligence sense – it is more of a mathematical model where the aggregate agent behaviour is controlled by global equations. Nonetheless, once the aggregate agent behaviour is known, it can be super-imposed upon individual (albeit non-independent) agents. In our implementation of the Lux and Marchesi model, we create N=500 independent agents and randomly assign and update their status as fundamentalists and chartists so that the total number of each class of agents matches the corresponding global state variable.

With these "slave" agents in place, it is possible to implement a "true" multi-agent model in which agent actions are controlled entirely at the agent level. The actions of the social investors are such that they base their investment decisions solely on the popularity of the investment activity itself. Specifically, a social investor will observe a random sample of other investors/agents and mimic their behaviour. If a majority of the other investors/agents are buying, the social investor will also buy. Conversely, if a majority of the sampled/observed investors are selling, the social investor will also sell.

After the social investors have acted, their collective behaviour is summarized and converted into a change in excess demand (*ED*). The overall performance of the hybrid multi-agent model is thus somewhat rigid in that each time step involves having the aggregate equations evaluated, the "simulated" agents updated, the "independent" agents activated, and their collective behaviour summarized. Nonetheless, the observations that are made possible with the new model are very insightful and encouraging.

7   The Effects of Social Investors

Many economists are aware that market bubbles and manias are often accompanied by an increase in market participation (e.g. [15,16]). For example, the introduction of on-line (day) trading is often associated as part of the causes of the recent internet bubble. However, this qualitative observation can be difficult to model and test quantitatively.

We have implemented a simple agent behaviour that models to an extent how new investors entered the market in the recent internet bubble. According to Spotton Visano [16], many of the new market participants during the internet bubble could be classified as "social investors" – people who bought stocks mostly to participate in the fad of owning internet stocks. As the fad grew, there was more and more pressure on non-participants to participate.

In our hybrid multi-agent model, social investors buy and sell based on the number of other investors they see buying and selling. For example, some "trend setters" will buy or sell when they see a relatively small number of other people engaging in that activity, and some "laggards" will only buy or sell when they see a relatively large number of other people engaging in that activity.

Qualitatively, the actions of social investors will clearly amplify any buying or selling trend. Further, the actions of chartists and social investors can create a positive feedback loop that drives prices to extremes. Quantitatively, our model shows that an increase of only 200 new investors can cause the previously stable market (see section 5) to go unstable (see Figure 2).

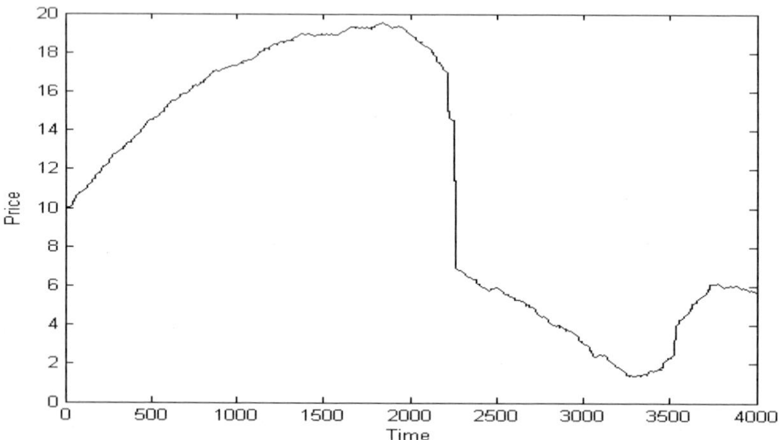

Fig. 2. The effects of social investors can lead to instability – e.g. a market bubble

8   Discussion

The goal of an economic model is to represent the aggregate behaviour of individual actors engaged in an economic activity. In many situations, the behaviours of these individuals may be well understood at a qualitative level, but the behaviour may be too complex to describe quantitatively in precise mathematical equations. A convincing demonstration of an economic model is to show that it can accurately describe (e.g. reproduce) data observed in the real world. Since qualitative models can rarely produce this demonstration, they are often less highly regarded than quantitative models.

The hybrid multi-agent model developed in this paper has the potential to integrate the key features of both quantitative and qualitative models. The first half of the hybrid model uses aggregating equations to control the agents, and this control ensures that specific collective behaviours which have been quantitatively observed can be embedded in the model. The second half of the hybrid model allows some more qualitative behaviours of individuals to be programmed into the independent agents. The overall hybrid multi-agent model allows quantitative testing of qualitative model features.

Specifically, the current model implemented for social investors suggests that an increase in market participation of 40% percent can cause a previously stable financial market to go unstable (e.g. simulate a market bubble). The range of stability for the t parameter which represents the amount of assets moved by chartist investors is around 100% (see Tables 1 and 2). A large influx of capital can clearly destabilize a market. However, the capital influx that accompanies our model for social investors is relatively small compared to other estimates (e.g. the t parameter) of the magnitude of capital flows required to destabilize a market. This result suggests that the actual behaviour of the social investors can be as important as the capital influx that they also represent.

Future work will involve collecting the time path data of increased market participation and price responses for the recent internet bubble. We will then attempt to refine our model of social investors to recreate both the time path and the levels of increased market participation. The ultimate objective is to create an accurate reproduction of the quantitative data observed during the recent internet bubble by using a more qualitative social investor model.

9   Summary

A traditional, highly quantitative economic model has been converted into hybrid multi-agent model through the introduction of agents that are "slaves" to the aggregating mathematical equations. Qualitative features of a new economic model were then programmed into independent agents at the individual level. The result is a unique opportunity to test a qualitative economic model within a framework that has previously been demonstrated to be quantitatively accurate.

Acknowledgements

This work has received funding support from the Natural Sciences and Engineering Research Council of Canada

References

1. Chen, S., Spotton Visano, B., Kong, Y.: Introducing Social Investors into Multi-Agent Mod-els of Financial Markets. In: Ali, M., Dapoigny, R. (eds.) IEA/AIE 2006. LNCS (LNAI), vol. 4031, pp. 44–53. Springer, Heidelberg (2006)
2. Cont, R., Bouchard, J.-P.: Herd Behavior and Aggregate Fluctuations in Financial Markets. Macroeconomic Dynamics 4, 170–196 (2000)
3. Eguiluz, V.M., Zimmermann, M.G.: Transmission of Information and Herd Behavior: An Application to Financial Markets. Physical Review Letters 85, 5659–5662 (2000)
4. Fama, E.F.: The Behavior of Stock Market Prices. Journal of Business 38, 34–105 (1965)
5. Fama, E.F.: Efficient Capital Markets: A Review of Theory and Empirical Work. Journal of Finance 25, 383–416 (1970)
6. Fama, E.F.: Foundations of Finance. Basic Books, New York (1976)
7. Fama, E.F.: Efficient Markets: II. Journal of Finance 46(5), 1575–1617 (1991)
8. Froot, K.A., Scharfstein, D.S., Stein, J.C.: Herd on the Street: Informational Inefficiencies in a Market with Short-Term Speculation. Journal of Finance 47, 1461–1484 (1992)
9. Keynes, J.M.: The General Theory of Employment, Interest and Money. Reprinted Prometheus Books (1936, 1997)
10. De Long, J.B., Schleifer, A., Summers, L.H., Waldman, R.J.: Noise Trader Risk in Financial Markets. Journal of Political Economy 98, 703–738 (1990)
11. De Long, J.B., Schleifer, A., Summers, L.H., Waldman, R.J.: Positive Feedback Investment Strategies and Destabilizing Rational Speculation. Journal of Finance 45(2), 379–395 (1990)
12. Lux, T.: The socio-economic dynamics of speculative markets: Interacting agents, chaos, and the fat tails of return distribution. Journal of Economic Behavior and Organization 33, 143–165 (1998)
13. Lux, T., Marchesi, M.: Scaling and criticality in a stochastic multi-agent model of a financial market. Nature 397, 498–500 (1999)
14. Lux, T., Marchesi, M.: Volatility Clustering in Financial Markets: A Microsimulation of Interacting Agents. International Journal of Theoretical and Applied Finance 3(4), 675–702 (2000)
15. Lynch, A.: Thought Contagions in the Stock Market. Journal of Psychology and Financial Markets 1, 10–23 (2000)
16. Spotton Visano, B.: Financial Crises: Socio-economic causes and institutional context. Routledge, London (2006)
17. Williams, J.B.: The Theory of Investment Value. Reprinted Augustus M. Kelley, New York (1938, 1965)

A Teleo-Reactive Architecture for Fast, Reactive and Robust Control of Mobile Robots

Gerhard Gubisch, Gerald Steinbauer, Martin Weiglhofer, and Franz Wotawa[*]

Institute for Software Technology, Graz University of Technology
Inffeldgasse 16b/II, A-8010 Graz, Austria
{gubisch,steinbauer,weiglhofer,wotawa}@ist.tugraz.at

Abstract. One of the elementary tasks of an autonomous mobile robot is the execution of different behavior patterns in order to fulfill a given task. The complexity of this problem is especially high if the robot operates in a dynamic, unpredictable environment and requires the parallel control of multiple actuators. In this paper we present a novel architecture for robust and fast mobile robot control. The architecture is based on Teleo-Reactive Programs. We discuss the benefits and drawbacks of such programs, extend the basic definition for the parallel control of multiple actuators, and propose a new language and a compiler for extended Teleo-Reactive Programs. These tools simplify the creation of new behavior patterns and increase the runtime performance. Finally, we discuss implementation issues of the architecture when applying it to RoboCup Middle-Size soccer robots.

Keywords: autonomous agents, control architecture, teleo-reactive programs, parallel actions, teleo-reactive program compilation.

1 Introduction

The execution of different behavior patterns in order to achieve a given task is one of the fundamental prerequisites of an autonomous mobile robot. Once a robot has derived a plan to achieve its task, some mechanism is needed to execute the plan. Such a mechanism has to be flexible in order to allow the execution of different plans, sub-plans or behavior patterns. This requires an appropriate description or programming language. In addition, the mechanism has to be robust against failure. Even in situations which are new to the robot, the execution of behavior patterns should not fail.

There is a great number of proposed mechanisms to organize, structure and describe the task execution of autonomous robots. On the highest level these mechanisms can be divided into three major groups: (1) the reactive paradigm, (2) the deliberative paradigm and (3) the hybrid paradigm. Mechanisms of the first group commonly use sets of simple reactive behavior and setup more complex behavior patterns by blending these simple ones. The advantage of these

---

[*] Authors are listed in alphabetical order.

N.T. Nguyen et al. (Eds.): IEA/AIE 2008, LNAI 5027, pp. 541–550, 2008.

mechanisms is their quick response to changes in the sensory input. The second group uses planning and reasoning capabilities in order to derive sequential plans. Mechanisms of this group are able to handle very complex tasks but suffer from performance issues when deriving appropriate plans. The last group merges the advantages of the first two. It provides fast reaction on sensory input and the capability to plan in domains of greater complexity.

In this paper we present a framework to organize and execute behavior patterns in a flexible and robust way using the hybrid paradigm. The organization of the reactive part is based on Teleo-Reactive (TR) Programs proposed by Nilsson [1]. TR-Programs are ordered lists of condition-action pairs, which ensure robustness in dynamic environments. Because basic TR-Programs are not able to deal with parallel actions, we introduce extended TR-Programs. Such TR-Programs serve as actions for a higher-level planning module. In order to improve the runtime performance and ease the use of extended TR-Programs we define a description language for the TR-Programs. Furthermore we show how a compiler can convert an extended TR-Program into native C++ code.

This paper continues as follows: In the next section we discuss TR-Programs and introduce extended TR-Programs. In Section 3 we present the design of the proposed framework, our language for extended TR-Programs and a compiler for converting extended TR-Programs to C++. Section 4 discusses an implementation of the framework for our RoboCup Middle-Size soccer robots. Section 5 shows an overview of related research. Finally, we draw our conclusions in Section 6.

2   Teleo-Reactive Programs

Teleo-Reactive Programs are a formalism to control mobile robots in dynamic environments. They address the problem of plan execution in a real world environment. In such dynamic environments the effect of an executed action may be changed or canceled by exogenous events. Thus, the execution of a plan will fail if the control software of the robot relies on the successful execution of an action. Teleo-Reactive Programs provide a solution to this problem. According to [1] a Teleo-Reactive Sequence is an ordered set of production rules, where K_i denotes a first order logic condition and a_i denotes an executable action:

$$K_1 \rightarrow a_1, \ldots, K_i \rightarrow a_i, \ldots, K_m \rightarrow a_m.$$

Formally a Teleo-Reactive Program can be defined as follows:

Definition 1 (Teleo-Reactive Sequence). *A Teleo-Reactive Sequence τ is a finite ordered list of m condition-action pairs (K_i, a_i) with $i \in \{1, \ldots, m\}$ and $a_i \in \mathcal{A}$ where $\mathcal{A} = \mathcal{A}_{disc} \cup \mathcal{A}_{dura} \cup \mathcal{TS}$ is the union of the disjoint sets of discrete actions $\mathcal{A}_{disc}$, durative actions $\mathcal{A}_{dura}$ and all Teleo-Reactive Sequences $\mathcal{TS}$:*

$$\tau = \langle (K_1, a_1), \ldots, (K_i, a_i), \ldots, (K_m, a_m) \rangle$$

Definition 2 (Teleo-Reactive Program). *A Teleo-Reactive Program is a Teleo-Reactive Sequence with variables. When the sequence is called, the variables are bound to either constant values or to entities that are computed continuously.*

The execution of such a sequence is simple. The interpreter scans the production rules from left to right. It chooses an action for execution if the according condition is the first one which is satisfied. TR-Sequences can be organized hierarchically, i.e. the actions a_i of a TR-Sequence can be Teleo-Reactive Sequences themselves. The primitive actions of a TR-Sequence can be either discrete or durative. A durative action a_i is executed continuously as long as K_i remains the first true condition in the list. In contrast to that, a discrete action is called once, as soon as the first true condition in the list is the action's condition.

Assume, that S holds the initial truth values of the predicates which are used to formulate the conditions. $effect(a_i)$ returns the effect in terms of predicate truth values when executing action a_i. $A \oplus B = B \cup \{l | l \in A \wedge \neg l \notin B\}$ represents a state update operator and $\Phi(K_i, S) = (\forall_{j<i} K_j \not\subseteq S) \wedge K_i \subseteq S$ represents the condition check. $obs()$ denotes a function which returns the currently observed state. Then the formal semantics of a Teleo-Reactive Sequence $\tau = \langle (K_1, a_1), \ldots, (K_i, a_i), \ldots, (K_m, a_m) \rangle$ is given as follows (where $[\![\ ]\!]$ denotes the interpretation function):

$$[\![\tau]\!](S) = [\![\langle (K_1, a_1), \ldots, (K_m, a_m) \rangle]\!]([\![(K_i, a_i)]\!](S)) \text{ if } \Phi(K_i, S)$$

$$[\![(K_i, a_i)]\!](S) = \begin{cases} [\![a_i]\!](S) & \text{if } a_i \in \mathcal{TS} \\ [\![a_i]\!]_{disc}(S) & \text{if } a_i \in A_{disc} \\ [\![(K_i, a_i)]\!]_{dura}(S) & \text{if } a_i \in A_{dura} \end{cases}$$

$$[\![(K_i, a_i)]\!]_{dura}(S) = \begin{cases} S & \text{if } effect(a_i) \subseteq S \vee \neg\Phi(K_i, S) \\ [\![(K_i, a_i)]\!]_{dura}([\![a_i]\!]_{dura}) & \text{otherwise} \end{cases}$$

$$[\![a_i]\!]_{disc}(S) = S \oplus effect(a_i)$$

$$[\![a_i]\!]_{dura}(S) = S \oplus obs()$$

The robustness of the execution of TR-Programs comes from two properties. The *regression* property ensures that the conditions in the list are regressive. That means, that each action a_i should activate a condition K_j with $j < i$. The *regression* property ensures that the agent proceeds towards the goal. A TR-Program is *complete* if the disjunction of all condition forms a tautology, which ensures, that there is always one action that can be executed. A TR-Program which has both properties is called a *universal* TR-Program.

Beside the advantages of TR-Programs there is one major drawback that comes with the original formalism, which is the lack of support for simultaneous action execution. Assume the two scenarios illustrated in Figure 1. The appliance of TR-Programs will fail if an agent has to start action a_i at time t while the currently active action a_j should not be stopped before t' with $t' > t$. For example action a_2 runs simultaneously with action a_1 between t_1 and t_2 in Figure 1. One practical example of such a setting is a robot equipped with a gripper operating in a ware-house environment. The task of the robot is to pick up packages from a moving conveyor belt. While the robot waits for the

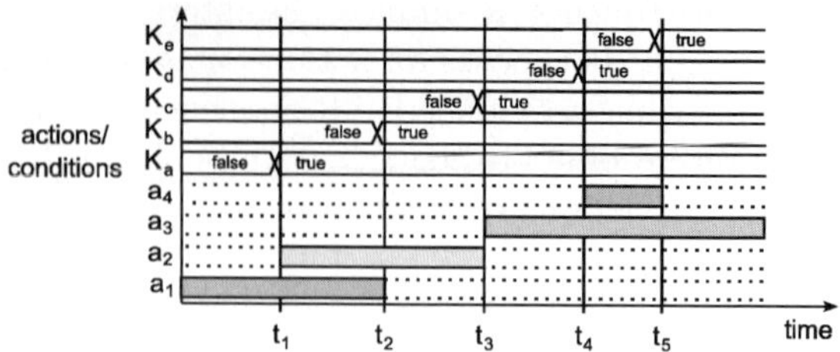

Fig. 1. Example of the simultaneous action problem

package it pre-positions its gripper (action a_1). If the package appears on the conveyor belt the robot starts moving parallel to the package (action a_2) and simultaneously grabbing the object of interest. When the packages has been taken, the gripper can be frozen (time t_2) while the robot drives towards it final position (action a_2). Another problematic setting is, if action a_j should be started at time t_1 and stopped at t_2 while action a_i is active all the time (e.g. a_3 and a_4 in Figure 1). That is, for example if a soccer robot should dribble (action a_3) and kick (action a_4). If the robot stops dribbling in order to prepare kicking, the ball will roll away from the robot. Thus, the robot has to kick while it concurrently dribbles.

2.1   Extended Teleo-Reactive Programs

To address the problem of simultaneous action execution we extend the basic definition of a TR-Programs. Therefore, we introduce an additional operator that can be used within the action parts of a TR-Sequence.

Definition 3 (Parallel Composition Operator). *Given two actions a_i and a_j with $i \neq j$, then the composition with the $||$-operator $a_i||a_j$ is again a valid action denoting the parallel execution of the two actions. The parallel execution of actions a_i and a_j still has to satisfy the regression property.*

In the following we will write A_i to denote either a single action a_i or a parallel composition of n actions $a_{i1}||a_{i2}||\ldots||a_{in}$. We use lower case letters a_i for single actions. $\mathcal{A}$ denotes the set of all actions.

Definition 4 (Extended Teleo-Reactive Sequence). *An extended Teleo-Reactive Sequence τ_e is a finite ordered list of m condition-action pairs (K_i, A_i) where $A_i = a_i \wedge a_i \in \mathcal{A}$ or $A_i = a_{i1}||\ldots||a_{in}$ with $\forall_{j=1\ldots n} a_{ij} \in \mathcal{A}$. The semantics of an extended Teleo-Reactive Sequence is given by $[\![\ ]\!]_e$.*

Definition 5. *An extended Teleo-Reactive Program is an extended Teleo-Reactive Sequence with variables. When the sequence is called, the variables are bound to either constant values or to entities that are computed continuously.*

The use of the $\|$-operator extends the semantics $[\![\ ]\!]$ for a Teleo-Reactive Sequence τ_e to the semantics $[\![\ ]\!]_e$ as follows:

$$[\![\tau_e]\!]_e(S) = [\![\langle (K_1, A_1), \ldots, (K_m, A_m) \rangle]\!]_e([\![(K_i, A_i)]\!]_e(S)) \text{ if } \Phi(K_i, S)$$

$$[\![(K_i, A_i)]\!]_e(S) = \bigcup_{a_i \in A_i} [\![(K_i, a_i)]\!](S)$$

Note, that any basic Teleo-Reactive Program can be interpreted by $[\![\ ]\!]_e$. Thus, the set of all basic Teleo-Reactive Programs $\mathcal{TRP}$ is a subset of all extended Teleo-Reactive Programs $\mathcal{TRP}_{ext}$, i.e., $\mathcal{TRP} \subset \mathcal{TRP}_{ext}$.

An extended Teleo-Reactive Program encoding the action sequence of Figure 1 looks like following:

$$K_e \to a_3, \ K_d \to a_3\|a_4, \ K_c \to a_3, \ K_b \to a_2, \ K_a \to a_1\|a_2, \ true \to a_1$$

Extended TR-Programs are appropriate for the description of the behavior of a robot for a wide range of tasks. But there are two issues that have to be solved when applying TR-Programs for mobile robot control. First, for complex high level tasks some deliberative component is needed in order to enable the robot to fulfil the task. TR-Programs are valuable for the execution of the behavior but the gap to the deliberative component has to be filled. Second, the execution of Teleo-Reactive Programs must be fast such that reactions to changes in the environment are taken into account immediately. We will now introduce a framework for mobile robot control, which addresses these two issues.

3   Organization and Specification of Behaviors

Figure 2 shows an overview of our architecture for robust control of mobile robots. The central elements within this architecture are extended Teleo-Reactive Programs that are translated to native C++ code. During the runtime a high level planning module selects the currently best Teleo-Reactive Program for a

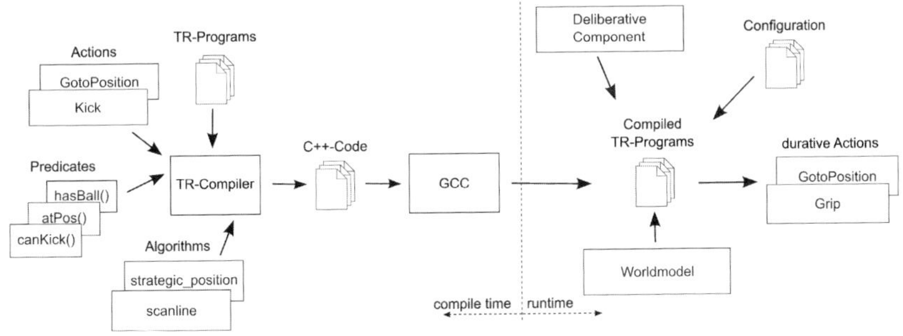

Fig. 2. Schematic overview of the proposed framework

given situation from a list of predefined TR-Programs. Thus, the Teleo-Reactive Programs are actions for a high level planning module.

The Teleo-Reactive compiler uses predicates, actions and algorithms, and translates a given extended Teleo-Reactive Program into C++. This code is compiled by a standard C++-Compiler into executable object code and linked into the robot control software. The translation of extended TR-Programs from a native language to object code has two major advantages. First, it simplifies the process of writing a extended Teleo-Reactive Program where the programmer does not have to care about complex features of modern programming languages. Second, we have experienced a significant improvement in the run-time performance when executing compiled Teleo-Reactive Programs instead of interpreting Teleo-Reactive Programs.

The reasoning within the TR-Program happens over values from the configuration, over data from the world model and over parameters retrieved from the planning module. Every durative action is implemented in a separate flow of control, i.e., a separate thread. The action-interfaces used by the TR compiler communicate with that thread by sending start commands and stop commands with parameters. Beside the advantage of having several actions executed simultaneously, this separation of actions has an additional benefit: Because there is only one instance of every action, the action can remember previous parameter values and can benefit from the history of parameters.

3.1   Teleo-Reactive Program/C++ Transformation

Algorithm 3 translates any non-hicrarchical extended Teleo-Reactive Program into a C++ program. An example is illustrated in Figure 4. As Figure 4 shows, the resulting C++ code consists of two functions. The main loop calls the `evaluate` function continuously. The `evaluate` function contains a list of if-then statements. Each condition-action pair corresponds to one if-then-statement. The condition of a (K_i, A_i)-tuple forms the condition in the if-clause. The *then*-branch is built by starting and stopping the actions of A_i (functions *start()* and *stop()*). These functions start and stop durative actions in a separate thread.

```
function transform(⟨(K₁, A₁),...,(Kₘ, Aₘ)⟩)
  A := ⋃_{i=1,...,m} Aᵢ;
  writeln "void main() { while(true) evaluate(); }"
  writeln "void evaluate() {"
  for i = 1 to m do
    writeln "if (Kᵢ) {"
    for all aⱼ ∈ A \ Aᵢ do writeln "aⱼ.stop();" done
    for all aₖ ∈ Aᵢ do writeln "aₖ.start();" done
    writeln "return; }"
  done
  writeln "}"
```

Fig. 3. Algorithm for the translation of extended Teleo-Reactive Programs into C++

Scored $\rightarrow$ nil, InRange(Goal) $\rightarrow$ DribbleTo(Goal) || Kick(), true $\rightarrow$ DribbleTo(Goal)

```
void main() { while(true) evaluate(); }
void evaluate() { if(Scored.eval()){DribbleTo.stop();Kick.stop();return;}
if(InRange.eval(Goal)){DribbleTo.start(Goal);Kick.start();return;}
if(true){DribbleTo.start(Goal);Kick.stop();return;} }
```

Fig. 4. Translation of an extended Teleo-Reactive Program for a scoring behavior (top) into C++ code (bottom)

Note, that the functions are called multiple times, where the parameters to those functions may be changed. Thus, start functions should start the thread only if it is not running yet. If the thread is already running, the functions should only exchange the old parameters with the new ones. For discrete actions, the start function runs the action once and refuses execution if called multiple times until the stop function has been invoked. The resulting C++ program does not interrupt durative actions and start them immediately again, which would break a continuous execution. Thus the C++ program starts an action a_i for a condition-action pair (K_i, A_i) if $a_i \in A_i$. An action a_j is stopped in the *then*-branch of a condition-action pair (K_k, A_k) iff $a_j \notin A_k$.From the semantical point of view, the two versions of TR-Programs in Figure 4 are equivalent. Both versions of the TR-Program will execute A_i if $(\forall_{j<i} \neg K_j) \wedge K_i$. If the Teleo-Reactive Program is *complete*, i.e., $K_1 \vee K_2 \vee \cdots \vee K_i \vee \cdots \vee K_m$ is a tautology, there will be always one action that is selected for execution in both versions of the TR-Program. If the Teleo-Reactive Program satisfies the *regression* property, the C++ version will satisfy this property as well, because we do not change the order of the condition-action pairs.

3.2   Teleo-Reactive Language

In this section we propose a programming language for TR-Programs, which is related to the imperative programming paradigm. According to the grammar of Figure 5, a TR-Program comprises two sections. One section contains the global variables, i.e., variables that are used as parameters in conditions or in more than one action block. The other section comprises the list of condition-action pairs that forms the body of the TR-Program. Conditions are built by combining the predicates of the control framework with the boolean operators *and, or* and *not*. In contrast to the Teleo-Reactive Language defined in [2], this grammar provides a more flexible form of writing actions. Instead of having a single object which is called for execution, an action is built by a code block. This code block can either be the name of one of the basic actions, or it can be a code block that uses algorithms, local variables and action objects. An algorithm does not execute any action but calculates parameters needed by some action. This is, why we propose to split up actions and algorithms. Each action and each algorithm should provide an atomic piece of operation. In that way new behavior can be composed without adding new functionality to the framework.

```
program ::= TR-PROGRAM : globals_section tr_stmt_section
globals_section ::= GLOBAL : ( var_decl+ | ε )
var_decl ::= type id = param_expr ;
param_expr ::= float | integer | ''string'' | param | funcall | var
param ::= object(id) | param(id) | config(id(.id)*) | random(paramlist)
tr_stmt_section ::= TELEO-REACTIVE : tr_stmt+
tr_stmt ::= task_name : condition :  action*  ;
condition ::= predicate ((and|or) predicate)*
predicate ::= true | false | (!|ε) funcall | (!|ε) ( condition )
action ::= var_decl | function_call;
funcall ::= id ( paramlist | ε )
paramlist ::= param_expr (, param_expr )*
```

Fig. 5. Grammar of the Teleo-Reactive language

In addition, the modular action block allows to use more than one basic action within such a block. The given basic actions are executed in parallel using the semantics of extended Teleo-Reactive Programs.

4   Applying the Framework to Mobile Soccer Robots

This section discusses an implementation of the proposed architecture for our RoboCup Middle-Size soccer robots. The planning module of Figure 2 is realized as a hierarchical state machine, which uses extended TR-Programs as actions.

One extended TR-Program is mapped to one C++ class. The list of if-then statements is encoded in an execute method. The main loop which calls this execute method is located in a controller class. This controller is responsible for switching between TR-Programs selected by the hierarchical state machine.

Our compiler[1] is implemented in C++ using of the Boost Spirit Library[2] for parsing, and implements simple type checking. For our mobile soccer robots, the framework is currently equipped with two predicates (`IsAtPosition(pos)` and `IsAtScoringPosition()`), two actions (`GotoPosition(pos)` and `KickTheBall`), and the four algorithms (`Scanline`: calculate a heading of the robot, where there is a maximum distance along the soccer field width between two obstacles, `CalcKickerParams`: determine currently optimal kick strength, `CalcStrategicPosition`: calculate a global position and a heading, which is strategically advantageous based on the work of [3], `CalcGrabBallPosition`: calculate position and heading for graping the ball such that the robot does not push the ball out of the field, `CalcGoalBlockingPosition`: calculates an intercept position for the goalkeeper if the ball rolls towards the goal).

Currently we use 15 different teleo-reactive programs for our RoboCup Middle-Size soccer robots. The average number of used condition-action pairs is 2.13 per TR-program. At maximum we use 4 condition-action pairs per TR-program. The smallest TR-program, which prevents the robot from doing anything (i.e. the idle TR-program) comprises only one condition-action pair. In four cases we make use of parallel actions. These TR-programs are basically all programs where some ball handling actions are involved.

---

[1] http://www.ist.tugraz.at/staff/weiglhofer/projects/trcompiler
[2] http://www.boost.org/libs/spirit

5   Related Research

Brooks proposed in [4] to blend simple behaviors, which provide a fast coupling of sensors and actuators, in order to get more complex behaviors. The basic behaviors are always active, receive their sensory input and immediately calculate their desired output for the actuators. An arbiter takes care about which output or which mixture of outputs are feed to the actuators. In difference to that, extended Teleo-Reactive programs only execute actions concurrently if required. Furthermore, the outcome of the actions are not merged by the use of an arbiter.

The Miro robot software framework provides a so called BAP framework in order to organize and execute behaviors [5]. The framework allows to arrange continuous and event-driven behaviors into behavior patterns and to blend the individual behaviors trough the use of different arbiters.

The authors of [6] presented an approach for robust plan execution in dynamic environments. The approach is based on a hybrid architecture and uses classical STRIPS planning. The behavioral level is organized using the framework of Miro. The robustness of the plan execution derives from the use of plan invariants, which are conditions that have to be true throughout the execution of the entire plan. Such condition can be used to monitor plan execution in order to detect infeasible or faulty plans.

In [7] Beetz presented a control architecture for mobile robots, which comprises a plan-based high-level control. The controller monitors the execution of plans by the use of prediction models of the behavior of actions. In the case of a problem the controller can react by modifying plans on the fly. Furthermore, the controller is able to execute concurrent plans and may postpone the execution of plans until some conditions are satisfied again.

In [8] Nilsson proposed the triple-tower architecture for the control of autonomous robots. The architecture is guided by the hybrid paradigm and comprises three towers for sensing, reasoning and acting. The acting tower is responsible for the execution of behaviors and comprises one or more TR-Programs. The higher level decision process is implemented by the reasoning tower which performs logical reasoning about the state of the world and the agents task.

The Task Description Language (TDL) proposed by Simmons [9] is a task-level programming language for robots. It is a extension to the C++ language and supports task decomposition, synchronization and exception handling. The authors provide a compiler to convert the TDL program into a native C++ code.

6   Conclusion

In this paper we have presented a novel architecture for fast, reactive and robust control of mobile robots. The architecture is based on an extension of TR-Programs. Beside the benefits of basic TR-Programs, extended TR-Programs allow the robust execution of concurrent actions. Furthermore, we introduced a description language for extended TR-Programs and showed how to transform extended TR-Programs to native C++ code. We have implemented the proposed architecture for our autonomous mobile soccer robots which led to promising results. By the use of this architecture our robots are able to react fast to changes in the environment. The main advantages of our architecture based on compiled extended TR-Programs can be summarized as:

Fast and robust execution: Because of the indirect compilation to object code the time consumed by program management during the execution of TR-Programs is negligibly small. The execution is robust in highly dynamic environments, where exogenous events may cancel effects of actions.

Simultaneous actions: Our approach is able to control multiple actuators in parallel by executing actions simultaneously.

Simple behavior pattern creation By providing the user an intuitive language it is easy to create new behavior patterns.

Further Research. Currently, we require that parallel actions do not contradict with each other. We need to investigate in some technique that allows to detect such contradicting actions.

References

1. Nilsson, N.J.: Teleo-reactive programs for agent control. JAIR 1, 139–158 (1994)
2. Nilsson, N.J.: Toward agent programs with circuit semantics. Technical Report STAN-CS-92-1412, Standford University (January 1992)
3. Tews, A., Wyeth, G.: Thinking as one: Coordination of multiple mobile robots by shared representations. In: IROS, pp. 1391–1396 (2000)
4. Brooks, R.A.: A robust layered control system for a mobile robot. IEEE Jornal of Robotics and Automation RA-2(1), 14–23 (1986)
5. Utz, H.: Advanced Software Concepts and Technologies for Autonomous Mobile Robotics. PhD thesis, University of Ulm, Neuroinformatics (2005)
6. Fraser, G., Steinbauer, G., Wotawa, F.: Plan execution in dynamic environments. In: 18th International Conference on Industrial and Engineering Applications of Artificial Intelligence and Expert Systems, Bari, Italy, pp. 208–217. Springer, Heidelberg (2005)
7. Beetz, M.: Plan-Based Control of Robotics Agents, Improving the Capabilities of Autonomous Robots. LNCS (LNAI), vol. 2554. Springer, Heidelberg (2002)
8. Nilsson, N.J.: Teleo-reactive programs and the triple-tower architecture. Electronic Transactions on Artificial Intelligence 5, 99–110 (2001)
9. Simmons, R., Apfelbaum, D.: A task description language for robot control. In: Conference on Intelligent Robotics and Systems, pp. 1931–1937 (1998)

Evolutionary Public-Key Cryptographic Circuits

Nadia Nedjah[1] and Luiza de Macedo Mourelle[2]

[1] Dept. of Electronics Engineering and Telecommunications
[2] Dept. of Systems Engineering and Computation
State University of Rio de Janeiro, Brazil

Abstract. In this paper, we evolve digital circuits for public-key cryptosystems. The methodology used is based on genetic programming. The evolutionary process attempts to minimise the hardware area required to implement modular multiplication and exponentiation. It does so while it also attempts to optimise the encryption and decryption time, by considering multiple objectives. We show that the evolved designs are shielded against side-channel leakage. We compare our results against existing and well-known designs, which were produced by human designers.

1 Introduction

Modular exponentiation is a cornerstone operation in several public-key cryptosystems such as RSA [1]. It consists of several successive modular multiplications. Modular multiplication is time consuming for large operands. Engineering fast public-key cryptography hardware needs either optimising the time consumed by a single modular multiplication or reducing the total number of modular multiplication performed or both of them. The so far engineered hardware designs using modular exponentiation as encryption process suffer from a very serious drawback that is called *side-channel leakage*. As the designs for modular exponentiation are regular and repetitive one can trace the data transfers between operations, which usually reveal the beginning of every long integer operation very clearly [2]. This allows one with an extra little effort to discover the private key of the cryptosystem.

Designing a hardware that fulfils a certain function consists of deriving from specific input/output behaviours, an architecture that is *operational* (i.e. produces all the expected outputs from the given inputs) within a specified set of constraints. Besides the input/output behaviour of the hardware, conventional designs are essentially based on knowledge and creativity, which are two human characteristics and too hard to be automated. Evolutionary hardware is a design that is generated using simulated evolution as an alternative to conventional-based electronic circuit design. *Genetic evolution* [3], [4] is a process that evolves a set of genotypes, i.e. *population*, producing a new population at each iteration process. Here, individuals are hardware designs. The more the design obeys the constraints, the more it is used in the reproduction process. The design constraints can be expressed in terms of hardware area and/or response time requirements. The freshly produced population is yield using some *genetic operators* such as *crossover* and *mutation* that attempt to simulate the natural breeding

N.T. Nguyen et al. (Eds.): IEA/AIE 2008, LNAI 5027, pp. 551–560, 2008.

process in the hope of generating new design that are *fitter* i.e. respect more the design constraints. Genetic evolution is usually implemented using *genetic algorithms.*

Genetic programming [3], [4] is way of producing a program using genetic evolution. So the individuals are programs. The main goal of genetic programming is to provide a domain-independent problem-solving method that automatically yields computer programs from expected input/output behaviours. Exploiting genetic programming, we automatically create novel cryptography circuits that exhibit creativity and inventiveness. Here, the individuals are *register-transfer level* specifications of the hardware. All existing synthesis tools synthesise this kind of specifications very quickly, and so an equivalent re-configurable hardware can be obtained within reasonable time.

The remainder of this paper is organised in five parts. In Section 2, we give an overview of public-key cryptography. In particular, we introduce basic encryption and decryption used by RSA-based cryptosystems. In Section 3, we describe the principles of genetic programming. In Section 4, we describe the methodology we employed to evolve new compact and fast cryptographic hardware. In Section 5, we compare the discovered novel hardware against existing most popular ones. Finally, in Section 6, we discuss the pros and cons of evolutionary hardware for cryptography and draw some conclusions.

2 Public-Key Cryptosystems

Cryptography is the science of keeping secrets secret. Its main task is to provide confidentiality by encryption methods. The original message, which can be some text, numerical data or any other kind of information, is usually called *plaintext* and the encrypted plaintext is called *ciphertext*. Information transmission between two parties through public channels occurs after plaintext t is encrypted into ciphertext c so that an eventual adversary third party in possession of c cannot derive any information about t. Cryptosystems must provide an encryption and a decryption algorithm. Existing cryptosystems can be classified into *symmetric* and *asymmetric* systems. Both encryption and decryption processes in symmetric cryptosystems depend on the same secret key while in asymmetric ones there exist a *public* key on which depends the encryption algorithm and another *private* key used by the decryption process.

A Rivest-Shamir-Adleman or simply RSA-based cryptosystem [1] is asymmetric. It consists of triple $\langle M, e, d \rangle$, which consists of the *modulus, public* and *private* key respectively. The modulus and the public key of the system are made public while the private key is kept secret. To build an RSA-based cryptosystem, one needs to: *(i)* Create two primes p and q; *(ii)* Compute $M = p.q$; *(iii)* Calculate the value of *Euler totient function* defined for M as $N = \Phi(M) = (p-1)(q-1)$; *(iv)* Choose e, such that the greatest common divisor of N and e is 1, i.e. $gcd(e, N) = 1$, with $e \neq 1$ and $e \neq N$; *(v)* Compute d such that $e.d \equiv 1 \bmod N$. This can be done using the *extended Euclidean algorithm.*

Note the public and private keys of a given cryptosystem are non-negative integer smaller than its modulus, i.e. for the system defined by $\langle M, e, d \rangle$, we have $0 \leq e, d \leq M-1$. With modulus of reasonable length, i.e. about 1024 bits, solving the factoring problem i.e. discovering p and q, which will lead to discovering the private key is impossible considering the computation power and the factoring algorithms one disposes of nowadays.

Both the encryption and decryption algorithms in RSA-based cryptosystems are implemented using the same algorithm: modular exponentiation. That is, the ciphertext C is obtained from plaintext T by $C = T^e \bmod M$ and T is obtained from C by $T = C^d \bmod M$. This characteristic is very attractive and so it increased the popularity of RSA-based cryptosystems. Note that the plaintext and its corresponding ciphertext in a given RSA-based cryptosystem are non-negative integers smaller than the modulus.

The practicality of cryptosystem depends heavily on how fast the encryption and essentially decryption process can be done. Therefore, the practicality of RSA-based cryptosystems depends essentially on how fast modular exponentiation of large integers can be performed.

Modular exponentiation can be implemented as a repetition of modular multiplications. So far, most published research attempt to either optimise the implementation of modular multiplication, minimise the number of required modular multiplications or do both [5], [6], [7], [8], [9]. Here, we use evolutionary computation, namely genetic programming, to discover new efficient and creative hardware for RSA-based cryptosystems.

3   Genetic Programming

Genetic programming [3] is an extension of genetic algorithms. The chromosomes are computer programs and the genes are instructions. In general, genetic programming offers a mechanism to get a computer to provide a solution of problem without being told exactly how to do it. In short, it allows one to automatically create a program. It does so based on a high level statement of the constraints the yielded program should obey to. The input/output behaviour of the expected program is generally considered as an omnipresent constraint. Furthermore, the generated program should use a minimal number of instructions and have an optimal execution time.

Starting form random set of computer programs, which is generally called *initial population*, genetic programming breeds a population of programs through a series of steps, called *generations*, using the Darwinian principle of natural *selection*, recombination also called *crossover*, and *mutation*. Individuals are selected based on how much they adhere to the specified constraints. Each program is assigned a value, generally called its *fitness*, which mirrors how *good* it is in solving the program. Genetic programming [3] proceeds by first, randomly creating an initial population of computer programs; then, iteratively performing a generation, which consists of going through two main steps, as far as the constraints are not met. The first step in a generation assigns for each computer program in the current population a fitness value that measures its adherence to the constraints while the second step creates a new population by applying the three genetic operators, which are *reproduction, crossover* and *mutation* to some selected individuals. *Selection* is done with on the basis of the individual fitness. The fitter the program is, the more probable it is selected to contribute to the formation of the new generation. *Reproduction* simply copies the selected individual from the current population to the new one. *Crossover* recombines two chosen computer programs to create two new programs using single-point crossover or two-points crossover

[3]. Mutation yields a new individual by changing some randomly chosen instruction in the selected computer program. The number of genes to be mutated is called *mutation degree* and how many individuals should suffer mutation is called *mutation rate*.

4   Evolving Multi-objective Hardware for Digital Circuits

There three main aspects in implementation of genetic programming [3]: *(i)* program encoding; *(ii)* crossover and mutation of programs; *(iii)* program fitness. In this section, we explain how we treat these three aspects in our implementation.

4.1   Circuit Specification = Programs

Encoding of individuals is one of the implementation decisions one has to take in order to use evolutionary computation. It depends highly on the nature of the problem to be solved. There are several representations that have been used with success: *binary encoding* which is the most common mainly because it was used in the first works on genetic algorithms, represents an individual as a string of bits; *permutation encoding* mainly used in ordering problem, encodes an individual as a sequence of integer; *value encoding* represents an individual as a sequence of values that are some evaluation of some aspect of the problem; and *tree encoding* represents an individual as tree. Generally, the tree coincides with the *concrete* as opposed to *abstract tree* of the computer program, considering the grammar of the programming language used.

Table 1. Gates allowed and the corresponding characteristics

Name	Gate Eq.	Delay	Name	Gate Eq.	Delay
NOT	1	0.0625	NAND	1	0.13
AND	2	0.209	NOR	1	0.156
OR	2	0.216	XNOR	3	0.211
XOR	3	0.212	MUX	3	0.212

Here a design is specified using register transfer level equations. Each instruction in the specification is an output signal assignment. A signal is assigned the result of an expression wherein the operators are those that represent basic gates in CMOS technology of VLSI circuit implementation and the operands are the input signals of the design. The allowed operators are shown in Table 1. Note that all gates introduce a minimal propagation delay as the number of input signal is minimal, which is 2.

For instance, a 2-bit multiplier has 4-bit result signal so an evolved register transfer level specification is as follows, wherein the input operands are $X =<x_1x_0>$ and $Y =<y_1y_0>$ and the output is the product $P =<p_3p_2\ p_1p_0>$. We encode specifications using an array of concrete trees corresponding to its signal assignments. The ith. tree represents the evaluation tree of the expression on the left-hand side of the ith. signal assignment. Leaf nodes are labelled with a literal representing a single bit of an input signal while the others are labelled with an operand. The individual corresponding to above specification is shown in Figure 1.

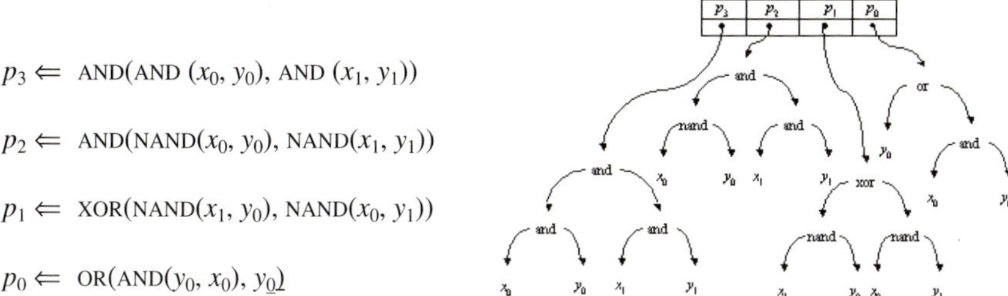

$$p_3 \Leftarrow \text{AND}(\text{AND}(x_0, y_0), \text{AND}(x_1, y_1))$$

$$p_2 \Leftarrow \text{AND}(\text{NAND}(x_0, y_0), \text{NAND}(x_1, y_1))$$

$$p_1 \Leftarrow \text{XOR}(\text{NAND}(x_1, y_0), \text{NAND}(x_0, y_1))$$

$$p_0 \Leftarrow \text{OR}(\text{AND}(y_0, x_0), y_0)$$

Fig. 1. Chromosome for Evolved multiplier

4.2 Circuit Specification Reproduction

Crossover recombines two randomly selected individuals into two fresh off-springs. It may be *single-point* or *double-point* or *uniform* crossover [3]. Crossover of circuit specification is implemented using a single, double and variable double-point crossover [3]. The single-point crossover is described in Figure 2 and double-point crossover in Figure 3. The impact of the type of crossover is shown in Figure 4.

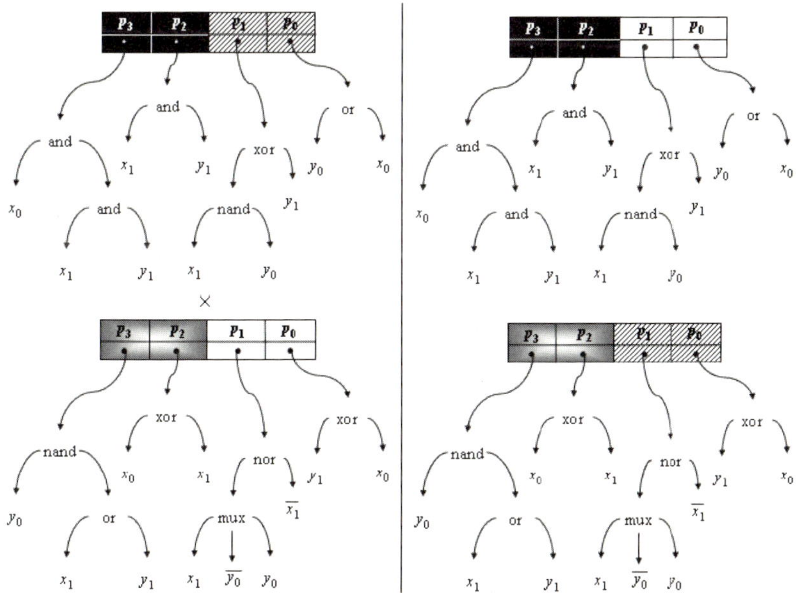

Fig. 2. Single-point crossover of circuit specification

One of the important and complicated operators for genetic programming is the *mutation*. It consists of changing a gene of a selected individual. The number of individuals that should suffer mutation is defined by the *mutation rate* while how many genes should be altered within a chosen individual is given by the *mutation degree*.

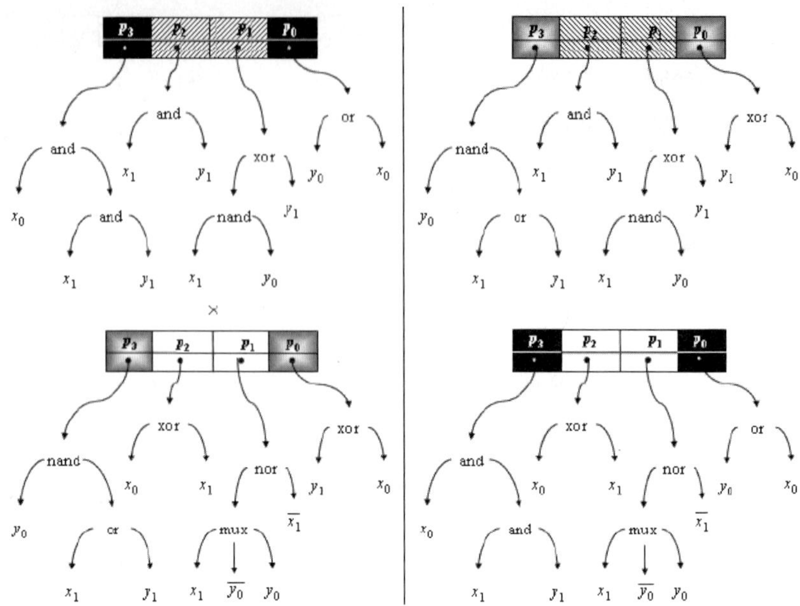

Fig. 3. Double-point crossover of circuit specification

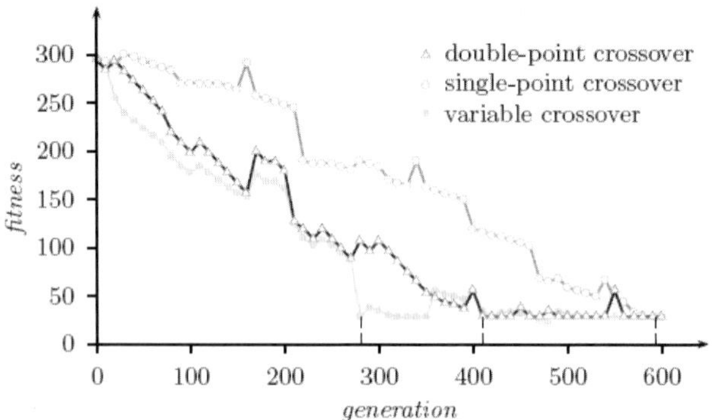

Fig. 4. Impact of the type of crossover

Here, a gene is the expression tree on the left hand side of a signal assignment symbol. Altering an expression can be done in two different ways depending on the node that was randomised and so must be mutated. A node represents either an operand or operator. In the former case, the operand, which is a bit in the input signal, is substituted with either another input signal or *simple* expression that includes a single operator. The decision is random. In the case of mutating an operand node to an operator node, the randomised operator node may be mutated to an operator node or to an operator of smaller (AND to NOT), the same (AND to XOR) or bigger arity (AND to MUX). In the last case, a new operand is randomised to fill in the new operand. The node mutation operator is illustrated in Figure 5.

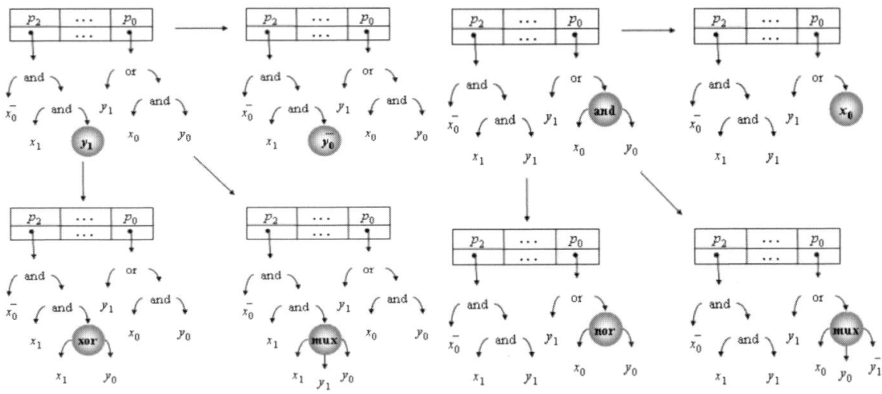

Fig. 5. Impact of the mutation operator

4.3 Circuit Specification Multi-objective Evaluation

Another important aspect of genetic programming is to provide a way to evaluate the adherence of evolved computer programs to the imposed constraints. In our case, these constraints are of three kinds. First of all, the evolved specification must obey the input/output behaviour, which is given in a tabular form of expected results given the inputs. This is the truth table of the expected circuit. Second, the circuit must have a reduced size. This constraint allows us to yield compact digital circuits. Thirdly, the circuit must also reduce the signal propagation delay. This allows us to reduce the response time and so discover efficient circuits. In order to take into account both area and response time, we evaluate circuits using the weighted sum approach [10], [11].

We estimate the necessary area for a given circuit using the concept of *gate equivalent*. This is the basic unit of measure for digital circuit complexity. It is based upon the number of logic gates that should be interconnected to perform the same input/output behaviour. This measure is more accurate than the number of gates.

When the input to an electronic gate changes, there is a finite time delay before the change in input is seen at the output terminal. This is called the propagation delay of the gate and it differs from one gate to another. Of primary concern is the path from input to output with the highest total propagation delay. We estimate the performance of a given circuit using the worst-case delay path.

Let C be a digital circuit that uses a subset (or the complete set) of the gates given in Table 1. Let $Gates(C)$ be a function that returns the set of all gates of circuit C and $Levels(C)$ be a function that returns the set of all the gates of C grouped by level. Notice that the number of levels of a circuit coincides with the cardinality of the set expected from function $Levels$. On the other hand, let $Val(X)$ be the Boolean value that the considered circuit C propagates for the input Boolean vector X assuming that the size of X coincides with the number of input signal required for circuit C. The fitness function, which allows us to determine how much an evolved circuit adheres to the specified constraints, is given as follows:

$$fitness\,(C) \;=\; \sum_{j=1}^{n}\left(\sum_{i\,|\,Val(X_i)\neq Y_{i,j}} Penalty\right) +$$

$$\Omega_1 \times \sum_{g\in Gates(C)} GateEq\,(g) \; +$$

$$\Omega_2 \times \sum_{L\in Levels(C)} \sum_{g\in L} Max\,Delay\,(g)$$

Where in X represents the input values of the input signals while Y represents the expected output values of the output signals of circuit C, n denotes the number of output signals that circuit C has, function $Delay$ returns the propagation delay of a given gate as shown in Table 1 and Ω_1 and Ω_2 are the weighting coefficients that allow us to consider both area and response time to evaluate the performance of an evolved circuit, with $\Omega_1 + \Omega_2 = 1$. For implementation issue, we minimised the fitness function below for different values of Ω_1 and Ω_2.

5 Evolutionary vs. Conventional Designs for RSA Cryptosystems

Several efficient designs for RSA cryptosystems were developed [5], [6], [9], [12]. In the following, we compare two conventional designs: one sequential and the other parallel to the evolutionary design obtained. For this purpose, we evolved a specification for $M = 13$, $E = 11$. The specification of the evolved RSA-based cryptographic hardware is given below, wherein the signals T_0 to T_3 are the bits constituting the plaintext from the less to most significant bit.

$$\text{CIPHER}_3 \Leftarrow \text{NUX}\,(\text{AND}\,(\text{NAND}\,(T_2, \overline{T_0})\,),\text{NAND}\,(\overline{T_1}, T_2)\,)\,),\text{NOR}\,(\text{NOR}\,(\text{NOR}\,(\overline{T_0}, \overline{T_2})\,),\overline{T_0})\,,$$
$$\text{AND}\,(\text{NAND}\,(T_2, \overline{T_0})\,),\overline{T_1})\,)\,),\text{NOR}\,(\text{MUX}\,(\overline{T_3}, \overline{T_1},\text{NOR}\,(\text{NOR}\,(\overline{T_0}, \overline{T_2})\,),\overline{T_0})\,)\,),T_3)\,)$$

$$\text{CIPHER}_2 \Leftarrow \text{NUX}\,(\text{NOR}\,(\text{MUX}\,(\overline{T_3}, 6,\text{NOR}\,(\text{NOR}\,(\overline{T_0}, \overline{T_2})\,),\overline{T_0})\,)\,),T_3)\,,\;\text{MUX}\,(\overline{T_3}, \overline{T_1},$$
$$\text{NOR}\,(\text{NOR}\,(\overline{T_0}, \overline{T_2})\,),\overline{T_0})\,)\,),\text{NAND}\,(\overline{T_2}, T_1)\,)$$

$$\text{CIPHER}_1 \Leftarrow \text{MUX}\,(\text{NOR}\,(\text{NOR}\,(\overline{T_0}, \overline{T_2})\,),\overline{T_0})\,,\text{NOR}\,(\text{NOR}\,(\text{NOR}\,(\overline{T_0}, \overline{T_2})\,),\overline{T_0})\,,$$
$$\text{AND}\,(\text{NAND}\,(T_2, \overline{T_0})\,),\overline{T_1})\,)\,),\overline{T_3})$$

$$\text{CIPHER}_0 \Leftarrow \text{AND}\,(\text{NAND}\,(\overline{T_1}, T_2)\,,\text{MUX}\,(\text{NOR}\,(\text{NOR}\,(\overline{T_3}, \overline{T_1})\,,\text{NOR}\,(\overline{T_0}, \overline{T_2})\,)\,),T_3,$$
$$\text{NOR}\,(T_0, T_1)\,)\,)$$

We generated automatically from the *XILINX^{TM}* Project Manager [13] the evolved circuit schematics using look-up tables. The basic unit is a four inputs and one output look-up table. The circuit requires 4 look-up tables as shown in Figure 6. We obtained and compared the size and response time for the evolved circuit with those corresponding to the sequential and parallel binary exponentiation implementations. Table 2 lists the collected data for $M = 13$ and $E = 11$.

The size of the circuits is expressed in terms of gate equivalent and the response time is ns. The data provide in Table 2 show clearly that the evolved circuit is far better than the conventional designs: It requires much less hardware area and encrypts/decrypts much faster. Furthermore, it is shielded against side-channel leakage as it has no repetitive behaviour, as it is the case for conventional designs. However, the evolved circuit is not scalable. When a new cryptosystem with new modulus and/or key is needed, a new design need be evolved from scratch.

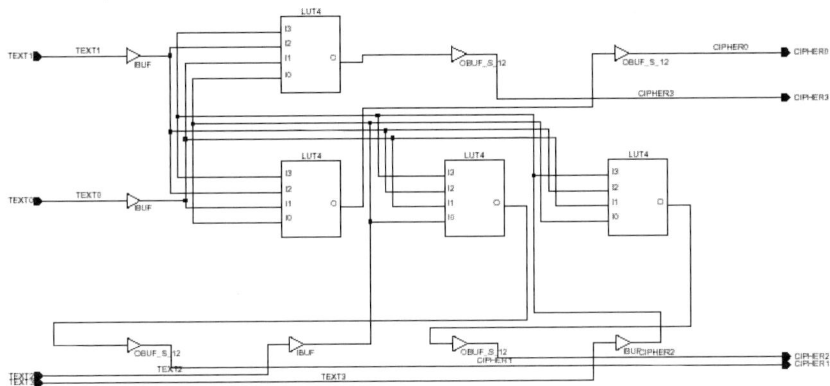

Fig. 6. Circuit schematics using look-up tables for the evolved circuit

Table 2. Conventional vs. evolutionary designs

	Size	**Time (ns)**
Sequential Binary	524	7.321
Parallel Binary	992	4.992
Evolved circuit	24	1.313

6 Conclusions

In this paper, we proposed a methodology based on genetic programming to automatically generate data-flow based specifications for hardware designs of public-key cryptosystems such as RSA-based encryption system. Our aim was evolving minimal hardware specifications, i.e. hardware that minimises both space (i.e. required gate number) and time (i.e. encryption and decryption time), for modular exponentiation. The advantages of such evolved cryptosystems are shielded against side-channel leakage. However, the designs are not scalable, i.e. for new modulus or keys, one need to evolve a new design. We compared our results against existing and well-known designs, which are based on the binary modular exponentiation method.

References

1. Rivest, R., Shamir, A., Adleman, L.: A method for obtaining digital signature and public-key cryptosystems. Communications of the ACM 21, 120–126 (1978)
2. Messerges, T.S., Dabbish, E.A., Sloan, R.H.: Power analysis attacks of modular exponentiation in smartcards. In: Koç, Ç.K., Paar, C. (eds.) CHES 1999. LNCS, vol. 1717, pp. 144–157. Springer, Heidelberg (1999)

3. Koza, J.R.: Genetic Programming. MIT Press, Cambridge (1992)
4. Nedjah, N., Ajith, A., Mourelle, L.M. (eds.): Genetic systems programming: theory & practice. Studies in Computational Intelligence Book Series, vol. 13. Springer, Heidelberg, Berlin (2006)
5. Nedjah, N., Mourelle, L.M.: Two hardware implementations for the Montgomery multiplication: sequential vs. parallel. In: Proc. of 15th Symposium on Integrated Circuits and Systems Design, Porto Alegre, Brazil, pp. 3–8. IEEE Computer Society, Los Alamitos (2002)
6. Nedjah, N., Mourelle, L.M. (eds.): New trends in cryptographic systems, Nova Science, Hauppauge, NY. Intelligent Systems Engineering Book Series (2006)
7. Brickell, E.F.: A survey of hardware implementation of RSA. In: Brassard, G. (ed.) CRYPTO 1989. LNCS, vol. 435, pp. 368–370. Springer, Heidelberg (1990)
8. Blum, T., Paar, C.: Montgomery modular exponentiation on reconfigurable hardware. In: Proc. of the 14th IEEE Symposium on Computer Arithmetic, Australia (1999)
9. Tiountchik, A.: Systolic modular exponentiation via Montgomery algorithm. Electronic Letters 34(9), 874–875 (1998)
10. Fonseca, C.M., Fleming, P.J.: An overview of evolutionary algorithms in multi-objective optimisation. Evolutionary Computation 3(1), 1–16
11. Nedjah, N., Mourelle, L.M.: Real-World Multi-objective System Engineering, Intelligent Systems Engineering Book Series, Nova Science, Hauppauge, NY (2005)
12. Nedjah, N., Mourelle, L.M.: Reconfigurable hardware implementation of Montgomery modular multiplication and parallel binary exponentiation. In: Proc. of Euromicro Symposium on Digital System Design, Dortmund, Germany, pp. 226–235. IEEE Computer Society, Los Alamitos (2002)
13. Xilinx^{TM}, Inc., http://www.xilinx.com

Automatic Selection of Cutting Tools Geometry Using an Evolutionary Approach

Orlando Duran, Nibaldo Rodriguez, and Luiz Airton Consalter

Pontificia Universidad Catolica de Valparaiso
Av. Brasil 2241, Chile
FEAR Universidade de Passo Fundo, P. Fundo, RS, Brasil
{nibaldo.rodriguez,orlando.duran}@ucv.cl,lac@upf.br

Abstract. This paper presents the application of an evolutionary algorithm for the definition of the optimal cutting tool geometry in machining operations. In essence, the proposed approach points to the use of a genetic algorithm for selecting adequate cutting tool angles. This optimization approach was developed considering a Macro Optimization Model reported in the literature. To determine the most appropriate configuration of the genetic algorithm and its parameters a set of tests were carried out. The different algorithm settings were tested against data obtained from experimental test carried out and provided by the authors of the optimization model. A variety of simulations were carried out to validate the performance of the system and to show the usefulness of the applied approach. The definition of proposed approach also has presented the following main conclusion: through the utilization of the evolutionary approach, the selection of the appropriate cutting tool geometry is possible in real world environments.

Keywords: Machining, Tool Geometry Optimization, Evolutionary Computation.

1 Introduction

Process Planning is an activity that establishes a set of manufacturing operations and their sequence, and specifies the appropriate tools and process parameters in order to convert a part from its initial state to a final form. Computer Aided Process Planning (CAPP) can be considered the technological solution that provides a great assistance and could even replace the human expertise in the planning procedure. Therefore, CAPP technology can assure the integration between CAD and CAM platforms and a total consistency and correctness of the developed process plans. This paper propose an expert system based on an evolutionary approach to effectively perform cutting tool selection. There are a number of papers in the literature that suggest the use of soft computing and evolutionary approaches to represent the knowledge of manufacturing operations. An example was presented by Knapp and Wang [1] who used an ANN in process planning. Cutting tool selection using neural networks was introduced by Dini [2]. The inputs used by the ANN are machining type, cutting

N.T. Nguyen et al. (Eds.): IEA/AIE 2008, LNAI 5027, pp. 561–569, 2008.

conditions, clamping type, workpiece material, workpiece slenderness and the generated outputs are five parameters identifying the cutting tool. Monostori et all.[3] proposed a set of models to estimate and classify tool wear using neural networks based techniques. The authors presented variable input-output configurations of ANN models according to variable tasks. Liao and Chen [4] presented a model for creep feed grinding of aluminium with diamond wheels. Recently, there have been some attempts to determine in an automated way the optimal tool geometry for a given machining operation. Oral and Cakir [5] presented a software for automated selection of cutting tools. The selection is performed using the machinability data, workpiece information, machine tool data, work holding method and a set-up number. According to the same authors, an optimum tool sequence is characterized by a minimum number of tool changes and minimum tool travel time. Zhao et all. [6] proposed a knowledge based system that performs the selection of cutting tools and conditions for turning operations. The system, called CADEXCATS processes CAD data and through the application of a set of rules the system defines set-up details, detects complex geometries, recognizes grooves and other important features. Arezoo et all. [7] developed a knowledge based system for selection of cutting tools and conditions in turning operations. The proposed system selects the toolholder, insert and cutting conditions (feed, speed and depth of cut). The input to the system is based in a feature-based representation of the workpiece and the available cutting tools. Mookherjee and Bhattacharyya [8] presented an expert system, which automatically selects the turning tool/insert or milling insert, the material and the geometry, based on the requirement of the users. Toussaint and Cheng [9] propose a web-based engineering approach to developing a design support system using case-based reasoning (CBR) technology for helping in the decision-making process when choosing cutting tools. Some attempts have also been made to ease this selection process through the use of intelligent systems, which have been developed as part of computer aided process planning (CAPP) applications, or more recently integrated to some "top of the range" computer aided design/manufacturing (CAD/CAM) packages. Dereli and Filiz [10] have proposed an approach using genetic algorithms (GAs), which mathematically determines from the 3D features of a mechanical part the best tooling arrangement to optimize the tooling set. McMullen et al. [11] have focused on optimizing production sequences by limiting the number of tooling replacements. Their approach is concerned with finding relevant tooling sequences while trying to maintain tool-wear uniformity through correlation and heuristic methods. Habel and Slodky [12] have developed expert system modules to be integrated to a CAPP application to intelligently select tooling configurations by taking into account as many factors as possible. Similarly CAD/CAM packages have recently started to integrate flexible tooling management features by accessing tool catalogues or interfacing with external tool database.

Up to now, no article have considered technological factors when selecting effective cutting tools and their geometries. The tool selection procedures developed thus far use expert systems approaches based on productivity or accessibility factors and others different than the impact that the cutting edge geometry may cause in machinability, surface roughness, chip breaking and cutting temperature. Here we propose the application of an evolutionary algorithm for selecting cutting tool regarding technological aspects and defining the cutting tool geometry using an empirically obtained relationship between cutting tool angles and the cutting performance as the main objective function.

2   Proposed Approach

Cutting tools selection is a very important subtask involved in process planning systems. Indeed, tool geometry (Fig. 1) definition is a very complex decision process. This fact is ascribable to the large number of and to the wide variety of considerations that are involved in this domain. Today an extensive variety of tool geometries is available to suit different cutting situations. As a consequence, the process planner has to work with voluminous machining data handbooks before deciding on the best tool geometry for the machining task at hand. In addition, the rules for selection are often vague and contradictory; hence, it is almost impossible for engineers or machinists to check all available cutters to find the most appropriate one. As a consequence, cutting tool geometry has to be defined using optimization models. Kaldor and Venuvinod [13] proposed a macro level optimization of cutting tool geometry. They have defined a model to describe the interactions among the tool material, workpiece material and the tool geometry. The authors proposed a geometric number, that characterizes the ideal set of tool angles at which a given tool material functions best (in terms of the tool life) in the context of machining a given work material (equation 1).

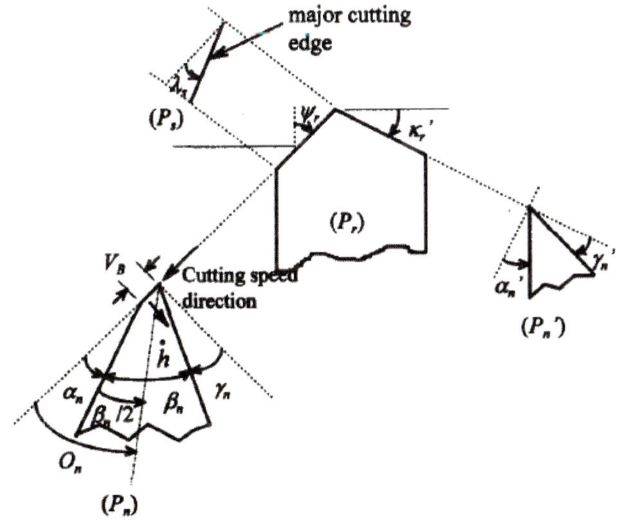

Fig. 1. Cutting geometry Model

$$\sigma_r = cos^2\lambda_s \frac{sin[\sigma + \frac{\beta_n}{2}]sin[\frac{\beta_n}{2}][\frac{\beta_n}{2} + \frac{1}{2}sin\frac{\beta_n}{2}] - cos[\alpha_n + \frac{\beta_n}{2}]cos[\frac{\beta_n}{2}][\frac{\beta_n}{2} - \frac{1}{2}sin\beta_n]}{[\frac{\beta_n}{2}]^2 - [\frac{1}{2}sin\beta_n]^2}$$

$$(1)$$

Where σ_r corresponds to a nondimensional stress factor that characterizes a cutting tool geometry; αn represents the tool normal clearance angle, βn represents normal wedge angle, γn represents tool normal rake angle and λn represents tool cutting edge inclination angle. Figure 2 shows the geometric specification of single point tools based on ISO 3002/1.

G number represents the ideal relationship between tool material and workpiece material. Kaldor and Venuvinod [13] examined over 80 published sources listing machinability data and relevant experimental results encompassing a wide range of cutting operations, tool and work materials and cutting conditions. They found that the following quantitative semi-empirical expression relating tool and work material properties can be assumed with a confidence greater than 95 %:

$$G = \log\{Sb/\{EU\}^2\} + 4.73 \tag{2}$$

Where G number represents the ideal relationship between tool material and workpiece material providing maximum tool life; Sb represents the bending strength of the tool material; E is the modulus of elasticity of the tool material and U corresponds to the specific cutting energy of the work material, all expressed in GPa. In consequence, the ideal tool geometry for a given cutting situation can be obtained through the minimization of the difference between G and σ_r.

3   Optimization Model

As it was mentioned above, to obtain the optimal tool geometry for a given cutting situation (tool and workpiece materials) one can minimize the difference between σ_r and G, subject to some technological restrictions such as allowed cutting edge angles, accordingly:

$$Minf(\lambda, \alpha, \gamma) = ABS(\sigma_r - G) \tag{3}$$

Subject to:
$-20 \leq \lambda_n \leq 20$
$0 \leq \alpha_n \leq 20$
$-20 \leq \gamma_n \leq 20$
$\beta_n = 90 - (\alpha_n + \gamma_n)$

To achieve the balance between exploitation and exploration capabilities of the genetic algorithm, and to determine the most appropriate configuration of the genetic algorithm and its parameters a set of tests were carried out. The different algorithm settings were tested against data obtained from [13]. Kaldor and Venuvinod listed the available carefully established empirical estimates of G. A sub set of these data is shown in table 1.

Table 1. Subset of empirical data used to set the genetic algorithm parameters

α	γ	λ	σ	α	γ	λ	σ	α	γ	λ	σ
10	-4	-8	1,82	10	16	0	2,82	13	5	0	2,42
18	-18	-16	1,82	13	15	0	2,96	8	24	4	2,79
6,2	-16	-20	1,25	5	8	0	1,83	8	8	0	2,07
0	-3	0	1,32	4,8	9,6	-2,6	1,85	8,9	18	-1,3	2,34
1	0	0	1,4	4,8	9,7	-2,6	1,86	5	6	0	1,78
0	3	0	1,41	4	15	0	1,94	8	15	0	2,34
5	-7,5	0	1,5	4,8	14	6,6	1,96	7	-0,7	-4	1,74
4,8	-6,1	-3,5	1,51	4,8	14	6,6	1,98	4,8	4,8	-1,3	1,73
4,8	-6,1	-3,5	1,51	6	14	6	2,08	4,8	4,8	-1,3	1,73
6	-6	6	1,56	8	9,8	5,7	2,11	6	0	0	1,7
4	0	0	1,58	7,9	10,4	4,1	2,14	9,8	-12	-7	1,63
3,5	3,5	3,5	1,61	5,8	15,5	4,1	2,18	10	-10	-13	1,62

Table 2. Mutation and Crossover parameters tested

Cross Prob.	Mutation Rate
0.1	0.1
0.3	0.3
0.5	0.5
0.7	0.7
0.9	0.9

The experiment included five levels of crossover probability (Pc) and five levels of mutation rate (Pm). At each GA trial run, the best order result obtained was recorded along with the average result and the average number of generations at which convergence is reached. The values of the control parameters tested and compared are reported in Table 2.

The average results of the best 10 runs for each set of parameters are shown in Table 3.

The parameters selected in this study are Crossover probability, 0.7 and Mutation rate, 0.3 because they have shown the best performance during the tests. The algorithm used the Roulette wheel method for parents selection. Figure 2

Table 3. Some of the best results obtained in test runs

Test Number	Average Error	Test Number	Average Error
9	4,33E-06	23	6,26E-06
14	4,93E-06	6	6,31E-06
8	5,04E-06	13	6,57E-06
24	5,74E-06	2	7,19E-06
7	6,12E-06	17	7,30E-06

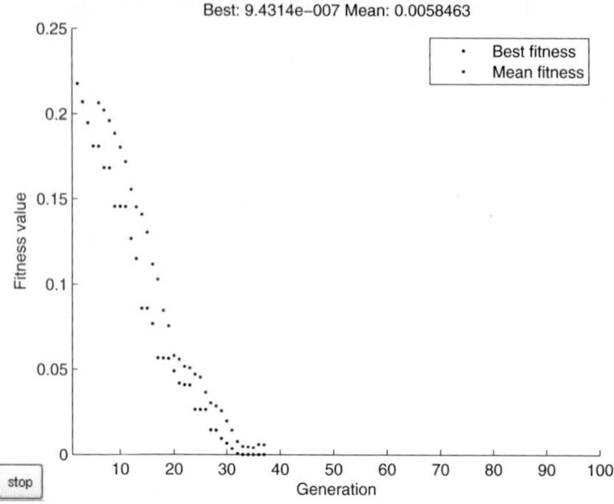

Fig. 2. Convergence process of the genetic algorithm with the selected parameters

shows the convergence process of the GA to the optimum using the selected parameters.

4   Application Example and Results

Each CAM system has a cutting-tool database and the appropriate cutting tool may be selected from it. A series of cutting tools can be identified from the cutting tool database. Based on the answer of the developed expert system, one or a set of cutting tool are selected from database for a given combination of tool material and workpiece material. Since no cutting tool in the database is likely

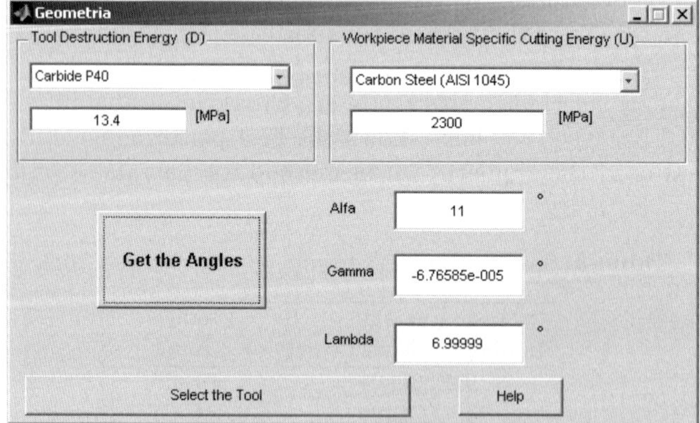

Fig. 3. Graphical user Interface - Input dialog box

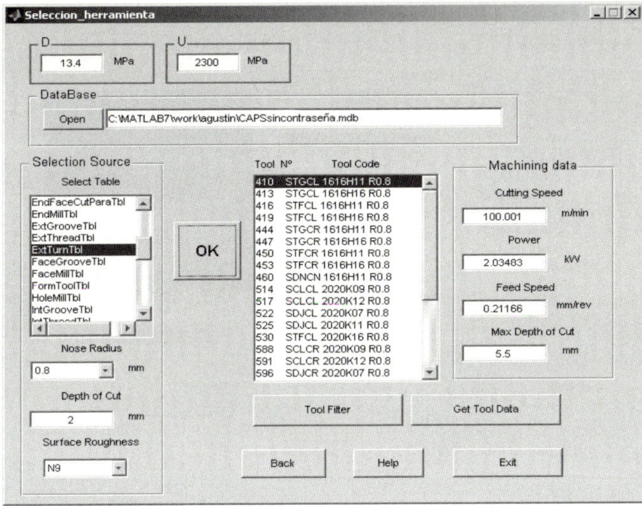

Fig. 4. Results of the genetic algorithm applied in a given tool database

to meet 100 percent of the σ_r, an Euclidean distance algorithm was implemented for the automatic search of the database. This search algorithm produces objects (cutting tools) that are geometrically close to the optimal one. Therefore, it can find one or more cutting tools in the database that meet the optimal geometric properties recommended by the G value or at least, a near approximation to it. To implement such an interaction a series of Matlab functions calls were written using the ODBC protocol. Figure shows the architecture of the proposed cutting tool selection expert system. The system is composed of a graphical user interface, a genetic algorithm-based expert system, a neural network module, an

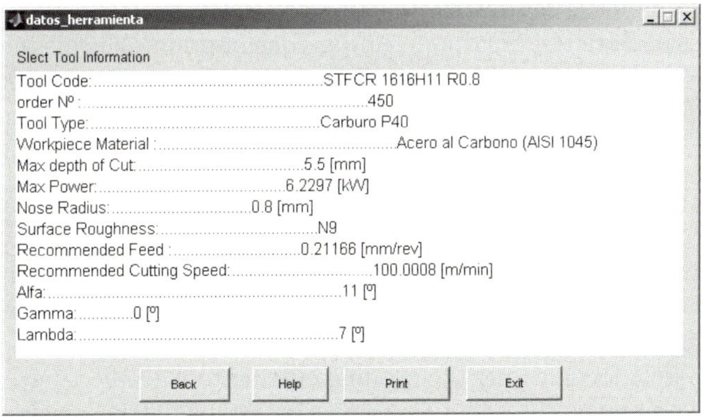

Fig. 5. Obtained results window

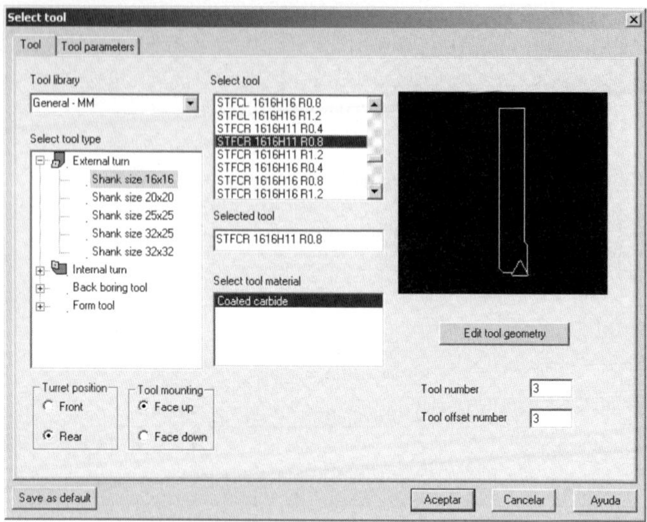

Fig. 6. Tool selection window of the commercial CAM system

interconnected machining tool database and an interface for a CAM software package. Figure 3 shows the dialog box whcre the user inputs the information about the workpiece material and identifies the type of tool material. The results of the searching algorithm are presented to the end user, which is in charge of the final selection of the specific tool among the candidates isolated by the expert system in coordination with the searching algorithm (Fig. 4. The system returns all the tools that meet the cutting angles recommended by the genetic algorithm. Several other parameters can be extracted or computed by the system. The cutting speed and feed, are calculated by an intelligent module that were implemented using neural networks approach. The maximum depth of cut is obtained by computing the effective cutting edge for the selected tool. This values are used for calculate the Maximum Power consumption. All this information is presented to the user in a dialog box (Figure 5). Finally, the user can select or define the appropriate tool from the CAM database (Fig. 6).

5   Conclusions

For promoting adaptative capability of Automated Process Planning systems, an intelligent system for selecting the optimal cutting conditions was applied. For promoting adaptative capability of Automated Process Planning systems, an intelligent system for selecting the optimal cutting tool geometry was developed. The system points to the identification of a list of cutting tools stored in a commercial CAM system database to aid the CAM operator to select the more appropriate cutting tool. The definition of proposed system also has presented the following conclusions: through the utilization of the evolutionary approach, the selection of the appropriate cutting tool geometry is possible in real world environments (integration with a cutting tool database); the system is capable of interact with several cutting tool databases; with a few input information the system can give the user several alternatives with different tool shapes or other tool characteristics. A variety of simulations were carried out to validate the performance of the system and to show the usefulness of the applied approach. Further evolution of the system is possible. This evolution points to enhance the interconnectivity of the system with other types of databases, rather than the MDB formats.

References

1. Knapp, G.M., Wang, Pin, H.: Acquiring, storing and utilizing process planning knowledge using neural networks. J. of Intelligent Manufacturing 3, 333–344 (1992)
2. Dini, G.: A neural approach to the automated selection of tools in turning. In: Proc. of 2nd AITEM Conf., Padova, September 18-20, pp. 1–10 (1995)
3. Monostori, L., Egresits, C.S., Hornyk, J., Viharos, Z.S.J.: Soft computing and hybrid AI approaches to intelligent manufacturing. In: Proc. of 11th Int. Conference on Industrial and Engineering Applications of Artificial Intelligence and Expert Systems, Castellon, pp. 763–774 (1998)
4. Liao, T.W., Chen, L.J.: A Neural Network Approach for Grinding Processes Modeling and Optimization. Int. J. of Machine Tools and Manufacture 34(7), 919–937 (1994)
5. Oral, A., Cakir, M.C.: Automated cutting tool selection and cutting tool sequence optimisation for rotational parts. Robotics and Computer-Integrated Manufacturing 20(2), 127–141 (2004)
6. Zhao, Y., Ridgway, K., Al-Ahmari, A.M.A.: Integration of CAD and a cutting tool selection system. Computers and Industrial Engineering archive 42(1) (April 17-34, 2002)
7. Arezoo, B., Ridgway, K., Al-Ahmari, A.M.A.: Selection of cutting tools and conditions of machining operations using an expert system. Computers in Industry 42(1), 43–58 (2000)
8. Mookherjee, R., Bhattacharyya, B.: Development of an expert system for turning and rotating tool selection in a dynamic environment. Journal of materials processing technology 113(1-3), 306–311 (2001)
9. Toussaint, J., Cheng, K.: Web-based CBR (case-based reasoning) as a tool with the application to tooling selection. Int. J. Adv. Manuf. Technol. 29, 24–34 (2006)
10. Dereli, T.R., Filiz, I.H.S.: Optimisation of process planning functions by genetic algorithms. Int. J. Comput. Ind. Eng. 36(2), 281–308 (1999)
11. McMullen, P.R., Clark, M., Albritton, D., Bell, J.: A correlation and heuristic approach for obtaining production sequences requiring a minimum of tool replacements. Int. J. Comput. Oper. Res. 30, 443–462 (2003)
12. Habel, J., Slodky, B.: The method of automated tool and cutting parameters selection for CAPP utilization. In: 10th International Conference FAIM 2000, Flexible Automation and Intelligent Manufacturing, Maryland, USA (2000)
13. Kaldor, S., Venuvinod, P.K.: Macro level Optimization of Cutting Tool Geometry. Journal of Manufacturing Science and Engineering 119, 1–9 (1997)

Optimal Sizing and Siting of Distributed Energy Resources Considering Public and Private Incentive Policies

Angelo Campoccia, Eleonora Riva Sanseverino, and Gaetano Zizzo

DIEET: Department of Electrical, Electronic and Telecommunication Engineering, University of Palermo, viale delle Scienze, Edificio 9,
90128 Palermo, Italy
zizzo@dieet.unipa.it

Abstract. The present work presents the formulation and solution approach for the problem of optimal sizing and siting of distributed energy resources based on Photovoltaic, PV, technology. The considered system is an isolated grid (small island) and the parts involved are the utility and the customers. As it happens in islands, the same utility generates and delivers energy to customers, for this reason, the installation of dispersed generation units is beneficial for reducing power losses, regularizing the voltage profile, but also for increasing the profit. The problem is solved by means of the Non dominated sorting Genetic Algorithm II, NSGA-II, identifying the optimal size and location of PV systems under different incentive policies supported by both the utility and the national government. Since a multiobjective approach has been used, the sizing and siting of PV units as well as the amount of financial support from the local distributor utility allowing higher benefits both for the utility and for the customers have been determined. The application section also quantifies the external costs associated with the most interesting design solutions.

Keywords: Distributed Generation, PV Systems, Multi-objective Optimization, Genetic Algorithms.

1 Introduction

Distributed Generation (DG) is the use of small generating sets, connected to the grid or feeding isolated micro-grids, based on technologies such as internal combustion engines, small and micro gas turbines, fuel cells, photovoltaic and wind plants. The use of DG leads to numerous advantages for the grid and the environment. DG is indeed a valid resource for demand management strategies, can play an important role on voltage regulation and control, can improve security of power supplies and can be used to obtain higher levels of end-user reliability than those obtainable with central generation. Thanks to the low rated powers of the DG units it is possible to install them at any bus of the Low Voltage (LV) and Medium Voltage (MV) distribution networks, in particular near to the load centres.

N.T. Nguyen et al. (Eds.): IEA/AIE 2008, LNAI 5027, pp. 570–579, 2008.

Moreover DG units can be set up modularly and their shorter construction time allows the development of the plants quickly enough to react to fluctuations in the market or peak-load-demand growth. Finally Renewable Energy Sources (RES) based DG allows to reduce emissions of green house gasses (GHGs). On the other hand, the installation of DG units in the network has technical, environmental and commercial problems that have to be faced properly for achieving the above-mentioned benefits. For example one of the main problems of RES-based DG units is the variability and the uncertainty of the energetic source. The work proposes an innovative formulation of the problem of the optimal size and location of DG units based on Photovoltaic (PV) technology, considering the possibility for the utility of supporting with private incentives the rise of new small size PV systems, taking, in this way, advantage of benefits deriving from the wide spread of DG units. The unknowns of the problem are:

- size and location of PV systems;
- the financial incentive given by the utility to its customers.

The solution algorithm used is the Non dominated sorting Genetic Algorithm II, (NSGA-II) [1], and the objectives of the problem are the minimization of the power losses in the grid, the minimization of the cost supported by the utility and the maximization of the gain of the customers. The reduction of power losses is indeed connected to the increase of the lifetime of components, to the voltage profile regulation, and thus to the improvement of the service quality. In the following, after a review on the works on the optimal sizing and siting of DG units (Section 2), the problem formulation (Section 3) and the NSGA-II algorithm (Section 4) are briefly presented. Finally an application example on a real existing grid (Section 5) and some considerations on the environmental benefits of the utility's strategy (Section 6) are provided.

2   Optimal Sizing and Siting of DG Units

The optimal sizing and siting of DG units appears to be a complicated issue that in the last years has been faced by many authors in different ways. Papers [2]-[5] are representative of the state of the art on this topic. Khator et al. [2] identify two major approaches in distribution systems planning: the single period approach and the multiperiod approach. Khator shows that only the second one is suitable for DG planning because the first one does not allow to take into account the increasing penetration of DG in the grid. Kuri et al. [3] face the planning problem taking into account the risks and the uncertainties of the power market. Carpinelli et al. [4] propose a methodology that solves the problem of the planning of DG for maximising the network performance by optimising some power quality indicators, like voltage quality and harmonic distortion, and by minimising the network costs. In [4] the problem of the optimal sizing and siting of DG is formulated as a constrained, multiobjective, and non-differentiable optimisation problem and is solved by means of a Genetic Algorithm (GA). Also Silvestri et al [5] use GA for solving the problem minimising the total cost of replacing components, building new substations and feeders, installing distributed generation, increasing the reliability and power quality and reducing power and energy losses. In all the cited works the DG optimal sizing and siting problem is formulated and solved considering the only point of view of the utility. The present work reformulates the problem considering the point of view both of the utility and of its customers that can also take advantages from the policy of the utility, consisting in the support of the installation of small DG units, as described in the following.

3   The Problem Formulation

Today, thanks to the national financing mechanism implemented in the world for supporting RES-based DG, many private end-users voluntarily realize little DG units, in particular Photovoltaic (PV) units, due to their consolidated technology. One of the most spread support mechanism in Europe for grid-connected PV systems is represented by the Feed'in Tariffs (FITs). With FITs a national government pays the whole energy produced by a PV system at a price that allows the owner of the production system to get back in few years the starting investment cost. Despite this support measure, the high initial installation cost of PV systems drives a big part of the potential self-producers (in particular domestic users) away from such a technology. FITs can not be added to other public incentives like capital subsidies that can support the self-producer in the starting phase of the investment. However the legal frameworks introducing FIT mechanism in the European countries do not exclude the possibility for the owner of the PV system of taking advantage of private capital subsidies, like, for example, subsidies from private citizens, banks or organizations of various kinds. This paper considers the possibility for the utility of exploiting for its own advantage this situation, supporting with private incentives the rise of new small size PV systems. In this case, the utility bears an expense for financing the customers' PV systems but at the same time takes advantage of the benefits of the wide spread of DG units.

The financial support is expressed by a coefficient β representing the percentage of the cost per installed kWp paid by the utility.

The utility needs to determine the optimal size and location of the PV systems and the amount of the financial support to be given to its customer that:

1.   minimise the power losses on the network's elements;
2.   minimise the costs of the utility;
3.   maximise the convenience for the PV systems' owners.

In this situation the optimisation problem is formulated considering two different points of view: the utility and the customers. The first wants to reduce the power losses in the network and to contain the investment costs; the seconds will install as many PV units as the subside given by the utility is high enough. The double point of view can drive the problem towards not easily predictable solutions. Once the fixed objectives and the possible solution strategy are identified, also the mathematical model to be adopted to represent the network must be defined. The model's features indeed influence the calculation times and the quality of the found solutions. It is indeed necessary to find a good compromise between speed and precision in order to attain reliable results in a reasonable solution time. The discrete nature of the optimisation variables and the adopted solution strategy suggest the use of a simplified model for the system. On this basis, a constant current model has been chosen for the loads representation while lines and transformers are represented through series impedances. A generic optimisation variable, namely a solution of the problem, includes a string containing the size and location of all the PV installations as well as the value of the coefficient β. The load flow algorithm is a backward/forward strategy and is implemented using a dynamic data structure allowing fast changes and evaluations in the network. In the following the analytical expressions and the relevant calculation hypotheses used are reported for the three objectives considered in the proposed formulation.

3.1 Power Losses

The power losses are associated with the resistive elements of lines and with HV/MV transformers. Losses at MV/LV transformers and losses caused by insulation of cable lines can be neglected because they are numerically small if compared to the line power losses. Other losses terms such as terms that are not varying with current can be neglected too. Under these assumptions the overall power losses considering lines and HV/MV transformers are:

$$\Delta P(h) = \sum_{i=1}^{N_b} \frac{R_i}{U_N^2}\left\{\left[P_i(h)-P_i^{FV}(h)\right]^2 + Q_i^2(h)\right\} + \sum_{i=1}^{N_{ss}} \frac{R_{t,i}}{U_N^2}\left\{\left[P_{t,i}(h)-P_{t,i}^{FV}(h)\right]^2 + Q_{t,i}^2(h)\right\} \tag{1}$$

where:

- N_b is the number of branches of the distribution network;
- N_{SS} is the number of transformers feeding the distribution network;
- U_N is the rated voltage value;
- R_i and $R_{t,i}$ respectively are the resistance of the ith branch and of the ith transformer feeding the distribution network;
- $P_i(h)$ and $Q_i(h)$ are the average real and reactive power flows on the ith branch at hour (h);
- $P_{t,i}(h)$ and $Q_{t,i}(h)$ are the average real and reactive power flows injected in the network through the ith transformer at hour h;
- $P_i^{FV}(h)$ and $P_{t,i}^{FV}(h)$ respectively are the average reduction of the real power flowing on the ith branch and on the ith transformer, due to the installation of the PV systems.

3.2 Yearly Costs of the Utility

The installation of the PV systems modifies the cash flow for the utility that yearly must bear a cost $C_{U,Y}$ that can be evaluated as the sum of various terms:

- part of the yearly installation cost $C_{INST,Y}$ of the PV systems of the customers;
- yearly cost of the energy losses in presence of PV systems C_{E1};
- yearly cost of the energy losses in absence of PV systems C_{E2};
- cost C_{PROD} that the utility does not bear for the production of a part of electric energy;
- cost C_S due to the reduction of the energy sold to the customers as consequence of the installation of the PV systems;
- FIT for the electricity produced by the proportion of plants owned, E_{FITD}

$$E_{FITD} = \beta \cdot FIT \cdot P_{TOT}^{FV} \cdot h_{eq} \cdot 365 .$$

The above-mentioned terms summed up give the cost $C_{U,Y}$:

$$C_{U,Y} = \beta \cdot C_{INST,Y} + C_{E1} - C_{E2} - C_{PROD} + C_S \tag{2}$$

$$C_{U,Y} = \beta \cdot C_{INST,Y} + C_{E1} - C_{E2} - C_{PROD} + C_S - E_{FITD} \tag{3}$$

In (2) and (3) β can vary between 0 and 1: when β is 1, it means that the contribution from the utility is full, when it is zero, it means that it is null.

3.3 Earnings of the Customers

Customers install the PV systems:

- paying an yearly cost for the installation;
- receiving the *FIT* for the electricity produced;
- receiving a contribution from the utility for the installation of the production system;
- paying yearly a maintenance cost depending on the peak power of the PV system;
- reducing the yearly expense for buying the electric energy bought by the utility.

Therefore the yearly earning of the customers is given by:

$$E_{C,Y} = -(1-\beta) \cdot C_{INST,Y} + E_{FIT} + E_{ES} - C_M \tag{4}$$

where:

- $E_{FIT} = FIT \cdot P_{TOT}^{FV} \cdot h_{eq} \cdot 365$ is the yearly earning due to the payment of the FIT for the electric energy produced;

- $E_{ES} = c_{kWh} \cdot P_{TOT}^{FV} \cdot h_{eq} \cdot 365$ is the earning due to the saving of electric energy;

- $C_M = 0.01 \cdot c_{kWp} \cdot P_{TOT}^{FV}$ is the maintenance cost.

In the previous equations: *FIT* is the value of the Feed-in-Tariff paid for the electric energy; P_{TOT}^{FV} is the total installed PV power; h_{eq} is the equivalent hours produced of the PV systems; c_{kWh} is the electricity cost paid by the customers; c_{kWp} is the market specific installation cost (€/kWp) of PV systems.

4 The Optimization Algorithm

The algorithm used for solving the optimization problem is the Non dominated Sorting Genetic Algorithm II, NSGA-II [1].

The concept of non-dominance is one of the basic concepts in multiobjective optimization. For a problem having more than one objective function to minimize (say, f_j, $j=1,\ldots,m$ and $m>1$) any two multidimensional solutions $\mathbf{x_1}$ and $\mathbf{x_2}$ can have one or two possibilities: one dominates the other or none dominates the other. A solution $\mathbf{x}_1$ is said to dominate the other solution $\mathbf{x}_2$, if both the following conditions are true:

a)   The solution $\mathbf{x}_1$ is no worse than $\mathbf{x}_2$ in all objectives, $f_j(\mathbf{x}_1) \leq f_j(\mathbf{x}_2)$, for all $j=1....m$.
b)   The solution $\mathbf{x}_1$ is strictly better than $\mathbf{x}_2$ in at least one objective, or $f_j^*(\mathbf{x}_1) < f_j^*(\mathbf{x}_2)$ for at least one $j^* \in \{1...m\}$.

If any of the above conditions is violated, the solution $\mathbf{x}_1$ does *not dominate* solution $\mathbf{x}_2$. If $\mathbf{x}_1$ dominates the solution $\mathbf{x}_2$, it is also customary to write $\mathbf{x}_2$ *is dominated* by $\mathbf{x}_1$, or $\mathbf{x}_1$ is *not dominated* by $\mathbf{x}_2$, or, simply, among two solutions, $\mathbf{x}_1$ is the *non-dominated* solution.

It is also important to observe that the concept of optimality in multiobjective optimization is related to a set of solutions, instead than to a single one. It is therefore possible to define Pareto local and global optimality for sets of solutions.

P is a locally optimal Pareto set, if for every member $\mathbf{x}$ in P, there exist no solution $\mathbf{y}$ in a small neighbourhood, which dominates every member in the set P.

P is a global Pareto-optimal set, if there exist no solution in the search space, which dominates every member in the set P.

From the above discussion, it is possible to point out that there are primarily two goals that a multi-criterion optimization algorithm must achieve:

1.   guide the search towards the global Pareto-optimal region;
2.   maintain population diversity in the Pareto-optimal front.

As NSGA (Non dominated Sorting Genetic Algorithm) [6], it divides the population in fronts of non-dominated solutions so that the search can be addressed towards interesting areas of the search space, where the global Pareto-optimal region is presumably located. NSGA-II varies from the NSGA in three main things. It is more efficient computationally, since the ranking of solutions is performed with a $O(kN^2)$ algorithm, instead of $O(kN^3)$, where k is the number of objectives (in our case, k is the sum of the number of objectives, m, and inequality constraints, s) and N is the population size; it significantly prevents the loss of good solutions once they have been found (elitism); it does not need any parameter specification. A Binary Tournament Selection operator is used to select the offspring population, whereas crossover and mutation operators remain as usual. Before selection is performed, the population is ranked on the basis of an individual's non-domination level and, to allow the diversification, a crowding factor is calculated for each solution.

5   Application Example

The study has been applied to the MV distribution network of the island of Lampedusa (Italy) managed by SE.LI.S. S.p.A. The Network has 69 nodes, of which 52 are load nodes, and is composed by a thermoelectric power plant supplying three cable lines (type RG7H1RX, Cross section: $3\times95\text{mm}^2$) and one aerial line (Copper conductors, Cross Section: $3\times35\text{mm}^2$). The rated voltage of the network is 10kV. The layout of the network is represented in Fig.1.

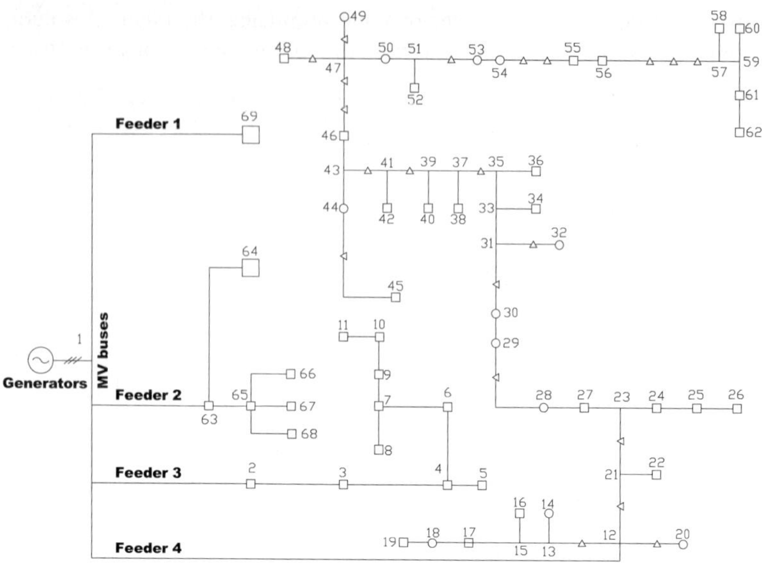

Fig. 1. Single-line scheme of the MV system supplying the Island of Lampedusa (Italy)

The input data are:

- the hourly average insulation of the island and the real average active and reactive power profiles for each load node, differentiated between summer and winter, and relative to 2006, provided by SE.LI.S.;
- the correlation between the capital subside paid by the utility and the installed PV power, assumed (for simplicity) linear;
- the market cost of PV system (about 7000 €/kW for small size units);
- the electric energy cost, equal to 0.21 €/kWh for SE.LI.S. for customers;
- the *FIT* value, equal to 0.44 €/kWh [7] for PV units partially integrated in building (most frequent case in Italy);
- the energy production cost from fossil source, equal to 0.06 €/kWh;
- the sum of the interest and the amortization rates, assumed equal to 8%.

Figure 2 shows the fifty best results at the last iteration. In Table 1, some of the fifty best results chosen on the basis of the value of the capital subside given by the

Table 1. Results of the simulations

Sol.	$C_{U,Y}$ (€)	$E_{C,Y}$ (€)	Power losses E_l (MWh)	PVinst (kWp)	β
1	16237.92	422338.94	747.15	784.5	0.041
2	22352.86	581426.75	721.96	1080.0	0.041
3	152908.47	455063.23	731.40	1087.5	0.286
4	362460.89	256410.31	719.80	1107.0	0.667
5	254666.27	397748.52	722.25	1167.0	0.444
6	405745.95	278536.29	718.45	1224.0	0.676
7	572530.21	161228.47	716.21	1312.5	0.889
8	27881.56	725163.22	717.03	1347.0	0.041

utility and of the installed PV power are summarized. The eight solutions in Table 1 show the most significantly different indicators chosen for optimization. It is interesting to compare the solutions 1, 2 and 8 (low beta) with the other solutions in the table and in particular the last two solutions (7 and 8).

These show similar values of PV power installed and thus of power losses. Larger contributions from the utility induce limited earnings for the customers, while smaller contributions from the utility induce larger benefits for the customers. This unexpected result is due to the effect of the combination of private and public incentives, the first ruled by the parameter β, the second ruled by the property of the plant. The public incentives are large and are proportional to the amount of energy produced by the PV plants; for this reason, the private measures, based on incentives on capital account, have a little effect. The utility with a small contribution can get optimized operation, low losses. The customer on the other hand owning almost entirely the plants gets large earnings.

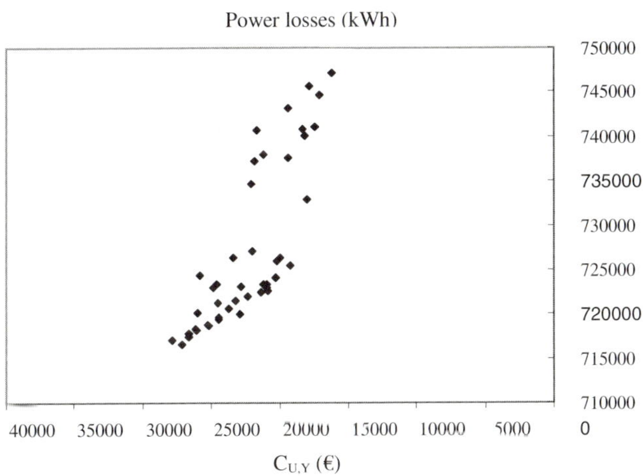

Fig. 2. Optimal solutions of the multiobjective problem

The solutions have been found using a software based on NSGA-II developed by DIEET. The software gives the optimal location and size of each DG unit for each of the fifty best solutions found but for practical reasons only the results related to solution eight (highest installed PV power) are shown in Table 2.

Table 2. Photovoltaic systems rated size and id of the installation nodes (solution n°1)

Node	1	2	3	4	5	6	7	8	9	10	11	13	15
P [kW]	12	3	36	37.5	1.5	52.5	73.5	18	10.5	19.5	10.5	12	6
Node	17	18	19	20	21	22	23	24	26	28	29	31	32
P [kW]	13.5	1.5	7.5	6	42	7.5	4.5	7.5	6	3	21	6	13.5
Node	35	36	37	39	40	42	44	46	47	49	51	52	54
P [kW]	22.5	21	10.5	9	15	4.5	7.5	19.5	27	6	39	60	28.5
Node	55	56	57	60									
P [kW]	88.5	105	116	1.5									

Table 3. Saved external costs

	Installed PV power [kW]	Energy yearly saved [MWh]	External cost yearly saved [€]
Min	784.5	1803.96	43294.99
Max	1347	3097.43	74338.24

6 Conclusion

Whatever it is the configuration of the private incentive, none or full, the results of the study show that for promoting the installation of small PV units by the customers, the utility must always bear yearly a notable expense (in the specific case variable between 16237.92 €/year and 572530.21 €/year). At the same time the PV systems' owner has a significant earning due to both the payment of the *FIT* and the capital subside from the utility (customers earn between 161228.47 €/year and 725163.22 €/year). Therefore another important result must be underlined: the promotion of the PV technology leads to significant benefits in terms of reduction of environmental impacts and of the associated costs for the community. Indeed the *"ExternE, Externalities of Energy"* Research Project of the European Commission [8]-[9] has recently presented a method for the monetary evaluation of the environmental impacts associated to the energy production. According to this study it is possible to transform the global warming, related to the production of CO_2 emissions, and the impacts due to the release of either substances (e.g. finc particles, SO_2, NO_X, CO, etc) or energy (noise, radiation, heat) into air, soil and water, into monetary values named "external costs". The "external costs" vary from country to country, depending on the technologies used for producing energy and various other socio-economic and technical factors. In the specific case considered in the application example, following the methodology defined in [8]-[9] an external cost equal to 24€/MWh has been found for the island of Lampedusa. Considering that the equivalent hours produced of the PV systems installed in the islands are equal to 6.30, the external costs saved by the global community installing the PV units are calculated and are reported in Table 3.

The values reported in Table 3 refer to the two extreme values (solutions 1 and 8) the solutions in Table 1 refer to. The Table shows that, besides the utility must bear very high cost for supporting PV DG, in many cases the saved external cost are significant. Finally it must be observed that as soon as these savings for the community will be translated into an economical equivalent by the governments, the utility will largely compensate its investments. Further studies will be addressed towards the analysis of other incentive measures and of other RES types having different unitary costs.

References

1. Deb, K., Agrawal, S., Pratap, A., Meyarivan, T.A.: Fast Elitist Non-Dominated Sorting Genetic Algorithm for Multi-Objective Optimization: NSGA-II. In: Proceedings of Parallel Problem Solving from Nature VI, Paris, France (2000)
2. Khator, S.K., Leung, L.C.: Power distribution planning: a review of models and issues. IEEE Transactions on Power Systems 12(3), 1151–1159 (1997)

3. Kuri, B., Li, F.: Distributed generation planning in the deregulated electricity supply industry. IEEE Power Engineering Society General Meeting 2, 2085–2089 (2004)
4. Carpinelli, G., Celli, G., Mocci, S., Pilo, F., Russo, A.: Optimisation of embedded generation sizing and siting by using a double trade-off method. IEE Proceedings on Generation, Transmission and Distribution 152(4), 503–513 (2005)
5. Silvestri, A., Berizzi, A., Buonanno, S.: Distributed generation planning using genetic algorithms. In: Proceedings of IEEE Powertech 1999, Budapest, p. 257 (1999)
6. Srinivas, N., Deb, K.: Multi-objective function optimization using nondominated sorting genetic algorithms. Evolutionary Computation 2(3), 221–248 (1994)
7. Criteri e modalità per incentivare la produzione di energia elettrica mediante conversione fotovoltaica della fonte solare, in attuazione dell'articolo 7 del decreto legislativo 29 dicembre 2003, n. 387. Ministry for Economical Development decree (February 19, 2007)
8. ExternE, Externalities of Energy, Methodology 2005 Update. European Commission, European Communities, Luxembourg (2005), http://www.externe.info/
9. ExternE, Externalities of Energy, Vol XX: National Implementation. European Commission, Directorate-General XII, Science, Research and Development (1999), http://www.externe.info/

Test Pattern Generator Design Optimization Based on Genetic Algorithm

Tomasz Garbolino[1] and Gregor Papa[2]

[1] Silesian University of Technology, PL-44100 Gliwice, Poland
tomasz.garbolino@polsl.pl
[2] Jožef Stefan Institute, SI-1000 Ljubljana, Slovenia
gregor.papa@ijs.si

Abstract. In this paper an approach for the generation of deterministic test pattern generator logic composed of D-type and T-type flip-flops is described. The approach employs a genetic algorithm to find an acceptable practical solution in a large space of possible implementations. In contrast to conventional approaches our genetic algorithm approach reduces the gate count of built-in self-test structure by concurrent optimization of multiple parameters that influence the final solution. Results of experiments with combinational benchmarks demonstrate the efficiency of the proposed evolutionary approach.

1 Introduction

Due to the growing complexity of modern integrated circuits and increasing testing demands, boundary-scan approach has been developed and is widely adopted in practice [9,14]. Limited number of input/output pins represents a bottleneck in testing of complex embedded cores where transfers of large amounts of test patterns and test results between the automatic test equipment (ATE) and the unit-under-test (UUT) are required. One alternative solution is to implement a built-in self-test (BIST) of the UUT with on-chip test pattern generation (TPG) and on-chip output response analysis logic. In this way, communication with external ATE is reduced to test initiation and transfer of test results. One disadvantage of BIST implementation is the area overhead, which leads to longer signal routing paths. Minimization of the BIST logic is needed to decrease this drawback.

In the past different TPG approaches have been proposed; ROM-based deterministic, algorithmic, exhaustive and pseudo-random. Most of proposed are pseudo-random structures with Linear Feedback Shift Register (LFSR) employing D-type flip-flops. In recent years, LFSR composed of D-type and T-type flip-flops is gaining popularity due to its low area overhead and high operating speed [6,7].

The aim of this work was the usage of deterministic test pattern generation for an on-line BIST structure, where functional units and registers that are not used for the computations of the target application during individual time slots are organized into a structure that is continuously tested in parallel with normal system operation.

N.T. Nguyen et al. (Eds.): IEA/AIE 2008, LNAI 5027, pp. 580–589, 2008.

2 TPG Structure

A TPG is initialized with a given deterministic seed and run until the desired fault coverage is achieved. The test application time using an LFSR is significantly larger than what is required for applying the test set generated using a deterministic TPG; vector set generated by a LFSR includes not only useful vectors but also many other vectors that do not contribute to the fault coverage. In our approach, the goal is to develop a TPG that would generate only the required test vectors (i.e., with no intermittent non-useful vectors).

The structure of the proposed n bit test pattern generator is composed of a Multiple-Input Signature Register (MISR) and modification logic. The MISR has a form of a ring that is composed of n flip-flops. Each flip-flop (either T-type or D-type) can also have inverter on their input (denoted as $\overline{D}$ or $\overline{T}$). Thus, the register may have one of $4n$ different structures. The inputs of the MISR are controlled by the modification logic, while the outputs of the MISR are fed back to the modification logic which is a simple combinational logic and acts like a decoder.

The modification logic allows that in the subsequent clock cycles the contents of the MISR assume the values specified by the target test pattern set. Hence MISR and the modification logic are application specific: they are synthesized according to the required test pattern set.

Particularly important parameter in the case of deterministic test pattern generators is the area overhead, which is influenced by:

– the structure of each MISR stage,
– the order of the test patterns in a test sequence,
– the bit-order of the test patterns.

The first one influences the complexity of both the MISR and the modification logic, while the remaining two impact the area of the modification logic only. The relationships are illustrated below.

Initial Structure and Test Vectors. Having the set of six 3-bit vectors the resulting structure of the TPG consists of D-type flip flops in all stages of the MISR (Figure 1a). Since all the flip flops are scannable and have asynchronous reset, the total area of the TPG manufactured in AMS (Analog Mixed-Signal) 0.35 μm technology is 1821 μm^2.

Flip-Flop Type Replacement. Replacing the second flip-flop with a T-type flip-flop having active low input, the new configuration of the TPG is presented in Figure 1b. While there is no T type flip flop with inverted input in the standard cell library of the AMS 0.35 μm technology, the negation is implemented by replacing the XOR gate with an XNOR. The total area of the TPG is 1784 μm^2.

Column Permutation. Permutation of columns of the test pattern sequence further decreases the area of the TPG. If we permute the second and the third column in the test sequence (as illustrated in Figure 1c), the TPG is simplified to the structure with the area of 1657 μm^2.

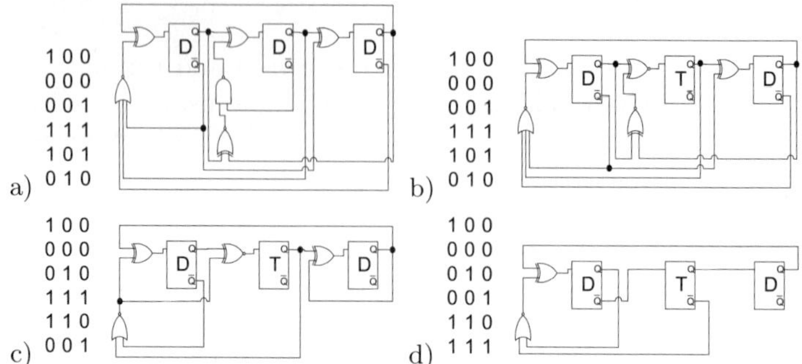

Fig. 1. TPG structure: a) initial structure, b) replaced flip-flop type, c) permutated columns, and d) permutated vectors

Vectors Permutation. Further we can permute test patterns in the test sequence. Exchanging the test patterns 4 and 6 in the test sequence simplifies the structure (Figure 1d) to the area of 1421 μm^2.

A change of the MISR structure, the order of the test patterns in a test sequence and the bit-order of the test patterns may result in a substantial area reduction of the TPG. The solution space is very broad: for an n-bit TPG producing the sequence of m test patterns there are $4nm!n!$ possible solutions; therefore, effective optimization procedure is required to find an acceptable practical solution.

3   Genetic Algorithm

Population-based evolutionary approach - implemented through genetic algorithm (GA) [1,8] - was used for optimization due to its intrinsic parallelism that allows searching within a broad database of solutions in the search space simultaneously. There is always some risk of converging to a local optimum, but efficient results of various research work obtained in other optimization problem areas [10,11,12,13,15] encouraged us to consider GA approach as a promising alternative in TPG synthesis optimization.

Our GA implementation used within the whole design process (Figure 2) involves optimization of multiple design aspects (type of flip-flops, order of patterns in test sequence, and bit-order of a test pattern). The details are described in the following subsections.

3.1   TPG Encoding

Three different chromosomes are used to encode the parameters of the TPG to be optimized. With three chromosomes, which do not interact with each other, we concurrently optimize the structure of the TPG, the order of the test patterns, and the bit order of test patterns. The first chromosome, which encodes the structure of n-bit TPG, looks like

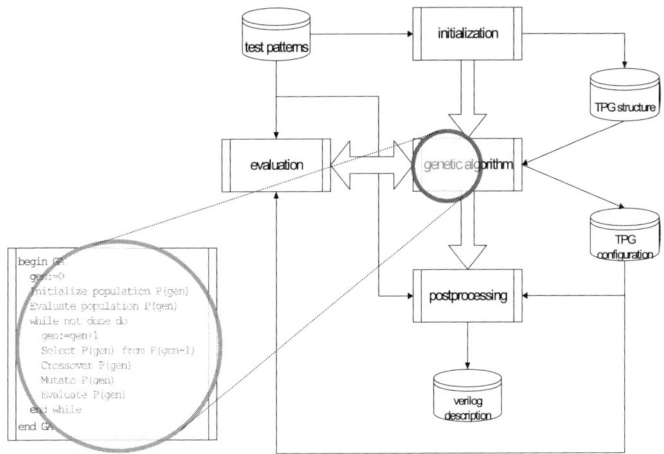

Fig. 2. GA within the whole design process

$$C_1 = t_1 i_1 t_2 i_2 \ldots t_n i_n, \tag{1}$$

where t_j $(j = 1, 2, \ldots, n)$ represents the type of the flip-flop (either D or T) and i_j $(j = 1, 2, \ldots, n)$ represents the presence of the inverter on the output of the j-th flip-fop.

The second and third chromosome, which encode the order of the test patterns, and the bit order of test patterns, look like

$$C_2 = a_1 a_2 \ldots a_m, \tag{2}$$

where m is the number of test vectors and a_j $(j = 1, 2, \ldots, m)$ is the label number of the test vector from the vector list, and

$$C_3 = b_1 b_2 \ldots b_k, \tag{3}$$

where k is the number of flip-flops in the structure and b_j $(j = 1, 2, \ldots, k)$ is the label number of the bit order of test patterns.

3.2   Population Initialization

The initial population consists of N chromosomes, of each type, that represent the initial structure. To ensure versatile population some chromosomes are mirrored. The values on the left side (beginning) of the structure chromosome are mirrored to the right side (ending); either type of registers or inverter presence or both values are mirrored. In case of other two, i.e. order of test patterns and their bit order, chromosomes, their initial reproduction included mirroring of orders between the beginning and the ending positions.

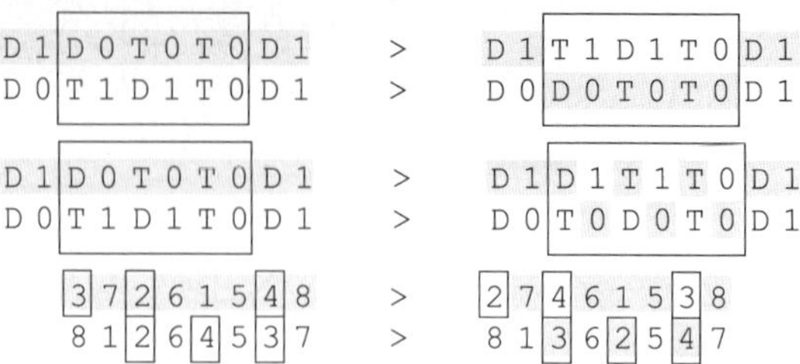

Fig. 3. Crossover: flip-flop types and inverter presence (top), inverter presence only (middle), pattern and bit order position (bottom)

3.3 Genetic Operators

In the selection process the elitism strategy is applied through the substitution of the least-fit chromosomes with the equal number of the best-ranked chromosomes.

With a two-point crossover scheme, chromosome mates are chosen randomly and with a probability p_c all values between two randomly chosen positions are swapped, which leads to the two new solutions that replace their original solutions. Figure 3(top) shows the example of crossover with crossover points on positions 1 and 4.

In the first chromosome, register type and inverter presence are considered as one indivisible block (i.e., two values for one position in the chromosome). Moreover, with some probability p_r only the values of inverters within the crossover points are swapped, as presented in Figure 3(middle).

The crossover in case of test patterns order and bit-order of the test patterns is performed with the interchange of positions that store the ordered numbers within the range; for an example within the range [2, 4], see Figure 3(bottom).

In the mutation process each value of the chromosome mutates with a probability p_m. However, since a high mutation rate resulted in a random walk through the GA search space, p_m has to be chosen to be somewhat low. Three different types of mutation are applied (see Figure 4 for details):

- D/T type change, where only flip-flop types were changed,
- inverter change, where inverter presences were changed,
- order change, where pattern order and bit order were changed.

The variable mutation probability p_m is decreasing linearly with each new population. Since each new population generally is more fit than the previous one, we overcome a possible disruptive effect of mutation at the late stages of the optimization, and speed up the convergence of the GA to the optimal solution in the final optimization stages.

3.4 Fitness Evaluation

After the recombination operators modify the solutions, the whole new population is ready to be evaluated. Here, the external evaluation tool is used to

```
D 1 [D] 0 [T] 0 T 0 D 1      >      D 1 [T] 0 [D] 0 T 0 D 1
D [1] D 0 T [0] T 0 D 1      >      D [0] D 0 T [1] T 0 D 1
    3 7 [2] 6 1 [5] 4 8      >      3 7 [5] 6 1 [2] 4 8
```

Fig. 4. Mutation: flip-flop types (top), inverter presence (middle), pattern orders and bit orders (bottom)

evaluate each new chromosome created by the GA, and two results are obtained for each solution:

- cost of the flip-flops in the register, and
- cost of the combinational next state function.

The first one represents the cost of all flip-flops that build the MISR, while the second one represents the cost of the modification logic that executes the next state function.

Evaluation Tool. On the basis of the equations for the register's next-state, values of the outputs of the modification logic for each vector but last in the test sequence can be derived. In that way ON-set and OFF-set of the modification logic are defined. Further, Espresso software [4] is used for Boolean minimization of the modification logic and its approximate cost estimation. This software takes a two-level representation of a two-valued (or multiple-valued) Boolean function as input, and produces a minimal equivalent representation (number of equivalent gates).

3.5   Termination

When a certain number of populations is generated and evaluated, the system is assumed to be in a non-converging state. The solutions on the Pareto front are taken to be the final implementation solution candidates. They are further evaluated by the experienced engineer to choose the one that best fits the given problem.

4   Results

The initial TPG structure is set through the desired sequence of test patterns. Then the GA tries to make new configuration while checking the allowed TPG structure and using the external evaluation tool. The evaluation tool calculates the cost of a given structure. After a number of iterations the best structure is chosen and implemented.

According to short pre-experimental tests we found the following GA parameters that give the results in an acceptable computing time; (1) for first three circuits: number of generations is 50, population size is 10, probability of crossover

Table 1. Results of modification logic size

circuit	test pattern width	number of test patterns	initial TPG	optimized TPG	improvement in %
c432	36	27	348	280	19.5
c499	41	52	312	164	47.4
c880	60	16	536	402	25.0
c1355	41	84	584	488	16.4
c1908	33	106	2077	1840	11.4
c6288	11	12	74	49	33.8

is 0.8, and probability of mutation is 0.01, (2) for the next three circuits: number of generations is 100, population size is 50, probability of crossover is 0.7, and probability of mutation is 0.05.

The results of the evaluation of the optimization process with the ISCAS test-benchmark combinational circuits is presented in Table 1. These combinatorial circuits are used to benchmark various test pattern generation systems. The ISCAS benchmark suite has been introduced in simple netlist format at the International Symposium of Circuits and Systems in 1985 (ISCAS'85), and was expanded with additional circuits at 1989 Symposium.

The test sets are transformed by the input reduction procedure proposed in [3]. The test pattern width (number of the inputs of the circuits) and the number of test patterns (number of different test vectors to cover all possible faults) are presented in the second and the third column, respectively, for each benchmark. The next two columns present the total cost (number of equivalent gates) of the modification logic reported by Espresso software for the initial and optimized TPG structure. The last column shows the achieved improvement.

Since this is off-line and one-time optimization procedure, optimization effectiveness was considered more important as optimization time. Therefore no report on total execution time is included (in fact it is measured in minutes).

As mentioned, the bit-order of the test patterns and the order of the test patterns in a test sequence influence the area of the modification logic. In this respect it is interesting to compare our results with the results of column matching algorithm [5]. Both approaches use MISR of similar complexity, but the main differences are in the design of the modification logic. The second and the third column of Table 2 show the results of the comparison of these two approaches for the same benchmark circuits.

The *complexity* values in Table 2 are expressed in terms of a total cost reported by Espresso software per bit of the produced test pattern:

$$complexity = \frac{total\_cost}{test\_pattern\_width * number\_of\_test\_patterns}. \tag{4}$$

Such new measure is needed since in our experiments we use different test pattern sets as those reported in [5] are.

Table 2. Comparison of GA approach through *complexity* in [5] and through *area_per_bit* in [2]

	complexity		*area_per_bit*	
circuit	[5]	GA	[2]	GA
c432	0.33	0.29	0.22	0.11
c499	0.13	0.08	0.21	0.10
c880	0.38	0.35	0.19	0.29
c1355	0.19	0.14	0.20	0.09
c1908	0.29	0.53	0.19	0.32
c6288	–	0.44	0.24	0.54

The comparison indicates that the proposed approach has a higher potential to provide solutions of TPG generating deterministic test patterns than column matching. There is also a big difference in testing time. In column matching solution all deterministic test patterns are embedded in a long test sequence composed of 5000 test vectors, which contains a lot of patterns not contributing to the fault coverage in the UUT. On the other hand, the GA based solution produces all deterministic test patterns as a one short test sequence that does not contain any superfluous vectors.

The fourth and the fifth column of Table 2 present the area of TPG logic for AMS 0.35 μm technology for the implementations reported in [2] and the GA based solutions, respectively. The area is expressed in terms of equivalent two input NAND gates. Like for *complexity* we need to apply a specific measure of the area overhead of the TPGs due to the fact that different deterministic patterns sets have been used for TPG synthesis. The proposed measure is expressed by the following equation:

$$area\_per\_bit = \frac{area}{test\_pattern\_width * number\_of\_test\_patterns}. \tag{5}$$

These experimental results indicate that for some benchmarks the proposed TPG and the GA optimization procedure provide solutions with lower area overhead than the TPG presented in [2] while for some other benchmarks the TPG in [2] are better. This may be due to the fact that we use Espresso software as a fast evaluation tool in the TPG optimization process and Synopsys software as a tool for synthesizing the final solution. Applying Synopsys software as both the evaluation tool and the final synthesis tool is likely to improve the results.

These evaluations and results illustrate the advantages of the proposed approach in comparison with the existing solutions. However, the employed benchmark circuits are relatively small. Realistic assessment of techniques for automatic deterministic test pattern generation requires more complex circuits. Since such examples are not reported in the referred papers, we perform GA optimization approach on some larger benchmark circuits. While the results regarding the *complexity* and the *area_per_bit* are in average comparable to the GA examples reported above, the computation time for larger circuits considerably increases and may represent a bottleneck in practical implementations. For example, the computation time for circuit s38417 is 140 times larger than for c880.

5   Conclusion

When a TPG fails to provide the desired fault coverage within the given test length, application specific deterministic TPGs are employed. Deterministic TPGs are more complex than pseudo random TPGs since they employ additional logic to prevent the generation of non-useful test patterns. Area overhead is one of the important issues in the design of deterministic TPGs. In this paper, a deterministic TPG is presented based on a feedback shift register composed of D- and T-type flip-flops and inverters, and some modification logic. The search for the optimal structure of the TPG is performed by a genetic algorithm. Promising initial results have been obtained on small and medium ISCAS test-benchmark circuits, while the computation time for larger circuits considerably increases and may represent a bottleneck in practical implementations. The future experiments and the search for more effective GA implementation should include faster evaluation tool.

References

1. Bäck, T.: Evolutionary Algorithms in Theory and Practice. Oxford University Press, Oxford (1996)
2. Bellos, M., Kagaris, D., Nikolos, D.: Test set embedding based on phase shifters. In: Bondavalli, A., Thévenod-Fosse, P. (eds.) EDCC 2002. LNCS, vol. 2485, pp. 90–101. Springer, Heidelberg (2002)
3. Chen, C.-A., Gupta, K.: Efficient BIST TPG design and test set compaction via input reduction. IEEE Transactions on Computer-Aided Design of Integrated Circuits and Systems 17, 692–705 (1998)
4. Espresso UC Berkeley (1988),
   `http://www-cad.eecs.berkeley.edu:80/software/software.html`
5. Fišer, P., Hlavička, J.: Column matching based BIST design method. In: Proceedings IEEE European Test Workshop, Corfu, Greece, pp. 15–16 (2002)
6. Garbolino, T., Hlawiczka, A.: A new LFSR with D and T flip flops as an effective test pattern generator for VLSI circuits. In: Hlavicka, J., Maehle, E., Pataricza, A. (eds.) EDDC 1999. LNCS, vol. 1667, pp. 321–338. Springer, Heidelberg (1999)
7. Garbolino, T., Hlawiczka, A., Kristof, A.: Fast and low area TPG based on T type flip ops can be easily integrated to the scan path. In: Proceedings IEEE European Test Workshop, Cascais, pp. 161–166 (2000)
8. Goldberg, D.: Genetic Algorithms in Search, Optimization, and Machine Learning. Addison-Wesley, Reading (1989)
9. Khalil, M., Robach, C., Novak, F.: Diagnosis strategies for hardware or software systems. Journal of electronic testing: Theory and Applications 18, 241–251 (2002)
10. Koroušić-Seljak, B.: Timetable construction using general heuristic techniques. Journal of Electrical Engineering 53(3-4), 61–69 (2002)
11. Oblak, K., Korošec, P., Kosel, F., Šilc, J.: Multi-parameter numerical optimization of selected thin-walled machine elements using a stigmergic optimization algorithm. Thin-walled structures 45(12), 991–1001 (2007)

12. Papa, G., Koroušić-Seljak, B.: An artificial intelligence approach to the efficiency improvement of a universal motor. Engineering applications of artificial intelligence 18(1), 47–55 (2005)
13. Papa, G., Šilc, J.: Automatic large-scale integrated circuit synthesis using allocation-based scheduling algorithm. Microprocessors and Microsystems 26(3), 139–147 (2002)
14. Parker, K.: The boundary-scan handbook, 3rd edn. Kluwer Academic Publishers, Dordrecht (2003)
15. Wu, C.L., Chau, K.W.: A flood forecasting neural network model with genetic algorithm. International Journal of Environment and Pollution 28(3-4), 261–273 (2006)

Solving Stochastic Path Problem: Particle Swarm Optimization Approach

Saeedeh Momtazi[1], Somayeh Kafi[1], and Hamid Beigy[1,2]

[1] Computer Engineering Department, Sharif University of Technology, Tehran, Iran
[2] Institutes for Studies in Theoretical Physics and Mathematics (IPM), School of Computer Science, Tehran, Iran
{momtazi, kafi, beigy}@ce.sharif.edu

Abstract. An stochastic version of the classical shortest path problem whereby for each node of a graph, a probability distribution over the set of successor nodes must be chosen so as to reach a certain destination node with minimum expected cost. In this paper, we propose a new algorithm based on Particle Swarm Optimization (PSO) for solving Stochastic Shortest Path Problem (SSPP). The comparison of our algorithm with other algorithms indicates that its performance is suitable even by the less number of iterations.

Keywords: Particle Swarm Optimization, Stochastic Shortest Path Problem, Swarm Intelligence.

1 Introduction

Given a directed graph G = (V; E), where V = {1, 2, …, n} denotes the set of nodes and E ⊂ V × V specifies the set of edges, the deterministic shortest path problem is to select at each node j, a successor node $\mu(j)$ so that $(j, \mu(j))$ is an edge, and the path formed by a sequence of successor nodes starting node v_s as source node and terminates at destination node v_d has minimum cost (i.e. minimum sum of edge costs), over all paths that start at v_s and terminate at v_d.

The stochastic shortest path problem (SSPP) is a generalization of classic shortest path problem whereby at each node, we must select a probability distribution over all possible successor nodes, out of a given set of probability distributions. The stochastic graph G can be defined by a triple G = (V; E; Q), where n × n matrix Q is the probability distribution describing the statistics of edge costs. In particular, the cost C_{ij} of edge (i, j) is assumed to be a random variable with q_{ij} as its probability density function. For a given edges' cost distributions and for a given source node, the path traversed as well as its cost are now random, but we wish that the path leads to destination node v_d with probability close to one and has minimum expected cost.

Solving the shortest path problem for deterministic graphs has an extensive background sind its results have been found to be a very useful tool in a great variety of contexts [1]. By presence of uncertainties in many applications such as link failure and variable travel time due to the congestion in a variety of distributed systems, the stochastic graphs are known as a more realistic model.

N.T. Nguyen et al. (Eds.): IEA/AIE 2008, LNAI 5027, pp. 590–600, 2008.

Different classes of stochastic shortest path problems are considered in the literature. The first work known in this area is due to Frank [2] where the shortest path over a probabilistic graph is determined. The most common criterion to determine the shortest path is the one that optimizes the expected value of a utility function. This criterion stems from the formulation presented by Von-Newman-Morgenstern where evaluations should be made under uncertainty [3]. Algorithms for linear and quadratic utility functions have been presented by Mirchandini and Soroush [3], Murthy and Sarkar [4], [5] and more recently by Deolinda Dias Rasteiro, Antonio Batel Anjo [6].

Ishwar Murthy and Sumit Sarkar [5] considered a stochastic shortest path problem which the costs of edges are independent random variables following a normal distribution. In this problem, the optimal path is one that maximizes the expected utility, where the utility function being piecewise linear and concave. Computational testing is done to evaluate the performance of their algorithms. Overall, their algorithms are very effective in solving large problems quickly.

Beigy and Meybodi introduce two algorithms based on distributed learning automata (DLA) for solving SSPP [7,8]. In the former [7], DLA is introduced and applied to the shortest path problem and in the latter [8], they introduce another DLA based algorithm which is faster than it. It requires fewer numbers of samples taken from the edges of the graph in order to decide which path from source to destination is shortest. The main difference between these algorithms is the definition of dynamic threshold, which is used for producing the reinforcement signal. It was shown that the shortest path is found with a probability as close as to unity by proper choice of the parameters of the proposed algorithms [14].

In this paper we introduce a new algorithm for solving the stochastic shortest path problem which is based on the particle swarm optimization method. Computer experiments are conducted to evaluate the performance of the proposed algorithm. The comparison of our algorithm with other algorithms indicates that its performance is suitable even by the less number of iterations.

The rest of this paper is organized as follows: Section 2 deals with a short summarization of particle swarm optimization (PSO) and its features. The proposed algorithm and preliminary experimental results are discussed in sections 3 and 4, respectively. Finally, in section 5, concluding remarks are made.

2 Particle Swarm Optimization

From the beginning of 90's, new optimization technique researches using analogy of swarm behavior of natural creatures have been started [9]. Dorigo developed ant colony optimization (ACO) mainly based on the social insect, especially ant, metaphor [10]. Eberhart and Kennedy developed particle swarm optimization based on the analogy of swarm of bird and fish school [11]. PSO simulates the behaviors of bird flocking. Suppose the following scenario: a group of birds are randomly searching food in an area. There is only one piece of food in the area being searched. No bird knows where the food is, but at each iteration they know how far the food is. One of the best strategies to find the food is to follow the bird which is nearest to the food. For using this strategy, PSO considers each bird (particle) in the search space as a single solution.

All particles have fitness values which are evaluated by the fitness function to be optimized, and have velocities which direct the flying of the particles. They are flown through the problem space by following the current optimum particles [12].

PSO is initialized with a group of random particles and then searches for optimum solution by updating generations. At each iteration, each particle is updated by following two "best" values. The first one is the best solution it has achieved so far and is called *pbest* and the second one is tracked by the particle swarm optimizer is the best value, obtained so far by any particle in the population and is called *gbest*. Finally, each particle updates its velocity and positions using equations (1) and (2).

$$velocity(k+1) = w*velocity(k) + c1*rand()*(pbest - p(k)) + c2*(gbest - p(k)), \quad (1)$$

$$p(k+1) = p(k) + velocity(k+1), \quad (2)$$

where *velocity* is the particle's velocity, *p* is the current particle's position, *pbest* and *gbest* are defined as stated before. *rand ()* is a random number between (0,1). *c1* and *c2* are learning factors. Usually *c1 = c2 = 2*. The inertia weight *w* is employed to control the impact of the previous history of velocities on the current velocity, thus to influence the trade-off between global and local exploration abilities of the *flying points*. The performance of each particle is measured according to a predefined fitness function, which is related to the problem being solved. In SSPP each particle is defined as a sequence of vertexes that represent a valid path in the stochastic graph and the fitness function is the cost of the path according to the cost of the edges. The detail of representation style for each particle, their fitness function, and its operators are discussed in the following section.

3   The Proposed Algorithm

In this section, we propose an algorithm based on particle swarm optimization for solving the SSPP. Our algorithm and its pseudo code are like the PSO. The novelty of the proposed algorithm is in definition of elements and operators. The pseudo code of the proposed algorithm is as follows:

```
Initialize particles
repeat
    for each particle u do
        Calculate fitness value of particle u, denoted by f(u)
        if (f(u) is better than f(pbest)) then
          Set u as the new pbest
        end
        Choose the particle with the best fitness value among all
        particles as the gbest
         for each particle u do
            Calculate particle velocity according equation (1)
            Update particle position according equation (2)
        end
    until (maximum iterations or minimum error criteria is attained)
```

In the rest of this section we describe the elements and operators of this algorithm.

3.1 Position

Let G = (V; E; Q) be the graph in which we are looking for shortest path from v_s to v_d. As we are looking for path, we can consider just sequences of $n\text{-}1$ nodes, all different nodes of graph except v_s. since we can add v_s in the first place of sequence, we don't use it during sequence generation. Also we just need the nodes that appear before v_d; for this reason just the sequence of nodes that appear before v_d are considered. Such a sequence is here seen as a "position". So the search space is defined as the finite set of all positions.

3.2 Objective Function

Let us to define a position as $p = (v_1, v_2,..., v_{n-1})$. This position is *acceptable* only if for all pairs (v_i, v_{i+1}) are edges of the graph. In order to define the *cost* function, a classical way it to just complete the graph, by *virtual* edges with an arbitrary large cost value enough to be sure no solution could contain such them. Now, on each position, a possible objective function can simply be defined by

$$p(x) = \left\{ \sum_{i=1}^{k-1} w_{i,i+1} \mid v_k = v_d \right\},\tag{3}$$

where $w_{i,i+1}$ is the cost of edge (v_i, v_{i+1}). This objective function has a finite number of values and its global minimum is indeed on the best solution.

3.3 Velocity

We want to define an operator *velocity;* when this operator is applied to a position, it gives another position. So, here, it is a permutation of n elements, that is to say a list of transpositions. A *velocity* is then defined by

$$velocity = \left\{ (i_k, j_k) \mid i_k, j_k \in \{v_1,..., v_n\} \right\}\tag{4}$$

which means exchanging numbers (i_1, j_1), then numbers (i_2, j_2) ... and the last numbers (i_n, j_n).

Note that the results of two such lists applied to any position are the same. To create the opposite of a velocity $(\neg velocity)$ we can do the same transpositions as in *velocity*, but in reverse order.

3.4 Move

Let p be a position and *velocity* a velocity. The position $p{'} = p + velocity$ is found by applying the first transposition of *velocity* to p, then the second one to the result and etc.

For example consider $p = (1,2,3,4,5)$ and $velocity = \{(1,2)(2,3)\}$. By applying *velocity* to p, we obtain successively $(2,1,3,4,5)$ and $(3,1,2,4,5)$.

3.5 Subtraction

Let p_1 and p_2 be two positions. The difference of p_1 and p_2 is defined as *velocity*, found by a given algorithm, so that applying *velocity* to p_1 gives p_2. The algorithm that we introduce for reaching this goal is as follow:

- Compare the elements of p_1 and p_2 one by one
- For each $v_x \in p_1$ and $v_y \in p_2$ which are in the same position in p_1 and p_2 and $v_x \neq v_y$ add (v_x, v_y) to *velocity*
- Apply the updated *velocity* to p_1

3.6 Addition

Let *velocity*$_1$ and *velocity*$_2$ be two velocities. In order to compute $velocity_1 \oplus velocity_2$, we construct a list which contains first the transpositions of velocity1, followed by the ones of velocity2. Optionally, we contract it to obtain a smaller equivalent velocity. In particular, this operation is defined so that

$$\| velocity_1 \oplus velocity_2 \| \leq \| velocity_1 \| + \| velocity_2 \|, \tag{5}$$

where $\oplus$ is the addition operation between two *velocities*.

3.7 Multiplication

Let c be a real coefficient and *velocity* be a velocity. There are different cascs, depending on the value of c. When c is zero, then we having $c * velocity = \phi$, when $c \in (0,1]$, we just truncate *velocity*. So we select the first $c\%$ of *velocity* elements, and when c is greater than one, it means we have $c = k + c', k \in n, c' \in [0,)$. So we define

$$c * velocity = \underbrace{velocity \oplus velocity \oplus ... \oplus velocity}_{k \; times} \oplus c' * velocity, \tag{6}$$

when c is negative, we write $c * velocity = (-c) * \neg velocity$ and we just have to consider one of the previous cases.

4 Experimental Result

To evaluate the performance of the proposed algorithm a set of experiment are conducted on three following stochastic graphs borrowed from [15]. The distribution of edge costs for these graphs are given in tables 1 through 3.

- Graph 1 is a graph with 10 nodes, 23 edges, $v_s = 1$, and $v_d = 10$
- Graph 2 is a graph with 10 nodes, 23 edges, $v_s = 1$, and $v_d = 10$
- Graph 3 is a graph with 15 nodes, 42 edges, $v_s = 1$, and $v_d = 15$

Table 1. Cost Distribution of Graph 1 with $v_s = 1$ and $v_d = 10$

Edge	Cost	Probability
(1,2)	7.0 7.3 9.4	0.2 0.5 0.3
(1,3)	2.5 3.5 8.2	0.5 0.4 0.1
(1,4)	4.2 4.8 6.1	0.2 0.3 0.5
(2,5)	2.6 3.1 5.5 8.8 9.0	0.1 0.2 0.4 0.2 0.1
(2,6)	5.8 7.0 9.5	0.3 0.3 0.4
(3,2)	1.5 7.3	0.4 0.6
(3,7)	6.5 7.4 7.5	0.4 0.5 0.1
(3,8)	5.9 7.2 9.8	0.6 0.3 0.1
(4,3)	2.1 3.2 8.5 9.8	0.3 0.2 0.3 0.2
(4,9)	8.9 9.6	0.7 0.3
(5,7)	3.2 4.8 6.7	0.2 0.2 0.6
(5,10)	6.3 6.9	0.5 0.5
(6,3)	6.6 8.5 9.8	0.8 0.1 0.1
(6,5)	0.6 1.5 3.9 5.8	0.1 0.4 0.3 0.2
(6,7)	0.2 4.8	0.4 0.6
(7,6)	6.1 6.3 8.5	0.2 0.3 0.5
(7,8)	1.6 1.8 4.0 5.2	0.2 0.3 0.3 0.2
(7,10)	1.6 3.4 7.1	0.1 0.5 0.4
(8,4)	9.0 9.6	0.5 0.5
(8,7)	2.1 4.6 8.5	0.3 0.4 0.3
(8,9)	1.7 4.9 5.3 6.5	0.1 0.4 0.4 0.1
(7,9)	0.3 3.0 5.0	0.1 0.4 0.5
(9,10)	0.6 1.2 5.4 6.6	0.1 0.1 0.3 0.5

Table 2. Cost Distribution of Graph 2 with $v_s = 1$ and $v_d = 10$

Edge	Cost	Probability
(1,2)	3.0 5.3 7.4 9.4	0.2 0.2 0.3 0.3
(1,3)	3.5 6.2 7.9 8.5	0.3 0.3 0.2 0.2
(1,4)	4.2 6.1 6.9 8.9	0.2 0.3 0.2 0.3
(2,5)	2.6 4.1 5.5 9.0	0.2 0.2 0.4 0.2
(2,6)	5.8 7.0 8.5 9.6	0.3 0.3 0.2 0.2
(3,2)	1.5 2.3 3.6 4.5	0.2 0.2 0.3 0.3
(3,7)	6.5 7.2 8.3 9.4	0.5 0.2 0.2 0.1
(3,8)	5.9 7.8 8.6 9.9	0.4 0.3 0.1 0.2
(4,3)	2.1 3.2 4.5 6.8	0.2 0.2 0.3 0.3
(4,9)	1.1 2.2 3.5 4.3	0.2 0.3 0.4 0.1

Table 2. (*continued*)

(5,7)	3.2 4.8 6.7 8.2	0.2 0.2 0.3 0.3
(5,10)	6.3 7.8 3.4 9.1	0.2 0.2 0.4 0.2
(6,3)	6.8 7.7 8.5 9.6	0.4 0.1 0.1 0.4
(6,5)	0.6 1.5 3.9 5.8	0.2 0.2 0.3 0.3
(6,7)	2.1 4.8 6.6 7.5	0.2 0.4 0.2 0.2
(7,6)	4.1 6.3 8.5 9.7	0.2 0.3 0.4 0.1
(7,8)	1.6 2.8 5.2 6.0	0.2 0.3 0.3 0.2
(7,10)	1.6 3.4 8.2 9.3	0.2 0.3 0.3 0.2
(8,4)	7.0 8.0 8.8 9.4	0.2 0.2 0.2 0.4
(8,7)	2.1 4.6 8.5 9.6	0.4 0.2 0.2 0.2
(8,9)	1.7 4.9 6.5 7.8	0.2 0.2 0.2 0.4
(7,9)	3.5 4.0 5.0 7.7	0.1 0.2 0.4 0.3
(9,10)	4.6 6.4 7.6 8.9	0.4 0.1 0.2 0.3

Table 3. Cost Distribution of Graph 3 with $v_s = 1$ and $v_d = 15$

Edge	Cost	Probability
(1,2)	16 25 36	0.6 0.3 0.1
(1,3)	21 24 25 39	0.5 0.2 0.2 0.1
(1,4)	11 13 26	0.4 0.4 0.2
(2,11)	24 28 31	0.5 0.3 0.2
(2,5)	11 30	0.7 0.3
(2,6)	13 37 39	0.6 0.2 0.2
(3,2)	11 20 24	0.6 0.3 0.1
(3,7)	23 30 34	0.4 0.3 0.2
(3,8)	14 23 34	0.5 0.4 0.1
(4,3)	22 30	0.7 0.3
(4,9)	35 40	0.6 0.4
(4,12)	16 25 37	0.5 0.4 0.1
(5,13)	28 35 37 40	0.4 0.3 0.2 0.1
(5,15)	25 32	0.7 0.3
(5,10)	27 33 40	0.4 0.3 0.3
(5,7)	15 17 19 26	0.3 0.3 0.3 0.1
(6,5)	18 25 29	0.5 0.3 0.2
(6,13)	21 23	0.5 0.5
(6,7)	11 31 37	0.5 0.5 0.1
(6,3)	18 24	0.7 0.3
(7,10)	19 23 37	0.6 0.2 0.2

Table 3. (*continued*)

(7,8)	15 22 24	0.3 0.3 0.3
(7,6)	12 23 31	0.5 0.3 0.2
(8,7)	14 34 39	0.6 0.2 0.2
(8,14)	14 15 27 32	0.3 0.3 0.2 0.2
(8,9)	13 31 32	0.8 0.1 0.1
(8,4)	13 23 34	0.4 0.3 0.3
(9,7)	10 17 20	0.6 0.3 0.1
(9,10)	16 18 36 39	0.3 0.3 0.2 0.2
(9,15)	12 13 25 32	0.4 0.3 0.2 0.1
(9,14)	19 24 29	0.4 0.3 0.3
(10,13)	14 20 25 32	0.3 0.3 0.2 0.2
(10,15)	15 19 25	0.4 0.3 0.3
(10,14)	23 34	0.9 0.1
(11,13)	13 31 25	0.6 0.3 0.1
(11,5)	18 19 20 23	0.3 0.3 0.3 0.1
(11,6)	10 19 39	0.5 0.4 0.1
(12,8)	15 36 39	0.5 0.3 0.2
(12,9)	16 22	0.7 0.3
(12,14)	10 13 18 34	0.3 0.3 0.3 0.1
(13,15)	12 31	0.9 0.1
(14,15)	14 19 32	0.5 0.3 0.2

The number of iterations for each run is set to 50. We ran the algorithm 12 times for each graph by 25, 50, 100 and 150 swarm sizes. Tables 4 through 6 show the results of our experiments in each graph. Each row of table shows the swarm size.

Table 4. The Result of Algorithm on Graph 1 with Different Swarm Sizes

Swarm Size	Converged Path	Cost of the Converged Path	Number of Convergence	Percentage of Convergence
25	1 3 7 10	14.369	8	67.33%
	1 4 9 10	18.482	2	16.0%
	1 3 8 7 10	19.81	1	8.33%
	1 3 2 5 7 10	22.171	1	8.33%
50	1 3 7 10	14.92	12	100%
100	1 3 7 10	15.061	12	100%
150	1 3 7 10	14.873	12	100%

Table 5. The Result of Algorithm on Graph 2 with Different Swarm Sizes

Swarm Size	Converged Path	Cost of the Converged Path	Number of Convergence	Percentage of Convergence
25	1 4 9 10	15.6710	4	33.33%
	1 3 7 10	18.1515	3	25.0%
	1 2 5 10	17.5327	4	33.33%
	1 3 8 7 10	22.6778	1	8.33%
50	1 4 9 10	15.3545	11	91.66%
	1 2 5 10	14.7778	1	8.33%
100	1 4 9 10	15.7380	12	100%
150	1 4 9 10	15.3053	11	91.66%
	1 3 2 5 10	17.4222	1	8.33%

Table 6. The Result of Algorithm on Graph 3 with Different Swarm Sizes

Swarm Size	Converged Path	Cost of the Converged Path	Number of Convergence	Percentage of Convergence
25	1 2 5 15	63.292	4	33.33%
	1 4 9 15	68.0357	2	16.66%
	1 4 3 8 14 15	89	1	8.33%
	1 4 3 8 9 15	92.5714	1	8.33%
	1 3 7 10 15	94.2222	1	8.33%
	1 4 12 14 15	86.864	2	16.66%
50	1 2 5 15	61.1428	8	66.6%
	1 4 9 15	63.6461	4	33.3%
100	1 2 5 15	62.7442	6	50.0%
	1 4 9 15	68.0933	2	16.66%
	1 4 12 9 15	62	2	16.66%
	1 3 8 14 15	77.6667	1	8.33%
	1 4 12 14 15	65.4423	1	8.33%
150	1 2 5 15	63.0834	9	75.0%
	1 4 9 15	67.5215	3	25.0%

In tables 7 and 8, we compare the result of our algorithm on the above graphs by the results of the algorithms reported in [7][8][13]. Each row of the table shows the results for each graph. Columns contain paths and costs identified by our algorithm and other algorithms. The values in columns are mean of the values in runs of the algorithm which coverage to the correct path.

Table 7. Comparison of Our Algorithm with Dijkstra's by Running on Three Graphs

Graphs	PSO Shortest Path	PSO Shortest Cost	Dijkstra Shortest Path	Dijkstra Shortest Cost
Graph 1	1 3 7 10	14.84535	1 3 7 10	15.22
Graph 2	1 4 9 10	15.49471	1 4 9 10	16.1
Graph 3	1 2 5 15	62.46404	1 2 5 15	64.5

Table 8. Comparison of Our Algorithm with DLA Algorithm by Running on Three Graphs

Graphs	PSO Shortest Path	PSO Shortest Cost	DLA Shortest Path	DLA Shortest Cost
Graph 1	1 3 7 10	14.84535	1 3 7 10	15.1
Graph 2	1 4 9 10	15.49471	1 4 9 10	15.7
Graph 3	1 2 5 15	62.46404	1 2 5 15	63.2

An important point of our algorithm in comparison with DLA is the difference between numbers of iterations for each algorithm. In all cases we run the algorithm for 50 iterations and most of them reach the correct path, but DLA reach these result by 9769, 9846 and 9718 iterations for graphs 1, 2 and 3, respectively.

5   Conclusion

In this paper we proposed a new method for solving the stochastic shortest path problem. Since the population based techniques have good effects in stochastic applications, we use one of these methods. Our approach is based on particle swarm optimization which is an important parts of swarm intelligence by focused on the birds behavior. For implementing this idea we simulated all operators which are used in the PSO equation, by some suggested simple algorithms. These operators are move, addition, subtraction, multiplication. For evaluating our proposed algorithm, the result of it is compared with Dijkstra[13] and DLA[7][8] algorithms.

References

1. Deo, N., Pang, C.: Shortest Path Algorithms: Taxonomy and Annotation. Networks 14, 275–323 (1984)
2. Frank, H.: Shortest paths in probabilistic graphs. Operations Research 17, 583–599 (1969)
3. Loui, R.P.: Optimal paths in graphs with stochastic or multidimensional weights. Communications of the ACM 26, 670–676 (1983)
4. Murthy, I., Sarkar, S.: A relaxation based pruning technique for a class of stochastic shortest path problems. Transportation Science 30, 220–236 (1996)
5. Murthy, I., Sarkar, S.: Stochastic shortest path problems with piecewise linear concave utility functions. Management Science 44, 125–136 (1998)
6. Rasteiro, D.M., Anjo, A.B.: Metaheuristics for stochastic shortest path problem. In: Proceedings of 4th MetaHeuristics International Conference (MIC), Porto, Portugal (2001)

7. Meybodi, M.R., Beigy, H.: Solving Stochastic Shortest Path Problem Using Distributed Learning Automata. In: Proceedings of 6th Annual International Computer Society of Iran Computer Conference CSICC, Isfehan, Iran, February 2001, pp. 70–86 (2001)
8. Beigy, H., Meybodi, M.R.: A. New Distributed Learning Automata Based Algorithm For Solving Stochastic Shortest Path Problem. In: Proceeding of Joint Conference on Information Sciences (JCIS), North Carolina, USA, pp. 339–343 (2002)
9. Fukuyama, Y.: Fundamentals of particle swarm optimization techniques. In: IEEE PES Tutorial on Modern Heuristic Optimization Techniques with Application to Power Systems, ch. 5 (January 2002)
10. Colorni, A., Dorigo, M., Maniezzo, V.: Distributed Optimization by Ant Colonies. In: Proceeding of First European Conference on Artificial Life, pp. 134–142. MIT Press, Cambridge (1991)
11. Kennedy, J., Eberhart, R.: Particle Swarm Optimization. In: Proceedings of IEEE International Conference on Neural Networks (ICNN), vol. IV, Perth, Australia, pp. 1942–1948 (1995)
12. Eberhart, R.C., Kennedy, J.: A New Optimizer using Particle Swarm Theory. In: Proceeding of the Sixth International Symposium on Micro Machine and Human Science, Nagoya, Japan, pp. 39–43 (1995)
13. Dijkstra, E.W.: A note on two problems in connection with graphs. Numerische Mathematics, pp. 269–271 (1959)
14. Beigy, H., Meybodi, M.R.: Utilizing Distributed Learning Automata to Solve Stochastic Shortest Path Problems. International Journal of Uncertainty, Fuzziness and Knowledge-Based Systems 14, 591–615 (2006)
15. Alexopoulos, C.: State Space Partitioning Methods for Stochastic Shortest Path Problems. Networks 30, 9–21 (1997)

Meta-heuristic Algorithm for the Transshipment Problem with Fixed Transportation Schedules

Zhaowei Miao[1,*], Ke Fu[2], Qi Fei[3], and Fan Wang[4]

[1] School of Management, Xiamen University, Fu Jian, China
miaozhaowei@gmail.com
[2] Lingnan College, Sun Yat-sen University, Guangzhou, China
[3] Department of IELM, Hong Kong University of Science and Technology,
Clear Water Bay, Kowloon, Hong Kong
[4] School of Business, Sun Yat-Sen University, Guangzhou, China

Abstract. In this work, we develop an efficient meta-heuristic genetic algorithm for a different type of transshipment problem with supplier and customer time windows, where flow through the crossdock (a kind of transshipment center) is constrained by fixed transportation schedules and crossdocks capacities, and which was proved to be **NP**-complete in the strong sense. And computational experiments are conducted to show the proposed heuristic outperforms CPLEX.

Keywords: genetic algorithm, transshipment, scheduling, supply chain.

1   Introduction

A major challenge in making supply meet demand is to coordinate transshipments across the supply chain to reduce costs and increase service levels in the face of demand fluctuations, short lead times, warehouse limitations and transportation and inventory costs. In particular, transshipment through crossdocks, where just-in-time objectives prevail, requires precise scheduling between suppliers, crossdocks and customers. Crossdocks can be complex and difficult to manage, involving a large number of transshipment points and vehicles. The well-known success of Wal Mart in crossdocks requires coordinating 2000 dedicated trucks over a large network of warehouses, crossdocks and retail points. Advantages of crossdocks can accrue from the reduction of warehousing costs, inventory-holding costs, service cycle times and transportation costs.

Transshipment is concerned with how much to ship between which locations on which routes and at what times. Successful implementation of hybrid push-pull strategies (see, e.g., Simchi-Levi et al. [14]) in a supply chain depends on available transshipment points and how well they can be exploited, especially

---

* Corresponding author.

N.T. Nguyen et al. (Eds.): IEA/AIE 2008, LNAI 5027, pp. 601–610, 2008.

when deploying flexible and quick-to-react supply chains which aim at high levels of service. Associated with this are replenishment and inventory policy issues which impact costs in managing supply and demand. Here, a common response has been the implementation of multilocation systems governing stock movement at the same (mostly retail) level in the chain (see, e.g., Grahovac and Chakravarty [8], Herer and Tzur [9], Herer et al. [10], Axsater [2], [3]) where transshipments are lateral, e.g., between retailers. As a distribution strategy, transshipment centers have been used as crossdocks through which goods can be distributed continuously from suppliers to customers where the objective is to minimize inventory holdovers.

In classical models, where transshipment is studied in the context of network flow (e.g., Aronson [1], Hoppe and Tardos [11]), there has been no work which includes time constraints. This is a critical factor when shipments flow through crossdocks, which have become synonymous with rapid consolidation and processing. Napolitano [13] has described manufacturing, transportation, distribution, retail and opportunistic crossdocking, all of which have the common feature of consolidation and short cycle times made possible by known pick-up and delivery times. Crossdocking networks are, in fact, difficult to manage and require significant start-up investment, where strategies are effective only for large distribution systems (Simchi-Levi et al. [15]) with sufficient volumes of goods for fully loaded vehicles. In view of the inverse relationship between inventory and transportation costs, where larger lot sizes can reduce delivery frequency and transportation costs but increase inventory costs, transshipment from suppliers to customers through crossdocks can reduce costs only when shippers are able to operate effectively within supply and delivery time constraints and transportation schedules at all points in the supply chain. Studies on crossdock operations can be found in Bartholdi et al. [4], [5], [6], Donaldson et al. [7] and Ratcliff et al. [14].

In this work, we develop an efficient heuristic algorithm for a different type of transshipment problem, whose complexity has been studied in Lim et al. [12], considering general transshipment networks where transportation is available at fixed schedule, and where both shipping and delivery can be executed only within specified time windows at supply and demand locations. Supplier time windows allow, for example, flexibility in planning for best shipout times to fit production and operating schedules. Time windows at demand points satisfy customer requirements, for example, when service deadlines must be met. Further, inventory holding costs are included at crossdocks as these are burdens that arise in any transshipment strategy. We develop an efficient genetic algorithm to solve it, and conduct computational experiments to show the proposed heuristic outperforms ILOG CPLEX solver.

The paper is organized as follows. In section 2, we describe the problem and its complexity, and in sections 3 and 4, an efficient genetic algorithm is developed, and computational experiments are conducted. Finally a conclusion is provided in Section 5.

2   Transshipment Problem with Fixed Transportation Schedules

2.1   Problem Description

The problem studied here extends the well-known transshipment problem to include constraints imposed by time and inventory considerations which arise in applications. The following assumptions are made. First, a supplier is allowed to ship goods to crossdocks only within a specified time window, and likewise, a customer can receive shipments from the crossdocks only within a given time window. Second, shipped goods can be delayed at crossdocks. Third, shipping schedules offered by transportation providers is fixed one in which departure and arrival times are fixed, such as a schedule in the railway network or in airline operations. We assume that each schedule has a set of associated shipping costs and route capacities. In the temporal dimension, constraints on shipping and delivery can be generalized to reflect operational requirements. Fourthly, the setup cost of each transportation sometimes is very high in real world, so in order to reduce setup cost as much as possible, it requires each supplier can make only one shipment to some crossdock within its specified time window, and each customer can receive goods only one time from some crossdock within its time window, which we call single shipment and single delivery case. Finally, the objective of our problem is to satisfy all the customers by the suppliers with minimize shipping and inventory holding costs without violating time windows of suppliers and customers and capacity constraints of crossodocks and routes through the fixed schedules transportation system.

The underlying problem can be represented by a network. Let $\Sigma := \{1, ..., n\}$ be the set of supply nodes (suppliers) where, for each $i \in \Sigma$, s_i units of goods are available which can be shipped (released) in the time window $[b_i^r, e_i^r]$, $\Delta := \{1, ..., m\}$ be the set of demand nodes (customers) where each $k \in \Delta$ requires d_k units of goods which must be delivered (accepted) within the time window $[b_k^a, e_k^a]$, and $\mathbf{X} := \{1, ..., l\}$ be the set of crossdocks, where each $j \in \mathbf{X}$ has inventory capacity c_j and holding cost h_j per unit per time. Take S_1 to denote all fixed scheduled routes between points in Σ and points in $\mathbf{X}$, i.e., routes serviced by transport providers, each with a scheduled departure (begin) and arrival (end) time, capacity and unit transportation cost. Similarly, let S_2 denote the set of fixed schedules between the crossdocks $\mathbf{X}$ and customers, Δ. We can assume here that total supply is equal to the total demand since the unbalanced problem is easily transformed using dummy nodes. Figure 1 illustrates networks representing a fixed schedule transshipment problem for the single shipping - single delivery case, in which each vertical pair of lines duplicates the time horizon of the schedules (S_1 and S_2), and directed arcs between the lines with tails and heads fixed at time points in the range represent fixed schedules.

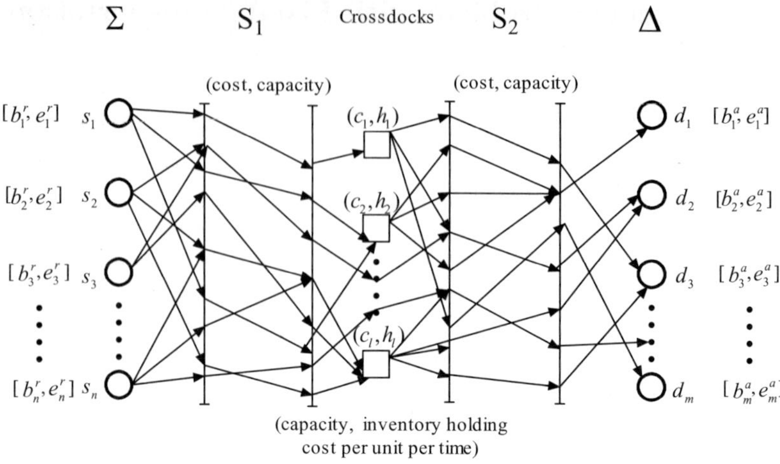

Fig. 1. Transshipment Problem with Fixed Transportation Schedules

2.2   Complexity Analysis

In order to be convenient for understanding the complexity of this problem, the proof (see [12]) is given again as following:

Proposition 1. *The transshipment problem with fixed transportation schedules of single shipping - single delivery case is **NP**-complete in the strong sense, even if supply and demand time windows and route capacities are relaxed.*

Proof. We use a reduction from the **3-PARTITION** problem, which is **NP**-complete in the strong sense: Given a positive integers, w, D and $\Gamma = \{1, 2, ..., 3w\}$ with a positive integer values $\gamma(i)$ where, for each $i \in \Gamma$, $\sum_{i \in \Gamma} \gamma(i) = wD$ and $D/4 < \gamma(i) < D/2$, can Γ be partitioned into w disjoint sets $\Gamma_1, \Gamma_2, ..., \Gamma_w$ such that $|\Gamma_j| = 3$ and $\sum_{i \in \Gamma_j} \gamma(i) = D$ for $j = 1, ..., w$? An arbitrary instance of **3-PARTITION** can be reduced polynomially to an instance of the problem. Let there be $3w$ suppliers in Σ, and w customers $\Delta = \{1, 2, ..., w\}$. For each $i \in \Sigma$, let the supply be s_i with $s_i = \gamma(i)$, and schedules be $(\alpha - 1, \alpha)$, $\alpha = 1, 2, ..., w$, where $\alpha - 1$ is departure time and α is arrival time from i. For each $j \in \Delta$, take the demand to be D and the scheduled route to be $(j, j + 1)$, where j is departure time from the crossdock χ defined next, and $j + 1$ is arrival time at customer j. Exactly one crossdock, χ, say, with zero capacity exists linking suppliers and customers, where shipping costs and travel times from the suppliers to crossdock χ are zero for all routes. We can now show that a feasible schedule exists if and only if **3-PARTITION** has a feasible solution. On one hand, if **3-PARTITION** has a feasible solution $\Gamma_1, ..., \Gamma_w$, then we can ship all goods provided by suppliers in Σ_i (letting $\Sigma_i = \Gamma_i$) to crossdock χ at time j through schedule $(j, j + 1)$, which satisfies the demand D, where $j = 1, 2, ..., w$. It is easy to verify that such a schedule is feasible. On the other hand, if a feasible schedule exists, we can construct the partition by setting Σ_j to be the subset of $i \in \Sigma$ where there is positive flow from i to χ at time j, for $1 \leq j \leq w$. Because the inventory capacity is zero and the demands are D at time j, we have $\sum_{i \in \Sigma_j} s_i = D$. Since $D/4 < s_i < D/2$ for $i \in \Sigma$, we have $|\Sigma_j| = 3$. In view of the single shipping constraint, Σ_1, ..., Σ_w must be a feasible partition for the instance of **3-PARTITION** and this completes the proof. $\square$

3   Meta-heuristics: Genetic Algorithm

Genetic algorithms have become a well-known and powerful meta-heuristic approach for hard combinatorial optimization problems. Genetic algorithms are based on the ideas of natural selection, and have been applied to numerous combinatorial optimization problems successfully. In this section, we first describe the essential components of our proposed GA for the transshipment problems with fixed transportation schedules, eg. solution representation, the crossover operator, etc. Then we outline the framework of the GA.

3.1   Components of GA

Solution Representation: The chromosome is an important component in GA and has great influence on the algorithm output. In the basic GA, a chromosome is usually encoded as a sequence and represents a solution. Here each chromosome is represented as a sequence $SOL = (\chi_1, \ldots, \chi_n, \chi_{n+1}, \ldots, \chi_{n+m})$, where n and m are the number of suppliers and that of customers respectively, moreover, χ_i $(i = 1, 2, \ldots, n)$ represents supplier i ships cargos to crossdock χ_i, and χ_j $(j = n + 1, n + 2, \ldots, n + m)$ represents customer $j - n$ receives cargos from crossdock χ_j. To begin, sequences are generated randomly. However, given such a chromosome sequence, we can not guarantee the feasibility of the solution, because the time windows of suppliers and customers may conflict each other when proper transportation schedules do not exit, or the capacity constraints of crossdocks or routes may be violated in the cargo transferring process. In case when a generated chromosome sequence from the initial population is infeasible, we simply drop the sequence and generate a new one.

Crossover: Each offspring is generated from its parents with some probability. Let the parents be $PAR_1 = (\chi_1, \ldots, \chi_n, \chi_{n+1}, \ldots, \chi_{n+m})$ and $PAR_2 = (\chi'_1, \ldots, \chi'_n, \chi'_{n+1}, \ldots, \chi'_{n+m})$, then, an offspring of PAR_1 and PAR_2 is given by $OFFS = (rand\ (\chi_1, \chi'_1), \ldots, rand\ (\chi_n, \chi'_n), rand\ (\chi_{n+1}, \chi'_{n+1}), \ldots, rand\ (\chi_{n+m}, \chi'_{n+m}))$ with $\mathrm{Prob}\ (rand\ (\chi_i, \chi'_i) = \chi_i) = \frac{OBJ(PAR_2)}{OBJ(PAR_1)+OBJ(PAR_2)}$ and $\mathrm{Prob}\ (rand\ (\chi_i, \chi'_i) = \chi'_i) = \frac{OBJ(PAR_1)}{OBJ(PAR_1)+OBJ(PAR_2)}$ for $i = 1, 2, \ldots, n + m$, where $OBJ(\cdot)$ is the objective value of current solution. Using this probability scheme defined above, the genes in a parent with less cost can be saved with a large probability.

Mutation: We choose mutation operator called ' 2-Swap Mutation', which selects two mutation sites at random and swaps the values at these two sites. An example is as follows.

Fig. 2. The 2-Swap Mutation Operator

3.2 GA Framework

With these components, we now outline GA framework in following. In this algorithm, #pop denotes the number of population, #crossover denotes the number of crossover we will do , #iter denotes the maximum number of iterations and p_1 denotes the probability of mutation.

> **Initialize** Population with size $\sharp pop$
> **for** $iter \leftarrow 1$ to $\sharp iter$ **do**
>   **for** $off \leftarrow 1$ to $\sharp crossover$ **do**
>   Randomly select $Parent_1$ and $Parent_2$
>   Crossover $Parent_1$ and $Parent_2$ to produce a new offspring $Offs$
>   **end for**
>   **for** each newly-produced individual $Indv$ **do**
>   mutate $Indv$ with probability p_1
>   **end for**
>   evaluate each individual
>   select the best $\sharp pop$ individuals from all the individuals
>   update current best solution
> **end for**

4 Computational Experiments and Results Analysis

The algorithm runs on Intel P4 2.4GHz machine with 1G memory. As comparison, we use ILOG CPLEX solver to solve the proposed problem. The test generation process, parameter settings of GA, and detailed computational results are presented in the following subsections.

4.1 Test Data Generation and Experimental Parameter Setting

Because crossdocks problems are relatively new, there are no benchmarks test sets available. As a result, we generated our own data to be as realistic as possible. The test data generation program requires three parameters: The number of suppliers n, the number of customers m, and the number of crossdocks l. The time horizon is fixed at 48 hours (2 days) in test sets, as this is usually almost the longest time shipments by railways between two cities. So the n start points of supplier i time window $b_i^r (1 \leq i \leq n)$ were uniformly generated in the interval $[0, 12]$. The end points of supplier i time window e_i^r were uniformly generated as $e_i^r = Unif[12, 36]$. For customers, their time windows are generated as $(Unif[12, 24], Unif[24, 48])$. Meanwhile, all the fixed transportation schedules from suppliers to crossdocks are generated as $(begin, end) = (Unif[0, 12], Unif[12, 24])$, and those from crossdocks to customers are generated as $(Unif[12, 36], Unif[36, 48])$. Next, because pickups usually follow deliveries within short times, we take the inventory-handling cost at crossdocks to be small relative to transportation costs. This reflects the fact that handling costs are usually smaller than transportation costs. Based on this, the transportation cost per unit cargo of each fixed scheduled route is uniformly generated in the interval $[10, 30]$ and inventory-handling cost per unit per hour is uniformly generated in the interval $[1, 3]$, which is almost $\frac{1}{10}$ of transportation cost. At last, the amount of supplied cargo s_i (demanded cargo d_k)is randomly generated in the interval $[100, 500]$. The capacity of each crossdock is set to $CC = \lceil \alpha \sum_{1 \le i \le n} s_i \rceil$, where α is generated in the interval $[0.5, 0.8]$. Also capacity of each route is set to $CR = \lceil \frac{\beta \sum_{1 \le i \le n} s_i}{n} \rceil$, where β is generated in the interval $[2, 5]$.

The following values of parameters are used: $\sharp iter = 10^4$, $\sharp pop = 300$, $\sharp crossover = 500$. The mutation probability p_1 is taken to be 0.2. The maximum iteration is 10^5 and the termination condition was when the best solution did not improve within 500 iterations.

4.2   The Results

We designed two categories (normal and large) of instances to test the algorithm. The detailed results are presented in Table 1 and 2. Each category has 40 test cases, sorted into 8 groups where each group has 5 cases. The first row of the each table specifies the instance size. $n \times m \times l$ denotes that there are n suppliers, m customers and l crossdocks for this instance group. The rest of the rows provide the results of CPLEX and GA. Each result cell contains two values: the average objective value and the average computational time in seconds.

1. **Normal Scale Instances**

Eight normal scale instance groups are generated with the sizes $(n \times m \times l)$ ranging from $4 \times 6 \times 2$ to $8 \times 12 \times 4$. We use these instances to test the performance of CPLEX solver and our heuristic algorithm. The results are shown in Table 1. We find that CPLEX can get the optimal solutions for the four smallest instance groups within the time limit of 3600 seconds. For these four instance groups, our heuristic algorithm obtain the optimal solutions within a much shorter runtime as well. The CPLEX solver fails to get optimum within the time limit for all other instance groups, while our GA obtains good solutions quickly by solving all the test cases within an average no more than 1 minute.

2. **Large Scale Instances**

Eight large scale instance groups are generated and categorized into 8 groups with the size ranging from $10 \times 15 \times 5$ to $20 \times 30 \times 10$. The results can be found in Table 2. CPLEX fails to get optimal solutions within the time limit for all instance groups in Table 2, even to find feasible solutions. While the heuristic algorithm performs well, our GA obtains much better solutions than CPLEX in all cases within an average no more than 3 minutes.

Table 1. Results of CPLEX and GA on random instances with normal scale

Size	$4\times6\times2$	$5\times7\times2$	$5\times6\times3$	$6\times8\times3$
OBJ_{CPLEX}	58722	63513	55814	77345
$TIME_{CPLEX}$ (s)	1852	2183	3374	≥ 3600
OBJ_{GA}	58722	63513	55814	77345
$TIME_{GA}$ (s)	8.1	13.5	14.8	26.3
Size	$6\times9\times3$	$7\times9\times4$	$7\times11\times4$	$8\times12\times4$
OBJ_{CPLEX}	68242	109754	128637	134846
$TIME_{CPLEX}$ (s)	≥ 3600	≥ 3600	≥ 3600	≥ 3600
OBJ_{GA}	64351	90586	119896	115672
$TIME_{GA}$ (s)	29.2	38.4	39.9	51.4

Table 2. Results of CPLEX and GA on random instances with large scale

Size	$10\times15\times5$	$12\times20\times5$	$15\times20\times6$	$18\times20\times6$
OBJ_{CPLEX}	184560	257850	373650	765120
$TIME_{CPLEX}$	≥ 3600	≥ 3600	≥ 3600	≥ 3600
OBJ_{GA}	128592	203960	287590	306674
$TIME_{GA}$	73.4	88.3	101.7	137.9
Size	$18\times25\times8$	$20\times25\times8$	$20\times25\times10$	$20\times30\times10$
OBJ_{CPLEX}	695480	858850	805980	1087590
$TIME_{CPLEX}$	≥ 3600	≥ 3600	≥ 3600	≥ 3600
OBJ_{GA}	299730	337580	306972	389435
$TIME_{GA}$	132.4	155.3	159.5	167.2

Our heuristics outperformed CPLEX solver in terms of quality of solutions and computing times needed. The superiority of the heuristic method is more apparent in large test instances, in which GA totally overwhelmed CPLEX. From the observation of the experiments, we believe that our GA is effective and a suitable approach to tackle the transshipment problem with fixed transportation schedules.

5   Conclusions

The just-in-time (JIT) inventory management principle requires that there is just enough inventory that arrives to replace what has been used. As a result, warehousing large inventories has become less common, and can be, in some situations, detrimental to business. The implementation of crossdock operations repositions the focus from warehousing inventory to one of managing inventory through-flow in transit from suppliers to customers. In this process, the warehouses, as crossdocks, are transformed from inventory repositories to points of delivery, consolidation and pickup. In this paper, we study general crossdocks distribution networks where transportation is available at fixed schedule, and where both shipping and delivery can be executed only within specified time windows at supply and demand locations. Also in order to reduce setup cost as much as possible, it requires single shipment for each supplier and single delivery for each customer. And the objective of the problem is to satisfy all the customers by the suppliers with minimize shipping and inventory holding costs without violating time windows of suppliers and customers and capacity constraints of crossodocks and routes through the fixed schedules transportation system. Because this transshipment problem was proved to be **NP**-complete in the strong sense, we develop an efficient genetic algorithm to solve it. The results of computational experiments show that our heuristics outperformed CPLEX solver in terms of quality of solutions and computing times needed. The superiority of the heuristic method is more apparent in large test instances, in which GA totally overwhelmed CPLEX. From the observation of the experiments, we believe that our GA is effective and a suitable approach to tackle the transshipment problem with fixed transportation schedules.

With the current problem, the service time windows of suppliers and customers are hard time windows, i.e. predetermined and fixed, so a set of feasible transportation schedules is difficult to find, which inevitably causes lots of time consumed at last. One future study is to work on the soft time window scenario, i.e. the time windows that can be violated at a cost. In this scenario, we are able to slightly adjust the time windows to achieve feasible transportation schedules.

Acknowledgments. The author Dr. Zhaowei Miao thanks the support by Humanities and Social Science Project "Research on Green Logistics System Design and Optimization Strategies" with Project No. 07JC630047, National Ministry of Education, China. And the author Prof. Fan Wang thanks the support by National Natural Science Foundation of China (NSFC) under Project No. 60704048.

References

1. Aronson, J.E.: A survey on dynamic network flows. Annals of Operations Research 20, 1–66 (1989)
2. Axsater, S.: A new decision rule for lateral transshipments in inventory systems. Management Science 49, 1168–1179 (2003)
3. Axsater, S.: Evaluation of unidirectional lateral transshipments and substitutions in inventory systems. European Journal of Operational Research 149, 438–447 (2003)
4. Bartholdi III, J.J., Gue, K.R.: Reducing labor costs in an LTL crossdocking terminal. Operations Research 48(6), 823–832 (2000)
5. Bartholdi III, J.J., Gue, K.R., Kang, K.: Staging freight in a crossdock. In: Proceedings of the International Conference on Industrial Engineering and Production Management, Quebec City, Canada (2001)
6. Bartholdi III, J.J., Gue, K.R.: The best shape for a crossdock. Transportation Science 38(4), 235–244 (2004)
7. Donaldson, H., Johnson, E.L., Ratliff, H.D., Zhang, M.: Schedule-driven crossdocking networks, Georgia Institute of Technology, Research Report (1999)

8. Grahovac, J., Chakravarty, A.: Sharing and lateral transshipment of inventory in a supply chain with expensive low-demand items. Management Science 47(4), 579–594 (2001)
9. Herer, Y.T., Tzur, M.: The Dynamic Transshipment Problem. Naval Research Logistics Quarterly 48, 386–408 (2001)
10. Herer, Y.T., Tzur, M., Yücesan, E.: Transshipments: An emerging inventory recourse to achieve supply chain leagility. International J. of Production Economics 80, 201–212 (2002)
11. Hoppe, B., Tardos, E.: The quickest transshipment problem. In: Proceedings of the Sixth Annual ACM-SIAM Symposium on Discrete Algorithms, San Francisco, California, United States (1995)
12. Lim, A., Miao, Z., Rodrigues, B., Xu, Z.: Transshipment through crossdocks with inventory and time windows. Naval Research Logistics Quarterly 52(8), 724–733 (2005)
13. Napolitano, M.: Making the move to crossdocking, Warehousing Education and Research Council (2000)
14. Ratcliff, D.H., van de Vate, J., Zhang, M.: Network design for load-driven cross-docking systems, Georgia Institute of Technology, Research Report (1999)
15. Simchi-Levi, D., Kaminsky, P., Simchi-Levi, E.: Designing and Managing the Supply Chain, 2nd edn. McGraw-Hill - Irwin Publishers, Boston (2003)

A Dynamic Population Steady-State Genetic Algorithm for the Resource-Constrained Project Scheduling Problem

Mariamar Cervantes[1,2], Antonio Lova[3], Pilar Tormos[3], and Federico Barber[1]

[1] DSIC – Universidad Politécnica de Valencia, Spain
{mcervantes,fbarber}@dsic.upv.es
[2] Universidad de La Sabana, Bogotá - Colombia
{maria.cervantes}@unisabana.edu.co
[3] DEIOAC – Universidad Politécnica de Valencia, Spain
{allova, ptormos}@eio.upv.es

Abstract. Resource Constrained Project Scheduling Problem (RCPSP) is a well known problem that is easy to describe but very difficult to solve, and therefore, it has attracted the attention of many researchers over the last few decades. In this context, heuristics are the only option when solving realistically-sized projects. In this paper we develop a steady-state genetic algorithm that uses a dynamic population and four decoding methods. These features allow the algorithm to adapt itself to the characteristics of the problem. Finally, its performance is compared against the best project scheduling methods published so far. The results show that the proposed scheduling method is one of the best scheduling techniques when compared with results reported in the literature.

Keywords: project scheduling, resource constraints, genetic algorithm.

1 Introduction

The Resource Constrained Project Scheduling Problem (RCPSP) is a well-known problem which is widely studied in the literature. In recent years, many works have been published, including [6], which summarizes the research for this problem.

Assume a project is represented in activity-on-the-node format by a directed graph $G=\{N,A\}$ in which N is the set of activities that have to be processed and A is the set of precedence relationships. The non-preemtable activities are numbered from 0 to $n+1$, where the dummy activities 0 and $n+1$ mark the beginning and the end of the project. The duration of an activity is denoted by d_i where the duration is zero for dummy activities and non-zero for others. The start time of each activity is denoted by S_i ($0 \leq i \leq n+1$) and its finish time by F_i ($0 \leq i \leq n+1$). There are K renewable resource types, r_{ik} ($0 \leq i \leq n+1$, $1 \leq k \leq K$) being the resource requirements of activity i with respect to resource type k. The resource requirement of dummy activities is 0. R_k ($1 \leq k \leq K$) is the constant availability of resource type k throughout the duration of the project.

N.T. Nguyen et al. (Eds.): IEA/AIE 2008, LNAI 5027, pp. 611–620, 2008.

Based on the definitions of the variables and considering that $P(t)$ denotes the set of activities in process at time t, T being an upper bound on the feasible project duration, the RCPSP can be formulated as follows [3]:

$$\text{Minimize } S_{n+1} \; . \tag{1}$$

Subject to:

$$S_j - S_i \geq d_i \; (i, j) \in A \; . \tag{2}$$

$$\sum_{i \in P(t)} r_{ik} \leq R_k \quad t = 1, \cdots, T \; ; \quad k = 1, \cdots K \; . \tag{3}$$

$$S_i \geq 0, \; i \in N \; . \tag{4}$$

The objective function (1) minimizes the completion time of the dummy activity $n+1$ and thus the makespan of the project. Constraints (2) enforce the precedence constraints between activities. Constraints (3) ensure that for each resource k and each time period t, the resource demand of the set of activities that are currently being processed does not exceed the available capacity.

As the RCPSP is a generalization of the job shop problem, it belongs to the class of NP-hard problems [2]. Taking the combinatorial nature of the problem, the majority of scheduling algorithms are heuristics. With this background in mind, the main challenge is to obtain better solutions (e.g. reduce the project makespan) in less computational time. Several heuristic procedures can be applied and one of the most widely used is Genetic Algorithms because of its good performance.

In this paper we develop a steady-state genetic algorithm which builds individuals (e.g. project schedules) using four codification methods based on priority rules, and an improvement method. The codification methods are also used to evaluate the individuals that are generated via the application of the genetic operators.

The algorithm has two major innovative features which make it stand out when compared with previous works in the RCPSP [7]. First, it has a dynamic population which means that the number of individual increases as the search deepened. Secondly it uses a steady-state replacement strategy.

The computational experiments show that the performance of our algorithm can be consider one of the best, and in certain instances it obtains the optimal solution in the first iteration.

The remainder of this paper is organized as follows; firstly we review the methods that will be used in the generation and evaluation of individuals. In section 3 we describe in detail the genetic algorithm, including the new operators developed and their settings. Section 4 is devoted to describe the results obtained for the standard set of project instances with 30, 60 and 120 activities of the well known PSPLIB. In Section 5 we compare the effectiveness of the algorithm against the best project scheduling methods currently available. Finally, we highlight the main conclusions and directions of further research.

2 Representation and Decoding of Schedules

One of the key factors of genetic algorithms is the representation of solutions. When representations are easy to decode the computational time needed to obtain the schedule is low. Furthermore, it is possible to exploit the properties of the representation in order to design genetic operators that improve the performance of the algorithm.

In this work we use the *activity list* (AL) representation because it was determined that it performs the best to solve the RCPSP [1]. An AL can be seen as an array with one activity in each position. An AL is *precedence-feasible* when an activity never comes after the position of one of its successors.

In order to generate the activity list for the individuals of the initial population and the individuals that are introduced when the population grows, we use a priority rule based heuristic. A priority rule is a criterion to decide the order in which the activities are going to be scheduled and is based on activity's characteristics.

In addition we use the *Parameterised Regret-Biased Random Sampling* (RBRS [7]) in which a probability of being selected is assigned to each activity from the eligible set, depending on its priority value. An eligible activity is one whose predecessors are all in the partial schedule. Each pass of the method obtains a different schedule and the best one will be the final schedule.

The RBRS uses α as a parameter to control the amount of bias. When $\alpha=0$, there is a pure random activity selection. On the other hand, if α is large the activity selection is deterministic.

2.1 Schedule Generation Scheme

To decode the activity list generated by means of the priority rule and the RBRS we need to use a schedule generation scheme.

There are two different schedule generation schemes (SGS), *serial* and *parallel*, that can be applied in two scheduling directions (SD) *forward* and *backward*. Both schemes build feasible project schedules by stepwise extension of a partial schedule (a schedule where only a subset of activities has been scheduled).

In the Serial SGS we schedule the activities one by one, in the order given by the list. In the Parallel SGS the position number of the activity will indicate its priority to be scheduled, the activity with the lowest position being the activity with the highest priority [4]. Both scheduling schemes are presented in detail in [5].

Each SGS can be applied in two schedule directions (SD): Forward and Backward. A forward schedule is built from the first activity to the last one, and each activity is scheduled in the earliest time within the precedence and resource constraints. On the contrary, a backward schedule starts from the last activity and finishes in the first one, scheduling the activities as late as possible.

2.2 Improving Method: Backward-Forward Method

This procedure was proposed by Tormos and Lova in [11], and more recently used in [12] and [14] among many others. Once a feasible schedule has been obtained, the Forward-Backward Method employs the serial SGS in order to iteratively schedule the project by alternating between backward and forward scheduling (BF pass).

Starting from a Forward Schedule, the procedure creates an AL by sorting the activities in decreasing order of their finish times. Then the S-SGS is used to build a Backward Schedule. (Backward Pass). The b/f gene of the individual changes from *f* to *b* after the Backward Pass. Then, one BF pass implies the generation of 2 solutions.

The Forward Pass starts from a Backward Schedule, sorting the activities in increasing order of their start times. The S-SGS is used to build a Forward Schedule. In this case the b/f gene changes from B to F. Because the use of this procedure can not increase the schedule makespan, the new sequence replaces the original in both cases.

3   Genetic Algorithm Proposed

Genetic Algorithms (GA) is the metaheuristic procedure which achieves the best results when solving the RCPSP (see Tables 3, 4 and 5). However, in the most recent works like [1], [4], [7] or [14] among others, authors use different parameters' values for each set of problems and each number of maximum generated schedules, making the solution very dependent on the problem settings. Moreover, in real problems the maximum number of schedules generated is not known in advance, therefore, these assumptions are not practical.

This situation motivated us to build an adaptive algorithm to reduce the external settings by the user. In order to obtain this independence, we developed an original approach for the RCPSP by means of three factors: we used a dynamic population; the local search varies according to the quality of the solution and the degree of depth of the search; and the individuals generated by the genetic operators enter the population immediately. Fig 1 shows the structure of the new algorithm. In the following sections we explain the operators used.

```
GeneticAlgorithm
  CreatePopulation(Population,Pop_Size);
  Evaluation(Population, Local Search)
  While (NSched<MaxSched);
    Selection(Population,F,M);
    Crossover(F,M);
    Mutation(S,D);
    Evaluation(S,D,SelectiveLocalSearch)
    PopulationUpDate(Population,S,D);
    DinamicPopulation(Population,NSched,Pop_Size);
  end While
  Report BestSchedule
End
```

Fig. 1. Pseudo code for the Dynamic Population Steady State Algorithm

3.1   Encoding and Evaluation

We use the AL representation explained above. Each individual in the population is represented by an array with as many positions as activities in the project.

As in [2] each individual has a position (S/P): to code the SGS serial or parallel; and another (B/F) for the direction of the schedule: forward or backward. To compute a schedule we use the SGS and the scheduling direction specified in the genotype. The fitness of the individual is defined as the makespan of the schedule. That is, a lower fitness implies a better individual (and thus a higher chance to survival).

3.2 Initial Population

We start the genetic algorithm by building an initial population using priority rules to determine the order in which the activities will be selected for scheduling.

The generation of the initial population is a two stage procedure: First we perform a deterministic multi-pass priority rule-based method using S-SGS and P-SGS both backward and forward. For each feasible schedule the improvement method iteratively schedules the project by alternating between backward and forward scheduling (BF pass) until no improvement is achieved in two consecutive BF iterations.

The second stage randomly selects the SGS, the SD and the priority rule, and builds an individual by means of the RBRS, using $\alpha=2$, 3.5 and 10 for the sets J30, J60 and J120 respectively as in [8]. Based on the population sizes in [4], the initial population size is fixed at 2000/number_of_activities.

3.3 Selection and Crossover Operators

We use the standard 2-tournament selection operator. In this selection procedure, two individuals are chosen randomly, and the element with the lowest makespan is selected. Afterwards, we determine randomly whether a or b represents the father F. The other parent represents the mother M.

The crossover used in this work is the standard 2-point crossover operator which exploits the advantages of the codification chosen, randomly mating pairs of individuals of the population. The crossover operation is performed with a probability of P_{cross} If the operator is not performed they remain unaltered for the next stage. P_{cross} is set to 0.8.

3.4 Mutation Operator

We use the insertion operator for the activity list and the standard flip bit for the S/P and B/F genes.

The insertion operator works as follows: for each activity in the AL, a new position is randomly chosen between the highest position of its predecessors and the lowest position of its successors. The activity is inserted into the new position with a probability of $P_{muta}=0.05$.

The s/p and b/f genes could be altered with the same probability. That is, the p/f could change from p to s or from s to p, while the b/f gene could change from b to f or from f to b.

3.5 Selective Local Search

We use the improvement method described in section 2.2 to improve the quality of the individual. As in [12] the improving method is selectively applied to two types of schedules: We consider a schedule as a **Good Schedule** if its makespan is less than the mean of the solutions generated so far, and a **Very Good Schedule** if its makespan is less than (mean − best/2).

In this respect, the novelty of our approach is that the intensity of the local search is related to the number of schedules (NSched) generated so far. If the number of schedules generated so far is less than 5000 we use a simple B or F pass for good schedules and a BF pass for very good schedules. If the total solutions are greater than 5000 we use a maximum of two BF passes for good schedules and a maximum of 3BF passes for very good schedules.

When we say a maximum of 2 or 3 BF passes we mean that the process ends when no improvement is achieved in two consecutive BF iterations.

3.6 Replacement of the Individuals

Another innovative feature of this algorithm is that, instead of using generational replacement we develop a steady state strategy. In RCPSP literature all GAs use generational replacement [7], which means that the complete population is replaced by the offspring population. Alternatively, in the steady state strategy the new individuals are available to be selected in the next iteration.

The new individuals enter the population and replace the worst if (i) they are better than the worst and (ii) the AL of the new individual is different to the AL of all of the individuals in the population with the same fitness as the new individual. The second condition was developed to diminish the high selective pressure over the population that is generated by replacing the worst elements of the population [10].

3.7 Population Size

In previous works, authors use different population sizes for each set of problems and for each number of maximum schedules (1.000, 5.000 and 50.000). Therefore, the algorithm becomes dependent on the parameters of the problem that must be known in advance.

To overcome this problem we have designed an algorithm with a dynamic population size, meaning that the algorithm starts with a determined number of individuals and as the search is deepened, the size of the population grows.

In order to implement this feature we increase the population size by 25% of the previous population size each time that 1000 new schedules have been evaluated.

The new individuals are generated using the priority rule and RBRS described in section 2.2 and the selective local search described in section 3.6. These individuals are added to the population as soon as they are evaluated.

4 Computational Experiments and Results

In the experiments carried out in this study we use the standard set of project instances with 30, 60 and 120 activities (small-sized, medium-sized and large-sized projects respectively) from the well-known PSPLIB library [9] using an implementation in C compiled with Microsoft Visual C++ v.6.0,running on a 1 GB RAM, 3 GHz Pentium under Windows XP.

To characterize the algorithm, we calculate average deviation over the critical-path based lower bound (%ADLB). Since the optimal solutions for the small-sized projects are known, the lower bound is the optimal solution. As for the other two instance sets, some of the optimal solutions are not known the critical-path based lower bound has been used. In table 1, we present the main results of the steady-state and dynamic population genetic algorithm (SS-DP) for 1000, 5000 and 50000 schedules respectively.

Table 1. Results of the SS-DP Genetic Algorithm

	1,000		5,000		50,000	
	%ADBL	Std Dev	%ADBL	Std Dev	%ADBL	Std Dev
Small sized	0.16	0.58	0.04	0.26	0.01	0.11
Medium-sized	11.43	22.76	10.96	21.85	10.81	21.53
Large-sized	33.94	45.34	32.57	44.24	31.65	43.24

We see that the algorithm evolves successfully, finding better solutions as the number of schedules increases. In the three sets of problems, there are cases where the best solution found is the first one, all of them being the optimal. This is because of the initial population generating scheme, which enables the algorithm to find better solutions in early stages.

In order to evaluate the impact of the steady state replacement and dynamic population strategies we have designed three more algorithms (i) Generational Replacement and Static Population, (ii)Generational Replacement and Dynamic Population and (iii) Steady State Replacement and Static Population. The settings of the genetic operators are the same as the new algorithm proposed. The results can be seen on Table 2.

Table 2. %ADBL Algorithms for comparison

	(i)			(ii)			(iii)		
	1,000	5,000	50,000	1,000	5,000	50,000	1,000	5,000	50,000
Small sized	0.15	0.05	0.04	0.15	0.06	0.02	0.16	0.05	0.04
Medium-sized	11.42	11.03	10.84	11.42	11.01	10.87	11.43	10.98	10.85
Large-sized	34.29	33.31	32.54	34.00	33.16	32.54	33.94	32.75	31.98

As can be seen, the SS-DP Genetic Algorithm performs better when compared with the previous three algorithms, confirming that the new strategies used work through the entire search and the impact is bigger on the large-sized set, which is the most difficult to solve. In particular, the steady state (SS-GA) replacement seems to have more impact than the dynamic population. Both SS-GA outperform the generational ones.

5 Comparison with the Best Heuristics for the RCPSP

The results of the genetic algorithm show that it obtains an excellent performance when compared against the best five heuristics published and reported in [6] and they are ordered by the results obtained for 1,000 schedules.

Small-Sized Projects
The increase, with respect to the optimal solution when 1,000 schedules are generated, is 0.16%, optimally solving 92.29% of the instances. According to the results, the proposed algorithm ranks second. When 5,000 solutions are generated, the increase is 0.04%, coming in second in the ranking, optimally solving 97.29% of the instances. For 50,000 solutions we obtained 0.01% of deviation over the optimal solutions, optimally solving 99.17% of the instances. For the complete results see Table 3.

Table 3. Small-sized set

Heuristic	SGS	Reference	% ADLB		
			1,000	5,000	50,000
GA- TS - path relinking	P/S	Kochetov and Stolyar (2003)	0.10	0.04	0.00
GA- SS - DP	P/S	This paper	0.16	0.04	0.01
Comb-RBRS BF/FB	P/S	Tormos and Lova (2003b)	0.25	0.13	0.05
GA- fwd-backwd	P/S	Alcaraz et al. (2004)	0.25	0.06	0.03
GA - hybrid	S	Valls et al. (2003)	0.27	0.06	0.02
Scatter Search	S	Debels et al. (2007)	0.27	0.11	0.01

Medium-Sized Projects
With this set of project instances the SS-DP Genetic Algorithm improves its performance, ranking first on the list with 1,000 and 5,000 schedules obtaining 11.43% and 10.96 %ADBL respectively. For 50,000 schedules it obtains 10.8 1%ADBL as shown in Table 4.

Table 4. Medium-sized projects

Heuristic	SGS	Reference	%ADLB		
			1,000	5,000	50,000
GA- SS - DP	P/S	This paper	11.43	10.96	10.81
GA-hybrid	S	Valls et al. (2003)	11.56	11.10	10.73
GA, TS – path relinking	P/S	Kochetov and Stolyar (2003)	11.71	11.17	10.74
Scatter Search	S	Debels et al. (2007)	11.73	11.10	10.71
Comb-RBRS BF/FB	P/S	Tormos and Lova (2003b)	11.88	11.62	11.36
GA – fwd-backwd	P/S	Alcaraz et al. (2004)	11.89	11.19	10.84

Table 5. Large-sized projects

Heuristic	SGS	Reference	%ADLB		
			1,000	5,000	50,000
GA- SS - DP	P/S	This paper	33.71	32.57	31.65
GA - hybrid	S	Valls et al. (2003)	34.07	32.54	31.24
GA, TS - path relinking	P/S	Kochetov and Stolyar (2003)	34.74	33.36	32.06
RBRS BF/FB	P/S	Tormos and Lova (2003 b)	35.01	34.41	33.71
Population-based	S	Valls (2005)	35.18	34.02	32.81
Scatter Search	S	Debels et al. (2007)	35.22	33.10	31.57

Large-Sized Projects

The percentage of increase over the lower bound of the algorithms analyzed is reported in Table 5. The proposed algorithm obtains 33.71 %ADBL with 1.000 schedules, taking first place in the ranking. With 5.000 schedules the algorithm ranks second with 32.57 %ADBL and for 50.000 schedules it obtains 31.65 %ADBL.

6 Conclusions

In this paper a genetic algorithm has been developed with two innovative features that make it different when compared with previous works. Firstly, it has a dynamic population meaning that the number of individuals increases as the search deepens. Secondly it uses a steady-state replacement strategy.

The two features are complementary. The steady-state replacement generates high selective pressure. The dynamic population introduces variety to the population on a periodic basis.

We use the problem's characteristics and the degree of depth of the search to set the algorithm parameters, in particular the intensity of the local search.

We found that using good priority rules and the improving method when generating the initial population, the algorithm can find optimal solutions in the first schedule.

Finally, once the dynamic population steady-state algorithm heuristic has been set, we have compared the performance of our approach with the most recent heuristics and metaheuristics developed for RCPSP using the well known standard sets of instances PSPLIB. The results indicate that the proposed heuristic is the best for the medium-sized and large-sized set of problems, making our genetic algorithm competitive with the best scheduling methods published so far in the literature.

Acknowledgment. This work has been partially supported by the research projects TIN2004-06354-C02- 01 (Min. de Educación y Ciencia. Spain-FEDER). FOM-70022/T05 (Min. de Fomento. Spain) and FP6-021235-2. IST-STREP (UE).

References

1. Alcaraz, J., Maroto, C.: A Robust Genetic Algorithm for Resource Allocation in Project Scheduling. Annals of Operations Research, vol. 102, pp. 83–109. Kluwer Academic Publishers, Dordrecht (2001)
2. Blazewicz, J., Lenstra, J., Rinnooy Kan, A.H.G.: Scheduling Subject to Resource Constraints: Classification and Complexity. Discrete Applied Mathematics, vol. 5, pp. 11–24. Elsevier, Amsterdam (1983)
3. Christofides, N., Álvarez-Valdés, R., Tamarit, J.M.: Project Scheduling with Resource Constraints. A branch and bound approach. European Journal of Operational Research 29, 262–273 (1987)
4. Hartmann, S.: A Self-Adapting Genetic Algorithm for Project Scheduling under Resource Constraints. Naval Research Logistics, vol. 49, pp. 433–448. John Wiley & Sons, Chichester (2002)
5. Kolisch, R.: Serial and Parallel Resource-Constrained Project Scheduling Methods Revisited: Theory and Computation. European Journal of Operational Research 90, 320–333 (1996)
6. Kolisch, R., Hartmann, S.: Experimental Investigation of Heuristics for Resource- Constrained Project Scheduling: An Update. European Journal of Operational Research 174, 23–37 (2006)
7. Lancaster, J., Ozbayrak, M.: Evolutionary algorithms applied to project scheduling problems—a survey of the state-of-the-art. International Journal of Production Research 45, 425–450 (2007)
8. Lova, A., Tormos, P., Cervantes, M., Barber, F.: An Efficient Adaptive Heuristic for the Resource Constrained Project Scheduling Problem. In: Proceedings CAEPIA 2007, vol. II, pp. 259–268 (2007)
9. PSPLIB, http://129.187.106.231/psplib/
10. Smith, J.: On Replacement Strategies in Steady State Evolutionary Algorithms. Evolutionary Computation 15, 29–59 (2007)
11. Tormos, P., Lova, A.: A Competitive Heuristic Solution Technique for Resource-Constrained Project Scheduling. Annals Of Operations Research, vol. 102, pp. 65–81. Kluwer Academic Publishers, Dordrecht (2001)
12. Tormos, P., Lova, A.: An Efficient Multi-Pass Heuristic for Project Scheduling with Constrained Resources. International Journal of Production Research 41, 1071–1086 (2003a)
13. Tormos, P., Lova, A.: Integrating heuristics for RCPSP: One Step Forward. Technical Report. Universidad Politécnica de Valencia (2003b)
14. Valls., V., Ballestin, F., Quintanilla, M.S.: Justification and RCPSP: A Technique that Pays. European Journal of Operational Research 165, 372–386 (2005)
15. Valls, V., Ballestin, F., Quintanilla, M.S.: A Hybrid Genetic Algorithm for the RCPSP. Technical Report. Department of Statistics and Operations Research. University of Valencia (2003)

Access Control for XML Document

Yun Bai

School of Computing and Mathematics
University of Western Sydney
NSW 1797, Australia
ybai@scm.uws.edu.au

Abstract. The aim of this paper is to investigate the security issue of the XML documents. We discuss a protection mechanism for the XML documents; and investigate a knowledge based formal approach to ensure the security of web-based XML documents. Our approach starts by introducing a high level language to specify an XML document and its protection authorizations. We also investigate the syntax and semantics of the language. The flexible and powerful access control specification can effectively protect the documents from unauthorized attempts and malicious damages.

Keywords: KBS methodology, XML security, authorization policy, logic based specification.

1   Introduction

XML is becoming the favorable format for information exchange over the Internet, at the same time security issue has been more and more concerned. XML document security has been increasingly studied and has become an active research area. Fine grained access control for XML documents has been investigated by some researchers. Murata *et al.* [10] proposed a static analysis for XML access control. Given an access control policy and an access query, they use a static analysis to decide if to grant or deny such an access request. In this way, run-time evaluation is only needed when the static analysis is unable to decide. This pre-execution analysis improves the performance of the system response to a query. Damiani *et al.* [5] presented a language for specification of access control by exploiting the characteristics of XML to define and enforce access control directly on the structure and content of the document. They provide a flexible security mechanism for protecting XML documents. Devanbu *et al.* [6] proposed an authentication approach for XML documents. They use signature techniques to ensure the authenticity of the XML documents by having a server processing queries and certifying answers using a digital signature with an on-line private key. This approach allows untrusted servers to answer certain type of path queries over the Internet without the need for a trusted on-line signing key. It provides the security of XML documents over the Internet by using a signature based document authentication.

N.T. Nguyen et al. (Eds.): IEA/AIE 2008, LNAI 5027, pp. 621–630, 2008.

Access control or authorization specifications have long been an important issue in computer system security. The function of the authorization is to control access to the system, to prevent unauthorized attempt to the system resources.

Since knowledge based logic specification has a clear and precise semantics and powerful expressiveness, a variety of logic authorization specification approaches have been proposed [2,8,9,11]. Woo and Lam [12] proposed a formal approach using default logic to represent and evaluate authorizations. Bertino *et al.* [3], proposed a general framework on a logic formalism to model discretionary, mandatory access control and role-based access control models. Bettini *et al.* [4] formalized a rule-based security policy framework which included provisions and obligations, and investigated a reasoning mechanism within this framework in a general database scenario. Many of the works either concentrate on a specific application, or propose a general logic framework for authorizations, it's hard to capture the hierarchical structure and the access constraints of XML documents.

The aim of this paper is to address high level authorization specifications in XML document scenario. The works so far regarding XML document security generally lack a formal semantics to characterize different types of inheritance properties of authorization policies among the semi-structured elements of the document. This work is a preliminary investigation towards a knowledge based formal method on XML document security. We propose a formal logic language with a precise and declarative semantics to capture the security feature of XML documents. The flexible and powerful access control specification can effectively protect the documents from unauthorized attempts.

The rest of the paper is organized as follows. Section 2 specifies the features of the XML documents by a formal language, we discuss its syntax and semantics. Section 3 extends the language by incorporating access control rules into the XML document specification to provide the protection of the document. We also discuss the syntax and semantics of the extended language. Finally section 4 concludes the paper with some discussions for the future work.

2   XML Document Specification: Syntax and Semantics

XML is a markup language which defines a format for documents used in web-based applications. An XML document contains a sequence of nested elements. Each element is represented by a pair of begin and end delimiter tags such as <record> and </record>. An element has a set of attributes associated with it. The elements within a document form a tree structure as shown in Figure 1.

In the tree structure, we use rectangle node for the element and oval node for the attribute of the element. "Mary is an admin staff, her duty is assistance to the dean" is an instance of such a document frame. From the structure we observe that the elements of the document reside in a hierarchy of a tree structure and have inheritance properties. For instance, an *acad* staff has the general attributes (*name*, *salary*) a staff has, which are inherited from its parent element *staff*. Apart from the general inherited properties, it has its specific properties of *research* and *teaching*. Now we propose a logic language $\mathcal{L}$ to formally specify the XML document.

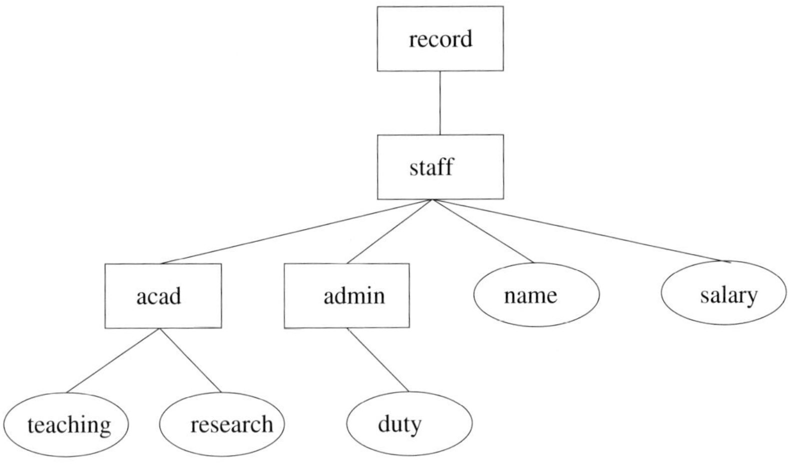

Fig. 1. XML document tree structure

2.1   Syntax of Language $\mathcal{L}$

The vocabulary of language $\mathcal{L}$ consists of:

1. A finite set of *element variables* $\mathcal{EV} = \{e, e_1, e_2, \cdots\}$ and a finite set of *element constants* $\mathcal{EC} = \{E, E_1, E_2, \cdots\}$. We will simply name $\mathcal{E} = \mathcal{EV} \cup \mathcal{EC}$ as *element set*.
2. Binary symbols $<$, $<<$ and $\in$.
3. Auxiliary symbol $\Rightarrow$.

For simplicity, we do not separate the element and its attributes. We use $A|B$ to indicate the attribute B of an element A. Together they are viewed as an object to be accessed by a user or an application program. We call such user or application program subject.

We use $<$ and $<<$ to denote the hierarchy relationship between two elements. $E_1 < E_2$ indicates that E_1 is an immediate child of E_2; $E_1 << E_2$ indicates that E_1 is at a lower but not immediate hierarchy of E_2. The different hierarchy definitions $<$ and $<<$ are used to solve conflicts of inherited authorizations. We also use $\in$ to represent membership relationship. For instance, "Mary $\in$ *admin*" represents that Mary is a member of *admin* staff. The symbol $\Rightarrow$ is used to map an element to its associated attributes.

The basic building blocks of an XML document are **elements** nested in the hierarchical file structure; the **relationships** among these elements indicating how they are related; and the **restrictions** on the elements to satisfy certain document requirements. Logic language $\mathcal{L}$ has a simple yet flexible syntax. It can be suitably used to formalize various features of the XML documents. In the language, the set of element *constants* represents element instances of the document and the set of element *variables* represents a general framework of elements in the document.

An *element proposition* is an expression of the form

$$E \Rightarrow \Pi_1,$$
$$\cdots,$$
$$\Rightarrow \Pi_m. \tag{1}$$

In (1) E is an element and $\Pi_1 \cdots \Pi_m$ are attributes of E. When the set Π is empty, it refers to the element itself.

A *relationship proposition* of $\mathcal{L}$ is an expression of one of the following three forms:

$$E < E_1, \tag{2}$$
$$E << E_1, \tag{3}$$
$$E \in E_1. \tag{4}$$

where E and E_1 are elements from the document, i.e., E and E_1 may be element constants or variables. Clearly, relationship propositions (2), (3) and (4) explicitly represent the hierarchy relations between two elements.

A *constraint proposition* is an expression of the form

$$\phi \textbf{ if } \phi_1, \cdots, \phi_k. \tag{5}$$

where $\phi, \phi_1, \cdots, \phi_k$ are element propositions. It specifies that ϕ is a derived element from elements $\phi_1, \cdots, \phi_k$. When the details of an element proposition is not interested in the context, we usually use the notation ϕ to denote it. A constraint proposition represents some relationship among different elements.

We use the *element proposition* to represent elements and their attributes; the *relationship proposition* to capture the hierarchical structure and membership feature of XML document; and the *constraint proposition* to represent different restrictions on different elements or attributes of an element. A proposition without variables is called a ground proposition.

For instance, the hierarchical structure and membership feature of an XML document can be represented by a *relationship proposition* such as: $Mary \in admin$ or $admin < staff$.

With the three propositions, an XML document can be formally defined as a finite set of **element propositions** specifying different kinds of data elements in the document, a finite set of **relationship propositions** expressing how these elements are related within the document and a finite set of **constraint propositions** restricting the elements to satisfy various document requirements.

We can now formally define our XML document as follows.

Definition 1. *An XML document D is a triplet (α, β, γ), where α is a finite set of ground element propositions, β is a finite set of ground relationship propositions, and γ is a finite set of constraint propositions.*

For instance, for the document frame in Figure 1, if we have "John is an academic staff; Mary is an admin staff" Using the definition, we have:

(1) the set of ground element propositions α consists of:

$$
\begin{aligned}
staff \;&\Rightarrow\; name(String), \\
&\Rightarrow salary(Integer), \quad\quad (6) \\
acad \;&\Rightarrow\; teaching(String), \\
&\Rightarrow research(String), \quad\quad (7) \\
admin \;&\Rightarrow\; duty(String). \quad\quad (8)
\end{aligned}
$$

(2) the set of ground relationship propositions β consists of:

$$
\begin{aligned}
John &\in acad, &\quad (9) \\
Mary &\in admin, &\quad (10) \\
acad &< staff, &\quad (11) \\
admin &< staff. &\quad (12)
\end{aligned}
$$

(3) the set of constraint propositions γ consists of:

$$
\begin{aligned}
x &\in acad \\
\textbf{if } x &\Rightarrow teaching(String), \\
x &\in staff, \quad\quad (13) \\
y &\in acad \\
\textbf{if } y &\Rightarrow research(String), \\
y &\in staff, \quad\quad (14) \\
z &\in admin \\
\textbf{if } z &\Rightarrow duty(String), \\
z &\in staff. \quad\quad (15)
\end{aligned}
$$

The constraints states that if x is a staff member and has attribute *teaching*, then x is an academic staff; if y is a staff member and has attribute *research*, then y is an academic staff; if z is a staff member and has attribute *duty*, then z is an administration staff.

2.2   Semantics of Language $\mathcal{L}$

In this subsection, we define the semantics of language $\mathcal{L}$ by following a classical logic definition. First, we define the structure of $\mathcal{L}$.

Definition 2. *A structure of $\mathcal{L}$ is a tuple $S = (U, \mathcal{F}_S, <_U, <<_U, \in_U)$, where*

1. *U is a nonempty set called the* domain *of S which represents the set of all actual elements and attributes in the XML document.*
2. *$\mathcal{F}_S$ is a set of functions, for each function symbol f in $\mathcal{F}_S$, f maps an element to its corresponding set of attributes.*

3. $<_U$ and $<<_U$ are partial orderings on U and $\in_U$ is a binary relation on U. We require that if $a \in_U b$ and $b <_U c$, then $a \in_U c$; if $a \in_U b$ and $b <<_U c$, then $a \in_U c$; if $a <_U b$ and $b <_U c$, then $a <<_U c$.

The above definition states that in a structure S, U represents all the possible *actual* elements in the document domain. That is, each item in U is a real object in our world. A function symbol f in $\mathcal{F}_S$ is corresponding to $\Rightarrow$ defined in $\mathcal{L}$ and maps an element to its set of attributes. The functions of ordering $<_U$ and $<<_U$ are to represent the semantics of relationship propositions in $\mathcal{L}$. For example, $a <_U b$ in the structure is the counterpart of proposition $A < B$, while A and B are elements in $\mathcal{L}$ and are mapped to a and b, which are the elements of U respectively. The semantics of the relationship propositions $<<$ and $\in$ in $\mathcal{L}$ are provided by $<<_U$ and $\in_U$ in S respectively in a similar way.

Now, we define the entailment relation and models of structure S.

Definition 3. *Let* $S = (U, \mathcal{F}_S, <_U, <<_U, \in_U)$ *be a structure of* $\mathcal{L}$. *We define entailment relation* $\models$ *as follows.*

1. *For ground relationship propositions,* $S \models E \in E_1$ *if* $E \in_U E_1$; $S \models E < E_1$ *if* $E <_U E_1$; *and* $S \models E << E_1$ *if* $E <<_U E_1$.
2. *For a ground element proposition*
   $$S \models \quad f_1(E) \Rightarrow \Pi_1,$$
   $$\cdots,$$
   $$f_m(E) \Rightarrow \Pi_m$$
   if for each f *where* f *is in* $\{f_1, \cdots, f_m\}$, $\{\Pi_1, \cdots, \Pi_m\}$ *are sets of attributes of* E.
3. *For a ground constraint proposition,* $S \models \phi$ **if** $\phi_1, \cdots, \phi_k$
   if $S \models \phi_1, \cdots, S \models \phi_k$ *implies* $S \models \phi$.
4. *For any proposition* ψ *including element variables,* $S \models \psi$
   if for every instance ϕ *of* ψ *(i.e.* ϕ *is obtained from* ψ *by substituted each variable in* ψ *with some element of* U), $S \models \phi$.

Now we can formally define the model of an XML document D as follows:

Definition 4. *A structure* M *of* $\mathcal{L}$ *is a* model *of an XML document* $D = (\alpha, \beta, \gamma)$ *if*

1. *For each proposition* ψ *in* $\alpha \cup \beta \cup \gamma$, $M \models \psi$.
2. *For each element proposition* ϕ, *if* $M \models \phi$, *then* $M \models \phi'$
   where ϕ' *is obtained from* ϕ *by omitting some attributes of* ϕ.
3. *For any relationship proposition* $E \in E_1$ *and element proposition* $f(E_1) \Rightarrow \Pi$, $M \models E \in E_1$ *and* $M \models f(E_1) \Rightarrow \Pi$ *imply* $M \models f(E) \Rightarrow \Pi$.
4. *For any relationship propositions* $E < E_1$ *and* $E_1 < E_2$, $M \models E < E_1$ *and* $M \models E_1 < E_2$ *imply* $M \models E << E_2$.

Condition 1 in the above definition is the basic requirement for a model. Condition 2 allows us to partially represent an element with only those attributes that are of interest in a given context. Condition 3 is a restriction to guarantee necessary inheritance of membership, whereas Condition 4 is needed for the purpose of element property and authorization inheritance in case of conflicts. Let Σ be an XML document and ϕ be a proposition. If for every model M of Σ, $M \models \phi$, we also call that ϕ *is entailed* by Σ, denoted as $\Sigma \models \phi$.

3 Access Control in XML Document Specification: Syntax and Semantics

This section is to extend the XML document specification language $\mathcal{L}$ to include authorization rules in order to control access to the document. A specific authorization rule is to define which subject holds what kind of access right for which object. In this context, a subject is either a user or an application program; an object is an element or attribute(s) of an element of the document; and an access right is an operation to be performed on the object.

3.1 Syntax of the Extended Language $\mathcal{L}$

The *vocabulary* of the extended $\mathcal{L}$ includes the original vocabulary together with the following additions:

1. A finite set of *subject variables* $\mathcal{SV} = \{s, s_1, s_2, \cdots\}$ and a finite set of *subject constants* $\mathcal{SC} = \{S, S_1, S_2, \cdots\}$. We denote $\mathcal{S} = \mathcal{SV} \cup \mathcal{SC}$.
2. A finite set of *access-rights variables* $\mathcal{AV} = \{r, r_1, r_2, \cdots\}$ and a finite set of *access-right constants* $\mathcal{AC} = \{R, R_1, R_2, \cdots\}$. We denote $\mathcal{A} = \mathcal{AV} \cup \mathcal{AC}$.
3. A ternary predicate symbol *holds* taking arguments subject, access-right, and object respectively.
4. Logic connectives $\wedge$ and $\neg$.

In the extended $\mathcal{L}$, an authorization fact that a subject S has access right R for element E (or its attribute A) is represented using a ground formula $holds(S, R, E)$ (or $holds(S, R, E|A)$). A ground formula is a formula free of variables. We use lower case letters for variables and capital letters for constants.

We define an *access fact* to be an atomic formula $holds(s, r, o)$ or its negation. An *access fact expression* is defined as follows: (i) each access fact is an access fact expression; (ii) if ψ is an access fact expression and ϕ is an element or relationship proposition, then $\psi \wedge \phi$ is an access fact expression; (iii) if ψ and ϕ are access fact expressions, then $\psi \wedge \phi$ is an access fact expression.

From the above definition,

$$holds(S, R, E) \wedge (E{<}{<}E_1),$$
$$\neg holds(S, R, E|A) \wedge (E{\in}E_2)$$

are access fact expressions.

Now, we define an *access proposition* of the extended $\mathcal{L}$ as:

$$\psi \text{ implies } \phi \text{ with absence } \gamma \tag{16}$$

This proposition says that ϕ is true if ψ is true under the condition that γ is not presented.

A special form of the above access proposition occurs when γ is empty. In this case, we can rewrite it as:

$$\psi \ \textbf{provokes} \ \phi \tag{17}$$

This is viewed as a *causal* or *conditional* relation between ψ and ϕ. Furthermore, when ψ is also empty, we rewrite it as:

$$\textbf{always} \ \phi \tag{18}$$

which specifies a constant condition that ϕ should always be true.

Now we can define an *authorization rule base* to control access to XML document. It is defined as a finite set of **data propositions** representing various elements and their attributes, and their relationships within the XML document; a finite set of **access propositions** specifying access permissions to the data elements; and a finite set of **constraints propositions** being complied by the data elements regulated by users or systems. Formally, it can be defined as:

Definition 5. *An* XML *document with access control rules in extended* $\mathcal{L}$ *is a pair* $\Lambda = (D, A)$, *where* $D = (\alpha, \beta, \gamma)$ *is the* XML *document as defined in Definition 1, and* A *is an* authorization description *on* D *to specify a set of system and user-defined access propositions.*

For example, some authorization rules for accessing an XML document can be specified as:

$$holds(s, r, e) \wedge (e_1 < e)$$
$$\textbf{implies} \ holds(s, r, e_1)$$
$$\textbf{with absence} \ \neg holds(s, r, e_1), \tag{19}$$

$$holds(s, r, e) \wedge (e_1 << e)$$
$$\textbf{implies} \ holds(s, r, e_1)$$
$$\textbf{with absence} \ \neg holds(s, r, e_1), \tag{20}$$

and

$$holds(s, r, e) \wedge (e_1 \in e)$$
$$\textbf{implies} \ holds(s, r, e_1)$$
$$\textbf{with absence} \ \neg holds(s, r, e_1). \tag{21}$$

The above three propositions express the hierarchy and membership authorization inheritance properties within an XML document.

The proposed high level specification language is expressive enough to represent authorizations in XML document environment. Within this specification, constraints, causal and inherited authorizations as well as general default authorizations can be properly justified.

3.2   Semantics of the Extended Language $\mathcal{L}$

Now we consider the semantics of the extended language $\mathcal{L}$. To define a proper semantics of our access proposition (16), we need to employ a *fix-point semantics* that shares the spirit of fix-point semantics used for *extended logic programs* [1,7].

Formally, a *structure S^Λ* of the extended $\mathcal{L}$ is a pair (S^D, S^A), where S^D is a structure of $\mathcal{L}$ as defined in Definition 2 and S^A is a finite set of ground literals with forms $holds(S, R, E)$, $holds(S, R, E|A)$, $\neg holds(S, R, E)$ or $\neg holds(S, R, E|A)$.

Now we can define the entailment relation $\models_\lambda$ of the extended $\mathcal{L}$.

Definition 6. *Let $S^\Lambda = (S^D, S^A)$ be a structure of the extended $\mathcal{L}$. We define the entailment relation $\models_\lambda$ of the extended $\mathcal{L}$ as follows.*

1. *For an XML document proposition ψ, $S^\Lambda \models_\lambda \psi$ iff $S^D \models \psi$.*
2. *For a pure ground access fact expression $\psi \equiv F_1 \wedge \cdots \wedge F_k$, where each F_i is a ground access fact, $S^\Lambda \models_\lambda \psi$ iff for each i, $F_i \in S^A$.*
3. *For a ground access fact expression ψ, $S^\Lambda \models_\lambda \psi$ iff for each relationship or element proposition ϕ occurring in ψ, $S^D \models \phi$, and for each ground access fact ϕ' occurring in ψ, $\phi' \in S^A$.*
4. *For an access fact expression ψ, $S^\Lambda \models_\lambda \psi$ iff for each ground instance ψ' of ψ, $S^\Lambda \models_\lambda \psi'$.*

Now we are in the position to formally define a model of $\Lambda = (D, A)$.

Definition 7. *Consider an extended database $\Lambda = (D, A)$ and a structure $S^\Lambda = (S^D, S^A)$. Let A' be an authorization description obtained from A in the following way:*

*(i) by deleting each access proposition ψ **implies** ϕ **with absence** γ from A if for some F_i in γ, $F_i \in S^A$;*
*(ii) by translating all other access propositions ψ **implies** ϕ **with absence** γ to the form ψ **provokes** ϕ, or to the form **always** ϕ if ψ is empty.*

Definition 8. *Consider an extended XML document $\Lambda = (D, A)$ and a structure $S^\Lambda = (S^D, S^A)$. Let A' be an authorization description obtained from A as described in Definition 7. $S^\Lambda = (S^D, S^A)$ is a* model *of $\Lambda = (D, A)$ if and only if*

(i) S^D is a model of D;
(ii) S^A is the smallest set satisfying the following conditions:
   *(a) for each access proposition **always** ϕ in A', $S^\Lambda \models \phi$;*
   *(b) for each access proposition of the form ψ **provokes** ϕ in A', if $S^\Lambda \models \psi$, then $S^\Lambda \models \phi$.*

4   Conclusion

In this paper, we proposed a knowledge based logic language for XML document security, discussed the syntax and semantics of the language, investigated XML document and the authorization rules for accessing it. The flexible and powerful access control specification can effectively protect the documents from unauthorized attempts and malicious damages. We are currently investigating the mapping of the authorization rules to logic programs and the implementation of logic programs.

References

1. Bai, Y., Varadharajan, V.: A Language for Specifying Sequences of Authorization Transformations and Its Applications. In: Han, Y., Quing, S. (eds.) ICICS 1997. LNCS, vol. 1334, pp. 39–49. Springer, Heidelberg (1997)
2. Bertino, E., Buccafurri, F., Ferrari, E., Rullo, P.: A Logic-based Approach for Enforcing Access Control. Computer Security 8(2-2), 109–140 (2000)
3. Bertino, E., Catania, B., Ferrari, E., Perlasca, P.: A Logical Framework for Reasoning about Access Control Models. ACM Transactions on Information and System Security 6(1), 71–127 (2003)
4. Bettini, C., Jajodia, S., Wang, X.S., Wijesekera, D.: Provisions and Obligations in Policy Management and Security Applications. In: Proceedings of the Very Large Database Conference, pp. 502–513 (2002)
5. Damiani, E., Vimercati, S., Paraboschi, S., Samarati, P.: A Fine Grained Access Control System for XML Documents. ACM Transactions on Information and System Security, 160–202 (2002)
6. Devanbu, P., Gertz, M., Kwong, A., Martel, C., Nuckolls, G., Stubblebine, S.G.: Flexible Authentication of XML Documents. In: Proceedings of the ACM Conference on Computer and Communications Security, pp. 136–145 (2001)
7. Gelfond, M., Lifschitz, V.: Classical Negation in Logic Programs and Disjunctive Databases. New Generation Computing 9, 365–385 (1991)
8. Jajodia, S., Samarati, P., Sapino, M.L., Subrahmanian, V.S.: Flexible Support for Multiple Access Control Policies. ACM Transactions on Database Systems 29(2), 214–260 (2001)
9. Li, N., Grosof, B., Feigenbaum, J.: Delegation Logic: A Logic-based Approach to Distributed Authorization. ACM Transactions on Information and System Security 6(1), 128–171 (2003)
10. Murata, M., Tozawa, A., Kudo, M.: XML Access Control Using Static Analysis. In: Proceedings of the ACM Conference on Computer and Communications Security, pp. 73–84 (2003)
11. Wang, L., Wijesekera, D., Jajodia, S.: A logic-based framework for attribute based access control. In: Proceedings of the ACM Workshop on Formal Methods in Security Engineering, pp. 45–55 (2004)
12. Woo, T.Y.C., Lam, S.S.: Authorization in Distributed systems: A Formal Approach. In: Proceedings of IEEE Symposium on Research in Security and Privacy, pp. 33–50 (1992)

Extending Knowledge Base Update into First-Order Knowledge Bases

Ewa Madalińska-Bugaj[1] and Witold Łukaszewicz[2]

[1] Institute of Informatics, Warsaw University
[2] University of Computer Science and Economics
TWP, Olsztyn, Poland

Abstract. In this paper, we introduce a new belief update operator. In contrast to all existing approaches to this problem, which are based on propositional or description logics, our proposal admits representing knowledge bases in full first-order logic. In consequence, our proposal is much more expressive than the existing ones.

1 Introduction

Belief update is the task of modifying a knowledge base when an action is performed. More specifically, given a knowledge base KB, representing the world under consideration, and a formula α, representing an effect of an action, the task is to specify a new knowledge base, $KB * \alpha$, representing the world after performing the action.

The first formalization of belief update, known in the literature as a *possible model approach* (PMA, for short), has been given in [11] (see also [12,13]).[1]

A number of researchers ([2], [7]) have observed that the classical PMA may lead to unintuitive results, particularly when disjunctive update is involved. Assume, for instance, that all we know about the considered world is p and the effect of an action performed is $p \vee q$. That is $KB = p$ and $\alpha = p \vee q$. Applying the PMA operator, we get $KB * \alpha = p$. However, intuition dictates that the description of the new state of the world should be $p \vee q$ rather than p. The reason is that if p was accepted as the description of the new state, then this would imply that our knowledge about the current state makes an unpredictable action predictable.

A number of different knowledge base update operators have been proposed in the literature. Ten of them are examined by Herzig and Rifi in [8]. The conclusion they come to is that only two of the considered operators are satisfactory. One of them is MPMA, introduced in [5] (see also [6]).

The main difference between the MPMA and the PMA is the following. The PMA is based on minimal change policy. More specifically, given a knowledge base KB and an update formula α, $KB * \alpha$ is to be as similar to KB as possible.

---

[1] Katsuno and Mendelzon [9] proposed eight postulates which, as they claimed, should be satisfied by any belief update operator. Actually, Winslett's PMA satisfies all these postulates.

N.T. Nguyen et al. (Eds.): IEA/AIE 2008, LNAI 5027, pp. 631–640, 2008.

The MPMA can be succinctly described as the relativization or weakening of the minimal change policy to a subset of atoms in the language rather than to all atoms. The technique is similar to the use of varied predicates in circumscription.

All approaches to belief update are based on propositional logic what significantly restricts the use of these formalisms in practical applications.[2] In this paper we generalize the MPMA update operator by admitting first-order knowledge bases and restricted first-order update formulae. This allows us to consider scenarios which cannot be properly formalized in existing approaches to belief update.

The paper is organized as follows. In the next section, we present a number of basic notions used in the sequel. Section 3 is devoted to the notion of an eliminant in first-order logic which plays a crucial role in our approach. In section 4 our update operator, referred to as FOMPMA, is introduced and in section 5 we illustrate it by presenting several examples. In section 6 the FOMPMA is analyzed in the context of Katsuno and Mendelson postulates. Finally, the last section contains concluding remarks and future work.

2   Basic Notions

We assume a first-order language with equality. Formulae are constructed in the usual way using sentential connectives $\neg, \wedge, \vee, \Rightarrow, \Leftrightarrow$, quantifiers $\forall, \exists$, Boolean constants $\top$ (true), $\bot$ (false) and the equality sign $=$.

A sentence is a formula containing no free variables.

Let $\mathcal{L}$ be a first-order language with equality. The objects under consideration, referred to as *knowledge bases*, are finite sets of sentences stated in $\mathcal{L}$. Since each such a set is logically equivalent to the conjunction of its members, a knowledge base may be always viewed as a single first-order sentence. In the sequel, we shall never distinguish between a knowledge base KB and the sentence being the conjunction of all members of KB.

An *atom* is a formula of the form $P(\vec{t})$, where P is an n-ary predicate symbol and $\vec{t}$ is an n-tuple of terms. A *literal* is an atom or its negation. A literal is said to be *ground* if it contains no variables.

If $\vec{t} = (t_1, \ldots, t_n)$ and $\vec{t'} = (t'_1, \ldots, t'_n)$ are tuples of terms then $\vec{t} = \vec{t'}$ is an abbreviation for $t_1 = t'_1 \wedge \ldots \wedge t_n = t'_n$.

If A is a formula and $P(\vec{t})$ is a ground atom, then we write $A[\top/P(\vec{t})]$ (resp. $A[\bot/P(\vec{t})]$) to denote the formula obtained from A by replacing all occurrences of $P(\vec{t})$ by $\top$ (resp. $\bot$).

A *structure* of a first-order language with equality $\mathcal{L}$ is a pair $M = \langle D, m \rangle$, where D is a non-empty *domain* of the structure and m is a function that assigns an n-ary relation on D to each n-ary $(n \geq 0)$ predicate symbol and assigns an n-ary function on D to each n-ary $(n \geq 0)$ function symbol .

Let $M = \langle D, m \rangle$ be a structure of a language $\mathcal{L}$. We write $|M|$ to denote the domain of a structure M. $M|C|$, where C is a predicate or function symbol, stands for $m(C)$.

---

[2] The exception is [4], where belief update is lifted to description logic.

3   Eliminants in First-Order Logic

Our approach is heavily based on a notion of an *eliminant*. This concept has been originally defined for propositional logic in [1] (see also [3]). Here we need its first-order generalization. Our presentation follows [10].

Suppose that we are given a first-order formula A and a ground atom $P(\vec{t})$. Intuitively, an eliminant of $P(\vec{t})$ in A is a formula which entails all sentences entailed by A that are "irrelevant" to $P(\vec{t})$ and says nothing about $P(\vec{t})$.

We write $SEP(A, P(\vec{t}))$ to denote the result of replacing each occurrence of the form $P(\vec{t'})$ in A by

$$[\vec{t} = \vec{t'} \wedge P(\vec{t})] \vee [\vec{t} \neq \vec{t'} \wedge P(\vec{t'})].$$

It is obvious that A and $SEP(A, P(\vec{t}))$ are equivalent. Each first order formula may be rewritten in the above form.

Definition 1. An *eliminant* of a ground atom $P(\vec{t})$ in a first-order formula A, denoted by $\exists P(\vec{t}).A$, is the formula

$$SEP(A, P(\vec{t}))[\top/P(\vec{t})] \vee SEP(A, P(\vec{t}))[\bot/P(\vec{t})].^3$$

∎

Example 2. Let $A = \exists x.\exists y.x \neq y \wedge Green(x) \wedge Green(y)$. We compute the eliminant of $Green(h)$ in A.

$$SEP(A, Green(h)) = \exists x \exists y.x \neq y \wedge [h = x \wedge Green(h) \vee h \neq x \wedge Green(x)]$$
$$\wedge [h = y \wedge Green(h) \vee h \neq y \wedge Green(y)].$$

$$SEP(A, Green(h))[\top/Green(h)] = \exists x \exists y.x \neq y \wedge [h = x \vee h \neq x \wedge Green(x)]$$
$$\wedge [h = y \vee h \neq y \wedge Green(y)].$$

$$SEP(A, Green(h))[\bot/Green(h)] = \exists x \exists y.x \neq y \wedge$$
$$[h \neq x \wedge h \neq y \wedge Green(x) \wedge Green(y)].$$

It is easily seen that

$$SEP(A, Green(h))[\bot/Green(h)] \Rightarrow SEP(A, Green(h))[\top/Green(h)].$$

Thus

$$\exists Green(h).A = \exists x \exists y.x \neq y \wedge [h = x \vee h \neq x \wedge Green(x)] \wedge$$
$$[h = y \vee h \neq y \wedge Green(y).]$$

After simplifying we get

$$\exists y.h \neq y \wedge Green(y).$$

∎

---

[3] In [10] eliminants are called forget operators and an eliminant of $P(\vec{t})$ in A is denoted by $forget(A, P(\vec{t}))$. Our terminology and notation is from [3].

The notion of an eliminant can be generalized as follows. Let A be a first-order formula and let $\overrightarrow{P} = (P_1(\overrightarrow{t_1}), \cdots, P_n(\overrightarrow{t_n}))$ be an n-tuple of ground atoms. An eliminant of $P_1(\overrightarrow{t_1}), \cdots, P_n(\overrightarrow{t_n})$ in A, written $\exists \overrightarrow{P}.A$ is $\exists P_1(\overrightarrow{t_1}) \cdots \exists P_n(\overrightarrow{t_n}).A$.

Lin and Reiter ([10]) provide a semantic characterization of an eliminant in the case when one atom is eliminated. Their result can be generalized as follows.

Let $\mathcal{L}$ be a first-order language with equality and suppose that M_1 and M_2 are two first-order structures of $\mathcal{L}$. We say that M_1 and M_2 are equal except (possibly) of ground atoms $\overrightarrow{P} = (P_1(\overrightarrow{t_1}), \cdots, P_n(\overrightarrow{t_n}))$, written $M_1 \sim_{\overrightarrow{P}} M_2$, iff

1. M_1 and M_2 have the same domain and interpret every function symbol the same.
2. For any predicate symbol Q distinct from $P_1, \ldots, P_n$, $M_1[Q] = M_2[Q]$.
3. Let $\overrightarrow{u_1} = M_1[\overrightarrow{t_1}], \cdots, \overrightarrow{u_n} = M_1[\overrightarrow{t_n}]$. Then for any tuple $\overrightarrow{d_i}$ of the elements in the domain that is distinct from $\overrightarrow{u_i}$, $\overrightarrow{d_i} \in M_1[P_i]$ iff $\overrightarrow{d_i} \in M_2[P_i]$.

The following result holds.

Theorem 3. Let A be a formula and $\overrightarrow{P} = (P_1(\overrightarrow{t_1}), \ldots, P_n(\overrightarrow{t_n}))$ be a tuple of ground atoms. $A' = \exists \overrightarrow{P}.A$ iff for any structure M', M' is a model of A' if there is a model M of A such that $M \sim_{\overrightarrow{P}} M'$.   ∎

4   Defining Knowledge Base Update

We start with some preliminary notions.

By a *boolean combination of ground atoms* we mean a first-order formula constructed using ground atoms and boolean connectives.

Let α be a boolean combination of ground atoms and let $P(\overrightarrow{t})$ be a ground atom occurring in α. We say that $P(\overrightarrow{t})$ is *redundant* in α if a truth-value of α is independent of a truth-value of $P(\overrightarrow{t})$. More precisely, $P(\overrightarrow{t})$ is redundant in α iff $\alpha[\perp/P(\overrightarrow{t})]$ is equivalent to $\alpha[\top/P(\overrightarrow{t})]$.

Example 4. Let $\alpha = (P(a) \wedge P(b)) \vee (P(a) \wedge \neg P(b))$. Since $\alpha[\perp/P(b)] = P(a)$ and $\alpha[\top/P(b)] = P(a)$, the atom $P(b)$ is redundant in α. On the other hand, $\alpha[\perp/P(a)] = \perp$ and $\alpha([\top/P(a)] = \top$. Thus the atom $P(a)$ is not redundant in α.[4]   ∎

We are now ready to define our knowledge base update operator FOMPMA.

Definition 5. Let a knowledge base KB be a closed first order formula and update formula α be a Boolean combination of ground atoms. Denote by $ATM(\alpha)$ the set of all non-redundant atomic formulae appearing in α. Then

$$KB \star \alpha \equiv \exists\, ATM(\alpha).KB \wedge \alpha.$$

     ∎

---

[4] It can be shown that $P(\overrightarrow{t})$ is redundant in α if α can be replaced by an equivalent formula containing no occurrence of $P(\overrightarrow{t})$. In Example 4, α is equivalent to $P(b)$.

The intuition standing behind our knowledge base update is quite simple. First, we select non-redundant atoms in the update formula α. Next, we weaken the considered knowledge base KB by eliminating all these atoms. Finally, we strengthen the knowledge base $\exists\, ATM(\alpha).KB$ by combining it with the update formula.

In view of Theorem 3, we immediately have the following semantic characterization of our update operator.

Theorem 6. Let KB be a knowledge base and α be an update formula. Let $\overrightarrow{P} = (P_1(\overrightarrow{t_1}), \ldots, P_n(\overrightarrow{t_n}))$ be a tuple of all non-redundant ground atoms occurring in α. M' is a model of $KB * \alpha$ iff M' is a model of α such that there exists a model M of KB such that $M \sim_{\overrightarrow{P}} M'$.   ∎

The next theorem shows that FOMPMA preserves consistency.

Theorem 7. Let KB be a consistent knowledge base and let α be a consistent update formula. Then $KB * \alpha$ is consistent.

Proof. Since KB (resp. α) is consistent, there exists a structure M_{KB} (resp. M_α) which is a model of KB (resp. α). Let $\overrightarrow{P} = (P_1(\overrightarrow{t_1}), \ldots, P_n(\overrightarrow{t_n}))$ be a tuple of all non-redundant ground atoms occurring in α. We define a structure M as follows:

(1) $|M| = M_{KB}$.
(2) $M[f] = M_{KB}[f]$, for each function symbol f.
(3) $M[Q] = M_{KB}[Q]$, for any predicate symbol Q distinct from $P_1, \ldots, P_n$.
(4) Let $\overrightarrow{u_1} = M_{KB}[\overrightarrow{t_1}], \cdots, \overrightarrow{u_n} = M_{KB}[\overrightarrow{t_n}]$. For any tuple $\overrightarrow{d_i}$ of the elements in the domain that is distinct from $\overrightarrow{u_i}$, $\overrightarrow{d_i} \in M[P_i]$ iff $\overrightarrow{d_i} \in M_{KB}[P_i]$;
(5) Let $\overrightarrow{u_1}, \cdots, \overrightarrow{u_n}$ be as before and let $\overrightarrow{v_1} = M_\alpha[\overrightarrow{t_1}], \cdots, \overrightarrow{v_n} = M_\alpha[\overrightarrow{t_n}]$. $\overrightarrow{u_i} \in M[P_i]$ iff $\overrightarrow{v_i} \in M_\alpha[P_i]$

It is easily seen that M is well-defined and $M \sim_{\overrightarrow{P}} M_{KB}$. Thus, by Theorem 6, M is a model of $\exists.\overrightarrow{P}.KB$. On the other hand, in view of (5) in the specification of the structure M, M is a model of α. Thus M is a model of $KB * \alpha$, and hence $KB * \alpha$ is consistent.   ∎

5   Examples

In this section we provide a number of examples illustrating our approach.

Example 8. Suppose that there are at least two green objects in the world and the performed action is to paint an object h into red. That is, $KB = \{\exists x.\exists y.x \neq y \wedge Green(x) \wedge Green(y)\}$ and $\alpha = Red(h) \wedge \neg Green(h)$. Since Red does not occur in KB, $\exists Red(h).KB$ is equivalent to KB. Thus, there remains to eliminate $Green(h)$. In view of Example 2

$$\exists Green(h).KB = \exists y.h \neq y \wedge Green(y).$$

Thus

$$KB * \alpha = \exists y.h \neq y \wedge Green(y) \wedge Red(h) \wedge \neg Green(h).$$

This agrees with our intuition.   ∎

Example 9. Suppose that all objects in the world under consideration are blue and suppose that the performed action is to paint an object h into yellow. That is, $KB = \{\forall x.Blue(x)\}$ and $\alpha = Yellow(h) \wedge \neg Blue(h)$. Since $Yellow$ does not occur in KB, $\exists Yellow(h).KB$ is equivalent to KB. Thus, we have to eliminate $Blue(h)$ in KB.

$$SEP(KB, Blue(h)) = \forall x.(h = x \wedge Blue(h) \vee h \neq x \wedge Blue(x)).$$

$$SEP(KB, Blue(h))[\top/Blue(h)] = \forall x.(h = x \vee h \neq x \wedge Blue(x)) \qquad (1)$$

$$SEP(KB, Blue(h))[\bot/Blue(h)] = \forall x.(h \neq x \wedge Blue(x)). \qquad (2)$$

Since (2) implies (1),

$$SEP(KB, Blue(h))[\top/Blue(h)] \vee SEP(KB, Blue(h))[\bot/Blue(h)] =$$
$$\forall x.(h = x \vee h \neq (x) \wedge Blue(x))$$

what is equivalent to

$$\forall x.x \neq h \Rightarrow Blue(x).$$

Thus $KB * \alpha = \forall x.x \neq h \Rightarrow Blue(x) \wedge Yellow(h) \wedge \neg Blue(h)$. This result agrees with our intuition.   ∎

Example 10. Suppose that there are at least two distinct objects: one is red and the other is green. The performed action is to paint an object h into yellow. That is, $KB = \{\exists x.\exists y.x \neq y \wedge Red(x) \wedge Green(y)\}$ and $\alpha = Yellow(h) \wedge \neg Red(h) \wedge \neg Green(h)$. Now we need to eliminate $Red(h)$ and $Green(h)$. First, we eliminate $Red(h)$ in KB.[5]

$$SEP(KB, Red(h)) = \exists x \exists y.x \neq y \wedge$$
$$[h = x \wedge Red(h) \vee h \neq x \wedge Red(x)] \wedge Green(y).$$

$$SEP(KB, Red(h))[\top/Red(h)] = \exists x \exists y.x \neq y \wedge Green(y) \wedge$$
$$[h = x \vee h \neq x \wedge Red(x)]. \qquad (3)$$

$$SEP(KB, Red(h))[\bot/Red(h)] = \exists x \exists y.x \neq y \wedge Green(y) \wedge$$
$$[h \neq x \wedge Red(x)]. \qquad (4)$$

Since (4)⇒(3),

$$SEP(KB, Red(h))[\top/Red(h)] \vee SEP(KB, Red(h))[\bot/Red(h)] =$$
$$\exists x \exists y.x \neq y \wedge Green(y) \wedge [h = x \vee h \neq x \wedge Red(x).]$$

---

[5] If a number of ground atoms are to be eliminated in a formula, the order in which they are eliminated is irrelevant.

After simplifying we get

$$\exists x \exists y.x \neq y \wedge Green(y) \wedge [h = x \vee Red(x)]. \tag{5}$$

We now eliminate $Green(h)$ in (5).

$$SEP((5), Green(h)) = \exists x \exists y.x \neq y \wedge [h = x \vee Red(x)] \wedge$$
$$[y = h \wedge Green(h) \vee y \neq h \wedge Green(y)].$$

$$SEP((5), Green(h))[\top/Green(h)] = \exists x \exists y.x \neq y \wedge$$
$$[h = x \vee Red(x)] \wedge$$
$$[y = h \vee y \neq h \wedge Green(y)]. \tag{6}$$
$$SEP((5), Green(h))[\bot/Green(h)] = \exists x \exists y.x \neq y \wedge$$
$$[h = x \vee Red(x)] \wedge$$
$$y \neq h \wedge Green(y)]. \tag{7}$$

Since (7)$\Rightarrow$ (6),

$$SEP((5), Green(h))[\top/Green(h)] \vee SEP((5), Green(h))[\bot/Green(h)]$$

is equivalent to (6), and after simplifying we get

$$\exists x \exists y.x \neq y \wedge [h = x \vee Red(x)] \wedge [y = h \vee Green(y)].$$

Thus $KB * \alpha = \exists x \exists y.x \neq y \wedge [h = x \vee Red(x)] \wedge [y = h \vee Green(y)] \wedge Yellow(h) \wedge \neg Red(h) \wedge \neg Green(h).$ ∎

Example 11. Suppose that there are only two colours, namely red and green, in the world under consideration and assume that all objects are painted red. The performed action is to paint an object h. Formally, we have $KB \equiv \forall x.Red(x)$, and update formula $\alpha \equiv Red(h) \vee Green(h)$ (since we have two colours). Since $Green$ does not occur in KB, we need eliminate only $Red(h)$.

$$SEP(KB, Red(h)) = \forall x.(x = h \wedge Red(h) \vee (x \neq h \wedge Red(x))$$
$$\exists Red(h).KB = \forall x.((x \neq h) \Rightarrow Red(x)) \tag{8}$$

Thus

$$KB * \alpha = \forall x.((x \neq h) \Rightarrow Red(x)) \wedge (Red(h) \vee Green(h))$$
$$= \forall x.Red(x) \vee \forall x.((x \neq h) \Rightarrow Red(x)) \wedge Green(h) \tag{9}$$

∎

6   Properties of Update Operator

Katsuno and Mendelzon [9] formulated theoretical properties which should be satisfied by each update operator. They presented them in the form of eight postulates. In this section, we analyse the FOMPMA in the context of these postulates. Katsuno and Mendelzon's postulates are the following.

(1) $KB \star \alpha$ implies α.

(2) If KB implies α, then $KB \star \alpha$ is equivalent to KB.

(3) If both KB and α are satisfiable, then $KB \star \alpha$ is also satisfiable.

(4) If $KB_1 \equiv KB_2$ and $\alpha_1 \equiv \alpha_2$, then $KB_1 \star \alpha_1 \equiv KB_2 \star \alpha_2$.

(5) $(KB \star \alpha_1) \wedge \alpha_2$ implies $KB \star (\alpha_1 \wedge \alpha_2)$.

(6) If $KB \star \alpha_1$ implies α_2 and $KB \star \alpha_2$ implies α_1, then $KB \star \alpha_1 \equiv KB \star \alpha_2$.

(7) If KB is complete, $i.e.$ has at most one model, then $(KB \star \alpha_1) \wedge (KB \star \alpha_2)$ implies $KB \star (\alpha_1 \vee \alpha_2)$.

(8) $(KB_1 \vee KB_2) \star \alpha \equiv (KB_1 \star \alpha) \vee (KB_2 \star \alpha)$.

As remarked earlier, FOMPMA is a first-order generalization of MPMA ([5]). Thus, as expected, properties of the FOMPMA operator are similar to those of the MPMA operator.

It is obvious that FOMPMA satisfies postulates (1), (3), (4) and (8).

It is easily seen (Example 11) that postulate (2) does not generally hold. This is also the case as regards postulates (5),(6) and (7). To see that (5) does not generally hold take $KB = \neg On(m) \wedge On(b)$ (here On, m and b stand for "lies on a table", "magazine" and "book", respectively), $\alpha_1 = \neg On(b) \vee On(m)$ and $\alpha_2 = On(b) \vee On(m)$. It is easy to calculate that

$$(KB \star \alpha_1) \wedge \alpha_2 \equiv On(m)$$
$$KB \star (\alpha_1 \wedge \alpha_2) \equiv On(b) \wedge On(m).$$

Thus

$$(KB \star \alpha_1) \wedge \alpha_2 \Rightarrow KB \star (\alpha_1 \wedge \alpha_2)$$

does not hold.

As a counterexample for (6) take KB as before, $\alpha_1 = On(b) \vee On(m)$ and $\alpha_2 = \top$.

$$KB \star \alpha_1 = On(b) \vee On(m) \text{ implies } \alpha_2$$
$$KB \star \alpha_2 = \neg On(m) \wedge On(b) \text{ implies } \alpha_1$$

but they are not equivalent.

To see that (7) need not to hold, take $KB = On(m) \wedge On(b) \wedge On(n)$, where n stands for a "newspaper", $\alpha_1 = On(b) \wedge On(m) \vee On(n)$ and $\alpha_2 = On(b) \wedge \neg On(m) \vee On(n)$. It is easily seen that

$$(KB \star \alpha_1) \wedge (KB \star \alpha_2) = n$$
$$KB \star (\alpha_1 \vee \alpha_2) = (On(b) \vee On(n)) \wedge On(m)$$

and the required implication does not hold.

As in MPMA, the analogical weaker forms of the postulates (5), (6) and (7) hold for FOMPMA.

Theorem 12 (postulate 5). If $ATM(\alpha_1) \subseteq ATM(\alpha_1 \wedge \alpha_2)$, then $(KB \star \alpha_1) \wedge \alpha_2$ implies $KB \star (\alpha_1 \wedge \alpha_2)$.

Proof. Denote $ATM(\alpha_1)$ and $ATM(\alpha_1 \wedge \alpha_2)$ by P and Q, respectively. $(KB \star \alpha_1) \wedge \alpha_2 = \alpha_1 \wedge \exists P.KB \wedge \alpha_2$ which implies (because $P \subseteq Q$) $\alpha_1 \wedge \exists Q.KB \wedge \alpha_2$. Thus the last formula is just $KB \star (\alpha_1 \wedge \alpha_2)$. ∎

Theorem 13 (postulate 6). Let $ATM(\alpha_1) = ATM(\alpha_2)$. If $KB \star \alpha_1$ implies α_2 and $KB \star \alpha_2$ implies α_1, then $KB \star \alpha_1 \equiv KB \star \alpha_2$.

Proof. Denote $ATM(\alpha_1)$ and $ATM(\alpha_2)$ by P. Since $KB \star \alpha_1$ implies α_2 and $KB \star \alpha_2$ implies α_1, we infer that the formulae $\alpha_1 \wedge \exists P.KB \Rightarrow \alpha_2$ and $\alpha_2 \wedge \exists P.KB \Rightarrow \alpha_1$ are tautologies. Hence $\alpha_1 \wedge \exists P.KB \Leftrightarrow \alpha_2 \wedge \exists P.KB$ is also a tautology, what proves the theorem. ∎

Theorem 14 (postulate 7). If $ATM(\alpha_1) \subseteq ATM(\alpha_1 \vee \alpha_2)$ and $ATM(\alpha_2) \subseteq ATM(\alpha_1 \vee \alpha_2)$, then $(KB \star \alpha_1) \wedge (KB \star \alpha_2)$ implies $KB \star (\alpha_1 \vee \alpha_2)$.[6]

Proof. Denote $ATM(\alpha_1)$, $ATM(\alpha_2)$ and $ATM(\alpha_1 \vee \alpha_2)$ by P, Q and R, respectively. $(KB\star\alpha_1) \equiv \alpha_1 \wedge \exists P.KB$, $(KB\star\alpha_2) \equiv \alpha_2 \wedge \exists Q.KB$ and $KB \star (\alpha_1 \vee \alpha_2) \equiv (\alpha_1 \vee \alpha_2) \wedge \exists R.KB$. Since $P \subseteq R$ and α_1 implies $\alpha_1 \vee \alpha_2$, $\alpha_1 \wedge \exists P.KB$ implies $(\alpha_1 \vee \alpha_2) \wedge \exists R.KB$ and so, $KB \star \alpha_1$ implies $KB \star (\alpha_1 \vee \alpha_2)$. Similarly, we show that $KB \star \alpha_2$ implies $KB \star (\alpha_1 \vee \alpha_2)$. Hence $(KB \star \alpha_1) \wedge (KB \star \alpha_2)$ implies $KB \star (\alpha_1 \vee \alpha_2)$. ∎

7   Conclusion and Future Work

In this paper, we introduced a new update operator. In contrast to the existing update operators, which are based on propositional or descriptive logics, our proposal admits knowledge bases stated in full first-order logic. In consequence, we can deal with scenarios which cannot be properly represented using the existing update operators.

There are two topics that we left for further research. Firstly, we would like to extend our approach by admitting integrity constraints. Secondly, we would like to compare FOMPMA with reasoning about action paradigms.

References

1. Boole, G.: An Investigation of the Laws of Thought. London, Walton (1894), Reprinted by Dover Books, New York (1954)
2. Brewka, G., Hertzberg, J.: How to Do Things with Worlds: on Formalizing Actions and Plans. Journal of Logic and Computation 3(5), 517–532 (1993)
3. Brown, F.M.: Boolean Reasoning. Kluwer Academic Publishers, Dordrecht (1990)
4. Liu, H., Lutz, C., Milicic, M., Wolter, F.: Updating Description Logic Aboxes. In: Proceedings of the 10th International Conference on Principles of Knowledge Representation and Reasoning, KR-2006, pp. 46–56 (2006)
5. Doherty, P., Łukaszewicz, W., Madalińska-Bugaj, E.: The PMA and Relativizing Minimal Change for Action Update. In: Proceedings of the 6th International Conference on Principles of Knowledge Representation and Reasoning, KR–1998, pp. 158–169 (1998)
6. Doherty, P., Łukaszewicz, W., Madalińska-Bugaj, E.: The PMA and Relativizing Minimal Change for Action Update. Fundamenta Informaticae 44(1-2), 95–131 (2000)

---

[6] The assumption that KB is complete is not necessary here.

7. Hertzig, A.: The PMA Revisited. In: Proceedings of the 5th International Conference on Principles of Knowledge Representation and Reasoning, KR 1996, pp. 40–50. Morgan Kaufmann Publishers, Inc., San Francisco (1996)
8. Herzig, A., Rifi, O.: Propositional Belief Base Update and Minimal Change. Artificial Intelligence Journal 115(1), 107–138 (1999)
9. Katsuno, H., Mendelzon, A.O.: On the Difference between Updating a knowledge base and revising it. In: Proceedings of the 2nd International Conference on Principles of Knowledge Representation and Reasoning KR 1991, pp. 387–395. Morgan Kaufmann Publishers Inc., San Francisco (1991)
10. Lin, F., Reiter, R.: Forget It! In: AAAI Fall Symposium on Relevance, New Orleans (November 1994), Electronic version `http://www.cs.ust.hk/~flin/papers.html`
11. Winslett, M.: Reasoning about Action Using a Possible Model Approach. In: Proceedings AAAI 1988, St. Paul, MN, pp. 89–93 (1988)
12. Winslett, M.: Updating Logical Databases. Cambridge Tracks in Theoretical Computer Science. Cambridge University Press, Cambridge (1990)
13. Winslett, M.: Updating Logical Databases. In: Gabbay, D., Galton, A., Robinson, J.A. (eds.) Handbook of Logic in Artificial Intelligence and Logic Programming. Epistemic and Temporal Reasoning, vol. 4, pp. 133–174. Oxford University Press, Oxford (1995)

Shared Context for Knowledge Distribution:
A Case Study of Collaborative Taggings

Jason J. Jung

Department of Computer Engineering
Yeungnam University
Dae-Dong, Gyeongsan, Korea 712-749
j2jung@intelligent.pe.kr

Abstract. Many existing knowledge management systems have been employing blogging services which is capable of providing various services to people. However, content delivering service among bloggers is not taking into account context (or semantics) of the contents, so that the service can spread irrelevant information into blogs. In order to solve this problem, this study proposes a blog context overlay network architecture for context matching between blogs. It is referred to as detecting "shared" context Thus, we can identify a community of practice (CoP) on blogosphere, with respect to contexts. As a result, newly generated knowledge can be proactively diffused to the blogs of which context is relevant to the knowledge, before the bloggers' queries are asked.

Keywords: Community of practice, context-based computing, knowledge sharing, shared context.

1 Introduction

Most of knowledge management systems (KMS) have serious problems to support efficient interactions between people. To deal with the problems, information systems have been recently trying to employ the emerging Web 2.0 platforms, e.g., blogs and wikis. We need to note that such platforms are providing two important services in common; i) participation and ii) sharing. In the context of blog-based KMS, we can address them, as follows.

Knowledge Publication. People can post their own experiences and know-hows obtained during conducting their jobs and tasks. More importantly, the knowledge can be tagged with some keywords. These tags can be regarded as a user-specified categorization system containing their knowledge and context. All tags are visualized as the so-called *tag cloud*, for better understanding.
Social Communications. People can declare their social relations (e.g., friends, family, colleagues, and so on), which are represented as blogrolls. These are playing an important role of channel for information flowing on blogosphere. Not only this social network establishment but also social interactions can be made among people. Mainly, the interactions are happened by comments. (In fact, more advanced comments are trackback.)

N.T. Nguyen et al. (Eds.): IEA/AIE 2008, LNAI 5027, pp. 641–648, 2008.

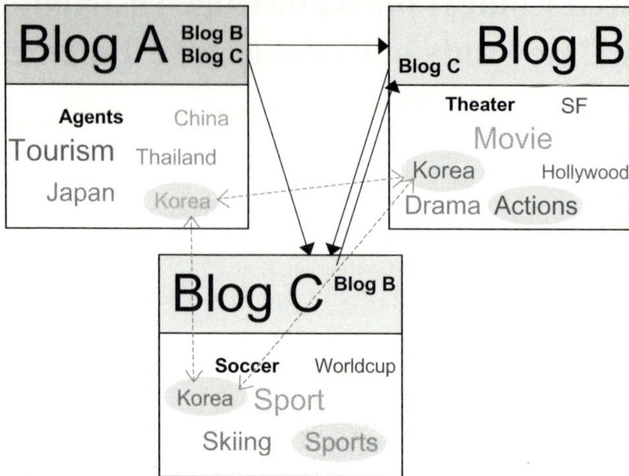

Fig. 1. Basic functionalities of blogs. It shows three main components of blogs, which are re-sources, blogrolls, and tags (tag clouds). The solid arrows are indicating blogrolls among blogs. More interestingly, the dotted ones are resulted from string matching between tags in different blogs.

In addition, blogs are providing a variety of syndication services, e.g., RSS (RDF Site Summary[1]). It is represented as a family of web feed formats used to publish fre-quently updated content such as blog entries and news headlines. This is similar to the subscription of mailing lists. Hence, bloggers do not have to access to every blogs by periods, in order to find out new updates.

This automatic synchronization has to employ a certain estimation process to find out thematic relatedness between bloggers for better performance. For example, it can utilize not only blogrolls but also tag matching. They are depicted solid arrows ($A \rightarrow B, A \rightarrow C, C \rightarrow B, B \rightarrow C$) and dotted arrows ($\langle A : Korea, B : Korea, C : Korea, Equivalence\rangle$) in Fig. 1, respectively.

However, the problem is that the RSS-based services are spreading information to people, without considering contexts. In other words, this problem can be divided two sub-problems, as follows.

- Contextually irrelevant information may be reached to people. It is very similar to the *spam* mails. It means that in Fig. 1, resources in blog A are not guaranteed to be relevant to the blog B or C, even if there have equivalent tags $Korea$ in common.
- It is difficult for people to receive contextually relevant information by finding out the contextually equivalent tags among blogs. In Fig. 1, two tags *Actions* in blog B and *Sports* in blog C may be matched with $Equivalence$ relation.

In order to solve these problems, we propose a novel architecture, called *blog context overlay network* (BCON) [1,2], to control information propagation through RSS channels on blogosphere. Thereby, we want to focus on a set of tags representing the

---

[1] http://web.resource.org/rss/1.0/

corresponding blogs' contexts, and present context matching algorithm for analyzing contextual relatedness between both blogs. The most important aim of this algorithm is to uncover the hidden relationships between people whose contexts are most similar, even though they have been directly known with each other yet. Moreover, we want to organize a set of cohesive blog group (i.e., the contextually similar people), and refer to this blog set as a blog community of practice (BCoP).

In the following Sect. 2, we will show mathematical formalization of blogs, and describe how to match the blogs' contexts. Sect. 3 explain query-free knowledge distribution on the proposed BCON platform. In Sect. 4, we show the experimental results obtained from evaluation process. Finally, in Sect. 5, we will draw a conclusion of this study.

2 Blog Context Overlay Network

Above all, we assume that our proposed BCON architecture in a blogosphere should be composed of a set of authorized blogs. In this section, we define a blog as a set of tuples. Context matching scheme is introduced to measure the similarity between blogs.

2.1 Mathematical Definition

First of all, a blog B_k is formulated as

$$B_k = \{P_{B_k}, T_{B_k}, R_{B_k}^{Tag}, R_{B_k}^{Blogroll}, R_{B_k}^{Comment}\} \tag{1}$$

where

- P_{B_k} is a set of posted resources (e.g., resources are including simple texts as well as images, movies, and so on),
- T_{B_k} is a set of tags represented by user-generated keywords,
- $R_{B_k}^{Tag} \subseteq P_{B_k} \times T_{B_k}$ is a set of linkages between tags and resources,
- $R_{B_k}^{Blogroll} \subseteq B_k \times B_{k'}$ means an explicit social network among bloggers, and
- $R_{B_k}^{Comment} \subseteq B_k \times B_{k'} \times spd$ indicates social interactions of which type is *comment*.

In practice, within a blogosphere, $R^{Blogroll}$ and $R^{Comment}$ are represented as asymmetric matrices. In case of the social interactions $R_{B_k}^{Comment}$, we want to record shortest path distance $spd(k, k')$ between both bloggers, by computing matrix multiplication [3]. If there are no path between B_k and $B_{k'}$, $spd(k, k') = M + 1$ where M is the number of blogs in a blogosphere. Of course, this formalization is rather simplified in this paper. But, important point is that these five components can cover main characteristics and features of other supplementary blog services. Overall, the generic blogosphere can be modeled as a three-layered architecture. Fig. 2 is simply depicting a blog context overlay network for context matching on blogosphere, which is composed of three layers; i) blog layer, i) tag layer, and i) context layer.

2.2 Context Matching

In this architecture, context matching process for social relation discovery is conducted by the following two phases;

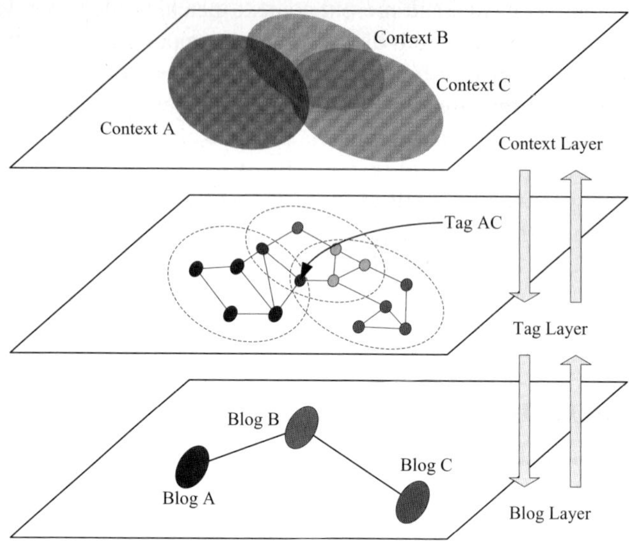

Fig. 2. A three-layered architecture for context matching on blogosphere

1. Bottom-up phase from blog layer to context layer, and
2. Top-down phase from context layer to blog layer

Even though we can build various social networks by using blogrolls as well as co-occurrence patterns (e.g., resources and tags), we want to find out contextual relationships among blogs. In order to compare contexts of two blogs, it is too difficult to directly analyze contents (e.g., posts) themselves in the blogs. Thereby, in this paper, we assume that context of a blog is implicitly represented as a set of corresponding tags. As a simple example, some posts about 'Scientific Fiction' in blogs are tagged with 'sf' in common.

For example, a tag sf in blog B_i, meaning 'Scientific Fiction', is contextually different from a tag sf in blog B_j, meaning 'San Francisco'. It means that context matching between blogs B_i and B_j can be replaced to between the corresponding tags $R_{B_i}^{Tag}$ and $R_{B_j}^{Tag}$. Hence, given a pair of blogs, we have to discover the best alignment condition between two tag sets, as finding out which two tag elements from both blogs are either contextually equivalent, opposite, or similar.

Let two blogs B_i and B_j matched with each other. We have to find out the best matching between two sets of tags, as maximizing summation of contextual similarities between tags. The matching mechanism is given by

$$Sim_C(B_i, B_j) = \max_{\langle t,t' \rangle \in Pairing(T_{B_i}, T_{B_j})} \sum_{t \in T_{B_i}, t' \in T_{B_j}} Sim_C(t, t') \qquad (2)$$

where $Sim_C \in [0, 1]$. Mainly, the following three types of features are applied to compute the contextual similarities.

- Background knowledge (i.e., ontologies for lexical semantics and directories for topics) $\mathcal{O}$. Meaning of each tag can be retrieved. This is only useful for simple semantics for dealing with synonyms and hypernyms. A variety of senses defined in ontologies (e.g., WordNet) can be applied to compare the tag contexts [4,5]. We can make a tag t_i relaxed with semantics given from ontologies.

$$\mathcal{O}(t_i) = \{\widetilde{t_i}|Synonym(t_i), Antonym(t_i), Hypernym(t_i), \ldots\} \tag{3}$$

Thus, context matching between two tags t_i and t_j can be approximated to matching between $\mathcal{O}(t_i)$ and $\mathcal{O}(t_j)$.

- Tag cohesiveness $COH_{\mathcal{T}}$. A set of tags in a certain blog might be represented in a same way. We refer to this cohesiveness as a *person* context. For example, if a person is interested in topic "Movie," then his context of tag sf is probably related to 'Scientific Fiction'. Thus, given a certain blog context overlay network, two-mode network can be constructed i) between tag layer and context layer, and ii) between tag layer and blog layer. Assume that a resource $p_i \in P_{B_k}$ is annotated with tag set $t_\alpha = \{t_\alpha, t_\beta, \ldots\}$, which can be easily acquired from i-th column of $R_{B_k}^{Tag}$. Similar to corresponding analysis [6,7] and association rule mining, we have to statistically find out which tags are contextually more cohesive than others by the following equation

$$COH_{\mathcal{T}}(B_i) = \Delta_{\widetilde{t_i} \in \mathcal{O}(t_i), \widetilde{t_j} \in \mathcal{O}(t_j)}(\widetilde{t_i}, \widetilde{t_j}). \tag{4}$$

- Social affinity $\mathcal{SA}$. Several sets of tags located within a social distance (e.g., blogrolls) might be represented in a similar way. We refer to this social affinity pattern as a *community consensual* context.

As a result of context matching between blogs, we can obtain a set of tag correspondences

$$\widetilde{\mathcal{M}}(B_i, B_j) = \{\langle t, t', o\rangle | t \in R_{B_i}^{Tag}, t' \in R_{B_j}^{Tag}, o \in \mathcal{O}\} \tag{5}$$

where a correspondence is attached with a semantic relation o which is derived from a WordNet ontology $\mathcal{O}$. (For simplicity, $\mathcal{O} = \{\equiv, \sqsubseteq, \sqsupseteq\}$, meaning semantic equivalence and subsumption.) Eventually, we can enhance $\widetilde{\mathcal{M}}$ with social affinity (e.g., blogrolls) as

$$\mathcal{M}(B_i, B_j) \longleftarrow \widetilde{\mathcal{M}}(B_i, B_j) \times \frac{1}{\log \rho_{ij}} \tag{6}$$

where ρ_{ij} is the social geodesic distance.

3   Knowledge Distribution over Blog Context Overlay Network

As next step of the BCON framework, we want to identify a community in which members are more cohesive than others by using contextual similarities among blogs. Particularly, we are considering dynamic identification [8], because the context might be changable over time. Knowledge which is newly published on blogosphere is automatically distributed to the members in a same community.

3.1 Dynamic "Community of Practice" Identification

Subsequently, we can build an weighted social network of which links and weights are contextual relations and similarity between blogs, respectively. Formation of CoPs can be built by applying Q-modular function to the contextual social network. The modularity function $Q^\diamond$ is formulated by

$$Q^\diamond(\mathcal{S}) = \sum_{i=1}^{k} \frac{\sum_{B_a \in g_i, B_b \in g_i, ADJ_{(ab)}=1} Sim_{\mathcal{C}}(B_a, B_b)}{|g_i|} \tag{7}$$

where all possible pairs of bloggers should be considered.

3.2 Knowledge Distribution on Tag Correspondences

In this work, two ways of knowledge distribution schemes have been proposed, as follows.

- Systematic broadcasting of new resource to all members in a same community, and
- Selective propagation along to tag correspondences

Once a resource has newly published and tagged with t in B_a, the resource can be automatically pushed into $\langle t, t', o \rangle_{t \in B_a, t' \in B_b}$ in B_b. More importantly, the resource can be translated by tag replacement strategy.

4 Experimental Results and Discussion

In order to evaluate performance of the proposed blogosphere, we have implemented collaborative tagging system applying for context matching process. We are exploiting WordPress blog open platform[2] and Blojsom platform[3]. We have invited 16 graduated students (U_1 to U_{16}), and asked them to manage their contents on their own blogs.

As shown in Table 1, we measured the contextual similarity ($Sim_{\mathcal{C}}$) between all possible pairs of bloggers. Hence, by using community identification equation Equ. 7 ($k = 3$), we have organized three communities with highly cohesive blogs, as follows.

- Community$_1$: U_1, U_8, U_{10}, U_{12}, U_{14} (i.e., $Q^\diamond(Community_1) = 0.792$)
- Community$_2$: U_2, U_3, U_6, U_7, U_{15}, U_{16} (i.e., $Q^\diamond(Community_2) = 0.817$)
- Community$_3$: U_4, U_5, U_9, U_{11}, U_{13} (i.e., $Q^\diamond(Community_3) = 0.792$)

We found out that the proposed community identification method is working very well, because the modularity value is relatively high. In particularly, although Community$_2$ have more members, the cohesiveness is higher than other communities.

As second experimentation, we have conducted human evaluation for RSS-based information recommendation. During 10 days, we kept tracking of bloggers' rating patterns, as shown Fig. 3. The precision (i.e., user satisfaction) of context-based RSS feeds in three communities has been increased over time in common. This is caused by the dynamic community identification process. The bloggers were able to be automatically involved into more relevant communities.

---

[2] WordPress. http://wordpress.org/
[3] Blojsom. http://wiki.blojsom.com/wiki/display/blojsom3/About+blojsom

Table 1. Contextual similarity for community identification

	U_1	U_2	U_3	U_4	U_5	U_6	U_7	U_8	U_9	U_{10}	U_{11}	U_{12}	U_{13}	U_{14}	U_{15}	U_{16}
U_1	-															
U_2	0.24	-														
U_3	0.32	**0.68**	-													
U_4	0.29	0.3	0.45	-												
U_5	0.42	0.25	0.24	**0.83**	-											
U_6	0.26	**0.74**	**0.78**	0.48	0.37	-										
U_7	0.18	**0.76**	**0.92**	0.26	0.45	**0.83**	-									
U_8	**0.86**	0.52	0.33	0.34	0.28	0.22	0.2	-								
U_9	0.41	0.42	0.21	**0.74**	**0.82**	0.35	0.52	0.44	-							
U_{10}	**0.82**	0.18	0.51	0.51	0.3	0.29	0.42	**0.85**	0.57	-						
U_{11}	0.29	0.23	0.52	**0.64**	**0.75**	0.49	0.18	0.56	**0.86**	0.1	-					
U_{12}	**0.91**	0.46	0.43	0.3	0.14	0.58	0.45	**0.72**	0.22	**0.72**	0.26	-				
U_{13}	0.27	0.37	0.18	**0.75**	**0.93**	0.37	0.37	0.3	**0.78**	0.05	**0.82**	0.4	-			
U_{14}	**0.68**	0.34	0.35	0.15	0.43	0.3	0.52	**0.68**	0.25	**0.85**	0.3	**0.83**	0.53	-		
U_{15}	0.35	**0.67**	**0.83**	0.39	0.5	**0.95**	**0.98**	0.28	0.36	0.52	0.25	0.43	0.3	0.44	-	
U_{16}	0.27	**0.84**	**0.73**	0.42	0.18	**0.84**	**0.88**	0.33	0.28	0.42	0.38	0.13	0.45	0.28	**0.82**	-

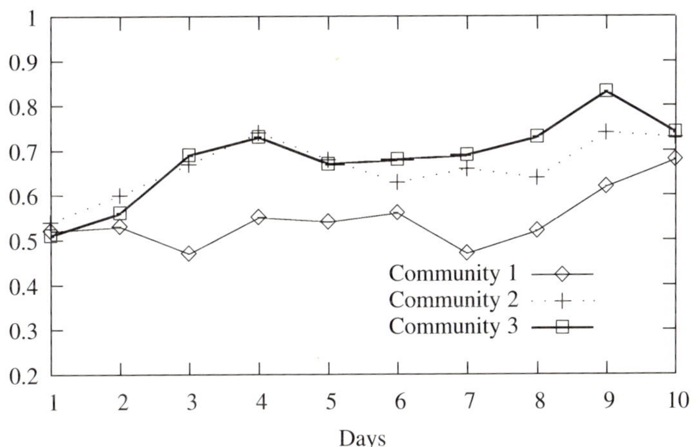

Fig. 3. Measuring user satisfaction with RSS feeds via BCON

5 Concluding Remarks and Future Work

As a conclusion, we have claimed a new measurement for contextual similarity between blogs. Similar to [9], we may consider only the concepts applied to the specific knowledge. As mentioned in [8], dynamic CoP identification is NP-hard and APX-hard problem. We might have to evaluate our heuristics computing the similarity. Furthermore, this similarity can be extended to contextual centrality, which means the potential power of bridging among blogs on social network.

As future work of semantic centrality, we have three main plans to investigate the followings issues *i*) *semantic subgroup discovery*, to organize the sophisticated user groups with enhancing Equ. 7, *ii*) *query propagation*, to determine the ordering (or route) of potential peers to which the queries will be sent, and *iii*) *semantic synchronization*, to maximize the efficiency interoperability by information diffusion. Furthermore, we have to consider to enhance the semantic centrality measurement $C^\diamond$ by combining with *i*) authoritative and hub centrality measurement, proposed in [10], and *ii*) the modified shortest paths $spd(n,t) = \frac{1}{C^\diamond(n)+C^\diamond(t)}$. Finally, based on [11], we have plan to visualize the semantic dynamics on the social network.

References

1. Jung, J.J., Euzenat, J.: Towards semantic social networks. In: Franconi, E., Kifer, M., May, W. (eds.) ESWC 2007. LNCS, vol. 4519, pp. 267–280. Springer, Heidelberg (2007)
2. Jung, J.J., Koo, C.M.: Contextual matching-based blog overlay network for information sharing on blogoshphere. Telecommunication Review 17(4), 651–659 (2007)
3. Wasserman, S., Faust, K.: Social Network Analysis. Cambridge University Press, Cambridge (1994)
4. Chan, Y.S., Ng, H.T.: Word sense disambiguation with distribution estimation. In: Kaelbling, L.P., Saffiotti, A. (eds.) Proceedings of the Nineteenth International Joint Conference on Artificial Intelligence (IJCAI 2005), Edinburgh, Scotland, UK, July 30-August 5, Professional Book Center, pp. 1010–1015 (2005)
5. Curtis, J., Cabral, J., Baxter, D.: On the application of the Cyc ontology to word sense disambiguation. In: Sutcliffe, G., Goebel, R. (eds.) Proceedings of the Nineteenth International Florida Artificial Intelligence Research Society Conference, Melbourne Beach, Florida, USA, May 11-13, 2006, pp. 652–657. AAAI Press, Menlo Park (2006)
6. Borgatti, S.P., Everett, M.G.: Network analysis of 2-mode data. Social Networks 19(3), 243–269 (1997)
7. Roberts, J.M.: Correspondence analysis of two-mode network data. Social Networks 22(1), 65–72 (2000)
8. Tantipathananandh, C., Berger-Wolf, T., Kempe, D.: A framework for community identification in dynamic social networks. In: Proceedings of the 13th ACM SIGKDD International Conference on Knowledge Discovery and Data mining (KDD 2007), pp. 717–726 (2007)
9. Mika, P.: Ontologies are us: A unified model of social networks and semantics. In: Gil, Y., Motta, E., Benjamins, V.R., Musen, M.A. (eds.) ISWC 2005. LNCS, vol. 3729, pp. 522–536. Springer, Heidelberg (2005)
10. Kleinberg, J.M.: Authoritative sources in a hyperlinked environment. Journal of the ACM 46(5), 604–632 (1999)
11. Jung, J.J.: Collaborative web browsing based on semantic extraction of user interests with bookmarks. Journal of Universal Computer Science 11(2), 213–228 (2005)

Modelling and Automated Analysis of Organisations from the Air Traffic Management Domain

Alexei Sharpanskykh

Vrije Universiteit Amsterdam, Department of Artificial Intelligence,
De Boelelaan 1081a, 1081 HV Amsterdam, The Netherlands
sharp@few.vu.nl

Abstract. A modern Air Traffic Organisation (ATO) represents a complex organisation that involves many parties with diverse goals performing for a wide range of tasks. Due to the structural and behavioural complexity of ATOs, mistakes and performance problems are not rare in such organisations. Some of these faults may seriously affect safety, causing incidents. Therefore, the possibility to perform detailed and reliable analysis is of primary importance for ATOs. To this end, the paper introduces an automated approach for modelling and analysis of complex ATOs. The developed model incorporates all important structural and behavioural aspects of an ATO.

1 Introduction

An Air Traffic Organisation (ATO) ensures a safe and efficient flow of aircraft both at airports and in the air. An ATO represents a complex organisation that involves many parties with diverse goals performing a wide range of tasks. Among the ATO's participants are airports, air navigation service providers (ANSP), airlines, regulators, and the government. Due to the high complexity, inconsistencies and performance bottlenecks often occur in ATOs. Some of these faults may result into performance issues, whereas others can seriously affect safety, causing incidents. Therefore, the possibility to perform detailed and reliable automated analysis aiming at detecting safety hazards in ATOs is of primary importance in the air traffic domain. Currently, formal risk assessment approaches [3] are based predominantly on fault/event trees used for sequential cause-effect reasoning for accident causation. However, such trees do not encounter for complex, non-linear dependencies and dynamics inherent in ATOs. Advantages of agent-based organisation modelling that allows investigating complex emergent dynamics of a system are increasingly recognized in the domain. In particular, agent-based modeling has been proposed as a means to assess safety risk of complex emergent dynamics of air traffic operations [7, 8]. These studies focus on the risk of air traffic operations and use a plain society of agents, without considering the organizational layer. Several approaches [4, 5] consider an influence of different organisational aspects on safety, however, without providing precise details. This paper presents the first attempt to create a formal agent-based organisational model of

N.T. Nguyen et al. (Eds.): IEA/AIE 2008, LNAI 5027, pp. 649–658, 2008.

an ATO using the developed previously organisation modelling and analysis framework [6] and the methodology from [9]. On the one hand, the framework allows specifying the prescriptive structural and behavioural dependencies of an organisation. On the other hand, it provides means to describe autonomous behaviour of the organisational actors. In contrast to many existing enterprise modelling approaches this framework has a formal basis, which enables reliable analysis of models. More specifically, to express structural relations, sorted predicate logic-based languages are used, whereas the Temporal Trace Language (TTL) [2] is used for specifying dynamic aspects of organisations. To decrease the complexity of modelling the framework distinguishes four interrelated views: the *performance-oriented view* describes organisational goal structures, performance indicators structures, and relations between them; the *process-oriented view* describes organisational functions, processes, resources and relations between them; the *organisation-oriented view* describes organisational roles, their authority, responsibility and interraction relations; the *agent-oriented view* describes agents' types with their capabilities, and principles of allocating agents to roles.

The framework proposes a number of analysis techniques, the application of some of which is demonstrated in this paper. Specifically, the constructed specification of the ATO is verified for correctness by applying the general and specific for particular views consistency verification techniques from [2, 6]. Further, the consequences of different types of agent behaviour that diverges from the prescriptive (formal) organisational specification are simulated.

The paper is organized as follows. Section 2 introduces the description of the ATO under consideration. The design process of a specification for the ATO is described in Section 3. The analysis results are given in Section 4. Section 5 concludes the paper.

2 Air Traffic Organisation in Focus

The ATO performs a variety of tasks: development and evaluation of new operations, movement of aircraft on the ground, incident reporting and investigation, etc. In this paper we focus particularly on the ATO tasks related to movement of aircraft on the ground. More specifically, the taxiing of an aircraft to a designated runway and the subsequent take off from this runway are considered.

During the taxiing an aircraft moves from one sector of the airport to another, until it reaches the runway designated for take off. The crew of an aircraft consists of the pilot-in-command and the second pilot. The monitoring and control over the traffic in a sector is performed by a dedicated ground controller. Also, the control over aircraft on a runway and in its surroundings is performed by a dedicated runway controller. During the taxiing control over an aircraft is handed over from one controller to another, depending on the physical position of the aircraft. Before crossing a runway on its way, the crew of a taxiing aircraft should request the controller responsible for the runway for clearance. Only when the clearance is provided, the aircraft is allowed to cross. The same holds for the take off operation. Controllers may be situated in the same or in different towers at the airdrome, each of which is guided by a Tower Controllers Supervisor.

3   Modelling the Air Traffic Organisation

To perform analysis of the ATO's structures and processes both the specification of the formal organisation and the specifications of agents and the principles of their allocation to the roles should be developed. To design such specifications a sequence of design steps is identified in [9][1]. The formal organisational specification is built by executing the steps 1-8 described below. Agents that cause performance variability in the ATO are specified at the step 9. In general, organisation modelling is a challenging task that requires a close investigation of organisational documents (e.g., policies, job prescriptions), interaction with organisational actors (e.g., by organising interviews and formulating questionnaires).

Step 1. The identification of the organisational roles
In this step organisational roles are identified, both simple and composite ones and subrole-relations are established. A *role* represents a set of functionalities of (part of) an organisation abstracted from specific actors who fulfil them. Each role can be composed by several other roles. A role composed of subroles is called a composite role. Each role has an input and an output interface facilitating in interaction with other roles. The environment is a special component of a model, which also has input and output interfaces. In the considered ATO, roles are identified at three aggregation levels, some of which are presented in Fig. 1 and 2.

Step 2. The specification of the interactions between the roles
In this step, interaction relations between roles, roles and the environment are identified. To specify interaction relations, the interfaces of the roles and the environment are formalised by interaction ontologies. Generally speaking, an input ontology determines what types of information are allowed to be transferred to the input of a role (or of the environment), and an output ontology predefines what kinds of information can be generated at the output of a role (or of the environment). Relations between roles are represented by interaction and interlevel links. An interaction link is an information channel between two roles at the same aggregation level. An interlevel link connects a composite role with one of its subroles. It represents information transition between two adjacent aggregation levels. The interaction relations for the ATO have been identified and formalised at each aggregation level (see Fig. 1 and 2).

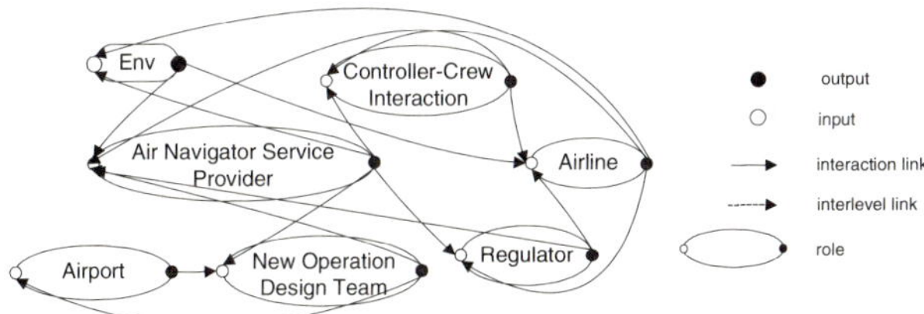

Fig. 1. The composite role Air Navigator Service Provider considered at the aggregation level 2

---

[1] Although the specifications are based on the formal languages, for better readability in this paper they are given in textual form, for the complete formal specifications we refer to [6].

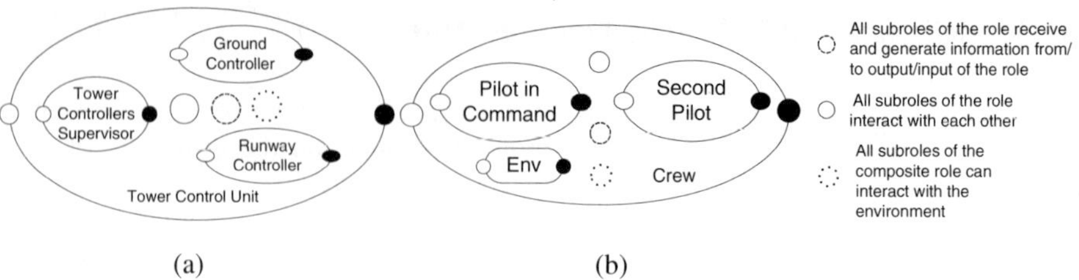

Fig. 2. Interaction relations at the aggregation level 3: (a) within the Tower Control Unit (sub-role of the ANSP) and (b) within Crew role (subrole of the Airline)

Step 3. The identification of the requirements for the roles
In this step the requirements on knowledge, skills and personal traits of the agent implementing a role at the lowest aggregation level are identified. Knowledge-related requirements define facts and procedures that must be well understood by an agent. Skills describe developed abilities of agents to use their knowledge for tasks performance. For example the following requirements for the air traffic controller role are defined: (1) passed a medical examination; (2) 2 or 4 year college degree before initiation of training; (3) thorough knowledge of the air traffic management system and the flight regulations; (4) computer training; (5) air traffic control training; (6) excellent listening and communication skills; (7) quick decision-making skills.

Step 4. The identification of the organisational performance indicators and goals
In this step, organisational goals, performance indicators (PIs) and relations between them and organisational roles are identified. A *PI* is a quantitative or qualitative indicator that reflects the state/progress of the company, unit or individual. PIs can be hard (e.g., taxiing time) or soft, i.e., not directly measurable, qualitative (e.g., level of collaboration between controllers). PIs can be related through various relationships. The following relations are considered in the framework: (strongly) positive/negative causal influence of one PI on another, positive/negative correlation between two PIs, aggregation – two PIs express the same measure at different aggregation levels.

Goals are objectives that describe a desired state or development and are defined as expressions over PIs. The characteristics of a goal include, among others: *priority*; *horizon* – for which time point/interval should the goal be satisfied; *hardness* – hard or soft (for which instead of satisfaction, degrees of *satisficing* are defined). A goal can be refined into subgoals forming a hierarchy. Some examples of the goals and PIs of the ATO are given in Table 1. Here goals 25, 26, 27, 28, 16 and 21 are subgoals of goal 10, and the PIs, on which these subgoals are based, are related to the PI of goal 10 by the aggregation relation. Goals are related to roles. For example, goal 10 is associated with Airline, Tower Control Unit and Safety Investigation Unit roles.

Step 5. The specification of the resources
In this step organisational resource types and resources are identified, and characteristics for them are provided, such as: *name, category*: discrete or continuous, *measurement unit, expiration duration*: the time interval during which a resource type can be used; *location*; *sharing*: some processes may share resources. Examples of resource types of the ATO are: airport's diagram, aircraft, incident classification database, clearance to cross a runway, an incident investigation report.

Table 1. Examples of goals and PIs of the ATO

#	Goal	Based on the PI
10	It is required to maintain a high level of safety of execution of tasks related to the air traffic management	the level of safety of execution of tasks related to the air traffic management
16	It is required to maintain a high level of robustness and unambiguousness of the control (coordination) structure for the execution of tasks	the level of robustness and unambiguousness of the control (coordination) structure for the execution of tasks
20	It is required to maintain a sufficient level of autonomy of decision making and the operation execution for the roles involved into the air traffic management	The level of autonomy of decision making and the operation execution for the roles involved into the air traffic management
21	It is required to maintain unambiguousness, consistency, correctness and timeliness of information exchanged between agents	the unambiguousness, consistency, correctness and timeliness of information exchanged between agents
23	It is desired to increase the volume of passengers, departing/arriving from/to an airport	the volume of passengers, departing/arriving from/to an airport
25	It is required to maintain a high level of conformance of all roles involved into the air traffic management to the formal norms and regulations defined for their tasks	the level of conformance of all roles involved into the air traffic management to the formal norms and regulations defined for their tasks.
26	It is required to maintain a high (sufficient) level of proficiency of pilots	the level of proficiency of pilots
27	It is required to maintain a high (sufficient) level of proficiency of controllers	the level of proficiency of controllers
28	It is required to maintain the high quality and reliability of the hardware used in the air traffic control management	the quality and reliability of the hardware used in the air traffic control management

Step 6. The identification of the organisational tasks, the relations between the tasks, and relations between the tasks, the resources and the goals
A *task* represents a function performed in the organisation and is characterized by *name*, *maximal* and *minimal duration*. Tasks can be decomposed into more specific ones using AND- and OR-relations forming hierarchies. Each task performed in an organisation should contribute to the satisfaction of one or more organisational goals. Examples of the ATO's tasks in relation to goals and resources are given in Table 2.

Step 7. The specification of the authority relations
In this step authority (i.e., informal power) relations of an organisation are identified: superior-subordinate relations on roles with respect to tasks, responsibility relations, control for resources, authorization relations. Organisational roles may have different rights and responsibilities with respect to different aspects of task execution, such as execution, passive monitoring, consulting, making technological decisions (i.e., decisions that concern technical questions related to the task content) and making

managerial decisions (i.e., decisions that concern general organisational issues related to the task). Examples of responsibility relations in the air traffic organisational model are presented in Table 3.

Table 2. Examples of the tasks of the ATO in relation to goals and resources

#	Task name	Uses	Produces	Durations
1	Taxiing the aircraft to the designated runway	All resources of the subtasks	All resources of the subtasks	Depends on the durations of subtasks
1.1	Taxiing the aircraft on a taxiway	airport's diagram, the taxi instructions, compass, radar, aircraft	-	Depends on a particular taxiway
Goal: 29, 30, 31, 32, 33, 34, 20				
1.2	Switching to the frequency of another controller	data about the new frequency	-	Min: 1 sec Max: 5 sec
Goal: 30, 31, 33				
1.3	Inquiry for the clearance for crossing an active runway	observations, the taxi instructions, communication R/T system	a request for clearance	Min: 2 sec Max: 5 sec
Goal: 30, 31, 33				
1.4	Making and communicating the decision on a request for crossing a runway	data about the current state of the runway, a request for for clearance to cross, communication R/T system	'position and hold' or 'clearance is provided'	Min: 3 sec Max: 11 sec
Goal: 35, 36, 32, 34, 20				
1.5	Crossing a runway	clearance to cross, airport's diagram, taxiing instructions, radar	'clear of the runway'	Min: 30 sec Max: 60 sec
Goal: 30, 31, 34, 33, 20				

Table 3. The responsibility relations of the roles on different aspects of some identified tasks

Task	Execution	Monitoring	Consulting	Technological decisions	Managerial decisions
1.1	Crew	Ground Controller, Tower Controllers Supervisor	Ground Controller	Crew	Ground Controller, Tower Controllers Supervisor
1.2	Crew		Ground Controller	Crew	
1.3	Crew				

Step 8. The specification of the flows of control
In this step dynamic structures (called workflows or flows of control) are defined that represent temporal execution sequences of processes of an organisation in particular scenarios. A workflow example for the ATO is given in Fig. 3.

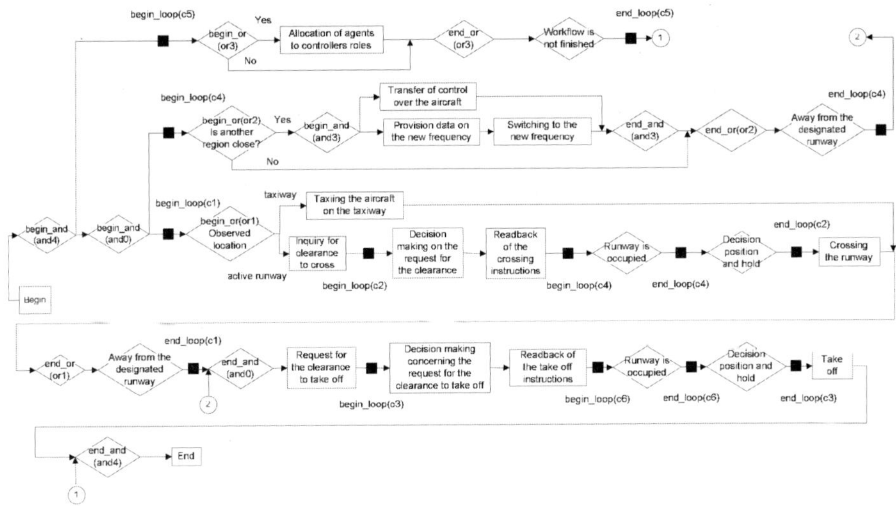

Fig. 3. Workflow for an aircraft taxiing to and taking-off from a designated runway

Step 9. The specification of the characteristics and behaviour of agents, and the agent allocation principles.

Performance variability in an organisation is represented by specifications of agents that are allocated to organisational roles. A prerequisite for the allocation of an agent to a role is the existence of a mapping between the capabilities and traits of the agent and the role requirements. For the ATO a number of agent types have been identified, such as Controller, Pilot, and Manager. Then, particular agents of these types with varying capabilities and traits have been defined. For example, the agent allocated to Tower Controllers Supervisor role in comparison to the agent allocated to some Ground Controller role has a higher level of development of the technical and interpersonal skills and additionally has the developed managerial skills. The behaviour of an agent is considered as goal-driven. Goals of an agent may be in line with the organisational goals or may, sometimes, contradict them. Other internal states of agents allocated to organisational roles are represented as beliefs. A belief of an agent is created based on: an observation from the environment; a communication provided to/obtained from another agent, and an action performed by the agent in the environment.

Step 10. The identification of the generic and domain-specific constraints

In this step generic and domain-specific constraints imposed on a formal organisational specification are identified. Generic constraints need to be satisfied by any organisational specification. Domain-specific constraints are dictated by the application domain and may be changed by the designer. A set of constraints imposed on an organisational specification is expressed using the formal languages of the framework. An organisational specification is *correct* if every constraint in the corresponding set is a logical consequence of this specification. The framework provides means for automated checking of the correctness of a specification. Consider examples of the domain-specific constraints of the ATO obtained from the formal regulations of a controller and of a pilot:

C1: When an aircraft is approaching to an active runway, the pilots should cease all processes not related to the taxiing.

C2: The pilots of a crew should verbally share information about the instructions of controllers.

C3: A controller may guide maximum two aircrafts at the same time.

C4: A controller is not allowed to issue any new clearances for some runway until this runway is vacated by the aircraft that had received the last clearance from the controller.

C5: Perform the allocation of agents-controllers to the aircraft monitoring processes in such a way that the number of processes executed at the same time by each controller is less than two.

4 Analysis Results

In this Section first the results of the correctness verification of the designed ATO specification are presented (Section 4.1). Then, the analysis by simulation of a combined specification with agents allocated to the roles is described (Section 4.2).

4.1 Correctness Verification

As a result of the automated analysis a number of inconsistencies have been identified. In particular, several (potential) conflicts have been found in the goal structure: between goals 27 and 37; between goals 38 and 37; between goals 20 and 25; and between goals 23 and 25. The goals that are in conflict cannot be satisfied at the same time. For example, goal 25 ensures adherence of the roles to the safe-related norms, which may not always be optimal from the performance point of view (goal 23). Besides execution of tasks, the formal authority relations influence the satisfaction of organisational goals. For example, to achieve the satisfaction of the goal 20, the crews and the controllers should be provided sufficient decision making power with respect to their tasks.

To ensure that constraint C5 defined in step 10 of Section 3 is satisfied, the organisation should have a sufficient number of properly trained agents to be allocated to all the roles of the organisation. The analysis based on the amount of agents currently employed by the organisation identified many situations in which the same agent-controller should be allocated to more than two aircraft's monitoring processes, thus violating constraints C3 and C5, and sacrificing the satisfaction of goals 10 and 24. Sometimes the management to keep the satisfaction of C5, allocates not (completely) qualified agents to the controller roles, thus, causing the dissatisfaction of goal 10. Obviously, the satisfaction of the important safety-related goal 10 is sacrificed in both solutions. The lack of the consideration for the safety-related goals may cause incidents or even accidents.

4.2 Analysis by Simulation

Using the developed model of the ATO, simulation of different scenarios can be performed, one of which is described in this Section. Based on the joint decision of the Airport's Management, the ANSP and the largest airlines, the new runway runway1 has been introduced. Due to its physical position, most of the aircraft taxiing to other runways need to cross runway1 on its way (runway1 can be crossed at one place only, whereas may be approached using two taxiways situated in two different sectors of the airport). The purpose of this study was to investigate the safety issues that may be caused by the introduction of runway1. Both the normal and the critical configurations have been investigated. In the normal configuration the number of aircraft guided by each controller is less than 3, whereas in the critical - the number ≥ 6 and constraint C5 cannot be satisfied for some controllers. The number of agents-controllers in both configurations is limited to 4, 1 of which is always allocated to Tower Controllers Supervisor role. This agent sees to the satisfaction of constraint C5. It is assumed that the agents are properly qualified for their roles. The behaviour of the allocated agents is defined by the ATO formal specification extended with the behavioural deviations, some of which are identified in [8] (e.g., incorrect situation awareness, mistakes) associated with the probability values. Some of these values are dependant on the agents' workload: the higher the agent's workload, the more chance of its error. In the study only serious occurrences were considered, such as an incursion of aircraft on a runway. One hundred simulation trials with the simulation time 3 years and simulation step 1 hour have been performed in the LeadsTo simulation environment [1]. The obtained simulation traces have been analyzed using the checking environment [2]. By the analysis the following results have been obtained:

(1) The agent allocated to Controller Runway1 role in all traces most of the time was monitoring at least 4 aircraft (i.e., was overloaded).
(2) The ground controller of the sector 1 was also overloaded, guiding in average three aircrafts at the same time.
(3) The incursion event on the runway1 occurred in 36 traces from 100.
(4) The number of incursions caused by the combination of the events a (the crew mistakenly recognized the runway as a taxiway) and c (the responsible ground controller forgot to inform the crew about the frequency change because of the high workload) is 30.
(5) The number of incursions caused by mistakes of the runway controller in the calculation of the separation distance between aircrafts is 5.
(6) There is only one incursion caused by a crew mistakenly reacting to the clearance for some other crew.

In the future a precise validation of the obtained results will be performed.

5 Conclusions

The paper presents the first attempt to create a formal agent-based organisational model of an ATO using the framework of [6]. A typical ATO has high structural and behavioural complexities that present a challenge both for modelling and analysis of such an organisation. All important aspects of the considered organisation have been identified using four interrelated views, i.e. performance-oriented, process-oriented, organization-oriented and agent-oriented. The modelling framework used allows scalability by specifying an organisational model at different aggregation levels and identifying relations between these levels. However, for complex organisations (such as ATOs) specifications of lower aggregation levels still may be very elaborated.

Using the automated analysis techniques from [2, 6] missing and conflicting parts of the ATO model can be identified. Some examples of application of these techniques are provided in the paper. The scalability of analysis is achieved by applying dedicated techniques for verification of specifications of particular organisational views and by distinguishing aggregation levels. Another analysis type demonstrated in the paper is by simulation. It allows to evaluate how different types of divergent agent behaviour in simulation models may result into delays in executions of processes up to the level of incidents. In comparison with the simulation approach of [7, 8], the novel approach considers the organisational layer of the ATO explicitly, however at the expense of not simulating beyond the incidents.

Interesting follow-up research is to evaluate the validity of the developed model, and to integrate our organisational simulation model with the accident risk simulation model of [7, 8].

Acknowledgement

The author would like to acknowledge Sybert Stroeve and Henk Blom (the Dutch National Aerospace Laboratory, NLR, Amsterdam) and Barry Kirwan (Eurocontrol, Bretigny) for their cooperation. This research has partly been funded through an Eurocontrol Innovative Research grant.

References

1. Bosse, T., Jonker, C.M., van der Meij, L., Treur, J.: A Language and Environment for Analysis of Dynamics by Simulation. International Journal of Artificial Intelligence Tools 16, 435–464 (2007)
2. Bosse, T., Jonker, C.M., van der Meij, L., Sharpanskykh, A., Treur, J.: Specification and Verification of Dynamics in Cognitive Agent Models. In: Proceedings of the 6th Int. Conf. on Intelligent Agent Technology, IAT 2006, pp. 247–255. IEEE Computer Society Press, Los Alamitos (2006)
3. Eurocontrol: Air navigation system safety assessment methodology. SAF.ET1.ST03.1000-MAN-01, edition 2.0 (2004)
4. Le Coze, J.: Are organizations too complex to be integrated in technical risk assessment and current safety auditing? Safety Science 43, 613–638 (2005)
5. Reason, J., Hollnagel, E., Paries, J.: Revisiting the Swiss cheese model of accidents. Eurocontrol, EEC Note no. 13/06 (2006)
6. Sharpanskykh, A.: On Computer-Aided Methods for Modeling and Analysis of Organizations. PhD Dissertation. Vrije Universiteit Amsterdam (2008)
7. Stroeve, S.H., Blom, H.A.P., Bakker, G.J.: Safety risk impact analysis of an ATC runway incursion alert system, Eurocontrol Safety R&D Seminar, Barcelona (2006)
8. Stroeve, S.H., Blom, H.A.P., Van der Park, M.N.J.: Multi-agent situation awareness error evolution in accident risk modelling. In: Proceedings of 5th ATM R&D Seminar, pp. 410–420 (2003)
9. Stroeve, S.H., Sharpanskykh, A., Blom H.A.P.: Organizational safety modelling and analysis of an air traffic application: Eurocontrol CARE Innovative research III. National Aerospace Laboratory NLR, report CR-2007-457 (2007)

Visualized Technique for Trend Analysis of News Articles

Masahiro Terachi[1], Ryosuke Saga[1], Zhongqi Sheng[1,2], and Hiroshi Tsuji[1]

[1] Osaka Prefecture University, Graduate School of Engineering,
1-1, Gakuencho, Nakaku, Sakai, Japan, 559-8531
[2] Northeastern University, School of Mechanical Engineering,
3-11, Wenhua Road, Shenyang, Liaoning, China, 110004
{Terachi,Saga,Sheng}@mis.cs.osakafu-u.ac.jp,Tsuji@cs.osakafu-u.ac.jp

Abstract. In order to visualize keyword trends in texts of news articles, this paper proposes a method named FACT-Graph by extending co-occurrence graph. The method uses four classes of keywords, considers three patterns of class transitions, and expresses three types of co-occurrence relationships between two analysis periods. Classes of keywords are characterized by the shapes of their nodes, the transition patterns of keyword classes are shown by the colors of the nodes, and the co-occurrences relationships between two keywords are represented by the types of edges their nodes have. FACT-Graph is applied to a sample of 220,000 newspaper articles and is found to be effective in visualizing keyword trends embedded in volumes of text data.

Keywords: Text Mining, Trend Analysis, Visualized Technique, Co-occurrence Graph, TF-IDF.

1 Introduction

With the improving of computer performances and the lowering of hardware prices, computers have been widely used in every area of modern society, and a large amount of electrical data representing all kinds of information has been generated. Text mining, sometimes referred to as text data mining, is the process of extracting high quality information from a vast array of text data and has received a lot of attention in recent years. Keywords are words with special meanings that briefly describe the key information in articles. A lot of research has been done on text mining of keywords [1]-[3], and some has focused on analyzing keyword trends and visualizing keyword relationships [4]-[7].

However, there are problems in trend visualization analysis. To simultaneously investigate several changing keyword trends, some graphs must be compared side by side, which makes it difficult to master trend information accurately. Some keywords that occur less frequently are paid little attention even though they are actually important in describing articles.

We introduce a trend analysis method in this paper, which works by identifying four classes of keywords. To solve the simultaneous visualization and low

N.T. Nguyen et al. (Eds.): IEA/AIE 2008, LNAI 5027, pp. 659–668, 2008.

frequency problems, we propose FACT-Graph (Frequency And Co-occurrence-based Trend-Graph) by extending the traditional co-occurrence graph, which visualizes trend analysis and simultaneously examine keyword class and keyword co-occurrence relationship information. We apply FACT-Graph to 220,000 newspaper articles and report here the analysis results and discuss the merits of FACT-Graph.

2   Visualization Trend Analysis Based on FACT-Graph

2.1   Overview of Visualization Trend Analysis

The aim of this research is to mine the trend knowledge indicated by keywords from the text data with date information. An overview of the proposed method is shown in Fig.1. First, FACT-Graph extracts the morphemes from text data and builds a term database. Then, based on the frequency of each term, it calculates the weight value of every term in the article using the TF-IDF algorithm [8]. Finally, FACT-Graph extracts the keywords from the term database and obtains a keyword database used for trend analysis. There are problems in previous trend analysis methods [9], which are briefly introduced in the third part of chapter 2.2. FACT-Graph utilizes information about co-occurrence relationships among keywords between two periods to solve those problems.

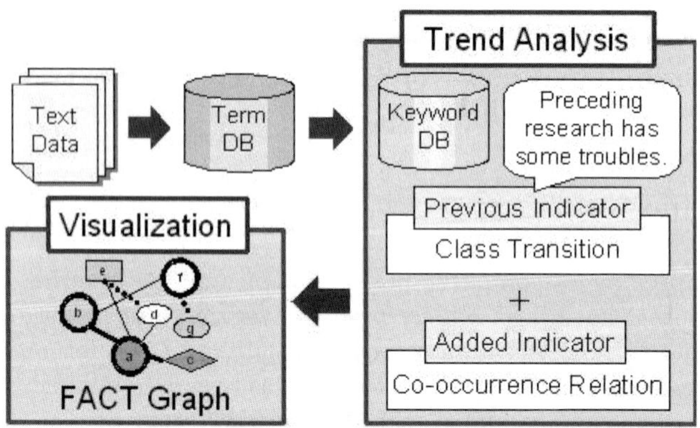

Fig. 1. Flowchart of Visualization Trend Analysis

2.2   Previous Analysis Methods

(1)   Definition of Keyword Class

FACT-Graph considers the meanings of keywords in time series. Unlike conventional methods that choose keywords based on frequency, FACT-Graph considers more on the keywords with change even if those keywords emerge gradually, calculating the TF (Term Frequency) values and DF (Document Frequency) values for all keywords in given analysis period. Then, based on the threshold values given by the user, the keywords are divided into four classes, as illustrated in Table 1. Some keywords may belong to different classes in different analysis periods.

Both TF and DF values are high for the keywords belonging to class A, which may express the basic content and indicate the themes of the documents. The keywords belonging to class B play a supplementary role, and the keywords belonging to class C attract attention in some articles. The keywords belonging to class D are paid little attention in the analysis period. FACT-Graph treats keywords that are present only in one analysis periods in the same way as the keywords belonging to class D.

Table 1. Definition of Keyword Class

		Document Frequency	
		High	Low
Term	High	Class A	Class C
Frequency	Low	Class B	Class D

(2)   Classification of Class Transition

A keyword's class may change as time series change. In Table 2, the implications of all kinds of class transitions are summarized. For example, the keywords belonging to class A in two analysis periods are seen as important topics. Keywords that occurred infrequently and were seen as unimportant topics in early periods may become the new important topics as they increase in frequency in later periods. These include keywords whose class changed from class D to class A. In contrast, some keywords may change from important topics to unimportant topics.

Table 2. Transition of Class Type

		Current Period			
		Class A	Class B	Class C	Class D
	Class A	Hot	Cooling	Bipolar	Fade
Previous	Class B	Common	Universal	-	Fade
Period	Class C	Broaden	-	Locally Active	Fade
	Class D	New	Widely New	Locally New	Negligible

For the keywords in class C that appear frequently only in certain specific documents, there may be many related characteristic keywords. If they appear in many more documents as time goes on, which move from class C to class A, or still occur as keywords belonging to class C as time series change, they probably include information important to the documents.

(3)   Problems and Solutions

The relationships among the keywords cannot be obtained simply by analyzing class transitions. That is to say, though the classes of keywords are based on class transitions over time, it is still difficult to master trend information without referring to the trend of other keywords. The topics indicated by some keywords can be easily mastered, but it may also be hard to identify the topics indicated by some keywords without considering keywords related to them. Under these circumstances, referring them one by one is more time consuming, which is often infeasible.

There are also keywords that appear infrequently but reflect concepts important to the document. Some of these keywords may be important for trend analysis, but in analysis of class transition, those keywords are paid little attention. We combine the data used in analysis of transition between classes and the information about co-occurrence of keywords, and propose a visualization method based on extension of co-occurrence graphs. Three strategies are used to solve the two problems discussed above:

- Overlook changes in trends
- Analyze topics consisting of multiple keywords
- Find important keywords with low appearance frequencies

2.3   FACT-Graph Visualization Method

(1)   Co-occurrence Graph

Recently, the techniques of extracting and visualizing keywords by utilizing the co-occurrence of keywords in the field of chance discovery have received a lot of attention [10][11]. To show the co-occurrence degree, some coefficients such as *Jaccard* coefficient and *Simpson* coefficient are used. In this research, *Jaccard* coefficient is selected, which is defined as $Jaccard(a,b) = count(a \cap b)/count(a \cup b)$, where $count(a \cap b)$ is the number of documents in which both a and b appear, $count(a \cup b)$ is the number of documents in which either a or b appears.

FACT-Graph operates as follows. First, the co-occurrence coefficients of keywords are individually calculated. Then, the edges are plotted between the nodes with the co-occurrence coefficient that exceeds the given threshold. Finally, a graph like that in Fig.2 is obtained, which is called co-occurrence graph. The cluster of nodes with adjacent edges in the co-occurrence graph suggests that the document concerns specific concepts, and it is thought that those keywords connect those concepts, which is important to documents in the field of chance discovery.

(2)   FACT Graph

The elements for trend analysis are added to the co-occurrence graph and the extended co-occurrence graph is proposed, which is called FACT graph. Using the FACT graph, it is easy to analyze the class transitions of every keyword. Moreover, the concept of some sub-graph in the document can be found by paying attention to the kind of edges. Also, using macro analysis makes it possible

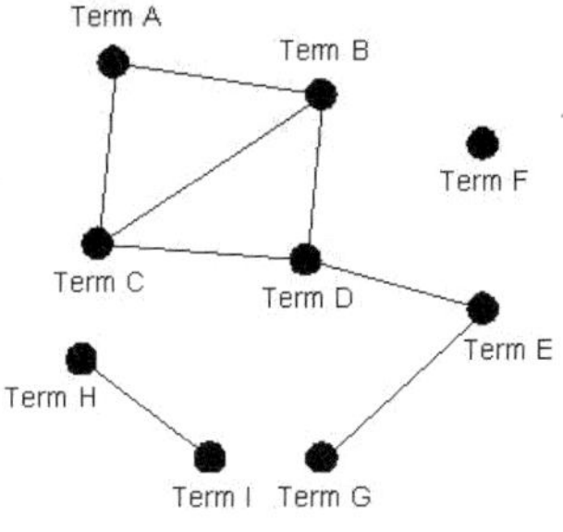

Fig. 2. Co-occurrence Graph

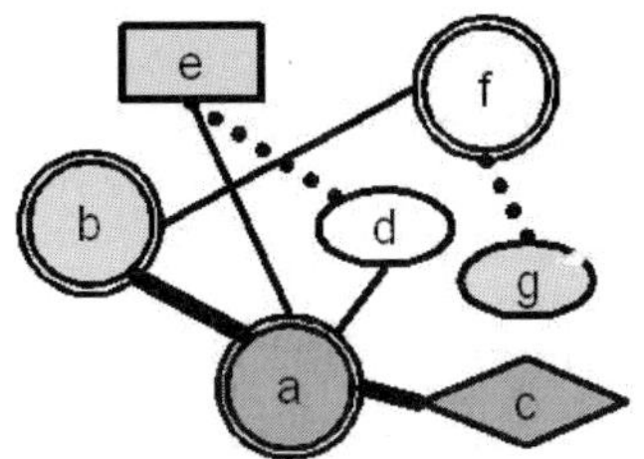

Fig. 3. FACT Graph

to analyze trends. FACT-Graph first classifies text data by the analysis period in the time series. Then, the keywords from the text data for every period are individually extracted by the TF-IDF algorithm. Finally, the keywords are classified into four classes based on the TF and DF thresholds. By referring to keyword classes in the previous analysis period, FACT-Graph formulates a table that corresponds to a class transition such as Table 2.

However, showing every element of Table 2 in the graph is very complex, and it is also very difficult to identify the change in the trend simply by looking at it. Therefore, three simple patterns are defined by dividing transition patterns roughly as shown in Table 3. In pattern 1, the keyword trends do not change and are stable from the previous analysis period. In pattern 2, the keywords tend to increase in frequency, which shows that those keywords are paid more attention to compared with previous analysis period. In pattern 3, by contrast, the keywords tend to decrease in frequency, so they are thought to be less important than in previous analysis period. The transitions between class B and class C are classified into pattern 1 as an exception, which seldom occur.

Table 3. Definition of Transition Pattern

Pattern 1	Pattern 2	Pattern 3
Class A $\Rightarrow$ Class A	Class B $\Rightarrow$ Class A	Class A $\Rightarrow$ Class B
Class B $\Rightarrow$ Class B	Class C $\Rightarrow$ Class A	Class A $\Rightarrow$ Class C
Class C $\Rightarrow$ Class C	Class D $\Rightarrow$ Class A	Class A $\Rightarrow$ Class D
Class D $\Rightarrow$ Class D	Class D $\Rightarrow$ Class B	Class B $\Rightarrow$ Class D
Class B $\Rightarrow$ Class C	Class D $\Rightarrow$ Class C	Class C $\Rightarrow$ Class D
Class C $\Rightarrow$ Class B		

For each analysis period, the degrees of co-occurrence relationships between keywords are individually calculated. A list of the pairs of keywords with co-occurrence relationship degree exceeded given thresholds is made, and one of the following attributes is assigned to every pair of keywords referring to the co-occurrence relationship of the keywords in the previous analysis period.

- There was a co-occurrence relationship in previous period and the co-occurrence relationship continues in current period.
- There was no co-occurrence relationship in previous period but there is one in current period.
- There was a co-occurrence relationship in previous period but not in current period.

◎	Double Circle	Class A
▭	Rectangle	Class B
◇	Diamond	Class C
◯	Ellipse	Class D
	Pale Shading	Pattern 1
	Deep Shading	Pattern 2
▭	White	Pattern 3
▬	Heavy Line	Co-occurrence relation continues
─	Fine Line	Co-occurrence relation starts
------	Dashed	Co-occurrence relation ends

Fig. 4. Implication of Symbol

As shown in Fig.3, FACT graph is created for every concerned analysis period by using information obtained above. In the graph, the class of each keyword in the current period is expressed by the shape of the node, and the transition pattern for the analysis period is shown by the color (shade) of the node. The implications of nodes and edges are shown in Fig.4. There are some pairs of keywords in which neither keyword is keyword any longer in current analysis period though it had co-occurrence relationship with other keyword in previous analysis period. This kind of keywords is classified into class D especially and the third kind of edge (Co-occurrence relation ends) is added to FACT graph.

Table 4. Properties of Dataset

No.	Item	Value
1	Publication Year	1998-1999
2	Number of Total Articles	220,078
3	Total Appearance Number of Terms	5,014,428
4	Variety of Terms	116,966
5	Average Number of Articles per Month	9,167
6	Average Number of Terms per Article	22.8

3   Case Study

3.1   Outline of Datasets

In this case study, text data of news articles from *Mainichi Newspaper* for the
24 months of calendar years 1998 and 1999 is used. The data of every month is
analyzed, and some of the properties are listed in Table 4. We focus on the topics
in the newspaper articles, so the morphemes are filtered first. Only the nouns
and unknown words are extracted, and ChaSen[1] is used as the morphological
analysis tool. The kind of co-occurrence coefficient, the number of keywords extracted for every analysis period, and the thresholds of TF and DF values used
to decide the class of keywords are shown in Table 5. These parameters are set
based on our experience and the user should adjust them by referring to the
visualization results. In the visualization phase, Graphviz[2] is used to plot the
FACT graph. Fig.5, Fig.6 and Fig.7(partial graphs for clearly showing) are used
as examples to demonstrate how FACT-Graph works. The case study and the
selection of noteworthy words is just one example, showing that FACT-Graph
is effective.

Table 5. Settings of Experiment Conditions

No.	Item	Value
1	Kind of Co-occurrence Coefficients	Jaccard
2	Threshold of Co-occurrence Coefficient	0.1
3	Number of Keywords Extracted per Month	50
4	Threshold of Term Frequency	400
5	Threshold of Document Frequency	200

3.2   Overlooking Change in Trends

Transitions of keywords between classes and changes in co-occurrence relationships can be understood based on a comprehensive view of FACT graph. Trends
can be analyzed for an individual keyword or for a specific cluster.

It can be seen in Fig.5 that there are co-occurrence relationships among keywords concerning Japanese politics, which form one cluster. *Hashimoto* is the
Prime Minister's family name and *Liberal-Democratic Party* was the majority party in the government at the time. Either TF or DF values of keywords
Hashimoto and *Liberal-Democratic Party* are high, so these two keywords are
put in class A and pattern 1 because the trends are steady. Thus, it can be
concluded that these keywords stand for topics concerning Japanese politics. In
this cluster, the keyword *Democratic Party* is classified into class C and is also
a keyword in pattern 2. Therefore, it can be concluded that *Democratic Party*
has appeared concentrating for domestic politics and been paid more attention

---

[1] http://chasen.naist.jp/hiki/ChaSen/
[2] http://www.graphviz.org/

to. Actually, noticing this change and referring the corresponding articles, it can be found that just at that time the new *Democratic Party* was set up, and this change reflects such a trend in domestic politics.

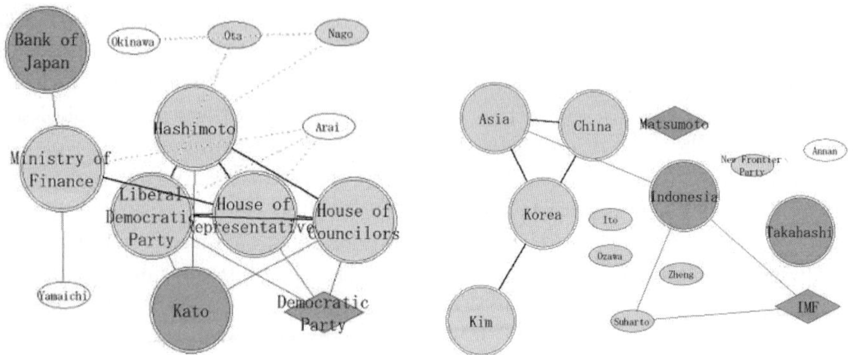

Fig. 5. Overall Trend Analysis   **Fig. 6.** Related Keywords Analysis

3.3 Analyzing Topics Consisting of Multiple Keywords

An individual keyword can be analyzed by using the co-occurrence relationships among two or more keywords and the trend in the example for the political climate of *Indonesia* is found.

Though the keyword *Indonesia* in Fig.6 is a keyword in pattern 2, it is not easy to imagine what trend it indicates by the keyword alone. However, it is clear that the keyword *Indonesia* indicates a topic related to Asian monetary crisis while referring to the keywords *Asia* and *IMF* together, for which there are co-occurrence relationships with *Indonesia*. There are co-occurrence relationships between these keywords and the keyword *Indonesia* in January of 1998 though the co-occurrence relationships disappear temporarily in February. The co-occurrence relationships with the keyword *Suharto* appear for the first time, making it clear that the scale of the topic is growing. The connection between the monetary crisis and the collapse of the *Suharto* regime can be seen in this graph.

3.4 Finding Important Keywords with Lower Appearance Frequencies

It can be seen that some keywords play important roles at that period though they occur less frequently.

The keywords *Nago* and *Ota* in Fig.7 are classified into class D in the previous and current analysis periods, so they have not transition between classes and occur infrequently. However, because there are co-occurrence relationships with the cluster concerning Japanese politics described above, it is possible that there are some unknown elements deeply related to domestic politics. As a matter of

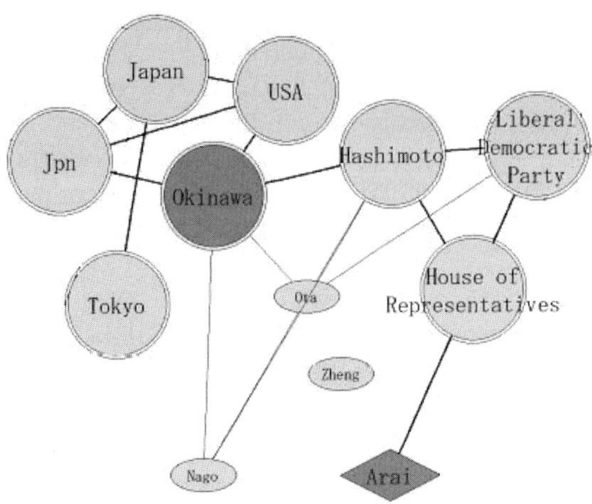

Fig. 7. Low Frequency Keywords Analysis

fact, the *Nago* mayoral election took place in February of the same year, when the problem of American military bases was in the news and when the governor of *Okinawa* Prefecture was *Masahide Ota*.

4   Discussion

KeyGraph is a keyword visualization technique that uses the co-occurrence graph[10]. In KeyGraph, words with high TF values are extracted first. Then, words that have strong co-occurrence relationships with them are extracted later. Because the degree of co-occurrence has already been used in the keyword extraction phase, KeyGraph can extract words with strong co-occurrence relationships but low frequencies and add them to the set of objects for analysis. In contrast, FACT-Graph uses the TF-IDF algorithm to extract all keywords. Keywords with low weights might not be extracted, making it impossible to relate keywords with lower frequency because FACT-Graph calculates the co-occurrence level for the extracted keywords.

One particularity of FACT-Graph is the definition of classes of keywords on the basis of frequency information. This makes it possible for FACT-Graph to identify this information about frequency change. In the trend analysis, changes are easily imaged. FACT-Graph can also illustrate changes in trends between two analysis periods in one graph, although KeyGraph does it in two graphs.

5   Conclusions

We proposed a method of analyzing relationships between multiple words and analyzing keywords that appear infrequently by taking account of transitions between keyword classes and changes in co-occurrence relationships. The method,

FACT-Graph, is designed to visualize trend analysis of keywords by extending the co-occurrence graph. We demonstrated FACT-Graph's effectiveness by applying it to newspaper article data. In the future, we plan to develop an interactive interface that can modify the conditions of analysis such as thresholds, define compound keywords and exclude unnecessary keywords, while taking account of FACT-Graph's output. We will carry out deep comparing analysis with other related methods to further evaluate the effectiveness of FACT-Graph.

Acknowledgments. The authors would like to express sincere thanks to NTCIR-6 projects who provide experimental article data. This work is partially supported by JST "Research for Promoting Technological Seeds 2007".

References

1. Yamamoto, H., Ohmi, S., Tsuji, H.: Entropy-based Indexing Term Selection for N-gram Text Search System. In: IEEE International Conference on Systems, Man & Cybernetics, pp. 4852–4857 (2003)
2. Kageyama, A., Tsuji, H.: Web-based Characteristics Analysis for Industrial Departments in Universities. World Multi-conference on Systemics, Cybernetics and Informatics 10, 23–28 (2004)
3. Yamada, K., Komine, H., Kinukawa, H., Nakagawa, H.: Abstract of Abstract: A New Summarizing Method based on Document Frequency and Clause Length. In: The 8th World Multi-Conference on Systemics, Cybernetics and Informatics, Orland (2004)
4. Matsuo, Y., Ishizuka, M.: Keyword Extraction from a Document using Word Co-occurrence Statistical Information. JASI Journal 17(3), 217–223 (2002)
5. Lent, B., Agrawal, R., Srikant, R.: Discovering Trends in Text Databases. In: Proc. 3rd Int. Conf. On Knowledge Discovery and Data Mining (1997)
6. Havre, S., Hetzler, B., Nowell, L.: ThemeRiver: In Search of Trends, Patterns, and Relationships. IEEE Transactionson on Visualization and Computer Graphics 8, 9–20 (2002)
7. Feldman, R., Aumann, Y., Zilberstein, A., Ben-Yehuda, Y.: Trend Graphs: Visualizing the Evolution of Concept Relationships in Large Document Collections. In: Żytkow, J.M. (ed.) PKDD 1998. LNCS, vol. 1510, pp. 38–46. Springer, Heidelberg (1998)
8. Salton, G., Yang, C.S.: On the Specification of Term Values in Automatic Indexing. Journal of Documentation 29(4), 351–372 (1973)
9. Terachi, M., Saga, R., Tsuji, H.: Trends Recognition in Journal Papers by Text Mining. In: IEEE International Conference on Systems, Man & Cybernetics, pp. 4784–4789 (2006)
10. Ohsawa, Y., Benson, N.E., Yachida, M.: KeyGraph: Automatic Indexing by Co-occurrence Graph based on Building Construction Metaphor. In: Proc. Advanced Digital Library Conference, pp. 12–18 (1998)
11. Oguma, J., Utsumi, A.: Document clustering that uses co-occurrence information on word. JSAI 19(1), 153–155 (2005)

Solving SQL Constraints by Incremental Translation to SAT

Robin Lohfert, James J. Lu, and Dongfang Zhao

Mathematics and Computer Science, Emory University, Atlanta, GA 30322-1950, U.S.A.
{rlohfer,jlu,dzhao3}@mathcs.emory.edu

Abstract. The need to model and solve constraints over large sets of relational data occurs frequently in practice. Naively and inefficiently, solutions to the problem may be implemented in ad-hoc and difficult to maintain procedural code that accesses the data through embedded SQL programming. More elegant solutions involve the use of declarative programming languages that integrates constraint modeling with database access in transparent ways. One of the more interesting constraint languages for relational databases is the language CONSQL, proposed by Cadoli and Mancini, in which SQL and its relational algebraic foundation form the basis for expressing constraints. The current paper explores the feasibility of solving finite-domain CONSQL constraints via a SAT solver backend.

Keywords: intelligent database systems, satisfiability, constraint analysis, heuristics.

1   Introduction

Problem Context. Modeling and solving constraints over large sets of relational data is important in practice. The naive approach to developing such an application is to implement ad-hoc procedural code that accesses the data through embedded SQL programming. A more elegant and reusable approach is to use declarative programming languages that integrate constraint modeling with database access in transparent ways. While numerous constraint database languages exist, one of the more intriguing recent proposals is the language CONSQL, by Cadoli and Mancini [6], in which SQL and its relational algebraic foundation are adopted as the basis for expressing constraints over relational data.

The key concept in CONSQL is the non-deterministic GUESS operator that declares a set of relations to have an arbitrary extension. A set of constraints, written in usual SQL syntax over both existing and guess relations, specifies conditions that the guess relations must satisfy. The following partial example illustrates the idea. It specifies a lineup for a tennis team competing against another team. The lineup is made up of five doubles pairs. Each doubles pair consists of two players, and no player may play more than once. We assume a base relation, roster(name,phone), which lists the available players on the team. The cardinality of roster is assumed greater than 10.

N.T. Nguyen et al. (Eds.): IEA/AIE 2008, LNAI 5027, pp. 669–676, 2008.

```
1 GUESS TABLE lineup AS
2 SELECT r1.name player1, r2.name player2
3 FROM roster r1, roster r2
4 CHECK (10 = (SELECT COUNT(*)
5              FROM (SELECT player1 FROM lineup
6                    UNION
7                    SELECT player2 FROM lineup)))
```

Lines 1, 2, and 3 declare the guess relation, lineup(player1,player2), to be an arbitrary extension of $\pi_{\text{name}}(\text{roster}) \times \pi_{\text{name}}(\text{roster})$. Each tuple of the lineup relation indicates a partnership between player1 and player2. The constraint, from lines 4 to 7, specifies that the total number of names that appear in the lineup must equal 10. This captures the restriction that each player on the roster may play at most once (assuming that all roster members have distinct names). Suppose that the null value may not appear in the extension. The constraint also specifies the required five doubles teams.

A straightforward but infeasible approach to populating the guess relations is guess-and-check. A better approach, as taken in [6], is to couple the database query engine with a (home-grown or off-the-shelf) constraint solver. But even with carefully designed integrated solvers, practical applications to large-scale problems present significant engineering challenges due to the conflicting needs to perform large-scale database accesses and to compute large combinatorial searches.

In this paper, we explore the feasibility of computing extensions of guess relations with constraints over finite domains using a high-performance SAT solver in the backend. SAT solvers possess certain advantages over general constraint solvers given the low-level nature of its language for representing problems [2]. Under such design, the task of the CONSQL engine is to encode an input problem specification to an equivalent set of clauses, and to decode results produced by the SAT solver back to appropriate tuples for the guess relations. For both processes, appropriate SQL statements to the existing base tables would need to be generated: queries during encoding and updates during decoding.

While this simple design works in principle, for even modest size problems, the size of the encoded SAT instances is often overwhelming. For example, a problem to compute the teaching schedule for a university department consisting of 20 professor, 35 courses, and a small number of time slots and classrooms (6 each) quickly generates close to 3,000,000 clauses. For a slightly more complex input with 12 time slots and 8 classrooms, the set of constraints encodes to nearly 20,000,000 clauses. As a point of perspective, the typical size of a problem in a 2003 SAT systems competition number in the tens of thousands (http://www.lri.fr/~simon/satex/satex.php3). While many of these massive clause sets can still be solved quickly, their lengthy encoding time makes the application of CONSQL prohibitive. Thus, we address the following problem.

Problem Statement. To find a way to extend the range of problems that a SAT-solver based CONSQL engine can handle.

We adopt a simple, incremental technique in which the given problem instance P is solved by first encoding and solving a subproblem P'. Solutions of P' are then used to guide the search for a solution to the remaining problem of P. A more precise formulation is given next.

Approach. Suppose $P = (Q, R)$ is a CONSQL input problem where Q is the set of guess relations, and R a set of constraints over the base and guess relations. Without loss of generality, we assume that problems are *covered*: all attributes that appear in the guess relations Q also appear in R. Let $A_R = \{a_1, ..., a_n\}$ denote the set of all attributes that appear in R. The set of variables, V_P, in a SAT encoding of P corresponds to the set of all possible tuples of A_R that are consistent with possible tuples of base relations. For simplicity, "variables in V_P" and "tuples of A_R" are used interchangeably. Given a model S of the SAT encoding, the extension of a guess relation $r \in Q$ corresponds to $\pi_r(S)$.

The subproblem P' is a CONSQL problem (Q', R') where each relation in Q' is a projection of some relation in Q, and $R' \subseteq R$ is the set of constraints over attributes related to Q'. Note that given a solution S' of P', the problem that "remains" of P is $P'' = (Q'', R'')$ where $Q'' = Q$, $R'' = (R - R')$, and the set of variables $V_{P''} \subseteq V_P$ satisfies the following. For each $v'' \in V_{P''}$, there exists a $v' \in S'$ such that $v' = \pi_{A_{R'}}(v'')$. Clearly if $|S'| > 0$, then $|V_{P''}| < |V_P|$. This is the sense in which S' may be used to guide and speed up the computation of an overall solution to P. Moreover, solvability is not affected.

Proposition 1. *If there is a solution S to P, then there is at least one solution S' to P' such that* $\pi_{A'_{R'}}(S) = S'$.

The approach may be generalized by breaking P into several subproblems (i.e., increments), but to be effective, "good" choices of attributes for each increment must be made. Intuitively, preference should be given to those subproblems whose solutions constrain the search space for P as much as possible. Moreover, we would like a large number of solutions to the subproblem to be sub-solutions of P. We present a heuristic in Section 3 that works well based on preliminary experiment.

2   Related Work

Propositional satisfiability and constraint satisfaction are well-established areas of research. An excellent recent survey that relates the two fields is the paper [5]. On the other hand, research into integrating constraint solving with databases is rooted primarily in deductive databases [13] and constraint logic programming [9]. A natural extension of these areas is constraint databases [10] that generalizes relational databases with quantifier free constraints. Recently, investigations into integrating constraints into relational database systems have been made [7].

The idea of adapting SQL to express constraint satisfaction problems was proposed by Cadoli and Mancini [6] on the observations that 1) most practical contexts for constraint problems involve large relational databases, and 2) SQL is a well-understood language that can be used to express a variety of constraints. However, as CONSQL is sufficiently expressive to represent all problems in NP, careful attention must be paid to ensure an implementation that is capable of handling a wide-range of problems with reasonable efficiency.

Most work on improving the practical reaches of SAT solvers have focused on exploring the structural properties of the graph representation of clauses [11,4,1]. An idea much closer to our work is the research by Barrett, Dill, and Stump [3], where a series of related SAT problems are used to incrementally check for first-order satisfiability.

3   Heuristic Problem Decomposition

Given $P = (Q, R)$, we determine the attributes to keep for the subproblem $P' = (Q', R')$ by analyzing the constraint R. While a full "natural language" analysis would be ideal, it requires the presence of information that may not be available. Hence, we use the SQL sentence "R" as an approximation to, quickly, identify important attributes. Borrowing a basic idea from heuristic query optimization [12], an attribute a that strongly connects to other attributes should be included among the attributes of P' since fixing values for a will restrict the possible values for a large number of other attributes.

The strength of how an attribute a relates to other attributes may be reasoned in several ways. The one we focus on is the number and ways in which a is referenced in R. We call this property the *connectedness* of a.

As in [6], a constraint is any relational algebraic expression. In our work we also consider extensions such as the aggregate operator $\mathcal{F}$ [8]. We represent the connectedness of pairs of attributes of R with $A_R = \{a_1, ..., a_n\}$ by a symmetric matrix, $[\![R]\!]$, whose entries are real numbers in the unit interval. The value $[\![R]\!][i, j]$ indicates the strength of the connection between a_i, a_j. We call this the *c-matrix* of R. The symmetry of $[\![R]\!]$ reflects our current view that, generally, connections are bi-directional, but this is a point of ongoing investigation. The connectedness of an attribute a_i is then defined by Equation 1.

$$\Sigma_{j=1}^n [\![R]\!][i, j] \tag{1}$$

To determine the strength of connection between a pair of attributes a_i and a_j, we note that if they appear in the same comparison (e.g., $a_i = a_j$), then the strength of connection should be higher than if they are indirectly related (e.g., $a_i < a_k \wedge a_k = a_j$). Moreover, the "weakening" effect of operators should vary according to their semantics.

To formalize, we associate, for each operator O in the language, a weakening factor $\lambda_O \in [0, 1]$. A set of mutually-recursive, syntax-directed rules are used to specify $[\![R]\!]$. As an example of one base case, given a comparison $a\Theta b$ where a and b are attributes, the c-matrix $[\![a\Theta b]\!]$ is defined to be a c-matrix that is zero everywhere except $[i, j] = [j, i] = \lambda_\Theta$:

$$[\![a_i \Theta a_j]\!] = \lambda_\Theta (\mathbf{e}_i \mathbf{e}_j^T + \mathbf{e}_j \mathbf{e}_i^T)$$

Here $\mathbf{e}_i$ (respectively $\mathbf{e}_j$) is the unit vector containing all zeros except 1 in the ith (respectively jth) entry, and $\mathbf{e}_i^T$ (respectively $\mathbf{e}_j^T$) is its transpose.

The c-matrices of more complex constraint expressions are computed bottom-up, by combining the c-matrices of sub-expressions through the function $\Diamond$ that takes a real number in [0,1], a set of c-matrices, and that outputs a c-matrix. Computation of $\Diamond$ is given by the algorithm `combine` below, and is based on the following intuition. If attributes a_i and a_j are indirectly related through an operator O (e.g., $\wedge$), then there exists a k such that both $[\![R]\!][i, k]$ and $[\![R]\!][j, k]$ are non-zero. The strength of connection between a_i and a_j are then the average of $[\![R]\!][i, k]$ and $[\![R]\!][j, k]$, weakened by λ_O, unless a larger value already exists for $[\![R]\!][i, j]$ (possibly due the existence of other constraints that relate a_i and a_j). Each matrix in the input $\mathcal{M}$ is assumed to be an $n \times n$ c-matrix.

Algorithm (`combine`)
   Input: λ: real; $\mathcal{M}$: c-matrices
   Output: a c-matrix
   1. $M' \leftarrow M'' \leftarrow \text{zeros}(n)$ /* two temporary nxn zero matrices */
   2. $M' \leftarrow \text{pMax}\mathcal{M}$ /* pMax the pointwise maximum function of a set of matrices */
   3. For $1 \leq i, j, k \leq n$ where i, j and k are pairwise distinct do
       If $M'[i, k] \neq 0$ and $M'[j, k] \neq 0$,   /* compute indirect connections */
          $M''[i, j] \leftarrow M''[j, i] \leftarrow \max\{M'[i, j], \lambda \frac{M'[i,k]+M'[j,k]}{2}\}$
   4. return $\text{pMax}(M', M'')$

A complete specification of $[\![\ ]\!]$ is ongoing and will be reported [15]. Two examples of a recursively defined c-matrices are below.

$$[\![R_1 \wedge R_2]\!] = \Diamond(\lambda_\wedge)\{[\![R_1]\!], [\![R_2]\!]\}$$
$$[\![\sigma_{R_1}(T)]\!] = \Diamond(\lambda_\sigma)\{[\![R_1]\!], [\![T]\!]\}$$

Note that boolean expressions and relational algebraic expressions are not type differentiated in the specification. For our purpose, such mixing is immaterial since we do not concern ourselves with the operational semantics of expressions with respect to data retrieval. Rather, we are interested in the constraint "implied" or "suggested" when constraints appear together in a given context. For example, the most pertinent information conveyed by the constraint $(\sigma_{\texttt{player1=player2}}\texttt{lineup}) = \emptyset$ is that the attributes `lineup.player1` and `lineup.player2` directly restrict each other, and are thus strongly connected.

Given $[\![R]\!]$, a simplistic approach to dividing the given problem $P = (Q, R)$ into a sequence $P_0, ..., P_m$ of subproblem increments is by grouping the attributes of A_R into sets $A_0, ..., A_m$ according to the connectedness values given by Equation 1. For now, m is a user-determined value. The initial group A_0 consists at least two attributes. Then for each $0 \leq i \leq m$, $P_i = (Q_i, R_i)$ where Q_i is the set of sub-relations of Q restricted to the set $\cup_{j=0}^{i} A_j$, and R_i to those constraints in R that contain only attributes in the same set, but excluding constraints in $R_0, ..., R_{i-1}$. Note that Q_i may be empty. This happens when $\cup_{j=0}^{i} A_j$ only contains attributes that do not appear in Q (but are in base relations). In the preliminary experiments discussed next, we further combine attributes that co-occur in base relations. This is to reduce the number of increments that need to be solved.

4   Preliminary Experiments

We apply the heuristic decomposition technique to a university scheduling problem. The base relations consist of

```
professor(name, rank, department, research areas, # courses)
course(name, department, term-offered, topics)
room(name, capacity)   /* sample: (Math-200, 35) */
slot(name, duration)   /* sample: (MWF-10AM, 50) */
semester(year, term)
```

Some of the more interesting constraints imposed include 1) "Each professor has an assigned number of classes to teach each semester, and usually have preferences for teaching time (e.g., Tuesday/Thursday afternoons)." 2) "Course topics should match professors research interest and expertise." 3) "The same course offered in consecutive terms should not be taught by the same professor."

The problem is to compute an extension for a teaching schedule relation for the academic year. The schema of the guess relation is

```
schedule(professor.name, course.name, slot.name,
         room.name, semester.term).
```

To begin, a weakening factor for each operator had to be defined. For these experiments, we assign the following values. (The symbol Θ stands for any comparison operator.)

Operator	Θ	$\wedge$	$\vee$	$-$	σ	$\bowtie$	$\mathcal{F}$
Value	1	0.8	0.6	0.6	0.4	0.4	0.5

Based on these, the connectedness of the attributes were computed and ordered to determine the subproblems. If a_i has a high connectedness value and a_j appears in the constraint and is in the same base relation as a_j, then a_j is grouped with a_i even if a_j's connectedness value may be lower. This reduces the number of increments that needs to be solved with minimal increase in the size of the encoding for each increment, since the size of the variable set is restricted by the the tuples that occur in the base relations.

A set of sample problems are created based on a combination of real and artificial tuples. For the results shown in Figure 1, each problem is named along with, in parenthesis, the number of data instances for each of the attributes of the guess relations. For example, P2(20,35,12,8,1) indicates 20 professors, 35 courses, , 12 time slots, and so on. In the first three test problems, the relation semester is not used. The column Sol indicates whether the problem has a solution. The column STD shows the

Data	Sol	STD	STD-Time	HD	HD-Time
D1(5,3,4,4)	Yes	9,754	0.121 (0.08,0.00)	17 + 10 + 13	0.145
D2(20,35,12,8)	Yes	5,571,459	44.678 (42.53,2.14)	173 + 92 + 579	1.218
D3(20,35,12,8)	Yes	692,255	5.553 (5.33,0.22)	85 + 92 + 579	2.829
D4(20,37,12,8,2)	No	23,571,459	34.029 (30,26,3.76)	1127 + N/A	3.307
D5(20,37,12,4,2)	No	Unknown	Err	1173 + 116 + 333	3.973
D6(20,37,11,5,2)	No	Unknown	Err	1173 + N/A	2.946
D7(20,37,12,8,2)	Yes	Unknown	Err	1173 + 116+ 637	1.748

Fig. 1. Experiments

number of clauses produced using a straightforward encoding of the problems. The column STD-TIME indicates the total time required to solve the problem, broken down parenthetically to the time required to encode the problem as a SAT instance, and the time taken to solve the SAT instance using SATO [14].

When applying the heuristic problem decomposition technique, attributes with the highest connectedness values were `semester.term` (when available), `professor.name`, and `course.name`. These along with attributes that co-occur in base relations defined the initial subproblem. As mentioned, each problem is solved in three increments. The column HD shows the number of clauses that the technique encodes as the sum of the number of clauses over the three increments. Other than the initial subproblem, each value shows the number of clauses in the final iteration (lead to either success or failure). Observe that the detection of unsolvability may occur at different stages. Problem D5, for instance, unsolvability was detected only after all attempts to extend solutions of the first two increments failed. Problem D6, on the other hand, unsolvability was determined in the second increment. The column HD-Time indicates the total time required to solve the problem including the time for choosing increments, the encoding time over all increments, and the solving time over all increments.

Results of the experiments show, clearly, the potential benefit of incremental encoding and the feasibility of using a SAT solver as the backend to a CONSQL engine. In all cases, incremental encoding dramatically reduces the number of encoded clauses and as a result, the time to a solution (except for the smallest problem). The improvement holds for both solvable as well as unsolvable problems. As mentioned earlier, the SAT instances are not necessarily difficult to solve, but the amount of encoding time required makes it prohibitive in many cases to adopt an eager approach (i.e., a single encoding of the entire problem).

5   Conclusion and Ongoing Work

The primary contribution of our work is in showing that, with some engineering, a SAT-based CONSQL engine is feasible. The use of incremental encoding to expand the range of problems that can be efficiently solved has been shown useful for checking first-order satisfiability [3]. What we have demonstrated is how the technique may be adapted to computing constraint problems over relational databases. We briefly describe ongoing work.

1. The computation of $[\![R]\!]$ is driven by the form of the given constraint and as such, may vary for two constraints that are syntactically dissimilar but semantically equivalent. To compute connectedness that are invariant with respect to the syntactic representation of constraints, a possible solution is to preprocessing constraints into a "normal form". To that end, query rewrite rules employed by query optimizers may provide a useful starting point.
2. Results reported in this paper have been obtained with a "simulated database" where data reside in text files and CONSQL constraints are specified in ad-hoc (Lisp like) syntax. A prototyping effort is underway to implement a SATO-backed CONSQL engine within a relational database system. Along with this, a formal specification of CONSQL to clausal encoding in propositional logic is under study.

Longer term extensions include support for encoding numerical data. As [5] points out, the use of incremental encoding is particularly useful for handling numerical data.

References

1. Amir, E., McIlraith, S.: Solving Satisfiability using Decomposition and the Most Constrained Subproblem. In: Proceedings of the Workshop on Theory and Applications of Satisfiability Testing (2001)
2. Bacchus, F.: CSPs: Adding Structure to SAT. In: Biere, A., Gomes, C.P. (eds.) SAT 2006. LNCS, vol. 4121, p. 10. Springer, Heidelberg (2006)
3. Barrett, C.W., Dill, D.L., Stump, A.: Checking Satisfiability of First-Order Formulas by Incremental Translation to SAT. In: Brinksma, E., Larsen, K.G. (eds.) CAV 2002. LNCS, vol. 2404, pp. 236–249. Springer, Heidelberg (2002)
4. Bjesse, P., Kukula, J.H., Damiano, R.F., Stanion, T., Zhu, Y.: Guiding SAT Diagnosis with Tree Decompositions. In: Giunchiglia, E., Tacchella, A. (eds.) SAT 2003. LNCS, vol. 2919, pp. 315–329. Springer, Heidelberg (2004)
5. Bordeaux, L., Hamadi, Y., Zhang, L.: Propositional Satisfiability and Constraint Programming: A comparative survey. ACM Computing Survey 38(4) (2006)
6. Cadoli, M., Mancini, T.: Combining relational algebra, SQL, constraint modelling, and local search. Theory Pract. Log. Program. 7(1–2), 37–65 (2007)
7. Cai, M.: Integrating Constraint and Relational Database Systems. In: Kuijpers, B., Revesz, P.Z. (eds.) CDB 2004. LNCS, vol. 3074, pp. 180–188. Springer, Heidelberg (2004)
8. Elmasri, R., Navathe, S.B.: Fundamentals of Database Systems, 2nd edn. Benjamin/Cummings (1994)
9. Jaffar, J., Maher, M.J.: Constraint Logic Programming: A Survey. Journal of Logic Programming 19/20, 503–581 (1994)
10. Kanellakis, P.C., Goldin, D.Q.: Constraint Programming and Database Query Languages. In: Hagiya, M., Mitchell, J.C. (eds.) TACS 1994. LNCS, vol. 789, pp. 96–120. Springer, Heidelberg (1994)
11. Li, W., van Beek, P.: Guiding Real-World SAT Solving with Dynamic Hypergraph Separator Decomposition. In: Proceedings of ICTAI, pp. 542–548. IEEE Computer Society, Los Alamitos (2004)
12. Ramakrishnan, R., Gehrke, J.: Database Management Systems. McGraw-Hill Higher Education, New York (2000)
13. Zaniolo, C.: Deductive databases - theory meets practice. In: Bancilhon, F., Tsichritzis, D.C., Thanos, C. (eds.) EDBT 1990. LNCS, vol. 416, pp. 1–15. Springer, Heidelberg (1990)
14. Zhang, H., Stickel, M.: Implementing the Davis-Putnam Procedure. Journal of Automated Reasoning 24, 277–296 (2000)
15. Zhao, D.: Analyzing SQL Constraints. Master's thesis, Emory University (August 2008)

Using Place and Transition Fault Net Models for Sequential Diagnosis Time Assessment in Discrete Event Systems

Iwan Tabakow

Institute of Applied Informatics, Wroclaw University of Technology, Poland
iwan.tabakow@pwr.wroc.pl

Abstract. The diagnosis-time assessment is studied below in the case of discrete event systems. It is assumed that any such system is described by a live, bounded, and reversible place-transition Petri net. There are assumed some deterministically given delays associated with the transitions of N and hence N is assumed to be deterministic timed. For this purpose two different type of (single) fault models are used, i.e. place fault and transition fault models and the corresponding diagnosis process is assumed to be sequential. Hence, the diagnosis-time assessment is realised by computing the absolute value of the time difference between the minimum cycle time of N and the worst-case fault-isolation time according to the obtained diagnostic tree.

1 Introduction

The use of Petri net models in diagnosis and reliable design of event-driven systems is a subject of interest to researchers since more than twenty years. In general, the most of the studies in this area focus attention on dynamical analysis concerning specification and implementation of some fault detection, fault diagnosis and/or fault recovery procedures, e.g. using partially stochastic Petri nets [1], encoded Petri net states for non-concurrent fault identification [16], using trace analysis [7], or also an online computation of the set of possible fault events required to explain the last observed event [2]. In the last paper, an algorithm of detecting occurrences of fault events associated to unobservable transitions was presented. A review of the recent research was also given in [2]. In general, some special (compiled or also interpreted) agents, i.e. algorithms called "diagnosers" were introduced. The fault detection and/or isolation are realised as an off- or online computation process. It can be noted that the above compiled and interpreted diagnosers correspond to the notions of combinational and sequential fault diagnosis, respectively [11,12,14]. The main advantages of the considered works are related to the possibility of formulating fault diagnosis with application to any discrete event system. However, some disadvantages seem to be the lack of information concerning the inherent fault distinguishability properties of the considered system. And so, the study of the system fault indistinguishability properties seems to be important because of the following two reasons. First, we have an additional possibility of describing the critical components of the considered system. Second, there exists a possibility of using some simple and at the same time exact tools

N.T. Nguyen et al. (Eds.): IEA/AIE 2008, LNAI 5027, pp. 677–686, 2008.

for improving the system (self-) diagnosis capabilities in the early stages of its design [10 -14].

This paper describes a method of diagnosis-time assessment in discrete event systems. Any such system is modelled by a live, bounded, and reversible place-transition Petri net N. Also there are assumed some deterministically given delays associated with the transitions of N and hence N is assumed to be deterministic timed. For this purpose two different type of (single) fault models are used, i.e. place fault and transition fault models and the corresponding diagnosis process is assumed to be sequential. Hence, the diagnosis-time assessment is realised by computing the absolute value of the time difference between the minimum cycle time of N and the worst-case fault-isolation time according to the obtained diagnostic tree. The notions of D-partition of the set of places P of a given place-transition net N and net k-distinguishability are first introduced. Then the corresponding net place invariants are computed. The system k-distinguishability measure is obtained in a unique way from the place-invariant matrix. For a large value of k, the system model is extended by using some set of additional places called test points and at the same time preserving the original net properties. In accordance with the above assumption of sequential fault diagnosis, the process of fault isolation is carried step by step, where each step depends on the result of the diagnostic experiment at the previous step. A preliminary version of this approach was given in [15] where only the single place fault model was assumed. The complexity of the proposed method depends on the effectivity of the existing algorithms for computation of the P-cover, i.e. the set of P-invariants covering N.

2 Basic Notions

In general any place-transition net $N =_{df} (T, P, A, M_0, K, W)$, where (T, P, A) is a finite net containing sets of *transitions* , *places*, and *arcs* called also *edges*, $K : P \rightarrow (IN_\omega - \{0\})$ and $W : A \rightarrow \mathbb{N}$ are the corresponding *place capacity* and *edge multiplicity* (called also *weight*) functions, respectively. In particular, N is *ordinary* iff $W(a) = 1$ (for any $a \in A$). The *initial marking vector* $M_0 : P \rightarrow IN_\omega$, where $\mathbb{N}$ denotes the set of all natural numbers, $IN =_{df} \mathbb{N} \cup \{0\}$, $IN_\omega =_{df} IN \cup \{\omega\}$, and ω is an infinite number such that: $\omega + k = \omega$ and $k < \omega$ (for any $k \in IN$) [5,8,9]. The *forward marking class* of N, i.e. $[M_0 > =_{df} \{M \in IN_\omega{}^P / \exists \tau \in T^* (M_0[\tau >M)\}$.

In the next considerations we shall assume N is a live and bounded net. In the case of manufacturing systems the *net reversibility property* is also required. Moreover, for simplicity it is assumed below that N is pure (i.e. it has no self-loops) and simple (there are no different vertices in N having the same pre- and post-sets). The net P-*invariants* (*T-invariants*) are computed using $\underline{N} \cdot \underline{i} = \underline{0}$ ($\underline{N}^T \cdot \underline{x} = \underline{0}$), where $\underline{N}$ is the *PN-connectivity matrix* of N (having $|T|$ rows and $|P|$ columns). We have: $\underline{N} = \underline{N}^+ - \underline{N}^-$, where $\underline{N}^+$ and $\underline{N}^-$ are the corresponding *output* and *input matrices* for N. The *support* of any P-invariant $\underline{i}$ wrt N is defined as follows: $\text{supp}(\underline{i}) =_{df} \{p \in P / \underline{i}(p) \neq 0\} \subseteq$ P. Let $\mathbf{I}$ be the set of all (positive) P-invariants of N and $\mathbf{J} \quad \subseteq \mathbf{I}$ is a subset. The

P-invariant matrix of N wrt $\mathbf{J}$ is introduced as follows: $\underline{\mathbf{J}} : \mathbf{J} \times P \to IN$, where $\underline{\mathbf{J}}(\underline{i},p) =_{df} \underline{i}(p) \in IN$.

For convenience only, we shall assume below that the P-cover $\mathbf{J}$ of N is a set of all positive and minimal P-invariants. Any such set is assumed to be a set of linearly independent P-invariants. And in fact, any P-invariant matrix $\underline{\mathbf{J}}$ can be considered as an information system. Hence, we shall assume that the set of P-invariants $\mathbf{J}$ (i.e. 'attributes' of this information system) is a reduced set [5]. Also we shall use the notion of the *revised P-invariant matrix* of N, defined as: $\underline{\rho} : \mathbf{J} \times P \to \{0.1\}$, where $\underline{\rho}(\underline{i},p) =_{df} 1$ iff $\underline{i}(p) \neq 0$ [3]. Let $x \in T \cup P$. The *pre-set* (*post-set*) associated with x is defined as follows: $^{\bullet}x =_{df} \{y \in T \cup P / (y,x) \in A\}$ ($x^{\bullet} =_{df} \{y \in T \cup P / (x,y) \in A\}$). For any nonempty $X \subseteq T \cup P$: $^{\bullet}X =_{df} \bigcup_{x \in X} {}^{\bullet}x$ and $X^{\bullet} =_{df} \bigcup_{x \in X} x^{\bullet}$ Any ordinary net is a *marked graph* iff $| {}^{\bullet}p | = | p^{\bullet} | = 1$ (for any $p \in P$). For simplicity, it is assumed below N have a P-cover. Otherwise, this method is also applicable. In the last case some additional test points is necessary to be introduced. Moreover, it can be observed that a selection of a minimal (or in general: optimal) P-cover may not guarantee a better net fault distinguishability. The net's places are interpreted below as representing resource states or operations and the transitions as representing start or completion of the corresponding discrete event [17].

3 Net k-Distinguishability and Simulation

Let $[M_0 >_{\alpha} =_{df} [M_0 > \cup \{M_{\alpha}\}$, where M_0 is the initial marking and M_{α} be a marking of N such that $M_{\alpha} \notin [M_0 >$. We shall say M_{α} is a *faulty marking*. Since $M \cdot \underline{i} = M_0 \cdot \underline{i}$ (for any $M \in [M_0 >$ and $\underline{i} \in \mathbf{J}$) [8] then $\Delta M \cdot \underline{i} = 0$, where $\Delta M =_{df} M - M_0$. The last property is satisfied for any P-invariant $\underline{i} \in \mathbf{J}$. Hence we can obtain $\underline{\mathbf{J}} \cdot \Delta M^T = \underline{0}$. Therefore for $M \in [M_0 >_{\alpha}$ the above equation may be violated. Thus we have: $\underline{\mathbf{J}} \cdot \Delta M^T = \underline{a} \in \{0,1\}^{|\mathbf{J}|}$ (for any $M \in [M_0 >_{\alpha}$, obviously $\underline{a} = \underline{0}$ iff $M \in [M_0 >$). Without losing any generality, below $(\underline{a})_s \neq 0$ are interpreted as $(\underline{a})_s = 1$ ($s \in \{1,..., |\mathbf{J}|\}$). Hence, in accordance with [4], any $(\underline{a})_s = 1$ will correspond to some subset of places $\mathrm{supp}(\underline{i}_s) \subseteq P$ having a (potentially) faulty behaviour. Let $\Omega(\underline{a}) =_{df} \bigcap_{(\underline{a})_s=1} \mathrm{supp}(\underline{i}_s) \cap \bigcap_{(\underline{a})_s=0} \mathrm{supp}(\underline{i}_s)' \subseteq P$, where $\mathrm{supp}(\underline{i}_s)' =_{df} P - \mathrm{supp}(\underline{i}_s)$ is the corresponding set complement operation (provided there is no ambiguity we shall use below the same designation " ´ " as an index, e.g. to denote M', i.e. the marking M for N', where N' is the net simulator corresponding to N, in a similar manner Ω' is used for Ω of N'). The notions of D-partition and net k-distinguishability are first given below [10-14].

Definition 1
By a *D-partition of the set of places* P of a given place-transition net N wrt the P-cover $\mathbf{J}$ of N, denoted by $\Omega(N,\mathbf{J})$, or Ω if N and $\mathbf{J}$ are understood, we shall mean the (multi) family $\Omega =_{df} \{\Omega(\underline{a}) / \underline{a} \in \{0,1\}^{|\mathbf{J}|}\}$.

Proposition 1
(a) $\Omega(\underline{0}) = \varnothing$,
(b) $\forall \, \underline{a},\underline{b} \neq \underline{0} \, (\underline{a} \neq \underline{b} \Rightarrow \Omega(\underline{a}) \cap \Omega(\underline{b}) = \varnothing)$, and
(c) $\bigcup\limits_{\underline{a} \in \{0,1\}^{|\mathbf{J}|}} \Omega(\underline{a}) = P.$ □

Definition 2
The Petri net N is a *k-distinguishable net under* Ω iff

(i) $\exists \, \Omega(\underline{a}) \in \Omega \, (|\Omega(\underline{a})| = k)$ and
(ii) $\forall \, \Omega(\underline{a}) \in \Omega \, (|\Omega(\underline{a})| \leq k)$.

With any P/T-net N it can be associated a new net, say N´, such that any transition $t \in T$ of N is transformed to a subnet $(\{t^+,t^-\},\{p^t\},\{(t^+,p^t),(p^t,t^-)\})$ in N´. Any such transformation is closed in the class of P/T-nets. The size of N´, i.e. $s(N´) = s(N) + 4 \cdot |T|.$, where $s(N) =_{df} |T| + |P| + |A|$ by definition is the *size* of the original net N. Provided there is no ambiguity, the additional places p^t of N´ will be denoted below by p(t) (for any $t \in T$). The following values are assumed for the edge multiplicity function related to p(t): $W(t^+,p(t)) = W(p(t),t^-) = 1$ (for any $t \in T$). Any other values of W remain the same as in N. An example net N´ is shown in Figure 1(b) below (see Example 1).

In accordance with the above given construction any marking M in N will correspond to exactly one marking M´ in N´. Also different markings in N will correspond to different markings in N´. So there exists some injective mapping, e.g. ψ from $[M_0 >$ in N to $[M_0´>$ in N´. In general, the following definition can be introduced (very similar to the well-known classical notion).

Definition 3
We shall say that N´ is a *net simulator* of N (or *simulates* N) iff for any marking sequence $M_0, M_1, ..., M_k, ...$ in N there exists a marking sequence $M_0´, M_1´, ..., M_r´, ...$ in N´ such that: (1) $M_0´ = \psi(M_0)$, (2) If the above two sequences are finite having final markings M_k and $M_r´$ then $M_r´ = \psi(M_k)$ and (3) For any two neighbouring markings M_i, M_{i+1} in the first sequence there exist two markings $M_u´, M_v´$ in the second sequence such that $i \leq u < v$, $M_u´ = \psi(M_i)$, and $M_v´ = \psi(M_{i+1})$.

Since $|\,{}^\bullet p(t)\,| = |\,p(t)^\bullet\,| = 1$ (for any $t \in T$), the following proposition is satisfied.

Proposition 2

Let N be a marked graph. Then N´ is a marked graph.   □

According to Definition 3, the net N´ obtained under the above given transition transformation is a well-defined net simulator of N. Moreover, any such transformation will preserve the basic inherent properties of N (a more formal treatment is omitted). Let N´ be a net simulator of N and $\underline{i}$´ be a P-invariant of N´. It was shown that $\underline{i}$´ can be directly obtained by means of the corresponding P-invariant $\underline{i}$ of N. Hence there exists a strongly defined relationship between the P-covers of N´ and N. The above given Definition 2 is generalised as follows [9].

Definition 4
Let N be a place-transition net. Then N is a *k-distinguishable net* iff $\exists$ N´ (N´ is a net simulator of N and N´ is a k-distinguishable net under Ω´).

The *support* of any D-partition is defined as follows: $\mathrm{supp}(\Omega) =_{df} \{\ \Omega(\underline{a}) \in \Omega\ /\ \Omega(\underline{a}) \neq \varnothing\}$. Let $\pi(P)$ be the partition generated by the set of subsets of places (i.e. classes), such that each class consists of places having identical columns in the revised P-invariant matrix $\underline{\rho}$ of N. The following proposition is satisfied [3] (a more formal proof is given in [11]).

Proposition 3

$$\mathrm{supp}(\Omega) = \pi(P). \qquad\qquad\qquad \square$$

In accordance with Proposition 3, the system k-distinguishability measure can be obtained in a unique way from the place-invariant matrix.

4   Test Points and Fault Models

For a large value of k, the system model is extended by using some set of additional places called test points and at the same time preserving the original net properties. The notion of test point is introduced as follows [12].

Definition 5

Let $p_{k_0} \in P$ be a given place of N such that the pre-set $^{\bullet}p_{k_0} =_{df} \{t_1\}$ and the post-set $p_{k_0}^{\bullet} =_{df} \{t_2\}$, where t_1 and t_2 are two different transitions of N. The additional place $p_{k_0}' \in {}^{\bullet}t_1 \cap t_2^{\bullet}$ is said to be a *test point associated with* p_{k_0} iff the initial marking $\hat{M}_0$ of the obtained net $\hat{N}$ is specified as follows: $\hat{M}_0(p) =_{df}$ if $p = p_{k_0}'$ then $\max\{M(p_{k_0})\ /\ M \in [M_0>\} - M_0(p_{k_0})$ else $M_0(p)$ fi (for any $p \in \hat{P} =_{df} P \cup \{p_{k_0}'\}$).

A generalisation of Definition 5 for *non-ordinary place-transition nets* (i.e. nets having some edges $a \in A$ with weights $w(a) \neq 1$) is omitted here. Any such generalisation of the last definition for place-transition nets, which are not ordinary, would require an isomorphism between the corresponding reachability graphs RG(N) and RG($\hat{N}$). Moreover, any additional test point will not change the original boundedness, liveness, and reversibility net properties [13,14].

682   I. Tabakow

Any place $p \in P$ of N having an incorrect behaviour is said to be a *faulty place* (denoted also by p_α). The single faulty place model will be assumed below (called in short: *p-fault model*). Moreover, in accordance with Definition 4 the above presented p-fault model can be generalised to the set of all vertices $x \in P \cup T$ of N. In particular, assuming that P is fault-free, the single faulty transition model can be obtained (called in short: *t-fault model*).

Definition 6
The Petri net N is a *p-fault k-distinguishable net* (a *t-fault k-distinguishable net*) iff N is a k-distinguishable net under Ω assuming the p-fault model (t-fault model).

   Obviously, the process of test point placement is finite, i.e. the following proposition is satisfied.

Proposition 4
Let N be a p-fault 1-distinguishable net (a t-fault 1-distinguishable net) and $p_{k_0}{}'$ is a

test point associated with p_{k_0} in N. Then $\hat{N}$ is also a p-fault 1-distinguishable net (a

t-fault 1-distinguishable net).

Proof
Let N be a p-fault 1-distinguishable net (a t-fault 1-distinguishable net). Since by assumption $\underline{J}$ is a P-cover of N there are no zero-columns in $\underline{J}$. Obviously, the column

corresponding to $p_{k_0}{}'$ will be different from the rest and hence the new obtained ma-

trix $\hat{\underline{J}}$ has all columns different. So, in accordance with Proposition 3 $\hat{N}$ is also a p-

fault 1-distinguishable net (a t-fault 1-distinguishable net). $\qquad\qquad\square$

5 P- and T-Fault Diagnosis-Time Assessment

Suppose we are interested in finding how fast each transition can initiate firing in a periodically operated timed Petri net, where a period ζ is defined as the time to complete a firing sequence leading back to the initial marking after firing each transition at least once. ζ is called a *cycle time*. Hence, it is assumed that N is consistent. Without loss of generality, we shall assume below that there is a delay of at least d_i [sec] associated with $t_i \in T$. This means that when t_i is enabled, $n_{ij}^- =_{df} W(p_j,t_i)$ tokens will be reserved in place p_j for at least d_i [sec] before their removal by firing t_i [5]. The above introduced delay can be presented as a mapping $d : T \rightarrow IN$ and so $d_i = d(t_i)$ (for any $t_i \in T$). Let D be the diagonal matrix of d_i ($i = 1, 2, ..., |T|$) and $\underline{x}$ be a minimal positive T- invariant covering all transitions of T. The following lower bound of the cycle ζ or the *minimum cycle time* was given (a more formal treatment is

omitted) [5]: $\displaystyle \zeta_{min} = \max\left\{ \frac{\underline{i} \cdot (\underline{N}^-)^T \cdot D \cdot \underline{x}}{\underline{i} \cdot M_0} / \underline{i} \in \mathbf{J} \right\}$. Let $\underline{i}_s \in \mathbf{J}$ and $P_s =_{df} \text{supp}(\underline{i}_s) \subseteq$

P. The *subset of transitions associated with* $\underline{i}_s$ is defined as follows: $T_s =_{df}\ {}^\bullet P_s \cup P_s^\bullet$ $\subseteq T$. The *total delay* obtained using $\underline{i}_s$ can be defined as follows: $\delta_s = \delta(\underline{i}_s) =_{df} \sum_{t \in T_s} d(t)$. Any sequential diagnosis procedure can be graphically represented as diagnostic tree. The cost of this tree (in short: CDT) can be defined as follows [11]: $\text{CDT} =_{df} \sum_{p \in P} \text{Prob}\{p\} \cdot c(p)$, where $c(p) =_{df} \sum_{\tau \in \Theta(p)} c(\tau)$. By $\Theta(p) \subseteq \Theta$ it is denoted the subset of tests isolating (or locating) fault in p. The *time of isolating* p is denoted by $\Delta(p)$ ($p \in P$). Since there is one-to-one correspondence between $\tau_s \in \Theta$ and $\underline{i}_s \in J$, the above costs $c(p)$ and $c(\tau)$ can be interpreted as $\Delta(p)$ and δ_s respectively, where $\Delta(p) =_{df} \sum_{\tau \in \Theta(p)} \delta_s$.

Let $\Delta^* =_{df} \max\{\Delta(p) / p \in P\}$ be the *worst-case fault-isolation time*. The *diagnosis-time assessment* (in short: DTA) can be realised by computing the absolute value of the time difference between the minimum cycle time of N and the worst-case fault-isolation time according to the obtained diagnostic tree. And hence, the following measure was given in [15]: $\text{DTA} =_{df} \text{abs}(\zeta_{min} - \Delta^*)$.

Example 1
Consider the Petri net N of Figure 1(a) below corresponding to the example manufacturing system given in [17] (a system consisting of two different machines, a robot, and a buffer.). The obtained net simulator N´ is shown in Figure 1(b). Without losing any generality, the t-fault sequential model (related to N´) is illustrated. According to [14], N is a p-fault 1-distinguishable net and a t-fault 2-distinguishable net. Here, the additional places p_{1i} correspond to $p(t_i)$ ($i = 1,2,...,6$).

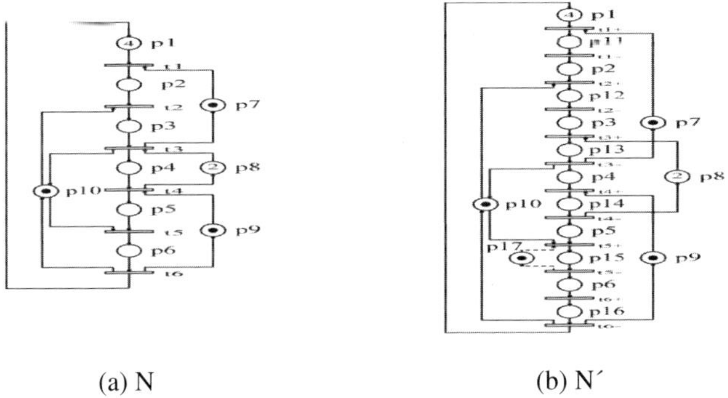

(a) N   (b) N´

Fig. 1. The Petri net model (a) and the corresponding net simulator (b)

And so, to distinguish between faults in t_5 and t_6, an additional test point p_{17} is placed (as it is shown in Figure 1(b), using dashed line). The extended P-invariant

$$\text{submatrix of } N',\ \hat{\underline{J}}\ '/\,T = \begin{bmatrix} 1 & 1 & 1 & 1 & 1 & 1 & 0 \\ 1 & 1 & 1 & 0 & 0 & 0 & 0 \\ 0 & 1 & 1 & 0 & 1 & 1 & 0 \\ 0 & 0 & 1 & 1 & 0 & 0 & 0 \\ 0 & 0 & 0 & 1 & 1 & 1 & 0 \\ 0 & 0 & 0 & 0 & 1 & 0 & 1 \end{bmatrix} \begin{array}{l} 6d \\ 3d \\ 4d \\ 2d \\ 3d \\ 2d \end{array}$$

. The time delays $\delta_s =$

$\delta_s(\ \hat{\underline{i}}_s\ '/\,T)$ associated with any row are also given (assuming all of $d_i = d$, $i = 1,2,...,6$). It can be observed that any δ_s corresponds to the number of ones in the corresponding row. But in general, this property is not satisfied (e.g. for the P-invariant $\underline{i} = (0,0,1,0,0,1,0,0,0,1)$ of N we have: $\delta(\underline{i}) = 4d$). But it holds in the class of timed marked graphs.

Since $\hat{\underline{J}}\ '/\,T$ has all columns different, any single faulty transition can be identified. The set of P-invariants, i.e. rows of $\hat{\underline{J}}\ '/\,T$ can be considered as attributes of an information system [6]. It can be shown that $\hat{\underline{J}}\ '/\,T$ is a set of independent attributes (this is omitted). For simplicity, we shall assume below a uniform fault distribution, i.e. a constant probability. Since test costs are different, the following construction of the obtained diagnostic tree (in short: D-tree) was used.

In any step of fault isolation it is selected a row in $\hat{\underline{J}}\ '/\,T$ with minimal time delay δ. If there are two or more such rows, then an additional requirement is the possibility of dividing the actual fault set into two equal parts. In the case when the last obtained set is not singleton, the choice is arbitrary. Hence, the obtained tree is shown in Figure 2 below, where any i_s' corresponds to $\Delta\hat{M}/T\cdot\hat{\underline{i}}_s\ '/T = 0?$, $s = 2,...,6$).

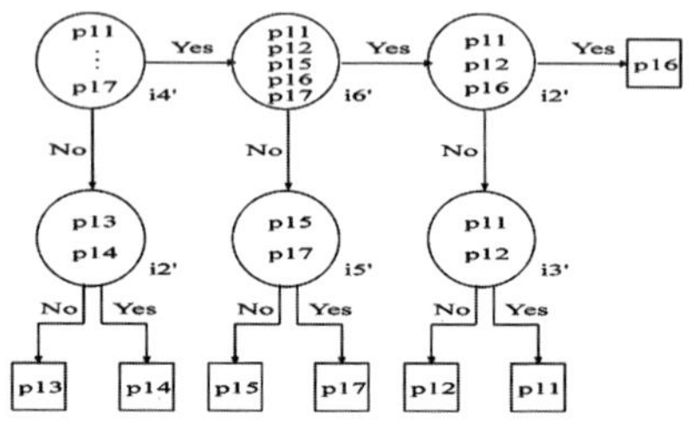

Fig. 2. An example D-tree

Since the minimum cycle time for N, $\zeta_{min} = \max\left\{\dfrac{d_1+d_2+d_3+d_4+d_5+d_6}{4},\right.$

$\left.\dfrac{d_1+d_2+d_3}{1},\dfrac{d_2+d_3+d_5+d_6}{1},\dfrac{d_3+d_4}{2},\dfrac{d_4+d_5+d_6}{1}\right\}/d_i = d = 4d$ and $\Delta^*{}_{/t-fault}$

$= 11d$ then $DTA_{/t-fault} = 7d$. Similarly, in the case of the p-fault model it can be obtained: $\Delta^{*}_{/p-fault} = 18d$ and $DTA_{/p-fault} = 14d$. And finally, the following table has been obtained (the value for CDT is also illustrated). $\qquad\square$

DTA [sec]	p-fault model	t-fault model	$\dfrac{DTA_{/p-fault}}{DTA_{/t-fault}}$
Δ^{*}	14.00d	07.00d	02.00
CDT	08.70d	03.57d	≈ 02.44

6 Conclusions

The above-considered approach gives a possibility of diagnosis-time assessment of discrete event systems in the case of sequential fault isolation. The choice of diagnosis strategies, i.e. combinational or also sequential is depending on the used time requirements for testing. An additional cost-minimisation can be obtained by assuming the considered test point set as a "hardcore". The complexity of the proposed method depends on the effectivity of the existing algorithms for computation of the P-cover, i.e. the set of P-invariants covering N. The proposed approach can be extended for higher level Petri nets, e.g. such as coloured or also to the class of nondeterministic timed nets (i.e. stochastic nets if the delays are probabilistically specified). A more optimistic measure of this time assessment can be obtained by using the cost-value of the corresponding diagnostic tree. The using of additional test points may implicate different values for the obtained minimum net-cycle time. In general, the diagnosis-time assessment in the case of the p-fault model seems to be greater than this one in the case of using t-fault model.

References

1. Aghasaryan, A., Fabre, E., Benveniste, A., Boubour, R., Jard, C.: Fault detection and diagnosis in distributed systems: an approach by partially stochastic Petri nets. Discrete Event Dynamic Systems 8(2) (Special issue on Hybrid Systems), 203–231 (1998)
2. Basile, F., Chiacchio, P., De Tommasi, G.: An efficient approach for online diagnosis of discrete event systems. IEEE Trans. on Automatic Control, 26 (submitted, 2007)
3. Immanuel, B., Rangarajan, K.: System diagnosis and k-distinguishability in Petri nets. Private communication, India, p. 14 (2001)
4. Murata, T.: Petri nets and their applications. Journal Soc. Instrum. Control Eng. 22, 65–72 (1983)
5. Murata, T.: Petri nets: properties, analysis and applications. Proceedings of the IEEE 1(4), 541–580 (1989)
6. Pawlak, Z.: Rough Sets, Theoretical Aspects of Reasoning about Data, p. 229. Kluwer Academic Publishers, Dordrecht (1991)

7. Pietschker, A., Ulrich, A.: A light-weight method for trace analysis to support fault diagnosis in concurrent systems. Journal of Systemics, Cybernetics and Informatics 1(6), 6 (2003)
8. Reisig, W.: Petri Nets. An Introduction, pp. 15, 62–66. Springer, Heidelberg (1985)
9. Reisig, W.: A Primer in Petri Net Design, pp. 25–33. Springer, Heidelberg (1992)
10. Tabakow, I.G.: Using Petri net invariants in system diagnosis. Petri Net Newsletter 58, 21–31 (2000)
11. Tabakow, I.G.: Using place invariants to isolate faults in concurrent systems. Petri Net Newsletter 68, 10–20 (2005)
12. Tabakow, I.G.: Fault Diagnosis of Discrete Event Systems Using Place Invariants. In: Khosla, R., Howlett, R.J., Jain, L.C. (eds.) KES 2005. LNCS (LNAI), vol. 3682, pp. 541–547. Springer, Heidelberg (2005)
13. Tabakow, I.G.: Fault Distinguishability of Discrete Event Systems. In: Alexandrov, V.N., van Albada, G.D., Sloot, P.M.A., Dongarra, J. (eds.) ICCS 2006. LNCS, vol. 3993, pp. 168–175. Springer, Heidelberg (2006)
14. Tabakow, I.G.: Using Place Invariants and Test Point Placement to Isolate Faults in Discrete Event Systems. Journal of Universal Computer Science 13(2), 224–243 (2007)
15. Tabakow, I.G.: Diagnosis-time assessment in discrete event systems using timed Petri nets. In: The Sixteenth International Conference on System Science, Wrocław Poland, vol. 1, pp. 247–254 (2007)
16. Wu, Y., Hadjicostis, C.N.: Non-concurrent fault identification in discrete event systems using encoded Petri net states. In: Proceedings of the 41st IEEE Conference on Decision and Control, Las Vegas, Nevada USA, December 10–13, 2002, vol. 4, pp. 4018–4023 (2002)
17. Zhou, M.C., DiCesare, F.: Petri net synthesis for discrete event control of manufacturing systems, p. 233. Kluwer Academic, Dordrecht (1993)

A CBR-Based Approach for Ship Collision Avoidance

Yuhong Liu[1], Chunsheng Yang[2], and Xuanmin Du[3]

[1] Merchant Marine College of Shanghai Maritime University,
Shanghai 200135, China
[2] Institute for Information Technology, National Research Council Canada
[3] Shanghai Marine Electronic Equipment Research Institute
Shanghai 201108, China

Abstract. In this paper, we propose a novel CBR-based approach for ship collision avoidance. After the introduction of the CBR-based decision-making support, we present two abstraction principles, selecting view points and describing granularity, to create collision avoidance cases from real-time navigation data. Several issues related case creation and CBR-based decision-making support are discussed in details, including case presentation, case retrieval and case learning. Some experimental results show the usefulness and applicability of CBR-based approach for ship collision avoidance.

Keywords: case-based reasoning; ship collision avoidance; case retrieval; case learning.

1   Introduction

Ship collision avoidance plays an important role in navigation safety. Many works [1,2,3,4,5,6] tried to apply rule-based reasoning or model-based reasoning techniques to solve this challenging problem. However, it is difficult to apply these research results to practical navigation system, since the exciting techniques cannot fully simulate the human ship-handling behavior and experience, which is the most important factor in ship-handling for collision avoidance. For instance, it is captains' navigation experiences rather than theories that be available or usable for collision avoidance in many complicated encounter situations.

Case-based reasoning (CBR) is one of the reasoning paradigms and is a feasible and efficient way to the problems which are difficult to be solved in traditional methods such as model-based reasoning. A CBR-based system solves a new problem by retrieving a similar one from a case base. We believe that CBR is a solid solution for the collision avoidance problem [7, 8, 9, 10, 11, 12], because cases can well document human collision avoidance experiences. In this work, we propose a novel CBR-based approach for collision avoidance, focusing on case creation and CBR-based decision-making support for collision avoidance. In our previous work [13,14], we have developed a tool for evaluating ship ship-handling procedures [13, 14] for collision avoidance in ship-handling simulator. The tool is able to evaluate the ship-handling results by conducting a series of mathematical and logical analyses. Some good ship-handling results can be used for case creation. In this work, we integrate this tool into

N.T. Nguyen et al. (Eds.): IEA/AIE 2008, LNAI 5027, pp. 687–697, 2008.

a CBR-based collision avoidance framework as a means for learning cases from ship-handling simulations.

In this paper, a framework of the CBR-based decision support for ship collision avoidance is first introduced in Section 2. Then, the primary principles for extracting information of cases from ship-handing data are discussed in Section 3. In Section 4, the case representation method with combination of object-oriented and frame characteristics, and a hierarchical indexing tree are discussed in detail. The nearest neighbor case retrieval method and the case learning method are presented in Section 5 and 6, respectively. The experimental results are presented in Section 7 to demonstrate the feasibility and applicability of the proposed approach. Finally, the conclusions and future work are discussed in Section 8.

2   CBR-Based Framework for Collision Avoidance

In this section, we present the proposed CBR-based framework for ship collision avoidance. The framework shown as Fig.1 consists of three main process: problem generation, case retrieval and update, and case learning. The following is the brief description of each process.

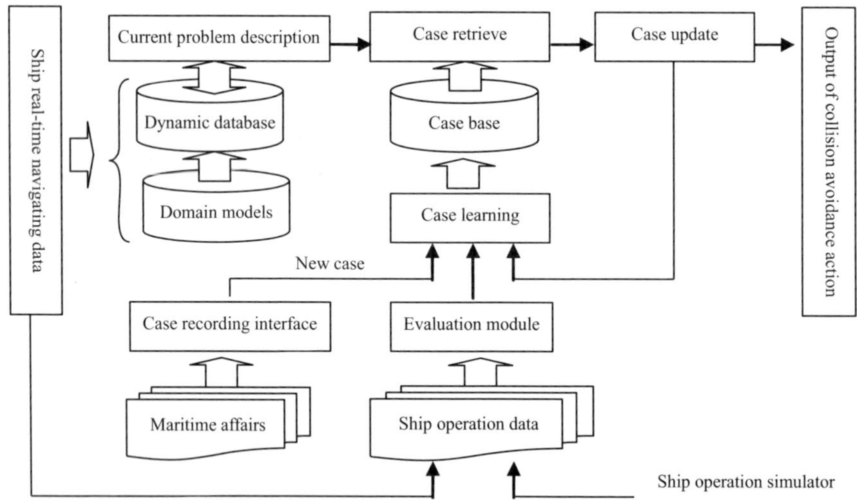

Fig. 1. CBR-based decision support framework for ship collision avoidance

A.   *Problem Generation*

The problem generation process creates a problem description for collision avoidance from real-time navigation data. In this work, the ship-handling operation is simulated using a simulator. The navigation data from the simulator can be treated as real-time ship-handling data. These data include static information (such as ship type, ship length and sea gauge), dynamic information (such as course, speed and position), and navigation information (such as the relative course and speed, azimuth, distance,

DCPA, TCPA, encounter situation and collision risk). Navigation information is derived from the real-time navigation data by using domain models which are stored in the domain model base in the form of procedures. All data are stored in the dynamic database in a given data format and can be used to form the current problem description as soon as the decision support model is activated.

B. Case Retrieval and Update

The cases are stored in a case base with a given presentation format and an index structure. Once a collision problem is defined from the problem generation process, a case retrieval algorithm is used to retrieve similar cases from the case base. The case with maximal similarity is selected as the proposed solution for the current collision problem. A pre-operation process is adopted to determine if the proposed solution is applicable for the current problem. If the pre-operation result is satisfying, no update is needed. Otherwise the proposed solution is updated for solving the current problem.

C. Case Learning

Case learning is an important process in the framework. The main task is to create cases from real-time ship-handling simulations. For real-time ship-handling data, we apply the developed evaluation tool to create cases by adding some remarks on the operation data, processing playback, and analyzing data.

3 Case Abstraction Principles

Ship collision avoidance is a dynamic process having a close relationship with the sea, the ship, the human, and the environment, and involving much information and changes during a period. A ship-handling procedure records ship operations over a long period. It contains all information related to ship navigation. When we create cases from a given resource such as ship-handling operation, we have to extract useful and necessary information. Therefore, we proposed two abstraction principles, selecting view points and describing granularity, in order to simplify and describe the collision avoidance procedures. Selecting view points transforms a dynamic process into a static scene. To describe this principle, we give the following definitions.

Definition 1, Encounter Scene (ES): a well-defined data structure. It is used to record the environment information (EI), the basic information (BI) of each ship, the relative information (RI) between own ship and each target ship and the proposed actions (PA) at a given time point. That is:

$$ES = < EI, BI, RI, PA >\qquad(1)$$

Definition 2, View Point (VP): during the ship collision avoidance, we label one of the encountering ships as the own ship (OS) and the others as target ships (TS). And then we select a time point T and record the encounter scene (ES) at this moment. VP is denoted as:

$$VP = < OS, TS, T, ES >\qquad(2)$$

Definition 3, Describing Granularity (DG): the precision of case description, which is decided by the case attribute number (AN) and attribute value type (VT). That is:

$$DG = <AN, VT > \qquad (3)$$

Where: VT may be a precise value (PV), a fuzzy value (FV) or a default value (DV). When DV= {NULL}, the value of this attribute has nothing to do with case matching.

For a given VP, each type of information in ES is defined as an attribute in a case. The describing granularity is to determine the number and value type of the case attribute. DG impacts directly on storage space, retrieval time and applicability of a CBR-based system. In general, the bigger the DG, the smaller the storage spaced and the quicker the retrieving time, but the applicability may not be satisfied. As a result, we have to choose a trade-off DG value when we build a case base for a CBR-based application.

4   Case Representation and Organization

According to case abstraction principles above, we can represent the case by combining the characteristics of object-oriented methods and frame knowledge representation methods. Five kinds of attribute classes and their relationships are defined and shown in Fig. 2.

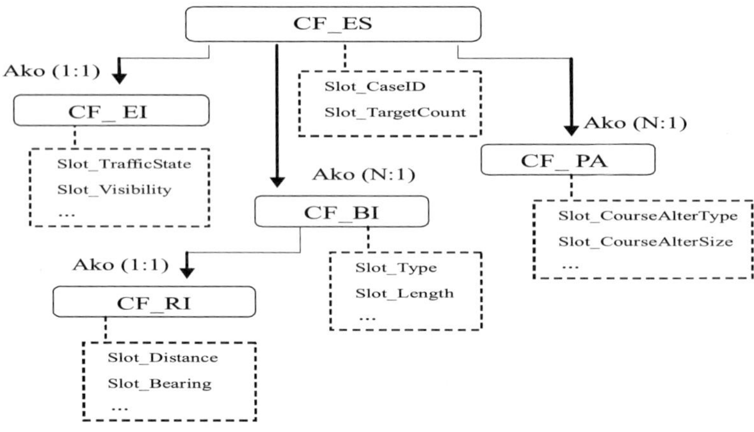

Fig. 2. Case representation: classes and attributes

CF_ES is the class of ES with four sub-classes, CF_EI, CF_BI, CF_RI and CF_PA, which corresponds to the EI, BI, RI and PA defined in equation (2). Each class has some attributes in a frame representation format. Ako (N: M) is the abbreviation for a-kind-of and is used to describe the relationship between two classes. That means M objects of the super-class will have some relationships with N objects of the sub-class.

The organization of a case base has an important impact on case retrieving efficiency. We create a hierarchical indexing tree for organizing the case base. The indexing tree is ordered with attributes in terms of their importance. These attributes are the number of encounter ships (Slot_TargetCount), visibility at sea (Slot_Visibility), two ship encounter situation (Slot_Situation) and water area condition (Slot_TrafficState). In a top-down way, the indexing tree shown in Fig. 3 is organized by decreasing importance and each node of the indexing tree corresponds to one of the attribute values. Since each case belongs to one of the nodes in the tree, such index facilitates case retrieval.

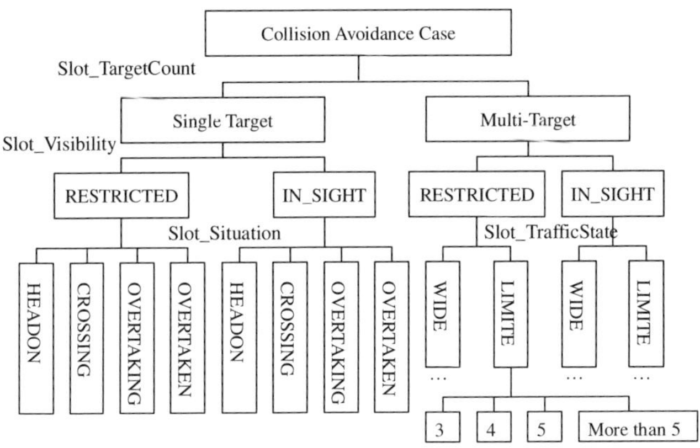

Fig. 3. The hierarchical indexing tree of a case base for collision avoidance

5   Case Retrieval

Given a description of a collision problem, we use a retrieval algorithm to retrieve the most similar cases from the case base that is indexed with a hierarchical indexing tree above. Our case retrieval algorithm is a Nearest-neighbor-based approach, which assesses the similarity between the stored cases and the problem description by a weighted sum of attributes. We describe the algorithm as follows:

If $V_{ck}^i \in [0,1]$ is defined as the similarity between a current problem c and a stored case k in the ith attribute, x_c^i and x_k^i are the value for the ith attribute in c and k respectively. With different value types, PV, FV or DV, there are four kinds of functions to calculate attribute similarity.

1) Similarity between two precise values: for two precise values x_c^i and x_k^i, the equal or unequal judgement method is not adopted. Instead, a more flexible similarity function is introduced.

$$V_{ck}^i = 1.0 - \frac{\left| x_c^i - x_k^i \right|}{\lambda_i} \tag{4}$$

where: λ_i is a threshold for the ith attribute.

2) Similarity between a precise value and a fuzzy value: for two values x_c^i and x_k^i, if one is a precise value x, and the other is a fuzzy value with a fuzzy set U, then the fuzzy membership function $\mu_U(x)$ is selected as the similarity function.

$$V_{ck}^i = \mu_U(x) \tag{5}$$

3) Similarity between two fuzzy values: for two fuzzy values x_c^i and x_k^i with two fuzzy set A and B, their approximate relation matrix can be calculated through equation (6) and (7).

$$V_{ck}^i = \rho \cdot \left[A \circ B + (1 - A \otimes B) \right] \tag{6}$$

where:

$$\begin{cases} A \circ B = \bigvee_{x \in X} (A(x) \wedge B(x)) \\ A \otimes B = \bigwedge_{x \in X} (A(x) \vee B(x)) \\ \rho = \dfrac{1}{2}(1 - |CG_A - CG_B|) \end{cases} \tag{7}$$

CG_A and CG_B are the centre of gravity of A and B.

4) Similarity between default value and non-default value: for two values x_c^i and x_k^i, if one is the default value NULL, and the other is a non-default value, then similarity function will be the default value because default value NULL can be any value in the algorithm:

$$V_{ck}^i = 1.0 \tag{8}$$

Finally, S_{ck}, the similarity between a current problem c and a stored case k, can be obtained by equation (9)

$$S_{ck} = \frac{\displaystyle\sum_{i=1}^{m} \omega_i \cdot V_{ck}^i}{\displaystyle\sum_{i=1}^{m} \omega_i} \tag{9}$$

where: $\omega_i \in [0,1]$ is the weight of the ith attribute and m is a total of attributes in a given case.

6   Case Learning

Since ship navigation data can be collected from the ship-handling simulator, we could create or learn some cases for collision avoidance by analyzing these data. To this end, we applied the developed evaluation tool in our previous work [13][14] as a method for learning cases. By evaluating the ship-handing results, our case learning procedure shown in Fig. 4 consists mainly of three processes:

Automatic case creating: For the operation of collision avoidance with excellent results, a new case is created. To obtain the attribute values for the new case from the initial data, several steps are involved, including evaluating ship action time, action type and action size; extracting ship basic information (BI) and collision avoidance action (PA); calculating relative information (RI) between two ships; and determining the view point (VP). Using the obtained values, a new case is automatically created and added to the case base.

Manual case revising: In learning cases, not all of the attribute values can always be obtained automatically from the initial data. Some values such as the environment information (EI) and ship static data are not involved in the initial data. In such a situation, a manual case revision is necessary. Therefore, we developed a user interface to help input some information manually when necessary.

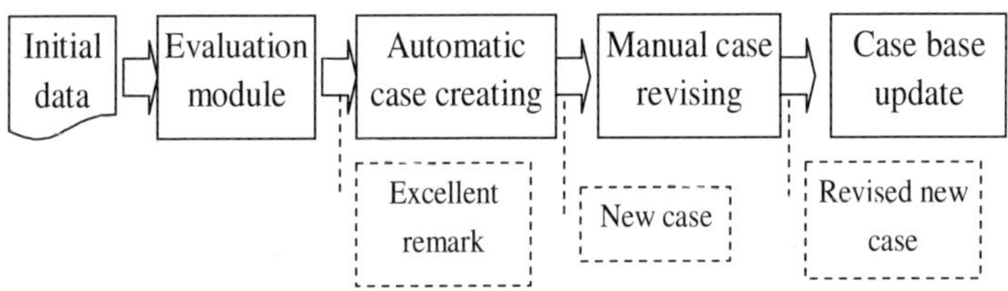

Fig. 4. The processes for learning cases from navigation data

Case base update: When adding a new case to a case base, we have to check the integrity and consistency. At the same time, the indexing tree needs to be updated automatically. The following is the description of the case base updating method. If we define $C = \{c_1, c_2, \cdots, c_M\}$ as a case set where M is the total number of cases, define $A = \{a_1, a_2, \cdots, a_N\}$ and $B = \{b_1, b_2, \cdots, b_L\}$ as a set of case condition attributes and a set of case conclusion attributes, respectively, where N and L are the number of attributes. For a case $c_i \in C$ $(i = 1, 2, \cdots, M)$, $x_i^{a_j}$ and $x_i^{b_k}$ are the attribute values for attribute $a_j \in A$ $(j = 1, 2, \cdots, N)$ and $b_k \in B$ $(k = 1, 2, \cdots, L)$. We also define

$$S_{ck}^A = \frac{1}{N} \sum_{i=1}^{N} V_{ck}^i \text{ and } S_{ck}^B = \frac{1}{L} \sum_{i=1}^{L} V_{ck}^i$$ as the condition similarity and conclusion similarity

between case c and k, where V_{ck}^i can be obtained through equation (4), (5) or (6).

Definition 4, Identical Case: for two cases $c_1 \in C$ and $c_2 \in C$, if there are $S_{12}^A \geq \lambda_A$ and $S_{12}^B \geq \lambda_B$, where λ_A and λ_B are two thresholds within $[0, 1.0]$ predefined based on domain knowledge, then c_1 and c_2 are regarded as identical cases.

Definition 5, Incompatible Case: for two cases $c_1 \in C$ and $c_2 \in C$, if $S_{12}^A \geq \lambda_A$, but $\exists b_k \in B$ $(k = 1, 2, \cdots, L)$ with $x_1^{b_k}$ and $x_2^{b_k}$ having incompatible values, then c_1 and c_2 are regarded as incompatible case.

Definition 6, Inclusive Case: for two identical cases $c_1 \in C$ and $c_2 \in C$, if $\exists a_j \in A$ with $x_1^{a_j} = NULL$ while $x_2^{a_j} \neq NULL$, then c_1 and c_2 are regarded as an inclusive case, called that c_1 includes c_2 or c_2 is included in c_1.

Definition 7, Case Base Consistency: if neither an identical case nor an incompatible case exists in the case base, then the case base has consistency.

Definition 8, Case Base integrity: if no inclusive case exists in the case base, then the case base has integrality.

Based on these definitions of the integrity and consistency, we have 4 possible operations for updating a case base: (a) if there exists an identical case against the new case, then the new case will not to be added to the case base; (b) if there exists incompatible case against the new case, then one of them will be kept in the case base; (c) if there exists a case which includes the new case, then the new case will not to be added; (d) if there exists a case which is included in the new case, then the new case will be added and the other one should be deleted.

7   Experiments and Results

We implemented a prototyping system for the proposed CBR-based approach in a VC^{++} platform. We conducted some experiments for validating the applicability of the approach. For validating the approach, we focused on case learning ability and decision-making support ability by retrieving the similar cases from the case base. We present some results in this section.

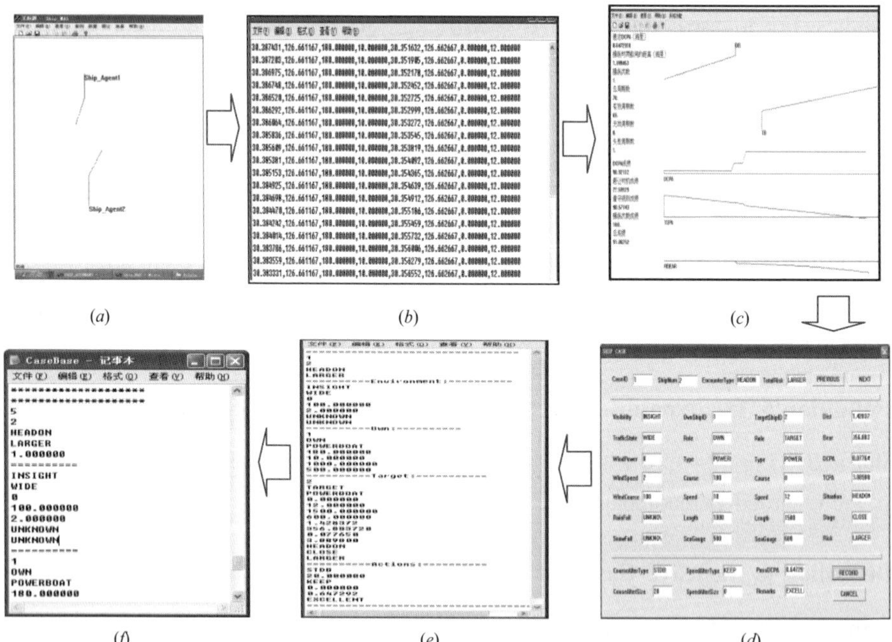

Fig. 5. An example of case learning procedure

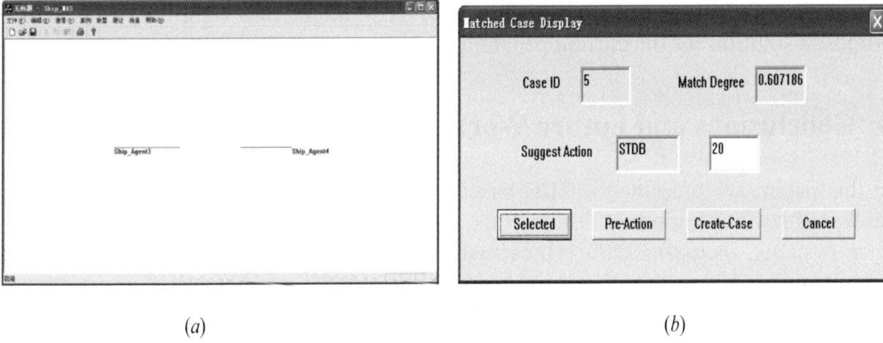

Fig. 6. An example of case retrieving

Fig 5 illustrates a case learning procedure from navigation data which is collected from a two-ship encounter simulation. Fig. 5(*a*) displays the collision avoidance procedures between two ships. Each ship is treated as an intelligent agent with calculating, reasoning, learning and communicating abilities Ship_Agent1 has the initial course 180° and speed 10 kn. Ship_Agent2 has the initial course 0° and speed 12 kn. The two ships are in a head on situation with certain collision risk. In order to avoid the collision risk, each ship takes an action: turn right (denoted as STDB in the case conclusion attribute). Ship_Agent1changes course to 200°, and Ship_Agent2 changes course to 30°. Fig. 5(*b*) shows the basic navigation data (latitude, longitude, course and speed) of these two ships, recorded in a file every 5 minutes. Using the recorded data, the evaluation tool can analyze their trajectories and obtain the necessary information for creating cases. Fig. 5(*c*) shows these evaluating results, which include the ship navigation trajectories, the variation curves of DCPA, TCPA and azimuth. After selecting Ship_Agent1 as an own ship and Ship_Agent2 as a target ship, the evaluation tool gives the remarks on the ship navigation in a form of grade. In this case, the total grade is 91.06252. Using the obtained information, the case learning algorithm creates a case for that collision avoidance procedure. Fig. 5(d) shows a case that has 27 attributes: 5 attributes for the case conclusion and 22 attributes for the case condition. Using the interface, some attribute values can also be input, revised and recorded if necessary. Fig. 5(*e*) shows that the revised new case is stored in a temporal file. Fig. 5(*f*) demonstrates that the new case has been added into the case base and assigned to an ID number 5 in the indexing tree.

Fig. 6 is a case retrieval example. In this experiment, the system retrieved a similar case from the case base for a new collision problem. Fig. 6(*a*) is a new encounter situation, in which two ships are head on to each other. They are noted as Ship_Agent3 and Ship_Agent4. Ship_Agent3 has course 90° and speed 12 kn. Ship_Agent4 has course 270° and speed 10kn. In order to make decisions on collision avoidance, Ship_Agent3 is selected as an own ship and the current problem description is formed. Fig. 6(*b*) shows that a case is retrieved from a case base bin terms of the computed similarity. In this experiment, the case with ID 5 is retrieved since it has the maximal similarity 0.607186. Therefore, its solution (turn right 20°) is used as a proposed solution for the current problem.

8 Conclusions and Future Work

In this paper, we presented a CBR-based approach for ship collision avoidance. We discussed several important issues in the development of CBR-based collision avoidance systems, including case representation, case base indexing, case retrieval, and case learning. Using the developed prototyping system, we conducted some experiments for validating the usefulness and applicability of the proposed approach. The experiments demonstrated that the system can provide an effective way for learning cases from the real-time ship-handling data automatically. The created case can be retrieved as a solution for a similar collision problem.

Although the experiment results showed the usefulness and applicability, we still have to conduct large-scale exclusive experiments for different navigation environments and more complicated encounter simulations in order to evaluate the approach effectively. Some work is on going; we will report the results in other paper. From the viewpoint of case learning ability, we have to develop a technique for learning cases from maritime affairs records which were/are collected in ship navigation over many years. These records reflect either instructive and successful case or edifying and failing cases. They are valuable resources to generate cases for CBR-based collision avoidance systems. Therefore, learning cases from maritime affaire records will be our future work.

Acknowledgments

This research is supported by HuoYingdong educational fund grant (No.0254-05-FN580001) and Shanghai academic project (No. T0603).

References

1. Sato, Y., Ishii, H.: Study of collision-avoidance system for ships. Control Engineering Practice 6, 1141–1149 (1998)
2. Liu, Y., Yang, W.: The structure Design of an Intelligent Decision Support System for Navigation Collision Avoidance. In: IEEE The Third International Conference on Machine Learning and Cybernetics, August 2004, vol. 1, pp. 302–307 (2004)
3. Liu, Y.: A design and Study on Intelligence Collision Prevention Expert System for Navigation. Ph.D. thesis, Harbin Engineering University, china (July 1999)
4. Yang, C.: An Expert System for Collision Avoidance and Its Application. Ph.D. thesis, Hiroshima University, Japan (September 1995)
5. Hwang, C.: The Integrated Design of Fuzzy Collision Avoidance and H∞- Autopilots on ships. The Journal of navigation 55(1), 117–136 (2002)
6. Liu, Y., Du, X., Yang, S.: The Design of a Fuzzy-Neural Network for Ship Collision Avoidance. In: Yeung, D.S., Liu, Z.-Q., Wang, X.-Z., Yan, H. (eds.) ICMLC 2005. LNCS (LNAI), vol. 3930, pp. 804–812. Springer, Heidelberg (2006)

7. Watson, I., Marir, F.: Case-Base Reasoning: A Review. Knowledge Engineering Review 9(4) (1994)
8. Yang, C., Orchard, B., Farley, B., Zaluski, M.: Automated Case Base Creation and Management. In: Chung, P.W.H., Hinde, C.J., Ali, M. (eds.) IEA/AIE 2003. LNCS, vol. 2718, Springer, Heidelberg (2003)
9. Therani, M., Zhao, J., Marshall, B.: A case-based reasoning framework for workflow model management. Data & Knowledge Engineering 50, 87–115 (2004)
10. Avesani, P., Ferrari, S., Susi, A.: Case-Based Ranking for Decision Support Systems. In: Ashley, K.D., Bridge, D.G. (eds.) ICCBR 2003. LNCS, vol. 2689, pp. 35–49. Springer, Heidelberg (2003)
11. McSherry, D.: Similarity and Compromise. In: Ashley, K.D., Bridge, D.G. (eds.) ICCBR 2003. LNCS, vol. 2689, pp. 291–305. Springer, Heidelberg (2003)
12. Nordlund, J., Schafer, H.: Case-Based Reasoning in a support System. Master's thesis, UMEA University, Sweden (April 2006)
13. Liu, Y., Hu, S.: An Evaluation System for Single-Target Ship Collision Avoidance Based on Data Fusion. Navigation of China 65(4), 40–45 (2005)
14. Liu, Y., Liu, H.: Case Learning Based on Evaluation System for Vessel Collision Avoidance. In: IEEE The Fifth International Conference on Machine Learning and Cybernetics, vol. 4, pp. 2064–2069 (2006)

Multiphase Data Exchange in Distributed Logic-Algebraic Based Processing

Leszek Borzemski and Mariusz Fraś

Wroclaw University of Technology, Institute of Information Science and Engineering,
Wybrzeze Wyspianskiego 27, 50-370 Wroclaw, Poland
{Leszek.Borzemski, Mariusz.Fras}@pwr.wroc.pl

Abstract. The problems formulated for a class of expert systems with knowledge representation in the form of facts can be solved applying the logic-algebraic (LA) method. Parallel processing of logic-algebraic algorithms addresses issue of data exchange. During so called task composition step the data processed on each processor has to be distributed to all other processors. In the paper we introduce a multiphase data exchange used for information dissemination in LA parallel computations. For the assumed processing system model we derive the analytical formulae for the task composition completion time in balanced and non-balanced data distribution.

Keywords: knowledge-based system, distributed processing, data exchange.

1 Introduction

Expert systems that are used in practical applications address the performance as one of the key issue. The possible approach to improve computations in expert systems is to utilise modern computer system architectures and to develop parallel execution of expert tasks. In the area of artificial intelligence (AI) typical parallel processing issues such as discovering of parallelism, granularity of tasks and task allocation problems were exploited [e.g. 6, 11]. In recent years the researches have concentrated on applying parallel solutions for different areas of AI-based systems such as logic programming languages [9] or constraint programming [12], as well as on adapting AI solutions for parallel and distributed computing [e.g. 5, 10, 13].

For a class of control, identification and recognition systems an appropriate object expert system with knowledge representation in the form of facts describing object under consideration, and a logic-algebraic method based on logic algebra fundamentals are developed [3]. The LA method is applied for different problems such as decision-making in complex operation systems or pattern recognition. The LA computations can be performed applying the parallel processing architecture [2].

One important issue related to parallel and distributed systems is information dissemination when doing parallel computations, e.g. to synchronize processing and/or exchange data. Parallel processing of LA algorithms also addresses this issue. Complete exchange, also named all-to-all personalized communication, is one of well known communication schemes in parallel computing. It requires each of Q processors

N.T. Nguyen et al. (Eds.): IEA/AIE 2008, LNAI 5027, pp. 698–707, 2008.

to send a unique message to each of the remaining Q-1 processors [1]. In LA parallel system each processor sends (during so called task composition step), a data of different size to the processors that have no yet got such data. The ultimate goal is to distribute all data to all processors.

The data exchange problems have been widely studied in the literature under a variety of assumptions and for specific topologies, such hypercubes, meshes, tori [e.g. 1] multi-dimensional networks [e.g. 7] and Grids [e.g. 8]. In our work we concentrate on the analysis of the communication problem in our specific case. We propose a general processing system model that conforms to general distributed network. Unlike in [8], where scheduling of communication operations is discussed, we assume that no information of exchanged messages sizes is available to processing units taking into account that every extra communication may have significance because of communication system parameters and size of messages.

2 Logic-Algebraic Method

The knowledge representation of the discussed object expert systems is described as a set of simple formulae α and sequence of logical facts $F(\alpha)$ composed of subsequences of α and logical operators [3]. Simple formula is a property of the object under consideration in the form of logical sentence (for instance "the temperature t is above threshold t_0", "operation O_1 follows operation O_2", etc.). The facts describe known relationships of the simple formulae. For the given object we distinguish input formulae α_x (i.e. formulae considering input properties of the object) and input fact $F_x(\alpha_x)$, as well as output formulae α_y and output fact $F_y(\alpha_y)$. There are considered two basic problems for such knowledge representation: the analysis problem – for the given $F_x(\alpha_x)$ finding the best output fact $F_y(\alpha_y)$ such that implication $F_x \Rightarrow F_y$ is true, and the decision-making problem – for the given $F_y(\alpha_y)$ finding the best input fact $F_x(a_x)$ such that implication $F_x \Rightarrow F_y$ is true. The logic-algebraic method defines equivalent problems specifying the appropriate sets $S_a=\{a: F(a)=1\}$, $S_x=\{a: F_x(a_x)=1\}$, $S_y=\{a: F_y(a_y)=1\}$ to be determined, where a is 0-1 sequence of logical values of the corresponding simple formulae [3]. The sets are determined using recursive procedure based on the decomposition of facts that is partitioning of set of facts into appropriate subsets $\overline{F}_j$:

$$F_x(a_x) \wedge F(a) = \overline{F}_1(\overline{a}_0, \overline{a}_1) \wedge ... \wedge \overline{F}_j(\overline{a}_{j-1}, \overline{a}_j) \wedge ... \wedge \overline{F}_J(\overline{a}_{J-1}, \overline{a}_J) \ , \tag{1}$$

where: $\overline{a}_{j-1}, \overline{a}_j$ - appropriate subsequences of logical variables of values of simple formulae; $\overline{a}_0 = a_y$; $\overline{F}_j$ - subsequence of facts (conjunction), J – the number of decomposition stages. The recursive procedure determines at j-th decomposition stage appropriate subsets $\overline{S}_{j-1}$ of sequences $\overline{a}_{j-1}$ according to the formula:

$$\overline{S}_{j-1} = \left\{ \overline{a}_{j-1} \in S_{j-1} : \bigvee_{\overline{a}_j \in \overline{S}_j} \left[\overline{F}_j \left(\overline{a}_{j-1}, \overline{a}_j \right) = 1 \right] \right\}, \qquad (2)$$

where: S_{j-1} - the set of all possible sequences $\overline{a}_{j-1}$, $\overline{S}_J = S_J$, $\overline{S}_0$ - the ultimate solution for the expert problem formulated on the basis of LA approach. The formula (2) describes the basic processing to be done. Thus on each j-th stage the sequences $\overline{a}_{j-1}$ are computed for processing on the next stage. To improve processing the sequences $\overline{a}_{j-1}$ can be computed in parallel on distributed system [2]. This, however force to distribute computed sequences to all processing units – creates a total data exchange phase.

3 Distributed Processing System Model

The model of processing system must conform to our specific problem, however the general architecture of computations match wide class of particular processing tasks so we define it in general manner. The considered processing system model is the following:

1. The processing is performed step by step at so called computation stages. The results of processing at given stage is the input data for processing at next stage.
2. The task to be processed at given stage is related to the state vector $A=[a_1, a_2, ..., a_n, ..., a_N]$. The processing consists in finding the values $A^{(i)}=[a_1^{(i)}, a_2^{(i)}, ..., a_n^{(i)}, ..., a_N^{(i)}]$ of the state vector that satisfy the solution of given problem ψ.
3. At the stage j the problem ψ_j is determined by results obtained at previous stage j-1. The goal is to find the set of solutions $S_j = \{ A_j^{(i)}: \psi_j(A_j^{(i)}, S_{j-1})$ is satisfied$\}$, where S_{j-1} – the set computed at the stage j-1.
4. The processing is performed in parallel with distributed processing units (processing nodes or agents). Each unit computes the subset $S_{j,q}$ of the set S_j and $S_j = \bigcup_{q=1,...Q} S_{j,q}$, where Q – the number of processing units.
5. The results of processing on each processing unit at given computation stage (i.e. m_q bytes of data of the set $S_{j,q}$) are distributed to all other units – it is so called task composition step.
6. The communication model assumes as in other papers [1, 7] that two parameters are used in modeling communication costs: τ_s – start-up latency and τ_t – throughput parameter of communication links (transfer rate).
7. The communication model is based on a single communication operations therefore similarly to [14] no gap parameter is used and the time to transmit m-byte message is $\tau_s + m \cdot \tau_t$.
8. Each processing unit is allowed to participate in only one send or receive message operation at a time.

This general model of processing corresponds to different parallel and distributed computing systems and tasks – various multiphase computations in clusters as well as Grid computing or cooperative multiagent systems where processed local data must be used in further processing by other agents. In our case the state vector corresponds to sequence $\bar{a}_{j-1}$, problem ψ_j corresponds to condition in formula (2). In this paper we assume that all communication links have the same performance parameters.

The presented processing model tested for LA computations (without considering task composition issues) showed its unquestionable superiority over uniprocessor computations [2]. Comparing to this model the pipeline processing proposed in [4] has two major disadvantages: it assumes strong assumptions on computed task characteristics and can be applied only in closely-coupled multiprocessor – the communication issues are not even considered. The proposed distributed processing model has no such restrictions.

In the next section we focus on the task composition step of the general computational procedure at a given stage of computation. We propose the task composition model for balanced and non-balanced distributions of sequences to be exchanged. The model is used for deriving analytical formulae for the estimation of the completion time of task composition step between two stages of computations in the LA method.

4   The Multiphase Data Exchange

The complete distribution of calculated sequences $\bar{a}_{j-1}$ (hereafter 'sequences' for short) is based on the multiphase exchange procedure. Note that the index j used up to now for indexing stage of computation in this section is used in different meaning.

First, we consider he number of processing units (processors for short) $Q = 2^r$, where r is a positive integer. For the set $V=\{P_1, P_2, ..., P_Q\}$ of Q processors we define partitioning $\mathbf{V}_i$ of the set V during i-th phase done in following manner:

Step 1: $\mathbf{V_1} = \{V_{1,1}, V_{1,2}, ..., V_{1,Q}\}$, where $V_{1,j} = \{P_j\}$, $j \in \overline{1,Q}$, i.e. V_1 is the set of one-element subsets of processors, $\|\mathbf{V_1}\| = Q$.

Step 2: for $i \in \overline{2,R}, R = \log_2 Q$ $\mathbf{V}_i$ is defined as:

$$\mathbf{V}_i = \{V_{i,1}, V_{i,2}, ..., V_{i,R_i}\}, \text{ where } V_{i,j} = V_{i-1,2j-1} \cup V_{i-1,2j}, \ j \in \overline{1,R_i}, R_i = \|\mathbf{V}_i\| = \frac{Q}{2^{i-1}}.$$

$V_{i,j}$ is the sum of proper sets from phase i-1 During successive phases we specify partitioning $\mathbf{V}_i$ until exist possibility of merging subsets, i.e. we have $R = \log_2 Q$ phases of partitioning (see example for eight processors in Fig. 1).

We define operation $s(V_{i,j_1}, V_{i,j_2})$ that denotes the simultaneous exchange (transfer) of computed sequences by the pairs of processors (P_k, P_l): $P_k \in V_{i,j_1}$, $P_l \in V_{i,j_2}$, $j_1, j_2 \in [1, R_i]$.

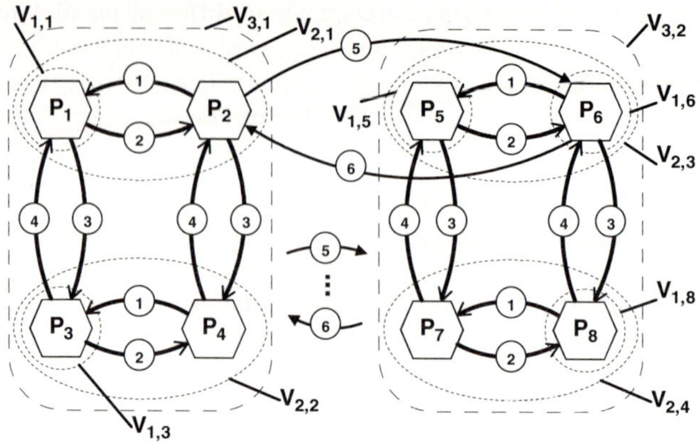

Fig. 1. The schema of the complete exchange of sequences for $Q = 2^r = 8$, $R = 3$

The procedure of complete exchange of sequences computed by all processors is the following:

1. For i=1 to R do
2.   Perform partitioning $\mathbf{V}_i$
3. $R_i = Q / 2^{i-1}$
4.   For j=1 to $R_i /2$ do
5.   Execute operation s($\mathbf{V}_{i,2j}$, $\mathbf{V}_{i,2j-1}$)

The above schema of performing distribution of computed sequences (Fig. 1) has the following property: before each i-th phase of the procedure all processors belonging to the set $\mathbf{V}_{i,j}$ have the same set of sequences.

The efficient implementation of the procedure of complete distribution can be done when we label each processor with binary identifier. During each i-th phase every processor P_k with identifier p_k calculate the identifier p_l of the corresponding processor P_l for the bidirectional data transfer operation s(P_k, P_l) according to the formula $p_l = p_k$ **xor** 2^{i-1}. The following pseudo-code describes procedure of complete exchange of sequences:

```
procedure complete_exchange;
   begin
   for i=1 to log2Q do
   begin
       for k=1 to Q do in parallel
       begin
           if (pk and 2i-1) equal 0
           begin
             pl = pk xor 2i-1;
             execute s(pk,pl);
           end;
```

```
        end;
    end;
end.
```

The completion time of operation $s(P_k, P_l)$ is estimated as $T(P_k, P_l) = 2 \cdot \tau_s + (m_k + m_l) \cdot \tau_t$, where: m_k, m_l – the number of sequences transmitted from processors P_k and P_l respectively.

The time T_K of completion of task composition at given stage of computations depends on the distribution of total number N of computed sequences on processors. For balanced distribution each processor has assigned the same number of sequences $n_i = N / Q$, $i \in \overline{1, Q}$ and then time T_K is given by:

$$T_K = 2 \cdot \log_2 Q \cdot \tau_s + \tau_t \cdot N \cdot \sum_{i=1}^{\log_2 Q} \frac{2^i}{Q}. \tag{3}$$

When the distribution is extremely non-balanced, i.e. when all N calculated sequences are on a single processor, the time T_K is estimated as:

$$T_K = 2 \cdot \log_2 Q \cdot \tau_s + \log_2 Q \cdot N \cdot \tau_t. \tag{4}$$

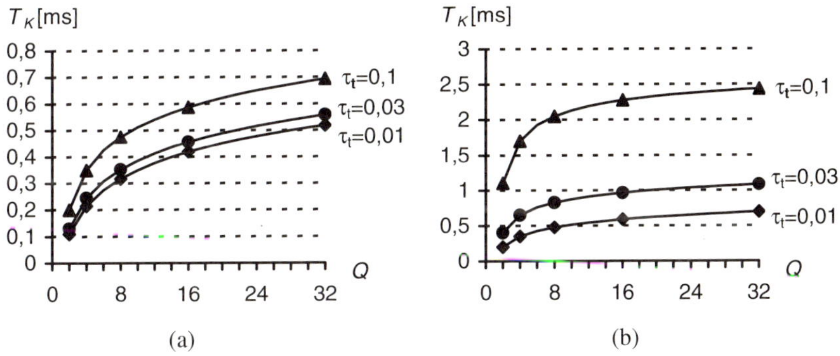

Fig. 2. The task composition time T_K versus the number of processor Q for the case of balanced distribution of sequences in a parallel system with: $\tau_s = 50\mu s$, $\tau_t = 0,01\mu s$, $0,03\mu s$, and $0,1\mu s$, and for $N=1000$ (a) and $N=10000$ (b)

Fig. 2 shows (for communication parameters characteristic to cluster computing) that for larger number of sequences the task composition time T_k does not increase so fast and nearly levels off when performing computations on larger number of processors. The impact of change of throughput of communication links is greater not only for larger number of sequences but also for larger τ_t / τ_s ratio.

The generalized task composition procedure for the number of processors $Q \neq 2^r$, where r is a positive integer, is defined addition two supplementary phases to the process of complete distribution of sequences (Fig. 3).

The procedure is identical as presented earlier with exception of the following:

- procedure of partitioning is performed for the maximal number of processors Q' such that $Q' = 2^r$ and $Q' < Q$, Q' processors make up the set V',
- remaining Q'' processors constitute the set V'',
- there is the initial phase of exchange of sequences for the transmission of sequences (in pairs) from processors from the set V'' to processors from the set V',
- there is the terminal phase of exchange of sequences for the transmission of sequences (in pairs) from processors from the set V' to processors from the set V''.

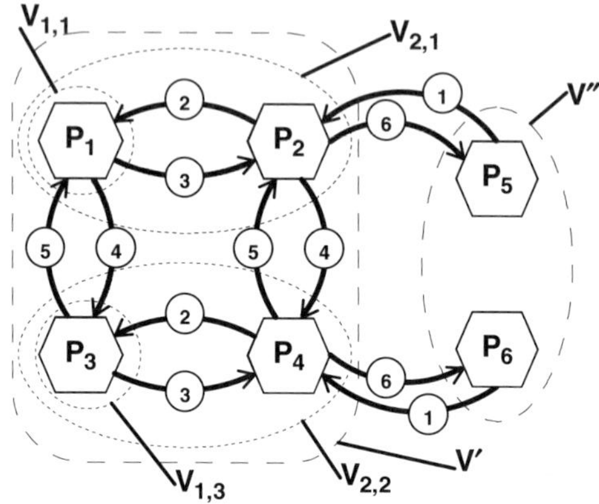

Fig. 3. The schema of the complete distribution of sequences in the system with $Q \neq 2^r$ processors

For the generalized procedure, in the case of extremely non-balanced distribution of sequences the time T_K is given by:

$$T_K = 2 \cdot (\log_2 Q' + 1) \cdot \tau_s + (\log_2 Q' + 2) \cdot N \cdot \tau_t . \tag{5}$$

To evaluate the time T_K for balanced distribution of sequences it is necessary to precise the specify precisely how to assign processors into pairs while exchanging sequences in the initial phase. To minimize the completion time of task composition T_K at given stage of computations we define the following procedure:

1. $p_l = Q' + 1$
2. $v_{\min} = Q'$
3. For $i = \log_2 Q'$ to 1 do
4.   For $j = 1$ to R_i do
5.   If $v_{i,j} < v_{\min}$ then $v_{\min} = v_{i,j}$
6.   If $v_{\min} = 0$ then do
7. $p_k = (j - 1) \cdot 2^{i-1} + 1$
8. $v_{i,j} = v_{i,j} + 1$
9.   go to step 10
10. If $p_l < Q$ then $p_l = p_l + 1$ and go to step 2
11. Finish

In the above procedure the following notation is used: $v_{i,j}$ – the number of selected processors from the subset $V_{i,j}$ of set V' that already formed pairs with processors from the set V'', $v_{i,j}$ is initially 0 for all i,j; v_{min} – auxiliary variable; p_k – the processor from the set V' selected to form a pair with consecutive p_l processor from the set V''.

To speed up the computations we can pre-define assignment tables for given number of processors as shown in Fig 4.

17	18	19	20	21	22	23	24	25	26	27	28	29	30	31
1	9	5	13	3	11	7	15	2	10	6	14	4	12	8

Fig. 4. Assignment table for 17 to 31 processors. First row: the identifiers of processors from the set V''. Second row: identifiers of corresponding processors from the set V'.

After applying the above schema of forming pairs in the initial phase, the task composition time T_K can be calculated as follows:

$$T_K = 2 \cdot (\log_2 Q' + 1) \cdot \tau_s + \tau_t \cdot N \cdot \sum_{i=0}^{\log_2(Q'-1)} \frac{Q + 2^i - 1 - (Q-1)\bmod 2^i}{Q \cdot 2^i}. \tag{6}$$

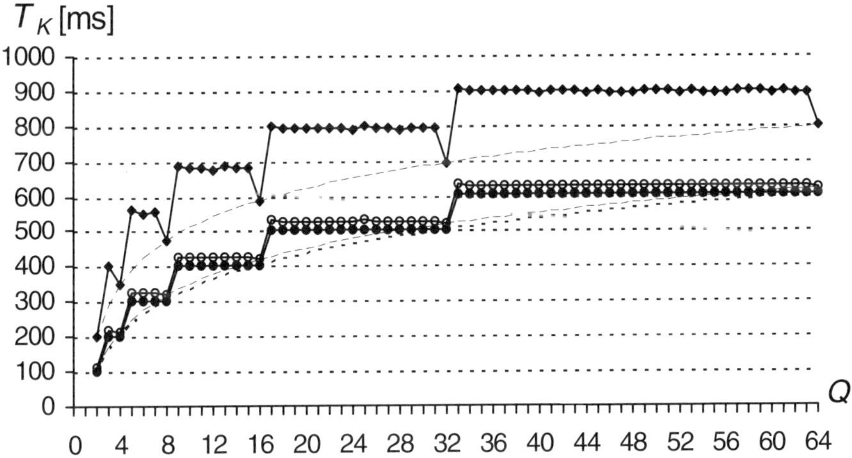

Fig. 5. The task composition time T_K versus the number of processor Q for generalized exchange of sequences procedure: $\tau_s = 50$ms, $\tau_t = 1\mu$s (1Mb/s), N=1k, 10k, 100k

The Fig. 5 shows completion time of data exchange for parameters characteristic for Grid computing. It is obvious that, the best performance is achieved when parallel system has $Q = 2^r$ processors. Additionally we can notice that for proposed data exchange procedure adding consecutive processors does not continuously increase the task composition time but even slightly may decrease it. The largest rise appears when (2^r+1)-th processor is added. For quite large message size range the increase completion time of data exchange is very low.

5 Conclusions

The multiphase complete exchange model for parallel logic-algebraic expert system presented in this paper was introduced. We derived the analytical equations for estimation of the completion time of the task composition step that is realized each time between every two stages of computations in the LA method. We show how the multiphase data exchange is organized at the task composition step in parallel execution structure. Two cases are considered, namely extremely non-balanced and balanced distributions of sequences. The analytical equations are derived to calculate the completion time of the task composition between two stages of computations in the LA method. These equations can be used in the design of a multiprocessor system for discussed processing tasks that use presented data exchange algorithm.

The preliminary simulation experiments, performed with developed system SymLog that is the expert system as well as the event-driven simulation system for studying execution issues of LA algorithms, showed that proposed processing architecture is efficient and promising good performance in real-life environment. The system is now planed to be implemented in multiprocessor (multicore) system – the IBM BladeCenter servers based cluster – configured with different communication network systems (100Mb, 1000Mb and 10GbE).

References

1. Bokhari, S.H.: Multiphase Complete Exchange on Paragon, SP2, and CS 2. IEEE Parallel and Distributed Technology, Fall 1996 (1996)
2. Borzemski, L., Fraś, M.: Parallel computations for logic-algebraic based expert systems. In: Apolloni, B., Howlett, R.J., Jain, L. (eds.) KES 2007, Part I. LNCS (LNAI), vol. 4692, Springer, Heidelberg (2007)
3. Bubnicki, Z.: Logic-algebraic method for a class of knowledge based systems. In: Computer Aided Systems Theory. LNCS, Springer, Heidelberg (1997)
4. Bubnicki, Z.: Structures of Distributed Expert Systems with Parallel Processing. In: Proceedings of the 12th International Conference on Systems Engineering, vol. 1 Coventry (1997)
5. Choi, S.-Y., Cha, J.-S., Shin, M.-C.: Artificial Intelligent Application to Service Restoration Considering Load Balancing in Distribution Networks. In: Gabrys, B., Howlett, R.J., Jain, L.C. (eds.) KES 2006. LNCS (LNAI), vol. 4253, Springer, Heidelberg (2006)
6. Dewan, H.M., Stolfo, S.J., Woodbury, L.: Scalable parallel and distributed expert database systems with predictive load balancing. Journal of Parallel and Distributed Computing 22(3) (September 1994)
7. Dimakopoulos, V.V., Dimopoulos, N.J.: A Theory of Total Exchange in Multidimensional Interconnection Networks. IEEE Transactions on Parallel and Distributed Systems 9(7) (1998)
8. Fujiwara, A., Jinno, Y., Ito, M.: Efficient scheduling algorithms for total exchange on GRID environment. In: Proceedings of the International Conference on Parallel and Distributed Processing Symposium PDPTA 2003, vol. 1, CSREA Press, Las Vegas (2003)

9. Gupta, G., Pontelli, E., Khayri, A.M., Ali, C.M., Hermenegildo, M.V.: Parallel Execution of Prolog Programs: A Survey. ACM Transactions on Programming Languages and Systems (TOPLAS) 23(4) (2001)
10. Ishikawa, H., Shioya, Y., Omi, T., Ohta, M., Katayama, K.: A Peer-to-Peer Approach to Parallel Association Rule Mining. In: Negoita, M.G., Howlett, R.J., Jain, L.C. (eds.) KES 2004. LNCS (LNAI), vol. 3213, Springer, Heidelberg (2004)
11. Neiman, D.E.: Issues in the Design and Control of Parallel Rule-Firing Production Systems. Journal of Parallel and Distributed Computing 23(3) (December 1994)
12. Pontelli, E.: Parallel and distributed execution of constraint programs. ACM SIGSOFT Software Engineering Notes 25(1) (2000)
13. Srinivasa, R., Reynolds, P.F., Williams, C.: Parallel Rule-Based Systems on Isotach Networks. In: Int. Conf. on Parallel and Distributed Computing and Systems, IASTED, Cambridge, Massachusetts (1999)
14. Xu, H., Hwang, K.: Modeling Communication Overhead: MPI and MPL Performance on the IBM SP2. IEEE Parallel and Distributed Technology (Spring 1996)

Visualization of Financial Trends Using Chance Discovery Methods

Tzu-Fu Chiu, Chao-Fu Hong, and Yu-Ting Chiu

Department of Industrial Management, Aletheia University, Taipei, Taiwan, R.O.C.
chiu@email.au.edu.tw
Department of Information Management, Aletheia University, Taipei, Taiwan, R.O.C.
cfhong@email.au.edu.tw
Department of Information Management, National Central University, Taoyuan, Taiwan, R.O.C.
gloria@mgt.ncu.edu.tw

Abstract. Due to the concern of business performance and the consideration of possible investment, stakeholders inside and outside the business need to understand the financial status of a company. Usually, reading and interpreting the public offering financial statements is a common way to obtain an overall financial situation of a company. Apart from reading them directly, some visualization methods were employed so as to assist the less-professional stakeholders to understand the financial status more intuitively and painlessly. Chance discovery is one of the visualization methods which may be suitable to be applied in the financial trend detection area. In this study, a financial data visualization framework has been proposed to produce the serial KeyGraph for explaining the financial situations of two companies. Subsequently, an integrated map of financial trend was generated for depicting the overview of the accumulative five-year scenario. Finally, the visualization of financial trend was attained using serial KeyGraph and integrated map.

Keywords: Chance Discovery, Visualization, Financial Trend.

1   Introduction

Financial distress affects stakeholders of the company and even the whole society. Thus, detecting the financial trends of a company for assisting the stakeholders becomes an important issue nowadays.

Most traditional financial prediction models used static data rather than dynamic data to predict the financial trend, especially to predict the financial distress [1]. According to Balcaen and Ooghe [2], some of the popular models were established using statistic methodologies; and a common problem in the classical models is the neglect of the time dimension in illustrating the failure of a company. Besides, it is not easy for people without professional knowledge in finance to understand the predicted results intuitively.

N.T. Nguyen et al. (Eds.): IEA/AIE 2008, LNAI 5027, pp. 708–717, 2008.

Thus, this study aims at using financial data to observe not only static status in the financial statements, but the continuous changes and shifts in the time sequence. In other words, the time dimension will be considered in this study. The visualized diagrams will be generated for stakeholders and managers to understand the financial trends, and discover the business strategic operations.

2   Related Work

This section will be divided into three subsections to express the related work. They are Traditional financial prediction, Chance discovery, and Visualization tool: KeyGraph.

2.1   Traditional Financial Prediction

Since 1960s, models with different analysis methods had been proposed by Ohlson, Beaver, and Altman [1,3,4] to predict the financial distress of firms. However, the accuracy of model declined as the applied time period is different from the developed one [5]. These statistic models predict the static status rather than dynamic situations. Thus, they are weak in predicting the dynamic variations of a company during a long period of time. According to Balcaen and Ooghe, there are four categories of problems in the statistic prediction models [2]. Among them, the category "Neglect of the time dimension of failure" is more related to this study. The argument of this category is that a steady state (i.e. stable all the time) is assumed to observe failure rather than a progressive process.

It seems that a certain kind of model is needed to include a time dimension rather than a static status to detect the financial trend dynamically. Thus, this study intends to propose a graphical framework, named financial data visualization framework, to achieve this attempt. In the following section (i.e., section 3), the proposed framework will be introduced and described in detail.

2.2   Chance Discovery

A chance is a new event or situation which might be an opportunity or a risk [6]. In addition, a chance means a rare or unnoticed event which can be significant for making decisions [7], especially some important phenomena are in their initial developing stage. Originally, chance discovery is to discover chances and explain their importance [6]. Chance discovery is increasingly used to mine text and other data for the connection of rare events to more statistically regular events (i.e., frequent events) in the hopes of teasing out a meaningful trend [8].

Chance discovery could also be viewed as a new method to solve problems in the finance domain. Goda proposed that chance discovery can be adopted in credit card management [9]. The correlations in a Directed KeyGraph were used to estimate the effect upon possible starting-spot for leading the chain reaction of bankruptcy.

2.3   Visualization Tool: KeyGraph

KeyGraph is an important method in chance discovery to visualize data, and express the concrete of unnoticed or rare events under the common or regular events [6]. KeyGraph is derived from three basic components: : document, sentence, and word[10]. The algorithms for generating a KeyGraph can refer to [11]. In a KeyGraph, a hub is a node with lower frequency and bridges two clusters together. A hub with higher key value becomes a chance and is denoted with red circle. Besides, a chance in this study can possibly be identified because of its continuous appearance in a time sequence. It is attempted to extend the original KeyGraph to Serial KeyGraph so as to observe the financial situations of a company through the time dimension.

3   Financial Data Visualization Framework

The financial data visualization framework is organized as in Fig. 1. It will be divided into five phases and described in the following subsections. They are: descriptive rules, financial report collection and data preprocessing, code transformation, serial KeyGraph and integrated map of financial trend, and explanation.

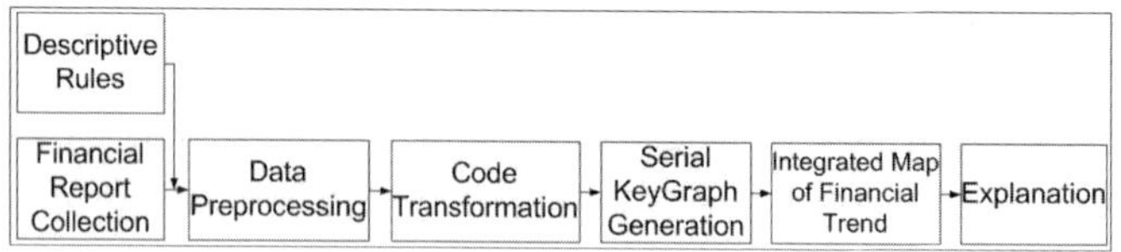

Fig. 1. Financial data visualization framework

3.1   Descriptive Rules from Literature Review

In the framework, the first phase is to review the relevant literature and gather the descriptive rules. The rules are constructed for observing the occasion of financial distress and failure of a company, and are used to examine the synthetically business status [12]. There are six descriptive rules found for this study. According to Beaver and Blum, a business firm can be viewed as a reservoir, and might have financial distress with less inflows and greater outflows [3,13]. Thus, the first descriptive rule is that a firm with poor ability of refunding but high financial leverage might be failed easily. The second one is: While total liabilities are less than total assets, a firm might encounter the financial failure [14]. Also according to Lee et al. [14], the third rule is: a firm would fail as sharking its firm size but still not performing well. Furthermore, Lensberg et al. [15] indicated that a firm might bankrupt because of low profits and poor ability of refunding liabilities [15]. This is the forth rule. The fifth one is: a firm might bankrupt with low profits and small firm size [15]. Finally, the sixth one: a firm with weak ability of liquidity, inefficiency of using assets, and great extent of using financial leverage would result in financial failure.

These six descriptive rules concern more about the signs and hints for leading failure. However, the aim of this study is to examine the financial situation of a company, it would be appropriate to investigate a firm from both the negative and positive aspects. Thus in a KeyGraph, any descriptive rule will be identified as an existence if all the required features are shown and linked (directly or indirectly); otherwise, as a nonexistence. Moreover, the existent rule will be recognized as a satisfied one if all its features are in the same negative direction. On the other hand, if any of the features is in the opposite direction, the rule will be an unsatisfied one.

3.2   Financial Report Collection and Data Processing

The second phase in the financial data visualization framework is to collect the financial statements and perform the data preprocessing. While doing data collection, nine features are selected corresponding to the descriptive rules and the relevant literature [1]. These features (as in Table 1) are used to observe the existence of rules and to produce chances in the KeyGraph. Each feature is influenced causally by corresponding financial activities.

In data preprocessing step, the value of each feature (i.e., financial ratio) is calculated and standardized. It is assumed that the value of each feature fits the standard normal distribution. After standardization, every feature is transformed into codes using every 0.5 standard deviation. For example, if $0<z$ (standard deviation) ≤ 0.5, it will be transformed into the code value 0.5. This is a preparing stage for the "Code Transformation" phase.

3.3   Code Transformation

Before generating Serial KeyGraph, the third phase named "Code Transformation" needs to be conducted in advance. In this transformation, the code of each feature acquired in the above phase is coded again to obtain a probability value. The previous code will be substituted by the corresponding probability according to the Standard Normal Distribution probability table [16]. For example, if the code value is 0.5 (i.e. $0<z\leq 0.5$), the probability value will be 0.1915. Similarly, code value 1.5 (i.e. $1<z\leq 1.5$) will be converted to probability value 0.0919, and so on. A feature with code value closer to the mean is transformed to a higher probability while the one with code value far from the mean is given a lower probability. Hence, the obtained probability value of each feature can be viewed as the occurrence frequency of each term in the field of chance discovery. The necessity of executing this code transformation is to match the principles in chance discovery, and to observe the consecutive changes along the time dimension. In other words, this study tried to find a way so that the meaning of features in finance can correspond to the frequency in chance discovery.

3.4   Serial KeyGraph and Integrated Map of Financial Trend

Since the frequency (i.e., integer ($probability\_value * 100$)) of each feature is gained, the serial KeyGraph will be generated according to the algorithm of

KeyGraph [11]. The serial KeyGraph is a series of KeyGraphs generated in sequence to observe a target firm during a selected period of time.

According to the definition of KeyGraph, hubs are viewed as the candidates of chances. In this study, the way of choosing a chance is extended to consider a continuously appeared hub as a chance which can be used to examine the financial situation and manipulation of a firm. Using six descriptive rules, it is intended to check the good or poor conditions initially. The amount of satisfied or unsatisfied rules can be used to detect financial trends and changes subsequently. Accordingly, four possible financial conditions can be found in the KeyGraph: steady, growing, returning back from turbulence, declined/dangerous, and becoming failed.

Finally, an integrated map of financial trend will be employed to sum up the serial scenarios for presenting an overview of the financial trend within the whole period of time.

3.5   Explanation

In the KeyGraph, a green node denotes a positive effect; on the contrary, the yellow node denotes a negative effect. Nodes in the same color mean a sustained expression of highlighting the shifts in the same direction. As chances represent serious status, a diagram with more chances means that the situation is significantly good or poor.

It becomes easier and friendlier for users to check the dynamic changes via visualized expression than textual expression. Generally, it is better to have certain amount of nodes (either in the same direction or not) than too few nodes during a year because nodes represent the financial operations. The diagrams can be read and explained easily by the stakeholders and managers to realize the condition of a company conveniently. It can also be used to detect the financial status of a company, or to provide advices for financial manipulations of the next year.

4   Experiment and Explanation

The experiment was executed according to the financial data visualization framework. The contents of nine features are listed in Table 1. The short forms of feature description are: *Firm, leverage, Performance, Liquidity, Liability>Asset, ROA, Refunding, Negative_NI,* and *NI* for marking in the diagrams.

This study aims at investigating financial situation in the "optical storage media companies"in the electronic industry in Taiwan. CMC Magnetics Corporation and Megamedia Corporation were selected as the target firms for the experiment. CMC is an example of non-distressed company while Megamedia is an example of distressed company as its listing was terminated in 2005. Subsequently, seasonal financial statements from 1997 to 2004 were collected from the Taiwan Economic Journal (TEJ) Data Bank. The collected data was then divided into two parts in sequence. The first part (i.e., from 1997 to 1999) formed a calculating basis for the standardization, and the second part provided the initial value for generating the transformed codes.

Table 1. Experimental features and relevant descriptions

Feature and Formulae	Description	Pref.
$F1 = \log(TotalAset/GNP)$	Firm size	H
$F2 = TotalLiability/TotalAsset$	Extent of using financial leverage	L
$F3 = WorkingCapital/TotalAsset$	Performance of current capital	H
$F4 = Cur.Liabiilty/Cur.Asset$	Inverse of liquidity	L
$F5 = 1$ while total liability exceeds total asset; and $F5 = 0$ otherwise	Relationship between liabilities and assets	Z
$F6 = NetIncome/TotalAsset$	Return of assets (ROA)	H
$F7 = FundByOperation/TotalLiability$	Ability for refunding total liabilities	H
$F8 = 1$ while net income was negative and last for two seasons; and $F8 = 0$ otherwise	State of net income	Z
$F9 = (NI_t - NI_{t-1}/|NI_t| + |NI_{t-1}|)$ where NI_t is netincome of the nearest period t	Growth of net income	H

H: The higher the better; L: The lower the better; Z: Zero the best.

4.1   Serial KeyGraph in the Experiment

According to the concepts of chance discovery [10], the code of each feature obtained from the "Code Transformation" phase can be viewed as the occurrence frequency of a term. The feature frequency was then entered into the "Serial KeyGraph Generation" phase to create the annual KeyGraph. Successively, the serial KeyGraphs for CMC and Megamedia were generated and shown in Fig. 2 and Fig. 3. Each serial KeyGraph contains five annual KeyGraphs to illustrate the financial situation and performance. In the diagrams, green nodes denote a positive condition, and yellow nodes denote a negative condition. Lines in diagrams mean the associations between every two nodes.

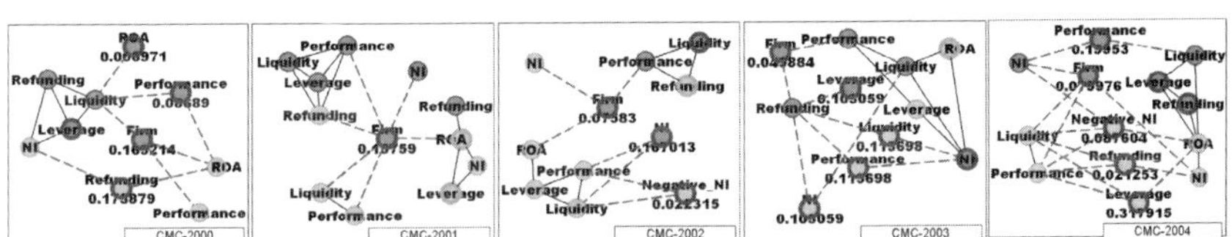

Fig. 2. Serial KeyGraph of CMC

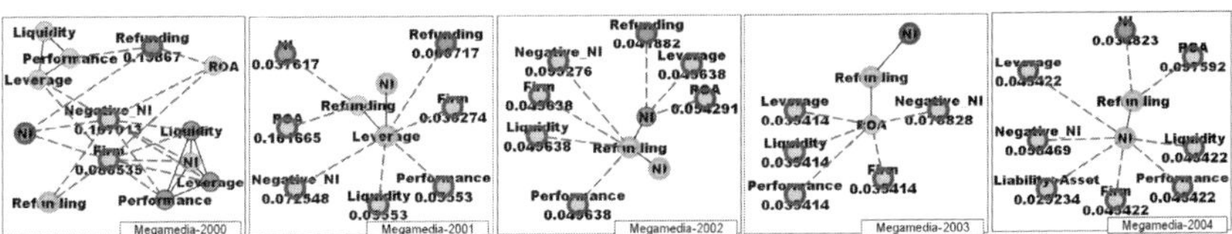

Fig. 3. Serial KeyGraph of Megamedia

The 2003 KeyGraphs of CMC and Megamedia were selected randomly as examples to show how to examine the diagrams for explaining the financial situation in a separate year. Firstly, the 2003 KeyGraph of CMC (Fig. 4(a)) was used to explain the financial situation of the company.

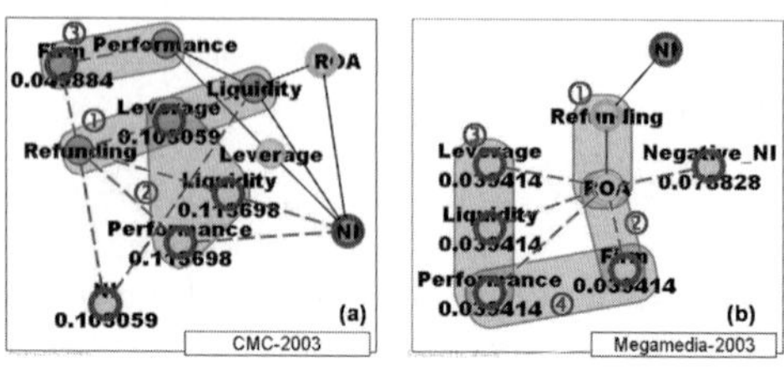

Fig. 4. KeyGraph for CMC and Megamedia in 2003

In Fig. 4(a), Area① containing three features, namely *Refunding, Leverage* (also a positive chance) and *Liquidity*, supported the unsatisfied first descriptive rule (because of the uneven directions) and was described as: "Total refunding ability of CMC was extremely good". Area② containing three features, supported the unsatisfied sixth rule and was described as: "The firm was a bit weakened in its performance, but the leverage was good in the meantime". Area③ containing two features, supported the unsatisfied third rule and was described as: "The operating efficiency of CMC was excellent". In addition, there were two positive and three negative chances in Fig. 4(a), which could be described as: "The positive and negative forces within chances are about balanced".

Consequently, the scenario of KeyGraph in Fig. 4 (a) was: "The firm size of CMC was growing rapidly because of the greater loan and investment, but the net income and ability of liquidity were poor in 2003".

Secondly, the 2003 KeyGraph of Megamedia (in Fig. 4(b)) was used to explain the financial situation of the company. Area① in Fig. 4(b), containing two features (i.e. *Refunding* and *ROA*), supported the satisfied forth rule (because of the even directions) and was described as: "The ability of gaining profit was weak within Megamedia". Area② containing two features (with one negative chance), supports the satisfied fifth rule and was described as: "The operating performance of this firm was getting worse seriously". Area③, containing three features, supported the satisfied sixth rule and was described as: "The financial structure was thoroughly becoming weak, unstable, and unsecured in this firm". Area④, containing two features (both negative chances), supported the satisfied third rule and was described as: "The operating efficiency of Megamedia was extremely poor". Moreover, there were one positive and five negative chances in Fig. 4(b), which could be described as: "The negative forces were greater than positive ones and the status was turning worse quickly".

Consequently, the scenario of KeyGraph in Fig. 4(b) was: "The financial situation of this company was exceedingly declined, even it tried hard to increase the book value of *Net Income* in 2003".

Table 2. Summry of satisfied/unsatisfied rules and positive/negative chances

company		CMC					Megamedia				
year		00	01	02	03	04	00	01	02	03	04
satisfied	R1	Δ	Δ		Δ	Δ		v			
unsatisfied	R2										v
rules	R3	Δ	Δ	Δ	Δ	Δ	Δ	v	v	v	v
	R4	v	Δ				Δ	v	Δ	v	v
	R5	Δ	Δ	Δ			v			v	
	R6	Δ			Δ	Δ	v	v		v	v
num. of	pos.	3	1	2	2	2	1	2	1	0	1
chances	neg.	1	0	1	3	3	2	5	6	5	7

v: satisfied rule (poor condition). Δ: unsatisfied rule (good condition).
pos.: number of positive chance. neg.: number of negative chance.

In order to produce the successive scenarios of serial KeyGraph, the information of recognition of the satisfied and unsatisfied rules and the number of positive and negative chances from 2000 to 2004 was summarized in Table 2.

Following the way used above for explaining a separate KeyGraph, every KeyGraph in the serial KeyGraph would be described successively.

Firstly, according to Fig. 2 and Table 2, the successive scenarios of CMC from 2000 to 2004 will be presented as follows. In 2000, the scenario was: "The status was good, and some of the features were in an extremely good condition." The scenario of 2001 was: "It was a fluctuating year with uneven positive and negative features, and some financial manipulations occurred for expending the firm size." The scenario of 2002 was: "As an extremely negative chance (i.e. *Negative_NI*) was shown, a tendency of becoming declined was rising." In 2003 and 2004, the scenario was: "The financial situations came back to steady and healthy after the past worse year, and the positive forces were apparently larger than the negative ones."

Secondly, according to Fig. 3 and Table 2, the successive scenarios of Megamedia would be presented. In 2000, the scenario was: "The status was fluctuating, and the features were uneven with positive and negative directions." The scenario of 2001 was: "The financial situation was turning weaker, and there were too few positive features to pull it back." The scenario of 2002 was: "The situation was getting worse, and the positive features decreased while the negative ones increased." The scenario of 2003 was: "The situation was getting seriously worse with four poor conditions (no good ones) and five negative chances (no positive ones)." The scenario of 2004 was: "The financial situation was appearing extremely unhealthy, and the distress might happen at any time, as the number of negative chance abruptly jumped to seven with only a positive one."

4.2   Integrated Map of Financial Trend

After explaining the serial KeyGraphs of CMC and Megamedia, the five-year information within Table 2 could also be utilized to generate an integrated map

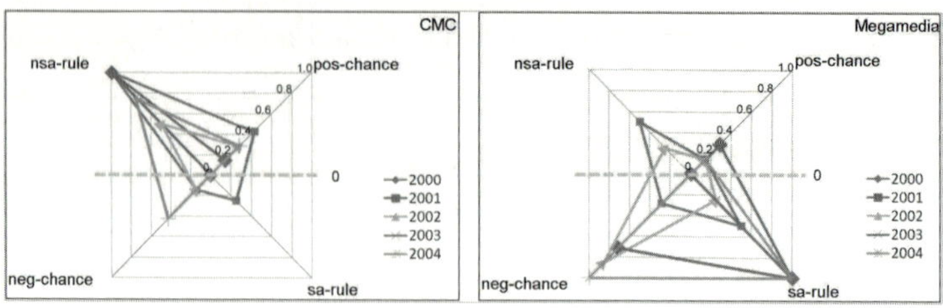

Fig. 5. Integrated map of financial trend for CMC and Megamedia

of financial trend as shown in Fig. 5 to provide an overview picture of the accumulative five-year scenario. Two axes of Fig. 5 are the number of satisfied and unsatisfied rules and the number of positive and negative chances.

According to Fig. 5, most of CMC's financial operations were above the zero line; the surrounded area of every year was appearing stable. That is, the financial trend of CMC was steady and healthy with acceptable manipulations. In contrast, most of Megamedia's financial operations were below the zero line; the surrounded areas of most years were getting bigger under the zero line. Hence, the financial trend of Megamedia was declined and dangerous with some strange manipulations.

5   Conclusion

Within the experiment, the source data of financial statements was coded into the term frequency for chance discovery. Afterwards, the term frequency was employed to produce the serial KeyGraph for CMC and Megamedia companies. Finally, the integrated map of financial trend was generated according to the summarized information from serial KeyGraph. Referring to the serial KeyGraphs (i.e., Fig. 2 and Fig. 3) and the integrated map of financial trend (i.e., Fig. 5), the overall scenario of CMC could be described as: "it was steady and healthy with a mild growth from 2000 to 2004"; while Megamedia could be depicted as: "it was poor and becoming dangerous with an obvious decline from 2000 to 2004". Thus the visualization of financial trend becomes attainable and plausible using chance discovery methods upon the financial statement data.

Furthermore, by comparing Fig. 2 with Fig. 3, the financial situations of CMC in 2001 and Megamedia in 2000 were both fluctuating, but the subsequent development differed drastically. CMC returned back to normal from 2003 eventually while Megamedia kept dropping down irresistibly. The key point of the obvious difference could be the financial manipulating strategy and crisis handling ability.

The future work of this study is suggested to include more relevant data (e.g. assessment reports of accountant or financial reports from newspaper or media) to enrich the discovery of the financial status and trend. Expectedly, the additional data sources and analyzed results may ensure the feasibility of applying visualization methods in the finance area.

References

1. Ohlson, J.A.: Financial Ratios and the Probabilistic Prediction of Bankruptcy. Journal of Accounting Research, 109–131 (1980)
2. Balcaen, S., Ooghe, H.: 35 years of studies on business failure: an overview of the classical statistical methodologies and their related problems. British Accounting Review 38, 63–93 (2006)
3. Beaver, W.H.: Financial Ratios as Predictors of Failure. Journal of Accounting Research 4, 71–111 (1966)
4. Altman, E.I.: Financial Ratios, Discriminant Analysis and the Prediction of Corporate Bankruptcy. Journal of Finance, 589–609 (September 1968)
5. Grice, J.S., Dugan, M.T.: The Limitation of Bankruptcy Prediction Models: Some Cautions for the Researcher. Review of Quantitative Finance and Accounting 17, 151–166 (2001)
6. Ohsawa, Y., Fukuda, H.: Chance Discovery by Stimulated Groups of People. Application to Understanding Consumption of Rare Food. Journal of Contingencies and Crisis Management, 129–137 (2002)
7. Ohsawa, Y.: Chance Discovery: The Current States of Art. In: Ohsawa, Y., Tsumoto, S. (eds.) Chance Discovery in Real World Decision Making, pp. 3–20. Springer, Heidelberg (2006)
8. Goldberg, D.E., Sastry, K., Ohsawa, Y.: Discovering Deep Building Blocks for Competent Genetic Algorithms Using Chance Discovery via KeyGraphs. In: Ohsawa, Y., McBurney, P. (eds.) Chance Discovery, pp. 276–301. Springer V, Heidelberg (2003)
9. Goda, S., Ohsawa, Y.: Chance Discovery in Credit Risk Management - Estimation of Chain Reaction Bankruptcy Structure by Directed KeyGraph. In: Proceedings of the 20th International Conference on Industrial, Engineering and Other Applications of Applied Intelligent Systems, pp. 896–904 (2007)
10. Ohsawa, Y.: KeyGraph: Visualized Structure Among Event Clusters. In: Ohsawa, Y., McBurney, P. (eds.) Chance Discovery, pp. 262–275. Springer, Heidelberg (2003)
11. Ohsawa, Y., Benson, N.E., Yachida, M.: KeyGraph: Automatic Indexing by Co-occurrence Graph based on Building Construction Metaphor. In: Proceedings of the Advanced Digital Library Conference (IEEE ADL 1998), pp. 12–18 (1998)
12. Hong, C.F., Chiu, T.F., Chiu, Y.T., Lin, M.H.: Using Conceptual Scenario Diagrams and Integrated Scenario Map to Detect the Financial Trend. In: Proceedings of the 20th International Conference on Industrial, Engineering and Other Applications of Applied Intelligent Systems, pp. 886–895 (2007)
13. Blum, M.: Failing Company Discriminant analysis. Journal of Accounting Research 12, 72–102 (1974)
14. Lee, C.F., Finnerty, J.E., Norton, E.A.: Foundations of Financial Management. West Publishing Company, MN (1997)
15. Lensberg, T., Eilifsen, A., McKee, T.M.: Bankruptcy theory development and classification via genetic programming. European Journal of Operational Research, 169, 677–697 (2006)
16. Anderson, D., Sweeney, D., Williams, T.: Statistics for Business and Economics. South-Western College Publishing (2007)

A Survey on Reviewer Assignment Problem

Fan Wang[1], Ben Chen[1,*], and Zhaowei Miao[2]

[1] School of Business, Sun Yat-Sen University, Guangzhou, P.R. China
chenben819@gmail.com
[2] Management School, Xiamen University, Xiamen, P.R. China

Abstract. Research into Reviewer Assignment Problem (RAP) is still in its early stage but there is great world-wide interest, as the foregoing process of peer-review which is the brickwork of science authentication. The RAP approach can be divided into three phases: identifying assignment procedure, computing the matching degree between manuscripts and reviewers, and optimizing the assignment so as to achieve the given objectives. Methodologies for addressing the above three phases have been developed from a variety of research disciplines, including information retrieval, artificial intelligent, operations research, etc. This survey is not only to cover variations of RAP that have appeared in the literature, but also to identify the practical challenge and current progress for developing intelligent RAP systems.

Keywords: reviewer assignment; information retrieval; conference system.

1 Introduction

Assigning submitted manuscripts to reviewers known as Reviewer Assignment Problem (RAP), is an important but tough task for journal editors, conference program chairs, and research councils. The essence of RAP can be divided into three phases: (1) identifying the assignment procedure, (2) computing the match between manuscripts and reviewers, and (3) optimizing the assignment so as to maximize the match within the feasible restriction.

Reviewer assignment, traditionally handled by a single person (or at most a few people), is approached to satisfy four conditions: matching manuscripts and reviewers, fulfilling manuscript slots, balancing reviewers' workload and avoiding conflicts of interest. As reviewer assignment must be completed under severe timing constraints, along with a very large number of submissions arriving near an announced deadline, it makes RAP a stressed dual problem of time and labor intensive. In response to the need of automatic mechanism, a number of studies have addressed the assignment solutions since Dumais and Nielsen's [14] breakthrough.

---

* Corresponding Author. This research is supported by National Natural Science Foundation of China under Project No. 60704048. The author Dr. Zhaowei Miao thanks the support by Humanities and Social Science Project (No. 07JC630047) of National Ministry of Education, China.

N.T. Nguyen et al. (Eds.): IEA/AIE 2008, LNAI 5027, pp. 718–727, 2008.

In general, RAP described in this paper, should be relevant whenever one has two large sets of objects that need to be matched such that each object in one set gets assigned a small number of objects from the other, and have many practical applications, such as resource allocation (matching funding agencies to research projects[10], scheduling on parallel machines [13], assigning managers to construction projects [27], classroom assignment [8]), staff scheduling (assigning graduating students to interviewer, assigning press releases to newspaper reporters, matching staff to projects in consulting companies [7], crew scheduling in airline companies [19], posting military servicemen [3,25]), and construction decision making (corrective action recommendation for material management [38]).

This wide range of real-world applications has constituted a major motivation for scholars in developing solutions for RAP. Reviewer assignment has been discussed as a process of peer-review in the voice of improving review mechanism. One of the earliest papers that addressed an assignment solution is by Dumais and Nielsen [14], who presented the matching degree computation by Latent Semantic Indexing (LSI), which was refined by Yarowsky and Florian [41] on using reviewers' online publication instead of their autobiography. Different from content-based Information Retrieval (IR), Watanabe *et al.* [39] raised the matching degree computation by constructing collaborative network, which leads to the hybrid approach of the two technologies. On the other hand, Operations Research (OR) has been used to build the assignment models and design algorithms of optimization.

RAP, which has been widely approached along different disciplines, can be applied into various application fields and represented by multifarious items, thus making it more difficult to search for previous work on the topic. This paper is intended to provide a comprehensive survey according to the researches which have appeared in the literature sorting by the three phases of RAP. The value of such a study is in providing an opportunity to reflect on what has been achieved, to identify gaps that need to be addressed, and to set direction for future research.

The reminder of this paper is organized as follows. Section 2 provides a review on the assignment procedure. Section 3 presents IR technology for computing matching degree between manuscripts and reviewers. Section 4 is a summary on the methodologies for optimization modeling. Finally, conclusions are presented and suggestions are made for further research.

2 Reviewer Assignment Procedure

Researches defended on reviewer assignment procedure involve the specification of four issues: assignment criteria, assignment processes, solutions of qualified reviewer identification, and its influence in the peer-review model.

The assignment criteria play an important role in the methodology and procedure of reviewer assignment, and indirectly affect the peer-review quality. Fixed assignment criteria are widely used in the science community, which require authors to select keywords from one list of disciplines or prorate the keywords. Fixed lists make up of two or three columns sometimes (e.g. "Methodology", "Application" and "Others" [33]), which makes the chosen keywords more comprehensively. As it is argued that the update of fixed lists cannot catch up with the development of disciplines, the unfixed criteria are also used in some conference procedure, especially when the discipline information is not integrated or hard to represent by several keywords. In that case, IR technology is applied to compute the similarity between manuscripts and reviewers' biographies [14]. In the mean while, data mining is used to extract the keyword-list by doing unsupervised clustering or supervised learning by using pervious accepted papers as training set [5].

Reviewer assignment is the foregoing process of peer-review in the manuscripts selection procedure, which directly influences the review result and evaluation aggregating. Conference chair usually works on the reviewer assignment with the registered information of manuscripts and reviewers, and then solution is addressed within the certain community. Meanwhile, in the project selection of national funding committee (e.g. NSF), the assignment is firstly run for an optimal solution, and new reviewers are invited in case no satisfied solution exists. As the potential reviewer pool is large, committee chair never worries about reviewers' workload intensive [21,36]. Moreover, some large science communities (e.g. AAAI) ask reviewers to bid on manuscripts by scanning abstracts, which is taken into consideration for the assignment. The bid behavior had been studied as human-factor noise which influences the preference very much rather than disciplines of manuscripts [31].

Subjects of domain and *conflicts of interest* are the two main factors in identifying qualified reviewers. Collecting information of these two factors, known as building of knowledge-database, attracts attention of many conference chairs. Domain information can be submitted by authors and reviewers during registration; but information of conflict, including collaborative relation, student-advisor-relationship, colleague relation, is hard to collect. Geller [15] raised this problem to challenge the AI committee to call for an intelligent solution. Furthermore, Geller and Scherl [16] described how to search Internet to generate a potential-reviewers-list.

There exists a rich body of literature on peer-review that point out the inadequacies of the current systems. Weber [40] presented his manifestos for changing the journal review processes, since the assignment between manuscripts and reviewers works irrationally and inefficiently. Casati *et al.* [9] asked for more awareness on the open efficient review model and the reasonable assigning manuscripts to reviewers using information technology along with internet. Some scholars argued that the automatic reviewer assignment approaches bereaved their rights on classifying their own problems which were treated as the scientists' most precious possession [34]. And it is said that the taxonomy of disciplines is not changed momentarily, which makes some interdisciplinary researches and frontier of science will never be recognized by the corresponding committee.

3 Assignment Based on Information Retrieval

IR used on reviewer assignment focuses on the second phase of RAP, which is computing the matching degree between manuscripts and reviewers. This phase had been approached mainly in four ways: content-based IR, collaborative filtering, hybrid approach of the former two and data mining.

One of the earliest RAP solutions found in literature is by IR, since inefficiency of matching degree scoring manually was firstly raised. Using the content-based IR method known as LSI, Dumais and Nielsen [14] represented each manuscripts and reviewers' autobiography by a matrix containing nearly 100 item vectors of factors weight, the matching degree was computed as the dot product of the two matrixes. Then, assignment was done by picking several reviewers from those with high matching degree. A similar task was performed by Yarowsky and Florian [41], but reviewers' biographies were replaced by their publications which were submitted by themselves or downloaded from internet. Beginning with Dumais and Nielsen's [14] paper, there are nine papers addressed the solution by using IR techniques. Table 1 reveals that content-based methodologies are acceptable, as text is the most important factor for manuscripts and reviewers' biographies, but not the only one for assignment. Biswas and Hasan [5] compared the applicability of different content-based filtering and indicated that hybrid approaches might be a more comprehensive way.

Table 1. Review on the use of IR solutions for RAP

Study	Methodology	Techniques
Dumais and Nielsen [14]	Content-Based	Latent Semantic Indexing
Yarowsky and Florian [41]	Content-Based	VSM/Naive Bayes Classifier
Basu *et al.* [2]	Hybrid	N/A
Popescul *et al.* [30]	Hybrid	N/A
Watanabe *et al.* [39]	Collaborative Filtering	Scale-free Network
Hettich and Pazzani [21]	Data Mining	Data Mining
Rodriguez and Bollen [32]	Collaborative Filtering	Relative-rank Particle-swarm Algorithm
Biswas and Hasan [5]	Content-Based	VSM (Comparison Study)
Cameron *et al.* [6]	Hybrid	Semantic Web

Studies by IR develop with the progresses of the technology itself. Content-based IR looks only at the contents of an artifact (e.g., the words on a paper), whereas collaborative filtering, which also consider the opinions of other like-minded people with respect to these artifacts, has been used to recommend NetNews articles [26], movies [1,22], music[11], and even jokes [18]. Scale-free network, which can continuously expand with the addition of new vertices, is a useful mechanism of collaborative filtering. Watanabe *et al.* [39] had constructed a scale-free network whose vertices were keywords of reviewers' expertise and manuscripts' topic, and similarity between two keywords was the probability of connecting between the corresponding vertices. The matching degree is the weighted average of similarities between each pair of keywords of manuscripts and reviewers. Instead of keywords, Rodriguez and Bollen [32] had approached a co-authorship network with vertices representing experts, edges representing a tie between two experts, and weights representing the strength of tie.

With the application of collaborative filtering in other operations, a hybrid approach was achieved before collaborative filtering by using co-authors and authors of reference to approach the collaborative method in the paper of Basu *et al.* [2]. Their framework provides a more flexible alternative to simple keyword-based search algorithms and a less intrusive alternative to collaborative methods. Popescul *et al.* [30]

proposed a unified probabilistic framework for combining content-based and collaborative IR by extending Hofmann's [23] aspect model to incorporate the information source among scholar, manuscript and manuscript content. Semantic Web technology was also brought to collect data, represent researches' expertise and co-authorship, and find relevant reviewers in a peer-review setting [6]. As the increase of internet resource, data mining can be used to identify relative reviewers within an existing expert pool by mining online information through search engines, potential external reviewers can also be found in the online academic community.

In respond to the difficulty for a scientific community to agree upon taxonomy of keywords and maintain such a keyword database over time, Hettich and Pazzani [21] described the data mining method deployed at the U.S. NSF for assisting program directors in identifying reviewers for proposals. To the best of our knowledge, their paper is the only one work found in literature which combined IR and optimization to achieve RAP.

4   Reviewer Assignment Optimization

Optimization on reviewer assignment which mainly focus on the theory, modeling and algorithm of assigning manuscripts to reviewers, can be viewed as an enhanced version of the Generalized Assignment Problem (GAP). However, most of these studies are not based on the matching degree evaluated by IR, but simply in sense of similarity by the selected keywords. In making it easier to read, the notations used in the cited sources have, where necessary, been changed to try to keep consistent as those of traditional GAP.

The RAP optimization we study is the following. We are given a set $P = \{1,...,p\}$ of manuscripts and a set $R = \{1,...,r\}$ of reviewers; and a parameter c_{ij} denoting the "matching degree" of manuscript i for reviewer j, where $i \in P$ and $j \in R$. Parameter a_i is the certain number of reviewers that manuscript i should be assigned to; Parameter b_j is the certain number of manuscripts that reviewer j should be assigned to no more than; a given threshold T can be set as boundary of c_{ij} to identify reviewers' qualification.

The simplest version of RAP just distinguishes whether each reviewer and each manuscript can be matched or not, and represents the matching degree as a $p \times r$ matrix $C = c_{ij}$ ($i = 1,..., p$, $j = 1,..., r$), where c_{ij} is a binary parameter whose value equals 1 if there is overlap between reviewer's expertise and manuscript's topic and no conflicts of interest, otherwise 0. As the binary c_{ij} is too general to present the grade of matching, discrete matching degree becomes a more popular method. A typical but exhausted way is requiring reviewers to rate their preference according to the abstracts, with 1 for the lowest preference to 10 for the highest, sometimes p is used for the highest, where p is the total number of manuscripts. Once there is conflict of interest, c_{ij} is set to 0 [24]. Instead of rating for all the submissions, reviewers are usually required to score their expertise level on different disciplines (keywords) from the corresponding category, and matching degrees are acquired by a computation mechanism set by organizer [20]. The above computation methods are raised as increasing matching degree, which is appropriate to the optimizations of maximizing assignment utility. In fact, the matching degree c_{ij} can easily be transformed as smaller value for higher preference, with the evaluation on the converse way, so as to be adapted for minimum optimization.

With the "matching degree" matrix C, a binary variable x_{ij}, whose value is 1 if manuscript i is assigned to reviewer j and 0 otherwise, is brought to present the integer programming (IP) formulation of the RAP (here we take the increasing matching degree as example):

$$\max \quad \sum_{i=1}^{p}\sum_{j=1}^{r} c_{ij}x_{ij} \tag{1}$$

Subject to

$$\sum_{j=1}^{r} x_{ij} = a_i \tag{2}$$

$$\sum_{i=1}^{p} x_{ij} \le b_j \tag{3}$$

$$x_{ij} \le \left\lfloor \frac{c_{ij}}{T} \right\rfloor \tag{4}$$

$$x_{ij} = 0 \quad or \quad 1 \tag{5}$$

Note that constraint (4) along with (5) force that reviewer would not be assigned to a manuscript whenever c_{ij} is smaller than the given threshold T. However, some conference chairs just require that at least one assigned reviewer is exactly expert for that manuscript, constraint (6) instead of (4), is brought into the mathematical model to ensure that at least one reviewer whose matching degree for manuscript i is greater than or equal to T [20].

$$\max_{1 \le j \le r} \left\{ c_{ij}x_{ij} \right\} \ge T \tag{6}$$

In case the above model does not have a feasible solution or takes too much running-time, the formulation will be reformed as a multi-objective (7) by relaxing constrains (2) and (3). The parameter $\alpha > 0$ is the penalty weight for missing reviewers ($\alpha = 0.5$ in the work of [23]), and $\beta \ge 0$ is for reviewers' over-workload (β is set to be 0 when the over-workload problem is not taken into consideration). These two free control parameters enable us to freely shape the solution structure. Once an optimal/feasible solution is found, the assignment procedure comes to the end, otherwise new reviewers are invited and the original model is run [24,36]. Reviewers' workload balancing can also be considered in the manner of (7) as a multi-objective problem.

$$\max \sum_{i=1}^{p}\sum_{j=1}^{r} c_{ij}x_{ij} - \alpha \cdot \sum_{i=1}^{p}\max\left\{0, a_i - \sum_{j=1}^{r} x_{ij}\right\} - \beta \cdot \sum_{j=1}^{r}\max\left\{0, \sum_{i=1}^{p} x_{ij} - b_j\right\} \qquad (7)$$

OR was brought into RAP in the latest decade. GAP formulation is the most popular method, as RAP plays a good incident for OR researchers to examine their algorithms. Network Flow Model and set-covering optimization were also discussed. The review presented in Table 2 shows that most of the researches are IP formulation of GAP with binary variables which indicate the assignment, and MIP models are lately raised by bringing continual variables into the objective function for constrains relaxation. Network Flow Model, whose polynomial-time algorithm has been proposed, also works well for RAP when manuscripts and reviewers are represented as nodes in bipartite graph, with weights of arcs connected nodes representing the matching degree; manuscripts slots and reviewers' workload limitation can be fulfilled by adding a source and a sink, and set the capabilities of all the arcs. Studies that focus on modeling seldom consider algorithm, and usually solve the model by the professional mathematic software (e.g. ILOG CPLEX, MATALAB), thus the solution is only examined in communities related to computer science, while conference chair of arts communities cannot handle.

Table 2. Review on the RAP optimization

Study	Model	Algorithm
Hartvigsen *et al.* [20]	Network Flow	N/A(using SAS/OR)
Benferhat and Lang [4]	GAP(IP)	VCSP
Tian *et al.* [37]	GAP(IP)	N/A
Merelo-Guervós *et al.* [29]	GAP(IP)	Evolutionary
Merelo-Guervós and Castillo-Valdivieso [28]	GAP(IP)	Hybrid(Greedy/Evolutionary)
Cook *et al.* [12]	Set-Covering(IP)	Greedy
Janak *et al.* [24]	GAP(IP/MIP)	N/A(using CPLEX)
Goldsmith and Solan [17]	Survey	N/A
Sun *et al.* [36]	GAP(IP)	N/A
Schirrer *et al.* [33]	GAP(IP/MIP)/Network Flow	Memetic/(using XPress^{TM})

Note: GAP-General Assignment Problem; IP-Integer Programming; MIP-Mixed Integer Programming.

5   Concluding Remarks and Future Perspectives

The focal point of interest in this paper is to review the up-to-date research on RAP which has important practical interests in several field including resource allocation, staff scheduling, decision making, etc. This article outlined the existing discussion and solution for RAP, which focused on the three different phases: (1) recognizing assignment criteria and procedure, (2) computing the matching degree between manuscripts and reviewers, (3) approaching the assignment. Hence, discussions on the first phase, IR that computed the match, OR that optimized the assignment are addressed in the above ordinal sections. Moreover, all these researches based themselves mostly in one field.

Future research on this field can be extended towards a variety of directions. First, widely acceptable reviewer assignment criteria and procedure are required for a certain field to ensure the democracy and equity; study on this field should be raised along with peer-review. Then, solutions employ IR work really well in the situation of time and labor intensive, but new technology and supervised can be brought in to improve the match computation to be closer to the actual demand. Further, innovation in mathematical modeling and algorithm is encouraged, such as network solution and set covering methodology are brought in to enrich RAP which is a traditional GAP. Another further, empirical study or tracking research can be done to study reviewer performance (such as review efficiency, quality, etc), in order to take reviewer performance into the future assignment consideration.

Another future research direction, which could be of interest at all levels of research and practice, is the investigation of implementing RAP solution by popular office software. Seeing that previous research are all in respond to the predicament in science community and solution are addressed using a corresponding professional tool of the certain field (e.g. AI, Computer Science, Decision Science, OR, etc), additional resource should be called for to deal with RAP in arts community. On condition that RAP solution can be implemented by popular software tool (e.g. Excel), it will be more convenient for program chair of arts community to manage conference proceeding.

There is a clear need for more field work where studies involving actual stakeholders with their own problems may reveal ways of improving technologies, methodologies and models, or suggesting where new approaches may be needed. This paper has identified certain issues in RAP research approach and direction. While, as pointed out above, the literature review carried out has some limitations, it is intended that a follow-up study will examine the principle and performance of reviewer assignment module in the conference managing software (e.g. CyberChair, ConfMan, Conftool, AAA S/W, Puma, SIGACT). It is also expected that this historical analysis will be continuously updated and reported at regular intervals in the future.

References

1. Basu, C., Hirsh, H., Cohen, W.: Recommendation as Classification: Using Social and Content-based Information in Recommendation. In: 15th national/tenth conference on Artificial intelligence/Innovative applications of artificial intelligence, pp. 714–720. AAAI, USA (1998)
2. Basu, C., Hirsh, H., Cohen, W., Nevill-Manning, C.: Technical paper recommendation: A study in combining multiple information sources. Journal of Artificial Intelligence Research 14, 231–252 (2001)
3. Bausch, D.O., Brown, G.G., Hundley, D.R., Rapp, S.H., Rosenthal, R.E.: Mobilizing Marine Corps Officers. Interfaces 21(4), 26–38 (1991)
4. Benferhat, S., Lang, J.: Conference Paper Assignment. International Journal of Intelligent Systems 16, 1183–1192 (2001)

5. Biswas, H.K., Hasan, M.M.: Using Publications and Domain Knowledge to Build Research Profiles: an Application in Automatic Reviewer Assignment. In: 2007 International Conference on Information and Communication Technology, pp. 82–86 (2007)
6. Cameron, D., Aleman-Meza, B., Arpinar, B.: Collecting Expertise of Researchers for Finding Relevant Experts in a Peer-Review Setting. In: First International ExpertFinder Workshop (2007)
7. Caron, G., Hansen, P., Jaumard, B.: The assignment problem with seniority and job priority constraints. Operations Research 47(3), 449–454 (1999)
8. Carter, M.W., Tovey, C.A.: When is the classroom assignment problem hard? Operations Research 40(1), S28–S39 (1992)
9. Casati, F., Giunchiglia, F., Marchese, M.: Publish and perish: Why the Current Publication and Review Model is Killing Research and Wasting Your Money, http://www.acm.org/ubiquity/views/v8i03_fabio.html
10. Cohen, P.R., Kjeldsen, R.: Information retrieval by constrained spreading activation in semantic network. Information Processing & Management 23(4), 255–268 (1987)
11. Cohen, W., Fan, W.: Web-collaborative Filtering: Recommending Music by Crawling the Web. Computer Networks 33(1-6), 685–698 (2000)
12. Cook, W.D., Golany, B., Kress, M., Penn, M., Raviv, T.: Optimal Allocation of Proposals to Reviewers to Facilitate Effective Ranking. Management Science 51(4), 655–661 (2005)
13. Dell'Amico, M., Martello, S.: The k-cardinality assignment problem. Discrete Applied Mathematics 76(1-3), 103–121 (1997)
14. Dumais, S., Nielsen, J.: Automating the assignment of submitted manuscripts to reviewers. Research and Development in information Retrieval, 233–244 (1992)
15. Geller, J.: How IJCAI 1999 can prove the value of AI by using AI. In: 15th International Joint Conference on Artificial Intelligence, pp. 55–58 (1997)
16. Geller, J., Scherl, R.: Challenge: Technology for Automated Reviewer Selection (1997), http://njit.edu/~geller/finalchall.ps1997
17. Goldsmith, J., Solan, R.H.: The AI Conference Paper Assignment Problem, http://www.cs.uic.edu/~sloan/my-papers/GodlsmithSloanPaperAssignment.pdf
18. Gupta, D., Digiovanni, M., Narita, H., Goldberg, K.: Jester 2.0: A new Lineartime Collaborative Filtering Algorithm Applied to Jokes. In: Workshop on Recommender Systems at ACM SIGIR 1999 (1999)
19. Hansen, P., Wendell, R.E.: A note on airline commuting. Interfaces 11(12), 85–87 (1982)
20. Hartvigsen, D., Wei, J.C., Czuchlewski, R.: The Conference Paper-Reviewer Assignment Problem. Decision Sciences 30(3), 865–876 (1999)
21. Hettich, S., Pazzani, M.J.: Mining for Proposal Reviewers: Lessons Learned at the National Science Foundation. In: 12th ACM SIGKDD international conference on Knowledge discovery and data mining, pp. 862–871. ACM Press, New York (2006)
22. Hill, W., Stead, L., Rosenstein, M., Furnas, G.: Recommending and Evaluating Choices in a Virtual Community of Use. In: SIGCHI conference on Human factors in computing systems, pp. 195–201. ACM Press/Addison-Wesley Publishing Co., New York (1995)
23. Hofmann, T.: Probabilistic Latent Semantic Analysis. In: 15th Conference on Uncertainty in Artificial Intelligence, pp. 289–296 (1999)
24. Janak, S.L., Taylor, M.S., Floudas, C.A., Burka, M., Mountzizris, T.J.: Novel and Effective Integer Optimization Approach for the NSF Panel-Assignment Problem: A Multiresource and Preference-Constrained Generalized Assignment Problem. Ind. Eng. Chem. Res. 45(1), 258–265 (2006)
25. Klingman, D., Phillips, N.: Topological and computational aspects of preemptive multicriteria military personnel assignment problems. Manage. Sci. 30(1), 1362–1375 (1984)

26. Konstan, J., Miller, B., Maltz, D., Herlocker, L., Gordon, L., Riedl, J.: Grouplens: Applying Collaborative Filtering to Usenet News. Communications of the ACM 40(3), 77–87 (1997)
27. LeBlanc, L.J., Randels, D., Swann, T.K.: Heery International's Spreadsheet Optimization Model for Assigning Managers to Construction Projects. INTERFACE 30(6), 95–106 (2000)
28. Merelo-Guervós, J.J., Castillo-Valdivieso, P.: Conference Paper Assignment Using a Combined Greedy/ Evolutionary Algorithm. In: Yao, X., Burke, E.K., Lozano, J.A., Smith, J., Merelo-Guervós, J.J., Bullinaria, J.A., Rowe, J.E., Tiňo, P., Kabán, A., Schwefel, H.-P. (eds.) PPSN 2004. LNCS, vol. 3242, pp. 602–611. Springer, Heidelberg (2004)
29. Merelo-Guervós, J.J., García-Castellano, F.J., Castillo, P.A., Arenas, M.G.: How Evolutionary Computation and Perl saved my conference. In: Sánchez, L. (ed.) Segundo Congreso Español sobre Metaheurísticas, Algoritmos Evolutivos y Bioinspirados, pp. 93–99 (2003)
30. Popescul, A., Ungar, L.H., Pennock, D.M., Lawrence, S.: Probabilistic Models for Unified Collaborative and Content-base Recommendation in Sparse-Data Environments. In: 17th Conference on Uncertainty in Artificial Intelligence, pp. 437–444. Morgan Kaufmann Publishers Inc., San Francisco (2001)
31. Rodriguez, M.A., Bollen, J., Van de Sompel, H.: Mapping the Bid Behavior of Conference Referees. Journal of Informetrics 1(1), 62–82 (2007)
32. Rodriguez, M.A., Bollen, J.: An Algorithm to Determine Peer-Reviewers. Arxiv preprint cs.DL/0605112 (2006)
33. Schirrer, A., Doerner, K.F., Hartl, R.F.: Reviewer Assignment for Scientific Articles using Memetic Algorithms. OR/CS Interfaces Series 39, 113–134 (2007)
34. Scott, A.: Peer review and the relevance of science. Futures 39, 827–845 (2007)
35. Shardanand, U., Maes, P.: Social Information Filtering: Algorithms for Automating "Word of Mouth". In: SIGCHI conference on Human factors in computing systems, pp. 210–217. ACM Press/Addison-Wesley Publishing Co., New York (1995)
36. Sun, Y.H., Ma, J., Fan, Z.P., Wang, J.: A Hybrid Knowledge and Model Approach for Reviewer Assignment. In: 40th Annual Hawaii International Conference on System Sciences, p. 47. IEEE Computer Society, Washington (2007)
37. Tian, Q., Ma, J., Liu, O.: A Hybrid Knowledge and Model System for R&D Project Selection. Expert Systems with Applications 23(3), 265–271 (2002)
38. Veronika, A., Riantini, L.S., Trigunarsyah, B.: Corrective Action Recommendation For Project Cost Variance in Construction Material Management. In: Kanok-Nukulchai, W., Munasinghe, S., Anwar, N. (eds.) 10th East Asia-Pacific Conference on Structural Engineering and Construction 2005, pp. 23–28 (2006)
39. Watanabe, S., Ito, T., Ozono, T., Shintani, T.: A Paper Recommendation Mechanism for the Research Support System Papits. In: International Workshop on Data Engineering Issues in E-Commerce, pp. 71–80 (2005)
40. Weber, R.: The Journal Review Process: a Manifesto for Change. Communications of the Association for Information Systems 2(2-3) (1999)
41. Yarowsky, D., Florian, R.: Taking the load off the conference chairs: towards a digital paper-routing assistant. In: 1999 Joint SIGDAT Conference on Empirical Methods in NLP and Very-Large Corpora (1999)

A Declarative Framework for Constrained Search Problems

Paweł Sitek and Jarosław Wikarek

Technical University of Kielce, Control and Management Systems Section,
Al. Tysiąclecia Państwa Polskiego 7, 25-314 Kielce, Poland
`{sitek, j.wikarek}@tu.kielce.pl`

Abstract. Constrained search problems (eg. scheduling, planning, resource allocation, placement, routing etc.) appear frequently at different levels of decisions. They are usually characterized by many types of constraints, which make them unstructured and difficult to solve (NP-complete). Traditional mathematical programming approaches are deficient because their representation of constraints is artificial (using 0-1 variables). Unlike traditional approaches, constraint logic programming (CLP) provides for a natural representation of heterogeneous constraints. In CLP we state the problem requirements by constraints; we do not need to specify how to meet these requirements. In this paper we propose a declarative framework for decision support system (DSS) for constrained search problems implemented by CLP and relational SQL database. We illustrate this concept by the implementation of a DSS for scheduling problems with external resources in different production organization environments.

Keywords: DSS, Scheduling, Constraint Logic Programming.

1 Introduction

Today's highly competitive business environment makes it an absolute requirement on behalf of the managers to continuously make the best decisions in the shortest possible time. *Learning from mistakes* has left its place to *one strike and you're out* reality. That is, there is no room for mistake in making decisions in this global environment. Success depends on quickly allocating the organizational resources towards meeting the actual needs and wants of the customer. Decision problems involve various numeric and non-numeric constraints, some of which are conflicting with each other. Occasionally, decision-makers do not have complete information on the situation. Thus they perform *what-if* and goal-seeking analyses involving constraints. In order to succeed in such an unforgiving environment, managers and decision makers need integrated *intelligent* decision support systems (DSS) that are capable of using a wide variety of models along with data and information resources available to them at various internal and external repositories. In this paper we present the use of constraint logic programming as a tool for such decision support systems in constrained search problems, focusing on the model representation and analyses.

N.T. Nguyen et al. (Eds.): IEA/AIE 2008, LNAI 5027, pp. 728–737, 2008.

The original contribution of our approach consists of a declarative framework for constrained search problems, developed within the constraint logic paradigm together with relational SQL database, and the development of a constraint logic solver for scheduling problems with external resources in different production organization environments.

2   Constrained Search Problems

Constrained search problems (e.g., scheduling, planning, resource allocation, placement, routing) appear frequently at different levels of decision. They are usually characterized by technical, environmental or manpower constraints, which make them unstructured, and in most of the cases are difficult to solve (NP-complete). Traditional mathematical programming approaches (linear programming, integer and mixed integer programming) are deficient in the following ways: their representation of constraints is artificial (commonly using 0-1 variables), their computing time in the presence of many constraints is very long (due to combinatorial explosion), and they cannot process various constraints applied to the main problem. Thus, the most used approach consists in developing specific software, written in a procedural language like PASCAL, BASIC or C, to solve each particular problem. However, the use of procedural languages brings the following well known disadvantages: the development time of the programs is very long and the programs are very complex, hence difficult to maintain and adapt to rapid changes of requirements.

Unlike traditional approaches, constraint logic programming CLP provides for a natural representation of heterogeneous constraints and allows domain-specific heuristics to be used on top of generic solving techniques.

3   Declarative Programming – SQL, CLP

Declarative programming is a term with two distinct meanings, both of which are in current use. According to one definition, a program is *declarative* if it describes *what* something is like, rather than *how* to create it. For example, HTML, XML web pages are declarative because they describe *what* the page should contain — title, text, images — but not *how* to actually display the page on a computer screen. This is a different approach from imperative programming languages such as PASCAL, C, and Java, which require the programmer to specify an algorithm to be run. In short, imperative programs explicitly specify an algorithm to achieve a goal, while declarative programs explicitly specify the goal and leave the implementation of the algorithm to the support software (for example, an SQL *select* statement specifies the properties of the data to be extracted from a database, not the process of extracting the data). According to a different definition, a program is *declarative* if it is written in a purely functional programming language, logic programming language, or constraint programming language. The phrase *declarative language* is sometimes used to describe all such programming languages as a group, and to contrast them against imperative languages.

These two definitions overlap somewhat. In particular, constraint programming and, to a lesser degree, logic programming, focus on describing the properties of the desired solution (the *what*), leaving unspecified the actual algorithm that should be used to find that solution (the *how*). However, most logic and constraint languages are able to describe algorithms and implementation details, so they arc not strictly declarative by the first definition.

CLP is a declarative modelling and procedural programming environment that integrates qualitative/heuristic knowledge representation of logic and quantitative/algorithmic reasoning into single paradigm. CLP as a declarative modelling and procedural programming environment is increasingly realized as an effective tool for decision support systems [4, 5, 6]. Constraint Logic Programming is suitable for Decision Support Systems (DSS) because [1,3]:

- CLP is a very good tool for the developments of knowledge base that has expertise and experience represented in terms of logic, rules and constraints. This tool allows the knowledge base to be built in an incremental and accumulating way (it is suitable for ill-structured or semi-structured decision analysis problems).
- Constraints naturally represent decisions and their inter-dependencies. Decision choices are explicitly modelled as the domains of constraint variables.
- CLP can serve as a good integrative environment for the decision analysis that has different kinds of model.
- Decision analysis requires a number of computational facilities which this tool can provide.

4   Declarative Framework for Constrained Search Problems

There is a growing need for decision support tools capable of assisting a decision maker in the constrained search problems. The most important of them are scheduling problems and scheduling problems with resource allocation. The diversity of scheduling problems, the existence of many specific constraints (precedence, resource, capacity, etc.) in each problem and the efficient constraint based scheduling algorithms make constraint logic programming a method of choice for the resolution of complex practical problems. In constraint programming approach to decision support in scheduling problems, the problem to be solved is represented in terms of decision variables and constraints on these variables [2]. Depending on the particular applications the variables of scheduling problems (job-shop, flow-shop, open-shop, and project shop) can be:

- The start time and the end time of each operation.
- The set of resources assigned to each operation (if this set is not fixed).
- The capacity of a resource that is assigned to an operation (e.g. the number of workers from a given team assigned to operation).
- The processing times (constant, variable increasing/decreasing function of starting times or allocated resources, etc.).

The constraints of a scheduling problem include:

- Temporal and precedence constraints which define the possible values for the start and end times of operations and the relations between the start and end time of two operations.

- Resource constraints which define the possible set of resources for each operation.
- Capacity constraints which limit the available capacity of each resource over time.
- Problem-specific constraint which correspond to particular features of operations and resources.

Additional variables and constraints can be included to represent optimization criteria, preferences of the user of scheduling system, etc.

4.1   Assumptions of DSS Based on CLP

The presented in (section 3) advantages and possibilities of CLP environment for decision support make it interesting for decision support in constrained search problems. Building decision support system for scheduling, covering a variety of production organization forms, such as job-shop, flow-shop, project, multi-project etc., is especially interesting. The following assumptions were adopted in order to design the presented scheduling processes of decision support system (see fig.1):

- Problem-specific constraint which correspond to particular features of operations and resources.
- The system should possess data structures that make its use possible in different production organization environments (see fig.2).
- The system should make it possible to schedule the whole set of tasks/jobs simultaneously, and after a suitable schedule has been found, it should be possible to add a new set of tasks later, and to find a suitable schedule for both sets without the necessity to change initial schedules.
- The system should regard:
    - o   additional resource types apart from machines, e.g. people, tools, etc,
    - o   temporary inaccessibility of all resource types,
    - o   resource or time depending processing times, etc.
- The decisions of the systems are the answers to appropriate questions formed as CLP predicates.

The range of the decisions made by the system depends on data structures and asked questions. Thus, the system is very flexible; as it is possible to ask all kinds of questions (write all kinds of predicates).

In this version of DSS the exemplified questions which can be asked are following:

- What is the minimum number of people necessary for assigned makespan and proper schedule? (predicate $opc\_d(L,C)$).
- What is the minimum makespan at the assigned number of people and proper schedule? (predicate $opc\_g(L,C)$).
- Is it possible to order new tasks for the determined makespan? (predicate $opcd\_s(L,C)$).
- What is minimum makespan at the assigned number of people for new tasks? (predicate $opcd\_g(L,C)$).

- What is the minimum number of people necessary for assigned makespan for new tasks? (without changing the schedule of basic set of tasks) (predicate *opcd_d(L,C)*).
- Is it possible to order tasks for the determined makespan? (predicate *opc_s(L,C)*).

L – number of workers (manpower), $C = C_{max}$ – makespan

INPUTS	QUESTIONS FOR THE DSS
FIRST TYPE	What is the minimum number of workers necessary for assigned makespan and proper schedule? What is the minimum makespan at the assigned number of workers and proper schedule?
SECOND TYPE	Is it possible to order new tasks. for the determined makespan? · Is it possible to order tasks for the determined makespan ? Is it possible to order tasks for the determined makespan where the processing time of job depends on allocated number of workers?

⇩

ADDITIONAL INFORMATION		CLP ENGINE OF DSS SYSTEM

* EXISTING SCHEDULES
 * COMPANY'S RESOURCES
   (MANPOWER
 * CUSTOMER'S REQUIREMENT
 * ....
	⇨	PREDICATES:
		 * FOR ASKED QUESTIONS
		 * FOR DATA TRANSFORMATION
		 * FOR AUTOMATED GENERATION
		   PREDICATED FOR ASKED
		   QUESTIONS
		 * ....

⇩

OUTPUTS:
* YES / NO   * NUMBER OF RESOURCES   * SCHEDULES   * MAKESPANS   * ....

Fig. 1. Concept of DSS for scheduling problems based on declarative framework

These questions are just examples of questions that the present system can be asked. New questions are new predicates that need to be created in CLP environment. Two types of questions are asked in the system:

- About the existence of the solution (eg., is it possible to carry out a new task in the particular time?, etc.).
- About a particular kind of the solution: find a suitable schedule fulfilling the performance index, find the minimum scheduling length-makespan, find the minimum number of people to carry out the task, etc.

4.2 Data Structures

Data structures were designed in such a way that they could be easily used to decision problems in a variety of scheduling environments, which is job-shop, flow-shop, project or multi-project. The obtained flexibility resulted from the use of relational data model.

Figure 2 presents the ERD (Entity Relationship Diagram) of the database that was designed to meet the requirements of cooperation with CLP environment and to have the following possibilities:

- Storing the data for scheduling problems and distribution of loads for different types of production organisation.
- Storing information about additional resources (e.g. labour force, tools or AGV vehicles).
- Saving the content and parameters of CLP predicates calls.
- Generating ready scripts for a CLP engine on the basis of the existing data.
- Saving the results obtained with a CLP solver, necessary for further calculations, visualisations or creating reports.
- Saving data about other problems within the family of constrained search problems.

5 Implementation of DSS Based on CLP for Scheduling Problems in Eclipse

We propose ECL^{i}PS^e [7] as a platform to decision support in scheduling problems. ECL^{i}PS^e is a software system - based on the CLP paradigm - for the development and

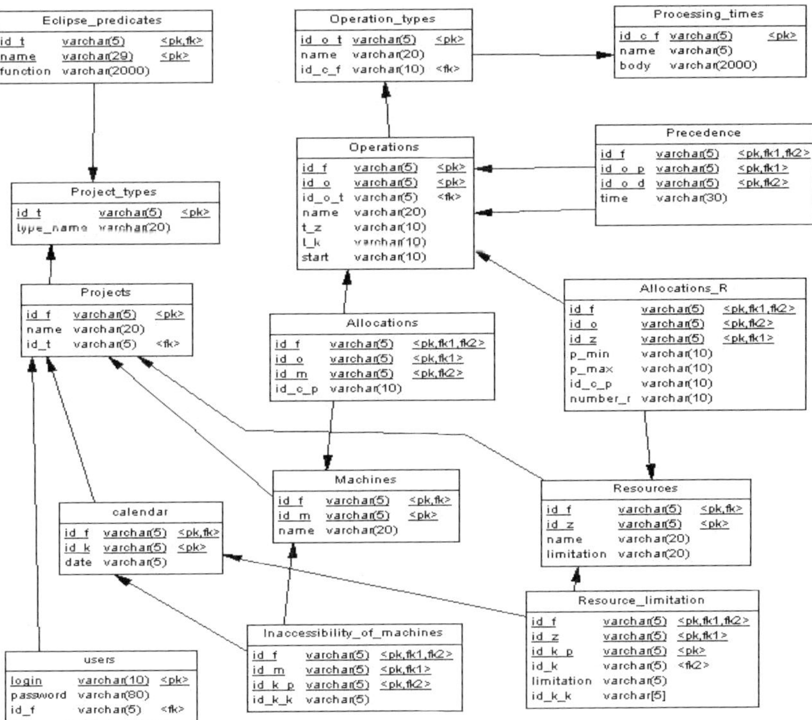

Fig. 2. The main part of database of DSS for constrained search problems (Entity Relationship Diagram)

deployment of constraint programming applications. It is also ideal for developing aspects of combinatorial problem solving, e.g. problem modeling, constraint programming, mathematical programming, and search techniques. Its wide scope makes it a good tool for research into hybrid problem solving methods. ECL^{i}PS^e comprises several constraint solver libraries, a high-level modeling and control language, interfaces to third-party solvers, an integrated development environment and interfaces for embedding into host environment. The ECL^{i}PS^e programming language is largely backward-compatible with Prolog and supports different dialects.

The novelty of the proposed approach is in the integration of the CLP methodology with a commonly used relational database model. The scripts started by a CLP engine are generated automatically on the basis of data in the database (numerical values and CLP body predicates). The proposed solution makes it possible to easily develop the system (developing and saving in the database the content of additional CLP predicates) and to integrate it with other computer systems based on a relational SQL database. Owing to the developed database structure (Fig. 2) solving other problems of the constrained search problems class is possible.

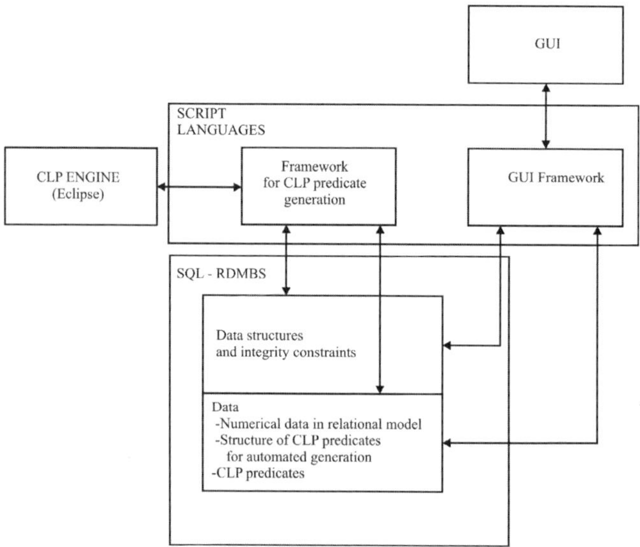

Fig. 3. Implementation of the declarative framework of DSS

6 Illustrative Examples

After the complete implementation of the DSS into ECL^{i}PS^e and SQL database environments, computation experiments were carried out. As an example the job-shop scheduling problem with manpower resources was considered. The parameters of computational example (Example_1) size 5x5 are presented in table 1. In the classical scheduling theory processing times are constant. However, there are many situations where processing time of an operation/activity depends on the starting time of the job in queue or the amount of allocated additional resource (e.g. people) (Example_2) etc. The job data structures are shown in Fig. 4a and Fig. 4b.

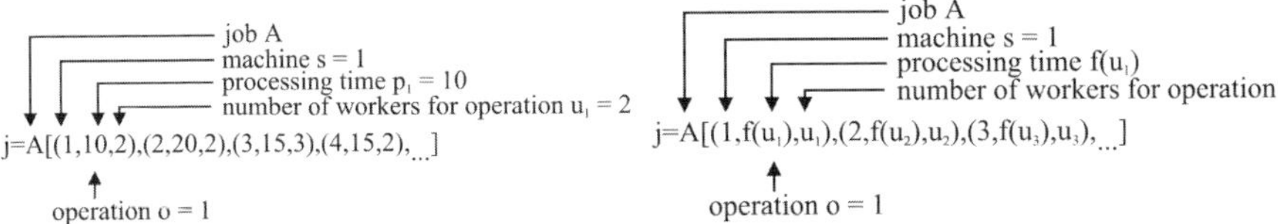

Fig. 4a. Description of task (job) data structure for job-shop computational example (Example_1) – the constant processing times

Fig. 4b. Description of task (job) data structure for job-shop computational example (Example_2) – the processing times depend on allocated number of workers

Table 1. (Example_1) – constant processing times

$j \in \{A,B,C,D,E\}$, $o \in \{1,2,3,4,5\}$, $s \in \{1,2,3,4,5\}$
j=A[(1,10,2), (2,20,2), (3,15,3), (4,15,2), (5,15,1)]
j=B[(1,10,1), (2,20,1), (3,15,2), (4,15,1), (5,20,1)]
j=C[(5,15,2), (4,20,2), (3,15,1), (2,10,2), (1,20,2)]
j=D[(1,10,3), (3,15,2), (2,20,2), (4,20,1), (5,10,2)]
j=E[(5,15,2), (4,10,1), (3,15,2), (2,10,2), (1,20,1)]
j – jobs, o – operation, s - machines

For the computational example (Example_1) the following questions (write following predicates) were asked: $opc\_g(\_,\_)$ (see fig.5), $opc\_d(\_, 120)$ (see fig.6), $opc\_s(4,155)$ - No, $opc\_s(4,170)$ - Yes.

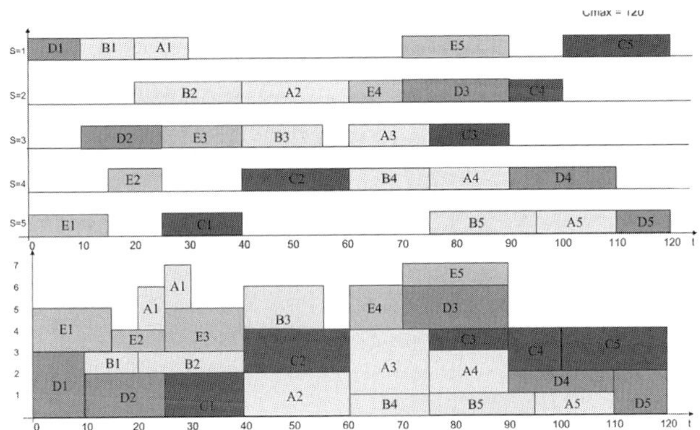

Fig. 5. Gantt's charts for answer to the question implemented in predicate $opc\_g(\_,\_)$, $C_{max}^{*}=120$, L=7 (Example_1)

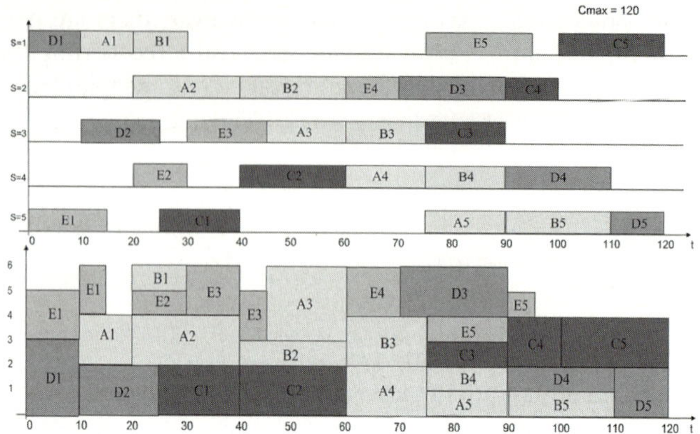

Fig. 6. Gantt's charts for answer to the question implemented in predicate $opc\_d(\_,120)$, $L_{min}=6$, $C_{max}= C_{max}^{*}=120$ (Example_1)

The second computational example was carried out with processing times of operation/activity depended on allocated additional resource (workers). The parameters of computational Example_2 are presented in tab.1 without processing times and number of allocated people. The processing time is a function of allocated workers $f(p_j,a_j,u_j)$ fig. 8. There is a simple linear function in this example. It can be any function in general case. For the computational example (Example_2) the following questions (write following predicates) were asked: $opc\_g(\_,\_)$ (see fig.7), $opc\_d(\_,\,89)$ - Yes, $opc\_s(12,110)$ - Yes.

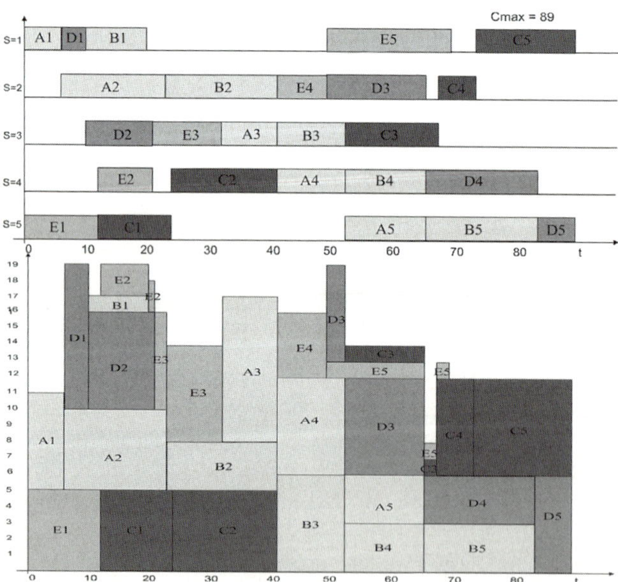

Fig. 7. Gantt's charts for answer to the question implemented in predicate $opc\_g(\_,\_)$, $C_{max}^{*}=89$, $L=19$ (Example_2)

<table>
<tr><td>

$f(p_j,a_j,u_j) = p_j - a_j*(u_j - x_j)$
and
$f(p_j,a_j,u_j) > 0$,
$a_j = 1, x_j \le u_j \le 3*x_j$

</td><td>

where :
p_j - processing time from Example_1
u_j - number of allocated workers
x_j - number of allocated workers from Example_1
a_j - acceleration factor

</td></tr>
</table>

Fig. 8. Processing time for Example_2

7 Conclusion

The proposed approach can be considered to be a contribution to constrained search problems and especially to scheduling problems with additional/external resources. In many enterprises this kind of resources can have influence on production and delivery schedules. That is especially important in the context of cheap, fast and user friendly decision support in SMEs (Small and Medium Sized Enterprises). Great flexibility of the presented approach and practically unlimited possibilities of asking questions through creating predicates cannot be overestimated. What is more, the whole decision system can be built in one modeling and programming declarative environment, which lowers costs and adds to the solution effectiveness. The CLP-tools fulfill the need of intelligent production management structures and can be based successfully in cases of scheduling problems with external resources. The proposed approach seems to be a viable alternative option for supporting quite a number of decision making processes. The originality of our approach, which achieves the transition from custom imperative programming to declarative programming in a field of constrained search problems, consists in the data structure and CLP implementation.

References

1. Liao, S.Y., Wang, H.Q., Liao, L.J.: An extended formalism to constraint logic programming for decision analysis. Knowledge-based Systems 15, 189–202 (2002)
2. Le, P.C.: Three Mechanisms for Managing Resource Constraints in a Library for Constraint-Based Scheduling Proceedings. In: INRIA/IEEE Conference on Emerging Technologies and Factory Automation (1995)
3. Young, R.U.: Constraint logic programming framework for integrated decision supports. Decision Support Systems 22, 155–170 (1998)
4. Bisdorff, R., Laurent, S.: Industrial linear optimization problem solved by constraint logic programming. European Journal of Operational Research 84(1), 82–95 (1995)
5. Lamma, E., Mello, P., Milano, M.: A distributed constrained-based scheduler. Artificial Intelligence in Engineering 11, 91–105 (1997)
6. Lee, H.G., Yu, L.G.: Constraint logic programming for qualitative and quantitative constraint satisfaction problems. Decision Support Systems 16(1), 67–83 (1996)
7. Apt, K.R., Wallace, M.G.: Constraint Logic Programming using ECLiPSe, Cambridge (2007)

Addition and Deletion of Agent Memories to Realize Autonomous Decentralized Manufacturing Systems

Yamamoto Hidehiko

Gifu University, Faculty of Engineering, Dept. of Human and Information Systems Engineering
1-1, Yanagido, Gifu, Japan
`yam-h@gifu-u.ac.jp`

Abstract. This paper describes a method to control Autonomous decentralized Flexible Manufacturing System (AD-FMS) by using a memory to determine a priority ranking for competing hypotheses. The aim is to increase the reasoning efficiency of a system the author calls reasoning to anticipate the future (RAF) which controls automatic guided vehicles (AGVs) in AD-FMSs. The system includes memory data of past production conditions and AGV actions. Using these memory data, the system reorders hypotheses by giving the highest priority ranking to the hypothesis that is most likely to be true. The system was applied to an AD-FMS that was constructed on a computer. The results showed that, compared with conventional reasoning, this reasoning system reduced the number of hypothesis replacements until a true hypothesis was reached.

Keywords: Intelligent Systems, Multi-Agent Systems, Planning and Scheduling, Production Systems, FMS, Production Planning, Autonomous Decentralized System, AGV.

1 Introduction

One approach to the operation of production plants in the 21st century is Autonomous decentralized flexible manufacturing systems (AD-FMSs) [1]–[4]. In a study on AD-FMS, the author examined the movements of automatic guided vehicles (AGVs) in terms of controlling which part should be taken next to which machining center during FMS operation [5]. In this study, a system called reasoning to anticipate the future (RAF) was developed that can determine the next action of the AGV at a given point in time by anticipating the next actions available to the AGV (next action) for several steps into the future and anticipating in advance the FMS operating status that will be produced in the near future. This RAF applies hypothetical reasoning to the number of next actions that can be considered for the AGV (competing hypotheses). However, if the number of agents included in the hypothetical reasoning process in the RAF is increased, the number of next actions that are considered as competing hypotheses also increases. As a result, the replacement of true and false hypotheses and number of repetitions of discrete production simulations produced by these replacements are increased, giving rise to the problem of decreased reasoning efficiency of the RAF. The present article reports a method to solve these problems.

N.T. Nguyen et al. (Eds.): IEA/AIE 2008, LNAI 5027, pp. 738–748, 2008.
© Springer-Verlag Berlin Heidelberg 2008

Reported methods to increase the efficiency of hypothetical reasoning include avoiding multiple searches of the same search trees, compiling knowledge from previously conducted reasoning, and applying learning functions using previous reasoning results. The approach in the present study is to express characteristic information of an AD-FMS as memory data that are added and deleted in order to establish a priority order among hypotheses competing to be selected as true. This method differs from conventional methods and seeks to make optimum use of the characteristics of AD-FMSs.

Research on predicting future situations has included statistical prediction [6] and a system in which the weight expressing the goodness of the expert predicted value is constantly updated [7]. The present method differs from conventional prediction methods in that it makes predictions based on memory, similarity [8][9], and discrete production simulations.

2　Autonomous Decentralized FMS

2.1　FMS Construction

The AD-FMS dealt with in this paper consists of internal agents including a parts warehouse for the supply of parts into the AD-FMS, a product warehouse where completed parts are kept, AGVs that transport single parts, and several machining centers (MCs), as shown in Fig. 1. The AGVs move at a constant speed along the line lattice in the figure. The MCs can process several types of parts, and the machining process and processing time for each are preset. In addition, there are several units of the same type of MC that do the same work. Groups of the same type of MC are called MC groups, and are designated as MC_1, MC_2, and so on. To distinguish between individual MCs in a group, a further designation is made with a hyphenated number after the group name, as MC_{1-1}, MC_{1-2}, and so on.

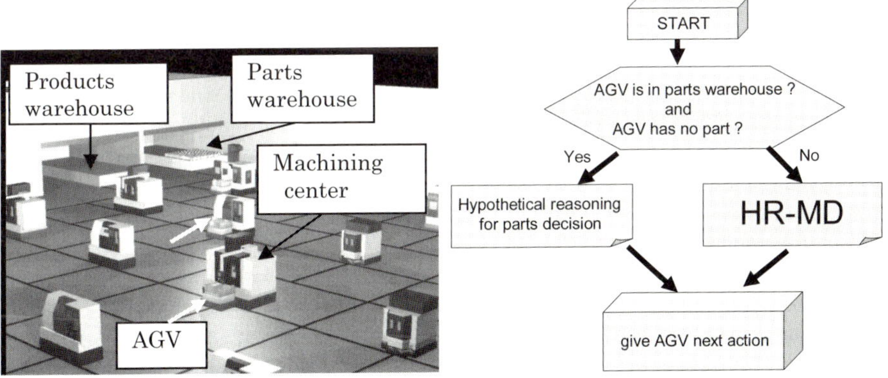

Fig. 1. AD-FMS example   **Fig. 2.** Flow of RAF

2.2 Reasoning to Anticipate the Future

In the AD-FMS in this study, production is carried out with each AGV determining its own actions through RAF. RAF can anticipate up to several future steps available to the AGV. Then, through predictions based on discrete production simulations of phenomena that may occur within these several future steps, RAF works backward to the present to decide which of the options the AGV should choose at the present point in time [5]. This process is controlled by the application of hypothetical reasoning to the several competing options (hypotheses) available to the AGV.

Fig. 2 shows the flow of RAF. RAF includes two parallel reasoning processes: hypothetical reasoning for moving decisions (HR-MD), which decides the destination of an AGV, and hypothetical reasoning for parts decisions, which decides which parts to input. Occurrence of a contradiction causes the reasoning to backtrack. The hypothetical reasoning for moving decisions that was applied in this study is described in the following.

To decide the next action of an AGV, HR-MD considers competing hypotheses for each destination MC, parts warehouse, and products warehouse, separates the competing hypotheses into true and false hypotheses, and finally decides the destination of that AGV. Specifically, it (1) sets a priority ranking for destinations of MC groups that perform the same machining process, (2) sets a priority ranking for parts warehouse and product warehouse destinations, and (3) sets a priority ranking for each MC within a group. It then sets a priority ranking for destinations available to the AGV in each of the competing hypothesis, in the order of likelihood of being adopted as a true hypothesis. This ranking is called a moving priority ranking (MP-ranking). Then, from among the competing hypotheses ranked by priority, one is selected as a true hypothesis from among the hypotheses with high priority rankings, and the remaining are considered false hypotheses. The hypothetical reasoning [10][11][12] then begins.

3 Memory Contents

In RAF, the reasoning and simulations are repeated continuously as true and false hypotheses are exchanged until contradictions are no longer found. Because of this, a problem occurs in that the number of exchanges of true and false hypotheses and number of production simulations that must be re-executed because of these exchanges, increase with greater numbers of MCs or AGVs. In the present study, therefore, good reasoning efficiency was defined as fewer exchanges or production simulations. To solve this problem of excessive exchanges, a method to rank competing hypotheses by oblivion and memory (ranking by oblivion and memory; ROM) is proposed to improve the reasoning efficiency of RAF. The ROM system is based on the idea that when a production situation occurs that is the same as one in the past, the same destination as in the past is more likely to be selected; that is, it has a high probability of being selected as the true hypothesis.

An important point in ROM is which memories are retained and how these data are used. In the following, therefore, we will first consider the contents of memory.

Humans often remember the past in the form of situation-phenomena; for example, "when… (situation), we were… (phenomena)." The memory contents used in ROM are similarly expressed in this form combining situation and phenomena. Specifically, a past production situation and the AGV destination selected at that time. Thus, the memory expresses 4 items: the 3 production situations of (a) moving priority ranking, (b) the location of the AGV, and (c) the location of the parts, together with (d) the AGV destination decided at that time (determined action). Next, the contents of these 4 items, as well as 3 terms using these 4 items, are defined as follows.

[Definition] (a) Moving priority ranking: the priority ranking determined for each destination available to the AGVs as reasoned by HR-MD.

[Definition] (b) AGV positions: the current position of each AGV or the destination it is moving toward. This corresponds to the parts warehouse, Product warehouse and each MC.

[Definition] (c) Parts positions: the place where each part existing in the AD-FMS is located. This corresponds to the parts warehouse, product warehouse, each MC and each AGV.

[Definition] (d) Decided action: the final destination selected for the AGV under the production situations of (a)~(c).

[Definition] Single memory: the memory set of (a), (b), (c) and (d).

[Definition] Whole memory: the set of all single memories, M_{number}.

[Definition] Oblivion degree: the values attached to all elements of whole memory, from 1 to M_{number}. The values are decided using a carry up method. For example, if a new memory corresponding to a single memory is assigned oblivion degree M_{number}, the single memory whose oblivion degree had been M_{number} is given a new oblivion degree of $M_{number} - 1$. This carry up method is carried out with other single memories in whole memory. As a result, the single memory whose oblivion degree had been 1 up to that point will be deleted from whole memory. The smaller the oblivion degree is, the sooner the memory is forgotten.

According to the above definitions, ROM can have many memories. Like humans, ROM has memories that are both easier and more difficult to forget.

The relation between whole memory and single memory is shown in Fig. 3. Examples of ROM memory contents (a) ~ (c) are shown in Table 1 to Table 3 and the signs used in these tables are described below.

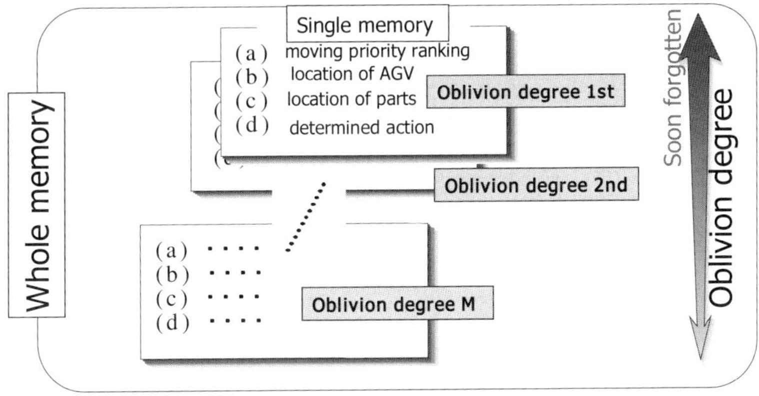

Fig. 3. Whole memory and single memory

$G(x)$: the currently available destinations for each AGV. The values of x are 1, 2,..., m'. $G(x)$ is also considered to be the following:

$$G(x) \in \left\{ Parts\_warehouse, Pr\,oducts\_warehouse, MC_{1-1}, MC_{1-2}, \cdots \right\}$$

$P'(x)$: MP-ranking f $G(x)$. The values of $P'(x)$ are 1, 2, 3, 4,...

$_{AGV}L(m)$: the current location or destination of AGV_m. The values of m are 1, 2,..., m'.

$$_{AGV}L(m) \in \left\{ Parts\_warehouse, Pr\,oducts\_warehouse, MC_{1-1}, MC_{1-2} \cdots \right\}$$

$_{Parts}L(s)$: the current place of part P_s. The values of s are 1, 2,..., s'.

$$_{AGV}L(s) \in \left\{ Parts\_warehouse, Pr\,oducts\_warehouse, MC_{1-1}, MC_{1-2}, \cdots, AGV_1, AGV_2, \cdots \right\}$$

Table 1. Memory (a) example

x	1	2	3	4	5	6	7
$G(x)$	MC_{1-1}	MC_{1-2}	MC_{1-3}	MC_{2-1}	MC_{2-2}	Parts Warehouse	Products Warehouse
$P'(x)$	4	1	3	2	5	7	6

Table 2. Memory (b) example

m	1	2	3	4
AGV_s	AGV_1	AGV_2	AGV_3	AGV_4
$_{AGV}L(m)$	Parts Warehouse	MC_{1-2}	MC_{2-2}	MC_{2-1}

Table 1 shows the contents of memory (a). The table indicates that the MP-rankings, $P'(x)$, for the destinations of the seven competing hypotheses, MC_{1-1}, MC_{1-2}, MC_{1-3}, MC_{2-1}, MC_{2-2}, parts warehouse and products warehouse are 4, 1, 3, 2, 5, 7, 6, respectively. Table 2 shows the contents of memory (b). It indicates that $_{AGV}L(m)$, the location of each AGV, is parts warehouse, MC_{1-2}, MC_{2-2} and MC_{2-1} respectively. Table 3 shows the contents of memory (c). It indicates that $_{Parts}L(s)$, the location of each part, is MC_{1-2}, AGV_1, MC_{2-1} and MC_{2-2} respectively.

Table 3. Memory (c) example

s	1	2	3	4	5
$Parts$	P_1	P_2	P_3	P_4	P_5
$_{Parts}L(s)$	MC_{1-1}	MC_{1-2}	AGV_1	MC_{2-1}	MC_{2-2}

4 ROM Functions

First, this section describes how the memories in ROM are used. ROM is included in the process of HR-MD and works to improve MP-ranking. In the HR-MD decision which is one of the hypothetical reasoning tasks in RAF described in section 2.2, MP-ranking for each AGV destination in the competing hypotheses is decided through three processes, <1> giving priority rankings to group MCs, <2> giving priority rankings to parts warehouse and products warehouse and <3> giving priority rankings to the selection orders for each MC. ROM improves the MP-ranking determined through three processes by rewriting the MP-ranking so that it is likely to be a realizable true hypothesis. New procedures to do this, which are carried out after the above three procedures, are included in ROM. These three new procedures are <4> refresh MP-ranking using memory, <5> refresh the oblivion degree, and <6> add a new memory and delete an existing memory. They are incorporated in HR-MD as shown in Fig. 4.

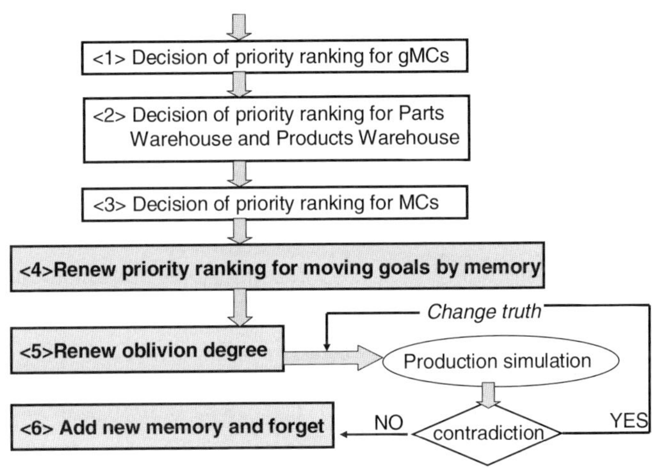

Fig. 4. ROM and HR-MD

Therefore, the MP-ranking decided in <1>~<3> is called a temporary MP-ranking and the ranking decided by the new three procedures, <4>~<6> of ROM, is called the final MP-ranking.

Second, this section first defines how the MP-ranking is refreshed using memory in <4>, which is one of the new three procedures of ROM.

[Definition] Refresh MP-ranking using memory: carry out the following three procedures.

[Procedure 4-1] Find the degree of similarity between the current production situation and the content of each M_{number} single memory in whole memory.

[Procedure 4-2] Find the single memory whose priority ranking is the highest and insert the determined action into the top position in the temporary MP-ranking.

[Procedure 4-3] Move the priority rankings in the second and lower positions down in the order.   □

In order to carry out Procedure 4-2, it is necessary to check out the similarity between the current production situation and the content of each M_{number} single memory in the whole memory. The similarity is obtained using the following three similarity degrees.

<similarity degree $_{move}A$>: the similarity in the MP-ranking
<similarity degree $_{agv}A$>: the similarity in the current positions of each AGV
<similarity degree $_{parts}A$>: the similarity in the current positions of each part

The similarity degree $_{move}A$ is the value expressing the difference between MP-ranking (a), which is in the memory, and the current temporary MP-ranking which is acquired during HR-MD. The similarity degree $_{agv}A$ is the value expressing the difference between AGV positions (b) and the current positions of each AGV in AD-FMS. The similarity degree $_{parts}A$ is the value expressing the difference between parts positions (c) and the current positions of each part in AD-FMS. The numerical values of the similarity degrees are calculated by adding 1 if the current production situation is the same as a situation in memory, and adding 0 if the current production situation is not the same as any in memory. Specifically, the similarity is expressed numerically with the following algorithm for similarity degree, from which the degree of similarity between each single memory in whole memory and the current production situation is obtained. The symbols used in the algorithm are described in the following.

- $G_{memory}(n)$: the destination of each AGV inmemory (a) in a single memory when $n=1, 2, \cdots , n'$. $G_{memory}(n)$ is expressed as follows.

$$G_{memory}(n) \in \{Partswarehouse, \Pr oductswarehouse, MC_{1-1}, MC_{1-2}, \cdots \}$$

- $P(n)$: the final MP-ranking of $G_{memory}(n)$. The values of $P(x)$ are 1, 2, 3, 4,……. .

- $_{AGV}L_{memory}(v)$: the location of each AGV in memory (b) in a single memory when $v=1, 2, \cdots , v'$. $_{AGV}L_{memory}(v)$ is expressed as follows.

$$_{AGV}L_{memory}(v) \in \{Parts\_warehouse, \Pr oducts\_warehouse, MC_{1-1}, MC_{1-2}, \cdots \}$$

- $_{Parts}L_{memory}(w)$: the current location of each part in memory (c) in a single memory when $w=1, 2, \cdots , w'$.

$_{Parts}L_{memory}(w)$ is expressed as follows.

$$_{Parts}L_{memory}(w) \in \{Parts\_Warehouse, \Pr oducts\_warehouse, MC_{1-1,}MC_{1-2}, \cdots , AGV_1, AGV_2, \cdots \}$$

[Algorithm for Similarity Degree]
Step 1: The initial values are set as follows: $x=1$, $_{move}A=0$, $_{parts}A=0$.
Step 2: Find $G(x)$ and $G_{memory}(n)$ corresponding to $P'(x)= P(n)$ and then carry out the following rule.

    if $(G(x)= G_{memory}(n))$, *then* (establish $_{move}A= {}_{move}A +1$ and go to Step 3)
    else (go to Step 3)
Step 3: Establish $x=x+1$ and carry out the following rule.
    if $(x>x')$, *then* (go to Step 4)
    else (return to Step 2)

Step 4: Establish $m=1$ and $v=1$.
Step 5: Carry out the following rule.

    If $(_{AGV}L(m)=\ _{AGV}L_{memory}(v))$, ***then*** (establish $_{agv}A=\ _{agv}A+1$ and go to Step 6)
    else (go to Step 6)

Step 6: Establish $m=m+1$ and $v=v+1$ and carry out the following rule.

    if $(m>m')$, ***then*** (go to Step 7)
    else (return to Step 5)

Step 7: Establish $s=1$ and $w=1$.
Step 8: Carry out the following rule.

    if $(_{Parts}L(s)=\ _{Parts}L_{memory}(w))$, ***then*** (establish $_{parts}A=\ _{parts}A+1$ and go to Step 9)
    else (go to Step 9)

Step 9: Establish $s=s+1$ and $w=w+1$ and carry out the following rule.

    if $(s>s')$, ***then*** (go to Step 10)
    else (return to Step 8)

Step 10: Consider the value of $_{move}A+_{agv}A+_{parts}A$ as the similarity degree of single memories and finish the algorithm.
        □

By using the algorithm for similarity degree in each single memory of M_{number} units, the similarity degree between the current production situation and the single memory for M_{number} units can be calculated. Next, [Procedure 4-2] is carried out. It selects the single memory with the highest similarity degree and inserts the determined action (d) of the single memory into the top position in the temporary MP-ranking. Third, [Procedure 4-3] moves the existing priority rankings down one place in order and, as a result, a new MP-ranking or the final MP-ranking can be decided.

Next, the followings definitions correspond to <5>, refreshing the oblivion degree.

[Definition] <5> Refresh the oblivion degree: Insert the single memory with a highest similarity degree into the lowest place, M_{number}, of the oblivion degree in the whole memory.
        □

Due to refreshing a single memory once selected is not easily removed from whole memory.

Finally, the function of <6>, which adds a new memory and deletes an existing memory, is defined as below.

[Definition] <6> Add a new memory and deletes an existing memory: The following two procedures are carried out.

[Procedure 6-1] The AGVs next action that is finally decided without contradictions is considered to be a new (d) determined action. The (a) MP-ranking, (b) AGV positions and (c) parts locations at this time including the new (d) determined action are memorized in the middle range of the oblivion degree among the whole memory as a new single memory.

[Procedure 6-2] Single memories whose oblivion degrees are higher than the new single memory are in turn moved up and, as a result, the single memory that has had the highest oblivion degree is deleted from the whole memory.
        □

Through this procedure <6>, whenever a real AGV's destination is decided, a new memory is added and at the same time a memory with a low frequency of selection as an AGV destination is deleted.

5 Simulation Experiments

The ROM proposed in the last chapter was applied to 3 types of AD-FMS created on computer in simulation experiments. The 3 AD-FMSs differed by number of MC groups, number of MCs, and number of AGVs. Style 1 had 9 types of parts, 8 MC groups, 1 of each MC, and 5 AGVs. Style 2 had 9 types of parts, 8 MC groups, 2 of each MC, and 5 AGVs. Style 3 had 9 types of parts, 8 MC groups, 3 of each MC, and 5 AGVs. The plant layouts for Styles 1, 2, and 3 are shown in Figs. 5, 6, and 7, respectively. Each distance between Machining Centers is 5 m.

On the assumption that unanticipated troubles occur during actual FMS operation, trouble conditions were set in which each AGV randomly broke down 3 times a day, each time for 5 minutes, and part processing time on each MC was randomly extended 10%. Ten different random number sequences were used as the random conditions for these troubles. The number of simple memories stored in the total memory of ROM was set at 20.

Operating results for Style 3 are summarized in Table 4. The table shows the number of hypotheses until the true hypothesis was selected (hypothesis selection number) during operation when the AD-FMS was operated for 24 hours with 10 types of trouble. For comparison, the table also shows the hypothesis selection number when using HR-MD with a temporary MP-ranking (conventional method). From the table, we see that the hypothesis selection number with ROM was reduced to less than half that with the conventional method for all of the 10 types of trouble. For example, the mean hypothesis selection number for Style 3 operation was 899,943.5 with the conventional method and 445,763.2 with ROM. Similarly, the hypothesis selection number was reduced by about half with the other 2 styles, Style 1 and 2 as well. This indicates that the MP-ranking of ROM is better than the temporary MP-ranking at ordering hypothesis in order of possibility of being selected as true, confirming that there is a reduction in the numbers of wasted true/false hypothesis replacements and production simulations that are executed.

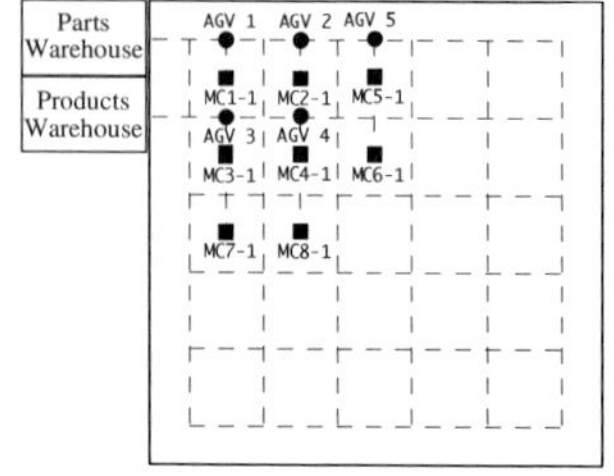

Fig. 5. Style 1 of AD-FMS

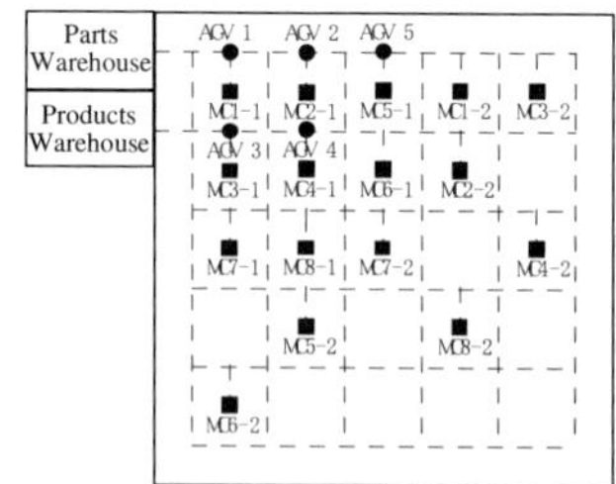

Fig. 6. Style 2 of AD-FMS

This simulation experiment compared not only hypothesis selection number but also production output. With Style 1, the mean production output was 454.5 units with the conventional method and 525.7 units with ROM. The respective figures were 460 and 698.5 with Style 2, and 476 and 754.4 with Style 3. In each case ROM gives a higher production output and improved reasoning efficiency without decreasing production efficiency.

6 Conclusions

The present study proposes a system called ROM that determines a hypothesis priority ranking using memory, to improve the reasoning efficiency of RAF. In this system, the AGV itself decides its movements in AD-FMS. ROM stores previous production situations and the action of the AGV decided at those times as memories. Using these memories, hypotheses are ranked according to possibility of being selected from among competing hypotheses as true, with the aim of improving the efficiency of the RAF. This ROM repeatedly adds new memories and deletes existing ones, so that the memory contents are constantly refreshed.

ROM was applied to AD-FMSs constructed on a computer and the number of hypothesis replacements until a true hypothesis was determined was compared with that from a conventional system. It was found that under all conditions ROM reduced the number of hypothesis replacements to half that with a conventional system, demonstrating the validity of this system.

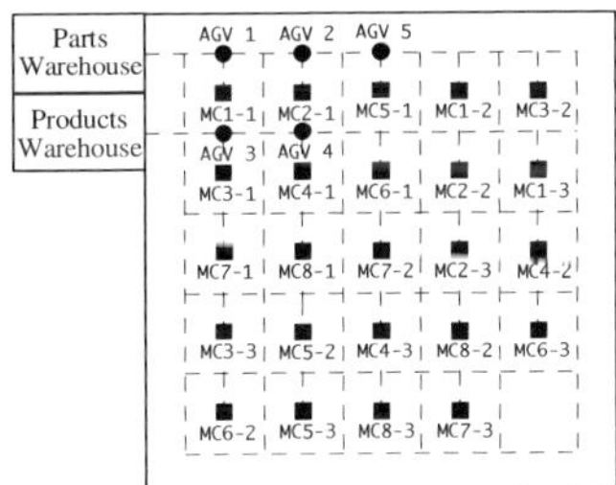

Fig. 7. Style 3 of AD-FMS

Table 4. Results of Style 3

Hypothesis selection number	Condition 1	Condition 2		Condition 9	Condition 10	average
Conventional method	893,532	905,398		891,872	898,715	**899,943.5**
ROM	452,539	445,126		444,910	444,599	**445,763.5**

References

1. Laengle, T., et al.: A Distributed Control Architecture for Autonomous Robot Systems. In: Workshop on Environment Modeling and Motion Planning for Autonomous Robots. Series in Machine Perception and Artificial Intelligence, vol. 21, p. 384. World Scientific, Singapore (1994)
2. Moriwaki, T., Hino, R.: Decentralized Job Shop Scheduling by Recursive Propagation Method. International Journal of JSME, Series C 45(2), 551 (2002)
3. Mitrouchev, P., Brun-Picard, D.: A New Model for Synchronous Multiagents Production among Clients and Subcontractors. International Journals of Simulation Model, 141–153 (2007)
4. Nishi, T., et al.: A distributed routing method for AGVs under motion delay disturbance. Robotics and Computer-Integrated Manufacturing 23(5), 517–532 (2007)
5. Yamamoto, H.: Decentralized Autonomous FMS Control by Hypothetical Reasoning including Discrete Simulator. In: Monostori, L., Váncza, J., Ali, M. (eds.) IEA/AIE 2001. LNCS (LNAI), vol. 2070, Springer, Heidelberg (2001)
6. Berger, J.O.: Statistic Decision Theory and Bayesian Analysis, 2nd edn. Springer, Heidelberg (1985)
7. Variant, L.: A Theory of the Learnable. Communication of the ACM 27(11), 11–34 (1984)
8. Janetzko, D., Wess, S., Melis, E.: Goal-driven similarity assessment. In: Ohlbach, H.J. (ed.) GWAI 1992. LNCS, vol. 671, p. 283. Springer, Heidelberg (1993)
9. Leake, D.B.: Adaptive similarity assessment for case-based explanation. International Journal of Expert Systems Research and Applications 8(2), 165 (1995)
10. Poole, D.: A methodology for using a default and abductive reasoning system. International Journal of Intelligent Systems 5(5), 521 (1990)
11. Provetti, A.: Hypothetical reasoning about actions: from situation calculus to event calculus. Computational Intelligence 12(3), 478 (1996)
12. Baldoni, M., Giordano, L., Martelli, A.: A modal extension of logic programming: Modularity, beliefs and hypothetical reasoning. Journal of Logic and Computation 8(5), 597 (1998)

Investigation of Influence of Grinding Regimes on Surface Tension State

Witold Halas[1], Victor Taranenko[2], Antoni Swic[2], and Georgij Taranenko[3]

[1] The State School of Higher Education in Chelm,
Pocztowa Str. 54, 22-100 Chelm, Poland
[2] Lublin University of Technology, Institute of Technological Systems of Information,
Nadbystrzycka Str. 36, 20-618, Lublin, Poland
[3] Sevastopol National Technical University,
Universyteckaya Str. 33, 99-053, Sevastopol, Ukraine

Abstract. The paper presents the methodology of investigation of influence of grinding regimes on surface layer tension state. The mathematical model of creating the final tension in part, based on full factorial experiment is described. The main values of factors are chosen close to practical regimes of grinding for a given materials and intervals for factors changes are calculated from the real process conditions. The estimated parameters and their accuracy are verified by means of Student and Fisher statistical criterion. As the result of investigation is determined that the final stresses of surface after grinding depends mainly on feed.

Keywords: investigation, influence, grinding, surface tension state.

1 Introduction

It is known that the grinding is characterized by the greatest heat emission in the process of machining. In some cases the instantaneous temperature of grinding reaches 1500 K. During the required cooling of the part under grinding it is almost impossible to avoid significant residual stresses. The main factors having effect on the value of stresses are the regimes of machining: feed, rotation speed, the depth of cutting [1, 2, 3], and grinding wheel material. However, taking into account that for different materials, the specific types of grinding wheels are recommended, this factor is assumed to be constant.

2 Methods and Equipment for Experimental Research

Experimental studies of residual stresses influence on the operation of grinding were conducted for the models made from steel Y8KH2NYAMA with a diameter of 24 mm, the length of 150 mm in a quantity of 24 pcs. The models were machined on 3M151B grinding machine. All the models were centered on the 2A450 jig-boring

N.T. Nguyen et al. (Eds.): IEA/AIE 2008, LNAI 5027, pp. 749–756, 2008.

machine. False centers were used as the fixtures for circular-grinding operation. Parts were exposed to the heat treatment of cementation with $h = 1,2... 1,5$ mm with the subsequent hardening to HRC 59 - 63 and preliminary circular-grinding operation. Then parts were cut along the axis of shaft on the electric spark machine LK -18 according to procedure [4]. The width of groove after cutting was 2 mm, the length was 125 mm. The process of cutting was done in the diesel fuel as a coolant. After cutting the grooves false centers were set up and the surfaces were ground with the regimes shown in table 1. Before etching the plane of the groove was insulated by the acid-proof varnish XMC26. After grinding, false centers were removed and the parts were exposed to layer by layer etching by hydrochloric and nitric acids, then thoroughly washed in alkaline solution and water and were left for two hours so they would have ambient temperature that was constant during all the measurements. The time of the etching of each layer was 10 min.

Table 1. Levels of factors and the intervals of variation

Levels of the factors	Designation	a_p, mm $\breve{x}_1$	v_c, m/s $\breve{x}_2$	f, mm/obr $\breve{x}_3$
Basic	0	0,03	0,5	250
Interval of the variation		0,02	0,333	100
Upper	+1	0,05	0,833	350
Lower	-1	0,01	0,166	150

After cutting the grooves and also after grinding and each cycle of etching the measurements of the bending deformations of the part ends were conducted. Furthermore, the longitudinal and bending deformations of the halves of ends were measured. Measurements were carried out on the two-coordinate instrument in the reflected light.

3 Mathematical Model of the Formation of Residual Stresses in the Detail

For the evaluation of grinding regime influence and for mathematical description of the process of forming the residual stresses in the mounts, the first order model was used in the following form:

$$\hat{y} = b_0 + b_1 x_1 + b_2 x_2 + b_3 x_3 + b_{12} x_1 x_2 + b_{13} x_1 x_3 + b_{23} x_2 x_3 + b_{123} x_1 x_2 x_3. \tag{1}$$

To obtain the value of coefficients in equation (1) a complete factor experiment of 2^3 types was used.

The levels of factors were selected close to the practical machining regimes for the certain material, and the intervals of variation - on the basis of the real limits of the fluctuation of factors values (table 1).

The matrix of planning the experiments with the calculated columns of interaction between factors is presented in table.2. Each experiment was repeated three times. The results of studies are given in table 3. Residual stresses were calculated from the equation (2)

$$\sigma_z(a) = 0,33\frac{E}{l^2}\left[\frac{df(a)}{da}(R-a)^2 - 6f(a)\cdot(R-a)\right] - 1,55(1-3\frac{a}{R})\sigma_u^H.\qquad (2)$$

Table 2. Matrix of planning experiments

Number of measurement	x_0	x_1 a_p, mm	x_2 v_c, m/s	x_3 f, mm/obr	x_1x_2 a_pv_c	x_1x_3 a_pf	x_2x_3 v_cf	$x_1x_2x_3$ a_pv_cf
1	+1	-1 0,01	-1 0,166	-1 150	+1	+1	+1	-1
2	+1	+1 0,05	-1 0,166	-1 150	-1	-1	+1	+1
3	+1	-1 0,01	+1 0,833	-1 150	-1	+1	-1	+1
4	+1	+1 0,05	+1 0,833	-1 150	+1	-1	-1	-1
5	+1	-1 0,01	-1 0,166	+1 350	+1	-1	-1	+1
6	+1	+1 0,05	-1 0,166	+1 350	-1	+1	-1	-1
7	+1	-1 0,01	+1 0,833	+1 350	-1	-1	+1	-1
8	+1	+1 0,05	+1 0,833	+1 350	+1	+1	+1	+1

Table 3. Results of experimental studies of residual stresses after the grinding

No. the model		df(a)/da				f(a)			
		Layers				Layers			
		1	2	3	4	1	2	3	4
1	0,025	+0,015	-0,05	+0,01	+0,015	+0,015	+0,01	+0,02	+0,035
2	0,04	-0,017	-0,072	+0,015	+0,022	-0,017	-0,089	-0,047	-0,052
3	0,017	-0,02	-0,042	+0,007	-0,003	-0,02	-0,062	-0,055	-0,058
4	0,072	-0,03	+0,04	+0,017	-0,007	-0,03	+0,01	+0,027	+0,02
5	0,047	-0,029	+0,16	+0,015	+0,003	-0,029	+0,131	+0,146	+0,149
6	0,025	-0,005	+0,067	-0,01	+0,022	-0,005	+0,062	+0,052	+0,074
7	0,025	+0,015	+0,005	+0,003	+0,02	+0,015	+0,02	+0,023	+0,043
8	0,02	-0,01	+0,015	+0,003	+0,01	-0,01	+0,005	+0,008	+0,018

Table 3. (*continued*)

№ the model		R-a				a				σ_z, MIIa			
		Layers				Layers				Layers			
		1	2	3	4	1	2	3	4	1	2	3	4
1	0,025	11,4	11,375	11,352	11,32	0,025	0,048	0,08	0,115	11,724	-50,31	7,26	5,52
2	0,04	11,82	11,78	11,69	11,62	0,04	0,132	0,202	0,255	2,547	-8,71	39,19	4,37
3	0,017	11,82	11,803	11,72	11,64	0,017	0,1	0,178	0,235	1,63	1,19	20,09	26,49
4	0,072	11,86	11,79	11,7	11,63	0,072	0,165	0,227	0,268	-1,37	-0,841	9,488	-2,992
5	0,047	11,83	11,78	11,7	11,64	0,047	0,122	0,195	0,252	1,07	63,96	-28,38	-36,31
6	0,025	11,38	11,35	11,32	11,3	0,025	0,055	0,082	0,12	8,898	26,861	-13,405	-2,124
7	0,025	11,4	11,375	11,355	11,32	0,025	0,045	0,08	0,12	11,722	4,528	17,619	5,945
8	0,02	11,39	11,37	11,33	11,3	0,02	0,055	0,085	0,123	31,852	1,221	3,53	7,747

The diagrams of stresses distribution over the section are shown on fig.1. The order of studies is randomized with the aid of the tables of random numbers [5]. The results of randomization are given in table 4.

The average value of the optimization parameter was determined from the equation [5]:

$$S_u^2 = \frac{1}{r-1}\Sigma_{u=1}^r (y_{u_n} - \hat{y}_u)^2 . \tag{3}$$

For example, for the first experiment it is equal:

$$y_1 = \frac{-50,5 + (-52,6) + (-47,83)}{3} = -50,31 . \tag{4}$$

Table 4. Randomization of the results of the experiment

No of model	σ_z, MIIa				$y_{u1} - \hat{y}_u$	$y_{u2} - \hat{y}_u$	$y_{u3} - \hat{y}_u$	$(y_{u1} - \hat{y}_u)^2$	$(y_{u2} - \hat{y}_u)^2$	$(y_{u3} - \hat{y}_u)^2$	S_u^2
	y_{u1}	y_{u2}	y_{u3}	$\hat{y}_u$							
1	-50,5	-52,6	-47,83	-50,31	-0,19	-2,29	+2,48	0,036	5,24	6,15	5,713
2	+43,4	+40,2	33,97	+39,13	+4,21	+1,01	-5,22	17,72	1,02	27,25	22,99
3	26,3	24,97	28,2	+26,49	-0,19	-1,52	+1,71	0,036	2,31	2,31	2,92
4	9,064	10,3	9,1	+9,488	-0,424	+0,812	-0,388	0,179	0,66	0,15	0,494
5	64,25	64,48	63,06	+63,96	+0,32	+0,55	-0,87	0,102	0,3	0,756	0,579
6	26,32	29,453	24,81	+26,861	-0,541	+2,592	-2,051	0,293	6,71	4,2	5,60
7	17,867	18,52	16,47	17,619	+0,248	+0,901	-1,149	0,06	0,812	1,32	1,096
8	34,95	30,194	30,412	+31,852	+3,098	-1,658	-1,44	9,59	2,749	2,07	7,205
				165,12							46,31

The dispersion of parallel experiments was determined from the equation:

$$S_u^2 = \frac{1}{r-1}\Sigma_{u=1}^r (y_{u_n} - \hat{y}_u)^2 . \tag{5}$$

For example, for the first experiment we have:

$$S_1^2 = \frac{0,036 + 5,24 + 6,15}{2} = 5,713. \tag{6}$$

To determine the possibility of conducting the regression analysis the uniformities of parallel experiments dispersions were calculated according to Kohren criterion:

$$G = \frac{S_{u\,max}^2}{\sum_{u=1}^{N} S_u^2} = \frac{22,99}{46,31} = 0,496. \tag{7}$$

The calculated value of criterion was compared with the tabular values for the degrees of freedom: numerator $f_1 = r - 1$ denominator $f_2 = N$ and in accordance with the selected level of significance $\alpha = 0,05$ [5]:

$$G_t = 0,5157 > G_c = 0,496.$$

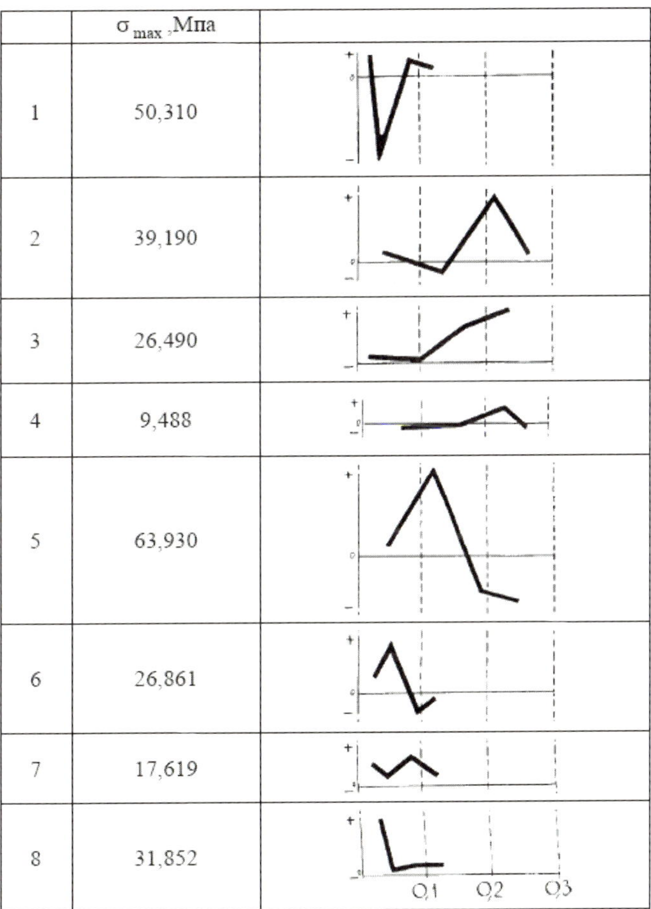

	$\sigma_{max},$Мпа	
1	50,310	
2	39,190	
3	26,490	
4	9,488	
5	63,930	
6	26,861	
7	17,619	
8	31,852	

Fig. 1. Residual stresses after the grinding of the mounts

Therefore, the hypothesis about the uniformity of the dispersions of parallel experiments can be used. Hence, the dispersion of reproducibility is equal:

$$S^2(y) = \frac{1}{N}\sum_{u=1}^{N} S_u^2 = \frac{46,31}{8} = 5,789 \,. \tag{8}$$

Error of the experiment:

$$S(y) = \sqrt{S^2(y)} = \sqrt{5,789} = 2,406 \,. \tag{9}$$

Then the coefficients of equation (1) were calculated. For example, for the coefficient b_1 we have:

$$b_1 = \frac{1}{N}\sum_{u=1}^{N} x_{1u}^2 y_u = 6,2 \,. \tag{10}$$

The same method was used to calculate other coefficients. After the calculation of all the coefficients equation (1) takes the form:

$$\hat{y} = 20,64 + 6,2x_1 + 0,722x_2 + 14,425x_3 - 6,9x_1x_2 - 11,916x_1x_3 - \\ - 11,052x_2x_3 + 19,725x_1x_2x_3 \tag{11}$$

4   Verification the Significance the Model Coefficients

Student's criterion was used to verify the statistical significance of coefficients. First of all, the dispersion of regression coefficient $S^2\{b_1\}$ was found. With the equal duplicating of experiments on the points with the number of repeated experiments it was determined from formula [6]:

$$S^2\{b_i\} = \frac{S^2\{y\}}{nr} = \frac{5,789}{8\cdot3} = 0,2412 \,, \tag{12}$$

with $f_E = n(r-1)$ the degrees of freedom

$$S\{b_i\} = \sqrt{0,2412} = 0,491 \,. \tag{13}$$

Value of t_i - criteria was determined from the formula [6]:

$$t_i = \frac{|b_i|}{S\{b_i\}} \,. \tag{14}$$

We have for our task:

t_0	t_1	t_2	T_3	t_{12}	t_{13}	t_{23}	t_{123}
42,036	12,627	1,47	29,378	14,052	24,26	22,509	40,173

The critical value of t_{Kp} was determined according to [5] with n(r-1)=16 degrees of freedom and assigned level of significance 5%. In our case t_{Kp} =1,74. If $t_c > t_{Kp}$, then hypothesis is rejected and b_i is recognized as significant. After testing the significance of coefficients and adequacy of the model according to Student and Fisher criteria it is established that after grinding the value of residual stresses depends mainly on the feed. The part rotation speed has the smallest influence to the residual stresses. The most favorable regimes of grinding are defined by experiment [4]:

$$a_p = 0,05mm, \quad v_c = 0,833m/s, \quad f = 150mm/min.$$

Otherwise it is considered as the statistically insignificant, i.e., $b_i = 0$. In our case such insignificant coefficient is b_2. After the exception of statistically insignificant coefficient the equation of regression takes the form:

$$\hat{y} = 20,64 + 6,2x_1 + 14,425x_3 - 6,9x_1x_2 - 11,916x_1x_3 - 11,052x_2x_3 + 19,725x_1x_2x_3. \quad (15)$$

5   Verification of Model Adequacy

The adequacy of obtained equation was verified. The results of calculating the dispersion of adequacy are given in table 5.

Table 5. Results of calculating the dispersion of the adequacy

№ the experience	$\bar{y}_u$	$\hat{y}_u$	$\bar{y}_u - \hat{y}_u$	$(\bar{y}_u - \hat{y}_u)^2$
1	-50,31	-49,578	-0,732	0,536
2	+39,19	+39,904	-0,714	0,509
3	+26,49	25,776	+0,714	0,509
4	+9,488	8,758	+0,73	0,533
5	+63,93	64,658	-0,728	0,529
6	+26,861	27,576	-0,715	0,511
7	+17,619	16,9	+0,719	0,517
8	+31,852	31,122	+0,73	0,533
				4,18

Hypothesis about the adequacy of equation (15) was verified from the equation [5]

$$S_{ad}^2 = \frac{r}{N-\lambda}\sum_{u=1}^{N}(\bar{y}_{u_n} - \hat{y}_u)^2, \quad (16)$$

where λ - the number of significant coefficients of equation, N - the number of independent experiments, r - number of parallel experiments,

$$S_{ad}^2 = \frac{3}{8-7} \cdot 4,18 = 12,54. \quad (17)$$

The adequacy of equation was evaluated with from F - Fisher criterion [5]:

$$F_c = \frac{S_{ad}^2}{S^2(y)} = \frac{12,54}{5,789} = 2,166 . \tag{18}$$

$F_t = 3$ respectively for the degrees of freedom of the $f_{ad} = 2, f_{0E} = 16$, and the level of significance 0,05. Because, with the fact that $F_c < F_t$, i.e., $2,1666 < 3,0$, equation (15) can be considered adequate.

Assuming

$$x_1 = \frac{a_p - 0,003}{0,02} mm , \quad x_2 = \frac{v_c - 500}{333} mm/s , \quad x_3 = \frac{f - 5,83}{1,67} mm/s \tag{19}$$

and substituting in expression (15) for optimization parameters their value from (19), we will obtain the equation of the natural values of factors [7]:

$$\sigma = -329,8 + 8060a_p + 55,82f - 11,33a_p v_c + 0,45v_c - 1241a_p f - 0,07v_c f + 1,77a_p v_c f . \tag{20}$$

6 Conclusion

On the basis of the obtained results and analysis of the equation of regression the following conclusion can be done: the value of residual stresses after grinding, depends mainly on feed, the part rotation speed has the smallest effect on residual stresses.

References

1. Matalin, A.A.: Totschnost mechanitscheskoy obrabotki i proektirovanje technologitscheskich processov L.: Maschinostroyenye (1970)
2. Starkov, W.K.: Obrabotka rezanyem. Upravlienye stabilinostiu i katschestvom v avtomatizirovannom proizvodstvie. M.: Maschinostroyenye (1989)
3. Yashericin, P.I.: Osnovy technologii mechanitscheskoy obrabotki i sborki v maschinostroyenii. M.: Vizshaja Shkola (1974)
4. Ovseyenko, A.P.: Opredelinye osewich ostatotchnych napryazenniy v cilindritcheskich sterznych metodom prodolnego razreza. Problemy protchnosti 7 (1981)
5. Yevdokimov, J.I., Kolesnikov, W.I., Teterin, A.N.: Planirovaniye i analiz eksperimientov pri reshenii zadatsch treniya i iznosa. M.: Nauka (1980)
6. Kacev, P.G.: Statistitcheskiye metody issledovanya rezushego instumenta. M.: Maschinostroyenye (1974)
7. Taranenko, V., Kvyatkovska, E.: Issledovanye vliyanya rezimov shlifovanya na napryazennoye sostoyaniye povierchnostiey. In: International Conference TOOLS 2002, 11.04.2002. Kočovce, Slovak Republic, p. 29, s. 6, CD-ROM (2002)

Estimating Flexibility Requirements in a Demand-Driven Lean/JIT Environment

Peter Nielsen and Kenn Steger-Jensen

Department of Production, Aalborg University, Fibigerstraede 16, 9220 Aalborg East, Denmark
`peter@production.aau.dk`

Abstract. Demand-driven JIT manufacturing is based on the assumption of a level stable demand rate. This is however not the reality experienced by most companies. To handle fluctuations from a level stable demand rate, the manufacturing system needs flexibility. This paper presents a method for using estimated multivariate density distributions of periodic demand rates to establish when flexibility is needed and how much. The method is applied to data from a JIT manufacture finding that the company in question had an unstable demand rate and needed a great deal of flexibility if a low delivery time should be guaranteed.

Keywords: JIT, flexibility, capacity matching.

1 Introduction

Since the introduction of The Toyota Production System, Just-in-Time (JIT) and Lean manufacturing has been a best practice driver and approach for many companies world wide. JIT is basically a philosophical tenet rooted in repetitive manufacturing, a fact many companies tend to forget. The object of manufacturing systems must be to match their external requirements, both the physical manufacturing system [1] and the Manufacturing Planning and Control (MPC) system [2].

The manufacturing strategy is often to try to level demand to achieve a flat demand rate and subsequently balance the manufacturing processes to handle this particular demand rate [3]. In a situation with a level known demand rate, establishing the lead time of the manufacturing system is trivial and no flexibility is needed. The simple truth is that few companies face a situation where they are able to achieve a steady and level demand rate of customer orders. Exogenous factors often add noise and customers can behave in a both systematic and erratic manner. For many companies delivery time is an important competitive priority. If a company uses a JIT paradigm to manufacture to customer orders, the manufacturing system needs to be flexible enough to (to some extend) adapt to these varying demand rates and achieve consistent delivery times. Often companies cope by using a standard delivery time regardless of the specific circumstances. This often means that either:

- The promised delivery time is inflated to ensure delivery by the promised due date.

N.T. Nguyen et al. (Eds.): IEA/AIE 2008, LNAI 5027, pp. 757–766, 2008.

- The due dates are occasionally missed due to lack of capacity in the manufacturing system.
- Cost of over capacity is incurred to ensure due dates can be upheld.

All of these approaches either lead to poor customer service or increased production costs, since they are manufacturing to order, often in low volume.

The issue addressed in this paper is line balancing and capacity planning under the condition that delivery time is a critical competitive priority, and the restriction is one of fixed due dates to customers, when, at the same time, facing a dynamic time dependent demand rate. The aim of the paper is to develop a method for determining how much flexibility is needed at a given time under these conditions. This paper will focus on the impact on capacity and resource load. The material availability's impact on the lead time, while an important issue, is outside the scope of this paper. Derived from the methods presented in this paper the subsequent development of a material planning approach should be straightforward.

The following assumptions and premises apply: 1) That the manufacturing system has adapted its overall capacity to match the total expected demand during any given planning period – i.e. focus is on allocation of resources at a particular point of time within a planning period. 2) That the demand pattern in a particular period are independent of the demand level or seasonality, and only depends on the product / product family. 3) The ability to maintain and promise a fixed short delivery time and adhere to promised due dates is a critical competitive priority.

The paper is structured as follows. First, background on demand-driven JIT manufacturing systems is presented. Secondly an approach for establishing flexible capacity profiles is addressed. Thirdly a discussion of the method based on results of analysis of demand rates from a case company is presented and capacity implications are inferred. Finally a conclusion and avenues of further research are presented.

2 Background

All businesses should have distinctive competencies that differentiates them from competitors. Competitive advantages are attainable through the underlying functional capabilities and through the company's focus on the competitive priorities based on its strategy. One of the most important contributors to a business strategy is the manufacturing strategy. In designing a manufacturing strategy, choices of chase vs. leveling strategy as well as the use of different and differentiated types of postponement are import [2,3]. The measure of the manufacturing strategy effectiveness is often based on four common manufacturing capability dimensions; cost, quality, delivery and flexibility. The growing competition and truly relentless pressures to increase customer satisfaction have forced manufacturers to become more demand-driven. This has triggered a dramatic shift in the focus of Lean planning processes away from production and inventory and towards a much more demand-driven approach. Taps and Steger-Jensen [4] presents relationships between manufacturing capabilities and competitive priorities. The implementation of a JIT manufacturing strategy is often driven by a desire to focus on the competitive priorities; delivery and flexibility, and subsequently on the derived manufacturing capabilities: Lead time, on-time delivery, capacity flexibility, process flexibility and product variety / mix flexibility [4]. The goals of JIT/Lean manufacturing can be summarized to the following three elements; eliminate disruptions, make the system flexible, eliminate waste, especially excess inventory. System flexibility is needed to handle a mix of products, often on a daily basis, and to handle changes at the level of output. This will also reduce the impact of the uncertainties the system must be able to handle. The more flexibility the JIT manufacturing system, the less product mix and volume variations impact the performance of the manufacturing system.

In some aspects unused capacity of the manufacturing system can be considered in somewhat the same manner that one would address the issue of inventory management of perishable goods [5,6]. If the capacity is expensive, one will seek high utilization, especially if capacity must be allocated prior to knowing demand [6]. This means that some sort of capacity matching must take place, either through adding flexibility to the system, actively using demand management or order splitting. Lin [7] suggests methods for using demand information to update the expected demand distribution and subsequently how to try to impact the demand rate through proactively changing prices. This is a reactive approach to effecting demand rates that is relevant if one is in a service industry such as the example put forth in Lin [7]. Both Weatherford and Bodily [6] and Lin [7] presents examples from the service industry where a fixed capacity is often encountered i.e. the upper limit of capacity is a known hard constraint. In most manufacturing systems the short term capacity (unless operating at the capacity limit) is somewhat flexible, e.g. a second shift can be introduced or overtime can be used. This means that most manufacturing companies have the ability to, at least to some extend, impact the short term capacity of the manufacturing system, although this often entails increased cost of operations.

A proper ERP system supporting the MPC paradigm of the company can help overcome the challenges of applying Lean to a demand-driven environment. The combination of real-time data collection and monitoring; the ability to map highly variable customer demand to a smooth manufacturing plan along with various operational capabilities such as real-time pull requirements and backflushing transactions, has placed ERP systems in the center of the new Lean evolution. The ERP system is an important tool to handle the increasing manufacturing design activities, daily operation activities and transactions, and to reduce delivery time, thereby moving beyond the relatively stable manufacturing environment to a dynamic demand-driven environment.

Demand smoothing is important since manufacturing lines are designed based on an average daily product mix. There are three levels of smoothing within a ERP system: No Level Loading, Level Loading, and Mixed Model. A mixed model map is a tool that displays the processes and products for a given line as well as the associated weighted times to complete the process. The mixed model map also displays the labor, machines and In-Process-Kanban resources needed to support forecast demand. This information is used to decide how to regroup events into line operations to balance the line. Mixed Model performs level loading for the whole product mix, and avoids batching. For example a mix of 100 A products and 50 B products could generate a pattern of AAB which would be repeated 50 times to schedule the total demand. This provides the most consistent pace through the main line, and will cause the least disruptions to the supply chain.

Mixed Model smoothing is a preferred method of demand smoothing, since it will minimize the gap between the design mix and the actual demands. This method is useful if customers are somewhat flexible in their delivery dates, and set-up times are insignificant. The other two methods can be summarized as follows. With level loading a daily rate level (demand ratio) is calculated, based on the mix of demand over the time horizon. This ratio is multiplied by the amount of available capacity each day to determine how much of each item will be scheduled on a given day. Items are then prioritized based on the sequencing criteria. With no level loading, the system performs no demand smoothing. Orders are scheduled solely based on the sequencing criteria and the line capacity. This method is useful when customers are not flexible regarding delivery dates. For example: a customer is running a JIT facility that needs delivery exactly at the requested date. But scheduling without level loading may create a mix of products that is very different from the mix line design. If products vary significantly in build time, set-up time, or the parts used, it will cause either large imbalances to the line, or shortages of material in Kanbans. If either no leveling or a mixed model approach is used and the demand rate varies significantly, it is obvious that knowledge of how the demand rate varies over time is critical to the performance. If no knowledge exists on how the demand rate varies over the planning horizon it is impossible to attune the manufacturing systems capacity. The consequence will be longer delivery times and potentially underutilization of the manufacturing capacity.

3   Addressing the Flexibility Problem

Consider the situation where the demand rate varies over time in a somewhat systematic manner. This is often situation experienced by companies, due to either company credit policies or specific customer ordering preferences e.g. use of periodic ordering. These can of course be somewhat alleviated by supply chain integration and planning measures. However if no such measures can be implemented, the manufacture will be forced to adapt internally to these conditions by either increasing flexibility, capacity or the delivery time to the customer. In practice the issue is reduced to when flexibility is needed – and how flexible must the system be. These issues are addressed in the following where a new method for establishing capacity flexibility requirements based on time dependent demand rate approximation is presented. The method presented addresses the following:

1) Develops time dependent demand rate estimates.
2) Based on demand rate estimates, capacity profiles can be developed to establish:
   a. When and how much flexibility is needed in the manufacturing system.
   b. Derive MPC implications for e.g. delivery time and manufacturing system performance.

3.1 The Demand Rate Estimation

The method uses historical demand data to estimate patterns for demand rates. This could be done by fitting a function of time and potentially other parameters describing the demand rate. However this is neither a generic nor reasonable approach since a demand rate function can 1) be highly nonlinear and unique, 2) include stochastic elements. A method that is both generic and able to handle stochastic elements is fitting a multivariate density distribution [8,9] to the two parameters; demand rate and time, using the kernel method. The kernel used is the standard bivariate normality density function [9], since it seems a reasonable assumption that demand rates would behave in this manner. To use this approach it must be assumed that we are dealing with a continuous distribution of demand rates and time. Given sufficient observations of demand rates and time points exists, this assumption should be reasonable. To avoid over-fitting, the model is fitted to the relative demand rate for a given time-frame rather than the absolute demand rate at a particular point of time. If significant seasonality is present then some periods will potentially weigh too heavy in the fitted density functions if non-standardized demand rates are used. Consider the example where the period in focus is a month with sales occurring arbitrarily on any day of the month, the expected mean daily demand rate would be (assuming 365 days a year $\approx$ 30.4 days/month) 0.033 units / day. For examples of fitted demand rate distributions refer to figure 1.

3.2 Implications for the MPC System

Subsequent to estimating a standardized demand rate distribution, the level of demand for a given period should be established. This will of course be subject to some uncertainty. However, if one aggregates sufficiently over time and matches the forecast horizons to the period length for which the demand rate distribution has been established, the forecast precision should (due to the nature of aggregation) be relatively high. A combination of a volume forecast for a period and an estimated demand rate distribution is subsequently used to develop a unique capacity profile for the given manufacturing system. This should enable companies to use a pure chase strategy but, due to the adjusted capacity profile, with some of the cost advantages usually associated with a leveling strategy. Using individual product capacity profiles also gives the possibility to better determine how to use mixed mode leveling by enabling a company to anticipate product mix shifts within given timeframes in a period.

4 Discussion

A prototype application implementing the demand rate estimation method has been developed and tested. An example based on actual demand data from a manufacturing company producing / assembling JIT to customer orders is used in the following. Three products accounting for the majority of the sales in a product family are examined. The product family is produced in a dedicated flow shop. The planning horizon for capacity in this particular system is one month; hence the period chosen for fitting is one month. The demand rate distributions should as a rule be fitted to a period matching the planning horizon of the manufacturing system.

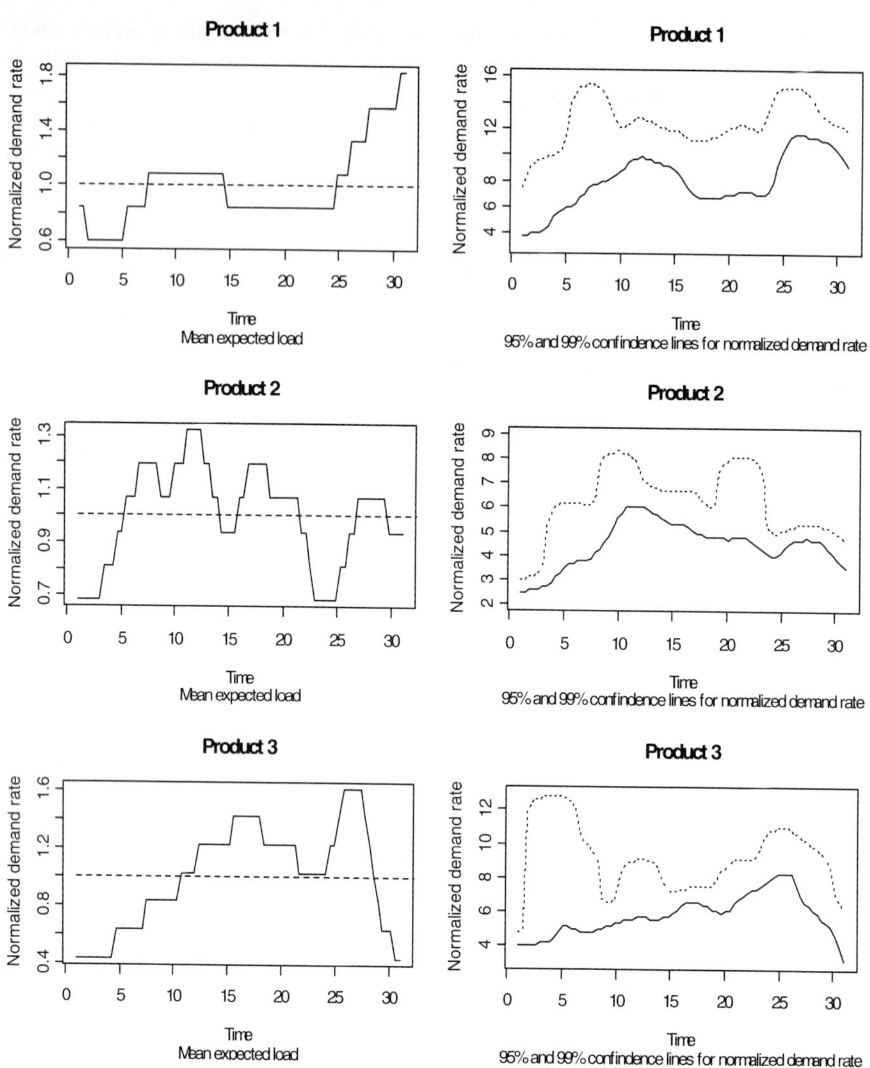

Fig. 1. The left hand graphs indicate the mean expected standardized demand rate at any given date in the month. The right hand graphs indicate the 95% and 99% confidence limits for the largest expected demand rates.

The graphs on the left side of figure 1 indicate the standardized demand rate where 1 corresponds to a demand rate equaling the mean expected demand rate for the given period. Looking at the standardized mean expected demand rates in figure 1, it is clear that all three products has a low demand rate in the beginning of the period. This is for all products followed by a higher than expected demand rate starting around day 6 and lasting until day 15-20 depending on the product. Up to the midway point of the month the mean standardized demand rates are positively correlated (0.59-0.78) and strongly positively correlated for the 95% largest demand rate (0.91-0.97). In demand-driven JIT MPC systems implemented today the assumption is either that demand rates within a planning period are uncorrelated or negatively correlated [3]. Negatively correlated demand rates within a period means that as the sales of one product momentarily rises the sales of others decrease. In a demand-driven JIT manufacturing system this is of particular importance since positively correlated demand rates will make the assumption of level demand rates incorrect, leading to either too little available capacity or too much. After the midway point the patterns diverge and become uncorrelated. Product 1 experiences a period of about ten days of a lower than average demand rate, followed by a surge in the demand rate lasting and increasing until the end of the month. Product 2 experiences a drop in the demand rate lasting for about five days until the demand rate stabilizes around the mean expected demand rate. Product 3 experiences a surge in the demand rate lasting for a few days, before incurring a dramatic decline in the demand rate towards the end of the period. The values found in table 1 can be used to establish minimum criteria for the needed flexibility of the manufacturing systems. The values in table 1 indicate that the mean expected demand rate requirements vary significantly. From a MPC perspective this indicates that the company would need the volume flexibility indicated in table 1 to be able to respond on a day-to-day basis to demand. These inferences can however not stand alone in evaluating the necessary flexibility of a manufacturing system.

Table 1. Minimum and maximum expected standardized demand rates for the three products, as well as the standard deviation of the same

	Min.	Max.	St. dev.
Product 1	0.59	1.83	0.30
Product 2	0.68	1.32	0.19
Product 3	0.44	1.62	0.36

Just like service levels in inventory management (defined as orders fulfilled from stock), it is possible to define a service level for a demand-driven JIT manufacturing system. The service level will be defined by the percentage of orders manufactured / assembled by the promised due date. The delivery time and the adherence to due dates being a direct result of the internal lead time. The lead time is in turn directly governed by the load on the manufacturing system (disregarding material constraints). In inventory management the service level is achieved by holding safety stock. The purpose of safety stock is to absorb demand above the expected level until replenishment occurs. In a JIT manufacturing system this could be thought of as the capacity beyond the ability to handle the average expected demand rate or buffer time added to the delivery time. While safety stock can be costly, excess manufacturing capacity is potentially even more so. To establish the flexibility capability in a JIT manufacturing system we have to make a number of deductions and definitions. Service level is defined as the percentage of customer orders fulfilled by the promised due date. The internal lead time of an order consists of two major elements: Processing / assembly time and waiting time. Processing / assembly time can be considered as independent of the degree of utilization of the system. Referring to the assumption of a manufacturing system in balance with the total demand for a period, waiting time can be found by looking at how much the demand rate on the date of receiving the order is above the normal standardized demand rate. If the demand rate on the particular date is lower than the expected rate, no waiting time is incurred. This assumes that the ordering date and due date differ. The right hand side graphs in figure 1 indicate the 95% and 99% confidence limits on the largest expected standardized demand rates. For example a value of 5 for the lower line at time 11, indicates that at time 11 with 95% certainty the largest expected demand rate will be five times the mean expected demand rate. This information enables us to clearly state the potential service level of the manufacturing system at any given point of time during the period. This can subsequently be used to find when e.g. an extra shift should be added to ensure a consistent service level for the whole period or when capacity should be adjusted downward. This particular information can also be used to calculate lead times to customers with a given certainty at different points of time in a period. The more prudent approach could however be to use it together with the capacity profile over the period to find the largest expected delivery time.

To utilize the demand rate information, the following must be done:

1. Establish desirable delivery time – i.e. lead time to customer. This corresponds to determining the desired system capability.
2. Determine manufacturing system capacity and potential flexibility – i.e. which demand rate of a given product mix can be handled in a given situation.
3. Use the demand rate profiles for all products to estimate a daily load on resources. If materials are included into the considerations, or product mix impacts the load, the individual demand rates should be considered.
4. Establish the desired service level i.e. deliveries on time. Here the assumption of sufficient capacity to cover the period comes into play.
5. Calculate the periodic capacity profile based on the desired flexibility found from the estimated demand rate distributions.

Consider the following example: Product 3 (Figure 1) takes 1 day to manufacture in the JIT line. The desired lead time to customer is 5 days. The manufacturing system is balanced to handle the standardized mean demand rate per day. The object is then to determine what should the capacity be, to be able to deliver orders with a 95% at time 5. Studying figure 1, the 95% largest expected standardized demand rate is approximately 5 at time 5, indicating that with 95% certainty the expected demand rate at time 5 will no more than five times the daily standard demand. At this point an assumption must be made, namely that the demand in following days is either negligible or at the level of the standard demand rate. If it is negligible then it is rather simple to find that the capacity the following 4 days should be increased with 25%. If it is at the level of standard demand rate – the capacity must be doubled for the next four days to achieve the promised delivery date. The problem that presents itself here is the lack of knowledge of the conditional probabilities for demand rates. This has yet to be implemented in the method, but could be a valuable tool for the updating of the capacity profile. The method enables companies to avoid hedging too much capacity to achieve a given delivery time. The fitted density functions underlying the graphs in figure 1 can be used to determine when and how much flexibility is needed in the manufacturing system. The demand rate estimates combined with a capacity profile can subsequently be used to develop a proactive either demand management approach or a proactive demand planning / resource allocation policy, not unlike the concept suggested in Lin [7]. The demand management approach is highly relevant if the manufacturing capacity is limited in flexibility and more so if the product load of the manufacturing system is very sensitive to product mix shifts. The approach of proactively adjusting capacity will be relevant if the manufacture has little or no ability to impact the customer ordering behavior. Clearly due to the potentially large demand rates in the case studied, it will be costly in capacity flexibility to promise a high service level with a very short delivery time. This can be seen from the fact that upwards to 15 times the standard daily demand rate can be expected using a 99% confidence level (figure 1 product 1 right hand graph). The ability to respond to half a month demand in a very short time can put tremendous pressure on the manufacturing system. A more reasonable approach if following a pure chase strategy, would be to use the information presented in figure 1 as an indicator for how much flexibility is needed in the day-to-day operations.

The method that has been presented in this paper can be the basis for a qualitative assessment of capacity needs in a manufacturing environment. To be truly effective the method should however be developed so it can be applied in an automated manner dynamically interacting with a planning system. To enable this, information of the individual resources making up the capacity and the different products load on these is needed. Provided with the proper information of capacity costs and costs of missing due dates it should pose no problem to use the demand rate estimates to derive capacity profiles for scheduling purposes.

The assumption of a level stable demand rate, that forms the backbone in a demand-driven JIT environment, is often wrong. The ability to asses the impact of deviating significantly from this assumption is however seldom present. The conclusion must be that the information gained by using density estimation methods for time dependent demand rates is a valuable tool for establishing capacity and flexibility requirements for the JIT manufacture. The main drawback of the suggested method is the need for a large amount of historical data. This can limit the methods applicability to well established products with a known demand history. Luckily this can be somewhat remedied by using e.g. a number of established products for scenario building. It is conccivable that a handful of demand patterns can be generalized to describe the behavior of a product family. If product mix shifts pose no significant problems for manufacturing system load, the aggregate demand rate should be used for fitting the demand rate density distribution. If product mix shifts significantly impact the load of the manufacturing system, then the demand rates will have to be evaluated individually.

5 Conclusions and Further Research

The aim of the paper was to establish a method that can be used to estimate the need for capacity flexibility in a demand-driven Lean/JIT manufacturing system. The issue addressed is critical since many companies are operating under a JIT paradigm without a level stable demand rate. The main issue in addressing the need for capacity flexibility, is establishing the time dependent demand rates. If these are known with some certainty either delivery times can be determined accordingly or the capacity can be adjusted to match expected requirements.

The method proposed in this paper numerically estimates a multivariate density distribution for time and demand rates. Subsequently this distribution is used to determine expected standardized mean demand rates and the largest probable demand rates. The method is applied to demand data from a demand-driven JIT manufacture, showing that the mean standardized demand varies significantly for all the examined products. Furthermore it is evident from the results, that the company in question needs a great deal of capacity flexibility to be able to cope with the potential peaks in demand rate. Based on a demand rate analysis it is possible to indicate when and how much flexibility is needed in the manufacturing system to be able to deliver on-time. The method thus enables JIT manufacturing companies to better match capacity to requirements. This will in turn enable demand-driven JIT manufactures to determine when they need flexibility and how much, potentially leading to lower manufacturing costs, more consistent delivery times and better customer service.

Further research should involve determining the conditional probabilities of demand rates in a given period. This step will be needed to establish a dynamic capacity adjustment mechanism as the one suggested in Lin [7]. Further research should also be conducted on making planning models that incorporate probabilities of demand rates rather than just level demand.

References

1. Hayes, R.H., Wheelwright, S.G.: Link manufacturing process and product life cycles. Harvard Business Review 57, 133–140 (1979)
2. Berry, W.L., Hill, T.: Linking Systems to Strategy. International Journal of Operations & Production Management 12, 3–15 (1992)
3. Vollmann, T., Berry, W., Whybark, D.: Manufacturing Planning and Control Systems, 4th edn. Irwin/McGraw-Hill, New York (1997)
4. Taps, S., Steger-Jensen, K.: Aligning Supply Chain Design with Manufacturing Strategies in Developing Regions. Production Planning & Control 18, 475–486 (2007)
5. Silver, E.A., Pyke, D.F., Peterson, R.: Inventory Management and Production Planning and Scheduling, 3rd edn. John Wiley & Sons, Chichester (1998)
6. Weatherford, L.R., Bodily, S.E.: A Taxonomy and Research Overview of Perishable-Asset Revenue Management: Yield Management, Overbooking, and Pricing. Operations Research 40, 831–844 (1992)
7. Lin, K.Y.: Dynamic pricing with real-time demand learning. European Journal of Operational Research 174, 522–538 (2006)
8. Krzanowski, W.J.: Principles of Multivariate Analysis - A User's Perspective. Oxford Statistical Science Series, vol. 3. Oxford University Press, Oxford (1988)
9. Silverman, W.: Density Estimation for Statistics and Data Analysis. Chapman and Hall, Boca Raton (1986)

Constraint Programming Approach to Time-Window and Multiresource-Constrained Projects Portfolio Prototyping

Irena Bach, Grzegorz Bocewicz, and Zbigniew Banaszak

Department of Computer Science and Management, Technical University of
Koszalin, 75-453 Koszalin, Poland
`zbigniew.banaszak@tu.koszalin.pl`

Abstract. Constraint Programming (*CP*) is an emergent software technology
for declarative description and effective solving of large combinatorial problems especially in the area of integrated production planning. In that context,
CP can be considered as an appropriate framework for development of decision
making software supporting small and medium sized enterprises (SMEs) in the
course of projects portfolio prototyping. The paper deals with problem considered multiresource problem in which more than one resource type may be
required by every activity in the project and the availability of each type is
time-windows limited. The problem belongs to a class of NP-complete ones.
The aim of the paper is to present a *CP* based projects portfolio prototyping
framework providing a prompt service to a set of routine queries stated both in
straight and reverse way, e.g., concerning the projects portfolio makespan implied by a given resources allocation, and the feasible resources allocation guaranteeing an assumed projects portfolio makespan. The way the responses to the
routine queries can be guaranteed while may be available in an on-line mode is
illustrated in the example enclosed.

Keywords: project scheduling, constraint programming, decision making,
knowledge engineering.

1 Introduction

For Small and Medium Size Enterprises (SMEs) with multiple production orders, an
optimal assignment of production steps to available resources is often economically
indispensable. The goal is to generate a plan/schedule of production for a given period
of time while minimizing of cost that is equivalent to maximization of profit. In that
context executives want to know how much a project will cost, what resources are
needed, what resources allocation can guarantee project due time completion, and so
on. So, SME's needs might be formulated in a form of standard, routine questions,
such as: Does the projects portfolio can be completed due to an arbitrary given deadline? Does the execution of the given projects portfolio meet the assumed resources
allocation within the arbitrary given period of time? Is it possible to undertake a new
project under given (constrained in time) resources availability while guaranteeing
disturbance free execution of the already executed projects? What values and of what

N.T. Nguyen et al. (Eds.): IEA/AIE 2008, LNAI 5027, pp. 767–776, 2008.

variables guarantee the project portfolio will completed with assumed values of a given set of performance indexes?

Most companies, particularly SMEs have to manage various projects which share a pool of constrained resources, taking into account various objectives at the same time. That is well known fact [1], [3], that about 80% of companies have to deal with multiple projects. This corresponds to statistics showing that about 90% of all projects occur in the multiproject context. Since the project management problems belong to the class of NP-complete problems, new methods and techniques addressing the impact of real-life constraints on on-line decision making are of great importance. Such methods, enhancing on-line project management, and supporting a manager in the course of decision making, e.g., in the course of evaluation whether a new project can be accepted to be processed in a multi-project environment of a manufacturing system at hand or not, could be included into Decision Support Systems (DSS) tools integrated into standard project management software.

Regardless of its character and scope of business activities, a modern enterprise has to build a project-driven development strategy in order to respond to challenges imposed by growing market complexity and globalization. Managers need to be able to use a modern DSS so as to make optimal business decisions from the strategic perspective of enterprise operation. In this context, this contribution covers various issues of decision making within the framework of Constraint Programming (CP). The paper can be seen as continuation of our former works concerning projects portfolio prototyping [2], [3] and CP-based approach to the project-driven manufacturing.

We first introduce the problem formulation, see the Section 2. Then we present some details of the modeling framework assumed, in particular we describe the formalisms employed, see the Section 3. In the Section 4, the straight and reverse approaches to projects portfolio scheduling and the relevant illustrative examples are discussed. We conclude with some results and lesson learned in the Section 6.

2   Problem Formulation

2.1   Illustrative Example of Decision Problem

Tree projects P_1, P_2, P_3, are considered (see the activity networks Fig. 1). Each project consists of 20 precedence and resource constrained non-preemptable activities that require two renewable resources. Assume the sequence $T_i = (t_{i,j},\dots,t_{i,k},\dots,t_{i,m})$ determines the k-th activities duration in the i-th project.

Up to two kinds of renewable resources can be allocated to each $O_{i,j}$ activity. Assume the $dp_{i,j,k}$ means an amount of the k-th resource allotted to $O_{i,j}$ in a unit time.

Therefore, besides of sequences determining the activities duration (1)

$$T_1 = (1,\ 2,\ 3,\ 4,\ 4,\ 6,\ 3, 2,\ 1,\ 4,\ 3,\ 1,\ 4,\ 3,\ 2,\ 3,\ 1,\ 4,\ 2,\ 4),$$
$$T_2 = (2,\ 1,\ 3,\ 5,\ 2,\ 5,\ 2,\ 1,\ 6,\ 3,\ 3,\ 4,\ 6,\ 3,\ 3, 2,\ 6,\ 3,\ 1,\ 4), \qquad (1)$$
$$T_3 = (1,\ 6,\ 4,\ 3,\ 3,\ 6,\ 3,\ 8,\ 5,\ 2,\ 4,\ 3, 5,\ 2,\ 4,\ 3,\ 4,\ 6,\ 2,\ 4).$$

the sequences (2) items of which determine the (fixed) discrete resource requirements of activities are considered.

$$
\begin{aligned}
DP_{1,1} &= (3,\ 1,\ 1,\ 1,\ 1,\ 1,\ 2,\ 1,\ 2,\ 1,\ 2,\ 3,\ 2,\ 1,\ 2,\ 3,\ 2,\ 3,\ 4,\ 3), \\
DP_{1,2} &= (1,\ 2,\ 1,\ 1,\ 2,\ 3,\ 3,\ 1,\ 1,\ 2,\ 1,\ 1,\ 1,\ 4,\ 2,\ 1,\ 2,\ 2,\ 1,\ 2), \\
DP_{2,1} &= (2,\ 2,\ 1,\ 1,\ 1,\ 3,\ 1,\ 2,\ 2,\ 2,\ 1,\ 1,\ 2,\ 4,\ 1,\ 2,\ 2,\ 2,\ 1,\ 2), \\
DP_{2,2} &= (2,\ 1,\ 2,\ 3,\ 1,\ 2,\ 1,\ 2,\ 1,\ 1,\ 2,\ 1,\ 2,\ 1,\ 3,\ 2,\ 2,\ 2,\ 1,\ 1), \\
DP_{3,1} &= (2,\ 1,\ 3,\ 1,\ 2,\ 1,\ 2,\ 2,\ 1,\ 1,\ 1,\ 2,\ 1,\ 1,\ 2,\ 1,\ 2,\ 2,\ 1,\ 2), \\
DP_{3,2} &= (1,\ 2,\ 2,\ 1,\ 1,\ 1,\ 2,\ 1,\ 1,\ 4,\ 2,\ 2,\ 2,\ 1,\ 2,\ 3,\ 2,\ 1,\ 3,\ 1).
\end{aligned}
\tag{2}
$$

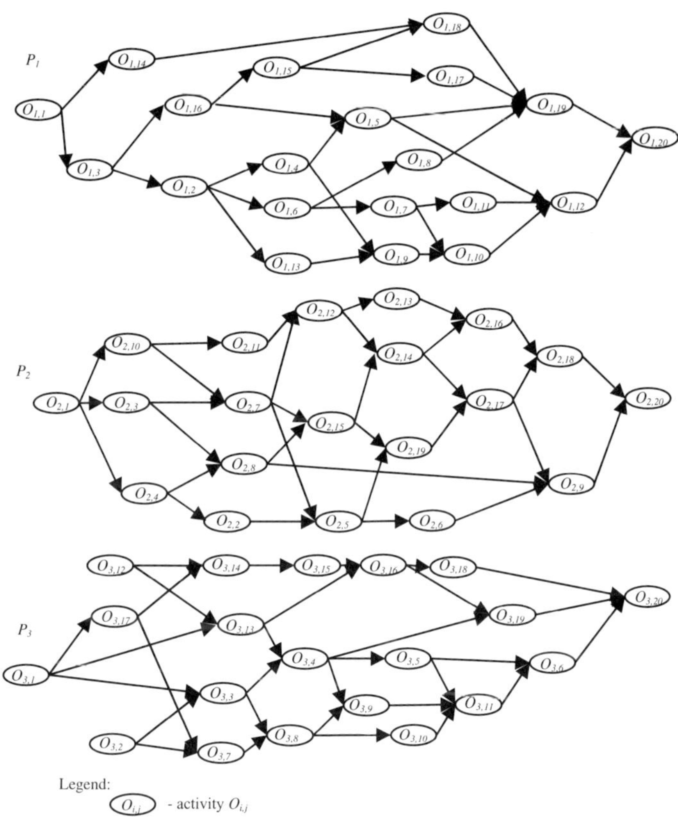

Fig. 1. Activity networks for P_1, P_2, P_3. projects

The total number of units of discrete resources (available within assumed time horizon H) is limited by sequences zo_1, zo_2 (3) items of which determine resources' limit available at time $v \in \{0,\dots,H\}$:

$$
zo_1 = (15,15,15,15,15,15,\ 5,15,15,15,13,13,13,13,13,13,13,13,13,13,10,10,\dots,10),
\tag{3}
$$
$$
zo_2 = (14,14,14,14,14,14,14,14,17,17,17,17,15,15,15,15,15,15,15,10,10,\dots,10).
$$

Assuming the given above resources availability as well as their allocations the following questions are considered: Does the projects portfolio can be completed due to an arbitrary given deadline 36 units of time? What resources allocation guarantee the projects portfolio will completed within the period do not exceeding 36 units of time? Response to these questions can be provided under the following assumptions.

2.2 Model of Decision Problem

Consider the discrete time horizon H, where: $\{0,1,\ldots,h,\ldots,H\}$, $h \subset N$, within of which the projects portfolio $P = \{P_1,P_2,\ldots,P_{lp}\}$ has to be completed. Given amount of renewable resources lz and their availability $Zo = (zo_1,zo_2,\ldots,zo_{lz})$; $zo_i = (zo_{i,1},zo_{i,2},\ldots,zo_{i,h})$ – the sequence items of which determine the availability of the i-th resource in a time unit within $\{0,1,\ldots,h,\ldots,H\}$. $zo_{i,j}$ – is the amount of the i-th resource at the j-th unit of time. Each project P_i consists of lo_i activities $P_i = \{O_{i,1},O_{i,2},O_{i,3},\ldots,O_{i,loi}\}$, where: $O_{i,j} = (x_{i,j}, t_{i,j}, Tp_{i,j}, Tz_{i,j}, Dp_{i,j})$ such that:

$x_{i,j}$ – means the starting time of the activity $O_{i,j}$, i.e., the time counted from the beginning of the time horizon H,

$t_{i,j}$ – the duration of the $O_{i,j}$-th activity,

$Tp_{i,j} = (tp_{i,j,1}, tp_{i,j,2}, \ldots, tp_{i,j,lz})$ – the sequence of time moments the activity $O_{i,j}$ requires new amounts of renewable resources: $tp_{i,j,k}$ – the time counted since the moment $x_{i,j}$ the $dp_{i,j,k}$ amount of the k-th renewable resource allotted to the activity $O_{i,j}$. That means a resource is allotted to an activity during its execution period: $0 \leq tp_{i,j,k} < t_{i,j}$; $k = 1,2,\ldots,lz$.

$Tz_{i,j} = (tz_{i,j,1}, tz_{i,j,2}, \ldots, tz_{i,j,lz})$ – the sequence of moments the activity $O_{i,j}$ releases the subsequent resources: $tz_{i,j,k}$ – the time counted since the moment $x_{i,j}$ the $dp_{i,j,k}$ amount of the k-th renewable resource was released by the activity $O_{i,j}$. That is assumed a resource is released by activity during its execution: $0 < tz_{i,j,k} \leq t_{i,j}$; $k = 1,2,\ldots,lz$, and $tp_{i,j,k} < tz_{i,j,k}$; $k = 1, 2, \ldots, lz$.

$Dp_{i,j} = (dp_{i,j,1}, dp_{i,j,2},\ldots, dp_{i,j,lz})$ – the sequence of the k-th resource amounts $dp_{i,j,k}$ are allocated to the activity $O_{i,j}$, i.e., $dp_{i,j,k}$ – the amount of the k-th resource allocated to the activity $O_{i,j}$. That assumes: $0 \leq dp_{i,j,k} \leq zo_k$; $k = 1, 2, \ldots, lz$.

Consequently, each activity $O_{i,j} = (x_{i,j}, t_{i,j}, Tp_{i,j}, Tz_{i,j}, Dp_{i,j})$ is specified by the following sequences of:

- starting times of activities in the project P_i:
$$X_i = (x_{i,1}, x_{i,2},\ldots, x_{i,lo_i}),\ \ 0 \leq x_{i,j} < h;\ i = 1, 2,\ldots, lp;\ j = 1, 2,\ldots, lo_i,$$

- duration of activities in the project P_i: $T_i = (t_{i,1},t_{i,2},\ldots,t_{i,lo_i})$,

- starting times the j-th resource is allocated to the k-th activity in the project P_i:
$$TP_{i,j} = (tp_{i,1,j}, \ldots,tp_{i,k,j},\ldots, tp_{i,lo_i,j}),$$

- starting times the j-th resource is released by the k-th activity in the P_i:
$$TZ_{i,j} = (tz_{i,1,j}, tz_{i,2,j},\ldots, tz_{i,lo_i,j}),$$

- amounts of the j-th resources allotted to the k-th activity in the project P_i:
$$DP_{i,j} = (dp_{i,1,j}, dp_{i,2,j},\ldots, dp_{i,lo_i,j}).$$

Moreover, the following constraints are assumed as well:

1) Activities Order Constraints

The projects are represented by activity-on-node networks, where activities state for nodes and arcs determine an order of activities execution. Consequently, the following constraints are considered:

- the k-th activity follows the i-th one:

$$x_{i,j} + t_{i,j} \leq x_{i,k}, \tag{4}$$

- the k-th activity follows other activities:

$$x_{i,j} + t_{i,j} \leq x_{i,k}, \; x_{i,j+1} + t_{i,j+1} \leq x_{i,k}, \; \ldots, x_{i,j+n} + t_{i,j+n} \leq x_{i,k}, \tag{5}$$

- the k-th activity is followed by other activities:

$$x_{i,k} + t_{i,k} \leq x_{i,j}, \; x_{i,k} + t_{i,k} \leq x_{i,j+1}, \; \ldots, \; x_{i,k} + t_{i,k} + \leq x_{i,j+n}. \tag{6}$$

For instance, in case of activity networks from Fig. 1 the constraints (4), (5), and (6) are as follows (see Table 1).

Table 1. Activities order constraints for activity networks from Fig. 1

Project P_1	Project P_2	Project P_3
$x_{1,3} \geq x_{1,1} + t_{1,1}$	$x_{2,3} \geq x_{2,1} + t_{2,1}$	$x_{3,3} \geq x_{3,1} + t_{3,1}$
$x_{1,4} \geq x_{1,1} + t_{1,1}$	$x_{2,4} \geq x_{2,1} + t_{2,1}$	$x_{3,3} \geq x_{3,2} + t_{3,2}$
...	...	...
$x_{1,20} \geq x_{1,12} + t_{1,12}$	$x_{2,20} \geq x_{2,9} + t_{2,9}$	$x_{3,20} \geq x_{3,6} + t_{3,6}$

2) Resource Availability Rate Constraints

The resources requested by an operation usually have to follow some proportion limits, i.e. limits determining the mutual rates the resources can be allocated to the activity $O_{i,j}$. The constraints considered are determined by the formulae (7):

$$dp_{i,j,1} + dp_{i,j,2} + dp_{i,j,3} + \ldots + dp_{i,j,lz} = rm_{i,j}, \tag{7}$$

where: lz – a number of renewable resources, $i=1,2,\ldots,lp$; $j = 1, 2, \ldots, lo_i$,
  lp – is a number of projects, lo_i – the number of the i-th projects' activities.

So, the sum of resources amount allocated to $O_{i,j}$ is limited by $rm_{i,j}$. In general case, to each P_i the following sequence corresponds $RM_i = (rm_{1,1}, rm_{1,2}, \ldots, rm_{i,loi})$.

3) Resource Conflict Constraints

In order to avoid deadlocks the constraints providing conflicts resolution, i.e., avoiding the occurrence of closed loop resources request, are considered. The constraints guarantee the sum of allocated amounts of a given resource do not exceed its current availability $zo_{i,j}$, at any moment within the assumed time horizon $\{0,1,\ldots,h,\ldots,H\}$. So, for each the k-th resource the following inequalities hold (8) at any time $v \in \{0,\ldots,H\}$,

$$\sum_{i=1}^{lp} \sum_{j=1}^{lo_i} \left[dp_{i,j,k} \cdot \bar{1}(v, x_{i,j} + tp_{i,j,k}, x_{i,j} + tz_{i,j,k}) \right] \leq zo_{k,v} \tag{8}$$

where: lp – a number of projects, lo_i – a number of activities contained by the i-th project, $dp_{i,j,k}$ – an amount of the k-th resource allocated by $O_{i,j}$,
  $\bar{1}(v,a,b)$ – the unit step function of the resource allocation
  $\bar{1}(v,a,b) = 1(v-a) - 1(v-b)$, where: $1(v)$ - a unit step function defined as follows (see Fig.2).

$$1(v) = \begin{cases} 0 & dla\ v < 0 \\ 1 & dla\ v \geq 0 \end{cases}$$

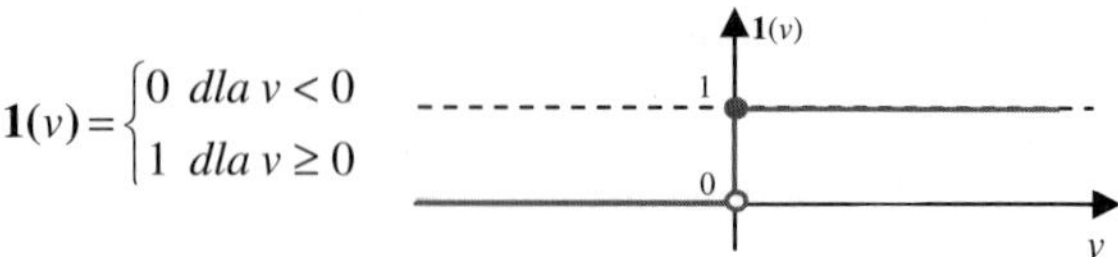

Fig. 2. A unit step function

That can be shown [5], the constraint (8) implies the set of inequalities (9) for the projects portfolio considered.

In constraints (9), the sum of requested resources is calculated only at moments corresponding to the ones $x_{i,j} + tp_{i,j}$, when resources are allocated to subsequent activities. Amount of available resources may change within the time horizon H. So, in order to avoid the amount of allocated resources exceeds the amount of available resources (similarly to (8)) the constraints associated to the moments $vp_{k,i}$ the resources availability changes, are introduced (10).

$$\begin{cases} \sum_{i=1}^{lp}\sum_{j=1}^{lo_i}\left[dp_{i,j,k}\cdot 1(x_{1,1}+tp_{1,1,k},x_{i,j}+tp_{i,j,k},x_{i,j}+tz_{i,j,k})\right]\leq zo_{k,x_{1,1}} \\[6pt] \sum_{i=1}^{lp}\sum_{j=1}^{lo_i}\left[dp_{i,j,k}\cdot 1(x_{1,2}+tp_{1,2,k},x_{i,j}+tp_{i,j,k},x_{i,j}+tz_{i,j,k})\right]\leq zo_{k,x_{1,2}} \\[6pt] \cdots \\[6pt] \sum_{i=1}^{lp}\sum_{j=1}^{lo_i}\left[dp_{i,j,k}\cdot 1(x_{1,lo_1}+tp_{1,lo_1,k},x_{i,j}+tp_{i,j,k},x_{i,j}+tz_{i,j,k})\right]\leq zo_{k,x_{1,lo_1}} \\[6pt] \sum_{i=1}^{lp}\sum_{j=1}^{lo_i}\left[dp_{i,j,k}\cdot 1(x_{2,1}+tp_{2,1,k},x_{i,j}+tp_{i,j,k},x_{i,j}+tz_{i,j,k})\right]\leq zo_{k,x_{2,1}} \\[6pt] \cdots \\[6pt] \sum_{i=1}^{lp}\sum_{j=1}^{lo_i}\left[dp_{i,j,k}\cdot 1(x_{lp,2}+tp_{lp,2,k},x_{i,j}+tp_{i,j,k},x_{i,j}+tz_{i,j,k})\right]\leq zo_{k,x_{lp,2}} \end{cases} \qquad (9)$$

for: $k = 1,2, \ldots, lz$, where: lz – a number of renewable resources.

$$\begin{cases} \sum_{i=1}^{lp}\sum_{j=1}^{lo_i}\left[dp_{i,j,k}\cdot 1(vp_{k,1},x_{i,j}+tp_{i,j,k},x_{i,j}+tz_{i,j,k})\right]\leq zo_{k,vp_{k,1}} \\[6pt] \sum_{i=1}^{lp}\sum_{j=1}^{lo_i}\left[dp_{i,j,k}\cdot 1(vp_{k,2},x_{i,j}+tp_{i,j,k},x_{i,j}+tz_{i,j,k})\right]\leq zo_{k,vp_{k,2}} \\[6pt] \cdots \\[6pt] \sum_{i=1}^{lp}\sum_{j=1}^{lo_i}\left[dp_{i,j,k}\cdot 1(vp_{k,q},x_{i,j}+tp_{i,j,k},x_{i,j}+tz_{i,j,k})\right]\leq zo_{k,vp_{k,q}} \end{cases} \qquad (10)$$

for $k = 1,2, \ldots, lz$, where: lz – a number of renewable resources $vp_{k,i}$ – its the i-th moment the available amount of the k-the resource changes, $zo_{k,(vp_{k,i}-1)} - zo_{k,vp_{k,i}} \neq 0$.

For the k-th resource the values $vp_{k,i}$ form the following sequence $Vp_k = (vp_{k,1},vp_{k,2}, \ldots, vp_{k,q})$ items of which are the moments corresponding to zo_k changes, q – a number of elements in the sequence Vp_k.

2.3 Problem Statement

The introduced model provides the formal framework enabling one to state the problem considered. Given the time horizon $\{0,...,H\}$, the projects portfolio P, the set of resources and their availabilities Zo within $\{0,...,H\}$. Given are sequences T_i, $TP_{i,j}$, $TZ_{i,j}$, $DP_{i,j}$. The following questions should be answered:

- Does a given resources allocation guarantee the project portfolio makespan do not exceed the deadline H? Response to this question results in determination of the sequences: $X_1,X_2,...,X_{lp}$.
- Does there exists such resources allocation guaranteeing the project portfolio makespan do not exceed the deadline H? Response to this question results in determination of the sequences: X_1, X_2,...,X_{lp} as well as the sequences $DP_{1,1}$, $DP_{1,2}$, ...,$DP_{1,lz}$, $DP_{2,1}$, $DP_{2,2}$, ...,$DP_{2,lz}$, ..., $DP_{lp,1}$, $DP_{lp,2}$, ...,$DP_{lp,lz}$.

The following remarks should be stated: - the problems considered are formulated in terms of variables, their discrete domains and the sets of constraints; - the sufficient conditions guaranteeing there exist a admissible solution to the above problems should be known; - the questions stated above correspond to the straight and reverse problems of multi-product scheduling.

3 Constraint Satisfaction Problem

Constraint programming (CP) is an emergent software technology for declarative description and effective solving of large combinatorial problems, especially in the areas of integrated production planning. Since a constraint can be treated as a logical relation among several variables, each one taking a value in a given (usually discrete) domain, the idea of CP is to solve problems by stating the requirements (constraints) that specify a problem at hand, and then finding a solution satisfying all the constraints [4]. From this perspective, CP can be considered as a pertinent framework for the development of decision making software aimed at supporting SMEs in the course of projects portfolio prototyping. Because of its declarative nature, it is particularly useful for applications where it is enough to state *what* has to be solved instead *how* to solve it.

More formally, CP is a framework for solving combinatorial problems specified by pairs: **<a set of variables and associated domains, a set of constraints restricting the possible combinations of the values of the variables>**. So, the constraint satisfaction problem (CSP) [4], [8], is defined as follows:

$$CS=((A, D), C) \tag{11}$$

where: $A = \{a_1, a_2,...,a_g\}$ – a finite set of discrete decision variables,

$D = \{D_i \,|D_i=\{d_{i,1}, d_{i,2},...,d_{i,j},...,d_{i,h}\}, i = 1,...,g\}$ – a family of finite variable domains, and the finite set of constraints

$C = \{C_i | i=1,...,L\}$ – a finite set of constraints limiting the decision variable values.

The solution to the CS is a vector $(d_{1,i}, d_{2,k},...,d_{n,j})$ such that the entry assignments satisfy all the constraints C. So, the task is to find the values of variables satisfying all the constraints, i.e., a feasible valuation. Generally, the constraints can be expressed by arbitrary analytical and/or logical formulas as well as bind variables with different non-numerical events.

The inference engine consists of the following two components: constraint propagation and variable distribution. Constraints propagation uses constraints to prune the search space. The aim of propagation techniques is to reach a certain level of consistency in order to accelerate search procedures by drastically reducing the size of the search tree. The constraints propagation executes almost immediately. What limits the size of the problem in practical terms is the variable distribution phase, which employs the backtracking-based search and is very time consuming as a result. Consequently, the crucial factor determining the practical usability of CP/CLP-based DSS is the provision of a variable distribution strategy that guarantees a feasible solution obtained in an on-line mode. Moreover, the declarative character of CP languages offers an attractive alternative to the currently available systems of computer-integrated management [6],[7], that employ operation research techniques.

4   Illustrative Example

For illustration of the capability of the CP-based approach let us consider the projects portfolio $P = \{P_1,P_2,P_3\}$ as stated in the Section 2.1. Let us assume the resources are allocated, and released at the moments corresponding to the beginning and completion of activities. Therefore, the sequences $TP_{1,1}, TP_{1,2}, TP_{2,1}, TP_{2,2}, TP_{3,1}, TP_{3,2}$ considered are as follows: $P_{1,2} = TP_{1,1} = TP_{2,2} = TP_{2,1} = TP_{3,2} = TP_{3,1} =$ (0,0,0,0, 0,0,0,0,0,0,0,0,0,0,0,0,0,0,0,0). Consequently: $TP_{1,1} = T_1$, $TP_{1,2} = T_1$, $TP_{2,1} = T_2$, $TP_{2,2} = T_2$, $TP_{3,1} = T_3$, $TP_{3,2} = T_3$. The considered sequences: $DP_{1,1}, DP_{1,2}, DP_{2,1}, DP_{2,2}, DP_{3,1}, DP_{3,2}$ are given in the Section 2.1.

4.1   The Straight Problem Case

For a given set of renewable resources and their availability $Zo = (zo_1, zo_2)$, see the Section 2.1, as well as the time horizon $\{0,...,36\}$, consider the question: Does a given projects portfolio can be completed within the time horizon $\{0,...,36\}$?

Response to this question requires the following sequences calculation: $X_1=(x_{1,1},x_{1,2},...,x_{1,20})$, $X_2= (x_{2,1}, x_{2,2},..., x_{2,20})$, $X_3= (x_{3,1}, x_{3,2},...,x_{3,20})$, where: $0 \leq x_{i,j} < 36$; $i = 1,2,3; j = 1,2,...,20$.

Of course, the sequences sought have to follow both the activities order and resource conflict constraints. In the case considered, 120 constraints (9) have been taken into account, each one consisting of 60 components.

That is assumed the starting times of activities ending the projects, i.e., $O_{1,20}, O_{2,20}, O_{2,20}$ have to follow the constraints (12):

$$x_{1,20}+t_{1,20} \leq H, \quad x_{2,20}+t_{2,20} \leq H, \quad x_{3,20}+t_{3,20} \leq H. \tag{12}$$

The stated above constraint satisfaction problem has been implemented in Oz Mozart environment. The first feasible solution:

$X_1 = (0, 4, 1, 6, 10, 6, 12, 12, 10, 15, 15, 19, 6, 1, 7, 4, 9, 9, 14, 20),$
$X_2 = (0, 10, 3, 2, 11, 19, 8, 10, 24, 5, 8, 11, 16, 15, 11, 24, 18, 26, 14, 30),$
$X_3 = (0, 0, 4, 12, 16, 26, 6, 9, 17, 17, 22, 0, 7, 13, 18, 22, 1, 25, 25, 32),$

has been obtained in 137 seconds, after the1993-th step (the processor used: AMD Athlon(tm)XP 2500+ 1.85 GHz and RAM 1,00 GB RAM).

4.2 The Reverse Problem Case

Given projects portfolio and sequences T_1, T_2, T_3 as well as $TZ_{1,1}$, $TZ_{1,2}$, $TZ_{2,1}$, $TZ_{2,2}$, $TZ_{2,1}$, $TZ_{2,2}$ see the Subsection 4.1. The resources availability limited by constraints (4) are determined by the following sequences:

$$RM_1 = (4, 3, 3, 5, 2, 3, 3, 2, 4, 4, 3, 2, 3, 4, 2, 5, 3, 3, 3, 4),$$
$$RM_2 = (4, 2, 3, 4, 2, 3, 3, 3, 4, 4, 3, 3, 3, 2, 2, 3, 4, 3, 4, 2),$$
$$RM_3 = (5, 2, 3, 4, 2, 3, 3, 3, 4, 4, 4, 2, 2, 4, 2, 3, 3, 3, 4, 4).$$

For a given set of renewable resources and their availability limits $Zo = (zo_1, zo_2)$, see the Section 2.1, as well as the time horizon $\{0,\dots,36\}$, consider the question: Does there exist the resource allocation guaranteeing the projects portfolio completion time will not exceed the assumed time horizon $\{0,\dots,36\}$?

Response to this question requires the following sequences calculation: X_1, X_2, X_3:

$$X_1 = (x_{1,1}, x_{1,2},\dots, x_{1,20}), \quad X_2 = (x_{2,1}, x_{2,2},\dots, x_{2,20}), \quad X_3 = (x_{3,1}, x_{3,2},\dots, x_{3,20}),$$

where: $0 \le x_{i,j} < 36$; $i = 1,2,3$; $j = 1,2,\dots,20$, and

$$DP_{1,1} = (dp_{1,1,1}, dp_{1,2,1},\dots, dp_{1,10,1}), \quad DP_{1,2} = (dp_{1,1,2}, dp_{1,2,2},\dots, dp_{1,10,2}),$$
$$DP_{2,1} = (dp_{2,1,1}, dp_{2,2,1},\dots, dp_{2,10,1}), \quad DP_{2,2} = (dp_{2,1,2}, dp_{2,2,2},\dots, dp_{2,10,2}),$$

where: $0 \le dp_{i,j,k} < 4$; $i = 1, 2$; $j = 1, 2, \dots, 10, k = 1,2$.

Of course, the sequences sought have to follow both the activities order and resource conflict constraints. The activities order constraints are given in the Table 1, and the resource availability constraints, determined due to (7) and taking into account sequences RM_1, RM_2, RM_3, are given in the Table 2.

Table 2. Resource availability constraints, determined due to (7)

Project P_1	Project P_2	Project P_3
$dp_{1,1,1}+dp_{1,1,2} = 4$	$dp_{2,1,1}+dp_{2,1,2} = 4$	$dp_{2,1,1}+dp_{2,1,2} = 5$
$dp_{1,2,1}+dp_{1,2,2} = 3$	$dp_{2,2,1}+dp_{2,2,2} = 2$	$dp_{2,2,1}+dp_{2,2,2} = 2$
...	...	...
$dp_{1,20,1}+dp_{1,20,2} = 4$	$dp_{2,20,1}+dp_{2,20,2} = 2$	$dp_{2,20,1}+dp_{2,20,2} = 4$

Resource conflict constraints follow the formulas: (9), (10).

The stated above constraint satisfaction problem has been implemented in Oz Mozart environment [9]. The first feasible solution:

$$X_1 = (0, 4, 1, 6, 10, 6, 12, 12, 10, 15, 15, 19, 6, 1, 7, 4, 9, 9, 14, 20),$$
$$X_2 = (0, 7, 2, 2, 8, 10, 5, 7, 21, 2, 5, 8, 12, 12, 8, 18, 15, 21, 11, 27),$$
$$X_2 = (0, 0, 1, 12, 15, 26, 6, 9, 17, 17, 22, 0, 7, 10, 12, 18, 1, 21, 21, 32),$$
$$DP_{1,1} = (3, 2, 1, 2, 1, 2, 1, 1, 2, 3, 2, 1, 2, 2, 1, 2, 2, 1, 2, 2),$$
$$DP_{1,2} = (1, 1, 2, 3, 1, 1, 2, 1, 2, 1, 1, 1, 1, 2, 1, 3, 1, 2, 1, 2),$$
$$DP_{2,1} = (2, 1, 2, 2, 1, 2, 2, 1, 2, 2, 1, 2, 1, 1, 1, 1, 2, 1, 1, 1),$$
$$DP_{2,2} = (2, 1, 1, 2, 1, 1, 1, 2, 2, 2, 2, 1, 2, 1, 1, 2, 2, 2, 3, 1),$$

$$DP_{3,1} = (3, 1, 2, 1, 1, 2, 2, 1, 1, 2, 1, 1, 1, 2, 1, 1, 2, 1, 1, 2),$$
$$DP_{3,2} = (2, 1, 1, 3, 1, 1, 1, 2, 3, 1, 3, 1, 1, 2, 1, 2, 1, 2, 3, 1),$$

has been obtained in 32 ms, after the102-th step (the processor used: AMD Athlon(tm)XP 2500+ 1.85 GHz and RAM 1,00 GB RAM).

5   Concluding Remarks

Proposed approach to projects portfolio prototyping provides the framework allowing one to take into account both: straight and reverse approach to multi-product project-like scheduling. This advantage can be seen as a possibility to response (besides of standard questions: Is it possible to complete a projects portfolio at a scheduled project deadline?) to the questions like: What values and of what variables guarantee the projects portfolio will completed due to assumed values of set of performance indexes?

Proposed approach provides the framework allowing one to take into account both: the sufficient conditions (guaranteeing the admissible solutions there exist) and choosing the best solution on the basis of chosen evaluation criteria. It can also be considered as a contribution to project-driven production flow management applied in make-to-order manufacturing as well as for prototyping of the virtual organization structures.

References

1. Archer, N., Chasemzadech, F.: An integrated framework for project portfolio selection. Int. Journal of Project Management 17(4), 207–216 (1999)
2. Banaszak, Z., Zaremba, M., Muszyński, W.: CP-based decision making for SME. In: Horacek, P., Simandl, M., Zitek, P. (eds.) Preprints of the 16th IFAC World Congress, Prague, Czech Republic (2005)
3. Banaszak, Z.: CP-based decision support for project-driven manufacturing. In: Józefowska, J., Węglarz, J. (eds.) Perspectives in Modern Project Scheduling. International Series in Operations Research and Management Science, vol. 92, pp. 409–437. Springer, New York (2006)
4. Barták, R.: Incomplete Depth-First Search Techniques: A Short Survey. In: Figwer, J. (ed.) Proceedings of the 6th Workshop on Constraint Programming for Decision and Control, pp. 7–14 (2004)
5. Bocewicz, G., Banaszak, Z., Wójcik, R.: Design of admissible schedules for AGV systems with constraints: a logic-algebraic approach. In: Nguyen, N.T., Grzech, A., Howlett, R.J., Jain, L.C. (eds.) KES-AMSTA 2007. LNCS (LNAI), vol. 4496, pp. 578–587. Springer, Heidelberg (2007)
6. Kis, T., Ërdos, G., Markus, A., Vancza, J.: A Project-Oriented Decision Support System for Production Planning in Make-to-Order Manufacturing. ERCIN News 58, 44–52 (2004)
7. Martinez, E.C., Duje, D., Perez, G.A.: On performance modeling of project-oriented production. Computers and Industrial Engineering 32, 509–527 (1997)
8. Puget, J.-F.: A C++ Implementations of CLP. In: Proceeding of SPICS 1994 (1994)
9. Schulte, C.H., Smolka, G., Wurtz, J.: Finite Domain Constraint Programming in Oz, DFKI OZ documentation series, German Research Center for Artificial Intelligence, Stuhlsaltzenhausweg 3, D-66123 Saarbrucken, Germany (1998)

Adaptive *E–Learning*: An Architecture Based on *PROSA* P2P Network

V. Carchiolo, A. Longheu, G. Mangioni, and V. Nicosia

Dipartimento di Ingegneria Informatica e delle Telecomunicazioni
Facoltà di Ingegneria - Università degli Studi di Catania
Viale Andrea Doria 6, I95125 - Catania - Italy

Abstract. Effective *E–Learning* requires ability to adapt in order to provide students with personalised learning path, based on specified goals and personal profiles, as well as the possibility of re-evaluating learning paths during the learning process based on actually learned topics. Moreover, shared teaching materials spread over the network, requiring an effective and efficient management solution for their storage and retrieval. In this paper we propose an *E–Learning* architecture where personalisation and dynamic adaption is achieved through the construction of learning paths tailored to each student's knowledge and needs, also allowing dynamically re-evaluation of such paths during the learning process, according to personal test results and/or needs. In addition, we arrange teaching materials into *PROSA* (P2P Resource Organisation by Social Acquaintances), a P2P network that tries to mimic the way social links among peers are established and evolve, in order to build a self organising network for an effective and efficient resource sharing and retrieval.

1   Introduction

E–Learning [1] has been evolved from simple distance learning, being simply a way to spread teaching materials through the network, to a more structured environment, characterised by high interactivity between the user and the system, collaboration within students communities, and high flexibility in course personalisation. Moreover, the increasing amount of shared teaching materials available on the network asks for an effective and efficient solution in order to manage and access such materials to further organise them into a personalised learning path.

In this paper such an architecture for a personalised dynamic *E–Learning* is proposed; in particular, personalisation is provided by creating all the possible learning paths for a student, starting from his/her basic knowledge and directed toward the desired knowledge (topic of interest), filtering these paths by taking into account the students' capabilities and needs; the student will choose one of these tailored learning path. The system can also adapt dynamically to a student's needs: for instance, if a student does not possess initially declared knowledge, the system can detect this situation from the results of exercises and

N.T. Nguyen et al. (Eds.): IEA/AIE 2008, LNAI 5027, pp. 777–786, 2008.

can re-evaluates and suggests a new path; or the system may change the path if the student's preferences (e.g., his available time) are modified.

Moreover, teaching materials usually spread over a huge number of students and teachers, each sharing lessons and exercises, at the same time asking his/her acquaintances for new materials. Since this is typical behaviour of a peer-to-peer (P2P) network, we arrange teaching materials into *PROSA* (P2P Resource Organisation by Social Acquaintances), a P2P overlay network that tries to mimic the way social links among peers are established and evolve, in order to build a self organising network. A decentralized vision in *E–Learning* infrastructure, encoraunging sharing among small contents repository is also presented in Edutella [2]. Three types of nodes are defined within Edutella network: consumer, provider and hub. In our approach, no specific role has to be assigned to nodes, in particular hubs have not to be preliminarly established, since the *PROSA* network allows an efficient query routing thanks to its social inspired behaviour. Besides, Edutella purpose is to exchange information about learning objects, whilst in addition we also aim at crafting personalized and dynamic learning paths as discussed above.

Preliminary results coming from campus learning context scenario are promising for an effective and efficient resource sharing and retrieval within the *E–Learning* system.

The paper is organised as follows: in section 2 the architecture of the proposed *E–Learning* system is outlined, whereas in sections 3 and 4 details about the ability to adapt and the *PROSA* P2P underlying network are respectively provided. In section 5 we introduce an example of an application of the system in a concrete *E–Learning* context with real topics, together with preliminary results, finally presenting our conclusions in section 6.

2   Architecture of the *E–Learning* System

A schema of the proposed *E–Learning* architecture is outlined in fig. 1, consisting of four layers: Database, Adaption, Presentation/Authoring and Interface layer.

The Database layer includes three databases, the Domain Database (DDB), the Teaching Material Database (TMDB) and the Profile Database (PDB).

The DDB contains information about the courses. They consist of Course Nodes (CNs) and Course Units (CUs) provide a two levels hierarchical organization of concepts, specifically a CN is used to group several CUs into a course (a CN hence represents a subgraph of CUs). A CU is a logical unit representing a set of concepts to be learned. Each CU has a set of properties, i.e. title, description, requisites (the knowledge required to understand CU concepts), objectives (the knowledge that will be acquired by learning the CU), estimated required time, level of abstraction (highly theoretical, mostly practical ...), level at which topics are addressed (introductory, in-depth, for specialists ...), level of detail with which contents are addressed (general overview of problem, details of specific problems ...), and finally the list of the teaching materials (CM) available for the CU. Knowledge for requisites and objectives is actually represented

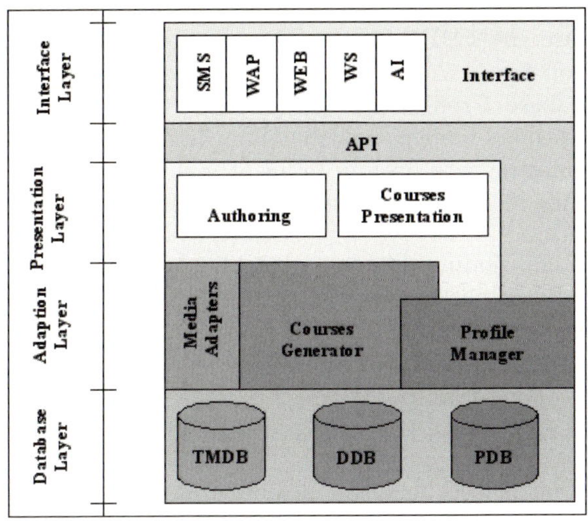

Fig. 1. Architecture of the *E–Learning* system

through a set of keywords extracted from a common ontology of a given domain of interest; it is however beyond the scope of this work to address ontologies issues. Also note that the level of detail and the general level at which topics are addressed may overlap, although there may be CUs on specialist topics with a low level of detail (e.g. a survey of a specialist problem). All the CUs stored in the DDB are organized in an AND/OR directed acyclic graph with the various CUs connected by arcs representing whether one is preliminary to another. An arc oriented from X to Y means that node X depends on node Y, i.e. all topics included in Y must be learned before topics of X can be understood. Two or more arcs involving the same node, for example the two arcs (Z,X) and (Z,Y) can represent alternative paths (either X or Y must be known in order to understand the topics in Z), or they may represent paths that are both necessary to understand the topics in the node Z to which they refer. These situations are defined as OR and AND arcs respectively. The second entity stored in the DDB is the CN, which represents a specific course (set of CUs). Each CN comes with a set of properties similar to those introduced above for CUs and with the list of all the CUs making up the course.

The second database, TMDB, contains all the CM used for courses/lessons (presentation, testing, …), and generally comprises multimedia and/or hypertext material. A given CU can be associated to different sets of CMs, that allows to learn the objectives of the associated CU, starting from its requisites. Sets can differ for their internal arrangement, for instance one set could consist of a single CM (e.g., a set of slides), whereas another could include several CMs (e.g., slides plus tutorial files and exercises). Such sets (i.e. all CMs they include) must be designed to share the same requisites/objectives. Note that contents (CUs) are separated from materials (CMs) to provide modularity when associating topics with concrete materials. To provide students with an effective and efficient retrieval architecture, the TMDB is actually implemented onto *PROSA*, described in detail in section 4.

The third database, Profile Database (PDB), contains all information about students (e.g. owned knowledge, available time, desired learning style and so on), used to build course tailored both in terms of topics and material.

The second layer includes the following modules:

– Media Adapters Module. It adapts teaching materials to the client device (PC, Pocket PC, SmartPhone, Mobile Phone and so on).
– Courses Generation Module. It is devoted to build courses and personalized learning paths, based on lessons/courses contained in the DDB and on information coming from the PDB.
– Profile Manager Module. It manages students profiles, stored in the PDB.

The Presentation/Authoring Layer includes a set of tools for the managements of courses, lessons and teaching materials (authoring), whereas the Courses Presentation Module, as soon as courses are built by the Courses Generation Module, retrieves the related teaching materials and arranges course units into learning paths according to each user's profile information.

Finally, the Interface Layer allows to implement several learning services, for instance the system can provide a WWW learning service (via the WEB module), or a learning interface based on Web Services (WS), or a set of interfaces for mobile devices. The modularity of the proposed framework helps to easy extend the functionalities of the system, e.g. adding new services or new media converters.

The media adapter module in the adaption layer, the authoring module in the presentation layer and the interface layer are out of the scope of this paper. Besides, here we omit all details about the algorithm for the generation of personalized courses, which involves the use of course generation and profile modules in the adaption layer, as well as the course presentation module in the presentation layer. All details can be found in [3].

3   Adaptivity in E-Learning

Adaptive systems, as defined in [4], *"cater information to the user and may guide the user in the information space to present the most relevant material, taking into account a model of the users goals, interests and preferences"*.

Adaptivity, now a key point for the success of an E-learning system, is present in several works. [5] proposes an author-defined storage for LMS (Learning Management Systems) capable of providing adaptivity: the student is presented with an overview of a document containing material tailored to the information stored in the *student model* (similar to the *student profile* defined in this paper). [6] provides adaptation by determining the most relevant learning path for every learner, also allowing course pages to be presented with a different look-and-feel according to user preferences (adaptive navigation). [7] also emphasises adaptation, named *appropriation*, proposing an approach to organise curriculum according to student's personal objectives (similar to the *desired knowledge* a student provides in our work when requiring a tailored learning path), and knowledge (to propose different views of curriculum). Construction of personalised learning paths can be found in several other works, e.g. [8,9,10]. A comparison of adaptive systems can be found in [11].

4   P2P and Social Networks: *PROSA*

Peer-to-peer (P2P) networks gained popularity and interest in the last ten years mainly due to the increasing low-cost available bandwidth as well as to the increasing resources sharing across the network, which requires a more effective solution than the classic client-server approach. In a P2P network each node indeed acts as a client if it is asking for a resource, while it becomes a server whenever it is asked a certain resource. Nodes in a P2P networks are functionally equivalent, and can collaborate in order to reach the common target: making available their resources in a fast and reliable way, to the higher number of nodes in the network, while being able to retrieve wanted resources themselves, even if some other nodes are down or unreachable. Starting from these considerations, many models have been proposed for P2P networks, the most common being *Unstructured Overlays* and **D**istributed **H**ash **T**ables (DHT) [12,13]; other recent works [14,15] focused their interest on introducing a certain amount of semantic in P2P overlays, allowing query to become more readable and understandable by users, while trying to maintain good performance in terms of resource availability, recall and robustness. In particular, social networks seem to be a valuable model to address both structural and semantics issues in P2P network.

Social networks are an abstract model for structure and dynamics of groups of connected or cooperating people. The most interesting thing in a social network is that queries for resources are routed in a fast and efficient way, naturally flowing to peers that can successfully answer them. In the case of a student, for example, he knows that it is better to ask his teacher for questions about math, whilst it is better to ask one of his classmates to collect information about his preferred football player. This is what we call *semantic routing*: in real life, humans are able to forward queries to other humans directly connected to them, choosing those that could probably give an answer back. The existence of such short paths is not limited to social networks. Several studies [16,17,18] underline the fact that almost all networks of cooperating elements naturally evolves to a *small-world* [19], i.e. a self organisation where any given pair of nodes are connected through a short path, even for large networks. The most appreciable characteristic of a small world is that messages from one node of the network to any other one can be delivered in a few steps, thanks to long-distance links. Since one of the main issues of many P2P overlay networks is that searching and retrieving documents is slow and inefficient, we proposed [20,21] a P2P overlay structure named *PROSA* (P2P Resource Organisation by Social Acquaintances) that tries to mimic the way social links among peers are established and evolve, in order to build an efficient and self-organising P2P network for resource sharing.

PROSA tries to face some important issues of P2P systems. First of all, query routing is based on a local evaluation of relevance between nodes and queries themselves: messages are not flooded to a great number of nodes, as in Gnutella [22,23], but just to nodes that can probably answer them. Second, the network organisation is entirely distributed and unsupervised: nodes naturally link to other nodes that share similar resources, once they *meet* them as a consequence of searching resources; it is not necessary to have super-peers in charge of deciding where to put each node and all nodes participate in building the structure of the network. Third, no overhead messages are needed in order to build or remove links among nodes: query messages are used to establish new links and to renew them, with no extra messages for network management. Finally, since routing and searching algorithms are based on social behaviours, simulations show that *PROSA* naturally evolve to a small-world network of peers, where each node can find needed resources just a few hops away [21]. Peers naturally get divided into *semantic groups*, i.e. emergent groups of nodes that result to be interested in a topic, that share resources in that topic and, thanks to the underlying link management algorithm, usually try to link each other. The structure of *PROSA* can dynamically change, following changes in peers preferences and attitudes: if a peer gets involved in different topics, it will link to other peers which can provide resources in those topics, just making queries and waiting for responses.

5   Application of *PROSA* in an *E–Learning* Context

A first application of *PROSA* P2P network in an *E–Learning* context has been implemented. In particular, we considered the concrete scenario of our academic context, where at the beginning of a new Academic year Faculty teachers define graduate programs and the set of courses they consist of, then the in-charge teacher details course contents, also providing materials. Several subject have been considered, in particular the DDB includes domains as Basic computer science, Computers architectures, Programming languages, Data structures, Web-oriented programming languages, Compilers/Interpreters and Algorithms.

Materials are actually either shared or searched by both students and teachers within the *E–Learning* context, in order to provide and/or collect teaching materials to be exploited when building personalised courses. This behaviour can be naturally mapped on that of a P2P network, gaining effectiveness and efficiency when teaching materials are shared; some advantages come from P2P basic networks [13], others are provided by PROSA, both described in the following.

A first advantage is that a connected repository from local teaching materials stored on the individual peers (students or teachers) has been created; indexing and categorisation of data can be accomplished locally by each peer exploiting the categorisation provided by CUs arranged into courses (CNs), thus preserving the same organisation of centralised database without its limitations. Another issue is the use of bandwidth, which is becoming more and more extensively required, still remaining a critical bottleneck within the classical client/server context. The use of P2P networks allow to address such issue by allowing a better load-balancing, indeed as soon as a peer finds and receive information (i.e. teaching materials) stored on another peer, he instantaneously acts as a new additional provider for that material, increasing its availability on the network, thus balancing the load as request increases. Additionally, the use of P2P networks accelerates the downloading and transport of big materials which are simultaneously requested by different entities. Finally, P2P networks can be effectively used as a scalable storage distributed network with high capacity and reliability (indeed various copies of the same file can be stored at different geographical locations, thus providing implicit backup).

The use of *PROSA* network allows to achieve additional advantages, in particular concerning the effectiveness and efficiency of teaching materials searching. Simulation results illustrated in the following have been obtained with networks of different sizes, where each node (student or teacher) performs an average of 15 searches for teaching material (queries), and requiring a maximum number of retrieved materials of $n_R = 10$. Figure 2 shows a comparison of average number of retrieved materials in a *PROSA* network; it compares *PROSA* with flooding and random walk approaches, where in the former a is forwarded across all the network, while in the latter each query is forwarded to one neighbour randomly chosen (note that nodes are *neighbours* when they exchange materials).

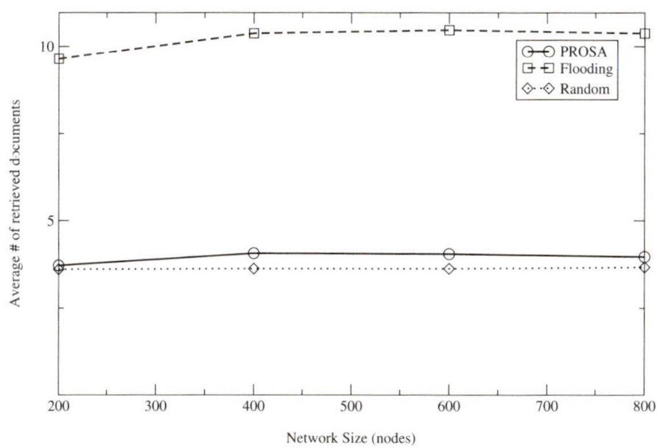

Fig. 2. Average number of retrieved documents

Flooding offers the best results, but it exploits much network bandwidth for query forwarding; *PROSA* is able to retrieve an average of 4 documents per query and this result is still better than that obtained by a random walk. An evaluation of the percentage of retrieved documents for *PROSA* shows that the highest percentage of answered queries is obtained by flooding the network, since about 94% of queries have an answer. In this case, however a valuable result is obtained also by *PROSA*: 84% to 92% of all queries are answered, while random walk usually returns results for less than 80% of issued queries. A relevant parameter is the query recall, i.e. the percentage of distinct retrieved documents over the total amount of distinct existing documents that match a query. The best performance is obtained, once again, flooding the network (results are not shown), but *PROSA* also has high recall: about 20% of queries obtain all matching documents, while 45% of queries are answered with at least one half of the total amount of matching documents. We also considered the recall for rare and common queries, being a query *rare* when the total number of matching documents is lower than the number of requested documents and *common* if it matches more than n_R. Figure 3 shows the cumulative normalised distribution of recall for rare queries (common queries are not shown). Results reported in figure 3 are really interesting: *PROSA* answers 35% of rare queries by retrieving all matching documents, while 75% of queries retrieve at least 50% of the total amount of matching documents; less than 10% of queries obtain less than 30% of matching documents. Performance of a random walk is worse than *PROSA*, whereas flooding is still the best. Considering common queries, *PROSA* is able to retrieve at least 10 documents for 20% of issued queries and, in every case, at least one document is found for 99% of queries, and at least 3 documents for 85% of queries.

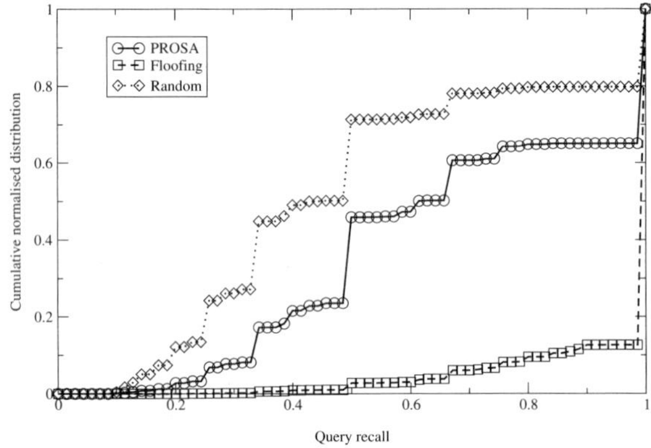

Fig. 3. Recall distribution for rare queries

The most relevant advantage offered by *PROSA* is however its efficiency, which can be measured through query deepness, defined as the average number of hops a query is forwarded far away from the source node. Figure 4 shows average deepness of successful queries for *PROSA*, flooding and random walk on the same *PROSA* network. Query deepness for *PROSA* is around 3 and is not heavily affected from the network size, while that of flooding and random walk is much higher (from 30 to 60 and from 120 to 600, respectively). This surprising result is due to the social network nature of *PROSA*, that allows to to exploit the

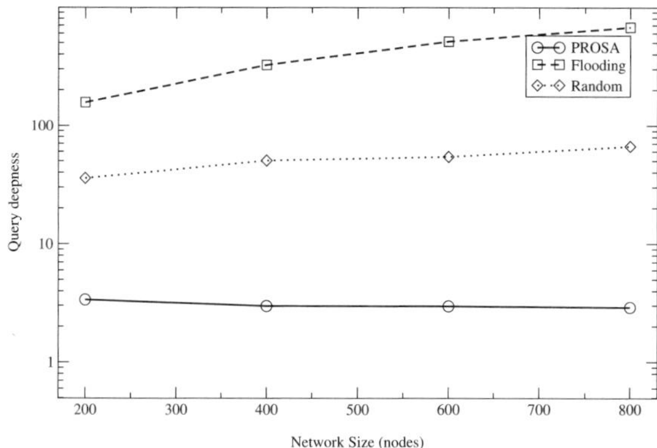

Fig. 4. Average query deepness

emerging small-world structure and to find a convenient and efficient route to forward queries along, avoiding a large number of forwards to non-relevant nodes.

6   Conclusions and Future Work

We introduced an architecture for *E–Learning* where *PROSA* P2P networks offer significant advantages for teaching materials search and retrieval, in addition to load balancing, accelerated download and virtually unlimited and reliable repository. Preliminary results coming from campus learning context scenario shows that *PROSA* achieves a good average number of retrieved documents and a good query recall, both for common and rare queries, while keeping query deepness at very low values; such results indicates that an effective and efficient resource sharing and retrieval within the *E–Learning* system can be obtained. Further works should investigate how to exploit *PROSA* for DDB implementation, and for supporting collaboration and working groups (communities).

References

1. Bergstedt, S., Wiegreffe, S., Wittmann, J., Moller, D.: Content management systems and e-learning-systems a symbiosis? In: ICALT 2003, Third IEEE International Conference on Advanced Learning Technologies, p. 155. IEEE Computer Society, Los Alamitos (2003)
2. Nejdl, W., Wolf, B., Qu, C., Decker, S., Sintek, M., Naeve, A., Nilsson, M., Palmér, M., Risch, T.: Edutella: a p2p networking infrastructure based on rdf, pp. 604–615. ACM Press, New York (2002)
3. Carchiolo, V., Longheu, A., Malgeri, M., Mangioni, G.: A model for a web-based learning system. Information Systems Frontiers 9(2-3), 267–282 (2007)
4. Brusilovsky, P., Kobsa, A., Vassileva, J. (eds.): Adaptive HyperText and Hypermedia. Kluwer Academic Publishers, Norwell (1998)

5. Sessink, O., Beeftink, R., Tramper, J., Hartog, R.: Author-defined storage in the next generation learning management systems. icalt 00, 57 (2003)
6. Weber, G., Brusilovsky, P.: ELM-ART: An adaptive versatile system for web-based instruction. IJAIED Special Issue on Adaptive and Intelligent Web-Based Systems 12, 351–384 (2001)
7. Rasseneur, R., Jacoboni, P., Tchounikine, P.: An approach to distance learning curriculum appropriation. icalt 00, 234 (2003)
8. Vassileva, J., Deters, R.: Dynamic courseware generation on the WWW. British Journal of Education Technologies 29(1), 5–14 (1998)
9. Brusilovsky, P., Vassileva, J.: Course sequencing techniques for large-scale web-based education. International Journal of Cont. Engineering Education and Lifelong Learning 13(1-2), 75–94 (2003)
10. Baldoni, M., Baroglio, C., Patti, V.: Web-based adaptive tutoring: An approach based on logic agents and reasoning about actions. Artificila Intelligence Review 22(1), 3–39 (2004)
11. Zarraonandia, T., Fernandez, C., Torres, J.: On the way of an ideal learning system adaptive to the learner and her context. In: ICALT 2005: Proceedings of the Fifth IEEE International Conference on Advanced Learning Technologies, pp. 641–643. IEEE Computer Society, Washington, DC, USA (2005)
12. Clarke, I., Sandberg, O., Wiley, B., Hong, T.W.: Freenet: A distributed anonymous information storage and retrieval system. In: Federrath, H. (ed.) Designing Privacy Enhancing Technologies. LNCS, vol. 2009, p. 46. Springer, Heidelberg (2001)
13. Steinmetz, R., Wehrle, K. (eds.): Peer-to-Peer Systems and Applications. Lecture Notes on Computer Science, vol. 3485. Springer, Heidelberg (2005)
14. Zhu, Y., Yang, X., Hu, Y.: Making search efficient on gnutella-like P2P systems. In: Proceedings of 19th IEEE International Parallel and Distributed Processing Symposium, 2005, IEEE Computer Society Press, Los Alamitos (2005)
15. Haase, P., Broekstra, J., Ehrig, M., Menken, M., Mika, P., Plechawski, M., Pyszlak, P., Schnizler, B., Siebes, R., Staab, S., Tempich, C.: Bibster - a semantics-based bibliographic peer-to-peer system. In: Proc. of the 3rd Int. Semantic Web Conference (2004)
16. Newman, M.E.J.: Models of the small world: A review. J. STAT. PHYS. 101, 819 (2000)
17. Newman, M.E.J., Park, J.: Why social networks are different from other types of networks. Physical Review E 68, 036122 (2003)
18. Albert, R., Barabasi, A.L.: Statistical mechanics of complex networks. Reviews of Modern Physics 74, 47 (2002)
19. Watts, D.J., Strogatz, S.H.: Collective dynamics of 'small-world' networks. Nature 393, 440–442 (1998)
20. Carchiolo, V., Malgeri, M., Mangioni, G., Nicosia, V.: Efficient searching and retrieval of documents in PROSA. In: Moro, G., Bergamaschi, S., Joseph, S., Morin, J.-H., Ouksel, A.M. (eds.) DBISP2P 2005 and DBISP2P 2006. LNCS, vol. 4125, Springer, Heidelberg (2007)
21. Carchiolo, V., Malgeri, M., Mangioni, G., Nicosia, V.: Social behaviours applied to P2P systems: An efficient algorithm for resources organisation. In: COPS 2006 – 2nd International Workshop on Collaborative P2P Information Systems (June 2006)
22. GNUTELLA website, http://www.gnutella.com
23. Sripanidkulchai, K.: The popularity of gnutella queries and its implications on scalability, http://www.cs.cmu.edu/~kunwadee/research/p2p/gnutella.html

Real-Time Car License Plate Recognition Improvement Based on Spatiognitron Neural Network

Dariusz Król and Maciej Maksym

Institute of Applied Informatics, Wrocław University of Technology
Wybrzeże S. Wyspiańskiego 27, 50-370 Wrocław, Poland
dariusz.krol@pwr.wroc.pl, maksym@maksym.info

Abstract. This article describes real-time car license plate recognition (CLPR) system based on spatiognitron neural network comparing to other ANPR/CLPR systems. Our neural network architecture is very efficient and improves whole recognition process. Spatiognitron neural network is inspired by biological neural structure – the mammalian primary visual cortex. This theory describes so called receptive fields, which are responsible for recognizing different kinds of features in the input image. This network also uses analog-like recognition method. In this method, the neural network responds in real-time. This is connected with reorganizing classical paradigm of image recognition process. The character of recognition stage is performed before the image segmentation. This approach seems to be more logical and it was certified in many quality tests of recognition process in commercial NeuroCar system.

Keywords: Car plate processing, character recognition, feature extraction, automated identification.

1   Introduction

Nowadays we can observe very rapid intelligent systems development. An automation of many ordinary processes in our life is noticeable everywhere. This tendency is based on replacing human's work with computer's work. There are many computer systems which do it with great result. One of them is a group of systems designed for image recognition. They are usually used in parking control systems, toll-pay systems and real-time highway camera monitoring. As one form of image recognition technology is car license plate recognition (CLPR) which can recognize the characters in the license plates. While the first commercial systems of CLPR appeared in 1980s, real outburst occurred in 1990s. Now we have hundreds systems available in the market. However, the research still continues.

Many methods have been proposed in order to solve the problem. In general, the following three major steps are used. Prior to character recognition, the license plate must be located from the vehicle images. Next, segmentation of characters from the found region must be done. At the end we start recognition process. A system for real-time CLPR consists of a camera, a computer, and software for image recognition.

N.T. Nguyen et al. (Eds.): IEA/AIE 2008, LNAI 5027, pp. 787–794, 2008.

Currently, most researchers prefer a hybrid detection algorithm, i.e. region-based method presented in [3], where several features are involved to make the algorithm more robust. A two-stage car plate character recognition method combining statistical and structural methods can be found in [7]. The NeuroCar system [6] is also a hybrid one.

This paper shows how skillfully the special neural network was used to manage car license plate recognition problem in different weather and light conditions. It shows also how important it is to achieve the best quality results, not only during identification process but also during other stages in recognition process.

The remainder of the paper is organized as follows. Section 2 presents car license plate recognition problem. Section 3 describes how to improve the quality of recognition using spatiognitron model. Section 4 illustrates the experimental settings and results. Finally, a conclusion and future work are presented in Section 5.

2   Car License Plate Recognition Problem

License plate recognition is a highly complex sequence of plates processing and analysis. Generally speaking, many external factors have negative influence on CLPR. For example (see Fig. 1): the weather and light conditions, vehicle's movement, license plate location in a whole frame, mechanical damages of license plate, etc. The solution for this problem is applying a suitable hardware and methods of plate recognition. That operation should minimize or even eliminate those problems and maximize the quality of whole recognition process.

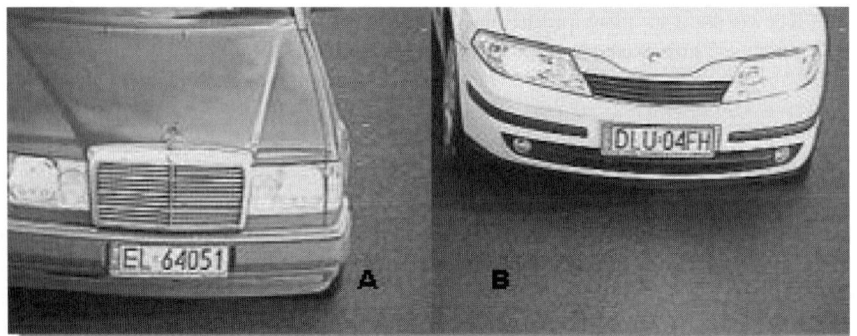

A ->   SYCOW-WRO-20061110-130044-260-PLW-EL_64051.JPG

B ->   SYCOW-WRO-20061110-130042-436-PLW-DLU_04FH.JPG

Fig. 1. Two input images with labels

This system can be divided into few main stages: image acquisition (digitalization), image preprocessing, license plate detection, segmentation, characters classification and recognition process verification. This is the most popular recognition schema.

Unfortunately, that schema causes most errors because of the wrong order of some recognition subprocesses. The main problem is the segmentation. We are not able to divide license plate into single characters properly before recognition process. A clue for this problem was found: reordering segmentation and identification processes with the aid of special architecture of neural network called spatiognitron [11]. This network represents a group of recognition techniques called segmentation free methods.

3   Quality Improvements Using Spatiognitron Model

Spatiognitron is a multilayered feed-forward neural network type with architecture similar to Neocognitron [11] and CMLP – Constrained Multilayered Perceptron. As we mentioned, this network responds in real-time and could be used for hand printing and machine printing recognition. The network uses so called scanning window in recognition process. This method treats input image as an infinite source for recognition and counts neural network response in each step of scanning window shift.

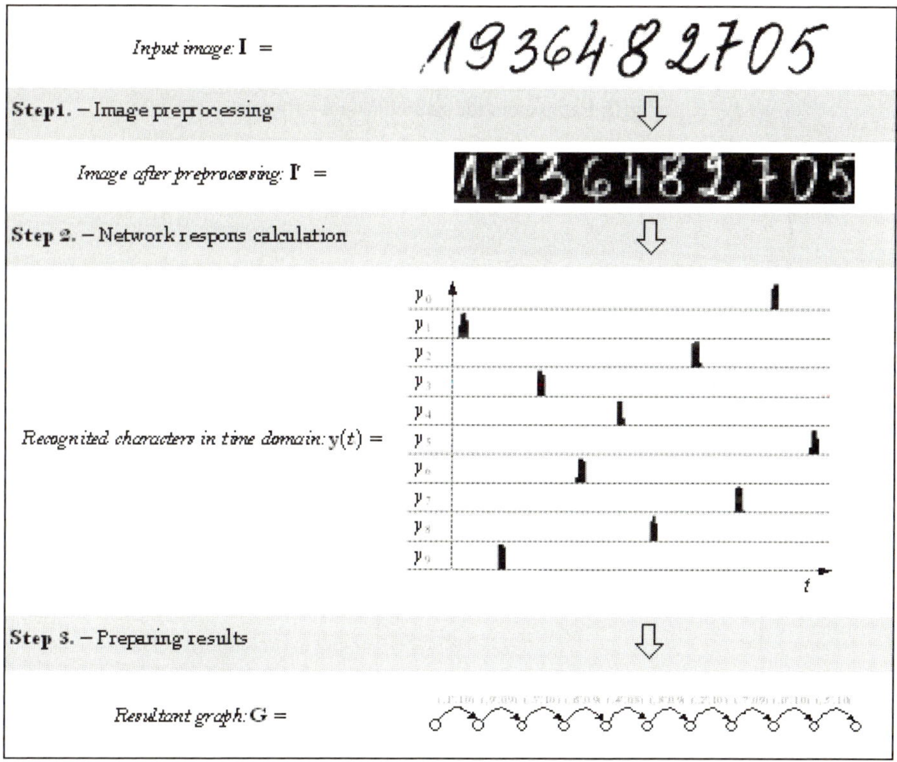

Fig. 2. Recognition process using spatiognitron schema

After processing the whole image, the results of the recognition are analyzed and transformed into resultant graph. The recognition process using spatiognitron is shown in Fig. 2.

In spatiognitron many elements of architecture are parameterized. To the most important parameters belong: Bipolar States, Layer Index, Spread Width, Spread Height, Cell Shift Vert, Cell Shift Horz, Slices, Window Width, Active Height, Sub Layers, Height Offset, Height Active, Height. The example is shown in Fig. 3.

```
Network Name      =   SAMPLE
Bipolar States =   1
Layer Index       =    0       1       2       3       4       5       6
Function          =   Input   Simple   Blur   Simple   Blur   Hidden  Output
Neurons           =    864    2560    4096    3456    1728     96      10
Sub Layers        =     1       1       2       2       4       4       1
Slices            =     1       4       8      12      12      24      10
Height            =    24      20      16      12       6       1       1
Height Offset     =     3       0       3       0       0       0       0
Height Active     =    18      20      10      12       6       1       1
Spread Width      =     1       5       2       5       2       6       1
Spread Height     =     1       5       2       5       2       6       1
Window Width      =     1       5       6      14      16      36      36
Cell Shift Vert=        1       1       2       1       2       1       1
Cell Shift Horz=        1       1       2       1       2       1       1
Trainable         =     0       1       1       1       1       1       1
Threshold         =     0       1       1       1       1       1       1
```

Fig. 3. Parameters for sample neural network

At the end of processing the system produces XML file with results of recognition (see Fig. 4).

```xml
<?xml version='1.0' encoding='utf-8'?>
<!-- Created by Neurocar ver. 0.1.X.X  Tue Sep 20 16:24:24 UTC+0200 2005' -->
<xVehicle xVersion="0.1" xID="100003212">
        <xInput>T001_input.jpg</xInput>
        <xType>normal</xType>
        <xCountry>pl</xCountry>
        <xPrefix>KR</xPrefix>
        <xNumber>49814</xNumber>
        <xReliability>0,79292</xReliability>
</xVehicle>
```

Fig. 4. XML file with information about car license plate

Spatiognitron has some very useful features in recognition process such as: tolerance for image/plate distortions, the same rotations and deformations as same as the LeNet neural network [5]. Those features let spatiognitron to be used in miscellaneous and very challenging real-time license plate recognition systems like highway systems.

Recognition quality improvement with this type of neural network is very impressive. The ratio of properly recognized vehicles to all recognized vehicles reached in total above 95 percent. This result places NeuroCar system beside different CLPR systems. By comparison, we can look at three other CLPR systems described in [1], [4], [8]. The difference in quality of the recognition is visible. These systems achieve merely: from 33 to 78 percent, only 47 percent, and 85 percent. This comparison can be found in [6]. As we can see, NeuroCar with spatiognitron achieves the best results but it is not only the contribution of his neural network. After many quality tests and experiments, we are absolutely sure that the main thing is to perceive recognition process as integrity. Even the best identification module is going to fail because of, for example, not efficient enough image preprocessing module or license plate local-ization algorithm. How strong recognition subprocesses effects on each other is shown in next Section.

4   Experiments

We designed and prepared nine experiments divided into about fifty single tests. The training set contained 2333 frames from NeuroCar system (533 single vehicles). Fig. 5 shows an example. This data set contained frames from video stream directly from NeuroCar system operated on national road no. 8 near Syców, about 55 km from our university. These images were captured in differential conditions so could contain distortions and be blurred or too much bright. This guarantees more objective results of the experiments.

SYCOW-WAW-20061127-095422-843-PLB-KZL_9916

SYCOW-WAW-20061127-095422-878-PLB-KZL_9916

SYCOW-WAW-20061127-095422-926-PLB-KZL_9916

SYCOW-WAW-20061127-095422-962-PLB-KZL_9916

Fig. 5. Original images – from 1 to 8 per one vehicle

The main goal of the experiments was the efficiency and quality recognition process in NeuroCar system, depending on various system parameters. In the experiments, the use of artificial neural nets in more than one subprocess of the recognition process was also considered.

The first three experiments showed a very important feature of car license plate system: image preprocessing is able to improve recognition quality from 22 percent up to 94 percent. Those optimistic results are relevant to the very first tests. These tests were based on applying contrast correction on the processing image/frame. Next experiments (the 2nd and 3rd) were based on changing the scale of the source image. These tests showed the best x and y scale factor. Applying this scale recognition quality improved about 1 percent.

Fig. 6. Maximum distortions with correct license plate character recognition

As it was said in previous Section, spatiognitron has good tolerance of image distortion. The fourth experiment was checking exactly that problem. The tests were analyzing spatiognitron tolerance of skew operation. The results were impressive: spatiognitron was able to make a properly recognition of images with angle of skew, which equals about 15 degrees. It is shown in Fig. 6.

There is another experiment which shows that not only identification process is important. We analyzed the neural network results depending on different syntax check parameters. Implementation of license plate syntax analyzer improves recognition quality from 70 percent up to 95 percent. It is shown in Fig. 7.

During quality test we took notes of some recognition problems. Despite the fact that spatiognitron uses receptive fields based on *Time-Delay Neural Network* and is very tolerant of different distortions, in some cases it was not able to recognize license plate number or did it with failures. The reason was localization of license plate clamping screws. In some configurations with plate characters, these screws could cheat the spatiognitron. It is shown in Fig. 8. This problem sometimes occurs; nevertheless spatiognitron is still a very good working neural network. These rare cases were also difficult to correct recognition for us.

All the experiments showed that the analysis of recognition process is not easy. There are many dependencies and problems so you should put attention to each

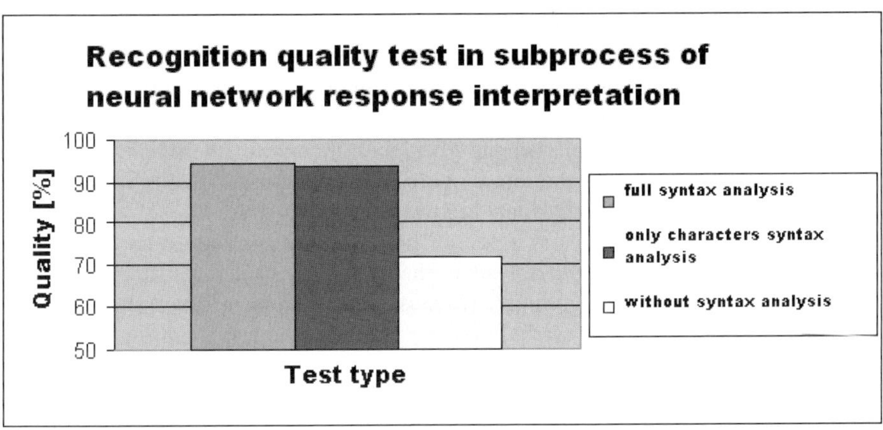

Fig. 7. Graph of recognition quality depending on neural interpretation parameters

Fig. 8. Examples of incorrect car plate character recognition

module/subprocess to make it the most suitable. The second important thing is to remember about treating recognition process as one solid operation.

5 Conclusions and Future Work

NeuroCar system and its spatiognitron neural network is an ideal answer for the increase the quality concerning car license plate recognition systems. Proposed unique neural network architecture and properly designed module of the whole recognition process, places this system at the top. 95 percent of recognition quality is enough for using NeuroCar system in professional highway or parking system.

We are going to continue our research of spatiognitron and NeuroCar system. Nowadays, there are few hypotheses about the possibility of using spatiognitron neural network in different recognition process stages like image processing or car license plate location. We have started preparing data for the test and designing special spatiognitron architecture to solve those problems. This way seems to be very up-and-coming [10].

Acknowledgments. The authors would like to thank Neurosoft CTO C.G. Dołęga for supporting this research.

References

1. Arth, C., Limberger, F., Bischof, H.: Real-Time License Plate Recognition on an Embedded DSP-Platform. In: Conference on Computer Vision and Pattern Recognition, pp. 1–8 (2007)
2. Casey, R., Lecolinet, E.: A Survey of Methods and Strategies in Character Segmentation. IEEE Transactions on Pattern Analysis and Machine Intelligence 18, 690–706 (1996)
3. Jia, W., Zhang, H., He, X.: Region-based license plate detection. Journal of Network and Computer Applications 30, 1324–1333 (2007)
4. Kwaśnicka, H., Wawrzyniak, B.: License Plates Localization and Recognition in camera pictures. In: 3rd Symposium on Methods of Artificial Intelligence, pp. 243–246 (2002)
5. LeCun, Y.: LeNet convolutional neural networks (28.07.2007),
   `http://yann.lecun.com/exdb/lenet/`
6. Maksym, M.: Using neural networks in 2D objects recognition. Wrocław University of Technology, Master Thesis (2007)
7. Pan, X., Ye, X., Zhang, S.: A hybrid method for robust car plate character recognition. Engineering Applications of Artificial Intelligence 18, 963–972 (2005)
8. Shapiro, V., Gluhchev, G., Dimov, D.: Towards a multinational car license plate recognition system. Machine Vision and Applications 17, 173–183 (2006)
9. Su, M.C., Hung, C.H.: A neural-network-based approach to detecting rectangular objects. Neurocomputing 71, 270–283 (2007)
10. Youssef, S.M., AbdelRahman, S.B.: A smart access control using an efficient license plate location and recognition approach. Expert Systems with Applications 34, 256–265 (2008)
11. Zamojski, W., Dołęga, C.: Spatiotemporal neural network for recognition of handwritten digit chains. In: Proceedings of the 6th Microcomputer School Neural Networks Theory and Applications, Brno, pp. 327–335 (1994)
12. Zheng, D., Zhao, Y., Wang, J.: An efficient method of license plate location. Pattern Recognition Letters 26, 2431–2438 (2005)

Handling Dynamic Networks Using Evolution in Ant-Colony Optimization

Christopher Roach and Ronaldo Menezes

Florida Institute of Technology, Computer Sciences
Computer Vision and Bio-Inspired Computing Laboratory
Melbourne, Florida, USA
croach@vt.edu, rmenezes@cs.fit.edu

Abstract. Ant Colony Optimization (ACO) is a popular meta-heuristic for solving combinatorial optimization problems. ACO uses the concept of ants foraging for food to find good solutions to these types of problems. ACO has been successfully applied to many problems, from the traveling salesman problem (TSP), to the problem of network routing. However, it has been pointed out that ACO does not perform as well as other heuristics in very dynamic problems. At first, this statement seems strange but a close look reveals that the nature strategy that inspires the ACO meta-heuristic has an important element that is lacking in ACO: evolution. This paper proposes a new algorithm, named Evolutionary Ant Colony Optimization (EACO), that combines ACO with elements of traditional Genetic Algorithms (GA), namely: selection, recombination, and mutation. Individual ants are endowed with a genotype that is allowed to evolve through generations of the population. In doing this, the EACO algorithm adds another element of optimization to the ACO algorithm that allows the individual agents (ants) in the algorithm to improve their behavior over several generations. Our results demonstrate that EACO can indeed overcome the hurdles faced by the original ACO.

1   Introduction

Biologically-Inspired Computing is the field of Computer Science that deals with the use of biological phenomena as the inspiration for new problem solving strategies. In this field of research, a popular group of algorithms have recently come to the forefront; their inspiration is taken from the interaction of individuals in groups of social organisms. This concept is referred to as Swarm Intelligence (SI).

SI algorithms use the idea that from a collection of simple agents, with no centralized decision structure, relatively complex behavior can emerge. One can see this idea in effect in the way that a colony of ants is able to find good paths to food sources, or in the way that birds are able to keep a tight, energy-efficient, pattern while flying.

A popular SI strategy that takes its inspiration directly from ant foraging behavior is the so-called Ant Colony Optimization (ACO) [6] meta-heuristic. ACO makes use of the method by which an ant colony forages for food, and in this process, find optimal solutions to certain kinds of problems in combinatorial optimization. In the ACO, artificial ants are sent out from their origin in an attempt to find a path to a destination. While doing so, each individual ant drops pheromone along their trail to entice other

N.T. Nguyen et al. (Eds.): IEA/AIE 2008, LNAI 5027, pp. 795–804, 2008.

ants to follow their chosen path. A shorter path will be traversed more often and have a higher concentration of pheromone. Thus, the majority of the ants will follow the path with the highest concentration of pheromone. The solution that emerges is in general an optimal (or close to optimal) solution to the problem. ACO has been successfully used to solve various computer science problems such as network routing [4] and the famous Traveling Salesman Problem [5].

The ACO heuristic, as well as several other swarm-intelligent algorithms are inspired directly by natural phenomena. However, these algorithms are lacking one characteristic that is present in their real world counterparts. Specifically, they are missing the ability to *evolve* [3]. In practice, this means that the ants do not posses the ability to inherit winning strategies from their ancestors. ACO is missing out on the optimization opportunities provided by evolution.

This paper proposes to remedy this shortcoming by incorporating techniques found in traditional GAs into ACO to allow stronger, more effective ants to help populate the next generation, and thus improve the colony's overall problem solving ability. This paper introduces a new hybrid approach, called Evolutionary Ant Colony Optimization (EACO), that is an amalgam of ACO and GA.

2   Background

2.1   Ant Colony Optimization

In the real world, ants search for food and, upon finding a new food source, they return to the nest, dispersing pheromone along the way. These pheromone deposits attract other ants in the colony, biasing their efforts towards the newly located food source (i.e. positive feedback). As several ants search for food, those who find shorter paths to food sources return home faster allowing their trails to be traversed by more ants in a smaller amount of time than the less efficient paths. The shortest path, therefore, gets the strongest concentration of pheromone and the ants in the colony are able to find the shortest route to a new food source. To avoid converging onto anything other than the most efficient paths, nature employs evaporation of the pheromone (i.e. negative feedback), thereby gradually removing the incentive for ants to visit inefficient paths and improving the chance an ant will find more optimal routes to food sources. Negative feedback also serves the purpose of making the colony behavior adaptable to environment changes (e.g. elimination of old paths to no-longer-interesting food sources). Dorigo *et al.* [6] utilized this behavior in their ACO algorithm and demonstrated that it is able to find optimal solutions to many combinatorial optimization problems.

2.2   Genetic Algorithms

Genetic algorithms (GA) are a branch of study in evolutionary computing developed in the late 60's by Holland [7] whose idea was to integrate the processes of evolution into computer science. The result was the definition of a new branch of research where operations taken from genetics are in the core of the process.

The idea behind GAs is the derivation of an optimal solution through the use of processes found in Darwinian evolution. This is done by randomly creating a population of solution candidates (i.e., a solution set) to a specific problem and evolving them through several generations to eventually derive the best possible solution. The evolution of new solution sets occurs through the use of *bio-operators* such as selection, recombination, and mutation. For all generations, each candidate in the solution set is checked against a fitness function. Those solutions passing the minimum fitness criteria are bred with each other through the use of the recombination *bio-operator* and resultant candidates are then mutated according to a probability measurement. This process continues until an optimal solution is found or until the maximum number of generations has been reached. Genetic algorithms have proven to be a powerful optimization tool particularly because the mutation operator can free a solution set that is stuck in a local optimum. Recombination (via crossover for instance) guarantees that good genotypes are passed on to future generations.

3   EACO Algorithm

3.1   Overview of the Algorithm

The EACO algorithm takes the idea of combining Ant-colony Optimization and Evolution a bit further than previous approaches [1,8,9,2,10]. Similar to White's proposal [10], the idea behind EACO is to endow each of the individual agents in ACO with characteristics and allow each of them to evolve, thereby enabling for two types of optimization to occur. First, the typical optimization of an ACO algorithm—namely, finding the optimal solution to the chosen problem. Second, the EACO algorithm gives the individual ants a chance to evolve, and thus, the agents themselves are allowed to become more optimized. This dual optimization allows the EACO algorithm to find better solutions in a shorter amount of time when problems are of a more dynamic nature; EACO has the ability to re-converge to a good solution even when the problem is constantly changing (e.g. a dynamic graph).

Where the EACO algorithm differs from White's algorithm however, is in two areas: *(i)* the characteristics of each ant, and mainly *(ii)* the point in the algorithm at which the bio-operators are used. In White's algorithm each ant was given two characteristics: sensitivity to pheromone and sensitivity to link cost. The EACO algorithm employs five characteristics in the genotype of its ant—lifespan, pheromone density, pheromone intensity, speed, and reproduction rate—which we argue to be a more realistic approach to an ant than the two used in White's experiments. More important than the introduction of new traits is the fact that in White's experiments, the algorithm was treated as more of a GA that used ACO to calculate the fitness of each ant. However, in EACO, the two paradigms (ACO and GA) are woven more tightly together and the process of evolution more closely resembles the natural process. EACO advocates the idea of a true, long-living, colony of ants in which genotypes are passed along generations chaining the phenotypes of the ants. In EACO, the re-population of the ant colony is done on a more continuous basis.

As a first step, a population of ants is created and released to explore the environment (as in ACO). As ants find better solutions, their fitness values are updated. Those ants that die (lifespan runs out) are removed from the population and new offspring are generated using GA's bio-operators (crossover and mutation). This should ensure a smooth and continuous operation of the ACO algorithm. It should also help reduce the execution time that past researchers have had in their experiments with GA and ACO since the ACO algorithm does not have to be run to completion each time before the GA runs and creates a new generation of ants.

Algorithm 1 describes the general idea behind our proposal. After creating the initial population of ants, the algorithm releases all of these ants into the environment updating the position of each ant in an iterative manner. At each iteration, the ant is moved along its chosen edge at the rate specified by the ant's speed until its next hop is reached. At that point, assuming the ant has not reached its final destination, a new node in the graph is chosen for its next hop according to the following probability:

$$p_{ij}^k(t) = \frac{a_{ij}(t)}{\sum_{l \in \mathcal{N}_i^k} a_{il}(t)}, \tag{1}$$

where N_i is the set of all nodes reachable from the current node i, N_i^k is a subset of N_i and includes all of the nodes reachable from node i and not currently in ant k's list of visited nodes, and $a_{ij}(t)$ is the value from the ant-decision table for traveling from node i to node j at time t. The ant-decision table is calculated according to the following formula:

$$a_{ij}(t) = \frac{[\tau_{ij}(t)]^\alpha [\eta_{ij}]^\beta}{\sum_{l \in \mathcal{N}_i} [\tau_{il}(t)]^\alpha [\eta_{il}]^\beta}, \quad \forall j \in \mathcal{N}_i \tag{2}$$

where $\tau_{ij}(t)$ is the amount of pheromone on edge (i, j) at time t and η_{ij} is the cost associated with moving from node i to node j (in our tests, we use the inverse of the cost associated with the edge in question). The α and β values are effectively weighting factors for the pheromone and cost associated with edge (i, j).

The pheromone for each edge in the graph is calculated according to the following formula:

$$\tau_{ij}(t) = (1 - \rho)\tau_{ij}(t - 1) + \Delta\tau_{ij}(t), \tag{3}$$

where ρ is the rate of pheromone evaporation such that $\rho \in (0, 1]$ and $\Delta\tau_{ij}(t)$ is the total pheromone deposited on edge (i, j) at time (t) by all ants in the colony. The change in pheromone is determined by the following formula:

$$\Delta\tau_{ij}^k(t) = \begin{cases} 1/L^k(t) & if (i, j) \in T^k(t) \\ 0 & if (i, j) \notin T^k(t) \end{cases}, \tag{4}$$

where $T^k(t)$ is the tour completed by ant k at time t and $L^k(t)$ is the total costs of this tour.

After updating the ant's position, the next step is to determine whether or not the problem has been solved. If the termination criteria has been met, the result is returned. If the termination criteria has not yet been met, the ant's age is updated and any ant whose life has expired is added to the $deadAnts$ list (when an ant dies, it allows for a new offspring to be generated in its place via the bio-operators). The ant's path is then

```
begin
    InitializePopulation(size);
    for n = 0 ... maxNumberOfIterations do
        finishedAnts ⟵ []; deadAnts ⟵ [];
        for each ant i ∈ Colony do
            UpdateAntPosition(i);
            if TerminationCriteriaMet() then
                return finalSolution;
            end
            // Update ant age, add to deadAnts if expired;
            UpdateAntAge(i, deadAnts);
            if FoundSolution(i) then
                // Add the ant to finishedAnts;
                finishedAnts ⟵ finishedAnts + i;
            end
        end
        UpgradePheromone(finishedAnts);
        for each ant i ∈ finishedAnts do
            // Update the ant's fitness and let it go again;
            fitness ⟵ CalculateFitness(getSolution(i));
            UpdateFitness(i,fitness); ResetAnt(i);
        end
        if Colony.currentSize() < size then
            diff ⟵ size - Colony.currentSize();
            for 1 ... diff do
                c ⟵ MateAnts();
                MutateChild(c); AddToColony(c);
            end
        end
        for each ant i ∈ deadAnts do
            RemoveAnt(i);
        end
    end
end
```

Algorithm 1. Sketch of EACO Algorithm

checked to see if a solution has been found. If a solution has been found, the ant is added to the $finishedAnts$ list. For ants that find solutions, the fitness of their solution is calculated and used in the selection of parents for the procreation process. This portion of the algorithm is primarily where the GA operations take place. If the colony size is less than the original size, it means that some ants have died while searching for a solution. Given that the population has a fixed size, for every space available in the colony, the algorithm generates an offspring—using the GA bio-operators—that is added to the colony. If the ant found a solution, but has not yet died, the ant is reset (i.e., path erased, solution cost is set to zero, and current node set to the source node) and it is set out again to find its way to the desired destination. The final portion of the algorithm removes all of the dead ants from the colony.

The EACO algorithm proposes five genotypical characteristics to be included in the ant. These together form the genetic code of the ant that is evolved through generations.

The five characteristics are: lifespan, pheromone quality, pheromone sensitivity, speed, and reproduction rate. The justification for these is related to observation in real ants.

4   Experimental Results

All the experiments we performed were for a problem of finding a shortest path based in the graph representing Romania (in Figure 1). The shortest path the algorithms were trying to identify is from the Arad to Bucharest. The shortest path is (Arad → Sibiu → Rimnicu Vilcea → Pitesti → Bucharest) with cost 418. The change that is applied to the graph to simulate a dynamic change is on the edge (Fagaras↔Bucharest); its value is changed from 211 to 150. This change causes the shortest path to be (Arad → Sibiu → Fagaras → Bucharest).

We have executed two experiments to test EACO. In the first experiment we ran each of the algorithms on a static graph and plotted their outcome over 50 tests. In the second experiment, we used the same graph and ran each algorithm a set number of iterations, then we made a minor change to the graph, and ran both algorithms again for the same number of iterations. The change made to the graph is to make another route the shortest path and the shortest path from before a local optimum. Essentially, what we are trying to convey in the second test is EACO's ability to re-converge faster to the new path.

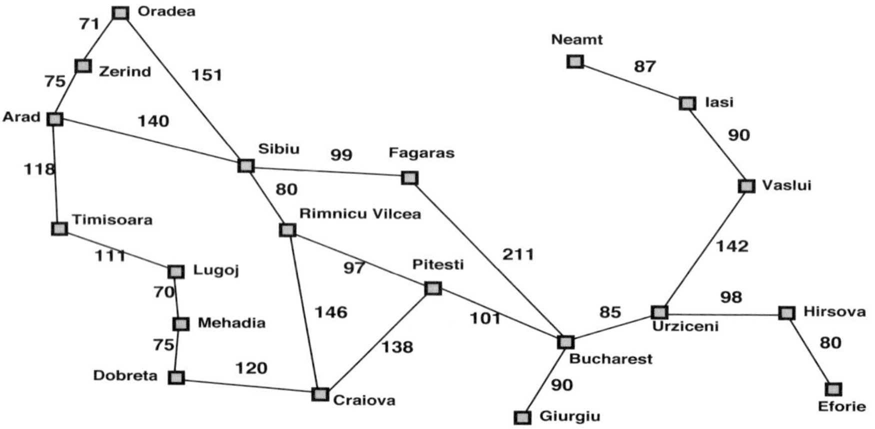

Fig. 1. Graph representing the map of Romania

In each experiment, we ran 50 tests. In the first experiment, we ran both algorithms a total of 10,000 iterations with 100 ants in the colony (these parameters were taken from previous works in ACO). In our first experiment, we run ACO and EACO on a static network, as expected ACO performed better than EACO in a static situation finding the optimal path 98% of the time in our tests versus 80% for EACO. We argued earlier that EACO is a variation of ACO suitable for dynamic environments. Therefore, our first experiment was to validate our ACO implementation with a static environment.

Table 1. EACO Parameters

α	β	evaporation %	mutation %	# ants	# iterations
1	0.1	1%	5%	100	10,000

In order to verify our results we have plotted the behavior of both ACO and EACO over time. Figure 2 relates to the finding of the best path. The algorithms were run for 10,000 iterations but the value of the best path was plotted every 100 iterations. Essentially, this figure shows how the algorithm converges on the *best path* in the map. The best path consists of the path in the graph that has the strongest pheromone. Basically the graph is traversed deterministically from source node to destination node. Note that in Figure 2 EACO does take longer to converge to the best path (418) which is what is expected given that it has more ants choosing alternative paths (due to the difference in the ant's genotypes). Yet, both of them do converge to the best path.

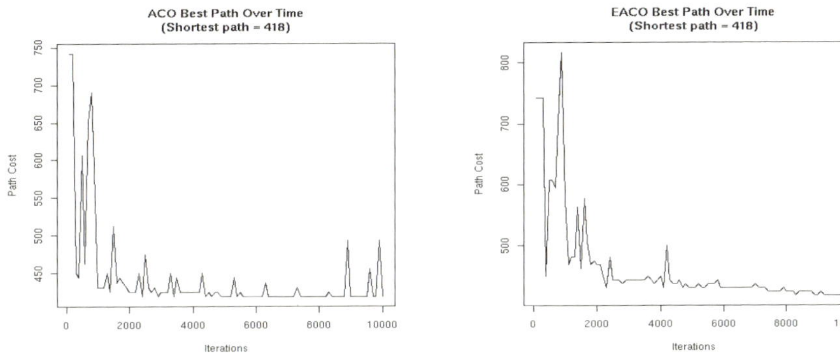

Fig. 2. This shows the best path at each 100 iterations of the execution

Figure 3 shows a plot of the path cost of every path found (whether good or bad) in each algorithm over the course of a single execution (or 10,000 iterations). The x-axis shows the total number of ants that have found a path, and the y-axis shows the cost of the path found by each ant. The dark line shows a moving average of 100 ants over the total number of paths found. Note that because this problem is static ACO does converge to the best path sooner than EACO.

We have previously argued that EACO is an approach suitable to dynamic environments therefore the results shown in a static setting were expected. In order to simulate a dynamic graph we devised a second experiment where again we ran each algorithm for 10,000 iterations with 100 ants. However, after 10,000 iterations a change was made to the graph to make the cost of the new shortest path 389 and the previous shortest path (path cost 418) a local optimum. After this change, we ran each algorithm again for another 10,000 iterations and plotted the outcome of each algorithm. As shown in Figure 4, EACO was better able to break out of the newly created local optimum in order to search the problem space for the newly created global optimum. In the second

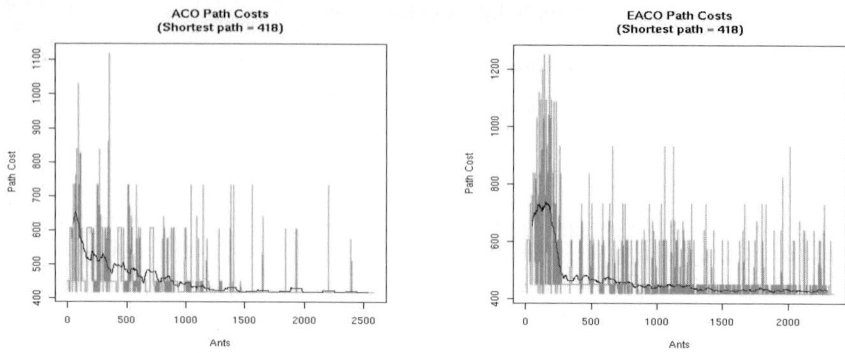

Fig. 3. This shows the cost of every path found by ACO/EACO

experiment, EACO was able to break out the local optimum 62% of the time and find the shorter path. ACO, however, was only able to break out of the local optimum 18% of the time and in each of the instances ACO found a worse path than it had previously. In short, after a change in the graph, EACO either stayed with the same path or got better, while ACO either stayed with the same path or got worse.

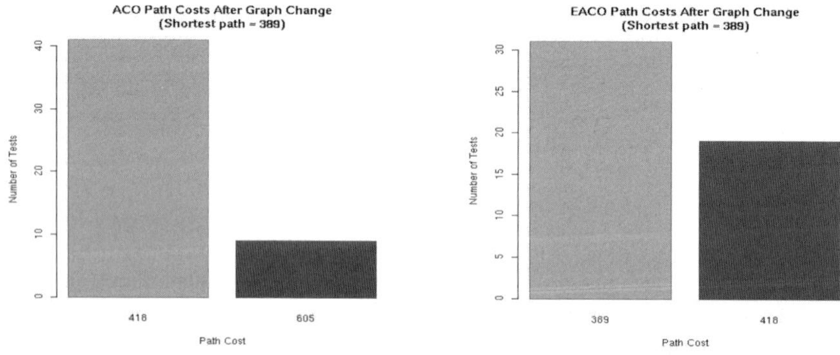

Fig. 4. In a simulation of a dynamic setting, ACO was not able to leave a local optimum and find the new best path (389) while EACO was able to find this path 62% of the runs

5   Related Work

There has been some research done on adding evolutionary techniques to ant-based algorithms. The first of these efforts was performed by Botee and Bonabeu [2]. In their approach, a GA was used to tune the parameters of the entire ACO algorithm—such as number of ants and sensitivity to pheromone. Problems existed in this method though since a single chromosome in the GAs population was made up of a list of all the parameters for the ACO algorithm that were being adjusted. Botee and Bonabeu used a population size of 40. Thus, with every iteration of the GA, the ACO algorithm was ran

40 times to find fitness values for each of the 40 individual chromosomes (i.e., sets of ACO parameters) in the GA. The major problem with this algorithm is speed, given the need to run the ACO algorithm N times with each GA iteration, where N is the size of the population.

Another group of researchers [10], chose to go another route and associate the parameters they wished to alter with the individual ants themselves. In this experiment, each individual ant had associated with it two different characteristics that determined the ant's sensitivity to pheromone and link cost. Thus, each ant acted differently when they came across a choice for the next link in their path. Those ants that chose their paths more wisely had a better fitness, and therefore, a better chance to pass their traits on to the next generation of ants, thereby, strengthening the overall effectiveness of the colony. A few problems still persist in White's experiments. The main one being that their experiments still used very discrete steps, like that of a traditional GA. What this means is that ACO has to be run to completion (i.e., all ants have found a path to their destination, or a desired number of iterations have been obtained) in order to obtain fitness values for each of the ants for the subsequent selection, recombination, and mutation steps. Running the entire ACO algorithm for each iteration of the GA leads to a much longer execution cycle.

6   Conclusion

A couple of limitations of this study that we would like to address in future works deal with the scope of the tests performed and with the amount of information of the convergence of the algorithm that we were able to obtain. To address the first limitation, we would like to test our algorithm in future works using the dynamic TSP problem with graphs taken from the TSPLIB (a library of sample instances for TSP). This will make it easier for us to compare the efficacy of our algorithm versus other SI and Evolutionary algorithms since TSP is the canonical problem for combinatorial optimization algorithms.

The second limitation that we found while conducting the experiments was that we had no real profile of the systems convergence. Upon noticing this particular piece of missing information, we came across a rather interesting alteration that could be made to the algorithm to improve its performance. By studying the level of self-organization in EACO, in particular the GA portion, we could find the best parameters for the algorithm given the dynamic nature of the system. In other words, by reducing the level of mutation and crossover in the system we become more like ACO and thus more effective in a static system and by increasing the levels of mutation and crossover in the system we become more effective in a dynamic system. To take this one step further, what if we did not determine these values ourselves, but instead let the algorithm determine what levels of mutation and crossover it needed depending on the dynamic nature of the graph. Thus EACO may use a self-organized approach in which the exact values of our GA parameters are based on how successful the ants are (based on the fitness function for individual ants). If the indication is that ants are not being that successful our algorithm can increase the mutation rate. Conversely, if the ants are doing well (on average) it can decrease the mutation rate so that the system does not move away from convergence.

This paper has demonstrated that the introduction of evolution in an ant-based process produces results that are comparable to standard ant-based approaches such as ACO. More importantly, we have demonstrated that the diversity of the ants in the population introduced in EACO makes our approach a stronger candidate for dynamic environments. Our experiments have already shown that EACO has a better tendency to free itself from local optima. In this process we are working on identifying a suitable real application where EACO would be most beneficial; it seems that applications such as network routing would be ideal. In this paper we used a simple shortest path problem in the static version of our experiments and a modified version where newer, shorter paths can appear after the algorithm converges. EACO has performed extremely well in these scenarios.

References

1. Angeline, P.J.: Using selection to improve particle swarm optimization. In: Proceedings of the 1998 IEEE World Congress on Computation Intelligence, pp. 84–89. IEEE Press, Los Alamitos (1998)
2. Botee, H.M., Bonabeau, E.: Evolving ant colony optimization. Advanced Complex Systems 1, 149–159 (1998)
3. Bourke, A.F., Franks, N.R.: Social Evolution in Ants. Princeton University Press, Princeton (1995)
4. Caro, G.D., Dorigo, M.: AntNet: a mobile agents approach to adaptive routing. Technical Report IRIDIA/97-12, Université Libre de Bruxelles, Belgium (1997)
5. Dorigo, M., Gambardella, L.: Ant colonies for the traveling salesman problem. BioSystems 43, 73–81 (1997)
6. Dorigo, M., Stützle, T.: Ant Colony Optimization. MIT Press, Cambridge (2004)
7. Holland, J.H.: Adaptation in natural and artificial systems. MIT Press, Cambridge (1992)
8. Robinson, J., Sinton, S., Rahmat-Samii, Y.: Particle swarm, genetic algorithm, and their hybrids: Optimization of a profiled corrugated horn antenna. In: Proceedings of Antennas and Propagation Society International Symposium, vol. 1, pp. 314–317 (2002)
9. Settles, M., Soule, T.: Breeding swarms: A GA/PSO hybrid. In: Proceedings of the Genetic and Evolutionary Computation Conference, Seattle, Washington, USA (July 2004)
10. White, T., Pagurek, B., Oppacher, F.: ASGA: Improving the ant system by integration with genetic algorithms. In: Genetic Programming 1998: Proceedings of the Third Annual Conference, pp. 610–617. Morgan Kaufmann, San Francisco (1998)

Rule Bases Integration on the Example of a Fuzzy Model of WIG20

Izabela Rejer

University of Szczecin, Mickiewicza 64, 71-101 Szczecin, Poland
irejer@uoo.univ.szczecin.pl

Abstract. Sometimes, when a fuzzy model is created, two knowledge sources are available – a data set describing the behavior of an analyzed system and a set of expert rules. In such case three possible approaches to the modelling process are possible: utilize a data set, utilize a set of expert rules or utilize both knowledge sources simultaneously. According to the author of this paper, the third approach is the most reasonable because by joining expert rules with rules created on the basis of a data set, fuzzy model inherits the specific advantages of both rule sets. The aim of this paper is to verify this statement and to illustrate (on a real example) the superiority of a model composed of expert and "data" rules over a model composed only of expert rules and a model composed only of "data" rules. The paper presents a writer's method of combining two rule bases and its application for building a combined fuzzy model of a real economic problem.

Keywords: rule bases integration, interpolation and extrapolation of a fuzzy model, expert fuzzy model.

1 Introduction

There are two general approaches which can be used when a fuzzy model is to be created – create model automatically on the basis of numeric data or build model manually with assistance of a domain expert. Of course, the first approach can be used when numeric data are available and the second - when it is possible to find a domain expert which is willing to cooperate. Sometimes, however, both knowledge sources are available and a question arises which of them should be applied in the process of creating a fuzzy model? Of course, the best solution is to utilize both knowledge sources because by joining expert rules with rules created on the basis of a data set, the fuzzy model inherits the specific advantages of both rule sets, it is high precision of the 1st rule set and wide range of application of the 2nd rule set.

There are a lot of approaches which can be used to join expert and data knowledge like: gray-box modelling [3], semi-mechanistic modelling [1], maintaining a set of rule bases joined with meta-rules [9], creating a rule base composed of rules chosen from different rule bases [5] etc. None of these approaches, however, can be used in order to build a model which will be credible in the whole, physically possible, input domain of the analyzed system, like an expert model and, simultaneously, will be

N.T. Nguyen et al. (Eds.): IEA/AIE 2008, LNAI 5027, pp. 805–814, 2008.

highly precise in the region covered by data points used in the estimation process, like a model created automatically on the basis of a data set. Therefore, there is a need to establish other methods to join expert knowledge with knowledge derived from a data set, methods which could be used to create models fulfilling aforementioned criteria of credibility and precision. One of these methods is described in the paper.

The main aim of this paper is to present the advantages of the model utilizing simultaneously expert knowledge and knowledge derived from a data set. In order to fulfill this aim, performance of three fuzzy models of the dependency existing between the Polish stock exchange index *WIG20* and two macroeconomic factors: *money supply* and *unemployment rate* is compared in the article. First model, described in Sect. 2, was created on the basis of a data set, second model, described in Sect. 3, was created with expert knowledge and the last model, described in Sect. 4, is a combination of rule bases of both previous models. The comparison of the models performance is presented in Sect 5.

2 Fuzzy Model of WIG20 Built on the Basis of a Data Set

The first fuzzy model of the analyzed dependency was built on the basis of monthly data from years 1995-2007. The output variable of the model was *WIG20* in month k and the input variables were *money supply* and *unemployment rate* in month $(k-2)$. Since the variable *money supply* was nominated in zlotys, its values had to be corrected with the inflation rate according to the formula:

$$K_o = (1 + \frac{(I_p - 100)}{100}) * K_p , \tag{1}$$

where: Ko – correction in current month, Kp – correction in previous month, Ip – inflation rate in previous month.

The whole data set, composed of 145 data points, was divided into two sets: training set (133 data points) and testing set (12 data points). While the training set was created in order to estimate the fuzzy model parameters, the testing set was created in order to compare the performance of all three fuzzy models described in the paper. It should be underlined here that, due to low dimensionality of the analyzed dependency, there was no need to reserve data points for testing the performance of the model described in this section.

To prepare data from the training set for estimating fuzzy model parameters, all variables (input and output) were normalized to the interval <0, 1>, according to the following equation [4]:

$$x_{zn} = \frac{x_{rz} - x_{min}}{x_{max} - x_{min}} , \tag{2}$$

where: x_{zn} – normalized value of variable x, x_{rz} – real value of variable x, x_{min} – minimal x value, x_{max} – maximal x value.

The architecture of the discussed fuzzy model was as follows:

- model type – Larsen model,
- input membership functions - asymmetrical triangular functions (4 functions per each input variable),
- output membership functions – 16 singleton functions,
- inference method – PROD-MAX,
- defuzzification method – height method.

In order to estimate the model parameters (it is central points of input and output membership functions), the model was trained with a fuzzy-neural network. The training process was carried out by 1000 epochs according to the backpropagation algorithm with momentum rate. The models parameters obtained after the training session are shown in Fig. 1 and in Tab. 1. Figure 1 presents sets of membership functions assigned to both input variables (Fig. 1a) and the rule net created in the input space (Fig. 1b) and Tab. 1 presents the model rule base.

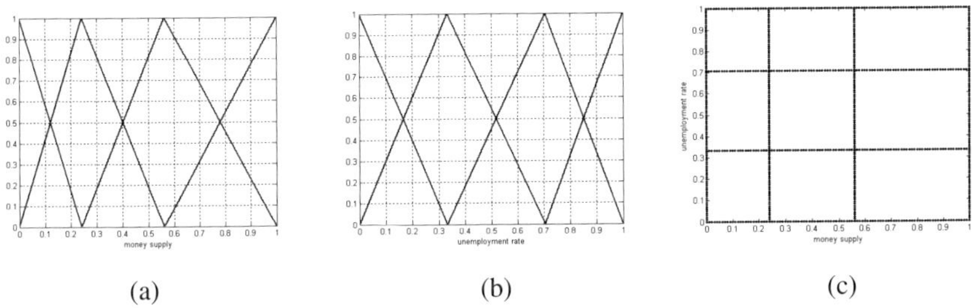

(a)   (b)   (c)

Fig. 1. Model 1 – a) membership functions assigned to input variable *money supply*; b) membership functions assigned to input variable *unemployment rate*; c) rule net

Table 1. Model 1 – rule base (columns – *unemployment rate*, rows – *money supply*)

	0	**0.33**	**0.71**	**1**
0	0	0.07	0	0
0.24	0.42	0.5	0.34	0
0.56	0	0.57	0	0.36
1	0	0.57	1	0.68

The approximated accuracy of the model was calculated according to the classic error measure – a mean absolute error (MAE) [2]:

$$MAE = \frac{\sum_{i=1}^{n}\left|z_i^* - z_i\right|}{n} * 100\% ,\tag{3}$$

where: MAE – mean square error, z_i^* – empirical values, z_i – theoretical values, n – number of data points.

MAE of the model was equal to 5.91%. Such small error meant that the model was very well fitted to the data points used in the estimation process. In order to determine whether the model was not overfitted, the graphic analysis of the model surface was performed (Fig. 2). As it can be noticed in Fig. 2, the model surface is situated between data points used in the estimation process which means that the model properly generalizes data from the training set.

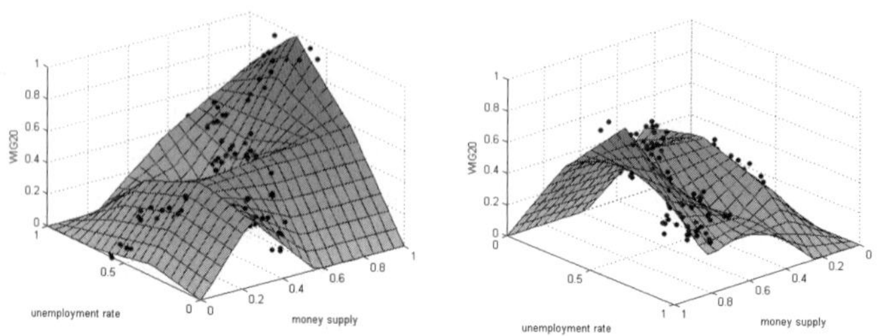

Fig. 2. Model 1 – model surface from two different points of view

3   Expert Fuzzy Model of WIG20

The second fuzzy model of the analyzed dependency was built with an assistant of a domain expert (prof. dr hab. Waldemar Tarczyński, Rector of the University of Szczecin). The first task of the expert was to describe all three variables (input and output) with sets of linguistic labels. After the analysis he decided to assign the same five labels to each variable (very small, small, medium, large and very large). Next, the expert was asked to assign numeric intervals to each label of each variable. Expert answers for this question were then converted into three sets of membership functions – one set per each variable (Fig. 3). The third expert task was to determine rules of the analyzed dependency by combining linguistic labels of input variables with linguistic labels of output variable. Results of expert evaluation are gathered in Tab. 2.

Expert membership functions and expert rule base were used to create the second model of the dependency existing between variables *money supply, unemployment*

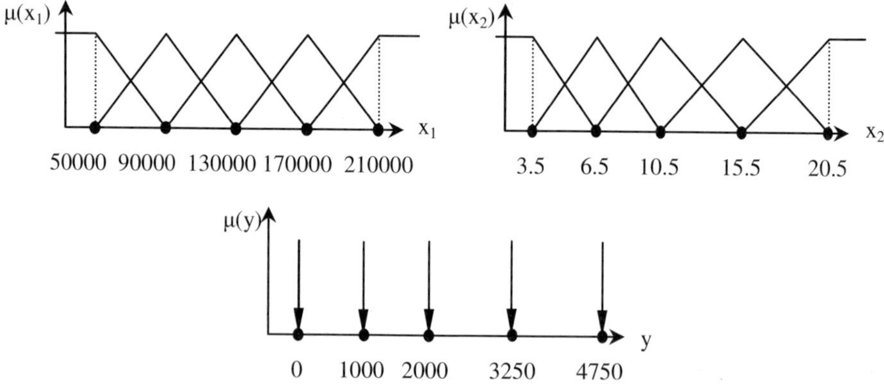

Fig. 3. Model 2 – membership functions assigned to succeeding variables: x_1 – *money supply*, x_2 – *unemployment rate*, y – *WIG20*

rate and *WIG20*. The architecture of this model was almost the same as discussed in Sect. 2. The only difference was in the number of membership functions assigned to each variable (five functions instead of four). In order to ensure the compatibility with the model created on the basis of the data set, the membership functions parameters of all variables given by the expert were normalized to the interval <0, 1>. The structure of the created model is presented in Fig. 4. In order to check the consistency of the expert model with real data, data from the training set were introduced to this model and MAE was calculated. It was equal to 8.57%.

Table 2. Model 2 – rule base (columns – *unemployment rate*, rows – *money supply*)

	V. small	**Small**	**Medium**	**Large**	**V. large**
V. small	medium	medium	small	v. small	v. small
Small	medium	medium	medium	small	v. small
Medium	large	large	medium	medium	small
Large	v. large	v. large	large	large	medium
V. large	v. large	v. large	v. large	large	medium

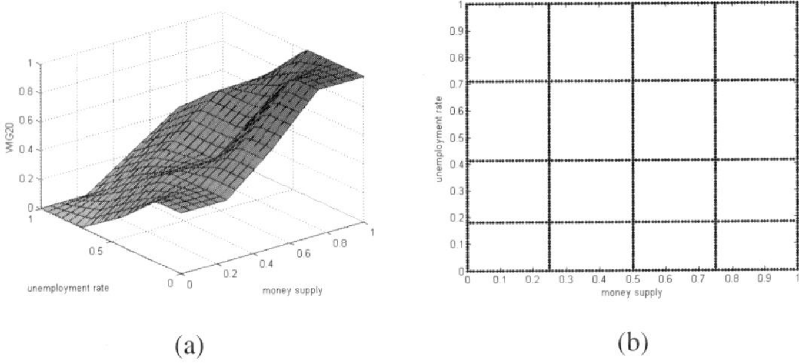

(a)   (b)

Fig. 4. Model 2 – a) model surface; b) model rule net

4   Combined Fuzzy Model of WIG20

In order to combine rule bases of two fuzzy models described in Sect. 2 and 3, a method of rule nets integration, proposed in the previous year by the author of this paper [6], was applied. The algorithm of this method is as follows:

1. Two fuzzy models of the analyzed system are created – an expert model and a model based on a data set (called: E-model and D-model, respectively).
2. Rule nets of both fuzzy models are integrated by joining pairs of sets of membership functions describing succeeding input variables.
3. An interpolation region of D-model is established.
4. Some rules conclusions are rewritten from D-model and E-model to the combined model: conclusions of rules situated inside the interpolation region of D-model are rewritten from D-model and conclusions of rules situated outside the interpolation region of D-model are rewritten from E-model.
5. Conclusions of remaining rules are calculated:

– conclusions of rules situated inside the interpolation region of D-model, supported by data points, are established in the training process,
– conclusions of rules situated inside the interpolation region of D-model but not supported by data points and conclusions of rules situated outside the interpolation region of D-model are established with methods of multi-dimensional neighborhood of rules or similar methods.

Ad. 1. The first step of the proposed algorithm is to built two fuzzy models of the same real system – a model based on a data set and a model defined by a domain expert. Both models have to be built on the basis of a grid partitioning of the input space.

Ad. 2. A rule net of a fuzzy model is created in the process of joining cores of one-dimensional membership functions describing succeeding input variables. Therefore, in order to perform the second step of the algorithm presented above, pairs of sets of one-dimensional membership functions describing succeeding input variables used in D-model and E-model are joined together. In this way one coherent set of membership functions per each input variable is created. Cores of these functions are then joined together and a rule net of the combined model is created.

Ad. 3. After creating the rule net in the input space, rules conclusions have to be established. There is no need to calculate conclusions for all rules – some of them are known from D-model and E-model. The question is, however, how to choose which of these two models generates proper conclusions for succeeding rules? For dealing with this task, a concept of interpolation region of D-model is applied. The idea of using the interpolation region as a decisional boundary stems from the fact that *while D-model produces credible results only for data situated inside its interpolation region, E-model gives results credible in the whole, physically possible, input domain but not as precise as D-model results.* That means that D-model should be applied only inside its interpolation region and E-model – only outside this region.

Hence, before establishing which conclusions from D-model and from E-model should be rewritten to the combined model, the interpolation region of D-model have to be determined. Although, the algorithm in its classic version utilizes the hypertube method to deal with this task [8], any other method of establishing the boundaries of the interpolation region can be applied as well.

Ad. 4. When the interpolation region is known, conclusions of rules situated inside this region are rewritten from D-model and conclusions of rules situated outside this region are rewritten from E-model.

Ad. 5. Only some rules of the combined model are contained in D-model and E-model which means that only some rules conclusions can be rewritten from both models. Conclusions of other, newly created rules have to be established in another way. Obviously, the assumptions from the 4th algorithm step should be hold, it is conclusions of rules situated inside the interpolation region of D-model should be established on the basis of a data set and conclusions of rules situated outside this region should be established on the basis of expert knowledge. In order to fulfill these assumptions:

– conclusions of all newly created rules situated inside the interpolation region of D-model, supported by data points, are trained with a fuzzy-neural network,
– conclusions of all newly created rules situated inside the interpolation region of D-model but not supported by data points and conclusions of all newly created rules situated outside the interpolation region of D-model are established: manually (with a domain expert assistance) or automatically (with methods of multi-dimensional neighborhood of rules or similar methods).

The algorithm described above was applied to combine rule bases of two fuzzy models from Sect. 2 and Sect. 3. Since real domains of variables used in both models were different, before the beginning of the integration process, they had to be unified (Tab. 3) and then once more normalized to the interval <0, 1>. The model created in the integration process is illustrated in Fig. 5:

–   Fig. 5a – presents sets of membership functions of the combined model (due to high closeness, membership functions no. 5 and 6 of the variable *money supply* and membership functions no. 8 and 9 of the variable *unemployment rate* were joined together);

–   Fig. 5b – presents the rule net of the combined model and the interpolation region of D-model (given by the hypertube);

–   Fig. 5c – presents the surface of the combined model.

The conclusions of rules from the rule base of the combined model are gathered in Tab. 4. MAE of the combined model, calculated over the training set, was equal to 2.65%.

Table 3. Domains of variables used in all three models

Variable	E-model	D-model	Combined model
Money supply	<50000; 210000>	<75241; 179697>	<50000; 210000>
Unemployment rate	<3.5%; 20.5%>	<9.5%; 20.6%>	<3.5%; 20.6%>
WIG20	<0; 4750>	<605; 3187>	<0; 4750>

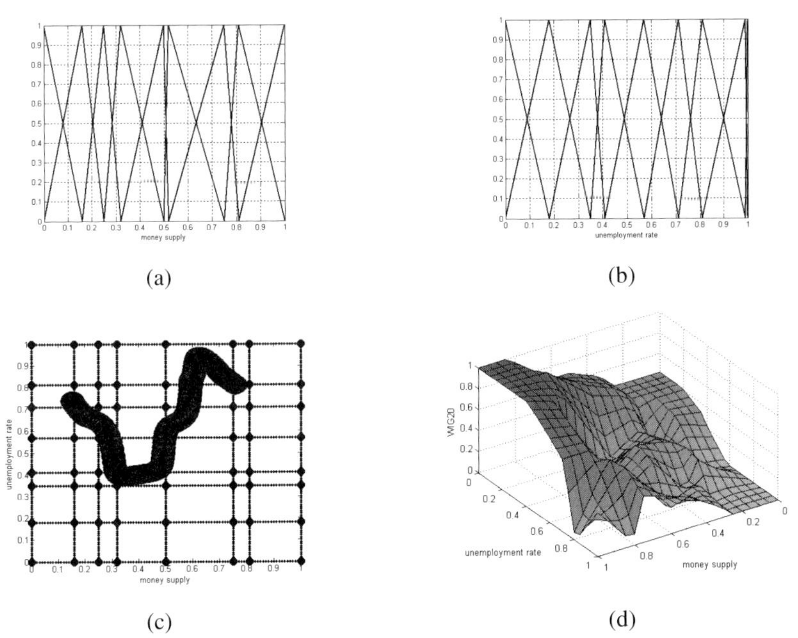

(a)

(b)

(c)

(d)

Fig. 5. Model 3 – a) membership functions of *money supply* (on the left) and *unemployment rate* (on the right); b) model rule net and the interpolation region of D-model; c) model surface

Table 4. Model 3 – rule base (columns – *unemployment rate*, rows – *money supply*)

	0	0.18	0.35	0.41	0.57	0.71	0.81	1
0	0.42	0.42	0.32	0.21	0.00	0.00	0.00	0.00
0.16	0.42	0.42	0.37	0.32	0.03	0.16	0.02	0.00
0.25	0.42	0.42	0.00	0.08	0.33	0.27	0.00	0.00
0.32	0.55	0.55	0.35	0.38	0.37	0.00	0.19	0.11
0.5	0.68	0.68	0.16	0.19	0.46	0.38	0.02	0.30
0.75	0.68	1.00	0.84	0.00	0.04	0.11	0.63	0.45
0.81	1.00	1.00	0.92	0.89	0.77	0.68	0.67	0.04
1	1.00	1.00	1.00	1.00	0.84	0.68	0.55	0.42

5 Models Comparison

The performance of models described in three previous sections was compared on the basis of the testing set created in the first stage of estimating D-model parameters. The testing set was composed of two subsets:

- a subset of six data points chosen randomly from the inner months (data from this subset were situated between data from the training set),
- a subset containing data points from six last analyzed months (data from this subset were situated outside the training set).

This supervised data selection was necessary to test the models performance in two opposite situations, it is in an interpolation situation (the first part of the testing set) and in an extrapolation situation (the second part of the testing set).

Testing results for all three models are presented in Tab. 5. As it can be noticed in this table, the performance of D-model was very well in case of data points coming from the first subset of the testing set (MAE = 2.62%) and very poor in case of data points coming from the second subset (MAE = 24.71%). On the opposite, the performance of E-model was very well in case of data points coming from the second subset (MAE = 3.15%) and average in case of data points coming from the first subset (MAE = 8.32%). These results support the fact mentioned in Sect. 4 that *while D-model produces credible results only for data situated inside its interpolation region, E-model gives results credible in the whole, physically possible, input domain but not as precise as D-model results.*

The most important part of Tab. 5 is obviously the last column which presents errors of the combined model. This time the model results are correct ones in case of both parts of testing set (MAE of the first part is equal to 2.69% and MAE of the second part is equal to 3.45%). These results mean that *the combined model, integrating rule bases of the expert model and the model built on the basis of the data set can be successfully used as well in interpolation situations as in extrapolation ones.*

It should be also underlined here, that taking into account the whole testing set composed of 12 data points, the performance of the combined model (MAE = 3.07) was in 77.54% better than the performance of the model built on the basis of the data set (MAE = 13.66%) and in 46.53% better than the performance of the expert model (MAE = 5.74%).

Table 5. Testing results

No.	Error of D-model	Error of E-model	Error of combined model
1	2,84%	5,09%	0,83%
2	4,67%	11,27%	3,38%
3	2,28%	7,99%	4,38%
4	3,27%	12,28%	1,28%
5	0,24%	9,62%	1,06%
6	2,41%	3,68%	5,18%
7	8,89%	6,42%	6,32%
8	18,21%	3,69%	4,24%
9	26,72%	1,55%	2,68%
10	32,21%	0,33%	0,90%
11	38,99%	4,21%	3,37%
12	23,22%	2,72%	3,20%

6   Conclusion

The comparison of testing results presented in Sect. 5 proves that rule bases integration is not just a waste of time but gives real practical advantages. First of all the overall testing error of the combined model was significantly smaller than errors of both preliminary models (more than 75% smaller in case of D-model and almost 50% smaller in case of E-model). Such significant reduction in error value is very important when a model is to be used in practical applications. Secondly, due to rule bases integration, the combined fuzzy model could be successfully used in both – interpolation and extrapolation situations. This feature of the rule bases integration is very important because it removes limitations of the applicability of a model based on a data set.

It should be underlined here that the method of rule bases integration applied in the paper is only one proposition for integrating rule bases of an expert model and a model built on the bases of a data set. The author of this paper proposed also two other methods for dealing with this task, one of them is described in [7].

References

1. Abonyi, J., Roubos, H., Babuka, R., Szeifert, F.: Interpretable Semi-Mechanistic Fuzzy Models by Clustering, OLS and FIS Model Reduction, ch. 10. In: Casillas, J., Cordon, O., Herrera, F., Magdalena, L. (eds.) Modeling and the interpretability-accuracy trade-off. Part I, Interpretability Issues. Studies in Fuzziness and Soft Computing, Physica-Verlag (2003)
2. Aczel, A.D.: Complete Business Statistics. Richard D. Irwin Inc., Sydney (1993)
3. Lindskog, P.: Fuzzy Identification from a Grey Box Modeling Point of View. In: Hellendoorn, H., Driankov, D. (eds.) Fuzzy Model Identification, pp. 3–50. Springer, Heidelberg (1997)
4. Masters, T.: Practical Neural Networks Recipes in C++. Academic Press Inc., London (1993)

5. Pham, T., Chen, G.: Some applications of fuzzy logic in rule-based expert systems. Expert Systems 19(4) (September 2002)
6. Rejer, I.: Integration of fuzzy rule bases. Polish Journal of Environmental Studies 16(5B) (2007)
7. Rejer, I.: An Approach to Integrating Rule Bases in a Fuzzy Expert System. In: Świątek, J., Borzemski, L., Grzech, A., Wilimowska, Z. (eds.) Information Systems Architecture and Technology, Wrocław University of Technology, Wrocław (2007)
8. Rejer, I., Mikołajczyk, M.: A Hypertube as a Possible Interpolation Region of a Neural Model. In: Rutkowski, L., Tadeusiewicz, R., Zadeh, L.A., Żurada, J.M. (eds.) ICAISC 2006. LNCS (LNAI), vol. 4029, Springer, Heidelberg (2006)
9. Wang, Ch., Hong, T., Tseng, S.: Integrating membership functions and fuzzy rule sets from multiple knowledge sources. Fuzzy Sets and Systems 112 (2000)

Fuzzy Analytical Hierarchy Process in Maintenance Problem

Mª Socorro García-Cascales[1] and Mª Teresa Lamata[2]

[1] Dpto de Electrónica, Tecnología de Computadoras y Proyectos. Universidad de Politécnica de Cartagena. Murcia, España
socorro.garcia@upct.es
[2] Dpto. Ciencias de la Computación e Inteligencia Artificial. Universidad de Granada. 18071-Granada. España
mtl@decsai.ugr.es

Abstract. This paper proposes the use of Multi-Criteria Analysis for management maintenance processes where only linguistic information was available because this was the type of data provided by the company. We are interested on the problems related to pieces with diverse degrees of dirt. In this direction, we propose and evaluate a maintenance decision problem in an engine factory that is specialized in production, sale and maintenance of four stroke engines; medium and slow speed. In our case, Multiple Criteria Decision-Making refers to making optimal decisions over a finite number of available alternatives and criteria.

Keywords: Multiple Criteria Decision-Making, fuzzy numbers, Maintenance Problem, AHP.

1   Introduction

The industrial organization needs to develop better methods for evaluating the performance of its projects. We are going to study a decision problem in maintenance in an engine factory (see fig 1), that is specialized in production, sale and maintenance of four-stroke diesel engines for naval applications, tank propulsion, electricity generating plants, turnkey cogeneration plants, and rail traction.

Since the company has a military character, it prefers to remain anonymous and not to provide details of itself.

One of the most important steps that must be carried out in an engine maintenance and repair process is to clean each individual component. In order to test and recondition each component, it is essential that all the parts be cleaned to the highest possible standards or the repair process will by unsuccessful.

Chlorinated products are currently used to clean the parts and there are two tanks for this purpose: the first contains trichloroethylene and is used as a general degreaser, and the second is a decarburizing tank for stripping paint and decarburisation.

The main feature of these products is that they are able to efficiently remove grease and are relatively economical. They do, however, have other drawbacks which lead us to question their suitability: Environmental disadvantages and health disadvantages.

N.T. Nguyen et al. (Eds.): IEA/AIE 2008, LNAI 5027, pp. 815–824, 2008.
© Springer-Verlag Berlin Heidelberg 2008

We therefore believe that it is necessary to study the problem of selecting a cleaning system by considering the environment assessment that this decision involves.

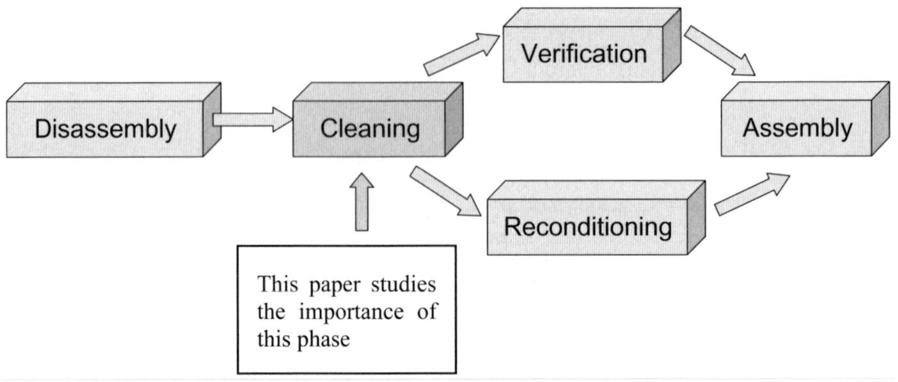

Fig. 1. Phases in the process of maintenance in a engine factory

A considerable number of works have been aimed at accommodating multiple criteria decision making (MCDM) models into engineering decision problems, in order to arrive at more concrete solutions [18]. Decision-making problems are those processes of finding the best option from all of the feasible alternatives. In almost all such problems the multiplicity of criteria for judging the alternatives is pervasive.

As it is well known, the Analytic Hierarchy Process (AHP) [16,17] is a simple MCDM to deal with unstructured and multi attribute problems which was developed by Saaty and consists of decomposing a complex problem into its components, organizing the components into levels to generate a hierarchical structure. The aim of constructing this hierarchy is to determine the impact of the lower level on an upper level, which is achieved by paired comparisons provided by the decision-maker. In this case the AHP was used in order to structuring and clarifying the preferences in a decision problem in maintenance. [1,3,5,10,11,19]

In classical MCDM methods [14,15], the ratings and the weights of the criteria are known precisely. But in many practical situations, the human preference model is uncertain and decision makers might be unable to assign exact numerical values to the comparison judgments. Given the subjective and qualitative nature of some service evaluation criteria, a decision maker finds it extremately difficult to express the strength of these preferences and to provide exact pair-wise comparison judgments.

Under many conditions, crisp data are inadequate to model real-life situations because human judgements including preferences are often vague and cannot be estimated with an exact numerical value.

The purpose of this paper is to contribute in a maintenance problem, as a structure of preference AHP with fuzzy numbers that interpret and describe better the human behaviour. [2,9]

The rest of the paper is organized as follows: The next section explain the necessary considerations on fuzzy numbers. In the following section, we describe the Fuzzy Analytic Hierarchy Process (FAHP) methodology related with the real problem in question which is study in the next one. Finally, in last section the most important conclusions and issues for further research are presented.

2 Fuzzy Set Theory

In order to overcome the above shortcoming, the fuzzy logic principle was introduced into the AHP for multi-criteria decision-making. This makes it possible to adopt the AHP in an environment where the input information or the relations between criteria and alternatives are uncertain or imprecise.

The fuzzy set theory, introduced by Zadeh (1965) [20] to deal with vague, imprecise and uncertain problems, has been used as a modelling tool for complex systems that can be controlled by humans but are hard to define precisely. A collection of objects (universe of discourse) X has a fuzzy set A described by a membership function f_A with values in the interval $(0,1)$: $f_A : X \rightarrow (0,1)$. Thus A can be represented as $A = \{f_A(x)/x,\ where\ x \in X\}$. The degree that u belongs to A is the membership function $f_A(x)$.

In this paper, with the support of the fuzzy set theory, triangular fuzzy numbers, which are parameterised by triplet numbers, are used to represent the importance and alternative performance of evaluation criteria as well as to construct the pair-wise comparison matrix. Therefore, the relative importance contribution in the adjacent upper level can be described as gradual and not abrupt, and this gives a more exact representation of the relationship between candidate alternatives and the evaluation criteria. The basic theory of the triangular fuzzy number is described as follows.

Definition 1. A real fuzzy number A is described as any fuzzy subset of the real line $\Re$ with membership function f_A which processes the following properties:

(a) $f_A(x)$ is a continuous mapping from $\Re$ to the closed interval $[0, 1]$;

(b) $f_A(x) = 0$, for all $x \in (-\infty, a]$;

(c) $f_A(x)$ is strictly increasing on $[a, b]$;

(d) $f_A(x) = w$, for all $x \in [b, c]$;

(e) $f_A(x)$ is strictly decreasing on $[c, d]$;

(f) $f_A(x) = 0$, for all $x \in (d, \infty]$,

where a, b, c, d are real numbers.

Definition 2. The fuzzy number A it will be triangular if its membership function is given by:

$$f_A(x) = \begin{cases} \dfrac{x-a}{b-a}, & a \leq x \leq b, \\[2mm] \dfrac{x-c}{b-c}, & b \leq x \leq c, \\[2mm] 0, & otherwise, \end{cases} \tag{1}$$

where a, b and c are real numbers. Then we designate A as the triangular fuzzy number. In this formula, c and a are the upper and lower values of the support of A, respectively, and b is the median value of A. The triangular fuzzy number is denoted as (a,b,c).

Definition 3. Let A and B be two positives triangular fuzzy numbers parameterized by the triplets (a_1, b_1, c_1) and (a_2, b_2, c_2) respectively [4]. Then

Fuzzy number addition $\oplus$

$$A \oplus B = [a_1 + a_2, b_1 + b_2, c_1 + c_2] \tag{2}$$

Fuzzy number multiplication $\otimes$

$$A \otimes B = [a_1 \times a_2, b_1 \times b_2, c_1 \times c_2] \tag{3}$$

Fuzzy number division $\varnothing$

$$A \varnothing B = \left[[a_1, b_1, c_1] \cdot [1/c_2, 1/b_2, 1/a_2] \right] \quad 0 \neq [a_2, b_2, c_2] \tag{4}$$

3   The Methodology of the Fuzzy-AHP

The Fuzzy-AHP extends Saaty's AHP by combining with fuzzy set theory. In the FAHP, fuzzy ratio scales are used to indicate the relative strength of the factors in the corresponding criteria, thereby constructing the fuzzy judgement matrix. The final scores of alternatives are represented in terms of fuzzy numbers. The optimum alternative is obtained by ranking the fuzzy numbers.

The working procedure of the FAHP is shown in Figure 2 and can be describes as follows:

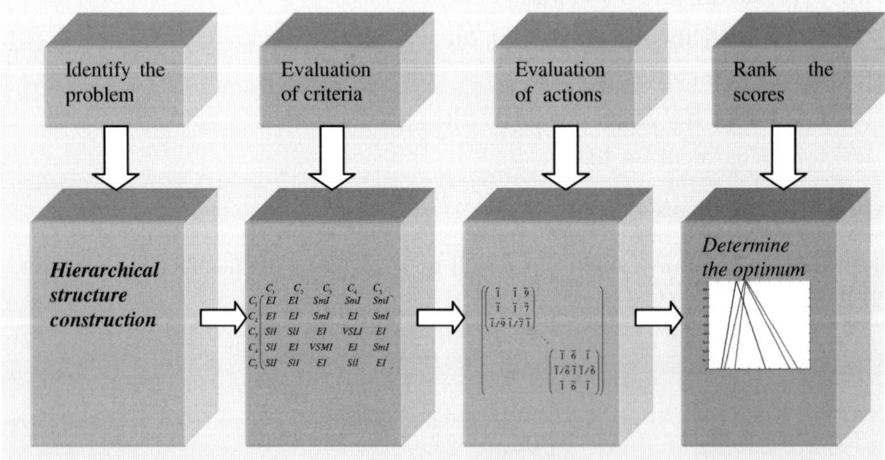

Fig. 2. Representation of the structure in the fuzzy analytic hierarchy process

Application of FAHP to a decision problem involves five steps:

Step 1: Hierarchical structure construction
   Structuring the decision problem into a hierarchical model.

- Define the problem clearly with specifications on its multi-criteria aspects.
- Determine the overall goal and sub-goals, identifying the evaluation criteria.
- Identify the candidate alternatives
- Construct the hierarchy, in which the overall goal (usually the selection of the best alternative) is situated at the highest level; elements with similar features (usually evaluation criteria) are grouped at the same interim level and decision variables (usually alternatives) are situated at the lowest level

Step 2: Constructing the evaluation of the linguistic terms.
   In this paper, all elements in the judgement matrix and weight vectors are represented by triangular fuzzy numbers, a fuzzy number $\tilde{x}$ expresses the meaning "about x". Each membership function is defined by three parameters (a, b, c). The meaning of fuzzy numbers $\tilde{1}$, $\tilde{3}, \tilde{5}, \tilde{7}$ and $\tilde{9}$ represent equal important, weak important, essential important, demonstrated important and extreme important, respectively. The values $\tilde{2}, \tilde{4}, \tilde{6}$ *and* $\tilde{8}$ represent the intermediate values for comparison. In this context, a fuzzy number is given by means of the following equations $\tilde{1} \equiv (1,1,1), \tilde{x} \equiv (x\text{-}1,\ x,\ x\text{+}1)\ \forall\ x=2,3,...,8$ and $\tilde{9} \equiv (8, 9, 9)$.

Step 3: Constructing the fuzzy judgement matrix A and weight vector W for the hierarchical structure.
   In this step, making pair-wise comparisons the elements of a particular level are compared with respect to a specific element in the immediate upper level [13,14]. Usually, an element which receives higher rating is viewed as superior (or more attractive) compared to another one that receives a lower rating. The comparisons are used to form a matrix of pair-wise comparisons called the judgement matrix A. Each entry a_{ij} of the judgements matrix are governed by the three rules: $a_{ij} > 0$; $a_{ij} = 1/a_{ji}$; $a_{ii} = 1$ for all i. The resulting weights of the elements may be called the local weights. (to be contrasted with final weights, discussed in Step 5)

Step 4: Calculating the final scores of candidate alternatives.
   Set the weight vector W made up of evaluation criteria as $\left[\tilde{w}_i\right]_{nx1}$. W^T is the transpose of the weight vector W and it can be shown as $\left[\tilde{w}_i\right]_{nx1}$. The fuzzy judgement matrix A is made up of candidate alternatives $[A_1, A_2, ...,A_m]$ and the evaluation criteria is given as $\left[\tilde{a}_i\right]_{mxn}$, then the final score S of alternatives can be calculated as follows [6]:

$$A = \left[\tilde{a}_{ij}\right]_{mxn} = \begin{bmatrix} \tilde{a}_{11} & \tilde{a}_{12} & \cdots & \tilde{a}_{1n} \\ \tilde{a}_{21} & \tilde{a}_{22} & \cdots & \tilde{a}_{2n} \\ \vdots & \vdots & \vdots & \vdots \\ \tilde{a}_{m1} & \tilde{a}_{m2} & \cdots & \tilde{a}_{mn} \end{bmatrix}, \quad W = \left[\tilde{w}_j\right]_{1xn} = \begin{bmatrix} \tilde{w}_1 & \tilde{w}_2 & \cdots & \tilde{w}_n \end{bmatrix}, \text{ and } W^T = \begin{bmatrix} \tilde{w}_1 \\ \tilde{w}_2 \\ \vdots \\ \tilde{w}_n \end{bmatrix},$$

Then

$$S = A \otimes W^T = \begin{bmatrix} \tilde{a}_{11} & \tilde{a}_{12} & \cdots & \tilde{a}_{1n} \\ \tilde{a}_{21} & \tilde{a}_{22} & \cdots & \tilde{a}_{2n} \\ \vdots & \vdots & \vdots & \vdots \\ \tilde{a}_{m1} & \tilde{a}_{m2} & \cdots & \tilde{a}_{mn} \end{bmatrix} \otimes \begin{bmatrix} \tilde{w}_1 \\ \tilde{w}_2 \\ \vdots \\ \tilde{w}_n \end{bmatrix} = \begin{bmatrix} \tilde{a}_{11} \otimes \tilde{w}_1 \odot \tilde{a}_{12} \otimes \tilde{w}_2 \odot \cdots \odot \tilde{a}_{1n} \otimes \tilde{w}_n \\ \tilde{a}_{21} \otimes \tilde{w}_1 \odot \tilde{a}_{22} \otimes \tilde{w}_2 \odot \cdots \odot \tilde{a}_{2n} \otimes \tilde{w}_n \\ \vdots \\ \tilde{a}_{m1} \otimes \tilde{w}_1 \odot \tilde{a}_{m2} \otimes \tilde{w}_2 \odot \cdots \odot \tilde{a}_{mn} \otimes \tilde{w}_n \end{bmatrix} = \begin{bmatrix} \tilde{s}_1 \\ \tilde{s}_2 \\ \vdots \\ \tilde{s}_m \end{bmatrix},$$

where $\tilde{w}_j$ is the relative importance of the jth evaluation criterion $\tilde{a}_{ij}$ is the relative importance of the ith alternative A_i corresponding to the jth evaluation criterion and $\tilde{s}_i$ is the final fuzzy score of candidate alternative A_i. Depending of the operator $\odot$ we can obtain different possible solutions.

Step 5: Ranking of the fuzzy numbers.

Since a fuzzy number represents the fuzzy synthetic decision reached for each alternative, we need to defuzzify these fuzzy numbers in order to compare the alternatives in a non-fuzzy ranking method. For this, in a previous work we proposed [7] the following expression.

$$I_{\beta,\lambda}(A_i) = \beta S_M(A_i) + (1-\beta)\lambda S_R(A_i) + (1-\beta)(1-\lambda)S_L(A_i) \tag{5}$$

when $S_R(A_i)$ represents the upper mean value, $S_L(A_i)$ is the lower mean value and $S_M(A_i)$ is the area to the middle point of core of the fuzzy number, β is the index of modality $\beta \in [0,1]$ that represent the importance of the central value front extreme values and λ is the decision maker's index $\lambda \in [0,1]$.

4 Empirical Study: A Real Problem in an Engine Factory

Due to the confidentiality of the information and taking into account the characteristics of the military company the decision-maker is not capable of defining in a strict way the importance of the criteria and how good the alternatives are. In this situation, we use quantities -linguistic terms- that are not exact but approximate and which are adjusted to the reality. Thus, we assume that the evaluations of the alternatives are represented by fuzzy numbers.

The problem consists of a certain type of part of a particular size and with a specific level of dirt that must be removed. The characteristics that affect the cleaning system are: type of dirt, size of part, number of parts to clean, and what the parts are made of. Faced with the problem of the parts having different levels of dirt and being of different shapes, the work process demands speed and flexibility. Criteria such as the total annual operation cost (C_1), system productivity (C_2), cleaning efficiency (C_3) and harmful effects (C_4) of the products used must be taken into account. The alternatives are:

    (A_1) Conventional cleaning: This group includes the industrial cleaning machines that apply pressurized cleaning solution to the part, and the applied product is basically water and detergent with a specific cleaning additive.

    (A_2) Chemical cleaning: This consists of the application of an aggressive chemical product to the part in order to dissolve dirt by immersion in a tank.

(A_3) Ultrasonic cleaning: This combines the action of a conventional detergent and the mechanical action of the shock waves and cavitations that occur in the recipient containing the part.

The global objective of the problem is to decide the best pasts cleaning system.

Taking into account the information and that exposed in the step 2 of the methodology the fuzzy judgement matrix A and weight vector W is constructing for the hierarchical structure.

Table 1. Pair-wise comparison of the criteria with respect to the goal. Computing the local priority vector.

	C_1	C_2	C_3	C_4	C_5	Average	Normalized
C_1	$\tilde{1}$	$\tilde{2}$	$\tilde{4}$	$\tilde{3}$	$\tilde{3}$	(1.6437,2.3521,2.9925)	(0.2013,0.3914,0.7055)
C_2	$\tilde{1}/\tilde{2}$	$\tilde{1}$	$\tilde{3}$	$\tilde{2}$	$\tilde{3}$	(1.0592,1.5518,2.1690)	(0.1297,0.2583,0.5114)
C_3	$\tilde{1}/\tilde{4}$	$\tilde{1}/\tilde{3}$	$\tilde{1}$	$\tilde{1}/\tilde{4}$	$\tilde{1}/\tilde{2}$	(0.3196,0.4014,0.5610)	(0.0392,0.0668,0.1323)
C_4	$\tilde{1}/\tilde{3}$	$\tilde{1}/\tilde{2}$	$\tilde{4}$	$\tilde{1}$	$\tilde{2}$	(0.7579,1.0592,1.4963)	(0.0928,0.1763,0.3528)
C_5	$\tilde{1}/\tilde{3}$	$\tilde{1}/\tilde{3}$	$\tilde{2}$	$\tilde{1}/\tilde{2}$	$\tilde{1}$	(0.4611,0.6444,0.9441)	(0.0565,0.1072,0.2226)
						(4.2415,6,0090,8.1629)	

Table 2. Pair-wise comparison of the alternatives with respect to the criteria. Computing the local priority vector.

C_1		A_1	A_2	A_3	Geometric Average	Normalized
	A_1	$\tilde{1}$	$\tilde{1}$	$\tilde{9}$	(2.0000,2.0801,2.0801)	(0.4592,0.4901,0.5127)
	A_2	$\tilde{1}$	$\tilde{1}$	$\tilde{7}$	(1.8171,1.9129,2.0000	(0.4172,0.4507,0.4929)
	A_3	$\tilde{1}/\tilde{9}$	$\tilde{1}/\tilde{7}$	$\tilde{1}$	(0.2404,0.2513,0.2752)	(0.0552,0.0592,0.0678)
C_2					(4.0575,4.2443,4.3552)	
	A_1	$\tilde{1}$	$\tilde{1}/\tilde{5}$	$\tilde{1}/\tilde{8}$	(0.2646,0.2924,0.3293)	(0.0493,0.0601,0.0754)
	A_2	$\tilde{5}$	$\tilde{1}$	$\tilde{1}/\tilde{6}$	(0.8298,0.9410,1.0627)	(0.1545,0.1933,0.2434)
	A_3	$\tilde{8}$	$\tilde{6}$	$\tilde{1}$	(3.2711,3.6342,3.9791)	(0.6090,0.7466,0.9115)
C_3					(4.3655,4.8677,5.3710)	
	A_1	$\tilde{1}$	$\tilde{1}/\tilde{7}$	$\tilde{1}/\tilde{5}$	(0.2752,0.3057,0.3467)	(0.0554,0.0719,0.0973)
	A_2	$\tilde{7}$	$\tilde{1}$	$\tilde{3}$	(2.2894,2.7589,3.1748)	(0.4612,0.6491,0.8907)
	A_3	$\tilde{5}$	$\tilde{1}/\tilde{3}$	$\tilde{1}$	(1.0000,1.1856,1.4422)	(0.2015,0.2790,0.4046)
C_4					(3.5646,4.2503,4.9637)	
	A_1	$\tilde{1}$	$\tilde{1}/\tilde{7}$	$\tilde{1}/\tilde{8}$	(0.2404,0.2614,0.2877)	(0.0550,0.0626,0.0725)
	A_2	$\tilde{7}$	$\tilde{1}$	$\tilde{1}$	(1.8171,1.9129,2.0000)	(0.4160,0.4583,0.5037)
	A_3	$\tilde{8}$	$\tilde{1}$	$\tilde{1}$	(1.9129,2.0000,2.0801)	(0.4380,0.4791,0.5239)
C_5					(3.9704,4.1743,4.3678)	
	A_1	$\tilde{1}$	$\tilde{6}$	$\tilde{1}$	(1.7100,1.8171,1.9129)	(0.4103,0.4920,0.5180)
	A_2	$\tilde{1}/\tilde{6}$	$\tilde{1}$	$\tilde{1}/\tilde{6}$	(0.2733,0.3029,0.3420)	(0.0656,0.0820,0.0926)
	A_3	$\tilde{1}$	$\tilde{6}$	$\tilde{1}$	(1.7100,1.8171,1.9129)	(0.4103,0.4920,0.5180)
					(3.6932,3.9371,4.1679)	

Table 3. Computing the global priority vector of C_j with the priority vectors for A_i

Local solution	A_1	A_2	A_3
C1	(0.0924,0.1918,0.3617)	(0.0840,0.1764,0.3478)	(0.0111,0.0232,0.0478)
C2	(0.0064,0.0156,0.0386)	(0.0200,0.0499,0.1245)	(0.0789,0.1928,0.4661)
C3	(0.0022,0.0048,0.0130)	(0.0181,0.0434,0.1178)	(0.0079,0.0186,0.0535)
C4	(0.0051,0.0111,0.0256)	(0.0386,0.0808,0.1777)	(0.0406,0.0845,0.1848)
C5	(0.0232,0.0528,0.1153)	(0.0037,0.0088,0.0206)	(0.0232,0.0528,0.1153)
	(0.1293,0.2760,0.5540)	(0.1645,0.3593,0.7884)	(0.1619,0.3718,0.8676)

Calculating the final scores of candidate alternatives. In particular, if in the expression (5), $\beta = 1/3$ and $\lambda = 1/2$ we obtain the index $I_{\beta,\lambda}(A_i)$ as mean of the three areas.

$$I_{1/3,1/2}(A_i) = \frac{1}{3}\left(S_L(A_i) + S_M(A_i) + S_R(A_i)\right) \tag{6}$$

Being the final results the followings:

Table 4. Final results

	Global Priority	Figure	$I_{1/3,1/2}(A_i)$	ranking
A_1	(0.1293,0.2760,0.5540)		0.2979	3
A_2	(0.1645,0.3593,0.7884)		0.3983	2
			0.4044	1
A_3	(0.1619,0.3718,0.8676)			

Ranking. We have used the fuzzy analytic hierarchy process to determine the weighted of subjective judgments and to derive the rankings of the alternatives

$$A_3 > A_2 > A_1$$

5   Conclusions

In this paper we have studied a problem of maintenance management, the selection of a cleaning system for pieces of four stroke engines. A linguistic decision process is proposed to solve the multi-criteria decision-making problem under fuzzy environment. Considering the fuzziness in the linguistic terms, these variables are used to assess the weights of all criteria and the ratings of each alternative in terms of every criterion.

We have proposed an analysis with linguistic labels (fuzzy numbers) because the company preferred not to give another type of data. As the table 4 show, we can admit that the order of the alternatives is the following

$$A_3 > A_2 > A_1$$

For the decision-maker the best option was $\mathbf{A_3}$ *the ultrasonic cleaning,* because it is the best solution for all the criteria specially for the healthiness criterion and the decision-maker do not take into account another counterpart of this alternative while *the chemical cleaning* A_2 is a good option to the decision-maker but it has the problem of the healthiness, and finally the conventional cleaning A_1 can not to solve any problem.

It is well known, the wide applicability of FAHP [12,21] is due to its simplicity, ease of use, and great flexibility. In this way, it is possible to be integrating with other different techniques to obtain the aggregation of the preferences, for instance, arithmetic mean, harmonic mean, and so one are possible.

Also it is possible a comparative study with the expression (5) when we consider different values in the index of modality and in the degree of optimism of the decision maker's given by means of the parameters β and λ, respectively. In this way, it is possible that the ranking of the alternatives is not the same.

The same problem is also possible to apply to other multicriteria analyses for the evaluation of the criteria and alternatives such as the classical pair-wise comparison method, the TOPSIS method or a combination of both [8]

Acknowledgements. This work is partially supported by the DGICYT and Junta de Andalucía under projects TIN2005-08404-C04-01 and TIC-00129-JA, respectively.

References

1. Al Harbi, K.M.A.: Application of the AHP in project management. International Journal of Project Management 19(1), 19–27 (2001)
2. Bellman, R., Zadeh, L.A.: Decision making in a fuzzy environment. Management Science 17, 141–164 (1970)
3. Chan, F.T.S., Chan, M.H., Tang, N.K.H.: Evaluation methodologies for technology selection. Journal of Materials Processing Technology 107, 330–337 (2000a)
4. Chen, S.M.: Evaluating weapon systems using fuzzy arithmetic operations. Fuzzy Sets and Systems 77, 265–276 (1996)
5. Cheng, C.-H., Yang, K.-L., Hwang, C.-L.: Evaluating attack helicopters by AHP based on linguistic variable weight. European Journal of Operation al Research 116(2), 423–435 (1999)
6. Deng, H.: Multicriteria analysis with fuzzy pairwise comparison. International Journal of Approximate Reasoning 21(3), 215–231 (1999)
7. García-Cascales, M.S., Lamata, M.T.: A modification of the index of Liou and Wang for ranking fuzzy number. International Journal of Uncertainty Fuzzyness and Knowledge-based Systems 15(4), 411–424 (2007)
8. García-Cascales, M.S., Lamata, M.T.: Solving a decisión problem with linguistic information. Pattern Recognition Letters (28), 2284–2294 (2007)
9. Hauser, D., Tadikamalla, P.: The analytic hierarchy process in an uncertain environment: a simulation approach. European Journal of Operational Research 91(1), 27–37 (1996)
10. Kablan, M.M.: Decision support for energy conservation promotion: an analytic hierarchy process approach. Energy Policy 32(10), 1151–1158 (2004)
11. Labib, A.W., O'Connor, R.F., Williams, G.B.: Effective maintenance system using the analytic hierarchy process. Integrated Manufacturing Systems 9(2), 87–98 (1998)
12. Lee, W.B., Lau, H., Liu, Z.Z., Tam, S.: A fuzzy analytic hierarchy process approach in modular product design. Expert Systems 18(1), 887–896 (2001)

13. Lipovetsky, S., Conklin, W.M.: Decision Aiding. Robust estimation of priorities in the AHP. European Journal of Operational Research 137, 110–122 (2002)
14. Lootsma, F.: Multi-Criteria Decision Analysis via Ratio and Difference Judgement. Kluwer Academic Publishers, Dordrecht (1999)
15. Luce, R.D., Raiffa, H.: Games and Decisions: Introduction and Critical Survey. John Wiley and Sons, New York (1967)
16. Saaty, T.L.: The Analytic Hierarchy Process. Mcgraw Hill, New York (1980)
17. Saaty, T.L.: Group Decision Making and the AHP. Springer, New York (1989)
18. Triantaphyllou, E.: Multi-Criteria decision making methods: A comparative study. Kluwer Academic, The Netherlands (2000)
19. Triantaphyllou, E., Mann, S.H.: Using the Analytic Hierarchy process for decision making in engineering applications: some challenges. International Journal of Industrial Engineering: Applications and Practice 2(1), 35–44 (1995)
20. Zadeh, L.A.: Fuzzy Sets. Information and Control 8, 338–353 (1965)
21. Zhu, K.-J., Jing, Y., Chang, D.-Y.: A discussion of extent analysis method and applications of fuzzy AHP. European Journal of Operational Research 116, 450–456 (1999)

Proposal for Agent Platform Dynamic Interoperation Facilitating Mechanism

Xiaolu Li, Takahiro Uchiya, Susumu Konno, and Tetsuo Kinoshita

Graduate School of Information Sciences, Tohoku University
littledeer@ka.riec.tohoku.ac.jp,
t-uchiya@nitech.ac.jp,
skonno@ka.riec.tohoku.ac.jp,
kino@riec.tohoku.ac.jp

Abstract. Interoperability among agent platforms is important for making full use of each platform's problem-solving capabilities. It is also crucial to the upper layer interoperations (re-organization, negotiation, etc.). Static interoperation as enabled by pre-configuration has been proposed and implemented, although no satisfactory mechanism for dynamic interoperation is available. We propose a mechanism to facilitate the dynamic interoperation between agents situated in different computers by discovering the underlying agent platforms and using that information to enable and support the interoperation process.

Keywords: Agent platform, Interoperability, Dynamic interoperation, Platform discovery.

1   Introduction

Many multi-agent platforms have been recently proposed and implemented. Many approaches related to the interoperability[1] [2] have been discussed. The following platforms are typical ones: JADE[3] is a popular FIPA[4] compliant platform, maintained by open source project; DASH[5] is specialized in intelligent knowledge processing; and SAGE[6] is a lightweight FIPA-compliant platform that is maintained by open source project.

Among those studies, FIPA's contribution is particularly worth mentioning. In fact, FIPA has made a great contribution to improving interoperability by making progress in many aspects[7]. However, the implementation details of specifications such as Message Transport Service (MTS), Agent Management Service (AMS), and Directory Facilitator (DF) are not restrictively set. Therefore, MTS, AMS, and DF related parts might be implemented with different protocols by different developers. Consequently, even if two MAS platforms are FIPA-compliant, they can not mutually connect when the system is started. Moreover, they can not start interoperation immediately without configuring the communication channel before runtime. Accordingly, the upper layer interaction or application can not perform automatically and dynamically.

N.T. Nguyen et al. (Eds.): IEA/AIE 2008, LNAI 5027, pp. 825–834, 2008.

An experiment conducted by AgentCities[1] achieved interoperation between the different agent platforms (All FIPA-compliant platforms) by introducing Ping-Agents into each platform, but that depends on *static* pre-configuration. Such an approach is effective only when all the attending computing resources for a certain application and how nodes mutually interact are known a priori. This is not flexible, especially in a constantly changing environment.

Two types of interoperation exist: *static* interoperation and *dynamic* interoperation. Achievement of what we have gained is only in the *static* interoperation domain. Here we define *dynamic* interoperation as "an interoperation capable of automatic re-configuration at runtime when agent components are changed". In contrast, the *static* interoperation is "an interoperation realized by pre-configuration of the system composition and is not capable of automatic re-configuration at runtime".

The problem that we must solve is to provide a mechanism for dynamic agent platform discovery, so that we can collect agent platform information. Without platform information, it will be difficult to re-configure the agent application using scattered agent resources because the platform is always providing a communication channel for agents.

For that reason, we propose a new mechanism to facilitate the *dynamic* interoperation process. The system comprises the following components:

- S1) Agent Platform Discovery Service
  - Collecting and storing of agent platform information
  - Exchanging and sharing of agent platform information
- S2) Agent Communication Facilitator
  - Agent platform information cache
  - Agent information cache
  - Agent service information cache

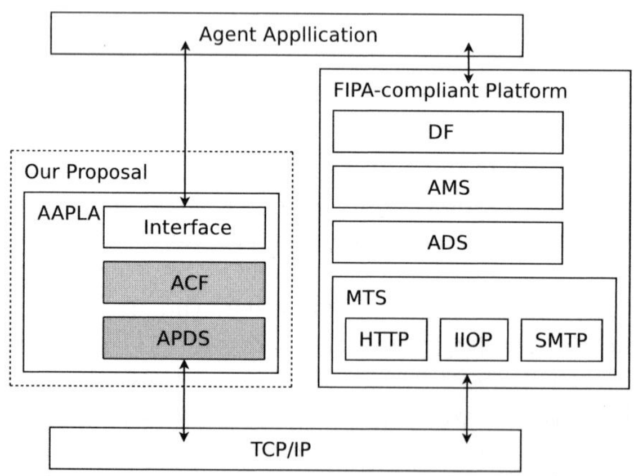

Fig. 1. Proposed AAPLA and FIPA-compliant Platform

2   Proposed Architecture

We name our proposed mechanism the Automatic Agent Platform Locator and Affiliator (AAPLA), the relationship between the AAPLA and FIPA-compliant platform is presented in Fig. 1.

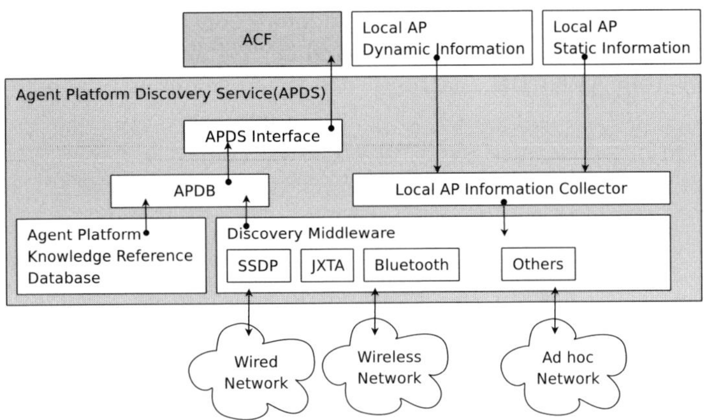

Fig. 2. Conceptual Scheme of APDS

2.1   Agent Platform Discovery Service

The Agent Platform Discovery Service (APDS) exchanges and shares information related to agent platforms, as shown in Fig. 2. It comprises the following parts:

- Local Agent Platform Information Collector (LPIC)
  The LPIC collects both *static* and *dynamic* information of the local platform. Subsequently, it formats and serializes the information and passes it to the Discovery Middleware (DM).
    - Platform Static Information: All the platform property information that will not change at runtime. For example: Basic property information such as the platform name, platform version information, implemented communication protocol, communication port number, etc.
    - Platform Dynamic Information: All platform property information that are changed during runtime, e.g., information related to the system load, currently available agent-providing services, number of agents, or even the QoS information of agent services.
- Discovery Middleware (DM)
  Actually, DM is responsible for proliferating and sharing both the *static* information and *dynamic* information. This module is an aggregation of a group of communicative modules. Communication modules can be implemented using one or more effective service discovery algorithms such as SSDP, JXTA, etc., which simplify expansion to other connection types to support future ubiquitous environments.

- Agent Platform Knowledge Reference Database (APKRDB)
  The APKRDB stores detailed static property information related to all known platforms, the information is large and not recommended to be transferred through DM because it consumes much more bandwidth.
- Agent Platform Database (APDB)
  A database (or simply a reference table) which stores all related information of currently available platforms in the inter-connected environment. It uses the basic property information gathered by DM, and seeks the full information set from APKRDB; moreover, it is dynamically maintained.

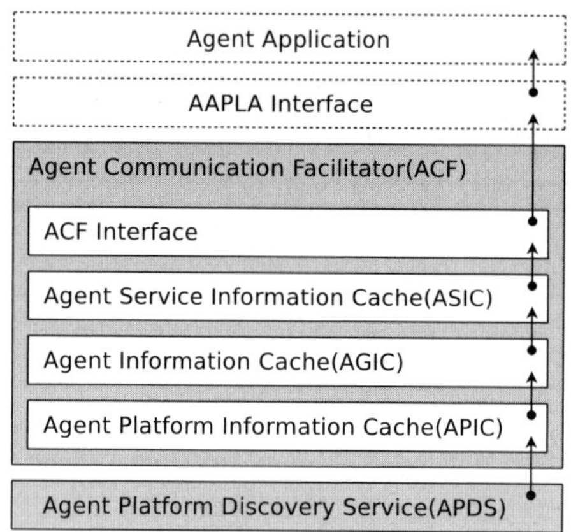

Fig. 3. Conceptual Scheme of ACF

2.2 Agent Communication Facilitator

The Agent Communication Facilitator (ACF) is responsible for transforming the discovered agent information into a recognizable form for local agents with the help of the APDS, as shown in Fig. 3. This transformation will simplify the interoperation process and remove the re-configuration steps during runtime.

- Agent Platform Information Cache (APIC)
  The APIC is responsible for processing and storing all the discovered platform information with which the local platform can interact. It always maintains the latest information. It will be filtered if the discovered platform can not be affiliated by the local platform, which will save processing time and reduce the processing load for the upper layers.
- Agent Information Cache (AGIC)
  The AGIC is responsible for processing and storing all agent information that the local agent can interact with. All agent information is gained from the platforms that is discovered and stored in the APIC. The AGIC always maintains the latest information of all known agents. It will be filtered to minimize the list size if the discovered agent information can not be used by the local agent (such as not-yet-supported-agent-type or any other reasons).

- Agent Service Information Cache (ASIC)
  The ASIC is responsible for processing and storing services provided by the agents who are discovered and stored in the AGIC.

After all processing by both the APDS and the ACF, we obtain all agent-provided-services in the inter-connected environment in AAPLA. For that reason, when we build our agent application with AAPLA, we need not know the location of the component agents or any other physical properties; developers can better focus on the application logic.

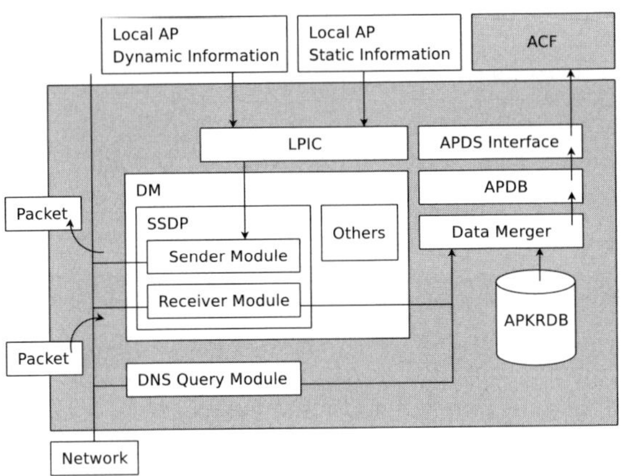

Fig. 4. APDS Implementation Design

3 Design and Implementation

Because several multi-agent platforms are based on their own original specifications, and are implemented with different languages, it is difficult to model a problem on various platforms. Therefore, we chose the FIPA-compliant platform SAGE as our testbed; we implemented our proposal in a LAN environment. The programming language is Java. Furthermore, DM is implemented with SSDP.

3.1 Design of APDS

Fig. 4 depicts the APDS design. When the platform is started, the attached AAPLA module starts too. Then the LPIC collects both the *static* information and the *dynamic* information of the platform; subsequently, the information is passed to the DM, which passes it to the communicative modules to proliferate and share the information with other AAPLA peers. The receivers of this information form complete platform information with reference to the APKRDB, and store the current available platform information into the APDB.

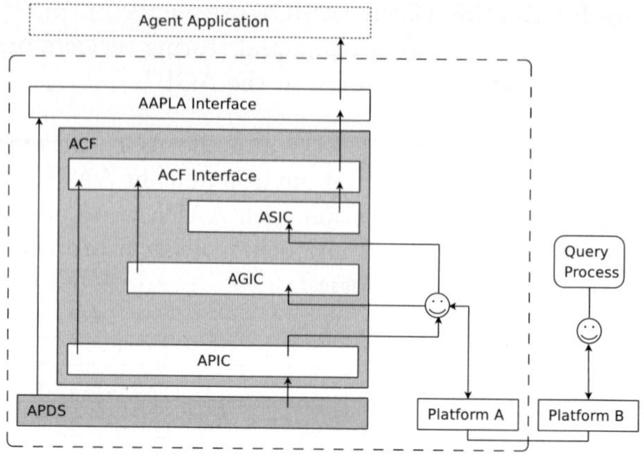

Fig. 5. ACF Implementation Design

3.2   Design of ACF

As depicted in Fig. 5, when an event arises from the APDS, it notifies that the other platform information is changed, this event is passed to the APIC, then the APIC composes the detailed access information of DF[1] for each discovered platform. In the following, we will show an example of how the basic information is used in the SAGE platform. First, when a platform is discovered, the platform name (such as "SAGE" or "JADE") is received along with the hostname and IP address of that platform. Then the ACF can compose the DF's name using the following rules. Furthermore, the transportation information can also be readily composed.

- DF Agent Name="DFAgent:"+reversed IP Address+"@"+hostname
- SAGE Agent Platform Transport=["http://"+IP Address+":666/acc"]

After these processes, "AAPLA agent" can communicate with the remote DF agent and achieve all the information related to agents and agent service on that platform.

In our ACF implementation, the query for remote agent information and agent service information is carried out through "AAPLA agent" which provides an agent interface and "talks" with remote DF agents. Because the AAPLA agent knows that the remote platform is FIPA-compliant, as mentioned in a previous example, it can compose a query message which can be understood by FIPA-compliant agents. After it receives the reply, the AAPLA agent stores the result (agent names of those situated in a remote platform) into the AGIC. This action triggers the AGIC to query for services provided by each agent. Before that occurs, the AGIC determines all the accessible or necessary agents. Then the AGIC uses the newly stored agent names as keywords to request their services. The AAPLA agent again plays the "talker" role to request agent services

---

[1] In the SAGE platform, DF is implemented as an agent.

information from the remote DF agent. At this time, the AAPLA receives the answer of *services name/agent name* pairs, and passes that information to the ASIC, which notifies all listeners to it. Any changes in the APDS notify the ACF timely; the ACF notifies its listeners as well.

4   Experiments and Evaluations

In this section, we will discuss the results of each experiment to verify each part's function.

4.1   Discovery Middleware Evaluation Experiment

- Purpose: To test the SSDP function of the DM.
- Experiment Description: Shut down or start up the test platforms; observe the received raw data at the observer platform.
- Result: We confirmed that the DM function is useful, and that the LPIC receives all information and proliferates it through the DM.
- Evaluation: All designed data are transferred and shared among nodes. Information such as "Hostname" and "IP Address" are obtained, which guarantees that the upper layer can compose the transport information for inter-agent communication.

4.2   Platform Discovery Evaluation Experiment

- Purpose: To test the agent platform discovery function.
- Experiment Description: Shutting down or starting up the test platforms, observe the state-changing information log at the observer platform.
- Result: We confirmed the timing by which a new platform is connected and disconnected. All this state information is maintained dynamically.
- Evaluation: Because of the SSDP implementation, the AAPLA-DM discovers each platform's information with average latency of 0.1 s, which can be improved by customizing the algorithm. Each platform's information is obtained and maintained at each APDS.

4.3   Platform Information Sharing Evaluation Experiment

- Purpose: Information sharing and storing function of the APDS.
- Experiment Description: Shut down or start up the test platforms; observe the state-changing information log at the observer platform.
- Result: As portrayed in Fig. 6, we confirmed that all necessary information related to the platform is collected correctly. The packed data transferred by the SSDP are parsed correctly.
- Evaluation: All information is received and the APDB is established with the reference to the APKRDB. The contents will be updated every time the test platform state changes. Then the upper layer can determine whether the communication message composition methods complied with the knowledge gained and stored in the APDS.

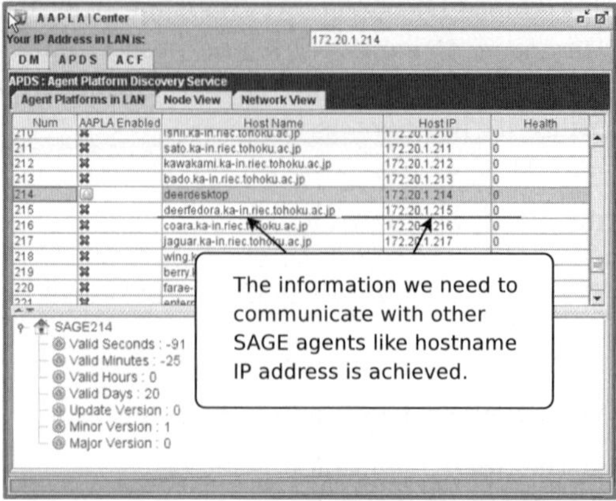

Fig. 6. APDS Output Screenshot

4.4   Agent Communication Facilitator Evaluation Experiment

- Purpose: To evaluate ACF functions.
- Experiment Description: Shut down or start up the platform at the test computer, observe the status changing of each ACF component.
- Result:
  - APIC: In the APIC module, all the discovered agent platform information is maintained. The DF agent information is composed using accurately maintained platform information.
  - AGIC: In the AGIC module, all the accessible agent information from the discovered platforms is maintained. The AGIC also maintains information related to how to access each agent.
  - ASIC: In the ASIC module, all usable services provided by the discovered agents from the AGIC are maintained. One service might be provided by multiple agents; one agent might provide multiple services. This information is also maintained by the ASIC.
- Evaluation: In this experiment, we confirmed the function of three major modules in the ACF. With the ACF, any application agent can readily access any remote agent in the ACF agent service list without knowing how to set the communication channel or underlying properties.

4.5   Agent Interoperation Experiment

- Purpose: To test the facilitatory function of the AAPLA.
- Experiment Description: We designed a simple test program (Agent Application) to test the AAPLA. The scenario process is depicted in Fig. 7.

  In fact, AAPLA peers are always proliferating and sharing information related to agent platforms, and maintain the available, accessible agent service list.

  Test program behavior is described as follows:

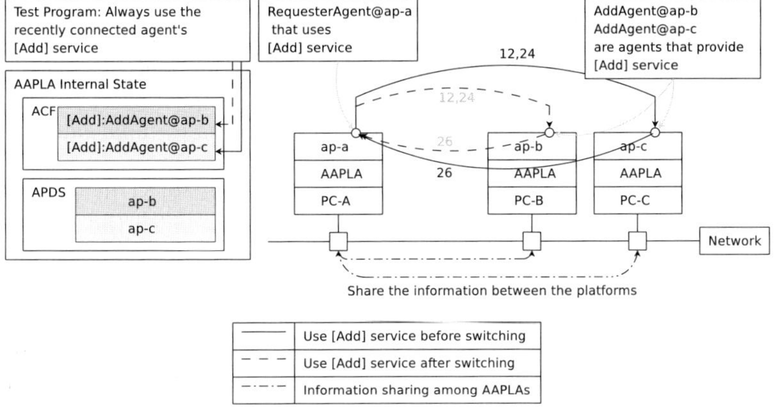

Fig. 7. AAPLA Overall Test Scenario Scheme

1. The calculation requester agent is situated in the agent platform *ap-a*. The requester agent (*RequesterAgent@ap-a*) has two numbers and wants to use AddAgent's [Add] service.
2. Platform *ap-b* is started and connected to the experiment LAN. Simultaneously, the platform information is proliferated and shared through the AAPLA.
3. Information related to the *AddAgent@ap-b* is notified to *ap-a*'s AAPLA.
4. The *RequesterAgent@ap-a* starts to use *AddAgent@ap-b* with the help of local AAPLA.
5. Then platform *ap-c* is started and connected to the experimental LAN.
6. Information related to *ap-c* is proliferated through AAPLA peers.
7. The *RequesterAgent@ap-a* switches to *AddAgent@ap-c* according to the policy of *"Always use the recently connected agent's service"*.
8. When *ap-c* shuts down, and disconnects from the experimental LAN, the *RequesterAgent@ap-a* falls back to use the [Add] service provided by *AddAgent@ap-b*.

- Result: We confirmed the procedures of test programs using the AAPLA service. When remote agents are ready for service, the remote AAPLA will start: the platform information, agent information and agent service information will be proliferated through AAPLA peers. The test program (the local agent application) will start to use the desired agent service with AAPLA's assistance. When the remote platform shuts down, the remote AAPLA shuts down as well. Consequently, a [Goodbye] packet will be sent to notify other AAPLA peers. Receiving this notification, the test program can switch to another service provider candidate if any exists.
- Evaluation: AAPLA encapsulates the underlying physical properties and provides a direct link to the accessible agent services in the inter-connected environment; this simplifies the developer's job and achieves *dynamic* inter-operation.

5   Conclusion and Future Work

In this paper, we presented a mechanism by proliferating and sharing platform information among the AAPLA peers, and pre-process agent access information to facilitate inter-agent communication, which helped us to build our agent application without concern related to the underlying physical environment properties. Building agent applications with AAPLA, it is unnecessary to hardcode any physical property such as IP addresses or hostnames in which the conventional agent application is unavoidable: this feature greatly improves applications' flexibility and portability.

For future work, we plan to extend our work to a global environment and modularize it as a regular part of other platforms. We also plan to conduct another evaluation of AAPLA structure from an application perspective in another medical care project.

References

1. AgentCities, `http://www.agentcities.org`
2. Suguri, H., Kodama, E., Miyazaki, M.: Assuring Interoperability of Heterogeneous Multi-Agent Systems. IEICE Trans., Inf. E86-D(10), 2095–2103 (2003)
3. Java Agent DEvelopment Framework (JADE): `http://jade.tilab.com/`
4. Foundation for Intelligent Physical Agents (FIPA): `http://www.fipa.org/`
5. Uchiya, T., Maemura, T., Li, X., Kinoshita, T.: Design and Implementation of Interactive Design Environment of Agent System. In: Okuno, H.G., Ali, M. (eds.) IEA/AIE 2007. LNCS (LNAI), vol. 4570, pp. 1088–1097. Springer, Heidelberg (2007)
6. Scalable Fault Tolerant Agent Grooming Environment (SAGE): `http://ias.comtec.co.jp`
7. Foundation for Intelligent Physical Agents (FIPA). Repository of FIPA Specifications (2003), `http://www.fipa.org/repository/`

A Formal Framework of Conversational Goals Based on Strategic Reasoning

Mohamed Mbarki[1], Jamal Bentahar[2], and Bernard Moulin[1]

[1] Laval University, Department of Computer Science and Software Engineering,
Canada
mohamed.mbarki.1@ulaval.ca, bernard.moulin@ift.ulaval.ca
[2] Concordia University, Concordia Institute for Information Systems Engineering
(CIISE), Canada
bentahar@ciise.concordia.ca

Abstract. In this paper, we propose a formal framework of strategic reasoning that agents use when interacting in a dialogue and trying to achieve their conversational goals. Such argumentation-based reasoning enables agents to generate a set of strategic goals depending on a set of constraints. Strategic goals are sub-goals, which are necessary to achieve a conversational goal. Some of these sub-goals are generated at the beginning of the interaction and they can be canceled or substituted by alternatives during the dialogue. An original characteristic of this framework is that it enables agents to persist in the achievement of their goals by considering alternatives and calculating the feasibility of each sub-goal. The set of constraints as well as sub-goals can be set at the beginning or during the dialogue.

1   Introduction

In multi-agent systems, agents are designed to perform particular tasks. Autonomy and intelligence are the most important characteristics of these agents, by which they should be able to generate and achieve their own goals. In the modern research into multi-agent systems, agents are equipped with reasoning capabilities expressed in computational logics [6,7]. Each agent has its own domain and certain goals to achieve what we call *operational goals*. To achieve their operational goals, agents often have to interact with each other. To participate in such interactions, agents need to create what we call *conversational goals*. Consequently, conversational goals must satisfy a set of *operational constraints*. Conversational goals must also satisfy a set of *conversational constraints* which are related to the conversational context. Time and budget constraints are examples of operational constraints, and respecting the religious and ideological beliefs of the addressee is an example of conversational constraints. The operational and conversational constraints may be revised during the dialogue. It is thus imperative to take into account these two types of constraints during the generation and the realization of conversational goals. Such constraints have been neglected in the most recent approaches based on goal modeling (e.g. [1,5]).

N.T. Nguyen et al. (Eds.): IEA/AIE 2008, LNAI 5027, pp. 835–844, 2008.

In this paper we present a formal framework to reason about conversational goals using sub-goals, prospective alternatives and constraints associated with each goal. The idea is to give agents the possibility to modify or reject their sub-goals and revise the set of constraints they decide to satisfy. This enables agents to decide about how to achieve their conversational goals considering the sub-goals and the sets of constraints to satisfy. Alternative sub-goals can also be considered in order to enable agents to persist in the achievement of their conversational goals, even in the case of the cancellation of one of them. Although the notion of persistence is important to ensure the conversation success, it has not been introduced in current communication models (e.g. [1],[3],[4] and [5]). In this context, the achievement of a conversational goal will depend on the realization of its sub-goals by taking into account operational and conversational constraints.

In this paper, we illustrate our model using an example of negotiation (of cars) between two agents. We suppose that an agent Ag_1 tries to convince another agent Ag_2 to buy a car. In this example, the seller's conversational goal, denoted B, corresponds to the objective of the conversation which is *the sale of a car*.

This paper is organized as follows. In Section 2, we introduce the agent model that defined the strategic reasoning in terms of strategic goals, constraints and possible alternatives. In Section 3, we present an argumentation-based reasoning which enables an agent to generate the sub-goals that are necessary for the achievement of its conversational goal. Before concluding, we present in Section 4 a formal framework which enables agents to persist in the trying to achieve their goals by the use of alternatives, and we show how agents can compute the feasibility of their sub-goals.

2   Agent Theory

Based on its mental states and other kinds of information (essentially provided by the social context and the conversational context), an agent can have a global vision to achieve its conversational goal. This vision is considered as a *strategy* that enables agents to generate a set of sub-goals, that we call *strategic goals*, which depend on a set of constraints. These strategic goals are selected and organized in order to achieve the conversational goal. Each strategic goal can be decomposed into a set of sub-goals which can themselves be decomposed recursively until elementary goals are reached. We call the generation of strategic goals: *strategic reasoning*. The choice of strategic goals is detailed in Section 3.

A strategic goal can have one or more alternatives, and the replacement of this goal by one of its alternatives enables an agent to achieve the same conversational goal, while satisfying different constraints. The subset of constraints to be satisfied and the subset of sub-goals to be realized in order to achieve the conversational goal determine the adopted strategy. Strategies are dynamic by nature and agents should adjust the adopted strategy while the conversation progresses. This can be achieved by taking into account the new constraints that can appear during the conversation. In this case, the new constraints to be satisfied should be consistent with the initial sub-set of constraints and criterions that need to be satisfied.

In our negotiation example , the seller agent can choose the strategy according to which the conversational goal B, which is *the sale of a car*, can be decomposed into three strategic goals B_1, B_2 and B_3. These sub-goals may be defined as follows: B_1 =*"know how much the buyer would like to invest in the purchase of a car as well as his preferences"*, B_2 = *"propose a car which may interest the buyer"* and B_3 = *"convince the buyer to accept this proposition"*.

The goal B_1 can be decomposed into two sub-goals B_{11} and B_{12}. The goal B_3 can also be decomposed into two sub-goals B_{31} and B_{32}. These new sub-goals are defined as follows: B_{11} = *"know which model of cars preferred by the buyer"*, B_{12} = *"know how much the buyer would like to invest"*, B_{31} = *"convince the buyer that the price of the proposed car is reasonable"* and B_{32} = *"convince the buyer that the proposed car consumes like small cars on the long distances"*.

In our example, we suppose that the seller is unable to convince the buyer to accept its offer (i.e. the seller is unable to achieve goal B_3 by using elementary actions) because a new conversational constraint occurs. In this case, the seller agent must persist in trying to achieve its goal by considering an alternative to goal B_2. For example, the seller agent may propose another car which may satisfy the new buyer's interest, and this new bid will be an alternative goal for B_2, named B_2'.

Moreover, if the seller agent finds during the dialogue that the buyer agent is not interested by the car gas consumption, then it may suggest an alternative to the strategic goal B_{32}, denoted B_{32}'. For example, the seller may try to convince the buyer that the spare parts for the proposed car are available and not expensive. The strategic goals B_2' and B_{32}' may be defined as follows: B_2'=*"propose another car which may satisfy a new buyer's interest"* and B_{32}'=*"convince the buyer that spare parts for this car are available and not expensive"*.

Our framework uses knowledge, goals and constraints. We introduce a formal language to manipulate these elements:

Definition 1 (knowledge, goal and constraint formulas). *Let $\mathcal{L}$ with typical element ϕ be a propositional language with negation and conjunction. The knowledge formulas $\mathcal{L}_\Gamma$ with typical element p, the goal formulas $\mathcal{L}_\mathcal{G}$ with typical element B and the constraint formulas $\mathcal{L}_\mathcal{C}$ with typical element c are defined as follows.*

- *if $\phi \in \mathcal{L}$, then $\Gamma\phi \in \mathcal{L}_\Gamma$, $\mathcal{G}\phi \in \mathcal{L}_\mathcal{G}$ and $\mathcal{C}\phi \in \mathcal{L}_\mathcal{C}$;*
- *if $p_1, p_2 \in \mathcal{L}_\Gamma$, $B_1, B_2 \in \mathcal{L}_\mathcal{G}$ and $c_1, c_2 \in \mathcal{L}_\mathcal{C}$ then $\neg p_1, p_1 \wedge p_2 \in \mathcal{L}_\Gamma$, $\neg B_1, B_1 \wedge B_2 \in \mathcal{L}_\mathcal{G}$ and $\neg c_1, c_1 \wedge c_2 \in \mathcal{L}_\mathcal{C}$.*

3   Argumentation-Based Strategic Goals

In our framework, the adoption of a set of strategic goals by an agent must be supported by internal arguments. For this reason, we define an *explanatory argument concept*, inspired by Amgoud and Kaci [1], and a *realization argument concept.* A given goal may be supported by these two types of arguments. The explanatory arguments justify the feasibility of the strategic goals in terms of beliefs. In contrast, the realization arguments determine the set of strategic goals necessary to achieve a conversational or a strategic goal[1]. We define in this section an argumentation-driven framework to generate the set of operational and conversational constraints related to a strategic goal. We also define the generation of strategic goals and their alternatives in order to achieve a conversational goal, while respecting the set of constraints related to this goal. In the rest of the paper, Γ indicates a possibly inconsistent knowledge base with no deductive closure, $\mathcal{C}$ indicates the set of constraints and $\mathcal{G}$ indicates a consistent set of goals. In addition we define two relations $\vdash_{\Gamma}$ and $\vdash_{\mathcal{C}}$, the former stands for classical inference and the latter stands for the need to achieve some sub-goals to achieve another goal.

Definition 2 (*Explanatory Argument*). *An explanatory argument of an agent Ag is a pair (H, B) where B indicates the Ag's goal and it is expressed as a formula in $\mathcal{L}_G$ and H is a subset of Γ such that: i) H is consistent, ii) $H \vdash_{\Gamma} B$, and iii) H is minimal (there is no subset of H which satisfies i and ii). An explanatory argument satisfying i and ii but not necessarily iii is called a non necessarily minimal argument. H is called the support of the argument which justifies the feasibility of the goal B in terms of beliefs.*

Definition 3 (*Realization Argument*). *A realization argument of an agent Ag is a triplet (G, B, C) where G is a finite set of Ag's strategic goals $(G \subseteq \mathcal{G})$, B indicates that Ag has the goal B $(B \in \mathcal{G})$, and C is a finite set of constraints $(C \subseteq \mathcal{C})$ such that : i) all the goals of G are supported by explanatory arguments, ii) G is consistent, iii) $G \vdash_{\mathcal{C}} B$, and iv) G is minimal (there is no subset of G which satisfies i, ii and iii). G is called the support of the argument which justifies the choice of the set of the strategic goals necessary for the realization of the goal B.*

G represents the strategic goals that Ag can use to achieve the goal B while satisfying a set of constraints C. Hence, the problem is: given an agent's goal B and a set of constraints C, what is the set of strategic goals G that need to be realized in order to achieve the goal B. By using explanatory and realization arguments, we can define the *strategic goals* and their possible *alternatives* in order to achieve a given conversational goal.

Definition 4 (*Strategic Goal*). *Let G be a finite set of Ag's goals, B be an Ag's conversational or strategic goal, C be a finite set of constraints, and $StrG(B)$ be a set of strategic goals (i.e. sub-goals) necessary to realize B. B' is a strategic goal of B $(B' \in StrG(B))$ iff there is a realization argument (G, B, C) such that: $G \subseteq \mathcal{G}$ and $B' \in G$.*

The fact that G is minimal makes B' necessary for the realization of B. However, B' may be substituted by another sub-goal called alternative goal.

---

[1] Agents can have plans specified by a set of rules, which enable them to select or revise their realization arguments.

Definition 5 (*Alternative Goal*). *Let G be a finite set of Ag's goals, B be an Ag's conversational or strategic goal, B_i be a strategic goal necessary for the realization of B, C be a finite set of constraints associated to B, C_i be a finite set of constraints associated to B_i, and $AltG(B_i/B)$ be a set of alternative goals of a strategic goal B_i. B_j is an alternative goal of B_i $(B_j \in AltG(B_i/B))$ iff:*

1. *(G, B, C) is a realization argument such that $B_i \in G$;*
2. *$(G \cup \{B_j\} - \{B_i\}, B, C \cup C_j - C_i)$ is also a realization argument of B such that C_j is the finite set of constraints associated to B_j.*

Proposition 1. *Let B_j be an alternative goal of a strategic goal B_i associated to a strategic or conversational goal B. B_j is also a strategic goal of B.*

Proof. According to the second condition of Definition 5, there is a realization argument $(G, B, C \cup C_j - C_i)$ of B such that $B_j \in G$ and C_i, C_j are respectively the sets of constraints associated to B_i and B_j. Consequently and according to Definition 4, B_j is a strategic goal of B. ∎

4   Constraint Generation and Goal Feasibility

Strategic reasoning enables agents to generate the strategic goals that ensure the realization of the conversational goal while respecting, at each step of the dialogue, the set of constraints associated with this goal. The initial operational and conversational constraints of a conversational goal are not generated by the agent which is committed to achieve this goal, but they are given by another agent (or the user) at the moment of the commitment. However, the initial constraints related to a strategic goal are calculated when this goal is generated. New constraints related to the strategic goals may be added during the dialogue progress. In this case, the set of constraints of the strategic goal that the agent tries to satisfy in the current step of the dialogue must be revised. This new set of constraints must be satisfied, otherwise the goal related to this set may not be achieved. With respect to the satisfaction of the set of constraints related to the conversational goal, there are two possible cases. If the new set of constraints related to the strategic goal is consistent with the set of constraints related to the conversational goal, the agent can keep the same strategy. In the second case, the agent must adjust its strategy by replacing the strategic goal by one of its alternatives. If some inconsistency persists, the agent must change its strategy completely. The dialogue terminates if the agent does not succeed in finding a new strategy, and we say that the realization of the conversational goal failed.

In our model, the set of agent's goals is represented by a tree in which the root represents the conversational goal (represented by square in Fig.1), the nodes represent strategic goals (also represented by squares), and the leaves represent elementary goals (represented by circles), which can be achieved by performing speech acts. This tree is built progressively while the dialogue progresses. To simplify the notation, an agent's conversational goal will be denoted by B and its strategic goals will be denoted by B_{ij}. The principal idea of the goals decomposition is that for each goal (conversational or strategic) we have:

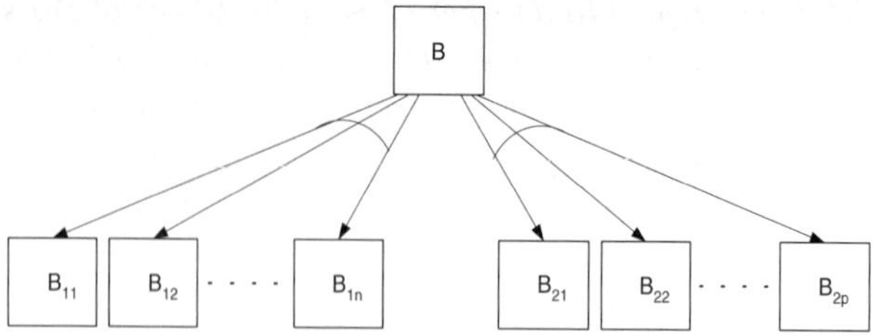

Fig. 1. Example of decomposition of a conversational or strategic goal

1. If the goal is elementary, then the agent tries to satisfy it by using tactical reasoning. This reasoning enables agents to choose the most relevant speech act in order to achieve an elementary goal. More details about this type of reasoning can be found in [2].

2. If the goal is decomposable, then the agent must determine, using an argumentative process, the sub-goals to achieve in order to achieve the initial goal. For each sub-goal, the agent may have several alternatives having different constraints. The achievement of these alternatives can provide the same result as the initial sub-goal. The set of strategic goals which may be used to achieve the same task are connected by a concave arc, as indicated in Fig.1. In this figure, the goal B may be decomposed into two goals B_{11} and B_{21}. For the goal B_{11}, we can have several alternatives $(B_{12}, \ldots, B_{1n})$ and its realization requires its achievement or the achievement of one of its alternatives (there is thus a disjunction). In the same way, the realization of B_{21} requires its achievement or the achievement of one of its alternatives: $B_{22}, \ldots,$ or B_{2p}. Finally, the realization of the initial goal B requires the achievement of a goal from the set $\{B_{11}, B_{12}, \ldots, B_{1n}\}$ and a goal from the set $\{B_{21}, B_{22}, \ldots, B_{2p}\}$ (there is thus a conjunction).

In a general way, the generation of the set of constraints related to a set of strategic goals is defined as follows.

Definition 6 (*Constraint Generation*). *Let B be a conversational or strategic goal and $\mathcal{E}$ be a function associating elementary goals to a set of constraints. The constraints associated to the set of the strategic goals $(StrG(B))$ of the goal B is given by the function Ctr which is defined in Table 1.*

In Definition 6, the function Ctr takes as an argument a set of goals (or a set of graphs) and returns a set of subsets of constraints representing the set of possible scenarios (i.e. each subset represents a scenario that an agent may consider). α and β are two sets of constraints. $B(1)$ represents the first strategic goal of the goal B and its possible alternatives. $\overline{B(1)}$ represents the remainder of the goals in the tree representing the goal B. In a general way, $B(i)$ represents the set including the i-th strategic goal of the goal B and its possible alternatives and $\overline{B(i)}$ represents the remainder of the goals of the tree representing the goal B. For example, in Fig.1 we have: $B(1) = \{B_{11}, B_{12}, \ldots, B_{1n}\}$ and

Table 1. Constraint Generation Function

$$\mathcal{C}tr(\emptyset) = \{\emptyset\}$$
$$\mathcal{C}tr(\{B\}) = \mathcal{E}(B) \text{ if } B \text{ is elementary}$$
$$\mathcal{C}tr(\{B\}) = \{ \bigcup_{\alpha \in \mathcal{C}tr(\{B(1)\})} \bigcup_{\beta \in \mathcal{C}tr(\{\overline{B(1)}\})} \alpha \cup \beta \} \text{ if } B \text{ is not elementary}$$
$$\mathcal{C}tr(\{B_1, B_2, \ldots, B_n\}) = \mathcal{C}tr(\{B_1\}) \cup \mathcal{C}tr(\{B_2\}) \cup \ldots \cup \mathcal{C}tr(\{B_n\})$$

$\overline{B(1)} = \{B_{21}, B_{22}, \ldots, B_{2p}\}$. Furthermore, we consider that the constraints related to an elementary goal are generated from the speech act performed to achieve this goal. For example, for the speech act: *"I sell you my watch for 5 dollars"*, the function $\mathcal{E}$ provides the set which contains the constraint: *"the price is equal to 5 dollars"*.

Definition 7 (*Goal Feasibility*). *Let B be a conversational goal and $C(B)$ be the set of its initial constraints. We say that B is a feasible goal or realizable if there is an element C_i of $\mathcal{C}tr(\{B\})$ such that: $C(B) \cup C_i$ is consistent.*

According to Definition 7, a conversational goal B cannot be achieved if there is no subset of constraints of the set $\mathcal{C}tr(\{B\})$ which is consistent with the set $C(B)$ (set of constraints associated with the agent conversational goal). In other words, an agent that is able to satisfy the constraints which appear during the dialogue would be able to achieve its conversational goal.

In our example of car negotiation (Section 2), the conversational goal is B, the set of the strategic goals of B is $StrG(B) = \{B_1, B_2, B_3, B'_2\}$, where B_2 and B'_2 are two alternative goals ($B'_2 \in AltG(B_2/B)$), the set of the strategic goals of B_1 is $StrG(B_1) = \{B_{11}, B_{12}\}$, and the set of strategic goals of B_3 is $StrG(B_3) = \{B_{31}, B_{32}, B'_{32}\}$, where B_{32} and B'_{32} are also two alternative goals ($B'_{32} \in AltG(B_{32}/B)$). The set of these goals is presented by a tree in Fig.2.

We also suppose that the set of initial operational and conversational constraints that the agent decides to satisfy is: $C(B) = \{c, c'\}$, $\mathcal{E}(B_{11}) = \{\{c_{11}\}\}$,

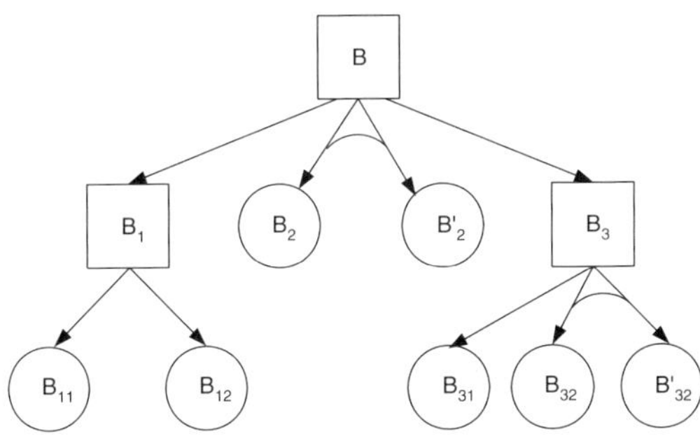

Fig. 2. Example of strategic reasoning

842   M. Mbarki, J. Bentahar, and B. Moulin

$\mathcal{E}(B_{12}) = \{\{c_{12}\}\}, \mathcal{E}(B_2) = \{\{c_2\}\}, \mathcal{E}(B_2') = \{\{c_2'\}\}, \mathcal{E}(B_{31}) = \{\{c_{31}\}\}, \mathcal{E}(\{B_{32}\})$
$= \{\{c_{32}\}\}$ and $\mathcal{E}(\{B_{32}'\}) = \{\{c_{32}'\}\}$. The constraints c and c' are defined as follows: $c = $ "*the price of the car must be equal or higher than 10.000 dollars*" and $c' = $ "*the buyer does not want to buy a car built in country X*".

According to Definition 6, the set of constraints associated with the strategic goals of B $(StrG(B))$ is defined as follows:

$$Ctr(\{B\}) = \{ \bigcup_{\alpha \in Ctr(\{B(1)\})} \bigcup_{\beta \in Ctr(\{\overline{B(1)}\})} \alpha \cup \beta \} \tag{1}$$

$$Ctr(\{B(1)\}) = Ctr(\{B_1\}) = \{ \bigcup_{\alpha \in Ctr(\{B_1(1)\})} \bigcup_{\beta \in Ctr(\{\overline{B_1(1)}\})} \alpha \cup \beta \}$$

$$= \{ \bigcup_{\alpha \in Ctr(\{B_{11}\})} \bigcup_{\beta \in Ctr(\{B_{12}\})} \alpha \cup \beta \}$$

$$= \{ \bigcup_{\alpha \in \mathcal{E}(\{B_{11}\})} \bigcup_{\beta \in \mathcal{E}(\{B_{12}\})} \alpha \cup \beta \}$$

$$= \{ \bigcup_{\alpha \in \{\{c_{11}\}\}} \bigcup_{\beta \in \{\{c_{12}\}\}} \alpha \cup \beta \}$$

$$= \{\{c_{11}, c_{12}\}\} \tag{2}$$

$$Ctr(\{\overline{B(1)}\}) = \{ \bigcup_{\alpha \in Ctr(\{B(2)\})} \bigcup_{\beta \in Ctr(\{\overline{B(2)}\})} \alpha \cup \beta \}$$

$$= \{ \bigcup_{\alpha \in Ctr(\{B_2, B_2'\})} \bigcup_{\beta \in Ctr(\{B_3\})} \alpha \cup \beta \}$$

$$= \{ \bigcup_{\alpha \in Ctr(\{B_2\}) \cup Ctr(\{B_2'\})} \bigcup_{\beta \in Ctr(\{B_3\})} \alpha \cup \beta \}$$

$$= \{ \bigcup_{\alpha \in \mathcal{E}(\{B_2\}) \cup \mathcal{E}(\{B_2'\})} \bigcup_{\beta \in Ctr(\{B_3\})} \alpha \cup \beta \}$$

$$= \{ \bigcup_{\alpha \in \{\{c_2\}, \{c_2'\}\}} \bigcup_{\beta \in Ctr(\{B_3\})} \alpha \cup \beta \} \tag{3}$$

$$Ctr(\{B_3\}) = \{ \bigcup_{\alpha \in Ctr(\{B_3(1)\})} \bigcup_{\beta \in Ctr(\{\overline{B_3(1)}\})} \alpha \cup \beta \}$$

$$= \{ \bigcup_{\alpha \in Ctr(\{B_{31}\})} \bigcup_{\beta \in Ctr(\{B_{32}, B_{32}'\})} \alpha \cup \beta \}$$

$$= \{ \bigcup_{\alpha \in Ctr(\{B_{31}\})} \bigcup_{\beta \in Ctr(\{B_{32}\}) \cup Ctr(\{B_{32}'\})} \alpha \cup \beta \}$$

$$= \{ \bigcup_{\alpha \in \mathcal{E}(\{B_{31}\})} \bigcup_{\beta \in \mathcal{E}(\{B_{32}\}) \cup \mathcal{E}(\{B_{32}'\})} \alpha \cup \beta \}$$

$$= \{ \bigcup_{\alpha \in \{\{c_{31}\}\}} \bigcup_{\beta \in \{\{c_{32}\}, \{c_{32}'\}\}} \alpha \cup \beta \}$$

$$= \{\{c_{31}, c_{32}\}, \{c_{31}, c'_{32}\}\} \tag{4}$$

According to the equations (3) and (4), we have:

$$Ctr(\{\overline{B(1)}\}) = \{ \bigcup_{\alpha \in \{\{c_2\}, \{c'_2\}\}} \bigcup_{\beta \in \{\{c_{31}, c_{32}\}, \{c_{31}, c'_{32}\}\}} \alpha \cup \beta \}$$

$$= \{\{c_2, c_{31}, c_{32}\}, \{c_2, c_{31}, c'_{32}\}, \{c'_2, c_{31}, c_{32}\}, \{c'_2, c_{31}, c'_{32}\}\} \tag{5}$$

According to the equations (1), (2) and (5), the set of constraints associated with the goal B becomes:

$$Ctr(\{B\}) = \{ \bigcup_{\alpha \in \{\{c_{11}, c_{12}\}\}} \bigcup_{\beta \in \{\{c_2, c_{31}, c_{32}\}, \{c_2, c_{31}, c'_{32}\}, \{c'_2, c_{31}, c_{32}\}, \{c'_2, c_{31}, c'_{32}\}\}} \alpha \cup \beta \}$$

$$= \{\{c_{11}, c_{12}, c_2, c_{31}, c_{32}\}, \{c_{11}, c_{12}, c_2, c_{31}, c'_{32}\},$$

$$\{c_{11}, c_{12}, c'_2, c_{31}, c_{32}\}, \{c_{11}, c_{12}, c'_2, c_{31}, c'_{32}\}\} \tag{6}$$

For illustration purposes we take in the sequel a simplified case in which we have only one constraint associated with B_{11} (i.e. $c_{12} = c_2 = c'_2 = c_{31} = c_{32} = c'_{32} = \{\emptyset\}$ and c_{11}="*the proposed car must be economic*").

Furthermore, we suppose that the seller believes that the buyer often drives from Quebec to Montreal and back, and that he has a small uncomfortable car. Consequently, the seller will try to achieve the goal B_{32} in order to convince the buyer that the proposed car is economic. Let us assume that during the dialogue the seller learns that the buyer does not travel regularly between Quebec and Montreal, and that he is currently working close to home. In this case, the seller is unable to convince the buyer by achieving the goal B_{32}, that the proposed car is has low gas consumption. Thereafter, the seller will give up the goal B_{32} and will try to persist in the realization of his conversational goal which is the sale of the proposed car by using the alternative goal B'_{32}. This goal aims at trying to convince the buyer that the spare parts for the proposed car are available and not expensive. If the buyer accepts the offer, then the set of constraints associated with the conversational goal B is equal to $\{\{c_{11}\}\}$. In this case, we have $C(B) \cup \{c_{11}\} = \{c, c', c_{11}\}$ is a consistent set. Consequently, the conversational goal B is achievable.

If the buyer refuses the offer unless the price is lower than *10.000 dollars*, the seller will have to add the constraint c'_{32} associated with the sub-goal B'_{32}. We have $c'_{32} = $ "*the price of the car must be lower than 10.000 dollars*".

Since the goal B_{32} is abandoned, the set of constraints including c_{32} will be removed from $Ctr(\{B\})$. The new set of constraints associated with the conversational goal B becomes: $Ctr(\{B\}) = \{\{c_{11}, c'_{32}\}\}$. In this case, the set $C(B) \cup \{c_{11}, c'_{32}\} = \{c, c', c_{11}, c'_{32}\}$ is inconsistent. Indeed, the constraints c and c'_{32} are contradictory. Consequently, the conversational goal B cannot be achieved and the seller will have to change his strategy if he wants to continue the dialogue.

5   Conclusion

This paper presents a formal framework based on strategic reasoning which allows agents to calculate a cognitive representation of the manner of achieving a conversational goal in terms of strategic goals. Agents' strategic goals are supported by two types of arguments: explanatory arguments which justify the choice of the goals, and realization arguments which provide the set of subgoals which are necessary to achieve these goals given a set of constraints. The second objective of this paper is to enable agents to persist in achieving their conversational goals by using alternative goals. The third objective is to provide agents by a formal method enabling them to know, at each moment, whether their goals can be achieved or not. We have illustrated each of these objectives by an example.

As future work, we integrating a rule-based planning system to the agent model. This will help in generating and revising explanatory and realization arguments. We are also interested in proposing a method enabling agents to select the most relevant and efficient strategy.

References

1. Amgoud, L., Kaci, S.: Approche basée sur l'argumentation pour la génération de buts bipolaires. In: Modèles Formels d'Intéraction (MFI 2005), Caen, May 2005, pp. 13–22 (2005)
2. Mbarki, M., Bentahar, J., Moulin, B.: Specification and Complexity of Strategic-Based Reasoning Using Argumentation. In: Maudet, N., Parsons, S., Rahwan, I. (eds.) ArgMAS 2006. LNCS (LNAI), vol. 4766, pp. 142–160. Springer, Heidelberg (2007)
3. Endriss, U., Maudet, N., Sadri, F., Toni, F.: Protocol conformance for logic-based agents. In: Proceedings of the 18th International Joint Conference on Artificial Intelligence, pp. 679–684 (2003)
4. Pitt, J.: Constitutive rules for agent communication languages. In: Proceedings of the International Joint Conference on Artificial Intelligence (IJCAI 2005), Acapulco, Mexico, pp. 691–698 (2003)
5. Shapiro, S., Lesperance, Y., Levesque, H.: Goal change. In: Proceedings of the International Joint Conference on Artificial Intelligence (IJCAI 2005), Denver, CO, pp. 582–588 (2005)
6. Toni, F., Torroni, P.: Computational Logic in Multi-Agent Systems. In: Toni, F., Torroni, P. (eds.) CLIMA 2005. LNCS (LNAI), vol. 3900, Springer, Heidelberg (2006)
7. van der Hoek, W., Jamroga, W., Wooldridge, M.: A logic for strategic reasoning. In: Proceedings of the International Joint Conference on Autonomous Agents and Multi-Agent Systems (AAMAS 2005), pp. 157–164. ACM Inc., New York (2005)

An Auction-Based System for Workforce Resource Allocation

Nadim Haque, Botond Virginas, Mathias Kern, and Gilbert Owusu

BT Group Chief Technology Office,
Orion Building, Adastral Park,
Martlesham Heath, Ipswich,
Suffolk, IP5 3RE, UK
{nadim.haque, botond.virginas, mathias.kern, gilbert.owusu} @bt.com
http://www.bt.com

Abstract. In this paper, we look at the problem of workforce redeployments where we consider the deployment of field engineers within a company organisation. Traditional methods for solving such problems have focused primarily on using centralised decision makers and optimisation algorithms which compute results in a solely centralised manner. Now, auctions have shown to have been used successfully for allocating resources in various applications and systems. Thus, in this paper, we propose a system that makes use of auctions as a mechanism for allocating the resources (field engineers) between different geographical parts of an organisation.

Keywords: agent-based system, auction, resource allocation.

1 Introduction

The service industry is built around the delivery of services to its customers. Typical examples are the National Health Service (NHS) which provides health care in the UK, or BT which delivers communication services to both domestic and business clients. The effective utilisation of available resources is central to the success of this industry and, hence, resource planning and management play a key role. Resource planning involves a wide variety of activities ranging from long-term capacity planning over mid-term deployment planning to short-term scheduling. Now, there is a need for companies to evolve in order to adapt to the dynamically changing requirements within their organisations. BT addresses this challenge with its Fieldforce Optimisation Suite (FOS) [5] which provides a unified and comprehensive resource planning approach. One aspect of this could include the redeployment of workforce employees from one part of a company to another where there may be a greater need for work to be carried out. Such a requirement may take place in order to improve upon the utilisation of the employees rather than if they remained static within an organisation. Now, in this paper, we describe the design of a system which is used to redeploy workforce field engineers, from one part of an organisation to another.

N.T. Nguyen et al. (Eds.): IEA/AIE 2008, LNAI 5027, pp. 845–854, 2008.

Previous attempts have been made to redistribute resources between various geographical domains within BT. These solutions are embedded within several prototype implementations. The methods employed in these implementations include centralised agent-based resource allocation using a multi-criteria optimisation algorithm [8], a distributed agent-based resource exchange with emerging allocation patterns [7] and agent-based distributed constraint satisfaction [6]. One of the major shortcomings common to these implementations is that they try to optimise an overall objective (quality of service of individual geographical regions) while individual participating domains might be losing in the process. Therefore, there is a conflict between the collaborative and competitive objectives of domains and regions.

The purpose of this work has been to investigate the feasibility of applying auctions to solve the problem of allocating field engineer resources across a workforce within an organisation. The novelty of our system lies in providing mechanisms to address the problem despite using a purely competitive method such as auctions. It is our belief that auctions can be used as an alternative to optimisation methods for solving such problems. Auctions have been successfully investigated in a number of areas where some of these include resource allocation in communications networks ([2] and [3]) as well as task allocation mechanisms for limited-capacity suppliers [1], amongst other work. We decided to investigate the use of auctions for two reasons. Firstly, auctions provide an intuitive way of viewing the problem of resource allocation since, in general, resources are allocated to the individual who places the highest value on them. Secondly, auctions can achieve successful allocations based only on information such as price of the resource alone.

The solution that we have proposed makes use of software agents [4]. There are several reasons for choosing agents. Firstly, the communicative nature of agents can allow them to achieve their own individual goals by interacting with other agents. Secondly, the autonomous behaviour exhibited by agents allows them to accomplish their duties on their own and without the input of a human controller. Thirdly, the reactive nature exhibited by agents allows them to respond to events in a timely manner without any unnecessary delay. This is particularly important when the availability of resources changes dynamically.

The remainder of this paper is structured in the following way: an overview describing our problem is set out in Section 2 along with details of the design of the system that we propose and the interaction between the various components. We also discuss our auction and a reward system that we consider. In Section 3, we briefly discuss the system and outline several experiments that we plan to conduct in order to empirically evaluate the performance of the system. Finally, the conclusions are given in Section 4 where we also outline ideas for future work.

2   Problem Description and System Design

In this section, we first describe the problem that we are dealing with, in Subsection 2.1. We then discuss the design of the resource allocation system that we propose. Here, we describe the various agent components within the system in Subsection 2.2. This is then followed by a description of how these components interact in Subsection 2.3. In Subsection 2.4, we discuss the auction component of the system and look more closely at the inputs provided to the auction and discuss how field engineer allocations are made. Finally, in Subsection 2.5, we look at a reward system that is used to provide an incentive to agents when a request is made for their engineer resources.

2.1   Problem Overview

In this work, we consider the deployment of workforce engineers from one part of an organisation to another in order to make use of under-utilised resources. For our work, there is a single geographical region which contains individual smaller sub-regions, each of which has several separate domains. A sub-region can be defined by the domains it contains as being geographically close together. Job demands originate from within domains. In each domain, there are also a number of local field engineers which reside there.

The domains which exist within a sub-region can be considered as being preferred working areas, with respect to each other. These domains are expected to communicate with each other in order to meet the job demands. There are a number of engineers which belong to each domain. Each field engineer has expertise in a number of different skill types, where there is a skill proficiency level associated with each of these skill types. Engineers have the following attributes: skill type(s), skill proficiencies (one for each skill type), home location (a domain), preferred working areas (other domains in the engineer's sub-region) and a calendar for reserving/booking jobs.

Now, in this work, we assume that optimisation algorithms have been used locally within each domain and that as many engineers as possible have been successfully deployed locally. From this point onwards, each domain will then typically have a set of surplus job demands that may still need to be processed, along with a set of surplus engineers who can be made available to other domains where there is a requirement for them. Thus, in our work, we focus upon the deployment of surplus field engineers in locations where there is a shortage of skills and/or workforce personnel. An example that comprises these components is shown in figure 1. This figure shows that, in the scenario that we consider, there is one geographical region which contains two separate sub-regions, where there are three domains within each sub-region.

2.2   The Agents

There are three different types of agents that exist within the system. These are: *buyer agent, seller agent* and the *region manager agent*. There is one buyer agent and one seller agent per domain. Each domain is responsible for submitting job demands, in order to obtain engineers and also to release any surplus engineers that they may have so that they can satisfy job demands in other domains. Thus, a buyer agent deals with submitting job demands to seller

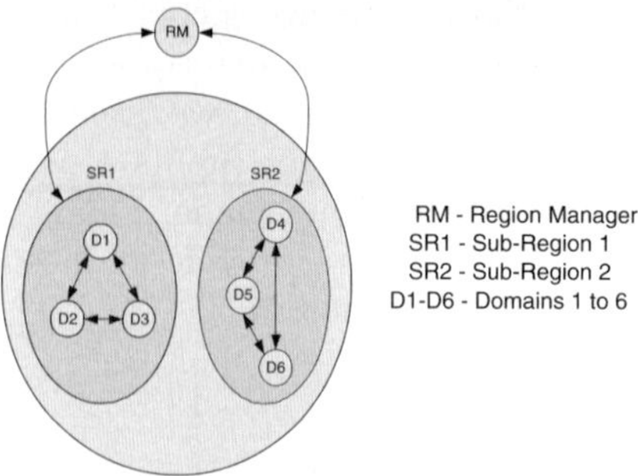

Fig. 1. Geographical region comprised of various components within an organisation

agents in other domains, within its sub-region, in an attempt to obtain engineers and a seller agent is responsible for lending out surplus engineers to the other domains. Therefore, *decentralised* communication (using auctions)[1] takes place directly between the buyer agents and seller agents in the first instance.

Within the region, there is one region manager, who is in charge of the region. The responsibility of the region manager is two-fold. Firstly, the region manager communicates with the buyer agents about the order in which they should submit job demands to the other domains. This is important since a buyer agent should not be allowed to continuously submit job demands because otherwise this would give it an unfair advantage over buyer agents in other domains when selecting engineers. The second role of the region manager is to collect all job demands from buyer agents, at the end of each day, which could not be matched to any available field engineer in its local sub-region. The region manager then conducts a set of *centralised* auctions[1] in order to find suitable and available field engineers for these remaining job demands. It attempts to achieve this by sending job demands to seller agents who are in the other sub-region to the one in which the job demand originated from.

2.3   Component Interaction

Figure 2 shows the communication that occurs between a buyer agent, *BA1*, in domain *D1* and seller agent 2, *SA2* in domain *D2*, and seller agent 3, *SA3* in domain *D3*, all three of which are within sub-region 1, *SR1*. In this figure, *BA1* starts off by directly sending a message to both *SA2* and *SA3* which contains its current job demand (*findSuitableEngineers*). On receipt of this job demand, each recipient seller agent checks to see if they have any engineers available that match the demand given by the buyer agent (*searchForEngineers*). The seller agents match all of the engineers that have the skill type requested by the buyer agent and which also have skill proficiencies which are equal to or greater than those desired by the buyer agent, for the skill type requested. The

---

[1] The use of auctions is discussed in Subsection 2.4.

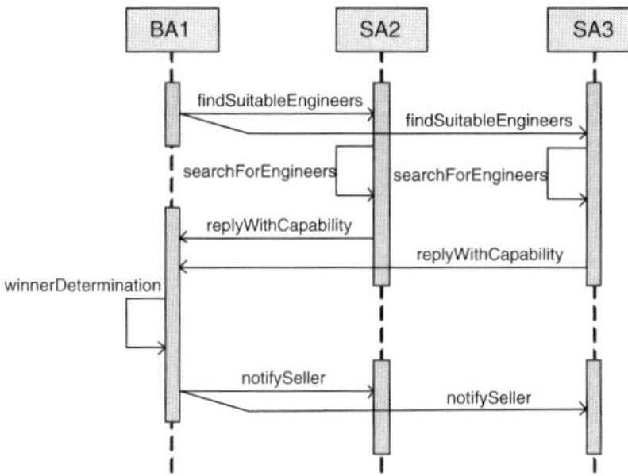

Fig. 2. Sequence diagram for communication between agents within the same sub-region, *without* using the region manager agent as a central agent

seller agents then put a price on each matching engineer and send this list of engineers back to the buyer agent (*replyWithCapability*).[2] Once *BA1* receives a response back from the seller agents, it then selects a winning engineer which can serve its purpose (*winnerDetermination*).[3] Finally, a message is sent from *BA1* to both *SA2* and *SA3* to notify the seller agents about the outcome of the buyer agent's selection (*notifySeller*). This process continues for each buyer agent, one at a time, until no buyer agent has any more job demands to submit for that particular day.

Once all of the job demands have been sent by the buyer agents for the current day being processed, the buyer agents then send their unresolved job demands to the region manager. Figure 3 shows the sequence of interactions that takes place between a buyer agent and seller agents, but via the region manager. In this scenario, the region manager acts as a central agent which controls the auction. Once the region manager has received the remaining job demands from all of the buyer agents (*giveRemainingDemand*), it then sorts these job demands by priority.[4] The region manager then selects the job demand with the highest importance value and contacts the appropriate seller agents to find a suitable resource. Now, the region manager contacts the seller agents which do not belong to the same sub-region in which the job demand originated from. The reason for this is that it would be unnecessary to contact the seller agents within the same sub-region since, earlier on, the buyer agent who submitted the job demand would have already contacted the seller agents within its sub-region during the original process that was shown in figure 2. Thus, in figure 3, we can assume that the buyer agent, *BA1*, belongs to sub-region 1, *SR1*, and that the seller agents, *SA4*, *SA5* and *SA6*, all belong to sub-region 2, *SR2*. This process continues until an attempt has been made to satisfy all of the job demands.

---

[2] The methodology by which the seller agents price their resources is discussed in Subsection 2.4.

[3] By default, the buyer agent selects the cheapest resource.

[4] Each job demand is assigned a value for job importance by its domain.

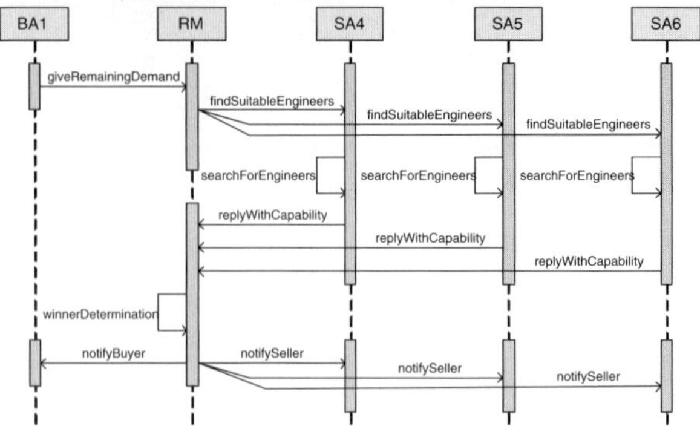

Fig. 3. Sequence diagram for communication between agents in different sub-regions, *with* the region manager agent acting as a central agent

2.4   Auction Design

As part of our design solution, we investigate the use of auctions for allocating field engineer resources. Now, for our system, we use the concept of reverse auctions. In the general case, reverse auctions work such that the agent conducting the auction receives all of the *bids* (or *asks*) from the participants and allocates (or offers) the good which was the cheapest in price. This is an appropriate auction mechanism to use in our system since it aims to minimise the costs incurred for the organisation. The input parameters into our auction are job demands (submitted by buyer agents) and a set of engineer data (submitted by seller agents) in response to the demands. A job demand comprises the following information: a *skill type* – the skill type required for the job, a *skill proficiency* – the minimum level required for the skill type, a *job location* (a domain) – the place where the job is to be carried out and a *date* – indicating the day on which the job should take place.

When a seller receives a job demand[5], it then filters its engineers and makes a list of the ones that match the requirements given in the job demand. A seller will then price each of its matched engineers before replying back with their details. The price is a function of three separate values: *distance* – distance between job location and the engineer's home location, *skill proficiency* – the engineer's proficiency level and *demand* – the number of times the engineer has been demanded previously. By combining these attributes, a price is obtained.[6] The higher the value for each of these attributes, the greater the overall price

---

[5] In the decentralised part of the system, a seller will receive job demands directly from a buyer agent whereas, in the centralised case, it receives job demands via the region manager.

[6] We propose that a weighted sum can be used to obtain a value for the price, making sure that the values used have been normalised beforehand. Different sets of weight values could be used for these attributes with an equal weighting being the default option. By changing the weights, we can investigate how the resource prices vary.

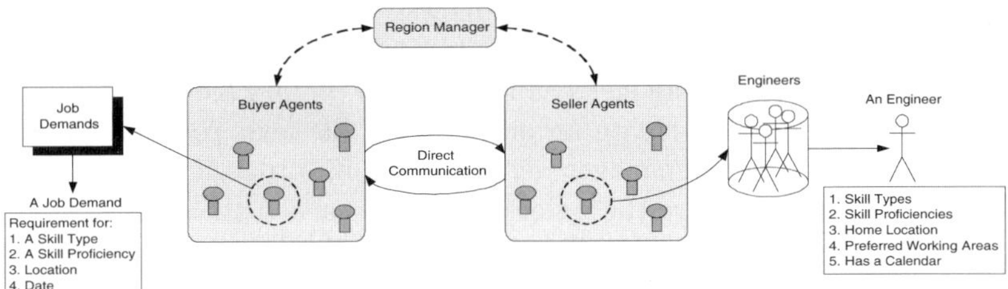

Fig. 4. High-level diagram of the system components

of the field engineer resource. This price reflects the cost associated with leasing
out the engineer to carry out the job to completion.

Once the matched field engineer data has been sent back to the requesting
agent, the auction can take place.[7] The output of conducting an auction is the
allocation of the cheapest priced field engineer. An advantage of using such a
price-based mechanism for allocating resources is that this could provide a suitable means for balancing surplus resources across different areas. For example, if
a field engineer is not used regularly, then the price for that engineer would typically be less than that for an engineer who has been allocated more frequently.
Therefore, if the price is less, then the chance of allocating that engineer, using
a reverse auction, would begin to increase, thus ensuring that there is a better
balance in the allocations across different domains. Figure 4 shows a high-level
diagram of the system.

2.5 Reward System

As discussed earlier, one role of the region manager is to ensure that the buyer
agents all have a chance to submit job demands to the seller agents in their
local sub-regions. It achieves this by doing the following. For each sub-region,
the region manager first sends a message to all of the buyer agents within that
sub-region which gives an order in which they are to submit job demands for
that particular round. Thus, we have a round-robin system where each buyer
agent takes it in turns to submit a job demand to the seller agents in its local
sub-region. Each buyer agent will have a list of job demands that need to be
resolved. These are ordered by the buyer agents before they take their turn in
submitting a job demand where this is based upon the priority of the job. After
each buyer agent has had a chance to submit a job demand, the region manager
is notified about this. The region manager then produces another round-robin
order and sends this to the buyer agents within that sub-region.

Now, as part of the system, we wanted to provide an incentive for agents to
give up their surplus resources from their domains. To achieve this, we introduced
a scoring system which is used when resources are released by agents from their

---

[7] In the case of figure 2, the buyer agent is responsible for determining the winning
engineer, whereas in figure 3, this is the responsibility of the region manager agent.

domains. The scoring system works as follows. When a seller agent has had a resource successfully allocated to another domain, it is rewarded a number of points. When the region manager has received the points scored by each seller agent, it then uses this to create an ordering for the next round-robin for the buyer agents. The region manager achieves this by ordering the round-robin based upon the scores where the seller agent who earned the highest score will have its domain first in the list. This means that the buyer agent within that domain will get a chance to submit a job demand first for the next round. This is beneficial because, typically, resources are scarce and domains are not guaranteed to obtain resources from other domains particularly if they don't submit their job demands early enough. Thus, there is a direct incentive for agents to release resources from within their domains, rather than keeping hold of them.

As a result of introducing this scoring system, we would expect the domains to be more willing to give up their surplus resources if they are to have a priority over being offered resources from other domains. Points can be gained by seller agents in a number of ways, for example, if a seller agent is successful in leasing one of its surplus engineers where extra points can be gained if the successfully allocated engineer has a higher skill proficiency and/or a larger variety of skills.

3   Discussion and Experiments

In this section, we provide a brief discussion of the system in Subsection 3.1 and outline a number of ongoing experiments in Subsection 3.2.

3.1   Discussion

The work in this paper described a system which allocates field engineers in an organisation. The system that was detailed in Section 2 consisted of two sets of interactions, one which involves direct communication between the buyer and seller agents, and the other which involves a centralised communication. The region manager conducts auctions only when job demands cannot be satisfied in local sub-regions. Thus, on average, we would expect engineers to travel shorter distances locally, initially, and only travel to other sub-regions as a last resort. This is desirable since it minimises the costs associated with the allocations.

We have chosen to use auctions for allocating resources. This is realistic since there is a price involved for transferring an engineer from one location to another. Also, as stated in Subsection 2.4, we would expect our system to perform well with respect to providing an even distribution of resources, thus ensuring fairness in the system. Our system also provides fairness in the allocation process. For example, we use a round-robin where each buyer agent in its domain takes turns in submitting job demands. By using a scoring system, we ensure that the domain which released more surplus engineers is most likely to submit its job demand earlier, giving it a better chance of securing an engineer from another domain.

Finally, several methods of scoring can be investigated in this work. For example, the region manager can use cumulative scores for each domain when deciding the order of the round-robin. Alternatively, scoring could be done for each round of job submissions where, at the end of each round, the order is established by the region manager and the scores are set to zero.

3.2 Experiments

We now outline various experiments that we plan to conduct on our system. It is our belief that by conducting these experiments, we will be able to draw positive conclusions. There are many experiments that could provide an insight into the performance of our system. The following list includes some of the more important experiments:

1. *Average Allocation Success Rate* – A key measurement that we wish to study in our work is the average allocation success rate. By doing this, we will be able to gain an insight into how well the system has performed globally with respect to the percentage of successfully allocated field engineer resources.
2. *Average Price per Successful Allocation* – For this experiment, we aim to look at the average price per successful allocation. By conducting this experiment, we would be able to see the average value at which the seller agents price their surplus field engineer resources. We would expect this price to change depending on the demand of the resource.
3. *Resource Balancing* – As part of our work, we also wish to look at resource balancing. By doing this, we will be able to analyse how well the surplus resources have been allocated across the different domains (i.e. if there is a fair and balanced distribution of the field engineers).
4. *Average Domain Points Scored* – For this experiment, we could investigate the average wealth per domain with respect to the number of points scored by each domain. This will tell us which domains are most successful and, from this, we can then perform further experiments to see why this is so.

4   Conclusions and Future Work

In this paper, we discussed the design of an auction-based resource allocation system for the deployment of field engineers in a workforce. Here, we looked at the decentralised and centralised processes within the entire system and discussed the auction mechanism that we considered. After outlining the system design and operational details, we provided a brief discussion and outlined a number of preliminary experiments that we plan to conduct in the near future in order to evaluate the performance of the system. The system that we have proposed can be applied to a number of different application areas. Examples of this include: police officers being redeployed from one area to another, doctors/medics moving from one hospital to another, depending on demand, and goods, such as vehicles, being moved from showrooms where there is relatively less demand for them to locations where the demand is greater. In all of these application domains, there is scope to exploit the use of auction-based mechanisms for allocating resources.

For future work, there are a number of aspects that could be investigated. Firstly, we would like to continue to design and carry out the experiments outlined in Section 3. Secondly, in addition to the system that we have currently proposed, we would like to investigate scenarios where engineers, who have already been redeployed, can be released and *redeployed again* to areas where there is a greater need for them (i.e. in emergency situations). Here, we would envisage developing a reward and/or penalty mechanism for releasing resources. Thirdly, we would also like to investigate how several engineers could work together in order to complete tasks. Finally, as part of future work, we would like to extend the notion of the engineers' preferred working areas. At present, we assume that all engineers are willing to work in all domains in the entire region, although they may have a preference of being deployed in their default sub-region.

Acknowledgments

The work in this paper is part of a Research Fellowship carried out by the main author in British Telecommunications' Intelligent Systems Research Centre.

References

1. Dash, R.K., Vytelingum, P., Rogers, A., David, E., Jennings, N.R.: Market-based task allocation mechanisms for limited capacity suppliers. IEEE Transactions on Systems, Man, and Cybernetics - Part A: Systems and Humans 37(3), 391–405 (2007)
2. Haque, N., Jennings, N.R., Moreau, L.: Resource allocation in communication networks using market-based agents. International Journal of Knowledge-Based Systems 18(4-5), 163–170 (2005)
3. Haque, N., Jennings, N.R., Moreau, L.: Scalability and robustness of a network resource allocation system using market-based agents. NETNOMICS: Economic Research and Electronic Networking 7(2), 69–96 (2005)
4. Jennings, N.R., Wooldridge, M.J.: Software agents. IEE Review, 17–20 (January 1996)
5. Owusu, G., Voudouris, C., Kern, M., Garyfalos, A., Anim-Ansah, G., Virginas, B.: On optimising resource planning in BT plc with FOS. In: IEEE International Conference on Service Systems and Service Management (IEEE/SSSM 2006), October 2006, vol. 1, pp. 541–546 (2006)
6. Tsang, E.P.K., Gosling, T., Virginas, B., Voudouris, C., Owusu, G.: Retractable contract network for distributed scheduling. In: Proceedings of the 2nd Multidisciplinary International Conference on Scheduling: Theory and Applications (MISTA 2005), New York, USA, July 18-21, 2005, pp. 485–500 (2005)
7. Ursu, M.F., Virginas, B., Voudouris, C.: Distributed resource allocation via local choices: General model and a basic solution. In: Negoita, M.G., Howlett, R.J., Jain, L.C. (eds.) KES 2004. LNCS (LNAI), vol. 3215, pp. 764–771. Springer, Heidelberg (2004)
8. Virginas, B., Owusu, G., Voudouris, C., Anim-Ansah, G.: A two stage optimisation system for resource management in BT. In: Proceedings of the Twenty-third Annual International Conference of the British Computer Society's Specialist Group on AI (AI 2003), pp. 109–121 (2003)

Scenario Description Language for Multi-agent Systems*

Armin Stranjak[1], Igor Čavrak[2], and Mario Žagar[2]

[1] Strategic Research Centre, Rolls-Royce plc, PO Box 31, Derby DE24 8BJ, UK
[2] University of Zagreb, Faculty of Electrical Engineering and Computing, Unska 3,
HR-10000 Zagreb, Croatia
`armin.stranjak@rolls-royce.com,{igor.cavrak;mario.zagar}@fer.hr`

Abstract. Increasing complexity of interactions among agents presents
a serious challenge in designing, building and maintaining of such systems. This paper analyses existing interaction description languages and
methods, and proposes a novel language based on descriptions of interaction scenarios. Program code generated from scenario descriptions, in
synergy with related platform components, simplifies design, implementation and maintenance phases of multi-agent systems characterized by
complex and interwoven communication.

Keywords: Multi-Agent System, Interaction, Scenario, Language.

1   Introduction

Agent-oriented paradigm advances a typically modular, client-server approach
by introducing concepts like autonomy, interaction and social behavior, to name
a few [1]. In such systems, agents are fulfilling their goals autonomously, by sensing environment and interacting with other agents if and when it is in their best
interest. In order to achieve conversation among agents, a conversation space
must be defined within which a dialogue, i.e. a sequence of messages exchanged
among agents, can be performed. To establish a meaningful agent communication, it is necessary to define a (set of) dialogue protocol(s). Protocols allow
agents to participate in conversations by prescribing shared protocol semantics
and defining conversation space within which agents are enabled to act, still
preserving their decision-making autonomy [2]. This space can be defined in a
form of a conversation description language.

This paper addresses a SDLMAS language, a generic interaction description
language independent of the target agent platform and implementation language.
The language is interaction-centric, focusing on message exchange sequences and
providing intuitive scenario descriptions. The language enforces a strict separation of scenario descriptions, followed by agents during interactions, and internal
agent logic, implementing agent reasoning. Complexity of managing numerous

---

* This work has been supported by the Croatian Ministry of Science, Education and
Sports under the research project "Software Engineering in Ubiquitous Computing".

N.T. Nguyen et al. (Eds.): IEA/AIE 2008, LNAI 5027, pp. 855–864, 2008.

parallel scenario executions, tracking of interaction states, conversation termina-
tions etc. are hidden from designers and developers within SDLMAS platform.
Similarity to sequence diagrams, simplicity but also high expressiveness allow
its quick adoption, as well as development of various tools for performing verifi-
cations and transformations to other models. To support execution of SDLMAS
scenarios, a tool for generating implementation source code and runtime framework components have also been developed.

2   Related Work

As a part of numerous methodologies appeared in a last decade or two, interactions are normally treated as an ingredient element of a wider context of issues
related to design, development and deployment of multi-agent systems. Models
[4] [5] [6] are often based on AUML [9], Petri Nets [8] or state-chart diagrams.
AUML are not expressive enough and do not capture the multi-lateral nature
of agent interactions [7]. In addition to this, AUML diagrams become hard to
read if interaction is not extremely simple and there is no clear mapping definition between interaction protocols and agent's internal actions. Petri Nets
are also not very suitable for interaction description as they are also hard to
read and lack of expressiveness and scalability [11] [10]. Although state-charts
are clearer in expressing interaction protocols, they still lack clear definition in
which way can be used to define a relationship between protocol execution and
agent's business logic. A textual form offers many advantages over given forms
as it can be handled in a more precise way, explicit syntax definition can be
provided and the mapping to the implementation language is easier to achieve.
There are numerous solutions provided as follows. MAP language [3] for dialogue
protocol definition is based on the principles found in Electronic Institutions [12]
but without need for administrative agents. Language semantics is inspired by
logic which is basis for communication and parallel systems [13]. Key concept of
the language is decomposition of a dialogue into scenes. A scene can be seen as
an interaction context within which agents are communicating with each other.
Another key concept is agent's role. Its role assumes a certain set of behaviors
that agent will undertake during interactions. MAP language allows agents to
establish asynchronous and simultaneous interactions, which might lead into un-
planned system's activities where introduction of well-structured protocol is not
sufficient to secure emergent behavior. It is important to note that this language
is not oriented on a message flow. AgentUML [14] language emerged as an attempt to represent agents' interactions and roles in a standardized way. It is
based on the UML standard in order to mitigate transition from object-oriented
to agent-based software paradigm. The main purpose is to offer standardized notation for analysis, design and implementation of agent systems. UML sequence
diagram is expanded in order to capture specifics of agent interactions while class
diagram is modified to incorporate concept of agent's roles and behaviors. Visual representation of agent dialogues is one of the advantages of the AgentUML.

In order to achieve practical usability, it is necessary to define the ways of its transformation into textual notation of protocols, and various language transitions are proposed [15] [16]. On the other hand, untidy diagrams are easily misunderstood especially if they define complex dialogue protocols. Furthermore, since AgentUML does not represent agent's states, it is not possible to define conditions under which messages can be received or sent. Although AUML is not practical for multi-agent system development, it influenced other language designs [15] [16] [17] [18] and modeling frameworks [20]. IOM/T language [19] emerged from a tendency to define interaction protocols in a textual notation. The language introduces formal way of mapping interaction protocol from AgentUML. One of the advantages of IOM/T is the way interaction protocol is defined. Instead of separate definitions of protocol-related agent's activities, the emphasis is on the message flow definition between agents. Unfortunately, the language lacks some important characteristics related to scenario descriptions of multi-agent systems. There is no explicit definition of message performative used in conversations. Cardinality of agent's instances is bound into protocol implementation inside of agent's internal logic. Consequently, it is not possible to change number of instances of particular agent without re-implementing internal implementation. Implementation of agent's internal logic is language-dependent on the JADE agent platform, which disables possibility of usage IOM/T language in another agent platform. Q Language [21] is another language for interaction protocol definition in a textual form. It is predominantly purposed for interaction with a user or another agents on behalf of a user, it is consequently not oriented on a message flow in sense that SDLMAS is. Typically, scenario description will be considered only from the point of view of one agent who is supposed to interact with other parties assuming their prior knowledge about the scenario they are supposed to follow.

3   Scenario Description Language

In this section we present the specification of SDLMAS and illustrate its syntax and semantics on an interaction example based on the ContractNet protocol [24]. A simplified sequence diagram of interactions is presented in Fig. 1 and a more detailed description in SDLMAS is presented in Figure 2. The scenario depicts an interaction where an agent playing a Buyer role collects proposals from a number of Supplier agents using the CNP protocol. In addition, each Supplier agent consults its Stock and, optionally, Production role agents in order to estimate the price and delivery time. If the proposal is accepted by the Buyer agent, Stock and Production agents are informed to allocate or start production, and the Transport role agent (only one in this system) is notified to schedule a shipment. This scenario includes two second-level CNP protocols intertwined both between themselves and with the first-level CNP protocol between the Buyer and the Seller roles.

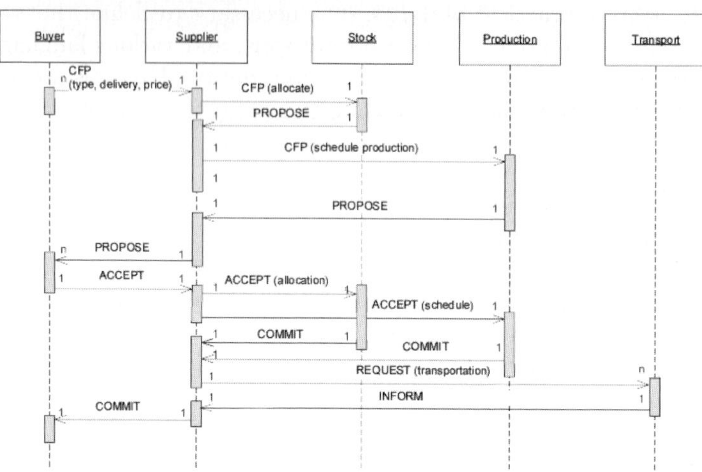

Fig. 1. Simplified sequence diagram of the OrderParts scenario

3.1   Language Properties

A SDLMAS is a declarative scenario description language and a platform for rapid design and development of multi-agent systems. The language describes conversation among agents (i.e. scenario) as a sequence of conversation actions, where actions define a conditional mapping between incoming and outgoing messages and agent business logic. The main language properties can be outlined in the following: (1) termination: the language introduces terminating performatives that denote end of conversation; (2) synchrony: a protocol is implicitly defined as a sequence of agent actions where order of these actions is important, achieving sequential approach in protocol definition; (3) uptake acknowledgement: implicit acknowledgement can be assumed for non-terminating performatives where an agent is supposed to reply according to defined protocol; (4) exception handling: at logical level, a terminating performative is an exception and its handling is an intrinsic part of a conversation protocol; (5) independence between language and agent platform: SDLMAS is designed not to interfere with implementation specificities but is only considered with the ways how agents will maintain dialogues; (6) message reception and transmission conditions: the language explicitly defines conditions for reception and transmission of messages as a part of conversation protocol definition; (7) relationship with the agent's business logic: an elementary action of the language is defined as a procedure that will be executed as a consequence of a satisfied condition following a message reception; (8) orientation of message flow: the language is oriented on system activity where agent actions are described sequentially in time domain.

3.2   Formal Model

Due to space restrictions, only the basic elements of the formal model will be briefly explained in this section. Scenario description for a multi-agent system

```
 1 agent @buyer : Buyer;                      42   msgSnd: (ACCEPT|#REJECT -><Supplier>);
 2 agent @supp  : Supplier;                   43 }
 3 agent $stock : Stock;                       44
 4 agent $prod  : Production;                  45 action Supplier in processAccept() {
 5 agent tAgent : Transport;                   46   msgRcv : (ACCEPT|#REJECT <- @buyer);
 6                                             47   msgSnd : (ACCEPT|#REJECT -> $stock) &
 7 scenario OrderParts {                       48             (ACCEPT|#REJECT -> $prod));
 8                                             49 }
 9 action Buyer in sendOrderCall() {           50
10   msgSnd : (CFP -> <Supplier>);             51 action Stock in allocateStock() {
11 }                                           52   msgRcv: (ACCEPT|#REJECT <- @supp);
12                                             53   msgSnd: (#ROLLBACK|#COMMIT -> @supp);
13 action Supplier in processOrderCall() {     54 }
14   msgRcv : (CFP <- @buyer);                 55
15   msgSnd : (CFP -> $stock);                 56 action Production in allocateProd () {
16 }                                           57   msgRcv: (ACCEPT|#REJECT <- @supp);
17                                             58   msgSnd: (#ROLLBACK|#COMMIT -> @supp);
18 action Stock in processStockRequest() {     59 }
19   msgRcv: (CFP <- @supp);                   60
20   msgSnd: (PROPOSE|#REFUSE -> @supp);       61 action Supplier in collectCommits() {
21 }                                           62   msgRcv: (#ROLLBACK|#COMMIT<- $prod) &
22                                             63             (#ROLLBACK|#COMMIT <- $stock);
23 action Supplier in processStockRsp () {     64   msgSnd: (#ROLLBACK -> @buyer) |
24   msgRcv: (PROPOSE|#REFUSE <- $stock);      65             (REQUEST -> tAgent);
25   msgSnd: (CFP -> $prod);                   66 }
26 }                                           67
27                                             68 action Transport in scheduleShpmnt() {
28 action Production in processPrdCall() {      69   msgRcv: (REQUEST <- @supp);
29   msgRcv: (CFP <- @supp);                   70   msgSnd: (INFORM|#REFUSE -> @supp);
30   msgSnd: (PROPOSE|#REFUSE -> @supp);       71 }
31 }                                           72
32                                             73 action Supplier in closeOrder() {
33 action Supplier in collectData() {          74   msgRcv: (INFORM|#REFUSE <- tAgent);
34   msgRcv: (PROPOSE|#REFUSE <- $prod);       75   msgSnd: (#ROLLBACK|#COMMIT -> @buyer);
35   msgSnd: (PROPOSE -> @buyer) |             76 }
36           ((#REFUSE -> @buyer) &            77
37            (#REJECT -> $prod) &             78 action Buyer in collectCommit() {
38            (#REJECT -> $stock));            79  msgRcv:(#ROLLBACK|#COMMIT<-<Supplier>);
38 }                                           80 }
39                                             81 }
40 action Buyer in collectProposals() {
41   msgRcv: (PROPOSE|#REFUSE<-<Supplier>);
```

Fig. 2. SDLMAS scenario description of the OrderParts scenario

using the SDLMAS language is based on the concept of dialogs. In SDLMAS, a dialog is defined as a set of agent type declarations $D^{(m)}$ and a set of scenario declarations $S^{(n)}$. Agent type declaration defines a participating agent and its type (i.e. scenario role). A role is understood as a standardized pattern of behavior required of all agents playing a part in a scenario (similar to [12]). A scenario is defined as a sequence of actions $a^{(k)}$ of a multi-agent system. Action a is defined as an execution of a procedure π (i.e. internal agent logic) of an agent type t only if all conditions defined within activity α are met.

Activity α defines two sets of conditions: message reception and message transmission conditions. The activity representing initial conversation activity defines only transmission conditions, while the last activity in a conversation defines only message reception conditions (as outgoing messages are no longer expected). All other activities defined within scenario contain both reception and transmission conditions. A message reception condition ρ defines circumstances under which a received message is to be passed to a procedure. A condition consists of a list of expected message performatives and their originating agents, and can form complex expressions using logical operators. This ability to define compound conditions for reception of messages enables system designers to describe complex and concurrent conversations among many agents, while retaining strict control over passing received messages to internal agent logic. Definition of message transmission condition σ is similar to the previously described reception condition ρ. This condition describes circumstances under which a message or a set of messages, resulting from an execution of a procedure, will be sent to corresponding agents.

The formal model allows us to prove several important scenario properties such as conversation termination, liveness, conversation consistency etc. and to implement static scenario verification.

3.3   Agents and Roles

Each agent in the SDLMAS system plays one or more roles. In scenario descriptions agents are represented with references. Four types of agent references are defined within SDLMAS: *verbatim*, *variable*, *anonymous* and *group* references. *Verbatim* reference is fixed at scenario definition and denotes exactly one (named) agent. *Variable* references, prefixed with $, are initially not bound to a particular agent and must be set 'internally' by the agent logic during a new conversation context (i.e. scenario instance) initialization. *Anonymous* references, prefixed with @, are initially not bound. Binding occurs 'externally', and is performed by the framework during creation of a new conversation context triggered by the reception of a scenario-triggering message. Variable and anonymous reference bindings exist as long as the enclosing conversation context exists. *Group* references, enclosed within < >, denote all agents of a particular type (role) present in the system at the moment an enclosing conversation context is created. Group reference membership can change as conversation with a particular group member can be terminated at any time during a scenario execution. Multiple conversation contexts active on the same agent have distinct bindings of variable, anonymous and group references.

3.4   Conversation Actions

Following declarations of agents and their types, a number of interaction scenarios can be defined. Each scenario is identified by a unique scenario name and built of a sequence of conversation actions implicitly defining an interaction protocol. A conversation action is defined in a scope of an agent type and consists of a procedure (connection to internal agent logic) and two elementary communication operations: message reception and transmission. The procedure is invoked only as a result of a successful reception of all required ingoing messages, and message transmission will occur as a result of a procedure execution and creation of prescribed outgoing message(s). Message reception and transmission constraints are defined with respect to message performatives and originating agents.

Lines 9-11 define the initial conversation action performed by an agent of type `Buyer` executing procedure `sendOrderCall()` and sending an ACL message with CFP set as a performative. This message is sent to all agents of type `Supplier` using group reference `<Supplier>` (line 10). On successful reception of the CFP message (line 14), each agent of type `Supplier` will create a new conversation context with anonymous reference `@buyer` referencing the message originator. This binding will persist until the end of the conversation context. All `Supplier` agents are still able to receive additional CFP-s and lead parallel conversations with other buyers, but those interactions are isolated in separate conversation contexts. After consultations with their `$stock` and `$prod` agents, `Supplier` agents will return a reply to the `Buyer` agent containing performative `PROPOSE` or `REFUSE` (lines 35,36). Agent `Buyer` will wait for replies from all `Supplier` agents (line 41) and, after processing the `collectProposals()` procedure, send appropriate responses only to `Suppliers` that returned messages containing the conversational performative `PROPOSE`.

3.5   Terminating and Conversational Performatives

Terminating performatives indicate an end of a conversation context and are prefixed with `#`. Non-terminating performatives are called conversational performatives. Returning an ACL message with the `REFUSE` performative set (line 36), a particular agent playing a `Supplier` role indicates the termination of a conversation with a `Buyer`. Corresponding performative on the reception side (line 41) must also be marked as terminating. This terminating performative relates only to a specific `Supplier` - `Buyer` interaction, not to the scenario as a whole, as the `Buyer` agent can have more than one conversation context active. A scenario is considered terminated when all conversation contexts are terminated.

4   SDLMAS Platform

Scenarios defined in SDLMAS language are transformed into program code for a target agent platform and language. Generated code, together with pre-existing libraries and components, forms a framework for implementation and execution of a multi-agent system whose interaction scenarios are defined in SDLMAS language. SDLMAS Platform is designed as an addition to existing agent platforms and depends on platform provided services such as FIPA-compliant messaging [22] and multi-threaded execution of agents.

4.1   System Components

Fig. 3 depicts the main SDLMAS platform system components: application agents implementing functionality of particular multi-agent system, the naming service agent, the management agent and the brokering component for FIPA compliant messaging. The message brokering component and the naming service agent must be provided by an underlying target agent platform.

Application Agents. In SDLMAS platform, internal agent structure is divided into three layers (Fig. 3.):

Target platform layer is part of the target agent platform and presents an interface between platform provided functionality (messaging, threading etc.) and a SDLMAS agent.

SDLMAS platform layer is divided into two sub layers. The 'lower' part of this layer is a platform-specific generic library providing support to scenario-dependent higher part of the layer and acting as an interface towards platform-specific communication layer. The 'upper' part of this layer is a scenario-dependent, but internal agent logic- and platform-independent. Handling conversation contexts,

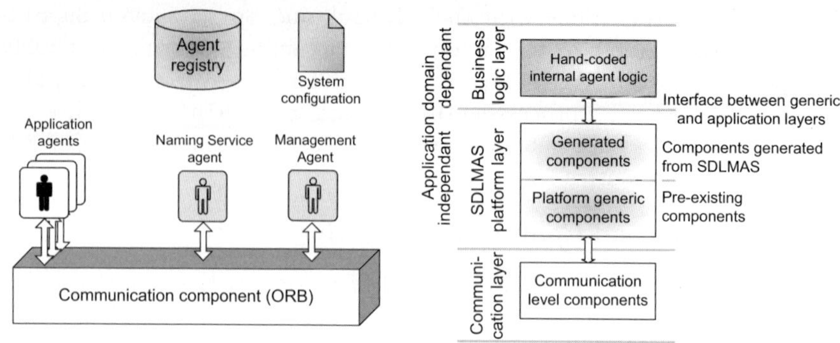

Fig. 3. SDLMAS platform main components and internal agent structure

tracking scenario compliance, enforcing message reception and transmission constraints, generating message timeouts and invoking business logic procedures are all preformed in this layer. Implementation code for the 'upper' layer, including timers, finite state automata, constraints etc., is generated according to provided SDLMAS scenarios.

Business logic layer is an application context dependent layer and presents the only part of the agent implementation that needs to be hand-coded. Business logic is implemented as a set of activities (method skeletons) within a conversation context (scenario class) invoked from the SDLMAS platform layer during the course of scenario execution. Care must be taken when developing business logic layer as individual agents can be concurrently involved in multiple and different scenario instances (conversation contexts).

Naming Service and Management Agents. Naming service agent is a centralized registry of all agents present in the system. Registration information is vital in the process of runtime name-agent binding when anonymous and group names are used in scenario definitions. Management agent provides a support for bootstrapping and initializing a multi-agent system according to provided global and agent-specific configurations.

4.2   Code Generation from Scenarios

SDLMAS compiler converts a set of scenario definitions into a set of entities. Generated entities are divided into two main categories: model-level entities, used among various system components, and scenario-level entities representing building blocks for implementation of agent communication behaviors. Code is generated (Fig. 4) according to supplied set of code template files, providing a simple mechanism for supporting various agent platforms and implementation languages. At the moment, only the JADE [25] agent platform is supported. In order to ease the development of SDLMAS based agent systems we have also created a SDLMAS Eclipse plug-in. The plug-in allows for fast scenario navigation, editing, verification and code generation in the same environment used for development of application-level agent logic.

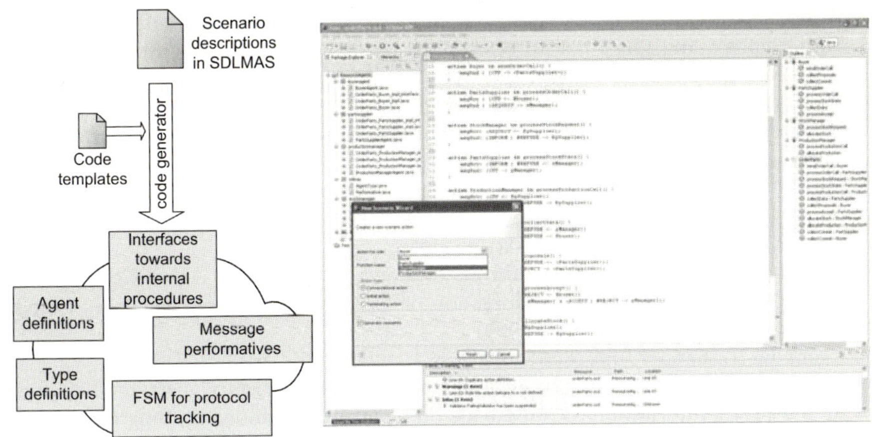

Fig. 4. Code generation and SDLMAS Eclipse plug-in

5 Conclusions

In this paper, we have addressed the problem of interaction complexity within multi-agent systems and analysed existing languages for interaction description. A new language, SDLMAS, aimed at describing interaction scenarios among agents was proposed. Its simplicity and expressiveness allow intuitive design of complex scenarios where a single agent can simultaneously participate in several conversations with different agents. SDLMAS enables generic approach to scenario building by defining anonymous and group names, binding those names to real agents at runtime. Strict separation of agent internal logic and interaction control mechanism is enforced, allowing clear separation of concerns between platform runtime and hand-coded agent logic. This clear separation also contributes to portability of SDLMAS to different agent platforms and pro gramming languages. Defined interaction scenarios are transformed into target language and agent platform code, and integrated into SDLMAS platform. SDLMAS platform forms a development and run-time environment for agents, ensuring adherence to and hiding of complexities related to tracking and coordinating possibly numerous simultaneously executing scenarios.

References

1. Jennings, N.R., Wooldridge, M.: Agent-Oriented Software Engineering. In: Garijo, F.J., Boman, M. (eds.) MAAMAW 1999. LNCS, vol. 1647, Springer, Heidelberg (1999)
2. Greaves, M., Holmback, H., Bradshaw, J.: What Is a Conversation Policy? Issues in Agent Communication (2000)
3. Walton, C.D.: Multi-Agent Dialogue Protocols (2003)
4. Gómez-Sanz, J.J., Fuentes, R.: Agent Oriented Software Engineering with INGENIAS. In: Mařík, V., Müller, J.P., Pěchouček, M. (eds.) CEEMAS 2003. LNCS (LNAI), vol. 2691, Springer, Heidelberg (2003)

5. Wood, M.F., DeLoach, S.A.: An Overview of the Multiagent Systems Engineering Methodology. In: The First International Workshop on Agent-Oriented Software Engineering, Limerick, Ireland (2000)
6. Wooldridge, M., Jennings, N.R., Kinny, D.: The Gaia Mcthodology for Agent-Oriented Analysis and Design. Autonomous Agents and Multi-Agent Systems Archive 3(3) (2000)
7. Paurobally, S., Cunningham, J.: Achieving Common Interaction Protocols in Open Agent Environments, Autonomous Agents and Multi-Agent Systems. In: AAMAS 2003, Melbourne, Australia (2003)
8. Cost, R., Chen, T., Finin, T., Labrou, Y., Peng, Y.: Modeling Agent Conversations With Colored Petri Nets. In: Workshop on Specifying and Implementing Conversation Policies, Seattle, USA (1999)
9. Agent UML, http://www.auml.org
10. Richters, M., Gogolla, M.: On Formalizing the UML Object Constraint Language. In: The 17th International Conference on Conceptual Modeling, Singapore (1998)
11. Paurobally, S., Cunningham, J., Jennings, N.R.: Developing Agent Interaction Protocols Using Graphical and Logical Methodologies. In: The Second International Joint Conference on Autonomous Agents and Multi-Agent Systems (AAMAS 2003), Melbourne, Australia (2003)
12. Estava, M., Rodriguez, J.A., Sierra, C., Garcia, P., Arcos, J.L.: APN 2001. LNCS (LNAI). Springer, Heidelberg (2001)
13. Milner, R.: Communication and Concurrency. Prentice-Hall International, Englewood Cliffs (1989)
14. Huget, M.P.: Agent UML Notation for Multiagent System Design. IEEE Internet Computing (July-August 2004)
15. Warmer, J., Kleppe, A.: OCL: The Constraint Language of the UML. Journal of Object-Oriented Programming (1999)
16. Winikoff, M.: Towards Making Agent UML Practical: A Textual Notation and a Tool. In: The Fifth International Conference on Quality Software (QSIC 2005), Melbourne, Australia (2005)
17. Dinkloh, M., Nimis, J.: A Tool for Integrated Design and Implementation of Conversations in Multiagent Systems. In: The Fourth International Joint Conference on Autonomous Agents and Multiagent Systems, Utrecht, The Netherlands (2005)
18. Huget, M.-P.: A Language for Exchanging Agent UML Protocol Diagrams, Technical Report ULCS-02-009, The University of Liverpool (2002)
19. Doi, T., Tahara, Y., Honiden, S.: IOM/T: An Interaction Description Language for Multi-Agent Systems. In: The Fourth International Joint Conference on Autonomous Agents and Multiagent Systems (AAMAS 2005), Utrecht, The Netherlands (2005)
20. Quenum, J.G., Aknine, S., Briot, J.-P., Honiden, S.: A Modelling Framework for Generic Agent Interaction Protocols. In: The 4th International Workshop on Declarative Agent Languages and Technologies, Hakodate, Japan (2006)
21. Ishida, T.Q.: A Scenario Description Language for Interactive Agents. IEEE Computer 35(11) (November 2002)
22. FIPA ACL message structure specification, http://www.fipa.org/specs/fipa00061/
23. AUML Inter. diagrams, http://www.auml.org/auml/documents/ID-03-07-02.pdf
24. Smith, R.G.: The Contract Net Protocol: High-level Communication and Control in a Distributed Problem Solver. IEEE Transactions on Computers 29(12) (1980)
25. Java Agent Development Framework, http://jade.cselt.it/

The CrocodileAgent: A Software Agent for SCM Procurement Gaming

Tvrtko Milicic, Vedran Podobnik, Ana Petric, and Gordan Jezic

University of Zagreb, Faculty of Electrical Engineering and Computing,
Department of Telecommunications, Unska 3, HR-10000 Zagreb, Croatia
{tvrtko.milicic, vedran.podobnik, ana.petric,
gordan.jezic}@fer.hr

Abstract. The Trading Agent Competition (TAC) is an international forum which promotes high-quality research regarding the trading agent problem. One of the TAC competitive scenarios is Supply Chain Management Procurement Challenge (SCM-PC) where three agents compete by buying components, assembling PCs from these components and selling the manufactured PCs to customers. The idea of SCM-PC is the development of agent-based systems that implement efficient business strategies, with special emphasis on the procurement processes. In this paper, we analyze the SCM-PC environment and describe the main features of the CrocodileAgent, our entry in the SCM-PC Competition.

1 Introduction

In the past, both the markets and choices available were much smaller than today, so the volatility of supply and demand functions was much more inert. Under such market conditions, companies did not need to make important decisions daily but they rather based business transactions on long-term partnerships. On the other hand, the accelerated economic globalization trend in the past decade is leading us closer to the existence of just one market - the global one. Consequently, the functions of supply and demand are becoming more and more dynamic and the possibilities of choice have risen to amazing levels. Under such market conditions, companies should also implement procurement strategies based on one-off settlements (spot market trading). The SCM-PC (*Supply Chain Management Procurement Challenge*) Game creates such environment which requests from trading agents to efficiently combine procurement based on both long-term contracts and spot market settlements.

Supply chain management (SCM) deals with planning and coordinating activities such as material procurement, product assembly, and the distribution of manufactured products. Dynamic supply chain management improves the competitiveness of companies since it has a direct impact on their capability of adjusting to the changing market demands quickly and efficiently [1]. Since the annual worldwide supply chain transactions are counted in trillions of dollars, even the slightest possibility of improvement cannot be neglected.

N.T. Nguyen et al. (Eds.): IEA/AIE 2008, LNAI 5027, pp. 865–875, 2008.

In this paper, we analyze the SCM-PC environment and describe the main features of the CrocodileAgent, an intelligent agent we developed to participate in the SCM-PC Competition. The paper is organized as follows. Section 2 describes the basic rules of the SCM-PC Game. Section 3 describes the CrocodileAgent's architecture and functionalities. In Section 4 CrocodileAgent's performances in the SCM-PC 2007 Competition are analyzed. Section 5 proposes directions for future work and concludes the paper.

2 The TAC SCM-PC Game

The Trading Agent Competition (TAC, http://www.sics.se/tac) is an international forum that promotes high-quality research on the trading agent problem. In the year 2007 TAC had four competitive scenarios.

The oldest of them, Supply Chain Management Game (TAC SCM), has been running as an annual tournament since 2003. It revolves around a PC (*Personal Computer*) assembly game, where trading agents from different teams compete for both customer orders for PCs and for PC components required to assemble these PCs. In addition to this baseline game, the 2007 tournament featured two new challenges: a *Procurement Challenge* and a *Prediction Challenge*. While the Procurement Challenge scenario requires trading agents to balance both long-term and one-off procurement contracts as they try to maximize profits and meet stochastic customer demand, in the Prediction Challenge scenario agents should make daily predictions over the course of a number of TAC SCM Games about four different types of prices: current and future computer prices, and current and future component prices. All three TAC SCM Games were motivated by the desire to develop automated strategies for buyer and seller trading agent in electronic markets (e-markets). The trading rules are fixed by the TAC SCM organizers, and competition entrants compete with one another by creating agents that seek to trade under these fixed rules. The fourth scenario, which was also introduced in the competition for the first time in 2007, is called the TAC Market Design scenario, or shortly CAT. In contrast to the TAC SCM based scenarios, the CAT environment is populated with the software trading agents created by the organizers of the competition, and as an entrant one must compete by defining rules for matching buyers and sellers and setting commission fees for providing this service. Entrants compete against each other in attracting buyers and sellers and making profits. This is achieved by having effective matching rules and setting appropriate fees that are a good trade-off between making profit and attracting traders.

In the SCM Procurement Challenge [2] scenario (see Figure 1), each of three manufacturer agents included in the game has its own PC manufacturing company. During the 100 SCM-PC days (one virtual day lasts 10 seconds), manufacturer agents compete for supply contracts from 10 different supplier agents. Each supplier produces one of four types of components (i.e., *CPUs*, *motherboards*, *memories* and *hard drives*). Long-term contracts are negotiated just once at the beginning of the game, consequently making agreed terms for long-term procurement valid till the end of the game. Each week, manufacturer agents may decide to make a purchase based on long-term contract. The quantities in such purchase can vary between the minimum quantities they committed to up to pre-specified maximum quantities. Each day, manufacturer agents may also decide to procure additional components outside of their long-term procurement contracts (this daily-based component purchase based on one-off settlements is called spot market procurement). All the manufacturer agents' factories are characterized by the same limited capacity, while customers' demands are randomly generated and require each manufacturer agent to satisfy an equal part. This allows agents to ignore the customer bidding dimension of their supply chain, making the SCM-PC simpler than the baseline TAC SCM scenario: in the SCM-PC, manufacturer agents are only expected to focus on making procurement decisions. At the end of the game, the manufacturer agent with the most money in the bank is declared the winner.

In order to participate in the game, an agent has to connect to the game server. The SCM-PC Game server has several functionalities. Namely, it simulates suppliers (i.e., PC component manufacturers), customers (i.e., PC buyers) and the bank. The game server also controls manufacturer agents' factories and warehouses. Each SCM-PC agent has a bank account and receives a daily report regarding its current bank balance. At the beginning of the game, the agent has no money and must hence loan money from the bank. For every day that the agent is in debt, the bank charges the agent interest while for every day that its bank account is positive, the bank pays interest to the agent.

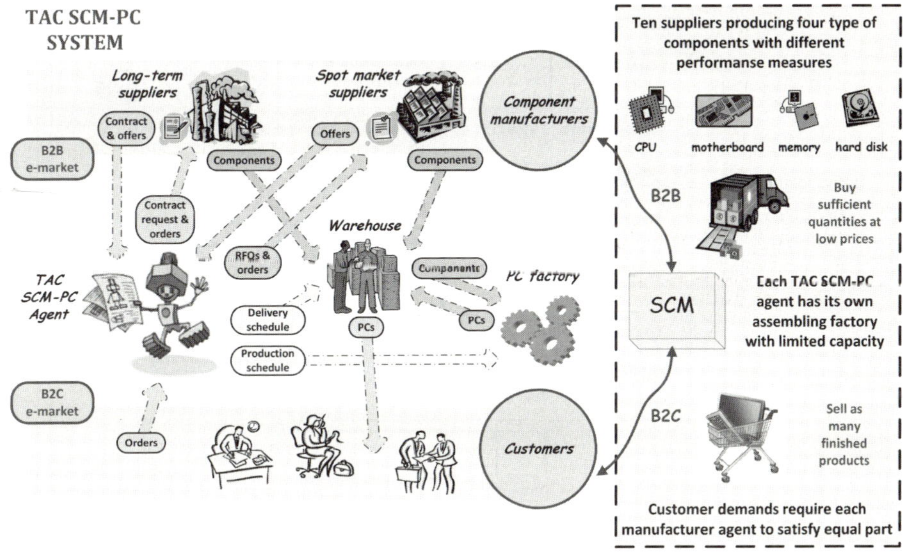

Fig. 1. The relationships in the TAC SCM-PC system

3   CrocodileAgent

The CrocodileAgent is an intelligent trading agent developed at the Department of Telecommunications, Faculty of Electrical Engineering and Computing, University of

Zagreb, Croatia. The CrocodileAgent [3, 4, 5] is long-standing participant in the baseline TAC SCM Competitions [6, 7, 8]. In the 2004 Competition the CrocodileAgent participated in TAC SCM Semi-finals, while in the 2005 and 2006 Competitions our TAC SCM agent took part in the quarter-finals. The CrocodileAgent ended its participation in 2007 Competition as the Second Finals winner, achieving its best result ever.

This section is going to present the CrocodileAgent's version for SCM-PC 2007. The CrocodileAgent's architecture (see Figure 2) is based on incorporating generic intelligent software agent model [9] into the IKB (*Information-Knowledge-Behaviour*) framework [10], a three layered agent-based framework for designing strategies in electronic trading markets.

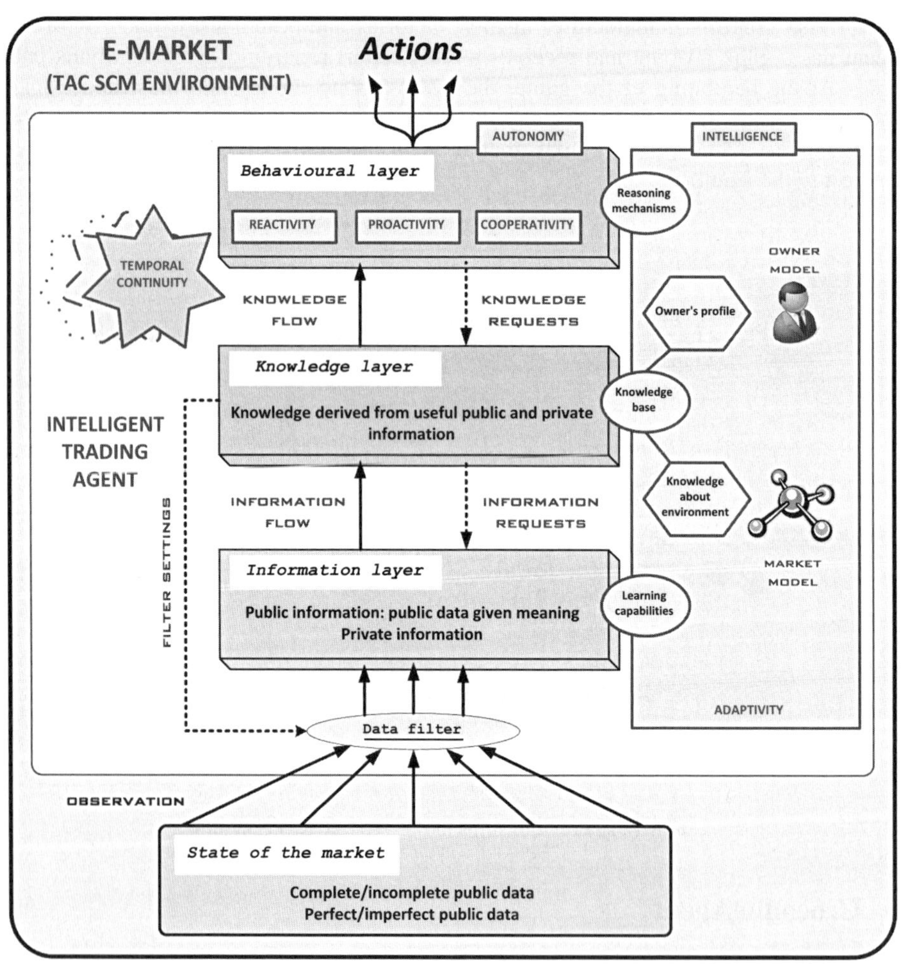

Fig. 2. The CrocodileAgent's architecture

3.1 Negotiating Long-Term Contracts

The most important parameters used in component purchase based on long-term contracts are:

- Q_{max} – the requested maximum weekly component quantity,

- Q_{max}^{real} – the contracted maximum weekly component quantity,

- Q_{min}^{real} – the contracted minimum weekly component quantity: $Q_{min}^{real} \in \left[0.77 \times Q_{max}^{real}, 0.95 \times Q_{max}^{real} \right]$ (the level of long-term contract flexibility is randomly determined for each component independently and announced at the beginning of the game),

- p_{nom} – the nominal component prices,

- p_{min} – the minimum price (i.e., the reserve price) for each of the components: $p_{min} \in \left[0.5 \times p_{nom}, 0.75 \times p_{nom} \right]$ (the reserve prices are randomly determined for each component independently and announced at the beginning of the game),

- p_{exec} – the maximal execution price (i.e., the maximal price that the trading agent is willing to pay for each component unit it purchases from the supplier),

- p_{exec}^{real} – the actual price every trading agent must pay per component unit purchased from supplier,

- q_{week} – the actually ordered weekly component quantity,

- N_{inv} – the number of components currently stored in the agent's warehouse.

On the game start (*day -1*) the CrocodileAgent negotiates quantity flexible long-term contracts for each component. After each long-term supplier announces p_{min} for each of the components it sells, the CrocodileAgent calculates Q_{max} for submitting a bid to the corresponding long-term supplier. The Q_{max} is determined only according to the p_{min} values: actual quantities linearly decrease from 270 (if $p_{min}=0.5 \times p_{nom}$) to 190 (if $p_{min}=0.75 \times p_{nom}$) for CPUs and from 370 (if $p_{min}=0.5 \times p_{nom}$) to 250 (if $p_{min}=0.75 \times p_{nom}$) for other components. After the Q_{max} quantities have been determined independently for all the components, CrocodileAgent submits a single quantity flexible bid for each of the components. In addition to the Q_{max} an agent must also specify the p_{exec}. The CrocodileAgent always sets $p_{exec}=p_{min}$.

Table 1. The relationship between q_{week} and N_{inv}

q_{week} / N_{inv}	CPUs	motheboards	memories	hard disks
max($0.77 \times Q_{max}^{real}$, Q_{min}^{real})	≥ 600	≥ 700	≥ 800	≥ 600
Q_{max}^{real}	≤ 300	≤ 400	≤ 500	≤ 400

On the following day (i.e., *day 0*) the CrocodileAgent receives the long-term contracts from the suppliers. Each of the suppliers allocated its resources based on its weekly nominal capacity: quantities were distributed among agents (Q_{max}^{real}) based on requested Q_{max}, starting with the highest bidder. The p_{exec}^{real} is determined according to the rules of the second-price sealed-bid auction. On the *day 0* trading agents also send its first component orders to the long-term suppliers: the CrocodileAgent submits all of its orders with $q_{week} = Q_{max}^{real}$. From this point till the end of the game the CrocodileAgent continues to send weekly orders to long-term suppliers. As the long-term contracts are quantity flexible the CrocodileAgent can every week for every component choose a different order quantity $q_{week} \in \left[Q_{min}^{real}, Q_{max}^{real}\right]$. The CrocodileAgent calculates the q_{week} independently for every component every week, according to the value of N_{inv} parameter. The q_{week} linearly increases from $\max(0.77 \times Q_{max}^{real}, Q_{min}^{real})$ to Q_{max}^{real}, where corresponding marginal N_{inv} values are given in Table 1. The referred N_{inv} values were determined after conducting a series of experiments.

3.2 Negotiating One-Off Contracts

There are two different aspects of spot market procurement: *day 0* component procurement and ordering components during the game. A close examination of the baseline TAC SCM Game rules [11] (which also define the SCM-PC spot market model) suggests that procurement of components at the very beginning of the game (*day 0* procurement) may provide an agent cheap components throughout the game (because there was no prior component demand). Although the concept of *day 0* procurement strategy has some similarities with long-term component contracting, these two procurement strategies are totally independent because each component is available from two different suppliers: one that only offers long-term contracts and one that only sells in the spot market.

***Day 0* procurement.** The most important parameters used in *day 0* component procurement are:

- $d_{del}[5]$ – requested delivery dates,
- $p_{min}[5]$ – the minimum prices (i.e., the reserve prices),
- $q_{CPU}[5]$ – requested CPU quantities,
- $q_{oth}[5]$ – requested quantities of other components than CPUs,
- p_{nom} – the nominal component prices.

Table 2. The actual parameter values in *day 0* RFQs

d_{del}	7	14	21	52	77
p_{min}	$1.07 \times p_{nom}$	$0.97 \times p_{nom}$	$0.92 \times p_{nom}$	$0.77 \times p_{nom}$	$0.69 \times p_{nom}$
q_{CPU}	300	350	400	450	450
q_{oth}	600	700	800	900	900

The goal of using the *day 0* procurement strategy is to acquire components for the beginning of the game and (if possible) provide the agent with cheap components in the second part of the game. The CrocodileAgent sends the day-maximum of five RFQs with the parameters set as shown in Table 2. The referred parameters were determined after conducting a series of experiments. Unfavourable situation happens when the chosen supplier cannot deliver the requested quantity on time. In that case the agent accepts partial offers.

Component purchase during the game. The most important parameters used in component purchase during the game are:

- N_{min} – the minimal quantity of components required to be in storage (i.e., 400 for CPUs and 700 for other components),
- N_{max} – the maximal quantity of components allowed in storage (i.e., 500 for CPUs and 1000 for other components),
- N_{ord} – the maximal amount of components that can be ordered each day (i.e., 150 for CPUs and 300 for other components),
- N_{tdy} – the quantity of a certain component used in PC production per day,
- N_{inv} – the number of components currently stored in the warehouse,
- p_{min} – the minimum prices (i.e., the reserve prices),
- p_{nom} – the nominal component prices.

It is important to point out that values of the parameters N_{min}, N_{max} and N_{ord} are not fixed values throughout the game. Actually, they are multiplied with *dayFactor*, which firstly increases linearly from 0.3 to 1.5 between days 0 and 60, while afterwards decreases linearly from 1.5 to 0.5 between days 61 and 95.

At the beginning of each day, the agent calculates the component quantity ordered, but not delivered, up to that moment for each component separately. Since the orders with an earlier delivery date will provide components earlier, the agent's ordered quantities of components are multiplied with a distance factor. The distance factor is a value between 0 and 1; the factor shrinks from 1 to 0 as the delivery date grows. When the delivery date reaches 30 days (from the current day) the distance factor becomes 0. The parameter obtained by performing this calculation is referred to as the *evaluatedQuantity*. Similarly, the *evaluatedLongTermQuantity* is calculated, which represents the quantity of all the ordered components that have a delivery date higher than 30 days.

For each component, the agent checks to see if the following condition is fulfilled:

$$N_{inv} + evaluatedQuantity \geq N_{max} . \tag{1}$$

The components are not ordered if condition (1) is fulfilled. However, in spite of condition (1), there are two situations where CrocodileAgent may send some RFQs to spot market suppliers. The first situation is the consequence of fact that, due to volatility of supplier capacity through the game, the prices offered in response to RFQs requesting near-immediate delivery are very unpredictable. To allow for the possibility of making low priced procurement (i.e., $p_{min} \approx 0.6 \times p_{nom}$) the CrocodileAgent sends, if the current date is before day 80 and N_{inv} is less than $1.1 \times N_{max}$, one RFQ with due in 2 days (the minimum possible) for small quantities (40 for all types of components). The *2-day* RFQs enable the agent to be opportunistic in taking advantage of short-term bargains on components without being dependent on the availability of such bargains [12]. The second reason for ignoring fulfilment of condition (1) covers the situation when the CrocodileAgent has not sent any RFQ for certain component during longer period of time (i.e., last 5 days). If the current date is before day 50 and the *evaluatedLongTermQuantity* is lower than its upper limit (i.e, $1.77 \times N_{max}$), the agent sends one RFQ with further delivery date (i.e., around 20 days) to ensure cheap components (i.e., $p_{min} \approx 0.6 \times p_{nom}$ and quantities are set to the N_{ord}) for the second part of the game.

If condition (1) is not fulfilled, the following condition is considered:

$$N_{inv} + N_{tdy} > N_{min}. \tag{2}$$

If condition (2) is not fulfilled the agent purchases components more aggressively with the purpose of getting the number of components in the warehouse above N_{min} as soon as possible (i.e., the agent sends five RFQs requesting near-immediate delivery and relaxes the p_{min} towards higher values). Otherwise, the CrocodileAgent also sends five RFQs, but with the purpose of maintaining the present quantity of components in the warehouse.

It is important to point out that these are only the main characteristics of the algorithm. Additionally, there are special mechanisms which calculate the p_{min} and exact quantities that need to be ordered. A simplified description of some of these mechanisms follows:

- The *lowComponentAlarm* contains several levels and marks the very low quantity of a certain component in the warehouse. In case the alarm is set, the agent is allowed to pay a higher price than usual for the component.
- The *demandPurchaseQuantityFactor* is modified according to customer demand. Sometimes during the game, the customer demand may rise rapidly. When this happens the agent uses more components to produce more PCs, so the parameter is increased to ensure that the agent does not run out of components and consequently looses potentially profitable PC orders.

4   TAC SCM-PC 2007 Competition

The SCM-PC competition was held for the first time in the year 2007 [13]. It was divided into two parts: qualifying rounds held from June 26th – 30th and final rounds held on July 23rd.

There were 5 teams competing in the qualifying rounds: **PhantAgent** from "Politehnica" University of Bucharest (Romania), **CMieux** from Carnegie Mellon University (USA), **kshitij** from Centre for Data Engineering, IIIT, Hyderabad (India), **Warrior** from Joint Wayne State University – University of Michigan team (USA) and the **CrocodileAgent**. Because of a small number of participants that were competing in the qualifying rounds, all of them went through to the final rounds. Kshitij team folded, so there were 4 teams competing in the finals. After 9 games played in the final rounds, the average CrocodileAgent's score was 6.399 M which was enough to place at the 3rd place. The rankings of the final rounds are shown in Table 3. Figure 3 shows the progress of average scores for all participants during the final rounds. We can see from this figure how average scores of other agents do not vary significantly during the competition. On the other hand, CrocodileAgent's average score continuously rises from game to game. The agent CMieux, who had the best average score in 8 games, lost the 1st place by not participating in only one game. In the same game, the PhantAgent won with the final score over 20 M and improved his final average score by 2 M which was enough to win in the competition. While the CrocodileAgent began the competition with a negative score in the first two games, afterwards it started to significantly improve its results. It won 2 games in the competition. By taking the 2nd place in the game that cost the CMieux its victory, with the score over 17 M, it came very close to taking the 2nd place in the final order.

Table 3. SCM-PC 2007 final rounds results

Position	Agent	Score	Games Played	Zero Games
1	PhantAgent	8 731 000	9	0
2	CMieux	7 405 000	9	0
3	CrocodileAgent	6 399 000	9	0
4	Warrior	4 200 000	9	0

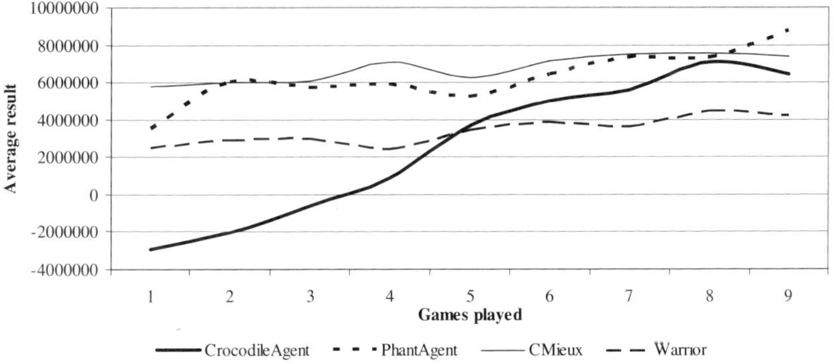

Fig. 3. Average scores of final rounds

The CrocodileAgent had the highest percentage of orders delivered on time and the highest factory utilization. These results are the outcome of boosting the low component management algorithm. The PhantAgent and the CMieux agents had approximately similar results in these segments, with only a small advantage of the PhantAgent, while the Warrior agent's performance in these segments was not very competitive. The problem with the CrocodileAgent was the fact that it had the most unused components left in its warehouse at the end of the game. The Warrior had the best results in the leftover component management, followed by CMieux and PhantAgent. Even though the CrocodileAgent sold the highest number of PCs it the games and implemented very efficient long-term purchase mechanisms, the agent placed 3rd in the final rounds due to very high component purchase prices during the spot market purchase.

5 Conclusions and Future Work

In this paper we presented the SCM-PC Competition and described the main features of the CrocodileAgent, our entry in that competition. The purpose of the SCM-PC Game is to evaluate the performance of mixed procurement strategies. Trading agents which compete in one SCM-PC Game are required to manage supply chain risks through combination of the long-term, quantity flexible procurement contracts and one-off, spot market settlements.

The SCM-PC 2007 was the first SCM-PC Competition. For future work we plan to thoroughly analyze CrocodileAgent's performance through a series of controlled experiments. On the basis of performed analysis improvements of CrocodileAgent's weaknesses are going to be designed and implemented. Moreover, we plan to enhance the CrocodileAgent's spot market trading mechanism with the ability of historical data analysis, allowing it to efficiently use information from previous games. In such a manner CrocodileAgent could not just react to the current state of the PC market, but also predict the fluctuations of customer demand and, consequently, minimize the quantity of unused components left in its warehouse at the end of the game.

Acknowledgements. This work was carried out within research projects 036-0362027-1639 "Content Delivery and Mobility of Users and Services in New Generation Networks", supported by the Ministry of Science, Education and Sports of the Republic of Croatia, and "Agent-based Service & Telecom Operations Management", supported by Ericsson Nikola Tesla, Croatia.

References

1. Benish, M., Sardinha, A., Andrews, J., Sadeh, N.: CMieux: Adaptive Strategies for Competitive Supply Chain Trading. In: Proc. of the 8th Int. Conf. on Electronic Commerce (ICEC), pp. 1–10. ACM Press, Fredericton (2006)
2. Sardinha, A., Benish, M., Andrews, J., Sadeh, N.: The 2007 Supply Chain Trading Agent Competition - Procurement Challenge. Technical Report CMU-ISRI-07-106 (2007), http://www.cs.cmu.edu/~alberto/papers/CMU-ISRI-07-106.pdf
3. Podobnik, V., Petric, A., Jezic, G.: The CrocodileAgent: Research for Efficient Agent-Based Cross-Enterprise Processes. In: Meersman, R., Tari, Z., Herrero, P. (eds.) OTM 2006 Workshops. LNCS, vol. 4277, pp. 752–762. Springer, Heidelberg (2006)
4. Petric, A., Podobnik, V., Jezic, G.: The CrocodileAgent 2005: An Overview of TAC SCM Agent. In: Fasli, M., Shehory, O. (eds.) TADA/AMEC 2006. LNCS (LNAI), vol. 4452, pp. 219–233. Springer, Heidelberg (2007)
5. Petric, A., Podobnik, V., Jezic, G.: The CrocodileAgent: Designing a Robust Trading Agent for Volatile E-Market Conditions. In: Nguyen, N.T., Grzech, A., Howlett, R.J., Jain, L.C. (eds.) KES-AMSTA 2007. LNCS (LNAI), vol. 4496, pp. 597–606. Springer, Heidelberg (2007)
6. Arunachalam, R., Sadeh, N.: The Supply Chain Trading Agent Competition. Electronic Commerce Research and Applications 4(1), 66–84 (2005)
7. Eriksson, J., Finne, N., Janson, S.: Evolution of a Supply Chain Management Game for the Trading Agent Competition. AI Communications 19(1), 1–12 (2006)

8. Wellman, M.P., Estelle, J., Singh, S., Vorobeychik, Y., Kiekintveld, C., Soni, V.: Strategic Interactions in a Supply Chain Game. Computational Intelligence 21(1), 1–26 (2005)
9. Podobnik, V., Trzec, K., Jezic, G.: Context-Aware Service Provisioning in Next-Generation Networks: An Agent Approach. International Journal of Information Technology and Web Engineering 2(4), 41–62 (2007)
10. Vytelingum, P., Dash, R.K., He, M., Jennings, N.R.: A Framework for Designing Strategies for Trading Agents. In: Proc. of the Int. Workshop on Trading Agent Design and Analysis (TADA), IJCAI: Edinburghpp, pp. 7–13 (2005)
11. Collins, J., Arunachalam, R., Sadeh, N., Eriksson, J., Finne, N., Janson, S.: The Supply Chain Management Game for the 2007 Trading Agent Competition. Technical Report CMU-ISRI-07-100 (2006), http://www.sics.se/tac/tac07scmspec.pdf
12. Pardoe, D., Stone, P.: An Autonomous Agent for Supply Chain Management. In: Adomavicius, G., Gupta, A. (eds.) Handbooks in Information Systems Series: Business Computing, Elsevier, Amsterdam (2007)
13. Sardinha, A., Benisch, M., Sadeh, N., Ravichandran, R., Podobnik, V., Stan, M.: The 2007 Procurement Challenge: A Competition to Evaluate Mixed Procurement Strategies. Technical Report CMU-ISRI-07-123 (2007),
http://www.cs.cmu.edu/~alberto/papers/CMU-ISRI-07-123.pdf

Author Index

Printing: Mercedes-Druck, Berlin
Binding: Stein+Lehmann, Berlin

Lecture Notes in Artificial Intelligence (LNAI)

Vol. 5032: S. Bergler (Ed.), Advances in Artificial Intelligence. XI, 382 pages. 2008.

Vol. 5027: N.T. Nguyen, L. Borzemski, A. Grzech, M. Ali (Eds.), New Frontiers in Applied Artificial Intelligence. XVIII, 879 pages. 2008.

Vol. 5012: T. Washio, E. Suzuki, K.M. Ting, A. Inokuchi (Eds.), Advances in Knowledge Discovery and Data Mining. XXIV, 1102 pages. 2008.

Vol. 5009: G. Wang, T. Li, J.W. Grzymala-Busse, D. Miao, A. Skowron, Y. Yao (Eds.), Rough Sets and Knowledge Technology. XVIII, 765 pages. 2008.

Vol. 4994: A. An, S. Matwin, Z.W. Raś, D. Ślęzak (Eds.), Foundations of Intelligent Systems. XVII, 653 pages. 2008.

Vol. 4953: N.T. Nguyen, G.S. Jo, R.J. Howlett, L.C. Jain (Eds.), Agent and Multi-Agent Systems: Technologies and Applications. XX, 909 pages. 2008.

Vol. 4946: I. Rahwan, S. Parsons, C. Reed (Eds.), Argumentation in Multi-Agent Systems. X, 235 pages. 2008.

Vol. 4944: Z.W. Raś, S. Tsumoto, D. Zighed (Eds.), Mining Complex Data. X, 265 pages. 2008.

Vol. 4938: T. Tokunaga, A. Ortega (Eds.), Large-Scale Knowledge Resources. IX, 367 pages. 2008.

Vol. 4933: R. Medina, S. Obiedkov (Eds.), Formal Concept Analysis. XII, 325 pages. 2008.

Vol. 4930: I. Wachsmuth, G. Knoblich (Eds.), Modeling Communication with Robots and Virtual Humans. X, 337 pages. 2008.

Vol. 4929: M. Helmert, Understanding Planning Tasks. XIV, 270 pages. 2008.

Vol. 4924: D. Riaño (Ed.), Knowledge Management for Health Care Procedures. X, 161 pages. 2008.

Vol. 4923: S.B. Yahia, E.M. Nguifo, R. Belohlavek (Eds.), Concept Lattices and Their Applications. XII, 283 pages. 2008.

Vol. 4914: K. Satoh, A. Inokuchi, K. Nagao, T. Kawamura (Eds.), New Frontiers in Artificial Intelligence. X, 404 pages. 2008.

Vol. 4911: L. De Raedt, P. Frasconi, K. Kersting, S. Muggleton (Eds.), Probabilistic Inductive Logic Programming. VIII, 341 pages. 2008.

Vol. 4908: M. Dastani, A. El Fallah Seghrouchni, A. Ricci, M. Winikoff (Eds.), Programming Multi-Agent Systems. XII, 267 pages. 2008.

Vol. 4898: M. Kolp, B. Henderson-Sellers, H. Mouratidis, A. Garcia, A.K. Ghose, P. Bresciani (Eds.), Agent-Oriented Information Systems IV. X, 292 pages. 2008.

Vol. 4897: M. Baldoni, T.C. Son, M.B. van Riemsdijk, M. Winikoff (Eds.), Declarative Agent Languages and Technologies V. X, 245 pages. 2008.

Vol. 4894: H. Blockeel, J. Ramon, J. Shavlik, P. Tadepalli (Eds.), Inductive Logic Programming. XI, 307 pages. 2008.

Vol. 4885: M. Chetouani, A. Hussain, B. Gas, M. Milgram, J.-L. Zarader (Eds.), Advances in Nonlinear Speech Processing. XI, 284 pages. 2007.

Vol. 4874: J. Neves, M.F. Santos, J.M. Machado (Eds.), Progress in Artificial Intelligence. XVIII, 704 pages. 2007.

Vol. 4870: J.S. Sichman, J. Padget, S. Ossowski, P. Noriega (Eds.), Coordination, Organizations, Institutions, and Norms in Agent Systems III. XII, 331 pages. 2008.

Vol. 4869: F. Botana, T. Recio (Eds.), Automated Deduction in Geometry. X, 213 pages. 2007.

Vol. 4865: K. Tuyls, A. Nowe, Z. Guessoum, D. Kudenko (Eds.), Adaptive Agents and Multi-Agent Systems III. VIII, 255 pages. 2008.

Vol. 4850: M. Lungarella, F. Iida, J.C. Bongard, R. Pfeifer (Eds.), 50 Years of Artificial Intelligence. X, 399 pages. 2007.

Vol. 4845: N. Zhong, J. Liu, Y. Yao, J. Wu, S. Lu, K. Li (Eds.), Web Intelligence Meets Brain Informatics. XI, 516 pages. 2007.

Vol. 4840: L. Paletta, E. Rome (Eds.), Attention in Cognitive Systems. XI, 497 pages. 2007.

Vol. 4830: M.A. Orgun, J. Thornton (Eds.), AI 2007: Advances in Artificial Intelligence. XIX, 841 pages. 2007.

Vol. 4828: M. Randall, H.A. Abbass, J. Wiles (Eds.), Progress in Artificial Life. XII, 402 pages. 2007.

Vol. 4827: A. Gelbukh, Á.F. Kuri Morales (Eds.), MICAI 2007: Advances in Artificial Intelligence. XXIV, 1234 pages. 2007.

Vol. 4826: P. Perner, O. Salvetti (Eds.), Advances in Mass Data Analysis of Signals and Images in Medicine, Biotechnology and Chemistry. X, 183 pages. 2007.

Vol. 4819: T. Washio, Z.-H. Zhou, J.Z. Huang, X. Hu, J. Li, C. Xie, J. He, D. Zou, K.-C. Li, M.M. Freire (Eds.), Emerging Technologies in Knowledge Discovery and Data Mining. XIV, 675 pages. 2007.

Vol. 4811: O. Nasraoui, M. Spiliopoulou, J. Srivastava, B. Mobasher, B. Masand (Eds.), Advances in Web Mining and Web Usage Analysis. XII, 247 pages. 2007.

Vol. 4798: Z. Zhang, J.H. Siekmann (Eds.), Knowledge Science, Engineering and Management. XVI, 669 pages. 2007.

Vol. 4795: F. Schilder, G. Katz, J. Pustejovsky (Eds.), Annotating, Extracting and Reasoning about Time and Events. VII, 141 pages. 2007.

Vol. 4790: N. Dershowitz, A. Voronkov (Eds.), Logic for Programming, Artificial Intelligence, and Reasoning. XIII, 562 pages. 2007.

Vol. 4788: D. Borrajo, L. Castillo, J.M. Corchado (Eds.), Current Topics in Artificial Intelligence. XI, 280 pages. 2007.

Vol. 4775: A. Esposito, M. Faundez-Zanuy, E. Keller, M. Marinaro (Eds.), Verbal and Nonverbal Communication Behaviours. XII, 325 pages. 2007.

Vol. 4772: H. Prade, V.S. Subrahmanian (Eds.), Scalable Uncertainty Management. X, 277 pages. 2007.

Vol. 4766: N. Maudet, S. Parsons, I. Rahwan (Eds.), Argumentation in Multi-Agent Systems. XII, 211 pages. 2007.

Vol. 4760: E. Rome, J. Hertzberg, G. Dorffner (Eds.), Towards Affordance-Based Robot Control. IX, 211 pages. 2008.

Vol. 4755: V. Corruble, M. Takeda, E. Suzuki (Eds.), Discovery Science. XI, 298 pages. 2007.

Vol. 4754: M. Hutter, R.A. Servedio, E. Takimoto (Eds.), Algorithmic Learning Theory. XI, 403 pages. 2007.

Vol. 4737: B. Berendt, A. Hotho, D. Mladenic, G. Semeraro (Eds.), From Web to Social Web: Discovering and Deploying User and Content Profiles. XI, 161 pages. 2007.

Vol. 4733: R. Basili, M.T. Pazienza (Eds.), AI*IA 2007: Artificial Intelligence and Human-Oriented Computing. XVII, 858 pages. 2007.

Vol. 4724: K. Mellouli (Ed.), Symbolic and Quantitative Approaches to Reasoning with Uncertainty. XV, 914 pages. 2007.

Vol. 4722: C. Pelachaud, J.-C. Martin, E. André, G. Chollet, K. Karpouzis, D. Pelé (Eds.), Intelligent Virtual Agents. XV, 425 pages. 2007.

Vol. 4720: B. Konev, F. Wolter (Eds.), Frontiers of Combining Systems. X, 283 pages. 2007.

Vol. 4702: J.N. Kok, J. Koronacki, R. Lopez de Mantaras, S. Matwin, D. Mladenič, A. Skowron (Eds.), Knowledge Discovery in Databases: PKDD 2007. XXIV, 640 pages. 2007.

Vol. 4701: J.N. Kok, J. Koronacki, R. Lopez de Mantaras, S. Matwin, D. Mladenič, A. Skowron (Eds.), Machine Learning: ECML 2007. XXII, 809 pages. 2007.

Vol. 4696: H.-D. Burkhard, G. Lindemann, R. Verbrugge, L.Z. Varga (Eds.), Multi-Agent Systems and Applications V. XIII, 350 pages. 2007.

Vol. 4694: B. Apolloni, R.J. Howlett, L. Jain (Eds.), Knowledge-Based Intelligent Information and Engineering Systems, Part III. XXIX, 1126 pages. 2007.

Vol. 4693: B. Apolloni, R.J. Howlett, L. Jain (Eds.), Knowledge-Based Intelligent Information and Engineering Systems, Part II. XXXII, 1380 pages. 2007.

Vol. 4692: B. Apolloni, R.J. Howlett, L. Jain (Eds.), Knowledge-Based Intelligent Information and Engineering Systems, Part I. LV, 882 pages. 2007.

Vol. 4687: P. Petta, J.P. Müller, M. Klusch, M. Georgeff (Eds.), Multiagent System Technologies. X, 207 pages. 2007.

Vol. 4682: D.-S. Huang, L. Heutte, M. Loog (Eds.), Advanced Intelligent Computing Theories and Applications. XXVII, 1373 pages. 2007.

Vol. 4676: M. Klusch, K.V. Hindriks, M.P. Papazoglou, L. Sterling (Eds.), Cooperative Information Agents XI. XI, 361 pages. 2007.

Vol. 4667: J. Hertzberg, M. Beetz, R. Englert (Eds.), KI 2007: Advances in Artificial Intelligence. IX, 516 pages. 2007.

Vol. 4660: S. Džeroski, L. Todorovski (Eds.), Computational Discovery of Scientific Knowledge. X, 327 pages. 2007.

Vol. 4659: V. Mařík, V. Vyatkin, A.W. Colombo (Eds.), Holonic and Multi-Agent Systems for Manufacturing. VIII, 456 pages. 2007.

Vol. 4651: F. Azevedo, P. Barahona, F. Fages, F. Rossi (Eds.), Recent Advances in Constraints. VIII, 185 pages. 2007.

Vol. 4648: F. Almeida e Costa, L.M. Rocha, E. Costa, I. Harvey, A. Coutinho (Eds.), Advances in Artificial Life. XVIII, 1215 pages. 2007.

Vol. 4635: B. Kokinov, D.C. Richardson, T.R. Roth-Berghofer, L. Vieu (Eds.), Modeling and Using Context. XIV, 574 pages. 2007.

Vol. 4632: R. Alhajj, H. Gao, X. Li, J. Li, O.R. Zaïane (Eds.), Advanced Data Mining and Applications. XV, 634 pages. 2007.

Vol. 4629: V. Matoušek, P. Mautner (Eds.), Text, Speech and Dialogue. XVII, 663 pages. 2007.

Vol. 4626: R.O. Weber, M.M. Richter (Eds.), Case-Based Reasoning Research and Development. XIII, 534 pages. 2007.

Vol. 4617: V. Torra, Y. Narukawa, Y. Yoshida (Eds.), Modeling Decisions for Artificial Intelligence. XII, 502 pages. 2007.

Vol. 4612: I. Miguel, W. Ruml (Eds.), Abstraction, Reformulation, and Approximation. XI, 418 pages. 2007.

Vol. 4604: U. Priss, S. Polovina, R. Hill (Eds.), Conceptual Structures: Knowledge Architectures for Smart Applications. XII, 514 pages. 2007.

Vol. 4603: F. Pfenning (Ed.), Automated Deduction – CADE-21. XII, 522 pages. 2007.

Vol. 4597: P. Perner (Ed.), Advances in Data Mining. XI, 353 pages. 2007.

Vol. 4594: R. Bellazzi, A. Abu-Hanna, J. Hunter (Eds.), Artificial Intelligence in Medicine. XVI, 509 pages. 2007.

Vol. 4585: M. Kryszkiewicz, J.F. Peters, H. Rybinski, A. Skowron (Eds.), Rough Sets and Intelligent Systems Paradigms. XIX, 836 pages. 2007.

Vol. 4578: F. Masulli, S. Mitra, G. Pasi (Eds.), Applications of Fuzzy Sets Theory. XVIII, 693 pages. 2007.

Vol. 4573: M. Kauers, M. Kerber, R. Miner, W. Windsteiger (Eds.), Towards Mechanized Mathematical Assistants. XIII, 407 pages. 2007.